A PEOPLE AND A NATION

◆

Brief Edition

A PEOPLE AND A NATION

A History of the United States

Brief Edition ◆ **Third Edition**

MARY BETH NORTON
Cornell University

DAVID M. KATZMAN
University of Kansas

PAUL D. ESCOTT
Wake Forest University

HOWARD P. CHUDACOFF
Brown University

THOMAS G. PATERSON
University of Connecticut

WILLIAM M. TUTTLE, JR.
University of Kansas

and

WILLIAM J. BROPHY
Stephen F. Austin State University

HOUGHTON MIFFLIN COMPANY   **BOSTON**
Dallas   Geneva, Illinois   Palo Alto   Princeton, New Jersey

Cover: Nan Phelps, *Riverfront Stadium: Phillies and Reds*. Courtesy Galerie St. Etienne, New York. Copyright © 1980, Nan Phelps.

Cover photograph researched by Rose Corbett Gordon.

Text photographs researched by Pembroke Herbert/Picture Research Consultants.

Insert credits appear on page I-39.

Printed in the U.S.A.

Library of Congress Catalog Card Number: 90-83004

ISBN: 0-395-47302-0

DEFGHIJ-D-9876543

Contents

17 ▶ THE MACHINE AGE, 1877–1920 305

18 ▶ THE CITY AND EVERYDAY LIFE, 1877–1920 321

19 ▶ GILDED AGE POLITICS, 1877–1900 345

Maps and Charts

Preface to the Brief Third Edition

This text is a condensation of the very successful Third Edition of *A People and a Nation*. We have preserved all the strengths of the full-length edition—its readability, its comprehensiveness, and, most important, its dynamic blend of social, political, diplomatic, and economic history—in a form approximately half as long. This condensation of the whole story of American history is ideally suited for short courses or courses in which additional readings are assigned.

The brief edition is available in both one-volume and two-volume formats. The two-volume format divides as follows: Volume A contains Chapters 1–15, beginning with a discussion of three cultures—Native American, African, and European—that intersected during the exploration and colonization of the New World and ending with a discussion of the Reconstruction era; Volume B contains Chapters 15–33, beginning its coverage at Reconstruction and extending to the present. The chapter on Reconstruction appears in both volumes to provide greater flexibility in matching a volume to the historical span covered by a specific course.

This brief edition is not a simple revision of the previous brief version: we have ensured that it reflects changes in content and organization incorporated into the full-length Third Edition (see the preface to the full-length edition, which follows). William J. Brophy, who prepared the condensation, collaborated closely with the six authors of the full-length edition to make all deletions with great care. Rather than simply cut entire sections, we took a line-by-line approach to the removal of material, paring down detail. Where two examples were given in the full-length edition, we deleted one; where many statistics were presented, we used a few. Although we abridged or deleted some excerpts from diaries and letters, we have retained many quotations and many individual accounts of everyday life. In the interest of concision, we also combined two chapters from the full-length edition—the chapter on the city from 1877 to 1920 and the chapter on everyday life during the same period.

Three aspects of this brief edition should be noted. First, we have used the occasion of a new edition to update the end-of-chapter bibliographies as well as the chapter that covers the Reagan and Bush years. Second, many pieces in the illustration and map program are new to the brief edition, including four maps, two figures, and numerous photographs. Finally, this edition includes four new full-color inserts that examine leisure in America during the years surrounding 1800, 1850, 1900, and 1950. The one-volume format contains all four inserts; each volume in the two-volume format includes two.

A full set of ancillaries is available with the brief edition. These include a *Study Guide* (in two volumes) by George C. Warren and Cynthia L. Ricketson; *Microstudy Plus,* an interactive computer study guide that gives students feedback on correct and incorrect answers; an *Instructor's Manual with Test Items* by George C. Warren; *Microtest,* a computerized test item file; map transparencies; and *Places in Time: Computer Exercises in Historical Geography,* a new computerized map study program.

Each volume of the *Study Guide* includes an introductory chapter on study techniques as well as learning objectives, a thematic guide, and various kinds of study questions for each chapter in the text. The *Instructor's Manual with Test Items* includes learning objectives, chapter outlines, lecture suggestions and topics, lists of audio-visual resources, and a variety of test questions for each chapter in the text. *Places in Time,* the new map study program designed for the Macintosh computer, uses maps to explore various issues—territory acquisition, population patterns, economic development, and so on—during four time periods—1763, 1860, 1920, and 1980. Each map is paired with a three-part exercise that focuses on map analysis, identification, and discussion. (A for-sale student workbook is also available.)

Though each of us feels answerable for the whole of *A People and a Nation,* we take primary responsibility for particular chapters: Mary Beth Norton, Chapters 1–7; David M. Katzman, Chapters 8–9, 11–12; Paul D. Escott, Chapters 10, 13–15; Howard P. Chudacoff, Chapters 16–20, 23; Thomas G. Paterson, Chapters 21–22, 25, 28, 30, and the material on foreign relations in 32 and 33; and William M. Tuttle, Jr., Chapters 24, 26–27, 29, and 31–33.

Finally, we want to thank the many people who have contributed their thoughts and labors to this work, including the staff at Houghton Mifflin Company.

W.J.B.

Preface to the Full-Length Third Edition

In preparing for the third edition, the authors of *A People and a Nation* met in Boston with Houghton Mifflin editors and art researchers. In several sessions we re-evaluated and discussed every aspect of the book—themes, organization, emphases, coverage, interpretation, scholarship, writing style, and illustrations. In these planning meetings, we analyzed many instructors' reports and profited from their advice. Our goals for this edition were to improve the organization of the book, delineate themes even more sharply, clarify specific passages, and incorporate the best of recent scholarship. Our basic approach to American history as the story of all the people remains the same, and in the third edition we have preserved and strengthened those characteristics of the second edition that students and faculty have found so attractive.

As teachers and students we are always recreating our past, restructuring our memory, rediscovering the personalities and events that have shaped us, inspired us, and bedeviled us. This book is our rediscovery of America's past—its people and the nation they founded and have sustained. This history is sometimes comforting, sometimes disturbing. As with our own personal experiences, it is both triumphant and tragic, filled with injury as well as healing. As a mirror on our lives, it is necessarily revealing—blemishes and all. As memory, it is the way we identify ourselves.

We draw on recent research, authoritative works, and our own teaching experience to offer a comprehensive book that tells the whole story of American history. Politics, government, diplomacy, wars, and economic patterns have been at the core of writing on American history for generations. Into this traditional fabric we weave social history in order to discuss both the public and private spheres of Americans. We investigate the everyday life of the American people, that of the majority of Americans—women—and that of minorities. We explore the many ways Americans have identified and still

Characteristics of the Book

identify themselves: gender, race, class, ethnicity, religion, work, sexual preference, geographic region, politics.

From the ordinary to the exceptional—the factory worker, the slave, the office secretary, the local merchant, the small farmer, the plantation owner, the ward politician, the president's wife, the film celebrity, the scientist, the army general—Americans have personal stories that have intersected with the public policies of their governments. Whether victors or victims, all have been actors in their own right, with feelings, ideas, and aspirations that have fortified them in good times and bad. All are part of the American story; all speak in *A People and a Nation* through excerpts from letters, diaries, oral histories, and other historical materials that we have integrated into this narrative history.

Several questions guided us in this third edition. On the official, or public, side of American history, we emphasize Americans' expectations of their governments and the practices of those local, state, and federal institutions. We look not only at politics but also at the culture of politics. We identify the mood and mentality of an era, searching for what Americans thought about themselves and their public officials. In our discussion of foreign relations, we ask why negotiations failed to prevent wars, why the United States became an expansionist, interventionist, global power, and how the domestic setting influenced diplomacy and vice versa.

Major Themes

In the social and economic areas, we emphasiz patterns of change in the population, geographi and social mobility, and people's adaptation to ne environments. We study the often friction-ridde interactions of people of different color, soc class, national origin, religious affiliation, sectio identity, and gender, and the efforts made, ofte reform movements, to reduce tensions. As well focus on the effects of technological developm on the economy, the worker and the workp and lifestyles.

In the private, everyday life of the family and the home, we pay particular attention to gender roles, childbearing and childrearing, and diet and dress. We ask how Americans have entertained themselves, as participants or spectators, through sports, music, the graphic arts, reading, theater, film, radio, and television. Throughout American history, of course, this private sphere of American life and public policy have interacted and influenced one another.

Students and instructors have commended the book for its discussion of these many topics in clear, concrete language, and they have commented on how enjoyable the book is to read. We have appreciated hearing, too, that we challenged them to think about the meaning of American history, not just to memorize it; to confront one's own interpretations and at the same time to respect the views of others; and to show how the historian's mind works to ask questions and to tease conclusions out of vast amounts of information. We especially welcome these responses because they tell us that we have met our goal: to convey the excitement and fascination we feel as teacher-scholars in recreating and understanding the past.

For this third edition, literally hundreds of changes—major and minor—have been made throughout the book. Among the major changes, the third edition is one chapter

Changes in the Third Edition

shorter than the second edition as a result of the merger of two chapters that covered the Hoover and Roosevelt periods. Now the Great Depression and the New Deal are presented in one [chapter] 1929–1941. In addition, half of the stories [that open the] chapters are new, and throughout we [have added] new examples to illustrate themes.

[A number] of other revisions deserve special [attention. Mary] Beth Norton, who had primary re[sponsibility for] Chapters 1–7, has introduced new [material on the] Spanish and French colonies and [the Indians] who fought in colonial wars and the [Revolution]. She has also revised the dis[cussion of] migration and slavery and of [Indian societ]ies. David M. Katzman, who had [responsibi]lity for Chapters 8–9 and 11–12, [expanded] coverage of the War of 1812, ag[ricultural adjustmen]t to a market-oriented econ-

omy, city and country life, public disorder, Indian removal, abolitionism, and Jacksonian politics. He has reworked the discussion of reform to link it more closely to social and economic changes, religion, and politics. He has also introduced new material on how people experienced the market economy, public space, the growing gender divisions in work, asylums, single women, and Hispanics in Texas and California. Paul D. Escott, who had primary responsibility for Chapters 10 and 13–15, has expanded the treatment of the spread of market relations among southern yeomen and the influence of slavery on national life and, in the chapter on Reconstruction, of black activism in the South, splits among Republicans in Congress, and Supreme Court cases.

Howard P. Chudacoff, who had primary responsibility for Chapters 16–21 and 24, has added new material on Indians and the cultural conflict between their subsistence societies and the market-oriented economy; post–Civil War land policy; child labor; eating habits; and women's history. He has expanded the discussion of immigration and family life, urban reform, the new consumer society, and the origins of feminism. Chapter 20 especially has been reworked to develop the theme of inclusion versus exclusion in politics. Thomas G. Paterson, who had primary responsibility for Chapters 22–23, 26, 29, and 31, and the foreign relations parts of 33 and 34, has sharpened the discussion of expansionism and imperialism and expanded the treatment of the origins of the First World War in Europe and the clash of "systems" before the Second World War. He has added new material on the everyday lives of soldiers, Eisenhower's domestic policies and views on race relations, and the grassroots nature of the civil rights movement. He has also reworked treatment of the world economy, termination policy toward Indians, and the Vietnam War—protest, lessons, and veterans. Paterson served as the coordinating author for *A People and a Nation* and also prepared the Appendix.

William M. Tuttle, Jr., who had primary responsibility for Chapters 25, 27–28, 30, and 32–34, has combined coverage of the Great Depression and the New Deal into one chapter. He has expanded discussion of the Second World War experience of soldiers, McCarthyism, women in higher education, the baby boom, and the 1970s economy. He also reworked treatment of the War on Poverty, the 1968 election, and the fragmentation of the Democratic party. New material on Asian-Americans appears in Chapter 33, and the foreign policy of Jimmy Carter has been relocated there. Finally, Chapter 34 on the Reagan years and the beginnings of the Bush administration has been thoroughly revised; besides carrying the story to the end of the 1980s, the last chapter includes new discussion of Reagan's popularity, AIDS, the Iran-contra scandal, feminization of poverty, and drugs.

We have also revised the "Important Events" lists and in this edition moved them toward the front of each chapter. The end-of-chapter bibliographies have been revised to reflect recent scholarship. The Appendix now includes the Articles of Confederation as well as updated information. New illustrations—many of them in color—have been introduced, and new maps have been added and other maps revised.

To make the book as useful as possible for students and instructors, several learning and teaching aids are available, including a *Study Guide* and *MicroGuide* (a computerized study **Study and** guide), an *Instructor's Manual,* a **Teaching** *Test Items* file, *Diploma III* (test **Aids** generator and class management software), and *Map Transparencies.* The *Study Guide,* which was prepared by George Warren and Cynthia Ricketson of Central Piedmont Community College, includes an introductory chapter on study techniques for history students, learning objectives and a thematic guide for each chapter in the text, exercises on evaluating and using information and on finding the main idea in passages from the text, map exercises where appropriate, new sections on organizing information for some chapters, and test questions (multiple choice and essay) on the content of each chapter. An answer key tells students not only which response is correct but also why each of the other choices is wrong. The *Study Guide* is available as *MicroGuide,* a computerized, tutorial version that also gives students feedback on incorrect as well as correct answers.

The *Instructor's Manual* contains chapter outlines, suggestions for lectures and discussion, and lists of audio-visual resources. The *Test Items* file, also by Professor Warren, offers more than 1,500 new multiple-choice and essay questions and more than 700 identification terms. The test items are available to adopters for IBM and Macintosh computers. In addition, there is a set of 93 full-color *Map Transparencies* available on adoption.

Acknowledgments Many instructors have read and criticized the several drafts of our manuscript. Their suggestions have made this a better book. We heartily thank:

John K. Alexander, *University of Cincinnati*
Sara Alpern, *Texas A & M University*
Dee Andrews, *California State University, Hayward*
Robert Asher, *University of Connecticut*
Edward L. Ayers, *University of Virginia*
Len Bailes, *El Paso Community College*
Delmar L. Beene, *Glendale Community College*
Michael Bellesiles, *Emory University*
Sidney R. Bland, *James Madison University*
Frederick J. Blue, *Youngstown State University*
Bill Cecil-Fronsman, *Washburn University*
William F. Cheek, *San Diego State University*
Michael S. Coray, *University of Nevada, Reno*
Donald T. Critchlow, *University of Notre Dame*
Bruce Dierenfield, *Canisius College*
Charles E. Dickson, *Clark State Community College*
Richard W. Etulain, *University of New Mexico*
Owen E. Farley, Jr., *Pensacola Junior College*
Lacy K. Ford, Jr., *University of South Carolina*
Donald E. Green, *Central State University*
L. Ray Gunn, *University of Utah*
Joseph M. Hawes, *Memphis State University*
Gary R. Hess, *Bowling Green State University*
Joseph P. Hobbs, *North Carolina State University*
Alan M. Kraut, *American University*
Monroe H. Little, Jr., *Indiana University, Purdue University at Indianapolis*
Cathy Matson, *University of Tennessee, Knoxville*
Michael N. McConnell, *University of Alabama, Birmingham*
Melissa L. Meyer, *University of Minnesota*
J. Bruce Nelson, *Dartmouth College*
Allan B. Spetter, *Wright State University*

Kathleen Xidis, *Johnson County Community College*

Charles A. Zappia, *San Diego Mesa College*

We also thank the following for their contributions to this third edition: Daniel H. Usner, Jr., Sharyn Brooks Katzman, Theodore A. Wilson, Eric Foner, Phillip Paludan, Nancy Fisher Chudacoff, Elizabeth Mahan, Ellen C. Garber, Kathryn N. Kretschmer, Samuel Watkins Tuttle, David Thelen, and Ronald Schlundt. We owe our special thanks to the many people at Houghton Mifflin who always set high standards, gave this book excellent guidance and care, and have become our friends.

T.G.P.

A PEOPLE AND A NATION

◆

Brief Edition

"It spread over the people as great destruction," the old man told the priest. "Some it quite covered [with pustules] on all parts—their faces, their heads, their breasts. . . . Great was its destruction. Covered, mantled with pustules, very many people died of them. And very many starved; there was death from hunger."

Four months earlier, Spanish troops led by Hernando Cortés had abandoned their siege of the Aztec capital of Tenochtitlán after failing in their first attempt to gain control of the city. The temples, desecrated during the siege, were cleaned and the images of the gods once again clothed with "godly ornaments"—turquoise mosaic masks and parrot and eagle feathers. But the European smallpox germs that would ensure the Spaniards' eventual triumph were already threatening the Aztecs. By the time the invaders returned, the epidemic described above had fatally weakened Tenochtitlán's inhabitants. Even so, the city held out for months. But in the Aztec year Three House, on the day One Serpent (August 1521), Tenochtitlán finally surrendered. The Spaniards had conquered Mexico, and on the site of the Aztec capital they built what is now Mexico City.

1

THE MEETING OF OLD WORLD AND NEW, 1492–1640

By the time Spanish troops occupied Tenochtitlán, the age of European expansion and colonization was already well under way. Over the next 350 years, Europeans would spread their civilization across the globe. Although they began by primarily seeking trade goods, they would eventually come to dominate native peoples in Asia and Africa, as well as in the New World of the Western Hemisphere. The history of the tiny colonies in North America that became the United States must be seen in this broader context of European exploration and exploitation.

After 1400, European nations sought to improve their positions relative to neighboring countries not only by fighting wars on their own continent, but also by acquiring valuable colonies and trading posts elsewhere in the world. At the same time, the warring tribes and nations of Asia, Africa, and the Americas attempted to use the alien intruders to their own advantage or, failing that, to adapt successfully to the Europeans' presence in their midst. All the participants in the resulting interaction of divergent cultures were indelibly affected. In the Americas and Africa, Europeans emerged politically dominant at the end of this long process of interaction. By no means, however, did they control every aspect of it.

Nowhere is that lack of European control shown more clearly than in the early history of the English settlements in North America. England's attempts to establish colonies on the mainland in the sixteenth century failed completely. In the early seventeenth century, the English succeeded only because neighboring Indians assisted the newcomers. The English colonists prospered by learning to grow such unfamiliar American crops as corn and tobacco and by developing extensive trading relationships with Native Americans. Eventually, they discovered a third source of prosperity—importing enslaved African laborers to work in their fields.

To achieve their first goal—feeding themselves—they had to adopt agricultural techniques suited both to the new crops and to an alien environment. Their second goal—maintaining lucrative trade networks—required them to deal regularly on a more or less equal basis with people who seemed very different from them and who were far more familiar with America than they were. The early history of the United States, in short, can best be understood as a series of complex interactions among different peoples and environments rather than as the simple story of a triumph by only one of those groups—the English colonists.

Societies of the Americas and Africa

In the Christian world, it was the year 1400; by the Muslim calendar, 802; and to the Mayas, who had the most accurate calendar of all, the era started with the date 1 Ahau 18 Ceh. Regardless of the name or reckoning system, the two-hundred-year period that followed changed the course of world history. For thousands of years, human societies had developed largely in isolation from each other. The era that began in the Christian fifteenth century brought the long-standing isolation to an end.

Although the civilizations had developed sepa-rately, they shared several basic characteristics. All had political structures governing their secular affairs, kinship customs regulating their social life, economic systems defining their modes of subsistence, and one or more sets of indigenous religious beliefs. In addition, they all organized their work assignments on the basis of the sexual division of labor. However, these various societies exhibited basic economic differences. Some were nomadic, surviving by moving continually in search of wild animals and edible plants; others combined regular seasonal movements with a limited reliance on agriculture. In many areas, the cultivation of food crops provided most of the essential food supply. Such agricultural civilizations did not have to devote all their energies to subsistence. Instead, they were able to accumulate wealth, produce ornamental objects, and create elaborate rituals and ceremonies.

The differences in cultural traditions became the focal point for the interactions that occurred in the fifteenth century and thereafter among the various societies. Basic similarities were obscured by the shock of discovering that not all people were the same color as oneself, that other folk worshiped other gods, or that some people defined the separate roles of men and women differently from the way one's own society did. Because three major human groups—Native Americans, Africans, and Europeans—met and mingled on the soil of the Western Hemisphere, their relationships can be examined in that context.

Because the earliest known humanlike remains, about 3 million years old, have been found in what is now Ethiopia, it is likely that human beings originated on the continent of Africa. During many millennia, people slowly dispersed to the other continents. Some crossed a now-submerged stretch of land that joined Asia and North America at the site of the Bering Strait. These forerunners of the Native American population, known as Paleo-Indians, arrived in the Americas more than thirty thousand years ago. The Paleo-Indians were nomadic hunters of game and gatherers of wild plants. Over many centuries, they spread through North and South America, probably moving as extended families, or bands. Tribes were

Paleo-Indians

1492	Christopher Columbus reaches Bahama islands	**1619**	First blacks arrive in Virginia
1518–30	Smallpox epidemic decimates Indian population of Central and South America	**1620**	Plymouth colony founded First group of English women arrives in Virginia
1521	Tenochtitlán surrenders to Cortés; Aztec empire falls to Spaniards	**1622**	Powhatan Confederacy attacks Virginia colony
1533	Henry VIII divorces Catherine of Aragon; English Reformation begins	**1625**	Charles I becomes king
		1630	Massachusetts Bay colony founded
1558	Elizabeth I becomes queen	**1634**	Maryland founded
1565	Establishment of St. Augustine	**1635**	Roger Williams expelled from Massachusetts Bay; founds Providence, Rhode Island
1587–90	Sir Walter Raleigh's Roanoke colony fails		
1603	James I becomes king	**1636**	Connecticut founded
1607	Jamestown founded	**1637**	Pequot war Anne Hutchinson expelled from Massachusetts Bay colony
1611	First Virginia tobacco crop		

composed of allied bands. Linguistic and cultural similarities linked tribes into even larger units, described by the name of the language they shared. East of the Mississippi River, the most important linguistic groups were the Algonkians and the Iroquoians, found primarily in the north, and the Muskogeans of the south.

Approximately 5,500 years ago, Indians living in central Mexico were already cultivating food crops. As knowledge of agricultural techniques spread, most Indian groups started to live a more sedentary existence. Some established permanent settlements; others moved several times a year among fixed sites. All the Native American cultures emphasized subsistence. Over the centuries, the North American Indians adapted their once-similar ways of life to specific and very different geographical settings. Thus they created the diversity of cultures

that the Europeans encountered when they first arrived (see map, page 4).

The Indian bands that lived in environments not well suited to agriculture—for example, the Great Basin (now Nevada and Utah)—continued the nomadic lifestyle of their ancestors. Bands of such hunter-gatherers were small because it was difficult to find sufficient food for more than a few people. These bands usually consisted of one or more related families, with men hunting small animals and women gathering seeds and berries. Where large game was more plentiful and food supplies therefore more certain, bands of hunters could be somewhat larger.

In more favorable environments, still larger groups of Indians combined agriculture in varying degrees with gathering, hunting, and fishing. Tribes living near the seacoasts, such as the Chinooks of

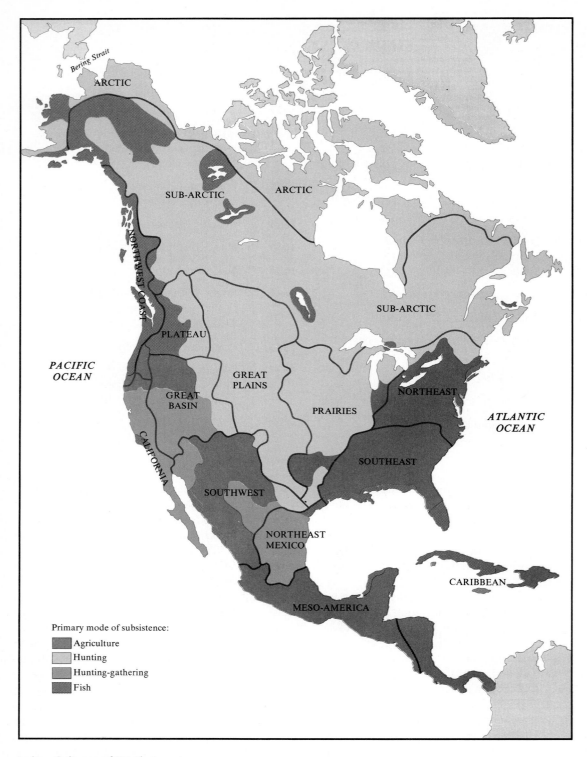

Primary mode of subsistence:

- Agriculture
- Hunting
- Hunting-gathering
- Fish

Indian Cultures of North America

John White, an artist who accompanied the exploratory mission Raleigh sent to America in 1585, sketched Pomeioc, a typical Algonkian village composed of houses made from woven mats stretched over poles, and surrounded by a defensive wooden palisade. *Library of Congress.*

the region that is now Washington and Oregon, consumed large quantities of fish and shellfish, in addition to growing crops and gathering seeds and berries. Tribes of the interior (for example, the Arikaras of the Missouri River valley) hunted large game animals while also cultivating fields of corn, squash, and beans. The Algonkian tribes, which inhabited much of what is now eastern Canada and the northeastern United States, also combined hunting and agriculture.

Societies that relied primarily on hunting large animals, such as deer and buffalo, for their food supply assigned that task to men, allotting food-processing and clothing-production chores to women. Before these nomadic bands acquired horses from the Spaniards, women—occasionally helped by dogs—also carried the family's belongings whenever the band relocated. Such a sexual division of labor was universal among hunting tribes,

Sexual Division of Labor in America

regardless of the linguistic group to which they belonged or their specific location.

By contrast, agricultural Indians differed in how they assigned cultivation of crops to the sexes. In what is now the southwestern United States, the Pueblo peoples defined agricultural labor as men's work. In the East, though, Algonkian, Iroquoian, and Muskogean peoples allocated agricultural chores to women. Among these eastern tribes, men's major assignments were hunting and clearing the land. In all the cultures, women gathered wild foods, prepared the food for consumption or storage, and cared for the children.

The southwestern and eastern agricultural Indians had similar social organizations. They lived in villages—sometimes sizable ones, with a thousand or more inhabitants. Pueblo villages were large, multistory buildings, constructed on terraces along the sides of cliffs or other easily defended sites. Most of the eastern villages were laid out defensively, often being surrounded by wood palisades and ditches. In these cultures, each dwelling housed an extended family defined matrilineally (through a female line of descent). Mothers, their married daughters, and their daughters' husbands and children all lived together. Matrilineal descent did not imply matriarchy, or the wielding of power by women; it was simply a means of reckoning kinship. The families in such dwellings were linked together into clans, again defined by matrilineal ties. On the other hand, nomadic bands of the Great Plains were most often related patrilineally— that is, through the male line.

In the southwestern and eastern cultures, the village supplied the most important political structures, but for the Plains dwellers, bands fulfilled that function. Among Pueblo and Muskogean peoples, the village council was the highest political authority; there was no government at the tribal level. That was also true of the nomadic hunters. The Iroquois, by contrast, had an elaborate political hierarchy, linking villages into tribes and tribes into a widespread confederation. In all the cultures, political power was divided between civil and war leaders, who had authority only so long as they retained the confidence of the people. Consensus rather than autocratic rule characterized the Indians' political systems.

Indian Politics and Religion

The political position of women varied from tribe to tribe. Women were more likely to assume leadership roles among the agricultural peoples than among nomadic hunters. For example, women could become the leaders of certain Algonkian bands, but they never held that position in the hunting tribes of the Great Plains. Iroquois women did not become chiefs, yet tribal matrons exercised political power. Probably the most powerful female chiefs were found in what is now the southeastern United States. In the mid-sixteenth century a female ruler, known as the Lady of Cofitachique, governed a large group of villages in the area that is now western South Carolina. Early English settlers on the Atlantic coast also noted the presence of female chiefs in nearby villages, most of them the wives, sisters, or widows of male leaders.

The Indian tribes varied in their religious beliefs even more than they did in their political systems. Yet they were all polytheistic, worshiping a multitude of gods. One common thread was their integration with nature. Thus the most important rituals related closely to each tribe's chief means of subsistence. The major deities of agricultural Indians and their chief festivals were linked to planting and harvest. On the other hand, the most important gods of hunting tribes were associated with animals, and their major festivals were related to hunting. The tribe's mode of subsistence and women's role in it helped to determine women's potential as religious leaders. Women held the most prominent positions in the agricultural societies (like the Iroquois) in which they were also the chief food producers.

The most highly centralized Indian civilizations on the North American continent inhabited what is now Mexico and Guatemala (Mesoamerica). The major Indian societies that the Spanish explorers encountered in the sixteenth century were the Aztecs and Mayas. The Aztecs, who entered central Mexico in the fourteenth century, were a warlike people who had consolidated their control over the entire region by the time of Cortés's arrival. The Mayas, who lived in what is now Guatemala and Mexico's Yucatan peninsula, were the intellectual leaders of Mesoamerica. They invented systems of writing and mathematics.

Aztecs and Mayas

Thus many different Indian cultures, comprising perhaps 4 to 6 million people, inhabited North America when Europeans arrived. Political systems varied among these cultures, as did means of sustenance. All told, these diverse groups spoke well over one thousand different languages. For obvious reasons, they did not consider themselves as one people.

Fifteenth-century Africa was also home to a variety of cultures adapted to different geographical settings (see map). In the north, along the Mediterranean Sea, lived the Berbers, a Muslim people of Middle Eastern origin. (Muslims are adherents of the Islamic religion, founded by the prophet Mohammed.) On the east coast of Africa, city-states dominated by Muslim merchants engaged in extensive trade with India, the Moluccas (part of modern Indonesia), and China. Through these ports passed a considerable share of the trade between the eastern Mediterranean and Far East;

Africa: Its Peoples

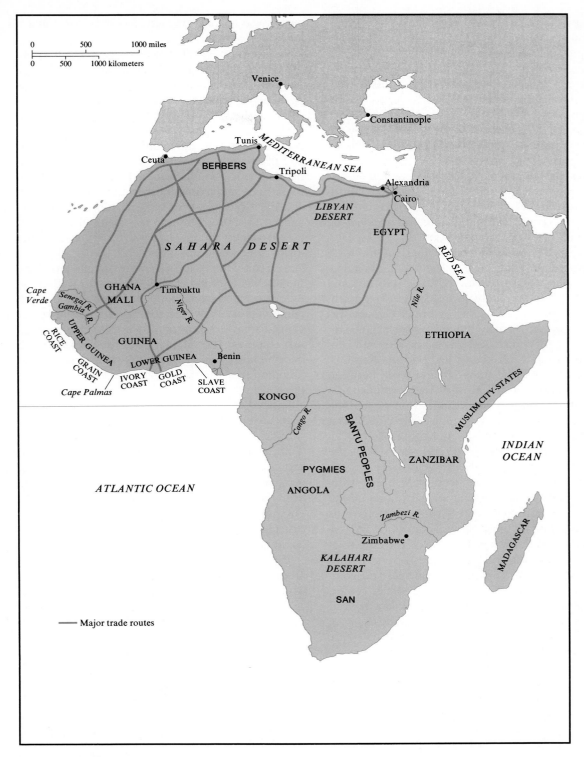

Africa and Its Peoples, ca. 1400

the rest followed the long land route across Central Asia known as the Silk Road.

In the African interior, south of the Mediterranean coast, lie the Sahara and Libyan deserts. Below the deserts, much of the continent is divided between tropical rain forests and grassy plains. People following quite different modes of subsistence lived in a wide belt south of the deserts. Below the Gulf of Guinea (see map), the fertile, forested landscape came to be dominated by Bantu-speaking peoples. About two thousand years ago, they had left their homeland in the region that now constitutes Nigeria and slowly migrated south and east across the continent, assimilating and conquering other ethnic groups as they went.

Most of the unwilling black migrants to North America came from West Africa, which the Europeans called Guinea, a land of tropical forests and small-scale agriculture. The north-

West Africa (Guinea) ern region, or Upper Guinea, was heavily influenced by Islamic culture. As early as the eleventh century, many of its inhabitants had become Muslims; more important, the trans-Saharan trade between Upper Guinea and the Muslim Mediterranean was black Africa's major connection to Europe and the Middle East. In return for salt, dates, and such manufactured goods as silk and cotton cloth, Africans exchanged ivory, gold, and slaves with the northern merchants. (Slaves, who were mostly criminals and wartime captives, were in great demand as household servants in the homes of the Muslim Mediterranean elite.) This commerce was controlled first by the great kingdom of Ghana (ca. 900–1100), and then by its successor, the empire of Mali. Black Africa and Islam intersected at Timbuktu, the city that was the intellectual and commercial hub of the trade. A cosmopolitan center, Timbuktu attracted merchants and scholars from all parts of North Africa and the Mediterranean.

Along the coast of West Africa and in the south, or Lower Guinea, most Africans continued to practice their indigenous religions, which revolved around rituals designed to ensure good harvests. The vast interior kingdoms of Mali and Ghana had no counterparts on the coast. Throughout Lower Guinea, individual villages composed of groups of kin were linked into small, hierarchical kingdoms. At the time of initial contact with Europeans, the region was characterized by decentralized political and social authority.

Just as the political structures varied, so too did the means of subsistence pursued by the different peoples of Guinea. In the northernmost part of Upper Guinea was the so-called Rice Coast, lying just south of the Gambia River. The people who lived there fished and cultivated rice. The Grain Coast, the next region to the south, was thinly populated and not readily accessible from the sea because it had only one good harbor. Its people concentrated on farming and animal husbandry. The Ivory Coast and the Gold Coast, in Lower Guinea, were each named by Europeans for the major trade goods they obtained there. The Gold Coast, comprising thirty little kingdoms known as the Akan States, later formed the basis of the great Asante kingdom. Initially many of the slaves destined for sale in the Americas came from the Akan States. By the eighteenth century, however, the next section of Lower Guinea supplied most of the slaves sold in the English colonies. The Adja kings of the region, which became known as the Slave Coast, encouraged the founding of slave-trading posts and served as middlemen in the trade.

Located east of the Slave Coast and west of the Niger River, the ancient kingdom of Benin was the strongest and most centralized coastal state in Guinea. Like Mali, it was a center of trade for West and North Africa. Those who lived in Benin along the delta of the Niger made much of their living from the water—like the peoples of the Rice Coast. They fished, made salt, and used skillfully constructed dugout canoes to carry on a wide-ranging commerce.

The societies of West Africa, like those of the Americas, assigned different tasks to men and women. In general, the sexes shared agricultural

Sexual Division of Labor in West Africa duties, but in some cultures women bore the primary responsibility for growing crops, whereas in others men assumed that chore. In addition, men hunted, managed livestock, and did most of the fishing. Women were responsible for childcare, food preparation, and cloth manufacture. Everywhere in West Africa women were the primary local traders.

Despite their different modes of subsistence and

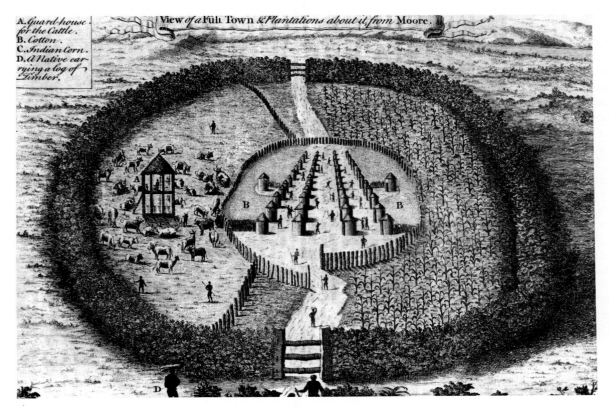

A West African village as drawn by a European observer. A wooden defensive palisade surrounds the circular houses made of woven plant materials. In this the African village resembles Pomeioc, the Indian village pictured on page 5. But note a major difference—a herd of livestock enclosed in a larger fence. Note also that the Africans are growing Indian corn, thus illustrating the exchange of plants between America and Africa (see page 14). *Library of Congress.*

deep political divisions, the peoples of West Africa had similar social systems. In the societies of West Africa, each sex handled its own affairs: just as male political and religious leaders governed the men, so females ruled the women. In the Dahomean kingdom, every male official had his female counterpart; in the Akan States, chiefs inherited their status through the female line, and each chief had a female assistant who supervised women's affairs. Religious beliefs likewise stressed the complementary nature of male and female roles. Both women and men served as heads of the cults and secret societies that directed the spiritual life of the villages.

The West Africans brought to the Americas, then, were agricultural peoples, skilled at tending livestock, hunting, fishing, and manufacturing cloth from plant fibers and animal skins. Both men and women were accustomed to working communally, alongside other members of their own sex. They were also accustomed to a relatively egalitarian relationship between the sexes. In the New World, they entered societies that used their labor but had little respect for their cultural traditions. Of the three peoples whose experience intersected in the Americas, their lives were the most disrupted.

Europe and Its Explorations

After 1400, Europe began to recover from centuries of decline. Northern Europe had long been an intellectual and economic backwater, far outstripped in importance by the states of the Mediterranean, especially the great Italian city-states like Venice and Florence. The cultural flowering known as the Renaissance began in those city-states in the fourteenth century and spread northward. At the same time, the pace of economic activity quickened. Near-constant warfare promoted feelings of nationalism within the combatant countries. All these developments helped to set the stage for extraordinary political and technological change after the middle of the fifteenth century.

Yet in the midst of that change the life of Europe's rural people remained basically untouched for at least another century. European societies were hierarchical, with a few wealthy aristocratic families wielding arbitrary power over the majority of the people. Accordingly, Europe's kingdoms resembled those of Africa or Mesoamerica but differed greatly from the more egalitarian, consensus-based societies found in America north of Mexico. Most Europeans, like most Africans or Native Americans, lived in small agricultural villages. European farmers, or peasants, had separate landholdings, but worked their fields communally. Because fields had to lie fallow every second or third year to regain their fertility, all the villagers shared the work and the crop annually. Otherwise, individual families could not be sure of a regular supply of food.

In European cultures, men did most of the field work, with women helping out chiefly at planting and harvest. At other times, women's duties consisted primarily of childcare and household tasks, including preserving food for the winter, milking cows, and caring for poultry. If a woman's husband was an artisan or storekeeper, she might assist him in business. Since Europeans usually kept domesticated animals to use for meat, hunting had little economic importance in their cultures.

Sexual Division of Labor in Europe

In African or Native American societies, women often played major roles in politics and religion. In Europe, however, men were dominant in all areas of life. A few women from noble families—for example, Queen Elizabeth I of England—achieved status or power, but the vast majority of European women were excluded from positions of political authority. In the Catholic church, men served as bishops and priests; women served as nuns. At the familial level, husbands and fathers expected to control the lives of their wives, children, and servants (a patriarchal system of family governance).

The traditional hierarchical social structure of Europe changed little in the fifteenth century. But the same era witnessed rapid and dynamic political change. In England, Henry VII founded the Tudor dynasty in 1485 and began uniting a previously divided land. In France, the successors of Charles VII unified the kingdom. Most successful of all, at least in the short run, were Ferdinand of Aragon and Isabella of Castile. In 1469, they married and combined their kingdoms, thus creating the foundation of a strongly Catholic Spain. In 1492, they defeated the Muslims, who had lived on the Iberian peninsula for centuries, and expelled all Jews from their domain.

Political and Technological Change

The fifteenth century also brought significant technological change to Europe. Movable type and the printing press, invented in the 1450s, made information more widely and more readily accessible than ever before. Adapting designs from Arab sailors, Europeans created more maneuverable ships, which could sail against the wind. Of key importance was the perfecting of navigational instruments, so that sailors could estimate their position on the high seas. These developments stimulated Europeans' curiosity about fabled lands and spurred them to think about reaching exotic places by ship. The widespread dissemination of Marco Polo's *Travels,* published in 1477, convinced many educated Europeans that they could trade directly with China via oceangoing vessels, instead of relying on the Silk Road or the Muslim merchants of East Africa.

Thus the European explorations of the fifteenth and sixteenth centuries were made possible by technological advances and by the financial might of newly powerful national rulers. The primary motivation for the exploratory voyages was a desire for direct access to the wealth of the East. Another motive was to spread Christianity around the world. The linking of materialist and spiritual goals might seem con-

Motives for Exploration

tradictory today, but fifteenth-century Europeans saw no conflict between the two.

The seafaring Portuguese, whose land was located on the southwestern corner of the continent of Europe, began the age of European expansion in 1415, when they seized control of Ceuta, a Muslim city in North Africa (see map, page 7). Prince Henry the Navigator, son of King John I, realized that vast wealth awaited the first European nation to tap the riches of Africa and Asia directly. Each year he dispatched ships southward along the western coast of Africa, attempting to discover a passage to the East. Not until after Prince Henry's death did Bartholomew Dias round the southern tip of Africa (1488) and Vasco da Gama finally reach India (1498).

Although West African states successfully resisted European penetration of the interior, they allowed the Portuguese to establish trading posts along their coasts. Charging the traders rent and levying duties on the goods they imported, the African chiefdoms benefited considerably from their new access to European manufactures. The Portuguese, who no longer had to rely on the long trans-Saharan trade route, earned immense profits by transporting African goods swiftly to Europe. Among their most valuable cargoes were slaves. When they carried African Muslim prisoners of war back to the Iberian peninsula, the Portuguese introduced the custom of black slavery into Europe.

Spain, with its reinvigorated monarchy, was the next country to sponsor exploratory voyages. Envious of Portuguese successes, Queen Isabella hoped to gain a foothold in Asia for her nation, and so she agreed to finance a voyage by Christopher Columbus, a Genoese sea captain. Like other experienced sailors, Columbus believed the world to be round. But Columbus was regarded as a crackpot because of his estimate of the world's size. He believed that Japan lay only three thousand miles from the southern European coast and therefore concluded that it would be easier to reach the East by sailing west than by making the difficult voyage around the southern tip of Africa.

On August 3, 1492, with three ships under his command—the *Pinta,* the *Niña,* and the *Santa Maria*—Columbus sailed west from the port of Palos in Spain. On October 12, he landed on an island in the Bahamas, which he named San Salvador and claimed for the king and queen of Spain. Because he thought he had reached the Indies, he called the inhabitants of the region Indians.

Columbus made three more voyages to the west, during which he explored most of the major Caribbean islands and sailed along the coasts of Central and South America. Until the day he died in 1506, Columbus continued to believe that he had reached Asia. Even before his death, others knew better. Because the Florentine Amerigo Vespucci, who explored the South American coast in 1499, was the first to publish the idea that a new continent had been discovered, a mapmaker in 1507 labeled the land America. By then, in 1494, Spain, Portugal, and Pope Alexander VI had signed the Treaty of Tordesillas, which confirmed Portugal's dominance in Africa and Brazil, in exchange for Spanish pre-eminence in the rest of the New World.

More than five hundred years earlier, Norse explorers had briefly colonized the area that is now Newfoundland, but the voyages of Columbus and his successors finally brought the Old and New Worlds together. England dispatched John Cabot (1497) to the new lands. Giovanni da Verrazzano (1524), and Jacques Cartier (1534) explored the North American coast for the French. Henry Hudson (1609 and 1610) did likewise for a Dutch company. (See map, page 12.) Although they were primarily searching for the legendary, nonexistent "Northwest Passage" through the Americas, their discoveries prompted European nations to explore the New World further for its own sake.

Only Spain moved immediately to take advantage of the discoveries. On his first voyage, Columbus had established a base on the island of Hispaniola. From there, Spanish explorers fanned out around the Caribbean basin. In the 1520s, Spain's dreams of wealth were realized when Cortés conquered the Aztec empire, killing its ruler, Moctezuma, and seizing a fabulous treasure of gold and silver. And Francisco Pizarro, who explored the western coast of South America, acquired the richest silver mines in the world by conquering and enslaving the Incas in 1535. Other conquistadores, such as Juan Rodriguez Cabrillo

Christopher Columbus

Conquistadores

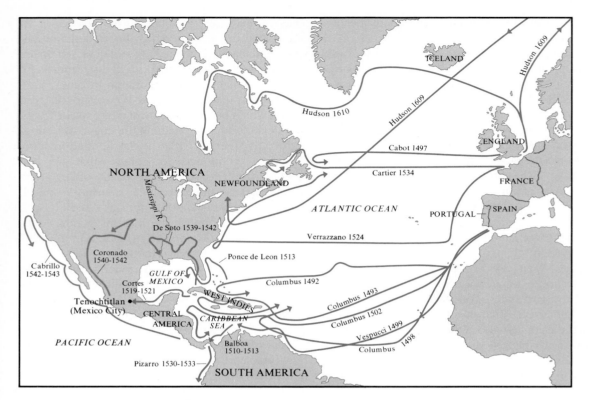

European Explorations in America

(who sailed along the California coast), Hernando de Soto (who discovered the Mississippi River), and Francisco Vásquez de Coronado (who explored the southwestern portion of what is now the United States), found little of value. Still, by 1550, Spain controlled the richest, most extensive empire Europe had known since ancient Rome.

Spain established the model of colonization that other countries later attempted to imitate, a model with three major elements. First, the crown maintained tight control over the colonies, establishing a hierarchical government that allowed little autonomy to New World jurisdictions. Second, most of the colonists sent from Spain were male. They married Indian—and later black—women, thereby creating the racially mixed population that characterizes Latin America to the present day. Third, the colonies' wealth was based on the exploitation of both the native population and slaves imported from Africa. The *encomienda* system, which granted tribute from Indian villages to individual

conquistadores as a reward for their services to the crown, ensured that the conquerors themselves did not have to engage in field work. Laws adopted in 1542 reformed the system, by forbidding Spaniards to enslave Indians. In response, the conquerors began to import Africans in order to increase the labor force under their direct control.

American civilizations suffered under Spanish rule. The Spaniards leveled Indian cities, building cathedrals and monasteries on sites once occupied by Aztec, Incan, and Mayan temples. Some conquistadores sought to erase all vestiges of the great Indian cultures by burning all the written records they found. With traditional ways of life in disarray, devastated by disease, and compelled to labor for their conquerors, many residents of Mesoamerica accepted the Christian religion brought to New Spain by Franciscan and Dominican missionaries. The friars devoted their initial energies to persuading the Indians to move into new towns and build Roman Catholic churches. There the Indians were exposed to European lifestyles, newly elaborated religious rituals, and attempts to assimilate Christianity and pagan beliefs. These conversion efforts met with remarkable success.

The Spanish missionaries who ventured into the territory that is now the United States were less able to win Indian converts, for native cultures there remained largely intact, despite the European invasion. After several failed attempts to colonize the Atlantic coast, the Spanish established St. Augustine, Florida, in 1565. Efforts to Christianize the Indians succeeded only after Franciscans forced them to move to mission towns; even then, many resisted the friars' message. Still, by the end of the sixteenth century, a chain of Spanish missions stretched across what is now northern Florida.

Unlike the Spanish, other European nations did not immediately start to colonize the coasts that their sailors had explored. They were interested in exploiting the natural wealth of the region, not in conquering territories. Their mariners, who came to fish in the rich waters off Newfoundland, learned that they could supplement their profits by exchanging cloth and metal goods like pots and knives for the Indians' beaver pelts. At first the Europeans conducted their trading from ships sailing along the coast, but later they established permanent outposts on the mainland, to centralize and control the traffic in furs. Among the most successful of these were the French trading posts at Quebec (1608) and Montreal (1642), on the St. Lawrence River; the Swedish settlement at Fort Christina (1638) on the Delaware River; and the Dutch forts of New Amsterdam and Fort Orange on the Hudson River, both founded in 1624, which together constituted the colony of New Netherland. All were inhabited primarily by male adventurers, whose chief aim was to send as many pelts as possible home to Europe.

Northern Traders

The northern Europeans' trading activities had a significant effect on native societies. The Europeans' insatiable demand for furs, especially beaver, was matched by the Indians' desire for European goods that could make their lives easier and establish their superiority over neighboring tribes. Some tribes concentrated so completely on trapping for the European market that they abandoned their traditional modes of subsistence. The Abenakis of Maine, for example, became partially dependent on food supplied by their neighbors to the south, the Massachusett tribe, because they devoted most of their energies to catching beaver to sell to French traders. The Massachusetts, in turn, intensified their production of foodstuffs, which they traded to the Abenakis in exchange for European metal tools.

The French in particular devoted considerable attention to converting Native Americans to Christianity. Jesuit missionaries in New France, known to the Indians as Black Robes, tried to persuade Native Americans to live near French settlements and to adopt European lifestyles and Roman Catholicism. When that effort failed, the Jesuits concluded that they could convert their new charges without insisting that the Indians alter their customary modes of existence. So the priests learned Indian languages and traveled to remote regions.

Jesuit Missions in New France

In their pursuit of conversions, the Jesuits sought to undermine the authority of village shamans (religious leaders) and to gain the confidence of leaders who could influence others. The Black Robes cleverly used a variety of weapons to attain the desired end. Seemingly immune to smallpox, they explained epidemics among the Native American peoples as God's punishment for sin. Drawing on a knowledge of European science, they predicted solar and lunar eclipses. Perhaps most important of all, they amazed the Indians by being able to communicate with each other over long distances and periods of time by employing marks on pieces of paper. The Indians' desire to learn how to harness the extraordinary power of literacy was probably the most critical factor in making them receptive to the Jesuits' message. Although the process took many years, the Jesuits slowly gained thousands of converts.

The Europeans' greatest impact on the Americas was unintended. The diseases carried from the Old World to the New by the alien invaders killed millions of Native Americans, who had no immunity to germs that had infested Europe, Asia, and Africa for centuries. The greatest killer was smallpox, which was spread by direct human contact. Other devastating diseases in-

Killer Diseases

cluded influenza and measles. The statistics are staggering. When Columbus landed on Hispaniola in 1492, more than 3 million Indians resided there. Fifty years later, only 500 were still alive.

Even in the north, where smaller Indian populations encountered only a few Europeans, disease ravaged the countryside. A great epidemic, most likely chicken pox, swept through the Indian villages along the coast north of Cape Cod in 1616–1618. The mortality rate may have been as high as 90 percent. Because of this dramatic depopulation of the area, just a few years later English colonists were able to establish settlements virtually unopposed by native peoples.

The Native Americans, though, took a revenge of sorts. They gave the Europeans syphilis, a virulent venereal disease. The first recorded case of the new disease in Europe occurred in Barcelona, Spain, in 1493, shortly after Columbus's return from the Caribbean. Although less likely to cause immediate death than smallpox, syphilis was extremely dangerous and debilitating. It spread quickly, even reaching China by 1505.

Columbus's voyages also brought about a broad mutual transfer of plants and animals between the Old World and the New. Europeans introduced large domesticated mammals to the Americas, and they obtained from the New World a variety of vegetables—particularly corn, beans, squash, and potatoes—that were more nutritious than Old World's wheat and rye. Thus, the diets of both peoples were enriched.

Exchange of Plants and Animals

The exchange of two other commodities significantly influenced European and American civilizations. In America, Europeans encountered tobacco, and smoking and chewing the "Indian weed" became a fad in the Old World. Tobacco cultivation was later to form the basis for the prosperity of the first successful English colonies in North America. But more important than tobacco's influence on Europe was the impact of the horse on some Indian cultures. Horses brought to America by the Spaniards inevitably fell into the hands of Native Americans. They were traded northward through Mexico into the Great Plains, where they eventually changed the lifestyles of some tribes—for example, the Apaches, Blackfeet, Comanches,

and Sioux, who made the horse a focal point of their existence.

England Colonizes the New World

English merchants and political leaders watched enviously as Spain's New World possessions immeasurably enriched that country. In the mid-sixteenth century, English "sea dogs," such as John Hawkins and Sir Francis Drake, began to raid Spanish treasure fleets. Their actions caused friction between the two countries and helped to foment a war that culminated in the defeat of the Spanish armada off the English coast in 1588. With the loss of the armada, Spain's fortunes began to ebb. England started to think about planting its own colonies in the Western Hemisphere, thereby preventing Spain from completely dominating the New World and simultaneously gaining direct access to valuable American commodities.

The first English colonial planners hoped to reproduce Spanish successes by dispatching to America men who would exploit the native peoples for their own and their nation's benefit. In the 1580s, a group including Sir Humphrey Gilbert and Sir Walter Raleigh promoted a scheme to establish

Raleigh's Roanoke Colony

outposts that could trade with the Indians and provide bases for attacks on New Spain. Approving the idea, Queen Elizabeth I authorized Raleigh and Gilbert to colonize North America. Gilbert failed to plant a colony in Newfoundland, and Raleigh was only briefly more successful. In 1587, he sent 117 colonists to the territory he named Virginia (for Elizabeth, the "Virgin Queen"). They established a settlement on Roanoke Island, in what is now North Carolina, but in 1590 a resupply ship could not find them. The colonists had vanished, leaving only the name of a nearby island carved on a tree.

Raleigh's failure ended English efforts at settlement in North America for nearly two decades.

When, in 1606, the English decided to try once more, they again planned colonies that imitated the Spanish model. However, success came only when they abandoned that model and sent large numbers of men and women to set up agriculturally based colonies in the New World. Before discussing the history of those colonies, it is important to examine the two major developments that prompted approximately 200,000 ordinary English men and women to move to North America in the seventeenth century—with encouragement from their government.

The first development was a significant change in English religious practice—a transformation that eventually led large numbers of English dissenters to leave their homeland. In 1533,

English Reformation Henry VIII, wanting a male heir, sought to annul his marriage to his Spanish-born queen, Catherine of Aragon. When the pope refused to approve the annulment, Henry left the Roman Catholic church, founded the Church of England, and, with Parliament's concurrence, proclaimed himself its head. At first the reformed Church of England differed little from Catholicism in its practices. Under Henry's daughter Elizabeth I, however, new currents of religious belief, which had originated on the European continent early in the sixteenth century, dramatically affected the English church.

The leaders of the continental Protestant Reformation were Martin Luther, a German monk, and John Calvin, a French cleric and lawyer. Combating the Catholic doctrine that priests had to serve as intermediaries between lay people and God, they both insisted that each person could interpret the Bible individually. Both Luther and Calvin rejected Catholic rituals, denied the need for an elaborate church hierarchy, and asserted that salvation came through faith alone, rather than, as Catholics believed, through faith and good works. Calvin, though, went further than Luther in stressing God's absolute omnipotence and emphasizing the need for people to submit totally to His will.

Elizabeth I tolerated religious diversity among her subjects as long as they generally acknowledged her authority as head of the Church of England. Accordingly, during her long reign (1558–1603) Calvin's ideas gained influence within the English church. By the late sixteenth century, many English Calvinists believed that the Reformation had not gone far enough. Because these English Calvinists said that they wanted to purify the church, they became known as Puritans.

Elizabeth I's Stuart successors, her cousin James I (1603–1625) and his son Charles I (1625–1649), were less tolerant of Puritans than she. As Scots,

Puritans they also had little respect for the traditions of representative government that had developed in England under the Tudors and their predecessors. The Stuarts insisted that a monarch's power came directly from God and that his subjects had no alternative but to obey him. A king's authority, they argued, was absolute. Both James I and Charles I believed that their authority included the power to enforce religious conformity among their subjects. Thus they authorized the persecution of Puritans, who were challenging many of the most important precepts of the English church. Consequently, in the 1620s and 1630s a number of English Puritans decided to move to America, where they hoped to put their religious beliefs into practice unmolested by the Stuarts or the church hierarchy.

The second major development that led English folk to move to North America was the onset of dramatic social and economic change caused by the

Social Change in England doubling of the English population in the 150-year period after 1530. All those additional people needed food, clothing, and other goods. The competition for goods led to high inflation, coupled with a fall in real wages as the number of workers increased. In these new economic and demographic circumstances, those with sizable landholdings frequently prospered. Others, particularly landless laborers or those with very small amounts of land, fell into unremitting poverty.

Well-to-do English people reacted with alarm to what they saw as the disappearance of traditional ways of life. The streets and highways were filled with steady streams of the landless and the homeless. Officials became obsessed with the problem of maintaining order and came to believe that England was overcrowded. They concluded that colonies established in the New World could siphon off England's "surplus population," thus easing the social strains at home. For similar reasons, many English people decided that they could improve their circumstances by migrating from a small, land-scarce, apparently overpopulated island to a large, land-rich continent.

The initial impetus for establishing what was to become England's first permanent colony in the Western Hemisphere came from a group of merchants and wealthy gentry. In 1606, envisioning the possibility of earning great profits from a New World settlement by finding precious metals and opening new trade routes, they set up a joint-stock company, the Virginia Company, to plant colonies in America.

Joint-stock companies had been developed in England during the sixteenth century as a mechanism for pooling the resources of a large number of small investors. These forerunners of modern corporations were funded through the sale of stock. Until the founding of the Virginia Company, they had been used primarily to finance trading voyages. For that purpose they worked well. No one person risked too much money, and investors usually received quick returns. But joint-stock companies turned out to be a poor way to finance colonies, because the early settlements required enormous amounts of capital and, with rare exceptions, failed to return much immediate profit. Accordingly, the colonies founded by joint-stock companies suffered from a chronic lack of capital.

Joint-Stock Companies

The Virginia Company was no exception to this rule. Chartered by King James I in 1606, the company tried but failed to start a colony in Maine and barely succeeded in planting one in Virginia. In 1607 it dispatched 144 men and boys to North America. Ominously, only 104 of them survived the voyage. In May of that year, they established the settlement called Jamestown. Many of the first migrants were gentlemen unaccustomed to working with their hands and artisans with irrelevant skills like glassmaking. They resisted living "like savages" and retained English dress and casual work habits despite their desperate circum-

Founding of Virginia

stances. Such attitudes, combined with the effects of chronic malnutrition and epidemic disease, took a terrible toll. Only when Captain John Smith, one of the colony's founders, imposed military discipline on the colonists in 1608 was Jamestown saved from collapse. But after Smith's departure, the colony experienced a severe "starving time" (the winter of 1609–1610), during which some colonists resorted to cannibalism. Although later conditions improved somewhat, by 1624 only 1,300 of the approximately 8,000 English migrants to Virginia remained alive.

That the colony survived at all was a tribute not to the English, but rather to a group of six Algonkian tribes known as the Powhatan Confederacy (see map). Powhatan, a powerful figure, was consolidating his authority over some twenty-five other small tribes in the area when the Europeans arrived. Fortunately for the Englishmen, Powhatan viewed them as potential allies. He found the English colony to be a reliable source of such items as steel knives and guns, which gave him a technological advantage over his Indian neighbors. In return, Powhatan's tribes traded corn and other foodstuffs to the starving colonists. The initially cordial relationship soon deteriorated, however. The colonists kidnaped Powhatan's daughter, Pocahontas, held her hostage, and forcibly married her off to one of their number, John Rolfe.

Powhatan Confederacy

Thereafter the relationship between the Jamestown colony and the coastal tribes was an uneasy one. English and Algonkian peoples had much in common: deep religious beliefs, a lifestyle oriented around agriculture, clear political and social hierarchies, and sharply defined sex roles. Yet both the English and the Indians usually focused on their cultural differences, not their similarities. English men saw Indian men as lazy because they hunted (hunting was a sport in English eyes) and did not work in the fields. Indian men thought English men effeminate because they did "women's work" of cultivation. In the same vein, the whites believed that Indian women were oppressed since they did heavy field labor.

Other differences between the two cultures caused serious misunderstandings. Although both

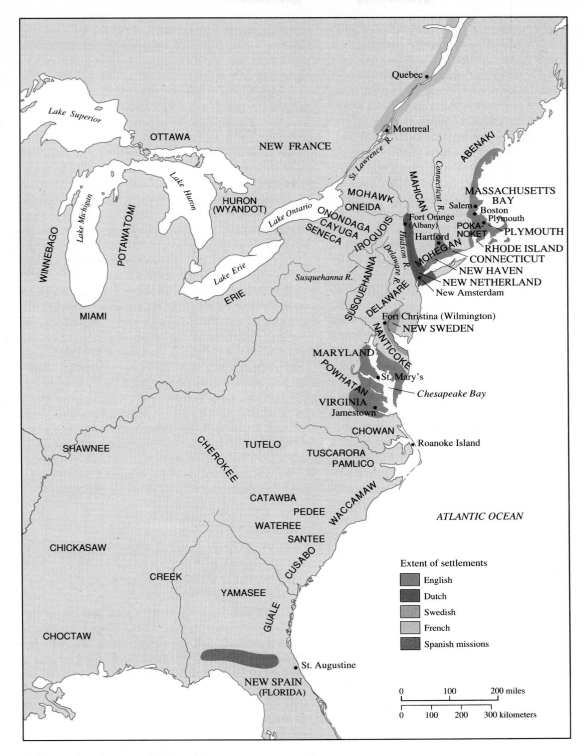

Lake Superior

OTTAWA

NEW FRANCE

Quebec

Montreal

Lake Michigan

Lake Huron

Lake Huron

St. Lawrence R.

ABENAKI

HURON
(WYANDOT)

POTAWATOMI

MOHAWK

ONEIDA

Connecticut R.

MASSACHUSETTS
BAY

WINNEBAGO

Lake Ontario

ONONDAGA

CAYUGA

SENECA

IROQUOIS

MAHICAN

Salem

Boston

Plymouth

Fort Orange
(Albany)

POKA-
NOKET

PLYMOUTH

Lake Erie

Hartford

MOHEGAN

RHODE ISLAND

CONNECTICUT

Lake Erie

ERIE

Susquehanna R.

SUSQUEHANNA

Hudson R.

Delaware R.

NEW HAVEN

NEW NETHERLAND

New Amsterdam

MIAMI

DELAWARE

Fort Christina (Wilmington)

NEW SWEDEN

NANTICOKE

MARYLAND

POWHATAN

St. Mary's

Chesapeake Bay

SHAWNEE

CHEROKEE

TUTELO

VIRGINIA

Jamestown

CHOWAN

Roanoke Island

TUSCARORA

PAMLICO

CATAWBA

PEDEE

WATEREE

WACCAMAW

ATLANTIC OCEAN

CHICKASAW

SANTEE

CUSABO

Extent of settlements

CREEK

YAMASEE

GUALE

English

Dutch

Swedish

French

Spanish missions

CHOCTAW

St. Augustine

NEW SPAIN
(FLORIDA)

0   100   200 miles

0   100   200   300 kilometers

European Settlements and Indian Tribes in America, 1650

societies were hierarchical, the nature of the hierarchies differed considerably.

Algonkian and English Cultural Differences Among the coastal Algonkian tribes, people were not born to positions of leadership, nor were political power and social status necessarily inherited through the male line. The English gentry inherited their position from their fathers, and English leaders tended to rule autocratically. By contrast, the authority of Indian leaders rested on the consent of their fellow tribesmen. Accustomed to the European concept of powerful kings, the English sought such figures within the tribes. Often (for example, when negotiating treaties) they willfully overestimated the ability of chiefs to make independent decisions for their people.

Furthermore, the Indians and the English had very different notions of property ownership. In most eastern tribes, land was held communally by the entire group. It could not be bought or sold absolutely. The English, on the other hand, were accustomed to individual farms and to buying and selling land. In addition, the English refused to accept the validity of Indian claims to traditional hunting territories, insisting that only land intensively cultivated could be regarded as owned or occupied by a tribe.

Above all, the English settlers believed unwaveringly in the superiority of their civilization. They expected the Indians to adopt English customs and to convert to Christianity. They showed little respect for traditional Indian ways of life, especially when they believed their own interests were at stake. That attitude was clearly revealed in the Virginia colony's treatment of the Powhatan Confederacy in subsequent years.

What upset the balance between the English and the Indians was the spread of tobacco cultivation. In tobacco, the settlers and the Virginia Company found the salable commodity for **Tobacco: The Basis of Virginia's Success** which they had been searching. John Rolfe planted the first crop in 1611. In 1620, Virginians exported 40,000 pounds of cured leaves, and by the end of that decade shipments had jumped dramatically, to 1.5 million pounds. The great tobacco boom had begun, fueled by high prices and substantial profits for planters. Although the price of tobacco fluctuated wildly from year to year, it became the foundation of Virginia's prosperity. With an economic base, the colony developed from an all-male outpost into an agricultural settlement inhabited by both men and women (the first group of English women arrived in 1620).

Successful tobacco cultivation required abundant land, since the crop quickly drained soil of nutrients. Planters soon learned that a field could produce only about three crops before it had to lie fallow for several years to regain its fertility. Thus the once-small English settlements began to expand rapidly: eager planters applied to the Virginia Company for large land grants on both sides of the James River and its tributary streams.

Opechancanough, Powhatan's brother and successor, watched the English colonists steadily encroaching on Indian lands and attempting to convert members of the tribes to Christianity. He recognized the danger his brother had overlooked. On March 22, 1622, the confederacy launched coordinated attacks all along the river. By the end of the day, 347 colonists (about one-quarter of the total) lay dead, and only a timely warning from two Christianized Indians saved Jamestown itself from destruction. The colony survived both this war and one waged by Opechancanough in 1644. His defeat in the latter war ended the Powhatan Confederacy's efforts to resist the spread of white settlement.

Life in the Chesapeake: Virginia and Maryland

In 1624, James I revoked the charter and made Virginia a royal colony, ruled by the king through appointed officials. At the same time, though, he allowed the company's "headright" system and a representative assembly to survive. Under the headright system, every new arrival was promised a land grant of fifty acres; those who financed the passage of others received headrights for each. The assembly, called the House of Burgesses, had been created in 1619. It gave the settlers a representative

Advocates of colonization hoped to establish a silk industry in the Chesapeake and published tracts illustrating the production of silk. This one shows a man and a woman working together, but at different tasks. All the attempts to create such industries failed, despite the promoters' efforts. *John Carter Brown Library, Brown University.*

system of government, with considerable local autonomy. The continuance of the House of Burgesses ensured that the political structure of England's American possessions would differ from that of New Spain, which was ruled autocratically by the Spanish monarchs.

By the 1630s, tobacco was firmly established in Virginia as the staple crop and chief source of revenue. It quickly became just as important in the second English colony planted on Chesapeake Bay: Maryland, chartered by the king in 1632 and given to the Calvert family as a personal possession (proprietorship). The Calverts intended the colony to serve as a haven for their fellow Roman Catholics, who were being persecuted in England. Cecilius Calvert, second Lord Bal-

Founding of Maryland

timore, became the first colonizer to offer freedom of religion to all Christian settlers. In that respect Maryland differed from Virginia, where the Church of England was the only officially recognized church. The two Chesapeake colonies, however, resembled each other in most ways. In Maryland, as in Virginia, tobacco planters spread along the riverbanks, establishing isolated farms instead of towns.

The planting, cultivation, and harvesting of tobacco were essentially unskilled tasks that had to be done by hand. When the headright system was adopted in Maryland in 1640, a prospective tobacco planter anywhere in the Chesapeake could simultaneously obtain both land and the labor to work it. Through good management a planter could use his profits to pay for the passage of more workers and thus gain title to more land.

There were two possible sources of laborers for the tobacco farms of the Chesapeake: Africa and England. Nearby tribes could not supply the needed workers, since the region was not densely populated. Beginning in 1619, a few Africans were carried to the Chesapeake. Their numbers were small and their status uncertain; some appear to have been slaves, but others were not. As late as 1670, blacks constituted only about 5 percent of Virginia's population. Chesapeake tobacco planters looked instead to England to supply their labor needs. Workers migrated from England as indentured servants: that is, in return for their passage they contracted to work for planters for periods ranging from four to seven years.

Indentured servants accounted for 75 to 85 percent of the approximately 130,000 English migrants to Virginia and Maryland during the seventeenth

Migrants to the Chesapeake

century. Roughly three-quarters of them were men between the ages of fifteen and twenty-four. Most had been farmers and laborers. They were what their contemporaries called the "common" or "middling" sort. Judging by their youth, though, most had probably not yet established themselves in England.

Many of the servants came from areas of England that were experiencing severe social disruption. Some had already moved several times within England before deciding to migrate to America. For such people the Chesapeake appeared to offer good prospects. Once they had fulfilled the terms of their indentures, servants were promised "freedom dues" consisting of clothes, tools, livestock, casks of corn and tobacco, and sometimes even land.

The migrants' lives were difficult. They typically worked six days a week, ten to fourteen hours a day, in a climate much warmer than they were accustomed to. Their masters could

Conditions of Servitude

discipline or sell them, and they faced severe penalties for running away. Even so, the laws did offer them some protection. For example, their masters were supposed to supply them with sufficient food, clothing, and shelter, and they were not to be beaten excessively. Servants who were especially cruelly treated could turn to the courts for assistance.

Servants and planters alike had to contend with epidemic disease. After surviving a process called "seasoning"—a bout with disease (probably malaria)—immigrants were confronted with dysentery, influenza, typhoid, and recurrences of malaria. As a result, approximately 40 percent of the male servants did not survive long enough to become freedmen.

For those who survived the term of their indentures, however, the opportunities for advancement were real. Until the last decades of the century, former servants were usually able to become independent planters (freeholders) and to live a modest but comfortable existence. Some even assumed such positions of political prominence as justice of the peace or militia officer. But after 1670, tobacco prices fell, good land became expensive, and Maryland dropped its legal requirement that servants receive land as part of their freedom dues. By 1700, the Chesapeake was no longer the land of opportunity it had once been.

Life in the seventeenth-century Chesapeake was hard for everyone. Before being cultivated, fields had to be cleared of trees. Most settlers lived in houses that were little more than shacks, had few material possessions, and consumed a diet based on pork and corn. Indeed, the lack of a nutritious diet magnified the health problems caused by epidemic disease.

The predominance of males, the incidence of servitude, and the high mortality rates combined to produce unusual patterns of family life. Female ser-

Family Life in the Chesapeake

vants normally were not allowed to marry during their terms of indenture, since masters did not want pregnancies to deprive them of workers. Many male ex-servants could not marry at all because there were so few women. On the other hand, nearly every adult free woman in the Chesapeake married, and the many widows commonly remarried within a few months of a husband's death. Yet because their marriages were delayed by servitude or broken by death, Chesapeake women bore only one to three children, in contrast to English women, who normally had at least five.

As a result of the demographic patterns that led to a low rate of natural increase, migrants made up a majority of the Chesapeake population through-

Chesapeake Politics out the seventeenth century. That fact had important implications for politics in Maryland and Virginia. Since migrants dominated the population, they also composed the vast majority of the membership of Virginia's House of Burgesses and Maryland's House of Delegates (established in 1635). In each colony, they also dominated the governor's council, which was simultaneously part of the legislature, the colony's highest court, and executive adviser to the governor.

English-born colonists naturally tended to look to England for solutions to their problems, and migrants frequently relied on English allies to advance their cause. The seventeenth-century leaders of the Chesapeake colonies engaged in bitter and prolonged struggles for power and personal economic advantage. These struggles often thwarted the Virginia and Maryland governments' ability to function effectively. Consequently, the existence of representative institutions failed to lead to political stability. Thus the people of the Chesapeake paid a high price for the area's unusual population patterns.

The Founding of New England

The economic motives that prompted English people to move to the Chesapeake colonies also drew men and women to New England. But Puritans had organized the New England colonies. Moreover, the northern landscape and climate were more conducive to diversified small farms than to large production units yielding staple crops. For both these reasons, the northern settlements turned out very differently from those in the South.

Religion was a constant presence in the lives of pious Puritans. As followers of John Calvin, they believed that an omnipotent God predestined souls to heaven or hell before birth and that Christians could do nothing to change their ultimate fate. One of their primary duties as Christians, though, was to assess the state of their own

Puritan Beliefs

souls. Thus they devoted themselves to self-examination and Bible study. Yet even the most pious could never be absolutely certain that they were numbered among the saved. Consequently, devout Puritans were filled with anxiety about their spiritual state.

Some Puritans (called Congregationalists) wanted to reform the Church of England rather than abandon it. Another group, known as Separatists, believed the Church of England to be so corrupt that it could not be salvaged. The only way to purify it, they believed, was to start anew, establishing their own religious bodies, with membership restricted to the saved, as nearly as they could be identified.

In 1620, some Separatists, many of whom had earlier migrated to Holland in quest of the right to practice their religion freely, obtained permission to settle in part of the territory controlled by the Virginia Company. In September 1620, more than one hundred people, only thirty of them Separatists, set sail from Plymouth, England, on the *Mayflower*. Two months later they landed in America, but farther north than they had intended. Because of the lateness of the season, they decided to stay where they were. They established their colony on a fine harbor and named it after the city from which they had sailed.

Founding of Plymouth

Even before they landed, the Pilgrims had to surmount their first challenge from the "strangers," or non-Puritans, who had sailed with them. Because they landed outside the jurisdiction of the Virginia Company, some of the strangers questioned the authority of the colony's leaders. In response, the Mayflower Compact, signed while everyone was still on board the ship, established a "Civil Body Politic" and a rudimentary legal authority for the colony. Later, after more towns had been founded and the population had increased, Plymouth created an assembly to which the landowning male settlers elected representatives.

A second challenge facing the Pilgrims in 1620 and 1621 was, quite simply, survival. Like the Jamestown settlers before them, they were poorly prepared to survive in the new environment. Their difficulties were compounded by the season of their arrival, for they barely had time to build shelters before winter descended on them. Only half of the *Mayflower*'s passengers were still alive by spring. But, again like the Virginians, the Pilgrims benefited from the political circumstances of their Indian neighbors.

The Pokanokets (also called Wampanoags), who controlled the area in which the Pilgrims had settled, had suffered terrible losses from an epidemic in 1616. To protect themselves from the powerful Narragansett Indians of the southern New England coast, the Pokanokets decided to ally themselves with the newcomers. In the spring of 1621, their leader, Massasoit, signed a treaty with the Pilgrims, and, during the colony's first difficult years, the Pokanokets supplied the English with essential foodstuffs. The settlers were also assisted by Squanto, an Indian whose village had been wiped out by the epidemic. Because he had been captured by traders and held prisoner in England for several years, Squanto spoke English. He served as the Pilgrims' interpreter, as well as their major source of information about the unfamiliar environment.

Before the 1620s had ended, a group of Congregationalists launched the colonial enterprise that would come to dominate New England. The

Founding of Massachusetts Bay

event that stimulated their interest in the New World was the accession of Charles I to the throne in 1625. Charles was more hostile to Puritan beliefs than his father had been. Consequently, some non-Separatists began to think of settling in America. A group of Congregationalist merchants sent out a body of settlers to Cape Ann, north of Cape Cod, in 1628. The following year, the merchants obtained a royal charter, constituting themselves as the Massachusetts Bay Company.

The new company quickly attracted the attention of Puritans of the "middling sort" who were becoming increasingly convinced that they could no longer practice their religion freely in England. Although still committed to the goal of reforming the Church of England, they came to believe that they should pursue it in America rather than at home. In a dramatic move, the Congregationalist merchants boldly decided to transfer the headquarters of the Massachusetts Bay Company to New England. The settlers would then be answerable to no one in the mother country and would be able to handle their affairs as they pleased.

The most important recruit to the new venture was John Winthrop, a pious but practical landed gentleman from Suffolk. In October 1629, the members of the Massachusetts Bay Company elected the forty-one-year-old Winthrop as their governor. With the exception of a few isolated years, he served in that post until his death in 1649. It thus fell to Winthrop to organize the initial segment of the great Puritan migration to America. In 1630, more than one thousand English men and women settled in Massachusetts—most of them in Boston, which soon became the largest town in British North America. By 1643, nearly twenty thousand compatriots had followed them.

Governor John Winthrop

Winthrop's was a transcendent vision. The society he foresaw in Puritan America was a true commonwealth, a community in which each person put the good of the whole ahead of his or her private concerns. In America, he asserted, "we shall build a city upon a hill, the eyes of all people are upon us." People in this "city upon a hill" were to live according to the precepts of Christian charity, loving and aiding friends and enemies alike. Of course, such an ideal was beyond human reach.

The Puritans' communal ideal was expressed chiefly in the doctrine of the covenant. They believed God had made a covenant—that is an agreement or contract—with them when they were chosen for the special mission to America. In turn, they covenanted with each other, promising to work together toward their goals. The founders of churches and towns in the new land often drafted formal documents setting forth the principles on which such institutions would be based. The same was true of the colonial governments of New England.

Ideal of the Covenant

The leaders of Massachusetts Bay likewise transformed their original joint-stock company charter into the foundation for a covenanted community based on mutual consent. Under pressure from the settlers, they gradually changed the General Court, officially merely the company's governing body, into a colonial legislature. They also opened the status of freeman, or voting member of the company, to all property-owning adult male church members residing in Massachusetts. Less than two decades after the first large group of Puritans had arrived in Massachusetts Bay, the colony had a functioning system of self-government composed of a governor and a two-house legislature. The General Court also established a judicial system modeled on England's.

The colony's method of distributing land helped to further the communal ideal. Groups of families, which often came from the same region of England,

New England Towns applied together to the General Court for grants of land to establish towns. The men who received the original town grant had the sole authority to determine how the land would be distributed. Understandably, they copied the villages from which they had come. First they laid out town lots for houses and a church. Then they gave each family parcels of land scattered around the town center: pasture here, a woodlot there, an arable field elsewhere. They also reserved the best and largest plots for the most distinguished among them (usually including the minister); people who had been low on the social scale in England were given much smaller and less desirable allotments. Even when migrants began to move beyond the territorial limits of the Bay Colony into Connecticut (1636), New Haven (1638), and New Hampshire (1638), the same pattern of town land grants was maintained.

Thus New England settlements initially tended to be more compact than those of the Chesapeake. Town centers grew up quickly, developing in three distinctly different ways. Some, chiefly isolated agricultural settlements in the interior, tried to sustain Winthrop's vision of harmonious community life based on diversified family farms. A second group, the coastal towns like Boston and Salem, became bustling seaports. The third category, in the Connecticut River valley, developed as commercialized agricultural towns.

The migration to the Connecticut valley ended the Puritans' relative freedom from clashes with neighboring Indians. The first English settlers in the valley moved there from Newtown (Cambridge), under the direction of their minister, Thomas Hooker. Connecticut was fertile, though remote from the other English towns, and the wide river promised ready access to the ocean. The site had just one problem: it fell within the territory controlled by the Pequot Indians.

The Pequots' dominance was based on their role as primary middlemen in the trade between New England Indians and the Dutch in New Netherland.

Pequot War The arrival of English settlers signaled the end of Pequot power over the regional trading networks, for their tributary bands could now trade directly with Europeans. Clashes between the Pequots and the English began even before the Connecticut valley settlements were established, but their founding tipped the balance toward war. After trying without success to galvanize other tribes to resist English expansion into the interior, the Pequots (after an English raid on their villages) attacked the new town of Wethersfield in April 1637, killing nine and capturing two of the colonists. In retaliation, a Massachusetts Bay expedition the following month attacked and burned the main Pequot town on the Mystic River. The Englishmen and their Narragansett Indian allies slaughtered at least four hundred people, mostly women and children. The few surviving Pequots were captured and enslaved.

Just five years later, the Narragansett leader Miantonomi realized that the Pequots had been correct in assessing the danger posed by the Puritan settlements. Miantonomi tried but failed to forge a pan-Indian alliance. He was killed in 1643 by other Indians, acting at the English colonists' behest.

For the next thirty years, the New England Indians tried to accommodate themselves to the spread of white settlement. They traded with the whites and sometimes worked for them, but for the most part they resisted acculturation or incorporation into English society. The Indians clung to their traditional farming methods, which did not employ plows, fertilizer, or fences; and women rather than men continued as the chief cultivators. The one European practice they did adopt was keeping livestock, for in the absence of game, domesticated animals provided excellent alternative sources of meat.

Although the official seal of Massachusetts Bay showed an Indian crying, "Come over and help us," most whites showed little interest in converting the Indians to Christianity. Only a few Puritan clerics, most notably John Eliot, seriously undertook missionary activities. Eliot insisted that converts reside in towns, farm the land in English fashion, assume

English names, wear European-style clothing and shoes, cut their hair, and stop observing a wide range of native customs. Since Eliot was demanding a total cultural transformation from his adherents, he understandably met with little success. At the peak of his efforts, only 1,100 Indians lived in the fourteen "Praying Towns" he established.

The Jesuits' successful missions in New France contrasted sharply with the Puritans' failure to convert many Indians. Three factors account for the

Puritan and Jesuit Missions Compared

difference. First, the small French outposts along the St. Lawrence did not substantially encroach on Indian lands and therefore did not alienate potential converts. Second, Catholicism, unlike Puritanism, employed attractive rituals, instructed converts that through good works they could help earn their own salvation, and supplied Indian women with inspiring role models—the Virgin Mary and the communities of nuns who resided in Montreal and Quebec. Third, and perhaps most important, the Jesuits understood that Christian beliefs were to some extent compatible with native culture. Quite simply, Catholics were willing to accept converts without requiring them to wholly embrace European lifestyles; Puritans were not.

But what attracted Indians to these alien religious ideas? One primary motive must have been a desire to use the Europeans' religion as a means of coping with the dramatic changes the intruders had wrought on Indian society. The combination of disease, alcohol, new trading patterns, and the loss of territory disrupted customary ways of life to an unprecedented extent. Many Indians must have concluded that the Europeans' own ideas could provide the key to survival in the new circumstances.

Life in New England

White settlers in New England adopted lifestyles that differed considerably from the lifestyles of both their Indian neighbors and their counterparts in the Chesapeake. Unlike the mobile Algonkians, English people lived year-round in the same loca-tion. Unlike the residents of the Chesapeake, New Englanders constructed sturdy, permanent dwellings intended to last for many years. They used the same fields again and again, believing it was less arduous to employ fertilizer than to clear new fields every few years. Furthermore, they had to fence their croplands to prevent them from being overrun by the cattle, sheep, and hogs that were their chief sources of meat. When New Englanders began to spread out over the countryside, it was often to find additional pasturage for their livestock.

In contrast to the Chesapeake migrants, Puritans commonly moved to America in family groups. The age range of New Englanders was wide and the

New England and the Chesapeake Compared

sexes were more balanced numerically, so the population could immediately begin to reproduce itself. Moreover, New England's climate was much healthier than the Chesapeake's. Indeed, New England proved to be even healthier than the mother country. Though adult male migrants to the Chesapeake lost about ten years from their English life expectancy, their Massachusetts counterparts gained about ten years.

Consequently, while Chesapeake population patterns gave rise to families that were few in number, small in size, and transitory, the demographic characteristics of New England made families there numerous, large, and long-lived. In New England, most men were able to marry; migrant women married young (at the age of twenty, on the average); and marriages lasted longer and produced more children, who were more likely to live to maturity. If seventeenth-century Chesapeake women could expect to rear one to three healthy children, New England women could anticipate raising five to seven.

The nature of the population had other major implications for family life. New England in effect created grandparents, since in England people

Family Life in New England

rarely lived long enough to know their children's children. And whereas early southern parents normally died before their children married, northern parents exercised a good deal of control over their adult children. Young men could not marry without acreage to cultivate, and because of the communal land-grant system, they were dependent on their fathers to supply them with that land. Daughters, too, needed the dowry of household goods that their parents would give them when they married. Yet parents needed their children's labor and were often reluctant to see them marry and start their own households. These needs at times led to conflict between the generations. On the whole, though, children seem to have obeyed their parents' wishes, for they had few alternatives.

Another important difference lay in the influence of religion on New Englanders' lives. The governments of Massachusetts Bay, Plymouth, Connecticut, and the other early northern colonies were all controlled by Puritans. Congregationalism was the only officially recognized religion; members of other sects had no freedom of worship except in Rhode Island. Some non-Puritans appear to have voted in town meetings, but with the exception of Connecticut, church membership was a prerequisite for voting in colony elections. All households were taxed to build meetinghouses and pay ministers' salaries. Massachusetts's Body of Laws and Liberties (1641) incorporated regulations drawn from the Old Testament into the legal code of the colony.

In the New England colonies, then, church and state were intertwined. Puritans objected to secular interference in religious affairs but at the same time expected the church to influence the conduct of politics. They also believed that the state had an obligation to support and protect the one true church—theirs. As a result, though they came to America seeking freedom of worship, they saw no contradiction in refusing to grant that right to others. Indeed, the two most significant divisions in early Massachusetts were caused by Massachusetts Bay's unwillingness to tolerate religious dissent.

Roger Williams, a Separatist, migrated to Massachusetts Bay in 1631. Williams soon began to express the eccentric ideas that the king of England had no right to give away land belonging to the Indians, that church and state should be kept entirely separate, and that Puritans should not impose their religious beliefs on others. Ban-

Roger Williams

ished from Massachusetts in 1635, Williams founded the town of Providence on Narragansett Bay. Because of his beliefs, Providence and other towns in what became the colony of Rhode Island adopted a policy of tolerating all religions, including Judaism.

The other dissenter, and an even greater challenge to Massachusetts Bay orthodoxy, was Anne Marbury Hutchinson. She was a follower of John Cotton, a minister who stressed the covenant of grace, or God's free gift of salvation to unworthy humans. In 1636, Hutchinson began holding women's meetings in her home to discuss Cotton's sermons. Soon men also started to attend. Hutchinson emphasized the covenant of grace more than did Cotton himself, and she even adopted the belief that the elect could communicate directly with God and be assured of salvation. Because her ideas offered Puritans the certainty of salvation instead of a state of constant tension, they had an immense appeal.

Anne Hutchinson

Hutchinson's ideas were a dangerous threat to Puritan orthodoxy, so in November 1637 she was brought before the General Court of Massachusetts, charged with defaming the colony's ministers. For two days she defended herself cleverly against her accusers. Finally, in an unguarded moment, Hutchinson declared that God had spoken to her "by an immediate revelation." That assertion assured her banishment to Rhode Island. Equally significant was her challenge to traditional gender roles. Her judges were almost as outraged by her "masculine" behavior as by her heretical beliefs. As one judge told her bluntly, "You have stept out of your place, you have rather bine a Husband than a Wife and a preacher than a Hearer; and a Magistrate than a Subject."

The New England authorities' reaction to Anne Hutchinson reveals the depth of their adherence to European gender-role concepts. To them, an orderly society required the submission of wives to husbands, as well as the obedience of subjects to rulers. English people intended to change many aspects of their lives by colonizing North America, but not the sexual division of labor or the assumption of male superiority.

In 1630, John Winthrop wrote to his wife, Margaret, who was still in England, "my deare wife, we are heer in a paradise." He was, of course, exaggerating. Yet America was a place where English men and women could free themselves from Stuart persecution or attempt to better their economic circumstances. Many died, but those who lived laid the foundation for subsequent colonial prosperity. That they did so by dispossessing the Indians bothered few besides Roger Williams. By the middle of the seventeenth century, Europeans had unquestionably come to North America to stay, a fact that signaled major changes for the peoples of both the Old and the New World.

European political rivalries, once confined to Europe, now spread around the globe, as the competing nations of England, Spain, Portugal, France, and the Netherlands vied for control of the peoples and resources of Asia, Africa, and the Americas. France and the Netherlands earned their profits from Indian trade rather than imitating the Spanish example and engaging in wars of conquest. Although they, too, at first relied on trade, the English colonies soon took another form altogether when so many English people of the "common sort" decided to migrate to North America. In the years to come, the European rivalries would grow even fiercer, and residents of the Americas—whites, Indians, and blacks alike—would inevitably be drawn into them. Those rivalries would continue to affect Americans of all races until after France and England fought—in the mid-eighteenth century—the greatest war yet known and the thirteen Anglo-American colonies won their independence.

Suggestions for Further Reading

General

Charles M. Andrews, *The Colonial Period of American History: The Settlements,* 3 vols. (1934–1937); Leslie Bethel, ed., *The Cambridge History of Latin America,* vol. 2: *Colonial Latin America* (1984); D. W. Meinig, *Atlantic America, 1492–1800* (1986); Gary B. Nash, *Red, White, and Black: The Peoples of Early America,* 2nd ed. (1982); Eric Wolf, *Europe and the People Without History* (1982).

Indians

Harold E. Driver, *Indians of North America,* 2nd ed. (1969); Brian Fagan, *The Great Journey: The Peopling of Ancient America* (1987); Alvin Josephy, Jr., *The Indian Heritage of America* (1968); Alice B. Kehoe, *North American Indians* (1981); Smithsonian Institution, *Handbook of North American Indians,* 8: California (1978), 9, 10: *The Southwest* (1979, 1983), 15: *The Northeast* (1978).

Africa

Philip Curtin et al., *African History* (1978); J. D. Fage, *A History of Africa* (1978); Robert July, *Precolonial Africa* (1975); Richard Olaniyan, *African History and Culture* (1982); Roland Oliver, ed., *The Cambridge History of Africa,* vol. 3: c. 1050–c. 1600 (1977).

England

Kenneth Andrews, *Trade, Plunder and Settlement: Maritime Enterprise and the Genesis of the British Empire, 1480–1630* (1984); Peter Laslett, *The World We Have Lost,* 3rd ed. (1984); Wallace Notestein, *The English People on the Eve of Colonization, 1603–1630* (1954); Michael Walzer, *The Revolution of the Saints* (1965); Keith Wrightson, *English Society, 1580–1680* (1982).

Exploration and Discovery

Alfred W. Crosby, Jr., *The Columbian Exchange: Biological and Cultural Consequences of 1492* (1972); Samuel Eliot Morison, *The European Discovery of America: The Southern Voyages, A.D. 1492–1616* (1974); *The Northern Voyages, A.D. 1500–1600* (1971); J. H. Parry, *The Age of Reconnaissance* (1963); David B. Quinn, *North America from Earliest Discovery to First Settlements* (1977); John Super, *Food, Conquest, and Colonization in Sixteenth Century Spanish America* (1988).

Early Contact Between Whites and Indians

James Axtell, *The Invasion Within: The Contest of Cultures in Colonial North America* (1985); James Bradley, *Evolution of the Onondaga Iroquois* (1987); William Cronon, *Changes in the Land: Indians, Colonists, and the Ecology of New England* (1983); Francis Jennings, *The Invasion of America: Indians, Colonialism, and the Cant of Conquest* (1975); Karen O. Kupperman, *Roanoke, The Abandoned Colony* (1984); Neal Salisbury, *Manitou and Providence: Indians, Europeans, and the Making of New England, 1500–1643* (1982); Tzvetan Todorov, *The Conquest of America* (1984); Alden T. Vaughan, *The New England Frontier: Puritans and Indians 1621–1675 ,* rev. ed. (1979).

Chapter 1: The Meeting of Old World and New, 1492–1640

Chesapeake

Lois Green Carr and Lorena Walsh, "The Planter's Wife: The Experience of White Women in Seventeenth-Century Maryland," *William and Mary Quarterly,* 3rd ser., 34 (1977), 542–571; Wesley Frank Craven, *The Southern Colonies in the Seventeenth Century, 1607–1689* (1949); David Galenson, *White Servitude in Colonial America: An Economic Analysis* (1981); Ivor Noel Hume, *Martin's Hundred: The Discovery of a Lost Colonial Virginia Settlement* (1979); Gloria L. Main, *Tobacco Colony: Life in Early Maryland, 1650–1720* (1983); Edmund S. Morgan, *American Slavery, American Freedom: The Ordeal of Colonial Virginia* (1975); Darrett Rutman and Anita Rutman, *A Place in Time: Middlesex County, Virginia, 1650–1750* (1984); Thad W. Tate and David L. Ammerman, eds., *The Chesapeake in the Seventeenth Century* (1979); Alden T. Vaughan, *American Genesis: Captain John Smith and the Founding of Virginia* (1975).

New England

Ben Barker-Benfield, "Anne Hutchinson and the Puritan Attitude Toward Women," *Feminist Studies,* 1 (1972), 65–96; Charles Cohen, *God's Caress: The Psychology of Puritan Religious Experience* (1986); David Cressy, *Coming Over: Migration and Communication Between England and New England in the Seventeenth Century* (1987); John Demos, *A Little Commonwealth: Family Life in Plymouth Colony* (1970); Philip J. Greven, Jr., *Four Generations: Population, Land, and Family in Colonial Andover, Massachusetts* (1970); Philip Gura, *A Glimpse of Sion's Glory: Puritan Radicalism in New England, 1620–1660* (1984); Stephen Innes, *Labor in a New Land: Economy and Society in Seventeenth-Century Springfield* (1983); Lyle Koehler, *A Search for Power: The "Weaker Sex" in Seventeenth-Century New England* (1980); Kenneth A. Lockridge, *A New England Town: The First Hundred Years* (Dedham, Massachusetts, 1636–1736) (1970); Edmund S. Morgan, *The Puritan Family,* rev. ed. (1966); Roger Thompson, *Sex in Middlesex: Popular Mores in a Massachusetts County, 1649–1699* (1986).

Olaudah Equiano was eleven years old in 1756 when black raiders seeking slaves for white traders kidnapped him from his village in what is now Nigeria. As a captive, he was passed from master to master, finally arriving at the coast, where an English slave ship lay at anchor. Terrified by the light complexions, long hair, and strange language of the sailors, he was afraid that "I had gotten into a world of bad spirits and that they were going to kill me." Equiano was placed below decks, where "with the loathsomeness of the stench and crying together, I became so sick and low that I was not able to eat, nor had I the least desire to taste anything."

After a long voyage, during which many of the Africans died of disease, the ship arrived in the West Indies. Equiano was not purchased in the West Indies because planters there preferred older, stronger slaves. Instead, he was carried to Virginia, where his new owner separated him from the other Africans and put him to work weeding and clearing rocks from the fields. "I was now exceedingly miserable and thought myself worse off than any of the rest of my companions," Equiano remembered, "for they could talk to each other, but I had no person to speak to that I could understand. In this state I was constantly grieving and pining and wishing for death rather than anything else."

2

AMERICAN SOCIETY TAKES SHAPE, 1640–1720

But Equiano did not remain in Virginia for long. Bought by a sea captain, Olaudah Equiano eventually became an experienced sailor. He learned to read and write English, purchased his freedom at the age of twenty-one, and later actively supported the English antislavery movement. Until he was purchased by the sailor, Equiano's experiences differed very little from those of other Africans who were forced into slavery in the English colonies of the New World. Like him, many were sold by black slavers and taken first to the West Indies, then to North America.

Equiano's life story, which he published in 1789, illustrates one of the major developments in colonial life during the years after 1640: the importation of more than 200,000 unwilling, captive Africans into North America. The introduction of the institution of slavery and the arrival of large numbers of West Africans reshaped colonial society. Indeed, the geographic patterns of that migration still influence the United States.

The other important trends in colonial life between 1640 and 1720 involved the English colonists' relationships with their mother country and with their American neighbors. Dramatic events in England during this period affected its New World colonies. The Puritan victory in the civil war, which began in 1642, the restoration of the Stuart monarchy in 1660, and finally the Glorious Revolution of 1688–1689 indelibly affected the residents of England's American possessions. By the end of the seventeenth century, the New World colonies were no longer isolated outposts but an integral part of a far-flung mercantile empire. Further, as the Anglo-American settlements expanded, they came into violent conflict not only with powerful Indian tribes, but also with the Dutch, French, and Spanish. By 1720, war was an all-too-frequent feature of American life.

The English Civil War, the Stuart Restoration, and the American Colonies

In 1640, Charles I, who had ruled England arbitrarily for the previous eleven years, called Parliament into session because he needed money and wanted to propose new taxes. But Parliament passed laws limiting his authority, and tensions heightened. In 1642, civil war broke out between royalists and the supporters of Parliament. Four years later, Parliament triumphed, and Charles I was executed in 1649. Oliver Cromwell, the leader of the parliamentary army, then assumed control of the government, taking the title of Lord Protector in 1653. After Cromwell's death in 1658, Parliament decided to restore the monarchy if Charles I's son and heir would agree to certain restrictions on his authority. In 1660, Charles II ascended the throne, having promised to seek Parliament's consent for any new taxes and to support the Church of England. Thus ended the tumultuous chapter in English history known as the Interregnum (Latin for "between reigns"), or the Commonwealth, period.

The civil war, the Interregnum, and the reign of Charles II (1660–1685) had major significance for the English colonies in the Americas. During the Civil War and the Commonwealth period, Puritans dominated the English government. Therefore the migration to New England largely ceased. During the subsequent reign of Charles II, six of the thirteen colonies that eventually would form the American nation were either founded or came under English rule: New York, New Jersey, Pennsylvania (including Delaware), and North and South Carolina (see map, page 30). All were proprietorships granted in their entirety to one man or a group of men who held title to the soil and controlled the government. Charles II gave these vast American holdings as rewards to men who had supported him during his years of exile.

One of the first to benefit was Charles's younger brother James, the duke of York. In March 1664, acting as though the Dutch colony of New Netherland did not exist, Charles II gave James the region between the Connecticut and Delaware rivers, including the Hudson valley and Long Island. James immediately organized an invasion fleet. In late August the vessels anchored off Manhattan Island (New Amsterdam) and demanded New Netherland's surrender. The colony's director-general, Peter Stuyvesant, complied without offering resistance.

Thus England acquired a tiny but heterogeneous possession. Though founded in 1624, New Netherland had remained small in comparison with its English neighbors. Holland, the world's dominant commercial power in the first half of the seventeenth century, was primarily interested in trade rather than colonization. As a trading post of the Dutch West India Company, whose chief economic interests lay elsewhere, New Netherland was considered relatively unimportant. Furthermore, the Dutch did not experience the economic, demographic, and religious pressures that caused English people to move to the New World, and so migration was sparse. Even a company policy of 1629 that offered a large land grant, or patroonship, to anyone who would bring fifty settlers to the province failed to attract takers. In the mid-1660s,

New Netherland Becomes New York

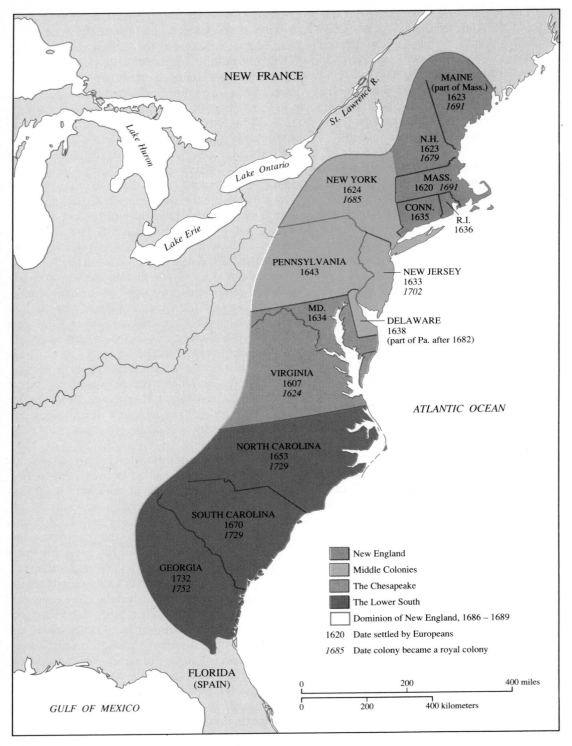

NEW FRANCE

Lake Huron

Lake Ontario

Lake Erie

St. Lawrence R.

MAINE
(part of Mass.)
1623
1691

N.H.
1623
1679

NEW YORK
1624
1685

MASS.
1620 *1691*

CONN.
1635

R.I.
1636

PENNSYLVANIA
1643

NEW JERSEY
1633
1702

MD.
1634

DELAWARE
1638
(part of Pa. after 1682)

VIRGINIA
1607
1624

ATLANTIC OCEAN

NORTH CAROLINA
1653
1729

SOUTH CAROLINA
1670
1729

GEORGIA
1732
1752

New England

Middle Colonies

The Chesapeake

The Lower South

Dominion of New England, 1686 – 1689

1620   Date settled by Europeans

1685   Date colony became a royal colony

FLORIDA
(SPAIN)

GULF OF MEXICO

| 0 | | 200 | | 400 miles |
| 0 | 200 | | 400 kilometers | |

The American Colonies in the Early Eighteenth Century

1642–46	English civil war
1649	Charles I executed
1651	First Navigation Act passed
1660	Stuarts restored to throne; Charles II becomes king
1662	Halfway Covenant drafted
1663	Carolina chartered
1664	English conquer New Netherland; New York founded; New Jersey established
1675–76	King Philip's (Metacomet's) War (New England)
1676	Bacon's Rebellion (Virginia)
1680–92	Pueblo revolt (New Mexico)
1681	Pennsylvania chartered; 1685 James II becomes king
1686–89	Dominion of New England
1688–89	James II deposed in Glorious Revolution; William and Mary ascend throne
1689–97	King William's War
1692	Witchcraft panic in Salem Village
1696	Board of Trade and Plantations established
1701	Iroquois adopt neutrality policy
1702–13	Queen Anne's War
1711–13	Tuscarora War (North Carolina)
1715	Yamasee War (South Carolina)
1732	Georgia chartered

when New Netherland became New York, it had only about five thousand inhabitants.

The Dutch made up the largest segment of this population. The rest consisted of Puritans who had left New England, migrants from several areas of Europe, Indians, and Africans. Because the Dutch West India Company had imported slaves into the colony, almost one-fifth of Manhattan's approximately fifteen hundred inhabitants were black at the time of the English conquest. Thus at that point, New York's urban population had a higher proportion of slaves than the population of the Chesapeake.

Recognizing the diversity of the population, the duke of York's representatives moved cautiously in their efforts to establish English authority. The Duke's Laws, a legal code proclaimed in March 1665, at first applied only to the Puritan settlements on Long Island; they were later extended to the rest of the colony. Dutch forms of local government were maintained and Dutch land titles confirmed. Religious toleration was guaranteed through a sort of multiple establishment: each town was permitted to decide which church to support with its tax revenues. Furthermore, the Dutch were allowed to maintain their customary legal practices. Much to the chagrin of English residents of the colony, the Duke's Laws made no provision for a representative assembly. James was suspicious of legislative bodies. He did not agree to the colonists' requests for an elected legislature until 1683.

The English takeover thus had little immediate effect on the colony. Its population grew slowly, barely reaching eighteen thousand by the time of the first English census in 1698.

Founding of New Jersey One of the chief reasons the English conquest brought so little change to New York was that the duke of York quickly regranted the land between the Hudson and Delaware rivers—East and West

Jersey—to his friends Sir George Carteret and John Lord Berkeley. That left his own colony confined between Connecticut to the east and the Jerseys to the west and south, depriving it of much fertile land and hindering its economic growth. He also failed to promote migration. Meanwhile, the Jersey proprietors promised settlers generous land grants, limited freedom of religion, and—without authorization from the Crown—a representative assembly.

Within twenty years, Berkeley and Carteret sold their interests in the Jerseys to separate groups of investors. The purchasers of all of Carteret's share (West Jersey) and portions of Berkeley's (East Jersey) were Quakers seeking a refuge from persecution in England. The Quakers, formally known as the Society of Friends, denied the need for an intermediary between the individual and God. Anyone, they believed, could receive the "inner light" and be saved, and all were equal in God's sight. They had no formally trained clergy; any Quaker, male or female, who felt the call could become a "public Friend" and travel from meeting to meeting to discuss God's word. Moreover, any member of the society could speak in meetings if he or she desired. Thus the Quakers were true religious radicals, in the mold of Anne Hutchinson.

The Quakers obtained their own colony in 1681, when Charles II granted the region between Maryland and New York to William Penn, one of the sect's most prominent members.

Pennsylvania: A Quaker Haven

Penn's father, Admiral William Penn, had originally served Oliver Cromwell but later joined forces with Charles II and lent the monarch a substantial sum of money. The younger Penn became a Quaker in the mid-1660s, much to his father's dismay. But despite Penn's radical political and religious beliefs, he and Charles II were close personal friends. Had it not been for their friendship (and the desire of Charles's advisers to rid England of religious dissenters), the despised Quakers would never have won a charter for an American settlement.

William Penn held the colony as a personal proprietorship, and the vast property holdings earned profits for his descendants until the American Revolution. However, Penn viewed the province not merely as a source of revenue, but also as a haven for his persecuted coreligionists. Penn offered land to all comers on liberal terms, promised toleration to all religions (though only Christians were given the right to vote), guaranteed such English liberties as the right to bail and trial by jury, and pledged to establish a representative assembly.

Penn's activities and the natural attraction of his lands for Quakers gave rise to a migration whose magnitude was equaled only by the Puritan exodus to New England in the 1630s. By mid-1683, more than three thousand people—among them Welsh, Irish, Dutch, and Germans—had already moved to Pennsylvania, and within five years the population reached twelve thousand. Philadelphia, carefully planned to be the major city in the province, drew merchants and artisans from throughout the English-speaking world. From mainland and West Indian colonies alike came Quakers seeking religious freedom. Pennsylvania's lands were both plentiful and fertile, and the colony soon began exporting flour and other foodstuffs to the West Indies. Practically overnight, Philadelphia acquired more than two thousand citizens and began to challenge Boston's commercial dominance.

A pacifist with egalitarian principles, Penn was determined to treat the Indians of Pennsylvania fairly. He carefully purchased tracts of land from the Delawares (or Leni-Lenapes), the dominant tribe in the region, before selling them to settlers. Penn also established strict regulations for the Indian trade and forbade the sale of alcohol to tribesmen. His Indian policy provides a sterling example of the complexity of the interaction among whites and Indians, because it prompted several tribes to move to Pennsylvania. Most important were the Tuscaroras, whose experiences are described later in this chapter. Likewise, Shawnees and Miamis chose to move eastward from the Ohio valley. By a supreme irony, however, the same toleration that attracted Indians to Penn's domains also brought non-Quaker Europeans, who showed little respect for Indian claims to the soil. In effect, Penn's policy was so successful that it caused its own downfall. The Scotch-Irish, Palatine Germans, and Swiss who settled in Pennsylvania in the first half of the eighteenth century clashed repeatedly over land with tribes that had also recently migrated to the colony.

The other proprietary colony, granted by Charles

II in 1663, encompassed a huge tract of land, stretching from the southern boundary of Virginia to Spanish Florida. The area had great strategic importance; a successful English settlement there would prevent the Spanish from pushing farther north. The proprietors named their new province Carolina in Charles's honor (in Latin his name was Carolus). The "Fundamental Constitutions of Carolina," which they asked the political philosopher John Locke to draft for them, set forth an elaborate plan for a colony governed by a hierarchy of landholding aristocrats and characterized by a carefully structured distribution of political and economic power. But Carolina failed to follow the course the proprietors laid out. Instead, it quickly developed two distinct population centers, which in 1729 split into two separate colonies.

Founding of Carolina

The Albemarle region that became North Carolina was settled by Virginians. They established a society much like their own, with an economy based on tobacco cultivation and the export of such forest products as pitch, tar, and timber. Because North Carolina lacked a satisfactory harbor, its planters continued to rely on Virginia's ports and merchants to conduct their trade, and the two colonies remained tightly linked. Although North Carolina planters held some slaves, they never became as dependent on slave labor as did the other population center in Carolina.

In 1670, Charleston, South Carolina, was founded by a group of settlers from Barbados, which was already overcrowded less than fifty years after English people had first moved there. The white Barbadians brought with them the slaves who had worked on their sugar plantations and the legal codes that had governed those laborers. Thus they irrevocably shaped the future of South Carolina and the subsequent history of the United States.

The Forced Migration of Africans

Since England had no tradition of slavery, why did English settlers in the New World begin to enslave Africans around the middle of the seventeenth century? The answer to that question lies in the combined effect of economics and racial attitudes.

The English were an ethnocentric people who believed firmly in the superiority of their values and civilization. Furthermore, they believed that fair-skinned peoples like themselves were superior to the darker-skinned races. Those beliefs alone did not cause them to enslave Indians and Africans, but the idea that other races were inferior to whites helped them to justify slavery and the slave trade.

Although the English had not previously practiced slavery, the Spanish and Portuguese had long enslaved African Muslims and other "heathen" peoples. Further, Christian doctrine could be interpreted as allowing enslavement as a means of converting such people to the "true faith." European colonizers needed a large labor force to exploit the riches of the New World, and few free people were willing to work as wage laborers in the difficult and dangerous conditions of South American mines or Caribbean sugar plantations.

The most obvious source of workers would have been the Indians native to the Americas. But their familiarity with the American environment made them difficult to enslave, and when captured, they often managed to escape. Africans, however, were a different story. Transported to alien surroundings far from home, frequently they could not communicate with their fellow workers. They were also the darkest (and thus, to European eyes, the most inferior) of all peoples. Black Africans, therefore, seemed to be ideal candidates for perpetual servitude.

The first English colonists in the Americas to utilize slave laborers extensively were those who settled in the Caribbean. In the 1640s, the English migrants to such islands as Barbados (colonized in 1627), Nevis (1628), and Antigua (1632) discovered that their soil and climate were ideally suited for the cultivation of cane sugar, previously a rare and expensive luxury food item. Caribbean planters made enormous profits by importing hundreds of thousands of African slaves to work in the cane fields. Until well into the eighteenth century, England's Caribbean colonies were far more valuable than those on the mainland.

Slavery Established

The English colonies to the north did not immediately move to the slave system because white indentured servants filled their labor needs. Lack of evidence makes it difficult to determine the legal status of blacks during the first few decades of English settlement, but apparently many of them were also indentured, which meant that they eventually became free. After 1640, some blacks were being permanently enslaved in each of the English colonies. Massachusetts, in 1641, was the first to mention slavery in its legal code. By the end of the century, the slaves' status was fixed. Barbados adopted a comprehensive slave code in 1661, and the mainland provinces soon did the same.

Between 1492 and 1770 more Africans than Europeans came to the New World. But just 4.5 percent of them (about 275,000 persons during the eighteenth century) were imported into the region that became the United States. By contrast, 42 percent of the approximately 9.5 million enslaved blacks were carried to the Caribbean, and 49 percent went to South America. The magnitude of this trade in slaves raises three important and related questions. First, what was its impact on West Africa and Europe? Second, how was the trade organized and conducted? Third, what was its effect on the blacks it carried?

The West African coast was one of the most densely inhabited regions of the continent. Despite the extent of forced migration to the Western Hemisphere, the area was not seriously depopulated by the trade in human beings. Even so, because American planters preferred to purchase male slaves, the sex ratio of the remaining population was significantly affected by the trade. The relative lack of men increased the work demands on women and encouraged polygyny (the practice of one man having several wives). In Guinea, the primary consequences of the trade were political. The coastal kings who served as middlemen in the trade used it as a vehicle to consolidate their power and extend their rule over larger territories. They controlled both the European traders' access to slaves and the inland peoples' access to European trade goods. The centralizing tendencies of the trade thus helped in the formation of such powerful eighteenth-century kingdoms as Dahomey and Asante.

West Africa and the Slave Trade

These West African kings played a crucial role in the functioning of the slave trade. Europeans set up permanent slave-trading posts in Lower Guinea under the protection of local rulers, who then supplied the resident Europeans with slaves to fill the ships that stopped regularly at the coastal forts. In Upper Guinea, there was a somewhat different trading pattern: Europeans would sail along the coast, stopping to pick up cargoes when signaled from the shore. Most persons sold into American slavery were wartime captives, criminals sentenced to enslavement, or persons seized for nonpayment of debts. A smaller proportion had been kidnapped.

Europeans were the chief beneficiaries of this traffic in slaves. The expanding network of trade between Europe and its colonies in the seventeenth and eighteenth centuries was fueled by the sale and transportation of slaves, the exchange of commodities produced by slave labor, and the need to feed and clothe so many bound laborers. Planters in the New World eagerly purchased slaves from Africa, dispatched shiploads of valuable staple crops to Europe, and bought large quantities of cheap food and clothing, much of it from elsewhere in the Americas. The European economy, previously oriented toward the Mediterranean and the Far East, shifted its emphasis to the Atlantic Ocean. By the late seventeenth century, commerce in slaves and the products of slave labor constituted the basis of the European economic system.

Given the economic importance of the slave trade, it is hardly surprising that European nations fought bitterly over control of it. The Portuguese, who initially dominated the trade, were supplanted by the Dutch. The Dutch in turn lost out to the English, who eventually controlled the trade through the Royal African Company, a joint-stock company chartered in 1672. Holding a monopoly on all English trade with black Africa, the company transported more than 120,000 slaves to England's American colonies. Yet even before the company's monopoly expired in 1712, many individual English traders had illegally entered the market for slaves. By the early eighteenth century, independent traders were carrying most of the Africans imported into the colonies and earning immense profits.

The experience of the Middle Passage (so named because it was the middle section of the so-called

A contemporary print illustrating how slave-ship captains tightly packed their human cargo so as to achieve the greatest possible profits from each voyage. *American Antiquarian Society.*

triangular trade among England, Africa, and the Americas) was often fatal for the Africans who made up a ship's cargo. An average of 10 to 20 percent of the slaves died en route, but on voyages that were unusually long or had outbreaks of epidemic diseases, the mortality rates rose much higher. In addition, some slaves usually died either before the ships left Africa or shortly after their arrival in the New World. Their white captors died at the same, if not higher, rates, chiefly through exposure to alien African germs.

The Middle Passage

On shipboard, men were usually kept shackled in pairs; women and children were released from any bonds once the ship was well out at sea. The slaves were fed a vegetable diet of beans, rice, yams, and corn cooked together in various combinations to create a warm mush. In good weather, they were allowed on deck for fresh air, because only healthy slaves commanded high prices. Many ships also carried a doctor, whose primary role was to treat the slaves' illnesses. The average size of a cargo was about 250 slaves, but since the size of ships varied, so too did the number of slaves carried.

Records of slave traders reveal numerous instances of Africans' resistance to captivity. Some committed suicide; others participated in shipboard revolts. Yet most of the Africans who embarked on the slave vessels arrived in the Americas alive and still in captivity; the whites saw to that, for only then could they make a profit.

At first, most of the slaves imported into the English colonies went to various Caribbean islands. But after about 1675, Chesapeake planters could no longer obtain an adequate supply of English workers. A falling birthrate and improved economic conditions in England decreased the number of possible migrants to the colonies. At the same time, new English set-

Slavery in the Chesapeake

tlements in North America started to compete with the Chesapeake for settlers. When the shortage of servants became acute in the mid-1670s, imports of Africans increased dramatically. As early as 1690, the Chesapeake colonies contained more black slaves than white indentured servants, and by 1710 one-fifth of the region's population was black.

Yet not all white planters could afford to devote so much money to purchasing workers. Those whites with enough money could acquire slaves and accumulate greater wealth, while less-affluent whites could not. Consequently, as time passed, white Chesapeake society became more and more stratified—that is, the gap between the rich and the poor steadily widened.

Besides causing demographic and economic change, the introduction of large numbers of Africans into the Chesapeake affected cultural values as well. Without realizing it, Chesapeake whites adopted African modes of thought about the use of time and the nature of work. Africans were more accustomed than European migrants to life in a hot climate, and whites soon learned the benefits of following African patterns of time usage—working early and late, taking a long rest in the heat of midday. And unlike the colonists in New England, where the Puritan condemnation of leisure-time activities prevailed, Chesapeake whites learned, again from blacks, the importance of recreation.

In South Carolina, the first slaves arrived with the initial white settlers. Indeed, one-quarter to one-third of South Carolina's early population was black. The Barbados whites **Blacks** quickly discovered that Africans **in South** had a variety of skills well suited **Carolina** to South Carolina's semitropical climate. African-style dugout canoes became the chief means of transportation in the colony, which was crisscrossed by rivers. Fishing nets copied from African models proved to be more efficient than those of English origin. The settlers also adopted African techniques of cattle herding. Since meat and hides were the colony's chief exports in its earliest years, blacks contributed significantly to South Carolina's prosperity.

The similarity of South Carolina's environment to West Africa's, coupled with the large number of blacks in the population, ensured that more aspects of West African culture survived in that colony than

elsewhere on the mainland of North America. Only in South Carolina did black parents continue to give their children African names; only there did a dialect develop that combined English words with African terms (known as Gullah, it has survived to the present day in isolated areas). African skills remained useful, and so techniques that in other regions were lost when the migrant generation died were here passed down from parents to children. In South Carolina, as in West Africa, black women were the primary traders, dominating the markets of Charleston as they did those of Gambia or Benin.

Significantly, the importation of large numbers of Africans near the end of the seventeenth century coincided with the successful introduction of rice as a staple crop in South Carolina. English people knew little about the techniques of growing and processing rice, but slaves from Africa's Rice Coast had spent their lives working with the crop. Although the evidence is circumstantial, it seems likely that the Africans' expertise enabled their English masters to cultivate the crop profitably. After rice had become South Carolina's major export, 43 percent of the Africans imported into the colony came from rice-producing regions, and blacks' central position in the colony's economy was firmly established.

South Carolina later developed a second staple crop, and it too made use of blacks' special skills. The crop was indigo, much prized in Europe as a blue dye for clothing. In the early 1740s, Eliza Lucas, a young white West Indian woman who was managing her father's South Carolina plantations, began to experiment with indigo cultivation. Drawing on the knowledge of white and black West Indians, she developed the planting and processing techniques later adopted throughout the colony. Indigo was grown on high ground, and rice was planted in low-lying swampy areas; rice and indigo also had opposite growing seasons. Thus the two crops complemented each other perfectly.

After 1700, white southerners were committed to black slavery as their chief source of labor; white northerners were not. Small-scale northern agriculture did not demand many bound **Slavery in** laborers. In northern urban areas, **the North** however, white domestic servants were hard to find and slaves were often used. In some northern colonial cities (notably Newport, Rhode Island, and New York City), black slaves accounted for more than 10 percent of the population.

The introduction of large-scale slavery in the South, coupled with its near-absence in the North, accentuated regional differences that had already begun to develop in England's American colonies. To the distinction between diversified agriculture and staple-crop production was now added a difference in the race and status of most laborers. That difference was one of degree, but it was crucial.

Relations Between Europeans and Indians

Everywhere in North America, European colonizers depended heavily on the labor of native peoples. But their reliance on Indians took varying forms in different parts of the continent. In the Northeast, France, England, and the Netherlands competed for the pelts supplied by Indian trappers. In the Southeast, England, Spain, and later France each tried to control a thriving trade with the tribes in deerskins and Indian slaves. Finally, in the Southwest, Spain attempted to exploit the agricultural and artisan skills of the Pueblo peoples.

In 1598, drawn northward by accounts that rich cities lay in the region, Juan de Oñate, a Mexican-born adventurer, led a group of about five hundred to colonize New Mexico. The emissaries from New Spain had three goals: to acquire personal wealth; to claim new territories for their monarch; and to convert the Indians to Catholicism. When it became apparent that New Mexico held little wealth and offered only a hard life, many of the first settlers returned to Mexico. In 1609, Spanish authorities decided to maintain only a small military outpost and a few Christian missions in the area, with the capital at Santa Fé (founded in 1610).

Franciscan friars set to work to convert the residents of the pueblos, with mixed success. The Pueblo peoples proved willing to add Christianity to their own religious beliefs but not to give up their indigenous rituals. Friars and secular colonists who held *encomiendas* also placed heavy labor demands on the In-

Popé and the Pueblo Revolt

dians. As the decades passed, conditions grew worse, for the Franciscans adopted brutal and violent tactics as they tried to wipe out all vestiges of the native religion. Finally, in 1680, the Pueblos revolted under the leadership of Popé, a respected shaman, and successfully drove the Spaniards out of New Mexico (see map, page 38). Although Spanish authority was restored in 1692, Spain had learned its lesson. From that time on, Spanish governors stressed cooperation with the Pueblos, and no longer attempted to reduce them to bondage or to violate their cultural integrity. The Pueblo revolt was the most successful and longest sustained Indian resistance movement in colonial North America.

When the Spanish expanded their territorial claims to the east (Texas) and the north (California), they followed the strategy they had used in New Mexico, establishing their presence through widely scattered military outposts and Franciscan missions. The army's role was to maintain order among the subject Indians and to guard the boundaries of the Spanish empire from possible incursions, especially by the French. The friars, of course, continued to concentrate on conversion efforts. By the late eighteenth century, Spain claimed a vast territory that stretched from California (initially colonized in 1769) through Texas (settled after 1700) to the Gulf Coast.

Along the eastern seaboard, Europeans valued the Indians as hunters and traders. The major Dutch settlements in North America were trading posts; the French settlements were trading posts allied to missions. In the earliest phase of settlement in each of the English mainland colonies, the primary exports were furs and skins obtained from neighboring Indians.

South Carolina provides a case in point. The Barbadians who colonized the region moved quickly to establish a vigorous trade in deerskins with nearby tribes. Between 1700 and 1710, South Carolina exported to Europe an average of 54,000 skins annually, a number that later climbed to a peak of 160,000. The trade gave rise to other exchanges that reveal the complexity of the economic relationships among Indians and Europeans. For example, white Carolinians carried those deerskins on horses, which they obtained from the Creek Indians, who had in turn acquired them from the Spaniards through trade and capture.

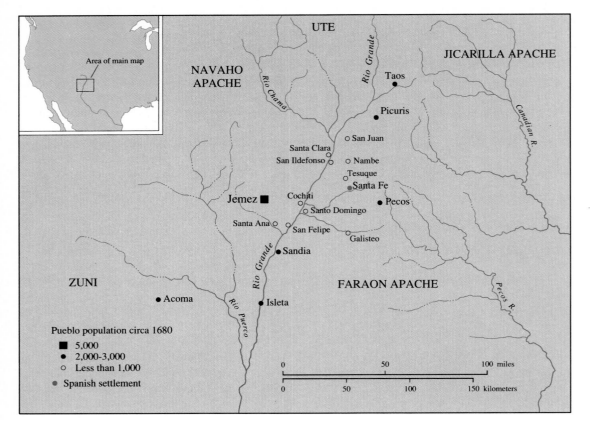

New Mexico, ca. 1680 *Source: From* Apache, Navaho, and Spaniard, *by Jack D. Forbes. Copyright © 1960, 1988 by the University of Oklahoma Press. Used by permission.*

Another important component of the Carolina trade was traffic in Indian slaves. The warring tribes of South Carolina (especially the Creeks) profited

Indian Slave Trade

from selling their captive enemies to the whites, who then either kept them in the colony as slaves or exported them to other mainland settlements or to the West Indies. There are no reliable statistics on the extent of the trade in Indian slaves, but in 1708 they made up 14 percent of the population of South Carolina.

A major conflict between white Carolinians and neighboring tribes added to the supply of Indian slaves. In 1711, the Tuscaroras, an Iroquoian people, attacked a settlement at New Bern, North Carolina, which had expropriated their lands without payment. The Tuscaroras had been avid slavers

and had sold to the whites many captives from the weaker Algonkian tribes. Those tribes seized the opportunity to settle old scores, joining with the English colonists to defeat their enemy in a bloody two-year war. In the end, more than a thousand Tuscaroras were themselves sold into slavery, and the remnants of the tribe drifted northward, where they joined the Five Nations Iroquois in New York.

The abuses of the slave trade led to the most destructive Indian war in the Carolinas. White traders regularly engaged in corrupt, brutal, and fraudulent practices. They were notorious for cheating the Indians, physically abusing them, and selling friendly tribesmen into slavery. In the spring of 1715, the Yamasees, aided by Creeks and a number of other tribes, retaliated by attacking the English colonists. At times, the Creek-Yamasee offensive came close to driving the intruders from the mainland altogether. But then colonial reinforcements arrived from the north, and the Cherokees joined the whites against their ancient enemies, the Creeks. The war pointed up both the difficulty of achieving unity among the tribes and the Indians' now-critical dependence on European weapons. When the tribal allies ran out of ammunition and could not repair their broken guns, their cause was lost. The Yamasees moved south to seek Spanish protection, and the Creeks retreated to villages in the west.

That the Yamasees could escape by migrating southward exposed the one remaining gap in the line of English coastal settlements, the area **Founding of** between the southern border **Georgia** of South Carolina and Spanish Florida. The gap was plugged in 1732 with the chartering of Georgia, the last of the colonies that would become part of the United States. Intended as a haven for debtors by its founder James Oglethorpe, Georgia was specifically designed as a garrison province. Since all its landholders were expected to serve as militiamen to defend English settlements, the charter prohibited women from inheriting or purchasing land in the colony. The charter also prohibited the use of alcoholic beverages and forbade the introduction of slavery. Such provisions reveal the founders' intention that Georgia should be peopled by sturdy, sober yeoman farmers who could take up their weapons against the Indians or Spaniards at a moment's notice. None of the conditions could be enforced, however, and all were abandoned by 1752, when Georgia became a royal colony.

In the Northeast, the Iroquois hoped to become the major supplier of pelts to the Europeans. They achieved that goal in the 1640s by practically exterminating the Hurons, their chief trading rivals. The scope of the Iroquois victory was made possible by the use of guns obtained from the Dutch. By defeating the Hurons, the Iroquois established themselves as a force that the Europeans could not ignore.

The Iroquois nation was not one tribe, but five: Mohawks, Oneidas, Onondagas, Cayugas, and Senecas. (In 1722, the Tuscaroras became the

Iroquois Confederacy sixth.) Under the terms of a defensive alliance forged early in the sixteenth century, key decisions of war and peace for the entire Iroquois Confederacy were made by a council composed of tribal representatives. Each tribe retained some autonomy, and no tribe could be forced to comply with a council directive against its will. The Iroquois were unique among Indians not only because of the strength and persistence of their alliance, but also because of the role played by their tribal matrons. The older women of each village chose its chief and could either start wars (by calling for the capture of prisoners to replace dead relatives) or stop them (by refusing to supply warriors with necessary foodstuffs).

The war with the Hurons was just the first of a series of conflicts with other tribes—conflicts known collectively as the Beaver Wars—in which the Iroquois fought to maintain a dominant position in the fur trade. In the mid-1670s, just when it appeared that they would be successful, the French stepped in to prevent an Iroquois triumph, which would have destroyed France's plans to trade directly with the Indians of the Great Lakes and Mississippi valley regions. During the next twenty years, the French launched repeated attacks on Iroquois villages. The English offered little assistance other than weapons to their Iroquois trading partners. Their people and resources depleted by constant warfare, the Iroquois in 1701 negotiated neutrality treaties with France, England, and their tribal neighbors. For the next half-century they maintained their power through trade and skillful, often successful diplomacy.

Military action against the Iroquois Confederacy was part of French Canada's plan to penetrate the heartland of North America. The plan also included **French** the explorations of Father Jacques **Expansion** Marquette, Louis Jolliet, and Robert Cavelier de La Salle in the Great Lakes and Mississippi valley regions. Officials in France approved the expeditions because they wanted to find a route to Mexico. La Salle, by contrast, hoped to make great personal profits by monopolizing the fur trade through establishing trading posts along the Mississippi River.

A French settler in Canada made this drawing of an Iroquois about 1700. The artist's fascination with his subject's mode of dress and patterned tattoos is evident. Such pictorial representations of "otherness" help to suggest the cultural gulf that divided the European and Indian residents of North America. *Library of Congress.*

Unlike the Spanish, these French adventurers did not attempt to subjugate the Indian peoples they encountered or even at first to claim the territory formally for France. Still, when France decided to strengthen its presence near the Gulf of Mexico by founding New Orleans in the early eighteenth century—to counter both the westward thrust of the English colonies and the eastward moves of the Spanish—the Mississippi posts became the glue of empire.

At each post lived a small military garrison and a priest, surrounded by powerful Indian nations (see map). The tribes permitted the French to remain among them because the traders gave them ready access to precious European goods. The French, for their part, sought political as well as economic ends, attempting to prevent the English from encroaching too far into the interior. Their goals, however, were limited; they did not engage in systematic efforts to convert the Indians of the region to Christianity.

The French learned to live in the midst of powerful tribes with relatively little friction because of the mutual needs of all parties to the arrangement. Matters were very different in the English colonies, where white colonists were interested in acquiring land. In Virginia, the conflict was especially acute because of the colonists' insatiable hunger for land on which to grow still more tobacco.

By the early 1670s, some Virginians were eagerly eyeing the rich lands north of the York River that had been reserved for Indians under earlier treaties. Using as a pretext the July **Bacon's Rebellion** 1675 killing of a white servant by some Doeg Indians, they attacked not only the Doegs, but also the powerful Susquehannocks. In retaliation, Susquehannock bands began to raid frontier plantations in the winter of 1676. The land-hungry whites rallied behind the leadership of Nathaniel Bacon, a planter who wanted, in his words, "to ruine and extirpate all Indians in general." Governor William Berkeley, however, hoped to avoid setting off a major war.

Berkeley and Bacon soon clashed. After Bacon forced the House of Burgesses to authorize him to attack the Indians, Berkeley declared Bacon and his men to be in rebellion. As the summer of 1676 wore on, Bacon alternately pursued Indians and battled with the governor's supporters. In September, he marched on Jamestown itself and burned the capital to the ground. But after Bacon died of dysentery the following month, the rebellion collapsed. A new Indian treaty signed in 1677 opened much of the disputed territory to whites.

Not coincidentally, New England, which had also been settled more than fifty years earlier, was wracked by conflict with Indians at precisely the same time. In both areas, the whites' original accommodation with the tribes no longer satisfied both parties. But in New England the Indians, rather than the whites, felt aggrieved.

In the mid-1670s, Metacomet (known to the whites as King Philip) set out to expel the whites from New England. Metacomet, whose father, Massasoit, had signed the treaty with the Pilgrims in 1621 was troubled because the whites had completely surrounded the ancestral lands of the Pokanokets (Wampanoags) on Narragansett Bay. He was also concerned about the impact of European culture and Christianity on his people. In late June 1675, Metacomet led his warriors in attacks on nearby white communities.

King Philip's War

Soon two other local tribes, the Nipmucks and the Narragansetts, joined Metacomet's forces. In the fall, the three tribes attacked settlements in the northern Connecticut River valley; in the winter and spring of 1676, they devastated well-established villages. Altogether, the alliance destroyed twelve of the ninety Puritan towns and attacked forty others. But the tide turned in the summer of 1676. The Indian alliance ran short of food and ammunition, and after Metacomet was killed in an ambush in August, the coalition crumbled. Many surviving Pokanokets, Nipmucks, and Narragansetts were captured and sold into slavery in the West Indies. The power of New England's coastal tribes was broken. From then on, they lived in small clusters, often working as servants or sailors.

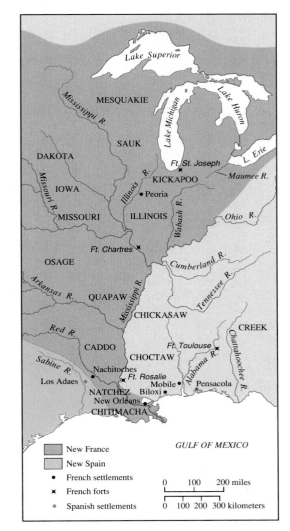

Louisiana, ca. 1720 *Source: Map from* France in America *by William J. Eccles. Copyright © 1972 by William J. Eccles. Reprinted by permission of Harper & Row, Publishers, Inc.*

New England and the Web of Imperial Trade

By the later years of the seventeenth century, the New England settlements had changed in three major ways since the early years of colonization. The population had grown dramatically; the nature of the residents' religious commitment had altered; and the economy had developed in unanticipated ways.

By 1700, New England's population had quadrupled to reach approximately 100,000. Such an increase placed great pressure on the available land,

Population Pressures and many members of the third and fourth generations of New Englanders had to migrate—north to New Hampshire or Maine, south to New York, or west beyond the Connecticut River—to find sufficient farmland for themselves and their children. Others abandoned agriculture and learned such skills as blacksmithing or carpentry.

Furthermore, second-generation Puritans did

not display the same religious fervor that had prompted their ancestors to cross the Atlantic.

Halfway Covenant
Many of them had not experienced the gift of God's grace, or "saving faith," which was required for full membership in the Congregational church. Yet they had been baptized as children, attended church services regularly, and wanted their own infants to be baptized, even though the sacrament of baptism was supposed to be available only to the children of church members. A synod of Massachusetts ministers, convened in 1662 to consider the problem, responded by establishing the Halfway Covenant. The clergymen declared that adults who had been baptized as children but were not full church members could have their children baptized. In return, such parents had to acknowledge the authority of the church and live according to moral precepts. "Halfway" members could neither vote in church affairs nor take communion.

By the 1660s, another change in church membership was evident: the proportion of women in the typical congregation was increasing. Indeed, by the end of the century, women constituted a majority in many churches. In response, Cotton Mather, the most prominent member of a family of distinguished ministers, began to deliver sermons outlining women's proper role in church and society—the first formal examination of that theme in American history. Mather urged women to be submissive to their husbands, watchful of their children, and attentive to religious duty.

The different rate of church membership for men and women in late-seventeenth-century New England suggests a growing division between pious women and their more worldly husbands. That split reflected significant economic changes—the third major way in which the Puritan colonies were being transformed.

New England's first commercial system had been based on two pillars: the fur trade and the constant flow of migrants. Through both these means, New Englanders could acquire the manufactured goods they needed. The fur trade gave them valuable pelts to sell in England, and the migrants were always willing to exchange clothing and other items for the earlier settlers' surplus seed, grains, and livestock. But New England's supply of furs was limited because the region lacked rivers giving ready access to the interior of the continent, and the migrants stopped coming after the English civil war began. Consequently, in 1640, that first economic system collapsed.

The Puritans then began a search for new salable crops and markets. They found such crops in the waters off the coast—fish—and on their own land—grain and wood products.

New England's Trading System
By 1643, they had also found the necessary markets: first the Wine Islands (Azores and Canaries) in the Atlantic and then the English colonies in the Caribbean. These islands lacked precisely the goods New England could produce in abundance: cheap food (corn and salted fish) to feed to slaves and wood to make barrels that would hold wine and molasses (the form in which sugar was shipped).

Thus developed the series of transactions that has become known, inaccurately, as the triangular trade. Since New England's products duplicated England's, the northern colonists sold their goods in the West Indies and elsewhere to earn the money with which to purchase English products. There soon grew up in New England's ports a cadre of merchants who acquired cargoes of timber and foodstuffs, which they then dispatched to the West Indies for sale. In the Caribbean the ships sailed from island to island, exchanging fish, barrel staves, and grains for molasses, fruit, spices, and slaves. Then the ships returned to Boston, Newport, or New Haven to dispose of their cargoes. The trading pattern was thus not a triangle but a shifting set of shuttle voyages (see map). Its sole constant was uncertainty, due to the weather, rapid changes of supply and demand in the small island markets, and the delicate system of credit on which the entire structure depended.

The Puritan New Englanders who ventured into commerce were soon differentiated from their rural counterparts by their ties to a wider transatlantic world and by their preoccupation with material endeavors.

Puritans and Anglicans
The gulf between commercial and farming interests widened after 1660, when Anglican merchants began to migrate to New England. Such men had little stake in the survival of Massachusetts Bay and

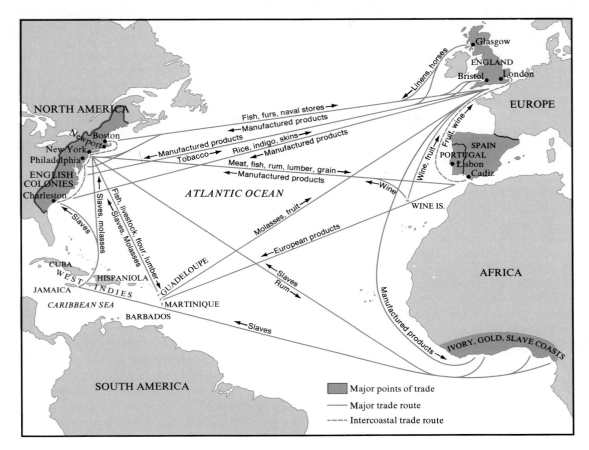

Atlantic Trade Routes

The map shows the following labels and trade route annotations:

NORTH AMERICA · Newport · Boston · New York · Philadelphia · ENGLISH COLONIES · Charleston

EUROPE · Glasgow · ENGLAND · Bristol · London · SPAIN · PORTUGAL · Lisbon · Cadiz · WINE IS.

AFRICA · IVORY, GOLD, SLAVE COASTS

ATLANTIC OCEAN

CUBA · WEST INDIES · JAMAICA · HISPANIOLA · GUADELOUPE · CARIBBEAN SEA · MARTINIQUE · BARBADOS

SOUTH AMERICA

Trade route labels: Linens, horses · Fish, furs, naval stores · Manufactured products · Rice, indigo, skins · Tobacco · Meat, fish, rum, lumber, grain · Manufactured products · Wine, fruit · Fruit, wine · Wine · Molasses, fruit · European products · Slaves · Rum · Fish, livestock, flour, lumber · Slaves, Molasses · Slaves, molasses · Slaves · Manufactured products

Legend:
Major points of trade
— Major trade route
- - - Intercoastal trade route

Connecticut in their original form, and some were openly antagonistic to Puritan traditions. As non-Congregationalists, they were denied the vote, and they resented their exclusion from the governing elite. Congregationalist clergymen returned their hostility in full measure and preached sermons called jeremiads, lamenting New England's new commercial orientation. But the ministers spoke for the past, not the future, because by the 1670s New England and the other American colonies were deeply enmeshed in an intricate international trading network.

The valuable American commerce also attracted the attention of English officials seeking a new source of revenue after the disruptions of the civil war. They realized that the colonies could make important contributions to England's economic well-being. Additional tax revenues could put the nation back on a sound financial footing, and English merchants wanted to ensure that they—not their Dutch rivals—reaped the benefits of trading with the English colonies. Accordingly, Parliament and the restored Stuart monarchs began to design a system of laws that would, they hoped, confine the profits of colonial trade primarily to the mother country.

They based their commercial policy on a series of assumptions about the operations of the world's economic system. Collectively, these assumptions are usually called *mercantilism*. The economic world was seen as a collection of national states, each government actively competing for shares of a finite amount of wealth. Each nation's goal was to become as economically self-sufficient as possible while maintaining a favorable balance of trade with other countries (that is, exporting more than it imported). Colonies had an important role to play in such a scheme. They could supply the mother country with valuable raw materials, and they could serve as a market for the mother country's manufactured goods.

Parliament applied mercantilist thinking to the American colonies in a series of laws known as the Navigation Acts. The major acts—passed in 1651, 1660, 1663, and 1673—established three main principles. First, only English or colonial merchants and ships could engage in trade in the colonies. Second, certain valuable American products (called enumerated goods) could be sold only in the mother country. Third, all foreign goods destined for sale in the colonies had to be shipped via England and were subject to English import duties. Some years later, a new series of laws declared a fourth principle: the colonies could not make or export items (such as wool clothing, hats, and iron) that competed with English products.

Navigation Acts

The intention of the Navigation Acts was clear: American trade was to center on England. The mother country was to benefit from colonial imports and exports. England had first claim on the most valuable colonial exports, and all foreign imports into the colonies had to pass through England first, enriching its customs revenues in the process. Moreover, English and colonial shippers were given a monopoly of the American trade. Even so, the American provinces produced many nonenumerated goods—such as fish, flour, and barrel staves—that could be traded directly to foreign purchasers as long as they were carried in English or American ships.

The English authorities soon learned that writing mercantilist legislation was easier than enforcing it. The many harbors of the American coast provided havens for smugglers, and colonial officials often looked the other way when illegally imported goods were offered for sale. In ports such as Curaçao in the Dutch West Indies, American merchants could easily dispose of enumerated goods and purchase foreign items on which duty had not been paid. Consequently, Parliament in 1696 enacted another Navigation Act designed to strengthen enforcement of the first four. This law established in America a number of vice-admiralty courts, which operated without juries. Since American juries had already demonstrated a tendency to favor local smugglers over customs officers, Parliament decided to remove Navigation Act cases from the regular colonial courts.

England took another major step in colonial administration in 1696 by creating the Board of Trade and Plantations, which from then on served as the chief organ of government concerned with the American colonies. (Previously, no one body had that responsibility.) It reviewed Crown appointments in America, scrutinized legislation passed by colonial assemblies, supervised trade policies, and advised successive ministries on colonial issues. Still, the Board of Trade did not have any direct powers of enforcement. It also shared jurisdiction over American affairs not only with the customs service and the navy, but also with the secretary of state for the southern department, the member of the ministry responsible for the colonies. In short, although the Stuart monarchs' reforms considerably improved the quality of colonial administration, supervision of the American provinces remained decentralized and haphazard.

Board of Trade

Even inefficient enforcement of the Navigation Acts was too much for many colonists, and they resisted the laws both by attempting to circumvent them and by formally protesting to the government in London. But protests had little effect, chiefly because policymakers in England were more concerned about preserving the revenues obtained from colonial trade than about any adverse impact the acts might have on the colonies.

Colonial Political Development and Imperial Reorganization

English officials who dealt with colonial administration in the 1670s and 1680s were confronted not only by resistance to the Navigation Acts, but also by a bewildering array of colonial governments. Massachusetts Bay still functioned under its original corporate charter, and its New England neighbors Connecticut and Rhode Island had been granted similar corporate status by Charles II in 1662 and 1663, respectively. Virginia was a royal colony, and New York became one when its proprietor ascended the throne in 1685 as James II. All the other mainland settlements were proprietorships.

Still, in political structure, the colonies shared certain characteristics. Most were ruled by a governor and a two-house legislature. In New England,

Colonial Political Structures the governors were elected by property-holding men or by the legislature; in the Chesapeake, they were appointed by the king or the proprietor. A council, elected in some colonies and appointed in others, advised the governor on matters of policy and sometimes served as the province's highest court. The council also had a legislative function: initially, its members met jointly with representatives elected by their districts to debate and vote on laws affecting the colony. But as time passed, the fundamental differences between the two legislative groups' purposes and constituencies led them to separate into two distinct houses. Thus developed the two-house legislature still used in almost all the states.

While provincial governments were taking shape, so too were local political institutions. In New England, elected selectmen governed the towns at first, but by the end of the century the town meeting, held at least annually and attended by most adult white townsmen, handled most matters of local concern. In the Chesapeake, the same function was performed by the judges of the county court and by the parish vestry, a group of laymen charged with overseeing church affairs, whose power also encompassed secular concerns.

By late in the seventeenth century, therefore, the American colonists were accustomed to exercising a considerable degree of local political autonomy. The tradition of consent was especially firmly established in New England. Everywhere in the English colonies, white males owning more property than a stated minimum (which varied from province to province) expected to have an influential voice in how they were governed, and especially in how they were taxed.

After James II became king, these expectations clashed with those of the monarch. The new king and his successors sought to bring order to the apparently chaotic state of colonial administration by tightening the reins of government and reducing the colonies' political autonomy. They began to chip away at the privileges granted in colonial charters and to reclaim proprietorships for the Crown. New Hampshire (1679), its parent colony Massachusetts (1691), New Jersey (1702), and the Carolinas (1729) all became royal colonies. The charters of Rhode Island, Connecticut, Maryland, and Pennsylvania were temporarily suspended as well but were ultimately restored to their original status.

The most drastic reordering of colonial administration was attempted in 1686 through 1689, and its chief target was Puritan New England. Reports from America had convinced English

Dominion of New England officials that New England was a hotbed of smuggling. Moreover, the Puritans refused to allow freedom of religion and insisted on maintaining laws that often ran counter to English practice. New England thus seemed an appropriate place to exert English authority with greater vigor. The charters of all the colonies from New Jersey to Maine (then part of Massachusetts) were revoked and a Dominion of New England was established in 1686. Sir Edmund Andros, the governor, was given immense power: all the assemblies were dissolved, and he needed only the consent of an appointed council to make laws and levy taxes.

New Englanders endured Andros's autocratic rule for more than two years. Then came the dramatic news that James II had been overthrown in a bloodless rebellion (known as the Glorious Revolution) and had been replaced on the throne by his daughter Mary and her husband, the Dutch prince William of Orange. Seizing the opportunity to rid themselves of the hated Dominion, New Englanders jailed Andros and his associates, proclaimed their loyalty to William and Mary, and wrote to England for instructions about the form of government they should adopt.

In other American colonies, too, the Glorious Revolution proved to be a signal for revolt. In Maryland, the Protestant Association overturned the government of the Catholic proprietor, and in New York, Jacob Leisler, a militia officer of German origin, assumed control of the government. Like the New Englanders, the Maryland and New York rebels allied themselves with the supporters of William and Mary. They saw themselves as carrying out the colonial phase of the English revolt against Stuart absolutism. The problem was that the new monarchs and their colonial administrators did not view American events in the same light.

Glorious Revolution in America

The Glorious Revolution occurred in the mother country because members of Parliament feared that once again a Stuart king was attempting to seize absolute power. James II, like his father, had levied taxes without parliamentary approval. He had also announced his conversion to Roman Catholicism. The Glorious Revolution affirmed the supremacy of Parliament and of Protestantism when Parliament offered the throne to the Protestants William and Mary. But it did not directly affect English policies toward America. William and Mary, like James II, believed that the colonies were too independent and that England should exercise tighter control over its unruly American possessions.

Consequently, the only American rebellion that received royal sanction was that in Maryland, which was approved primarily because of its anti-Catholic thrust. In New York, Jacob Leisler was hanged for treason, and Massachusetts (including the formerly independent jurisdiction of Plymouth) became a royal colony, complete with an appointed governor. The province was allowed to retain its town meeting system of local government and to elect its council, but the new charter issued in 1691 removed the traditional Puritan religious test for voting. An Anglican parish was even established in the heart of Boston.

Compounding New England's difficulties in a time of political uncertainty and economic change was a war with the French and their Indian allies. King Louis XIV of France allied himself with the deposed James II, and England declared war on France in the summer of 1689. In Europe, the conflict, which lasted until 1697, was known as the War of the League of Augsburg, but the colonists called it King William's War. The American phase of the war was fought chiefly on the northern frontiers of New England and New York.

In this period of extreme stress, there occurred an outbreak of witchcraft accusations in Salem Village (now Danvers), Massachusetts, a rural community adjoining the bustling port of Salem Town. Like their contemporaries elsewhere, seventeenth-century New Englanders believed in the existence of witches. If people could not find rational explanations for their troubles, they tended to suspect they were bewitched. Before 1689, 103 New Englanders, most of them middle-aged women, had been accused of practicing witchcraft, chiefly by neighbors who had suffered misfortunes they attributed to the suspected witch, with whom they usually had an ongoing dispute. Although most such accusations occurred singly, on occasion a witchcraft panic could result when one charge set off a chain reaction of similar charges. But nothing else in New England's history ever came close to matching the Salem Village cataclysm.

Witchcraft in Salem Village

The crisis began in early 1692, when a group of adolescent girls accused some older women of having bewitched them. Before the hysteria spent itself ten months later, nineteen people (including several men, most of them related to accused female witches) had been hanged, one person pressed to death by heavy stones, and more than one hundred people jailed. Historians have proposed various explanations for this puzzling episode, but to be understood, the panic must be put in the proper context—the context of political and legal disorder, of Indian war, and of religious and economic change. It must have seemed to Puritan New Englanders as though their entire world was collapsing. At the very least, they could have had no sense of security about their future.

Nowhere was that more true than in Salem Village, a farming town torn between old and new styles of life because of its position on the edge of a commercial center. And no residents of the village could have had a sharper feeling of insecurity than the girls who issued the initial accusations. Many of

No seventeenth-century New Englander ever drew a picture of a witchcraft trial or execution, but an artist did record a hanging of several witches in England, ca. 1650. The multiple executions of Salem witches in the summer of 1692 probably resembled this gallows scene. *By permission of the Folger Shakespeare Library.*

them had been orphaned in the recent Indian attacks on Maine; they were living in Salem Village as domestic servants. Their involvement with witchcraft began when they experimented with fortunetelling as a means of foreseeing their futures, in particular the identity of their eventual husbands. As the most powerless people in a town that was apparently powerless to affect its fate, they offered their fellow New Englanders a compelling explanation for the seemingly endless chain of troubles afflicting them: their province was under direct attack from the Devil and his legion of witches. Accordingly, it is not perhaps the number of witchcraft prosecutions that seems surprising but rather their abrupt cessation in the fall of 1692.

There were two reasons for the rapid end to the crisis. First, the accusers had grown too bold. When they started to charge some of the colony's most respected residents with being in league with the

Devil, members of the ruling elite began to doubt their veracity. Second, the new royal charter was fully implemented in late 1692, ending the worst period of political uncertainty and removing a major source of psychological stress. The war continued, and the Puritans were not entirely pleased with the charter, but at least order had formally been restored.

During the next three decades, Massachusetts and the rest of the English colonies in America accommodated themselves to the new imperial order. Most colonists did not like the class of alien officials who arrived in America determined to implement the policies of king and Parliament, but they adjusted to their demands and to the trade restrictions imposed by the Navigation Acts. They fought another imperial war—the War of the Spanish Succession, or Queen Anne's War—from 1702 to 1713, without enduring the psychological stress of the first, despite the heavy economic burdens the conflict imposed. Colonists who allied themselves with the royal government received patronage in the form of offices and land grants and composed "court parties" that supported English officials. Others, who were perhaps less fortunate in their friends or more principled in defense of colonial autonomy (opinions differ), made up the opposition, or "country," interest. By 1725 or so, most men in both groups were native-born Americans, members of elite families whose wealth derived from staple-crop production in the South and commerce in the North.

During the eighty years from 1640 to 1720, then, the European colonies in America changed dramatically. From a small outpost in Santa Fé, New Mexico, the Spanish had expanded their influence throughout the region as far east as Texas and—around the mid-century—as far north as California. The French had moved from a few settlements along the St. Lawrence to dominate the length of the Mississippi River and the entire Great Lakes region.

In 1640 there were just two isolated centers of English population, New England and the Chesapeake. In 1720, nearly the entire east coast of mainland North America was in English hands, and Indian power east of the Appalachian Mountains had been broken. What had been a migrant population was now mostly American-born; economies originally based on the fur trade had become far more complex and more closely linked with the mother country; and a wide variety of political structures had been reshaped into a more uniform pattern. Yet at the same time, the introduction of large-scale slavery into the Chesapeake and the Carolinas had irrevocably differentiated their societies from those of the colonies to the north.

By 1720, the essential elements of the imperial structure that would govern the English colonies until 1775 were in place. The regional economic systems originating in the late seventeenth and early eighteenth centuries continued to dominate North American life for another century—until after independence had been won. The period from 1640 to 1720, in other words, established the basic economic and political patterns that were to structure all subsequent changes in colonial American society.

▼

Suggestions for Further Reading

General

Charles M. Andrews, *The Colonial Period of American History,* vol. 4 (1938); Carl Bridenbaugh, *Cities in the Wilderness: The First Century of Urban Life in America, 1625–1742* (1938); Nicholas Canny and Anthony Pagden, eds., *Colonial Identity in the Atlantic World, 1500–1800* (1987); Wesley Frank Craven, *The Colonies in Transition, 1660–1713* (1968); W. J. Eccles, *The Canadian Frontier, 1534–1760,* rev. ed. (1983); Jack P. Greene and J. R. Pole, eds., *Colonial British America: Essays in the New History of the Early Modern Era* (1984); John J. McCusker and Russell R. Menard, *The Economy of British America, 1607–1789* (1985); Gary Walton and James Shepherd, *The Economic Rise of Early America* (1979).

New Netherland and the Restoration Colonies

Edwin Bronner, *William Penn's "Holy Experiment": The Founding of Pennsylvania, 1681–1701* (1962); Thomas J. Condon, *New York Beginnings: The Commercial Origins of New Netherland* (1968); Wesley Frank Craven, *New Jersey and the English Colonization of North America* (1964); Michael Kammen, *Colonial New York: A History* (1975); Oliver Rink, *Holland on the Hudson: An Economic and Social History of Dutch New York* (1986); Robert C. Ritchie, *The Duke's Province: A Study of Politics and Society in Colonial New York, 1660–1691* (1977); Robert M. Weir, *Colonial South Carolina: A History* (1983).

Africa and the Slave Trade

Philip D. Curtin, *The Atlantic Slave Trade: A Census* (1969); David Brion Davis, *The Problem of Slavery in Western Culture* (1966); David W. Galenson, *Traders, Planters, and Slaves: Market Behavior in Early English America* (1986); Herbert Klein, *The Middle Passage* (1978); Paul Lovejoy, ed., *Africans in Bondage: Studies in Slavery and the Slave Trade* (1986); James Rawley, *The Transatlantic Slave Trade: A History* (1981).

Blacks in Anglo-America

T. H. Breen and Stephen Innes, *"Myne Owne Ground": Race and Freedom on Virginia's Eastern Shore, 1640–1676* (1980); Allan Kulikoff, *Tobacco and Slaves: The Development of Southern Cultures in the Chesapeake, 1680–1800* (1986); Edgar J. McManus, *Black Bondage in the North* (1973); Edmund S. Morgan, *American Slavery, American Freedom: The Ordeal of Colonial Virginia* (1975); Peter H. Wood, *Black Majority: Negroes in Colonial South Carolina from 1670 Through the Stono Rebellion* (1974).

European-Indian Relations

Henry Bowden, *American Indians and Christian Missions: Studies in Cultural Conflict* (1981); Judith K. Brown, "Economic Organization and the Position of Women Among the Iroquois," *Ethnohistory,* 17 (1970), 151–167; Verner W. Crane, *The Southern Frontier, 1760–1732* (1929); Francis Jennings, *The Ambiguous Iroquois Empire* (1984); Elizabeth A. H. John, *Storms Brewed in Other Men's Worlds: The Confrontation of Indians, Spanish, and French in the Southwest, 1540–1795* (1975); Douglas Leach, *Flintlock and Tomahawk: New England in King Philip's War* (1958); Daniel Richter and James Merrell, eds., *Beyond the Covenant Chain: The Iroquois and Their Neighbors in Indian America, 1600–1800* (1987); J. Leitch Wright, Jr., *The Only Land They Knew: The Tragic Story of the American Indians in the Old South* (1981).

New England

Bernard Bailyn, *The New England Merchants in the Seventeenth Century* (1955); Paul Boyer and Stephen Nissenbaum, *Salem Possessed: The Social Origins of Witchcraft* (1974); Richard Bushman, *From Puritan to Yankee: Character and the Social Order in Connecticut, 1690–1765* (1967); John Demos, *Entertaining Satan: Witchcraft and the Culture of Early New England* (1982); Carol Karlsen, *The Devil in the Shape of a Woman: Witchcraft in Early New England* (1987); Perry Miller, *The New England Mind: From Colony to Province* (1953); Robert Pope, *The Half-Way Covenant: Church Membership in Puritan New England* (1969); Laurel Thatcher Ulrich, *Good Wives: Image and Reality in the Lives of Women in Northern New England, 1650–1750* (1982).

Colonial Politics

Lois Green Carr and David W. Jordan, *Maryland's Revolution of Government, 1689–1692* (1974); Richard P. Johnson, *Adjustment to Empire: The New England Colonies, 1675–1715* (1981); David S. Lovejoy, *The Glorious Revolution in America* (1972); Jack M. Sosin, *English America and Imperial Inconstancy: The Rise of Provincial Autonomy, 1696–1715* (1985); Jack M. Sosin, *English America and the Revolution of 1688: Royal Administration and the Structure of Provincial Government* (1982); Jack M. Sosin, *English America and the Restoration Monarchy of Charles II: Transatlantic Politics, Commerce, and Kingship* (1980).

Imperial Trade and Administration

Ronald Hutton, *Charles II* (1990); Michael Kammen, *Empire and Interest: The American Colonies and the Politics of Mercantilism* (1970); Robert C. Ritchie, *Captain Kidd and the War Against the Pirates* (1986); I. K. Steele, *Politics of Colonial Policy: The Board of Trade in Colonial Administration* (1968); Stephen Saunders Webb, *1676: The End of American Independence* (1984); Stephen Saunders Webb, *The Governors-General: The English Army and the Definition of the Empire, 1569–1681* (1979).

In June 1744, Dr. Alexander Hamilton, a Scottish-born physician living in Annapolis, Maryland, paid his first visit to Philadelphia. There he encountered two quite different worlds. One consisted of men of his own status, the merchants and professionals he called "the better sort." The other comprised ordinary folk from different ethnic backgrounds and religious beliefs. Hamilton thought of these people as "rabble." To Hamilton, the "better sort" engaged in informed conversation; the "rabble," he thought, spoke "ignorantly," regardless of the subject.

And what of the women in Philadelphia? Hamilton met few of them, aside from his landlady and one of her friends. "The ladies," he explained, "seldom appear in the streets, never in publick assemblies except at the churches or meetings." Hamilton was referring to women of "the better sort." He could hardly have walked the streets of the city without seeing many female domestic servants, market women, and wives of ordinary laborers going about their daily chores.

Despite his biases, Dr. Hamilton was an astute observer. The Philadelphians' chief employment, he wrote, "is traffick and mercantile business"; and the richest merchants of all were the Quakers. Members of that sect also controlled the colony's government. But, Hamilton noted, "the standing or falling of the Quakers in the House of Assembly depends upon their making sure the interest of the Palatines [Germans] in this province, who of late have turned so numerous that they can sway the votes which way they please." Hamilton deplored the impact on the city of the Great Awakening, a religious revival then sweeping the colonies. "I never was in a place so populous where the gout [taste] for publick gay diversions prevailed so little," he remarked.

Hamilton's observations applied to other places as well. Non-English migrants were settling in many regions of the mainland colonies. Their arrival enlarged the population, altered political balances worked out before 1720, and affected the religious climate by increasing the number of sects. Moreover, others shared Philadelphians' assessment of the importance of commerce. Indeed, by the 1750s, Americans of all descriptions were tied to an international commercial system.

Like other well-educated men of his time, Dr. Hamilton was heavily

3

GROWTH AND DIVERSITY, 1720–1770

The portrait of an eighteenth-century family shows the typical colonial childbearing pattern in the large number of "stairstep" children, born at approximately two-year intervals. *National Gallery of Art, Washington, D.C., Gift of Edgar William and Bernice Chrysler Garbisch.*

influenced by the Enlightenment, the major European intellectual movement of the day. The Enlightenment stressed reason and empirical knowledge. Enlightened thinkers believed above all in rationality. From this perspective came Hamilton's distaste for the Great Awakening, the hallmark of which was emotion. To a believer in the primacy of reason, the passions of the newly converted were more than foolish—they were idiotic.

The Enlightenment had affected Dr. Hamilton in yet another way: it had helped create the elite world of which he was a part. Wealthy, well-read Americans participated in a transatlantic intellectual community, lived in comfortable houses, and entertained at lavish parties. The world of the ordinary folk was different. Working daily from dawn to dark, they struggled just to make ends meet. And most of the "lesser sort" could neither read nor write. The colonies had always been composed of people of different ranks, but by the last half of the eighteenth century the social and economic distance between those ranks had widened noticeably.

Above all, after 1720 the colonies presented a picture of growth and diversity. Population increased dramatically, and the area settled by whites and blacks expanded until it filled almost all of the region between the Appalachian Mountains and the Atlantic Ocean. At the same time, the colonies became more diverse; the two original economies, the Chesapeake and New England, became four through the addition of the middle colonies and the Lower South. Before 1720, the colonies were still inhabited mainly by English, African, and Indian peoples; by 1770, a large proportion of the white population was of non-English origin. The urban population, though tiny by today's standards, grew considerably larger after 1720; and in the cities were found the greatest extremes of wealth and poverty. Such changes transformed the character of England's North American possessions. The colonies that revolted in unison against British rule after 1765 were very different from the colonies that revolted separately against Stuart absolutism in 1689.

Population Growth and Ethnic Diversity

One of the most striking characteristics of the mainland colonies in the eighteenth century was their rapid population growth. Only about 250,000 European and African-Americans resided in the colonies in 1700; thirty years later, that number had more than doubled, and by 1775 it had become 2.5 million. Although migration accounted for a considerable share of the growth, most of it resulted from natural increase. Once the difficult early decades of settlement in each colony had passed, the American population doubled approximately every twenty-five years. Such a rate of growth was then unparalleled in human history. It had a variety of causes, the chief one being the youthful marriage age of women (early twenties for whites, late teens for blacks). Since married women became pregnant every two or three years, women normally bore five to ten children. Because the colonies, especially those north of Virginia, were healthful places to live, a large proportion of the children born reached maturity and began families of their own. As a result, in 1775, about half the American population, white and black, was under sixteen years old.

Such a dramatic phenomenon did not escape the attention of contemporaries. As early as the 1720s, Americans began to point with pride to their fertility, citing population growth as evidence of the advantageous conditions in the colonies. In 1755, Benjamin Franklin published his *Observations Concerning the Increase of Mankind,* which predicted that in another century "the greatest Number of Englishmen will be on this Side the Water." Franklin's purpose in writing his *Observations* was to argue that Britain should prevent Germans from migrating to Pennsylvania. Since the English population in America was increasing so rapidly, he asked, "Why should Pennsylvania, founded by the English, become a Colony of *Aliens,* who will shortly be so numerous as to Germanize us instead of our Anglifying them?"

Whether a majority of Franklin's American-born contemporaries shared his fears is not known. But the eighteenth-century migration to the English colonies was massive; it comprised approximately 375,000 whites and 275,000 blacks. Because some of the whites (for example, convicts sentenced to exile by English courts) and all the blacks did not choose freely to come to the colonies, nearly half the migrants moved to America against their will.

Newcomers from Europe and Africa

Africans made up the largest single racial or ethnic group that came to the colonies during the eighteenth century. More important than the number of black migrants, however, is the fact that in the first half of the century the black population of the Chesapeake began to grow faster through natural increase than through importation. In the slaveholding societies of South America and the Caribbean, a surplus of males over females and appallingly high mortality rates produced very different slave population patterns. There, only large, continuing importations from Africa could maintain the enslaved work force at adequate levels. South Carolina, where rice cultivation was difficult and unhealthy and where planters preferred to purchase males, bore some resemblance to such colonies in that it too required a constant influx of Africans. But in the Chesapeake, the black population grew primarily through natural increase after 1740.

The largest group of white non-English immigrants to America was the Scotch-Irish, chiefly descended from Presbyterian Scots who had settled in northern regions of Ireland during the seventeenth century. Perhaps as many as 250,000 Scotch-Irish people moved to the colonies. Fleeing economic distress and religious discrimination, they were lured as well by hopes of obtaining land. The Scotch-Irish

Scotch-Irish, Germans, and Scots

1720–21 Smallpox inoculation controversy (Boston)

1720–40 Black population of Chesapeake begins to grow by natural increase

1739 Stono Rebellion
George Whitefield arrives in America; Great Awakening broadens

1739–48 King George's War

1741 Slave revolt scare (New York City)

1765–66 Hudson River land riots

1767–69 Regulator movement (South Carolina)

1771 North Carolina Regulators defeated at Battle of Alamance

often arrived in Philadelphia. They moved west and south from that city, settling chiefly in the western portions of Pennsylvania, Maryland, Virginia, and the Carolinas. Frequently unable to afford to buy any acreage, they squatted on land belonging to Indian tribes, land speculators, or colonial governments.

The German migrants numbered about 100,000. Most of them emigrated from the Rhineland between 1730 and 1755, usually arriving in Philadelphia. Not all, however, remained in Pennsylvania. Some moved west and then south along the eastern slope of the Appalachian Mountains, eventually finding homes in western Maryland and Virginia. Others sailed first to Charleston or Savannah and settled in the interior of South Carolina or Georgia. The German immigrants belonged to a wide variety of Protestant sects—primarily Lutheran, German Reformed, and Moravian—and therefore added to the religious diversity of the middle colonies.

The 50,000 or more Scots who came directly to America from Scotland should not be confused with the Scotch-Irish. Many early Scottish immigrants were supporters of Stuart claimants to the throne of England, or Jacobites. After the death of William and Mary's successor, Queen Anne, in 1714, the British throne passed to the German house of Hanover, in the person of King George I. In 1715 and again in 1745, Jacobite rebels attempted unsuccessfully to capture the Crown for the Stuart pretender, and many were exiled to America as punishment. Most of the Jacobites settled in North Carolina. Ironically, they tended to become loyalists during the Revolutionary War because of their strong commitment to monarchy.

The most concentrated period of immigration to the colonies fell between 1760 and 1775. Tough times in the home country led many to decide to seek a better life in America. In those fifteen years alone, more than 220,000 persons arrived—10 percent of the entire population of British North America. At least 125,000 of the migrants came from the British Isles: 55,000 Scotch-Irish, 40,000 Scots, and more than 30,000 English people. To them were added at least 12,000 Germans and 85,000 Africans. Late-arriving free immigrants had little choice but to remain in the cities or move to the far frontiers of settlement, for land elsewhere was fully occupied.

Because of the migration patterns of the different ethnic groups and the concentration of slaveholding in the South, half the colonial population south of New England was of non-English origin by 1775. Whether the migrants assimilated readily into Anglo-American culture depended on the patterns of settlement, the size of the group, and the strength of the migrants' ties to their common culture. For example, the Huguenots were French Protestants who settled in tiny enclaves in American cities but were unable to sustain either their language or their distinctive religious practices. Within two generations, they were almost wholly absorbed into Anglo-American culture. By contrast, the equally small group of colonial Jews maintained a separate identity. They established synagogues and strove to preserve their culture. Members of the larger groups of migrants (the Germans, Scotch-Irish, and Scots) found it easier to sustain Old World ways if they wished. Countless local areas of the colonies were settled almost exclusively by one or another of these groups.

Recognizing that it was to their benefit to keep other racial and ethnic groups divided, the dominant white elites on occasion deliberately fostered antagonisms among them. When the targets of their policies were European migrants, the goal was the maintenance of political and economic power. When the targets were Indians and blacks, as was the case in South Carolina, the stakes were considerably higher. South Carolina whites, a minority of the population, wanted to prevent Indians and blacks from making common cause against them. So that slaves would not run away to join the Indians, whites hired Indians as slave catchers. So that Indians would not trust blacks, whites used blacks as soldiers in Indian wars.

Although the dominant elites probably would have preferred to ignore the colonies' growing racial and ethnic diversity, they could not do so for long and still maintain their power. When these men decided to lead a revolution in the 1770s, they recognized that they needed the support of non-English Americans. Not by chance, then, did they begin to speak of "the rights of man," rather than "English liberties," when they sought recruits for their cause.

Economic Growth and Development

The eighteenth-century American economy was characterized more by sharp fluctuations than by a consistent long-term trend. Those fluctuations had two primary causes: the impact of European wars and variations in the overseas demand for American products. The only source of stability in the shifting economic climate was the dramatic increase in colonial population.

Each year the rising population generated greater demands for goods and services, which led to the development of small-scale colonial manufacturing and to the creation of a complex network of internal trade. As the area of settlement expanded, roads, mills, and stores were built to serve the new communities. A lively coastal trade developed; by the late 1760s, 54 percent of the vessels leaving Boston harbor were sailing to other mainland colonies. Such ships not only collected goods for export and distributed imports but also sold items made in America. The colonies thus began to move away from their earlier pattern of near-total dependence on Europe for manufactured goods. For the first time, the American population sustained sufficient demand to encourage manufacturing enterprises. The largest indigenous industry was iron making; by 1775, 82 American furnaces and 175 forges were producing more iron than was England itself. Almost all that iron was for domestic consumption.

The major energizing—yet destabilizing—influence on the colonial economy was foreign trade. Colonial prosperity still depended heavily on overseas demand for American products such as tobacco, rice, indigo, fish, and barrel staves, for it was through the sale of these items that the colonists earned the credit they needed to purchase English and European imports. If the demand for American exports slowed, the colonists' income dropped and so did their demand for imported goods.

Despite fluctuations, the economy grew during the eighteenth century. That growth produced higher standards of living for property-owning Americans. Early in the century, **Rising** households began to acquire such **Standard** amenities as crude earthenware **of Living** dishes, chairs, and knives and forks. (Seventeenth-century colonists had used only spoons.) Diet also improved; inventories reveal larger quantities and wider varieties of stored foods. After 1750, luxury items, such as silver plate, appeared in the homes of the wealthy, and the "middling sort" started to purchase imported English ceramics and teapots. Even the poorest property owners showed some improvement in the number and type of their household possessions.

Yet the benefits of economic growth were not evenly distributed: wealthy Americans improved their position relative to other colonists. The native-born elite families who dominated American society by 1750 were those who had begun the century with sufficient capital to take advantage of the changes caused by population growth. The rise of a group of monied families comprising urban merchants, large landowners, slave traders, and the owners of rum distilleries helped to make the social and economic structure of mid-eighteenth-century America more rigid than before. The new immigrants did not have the opportunities for advancement that had greeted their predecessors. Even so, there was little poverty among whites in the rural areas, where 90 percent of the colonists lived.

In the cities, however, the story was different. Families of urban laborers lived on the edge of destitution. In Philadelphia, for instance, a male laborer's average annual earnings **Urban** fell short of the amount needed to **Poverty** supply his family with the bare necessities. Even in a good year, other family members had to do wage work; in a bad year, the family could be reduced to beggary. By the 1760s, urban poor-relief systems were overwhelmed with applicants for assistance, and some cities began to build workhouses or almshouses to shelter the growing number of poor people. How could that have happened while the lot of the average American family was improving?

Three answers to that question suggest themselves. First, some poor, unskilled colonists were not able to accumulate sufficient resources to acquire property. Such people clustered in the cities, where they could more easily find work. Second, poverty seems to have been a stage that people passed through at certain times in their lives rather than a constant condition. Third, women, mostly widows, predominated among the urban poor. Since women in the eighteenth century, like women today, were paid about half the wages earned by men, it may be that urban poverty was primarily a sex-typed phenomenon, with poor white males being the exception rather than the rule.

Within this overall picture, it is important to distinguish among the various regions. In New England, three elements combined to exert a major influence on economic development: the quality of the land, the region's leadership in colonial shipping, and the impact of the imperial wars. New England's soil was rocky and thin, and farmers did not normally produce large surpluses to sell abroad. Farms were worked primarily by family members. New England had the lowest average wealth per freeholder in the colonies. But it also had its share of wealthy men: they were the merchants and professionals whose income was drawn from overseas trade.

Boston's central position in the New England economy and its role as a shipbuilding center ensured that it would be directly affected by any resumption of warfare. In 1739, **New** English vessels began clashing **England** with Spanish ships in the Carib- **and King** bean, setting off a conflict that **George's** would merge with the European **War** War of the Austrian Succession and become known in America as King George's War. Nominally, the war was fought to determine who would sit on the Austrian throne, but one of its causes was European commercial rivalries in the Americas. The war's first impact on Boston's economy was positive. Ships and sailors were in demand, and wealthy merchants profited from contracts to supply military expeditions.

But Boston suffered heavy losses of manpower. After France became Spain's ally, a Massachusetts force captured the French fortress of Louisbourg, which guarded the sea lanes leading to New France, but the colony had to levy heavy taxes on its residents to pay for the expensive effort. For decades, Boston's economy felt the continuing effects of King George's War. The city was left with unprecedented numbers of widows and children on its relief rolls, the boom in shipbuilding ended when the war did, and taxes remained high. As a final blow to the colonies, Britain gave Louisbourg back to France in the Treaty of Aix-la-Chapelle (1748).

Because of one key difference between the northern and middle colonies, the latter were more positively affected by King George's War and its aftermath. That difference was the greater fertility of the soil in New York and Pennsylvania, where commercial farming was the norm. With the outbreak of war, farmers in the middle colonies were able to profit from the increased demand for foodstuffs, especially in the West Indies. After the war, a series of poor grain harvests in Europe caused flour prices to rise even more rapidly. Philadelphia and New York, which could draw on large, fertile grain- and livestock-producing areas, took the lead in the foodstuffs trade, while Boston found its economy stagnating.

Prosperity of the Middle Colonies

The increased European demand for grain also had a significant impact on the Chesapeake. After 1745, some Chesapeake planters began to convert tobacco fields to wheat and corn because the price of grain was rising faster than that of tobacco. By diversifying their crops, they could avoid dependence on just one product for their income. But tobacco still ruled the region and remained the largest single export from the mainland colonies.

The continuing concentration on tobacco in the Chesapeake had two major results by the mid-eighteenth century. The first stemmed from the substitution of enslaved for indentured labor. The offspring of slaves were also slaves, whereas the children of servants were free. As the black population of the Chesapeake began to grow through natural increase between 1720 and 1740, the advantages for the slaveowners became evident. A planter who started with only a few slave families could watch the size of his labor force increase steadily without making additional major investments in workers. Not coincidentally, the first truly large Chesapeake plantations began appearing in the 1740s.

Natural Increase of Black Population

The second effect of tobacco cultivation on the Chesapeake was linked to patterns of trade. In the first half of the eighteenth century, wealthy planters served as middlemen in the tobacco trade. They collected and shipped tobacco grown by their less prosperous neighbors, extended credit to them, and ordered the English imports they wanted. This system changed in the 1740s, when Scottish merchants entered the tobacco trade. The Scots organized their efforts differently from their London-based competitors. They stationed representatives (called factors) in the Chesapeake to purchase tobacco, arrange for shipments, and sell imports. The arrival of the Scottish factors created genuine competition for the first time and thus pushed up tobacco prices. When the Chesapeake finally began to develop port towns later in the century, they grew up in centers of Scottish mercantile activity or in regions that had largely converted to grain production.

The Lower South, like the Chesapeake, depended on staple crops and slave labor, but its pattern of economic growth was distinctive. In contrast to tobacco prices, which rose slowly through the middle decades of the century, rice prices climbed steeply. The sharp increase was caused primarily by a heavy demand for rice in southern Europe. Because Parliament removed rice from the list of enumerated products in 1730, South Carolinians were able to do what colonial tobacco planters never could: trade directly with continental Europe. But dependence on European sales had its drawbacks, as rice growers discovered at the outbreak of King George's War in 1739. Trade with the continent was disrupted, rice prices plummeted, and South Carolina entered a depression. Still, by the 1760s, prosperity had returned; indeed, in that period, the Lower South experienced more rapid economic growth than the other regions of the colonies. Partly as a result, it had the highest average wealth per freeholder in Anglo-America by the time of the Revolution.

Lower South Trade Patterns

Each region of the colonies, then, had its own economic rhythm derived from the nature of its export trade. King George's War initially helped New England and hurt the Lower South, but in the long run those effects were reversed. In the Chesapeake and the middle colonies, the war initiated a long period of prosperity. The variety of these economic experiences points up a crucial fact about the mainland colonies: they did not compose a unified whole. They were linked economically into regions, but they had few political or social ties beyond or even within those regions. Despite the growing coastal trade, the individual colonies' economic fortunes depended not on their neighbors in America, but rather on the shifting markets of Europe and the West Indies.

Daily Life

The basic unit of colonial society was the household. Headed by a white male (or perhaps his widow), the household was the chief mechanism of production and consumption. Its members—bound by ties of blood or servitude—worked together to produce goods for consumption or sale. The white male head of the household represented it to the outside world, serving in the militia or political posts, casting the household's sole vote in elections. He managed the finances and held legal authority over the rest of the family—his wife, his children, and his servants or slaves. (Eighteenth-century Americans used the word *family* for people who lived together in one house, whether or not they were blood kin.) Such households were considerably larger than American families today; in 1790, the average per home was 5.7 whites. Most of those large families were nuclear—that is, they did not include extended kin like aunts, uncles, or grandparents.

More than 90 percent of all colonial families lived in rural areas. Therefore, nearly all adult white men were farmers, and all adult white women farm wives. In colonial **Sexual** America, household tasks were **Division of** allocated by sex. The master, **Labor Among** his sons, and his male servants **White** or slaves performed one set of **Americans** chores; the mistress, her daughters, and her female servants or slaves, an entirely different set. So rigid were the gender classifications that when households for some reason lacked a master or mistress, the appropriate jobs were not done. Only in emergencies and for brief periods of time would women do "men's work" or men do women's.

The mistress of the rural household was responsible for what were termed indoor affairs. She and her female helpers prepared the food, cleaned the house, did the laundry, and often made the clothing. The phrase "indoor affair" is somewhat deceptive. For instance, the preparation of food, an "indoor" function, involved planting and cultivating a garden, harvesting and preserving vegetables, salting and smoking meat, drying apples and pressing cider, milking cows and making butter and cheese, not to mention cooking and baking.

The head of the household and his male helpers, responsible for outdoor affairs, also had a heavy workload. They had to plant and cultivate fields, build fences, chop firewood, harvest and market crops, and butcher livestock. Only in the plantation South and in northern cities could even a few adult white males lead lives free from arduous physical labor.

Farm households were governed by the seasons and by the hours of daylight. Men and boys had the most leisure in the winter, when there were no **Rhythms of** crops that needed care. Women **Rural Life** and girls were freest in the summer, before embarking on autumn food preservation and winter spinning and weaving. Other activities, including education, had to be subordinated to seasonal work. The seasons also affected travel plans. Because the roads were muddy in the spring and fall, most visiting took place in the summer and, in the North, in the winter, when sleighs could be used.

Because most farm families were relatively isolated from their neighbors and had these heavy seasonal work obligations, rural folk took advantage of every possible opportunity for socializing. Men taking grain to be milled would stop at a crossroads tavern for a drink and conversation. Women gathering to assist at childbirth would drink tea and exchange news. Work itself also provided opportunities for visiting. Corn-husking bees, barn raisings, quilting parties, and other communal activities brought together neighbors from miles around, often for several days of work, followed by feasting, dancing, and singing in the evenings.

The few eighteenth-century colonial cities were just large towns by today's standards. The largest, Boston, had only seventeen thousand inhabitants in 1750. Still, city life differed considerably from rural life. City dwellers were not as tied to the seasons. Year-round they could purchase foodstuffs and wood at city markets and cloth at dry-goods stores. They could see friends whenever they wished. Wealthy urbanites had plenty of leisure to read, take walks around town, play cards, or attend dances, plays, and concerts.

Rhythms of Urban Life

City people also had much more contact with the world beyond their own homes than did their rural compatriots. By the 1750s, every major city had at least one weekly newspaper. Newspapers printed the latest "advices from London" (usually two to three months old) and news of events in other English colonies, as well as reports on matters of local interest. However, contact with the outside world also had drawbacks. Sailors sometimes brought contagious diseases into port with them, causing epidemics, which the countryside largely escaped.

Cities attracted many migrants from rural areas. Young men seeking to become apprentices, laborers in need of work, and widows looking for a means to support their families often moved into the cities. Widows could sell their services as nurses, teachers, seamstresses, servants, or prostitutes, or (if they had some capital) open shops, inns, or boarding houses. In rural areas, where the economy was based on agriculture and families produced many of their own necessities, there was little demand for the services that landless women and men could perform. In the cities, though, someone always needed another servant, blacksmith, or laundress.

Only widows and the very few never-married women could legally run independent businesses. An unmarried colonial woman had the same legal rights as a man (with the exception of voting), but an Anglo-American wife was subordinate to her husband in law as well as custom. Under the common-law doctrine of coverture, a married woman became one person with her husband. She could not sue or be sued, make contracts, buy or sell property, or draft a will. Any property she owned prior to marriage became her husband's after the wedding; any wages she earned were legally his; and all children of the marriage fell under his control.

Status of Women

Anglo-American men expected their wives to defer to their judgment. Most wives seem to have accepted secondary status without murmuring. When girls married, they were commonly advised to devote themselves to their husbands' interests. A Virginia woman remarked, for example, that it was wives' responsibility "to give up to their husbands" whenever differences of opinion arose between them.

The man's legal and customary authority extended to his children as well. Indeed, child rearing was the one task regularly undertaken by both sexes in colonial America. The father set the general standards by which children were raised and usually had the final word on such matters as education or vocational training. White parents normally insisted on unquestioning obedience from their offspring, and many freely used physical punishment to break a child's will. In the homes of America's elite families, most burdensome chores were performed by white or black servants, freeing parents to spend more time with their offspring and reducing the need for strict disciplinary measures.

A white man's authority could include black families, as well as his own kin. More than 95 percent of colonial blacks were held in perpetual bondage. In South Carolina, a majority of the population was black; in Georgia, about half; and in the Chesapeake, 40 percent. The trend toward consolidation of landholding and slave ownership after 1740 had a profound effect on the lives of African-Americans. In areas with high proportions of blacks in the population, most slaves resided on plantations with at least nine other bondspeople. Although many southern blacks lived on farms with only one or two other slaves, the majority had the experience of living and working in a largely black setting.

The concentration of the slave population also had a profound effect on whites. Plantation housing styles, for example, were more African than English in origin, with clusters of small buildings—serving

An Overseer Doing His Duty, by Benjamin H. Latrobe. Most slave women were field hands like these, sketched in 1798 near Fredericksburg, Virginia. White women were believed to be unsuited for heavy outdoor labor. *Maryland Historical Society, Baltimore.*

as kitchens, spinning rooms, and so forth—taking the place of one large structure. Just as blacks mimicked the whites' dances in their evening frolics, so too it became customary for whites to perform "Negro jigs" at the end of their cotillions. And words of African origin like *tote* and *okay* were readily incorporated into American English.

The size of such plantations allowed the specialization of labor. Encouraged by planters, whose goal was self-sufficiency, African-American men and women became highly skilled at tasks that whites believed appropriate to their sex. Each large plantation had its own male blacksmiths, carpenters, valets, shoemakers, and gardeners, and female dairymaids, seamstresses, cooks, and at least one midwife, who attended pregnant white and black women alike. These skilled slaves—between 10 and 20 percent of the black population—were essential to the smooth functioning of

Sexual Division of Labor Among Black Americans

the plantation. Most slaves, male or female, were assigned to work in the fields.

The typical Chesapeake tobacco plantation was divided into small "quarters" located at some distance from one another. White overseers supervised work on the distant quarters, while the planter personally took charge of the "home" quarter (which included the planter's house). Planters commonly assigned "outlandish" (African-born) slaves to do field labor in order to accustom them to plantation work routines and to enable them to learn some English. Artisans, on the other hand, were usually drawn from among the plantation's American-born blacks. In such families, skills like carpentry and midwifery were passed down from father to son and mother to daughter; such knowledge often constituted a slave family's most valuable possession.

All the English colonies legally permitted slavery, so discontented blacks had few places to go to escape bondage. Sometimes, recently arrived

Africans ran off in groups to the frontier, where they joined the Indians or attempted to establish traditional villages. Occasionally, slaves from South Carolina tried to reach Spanish Florida. But most slave runaways merely wanted to visit friends or relatives or to avoid their normal work routines for a few days or months. From the blacks' perspective, violent resistance had even less to recommend it than running away. Whites may have been in the minority in some areas, but they controlled the guns and ammunition.

African-Americans did try to improve the conditions of their bondage. Their chief vehicle for gaining some measure of control over their lives was the family. Planters' records reveal **Black** how members of extended-kin **Families** groups provided support, assistance, and comfort to each other. They asked to live on the same quarters, protested excessive punishment administered to relatives, and often requested special treatment for children. The extended-kin ties that developed among African-American families who had lived on the same plantation for several generations served as insurance against the uncertainties of existence under slavery. If a nuclear family was broken up by sale, there were always relatives around to help with child rearing and other tasks. Among colonial blacks, the extended family served a more important function than it did among whites.

By a variety of means, most black families managed to carve out a small measure of autonomy. On many plantations, slaves were allowed or required to plant their own gardens, hunt, or fish in order to supplement the standard diet of corn and salt pork. Some Chesapeake mistresses permitted their female slaves to raise chickens, which they could then sell or exchange for such items as extra clothing or blankets. In South Carolina, slaves were often able to accumulate personal property because most rice and indigo plantations operated on a task system. Once slaves had completed their assigned tasks for the day, they were free to work for themselves. In Maryland and Virginia, where by the end of the century whites had begun to hire out their slaves to others, blacks were sometimes allowed to keep a small part of the wages they earned. Such advances were slight, but against the bleak backdrop of slavery they deserve to be highlighted.

Yet blacks were always subject to white intrusions into their lives, since they had to serve white families rather than their own. In some households, **Black-White** masters and mistresses enforced **Relations** their will chiefly through physical coercion. On other plantations, masters were more lenient and respectful of slaves' property and their desire to live with other members of their families. But even in households where whites and blacks displayed genuine affection for one another, there were inescapable tensions. Such tensions were caused not only by whites' uneasiness about the slave system, but also by the dynamics of day-to-day relationships in which a small number of whites wielded arbitrary power over the lives of many blacks.

Thomas Jefferson was deeply concerned about that issue. In 1780, he observed, "The whole commerce between master and slave is . . . the most unremitting despotism on the one part, and degrading submission on the other. Our children see this, and learn to imitate it." What troubled Jefferson most was the impact of the system on whites. Before the Revolution, only a tiny number of Quakers took a different approach, criticizing slavery out of sympathy for blacks. The other white colonists who questioned slavery took Jefferson's approach, stressing the institution's adverse effect on whites.

By the third quarter of the eighteenth century, the daily work routines of most Americans had changed little from those of their Old World ancestors. Ordinary white folk lived in farm households, their lives governed by the sexual division of labor. Most African-Americans were held in perpetual bondage, but their work was performed as it had been in West Africa, communally in the fields. Even in colonial cities, life differed little from European cities in previous centuries. Yet if the routines of daily life seemed fixed and unchanging, the wider context in which those routines occurred did not. In both Europe and America, the eighteenth century was a time of great cultural and intellectual ferment. The movement known as the Enlightenment at first primarily influenced the educated elites. Ordinary people seemed little touched by it. But since enlightened thinking played a major part in the ideology of the American Revolution, it eventually had an important impact on the lives of all Americans.

Colonial Culture

The traditional form of colonial culture was oral, communal, and—for at least the first half of the eighteenth century—intensely local. The newer culture of the elite was print-oriented, individualized, and self-consciously cosmopolitan. Although the two are discussed separately here, they mingled in a variety of ways, for people of both descriptions lived side by side in small communities.

A majority of the residents of British America could neither read nor write. That had important consequences for the transmission and development of American culture. In the absence of literacy, the primary means of communication was conversation. Information tended to travel slowly and within relatively confined regions. Different locales developed divergent cultural traditions, and those differences were heightened by racial or ethnic variations.

Oral Culture

When Europeans or Africans migrated to the colonies, they brought with them assumptions about how society should work and how their own lives fitted into the broader social context. In North America, those assumptions influenced the way they organized their lives. Yet Old World customs usually could not be recreated intact in the New World, because people from different origins now resided in the same communities. Accordingly, the colonists had to forge new cultural identities for themselves, and they did so through public rituals.

Attendance at church was perhaps the most important such ritual in the colonies. In Congregational (Puritan) churches, seating was assigned by church leaders to reflect standing in the community. In early New England, men and women sat on opposite sides of a central aisle, arranged in ranks according to age, wealth, and

Religious Rituals

church membership. By the middle of the eighteenth century, wealthy men and their wives sat in privately owned pews. In eighteenth-century Virginia, seating in Anglican parishes also revealed the local status hierarchy. Planter families purchased their own pews. Where one sat in colonial churches, in other words, symbolized one's place in society and the values of the local community.

Other aspects of the service also reflected communal values. In most colonial churches, trained clergymen delivered formal sermons, but in Quaker services members of the meeting spoke informally to each other. Communal singing in Congregational churches added an egalitarian element to an otherwise status-conscious experience. The first book printed in the colonies was the *Bay Psalm Book* (1640), consisting of Old Testament psalms recast in short, rhyming, metrical lines so they could be easily learned and sung even by people who could not read. Such singing helped to reduce the ritual significance of hierarchical seating arrangements, bringing a kind of crude democracy into the church.

Communal culture also centered on the civic sphere. In New England in particular, colonial governments proclaimed official days of thanksgiving or days of fasting and prayer. Everyone in the community was expected to participate in the public rituals held on such occasions. Militia musters (known as training days), normally scheduled once a month, were similar moments that brought the community together, since all able-bodied men between the ages of sixteen and sixty were members of the militia.

Civic Rituals

In the Chesapeake, some of the most important cultural rituals occurred on court and election days. When the county court was in session, men would come from miles around to file suits, appear as witnesses, serve as jurors, or simply observe the goings-on. Attendance at court functioned as a method of civic education; from watching the proceedings men learned what behavior their neighbors expected of them. Elections served the same purpose, for freeholders voted in public. An election official, often flanked by the candidates for the office in question, would call each man forward to declare his preference. The voter would then be thanked politely by the gentleman for whom he had cast his oral ballot.

In such settings as church and courthouse, then, the elite and the ordinary folk alike participated in the oral culture that served as the cement holding their communities together. But the genteel residents of the colonies also took part in a newer kind of culture, one organized through the world of print and the message conveyed by reading, as well as by observing one's neighbors.

Literacy was certainly less essential in eighteenth-century America than it is today. People—especially women—could live their entire lives without ever being called upon to read a book or write a letter. Thus education beyond the bare rudiments of reading, writing, and "figuring" was usually regarded as a frill for either sex. Teaching slaves to read or write was forbidden as too subversive of the social order. Education was thus a sign of status. Only parents who wanted their children to be distinguished from less fortunate peers were willing to forgo their children's valuable labor to allow them to attend school. When parents did so, the education they gave their sons differed from that given their daughters. Girls received little intellectual training beyond the rudiments, though they might learn music, dancing, or fancy needlework. Boys studied with tutors or attended grammar schools that prepared them to enter college at the age of fourteen or fifteen.

The colonial system of higher education for males was therefore more fully developed than the basic instruction for either sex. The first American colleges were designed to train young men for the ministry. But during the eighteenth century, the curriculum and character of colleges changed considerably. Their students, the sons of the colonial elite, were now interested in careers in medicine, law, and business instead of the ministry. And the learned men who headed the colleges, though ministers themselves, were deeply affected by the Enlightenment.

In the seventeenth century, some European thinkers began to analyze nature in an effort to determine the laws that govern the universe. They employed experimentation and abstract reasoning to discover general principles behind such everyday phenomena as the motions of the planets and stars, the behavior of falling objects, and the characteristics of light and sound. Above all, Enlightenment philosophers emphasized acquiring knowledge through reason.

The Enlightenment had an enormous impact on well-to-do, educated people in Europe and America. It supplied them with a common vocabulary and a unified view of the world—a view stressing that the enlightened eighteenth century was better than all previous ages. It joined them in a common endeavor, the effort to make sense of God's orderly creation. Thus American naturalists supplied European scientists with information about New World plants and animals, so that they could be fitted into newly formulated universal classification systems.

Enlightenment rationalism affected politics as well as science. John Locke's *Two Treatises of Civil Government* (1691) challenged previous concepts of an unchanging and unchangeable political order. Government, declared Locke, was created by men and so could be altered by them. If a ruler broke his agreement with the people and refused to protect their rights, he could legitimately be ousted from power. Enlightenment theorists proclaimed that the aim of government was the good of the people, that a proper political order could prevent the rise of tyrants, and that even the power of monarchs was subject to God's natural laws.

These intellectual currents had a dramatic effect on the curriculum of the colonial colleges. Whereas in the seventeenth century Harvard courses had focused on the study of the ancient languages and theology, in the 1730s colleges began to introduce courses in mathematics, the natural sciences, law, and medicine. The young men educated in such colleges—and their sisters at home, with whom they occasionally shared their books and ideas—developed a rational outlook on life that differentiated them from their fellow colonists. This was the world of Dr. Alexander Hamilton and his associates. When he left Annapolis in 1744, he carried letters of introduction to "the better sort" in all the places he intended to visit. Such people had learned the value of reading, of regular correspon-

The Enlight-
enment

Attitudes
Toward
Education

dence with like-minded friends, and of conversation, which focused on recent books imported from Europe.

Well-to-do graduates of American colleges, along with others educated in Great Britain, formed the core of genteel culture in the colonies. Men and women from these families wanted to set themselves apart from ordinary folk. Beginning in the 1720s, they constructed grandiose residences and filled them with imported furnishings, entertained their friends at elaborate dinner parties and balls at which all present dressed in the height of fashion, cultivated polite manners, and saw themselves as part of a transatlantic and intercolonial network.

Elite Culture

In what ways did this genteel, enlightened culture affect the lives of most colonists? Certainly no resident of the colonies could have avoided some contact with members of the elite. Ordinary folk were expected to doff their hats and behave in a deferential fashion when conversing with their "betters." Some were economically dependent on genteel folk; for example, the elite's demand for consumer goods of all kinds led to the growth of artisan industries like furniture making and silversmithing. But the Enlightenment's most immediate impact on all Americans was in the realm of medicine.

Smallpox Inoculations

The key figure in the drama was the Puritan clergyman, Cotton Mather, who was a member of England's Royal Society, an organization of the intellectual elite. In a Royal Society publication, Mather read about the benefits of inoculation (deliberately infecting a person with a mild case of a disease) as a protection against the dreaded smallpox. In 1720 and 1721, when Boston suffered a major smallpox epidemic, Mather and a doctor ally urged people to be inoculated despite fervent opposition from Boston's leading physician. When the epidemic ended, the statistics bore out Mather's opinion: of those inoculated, fewer than 3 percent died; of those who became ill without inoculation, nearly 15 percent perished.

If the lives of genteel and ordinary folk in the eighteenth-century colonies seemed to follow different patterns, there was one man who in his per-

Benjamin Franklin, the Symbolic American

son appeared to combine their traits. That man was Benjamin Franklin. Born in Boston in 1706, he was the perfect example of a self-made, self-educated man. Apprenticed at an early age to his older brother James, a Boston printer, Franklin ran away to Philadelphia in 1723. There he eventually started his own publishing business, printing books, a newspaper, and *Poor Richard's Almanack*. The business was so successful that Franklin was able to retire from active control in 1748. He then devoted himself to intellectual endeavors and public service. Franklin's *Experiments and Observations on Electricity* (1751) was the most important scientific work by a colonial American; it established the terminology and the basic theory of electricity that is still in use today.

Franklin proposed the establishment of a new educational institution in Pennsylvania. The purpose of Franklin's "English School" was not to produce clerics or scholars, but to prepare young men "for learning any business, calling or profession." The College of Philadelphia (now the University of Pennsylvania), which he founded in 1755, was intended to graduate youths who would resemble Franklin himself—talented, practical men of affairs competent in a number of different fields.

Franklin and the student he envisioned thus fused the conflicting tendencies of colonial culture. Free of the Old World's traditions, the ideal American would achieve distinction through hard work and the application of common-sense principles. Like Franklin, he would rise from an ordinary family into the ranks of the genteel, thereby transcending the cultural boundaries that divided the colonists. The American would be a true child of the Enlightenment, knowledgeable about European culture yet not bound by its fetters, advancing through reason and talent alone. To him all things would be possible, all doors open.

The contrast with the original communal ideals of early New England could not have been sharper. Franklin's American was an individual, free to make choices about his future. John Winthrop's American had been a component of a greater whole that required his unquestioning submission. But the two visions had one point in common: both

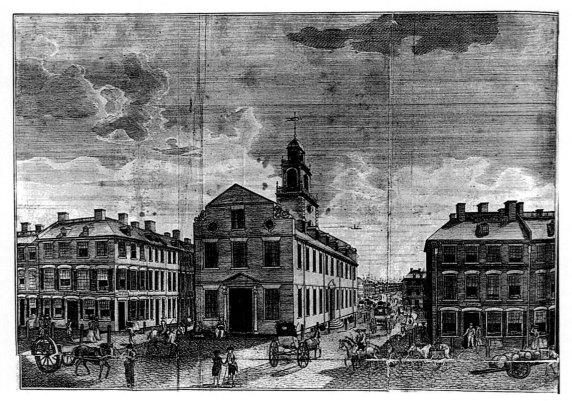

In 1713, the colony of Massachusetts constructed its impressive State House in Boston. Here met the Assembly and the Council. The solidity and imposing nature of the building must have symbolized for its users the increasing consolidation of power in the hands of the Massachusetts legislature. *Library of Congress.*

described only white males. Not until many years later would America formally recognize what had been true all along: that females and nonwhites had participated in creating the nation's cultural tradition.

Politics and Religion: Stability and Crisis at Midcentury

In the first decades of the eighteenth century, colonial political life developed a new stability. Despite the large migration from overseas, most mainland colonists were now native-born. Men from genteel families dominated the political structures in each province, for voters (white males who met property-holding requirements) tended to defer to their well-educated "betters" on election days.

Colonial political leaders sought to increase the powers of the elected assemblies relative to those of the governors and other appointed officials. Assemblies began to claim privileges associated with the British House of Commons, such as the right to initiate all tax legislation and to control the militia. The assemblies also developed effective ways of influencing British appointees, especially by threatening to withhold their salaries. In some colonies (for example, Virginia and South Carolina), the elite members of the assemblies usually presented a united front to royal officials, but in

Rise of the Assemblies

others (for example, New York), they fought with each other long and bitterly.

Yet eighteenth-century assemblies bore little resemblance to twentieth-century state legislatures. Much of their business was what today would be termed administrative; only on rare occasions did they formulate new policies or pass important laws. Unlike modern legislators, who act positively to improve the lives of their constituents, eighteenth-century assemblymen acted negatively, to prevent encroachments on the people's rights. In their minds, their primary function was to stop the governors or councils from enacting such measures as oppressive taxes, rather than to pass laws that would actively benefit their constituents.

By the middle of the century, politically aware colonists commonly drew analogies between their governments and the balance among king, lords, and commons found in Great Britain—a combination that was thought to produce a stable polity. Although the analogy was not exact, political leaders equated their governors with the monarch, their councils with the aristocracy, and their assemblies with the House of Commons. All three were thought essential to good government, but Americans did not regard them with the same degrees of approval. They saw the governors and appointed councils as representatives of England who posed a potential threat to colonial freedoms and customary ways of life. By contrast, they viewed assemblies as the people's protectors. The assemblies, for their part, regarded themselves as representatives of the people.

Again, such beliefs should not be equated with modern practice. Firmly controlled by dominant families, whose members were reelected year after year, the assemblies rarely responded to the concerns of their poorer constituents. Although settlement continually spread westward, assemblies failed to reapportion themselves to provide adequate representation for newer communities. Thus it is important to distinguish between the colonial ideal, which placed the assembly at the forefront in the protection of people's liberties, and the reality, in which the people protected tended chiefly to be the wealthy and the assembly members themselves.

At midcentury, the political structures that had stabilized in a period of relative calm confronted a series of crises. None affected all the mainland provinces, but no colony escaped wholly untouched by at least one. The crises foreshadowed the greater disorder of the revolutionary era. Most important, they demonstrated that the political accommodations arrived at in the aftermath of the Glorious Revolution were no longer adequate to govern Britain's American empire.

One of the first—and greatest—of the crises occurred in South Carolina. Early one morning in September 1739, about twenty slaves gathered near the Stono River, south of Charleston. After seizing guns and ammunition from a store, they killed the storekeepers and some nearby planter families. Then, joined by other slaves from the area, they headed south toward Florida, hoping to find refuge in that Spanish colony. Later the same day, the militia caught up with the fugitives (who numbered about one hundred) and attacked them, killing some and dispersing the rest. More than a week later, the whites finally captured most of the remaining conspirators. Those not killed on the spot were later executed.

Stono Rebellion

The Stono Rebellion shocked white South Carolinians and residents of other colonies as well. Laws governing the behavior of blacks were stiffened throughout British America. But the most immediate response came in New York, which itself had suffered a slave revolt in 1712. There the news from the South, coupled with fears of Spain generated by the outbreak of King George's War, set off a reign of terror in the summer of 1741. Hysterical whites transformed a biracial gang of thieves and arsonists into conspirators who wanted to foment a slave uprising under the guidance of a supposed priest in the pay of Spain. By the end of the summer, thirty-one blacks and four whites had been executed for participating in the "plot." The Stono Rebellion and the New York "conspiracy" revealed both the deepest fears about the dangers of slaveholding and the inability of assemblies to prevent serious internal disorder. Events of the next two decades confirmed that inability.

By midcentury, much of the fertile land east of the Appalachians had been purchased or occupied. As a result, conflicts over land titles and conditions of landholding grew in number and frequency as

Land Riots   colonists competed for control of land good for farming. In 1746, for example, New Jersey farmers holding land under grants from the governor of New York (dating from the brief period when both provinces were owned by the duke of York) clashed violently with agents of the East Jersey proprietors. The proprietors claimed the land as theirs and demanded annual payments, called quitrents, for the use of the property. Similar violence occurred in the 1760s in the region that later became Vermont.

The most serious land riots of the period took place along the Hudson River in 1765 and 1766. Late in the seventeenth century, Governor Benjamin Fletcher of New York had granted several huge tracts in the lower Hudson valley to prominent colonial families. The proprietors in turn divided these estates into small farms, which they rented chiefly to poor Dutch and German migrants. After 1740, though, increasing migration from New England brought conflict to the great New York estates. The New Englanders squatted on vacant portions of the manors and resisted all attempts to evict them. In the mid-1760s, the Philipse family brought suit against the New Englanders, some of whom had lived on Philipse land for twenty or thirty years. New York courts upheld the Philipse claim and ordered the squatters to make way for tenants with valid leases. Instead of complying, the farmers organized a rebellion against the proprietors. For nearly a year, the insurgent farmers terrorized proprietors and loyal tenants, freed their friends from jail, and on one occasion battled a county sheriff and his posse. The rebellion was put down only after British troops dispatched from New York City captured its most important leaders.

Violent conflicts of a different sort erupted just a few years later in the Carolinas. The Regulator movements of the late 1760s (South Carolina) and early 1770s (North Carolina) pitted backcountry farmers against the wealthy eastern planters who controlled their provinces' governments. The frontier dwellers, most of whom were Scotch-Irish, protested their lack of an adequate voice in colonial political affairs. The South Carolinians for months policed the countryside in vigilante bands, contending that law enforcement

The Regulators

in the region was too lax. The North Carolinians, many of whose grievances had their origin in heavy taxation, fought and lost a battle with eastern militiamen at Alamance in 1771.

The most widespread crisis occurred not in politics but in religion. From the late 1730s through the 1760s, waves of religious revivalism—known collectively as the Great Awakening—swept over various parts of the colonies, primarily New England (1735–1745) and Virginia (1750s and 1760s). America was ripe for religious renewal at midcentury. Orthodox Calvinists were eager to combat Enlightenment rationalism, which denied innate human depravity. In addition, many recent immigrants and residents of the backcountry had no prior religious affiliation, thus presenting evangelists with a likely source of converts.

First Great Awakening

The first signs of what was to become the Great Awakening appeared in western Massachusetts, in Northampton Congregational Church, led by the Reverend Jonathan Edwards, a noted preacher and theologian. During 1734 and 1735, Edwards noticed a remarkable response among the young members of his flock to a message based squarely on Calvinist principles. Individuals, Edwards argued, could attain salvation only through recognition of their own depraved natures and the need to surrender completely to God's will. Such surrender brought an intensely emotional release from sin and came to be seen as a single identifiable moment of conversion.

The effects of such conversions remained isolated until 1739, when an English Methodist named George Whitefield arrived in America. For fifteen months, Whitefield toured the colonies, preaching to large audiences from Georgia to New England, and he became the chief generating force behind the Great Awakening. At first, regular clerics welcomed Whitefield, as well as native evangelist preachers. Soon, however, many clergymen began to realize that "revived" religion ran counter to their own approach to matters of faith.

George Whitefield

Opposition to the Awakening heightened rapidly, and large numbers of churches splintered in its wake. "Old Lights"—traditional clerics and their followers—engaged in bitter disputes with the "New Light" evangelicals. American religion, already characterized by numerous sects, became further divided as the major denominations split into Old Light and New Light factions and as new evangelical sects—Methodists and Baptists—quickly gained adherents. Paradoxically, the angry fights and the rapid rise in the number of distinct denominations eventually led to an American willingness to tolerate religious diversity.

The most important effect of the Awakening was its impact on American modes of thought. The revivalists' message directly challenged the colonial

Impact of the Awakening

tradition of deference. Itinerant preachers, many of whom were not ordained clergymen, claimed they understood the will of God better than orthodox clerics. The Awakening's emphasis on emotion rather than learning undermined the validity of received wisdom, and New Lights questioned not only religious, but also social and political, orthodoxy. For example, New Lights began to defend the right of groups and individuals to dissent from a community consensus and so challenged one of the most fundamental tenets of colonial political life up to that time.

Thus, at midcentury, the Great Awakening injected an egalitarian strain into American life and further disrupted traditional structures of existence. Although primarily a religious movement, the Awakening also had important social and political consequences. It called into question habitual modes of behavior in the secular, as well as the religious, realm. The Great Awakening, in short, helped to break Americans' ties to their limited seventeenth-century origins. So, too, did the newcomers from Germany, Scotland, Ireland, and Africa, who brought their languages, customs, and religions to North America. Also important were the changes in the economy that linked the colonies tightly to international markets, drawing them irrevocably into European wars and creating the wealthy class of merchants and landowners who dominated colonial life.

A century and a half after English people had first settled in North America, the colonies were only nominally English. In reality, they mixed diverse European, American, and African traditions into a novel cultural blend. That culture owed much to the Old World, but just as much, if not more, to the New. In the 1760s, Americans began to recognize that their interests were not necessarily identical with those of Great Britain or its monarch.

Suggestions for Further Reading

General

Wayne Craven, *Colonial American Portraiture* (1986); Jack P. Greene, *Pursuits of Happiness: The Social Development of the Early Modern British Colonies and the Formation of American Culture* (1988); Richard Hofstadter, *America at 1750: A Social Portrait* (1971).

Rural Society

T. H. Breen, *Tobacco Culture* (1985); Lois Green Carr et al., eds., *Colonial Chesapeake Society* (1988); Rhys Isaac, *The Transformation of Virginia, 1740–1790* (1982); Sung Bok Kim, *Landlord and Tenant in Colonial New York: Manorial Society, 1664–1775* (1978); James T. Lemon, *The Best Poor Man's Country: A Geographical Study of Early Southeastern Pennsylvania* (1972); Jackson Turner Main, *Society and Economy in Colonial Connecticut* (1985); Michael Zuckerman, *Peaceable Kingdoms: New England Towns in the Eighteenth Century* (1970).

Urban Society

Carl Bridenbaugh, *Cities in Revolt: Urban Life in America, 1743–1776* (1955); Christine L. Heyrman, *Commerce and Culture: The Maritime Communities of Colonial Massachusetts, 1690–1750* (1984); Gary B. Nash, *The Urban Crucible: Social Change, Political Consciousness, and the Origins of the American Revolution* (1979); Frederick B. Tolles, *Meeting House and Counting House: The Quaker Merchants of Colonial Philadelphia, 1682–1763* (1948).

Economic Development

Paul Clemens, *The Atlantic Economy and Colonial Maryland's Eastern Shore: From Tobacco to Grain* (1980); Alice Hanson Jones, *Wealth of a Nation to Be: The American Colonies on the Eve of the Revolution* (1980); John J. McCusker and Russell R. Menard, *The Economy of British America,*

1607–1789 (1985); Edwin J. Perkins, *The Economy of Colonial America* (1980); Gary M. Walton and James F. Shepherd, *The Economic Rise of Early America* (1979).

Politics

Bernard Bailyn, *The Origins of American Politics* (1968); Patricia U. Bonomi, *A Factious People: Politics and Society Colonial New York* (1971); Richard Bushman, *King and People in Provincial Massachusetts* (1985); Edward M. Cook, Jr., *The Fathers of the Towns: Leadership and Community Structure in Eighteenth-Century New England* (1976); Jack P. Greene, *The Quest for Power: The Lower Houses of Assembly in the Southern Royal Colonies, 1689–1776 (1963).*

Immigration

Bernard Bailyn, *The Peopling of British North America* (1986); Bernard Bailyn, *Voyagers to the West* (1986); Jon Butler, *The Huguenots in America* (1983); R. J. Dickson, *Ulster Immigration to Colonial America, 1718–1775* (1966); Ned Landsman, *Scotland and Its First American Colony* (1985); Sharon Salinger, *To Serve Well and Faithfully: Labor and Indentured Servants in Pennsylvania, 1682–1800* (1988).

Blacks

Ira Berlin, "Time, Space, and the Evolution of Afro-American Society in British Mainland America," *American Historical Review,* 85 (1980), 44–78; Thomas J. Davis, *A Rumor of Revolt: The "Great Negro Plot" in Colonial New York* (1985); Herbert Gutman, *The Black Family in Slavery and Freedom, 1750–1925* (1976); Gerald W. Mullin, *Flight and Rebellion: Slave Resistance in Eighteenth-Century Virginia* (1972); William Pierson, *Black Yankees: The Development of an Afro-American Subculture in Eighteenth-Century New England* (1988); Mechal Sobel, *The World They Made Together: Black and White Values in Eighteenth-Century Virginia* (1987).

Women and Family

J. William Frost, *The Quaker Family in Colonial America* (1972); Philip J. Greven, *The Protestant Temperament: Patterns of Child-rearing, Religious Experience, and the Self in Early America* (1977); Barry J. Levy, *Quakers and the American Family* (1988); Mary Beth Norton, *Liberty's Daughters: The Revolutionary Experience of American Women, 1750–1800* (1980); Marylynn Salmon, *Women and the Law of Property in Early America* (1986).

Colonial Culture and the Enlightenment

Daniel J. Boorstin, *The Americans: The Colonial Experience* (1958); Richard Beale Davis, *Intellectual Life in the Colonial South, 1585–1763 ,* 2 vols. (1978); Henry F. May, *The Enlightenment in America* (1976); Louis B. Wright, *The Cultural Life of the American Colonies, 1607–1763* (1957).

Education

James Axtell, *The School upon a Hill: Education and Society in Colonial New England* (1974); Bernard Bailyn, *Education in the Forming of American Society* (1960); Patricia Cline Cohen, *A Calculating People: The Spread of Numeracy in Early America* (1982); Lawrence A. Cremin, *American Education: The Colonial Experience, 1607–1783* (1970); Kenneth A. Lockridge, *Literacy in Colonial New England* (1974).

Science and Medicine

Jane Donegan, *Women and Men Midwives: Medicine, Morality, and Misogyny in Early America* (1978); John Duffy, *Epidemics in Colonial America* (1953); Raymond P. Stearns, *Science in the British Colonies of America* (1970).

Religion and the Great Awakening

Patricia U. Bonomi, *Under the Cope of Heaven: Religion, Society, and Politics in Colonial America* (1986); Carl Bridenbaugh, *Mitre and Sceptre: Transatlantic Faiths, Ideas, Personalities, and Politics, 1689–1775* (1962); J. M. Bumstead and John E. Van de Wetering, *What Must I Do to Be Saved? The Great Awakening in Colonial America* (1976); David S. Lovejoy, *Religious Enthusiasm in the New World* (1985); Harry S. Stout, *The New England Soul: Preaching and Religious Culture in Colonial New England* (1986); Patricia Tracy, *Jonathan Edwards, Pastor* (1980).

In late October 1769, the young Boston shopkeeper Betsy Cuming was visiting a sick friend when outside the house she heard "a voilint Skreeming Kill him Kill him." Betsy ran to the window and saw John Mein, a bookseller and newspaper publisher, being chased by "a larg Croud of those who Call themselves Gentleman." That same night, Mein fled to a vessel anchored in the harbor. He later sailed to England and never returned to the city.

Mein had aroused the wrath of the crowd by printing in his newspaper, the *Boston Chronicle,* lists of names of local merchants who had recently cleared imports through the Boston customs house. But why was the information Mein revealed so explosive? In the fall of 1769, many American merchants had signed an agreement not to import goods from Great Britain; Mein's lists indicated that some of the most vocal supporters of nonimportation (including the patriot leader John Hancock) had been violating the agreement. That was why the "gentlemen" of Boston had to silence the outspoken publisher.

John Mein was not the first, and he would be far from the last, resident of the colonies who found his life wholly disrupted by the growing political antagonism between England and her American possessions. Long afterward, John Adams identified the years between 1760 and 1775 as the period in which the true American Revolution had occurred. The Revolution, Adams declared, was completed before the fighting started, for it was "in the Minds of the people," involving not the actual winning of independence but rather a shift of allegiance from England to America. Today, not all historians would agree with Adams's assertion that that shift constituted the Revolution. But none would deny the importance of the events of those crucial years.

The story of the 1760s and early 1770s is one of an ever-widening split between England and America. In the long history of British settlement in the Western Hemisphere, there had been at times considerable tension in the relationship between individual provinces and the mother country. Still, that tension had rarely been sustained for long, nor had it been widespread, except in 1688 and 1689. In the 1750s, however, a series of

4

SEVERING THE BONDS OF EMPIRE, 1754–1774

A LIST of the Names of *those*
who AUDACIOUSLY continue to counteract the UNIT-
ED SENTIMENTS of the BODY of Merchants thro'out
NORTH-AMERICA ; by importing British Goods
contrary to the Agreement.
_____

John Bernard,
(In King-Street, almost opposite Vernon's Head.

James McMasters,
(On Treat's Wharf.

Patrick McMasters,
(Opposite the Sign of the Lamb.

John Mein,
(Opposite the White-Horse, and in King-Street.

Nathaniel Rogers,
(Opposite Mr. Henderson Inches Store lower End
King-Street.

William Jackson,
At the Brazen Head, Cornhill, near the Town-House.

Theophilus Lillie,
(Near Mr. Pemberton's Meeting-House, North-End.

John Taylor,
(Nearly opposite the Heart and Crown in Cornhill.

Ame & Elizabeth Cummings,
(Opposite the Old Brick Meeting House, all of Boston.

Israel Williams, Esq; & Son,
(Traders in the Town of Hatfield.

And, *Henry Barnes,*
(Trader in the Town of Marlboro'.
_____

*The following Names should have been inserted in
the List of Justices.*

County of Middlesex.	County of Lincoln.
Samuel Hendley	
John Borland	John Kingsbury
Henry Barnes	
Richard Cary	County of Berkshire.
County of Bristol.	Mark Hopkins
George Brightman	Elijah Dwight
County of Worcester.	Israel Stoddard
Daniel Bliss	

A blacklist printed in the *North American Almanac* for 1770 identified those Boston merchants who had ignored the nonimportation agreement. Among their number were both John Mein, the object of the mob's wrath the previous October, and Betsy (Elizabeth) Cuming, the narrator of the story, who—with her sister Anne—ran a small dry-goods store. *Library of Congress.*

events began to change the situation. It all started with the Seven Years' War (1754–1763).

Britain's overwhelming victory in that war forever altered the balance of power in North America. France was ousted from the continent, an event with major consequences for both the Indian tribes of the interior and the colonists. Northern Indians could no longer play European powers off against one another, and so they lost one of their major diplomatic tools. Anglo-Americans, for their part, no longer had to fear a French threat on their borders. The British colonies would never have dared to break with their mother country, some historians have argued, if an enemy nation and its Indian allies had controlled the interior of the continent.

The British victory in 1763, then, constituted a major turning point in American history because of its direct effect on white and Indian residents of North America. It also had a significant impact on Great Britain, one that soon affected the colonies as well. To win the war, Britain had gone heavily into debt. To reduce the debt, Parliament for the first time laid revenue-raising taxes on the colonies. That decision exposed differences in the political thinking of Americans and Britons.

During the 1760s, a broad coalition of white Americans, men and women alike, resisted new tax levies and attempts by British officials to tighten controls over the provincial governments. America's elected leaders became ever more suspicious of Britain's motives as the years passed. They laid aside intercolonial antagonisms to coordinate their response to the new measures, and they slowly began to reorient their political thinking. As late as the summer of 1774, though, most were still seeking a solution within the framework of the empire; few harbored thoughts of independence. When independence did become the issue, as opposed to loyal resistance, the coalition of the 1760s broke down. That, however, did not happen until after the battles of Lexington and Concord in April 1775. Before then, only a few Americans closely connected to colonial administration or the Church of England opposed the trend of resistance.

Renewed Warfare Among Europeans and Indians

The English colonies along the Atlantic seaboard were surrounded by hostile, or potentially hostile, neighbors: Indians everywhere, the Spanish in Florida and along the coast of the Gulf of Mexico, and the French along the great inland system of

1754	Albany Congress Seven Years' War begins		**1767**	Townshend Acts
1756	War officially declared		**1770**	Lord North becomes prime minister Repeal of the Townshend duties, except the tea tax Boston Massacre
1760	American phase of war ends George III becomes king			
1763	Treaty of Paris Pontiac's uprising Proclamation of 1763		**1772**	Boston Committee of Correspondence formed
1764	Sugar Act		**1773**	Tea Act Boston Tea Party
1765	Stamp Act Sons of Liberty formed		**1774**	Coercive Acts
1766	Repeal of the Stamp Act Declaratory Act			

rivers and lakes that stretched from the St. Lawrence to the Mississippi. The Spanish outposts posed little threat to the English, for Spain's days as a major power had passed, but the French were another matter. Their forts and settlements dominated the North American interior, facilitating trading partnerships and alliances with the tribes of the region. In none of the three wars fought between 1689 and 1748 was England able to shake France's hold on the American frontier. Under the Peace of Utrecht, which ended Queen Anne's War in 1713, the English won control of such peripheral northern areas as Newfoundland, Hudson's Bay, and Nova Scotia (Acadia). But Britain made no additional territorial gains in King George's War (see map, page 72).

During both Queen Anne's War and King George's War, the Iroquois Confederacy did not take sides. Instead, it skillfully played the Europeans off against one another. **Iroquois Neutrality** When the Iroquois went to war in those years, it was against a traditional southern enemy, the Catawbas. Since France repeatedly urged them to attack the Catawbas, who were allied with England, the Iroquois achieved three desirable goals. They kept the French happy and simultaneously consolidated their control over the entire interior region north of Virginia. In addition, these southern wars (by identifying a common enemy) enabled the confederacy to cement its alliance with its weaker tributaries, the Shawnees and Delawares. But even the careful Iroquois diplomats could not prevent the region inhabited by the Shawnees and Delawares (now western Pennsylvania and eastern Ohio) from providing the spark that set off a major war. That conflict spread from America to Europe and proved decisive in the contest for North America. Trouble began in 1752, when English fur traders ventured into the area known as the Ohio country. The French could not permit their English rivals to dominate the region. A permanent English presence in the Ohio country could challenge France's control of the western fur trade and even threaten its prominence in the Mississippi valley. Accordingly, in 1753 the French built fortified outposts at strategic points along the rivers of the Ohio country.

European Settlements and Indian Tribes, 1750

In response to the threat posed by the French, delegates from seven northern and middle colonies gathered in Albany, New York, in June 1754.

Albany Congress With the backing of administrators in London, they sought to coordinate the defenses of the colonies and to persuade the Iroquois to abandon their traditional neutrality. They did not succeed in either aim. The Iroquois saw no reason to change a policy that had served them well for half a century. And although the Albany Congress delegates adopted a Plan of Union (which provided for an elected intercolonial legislature with the power to tax), the plan was uniformly rejected by their provincial governments—primarily because those governments feared a loss of autonomy.

As they deliberated, the delegates to the Albany Congress did not know that the war they sought to prepare for was already beginning. The governor of Virginia, which claimed ownership of the Ohio country, had sent a small militia force westward to counter the French moves. But the militiamen arrived too late. The French had already taken possession of the strategic point—now Pittsburgh—where the Allegheny and Monongahela rivers meet to form the Ohio, and they were busily constructing Fort Duquesne. The inexperienced young colonel who commanded the Virginians attacked a French detachment, then allowed himself to be trapped by the French in his crudely built Fort Necessity at Great Meadows, Pennsylvania. After the twenty-two-year-old George Washington surrendered and signed a document of capitulation, he and his men were allowed to return to Virginia.

Washington had blundered grievously. He had started a war that would eventually encompass nearly the entire world. He had also ensured that most tribes in the Ohio valley would support France in the coming conflict. The Indians took Washington's mistakes as an indication of Britain's inability to win the war, and nothing that occurred in the next four years made them change their minds. In July 1755, a combined force of French and Indians ambushed General Edward Braddock, two regiments of British regulars, and some colonial troops a few miles south of Fort Duquesne. Braddock was killed and his men demoralized by their complete defeat. After news of

Seven Years' War

the debacle reached London, Britain declared war on France in 1756, thus formally beginning the conflict that is known as the Seven Years' War.

Although the early years of the war were disastrous for the British, the tide began to turn in 1757. In that year, William Pitt was named secretary of state. Under his leadership, the British mounted the effort that won them the war in North America. By agreeing to reimburse the colonies for their military expenditures and placing troop recruitment wholly in local hands, Pitt gained wholehearted American support for the war effort. (Pitt's approach contrasted sharply with earlier British actions, when the British had commandeered supplies from American farmers and merchants and quartered royal troops in private homes.) In 1758, the British recaptured the fortress at Louisbourg. Then, in a surprise night attack in September 1759, General James Wolfe's soldiers defeated the French on the Plains of Abraham and broke down the defenses of Quebec. A year later, the British took Montreal, the last French stronghold on the continent, ending the American phase of the war.

When the Treaty of Paris was signed in 1763, France ceded its major North American holdings to Britain. Spain, an ally of France toward the end of the war, gave Florida to the victorious English. Since Britain feared the presence of France on its western borders, it also forced the French to cede the region west of the Mississippi (Louisiana) to Spain. The English seacoast colonies no longer had to worry about the threat to their existence posed by France's extensive North American territories, and the British gained control of the fur trade of the entire continent.

Because most of the fighting had been in the Northeast, the war had especially pronounced effects on New Englanders. Perhaps one-third of all

American Soldiers Massachusetts men between the ages of sixteen and twenty-nine served in the provincial army. Wartime service left a lasting impression on these soldiers. For the first time, ordinary Americans came into extended contact with Britons—and they did not like what they saw. The provincials thought the redcoats haughty, profane Sabbath-breakers who arbitrarily imposed overly harsh punishments on anyone who broke the rules.

The New England soldiers also learned that British regulars did not share their adherence to principles of contract and consensus. Colonial regiments mutinied or rebelled en masse if they believed they were being treated unfairly, as happened, for example, when they were not allowed to leave at the end of their formal enlistments. One private grumbled in his journal in 1759, "Although we be Englishmen born, we are debarred Englishmen's liberty. . . . [The British soldiers] are but little better than slaves to their officers. And when I get out of their [power] I shall take care how I get in again." Later, when they were deciding to support the Revolution, such men would draw on their personal experience of British "tyranny."

The overwhelming British triumph stimulated some Americans to think expansively about the colonies' future. Persons like Benjamin Franklin, who had long touted the colonies' wealth and potential, predicted a new, glorious future for British North America. Such men were to form the core of the leadership of resistance to British measures in the years after 1763. They uniformly opposed any laws that would retard America's growth and persistently supported steps to increase Americans' control over their own destiny.

1763: A Turning Point

The great victory over France had an irreversible impact on North America. Its effect was felt first by the interior tribes. With France excluded from the continent altogether and the Spanish confined to the area west of the Mississippi, the diplomatic strategy that had served the tribes so well could no longer be employed. The consequences were immediate and devastating.

Even before the Treaty of Paris, southern Indians had to adjust to the new circumstances. After the British gained the upper hand in the American war in 1758, the Creeks and Cherokees lost their ability to force concessions from them by threatening to turn instead to the French or the Spanish. In desperation and in retaliation for British atrocities, the Cherokees attacked the Carolina and Virginia fron-

tiers in 1760. Although initially victorious, the tribesmen were defeated the following year. Late in 1761, the two sides concluded a treaty under which the Cherokees allowed the construction of English forts in tribal territories and also opened a large tract of land to white settlement.

In the Ohio country, the Ottawas, Chippewas, and Potawatomis became angry when Great Britain, no longer facing French competition, raised the price of trade goods and ended the practice of paying rent for forts. In addition, the British allowed settlers to move into the Monongahela and Susquehanna valleys.

Pontiac, the war chief of an Ottawa village near Detroit, understood the implications of such British actions. Only unity among the western tribes, he realized, could possibly prevent total dependence on and subordination to the victorious British. Using his considerable powers of persuasion, in the spring of 1763 he forged an unprecedented alliance among Hurons, Chippewas, Potawatomis, Delawares, and Shawnees, even gaining the participation of some Mingoes (Pennsylvania Iroquois). Pontiac laid siege to the fort at Detroit while his war parties attacked and took possession of most of the other British outposts in the Great Lakes region.

Pontiac's Uprising

That was the high point of the uprising. The tribes raided the Virginia and Pennsylvania frontiers at will throughout the summer, killing at least two thousand whites. But they could not take the strongholds of Niagara, Fort Pitt (old Fort Duquesne), or Detroit. In early August, a combined force of Delawares, Shawnees, Hurons, and Mingoes was soundly defeated at Bushy Run, Pennsylvania, by troops sent from the coast. Conflict ceased when Pontiac broke off the siege of Detroit in late October, after most of his warriors had returned to their villages. A treaty ending the war was finally negotiated in 1766.

In the aftermath of the bloody summer of 1763, Scotch-Irish frontiersmen from Paxton Township, Pennsylvania, sought revenge on the only Indians within reach, a peaceful band of Christian converts living at Conestoga. In December, the whites raided the Indian village twice, killing twenty people. Two months later, hundreds of frontier dwellers known

Benjamin West, the first well-known American artist, engraved this picture of a prisoner exchange at the end of Pontiac's uprising, with Colonel Henry Bouquet supervising the return of whites captured during the war. In the foreground, a white child resists leaving the Indian parents he had grown to love. Many whites were fascinated by the phenomenon West depicted—the reluctance of captives to abandon their adoptive Indian families. *Rare Books and Manuscripts Division, New York Public Library, Astor, Lenox, and Tilden Foundations.*

to history as the Paxton Boys marched on Philadelphia to demand military protection against future Indian attacks. City officials feared violence and mustered the militia to repel the westerners, but the protesters presented their request in an orderly fashion and returned home.

Pontiac's uprising and the march of the Paxton Boys showed that Great Britain would not find it easy to govern the huge territory it had just acquired from France. In October, in a futile attempt to assert control over the interior, the ministry issued the Proclamation of 1763, which declared the headwaters of rivers flowing into the Atlantic from the Appalachian Mountains to be the temporary western boundary for colonial settlement. The proclamation was intended to prevent clashes between Indians and colonists by forbidding whites to move onto Indian lands until the tribes had given up their land by treaty. But many whites had already established farms or purchased property west of the proclamation line. Thus the policy was doomed to failure from the outset.

Other decisions made in London in 1763 and thereafter had a wider impact in British North America. The victory in the Seven Years' War both

Proclamation of 1763

created difficulties for the British government and offered it opportunities. The most pressing problem was Britain's immense war debt. The men who had to solve this problem were King George III and his new prime minister, George Grenville.

In 1760, George III, then twenty-two years old, assumed the English throne. A man of mediocre intellect and even more mediocre education, the young king was also an erratic judge of character. During the crucial period from 1763 to 1770, when the rift between England and the colonies kept widening, he replaced ministries with bewildering rapidity. Often acting stubbornly, the king viewed adherence to the status quo as the hallmark of patriotism.

George III

The man he chose as prime minister in 1763, George Grenville, confronted a financial crisis: England's burden of indebtedness had nearly doubled since 1754, from £73 million to £137 million. Obviously, Grenville's ministry had to find new sources of funds, and the English people themselves were already heavily taxed. Since the colonists had been major beneficiaries of the wartime expenditures, Grenville concluded that the Americans should be asked to pay a greater share of the cost of running the empire.

Grenville did not question Great Britain's right to levy taxes on the colonies. Like all his countrymen, he believed that the government's legitimacy derived ultimately from the consent of the people, but he defined consent far more loosely than did the colonists. Americans had come to believe that they could be represented only by men for whom they or their property-holding neighbors had actually voted. To Grenville and his English contemporaries, Parliament—king, lords, and commons acting together—by definition represented all English subjects, wherever they resided (even overseas) and whether or not they could vote. According to this theory of government, called *virtual representation,* the colonists were said to be virtually, if not actually, represented in Parliament. Thus their consent to acts of Parliament could be presumed.

Theories of Representation

Proceeding from the same theoretical starting point, the Americans and the English arrived at different conclusions in practice. In England, members of Parliament saw themselves as collectively representing the entire nation, composed of nobility and common folk. Only members of the House of Commons were elected, and the particular constituency that chose a member had no special claim on his vote. In the colonies, by contrast, members of the lower houses of the assemblies were viewed as individually representing the voters who had elected them.

The events following 1763 threw into sharp relief Americans' attitudes toward political power. The colonists had become accustomed to a government that wielded only limited authority over them and affected their daily lives very little. Consequently, they believed that a good government was one that largely left them alone, a view in keeping with the theories of a group of British writers known as the Real Whigs. These writers stressed the dangers inherent in a powerful government, particularly one headed by a monarch. They warned that political power was always to be feared, that rulers would try to corrupt and oppress the people, and that only the perpetual vigilance of the people and their elected representatives could preserve their fragile yet precious liberty.

Britain's attempts to tighten the reins of government and raise revenues from the colonies in the 1760s and early 1770s convinced many Americans that the Real Whigs' reasoning applied to their circumstances. Excessive and unjust taxation, they believed, could destroy their freedoms. They began to interpret British measures in the light of the Real Whigs' warnings and to see evil designs behind the actions of Grenville and his successors. In the mid-1760s, however, colonial leaders did not immediately accuse Grenville of an intent to oppress them. At first, they simply questioned the wisdom of the laws Grenville proposed.

The first such measures, the Sugar and Currency acts, were passed by Parliament in 1764. The Sugar Act revised the existing system of customs regulations; laid new duties on certain foreign imports into the colonies; established a vice-admiralty court at Halifax, Nova Scotia; and included special provisions aimed at stopping the widespread smuggling of molasses,

Sugar and Currency Acts

one of the chief commodities in American trade. Although the Sugar Act appeared to resemble the Navigation Acts, which the colonies had long accepted as legitimate, it broke with tradition because it was explicitly designed to raise revenue, not to channel American trade through Britain. The Currency Act, in effect, outlawed colonial issues of paper money. Americans could accumulate little hard cash, since they imported more than they exported; thus the act seemed to the colonists to deprive them of a useful medium of exchange.

Since the American economy was in the midst of a postwar depression, it is not surprising that both individual colonists and colonial governments decided to protest the new policies. But lacking any precedent for a united campaign against acts of Parliament, Americans in 1764 took only hesitant and uncoordinated steps. Eight colonial legislatures sent separate petitions to Parliament requesting repeal of the Sugar Act. They argued that the act placed severe restrictions on their commerce and that they had not consented to its passage. The protests had no effect. The law remained in force, and Grenville proceeded with another revenue plan.

The Stamp Act Crisis

The Stamp Act, Grenville's most important proposal, was modeled on a law that had been in effect in England for almost a century. It touched nearly every colonist by requiring tax stamps on most printed materials, but it placed the heaviest burden on colonial elites, who used printed matter more frequently than ordinary folk. Anyone who purchased a newspaper or pamphlet, made a will, transferred land, bought dice or playing cards, needed a liquor license, accepted a government appointment, or borrowed money would have to pay the tax. Never before had a revenue measure of such scope been proposed for the colonies. The act also required that tax stamps be paid for with hard money and that violators be tried in vice-admiralty courts, without juries. Finally, such a law broke decisively with the colonial tradition of self-imposed taxation.

The most important colonial pamphlet protesting the Sugar Act and the proposed Stamp Act was *The Rights of the British Colonies Asserted and Proved,* by James Otis, Jr., a brilliant young Massachusetts attorney. Otis starkly exposed the ideological dilemma that was to confound the colonists for the next decade. How could they justify their opposition to certain acts of Parliament without questioning Parliament's authority over them? On the one hand, Otis asserted that Americans were "entitled to all the natural, essential, inherent, and inseparable rights" of Britons, including the right not to be taxed without their consent. On the other hand, he was forced to admit that, under the British system, "the power of parliament is uncontrollable but by themselves, and we must obey."

Otis's Rights of the British Colonies

Otis's first contention, drawing on colonial notions of representation, implied that Parliament could not constitutionally tax the colonies because Americans were not represented in its ranks. Yet his second point both acknowledged political reality and accepted the prevailing theory of British government—that Parliament was the sole, supreme authority in the empire. Even unconstitutional laws enacted by Parliament had to be obeyed until Parliament decided to repeal them. Otis tried to find a middle ground by proposing colonial representation in Parliament, but his idea was never taken seriously on either side of the Atlantic. The British believed that the colonists were already virtually represented in Parliament, and the Americans realized that a handful of colonial delegates to London would simply be outvoted.

Otis wrote his pamphlet before the Stamp Act was passed. When Americans learned of its adoption in the spring of 1765, they did not at first know how to react. Few colonists publicly favored the law. But colonial petitions had already failed to prevent its adoption, and further lobbying appeared futile. Perhaps Otis was right, and the only course open to Americans was to pay the stamp tax, reluctantly but loyally.

Not all the colonists were resigned to paying the new tax. Among the dissenters was a twenty-nine-year-old lawyer serving his first term in the Virginia House of Burgesses. Patrick Henry later recalled that he was appalled by his fellow legislators' unwillingness to oppose the Stamp Act. Henry decided to act. "Alone, unadvised, and unassisted, on a blank leaf of an old law book," he wrote the Virginia Stamp Act Resolves.

Patrick Henry and the Virginia Stamp Act Resolves

Patrick Henry introduced his seven proposals in late May, near the end of the legislative session, when many members of the House of Burgesses had already departed for home. Henry's fiery speech in support of his resolutions led the Speaker of the House to accuse him of treason. (Henry quickly denied the charge, contrary to the myth that had him exclaiming in reply, "If this be treason, make the most of it!") The small number of burgesses remaining in Williamsburg adopted five of Henry's resolutions by a bare majority. Although they repealed the most radical resolution the next day, their action had far-reaching effects.

The four propositions adopted by the burgesses repeated the arguments that James Otis had already advanced. The colonists had never forfeited the rights of British subjects, they declared, and consent to taxation was one of the most important such rights. The other three resolutions went much further. The one that was repealed claimed for the burgesses "the only exclusive right" to tax Virginians. The final two asserted that residents of the colony did not have to obey tax laws passed by other legislative bodies (namely Parliament) and termed any opponent of that opinion "an Enemy to this his Majesty's Colony."

The burgesses' decision to accept only the first four of Henry's resolutions anticipated the position most Americans would adopt throughout the following decade. Though willing to contend for their rights, the colonists did not seek independence. They merely wanted some measure of self-government. Accordingly, they backed away from the assertions that they owed Parliament no obedience and that only their own assemblies could tax them.

During the next ten years, America's political leaders searched for a formula that would enable them to control their internal affairs, especially tax-

ation, but remain within the British Empire. The chief difficulty lay in British officials' inability to compromise on the issue of parliamentary power. The notion that Parliament could exercise absolute authority over all colonial possessions was basic to the British theory of government. In effect, the Americans wanted British leaders to revise their understanding of the workings of their government. That was simply too much to expect.

The ultimate effectiveness of Americans' opposition to the Stamp Act rested on more than ideological arguments over parliamentary power. What gave the resistance its primary force were the decisive and inventive actions of some colonists during the late summer and fall of 1765.

In August, the Loyal Nine, a Boston social club of printers, distillers, and other artisans, organized a demonstration against the Stamp Act. Hoping to show that people of all ranks opposed the act, they approached the leaders of the city's rival laborers' associations, based in the North End and the South End. The Loyal Nine convinced them to participate in the demonstration. After all, the stamp taxes would have to be paid by all colonists, not just affluent ones.

Loyal Nine

Early in the morning of August 14, the demonstrators hung an effigy of Andrew Oliver, the province's stamp distributor, from a tree on Boston Common. That night a crowd tore down a small building they thought was intended as the stamp office and built a bonfire near Oliver's house with the wood from the destroyed building. They then beheaded the effigy and added it to the flames. Members of the crowd broke most of Oliver's windows and threw stones at officials who tried to disperse them. The Loyal Nine's demonstration achieved its objective when Oliver publicly promised not to fulfill the duties of his office. Twelve nights later, another mob, reportedly led by the South End leader, Ebenezer MacIntosh, attacked the homes of several customs officers. This time the violence was almost universally condemned, for the mob completely destroyed Lieutenant Governor Thomas Hutchinson's townhouse.

The differences between the two Boston mobs of August 1765 exposed divisions that would continue to characterize colonial protests in the years that followed. The skilled craftsmen who composed the Loyal Nine and members of the educated elite like merchants and lawyers preferred orderly demonstrations confined to political issues. For the city's laborers, by contrast, economic grievances may have been paramount.

Colonists, like Britons, had a long tradition of crowd action in which disfranchised people took to the streets to redress deeply felt local grievances. But the Stamp Act controversy drew ordinary urban folk into the vortex of imperial politics for the first time. Matters that had previously been of concern only to genteel folk or to members of colonial legislatures were now discussed on every street corner. Sally Franklin observed as much when she wrote to her father, Benjamin, who was then serving as a colonial agent in London, that "nothing else is talked of, the Dutch [Germans] talk of the stompt act the Negroes of the tamp, in short every body has something to say."

The entry of lower-class whites, blacks, and women into the realm of imperial politics both threatened and afforded an opportunity to the elite white men who wanted to mount effective opposition to British measures. On the one hand, crowd action could have a stunning impact. Demonstrations against the Stamp Act occurred in cities and towns stretching from Halifax, Nova Scotia, to the Caribbean island of Antigua. They were so successful that by November 1, when the law was scheduled to take effect, not a single stamp distributor was willing to carry out the duties of his office. Thus the act could not be enforced. On the other hand, wealthy men recognized that mobs composed of the formerly powerless could endanger their own dominance of the society.

To channel resistance into acceptable forms, they created an intercolonial association, the Sons of Liberty. The first such group was established in New York in early November, and branches spread rapidly through the coastal cities. Composed of merchants, lawyers, prosperous tradesmen, and the like, the Sons of Liberty linked protest leaders from Charleston, South Carolina, to Portsmouth, New Hampshire, by early 1766.

Sons of Liberty

In Philadelphia, resistance leaders were dismayed when an angry mob threatened to attack Benjamin Franklin's house. The city's laborers believed Franklin to be partly responsible for the Stamp Act, since he had obtained the post of stamp distributor for a close friend. But Philadelphia's artisans—the backbone of the opposition movement there and elsewhere—were fiercely loyal to Franklin. They gathered to protect his home and family from the crowd. The house was saved, but the resulting split between the better-off tradesmen and the common laborers prevented the establishment of a successful workingmen's alliance like that of Boston.

During the fall and winter of 1765 and 1766, opposition to the Stamp Act proceeded on three separate fronts. Colonial legislatures petitioned Parliament to repeal the hated law and sent delegates to an intercolonial congress, the first since 1754. In October, the Stamp Act Congress met in New York to draft a unified but conservative statement of protest. At the same time, the Sons of Liberty held mass meetings in an effort to win public support for the resistance movement. Finally, American merchants organized nonimportation associations to put economic pressure on British exporters. By the 1760s, one-quarter of all British exports were being sent to the colonies, and American merchants reasoned that London merchants whose sales suffered severely would lobby for repeal. (Nonimportation also enabled colonial merchants to reduce bloated inventories.)

In March 1766, Parliament repealed the Stamp Act. The nonimportation agreements had the anticipated effect on London merchants. But boycotts, formal protests, and crowd actions were less important in winning repeal than was Grenville's replacement as prime minister in the summer of 1765. Lord Rockingham, the new head of the ministry, had opposed the Stamp Act, not because he believed that Parliament lacked power to tax the colonies, but because he thought the law unwise and divisive. Rockingham, however, linked repeal to passage of the Declaratory Act, which asserted Parliament's ability to tax and legislate for Britain's American possessions "in all cases whatsoever." As they celebrated the Stamp Act's repeal, few colonists saw the ominous implications of the Declaratory Act.

Repeal of the Stamp Act

BRITISH MINISTRIES AND THEIR AMERICAN POLICIES

Head of Ministry	Major Acts
George Grenville	Sugar Act (1764)
	Currency Act (1764)
	Stamp Act (1765)
Lord Rockingham	Stamp Act repealed (1766)
	Declaratory Act (1766)
William Pitt/Charles Townshend	Townshend Acts (1767)
Lord North	Townshend duties repealed, except the tea tax (1770)
	Coercive Acts (1774)
	Quebec Act (1774)

Resistance to the Townshend Acts

The colonists had accomplished their immediate aim, but the long-term prospects were unclear. Another change in the ministry, in the summer of 1766, revealed how fragile their victory had been. Charles Townshend, a Grenvillite, was named chancellor of the exchequer in a new administration headed by the ailing William Pitt. Townshend became the dominant force in the ministry and decided to renew the attempt to obtain additional funds from the colonies.

The taxes proposed by Townshend in 1767 were to be levied on trade goods such as paper, glass, and tea and thus seemed to be extensions of the existing Navigation Acts. But the Townshend duties differed from previous customs taxes in two ways. First, they were levied on items imported into the colonies from Britain, not from foreign countries. Thus they were at odds with mercantilist theory. Second, they were designed to raise money to pay the salaries of royal officials in the colonies. That posed a direct challenge to the colonial assemblies, which derived considerable power from threatening to withhold officials' salaries. In addition, Townshend's scheme provided for the establishment of an American Board of Customs Commissioners and for the creation of vice-admiralty

courts at Boston, Philadelphia, and Charleston. Townshend also proposed the appointment of a secretary of state for American affairs and the suspension of the New York legislature for refusal to comply with the Quartering Act of 1765, which required colonial governments to supply certain items to British troops who were stationed permanently in America.

The Townshend Acts drew a quick response. One series of essays in particular, *Letters from a Farmer in Pennsylvania* by the prominent lawyer John Dickinson, expressed a broad consensus. Dickinson contended that Parliament could regulate colonial trade but could not exercise that power for the purpose of raising revenue. By drawing a distinction between the acceptable regulation of trade and unacceptable commercial taxation, Dickinson avoided the complicated question of colonial consent to parliamentary legislation. But his argument implied that the colonies would have to assess Parliament's motives in passing any law pertaining to imperial trade before deciding whether to obey it. That was clearly an unworkable position.

The Massachusetts assembly responded to the Townshend Acts by drafting a circular letter to the other colonial legislatures, calling for unity and suggesting a joint petition of protest. Not the letter itself but the ministry's reaction to it united the colonies. When Lord Hillsborough, the first secretary of

Massachusetts Assembly Dissolved

state for America, learned of the circular letter, he ordered Governor Francis Bernard of Massachusetts to insist that the assembly recall it. He also directed other governors to prevent their assemblies from discussing the letter. Hillsborough's order gave the colonial assemblies the incentive they needed to forget their differences and join forces to meet the new threat to their prerogatives. In late 1768, the Massachusetts legislature met, debated, and resoundingly rejected recall by a vote of 92 to 17. Bernard immediately dissolved the assembly, and other governors followed suit when their legislatures debated the circular letter.

During the two-year campaign against the Townshend duties, the Sons of Liberty and other American leaders made a deliberate effort to involve ordinary folk in the formal resistance movement, not just in occasional crowd actions. In a June 1769 Maryland nonimportation agreement, for instance, the signers (who were identified as "Merchants, Tradesmen, Freeholders, Mechanics [artisans], and other Inhabitants") agreed not to import or consume items of British origin. Such tactics helped to increase the number of colonists who were publicly aligned with the protest movement.

Just as the pamphlets by Otis, Dickinson, and others acquainted literate colonists with the issues raised by British action, public rituals taught illiterate Americans about the reasons for resistance and familiarized them with the terms of the argument. When Boston's Sons of Liberty invited hundreds of the city's residents to dine with them each August 14 to commemorate the first Stamp Act uprising and the Charleston Sons of Liberty held their meetings in public, crowds gathered to watch and listen. The participants in such events were expressing their commitment to the cause of resistance and urging others to join them.

Women, who had previously regarded politics as outside their proper sphere, now took a part in resisting British policy. In towns throughout America, young women calling **Daughters of Liberty** themselves Daughters of Liberty met to spin in public in an effort to spur other women to make homespun and end the colonies' dependence on English cloth. These symbolic displays of patriotism served an important purpose. When young ladies from well-to-do families sat publicly at spinning wheels all day, eating only American food and drinking local herbal tea, and afterward listening to patriotic sermons, they were serving as political instructors.

Women also took the lead in promoting nonconsumption of tea. In Boston, more than three hundred matrons publicly promised not to drink tea, "Sickness excepted." The women of Wilmington, North Carolina, burned their tea after walking through town in a solemn procession. Housewives throughout the colonies exchanged recipes for tea substitutes or drank coffee instead. The best known of the protests (because it was satirized by a British cartoonist), the so-called Edenton Ladies Tea Party, actually had little to do with tea; it was a meeting of prominent North Carolina women who pledged formally to work for the public good and to support resistance to British measures.

But the colonists were by no means united in support of nonimportation. If the Stamp Act protests had occasionally revealed a division between artisans and merchants, on the **Divided Opinion on Boycotts** one hand, and common laborers, on the other, resistance to the Townshend Acts exposed new splits in the American ranks. The most important divided the former allies of 1765 and 1766, the urban artisans and merchants, and it arose from a change in economic circumstances. The Stamp Act boycotts had helped to revive a depressed economy. In 1768 and 1769, by contrast, merchants were enjoying boom times and had no financial incentive to support a boycott. As a result, merchants signed the agreements only reluctantly. However, artisans, who recognized that the absence of British goods would create a ready market for their own manufactures, supported nonimportation enthusiastically. They also used coercion to enforce nonimportation.

Such tactics were effective: colonial imports from England dropped dramatically in 1769, especially in New York, New England, and Pennsylvania. But they also aroused significant opposition, creating a second major division among the colonists. Some Americans who supported resistance to British measures began to question the use of violence to force others to join the boycott. In addition, wealthier and more conservative colonists were frightened by the threat to private property inherent in the campaign. Moreover, political activism by ordinary colonists challenged the ruling elite's domination.

Americans were relieved when the news arrived in April 1770 that a new prime minister, Lord North, had persuaded Parliament to repeal the Townshend duties, except the tea tax, on the grounds that duties on trade within the empire were bad policy. Although some political leaders argued that nonimportation should be continued until the tea tax was repealed, merchants quickly resumed importing. The rest of the Townshend Acts remained in force, but repeal of the taxes made the other laws appear less objectionable.

Repeal of the Townshend Duties

Growing Rifts

At first, the new ministry did nothing to antagonize the colonists. Yet on the very day that Lord North proposed repeal of the Townshend duties, a clash between civilians and soldiers in Boston led to the deaths of five Americans. The origins of the event, which patriots called the Boston Massacre, lay in repeated clashes between customs officers and the people of Massachusetts. The Townshend Acts' creation of an American Board of Customs Commissioners had been error enough, but a decision to base the board in Boston severely compounded the mistake.

From the day of their arrival in November 1767, the customs commissioners were frequent targets of mob action. In June 1768, their seizure of the patriot leader John Hancock's sloop *Liberty* on suspicion of smuggling caused a riot. The riot in turn led the ministry in London to station two regiments in Boston. This act confirmed Bostonians' worst fears; the redcoats were a constant reminder of the oppressive potential of British power.

Bostonians, accustomed to leading their lives with a minimum of interference from government, now found themselves hemmed in at every turn. Guards on Boston Neck, the entrance to the city, checked all travelers and their goods. Redcoat patrols roamed the city day and night, questioning and sometimes harassing passers-by. But the greatest potential for violence lay in the uneasy relationship between the soldiers and Boston laborers. Many redcoats sought employment in their off-duty hours, competing for unskilled jobs with the city's ordinary workingmen, and members of the two groups brawled repeatedly.

On March 2, 1770, workers at a ropewalk (a ship-rigging factory) attacked some redcoats seeking jobs; a pitched battle resulted when both groups acquired reinforcements. Three days later, the tension exploded. Early on the evening of March 5, a crowd began throwing hard-packed snowballs at sentries guarding the Customs House. Goaded beyond endurance, the sentries fired on the crowd against express orders to the contrary, killing four and wounding eight, one of whom died a few days later. Resistance leaders idealized the dead rioters as martyrs for the cause of liberty. The best-known engraving of the massacre, by Paul Revere, was part of the propaganda campaign. It depicts a peaceful crowd, an officer ordering the soldiers to fire, and shots coming from the window of the Customs House.

Boston Massacre

The leading patriots wanted to make certain that the soldiers did not become martyrs as well. Despite the political benefits the patriots derived from the massacre, it is unlikely that they approved of the crowd action that provoked it. Thus, when the soldiers were tried for the killings in November, they were defended by John Adams and Josiah Quincy, Jr., both unwavering patriots. All but two of the accused men were acquitted, and those convicted were released after having been branded on the thumb. Undoubtedly, the favorable outcome of the trials prevented London officials from taking further steps against the city.

For more than two years after the Boston Massacre and the repeal of the Townshend duties, a superficial calm descended on the colonies. Local incidents, like the burning of the customs vessel *Gaspée* in 1772 by Rhode Islanders, marred the relationship of individual colonies and the mother country, but nothing caused Americans to join in a unified protest. Even so, the resistance movement continued to gather momentum. The most outspo-

Paul Revere's engraving of the Boston Massacre, a masterful piece of propaganda. At right, the British officer seems to be ordering the soldiers to fire on a peaceful, unresisting crowd. The Customs House has been labeled Butcher's Hall. *Library of Congress.*

ken colonial newspapers, such as the *Boston Gazette,* the *Pennsylvania Journal,* and the *South Carolina Gazette,* published essays drawing on Real Whig ideology and accusing Great Britain of a deliberate plan to oppress America. Patriot writers played repeatedly on the word *enslavement.* Most white colonists had direct knowledge of slavery (either being slaveholders themselves or having slaveowning neighbors), and the threat of enslavement by Britain must have hit them with peculiar force.

Still, no one yet advocated complete independence from the mother country. Though the patriots were becoming increasingly convinced that

they should seek freedom from parliamentary authority, they continued to acknowledge their British identity and to pledge their allegiance to George III. They began, therefore, to try to envision a system that would enable them to be ruled by their own elected legislatures while remaining loyal to the king. But any such scheme was totally alien to Britons' conception of the nature of their government, which was that Parliament held sole undivided sovereignty over the empire. Furthermore, in the British mind, Parliament encompassed the king, as well as lords and commons, and so separating the monarch from the legislature was impossible.

In the fall of 1772, the North ministry began to

implement the portion of the Townshend Acts that provided for governors and judges to be paid from customs revenues. In early November, voters at a Boston town meeting established a Committee of Correspondence to publicize the decision by exchanging letters with other Massachusetts towns. Samuel Adams, the man who had proposed its formation, became the committee's head. Adams was fifty-one years old in 1772, thirteen years the senior of his distant cousin John and a decade older than most other leaders of American resistance. An experienced political organizer, Adams continually stressed the necessity of prudent collective action. Thus his Committee of Correspondence undertook the task of creating an informed consensus among all the citizens of Massachusetts.

Committees of Correspondence

Such committees, which were soon established throughout the colonies, represented the next logical step in the organization of American resistance. Until 1772, the protest movement was largely confined to the seacoast and primarily to major cities and towns. Adams realized that the time had come to widen the movement's geographic scope and try to involve the residents of the interior in the struggle. Accordingly, the Boston town meeting directed the Committee of Correspondence "to state the Rights of the Colonists and of this Province in particular," to list "the Infringements and Violations thereof that have been, or from time to time may be made," and to send copies to the other towns in the province.

Samuel Adams, James Otis, Jr., and Josiah Quincy, Jr., prepared the statement of the colonists' rights. Declaring that Americans had absolute rights to life, liberty, and property, the committee asserted that the idea that "a British house of commons, should have a right, at pleasure, to give and grant the property of the colonists" was "irreconcileable" with "the first principles of natural law and Justice . . . and of the British Constitution in particular." The list of grievances, drafted by another group of prominent patriots, complained of taxation without representation, the presence of unnecessary troops and customs officers on American soil, the use of imperial revenues to pay colonial officials, the expanded jurisdiction of vice-admiralty courts, and even the nature of the instructions given to American governors by their superiors in London. No mention was made of obedience to Parliament. Patriots—at least in Boston—had placed American rights first, and loyalty to Great Britain a distant second.

The response of the Massachusetts towns to the committee's pamphlet must have caused Samuel Adams to rejoice. Some towns disagreed with Boston's assessment of the state of affairs, but most aligned themselves with the city. From Braintree came the assertion that "all civil officers are or ought to be Servants to the people and dependent upon them for their official Support, and every instance to the Contrary from the Governor downwards tends to crush and destroy civil liberty." The town of Holden declared that "the People of New England have never given the People of Britain any Right of Jurisdiction over us." The citizens of Petersham commented that resistance to tyranny was "the first and highest social Duty of this people." Such beliefs made the next crisis in Anglo-American affairs the final one.

The Boston Tea Party

The only one of the Townshend duties still in effect by 1773 was the tax on tea. Although a continuing tea boycott was less than fully effective, tea retained its explosive symbolic character. In May 1773, Parliament passed an act designed to save the East India Company from bankruptcy. The company was of critical importance to the British economy and to the financial well-being of many prominent British politicians. Resistance leaders were immediately suspicious. Under the Tea Act, certain duties paid on tea were to be returned to the company. Tea was to be sold only by designated agents, which would enable the East India Company to avoid colonial middlemen and undersell any competitors, even smugglers. The net result would be cheaper tea for American consumers. But many colonists interpreted the new measure as a pernicious device to make them admit Parliament's right to tax them, since the less expensive tea would still be taxed under the Townshend law. Others saw the Tea Act

Tea Act

as the first step in the establishment of an East India Company monopoly of all colonial trade.

New York City, Boston, Charleston, and Philadelphia were singled out to receive the first shipments of tea. Only Boston was the site of a dramatic confrontation. There both sides—the town meeting, joined by participants from nearby towns, and Governor Thomas Hutchinson—rejected compromise.

The first of three tea ships, the *Dartmouth,* entered Boston harbor on November 28. Under the customs laws, a cargo had to be landed and the appropriate duty paid within twenty days of a ship's arrival. If that was not done, the cargo would be seized by customs officers. After a series of mass meetings, Bostonians voted to prevent the tea from being unloaded and to post guards on the wharf. Hutchinson, for his part, refused to permit the vessels to leave the harbor.

On December 16, 1773, one day before the cargo would have to be confiscated, more than five thousand people (about a third of the city's population) crowded into Old South Church. The meeting, chaired by Samuel Adams, made a final attempt to persuade Hutchinson to send the tea back to England. But Hutchinson remained adamant. At about 6 P.M. Adams reportedly announced "that he could think of nothing further to be done—that they had now done all they could for the Salvation of their Country." As if his statement were a signal, cries rang out from the back of the crowd: "Boston harbor a teapot tonight! The Mohawks are come!" Small groups pushed their way out of the meeting. Within a few minutes, about sixty men crudely disguised as Indians assembled at the wharf, boarded the three ships, and dumped the cargo into the harbor. By 9 P.M. their work was done: 342 chests of tea worth approximately £10,000 floated in splinters on the ebbing tide.

At the news of the Tea Party, the North ministry proposed—in March 1774—the first of the four laws that became known as the Coercive, or Intolerable, Acts. It called for closing the

Coercive and Quebec Acts

port of Boston until the tea was paid for and prohibiting all but coastal trade in food and firewood. Later in the spring, Parliament passed three other punitive measures. The Massachusetts Government Act altered the province's charter, substituting an appointed council for the elected one,

increasing the powers of the governor, and forbidding special town meetings. The Justice Act provided that a person accused of committing murder in the course of suppressing a riot or enforcing the laws could be tried outside the colony where the incident had occurred. Finally, a new Quartering Act gave broad authority to military commanders seeking to house their troops in private dwellings.

After passing the last of the Coercive Acts in early June, Parliament turned its attention to needed reforms in the government of Quebec. The Quebec Act, though unrelated to the Coercive Acts, thus became linked with them in the minds of the patriots. The law granted greater religious freedom to Catholics—alarming the Protestant colonists, who regarded Roman Catholicism as a mainstay of religious and political despotism. It also reinstated French civil law and established an appointed council as the governing body of the colony. To protect Indians from white settlement, the act annexed to Quebec the area east of the Mississippi River and north of the Ohio River. Thus that region, parts of which were claimed by individual seacoast colonies, was removed from their jurisdiction.

Members of Parliament who voted for the punitive legislation believed that the acts would be obeyed. But the patriots showed little inclination to bow to the wishes of Parliament. In their eyes, the Coercive Acts and the Quebec Act proved what they had feared since 1768: that Great Britain had embarked on a deliberate plan to oppress them. If the port of Boston could be closed, why not those of Philadelphia or New York? If the royal charter of Massachusetts could be changed, why not that of South Carolina? If troops could be forcibly quartered in private houses, did not that pave the way for the occupation of all of America? If the Roman Catholic church could receive favored status in Quebec, why not everywhere? It seemed as though the full dimensions of the plot against American rights and liberties had at last been revealed.

The Boston Committee of Correspondence urged all the colonies to join in an immediate boycott of British goods. But the other provinces were not yet ready to take such a drastic step. Instead, they suggested that another intercolonial congress be convened to consider an appropriate response to the Coercive Acts. Few people wanted to take hasty action; even the most ardent patriots still hoped for reconciliation with Great Britain. And so the colonies agreed to send delegates to Philadelphia in September.

During the preceding decade, momentous changes had occurred in the ways that politically aware colonists thought about themselves and their allegiance. Once linked unquestioningly to Great Britain, they had begun to develop a sense of their own identity as Americans. They had started to realize that their concept of the political process differed from that held by people in the mother country. They also had come to understand that their economic interests did not necessarily coincide with those of Great Britain. Colonial political leaders reached such conclusions only after a long train of events, some of them violent, had altered their understanding of the nature of their relationship with the mother country.

In the late summer of 1774, the Americans were committed to resistance but not to independence. Even so, they had started to sever the bonds of empire. During the next decade, they would forge the bonds of a new American nationality to replace those rejected Anglo-American ties.

Suggestions for Further Reading

General

Ian R. Christie and Benjamin W. Labaree, *Empire or Independence, 1760–1776: A British-American Dialogue on the Coming of the American Revolution* (1976); Marc Egnal, *A Mighty Empire: The Origins of the American Revolution* (1988); Merrill Jensen, *The Founding of a Nation: A History of the American Revolution, 1763–1776* (1968); Edmund S. Morgan, *The Birth of the Republic, 1763–1789* (1956).

Colonial Warfare and the British Empire

Fred Anderson, *A People's Army: Massachusetts Soldiers and Society in the Seven Years' War* (1984); Douglas Leach, *Roots of Conflict: British Armed Forces and Colonial Americans, 1677–1763* (1986); Howard H. Peckham, *The Colonial Wars, 1689–1762* (1963); Alan Rogers, *Empire and Liberty: American Resistance to British Authority, 1755–1763* (1974).

British Politics and Policy

John Brooke, *King George III* (1972); John L. Bullion, *A Great and Necessary Measure: George Grenville and the Genesis of the Stamp Act, 1763–1765* (1981); Bernard Donoughue, *British Politics and the American Revolution: The Path to War, 1773–1775* (1965); Lewis B. Namier, *England in the Age of the American Revolution*, 2nd ed. (1961); P. D. G. Thomas, *The Townshend Duties Crisis* (1987).

Indians and the West

Thomas P. Abernethy, *Western Lands and the American Revolution* (1959); Richard Aquila, *The Iroquois Restoration: Iroquois Diplomacy on the Colonial Frontier, 1701–1754* (1983); David H. Corkran, *The Cherokee Frontier: Conflict and Survival, 1740–1762* (1962); Francis Jennings, *Empire of Fortune: Crowns, Colonies and Tribes in the Seven Years' War in America* (1988); Howard H. Peckham, *Pontiac and the Indian Uprising* (1947); Jack M. Sosin, *Whitehall and the Wilderness: The Middle West in British Colonial Policy, 1760–1775* (1961).

Political and Economic Thought

Bernard Bailyn, *The Ideological Origins of the American Revolution* (1967); Jay Fliegelman, *Prodigals and Pilgrims: The American Revolution Against Patriarchal Authority, 1750–1800* (1982); Caroline Robbins, *The Eighteenth-Century Commonwealthman: Studies in the Transmission, Development, and Circumstance of English Liberal Thought from the Restoration of Charles II Until the War with the Thirteen Colonies* (1959); Clinton Rossiter, *Seedtime of the Republic: The Origin of the American Tradition of Political Liberty* (1953).

American Resistance

David Ammerman, *In the Common Cause: American Response to the Coercive Acts of 1774* (1974); Richard Beeman, *Patrick Henry: A Biography* (1974); Richard D. Brown, *Revolutionary Politics in Massachusetts: The Boston Committee of Correspondence and the Towns, 1772–1774* (1970); Dirk Hoerder, *Crowd Action in Revolutionary Massachusetts, 1765–1780* (1977); Rhys Isaac, *The Transformation of Virginia, 1740–1790* (1982); Benjamin W. Labaree, *The Boston Tea Party* (1964); Pauline R. Maier, *The Old Revolutionaries: Political Lives in the Age of Samuel Adams* (1980); Pauline R. Maier, *From Resistance to Revolution: Colonial Radicals and the Development of American Opposition to Britain, 1765–1776* (1972); Edmund S. Morgan and Helen M. Morgan, *The Stamp Act Crisis: Prologue to Revolution* (1953); Gary B. Nash, *The Urban Crucible: Social Change, Political Consciousness, and the Origins of the American Revolution* (1979); Peter Shaw, *American Patriots and the Rituals of Revolution* (1981); John W. Tyler, *Smugglers and Patriots: Boston Merchants and the Advent of the American Revolution* (1986); Hiller B. Zobel, *The Boston Massacre* (1970).

On November 20, 1837, Sarah Benjamin, then eighty-one years old, applied for a pension as the widow of a Revolutionary War soldier. She declared that she had married Aaron Osborn, a blacksmith, in Albany in 1780. After he enlisted, he insisted that she accompany him to the army. The narrative she dictated in 1837 is the only known autobiographical account left by one of the thousands of women who traveled with the revolutionary army as "camp followers."

For the first eighteen months of their service, Sarah and Aaron Osborn were stationed at West Point, on the Hudson River, where she did washing and sewing for the soldiers. Three other women were also attached to the company—an unmarried black woman and the wives of a sergeant and a lieutenant. This orderly existence changed abruptly in the fall of 1781, when their unit joined others marching hurriedly to Yorktown under the command of General George Washington.

5

A REVOLUTION, INDEED, 1775–1783

There, she reported, she "busied herself washing, mending, and cooking for the soldiers, in which she was assisted by the other females." At intervals she carried beef, bread, and coffee to the front lines. Once she met Washington himself, who asked whether she was afraid of the cannonballs. Osborn staunchly replied, "It would not do for the men to fight and starve too." One day she heard the British drums "beat excessively" and inquired what had happened. "The British have surrendered," she was told. She then watched the redcoats' ceremonial capitulation: the army "marched out beating and playing a melancholy tune, their drums covered with black handkerchiefs and their fifes with black ribbands tied around them."

The Osborns returned north with the army and stayed until the troops were disbanded in early 1784. Soon afterward, Aaron Osborn deserted his wife, leaving her with two young children. After he contracted a bigamous second marriage, she decided she too was free to remarry. Her second husband, John Benjamin, was also an army veteran, and in response to her 1837 petition the government awarded her a double pension in honor of her two husbands. Her own service earned her nothing.

The Revolution was more than just a series of clashes between British and patriot armies. It uprooted thousands of families like the Osborns, disrupted the economy, reshaped society by forcing many colonists into permanent exile, led Americans to develop new conceptions of politics, and created a nation from thirteen separate colonies. Thus it marked a significant turning point in Americans' collective history.

The struggle for independence required revolutionary leaders to accomplish three separate but closely related tasks. The first was political and ideological: they had to transform the 1760s consensus favoring loyal resistance into a coalition supporting independence. The second task was diplomatic. To win their independence, the patriot leaders knew they needed international recognition and aid, particularly assistance from France. Thus they dispatched to Paris Benjamin Franklin, the most experienced American diplomat. Franklin skillfully negotiated the Franco-American alliance of 1778, which was to prove crucial to the winning of independence.

Only the third task directly involved the British. George Washington, commander-in-chief of the American army, quickly realized that his primary goal should be not to win battles but rather to avoid losing them decisively. He understood that, as long as his army survived to fight another day, the outcome of any individual battle was more or less irrelevant. Accordingly, the story of the Revolutionary War reveals British action and American reaction, British attacks and American defenses. The American war effort was aided by the failure of British military planners to analyze accurately the problem confronting them. Until it was too late, they treated the war against the colonists as they did wars against other Europeans—that is, they concentrated on winning battles and did not consider the difficulties inherent in achieving their main goal, retaining the colonies' allegiance. In the end, the Americans' triumph owed more to their own endurance and to Britain's mistakes than to their military prowess.

Government by Congress and Committee

When the fifty-five delegates to the First Continental Congress convened in Philadelphia in September 1774, they knew that any measures they adopted were likely to enjoy support among many of their fellow countrymen and countrywomen. During the summer of 1774, open meetings held throughout the colonies had endorsed the idea of another nonimportation pact. The committees of correspondence that had been established in many communities publicized these meetings so effectively that Americans everywhere knew about them. Most of the congressional delegates were selected by extralegal provincial conventions, whose members were chosen at such local gatherings, since the royal governors had forbidden the regular assemblies to conduct formal elections. Thus the very act of designating delegates to attend the Continental Congress involved Americans in open defiance of British authority.

First Continental Congress

The colonies' leading political figures—most of them lawyers, merchants, or planters—were sent to the Philadelphia Congress. The Massachusetts delegation included both Samuel Adams and his younger cousin John, an ambitious lawyer. Among others, New York sent John Jay, a talented young attorney. From Pennsylvania came the conservative Joseph Galloway and his long-time rival John Dickinson. Virginia elected Richard Henry Lee and Patrick Henry, both noted for their patriotic zeal, as well as George Washington.

The congressmen faced three tasks when they convened on September 5, 1774. The first two were explicit: defining American grievances and developing a plan for resistance. The third—outlining a theory of their constitutional relationship with England—proved troublesome. The most radical congressmen, like Lee of Virginia, argued that the colonists owed allegiance only to George III and that Parliament was nothing more than a local legislature for Great Britain, with no authority over the colonies. By contrast, the conservatives—Joseph Galloway and his allies—proposed a formal plan of union that would have required the joint consent of Parliament and a new general American legislature to all laws pertaining to the colonies. After a heated debate, the delegates rejected Galloway's proposal, but they were not prepared to accept the radicals' position either.

Finally, they accepted a compromise position

1774	First Continental Congress	1778	French alliance with the United States
1775	Battles of Lexington and Concord		British evacuate Philadelphia
	Second Continental Congress	1779	Sullivan expedition against Iroquois villages
	Lord Dunmore's Proclamation		
1776	Thomas Paine, *Common Sense*	1780	British take Charleston
	British evacuate Boston		
	Declaration of Independence	1781	Cornwallis surrenders at Yorktown
	New York campaign	1782	Peace negotiations begin
1777	British take Philadelphia		
	Burgoyne surrenders at Saratoga	1783	Treaty of Paris

worked out by John Adams. The crucial clause that Adams drafted in the congressional Declaration of Rights and Grievances read in part: "From the necessity of the case, and a regard to the mutual interest of both countries, we cheerfully consent to the operation of such acts of the British parliament, as are bona fide, restrained to the regulation of our external commerce." Note the key phrases. "From the necessity of the case" declared that Americans had decided to obey Parliament only because they had decided that doing so was in the best interest of both countries. "Bona fide, restrained to the regulation of our external commerce" made it clear to Lord North that they would continue to resist taxes in disguise, like the Townshend duties. Most striking of all was the fact that such language, which only a few years before would have been regarded as irredeemably radical, could be presented and accepted as a compromise in the fall of 1774.

Declaration of Rights and Grievances

With the constitutional issue resolved, the delegates readily agreed on a list of the laws they wanted repealed (notably the Coercive Acts) and decided to implement an economic boycott while petitioning the king for relief. They adopted the Continental Association, which called for nonimportation of British goods (effective December 1, 1774), nonconsumption of British products (effec-

tive March 1, 1775), and nonexportation of American goods to Britain and the British West Indies (effective September 10, 1775, so that southern planters would have a chance to market their 1774 tobacco crop).

To enforce the Continental Association, Congress recommended the election of committees of observation and inspection in every county, city, and town in America. Since Congress specified that committee members be chosen by all persons qualified to vote for members of the lower house of the colonial legislatures, the committees were guaranteed a broad popular base. The seven to eight thousand members selected in all the colonies became the local leaders of American resistance.

Committees of Observation

Officially, these committees were charged only with overseeing the implementation of the boycott, but over the next six months they became de facto governments. They examined merchants' records and published the names of those who continued to import British goods. They also promoted home manufactures and encouraged Americans to adopt simple modes of dress and behavior. Since expensive leisure-time activities were symbols of vice and corruption, Congress urged Americans to forgo dancing, gambling, horse racing, cock fighting, and other forms of "extravagance and dissipation." In enforcing these injunctions, the committees gradually extended their authority over many aspects of American life.

The committees also attempted to identify opponents of American resistance, developed elaborate spy networks, and investigated reports of dissident remarks and activities. Suspected dissenters were first urged to convert to the colonial cause; if they failed to do so, the committees had them watched, restricted their movements, or tried to force them to leave the area. People engaging in casual political exchanges with friends one day could find themselves charged with "treasonable conversation" the next.

While the committees of observation were expanding their power during the winter and early spring of 1775, the established governments of the colonies were collapsing. Only in Connecticut, Rhode Island, Delaware, and Pennsylvania did regular assemblies continue to meet without encountering patriot challenges to their authority. In every other colony, popularly elected provincial conventions took over the task of running the government, sometimes entirely replacing the legislatures and at other times holding concurrent sessions. In late 1774 and early 1775, these conventions approved the Continental Association, elected delegates to the Second Continental Congress (scheduled for May), organized militia units, and gathered arms and ammunition. The British-appointed governors and councils, unable to stem the tide of resistance, watched helplessly as their authority crumbled. Courts were prevented from holding sessions; taxes were paid to agents of the conventions rather than to provincial tax collectors; sheriffs' powers were questioned; and militiamen refused to muster except by order of the local committees. In short, during the six months preceding the battles at Lexington and Concord, independence was being won at the local level, but without formal acknowledgment and, for the most part, without shooting or bloodshed. Not many Americans fully realized what was happening. The vast majority still proclaimed their loyalty to Great Britain and denied that they sought to leave the empire. Among the few who did recognize the trend toward independence were those who opposed it.

Provincial Conventions

Choosing Sides: Loyalists, Blacks, and Indians

The first protests against British measures, in the mid-1760s, had won the support of most colonists. Only in the late 1760s and early 1770s did a significant number of Americans begin to question both the aims and the tactics of the resistance movement. In 1774 and 1775, such people found themselves in a difficult position. Like their more radical counterparts, most of them objected to parliamentary policies and wanted some kind of constitutional reform. But their desire to uphold the legally constituted colonial governments and their fear of anarchy made them especially sensitive to the dangers of resistance. If forced to a choice, these colonists sympathized with Great Britain rather than with an independent America.

In 1774 and 1775, some conservatives began to publish essays and pamphlets critical of Congress and its allied committees. In New York City, a group of Anglican clergymen jointly wrote pamphlets and essays arguing the importance of maintaining a cordial connection between England and America. In Massachusetts, the young attorney Daniel Leonard, using the pseudonym Massachusettensis, engaged in a prolonged newspaper debate with Novanglus (John Adams). Leonard and the others realized that what had begun as a dispute over the extent of American subordination within the empire had now raised the question of whether the colonies would remain linked to Great Britain at all.

Some colonists heeded the conservative pamphleteers' warnings. About one-fifth of the white American population remained loyal to Great Britain, actively opposing independence. With notable exceptions, most people of the following types remained loyal to the Crown: British-appointed government officials; merchants whose trade depended on imperial connections; Anglican clergy everywhere and lay Anglicans in the North; former officers and enlisted men from the British army; non-English ethnic minorities, especially Scots; tenant farmers, particularly those whose landlords

Loyalists, Patriots, and Neutrals

sided with the patriots; members of persecuted religious sects; and many of the backcountry southerners who had rebelled against eastern rule in the 1760s and early 1770s. All these people had one thing in common: the patriot leaders were their long-standing enemies. Local and provincial disputes thus helped to determine which side a person chose in the imperial conflict.

The active patriots, who accounted for about two-fifths of the white population, came chiefly from the groups that had dominated colonial society, either numerically or politically. Among them were yeoman farmers, members of dominant Protestant sects, Chesapeake gentry, merchants dealing mainly in American commodities, city artisans, elected officeholders, and people of English descent. Wives usually, but not always, adopted their husbands' political beliefs.

The remaining two-fifths of the white population tried to avoid taking sides. This segment included sincere pacifist Quakers and those who simply wanted to be left alone. In the southern backcountry, many Scotch-Irish took a neutral position, for they had little love for either the patriot gentry or the English authorities.

To American patriots, that sort of apathy or neutrality was a crime as heinous as loyalism. Those who were not for them were against them; in their minds, there could be no conscientious objectors. By the winter of 1775–1776, the Second Continental Congress was recommending to the states that all "disaffected" persons be disarmed and arrested. The state legislatures quickly passed laws prescribing severe penalties for suspected loyalists. Many began to require all voters (or, in some cases, all free adult males) to take oaths of allegiance; the punishment for refusal was usually banishment or extra taxes. After 1777, many states confiscated the property of banished loyalists and used the proceeds for the war effort. Perhaps as many as 100,000 white loyalists were forced into exile, but they were not the only Americans to concern the patriots.

Slaves faced a dilemma at the beginning of the Revolution: how could they best achieve their goal of escaping perpetual servitude? Should they fight with or against their white masters? The correct choice was not immediately apparent, and so

The Blacks' Dilemma

blacks made different decisions. Some indeed joined the revolutionaries, but to most an alliance with the British appeared more promising. Thus news of slave conspiracies surfaced in different parts of the colonies in late 1774 and early 1775. All shared a common element: a plan to assist the British in return for freedom. A group of blacks petitioned General Thomas Gage, the commander-in-chief of the British army in Boston, promising to fight for the redcoats if he would liberate them. The governor of Maryland authorized the issuance of extra guns to militiamen in four counties where slave uprisings were expected. The most serious incident occurred during the summer of 1775, in Charleston, where Thomas Jeremiah, a free black harbor pilot, was brutally executed after being convicted of attempting to foment a slave revolt.

Concern over the slave population affected the level of revolutionary sentiment in the colonies. In the North, where whites greatly outnumbered blacks, revolutionary fervor was at its height. But in South Carolina, which was more than 60 percent black, and Georgia, where the racial balance was nearly even, whites were noticeably less enthusiastic about resistance. Georgia, in fact, sent no delegates to the First Continental Congress and reminded its representatives at the Second Continental Congress to consider its circumstances, "with our blacks and tories within us," when voting on the question of independence.

Racial Composition and Patriotic Fervor

The whites' worst fears were realized in November 1775, when Lord Dunmore, the governor of Virginia, offered to free any slaves and indentured servants who would leave their patriot masters to join the British forces. Dunmore hoped to use blacks in his fight against the revolutionaries and to disrupt the economy by depriving white Americans of their labor force. But fewer blacks than expected rallied to the British standard in 1775 and 1776 (there were at most two thousand), and many of them perished in a smallpox epidemic. Even so, Dunmore's proclamation led Congress in January 1776 to modify an earlier policy that had prohibited the enlistment of blacks in the Continental Army.

Although black Americans did not pose a serious threat to the revolutionary cause in its early

RUN away from *Hampton*, on *Sunday* laſt, a luſty Mulatto Fellow named ARGYLE, well known about the Country, has a Scar on one of his Wriſts, and has loſt one or more of his fore Teeth; he is a very handy Fellow by Water, or about the Houſe, &c. loves Drink, and is very bold in his Cups, but daſtardly when ſober. Whether he will go for a Man of War's Man, or not, I cannot ſay; but I will give 40 s. to have him brought to me. He can read and write.
NOVEMBER 2, 1775. JACOB WRAY.

An advertisement for a runaway slave suspected of joining Lord Dunmore—a common sight in Virginia and Maryland newspapers during the fall and winter of 1775 and 1776. *Virginia State Library and Archives.*

years, the patriots managed to turn rumors of slave uprisings to their own advantage. In South Carolina, they won adherents by promoting white unity under the revolutionary banner. The Continental Association was needed, they argued, to protect whites from blacks at a time when the royal government was unable to muster adequate defense forces. Undoubtedly, many wavering Carolinians were drawn into the revolutionary camp by fear that an overt division among the colony's whites would encourage a slave revolt.

A similar factor—the threat of Indian attacks—helped to persuade some reluctant westerners to support the struggle against Great Britain. In the years since the Proclamation of 1763, British officials had won the trust of the interior tribes by attempting to protect them from land-hungry whites. In 1768, the British-appointed superintendents of Indian affairs, John Stuart in the South and Sir William Johnson in the North, negotiated two treaties—signed at Hard Labor Creek, South Carolina, and at Fort Stanwix, New York—with the tribes. The treaties supposedly established permanent western borders for the colonies. But just a few years later, the British pushed the southern boundary even farther west to accommodate the demands of whites in western Georgia and Kentucky.

By the time of the Revolution, the Indians were impatient with white Americans' aggressive pressure on their lands. The relationship of the tribes

The Indians' Grievances and frontier whites was filled with bitterness, misunderstanding, and occasional bloody encounters. In combination with the tribes' confidence in Stuart and Johnson, such grievances predisposed most Indians toward an alliance with the British. Even so, the latter hesitated to make full and immediate use of their potential Indian allies. The superintendents were aware that tribal war aims and the Indians' style of fighting were not necessarily compatible with those of the British. Accordingly, they sought nothing more from the tribes than a promise of neutrality.

The patriots, recognizing that their standing with the tribes was poor, also sought the Indians' neutrality. In 1775, the Second Continental Congress sent a general message to the tribes describing the war as "a family quarrel between us and Old England" and requesting that they "not join on either side," since "you Indians are not concerned in it." A branch of the Cherokee tribe, led by Chief Dragging Canoe, nevertheless decided that the whites' "family quarrel" would allow them to settle some old scores. They attacked white settlements along the western borders of the Carolinas and Virginia in the summer of 1776. But a coordinated campaign by Carolina and Virginia militia destroyed many Cherokee towns, along with crops and large quantities of supplies. Dragging Canoe and his diehard followers fled west to the Tennessee River, where they established new outposts; the rest of the Cherokees agreed to a treaty that ceded more of their land to the whites.

The fate of the Cherokees—forced to fight alone without other Indian allies—foreshadowed the history of Indian involvement in the American Revolution.

Lack of Unity Among Indians During the eighteenth century, the Iroquois had forcefully established their dominance over neighboring tribes. But the basis of their power started to disintegrate with the British victory over France in 1763, and their subsequent friendship with Sir William Johnson could not prevent the erosion of their position during the years before 1775. Tribes long resentful of Iroquois power (and of the similar status of the Cherokees in the South) saw little reason to ally themselves with those from whose dominance they had just escaped, even to prevent white encroachment on their lands. Consequently, most tribes pursued a course that aligned them with neither side and kept them out of active involvement in the war.

Thus, although the patriots could never completely ignore the threats posed by loyalists, blacks, neutrals, and Indians, only rarely did fear of these groups seriously hamper the revolutionary movement. Occasionally, militia on the frontier refused to turn out for duty on the seaboard because they feared Indians would attack in their absence. Indeed, the practical impossibility of a large-scale slave revolt, coupled with tribal feuds and the patriots' successful campaign to disarm and neutralize loyalists, ensured that the revolutionaries would remain firmly in control as they fought for independence.

War Begins

On January 27, 1775, Lord Dartmouth, secretary of state for America, addressed a fateful letter to General Thomas Gage in Boston. Expressing his belief that American resistance was nothing more than the response of a "rude rabble without plan," Dartmouth ordered Gage to arrest "the principal actors and abettors in the provincial congress." If such a step were taken swiftly and silently, Dartmouth observed, no bloodshed need occur."

By the time Dartmouth's letter reached Gage, on April 14, the major patriot leaders had already left Boston. Spurred to action by the letter, Gage decided to send an expedition to confiscate provincial military supplies stockpiled at Concord.

Battles of Lexington and Concord Bostonians dispatched two messengers, William Dawes and Paul Revere (later joined by a third, Dr. Samuel Prescott), to rouse the countryside. Thus when the British vanguard approached Lexington at dawn on April 19, they found a straggling group of seventy militiamen—approximately half the adult male population of the town—drawn up before them on the town common. The Americans' commander, Captain John Parker, ordered his men to withdraw, realizing they could not halt the redcoat advance. But as they began to disperse, a shot rang out; the British soldiers then fired several volleys. When they stopped, eight Americans lay dead and another ten had been wounded. The British moved on to Concord, five miles away.

At Concord, British troops suffered their first casualties of the war when they were attacked by patriot militia at the North Bridge. Before the day ended, thousands of colonial militiamen harassed the British on their march back to Boston. The redcoats suffered 272 casualties (70 dead) and inflicted only 93 casualties on the patriots.

By the evening of April 20, perhaps as many as twenty thousand American militiamen had gathered around Boston, summoned by local committees that spread the alarm across the New England countryside. Many did not stay long, since they were needed at home for spring planting, but those who remained dug in along siege lines encircling the city. For nearly a year the two armies sat and stared at each other across those lines. The only battle occurred on June 17, when the British drove the Americans from trenches atop Breed's Hill in Charlestown. In that misnamed Battle of Bunker Hill, the British incurred their greatest losses of the entire war: more than 800 wounded and 228 killed. The Americans lost less than half that number. Elsewhere in the first eleven months of the war, the patriots captured Fort Ticonderoga, a British fort on Lake Champlain, acquiring much-needed cannon. In the hope of bringing Canada into the war on the American side, they also mounted a northern campaign that ended in disaster at Quebec in early 1776. Most significantly, the lull of the first year of the war gave both sides a chance to regroup, organize, and plan their strategies.

Lord North and his new American secretary, Lord George Germain, made three major assumptions about the war they faced. First, they concluded that patriot forces could **British** not withstand the assaults of **Strategy** trained British regulars. Accordingly, they dispatched to America the largest single force Great Britain had ever assembled anywhere: 370 transport ships carrying 32,000 troops and tons of supplies, accompanied by 73 naval vessels and 13,000 sailors. Such an extraordinary effort would, they thought, ensure a quick victory. Second, British officials and army officers persisted in comparing this war to wars they had fought successfully in Europe. Thus they adopted a conventional strategy of capturing major American cities. Third, they assumed that a clear-cut military victory would automatically bring about their goal of retaining the colonies' allegiance.

All these assumptions proved false. North and Germain, like Lord Dartmouth before them, vastly underestimated the Americans' commitment to armed resistance. Defeats on the battlefield did not lead the patriots to abandon their political aims and sue for peace. At one time or another during the war, the British controlled all major American ports, but with fifteen hundred miles of coastline, their actions did not halt essential commerce. Since less than 5 percent of the population lived in those cities, their loss did little damage to the American cause.

Most of all, the British did not grasp at first that a military victory would not necessarily bring a political victory. Securing the colonies permanently would require hundreds of thousands of Americans to return to their original allegiance. The conquest of America was thus a far more complicated task than the defeat of France twelve years earlier. The British needed not only to overpower the patriots, but also to convert them. They never fully realized that they were fighting an entirely new kind of conflict: the first modern war of national liberation.

The British at least had a bureaucracy ready to supervise the war effort. The Americans had only the Second Continental Congress, originally intended merely as a brief gathering **Second** of colonial representatives to con- **Continental** sider the British response to the **Congress** Continental Association. Instead, the delegates who convened in Philadelphia on May 10, 1775, found that they had to assume the mantle of intercolonial government. Yet as the summer passed, Congress slowly organized the colonies for war. It authorized the printing of money with which to purchase necessary goods, established a committee to supervise relations with foreign countries, and took steps to strengthen the militia. Most important of all, it created the Continental Army and appointed its generals.

Until Congress met, the Massachusetts provincial congress had taken responsibility for organizing the massive army of militia encamped at Boston. Because the cost of maintaining that army was too great, Massachusetts asked the Continental Congress to assume control of the army. Until then, the war had been a wholly northern affair. To ensure unity, Congress selected a non–New Englander to be the commander-in-chief. The only obvious and unanimous choice was a fellow delegate, George Washington of Virginia.

Washington was no fiery radical, nor was he a reflective political thinker. He had not played a prominent role in the prerevolutionary agitation, but his devotion to the Ameri- **George** can cause was unquestioned. **Washington:** He was dignified, conservative, **A Portrait of** and respectable—a man of un- **Leadership** impeachable integrity. Though unmistakably an aristocrat, Washington was unswervingly committed to representative government. Moreover, he both looked and acted like a leader. Six feet tall in an era when most men were five inches shorter, he had a stately and commanding presence. Other patriots praised his judgment, steadiness, and discretion, and even a loyalist admitted that Washington could "atone for many demerits by the extraordinary coolness and caution which distinguish his character."

Washington needed all the coolness and caution he could muster when he took command of the army outside Boston in July 1775. It took him months to impose hierarchy and discipline on the unruly troops and to bring order to the supply system. But by March 1776, the army was prepared to act. As it happened, an assault on Boston proved unnecessary. Sir William Howe, who had replaced Gage, had been considering an evacuation for some time; he wanted to transfer his troops to New York City. The patriots' bombardment of Boston early in the month decided the matter. On March 17, the British and more than a thousand of their loyalist allies abandoned Boston forever.

That spring of 1776, as the British fleet left Boston for the temporary haven of Halifax, Nova Scotia, the colonies were moving inexorably toward the unthinkable—a declaration of independence. But already in January 1776, a pamphlet had appeared, written by a man who both thought the unthinkable and advocated it.

Thomas Paine's *Common Sense*

Thomas Paine's *Common Sense* exploded on the American scene like a bombshell. Within three months of publication, it sold 120,000 copies. The author, a radical English printer who had lived in America only since 1774, called stridently and stirringly for independence. More than that: Paine rejected the notion that a balance of monarchy, aristocracy, and democracy was necessary to preserve freedom and advocated instead the establishment of a republic. Instead of acknowledging the benefits of a connection with the mother country, Paine insisted that Britain had exploited the colonies unmercifully. In place of the frequently heard assertion that an independent America would be weak and divided, he substituted an unlimited confidence in America's strength when freed from European control.

There is no way of knowing how many people were converted to the cause of independence by reading *Common Sense*. But by late spring, independence had clearly become inevitable. On May 10, 1776, the Second Continental Congress formally recommended that individual colonies "adopt such governments as shall, in the opinion of the representatives of the people, best conduce to the happiness and safety of their constituents in particular, and America in general." From that source grew the first state constitutions.

Then, on June 7, came confirmation of the movement toward independence. Richard Henry Lee of Virginia, seconded by John Adams of Massachusetts, introduced the crucial resolution: "that these United Colonies are, and of right ought to be, free and independent States, that they are absolved of all allegiance to the British Crown, and that all political connection between them and the State of Great Britain is, and ought to be, totally dissolved." Congress debated the resolution and directed a committee composed of Thomas Jefferson, John Adams, Benjamin Franklin, Robert R. Livingston of New York, and Roger Sherman of Connecticut to draft a declaration of independence. The committee in turn assigned primary responsibility for writing the declaration to Jefferson, a Virginia lawyer widely read in history and political theory and well known for his apt and eloquent style.

Declaration of Independence

The draft of the declaration was laid before Congress on June 28. The delegates officially voted for independence four days later, then debated the wording of the declaration for two more days, adopting it with some changes on July 4. Since Americans had long since ceased to see themselves as legitimate subjects of Parliament, the Declaration of Independence concentrated on George III (see the Appendix). That focus also provided a single identifiable villain on whom to center the charges of misconduct.

The declaration's long-term importance, however, did not lie in its catalogue of grievances against George III but rather in its ringing statements of principle. These statements have served ever since as the ideal to which Americans aspire: "We hold these truths to be self-evident: That all men are created equal; that they are endowed by their Creator with certain unalienable rights; that among these are life, liberty and the pursuit of happiness; that, to secure these rights, governments are instituted among men, deriving their just powers from the consent of the governed; that whenever any form of government becomes destructive of these ends, it is the right of the people to alter or to abolish it, and to institute new government." The phrases have echoed down through American history like no others.

After listening to the first formal reading of the Declaration of Independence in New York City on July 9, 1776, a crowd of American soldiers and civilians pulled down a statue of George III that stood on the Bowling Green in the heart of the city. Most of the statue was later melted down into bullets, but a British officer rescued the head, which was later taken to London. *Library of Congress.*

The delegates in Philadelphia who voted to accept the Declaration of Independence did not have the advantage of our two hundred years of hindsight. When they adopted the declaration, they risked their necks: they were committing treason. Thus when they concluded the declaration with the assertion that they "mutually pledge[d] to each other our lives, our fortunes, and our sacred honor," they spoke no less than the truth. The real struggle still lay before them.

The Long Struggle in the North

On July 2, 1776, the day Congress voted for independence, the first of Sir William Howe's troops from Halifax landed on Staten Island. But Howe delayed his attack on New York City until mid-August, when additional troops arrived from England. The delay gave Washington sufficient time to march his army south to meet the threat. To defend New York, Washington had ten thousand Continentals, who had promised to serve until the end of the year, and seven thousand militiamen, who had enlisted for shorter terms. Neither he nor most of his men had ever fought a major battle against the British, and their lack of experience led to disastrous mistakes. The difficulty of defending New York City only compounded the errors.

Washington's problem was as simple as the geography of the region was complex (see map). To protect the city adequately, he would have to divide his forces among Long Island, Manhattan Island, and the mainland. But the British fleet under Admiral Lord Richard Howe, Sir William's brother, controlled the harbors and rivers that divided the American

Battle for New York City

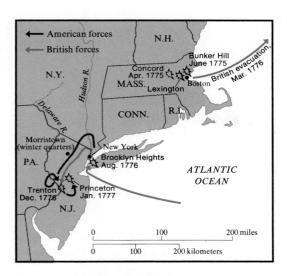

The War in the North, 1775–1777

forces. The patriots thus constantly courted catastrophe, for swift action by the British navy could cut off the possibility of retreat and perhaps even communication. But despite these dangers, Washington could not afford to surrender New York to the Howes without a fight. Not only did the city occupy a strategic location, but the region that surrounded it was known to contain many loyalist sympathizers. A show of force was essential if the revolutionaries were to retain any hope of persuading waverers to join them.

On August 27, Sir William Howe's forces attacked the American positions on Brooklyn Heights, pushing the untried rebel troops back into their defensive entrenchments. But Howe failed to press his advantage, even neglecting to send his brother's ships into the East River to cut off a retreat. Consequently, the Americans were able to escape. Washington then moved north on the island, retreating onto the mainland. But the nearly three thousand men he left behind in the supposedly impregnable Fort Washington on the west shore of Manhattan had to surrender to Howe in early November.

George Washington had defended New York, but badly. He had repeatedly broken a basic rule of military strategy: never divide your force in the face of a superior enemy. In the end, though, the Howe brothers' failure to move quickly prevented a decisive defeat of the Americans. Although Washington's army had been seriously reduced by casualties, the surrender of Fort Washington, and the loss of most of the militiamen (who had returned home for the harvest), its core remained. Through November and December, Washington led his men in a retreat across New Jersey. Howe followed at a leisurely pace, setting up a string of outposts manned mostly by Hessian mercenaries. After Washington crossed the Delaware River into Pennsylvania, the British commander turned back and settled into comfortable winter quarters in New York City.

The British controlled most of New Jersey, and hundreds of Americans accepted the pardons offered by the Howes. Occupying troops met little opposition, and the revolutionary cause appeared to be in disarray. "These are the times that try men's souls," wrote Thomas Paine in his pamphlet *The Crisis.*

In the aftermath of battle, as at its height, the British commanders let their advantage slip away. The redcoats stationed in New Jersey went on a rampage of rape and plunder. Because loyalists and patriots were indistinguishable to the British and Hessian troops, families on both sides suffered nearly equally. Houses were looted and burned, churches and public buildings desecrated. But nothing was better calculated to rally doubtful Americans to the cause than the wanton murder of innocent civilians and the rape of women.

The soldiers' marauding alienated potentially loyal New Jerseyites and Pennsylvanians, whose allegiance the British could ill afford to lose. It also spurred Washington's determination to strike back. With the enlistments of most of the Continental troops scheduled to expire on December 31, Washington decided to strike quickly. He first struck the Hessian encampment at Trenton early on the morning of December 26. The patriots captured more than nine hundred Hessians and killed another thirty; only three Americans were wounded. A few days later, Washington attacked Princeton. Having buoyed American spirits with the two victories, Washington set up winter quarters at Morristown, New Jersey.

Battle of Trenton

The campaign of 1776 established patterns that were to persist throughout much of the war. British forces, although usually numerically superior to the Americans, engaged in ponderous maneuvering, lacked familiarity with the terrain, and antagonized the populace. Furthermore, although Washington always seemed to lack regular troops—the Continental Army never numbered more than 18,500 men—he could usually count on the militia to join him at crucial times. American militiamen did not like to sign up for long terms of service or to fight far from home, but when their homes were threatened they would rally to the cause.

As the war dragged on, the Continental Army and the militia took on decidedly different characters. State governments, responsible for filling military quotas, discovered that most men willing to enlist for long periods in the regular army were young, single, and footloose. Farmers with families tended to prefer short-term militia duty. As the supply of whites willing to sign up with the Continentals diminished, recruiters in the northern states turned increasingly to blacks, both slave and free. Perhaps as many as five thousand blacks eventually served in the revolutionary army, and most of them won their freedom as a result. Camp followers, like Sarah Osborn, also rendered service to the army. These women, usually the wives and widows of poor soldiers, worked as cooks, nurses, and launderers for rations and low pay. The American army was unwieldy and difficult to manage, yet this shapelessness provided an almost unlimited reservoir of man and woman power.

The American Army

The officers of the Continental Army developed an intense sense of pride and commitment to the revolutionary cause. The hardships they endured, the battles they fought, the difficulties they overcame all helped to forge an esprit de corps that was to outlast the war. The realities of warfare were often dirty, messy, and corrupt, but the officers drew strength from a developing image of themselves as professionals who sacrificed personal gain for the good of the entire nation.

In 1777, the chief British effort was planned by the flashy "Gentleman Johnny" Burgoyne, a playboy general who had gained the ear of Lord George Germain. Burgoyne convinced Germain that he

Deborah Sampson (1760–1827), who disguised herself as a man and enlisted in the Continental Army as Robert Shurtleff. She served from May 1782 to October 1783, when her sex was discovered and she was discharged. In later years she gave public lectures describing her wartime experiences. After her death her husband became the only man to receive a pension as the "widow" of a revolutionary soldier. *Courtesy of The Rhode Island Historical Society.*

could lead an invading force of redcoats and Indians down the Hudson River from Canada, cutting off New England from the rest of the states. He proposed to rendezvous near Albany with a similar force that would move east from Niagara along the Mohawk River valley. The combined forces would then presumably link up with Sir William Howe's troops in New York City.

That Burgoyne's scheme would give "Gentleman Johnny" all the glory and relegate Howe to a supporting role did not escape Sir William's notice. While Burgoyne was plotting in London, Howe was

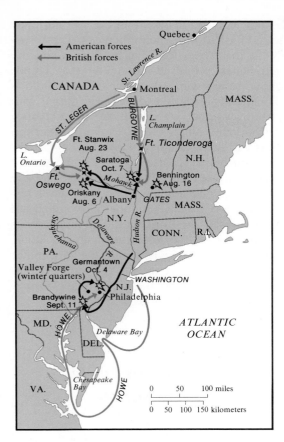

Campaign of 1777

the 1777 campaign was virtually over, and far to the north, Burgoyne was going down to defeat.

Burgoyne and his men set out from Montreal in mid-June 1777, floating down Lake Champlain into New York in canoes and flat-bottom boats. They easily took Fort Ticonderoga from its outnumbered and outgunned defenders. Trouble began, however, as Burgoyne started his overland march. Because of his clumsy artillery carriages and baggage wagons, Burgoyne's troops took twenty-four days to travel the twenty-three miles. Moreover, the eight hundred German mercenaries he sent to forage the countryside were nearly wiped out near Bennington. Yet Burgoyne failed to recognize the seriousness of his predicament and continued to dawdle. By the time he finally crossed the Hudson in mid-September, bound for Albany, his fate was sealed. After several bloody clashes with the American force commanded by Horatio Gates, Burgoyne was surrounded near Saratoga, New York. On October 17, 1777, he surrendered his entire force of more than six thousand men.

Burgoyne's Campaign in New York

Two months before, the fourteen hundred redcoats and Indians marching along the Mohawk River from Niagara toward Albany had also been turned back. The troops, under the command of Colonel Barry St. Leger, ambushed the patriots at Oriskany on August 6. The British claimed victory in the ensuing battle, one of the bloodiest of the war, but they and their Indian allies lost their taste for further fighting.

The Battle of Oriskany marked a split of the Iroquois Confederacy. In 1776, the Six Nations had formally pledged to remain neutral in the Anglo-American struggle. But two influential Mohawk leaders, Joseph Brant and Mary Brant, worked tirelessly to persuade their fellow Iroquois to join the British. Mary Brant, a powerful tribal matron, was also the widow of the Indian superintendent Sir William Johnson. Her younger brother Joseph, a renowned warrior, was convinced that the Six Nations should ally themselves with the British in order to prevent American encroachment on their lands. The Brants won over to the British the Senecas, Cayugas, and Mohawks. But the Oneidas preferred the American

Split of the Iroquois Confederacy

laying his own plans to take Philadelphia. Just as Burgoyne left Howe out of his plans, so Howe left Burgoyne out of his. Thus the two major British armies in America would operate independently in 1777, and the result would be a disaster (see map).

Howe accomplished his objective in an inexplicable fashion. Instead of marching his forces from New York, he waited for months and then transported them by sea. The six-week voyage brought him only forty miles closer to Philadelphia, debilitated his men, depleted his supplies, and gave Washington time to prepare a defense of the city. Washington engaged the enemy at Brandywine Creek and again at Germantown. Although the British won both engagements, the Americans handled themselves well. By the time the redcoats took Philadelphia in late September,

Howe Takes Philadelphia

side, bringing the Tuscaroras with them. At Oriskany, the three-hundred-year league of friendship was torn apart, as confederation warriors fought on both sides.

The collapse of Iroquois unity and the confederacy's abandonment of neutrality had important consequences for both whites and Indians in subsequent years. In 1778, Iroquois warriors allied with the British raided the frontier villages of Wyoming, Pennsylvania, and Cherry Valley, New York. Retaliating in the summer of 1779, the whites dispatched an expedition under General John Sullivan to burn Iroquois crops, orchards, and settlements. The destruction was so thorough that many bands had to leave their ancestral homeland to seek food and shelter with the British north of the Great Lakes. A large number of Iroquois people never returned to New York but settled permanently in British Canada.

For the Indians, Oriskany was the most significant battle of the northern campaign; for the whites, it was Saratoga. The news of Burgoyne's surrender brought joy to patriots, discouragement to loyalists, and prompted Lord North to authorize a peace commission to offer the Americans everything they had requested in 1774—in effect, a return to the imperial system of 1763. It was, of course, far too late for that. The patriots rejected the overture, and the peace commission sailed back to England empty-handed in mid-1778.

Most important of all, the American victory at Saratoga drew France formally into the conflict. Ever since 1763, the French had sought to avenge their defeat in the Seven Years' War, and the American Revolution gave them that opportunity. Even before Benjamin Franklin arrived in Paris in late 1776, France was covertly supplying the revolutionaries with military necessities.

Franklin worked tirelessly to strengthen ties between the two nations. By presenting himself as a representative of American simplicity, Franklin played upon the French image of Americans as virtuous yeomen. His effort culminated in February 1778, when the countries signed two treaties. In the Treaty of Amity and Commerce, France recognized American independence and established

Franco-American Alliance of 1778

trade ties with the new nation; the second treaty provided for a formal alliance between the two nations. In this Treaty of Alliance, France and the United States promised—assuming that France would go to war with Britain, which it soon did—that neither country would negotiate peace with the enemy without consulting the other. France also abandoned all its claims to North American territory east of the Mississippi River and to Canada.

The French alliance had two major benefits for the patriot cause. First, France began to aid the Americans openly, sending troops and naval vessels, in addition to arms, ammunition, clothing, and blankets. Second, the British could no longer focus their attention on the American mainland alone, for they had to fight the French in the West Indies and elsewhere. Spain's entry into the war in 1779 as an ally of France (but not the United States) further magnified Britain's problems.

The Long Struggle in the South

In the aftermath of the Saratoga disaster, Lord George Germain and the military officials in London reassessed their strategy. Maneuvering in the North had done them little good; perhaps shifting the field of battle southward would bring success. The new British commander-in-chief, Sir Henry Clinton, became convinced that a southern strategy would work. In late 1779, he sailed down the coast from New York with 8,500 troops to attack Charleston, the most important American city in the South (see map).

Although the Americans worked hard to bolster Charleston's defenses, the city fell to the British on May 12, 1780. General Benjamin Lincoln surrendered the entire southern army of 5,500 men to the invaders. The redcoats then spread throughout South Carolina. As hundreds of South Carolinians proclaimed their loyalty to the Crown, Clinton organized loyalist regiments. Yet the British triumph was less complete than it ap-

Fall of Charleston

The War in the South

dom. Indeed, slaves ran away from their patriot masters in such numbers that they seriously disrupted planting and harvesting in 1780 and 1781. Many of the thousands who ran away served the British well as scouts, guides, and laborers.

After the defeat at Camden, Washington gave command of the southern campaign to General Nathanael Greene of Rhode Island. Greene adopted a conciliatory policy toward loyalists and neutrals. He ordered his troops not to loot loyalist property and to treat captives fairly. Greene recognized that the patriots could win only by convincing the people that they could bring stability to the region. He thus helped the shattered provincial congresses of Georgia and South Carolina to begin re-establishing civilian authority in the interior.

Greene Rallies South Carolina

Greene also took a conciliatory approach to the southern Indians. With his desperate need for soldiers, he could not afford to have frontier militia companies occupied in defending their homes against Indian attacks. Since he had so few regulars (only sixteen hundred men when he took command), Greene had to rely on western volunteers. Therefore, he negotiated with the Indians. By the end of the war, only the Creeks remained British allies.

Even before Greene took command of the southern army in December 1780, the tide had begun to turn. In October, at King's Mountain, near the North Carolina–South Carolina border, a force of "overmountain men" from the settlements west of the Appalachians defeated a large party of redcoats and loyalists. Then, in January 1781, Greene's trusted aide Brigadier General Daniel Morgan brilliantly defeated the crack British regiment Tarleton's Legion at Cowpens, also near the border of the Carolinas. In March, Greene engaged the main body of British troops at Guilford Court House, North Carolina. Although the Americans lost, most of Cornwallis's army had been destroyed. He had to retreat to the coast in order to receive supplies and fresh troops from New York.

Cornwallis had already ignored explicit orders not to leave South Carolina unless the state was safely in British hands. He headed north into

peared. The success of the southern campaign depended on British control of the seas, for only by sea could the widely dispersed British armies remain in communication with one another. For the moment, the Royal Navy safely dominated the American coastline, but French naval power posed a threat to the entire southern enterprise. Moreover, the redcoats never managed to establish full control of the areas they seized. As a result, patriot bands operated freely throughout the state. Last but not least, the fall of Charleston did not dishearten the patriots; instead, it spurred them to greater exertions.

Nevertheless, the war in South Carolina went badly for the patriots. In August 1780, a reorganized southern army under the command of Horatio Gates was defeated at Camden by the forces of Lord Cornwallis, who had been placed in charge of the southern campaign. The British army was joined wherever it went by blacks seeking free-

Surrender at Yorktown Virginia, where he joined forces with a detachment of redcoats commanded by the American traitor Benedict Arnold. Instead of acting decisively with his new army of 7,200 men, Cornwallis withdrew to the edge of the peninsula between the York and James rivers; there he fortified Yorktown and, in effect, waited for the end. Seizing the opportunity, Washington quickly moved more than 7,000 troops south from New York City. When a French fleet under the Comte de Grasse arrived from the West Indies in time to defeat the Royal Navy vessels sent to rescue Cornwallis, the British general was trapped (see map, page 101). On October 19, 1781, Cornwallis surrendered to the combined American and French forces.

When news of the surrender reached England, Lord North's ministry fell. Parliament voted to cease offensive operations in America and authorized peace negotiations. But guerrilla warfare between patriots and loyalists continued to ravage the Carolinas and Georgia for more than a year, and in the North vicious retaliatory raids by Indians and whites kept the frontier aflame. The persistence of conflict between whites and Indians after the Battle of Yorktown, all too often overlooked in accounts of the Revolution, serves to underline the degree to which the Indians were the real losers in the war initiated by whites.

The fighting finally ended when Americans and Britons learned of the signing of a preliminary peace treaty at Paris in November 1782. The American negotiators—Benjamin Franklin, John Jay, and John Adams— **Treaty of Paris** ignored their instructions from Congress to be guided by France and instead struck a separate agreement with Great Britain. Their instincts were sound: the French government was more an enemy to Britain than a friend to the United States. In fact, French ministers worked secretly behind the scenes to try to prevent the establishment of a strong, unified, independent government in America. The new British ministry, headed by Lord Shelburne, was weary of war and made numerous concessions.

Under the treaty, signed formally on September 3, 1783, the Americans were granted unconditional independence and unlimited fishing rights off Newfoundland. The boundaries of the new nation were generous: to the north, approximately the present-day boundary with Canada; to the south, the 31st parallel; to the west, the Mississippi River. Florida, which the British had acquired in 1763, was returned to Spain. In ceding so much land unconditionally to the Americans, the British entirely ignored the territorial rights of their Indian allies. Once again, the tribes' interests were sacrificed to the demands of European power politics. Loyalists and British merchants were also poorly served by the British negotiators. The treaty's ambiguously worded clauses pertaining to the payment of prewar debts and the postwar treatment of loyalists caused trouble for years to come and proved impossible to enforce.

The long war finally over, the victorious Americans could look back on their achievement with satisfaction and awe. In 1775, with an inexperienced, ragtag army, they had taken on the greatest military power in the world—and eight years later they had won. They had accomplished their goal more through persistence and commitment than through brilliance on the battlefield. Actual victories had been few, but their army had always survived defeats and standoffs to fight again. Ultimately, the Americans had simply worn their enemy down.

Achieving independence in military terms, however, was only half the battle. The Americans still faced perhaps even greater challenges: establishing stable republican governments at the state and national levels, and ensuring their governments' continued existence in a world filled with bitter rivalries among the major powers—England, France, and Spain. Those European rivalries had worked to the Americans' advantage during the war, but in the decades to come they would pose significant threats to the survival of the new nation.

Suggestions for Further Reading

General

Edward Countryman, *The American Revolution* (1985); Stephen G. Kurtz and James H. Hutson, eds., *Essays on the*

American Revolution (1973); Edmund S. Morgan, *The Challenge of the American Revolution* (1976); Alfred F. Young, ed., *The American Revolution: Explorations in the History of American Radicalism* (1976).

Military

John Richard Alden, *The American Revolution, 1775–1783* (1964); John C. Dann, ed., *The Revolution Remembered: Eyewitness Accounts of the War for Independence* (1980); Don Higginbotham, *The War of American Independence: Military Attitudes, Policies, and Practice, 1763–1789* (1971); Piers Mackesy, *The War for America, 1775–1783* (1964); James K. Martin and Mark Lender, *"A Respectable Army": The Military Origins of the Republic, 1763–1789* (1982); Charles Royster, *A Revolutionary People at War: The Continental Army and American Character, 1775–1783* (1980).

Local and Regional

Edward Countryman, *A People in Revolution: The American Revolution and Political Society in New York, 1760–1790* (1981); Elaine F. Crane, *A Dependent People: Newport, R.I., in the Revolutionary Era* (1985); Jeffrey Crow and Larry Tise, eds., *The Southern Experience in the American Revolution* (1978); Thomas Doerflinger, *A Vigorous Spirit of Enterprise: Merchants and Economic Development in Revolutionary Philadelphia* (1986); Robert A. Gross, *The Minutemen and Their World* (1976); Ronald Hoffman, *A Spirit of Dissension: Economics, Politics, and the Revolution in Maryland* (1973); Ronald Hoffman, Thad W. Tate, and Peter Albert, eds., *An Uncivil War: The Southern Backcountry During the American Revolution* (1985); Stephen Rosswurm, *Arms, Country, and Class: The Philadelphia Militia and the "Lower Sort" During the American Revolution* (1988); John Selby, *The Revolution in Virginia, 1775–1783* (1988).

Indians and Blacks

Barbara Graymont, *The Iroquois in the American Revolution* (1972); Isabel T. Kelsey, *Joseph Brant, 1743–1807: Man of Two Worlds* (1984); Duncan J. MacLeod, *Slavery, Race, and the American Revolution* (1974); James H. O'Donnell III, *Southern Indians in the American Revolution* (1973); Benjamin Quarles, *The Negro in the American Revolution* (1961).

Loyalists

Bernard Bailyn, *The Ordeal of Thomas Hutchinson* (1974); Robert McCluer Calhoon, *The Loyalists in Revolutionary America, 1760–1781* (1973); William H. Nelson, *The American Tory* (1961); Mary Beth Norton, *The British-Americans: The Loyalist Exiles in England, 1774–1789* (1972); Janice Potter, *The Liberty We Seek: Loyalist Ideology in Colonial New York and Massachusetts* (1983).

Women

Richard Buel and Joy Buel, *The Way of Duty: A Woman and Her Family in Revolutionary America* (1984); Linda Grant DePauw and Conover Hunt, *"Remember the Ladies": Women in America, 1750–1815* (1976); Linda K. Kerber, *Women of the Republic: Intellect and Ideology in Revolutionary America* (1980); Mary Beth Norton, *Liberty's Daughters: The Revolutionary Experience of American Women, 1750–1800* (1980).

Foreign Policy

Jonathan Dull, *A Diplomatic History of the American Revolution* (1985); Felix Gilbert, *To the Farewell Address* (1961); Ronald Hoffman and Peter Albert, eds., *Peace and the Peacemakers: The Treaty of 1783* (1986); Ronald Hoffman and Peter Albert, eds., *Diplomacy and Revolution: The Franco-American Alliance of 1778* (1981); Lawrence Kaplan, ed., *The American Revolution and a "Candid World"* (1977); Richard B. Morris, *The Peacemakers: The Great Powers and American Independence* (1965); Richard W. Van Alstyne, *Empire and Independence: The International History of the American Revolution* (1965).

Patriot Leaders

Fawn M. Brodie, *Thomas Jefferson: An Intimate History* (1974); Verner W. Crane, *Benjamin Franklin and a Rising People* (1954); Marcus Cunliffe, *George Washington: Man and Monument* (1958); Noble Cunningham, *In Pursuit of Reason: The Life of Thomas Jefferson* (1987); James T. Flexner, *George Washington*, 4 vols. (1965–1972); Eric Foner, *Tom Paine and Revolutionary America* (1976); Claude A. Lopez and Eugenia Herbert, *The Private Franklin: The Man and His Family* (1975); Dumas Malone, *Jefferson and His Time*, 6 vols. (1948–1981); Peter Shaw, *The Character of John Adams* (1976).

On January 25, 1787, an army of fifteen hundred farmers in western Massachusetts advanced on the federal armory at Springfield. Inside the arsenal, General William Shepard prepared his group of one thousand militiamen to resist the assault. First, though, he warned the farmers that they would soon "inevitably" draw the fire of men who had been their officers during the Revolutionary War. "That is all we want, by God!" replied one of the rebels. The farmers moved toward the armory, urged on by the commands of Daniel Shays, one of their leaders. Shepard fired two cannon over the heads of the farmers. When that did not frighten them, he directed his men to shoot directly at the straggling ranks. Four men died; twenty were wounded; and the rebels withdrew from the field.

What had caused this violent clash between former comrades in arms? The Massachusetts farmers were angered by high taxes and the scarcity of money. Since the preceding summer, they had used committees and crowd actions—adopting the tactics used so successfully in the 1760s and early 1770s—to halt court proceedings in which the state was trying to seize property for nonpayment of taxes. Many of the insurgents were respected war veterans. Daniel Shays, their nominal leader, had been a captain in the Continental Army.

6

FORGING A NATIONAL REPUBLIC, 1776–1789

Clearly, the episode could not be dismissed as the work of an unruly rabble. What did the uprising mean for the future of the republic? Was it a sign of impending anarchy?

The protesters explained their position to the governor and council of Massachusetts. They proclaimed their loyalty to the nation but objected to the state's fiscal policies, which, they said, prevented them from providing adequately for their families. One rebel sympathizer explained, "Whenever any encroachments are made either upon the liberties or properties of the people, if redress cannot be had without, it is virtue in them to disturb government." The Massachusetts government, Shays asserted, was "tyrannical" and, like that of Great Britain, deserved to be overthrown.

To the state's elected leaders, the most frightening aspect of the uprising was the rebels' attempt to forge direct links with the earlier struggle for independence. The state legislature issued an address to the people, asserting that "in a republican government the majority must govern. If the minor part governs it becomes aristocracy; if every one opposed at his pleasure, it is . . . anarchy and confusion." Thus Massachusetts officials insisted that crowd actions, which had once been a justifiable response to British tyranny, were no longer legitimate. In a republic, reform had to come about through the ballot box rather than by force.

For many Americans, the confrontation at the Springfield armory symbolized the trials facing the new nation. That the rebels were dispersed easily, that their leaders (including Shays) were forced to flee to neighboring states for asylum, and that a newly elected Massachusetts legislature adopted conciliatory measures—all those facts were almost irrelevant to American political leaders' interpretation of the events in western Massachusetts. In Shays's Rebellion, they thought they discerned the first signs of disintegration of the republic they had worked so hard to establish.

Republicanism—the idea that governments should be based wholly on the consent of the people—had first been discussed by political theorists in ancient Greece and Rome. Republics, such writers declared, were desirable yet fragile forms of government. Unless their citizens were especially virtuous and largely in agreement on key issues, republics were doomed to failure. When they left the British Empire, Americans committed themselves to republicanism. Now they had to deal with the potentially unwelcome consequences of that decision. How could they best ensure political stability? How could they create a virtuous republic?

America's leaders worked hard to inculcate virtue in their fellow countrymen and countrywomen. After 1776, American literature, theater, art, architecture, and education all had explicitly moral goals. The education of women was particularly important, for as the mothers of the republic's children, they were primarily responsible for ensuring their nation's future. On such matters Americans could agree, but they disagreed on many other critical issues. Although almost all white men concurred that women, Indians, and blacks should be excluded from formal participation in politics, they found it difficult to reach a consensus on how many of their own number should be included. And

when should consent be sought: semiannually? annually? at intervals of two or more years? Further, how should governments be structured so as to reflect the people's consent most accurately? Americans replied to these questions in different ways.

Republican citizens had to answer many other questions as well. Should a republic conduct its dealings with Indian tribes and foreign countries any differently from other types of governments? Did republics, in other words, have an obligation to negotiate fairly and honestly at all times? And how could white republicans reconcile the conflict between slavery and Jefferson's words in the Declaration of Independence, "all men are created equal"? Some resolved the dilemma by freeing their slaves; others denied that blacks were "men" in the same sense as whites.

The most important task facing Americans in these years was the construction of a national government. Before 1765, the English mainland colonies had rarely cooperated on common endeavors. Many things separated them: their diverse economies, varying religious traditions and ethnic compositions, competing land claims, and differences in their political systems. But fighting the Revolutionary War brought them together and created a new nationalistic spirit. Wartime experiences broke down at least some of the boundaries that had previously divided Americans, replacing loyalties to state and region with loyalties to the nation.

Still, forging a national republic was neither easy nor simple. America's first framework for such a government, the Articles of Confederation, proved to be inadequate. But some of the nation's political leaders learned from their experiences and tried another approach when they drafted the Constitution in 1787. Some historians have argued that the Articles of Confederation and the Constitution reflected opposing political philosophies, the Constitution representing an "aristocratic" counterrevolution against the "democratic" Articles. The two documents are more accurately viewed as separate and successive attempts to solve the same problems. Both in part applied theories of republicanism to practical problems of governance; neither was entirely successful in resolving those difficulties.

Creating a Virtuous Republic

Many years after the Revolution, John Dickinson recalled that in 1776, when the colonies declared their independence from Great Britain, "there was no question concerning forms of Government, no enquiry whether a Republic or a limited Monarchy was best. . . . We knew that the people of this country must unite themselves under some form of Government and that this could be no other than the republican form." But how could that goal be implemented?

Three different definitions of *republicanism* emerged in the new United States. The first, held chiefly by members of the educated elite, was
Varieties of Repub-licanism based directly on ancient history and political theory. The histories of popular governments in Greece and Rome seemed to prove that republics could succeed only if they were small in size and homogeneous in population. Furthermore, unless the citizens of a republic were willing to sacrifice their own private interests for the good of the whole, the government would inevitably collapse. In return for sacrifices, though, a republic offered its citizens equality of opportunity. Under such a government, society would be ruled by a "natural aristocracy" of men whose rank would be based upon merit rather than inherited wealth or status.

A second definition, advanced both by members of the elite and by some skilled craftsmen, drew more on economic than political thought. Instead of perceiving the nation as an organic whole composed of people sacrificing to the common good, this version of republicanism followed the English theorist Adam Smith in emphasizing individuals' pursuit of rational self-interest. When republican men sought to improve their own economic and social circumstances, the entire nation would benefit. Republican virtue would be achieved through the advancement of private interests, rather than through their subordination to some communal ideal.

The third notion of republicanism was less influential because it was popular primarily with people who were illiterate or barely literate and who thus wrote little to promote their beliefs. But it involved a more egalitarian approach to governance than did either of the other two, both of which contained considerable potential for inequality. Some Americans (like Thomas Paine) emphasized the importance of widespread participation in political activities, wanted government to be responsive to their needs, and openly questioned the gentry's ability to speak for them. They can, in fact, be termed democrats in more or less the modern sense.

It is important to recognize that the three strands of republicanism were part of a unified whole and shared many of the same assumptions. For example, all three contrasted a virtuous, industrious America to the corrupt luxury of England and Europe. In the first version, that virtue manifested itself in frugality and self-sacrifice; in the second, it would prevent self-interest from becoming vice; in the third, it was the justification for including even propertyless white men in the ranks of voters.

As the citizens of the United States set out to construct their republic, they believed they were embarking on an unprecedented enterprise. With
Virtue and the Arts great pride in their new nation, they expected to exchange the vices of monarchical Europe for the virtues of republican America. They wanted to embody republican principles not only in their governments, but also in their society and their culture. They looked to painting, literature, drama, and architecture to convey messages of nationalism and virtue to the public.

But Americans faced a crucial contradiction at the very outset of their efforts. To some republicans, the fine arts themselves were manifestations of vice. What need did a frugal yeoman have for a painting—or, worse yet, a novel? Why should anyone spend hard-earned wages to see a play in a lavishly decorated theater? The first American artists, playwrights, and authors were thus trapped in a dilemma from which escape was nearly impossible. They wanted to produce works embodying virtue, but those very works, regardless of their content, were viewed by many as corrupting.

Still, they tried. William Hill Brown's *The Power of Sympathy* (1789), the first novel written in the

1776	Second Continental Congress directs states to draft constitutions	1787	Northwest Ordinance Constitutional Convention
1777	Articles of Confederation sent to states for ratification	1788	Hamilton, Jay, and Madison, *The Federalist* Constitution ratified
1781	Articles of Confederation ratified	1794	Battle of Fallen Timbers
1786	Annapolis Convention	1795	Treaty of Greenville
1786–87	Shays's Rebellion	1800	Weems, *Life of Washington*

United States, was a lurid tale of seduction intended as a warning to young women, who made up a large proportion of America's fiction readers. In Royall Tyler's *The Contrast* (1787), the first successful American play, the virtuous conduct of Colonel Manly was contrasted (hence the title) with the reprehensible behavior of the fop Billy Dimple. The most popular book of the era, Mason Locke Weems's *Life of Washington,* published in 1800, shortly after George Washington's death, was, the author declared, designed to "hold up his great Virtues . . . to the imitation of Our Youth."

Painting, too, was expected to embody high moral standards. Gilbert Stuart, one of the era's major artists, painted portraits of upstanding republican citizens. And John Trumbull's vast canvases depicted such milestones of American history as the Battle of Bunker Hill, Burgoyne's surrender at Saratoga, and Cornwallis's capitulation at Yorktown. Both men attempted to instill patriotic virtues in their viewers.

Architects likewise hoped to convey in their buildings a sense of the young republic's ideals, and most of them consciously rejected British models. When the Virginia government asked Thomas Jefferson, then ambassador to France, for advice on the design of a state capitol in Richmond, Jefferson unhesitatingly recommended copying a Roman building. "It is very simple," he explained, "but it is

noble beyond expression." Jefferson set forth ideals that would guide American architecture for a generation to come: simplicity of line, harmonious proportions, a feeling of grandeur. Nowhere were these rational goals of republican art manifested more clearly than in Benjamin H. Latrobe's plans for the majestic, domed United States Capitol in Washington, built in the early 1800s.

Despite the artists' efforts, or perhaps, some would have said, because of them, some Americans were beginning to detect signs of luxury and corruption by the mid-1780s. The end of the war and resumption of European trade brought a return to fashionable clothing styles and the abandonment of the homespun garments patriots had once worn with pride. Well-dressed elite families attended balls and concerts. Parties no longer seemed complete without gambling and card playing. Especially alarming to fervent republicans was the establishment in 1783 of the Society of the Cincinnati, a hereditary organization of Revolutionary War officers and their descendants. Many feared that the group would become the nucleus of a native-born aristocracy. All these developments directly challenged the image of the United States as a virtuous republic.

The deep-seated concern for the future of the infant republic focused Americans' attention on their children, the "rising generation." Education

Son: Do you want to kill the Colonel?
I feel chock full of fight.

A scene from Royall Tyler's *The Contrast,* as performed in New York City in 1787. The play both satirized English aristocrats and celebrated the virtuous simplicity of its American hero and heroine. *Harvard Theatre Collection.*

Educational Reform acquired new significance in the context of the republic. Since the early days of the colonies, education had been seen chiefly as a private means to personal advancement. Now, though, it would serve a public purpose. If young people were to resist the temptation of vice, they would have to learn the lessons of virtue at home and at school. In fact, the very survival of the nation depended on it. The early republican period was thus a time of major educational reform.

The 1780s and 1790s brought two significant changes in American educational practice. First, some northern states began to use tax money to support public elementary schools. Nearly all education in the colonies had been privately financed. In the republic, though, schools could lay claim to tax dollars.

Second, schooling for girls was improved. Americans' recognition of the importance of the rising generation led to the realization that mothers would have to be properly educated if they were to instruct their children adequately. Therefore Massachusetts, the first state to require towns to supply their citizens with free public elementary education, insisted that the schools be open to girls as well as boys. Throughout the United States, private academies were founded to give teenage girls from well-to-do families an opportunity for advanced schooling. No one yet proposed opening colleges to women, but a few fortunate girls could study history, geography, rhetoric, and mathematics.

The chief theorist of women's education in the early republic was Judith Sargent Murray of Gloucester, Massachusetts. In a series of essays published in the 1780s and 1790s, **Judith Sargent Murray on Education** Murray argued that women and men had equal intellectual capacities. Therefore, concluded Murray, boys and girls should be offered equivalent scholastic training. She further contended that girls should be taught to support themselves by their own efforts. Because she rejected the prevailing notion that a young woman's chief goal in life should be finding a husband, Judith Sargent Murray deserves the title of the first American feminist. (That distinction is usually accorded to better-known nineteenth-century women, such as Margaret Fuller or Sarah Grimké.)

Murray's direct challenge to the traditional colonial belief that (as one man put it) girls "knew quite enough if they could make a shirt and a pudding" was part of a general rethinking of women's position stemming from the Revolution. Male patriots who enlisted in the army or served in Congress were away from home for long periods of time. In their absence, their wives, who had previously handled only the "indoor affairs" of the household, had to shoulder the responsibility for "outdoor affairs" as well.

In many households, the necessary shift of responsibilities during the war caused men and women to rethink their notions of proper gender roles. Both John and Abigail Adams took great pride in Abigail's developing skills as a "farm-eress." Abigail Adams, like her female contemporaries, stopped calling the farm "yours" in letters to her husband and began referring to it as "ours"—a revealing change of pronoun. Both men and women realized that female patriots had made a vital contribution to winning the war. Thus, in the years after the Revolution, Americans began to develop new ideas about the role women should play in a republican society.

The best-known example of those new ideas came in a letter Abigail Adams addressed to her husband in March 1776. "In the new Code of Laws

Abigail Adams: "Remember the Ladies" which I suppose it will be necessary for you to make I desire you would Remember the Ladies," she wrote. "If perticuliar care and attention is not paid to the Laidies we are determined to foment a Rebelion, and will not hold ourselves bound by any Laws in which we have no voice, or Representation."

With these words, Abigail Adams took a step that was soon to be duplicated by other disfranchised Americans. She employed the ideology that had been developed to combat Great Britain's claims to political supremacy, but she applied it to purposes white male leaders had never intended. Abigail Adams did not ask that women be allowed to vote. But other women wanted to claim that right, as events in New Jersey proved. The men who drafted the state constitution in 1776 defined voters loosely as "all free inhabitants" who met certain property qualifications. They thereby unintentionally gave the vote to property-holding white spinsters and widows, as well as to free blacks. In the 1780s and 1790s qualified women regularly voted in New Jersey's local and congressional elections. They continued to exercise that right until 1807, when women and blacks were disfranchised by the state legislature on the grounds that their votes could be easily manipulated. Yet the fact that they had voted at all made plain their altered perception of their place in political life.

Such dramatic episodes were unusual. On the whole, the re-evaluation of women's position had its greatest impact on private life. The traditional

Woman's Role in the Republic colonial view of marriage had stressed the subordination of wife to husband. But in 1790, a female "Matrimonial Republican" asserted that "marriage ought never to be considered as a contract between a superior and an inferior, but a reciprocal union of interest. . . . The obedience between man and wife is, or ought to be mutual." This new understanding of the marital relationship seems to have contributed to a rising divorce rate after the war. Dissatisfied wives proved less willing to remain in unhappy marriages than they had been previously. At the same time, state judges became more sympathetic to women's desires to be freed from abusive or unfaithful husbands. Even so, divorces were still rare; most marriages were for life, and married women continued to suffer serious legal handicaps.

After the war, then, most white Americans still assumed that women's place was in the home and that their primary function was to be good wives and mothers. They accepted the notion of equality, broadly defined, but within the context of men's and women's separate roles in life. Seeing such differences between the male and female characters eventually enabled Americans to resolve the conflict between the two most influential strands of republican thought. Because married women could not own property or participate directly in economic life, women in general came to be seen as the embodiment of self-sacrificing, disinterested republicanism. Through female-run charitable and other social welfare groups, they assumed responsibility for the welfare of the community as a whole. Thus men were freed from any naggings of conscience as they pursued their economic self-interest (that other republican virtue), secure in the knowledge that their wives and daughters were fulfilling the family's obligation to the common good. The ideal republican man, therefore, was an individualist, seeking advancement for himself and his family; the ideal republican woman, by contrast, always put the well-being of others ahead of her own.

Together white men and women established the context for the creation of a virtuous republic. But nearly 20 percent of the American population was black. How did approximately 700,000 African-Americans fit into the developing national plan?

Emancipation and the Growth of Racism

Revolutionary ideology exposed one of the primary contradictions in American society. Both blacks and whites saw the irony in slaveholding Americans' claims that one of their aims in taking up arms was to prevent Britain from "enslaving" them.

As early as 1764, James Otis, Jr., had identified the basic problem in his pamphlet *The Rights of the British Colonies Asserted and Proved.* If, according to natural law, all people were born free and equal, that meant *all* humankind, black and white. "Does it follow that 'tis right to enslave a man because he is black?" Otis asked. The same theme was later voiced by other revolutionary leaders. In 1773, the Philadelphia doctor Benjamin Rush warned that "the plant of liberty is of so tender a nature that it cannot thrive long in the neighborhood of slavery." Common folk, too, noticed the contradiction. When a Connecticut soldier saw Washington's plantation, he observed in his journal: "Alas! That persons who pretend to stand for the rights of mankind . . . can delight in oppression, & that even of the worst kind!"

African-Americans themselves were quick to recognize the implications of revolutionary ideology. In 1779, a group of slaves from Portsmouth, New Hampshire, asked the state legislature "from what authority [our masters] assume to dispose of our lives, freedom and property" and pleaded "that the name of slave may not more be heard in a land gloriously contending for the sweets of freedom." That same year, several black residents of Fairfield, Connecticut, petitioned the legislature for their freedom, characterizing slavery as a "dreadful Evil" and "flagrant Injustice."

Both legislatures responded negatively. But the postwar years did witness the gradual abolition of slavery in the North. Vermont abolished slavery in its 1777 constitution. Massachu-

Gradual Emancipation setts courts decided in the 1780s that the clause in the state constitution declaring that "all men are born free and equal, and have certain natural, essential, and unalienable rights" prohibited slavery in the state. Pennsylvania passed an abolition law in 1780; four years later, Rhode Island and Connecticut provided for gradual emancipation, followed by New York (1799) and New Jersey (1804).

No southern state adopted similar general emancipation laws, but the legislatures of Virginia (1782), Delaware (1787), and Maryland (1790 and 1796) did decide to change laws that had restricted masters' ability to free their slaves. South Carolina and Georgia never considered adopting such acts, and North Carolina insisted that all manumissions (emancipations of individual slaves) be approved by county courts.

Thus revolutionary ideology had limited impact on the well-entrenched economic interests of large slaveholders. Only in the North, where there were few slaves, could state legislatures vote to abolish slavery with relative ease. Even there, legislators' concern for property rights led them to favor gradual emancipation over immediate abolition. Most states provided only for the freeing of children born after passage of the law. And even those children were to remain slaves until ages ranging from eighteen to twenty-eight. Still, by 1840 in only one northern state—New Jersey—were black persons legally held in bondage.

Despite the slow progress of abolition, the free black population of the United States grew dramatically in the first years after the Revolution. Before the war there had been few free

Growth of the Free Black Population blacks in America. Most prewar free blacks were mulattos, born of unions between white masters and enslaved black women. But wartime disruptions radically changed the size and composition of the free black population. Slaves who had escaped from plantations during the war, others who had served in the American army, and still others who had been emancipated by their owners or by state laws were now free. By 1790, there were nearly 60,000 free people of color in the United States; ten years later, they numbered more than 108,000, nearly 11 percent of the total black population.

In the 1780s and later, freed people often made their way to the port cities of the North. Boston and Philadelphia, where slavery was abolished sooner than it was in New York City, were particularly popular destinations. Women outnumbered men among the migrants by a margin of three to two. Like female whites, black women found more opportunities for employment, particularly as domestic servants, in the cities than in the countryside. Some black men also worked in domestic service, but larger numbers were employed as unskilled laborers or seamen. A few of the women and a sizable proportion of the men (nearly one-third of those in Philadelphia in 1795) were skilled workers or retailers. As soon as possible, these freed people established independent two-parent nuclear families instead of continuing to live in white households. They also began to cluster their residences in certain neighborhoods, probably as a result of both discrimination by whites and a desire for black solidarity.

Emancipation did not bring equality. Even whites who recognized African-Americans' right to freedom were unwilling to accept them as equals.

Discrimination Against Blacks Laws discriminated against emancipated blacks—South Carolina, for example, did not permit free blacks to testify against whites in court. Public schools often refused to educate free black children. Freedmen found it difficult to purchase property and find good jobs. And whites rarely allowed them an equal voice in church affairs.

Gradually, free blacks developed their own separate institutions, often based in the neighborhoods in which they lived. In Charleston, mulattos formed the Brown Fellowship Society, which provided insurance coverage for its members, financed a school for free children, and helped to support black orphans. In 1794, blacks in Philadelphia and Baltimore founded societies that eventually became the African Methodist Episcopal (AME) denomination. AME churches later sponsored schools in a number of cities and, along with African Baptist, African Episcopal, and African Presbyterian churches, became cultural centers of the free black community.

Their endeavors were all the more important because the postrevolutionary years ironically witnessed the development of a coherent racist theory

Development of Racist Theory in the United States. Whites had long regarded blacks as inferior, but the most influential writers on race had attributed that inferiority to environmental rather than hereditary factors. After the Revolution, white southerners needed to defend their holding other human beings in bondage against the notion that "all men are created equal." Consequently, they began to argue that blacks were less than fully human and that the principles of republican equality applied only to whites.

Their racism had several intertwined elements. First was the insistence that, as Thomas Jefferson suggested in 1781, blacks were "inferior to the whites in the endowments both of body and mind." Second came the belief that blacks were congenitally lazy, dishonest, and uncivilized (or uncivilizable). Third, and of crucial importance, was the notion that all blacks were sexually promiscuous and that black men lusted after white women. The specter of interracial sexual intercourse involving black men and white women haunted early American racist thought. The reverse situation, which occurred with far greater frequency (as white masters sexually exploited their female slaves), aroused little comment.

African-Americans did not allow these developing racist notions to pass unnoticed. Benjamin Banneker, a free black surveyor, astronomer, and mathematical genius, directly challenged Thomas Jefferson's belief in blacks' intellectual inferiority. In 1791, Banneker sent Jefferson a copy of his latest almanac (which included his astronomical calculations) as an example of blacks' mental powers. Jefferson's response admitted Banneker's capability but implied that he regarded Banneker as an exception.

At its birth, then, the republic was defined by

A woodcut portrait of Benjamin Banneker adorned the cover of his almanac for 1795. *Maryland Historical Society, Baltimore.*

sibility that they might combine with freed blacks to question the rule of the "better sort." That was one reason why, in the postrevolutionary years, the division of American society between slave and free was transformed into a division between blacks—some of whom were free—and whites. The white male wielders of power ensured their continued dominance in part by making certain that race replaced enslavement as the primary determinant of African-Americans' status.

Designing Republican Governments

On May 10, 1776, the Second Continental Congress directed the states to devise new republican governments to replace the provincial congresses and committees that had met since 1774. Thus Americans initially concentrated on drafting state constitutions and devoted little attention to their national government. At the state level, they immediately faced the problem of defining just what a constitution was. The British constitution could not serve as a model because it was an unwritten mixture of law and custom; Americans wanted tangible documents specifying the fundamental structures of government. Several years passed before the states agreed that their constitutions, unlike ordinary laws, could not be drafted by regular legislative bodies. Following the lead established by Massachusetts in 1780, they called conventions for the sole purpose of drafting constitutions. Thus the states sought direct authorization from the people—the theoretical sovereigns in a republic—before establishing new governments.

Those who wrote the state constitutions concerned themselves primarily with outlining the distribution and limitations of government power. As

Drafting of State Constitutions colonists, Americans had learned to fear the power of the governor—in most cases the appointed agent of the king or the proprietor—and to trust the legislature. Accordingly, the first state constitutions typically

whites as an exclusively white enterprise. Indeed, some historians have argued that the subjection of

A Republic for Whites Only blacks was a necessary precondition for equality among whites. They have pointed out that identifying a common racial antagonist helped to create white solidarity and to lessen the threat to gentry power posed by the enfranchisement of poorer whites. It was less dangerous to allow whites with little property to participate formally in politics than to open the pos-

provided for the governor to be elected annually (usually by the legislature), limited the number of terms any one governor could serve, and gave him little independent authority. At the same time, the constitutions expanded the powers of the legislature. All the states except Pennsylvania retained the two-house organization common in the colonial years and provided that members of the upper house would have longer terms and be required to meet higher standards of property holding. But they also redrew the lines of electoral districts to reflect population patterns more accurately and increased the numbers of members in both the upper and the lower houses. Finally, most states lowered property qualifications for voting. Thus the revolutionary era witnessed the first deliberate attempt to broaden the base of American government.

The authors of the state constitutions knew that governments designed to be responsive to the people would not necessarily provide sufficient protection if tyrants were elected to office. Consequently, they included limitations on government authority in the documents they composed. Seven of the constitutions contained formal bills of rights, and the others had similar clauses. Most of them guaranteed citizens freedom of the press and of religion, the right to a fair trial, the right of consent to taxation, and protection against general search warrants. An independent judiciary was charged with upholding such rights.

In sum, the constitution makers put far greater emphasis on preventing state governments from becoming tyrannical than on making them effective wielders of political authority. Their approach to the process of shaping governments was understandable, given the American experience with Great Britain. But establishing such weak political units, especially in wartime, practically ensured that the constitutions would soon need revision. Invariably, the revised versions increased the powers of the governor and reduced the scope of the legislature's authority. Only in the 1780s did Americans start to develop a formal theory of checks and balances as the primary means of controlling government power. Once they realized that legislative supremacy did not in itself guarantee good government, Americans attempted to achieve that goal by balancing the powers of the legislative, executive, and judicial branches against one another.

The constitutional theories that Americans applied at the state level did not at first influence their conception of the nature of a national government. The powers and structure of the Continental Congress evolved by default early in the war, since Americans had little time to devote to legitimizing their de facto government while organizing the military struggle against Britain. Not until late 1777, after Burgoyne's defeat at Saratoga, did Congress send the Articles of Confederation to the states for ratification.

The chief organ of national government was a unicameral (one-house) legislature in which each state had one vote. Its powers included the conduct of foreign relations, the settlement of disputes between states, control over maritime affairs, the regulation of Indian trade, and the valuation of state and national coinage.

Articles of Confederation

The Articles did not give the national government the ability to tax effectively or to enforce a uniform commercial policy. The United States of America was described as "a firm league of friendship" in which each state "retains its sovereignty . . . and every Power . . . which is not by this confederation expressly delegated to the United States, in Congress assembled."

The Articles required the unanimous consent of the state legislatures for ratification or amendment, and a clause concerning western lands turned out to be troublesome. The draft accepted by Congress allowed the states to retain all land claims derived from their original colonial charters. Because Maryland did not want to be overpowered by states with land claims deriving from their colonial charters, the state refused to accept the Articles until 1781. Only when Virginia promised to surrender its western holdings to national jurisdiction did Maryland accept the Articles (see map, page 114). Other states followed Virginia, establishing the principle that western lands would be held by the nation as a whole.

The fact that a single state could delay ratification for three years was a portent of the fate of American government under the Articles of Confederation. The authors of the Articles had not given

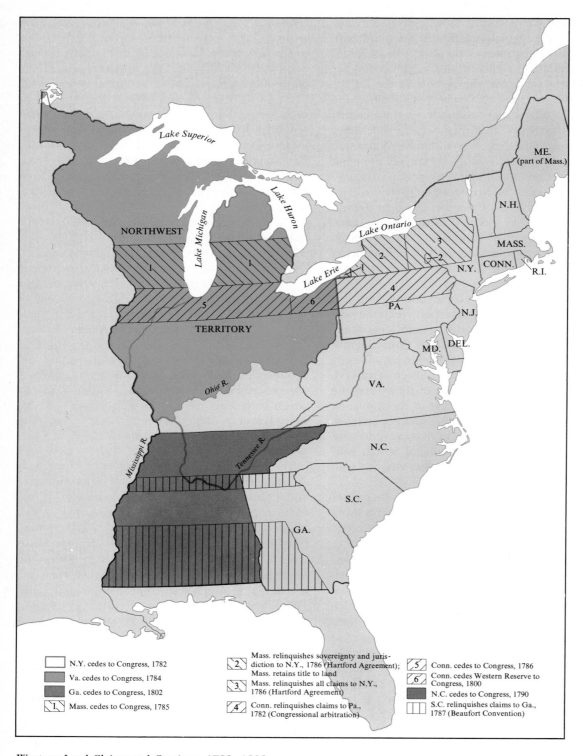

Western Land Claims and Cessions, 1782–1802

Map labels: Lake Superior, Lake Michigan, Lake Huron, Lake Ontario, Lake Erie, NORTHWEST TERRITORY, Ohio R., Mississippi R., Tennessee R.

State labels: ME. (part of Mass.), N.H., MASS., CONN., R.I., N.Y., N.J., PA., MD., DEL., VA., N.C., S.C., GA.

Legend:

N.Y. cedes to Congress, 1782

Va. cedes to Congress, 1784

Ga. cedes to Congress, 1802

1 Mass. cedes to Congress, 1785

2 Mass. relinquishes sovereignty and jurisdiction to N.Y., 1786 (Hartford Agreement); Mass. retains title to land

3 Mass. relinquishes all claims to N.Y., 1786 (Hartford Agreement)

4 Conn. relinquishes claims to Pa., 1782 (Congressional arbitration)

5 Conn. cedes to Congress, 1786

6 Conn. cedes Western Reserve to Congress, 1800

N.C. cedes to Congress, 1790

S.C. relinquishes claims to Ga., 1787 (Beaufort Convention)

adequate thought to the distribution of power within the national government or to the relationship between the Confederation and the states. The Congress they created was simultaneously a legislative body and a collective executive, but it had no independent income and no authority to compel the states to accept its rulings. What is surprising, in other words, is not how poorly the Confederation functioned in the following years, but rather how much the government was able to accomplish.

Trials of the Confederation

During and after the war, the most persistent problem faced by the American governments, state and national, was finance. Because of a reluctance to levy taxes, both Congress and the states tried to finance the war by printing currency. Even though the money was backed by nothing but good faith, it circulated freely and without excessive depreciation during 1775 and most of 1776. But in late 1776, as the American army suffered major battlefield reverses, prices began to rise and inflation set in. The value of the currency rested on Americans' faith in their government, a faith that was sorely tested in the years that followed. Both Congress and the states attempted to control inflation, but in 1780 it took forty paper dollars to purchase one silver dollar. A year later, Continental currency was worthless.

Financial Problems

Although many suffered from inflation, especially those on fixed incomes, some benefited from such economic conditions. Military contractors, large-scale farmers, and investors could make sizable profits. More risky, but potentially even more profitable, was privateering against enemy shipping. Privateering attracted venturesome sailors and wealthy merchants alike.

Accumulation of private wealth in the country, however, did not help Congress with its financial problems. In 1781, faced with the total collapse of the monetary system, the delegates undertook major reforms. After establishing a department of finance under the wealthy Philadelphia merchant Robert Morris, they asked the states to amend the Articles of Confederation so that Congress could levy a duty on imported goods. Morris put national finances on a solid footing, but the customs duty was never adopted.

Congress also faced major diplomatic problems at the close of the war. Chief among them were issues involving the peace treaty itself. Article 4, which promised the repayment of prewar debts (most of them owed by Americans to British merchants), and Article 5, which recommended that states allow loyalists to recover their confiscated property, aroused considerable opposition. States passed laws denying British subjects the right to sue for recovery of debts or property in American courts, and since most of the purchasers of the confiscated loyalist property were prominent patriots, state governments had no desire to enforce Article 5.

Weakness in Foreign Affairs and Commerce

The failure of state and local governments to comply with Articles 4 and 5 gave Britain an excuse to maintain military posts on the Great Lakes long after it was supposed to withdraw its troops. Furthermore, the inability of Congress to convince the states to implement the treaty pointed up its lack of power. Concerned nationalists argued publicly that enforcement of the treaty, however unpopular, was a crucial test for the republic. "Will foreign nations be willing to undertake anything with us or for us," asked Alexander Hamilton, "when they find that the nature of our governments will allow no dependence to be placed on our engagements?"

The weakness of Congress was especially evident in the realm of trade because the Articles of Confederation specifically denied it the power to establish a national commercial policy. Immediately after the war, Britain, France, and Spain restricted American trade with their colonies. When Britain closed the West Indies to American goods and flooded the United States with British products, Congress watched helplessly. Although Americans reopened trade with northern European countries and started a profitable trade with China in 1784, neither substituted for access to closer and larger markets.

Congress also had difficulty in dealing with the

threat posed by Spain's presence on the southern and western borders of the United States. Determined to prevent the new nation's expansion, Spain in 1784 closed the Mississippi River to American navigation. It thus deprived the growing settlements west of the Appalachians of their major access route to the rest of the nation and the world. If Spain's policy were not reversed, westerners might have to accept Spanish sovereignty as the necessary price for survival. Congress opened negotiations with Spain in 1785 but could not win the necessary concessions on navigation.

Diplomatic problems of another sort confronted congressmen when they considered the status of the land on the western borders of the United States. In the Treaty of Paris (1783), Britain ceded all land east of the Mississippi (except for that held by Spain) to the United States. The Indian tribes, however, had made no such cession. To eliminate that problem, representatives signed treaties of questionable legality with Iroquois at Fort Stanwix, New York, in 1784 and with the Choctaws, Chickasaws, and Cherokees at Hopewell, South Carolina, in 1785 and 1786. When whites poured over the southern Appalachians, the Creek tribe—which had not agreed to the Hopewell treaties—declared war. Only in 1790, when the Creek chief Alexander McGillivray traveled to New York to negotiate a treaty, did the tribe finally come to terms with the United States.

Encroachment on Indian Lands

In 1786, the Iroquois Confederacy formally repudiated the Fort Stanwix treaty and threatened new attacks on frontier settlements, but both whites and Indians knew that the threat was an empty one. The flawed treaty was permitted to stand by default. At intervals during the remainder of the decade, the state of New York purchased large amounts of land from individual Iroquois tribes. By 1790, the once-proud Iroquois Confederacy was confined to a few scattered reservations. In the West, tribes like the Shawnees, Chippewas, Ottawas, and Potawatomis formed their own confederacy and demanded direct negotiations with the United States. Their aim was to present a united front, so as to avoid the piecemeal surrender of land by individual tribes.

Congress, though, ignored the western Indian confederacy and organized the Northwest Territory, bounded by the Mississippi River, the Great Lakes, and the Ohio River. Ordinances passed in 1784, 1785, and 1787 outlined the process through which the land could be sold to settlers and formal governments organized. To ensure orderly development, Congress in 1785 directed that the land be surveyed into townships 6 miles square, each divided into thirty-six sections of 640 acres (1 square mile). Revenue from the sale of the sixteenth section of each township was to be reserved for the support of public schools—the first instance of federal aid to education in American history. The minimum price per acre was set at $1, and the minimum sale was to be 640 acres. Congress was not especially concerned about helping the small farmer: the minimum outlay of $640 was beyond the reach of most Americans. The proceeds from the land sales were the first independent revenues available to the national government.

The most important ordinance was the third, passed in 1787. The Northwest Ordinance contained a bill of rights guaranteeing settlers in the territory freedom of religion and the right to a jury trial, prohibiting cruel and unusual punishments, and abolishing slavery. It also specified the process by which residents of the territory could eventually organize state governments and seek admission to the Union "on an equal footing with the original States." Early in the nation's history, therefore, Congress laid down a policy of admitting new states on the same basis as the old and assuring residents of the territories the same rights as citizens of the original states.

The Northwest Ordinance

In a sense, though, the ordinance was purely theoretical at the time it was passed. The Miamis, Shawnees, and Delawares refused to acknowledge American sovereignty and insisted on their right to the land. They opposed white settlement violently, attacking pioneers who ventured too far north of the Ohio River. In 1788, the Ohio Company, to which Congress had sold a large tract of land at reduced rates, established the town of Marietta at the juncture of the Ohio and Muskingum rivers. But the Indians prevented the company from extending settlement very far into the interior. After General Arthur St. Clair, the first governor of the Northwest Territory, failed to negotiate a meaningful treaty with the tribes in early 1789, it was apparent that the United States and the Miami-led western confederacy would clash.

Little Turtle, the war chief of the Miami Confederacy, defeated General Josiah Harmar (1790) and then St. Clair himself (1791) in major battles near the present border between Indiana and Ohio. More than six hundred of St. Clair's men were killed and scores more wounded; it was the whites' worst defeat in the entire history of the American frontier. In 1793, the Miami Confederacy declared that peace could be achieved only if the United States recognized the Ohio River as the boundary between white and Indian lands. But the government refused to relinquish its claim to the Northwest Territory. A new army under the command of General Anthony Wayne defeated the tribesmen in 1794 at the Battle of Fallen Timbers (near Toledo, Ohio). This victory made serious negotiations possible.

War in the Northwest

The Treaty of Greenville (1795) gave each side a portion of what it wanted. The United States gained the right to settle much of what was to become the state of Ohio, the tribes retaining only the northwest corner of the region. The Indians received the acknowledgment they had long sought: American recognition of their rights to the soil. At Greenville, the United States formally accepted the principle of Indian sovereignty, by virtue of residence, over all lands the tribes had not yet ceded. Never again would the United States government claim that it had acquired Indian territory solely through negotiation with a European or American country.

The problems the United States encountered in ensuring safe settlement of the Northwest Territory pointed up, once again, the basic weakness of the Confederation government. Not until a new constitution was adopted could the United States muster sufficient force to implement all the provisions of the Northwest Ordinance. Thus, although the ordinance is often viewed as one of the few major accomplishments of the Confederation Congress, it must be seen within a context of political impotence.

From Crisis to a Constitution

The most obvious deficiencies of the Articles of Confederation involved overseas trade and foreign affairs. Congress could not impose its will on the states to establish a uniform commercial policy or to ensure the enforcement of treaties. The problems involving trade were particularly serious. Less than a year after the war ended, the American economy slid into a depression. Exporters of staple crops and importers of manufactured goods were adversely affected by the postwar restrictions that European powers imposed on American commerce. Although recovery had begun by 1786, the war's effects proved impossible to erase entirely.

The war had wrought permanent change in the American economy. The near-total cessation of commerce in nonmilitary items during the war years proved a great stimulus to domestic manufacturing. Consequently, despite the influx of European goods after 1783, the postwar period witnessed the stirrings of American industrial development—for example, the first American textile mill began production in Pawtucket, Rhode Island, in 1793. Moreover, foreign trade patterns shifted from Europe and toward the West Indies. Foodstuffs shipped to the French and Dutch Caribbean islands became America's largest single export.

Economic Change

Recognizing the inability of the Confederation Congress to deal with commercial matters, Virginia invited the other states to a convention at Annapolis, Maryland, to discuss trade policy. Although eight states named representatives to the meeting in September 1786, only five delegations attended. Those present realized that they were too few in number to have any real impact on the political system. They issued a call for another convention, to be held in Philadelphia in nine months, "to devise such further provisions as shall . . . appear necessary to render the constitution of the federal government adequate to the exigencies of the Union." The other states did not respond immediately to the summons to another general meeting, but then Shays's Rebellion occurred.

The reaction to Shays's Rebellion hastened the movement toward comprehensive revision of the Articles of Confederation. In February 1787, after most of the states had already appointed delegates, the Confederation Congress belatedly endorsed the convention. In May, fifty-five men, representing all the states except Rhode Island, assembled in Philadelphia to begin their deliberations.

The vast majority of the delegates to the Constitutional Convention were men of property and substance. Among their number were merchants, planters, physicians, generals, governors, and especially lawyers. Most had been born in America, and many came from families that had arrived in the seventeenth century. In an era when only a tiny proportion of the population had any advanced education, more than half had attended college. A few had been educated in Britain, but most were graduates of American institutions. The youngest delegate was twenty-six, the oldest—Benjamin Franklin—eighty-one. Like George Washington, whom they elected chairman, most were in their middle years. Of the dozen men who did the bulk of the convention's work, James Madison of Virginia was the most important. He truly deserves the title Father of the Constitution.

Constitutional Convention

Madison was unique among the delegates in his systematic preparation for the Philadelphia meeting. Through Jefferson in Paris he bought more than two hundred books on history and government and carefully analyzed their accounts of past confederacies and republics. In April 1787, a month before the Constitutional Convention began, he summed up the results of his research in a lengthy paper, entitled "Vices of the Political System of the United States." After listing the eleven major flaws he perceived in the current structure of the government, Madison set forth the principle of checks and balances.

James Madison

The government, he believed, had to be constructed in such a way that it could not become tyrannical or fall wholly under the influence of a particular interest group. He regarded the large size of a potential national republic as an advantage in that respect. Rejecting the common assertion that republics had to be small to survive, Madison argued that a large, diverse republic was in fact to be preferred. Because the nation would include many different interest groups, no single interest group would be able to control the government. Political stability would result from compromises among the contending parties.

Madison's conception of national government was embodied in the so-called Virginia Plan, introduced on May 29 by his colleague Edmund Randolph. The plan provided for a two-house legislature—one house elected directly by the people and the other selected by the first, with proportional representation in both houses, an executive elected by Congress, a national judiciary, and congressional veto over state laws. The Virginia Plan gave Congress the broad power to legislate "in all cases to which the separate states are incompetent." Had it been adopted intact, it would have created a government in which national authority reigned unchallenged and state power was greatly diminished.

Virginia and New Jersey Plans

But the convention included many delegates who, while recognizing the need for change, believed that the Virginians had gone too far in the direction of national consolidation. The disaffected delegates united under the leadership of William Paterson. On June 15, Paterson presented an alternative scheme, the New Jersey Plan, calling for modifications in the Articles of Confederation rather than a complete overhaul of the government. Paterson proposed retaining the unicameral Confederation Congress but giving it new powers of taxation and trade regulation. Although the delegates rejected Paterson's narrow interpretation of their task, he and his allies won a number of major victories.

The delegates began their work by discussing the structure and functions of Congress. They readily agreed that the new national government should have a two-house (bicameral) legislature. But then they discovered that they differed widely in their answers to three key questions: Should representation in both houses of Congress be proportional to population? How was representation in either or both houses to be apportioned among the states?

And, finally, how were the members of the two houses to be elected?

The last issue was the easiest to resolve. In the words of John Dickinson, the delegates thought it "essential" that members of one branch of Congress be elected directly by the people and "expedient" that members of the other be chosen by the state legislatures. Since the legislatures had selected delegates to the Confederation Congress, they would expect a similar privilege in the new government.

Considerably more difficult was the matter of proportional representation. The delegates accepted without much debate the principle of proportional representation in the lower house. The nature of representation to the Senate, however, was another matter. Delegates from the smaller states argued for equal representation; those from the large states favored proportional representation. For weeks, the convention was deadlocked on the issue, neither side being able to obtain a majority. A committee appointed to work out a compromise recommended equal representation in the Senate, coupled with a proviso that all appropriation bills had to originate in the lower house. The dispute was finally resolved when the convention agreed that the two senators from each state could vote as individuals rather than as a unit.

Another critical question remained: how was representation in the lower house to be apportioned among the states? Delegates from states with

Slavery and the Constitution large numbers of slaves wanted all people, black and white, to be counted equally; delegates from states with few slaves wanted only free people to be counted. The issue was resolved by using a formula developed by the Confederation Congress in 1783 to allocate financial assessments among the states: three-fifths of the slaves would be included in the population totals. (The formula reflected the delegates' judgment that slaves were less efficient producers of wealth than free people, not that they were 60 percent human and 40 percent property.) The three-fifths compromise was unanimously accepted by the convention.

Although the words *slave* and *slavery* do not appear in the Constitution (the framers used euphemisms like "other persons"), direct and indirect protections for slavery were deeply embedded in the document. The three-fifths clause, for example, ensured not only that white southern voters would be represented in Congress out of all proportion to their numbers, but also that they would have a disproportionate influence in the selection of the president, since the number of each state's electoral votes was determined by the size of its congressional delegation. Congress was prevented from outlawing the slave trade for at least twenty years. Furthermore, by guaranteeing that the national government would help any states threatened with "domestic violence," the Constitution promised aid in putting down slave revolts.

Once agreement was reached on the problems of slavery and representation, the delegates resolved the other issues more easily. They agreed to enumerate the powers of Congress but to allow it to pass all laws "necessary and proper" to carry out its functions. Foreign policy was placed in the hands of the executive, who was also made the commander-in-chief of the armed forces. The idea of a legislative veto over state action was rejected, but an implied veto was included. Moreover, the Constitution, national laws, and treaties were made the supreme law of the land. Finally, the delegates established the electoral college and a four-year term for the chief executive, who could seek re-election.

The key to the Constitution was the distribution of political authority—separation of powers among the executive, legislative, and judicial branches of

Separation of Powers the national government, and division of powers between the states and the nation. The system of checks and balances would make it difficult for the government to become tyrannical. At the same time, though, the elaborate system would sometimes prevent the government from acting quickly and decisively. Furthermore, the line between state and federal powers was so ambiguously drawn that it would take a civil war to fully resolve the issue.

The convention held its last meeting on September 17, 1787. Of the forty-two delegates, only three

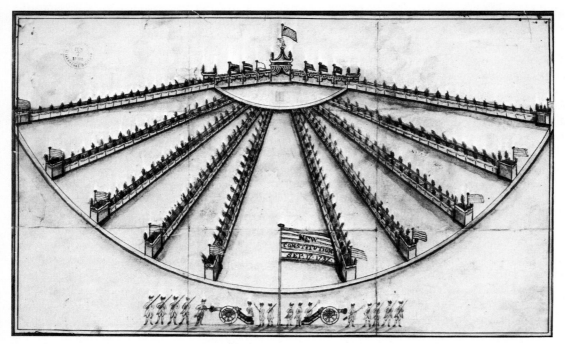

In July 1788, New York City's leaders celebrated their state's ratification of the Constitution at an elaborate banquet served in a pavilion erected for the occasion. Their hopes for an orderly government were symbolized by the orderly arrangement of the tables, separate but linked into a semicircle by the central structure displaying flags and banners. *The New-York Historical Society.*

refused to sign the Constitution. (Two of the three declined because of the lack of a bill of rights.) Though the delegates had accepted the Constitution, the question remained as to whether the states would ratify it.

Opposition and Ratification

The ratification clause of the Constitution provided for the new system to take effect once it was approved by special conventions in at least nine states. The delegates to each state convention were to be elected by the qualified voters. Thus the national Constitution, unlike the Articles of Confederation, would rest directly on popular authority.

As the states began to elect delegates to the special conventions, discussions of the proposed government grew more heated. Federalists, who supported the Constitution, and Antifederalists, who opposed it, wrote newspaper essays and pamphlets vigorously defending or attacking the convention's decisions. The extent of the debate was unprecedented.

The Antifederalist camp included those who emphasized the threat to the states embodied in the new national government and those who stressed the dangers to individuals posed by the lack of a bill of rights. All Antifederalists saw the states as the chief protectors of individual rights and their weakening as the onset of arbitrary power. Fearing a too powerful central government, they rejected the Federalists' emphasis on the need for national leadership by a disinterested elite. Their arguments against the Constitution often consisted of lists of potential abuses of the national government's authority. The Antifederalists were

Anti-federalists

the heirs of the Real Whig ideology of the late 1760s and early 1770s, which stressed the need for the people's constant vigilance to avert oppression.

Indeed, some of the Antifederalists were the very men who had originally promulgated those ideas; for example, Samuel Adams and Richard Henry Lee were both leaders of the opposition to the Constitution. Antifederalist ranks were also peopled by small farmers, who hoped to guard their property against excessive taxation, and by ambitious, upwardly mobile men, who knew that they would reap financial benefits from a less tightly controlled economic and political system that the Constitution promised to establish.

With each passing month, the Antifederalist attack focused more sharply on the Constitution's lack of a bill of rights. Even if the states were weakened by the new system, the Antifederalists believed, the people could still be protected from tyranny if their rights were specifically guaranteed. *Letters of a Federal Farmer,* perhaps the most widely read Antifederalist pamphlet, listed the rights that should be protected: freedom of the press and of religion, the right to trial by jury, and guarantees against unreasonable search warrants.

As the state conventions met to consider ratification, the lack of a bill of rights loomed larger and larger as a flaw in the new form of government.

Ratification of the Constitution

Four of the first five states to ratify did so unanimously, but serious disagreement then began to surface. Massachusetts ratified by a majority of only 19 votes out of 355 cast. In New Hampshire, the Federalists won by a majority of 57 to 47. When New Hampshire ratified, in June 1788, the requirement of nine states had been satisfied. But New York and Virginia had not yet voted, and everyone realized that the new Constitution could not succeed unless those key states accepted it.

In Virginia, despite a valiant effort by the Antifederalist Patrick Henry, the pro-Constitution forces won 89 to 79. In New York, James Madison, John Jay, and Alexander Hamilton campaigned for ratification by publishing *The Federalist,* a political tract that explained the theory behind the Constitution and masterfully answered its critics. Their reasoned arguments, coupled with the promise that a bill of rights would be added to the Constitution, helped win the battle. On July 26, 1788, New York ratified the Constitution by the slim margin of 3 votes. The new government was a reality, even though the last state (Rhode Island, which had not participated in the convention) did not formally join the Union until 1790.

The experience of fighting a war and of struggling for survival as an independent nation in the 1780s had altered the political context of American life. Whereas at the outset of the war most politically aware Americans believed that "that government which governs best governs least," by the late 1780s many had changed their minds. These were the drafters and supporters of the Constitution, who won their point when the Constitution was adopted, however narrowly.

Leading Federalists and Antifederalists did share one key common characteristic: they were all white males. The era of the formation of the Union was also the age of the systematic formulation of American racist thought, and the two processes were intimately linked. One way to preserve the freedom of all whites was to ensure the continued subjection of all blacks, slave or free. Likewise, one way to preserve the unchallenged economic independence of white men was to ensure the economic and political dependence of white women. Independence had been fought for and won by many Americans—white, black, and red, male and female—but in the new republic only white males would hold political power.

Suggestions for Further Reading

General

Richard Beeman et al., eds., *Beyond Confederation: Origins of the Constitution and American National Identity* (1987); Staughton Lynd, *Class Conflict, Slavery, and the United States Constitution: Ten Essays* (1967); Forrest McDonald, *Novus Ordo Seculorum: The Intellectual Origins of the Constitution* (1985); Forrest McDonald, *E Pluribus Unum: The Formation of the American Republic, 1776–1790* (1965); Edmund S. Morgan, *Inventing the People: The Rise of Popular Sover-*

eignty in England and America (1988); *William and Mary Quarterly,* 3rd ser., 44, No. 3 (July 1987), *The Constitution of the United States;* Gordon S. Wood, *The Creation of the American Republic, 1776–1787* (1969).

Continental Congress and Articles of Confederation

H. James Henderson, *Party Politics in the Continental Congress* (1974); Merrill Jensen, *The Articles of Confederation,* 2nd ed. (1959); Merrill Jensen, *The New Nation: A History of the United States During the Confederation, 1781–1789* (1950); Jerrilyn G. Marston, *King and Congress: The Transfer of Political Legitimacy, 1774–1776* (1987); Jack N. Rakove, *The Beginnings of National Politics: An Interpretive History of the Continental Congress* (1979).

State Politics

Willi Paul Adams, *The First American Constitutions: Republican Ideology and the Making of the State Constitutions in the Revolutionary Era* (1980); Ronald Hoffman and Peter Albert, eds., *Sovereign States in an Age of Uncertainty* (1981); Jackson Turner Main, *Political Parties Before the Constitution* (1973); Jackson Turner Main, *The Sovereign States, 1775–1783* (1973); J. R. Pole, *Political Representation in England and the Origins of the American Republic* (1966); David P. Szatmary, *Shays' Rebellion: The Making of an Agrarian Insurrection* (1980).

The Constitution

Charles A. Beard, *An Economic Interpretation of the Constitution of the United States* (1913); Forrest McDonald, *We the People: The Economic Origins of the Constitution* (1958); Jackson Turner Main, *The Anti-Federalists: Critics of the Constitution, 1781–1788* (1961); Frederick W. Marks III, *Independence on Trial: Foreign Affairs and the Making of the Constitution* (1973); Clinton Rossiter, *1787: The Grand Convention* (1973); Robert A. Rutland, *The Ordeal of the Constitution: The Antifederalists and the Ratification Struggle of 1787–88* (1966).

Education and Culture

Lawrence A. Cremin, *American Education: The National Experience, 1783–1876* (1981); Joseph M. Ellis, *After the Revolution: Profiles of Early American Culture* (1979); Russell B. Nye, *The Cultural Life of the New Nation: 1776–1803* (1960); Kenneth Silverman, *A Cultural History of the American Revolution* (1976).

Women

Charles Akers, *Abigail Adams: An American Woman* (1980); Linda K. Kerber, *Women of the Republic: Intellect and Ideology in Revolutionary America* (1980); Mary Beth Norton, *Liberty's Daughters: The Revolutionary Experience of American Women, 1750–1800* (1980); Lynn Withey, *Dearest Friend: A Life of Abigail Adams* (1980).

Blacks and Slavery

Ira Berlin and Ronald Hoffman, eds., *Slavery and Freedom in the Age of the American Revolution* (1983); David Brion Davis, *The Problem of Slavery in the Age of Revolution, 1770–1823* (1975); Carol V. R. George, *Segregated Sabbaths: Richard Allen and the Emergence of Independent Black Churches, 1760–1840* (1973); Winthrop Jordan, *White over Black: American Attitudes Toward the Negro, 1550–1812* (1968); Gary Nash, *Forging Freedom: The Formation of Philadelphia's Black Community, 1720–1840* (1988); Donald L. Robinson, *Slavery in the Structure of American Politics, 1765–1820* (1971); Arthur Zilversmit, *The First Emancipation: The Abolition of Slavery in the North* (1967).

Indians

Harvey L. Carter, *The Life and Times of Little Turtle* (1987); Dorothy Jones, *License for Empire: Colonialism by Treaty in Early America* (1982); Bernard Sheehan, *Seeds of Extinction: Jeffersonian Philanthropy and the American Indian* (1973); Anthony F. C. Wallace, *The Death and Rebirth of the Seneca* (1969).

Abigail Adams was furious. "I am at a loss to know how the people who were formerly so much alive to the usurpation of one Nation can crouch so tamely to a much more dangerous and dareing one," she wrote to her sister in January 1798. France, she asserted, "aims not only at our independance and libe[r]ty, but a total annihilation of the Christian Religion." Yet every state except Connecticut had elected French sympathizers to Congress.

Abigail Adams's anger stemmed from the way in which American opinion had divided over the French Revolution, which had begun in 1789. She and her husband, along with many others, viewed the violent tactics of the French revolutionaries with deep alarm and saw the former ally of the United States as the major threat to freedom in the world, even though other Americans continued to sympathize with the French. "There is no end to their audaciousness," she informed her sister in the spring of 1798; "French emissaries are in every corner of the union sowing and spreading their Sedition."

Opinionated and fiercely loyal to her husband, John, elected president of the United States in 1796, Abigail Adams found herself in the middle of the first truly heated partisan battle in the new republic. She knew her husband had devoted his life to the nation's welfare. What then could be the source of the bitter invective directed at him by his opponents, the political faction now called Republicans? For her and her husband, there was only one answer: the criticism must have been instigated by France, whose revolutionary government saw the Adams administration as its enemy.

The failure of Americans' quest for unity and unqualified independence during the 1790s was nowhere more evident than in the political battles that absorbed Abigail Adams's attention. The fight over the Constitution was the precursor of an even wider division over the major political, economic, and diplomatic questions confronting the young republic. To make matters worse, Americans had not anticipated the political disagreements that would mark the decade. Believing that the Constitution would resolve the problems that had arisen during the Confederation period, they expected the new government to rule by consensus. They could not

7

POLITICS AND SOCIETY IN THE EARLY REPUBLIC, 1789–1800

understand or fully accept the division of America's political leaders into two factions—not yet political parties—known as Federalists and Republicans.

Attaining prosperity and expanding were not easy tasks either. The United States economy depended on the export trade. When warfare between England and France resumed in 1793, Americans found their commerce disrupted once again. Moreover, the strength of the Miami Confederacy blocked the westward expansion of white settlement north of the Ohio River until after the Treaty of Greenville in 1795. South of the Ohio, settlements were established west of the mountains as early as the 1770s, but the geographical barrier of the Appalachians tended to isolate them from the eastern seaboard. Not until the first years of the nineteenth century did the frontier settlements become more fully integrated into American life through the vehicle of the Second Great Awakening, a religious revival that swept both east and west.

Building a Workable Government

In 1788, Americans celebrated the ratification of the Constitution with a series of parades, held in many cities on the Fourth of July. The processions were carefully planned to symbolize the unity of the new nation and to recall its history to the minds of the watching throngs. Like prerevolutionary protest meetings, the parades served as political educators for literate and illiterate Americans alike. Men and women who could not read learned about the significance of the new Constitution in the life of the nation. They were also instructed about political leaders' hopes for industry and frugality on the part of a virtuous American public.

The nationalistic spirit expressed in the ratification processions carried over into the first session of Congress. In the congressional **First** elections held late in 1788, only a **Congress** few Antifederalists ran for office, and even fewer were elected. Thus the First Congress consisted chiefly of men who supported a strong national government. Since the Constitution had deliberately left many key issues undecided, the nationalists' domination of Congress meant that their views on those points quickly prevailed.

Congress faced four immediate tasks when it convened in April 1789: raising revenue to support the new government, responding to the state ratification conventions' call for the addition of a bill of rights to the Constitution, setting up executive departments, and organizing the federal judiciary. The last task was especially important. The Constitution established a Supreme Court but left it to Congress to decide whether to have other federal courts as well.

James Madison, who had been elected to the House of Representatives, soon became as influential in Congress as he had been at the Constitutional Convention. Only a few months into the first session, he persuaded Congress to impose a 5-percent tariff on certain imported goods. Thus, the First Congress quickly achieved what the Confederation Congress never had: an effective national tax law. The new government would have problems, but lack of revenue in its first years was not one of them.

Madison also took the lead on the issue of constitutional amendments, introducing nineteen proposed amendments, of which Congress accepted twelve and the states ten. The two **Bill of Rights** not ratified by the states dealt with the number of congressmen and their salaries. The other ten amendments officially became part of the Constitution on December 15, 1791. Not for many years, though, did they become known collectively as the Bill of Rights.

The First Amendment specifically prohibited Congress from passing any law restricting the people's right to freedom of religion, speech, press, peaceable assembly, or petition. The next two arose directly from the former colonists' fear of standing armies as a threat to freedom. The Second Amendment guaranteed the people's right "to keep and bear arms" because of the need for a "well regulated Militia." The Third Amendment defined the circumstances in which troops could be quartered in private homes. The next five pertained to judicial procedures. The Fourth Amendment prohibited

1789	George Washington inaugurated Judiciary Act of 1789 French Revolution begins	**1795**	Jay Treaty
1790	Alexander Hamilton's *Report on* *Public Credit*	**1796**	First contested presidential election: John Adams elected president, Thomas Jefferson vice president
1791	First ten amendments (Bill of Rights) ratified	**1798**	XYZ affair Alien and Sedition Acts Virginia and Kentucky resolutions
1793	France declares war on Britain, Spain, and Holland Neutrality Proclamation Democratic-Republican societies founded	**1798–99**	Quasi-War with France
		1800	Franco-American Convention Jefferson elected president Second Great Awakening begins Gabriel's Rebellion
1794	Whiskey Rebellion		

"unreasonable searches and seizures"; the Fifth and Sixth established the rights of accused persons; the Seventh specified the conditions for jury trials in civil, as opposed to criminal, cases; and the Eighth forbade "cruel and unusual punishments." Finally, the Ninth and Tenth Amendments reserved to the people and the states other unspecified rights and powers. In short, the authors of the amendments made clear that in listing some rights explicitly they did not mean to preclude the exercise of others.

While debating the proposed amendments, Congress also concerned itself with the organization of the executive branch. It readily agreed to continue the three administrative departments established under the Articles of Confederation: War, Foreign Affairs (renamed State), and Treasury. Congress also instituted two lesser posts: the attorney general—the nation's official lawyer—and the postmaster general. The only serious controversy arose over whether the president alone could dismiss officials whom he had originally appointed with the consent of the Senate. After some debate, the House and Senate agreed that he had such authority. Thus was established the important principle

that the heads of the executive departments are responsible to the president.

Aside from the constitutional amendments, the most far-reaching piece of legislation enacted by the First Congress was the Judiciary Act of 1789.

Judiciary Act of 1789

That act provided for the Supreme Court to have six members: a chief justice and five associate justices. It also defined the jurisdiction of the federal judiciary and established thirteen district courts and three circuit courts of appeal. The act's most important provision may have been Section 25, which allowed appeals from state courts to the federal court system when certain types of constitutional issues were raised. This section was intended to implement Article VI of the Constitution, which stated that federal laws and treaties were to be considered "the supreme Law of the Land." If Article VI was to be enforced uniformly, the national judiciary clearly had to be able to overturn state court decisions involving the Constitution, federal laws, or treaties.

During the first decade of its existence, the Supreme Court handled few cases of any importance.

But in a significant 1796 decision, *Ware* v. *Hylton,* the Court—acting on the basis of Section 25 of the Judiciary Act of 1789—for the first time declared a state law unconstitutional. That same year, it also reviewed the constitutionality of an act of Congress, upholding its validity in the case of *Hylton* v. *U.S.* The most important case of the decade, *Chisholm* v. *Georgia* (1793), established that states could be freely sued in federal courts by citizens of other states. This decision, unpopular with the state governments, was overruled five years later by the Eleventh Amendment to the Constitution.

Domestic Policy Under Washington and Hamilton

George Washington did not seek the presidency. When in 1783 he returned to Mount Vernon, his plantation on the Potomac River, he was eager for the peaceful life of a Virginia planter. Yet his fellow countrymen never regarded Washington as just another private citizen. Americans agreed that only George Washington had sufficient prestige to serve as the republic's first president. The unanimous vote of the electoral college was just a formality.

Election of the First President

During his first months in office, Washington acted cautiously, knowing that whatever he did would set precedents for the future. For example, he concluded that he should exercise his veto power over congressional legislation very sparingly—only, indeed, if he was convinced that a bill was unconstitutional. His first major task as president was to choose the men who would head the executive departments. For the War Department, he selected an old comrade-in-arms, Henry Knox. His choice for the State Department was his fellow Virginian Thomas Jefferson, who had just returned to the United States from his post as minister to France. For the crucial position of secretary of the treasury, the president chose the brilliant, intensely ambitious Alexander Hamilton.

Two traits distinguished Hamilton from most of

John Trumbull painted "Washington at Verplanck's Point" in the spring of 1790, when George Washington was completing his first year as president. Washington's stepgrandson later wrote that this portrait was "the most perfect extant" of its subject, whom Trumbull depicted wearing a Continental Army uniform. *The Henry Francis du Pont Winterthur Museum.*

his contemporaries. First, he displayed an undivided, unquestioning loyalty to the nation as a whole. As a West Indian who had lived on the mainland only briefly before the war, Hamilton had no ties to an individual state. He showed little sympathy for, or understanding of, demands for local autonomy. Thus the aim of his fiscal policies was always the consolidation of power at the national level. Further, he never feared the exercise of centralized executive authority, as did his older counterparts who had clashed repeatedly with colonial governors.

Alexander Hamilton

Second, he regarded his fellow human beings

with cynicism. Perhaps because of his own poverty in his early years and his overriding ambition, Hamilton believed people to be motivated primarily, if not entirely, by self-interest—particularly economic self-interest. He placed absolutely no reliance on people's capacity for virtuous and self-sacrificing behavior. That outlook set him apart from those republicans who foresaw a rosy future, in which public-spirited citizens would pursue the common good rather than their own private advantage.

In 1789, Congress ordered the new secretary of the treasury to study the state of the public debt and to submit recommendations for supporting the government's credit. Hamilton discovered that the country's remaining war debts fell into three categories: those owed by the national government to foreign governments and investors, mostly to France (about $11 million); those owed by the national government to merchants, former soldiers, holders of revolutionary bonds, and the like (about $27 million); and, finally, similar debts owed by state governments (roughly estimated at $25 million). With respect to the national debt, there was little disagreement: politically aware Americans recognized that if their new government was to succeed it would have to repay at full face value the financial obligations the nation had incurred while winning independence.

The state debts were quite another matter. Some states—notably Virginia, Maryland, North Carolina, and Georgia—had already paid off most of their war debts. They would oppose the national government's assumption of responsibility for other states' debts, since their citizens would be taxed to pay such obligations. Massachusetts, Connecticut, and South Carolina, on the other hand, still had sizable unpaid debts and would welcome a system of national assumption. The possible assumption of state debts also had political implications. Consolidation of the debt in the hands of the national government would help to concentrate economic and political power at the national level.

Hamilton's first *Report on Public Credit,* sent to Congress in January 1790, reflected both his national loyalty and his cynicism. He proposed that

National Debt

Hamilton's First *Report on Public Credit*

Congress assume outstanding state debts, combine them with national obligations, and issue new securities covering both principal and accumulated unpaid interest. Current holders of state or national debt certificates would have the option of taking a portion of their payment in western lands. Hamilton's aims were clear: he wanted to expand the financial reach of the United States government and reduce the economic power of the states. He also wanted to ensure that the holders of public securities— many of them wealthy merchants and speculators —would have a significant financial stake in the survival of the national government.

Hamilton's plan stimulated lively debate in Congress. The opposition coalesced around his former ally James Madison. Well aware that speculators had purchased large quantities of debt certificates at a small fraction of their face value, Madison proposed that the original holders of the debt also be compensated by the government. Madison's plan, though fairer than Hamilton's—because it would have directly repaid those people who had actually supplied the revolutionary governments with goods or services—would have been difficult, perhaps impossible, to administer. The House of Representatives rejected it.

At first, the House also rejected the assumption of state debts. Since the Senate, by contrast, had adopted Hamilton's plan largely intact, a series of compromises followed. Hamilton agreed to some changes in the assumption plan that would benefit Virginia in particular. The assumption bill also became linked in a complex way to another controversial issue: the location of the permanent national capital. Both northerners and southerners wanted the capital in their region. The traditional story that Hamilton and Madison agreed over Jefferson's dinner table to exchange assumption of state debts for a southern site is not supported by the surviving evidence, but a political deal was undoubtedly struck. The Potomac River was designated as the site for the capital. Simultaneously, the four congressmen from Maryland and Virginia whose districts contained the most likely locations for the new city switched from opposition to support for assumption. The first part of Hamilton's financial program became law in August 1790.

Four months later, Hamilton submitted to Congress a second report on public credit, recommending the chartering of a national bank.

First Bank of the United States

Hamilton modeled his bank on the Bank of England. The Bank of the United States was to be capitalized at $10 million, of which only $2 million would come from public funds. Private investors would supply the rest. The bank's charter was to run for twenty years, and one-fifth of its directors were to be named by the government. Its bank notes would circulate as the nation's currency; it would also act as the collecting and disbursing agent for the Treasury and lend money to the government. Most political leaders recognized that such an institution would benefit the country. But there was another issue: did the Constitution give Congress the power to establish such a bank?

James Madison, for one, answered that question with a resounding no. He pointed out that the delegates at the Constitutional Convention had specifically rejected a clause authorizing Congress to issue corporate charters. Consequently, he argued, that power could not be inferred from other parts of the Constitution.

Disturbed by Madison's contention, Washington decided to request other opinions before signing the bill. Edmund Randolph, the attorney general, and Thomas Jefferson, the secretary of state, agreed with Madison that the bank was unconstitutional. Jefferson referred to Article I, Section 8, of the Constitution, which gave Congress the power "to make all Laws which shall be necessary and proper for carrying into Execution the foregoing Powers." The key word, Jefferson argued, was "necessary": Congress could do what was needed, but not what was merely desirable, without specific constitutional authorization. Thus Jefferson formulated the strict-constructionist interpretation of the Constitution.

Washington asked Hamilton to reply to these negative assessments of his proposal. Hamilton's *Defense of the Constitutionality of the Bank,* presented to Washington in February 1791, was a brilliant exposition of what has become known as the broad-constructionist view of the Constitution. Hamilton argued forcefully that Congress could choose any means not specifically prohibited by the Constitution to achieve a constitutional end. In short, if the end was constitutional and the means was not unconstitutional, then the means was also constitutional. Washington was convinced and signed the bill.

In December 1791, Hamilton presented to Congress his *Report on Manufactures,* the third and last of his prescriptions for the American economy. In it, he outlined an ambitious plan for encouraging and protecting the country's infant industries, such as shoemaking and textile manufacturing. Hamilton urged Congress to promote the immigration of technicians and laborers, enact protective tariffs, and support industrial development. Most congressmen, being convinced that America's future was agrarian, rejected Hamilton's report.

That same year, Congress did accept another part of Hamilton's financial program, an excise tax on whiskey. Congressmen both recognized the need

Whiskey Rebellion

for additional government revenues and hoped to reduce the national consumption of distilled spirits. The new tax most directly affected western farmers, who sold their grain crops in the form of distilled spirits as a means of avoiding the high costs of transporting wagonloads of bulky corn over the mountains.

News of the excise law set off protests in frontier areas of Pennsylvania. But matters did not come to a head until July 1794, when western Pennsylvania farmers resisted a federal marshal and a tax collector who were trying to enforce the law. About seven thousand rebels convened on August 1 to plot the destruction of Pittsburgh but decided not to face the heavy guns of the fort guarding the town. Unrest nevertheless continued for months on the frontiers of Pennsylvania, Maryland, and Virginia. Crowds of men drafted petitions protesting the excise, raised liberty poles (in deliberate imitation of the 1760s), and occasionally harassed tax collectors. But the Whiskey Rebellion remained largely leaderless and unorganized. Washington, determined to prevent another Shays's Rebellion, ordered the insurgents to disperse by September 1

Leisure in America, **1800**

SIMPLE PLEASURES

In almost all early American societies, the tasks of daily life demanded great investments of energy and time. Struggles for food, shelter, personal security, or political stability necessarily took precedence over frivolous pursuits. Nevertheless, the need to balance work with play is a human trait, and leisure had its place in even the most rigorous societies.

In Indian communities, ritual provided opportunities for recreation. In 1736, a German artist, Philip Georg Friedrich von Reck, painted several watercolors of the Yuchi, a tribe that occupied the coastal regions of South Carolina and Georgia, including this festival scene. Indians in the southeastern colonies were typically agriculturalists; their largest ceremonies usually coincided with the late-summer harvest and incorporated singing, dancing, the lighting of sacred fires, the creation of new clothes and household items, and the destruction of last year's goods. Although these thanksgiving rituals certainly served a religious purpose, they also afforded participants a well-earned physical and emotional release.

Colonial children, like their more modern counterparts, enjoyed playing with dolls, though eighteenth-century toys tended to be made simply, from available materials. Indians probably taught the colonists how to make little corncob figures, using wrapped or woven cornhusks for head, limbs, clothes, and doll-sized accessories.

Not surprisingly, romance, a perennial leisure-time activity, flourished in the colonies. The valentine above is thought to have been one of the first made in America, given to Elizabeth Sandwith, a Philadelphia Quaker, in 1753. Not only did Elizabeth's industrious suitor skillfully wield scissors to snip this intricate design from painted paper, he filled the valentine's interior scallops and arcs with lines of verse dedicated to her. (Elizabeth must have been pleased but not entirely persuaded; she married someone else eight years later.)

Families with money enjoyed portraying themselves surrounded by the pleasures of a European-style culture. For instance, the portraits of self-possessed young ladies often included handsome harps or pianofortes. The pianoforte was a relatively new invention, and some mechanical difficulties—for instance, the ease with which the strings and hammers might break— had yet to be resolved; nevertheless, pianofortes were fairly common items in well-to-do American homes by the end of the century.

Elaborate needlework pictures, in themselves a leisure-time pursuit, also hint at the degree of elegance and luxury some wealthy colonists aspired to. The lush example below was stitched by a thirty-year-old Salem, Massachusetts, woman. Though wonderfully detailed, its idyllic depiction may be more a reflection of the popular pictorial motifs of the period than a faithful representation of a garden party's ambience.

Above: Philippe Abraham Peticolas, *Musical Ladies* (watercolor-on-ivory miniature), 1798. Below: Needlework picture, stitched by Love Rawlins, ca. 1740

A social scene of a more modest character appears on the painted pie plate from Pennsylvania, shown left. The charm of the plate's craftsmanship reminds us, too, of the pleasures that baking and small domestic decorations must have afforded some eighteenth-century women.

Finally, contemporary depictions of slaves help prove that men and women create diversion in the midst of severe repression, that fun and relaxation are essential to human survival. From necessity, African-Americans invented simple entertainments. Juba dances could be performed without the use of any musical instruments; singing, foot tapping, hand clapping, and body slapping sometimes provided the only rhythmic accompaniment. Slave dances contrasted markedly with the slow steps practiced at plantation cotillions, and white observers often admired the dancers' remarkable ability and vitality.

Above: Pie plate, 1786. Below: Artist unknown, *The Old Plantation,* ca. 1790–1800.

and summoned nearly thirteen thousand militiamen. By the time the troops arrived, the disturbances were over.

The chief importance of the Whiskey Rebellion was the message it forcefully conveyed to the American public. The national government, Washington had demonstrated, would not allow violent organized resistance to its laws. In the new republic, change would be effected peacefully, by legal means.

By 1794, a group of Americans were already beginning to seek change systematically within the confines of electoral politics, even though traditional political theory regarded organized opposition—especially in a republic—as illegitimate. The leaders of the opposition, Jefferson and Madison, saw themselves as the true heirs of the Revolution. To emphasize their point, they and their followers in Congress began calling themselves Republicans. Hamilton and his supporters claimed to be the rightful interpreters of the Constitution and took the name Federalists. Each group contended that the other was a faction bent upon subversion. (By traditional definition, a faction was opposed to the public good.)

Partisan Politics and Foreign Policy

The first years under the Constitution were blessed by international peace. Eventually, however, the French Revolution, which began in 1789, brought about the resumption of hostilities between France, America's wartime ally, and Great Britain, America's most important trading partner.

At first, Americans welcomed the news that France was turning toward republicanism. But by the early 1790s, the reports from France were disquieting. Outbreaks of violence continued; ministries succeeded each other with bewildering rapidity; and executions were commonplace. The king himself was beheaded in early 1793. Although many Americans, including Jefferson and Madison, retained their sympathy for the French revolutionaries, others began to view France as a prime example of the perversion of republicanism. As might be expected, Hamilton fell into the latter group.

At that juncture, France declared war on Britain, Spain, and Holland. The Americans thus faced a dilemma. The 1778 Treaty of Alliance with France bound them to that nation "forever," and a mutual commitment to republicanism created ideological bonds. Yet the United States was connected to Great Britain as well. Aside from sharing a common history and language, America and England were economic partners. Indeed, since the nation's financial system depended heavily on import tariffs as a source of revenue and America's imports came primarily from Britain, the economic health of the United States required uninterrupted trade with the former mother country.

The political and diplomatic climate was further complicated in April 1793, when Citizen Edmond Genêt, a representative of the French government,

Citizen Genêt landed in Charleston. As Genêt made his leisurely way northward to New York City, he was wildly cheered and lavishly entertained at every stop. En route, he recruited Americans for expeditions against British and Spanish possessions in the Western Hemisphere and distributed privateering commissions with a generous hand. Genêt's arrival raised a series of key questions for President Washington. Should he receive Genêt, thus officially recognizing the French revolutionary government? Should he acknowledge an obligation to aid France under the terms of the 1778 Treaty of Alliance? Or should he proclaim American neutrality in the conflict?

For once, Hamilton and Jefferson saw eye to eye. Both told Washington that the United States could not afford to ally itself firmly with either side. Washington agreed. He received Genêt officially but also issued a proclamation informing the world that the United States would adopt "a conduct friendly and impartial toward the belligerent powers." However, the domestic divisions Genêt helped to widen were perpetuated by clubs called Democratic-Republican societies.

Americans sympathetic to France formed more than forty of these Democratic-Republican societies between 1793 and 1800. Their members saw themselves as heirs of the Sons of Liberty, seeking the same goal as their predecessors: protection of the people's liberties against encroachments by corrupt and evil rulers. To that end, they publicly protested government policies and warned the people of impending tyranny. Like the Sons of Liberty, the Democratic-Republican societies were composed chiefly of artisans and craftsmen of various kinds, although professionals, farmers, and merchants also joined.

Democratic-Republican Societies

The rapid growth of such groups, outspoken in their criticism of the Washington administration, deeply disturbed Hamilton and eventually Washington himself. Newspapers sympathetic to the Federalists charged that the societies were subversive agents of a foreign power. The climax of the attack came in the fall of 1794, when Washington accused the societies of having fomented the Whiskey Rebellion.

In retrospect, Washington's and Hamilton's reaction to the Democratic-Republican societies seems hysterical and overwrought. But it must be kept in mind that the Democratic-Republican societies were the first formally organized political dissenters in the United States. As such, they aroused the fear and suspicion of elected officials, who had not yet accepted the idea that one component of a free government was an organized loyal opposition.

That same year, George Washington decided to send Chief Justice John Jay to England to try to reach agreement on four major unresolved questions affecting Anglo-American affairs. The first point at issue was recent British seizures of American merchant ships trading in the French West Indies. The United States wanted to establish the principle of freedom of the seas and to assert its right, as a neutral nation, to trade freely with both sides. Second, Great Britain had not yet carried out its promise, made in the Treaty of Paris (1783), to evacuate its posts in the American Northwest. Third and fourth, the Americans hoped for a commercial treaty and sought compensation for the slaves who had left with the British army at the end of the war.

Jay Treaty

The negotiations in London proved difficult, since Jay had little to offer Britain in exchange for the concessions he wanted. In the end, Britain did agree to evacuate the western forts and ease the restrictions on American trade to England and the West Indies. No compensation for lost slaves was agreed to, but Jay accepted a provision establishing an arbitration commission to deal with the matter of prewar debts owed to British creditors. A similar commission was to handle the question of compensation for the seizures of American merchant ships. Under the circumstances, Jay did remarkably well: the treaty averted war with England. Nevertheless, most Americans, including the president, were dissatisfied with at least some parts of the treaty.

At first, potential opposition was blunted because the Senate debated and ratified the treaty in secret. Not until after it was formally approved on June 24, 1795, was the public informed of its provisions. The Democratic-Republican societies led protests against the treaty. Once President Washington signed the treaty, though, there seemed to be little the Republicans could do to prevent it from taking effect. Just one opportunity remained: Congress had to appropriate funds to carry out the treaty provisions.

When the House took up the money issue in March 1796, opponents of the treaty tried to prevent approval of the appropriations. They called on Washington to submit to the House all documents pertinent to the negotiations. In successfully resisting the House request, Washington established the doctrine of executive privilege—that is, the power of the president to withhold information from Congress if he believes circumstances warrant doing so. At first, the treaty's opponents appeared to be in the majority. But the desire of frontier residents to have British posts evacuated and of merchants to trade with the British Empire weakened the opposition. Finally, Federalist senators threatened to reject the treaty that Thomas Pinckney of South Carolina had negotiated with Spain unless the funds for the Jay Treaty were approved. Since Pinckney's Treaty had secured American navigation rights on the Mississippi, it was popular with southerners and westerners, for it would be an economic boost to their regions. For all these reasons the House approved the necessary funds by a vote of 51 to 48.

Analysis of the vote reveals both the regional nature of the division and the growing cohesion of the Republican and Federalist factions in Congress.

Republicans and Federalists Forty-four Federalists and seven Republicans voted in favor of the appropriations and forty-five Republicans and three Federalists voted against them. Southerners cast most of the votes against the bill. Except for two South Carolina Federalists, the bill's supporters came from New England and the middle states.

The small number of defectors revealed a new force at work in American politics: partisanship. Voting statistics from the first four Congresses show the ever-increasing tendency of members of the House of Representatives to vote as coherent groups, rather than as individuals. If factional loyalty is defined as voting together at least two-thirds of the time on national issues, the percentage of nonaligned congressmen dropped from 42 percent in 1790 to just 7 percent in 1796.

The growing division cannot be accurately explained in the terms used by Jefferson and Madison (aristocrats versus the people) or by Hamilton and Washington (true patriots versus subversive rabble). Nor do simple economic differences between agrarian and commercial interests provide the answer, since more than 90 percent of Americans in the 1790s lived in rural areas.

Yet certain distinctions can be made. Republicans, who were especially prominent in the southern and middle states, tended to be self-assured, confident, and optimistic about both politics and the economy. They did not fear instability and sought to widen the people's participation in government. Included in the Republican ranks were southern planters and small farmers, urban artisans, and non-English ethnic groups, especially Irish, Scots, and Germans.

By contrast, Federalists, who were concentrated in New England, were insecure, uncertain of the future. They stressed the need for order, authority, and regularity in the political world. Unlike Republicans, they had no grassroots political organization and put little emphasis on involving ordinary people in government. The nation was, in Federalist eyes, perpetually threatened by potential enemies, both internal and external, and best protected by a continuing alliance with Great Britain. The Federalists drew support from northern merchants and commercially oriented farmers, subsistence farmers in New England, and people of English stock.

The presence of the two organized groups—though not yet parties in the modern sense—made the presidential election of 1796 the first that was seriously contested. George Washington, tired of the criticism to which he had been subjected, decided to retire from office. (Presidents had not yet been limited to two terms by constitutional amendment.) In September, Washington published his famous Farewell Address, most of which was written by Hamilton. Washington outlined two principles that guided American foreign policy at least until the late 1940s: maintain commercial but not political ties with other nations and enter no permanent alliances. He also attacked the legitimacy of the Republican opposition.

Washington's Farewell Address

To succeed Washington, the Federalists in Congress put forward Vice President John Adams, with the diplomat Thomas Pinckney of South Carolina as his vice-presidential running mate. Congressional Republicans caucused and chose Thomas Jefferson as their presidential candidate; the lawyer, Revolutionary War veteran, and active Republican politician Aaron Burr of New York agreed to run for vice president.

Election of 1796

That the election was contested did not mean that its outcome was decided by the people. Under the Constitution, electors—not the people—voted. Though in most cases the people chose their electors, in 1796 more than 40 percent of the members of the electoral college were chosen by state legislatures. As the Constitution required members of the electoral college to vote for two persons without specifying the office, the system tended to work against the new parties. There was no way an elector could explicitly support one person for president and another for vice president. The man with the highest total became president; the second highest, vice president. Thus Adams, the Federalist with 71 votes, became the new president and Jefferson, the Republican with 68 votes, became vice president.

John Adams and Political Dissent

John Adams took over the presidency peculiarly blind to the partisan developments of the previous four years. As president, he never abandoned an outdated notion discarded by George Washington as early as 1794: that the president should be above politics, an independent and dignified figure who did not seek petty factional advantage. Thus Adams kept Washington's cabinet intact, despite its key members' allegiance to his chief rival, Alexander Hamilton. Adams often adopted a passive posture, letting others (usually Hamilton) take the lead, when he should have acted decisively. When Adams's term ended, the Federalists were severely divided and the Republicans had won the presidency. But Adams's detachment from Hamilton's maneuverings enabled him to weather the greatest international crisis the republic had yet faced: the so-called Quasi-War with France.

The Jay Treaty improved America's relationship with England, but it provoked retaliation from France. When French vessels began seizing American ships carrying British goods, Adams appointed three special commissioners to try to reach a settlement with France: Elbridge Gerry of Massachusetts, John Marshall of Virginia, and Charles Cotesworth Pinckney of South Carolina. At the same time, Congress increased military spending. The negotiations never materialized, however, because French agents demanded a bribe of $250,000 before talks could begin. The Americans retorted, "No, no; not a sixpence." When Adams received word of the incident in March 1798, he informed Congress of the impasse and recommended increased appropriations for defense.

Convinced that Adams had deliberately sabotaged the negotiations, congressional Republicans insisted that the dispatches be turned over to Congress. Aware that releasing **XYZ Affair** the reports would work to his advantage, Adams complied. He withheld only the names of the French agents, referring to them as X, Y, and Z. The revelation that the Americans had been treated with utter contempt stimulated a wave of anti-French sentiment in the United States. Cries for war filled the air. Congress formally abrogated the Treaty of Alliance and authorized American ships to seize French vessels.

Thus began the undeclared war with France. This Quasi-War was fought in the West Indies, between French privateers seeking to capture American merchant vessels and warships of the United States Navy. Although initial American losses of merchant shipping were heavy, by early 1799 the navy had established its superiority in Caribbean waters. Its ships captured a total of eight French privateers and naval vessels, easing the threat to America's vital West Indian trade.

The Republicans, who opposed war and continued to sympathize with France, could do little to stem the tide of anti-French feelings. The Federalists saw this climate of opinion as **Alien and** an opportunity to deal a death **Sedition Acts** blow to their Republican opponents. Now that the country seemed to see the truth of what they had been saying ever since the Whiskey Rebellion in 1794—that the Republicans were subversive foreign agents—the Federalists sought to codify that belief into law. In the spring and summer of 1798, the Federalist-controlled Congress adopted a set of four laws known as the Alien and Sedition Acts, intended to suppress dissent and prevent further growth of the Republican party.

Three of the acts were aimed at immigrants, whom the Federalists quite correctly suspected of being Republican in their sympathies. The Naturalization Act lengthened the residency period required for citizenship from five to fourteen years and ordered all resident aliens to register with the federal government. The Alien Enemies Act provided for the detention of enemy aliens in time of war. The Alien Friends Act, to be in effect for two years, gave the president almost unlimited authority to deport any alien he deemed dangerous to the nation's security. (Adams never used that authority. The Alien Enemies Act was not implemented either, since war was never formally declared.)

The fourth law, the Sedition Act, sought to control both citizens and aliens. It outlawed conspiracies to prevent the enforcement of federal

Matthew Lyon, the congressman convicted of violating the Sedition Act, had a fiery temper. In January 1798, before his arrest and trial, he engaged in this brawl with a congressman from Connecticut in the chamber of the House of Representatives. *Library of Congress.*

laws and set the maximum punishment for such offenses at five years in prison and a $5,000 fine. The act also tried to control speech. Writing, printing, or uttering "false, scandalous and malicious" statements "against the government of the United States, or the President of the United States, with intent to defame" became a crime punishable by as much as two years' imprisonment and a fine of $2,000.

In all, there were fifteen indictments and ten convictions under the Sedition Act. Most of the accused were outspoken Republican newspaper editors who failed to mute their criticism of the administration in response to the law. But the first victim—whose story may serve as an example of the rest—was a Republican congressman from Vermont, Matthew Lyon. The Irish-born Lyon was fined $1,000 and given a four-month prison sentence for declaring in print that John Adams had displayed "a continual grasp for power" and "an unbounded thirst for ridiculous pomp, foolish adulation, and selfish avarice."

Faced with the prosecutions of their major supporters, Jefferson and Madison sought an effective means of combating the Alien and Sedition Acts.

Virginia and Kentucky Resolutions

They turned to constitutional theory and the state legislatures. Carefully concealing their own role (it would hardly have been desirable for the vice president to be indicted for sedition), Jefferson and Madison each drafted a set of resolutions. Introduced into the Kentucky and Virginia legislatures respectively in the fall of 1798, the resolutions differed somewhat, but their import was the same. Since the Constitution was created by a compact among the states, they contended, the people speaking through their states had a legitimate right to judge the constitutionality of actions taken by the federal government. Both sets of resolutions pronounced the Alien and Sedition Acts null and void and asked other states to join in the protest.

Although no other state replied positively to the Virginia and Kentucky resolutions, they nevertheless had major significance. In the first place, they were superb political propaganda, rallying Republican opinion throughout the country. They placed the opposition party squarely in the revolutionary tradition of resistance to tyrannical authority. Second, the theory of union they proposed was expanded on by southern states' rights advocates in the 1830s and later.

Meanwhile, Adams's decision not to seek a declaration of war against France had split the Federalists, for Hamilton wanted a declared war. When the French government privately indicated that it regretted the treatment of the three American commissioners, Adams dispatched an envoy to Paris. The United States asked two things of France: nearly $20 million in compensation for ships the French had seized since 1793 and abrogation of the treaty of 1778. The Convention of 1800, which ended the Quasi-War, included the latter but not the former. The results of the negotiations, however, were not known until after the election of 1800. By then, the split in Federalist ranks had already cost Adams his re-election.

In sharp contrast, the Republicans entered the 1800 presidential race firmly united behind Jefferson and Burr. Although they won the election, their lack of foresight almost cost them dearly. The problem was caused by the system of voting in the electoral college. All Republican electors voted for both Jefferson and Burr, giving each of them 73 votes (Adams had 65). Because neither Republican had a plurality, the Constitution required that the contest be decided in the House of Representatives, with each state's congressmen voting as a unit. Federalist congressmen decided the election by selecting Jefferson on the thirty-fifth ballot. As a result of the tangle, the Twelfth Amendment to the Constitution (1804) changed the method of voting in the electoral college to allow for a party ticket.

Election of 1800

Westward Expansion, Social Change, and Religious Ferment

In the postrevolutionary years, the United States experienced a dramatic increase in internal migration. As much as 5 to 10 percent of the population moved each year, half of the movers relocating to another state. Young white men were the most mobile segment of the populace. The major population shifts were from east to west (see map): from New England to upstate New York and Ohio, from New Jersey to western Pennsylvania, from the Chesapeake to the new states of Kentucky and Tennessee, which entered the union in 1792 and 1796, respectively. Very few people moved north or south.

The first permanent white settlements beyond the mountains were established in western North Carolina in 1771. But not until after the defeat of the Shawnees in 1774 and the Cherokees in 1776 did significant numbers of settlers move west of the mountains and south of the Ohio River. By 1790, more than a hundred thousand residents lived in the future states of Kentucky and Tennessee. North of the Ohio River, white settlements grew more slowly because of the strength of the Miami Confederacy. But once the Treaty of Greenville was signed in 1795, the Ohio country, too, grew rapidly.

White Settlement in the West

The transplanted New Englanders did their best to recreate the societies they had left behind, laying out farms and towns in neat checkerboard patterns, founding libraries and Congregational churches. Early arrivals recruited others to join them through enthusiastic letters about Ohio's rich soil and potential for growth, setting off a phenomenon known in New England as Ohio Fever. The New Englanders, proud of their literate, orderly culture, viewed their neighbors with disdain. Ohioans, said one, were "intelligent, industrious, and thriving," whereas the Virginians who had settled across the river in Kentucky were "ignorant, lazy, and poor."

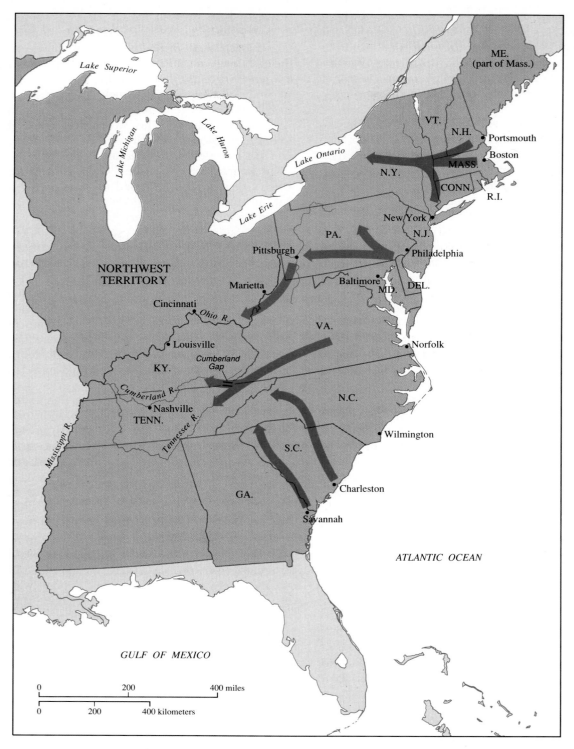

Western Expansion, 1785–1805

The westward migration of slaveholding whites, first to Kentucky and Tennessee, then to the rich lands of western Georgia, and eventually to the Gulf Coast, tore apart the web of family connections African-Americans had built up over several generations of residence in the Chesapeake. Even those few large planters who moved their entire slave force west could not have owned all the members of every family on their plantations. Far more commonly, the white migrants were younger sons of eastern slaveholders, whose inheritance included only a portion of the family's slaves, or small farmers who owned just one or two blacks. In the early years of American settlement in the West, the population was widely dispersed; accordingly, Chesapeake blacks, who had been raised in the midst of large numbers of kin, had to adapt to lonely lives on isolated farms. The approximately one hundred thousand African-Americans forcibly moved west by 1810 had to begin building new families there to replace those unwillingly left behind in the East.

Blacks in the West

The mobility of both blacks and whites created a volatile population mix in southern frontier areas. Since most of the migrants were young single men just starting to lead independent lives, western society was at first unstable. Like the seventeenth-century Chesapeake, the American West in the late eighteenth century was a society in which single women married quickly. The other side of the same coin was that the few women among the migrants lamented their lack of congenial female friends. Isolated, far from familiar surroundings, women and men both strove to create new communities to replace those they had left behind.

Perhaps the most meaningful of the new communities was that supplied by evangelical religion. Among the migrants to Kentucky and Tennessee were clergymen and committed lay members of the evangelical sects that arose in America after the First Great Awakening: Baptists, Presbyterians, and Methodists. At camp meetings, sometimes attended by thousands of people and usually lasting from three days to a week, clergymen exhorted their audiences to repent their sins and become genuine

Second Great Awakening

Christians. They stressed that salvation was open to all, downplaying the doctrine of predestination that had characterized orthodox colonial Calvinism. The emotional nature of the conversion experience was emphasized far more than the need for careful study and preparation. Such preachers thus brought the message of religion to the people in more ways than one. They were democratizing American religion, making it available to all, rather than to a preselected and educated elite.

The sources of the Second Great Awakening, which began around 1800 and revitalized Protestant Christianity in the United States, were embedded in late-eighteenth-century American society in the East, as well as the West. From the 1760s through the 1780s, religious concerns had been subordinated to secular affairs. Indeed, clerics had created a "civil religion" for the nation, in which the fervor of the veneration for the public sometimes surpassed the fervor of religious worship. Most churches, influenced by Enlightenment thought, had for decades stressed reason more than revelation. Circumstances were thus ripe for a movement of spiritual renewal that would appeal to the emotional side of people's natures.

Besides, America's largest Protestant denominations had to find new sources of financial and membership support after the Revolution. In the colonial period, most of the provinces had had established, or state-supported, churches. Many states dissolved their ties to churches during or immediately after the war, and others vastly reduced state support for established denominations.

Disestablishment of Religion

These changes meant that congregations could no longer rely on tax revenues and that all churches were placed on the same footing with respect to the government. Church membership became entirely voluntary, as did monetary contributions from members. If congregations were to survive, they had to generate new sources of support and increase the size of their membership. Revivals proved a convenient means of doing so. The revivals represented genuine outpourings of religious sentiment, but their more mundane function must not be overlooked.

An analysis of secular society can help explain

the conversion patterns of the Second Awakening. Unlike the First Great Awakening, when converts

Women and the Second Awakening

were evenly divided by sex, more women than men—particularly young women—answered the call of Christianity during the Second Awakening. The increase in female converts seems to have been directly related to major changes in women's circumstances at the end of the eighteenth century. In some areas of the country, especially New England, women outnumbered men after 1790. Thus eastern girls could no longer count on finding marital partners. The uncertainty of their social and familial position seems to have led them to seek spiritual certainty through religion. In the churches, they formed hundreds of female associations to aid widows and orphans, collect money for foreign missions, or improve the quality of maternal care. Thus American women collectively assumed the role of keepers of the nation's conscience, taking the lead in charitable enterprises and freeing their husbands from concern for such moral issues.

The religious ferment among blacks and whites in frontier regions of the Upper South contributed to racial ferment as well. People of both races at-

Blacks and the Second Awakening

tended camp meetings to hear black and white preachers. When revivals spread eastward into more heavily slaveholding areas, white planters became fearful of the egalitarianism implied in the evangelical message of universal salvation and harmony. At the same time, revivals created a group of respected black leaders—the preachers—and provided them with a ready audience.

Events in the West Indies gave whites ample reason for apprehension. In 1793, mulattos and blacks in the French colony of Saint Domingue (Haiti) overthrew European rule under the leadership of a mulatto, Toussaint L'Ouverture. In an attempt to prevent the spread of such unrest to their own slaves, southern state legislators passed laws forbidding white Haitian refugees from bringing their slaves with them. But North American blacks learned about the revolt anyway. And the preconditions for racial upheaval already existed in the South.

In Virginia, a revolt was planned by Gabriel Prosser, a blacksmith who argued that blacks should fight to obtain the same rights as whites and who

Gabriel's Rebellion

explicitly placed himself in the tradition of the French and Haitian revolutions. At revival meetings led by his brother Martin, a preacher, Gabriel recruited other blacks like himself—artisans who moved easily in both black and white circles and who lived in semifreedom under minimal white supervision. The artisan leaders then enlisted rural blacks in the cause. The conspirators planned to attack Richmond on the night of August 30, 1800, setting fire to the city, seizing the state capitol, and capturing the governor. Their plan showed considerable political sophistication, but heavy rain made it impossible to execute the plot as scheduled. Several whites then learned of the plan from their slaves and spread the alarm. Gabriel avoided capture for some weeks, but most of the other leaders of the rebellion were quickly arrested and interrogated. The major conspirators, including Prosser himself, were hanged, but in the months that followed other insurrectionary scares continued to frighten Virginia slaveowners.

Significantly, the Iroquois were affected by a religious revival at the same time as American whites and blacks were experiencing the Second Great

Handsome Lake

Awakening. Led by their prophet, Handsome Lake, the remaining American Iroquois, who were scattered on small reservations, embraced the traditional values of their culture and renounced such destructive white customs as drinking alcohol and playing cards. At the same time, though, they began abandoning their ancient way of life. With Handsome Lake's approval, Quaker missionaries taught the Iroquois Anglo-American styles of agricultural subsistence; men were now to be cultivators rather than hunters and women housekeepers rather than cultivators. Since the tribes had lost their hunting territories to white farmers, Iroquois men accepted the changes readily. But many women, especially the powerful tribal matrons, resisted the shift in the gender division of labor. They realized that when they surrendered control over food production they would jeopardize their status in the tribe. But Handsome Lake

Around 1790, an unknown artist painted Benjamin Hawkins, an Indian trader, and a group of Creeks at his trading post in northern Florida. Such commerce with the Indians, long a part of American life, continued to play an important role in the national economy during the early years of the republic.   *Courtesy of the Greenville County Museum of Art, S.C.*

branded as "witches" any women who opposed the changes too vigorously, and eventually he triumphed.

As the new century began, white, red, and black inhabitants of the United States were moving toward an accommodation to their new circumstances. Indians east of the Mississippi learned that they would have to give up some parts of their traditional culture to preserve others. Blacks and whites tried to create new lives in the West and adjust to changed economic circumstances in the East. Building on successful negotiations with both Britain (the Jay Treaty) and France (the Convention of 1800), the United States charted its own diplomatic course, striving to avoid dependence on the European powers. The 1790s spawned vigorous de-

bates over foreign and domestic policy and saw the beginnings of a system of political parties. Religious revivals again swept portions of the countryside, and again those revivals contributed to social unrest.

At the end of the decade, after years of struggle, the Jeffersonian interpretation of republicanism finally prevailed over Hamilton's approach. As a result, in the years to come the country would be characterized by a decentralized economy, minimal government (especially at the national level), and maximum freedom of action and mobility for individual white men. Jeffersonian Republicans, like white male Americans before them, failed to extend to white women, Indians, and blacks the freedom and individuality they recognized as essential for themselves.

Suggestions for Further Reading

National Government and Administration

Ralph Adams Brown, *The Presidency of John Adams* (1975); Forrest McDonald, *Alexander Hamilton* (1979); Forrest McDonald, *The Presidency of George Washington* (1974); John C. Miller, *The Federalist Era, 1789–1801* (1960); John R. Nelson, Jr., *Liberty and Property: Political Economy and Policymaking in the New Nation, 1789–1812* (1987); Merrill D. Peterson, *Thomas Jefferson and the New Nation* (1970); Garry Wills, *Cincinnatus: George Washington and the Enlightenment* (1984).

Partisan Politics

Lance Banning, *The Jeffersonian Persuasion: Evolution of a Party Ideology* (1978); Richard Buel, Jr., *Securing the Revolution: Ideology in American Politics, 1789–1815* (1972); William Nisbet Chambers, *Political Parties in a New Nation: The American Experience, 1776–1809* (1963); Joseph Charles, *The Origins of the American Party System* (1956); Richard Hofstadter, *The Idea of a Party System: The Rise of Legitimate Opposition in the United States, 1780–1840* (1970); Adrienne Koch, *Jefferson and Madison: The Great Collaboration* (1950); Norman K. Risjord, *Chesapeake Politics, 1781–1800* (1978); John Zvesper, *Political Philosophy and Rhetoric: A Study of the Origins of American Party Politics* (1977).

Foreign Policy

Jerald A. Combs, *The Jay Treaty* (1970); Alexander DeConde, *The Quasi-War: Politics and Diplomacy of the Undeclared War with France, 1797–1801* (1966); Alexander DeConde, *Entangling Alliance: Politics and Diplomacy Under George Washington* (1958); Felix Gilbert, *To the Farewell Address: Ideas of Early American Foreign Policy* (1961); Reginald Horsman, *The Diplomacy of the New Republic, 1776–1815* (1985); Lawrence Kaplan, *"Entangling Alliances with None": American Foreign Policy in the Age of Jefferson* (1987); William Stinchcombe, *The XYZ Affair* (1981); Paul A. Varg, *Foreign Policies of the Founding Fathers* (1963).

Civil Liberties

Leonard W. Levy, *Emergence of a Free Press* (1985); Leonard W. Levy, *Origins of the Fifth Amendment* (1968); Robert A. Rutland, *The Birth of the Bill of Rights, 1776–1791,* rev. ed. (1983); James Morton Smith, *Freedom's Fetters: The Alien and Sedition Laws and American Civil Liberties* (1956).

Women, Blacks, and the Family

Ira Berlin and Ronald Hoffman, eds., *Slavery and Freedom in the Age of the American Revolution* (1983); Nancy F. Cott, *The Bonds of Womanhood: "Woman's Sphere" in New England, 1780–1835* (1977); Toby Ditz, *Property and Kinship: Inheritance in Early Connecticut, 1750–1820* (1986); Gerald W. Mullin, *Flight and Rebellion: Slave Resistance in Eighteenth-Century Virginia* (1972).

Social Change and Westward Expansion

Andrew Cayton, *The Frontier Republic: Ideology and Politics in the Ohio Country, 1789–1812* (1986); Howard Rock, *Artisans of the New Republic: The Tradesmen of New York City in the Age of Thomas Jefferson* (1979); Malcolm Rohrbough, *The Trans-Appalachian Frontier: Peoples, Societies, and Institutions, 1775–1850* (1979); W. J. Rorabaugh, *The Alcoholic Republic: An American Tradition* (1979); Thomas Slaughter, *The Whiskey Rebellion* (1986); Charles G. Steffen, *The Mechanics of Baltimore: Workers and Politics in the Age of Revolution, 1763–1812* (1984); Sean Wilentz, *Chants Democratic: New York City and the Rise of the American Working Class, 1788–1850* (1984).

Religion

Catharine Albanese, *Sons of the Fathers: The Civil Religion of the American Revolution* (1976); Ruth Bloch, *Visionary Republic: Millennial Themes in American Thought* (1985); Fred J. Hood, *Reformed America, 1783–1837* (1980); William McLoughlin, *Revivals, Awakenings, and Reform* (1978).

"I have this morning witnessed one of the most interesting scenes a free people can ever witness," Margaret B. Smith, a Philadelphian, wrote on March 4, 1801, to her sister-in-law. "The changes of administration, which in every government and in every age have most generally been epochs of confusion, villainy and bloodshed, in this our happy country take place without any species of distraction, or disorder." On that day, Thomas Jefferson strolled from his New Jersey Avenue boarding house in the new federal capital of Washington, D.C., to take the oath as president at the Capitol. The precedent of an orderly and peaceful change of government had been established.

Jefferson's inauguration marked a change of style in government. Almost overnight, the formality of the Federalist presidencies of Washington and Adams disappeared as Jefferson set the tone for the Republican government. Jefferson abandoned the aristocratic wigs and breeches (knee-length trousers) of his predecessors and rejected the wealthy pretensions he associated with the Federalists. Republican virtue would be restored.

Carved out of Maryland and Virginia, the new district had been chosen because of its central location. Washington was thus beholden neither to the colonial past nor to any single state. The small government, which essentially collected tariffs, delivered mail, and defended the nation's borders, suited the republic. Even for the Federalists, the adoption of the Constitution had been more a result of dissatisfaction with the Articles of Confederation than a sign of confidence in central government. Though Jefferson, after his inauguration in 1801, cut the federal budget and operations, he and his Republican successors invigorated the federal government over the next two decades.

The transfer of power to the Republicans from the Federalists intensified political conflict and voter interest. Republican presidents sought to restrain government. Federalists prized a stronger national government with more centralized order and authority. With both factions competing for adherents and popular support, the basis was laid for the evolution of democratic politics. But factionalism, personal disputes, and suspicion of partisanship within each group prevented the development of modern political parties.

8

THE EMPIRE OF LIBERTY, 1801–1824

Events abroad and on the frontier encouraged and threatened the expansionism of the young nation. Seizing one opportunity, the United States purchased the Louisiana Territory, pushing the frontier farther west. But then from the high seas came war. Caught between the British and the French, the United States found itself a victim of European conflict, with its shipping rights as a neutral, independent nation ignored and violated. When the humiliation became too great, Americans took up arms in the War of 1812, both to defend their rights as a nation and to expand farther to the west and north.

The War of 1812 unleashed a wave of nationalism and self-confidence. War stimulated the development of domestic manufacturing and internal transportation. After the war, the federal government championed business and promoted road and canal building. The new spirit encouraged economic growth, western expansion at home, and assertiveness throughout the Western Hemisphere. By the 1820s, the United States was no longer an experiment; a new nation had emerged.

Rembrandt Peale's 1805 portrait of President Thomas Jefferson. Charles Willson Peale and his five sons helped establish the reputation of American art in the new nation. Rembrandt Peale was most famous for his presidential portraits; here he captures Jefferson in a noble pose without the usual symbols of office or power, befitting the Republican age. *The New-York Historical Society.*

Jefferson in Power

Jefferson delivered his inaugural address in the Senate chamber, the only part of the Capitol that had been completed. "We are all Republicans, we are all Federalists," he told the assembly in an appeal for unity. Confidently addressing those with little faith in the people's ability to govern themselves, he called America's republican government "the world's best hope."

Jefferson's Inaugural Address

The new president went on to outline his goals:

A wise and frugal government, which shall restrain men from injuring one another, which shall leave them otherwise free to regulate their own pursuits.
. . . Equal and exact justice to all men, of whatever state or persuasion, religious or political. . . .
The support of the state governments in all their rights, as the most competent administrators for our domestic concerns and the surest bulwarks against antirepublican tendencies.

At the same time, he assured Federalists that he shared some of their concerns:

The preservation of the general government in its whole constitutional vigor. . . . The honest payment of our debts and sacred preservation of the public faith.
. . . Encouragement of agriculture and of commerce as its handmaid.

Still, the Federalists and Republicans distrusted each other. Republicans considered the Federalists antidemocratic and antirepublican at heart. One of Jefferson's first acts was to extend the Republicans' grasp over the federal government. Virtually all officials appointed under Washington and Adams were loyal Federalists. To counteract Federalist power, Jefferson refused to recognize Adams's last-minute "midnight appointments" to local offices in the District of Columbia. He also dismissed Federalist customs collectors from New England ports, and awarded vacant treasury and judicial offices to Republicans. By July 1803, Federalists held only 130 of the 316 presidentially controlled offices. In restoring political balance in government, Jefferson used patronage to reward his friends, build a party organization, and compete with the Federalists.

The Republican Congress, too, proceeded to affirm its republicanism. Guided by Secretary of the Treasury Albert Gallatin and Representative John Randolph of Virginia, it put the federal government on a diet. Congress repealed all internal taxes, including the whiskey tax. Gallatin cut the army budget in half, to just under $2 million, and reduced the 1802 navy budget from $3.5 to $1 million. Moreover, Gallatin planned to reduce the national debt—Alexander Hamilton's engine of economic growth—from $83 million to $57 million, as part of a plan to retire it altogether by 1817.

More than frugality, however, separated Republicans from Federalists. Opposition to the Alien and Sedition laws of 1798 had helped unite Republicans. Now Congress let the acts expire in 1801 and 1802 and repealed the Naturalization Act of 1798. The 1802 act that replaced it required only five years of residency, acceptance of the Constitution, and the renouncing of foreign allegiance and titles.

The Republicans turned next to the judiciary, the last stronghold of unchecked Federalist power. During the 1790s, not a single Republican had been appointed to the federal bench. Moreover, the Judiciary Act of 1801, passed in the last days of the Adams administration, had created fifteen new judgeships (which Adams filled in his midnight appointments, signing appointments until his term was just hours away from expiring) and would reduce by attrition the number of justices on the Supreme Court from six to five. Since that reduction would have denied Jefferson any Supreme Court appointments until two vacancies had occurred, the new Republican-

Attacks on the Judiciary

dominated Congress, in one of its first moves, repealed the 1801 act.

Republicans also targeted opposition judges for removal. Federalist judges had refused to review the Sedition Act and prosecuted critics of the administration under the act. At Jefferson's suggestion, the House impeached (indicted) Federal District Judge John Pickering of New Hampshire; in 1804, the Senate removed him from office. Pickering had not committed any crime, although he was an alcoholic and was emotionally disturbed.

The day Pickering was convicted, the House impeached Supreme Court Justice Samuel Chase for judicial misconduct. Chase had repeatedly denounced Jefferson's administration from the bench. The Republicans, however, failed to muster the necessary two-thirds majority of senators to convict him. Their failure to remove Chase preserved the Court's independence by establishing the precedent that criminal actions, not political disagreements, were the proper grounds for impeachment. Although Jefferson did appoint three new Supreme Court justices, under Chief Justice John Marshall the Court remained a Federalist stronghold.

Marshall, a Virginia Federalist, was an astute lawyer with keen political sense. Under his domination, the Supreme Court retained a Federalist viewpoint even after Republican justices achieved a majority in 1811. Throughout his tenure (from 1801 until 1835), the Court upheld federal supremacy over the states and protected the interests of commerce and capital. More important, Marshall made the Court an equal branch of government in practice as well as theory. First, he made service on the Court a coveted honor. Second, he unified the Court, influencing the justices to issue single majority opinions rather than individual concurring judgments. Marshall himself became the voice of the majority. From 1801 through 1810, he wrote 85 percent of the 171 opinions, including every important decision.

John Marshall

Marshall also increased the Court's power. *Marbury* v. *Madison* (1803) was the landmark case that enabled Marshall to strengthen the Court. William Marbury had been designated a justice of the peace in the District of Columbia as part of Adams's midnight appointments. Marbury sued the new secre-

1801	John Marshall becomes chief justice Jefferson inaugurated	**1813**	Death of Tecumseh
		1814	Treaty of Ghent
1801–05	Tripoli War	**1814–15**	Hartford Convention
1803	*Marbury* v. *Madison* Louisiana Purchase	**1815**	Battle of New Orleans
		1816	Monroe elected president Second Bank of the United States chartered
1804	Jefferson re-elected		
1804–06	Lewis and Clark expedition	**1817**	Rush-Bagot Treaty
1805	Prophet emerges as Shawnee leader	**1819**	*McCulloch* v. *Maryland* Adams-Onís Treaty
1807	*Chesapeake* affair Embargo Act	**1819–23**	Financial panic; depression
1808	Madison elected president	**1820**	Missouri Compromise Monroe re-elected
1808–13	Prophet and Tecumseh: Indian resistance	**1823**	Monroe Doctrine
1812–15	War of 1812		

Marbury v. *Madison* tary of state, James Madison, for failing to certify his appointment so that Jefferson could appoint a Republican. In his suit, Marbury requested a writ of mandamus (a court order forcing Madison to appoint him).

At first glance, the case presented a political dilemma. If the Supreme Court issued a writ of mandamus, the president might not comply. After all, why should the president, sworn to uphold the Constitution, allow the Court to decide for him what was constitutional? However, if the Court refused to issue the writ, it would be handing the Republicans a victory. Marshall avoided both alternatives. Speaking for the Court, he ruled that Marbury had a right to his commission but that the Court could not compel Madison to honor it, because the Constitution did not grant the Court power to issue a writ of mandamus. Thus Marshall

declared unconstitutional Section 13 of the Judiciary Act of 1789, which authorized the Court to issue such writs. Marbury lost his job and the justices denied themselves the power to issue writs of mandamus, but the Supreme Court established its great power to judge the constitutionality of laws passed by Congress.

In succeeding years, Marshall fashioned the theory of judicial review. Since the Constitution was the supreme law, he reasoned, any act (federal or state) contrary to the Constitution must be null and void. And since the Supreme Court was responsible for upholding the law, the Court had a duty to decide whether a conflict existed between a legislative act and the Constitution. If such a conflict existed the Court would declare the act unconstitutional.

Marshall's decision rebuffed Republican criticism of the Court as a partisan instrument. He avoided a confrontation with the Republican-dominated Congress by not ruling on its repeal of the 1801 Judiciary Act. And he enhanced the Court's independence by claiming the power of judicial review.

While President Jefferson fought with the Federalist judiciary and struggled to reduce federal spending, Americans in search of land had trekked into the rich Mississippi and Ohio valleys. Western settlers—there were hundreds of thousands of them by 1800—depended on the Mississippi and Ohio rivers to get their products to New Orleans for export. Thus, whoever controlled the port of New Orleans had a hand on the throat of the American economy.

Louisiana Purchase

As long as Spain owned Louisiana, Americans had no fear. But in 1802, Napoleon acquired the vast territory in an ambitious bid to rebuild France's empire in the New World. The acquisition, Jefferson lamented, "works most sorely" on the United States. On the eve of ceding control to the French, Spain violated Pinckney's Treaty by denying Americans the privilege of storing their products at New Orleans before transshipment to foreign markets. Western farmers and eastern merchants thought a devious Napoleon had closed the port; they grumbled and talked war.

To relieve the pressure for war and to prevent westerners from joining Federalists in opposition to his administration, Jefferson simultaneously prepared for war and accelerated talks with the French. In January 1803, he sent James Monroe to France to join Robert Livingston in negotiating to buy New Orleans. Meanwhile, Congress authorized the call-up of eighty thousand militia if it proved necessary. Arriving in Paris in April, Monroe was astonished to learn that France had already offered to sell all 827,000 square miles of Louisiana to the United States for $15 million. On April 30, Monroe and Livingston signed a treaty to purchase the vast territory, whose borders were undefined and whose land was uncharted (see map).

The Louisiana Purchase doubled the size of the nation and opened the way for westward expansion across the continent. The acquisition was the single most popular achievement of Jefferson's presidency. But its legality was questionable. The Constitution gave him no clear authority to acquire new territory and incorporate it into the nation. Jeffer-

son considered requesting a constitutional amendment to allow the purchase, but finally he justified it on the grounds that he was exercising the president's implied powers to protect the nation. The people, he knew, would accept or reject the purchase on election day in 1804.

The president had a long-standing interest in Louisiana and the West. As secretary of state, he had commissioned a French emigré, André Michaux, to explore the Missouri River. Allegations of Michaux's complicity in the Genêt Affair aborted this mission. In 1803, Jefferson sent Meriwether Lewis and William Clark to the Pacific Ocean via the Missouri and Columbia rivers. Lewis and Clark, from 1804 to 1806, headed the nearly fifty-strong "Corps of Discovery," which was aided by trappers and American Indians along the way.

Lewis and Clark

The Lewis and Clark expedition, planned in secrecy before the Louisiana Purchase, reflected Jefferson's scientific curiosity and his interest in western commercial development, especially the fur and China trades. Other explorers soon followed Lewis and Clark, led in 1805 and 1806 by Lieutenant Zebulon Pike in search of the source of the Mississippi. Pike attempted to find a navigable water route to the Far West and sought the headwaters of the Arkansas River. He and his men reached the Rocky Mountains in present-day Colorado and wandered into Spanish territory to the south, where the Spanish arrested them and held them captive for several months in Santa Fe. After his release, Pike wrote an account of his experiences that set commercial minds spinning. He described a potential commercial market in southwestern Spanish cities, as well as the bounty of furs and precious minerals to be had. The vision of the road to the Southwest became a reality with the opening of the Santa Fe Trail in the 1820s.

Republicans Versus Federalists

Campaigning for re-election in 1804, Jefferson claimed credit for western expansion and the resto-

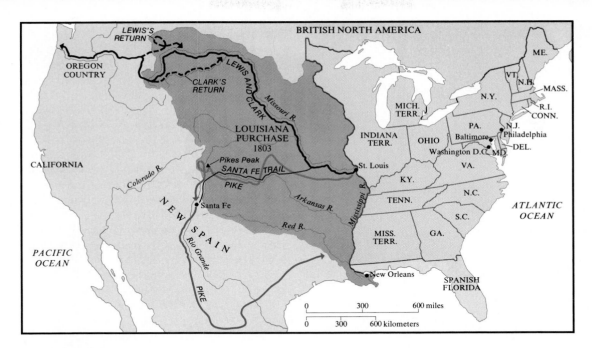

Louisiana Purchase

ration of republican values. He had removed the
Federalist threat to liberty by end-

**Election
of 1804**
ing the Alien and Sedition Acts
and the Judiciary Act. He had reduced the size and cost of govern-
ment by cutting spending. Despite his opponents'
charges, he had proved that Republicans supported
commerce by having Congress repeal Federalist excise and property taxes.

The Federalist candidate was Charles Cotesworth
Pinckney, a wealthy South Carolina lawyer and former Revolutionary War aide to General George
Washington. Pinckney had been Adams's vice-
presidential candidate in 1800, thereby inheriting
the Federalist leadership. Jefferson and his running
mate, George Clinton of New York, defeated Pinckney and Rufus King in the electoral college with 162
votes to 14.

Jefferson's re-election was both a personal and
an organizational triumph. The political dissenters
of the 1790s had used their Democratic-Republican
societies to win elections. More than anything else,
opposition to the Federalists had molded and
unified them. Indeed, it was in the parts of the

country where the Federalists were strongest—in
commercial New York and Pennsylvania in the
1790s and in New England in the 1800s—that the
Republicans had organized most effectively.

Until the Republican successes in 1800 and 1804,
most Federalists had disdained popular campaigning. They believed in government by the "best"
people—those whose education, wealth, and experience marked them as leaders. For candidates to
debate their qualifications before their inferiors—
the voters—was unnecessary and undignified. The
direct appeals of the Republicans struck the
Federalists as a subversion of the natural political
order.

After the resounding Federalist defeat in 1800, a
younger generation of Federalists began to imitate
the Republicans. They organized statewide and, led

**Younger
Federalists**
by men like Josiah Quincy, a
young congressman from Massachusetts, campaigned for popular
support. Quincy cleverly identi-
fied the Federalists as the people's party, attacking Republicans as autocratic planters. In attacking frugal government, the self-styled Younger

John Lewis Krimmel, *Election Day in Philadelphia* (1815). Citizens crowded outside the State House in Philadelphia on election day in 1815 to whip up support for their candidates and to await the results. The painting suggests the overwhelmingly white, male composition of the electorate. *The Henry Francis du Pont Winterthur Museum.*

Federalists played on fears of a weakened army and navy. Merchants depended on a strong navy to protect ocean trade while westerners, encroaching on Indian tribes, looked for federal support.

In the states where both factions organized and ran candidates, participation in elections increased markedly. In some states, more than 90 percent of the eligible voters cast ballots between 1804 and 1816. People became more interested in politics generally, especially at the local level; and as participation in elections increased, the states expanded suffrage. Nevertheless, the popular base remained restricted. Property qualifications for voting and holding office persisted, and in six states the legislatures still selected presidential electors in 1804.

Yet political competition, spurred on by a vigorous press that saw its primary role as partisan advocacy, prompted grassroots campaigning. The political barbecue symbolized the new style as the factions responded to increasing voter involvement in politics. During the barbecue, candidates and party leaders spoke from the stump. Oratory was a popular form of entertainment, and speeches were lengthy and uninhibited. Although both factions used the political barbecue, the Federalist party never fully mastered the art of wooing voters.

Older Federalists still opposed such blatant campaigning. And though they were strong in a few states like Connecticut and Delaware, the Federalists never offered the Republicans sustained competition. Divisions between Older and Younger

Chapter 8: The Empire of Liberty, 1801–1824

Federalists often hindered them, and the extremism of some Older Federalists tended to discredit the organization. A case in point was Timothy Pickering, a Massachusetts congressman who urged the secession of New England in 1803 and 1804. Pickering won some support among the few Federalists in Congress, but others opposed his plan for a northern confederacy. When Vice President Aaron Burr lost his bid to become governor of New York in 1804, the plan collapsed. Burr, more an opportunist than a loyal Republican, was to have led New York into secession, with the other states to follow.

Both political groups suffered from divisions and individuals' personal ambitions. For a long time, for instance, Aaron Burr and Alexander Hamilton had crossed swords in political conflict. It seemed to Burr that Hamilton always blocked his path. Hamilton had thwarted Burr's attempt to steal the election of 1800 from Jefferson, and in the 1804 New York gubernatorial race the Federalist Hamilton backed a rival Republican faction against Burr. Again a loser, Burr turned his resentment on Hamilton and challenged him to a duel. Hamilton accepted Burr's challenge and was killed. Indicted for murder, Burr became involved in a conspiracy to build an empire in the Southwest. After being tried and acquitted on the charge of treason, he fled to Europe.

Hamilton-Burr Duel

The controversies surrounding Burr highlight some of the limitations of the emerging political system. Personal animosities were as strong a force as ideology and political differences, and new, temporary factions flourished. Moreover, although politicians appealed for voter support, the electoral base remained narrow. As the election of 1804 revealed, the Federalists could offer only weak competition at the national level. And where Federalists posed no threat, Republicans fought among themselves.

Thus, although this period is commonly called the era of the first party system, parties as such were not fully developed. Competition encouraged party organization, but personal ambition, personality clashes, and local, state, and regional loyalties worked against it. Increasingly, external events intruded and occupied most of Jefferson's time in his second administration.

Preserving American Neutrality in a World at War

"Peace, commerce, and honest friendship with all nations, entangling alliance with none," President Jefferson had proclaimed in his first inaugural address. Jefferson's efforts to stand clear of European conflict were successful until 1805. Indeed, for two years after the renewal of the Napoleonic wars in May 1803, American commerce benefited from the conflict. As the world's largest neutral carrier, the United States became the chief supplier of food to Europe. American merchants also gained control of most of the West Indian trade, which was often transshipped though American ports to Europe.

Meanwhile, the United States victory over Tripolitan pirates on the north coast of Africa (the Barbary states) provided Jefferson with his one clear success in protecting American trading rights. In 1801, Jefferson had refused the demands of the sultan of Tripoli for payment to exempt American ships and sailors from being taken hostage. Instead, he sent a naval squadron to the Mediterranean to protect American merchant ships. The United States signed a peace treaty with Tripoli in 1805 but continued to pay tribute to other Barbary states until 1815, when the navy, under Captain Stephen Decatur, forced Algiers and Tunis to renounce attacks against Americans.

American merchants were more concerned about Anglo-French interference with trade. In October 1805, Britain tightened its control of the high seas with its victory over the French and Spanish fleets at the Battle of Trafalgar. Two months later Napoleon defeated the Russian and Austrian armies at Austerlitz. Stalemated, France and Britain waged commercial war, blockading and counterblockading each other's trade. As a trading partner of both countries, the United States paid a high price.

The British navy stepped up impressments of American sailors. Britain, whose navy was the world's largest, was suffering a severe shortage of sailors. Few men enlisted, and those already in service frequently deserted, discouraged by poor food and living

Impressment of American Sailors

conditions and brutal discipline. The Royal Navy resorted to stopping American ships and forcibly removing British deserters, British-born naturalized American seamen, and other unlucky sailors suspected of being British. It is estimated that six to eight thousand Americans were drafted in this manner between 1803 and 1812.

In February 1806, the Senate denounced British impressment as aggression and a violation of neutral rights. To protest the insult, Congress passed the Non-Importation Act, prohibiting importation from Great Britain of a long list of cloth and metal articles. In November, Jefferson suspended the act temporarily while William Pinckney, a Baltimore lawyer, joined James Monroe in London in an attempt to negotiate a settlement. The treaty Monroe and Pinckney carried home violated their instructions—it did not mention impressment—and Jefferson never submitted it to the Senate for ratification.

Less than a year later, the *Chesapeake* affair exposed American military weakness. In June 1807, the forty-gun frigate U.S.S. *Chesapeake* left Norfolk, Virginia. About ten miles out, still inside American territorial waters, it met the fifty-gun British frigate *Leopard*. When the *Chesapeake* refused to be searched for deserters, the *Leopard* repeatedly emptied its guns broadside into the American ship. Three Americans were killed and eighteen wounded, including the ship's captain. The British impressed four sailors—three of them American citizens, all of them deserters from the Royal Navy. Damaged and humiliated, the *Chesapeake* crept back into port.

Chesapeake Affair

Had the United States been better prepared militarily, the howl of public indignation that resulted might have brought about a declaration of war. But the United States was ill equipped to fight a war. Jefferson responded instead by strengthening the military and putting economic pressure on Great Britain. In July, he closed American waters to British warships to prevent similar incidents, and soon afterward he increased military and naval expenditures. On December 14, 1807, Jefferson again invoked the Non-Importation Act, and it was followed eight days later by a new law, the Embargo Act.

Intended as a short-term measure, the Embargo Act forbade virtually all exports from the United States to any country. Imports came to a halt as well, since foreign ships delivering goods had to leave American ports with empty holds. Smuggling blossomed overnight.

Embargo Act

Few American policies were as well intentioned but as unpopular and unsuccessful as Jefferson's embargo. The lucrative American merchant trade collapsed; between 1807 and 1808, exports fell by 80 percent. Federalist New England felt the brunt of a depression, and in the winter of 1808–1809, talk of secession spread through the region's port cities. Great Britain, in contrast, was only mildly affected by the embargo. Finally, the policy gave France an excuse to set privateers against the American ships that had managed to escape the embargo by avoiding American ports. The French argued that such ships must be British ships in disguise, since the embargo barred American ships from the seas.

In the election of 1808, the Republicans faced the Federalists, the embargo, and internal factional dissent. Jefferson followed Washington's example in renouncing a third term and supported James Madison, his secretary of state, as the Republican standard-bearer. Madison won the endorsement of the congressional caucus. Madison and his running mate, George Clinton, defeated the Federalist ticket of Charles C. Pinckney and Rufus King.

As for the embargo, it eventually collapsed under the pressure of domestic opposition. Jefferson withdrew the embargo in his last days in office, replacing it with the Non-Intercourse Act of 1809. The act reopened trade with all nations except Britain and France and authorized the president to resume trade with either country if it ceased to violate neutral rights. But the new act solved only the problems that had been created by the embargo; it did not convince Britain and France to change their policies.

Non-Intercourse Act

When the Non-Intercourse Act expired in the spring of 1810, Congress created a variant, labeled Macon's Bill Number 2. The bill reopened trade with both Great Britain and France, but it provided that if either nation ceased to violate American rights, the president could shut down American commerce with the other. Madison, eager to use the bill rather than go to war, was tricked at his own game. When Napoleon declared that French edicts against United States shipping would be lifted, Madison declared nonintercourse against Great Britain in March 1811. But Napoleon did not keep his word. The French continued to seize American ships, and nonintercourse failed a second time.

Britain, not France, was the main target of American hostility because the Royal Navy controlled the Atlantic. New York harbor was virtually blockaded by the British, so reopening trade with any nation had little practical effect. Angry American leaders tended to blame even Indian resistance in the West on British agitation, ignoring the Indians' legitimate protests against white encroachment and treaty violations. Frustrated and having exhausted all efforts to alter British policy, the United States in 1811 and 1812 drifted into war with Great Britain.

Meanwhile, unknown to the president and Congress, Great Britain was changing its policy. The Anglo-French conflict had ended much of British commerce with the European continent, and exports to the United States had fallen by 80 percent. Depression had hit the British Isles. On June 16, 1812, Britain opened the seas to American shipping. But two days later, before word had crossed the Atlantic, Congress declared war.

The War of 1812 was the logical outcome of United States policy after the renewal of war in Europe in 1803. The grievances enumerated in President Madison's message to Congress on June 1, 1812, were old ones: impressment, interference with neutral commerce, and British alliances with western Indians. Unmentioned was the resolve to defend American independence and honor—and the thirst of expansionists for British Canada.

Yet Congress and the country were divided. Much of the sentiment for war came from the War Hawks, land-hungry southerners and westerners led by Henry Clay of Kentucky and John C. Calhoun of South Carolina. Most representatives from the coastal states opposed war, since armed conflict with the great naval power threatened to close down all American shipping. The vote for war—79 to 49 in the House, 19 to 13 in the Senate—reflected these sharp regional differences. The split

would also be reflected in the way Americans fought the war.

The War of 1812

War was a foolish adventure for the United States in 1812; despite six months of preparation, American forces remained ill equipped. Because the army had neither an able staff nor an adequate force of enlisted men, the burden of fighting fell on the state militias, and not all the states cooperated. The navy did have a corps of well-trained, experienced officers but next to the Royal Navy, the ruler of the seas, the United States Navy was minuscule.

For the first time, the United States waged a general land war. It had an ill-equipped regular army, with only a few professionally trained soldiers; West Point had produced only eighty-nine regular officers by 1812. The army expanded by appointing political leaders to organize volunteer companies and by depending on the state militias. The government offered enlistees a $16 sign-up bonus, $5 monthly pay, a full set of clothes, and a promise of three months' pay and 160 acres of land upon discharge.

Recruiting an Army

Conditions in the army could be dismal. The Kentucky volunteers who constituted the majority of General William Henry Harrison's command at the Battle of the Thames were a ragtag group. Recruited as volunteers in the Kentucky militia, they were drafted into the regular army and sent to fight against Lower Canada. They marched twenty to thirty miles a day from Kentucky to join Harrison's forces in Ohio. They received no training, carried only swords and knives on the march, and were undisciplined.

In the South, Andrew Jackson's Tennessee volunteers were no better organized in their first fifteen months of service. Jackson had raised his militia in December 1812 with the promise that they would serve one year. By the late fall of 1813, his anti-Creek campaign was stalled, and his men were talking of disbanding and going home. Jackson refused to discharge the men. In March 1814, Jackson executed John Woods, a militiaman, for disobedience and mutiny. This broke the opposition in the ranks, and his men defeated the Creek nation at the Battle of Horseshoe Bend.

In Federalist New England, where the conflict was viewed as a Republican war, raising an army proved even more difficult. Those officials who agreed to raise volunteer companies, promised the men that they would serve only in a defensive role. Indeed, the inability of the United States to mount a successful invasion of Canada was due, in part, to the army's failure to assemble an effective force. State militias in New England and New York often declined to fight outside the borders of their own state.

Canada was important because it offered the United States the only readily available battlefront on which to challenge Great Britain. The mighty Royal Navy was useless on the waters separating the United States and Canada, since no river afforded it access from the sea. Canada, thousands of miles from British supply sources, was vulnerable.

Invasion of Canada

Begun with high hopes, the invasion of Canada ended as a disaster. The American strategy was to concentrate on the West, splitting Canadian forces and isolating the Shawnees, Potawatomis, and other tribes that supported the British. General William Hull marched his troops into Lower Canada, near Detroit. But the British anticipated the invasion, mobilized their Indian allies, moved troops into the area, and demanded Hull's surrender. When a pro-British, mostly Potawatomi, contingent captured Fort Dearborn, near present-day Chicago, Hull capitulated (see map). Farther to the west, other American forts surrendered. By the winter of 1812–1813, the British controlled about half of the Old Northwest.

The United States had no greater success on the Niagara front, where New York borders Canada. At the Battle of Queenstown, north of Niagara, the United States regular army met defeat because the New York state militia refused to leave the state. This scene was repeated near Lake Champlain, where American plans to attack Montreal were foiled when the militia declined to cross the border.

The navy provided the only bright note in the first year of the war: the U.S.S. *Constitution,* the U.S.S. *Wasp,* and the U.S.S. *United States* all bested British warships on the Atlantic. But their victories gave the United States only a brief advantage. In defeat, the British lost just 1 percent of their strength; in victory, the Americans lost 20 percent. The British admiralty simply shifted its fleet away from the American ships, and by 1813 the Royal Navy again commanded the seas.

In 1813, the two sides also vied for control of the Great Lakes, the key to the war in the Northwest. The contest was largely a shipbuilding race. Under Master Commandant Oliver Hazard Perry and shipbuilder Noah Brown, the United States outbuilt the British on Lake Erie and defeated them at the bloody Battle of Put-in-Bay on September 10. With this costly victory, the Americans gained control of Lake Erie.

Great Lakes Campaign

General William Henry Harrison then began the march that proved to be the most successful moment in the war for the United States. Harrison's force of forty-five hundred men, mostly Kentucky volunteers, crossed Lake Erie and pursued the British, Shawnee, and Chippewa forces into Canada, defeating them on October 5 at the Battle of the Thames. This victory gave the United States control of the Old Northwest.

An important by-product of the war at this stage was the defeat of effective Indian resistance to American expansion. In the decade before the War of 1812, the Shawnee leaders Prophet and Tecumseh had attempted to build a pan-Indian federation, but in the end they failed. With their failure died the most significant resistance to the federal government's treaty-making tactics.

Prophet's early experiences mirror the fate that befell many frontier tribes. Born in 1775, a few months after his father had died in battle, Prophet was raised by his sister and called Lalawethika (Noisemaker) as a young man. He was among the Shawnees defeated at the Battle of Fallen Timbers and expelled to Ohio under the 1795 Treaty of Greenville. Within the shrunken territory granted to the Shawnees under the treaty, game became scarce. Encroachment by whites and the periodic

Prophet

Chapter 8: The Empire of Liberty, 1801–1824

Major Campaigns of the War of 1812

ravages of disease brought further misery to Indian villages and tribes.

In 1804, Lalawethika became a tribal medicine man. But his medicine could not stop the white man's viral illness from ravaging his village. Lalawethika emerged from his own battle with ill-

ness in 1805 as a new man, called Prophet. Claiming to have died and been resurrected, he told a visionary tale of this experience and warned of damnation for those who drank whiskey. In the following years, Prophet traveled widely in the Northwest as a religious leader, attacking the de-

The Shawnee Chiefs Prophet (left) and Tecumseh (right). The two brothers led a revival of traditional Shawnee culture and preached Indian federation against white encroachment. In the War of 1812, they allied themselves with the British, but Tecumseh's death at the Battle of Thames (1813) and British indifference thereafter caused Indian resistance and unity to collapse. *Prophet: National Museum of American Art, Smithsonian Institution, Gift of Mrs. Joseph Harrison, Jr.; Tecumseh: Field Museum of Natural History, FMNH Neg. #A93851.*

cline of moral values among Indians, condemning intertribal battles, and stressing harmony and respect for elders. In essence he preached the revitalization of traditional Shawnee culture. Return to the old ways, he told the Indians of the Old Northwest, abandon white customs.

Prophet's message was a reassuring one to the tribes of the Old Northwest who felt unsettled and threatened by whites. Prophet won converts by performing miracles—he seemed to darken the sun by coinciding his activities with a solar eclipse—and used opposition to federal Indian policy to draw others into his camp.

The government and white settlers were alarmed by the religious revival led by Prophet. With his brother, Tecumseh, who was seven years older, he refused to leave lands claimed by **Tecumseh** the government. In 1808, Prophet and his brother began to turn from a message of spiritual renewal to one of resistance to American aggression. When he repudiated land cessions to the government made under the Treaty of Fort Wayne (1809), Tecumseh told Indiana's Governor William Henry Harrison in 1810 that "the only way to check and stop this evil is, for all the red men to unite in claiming a common and equal right in the land. . . . No part has a right to sell, even to each other, much less to strangers." Tecumseh then warned Harrison that the Indians would resist white occupation of the 2.5 million acres on the Wabash that they had ceded in the Treaty of Fort Wayne.

A year later, using a Potawatomi raid on an Illinois settlement as an excuse, Harrison attacked and demolished Tecumseh's headquarters on Tippecanoe Creek in Indiana Territory. Losses on both sides were heavy. When the War of 1812 started, Tecumseh joined the British in return for a promise of an Indian country in the Great Lakes region. Tecumseh, however, was killed in the Battle of the Thames in October 1813, and with his death Indian unity collapsed.

Outside the Old Northwest, the British set Americans back. In December 1812, the Royal Navy blockaded the Chesapeake and Delaware bays. By May 1814, the blockade extended southward from New England down the Atlantic coast and then westward along the Gulf of Mexico. It was so effective that between 1811 and 1814 American trade had declined nearly 90 percent.

British Naval Blockade

After their defeat of Napoleon in April 1814, the British stepped up the land campaign against the United States, concentrating their efforts in the Chesapeake Bay region. To retaliate for the burning of York (now Toronto) and divert American troops from Lake Champlain, where the British planned a new offensive, royal troops occupied Washington in August and set it ablaze. The attack on the capital, however, was only a raid. The major battle occurred at Baltimore, in September, where the Americans held firm. Francis Scott Key, witnessing the British fleet's bombardment of Fort McHenry in Baltimore harbor, was inspired to write the verses of "The Star-Spangled Banner." (In 1931, it became the national anthem.) Although the British inflicted heavy damage both materially and psychologically, they achieved no more than a stalemate. The British offensive at Lake Champlain proved equally unsuccessful. An American fleet forced a British flotilla to turn back at Plattsburgh on Lake Champlain, and the offensive was discontinued.

The last campaign of the war was waged in the South, along the Gulf of Mexico. It began when Andrew Jackson, a Tennessee militia general, defeated the Creek Indians at the Battle of Horseshoe Bend in March 1814. The battle ended the year-long Creek War. As a result, the Creeks had to cede two-thirds of their land and withdraw to southern and western Alabama. Jackson became a major general in the regular army and continued south toward the Gulf. To forestall a British invasion at Pensacola Bay, which guarded an overland route to New Orleans, Jackson seized Pensacola—in Spanish Florida—on November 7, 1814. After securing Mobile, he marched on to New Orleans and prepared for a British attempt to capture the city.

The Battle of New Orleans was the final military engagement. Early in December, the British fleet landed fifteen hundred men east of New Orleans, hoping to gain control of the Mississippi River. They faced an American force of regular army troops, plus a larger contingent of Tennessee and Kentucky frontiersmen and two companies of free black volunteers from New Orleans. For three weeks, the British and the Americans played cat and mouse, each trying to gain a major strategic position. Finally, on January 8, 1815, the two forces met head-on. Jackson and his mostly untrained army held their ground against two suicidal frontal assaults and a reinforced British contingent of six thousand. At day's end, more than two thousand British soldiers lay dead or wounded. The Americans suffered only twenty-one casualties. Andrew Jackson emerged a national hero. Ironically, the Battle of New Orleans was fought two weeks after the end of the war; unknown to Jackson, a treaty had been signed in Ghent, Belgium, on December 24, 1814.

Battle of New Orleans

The Treaty of Ghent did not mention the issues that had led to war. The United States received no satisfaction on impressment, blockades, or other maritime rights for neutrals. Likewise, British demands for an Indian buffer state in the Northwest and territorial cessions from Maine to Minnesota were not satisfied. Essentially, the treaty restored the prewar status quo. It provided for an end to hostilities with the British and with Indian tribes, as well as for the release of prisoners, the restoration of conquered territory, and arbitration of boundary disputes. Other questions—notably compensation for losses and fishing rights—would be negotiated by joint commissions.

Treaty of Ghent

Why did the negotiators settle for so little? Events in Europe had made peace and the status quo acceptable at the end of 1814, as they had not been in 1812. Napoleon's fall from power allowed the

United States to abandon its demands, since peace in Europe made impressment and interference with American commerce moot questions. Similarly, war-weary Britain, its treasury nearly depleted, ceased striving for a military victory.

The War of 1812 reaffirmed the independence of the young American republic. Although conflict with Great Britain continued, it never again led to war. The experience strengthened

Results of War of 1812 America's resolve to steer clear of European politics, for it was the British-French conflict that had drawn the United States into war. For the rest of the century, the United States shunned involvement in European political issues and wars. The war also convinced the American government to maintain a standing army of ten thousand men—three times its size under Jefferson.

The war had disastrous results for most Indian tribes. Although Indians were not a party to the Treaty of Ghent, the ninth article pledged the United States to end hostilities and to restore "all the possessions, rights, and privileges" that the tribes had enjoyed before the war. Treaties were signed in 1815 with midwestern tribal leaders, but they had little meaning. With the death of Tecumseh, the Indians lost their most powerful political and military leader; with the withdrawal of the British, they lost their strongest ally. The midwestern tribes thus lost the resources with which they could have resisted American expansion.

Possibly most important of all, the war stimulated economic change. The embargo, the Non-Importation and Non-Intercourse acts, and the war itself spurred the production of manufactured goods to replace banned imports. In the absence of commercial opportunities abroad, New England capitalists began to invest in manufactures. These changes had far-reaching effects (see Chapter 9).

The war also sealed the fate of the Federalist party. Its presidential nominee in 1812, De Witt Clinton, lost to James Madison despite a hard campaign by the Younger Federalists.

Hartford Convention The extremism of the Older Federalists—not the 1812 defeat—was the party's undoing. During the war, Older Federalists had revived talk of secession, and from December 15, 1814, to January 5, 1815, Federalist delegates from New England met in Hartford, Connecticut. With the war in a stalemate and trade in ruins, they plotted to revise the national compact or pull out of the republic. Moderates prevented a resolution of secession, but convention members endorsed radical changes in the Constitution. They wanted to restrict the presidency to one term and to require a two-thirds congressional vote to admit new states. These proposals were designed to weaken the Republicans.

The timing of the Hartford Convention proved fatal. The victory at New Orleans and news of the peace treaty made the convention, with its talk of secession and proposed constitutional amendments, look ridiculous, if not treasonous. Rather than harassing a beleaguered wartime administration, the Federalists retreated before a rising tide of nationalism. Though Federalism remained strong in a handful of states until the 1820s, the Federalists began to dissolve.

Postwar Nationalism and Diplomacy

With peace came a new sense of American nationalism. Self-confidently, the nation asserted itself at home and abroad as Republicans aped Federalists in encouraging economic development and commerce. In his message to Congress in December 1815, President Madison embraced Federalist doctrine by recommending military expansion and a program to stimulate economic growth. Wartime experiences, he said, had demonstrated the need for a national bank (the charter of the first Bank of the United States had expired) and for better transportation. To raise government revenues and perpetuate the wartime growth in manufacturing, Madison called for a protective tariff—a tax on imported goods. Though straying from Jeffersonian Republicanism, Madison did so within limits. Only a constitutional amendment, he argued, could give the federal government authority to build roads and canals that were less than national in scope.

The congressional leadership pushed Madison's nationalist program energetically. Representative John C. Calhoun and Speaker of the House Henry Clay, who named the program

American System

the American System, believed it would unify the country. They looked to the tariff on imported goods to stimulate industry. New mills would purchase raw materials; new millworkers would buy food from the agricultural South and West. New roads would make possible the flow of produce and goods, and tariff revenues would provide the money to build them. A national bank would facilitate all these transactions.

In 1816, Congress enacted much of the nationalistic program. The Second Bank of the United States was chartered. Like its predecessor, the bank had a twenty-year charter, was a blend of public and private ownership, and had one-fifth of its directors appointed by the government. The nation's first protective tariff was also passed. Duties were placed on imported cottons and woolens and on iron, leather, hats, paper, and sugar. Some New England representatives viewed the tariff as interference in free trade, and southern representatives (except Calhoun and a few others) opposed it because it raised the cost of imported goods to southern families. But the western and Middle Atlantic states backed it.

Congress did not share Madison's reservations about the constitutionality of using federal funds to build local roads. "Let us, then, bind the republic together," Calhoun declared, "with a perfect system of roads and canals." But Madison vetoed Calhoun's internal improvements bill, which provided for the construction of roads of mostly local benefit, insisting that it was unconstitutional. Internal improvements were the province of the states and of private enterprise. (Madison did, however, approve funds for the continuation of the National Road, which began in Maryland, to Ohio, on the grounds that it was a military necessity.)

James Monroe, Madison's successor as president, retained Madison's domestic program, supporting the national bank and tariffs and vetoing internal improvements on constitutional grounds. After he

easily defeated Rufus King, the last Federalist candidate, Monroe declared that "discord does not belong to our system." The American people were, he said, "one great family with a common interest." A Boston newspaper dubbed the one-party period the "Era of Good Feelings." For Monroe's first term, that label seemed appropriate.

Under Chief Justice John Marshall, the Supreme Court during this period became the bulwark of a nationalist point of view. In *McCulloch* v. *Maryland*

McCulloch v. Maryland

(1819), the Court struck down a Maryland law taxing a branch of the federally chartered Second Bank of the United States. Maryland had adopted the tax in an effort to destroy the bank's Baltimore branch. The issue was thus one of state versus federal power. Speaking for a unanimous Court, Marshall asserted the supremacy of the federal government over the states.

Having established federal supremacy, the Court in *McCulloch* v. *Maryland* went on to consider whether Congress could issue a bank charter. No such power was specified in the Constitution. But Marshall noted that Congress had the authority to pass "all laws which shall be necessary and proper for carrying into execution" the enumerated powers of the government. Therefore, Congress could legally exercise "those great powers on which the welfare of the nation essentially depends." If the ends were legitimate and the means were not prohibited, Marshall ruled, a law was constitutional. The bank charter was declared legal.

In *McCulloch* v. *Maryland,* Marshall combined Federalist nationalism with Federalist economic views. By asserting federal supremacy, he was protecting the commercial and industrial interests that favored a national bank. This was federalism in the tradition of Alexander Hamilton. The decision was only one in a series. In *Fletcher* v. *Peck* (1810), the Court voided a Georgia law that violated individuals' right of contract. Similarly, in *Dartmouth College* v. *Woodward* (1819), the Court nullified a New Hampshire act altering the charter of Dartmouth College, which, Marshall ruled, constituted a contract. In protecting such contracts, Marshall thwarted state interference in commerce and business.

John Quincy Adams, Monroe's secretary of state,

matched the self-confident Marshall Court in nationalism and assertiveness. From 1817 to 1825, he managed the nation's foreign policy brilliantly. Adams stubbornly pushed for expansion, fishing rights for Americans in Atlantic waters, political distance from the Old World, and peace. An ardent expansionist, he nonetheless placed limits on expansion, believing that it must come through negotiations, not war, and that newly acquired territories must not permit slavery. In appearance a small, austere man, Adams was a superb diplomat.

John Quincy Adams as Secretary of State

Despite being an Anglophobe, Adams worked to strengthen the peace with Great Britain. In April 1817, the two nations agreed in the Rush-Bagot Treaty to limit their Great Lakes naval forces to one ship each on Lakes Ontario and Champlain and two vessels each on the other lakes. The first disarmament treaty of modern times led to the demilitarization of the United States–Canadian border. Adams then pushed for the Convention of 1818, which fixed the United States–Canadian border from the Lake of the Woods in Minnesota west to the Rockies along the 49th parallel. When agreement could not be reached on the territory west of the mountains, the two nations settled on joint occupation of Oregon for ten years.

Adams's next move was to settle long-term disputes with Spain. During the War of 1812, the United States seized Mobile and the remainder of West Florida. Afterward, it took advantage of Spain's preoccupation with domestic and colonial troubles to negotiate for the purchase of East Florida. Talks took place in 1818, while General Andrew Jackson's troops occupied much of present-day Florida on the pretext of suppressing Seminole raids against American settlements across the border. Adams was furious with Jackson but defended his brazen act. The following year, Don Luís de Onís, Spanish minister to the United States, agreed on behalf of Spain to cede Florida to the United States without payment. In this Transcontinental, or Adams-Onís, Treaty, the United States also defined the southwestern boundary of the Louisiana Purchase. In return, the United

Adams-Onís Treaty

States government assumed $5 million's worth of claims by American citizens against Spain and gave up its dubious claim to Texas. Expansion was thus achieved at little cost and without war, and American territorial claims stretched from the Atlantic to the Pacific.

While these treaties with Great Britain and Spain temporarily resolved conflict between the United States and European nations, events to the south still threatened American interests. John Quincy Adams's desire to insulate the United States and the Western Hemisphere from European conflict led to his greatest achievement: the Monroe Doctrine.

The thorny issue of the recognition of new governments in Latin America had to be confronted. Between 1808 and 1822, the United Provinces of the Río de la Plata (present-day northern Argentina, Paraguay, and Uruguay), Chile, Peru, Colombia, and Mexico had all broken free from Spain. Although many Americans wanted to recognize the independence of these former colonies, Monroe and Adams moved cautiously. They sought to avoid conflict with Spain and its allies and to assure themselves of the stability of the revolutionary regimes. But in 1822, shortly after the Adams-Onís Treaty with Spain was safely signed and ratified, the United States became the first nation outside Latin America to recognize the new states.

Soon events in Europe again threatened the stability of the New World. Spain suffered a domestic revolt, and France occupied Spain in an attempt to bolster the weak Spanish monarchy against the rebels. The United States feared that France would seek to restore the new Latin American states to Spanish rule. Similarly distrustful of France, Great Britain proposed a joint United States–British declaration against European intervention in the hemisphere. Adams rejected the British overture; he insisted that the United States act independently in accordance with the principle of avoiding foreign entanglements.

The result was the Monroe Doctrine, a unilateral declaration against European interference in the New World. The president enunciated the famous doctrine in his last message to Congress on December 2, 1823. First, Monroe called for *non-colonization* of the Western

Monroe Doctrine

Hemisphere by European nations, a principle that expressed American anxiety not only about Latin America but also about Russian expansion on the West Coast. Second, he demanded *nonintervention* by Europe in the affairs of independent New World nations. Finally, Monroe pledged *noninterference* by the United States in European affairs, including those of Europe's existing New World colonies.

Monroe words, however, carried no force. Indeed, the policy could not have succeeded without the support of the British, who were already committed to keeping other European nations out of the New World. Europeans ignored the doctrine. It was the Royal Navy they respected, not American policy.

The Panic of 1819 and Renewed Sectionalism

Monroe's domestic achievements could not match the diplomatic successes that John Quincy Adams brought to his administration. In 1819, a financial panic interrupted the postwar nationalism and confidence and stimulated sectional loyalties. Neither the panic nor the resurgence of sectionalism hurt Monroe politically; without a rival political party to rally opposition, he won a second term in 1820 unopposed.

But hard times spread. The postwar expansion was built on loose money and widespread speculation. State banks extended credit and printed notes too freely, fueling a speculative **Hard Times** western land boom. When expansion slowed, the manufacturing depression that had begun in 1818 deepened. The Second Bank of the United States, in order to protect its assets, reduced loans, thus accelerating the contraction in the economy. Distressed urban workers lobbied for relief and began to take a more active role in politics. Farmers clamored for lower tariffs on manufactured goods. Hurt by a sharp decline in the price of cotton, southern planters railed at the protective Tariff of 1816, which had raised prices while their incomes were falling sharply.

Western farmers suffered too. Those who had purchased public land on credit could not repay their loans. To avoid mass bankruptcy, Congress delayed payment of the money, and western state legislatures passed "stay laws" restricting mortgage foreclosures. Many westerners blamed the panic on the Second Bank of the United States and its tightening of the money supply.

Even more divisive was the question of slavery. Ever since the drafting of the Constitution, most political leaders had avoided the issue. The one exception was the 1807 act closing **Slavery** the foreign slave trade after Janu- **Question** ary 1, 1808, which passed without much opposition. In February 1819, however, slavery finally crept onto the political agenda when Missouri residents petitioned Congress for admission to the Union as a slave state. For the next two and a half years the issue dominated all congressional action.

The debate transcended slavery in Missouri. At stake was the undoing of the compromises that had kept the issue quarantined since the Constitutional Convention. Five new states had joined the Union since 1812—Louisiana (1812), Indiana (1816), Mississippi (1817), Illinois (1818), and Alabama (1819). Missouri was on the same latitude as free Illinois, Indiana, and Ohio (a state since 1803), and its admission as a slave state would thus thrust slavery farther northward. It would also tilt the political balance in the Senate toward the states committed to slavery. In 1819, the Union consisted of an uneasy balance of eleven slave and eleven free states. If Missouri entered as a slave state, the slave states would have a two-vote edge in the Senate.

What made the issue so deeply felt was not the politics of admission to statehood but white people's emotional attitudes toward slavery. Many northerners had come to the conclusion that it was evil. Thus, when Representative James Tallmadge, Jr., of New York introduced an amendment providing for gradual emancipation in Missouri, it led to passionate and sometimes violent debate over moral and political concerns. The House, which had a northern majority, passed the Tallmadge amendment, but the Senate rejected it. The two sides were deadlocked.

A compromise emerged in 1820 under pressure

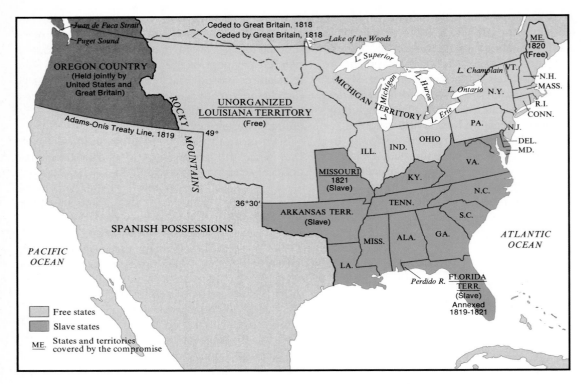

The Missouri Compromise and the State of the Union, 1820

from House Speaker Henry Clay: the admission of free Maine, carved out of Massachusetts, was linked with that of slave Missouri. In the **Missouri Compromise** rest of the Louisiana Territory north of 36°30′ (Missouri's southern boundary), slavery was prohibited forever (see map). Though the compromise carried, the issue ultimately undermined Republican unity and ended the Virginia dynasty that had begun with Jefferson's election in 1800.

Sectionalism and the question of slavery would ultimately threaten the Union itself. Still, the first decades of the nineteenth century were a time of nationalism and growth for the young republic. Political parties increased white, male involvement in government and channeled and limited partisan divisions. Moreover, a tradition of peaceful transition of power through presidential elections was established. A second war with Britain—the War of 1812—had to be fought to reaffirm American independence and to thwart Indian opposition to

United States expansion; thereafter, the nation was able to settle many disputes at the bargaining table.

The foreign policy problems confronting the infant republic from the turn of the century through the mid-1820s strikingly resemble those faced today by the newly established nations of the Third World. Mother countries often treat their former colonies as if they had not won their independence. Like Third World nations today, the young United States steered clear of alliances with the great powers, preferring neutrality and unilateralism.

After the war, all branches of the government, responding to the popular mood, pursued a vigorous national policy. The Supreme Court further advanced national unity by extending federal power over the states and encouraging commerce and economic growth. Moreover, disruption of trade during the war had promoted the manufacturing of goods in the United States. Developments in transportation further stimulated the economy, and old cities expanded in the market-oriented North as new ones sprouted up in the West on trade and transportation routes.

Along with nationalism and geographic expansion came the problem of sectionalism. While the manufacturers and commercial interests in the North were becoming increasingly connected with the agricultural producers in the West through transportation and trade, the South was developing its own economy and culture based on cotton crops, export markets, a plantation system, and slavery. Politicians kept the question of slavery off the national agenda as long as possible and worked out the Missouri Compromise as a stopgap measure. However, new land acquisitions and further westward expansion in the 1840s and 1850s, combined with a rising tide of reform, made the question of slavery unavoidable (see Chapters 12 and 13).

Suggestions for Further Reading

General

George Dangerfield, *The Awakening of American Nationalism, 1815–1828* (1965); John Mayfield, *The New Nation, 1800–1845* (1981); Marshall Smelser, *The Democratic Republic, 1801–1815* (1968).

Party Politics

Joyce Appleby, *Capitalism and a New Social Order: The Republican Vision of the 1790s* (1984); Noble E. Cunningham, Jr., *The Jeffersonian Republicans in Power: Party Operations, 1801–1809* (1963); David Hackett Fischer, *The Revolution of American Conservatism: The Federalist Party in the Era of Jeffersonian Democracy* (1965); Linda K. Kerber, *Federalists in Dissent* (1970); Richard P. McCormick, *The Presidential Game: The Origins of American Presidential Politics* (1982); James Sterling Young, *The Washington Community, 1800–1828* (1966).

The Virginia Presidents

Harry Ammon, *James Monroe: The Quest for National Identity* (1971); Noble E. Cunningham, Jr., *In Pursuit of Reason: The Life of Thomas Jefferson* (1987); Noble E. Cunningham, Jr., *The Process of Government Under Jefferson* (1978); Ralph Ketcham, *Presidents Above Party: The First American Presidency, 1789–1829* (1984); Forrest McDonald, *The Presidency of Thomas Jefferson* (1976); Merrill D. Peterson, *Thomas Jefferson and the New Nation* (1970); Merrill D. Peterson, *The Jefferson Image in the American Mind* (1960); Robert Allen Rutland, *James Madison: The Founding Father* (1987).

The Supreme Court and the Law

Richard E. Ellis, *The Jeffersonian Crisis: Courts and Politics in the Young Republic* (1971); Charles G. Haines, *The Role of the Supreme Court in American Government and Politics, 1789–1835* (1944); Morton J. Horowitz, *The Transformation of American Law, 1780–1860* (1977); R. Kent Newmyer, *The Supreme Court Under Marshall and Taney* (1968); Francis N. Stites, *John Marshall: Defender of the Constitution* (1981).

Expansion and the War of 1812

Roger H. Brown, *The Republic in Peril: 1812* (1964); Alexander De Conde, *This Affair of Louisiana* (1976); R. David Edmunds, *Tecumseh and the Quest for Indian Leadership* (1984); Clifford L. Egan, *Neither Peace nor War: Franco-American Relations, 1803–1812* (1983); Reginald Horsman, *The War of 1812* (1969); James P. Ronda, *Lewis and Clark Among the Indians* (1984); J. C. A. Stagg, *Mr. Madison's War: Politics, Diplomacy, and Warfare in the Early Republic, 1783–1830* (1983).

The Monroe Doctrine

Samuel F. Bemis, *John Quincy Adams and the Foundations of American Foreign Policy* (1949); Walter LaFeber, ed., *John Quincy Adams and American Continental Empire* (1965); Ernest R. May, *The Making of the Monroe Doctrine* (1976); Dexter Perkins, *Hands Off: A History of the Monroe Doctrine* (1941).

John Jervis's life bridged the old and the new. His roots lay in the farm country of upstate New York. Born at Huntington, Long Island, in 1795, he was taken to western New York in 1798 by his father. John learned to read and write during occasional attendance at common school. His father taught him to farm and handle an axe. But in 1817, he left behind much of that tradition and became involved in undertakings that would lead to a new and different nation. Hired to clear a cedar swamp for the Erie Canal, Jervis had to acquire skills not used on the farm. As he learned new skills, he advanced from axeman to surveyor to engineer and then to superintendent of a division. He was the most famous engineer to receive his training from the Erie Canal "School of Engineering."

When the 363-mile Erie Canal was completed in 1825, Jervis signed on as second-in-command of the Delaware and Hudson Canal project. Later, as a supervisor of an early railroad experiment, Jervis redesigned the locomotive's wheel assembly, and his design became standard throughout America. Jervis spent the next two decades building the 98-mile Chenango Canal and the freshwater system for New York City—consisting of the Croton Reservoir, a 33-mile aqueduct, and pumps. Later, he helped build other railroads, including the Michigan Southern, the Rock Island, and the Nickel Plate. In 1864, at the age of sixty-nine, Jervis returned home to Rome, New York, and organized an iron mill. He had spent his life constructing the mechanisms— canals and railroads—that would change America and connect its far-flung regions.

9

RAILS, MARKETS, AND MILLS: THE NORTH AND WEST, 1800–1860

The canals and railroads that John Jervis and others built were the most visible signs of economic development and the best-known links in the growing national economy from 1800 through 1860. The canal boat, the steamboat, the locomotive, and the telegraph were all agents of change and economic growth. They helped to open up the frontier and expand farm production for markets at home and abroad. They made it possible for New England mill girls to turn slave-produced southern cotton into factory-made cloth that was purchased by women from New York to San Francisco. Although transportation was the most visible change, less tangible but equally significant was the increased specialization in agriculture, manufacturing, and finance, which fostered a national, capitalist, market-oriented economy.

The dramatic transformation of the United States in the nineteenth century began in the first decades of the century and spread nearly everywhere. In 1800, most of the 5.3 million Americans earned a living working the land or serving those who did. Except in Kentucky and Tennessee, settlement had not stretched far to the west. By 1860, 31.4 million Americans had spread across the continent. A continental nation had been forged. Though still primarily agricultural, the economy was being transformed by commercial and industrial expansion.

Promotion of economic growth became the hallmark of government, especially in the nationalist mood after the War of 1812. Government sought to encourage individual freedom and choice by promoting an environment in which farming and industry could flourish. New financial institutions amassed the capital for large-scale enterprises like factories and railroads. Mechanization took root; factories and precision-made machinery successfully competed with home workshops and handmade goods, while reapers and sowers revolutionized farming.

Transportation and Regionalization

From 1800 through 1860, the North, South, and West followed distinctly different economic paths. Everywhere agriculture remained the foundation of the American economy. Nevertheless, industry, commerce, and finance came to characterize the North, plantations and subsistence farms the South, and commercialized family farms, agricultural processing, and implement manufacturing the West. This tendency toward regional specialization made the sections both different and more dependent on each other.

The revolution in transportation and communications was probably the single most important cause of these changes. The North's heavy investment in canals and railroads made the region the center of American commerce. With most of its capital invested in slave labor, the South built fewer canals, railroads, and factories and remained mostly rural and undeveloped.

Before the canal and railroad fevers, it was by no means certain that New England and the Middle Atlantic states would dominate American economic life. Indeed, the southward-**Change in** flowing Ohio and Mississippi **Trade Routes** rivers oriented the frontier of 1800—Tennessee, Kentucky, and Ohio—to the South. At first, westerners floated their products on flatboats down the rivers to New Orleans. In 1815, the steamboat *Enterprise* first carried cargo upstream on the Mississippi and the Ohio, further strengthening southern and western ties. This happened just eight years after Robert Fulton successfully introduced the steamboat by paddling up the Hudson River in the *Clermont*.

But the pattern changed in the 1820s. New arteries opened up east-west travel. The National Road, a stone-based, gravel-topped highway beginning in Cumberland, Maryland, reached Wheeling (then in Virginia) in 1818 and Columbus, Ohio, in 1833. More important, the Erie Canal, completed in 1825, forged an east-west axis from the Hudson River to Lake Erie, linking the Great Lakes with New York City and the Atlantic Ocean. Railroads and later the telegraph would solidify these east-west links. By contrast, only at one place—Bowling Green, Kentucky—did a northern railroad connect with a southern one. By 1850, the bulk of western trade flowed eastward. Thus, on the eve of the Civil War, the northern and Middle Atlantic states were closely tied to the former frontier of the Old Northwest.

Construction of the 363-mile-long Erie Canal was a visionary enterprise. Vigorously promoted by Governor De Witt Clinton, the Erie cost $7 million, much of it raised by loans from **Canals** British investors. The canal shortened the journey between Buffalo and New York City from twenty to six days and reduced freight charges from $100 to $5 a ton. By 1835, traffic was so heavy that the canal had to be widened from 40 to 70 feet and deepened from 4 to 7 feet.

The Erie Canal triggered an explosion of canal building. Other states and cities, sensing the advantage New York had gained, rushed to follow suit. By 1840, canals crisscrossed the Northeast and Midwest, and canal mileage in the United States reached 3,300—an increase of more than 2,000 miles in a single decade. Unfortunately for investors, none of these canals enjoyed the financial success achieved by the Erie. As a result, investment in canals began to slump in the 1830s. By 1850, more miles were being abandoned than built, and the canal era had ended.

Meanwhile, railroad construction boomed, and visionaries like John Jervis left canals for railroads. The railroad era in the United States began in 1830, when Peter Cooper's locomotive

Railroads *Tom Thumb* first steamed along 13 miles of track constructed by the Baltimore and Ohio Railroad. In 1833, a second railroad ran 136 miles from Charleston to Hamburg, South Carolina. By 1850, the United States had nearly 9,000 miles of railroad; by 1860, roughly 31,000.

The earliest railroads connected two cities or one city and its surrounding area. But in the 1850s, technological improvements, competition, economic recovery, and a desire for national unity prompted the development of regional and, eventually, national rail networks. By 1853, rail lines linked New York to Chicago, and a year later track had reached the Mississippi River. In 1860, the rails stretched as far west as St. Joseph, Missouri—the edge of the frontier. In 1853, seven short lines combined to form the New York Central system, and the Pennsylvania Railroad was unified from Philadelphia to Pittsburgh. Most lines, however, were still independently run, separated by gauge, scheduling, differences in car design, and a commitment to serve their home towns first and foremost.

Railroads did not completely replace water transportation. By the midcentury, steamships still carried bulk cargo more cheaply than railroads, except during freezing weather. The sealike Great Lakes permitted the construction of giant ships with propellers in place of paddle wheels; these leviathans carried heavy bulk cargoes like lumber, grain, and ore.

Gradually, steamships replaced sailing vessels on the high seas. In 1818, steam-powered packets made four round trips a year between New York and Liverpool, sailing on schedule

Steamboats rather than waiting for a full cargo as ships had done before then. The breakthrough came in 1848, though, when Samuel Cunard introduced regularly scheduled steamships to the Atlantic run between Liverpool and New York, reducing travel time from twenty-five days eastbound and forty-nine days westbound to between ten and fourteen days each way. Sailing ships quickly lost first-class passengers and light cargo to these swift steamships.

By far the fastest-spreading technological advance of the era was the magnetic telegraph. Samuel F. B. Morse's invention freed long-distance messages from the restraint of traveling no faster than the mes-

Telegraph senger. By 1853, only nine years after the construction of the first experimental line, 23,000 miles of telegraph wire spread across the United States; by 1860, 50,000. In 1861, the telegraph bridged the continent, connecting the east and west coasts. The new invention revolutionized news gathering, provided advance information for railroads and steamships, and altered patterns of business and finance. Rarely has an innovation had so great an impact so quickly.

The changes in transportation and communications between 1800 and 1860 were revolutionary. Railroads reduced the time of travel, were cheap to build over difficult terrain, and remained in use all year, unlike water transport, which was frozen out in winter. But time was the key factor. In 1800, it took four days to travel by coach from New York City to Baltimore and nearly four weeks to reach Detroit. By 1830, Baltimore was only a day and a half away, and Detroit, via the Erie Canal, was only a two-week journey. By 1857, Detroit was just an overnight train ride from New York City. The reduction in travel time saved money and facilitated commerce. During the first two decades of the century, wagon transportation cost 30 to 70 cents per ton per mile. By 1860, wheat moved from Chicago to New York for 1.2 cents per ton-mile. In sum, the transportation revolution had transformed the economy.

IMPORTANT EVENTS

1807	Fulton's steamboat, *Clermont*	**1837**	*Charles River Bridge* v. *Warren Bridge*
1812–15	War of 1812	**1839–43**	Hard times
1813	Boston Manufacturing Company founded	**1848**	Regularly scheduled steamship passage between Liverpool and New York
1818	National Road reaches Wheeling, Virginia	**1849**	California gold rush
1819–23	Depression	**1853**	British study American system of manufacturing
1824	*Gibbons* v. *Ogden*		
1825	Erie Canal completed	**1854**	Railroad reaches the Mississippi
1830	Baltimore and Ohio Railroad begins operation	**1857**	Hard times
1834	Mill workers strike at Lowell		

The Market Economy

Prior to the transportation revolution, most farmers in the early nineteenth century had geared production to family needs. They lived in interdependent communities and kept detailed account books of labor and goods exchanged with neighbors. Farm families tended to produce much of what they needed, but they traded agricultural surpluses for or purchased items that they could not produce. On such farms, men selling cordwood and women selling eggs, butter, cheese, and poultry produced the family's only cash. By the start of the Civil War, however, the United States had an industrializing economy, in which an increasing number of men and women worked for wages and in which most people outside the South—farmers and townspeople alike—increasingly purchased store-bought goods produced in workshops and factories.

In the market economy, crops were grown and goods produced for sale in the marketplace, at home or abroad. The money received in market transactions, whether from the sale of goods or of a person's labor, purchased items produced by other people. Such a system encouraged specialization. Formerly self-sufficient farmers began to grow just one or two crops or to concentrate on raising only cows, pigs, or sheep for market. Farm women gave up spinning and weaving at home and purchased fabric produced by wage-earning farm girls in Massachusetts textile mills.

Definition of a Market Economy

The United States experienced enormous economic growth. Improvements in transportation and technology, the division of labor, and new methods of financing all fueled expansion of the economy—that is, the multiplication of goods and services. In turn, this growth prompted new improvements. The effect was cumulative; by the 1840s, the economy was growing more rapidly than in the previous four decades. Per capita income doubled between 1800 and 1860, while the price of manufactured goods and food fell between 1809 and 1860. An expanding economy provided greater opportunities for wage labor.

Despite the great economic change and growth, the pace was uneven. Prosperity reigned during two long periods, from 1823 to 1835 and from 1843 to 1857. But there were also long stretches of economic contraction. During the time from Jefferson's 1807 embargo through the War of 1812, the growth rate was negative—that is, fewer goods and services were produced. Contraction and deflation occurred again during the hard times of 1819 through 1823, 1839 through 1843, and 1857. These periods were characterized by the collapse of banks, business bankruptcies, and a decline in wages and prices. For workers, the down side meant lower wages and higher unemployment rates.

Boom-and-Bust Cycles

Tens of thousands suffered during the hard times. In 1857, the Mercantile Agency—the forerunner of Dun and Bradstreet—recorded 5,123 bankruptcies, or nearly double the number in the previous year. Contemporary reports estimated 20,000 to 30,000 unemployed in Philadelphia and 30,000 to 40,000 in New York City. Female benevolent societies expanded their soup kitchens and distributed free firewood to the needy. In Chicago, charities reorganized to meet the needs of the poor; in New York, the city hired the unemployed to fix streets and develop Central Park. And in Fall River, Massachusetts, a citizens' committee disbursed public funds on a weekly basis to nine hundred families. The soup kitchen, the bread line, and public aid had become fixtures in urban America.

What caused the cycles of boom and bust that brought about such suffering? In general, they were a direct result of the new market economy. Prosperity stimulated greater demand for staples and finished goods. Increased demand led in turn to higher prices and still higher production, to speculation in land, and to the flow of foreign currency into the country. Eventually, production surpassed demand, leading to lower prices and wages; and speculation inflated land and stock values. The inflow of foreign money led first to easy credit and then to collapse when unhappy investors withdrew their funds.

Cause of Boom-and-Bust Cycles

Some early economists considered this process beneficial—a self-adjusting cycle in which unprofitable economic ventures were eliminated. In theory, people concentrated on the activities they did best, and the economy as a whole became more efficient. Advocates of the system argued also that it furthered individual freedom, since ideally each seller, whether of goods or labor, was free to determine the conditions of the sale. But in fact the system put workers on a perpetual roller coaster. They became dependent on wages—and the availability of jobs—for their very existence.

Government Promotes Economic Growth

The eighteenth-century political ideas that had captured the imagination of the Revolutionary War generation and found expression in the ideal of republican virtue were paralleled in economic thought by the writings of Adam Smith, a Scottish political economist. Smith's *The Wealth of Nations* first appeared in 1776, the year of the Declaration of Independence. Both works emphasized individual liberty, one economic, the other political. Both were reactions against forceful government: Jefferson attacked monarchy and distant government; Smith attacked mercantilism (government regulation of the economy to benefit the state). They believed that virtue was lodged in individual freedom and that the entire community would benefit most from individuals pursuing their own self-interest. As president, Jefferson put these political and economic beliefs into action by reducing the role of government.

Jefferson, however, recognized that government was nonetheless a necessary instrument in promoting individual freedom. Freedom, he believed, thrived where individuals had room for independence, creativity, and choices; individuals fettered by government, monopoly, or economic dependence could not be free. Committed to the idea that a republican democracy would flourish best in a nation of independent farmers and artisans and in an atmosphere of widespread political participation, Jefferson worked to realize those ideals. Beginning with the purchase of Louisiana in 1803, Republican policy, no less than that of the Federalists, turned to using the federal government to promote economic growth. Belief in limited government was not an end in itself, but only a means to greater individual freedom. The result was faith in a market economy in which government also played an active role.

Once Louisiana had been acquired, the federal government facilitated economic growth and geographic expansion by encouraging westward exploration and settlement and by promoting agriculture. The Lewis and Clark expedition from 1804 to 1806 was the beginning of a continuing federal interest in geographic and geologic surveying and the first step in the opening of western lands to exploitation and settlement.

To encourage western agriculture, the federal government offered public lands for sale at reasonable prices and evicted Indian tribes from their traditional lands. Because transportation was crucial to the development of the frontier, the government first financed roads and then canals and later subsidized railroad construction through land grants; it also surveyed about fifty railroad routes between 1827 and 1840. Even the State Department aided agriculture: its consular offices overseas collected horticultural information, seeds, and cuttings and published technical reports in an effort to improve American farming.

The federal government played a key role in technological and industrial growth. Federal arsenals pioneered new manufacturing techniques and helped to develop the machine-tool industry. The United States Military Academy at West Point, founded in 1802, emphasized technical and scientific subjects in its curriculum. The U.S. Post Office stimulated interregional trade and played a brief but crucial role in the development of the telegraph: the first telegraph line was constructed in 1844 under a government grant, and during 1845 the Post Office ran it. Finally, to create an atmosphere conducive to economic growth and individual creativity, the government protected inventions and domestic industries. Patent laws gave inventors a seventeen-year monopoly on their inventions, and

tariffs protected American industry from foreign competition.

The federal judiciary validated government promotion of the economy and encouraged business enterprise. In *Gibbons* v. *Ogden* (1824), the Supreme Court overturned a New York state law that had given Robert Fulton and Robert Livingston a monopoly on the New York–New Jersey steamboat trade. Ogden, their successor, lost his monopoly when Chief Justice John Marshall ruled that existing congressional licensing took precedence over New York's grant of monopoly rights to Fulton and Livingston. Marshall declared that congressional power under the commerce clause of the Constitution extended to "every species of commercial intercourse," including the transportation systems. In defining interstate commerce broadly, the Marshall Court expanded federal powers over the economy while limiting the ability of states to control economic activity within their borders.

Legal Foundations of Commerce

Federal and state courts, in conjunction with state legislatures, also encouraged the proliferation of corporations—groups of investors that could hold property and transact business as one person, with limited liability for the owners. In 1800, the United States had about three hundred incorporated firms. By 1830, the New England states alone had issued nineteen hundred charters. At first, each firm needed a special legislative act to incorporate, but after the 1830s applications became so numerous that incorporation was authorized by general state laws.

A further encouragement to economic development, corporate development, and free enterprise was the Supreme Court's ruling in *Charles River Bridge* v. *Warren Bridge* (1837) that new enterprises could not be restrained by implied privileges under old charters. The case involved issues of great importance. Should a new interest be able to compete against existing, older privileges, and should the state protect existing privilege or encourage innovation and the growth of commerce through competition?

In 1785, the Massachusetts legislature chartered the Charles River Bridge Company and in 1791 extended its charter to a seventy-year term. In return for assuming the risk of building the bridge between Charlestown and Boston, the owners received the privilege of collecting tolls. In 1828, the legislature chartered another company to build the Warren Bridge across the Charles, with the right to collect tolls for six years, after which the bridge would be turned over to the state and be toll-free. With the terminus of the new span only ninety yards away from its own bridge, the Charles River Bridge Company sued, claiming that the new bridge breached the earlier charter. Roger Taney, Marshall's successor as chief justice, speaking for the Court majority, noted that the original charter did not confer the privilege of monopoly and therefore exclusivity could not be implied. Focusing on the question of corporate privilege rather than the right of contracts, Taney ruled that charter grants should be interpreted narrowly and that ambiguities would be decided in favor of the public interest. New enterprises should not be restricted under old charters.

State governments far surpassed the federal government in promoting the economy. From 1815 through 1860, for example, 73 percent of the $135 million invested in canals was government money, mostly from the states. In the 1830s, the states started to invest in rail construction. Even though the federal government played a larger role in constructing railroads than in building canals, state and local governments provided more than half of southern rail capital. State governments also invested in corporation and bank stocks, providing those institutions with much-needed capital. Finally, state governments at a minimum equaled and may have exceeded private enterprise in their investments.

State Promotion of the Economy

From the end of the War of 1812 until 1860, the United States experienced uneven but sustained economic growth largely as a result of these government efforts. Although political controversy raged over questions of state versus federal activity—especially with regard to internal improvements and banking—all parties agreed on the general goal of economic expansion. Indeed, the major restraint on government action during these years was not philosophical but financial: both the government purse and the public purse were small.

The Rise of Manufacturing and Commerce

In 1851, hundreds of American products made their international debut at the London Crystal Palace Exhibition, the first modern world's fair. There the design and quality of American machines and wares astonished observers. American manufacturers returned home with dozens of medals. Most impressive to the Europeans were three simple machines: Alfred C. Hobb's unpickable padlocks, Samuel Colt's revolvers, and Robbins and Lawrence's six rifles with completely interchangeable parts. All were machine- rather than hand-tooled products of what the British called the American system of manufacturing. This American system so impressed the British—the leading industrial nation of the time—that in 1853 they sent a parliamentary commission to study it. Soon other nations were sending delegations across the Atlantic to bring back American machines.

The American system of manufacturing used precision machinery to produce interchangeable parts that needed no filing or fitting. In 1798, Eli Whitney promoted the idea of interchangeable parts when he contracted with the federal government to make ten thousand rifles in twenty-eight months. By the 1820s, the U.S. Ordnance Department, through the national armories at Springfield, Massachusetts and Harpers Ferry, Virginia, introduced machine-made interchangeable parts for firearms. From the arsenals, the American system spread, giving birth to the machine-tool industry—the mass manufacture of specialized machines for other industries. One by-product was an explosion in the production of inexpensive consumer goods of uniformly high quality.

American System of Manufacturing

Interchangeable parts and the machine-tool industry were uniquely American contributions to the industrial revolution. Both paved the way for America's swift industrialization after the Civil War. The process of industrialization began, however, in a simple and traditional way. In 1800, manufacturing was relatively unimportant to the American

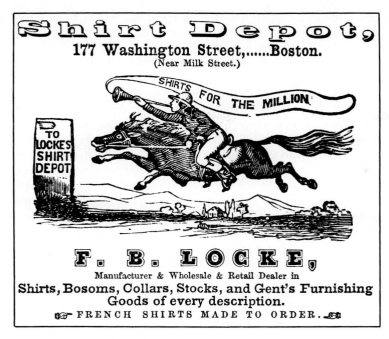

F. B. Locke adapted to the new market for ready-made clothing by becoming a manufacturer, wholesaler, and retailer of men's shirts. Though continuing to make shirts to order, the Shirt Depot's staple was mass-produced shirts, as this advertisement from the *Boston Directory, 1848–49* indicates. *Collection of Advertising History, Archives Center, National Museum of American History.*

economy. What manufacturing there was took place mostly in small workshops or homes. Journeymen and apprentices worked with and under master craftsmen; women working alone at home spun thread and wove cloth. Tailors, shoemakers, and blacksmiths made articles by hand for a specific customer.

The clothing trades illustrate well the nineteenth-century changes in manufacturing and distribution and the reliance on the market economy. The machine-tool industry produced new machinery that transferred textile and clothing production from kitchens and home workshops to mills and factories. Production, which had been based on artisan shops and female family labor, now depended on workers who were paid by the piece or by the hour. The manufactured product, first cloth, then cloth and finished clothing, was sold throughout the United States.

Clothing Trades

In the eighteenth century, most men wore clothes made at home, or they occasionally bought used clothing. Wealthy men had clothing made by tailors who cut unique garments to fit them. A tailor was a master craftsman whose journeymen and apprentices worked with him to produce goods made to order. By the 1820s and 1830s, clothiers and clothing manufacturers replaced most, though not all, of the old system. Typically, a journeyman cut the fabric panels in the factory, and the sewing was put out at piece rates to unskilled or semiskilled labor, often women working in their own homes. In 1832, Boston manufacturers employed three hundred journeymen tailors at $2 per day and a hundred boys and thirteen hundred women at 50 cents a day. Most of the women sewed straight seams at home. Previously women often had sewn an entire garment, but by the late 1850s, as many as seventeen different pairs of hands were involved in making a single pair of pants. Apprentices, if used at all, were no longer learning a trade but were a permanent source of cheap labor.

Merchants adapted to the changes in production. In the 1820s, clothiers appeared with stocks of ready-made clothes. T. S. Whitmarsh of Boston advertised in 1827 that "he keeps constantly for Sale, from 5 to 10,000 Fashionable ready-made Garments." Upon entering Whitmarsh's, a customer found row after row of ready-made apparel without a sign of tailors or a workshop. The merchant often bought the goods wholesale, though many merchants manufactured garments in their own factories apart from the retail stores. Lewis and Hanford of New York City boasted of cutting more than 100,000 garments in the winter of 1848–1849. The firm sold most of its clothing in the South and owned its own retail outlet in New Orleans. A New Orleans competitor, Paul Tulane, owned a New York factory that made goods for his Louisiana store. In the West, Cincinnati became the center of the new men's clothing industry.

The rise of cotton textile mills made possible the changes in the clothing industry. The first American textile mill, built in Pawtucket, Rhode Island, in 1790, used water-powered spinning machines constructed from British models by the English immigrant Samuel Slater. Slater employed women and children as cheap labor and sold thread from Maine to Maryland. Soon other mills sprang up, stimulated by the embargo on British imports from 1807 through 1815.

Early mills also used the "putting-out" system. Traditionally, women had spun their own thread and woven it into cloth for their own families; now many women received thread from the mills and returned finished cloth. The change was subtle but significant: although the work itself was familiar, women operated their looms for piece-rate wages and produced cloth for the market, not for their own use.

Textile manufacturing was radically transformed in 1813 by the construction of the first American power loom and the chartering of the Boston Manufacturing Company. The corporation was capitalized at $400,000—ten times the amount behind the Rhode Island mills—by Francis Cabot Lowell and other Boston merchants. Its goal was to eliminate problems of timing, shipping, coordination, and quality control inherent in the putting-out system. The owners erected their factories in Waltham, Massachusetts, combining all the manufacturing processes at a single location. They also employed a resident manager to run the mill, thus separating ownership from management. The company produced cloth so inexpensively that many women began to purchase rather than make their own cloth.

Waltham (Lowell) System

In the rural setting of Waltham not enough hands could be found to staff the mill, so the managers recruited New England farm daughters, accepting responsibility for their living conditions. To persuade young women to come, they offered cash wages, company-run boarding houses, and such cultural events as evening lectures—none of which was available on the farm. This paternalistic approach, called the Waltham (or Lowell) system, was adopted in other mills erected alongside New England rivers.

By the 1850s, though, another work force had entered the mills—Irish immigrants. With a surplus of cheap labor available, Lowell and the other mill towns abandoned their model systems. Within a few years, the typical mill had become a modern factory, and work relationships in American society had been radically altered.

Textile manufacturing changed New England. Lowell, the "city of spindles," symbolized early American industrialization as it grew from 2,500 people in 1826 to 33,000 in 1850. The textile industry became the most important in the nation before the Civil War, employing 115,000 workers in 1860, more than half of whom were women and immigrants. The key to its success was that the machines, not the women, spun the thread and wove the cloth. The workers watched the machines and intervened to maintain smooth operation. When a thread broke, the machine stopped automatically; the worker would find the break, piece the ends together, and restart the machine. The mills used increasingly specialized machines, relying heavily on advances in the machine-tool industry. Technology enabled American firms to compete successfully with British cotton mills. Here was the American system of manufacturing applied.

Textile mills were in the vanguard of industrialization, but manufacturing grew in many areas. The manufacture of woolen textiles, farm implements, machine tools, iron, glass, and finished consumer goods all became major industries. "White coal"— water power—was widely used to run the machines. Yet by 1860, the United States was still predominantly an agricultural nation; just over one-half of the work force was engaged in agriculture. Manufacturing accounted for only a third of total production, even though that fraction had doubled in twenty years.

Several factors stimulated industrial development. They included the need for home manufactures created by the War of 1812, population growth, government policy (protective tariffs, for example), the rise of commercial agriculture, and the transportation revolution. Commercial growth accompanied the rise of manufacturing and was in many ways essential to it.

Cotton, for instance, had once been traded by plantation agents who handled all the goods produced and bought by the owners, extending credit where needed. As cotton became a great staple export following the invention of the cotton gin in 1793, exports rose from half a million pounds in that year to 83 million pounds in 1815. Gradually, some agents came to specialize in finance alone: cotton brokers appeared, men who for a commission brought together buyers and sellers. Similarly, wheat and hog brokers sprang up in the West—in Cincinnati, Louisville, and St. Louis. The supply of finished goods also became more specialized. Wholesalers bought large quantities of a particular item from manufacturers, and jobbers broke down the wholesale lots for retail stores and country merchants.

Commercial specialization made some traders in the big cities, especially New York, virtual merchant princes. When the Erie Canal opened, the city became a standard stop on every major trade route—from Europe, the ports of the South, and the West. New York traders were the middlemen in southern cotton and western grain trading; in fact, New York was the nation's major cotton-exporting city. Merchants in other cities played a similar role within their own regions.

Specialization of Commerce

Newly rich traders invested their profits in processing and then manufacturing, further stimulating the growth of northern cities. Some cities became leaders in specific industries: Rochester became a milling center and Cincinnati—"Porkopolis"—the first meat-packing center.

Banking and other financial institutions played a significant role in the expansion of commerce and manufacturing and were also an important industry. Financial institutions (banks, insurance companies, and corporations) linked savers with those who wished to borrow money for equipment. The expiration of the first Bank of the United States in 1811, after Congress refused to renew its charter, acted as a stimulus to state-chartered banks, and in the next five years the number of banks more than doubled. Nonetheless, state banks proved inadequate to spur national growth. Consequently, in 1816 Congress chartered the Second Bank of the United States. But many farmers, local bankers, and politicians denounced the bank as a monster and in 1836 finally succeeded in killing it.

Banking and Credit Systems

The closing of the Second Bank in 1836 caused a nationwide credit shortage that, along with the Panic of 1837, stimulated major reforms in banking. Michigan and New York introduced charter laws promoting what was called *free banking*. Previously, every new bank had required a special legislative charter, and so each bank incorporation was in effect a political decision. Under the new laws, any proposed bank that met certain minimum conditions—capital invested, notes issued, and types of loans to be made—would automatically receive a state charter. Although banks in Michigan and New York were thus freer to incorporate, restrictions were placed on their practices, slightly reducing the risk of bank failure. Many other states soon followed suit.

Free banking proved a significant stimulus to the economy in the late 1840s and 1850s. New banks sprang up everywhere, providing merchants and manufacturers with the credit they needed. The free banking laws also served as a precedent for general incorporation statutes, which allowed manufacturing firms to receive state charters without special acts of the state legislature. Investors in

The young mill women who worked in this New England textile mill stopped work to pose for this early view, ca. 1850. New England farm daughters, and later Irish immigrants, comprised much of the nation's first factory workforce. *International Museum of Photography, George Eastman House.*

corporations, called shareholders, were granted *limited liability,* or freedom from responsibility for the company's debts. An attractive feature to potential investors, limited liability encouraged people to back new business ventures.

In the 1850s, with credit and capital both easily obtainable, the pace of industrialization increased. In the North, industry began to rival agriculture and commerce in dollar volume. Meanwhile, commercial farming, financed by the credit boom, integrated the early frontier into the northern economy. By 1860, six northern states—Massachusetts, New York, Pennsylvania, Connecticut, Rhode Island, and Ohio—were highly industrialized. The clothing, textile, and shoe industries employed more than 100,000 workers each, lumber 75,000, iron 65,000, and woolens and leather 50,000. Although agriculture still predominated even in these states, industrial employment would soon surpass it.

Mill Girls and Mechanics

Oh, sing me the song of the Factory Girl!
So merry and glad and free!
The bloom in her cheeks, of health how it
  speaks,
Oh! a happy creature is she!
She tends the loom, she watches the spindle,
And cheerfully toileth away,
Amid the din of wheels, how her bright eyes
  kindle,
And her bosom is ever gay.

This idyllic portrait of factory work appeared in the Chicopee, Massachusetts, *Telegraph* in 1850. It was a fitting song for the teenage, single women who first left the villages and farms of New England to work in the mills. The mill owners, believing that the degradation of English factory workers arose from their living conditions and not from the work itself, designed a model community, offering airy courtyards and river views, secure dormitories, prepared meals, and cultural activities.

Kinship ties, the promise of steady work, and good pay at first lured rural young women into the mills. Many pairs of sisters and cousins worked in the same mills and lived in the same boarding houses. They helped each other adjust, and letters home brought other kin to the mills. Girls then had few opportunities for work outside their own homes, and at the same time their families had less need for their labor. The commercial production of thread and cloth had reduced a good part of the work done in farm households by New England daughters, who averaged sixteen and one-half years of age when they entered the mills and usually stayed there only about five years. Few intended to stay longer. Most left the mills to marry and were replaced by other women interested in earning a wage.

By the 1840s, however, the paternalism of the Lowell system was beginning to be replaced by exploitation. In their race for profits, mill owners lengthened the workday, cut wages, and tightened discipline. They also introduced the speedup and the stretch-out to expand production. The speed-up increased the speed of the machines, and the stretch-out increased the number of machines a worker had to operate. These and other actions led to worker protests. In 1834, in reaction to a 25-percent wage cut, the mill women unsuccessfully "turned out" (struck) against the Lowell mills. Two years later, when boarding-house rates were raised, they turned out again. And in the 1840s, Massachusetts mill women joined forces with other workers to press for legislation mandating a ten-hour day.

Mill Girl Protests

What happened in the New England mills occurred in a less dramatic fashion throughout the nation. Work tasks and workplaces changed, as did relations between workers and supervisors. In the traditional workshops and households, work relationships were intensely personal. People worked within family settings and shared a sense of unity and purpose; men and women had a feeling of control over the quality, value (wages), and conditions of their labor.

The new textile mills, insurance companies, wholesale stores, and railroads, however, were the antithesis of the old workshop and household production tradition. Large factories lacked the reciprocity that had characterized earlier relationships. Factory workers lost their sense of autonomy, and impersonal market forces seemed to dominate. Stiff competition among mills in the growing textile industry led to layoffs and replacement of operatives with cheaper, less skilled workers or children. The formal rules of the factory contrasted sharply with the conditions in artisan or farm households. Supervisors separated the workers from the owners. The division of labor and the use of machines reduced the skills required of workers. And the coming and going of the large work forces was governed by the bell, the steam whistle, or the clock.

Changes in the Workplace

Changes in the workplace transformed workers. Initially, mill girls used kinship, village, and gender ties to build supportive networks in factories. In the 1840s and after, as Irish women came to predominate, more workers were strangers to each other before they entered the mills. Once employed, what they had in common—the bases for friendship and mutual support—were their work and job experiences. As a sense of distance from their employers increased, so did deep-seated differences among workers. Nationality, religion, education, and future prospects separated Irish and Yankee millworkers. For many Irish women, mill work was permanent employment, not a stage in their lives, as it was for their Yankee sisters.

Organized labor's greatest achievement during this period was gaining relief from the threat of conspiracy laws. When journeymen shoemakers organized in the first decade of the century, employers turned to the courts, charging criminal conspiracy. The cordwainers' (shoemakers') cases, which involved six trials from 1806 through 1815, left labor organizations in a tenuous position. Although the journeymen's right to organize was recognized, the courts ruled as unlawful any coercive action that harmed

Emergence of a Labor Movement

other businesses or the public. In effect, strikes were illegal. Eventually, a Massachusetts case, *Commonwealth* v. *Hunt* (1842), reversed that decision, when Chief Justice Lemuel Shaw ruled that Boston journeymen bootmakers could combine and strike. Conspiracy laws no longer thwarted unionization.

Yet permanent organizations were difficult to maintain. Outside the crafts, most workers were unskilled or, at best, semiskilled. Moreover, religion, race, and ethnicity divided workers. The early labor unions tended to be local in nature. The strongest resembled medieval guilds. They were created by journeymen craftsmen who sought to protect themselves against the competition of inferior workmen by regulating apprenticeship and establishing minimum wages. In the 1820s and 1830s, craft unions forged larger umbrella organizations in the cities, including the National Trades Union (1834). But in the hard times of 1839–1843, the movement fell apart amid wage reductions and unemployment. In the 1850s, the deterioration of working conditions strengthened the labor movement again. Workers won a reduction in hours, and the ten-hour day became standard. Though the Panic of 1857 wiped out the umbrella organizations, some of the new national unions for specific trade groups survived.

The impact of economic and technological change, however, fell more heavily on individual workers than on their organizations. As a group, the workers saw their share of the national wealth decline after the 1830s. Individual producers—craftsmen, factory workers, and farmers—had less economic power than they had had a generation or two before. And workers were increasingly losing control over their own work.

Commercial Farming

Beyond the town and city limits, agriculture (the nation was still overwhelmingly rural) remained the backbone of the economy. Indeed, it was rural population growth that transformed so many farm villages into bustling small cities. Moreover, the market orientation of farm families and their ability to feed the growing town and village populations made possible the concentration of population and the development of commerce and industry.

In 1800, New England and Middle Atlantic farmers worked as their fathers and mothers had. Life centered around a household economy in which the needs of the family and the labor it supplied mostly determined what was produced and in what amounts. But then canals and railroads began transporting grains eastward from the fertile Old Northwest. At the same time, northeastern agriculture developed some serious problems. Northeastern farmers had already cultivated all the land they could; expansion was impossible. Moreover, small New England farms with their uneven terrain did not lend themselves to the new labor-saving farm implements introduced in the 1830s—mechanical sowers, reapers, threshers, and balers. Many northeastern farms also suffered from soil exhaustion.

Northeastern Agriculture

In response to these problems and to competition from the West, many northern farmers either went west or gave up farming for jobs in the merchant houses and factories. Between 1820 and 1860, the percentage of people in the North living on farms declined from 71 to 40 percent. Those farmers who remained proved to be quite adaptable. By the 1850s, New England and Middle Atlantic farm families were successfully adjusting to western competition. Many abandoned the commercial production of wheat and corn and stopped tilling poor land. Instead, they improved their livestock, especially cattle, and specialized in vegetable and fruit production and dairy farming. They financed these changes through land sales or borrowing. In fact, their greatest potential profit was from rising land values, not from farming itself.

Increasingly, farm families everywhere adjusted to market conditions. In 1820, about one-third of the food produced was intended for market; by 1860, about two-thirds. As agriculture grew commercialized, women's production and earnings became essential to the survival of the family farm. As noted earlier, in New England, women did put-out work for income. In the Middle Atlantic states, especially near towns and cities, and in Ohio, women's dairy production was crucial to family income.

Butter and cheese making for local and regional markets replaced spinning and weaving as a major activity.

Most farm families seemed to welcome the opportunities offered by the market economy. Although they took pride in self-sufficiency and rural serenity, they shifted toward specialization and market-oriented production. The rewards in this period for such flexibility were great: produce sold at market financed land and equipment purchases and made credit arrangements possible. Many farm families flourished.

Americans saw great promise in railroads and industry, but they still valued agrarian life. State governments energetically promoted commercial agriculture in order to spur economic growth and sustain the values of an agrarian-based republic. Massachusetts in 1817 and New York in 1819 subsidized agricultural prizes and county fairs. New York required contestants to submit written descriptions of how they grew their prize crops; the state then published the best essays to encourage the use of new methods and to promote specialization.

Even so, the Old Northwest gradually and inevitably replaced the northeastern states as the center of American family agriculture. Farms in the Old Northwest were much larger than

Mechanization of Agriculture

northeastern ones and better suited to the new mechanized farming implements. The farmers of the region bought machines, such as the McCormick reaper, on credit and paid for them with the profits from their high yields. By 1847, Cyrus McCormick was selling 1,000 reapers a year. Using interchangeable parts, he expanded production to 5,000 a year. Similarly, John Deere's steel plow, invented in 1837, replaced the inadequate iron plow; steel blades kept the soil from sticking and were tough enough to break the roots of prairie grass. By 1856, Deere's 65 employees were making 13,500 plows a year.

Mechanized farming was the basis of expanded production. In the 1850s alone, wheat production surged 70 percent. By that time the area that had been the western wilderness in 1800 had become one of the world's leading agricultural regions. Midwestern farm families fed an entire nation and had food to export.

The Western Frontier

Integral to the development of the market economy was the steady expansion of the United States. In 1800, the edge of settlement had formed an arc from western New York through the new states of Kentucky and Tennessee, south to Georgia. By 1820, it had shifted to Ohio, Indiana, and Illinois in the North and Louisiana, Alabama, and Mississippi in the South. By 1860, settlement reached the Southwest and the West Coast. Unsettled land remained—mostly between the Mississippi River and the Sierra Nevada—but the old frontier and its native inhabitants, the Indians, had given way to white settlement. Still, the plains and mountain territories were only sporadically settled by whites.

The lore of the frontier and of pioneers forms a part of the mythology of America. James Fenimore Cooper used the frontier setting and ordinary peo-

Legends of Pioneers

ple in his Leatherstocking tales, a series of novels, the first of which appeared in 1823. The protagonist, Hawkeye (Natty Bumppo), was the first popular fictional hero in America. At heart a romantic, Hawkeye preferred the freedom of the virgin forest to domesticated society. Popular legends, songs, and dime novels in the nineteenth century, like movies, television, and paperbacks in the twentieth, glorified fur trappers, explorers and scouts, and pioneers. Major themes included pioneers crossing the arid plains and snow-covered Rockies to bring civilization to the wilderness; Mormons finding Zion in the Great American Desert; and gold seekers sailing on clipper ships to California.

Americans have only recently come to recognize that there are other sides to these familiar stories. Women, Indians, and blacks, as well as white men, were pioneers. Explorers and pioneers did not discover North America by themselves, nor did the wagon trains fight their way across the plains— Indians guided them along traditional paths and led them to food and water. Rather than civilizing the frontier, settlers at first brought a rather primitive economy and society, which did not compare favorably with the well-ordered Indian civilizations.

All those who sought furs, gold, and lumber spoiled the natural landscape in the name of progress and development.

No figure has come to symbolize the frontier more aptly than the footloose, rugged fur trapper, who roamed the wilderness in search of pelts. The

Fur Trade

trapper, with his backpack, rifle, and kegs of whiskey, spearheaded America's manifest destiny (see page 232), extending the United States presence to the Pacific Slope. Indeed, the history of trapping was in essence the history of the opening of the frontier. Early fur traders exploited friendly Indian tribes. Then pioneers—mountain trappers—monopolized the trade through the systematic organization and backing of trading companies. Soon settlements and towns sprang up along the trappers' routes. By the 1840s, with demand at a low ebb and the beaver nearing extinction, fur trading decreased and some trappers settled down. In Oregon in 1843, former trappers helped organize the first provisional government and pressured for United States statehood. In the mountain states, the mining and cattle frontiers lasted another half-century, following the development of the fur-trading frontier.

But not all regions followed that pattern. Anglos settled newly acquired California almost overnight. In January 1848, James Marshall, a carpenter,

California Gold Rush

spotted a few goldlike particles in the millrace at Sutter's Mill (now Coloma, California). Word of the discovery spread, and other Californians rushed to garner instant fortunes. By 1849, the news had spread eastward; hundreds of thousands of fortune seekers flooded in. Success in the market economy required capital, hard labor, and time; by contrast, gold mining seemed to promise instant riches. Most forty-niners never found enough gold to pay their expenses. "The stories you hear frequently in the States," one gold seeker wrote home, "are the most extravagant lies imaginable—the mines are a humbug. . . . the almost universal feeling is to get home." But many stayed, unable to afford the passage back home or tempted by the growing labor shortage in California's cities and agricultural districts. San Francisco, the gateway from the West Coast to the interior, became an instant city, ballooning from one

The gold rush brought treasure seekers—black and white, men and women, native and foreign born—to California. Few found their fortune in gold, but most stayed to settle the West Coast. *California State Library.*

thousand people in 1848 to thirty-five thousand just two years later.

About one-seventh of the travelers on the overland trails were women, many of whom found their domestic skills in great demand. They received

Frontier Women

high fees for cooking, laundering, and sewing. Inevitably, boarding houses and hotels were run by women, as men shunned domestic work. Not all women were entrepreneurs, however. Some wives, at their spouses' commands, cooked for and served their husbands' friends. The women did the work while their husbands built reputations as hosts.

Abigail Scott Duniway, a leading western crusader for women's suffrage and a veteran of the Overland Trail to Oregon, wrote of one woman's experience. She lived in a "neighborhood composed chiefly of bachelors," Duniway wrote in 1859, "who found comfort in mobilizing at meal time at the homes of the few married men of the township, and seemed especially fond of congregating at the hospitable cabin home of my good husband, who was never quite so much in his glory as when entertaining men at this fireside, while I, if not washing, scrubbing, churning, or nursing the baby, was preparing their meals in our lean-to kitchen."

Gold altered the pattern of settlement along the entire Pacific coast. Before 1848, most overland traffic flowed north over the Oregon Trail; few pioneers turned south to California or used the Santa Fe Trail. By 1849, a pioneer observed that the Oregon Trail "bore no evidence of having been much traveled this year." Instead, traffic was flowing south, and California was becoming the new population center of the Pacific Slope. One measure of the shift was the overland mail routes. In the 1840s, the Oregon Trail had been the major communications link between the Pacific and the Midwest. But the Post Office officials who organized mail routes in the 1850s terminated them in California, not in Oregon; there was no route farther north than Sacramento.

By 1860, California, like the Great Plains and prairies to the east, had become a farmers' and merchants' frontier linked to the market economy.

Land Grants and Sales

What made farm settlement possible was the availability of land and credit. Some public lands were granted as a reward for military service: veterans of the War of 1812 received 160 acres; veterans of the Mexican War could purchase land at reduced prices. Until 1820, civilians could buy government land at $2 an acre (a relatively high price) on a liberal four-year payment plan. More important, from 1800 to 1817, the government successively reduced the minimum purchase from 640 to 80 acres. However, when the availability of land prompted a flurry of land speculation that ended in the Panic of 1819, the government discontinued credit sales. Instead, it reduced the price further, to $1.25 an acre.

Some eager pioneers settled land before it had been surveyed and put up for sale. Such illegal settlers, or squatters, then had to buy the land they lived on at auction, and they faced the risk of being unable to purchase it. In 1841, to facilitate settlement, simplify land sales, and end property disputes, Congress passed the Pre-emption Act, which legalized settlement prior to surveying.

Since most settlers, squatters or not, needed to borrow money, private credit systems arose. Banks, private investors, country storekeepers, and speculators all extended credit to farmers. Railroads also sold land on credit—land they had received from the government as construction subsidies. Indeed, nearly all economic activity in the West involved credit, from land sales and the shipping of produce to railroad construction.

Towns and cities were the life lines of the agricultural West. Steamboats connected eastern markets and ports with river cities like Louisville, Cincinnati, and St. Louis and lake **Frontier Cities** cities such as Cleveland and Chicago. These western cities eventually developed into manufacturing centers when merchants shifted their investments from commerce to industry. Chicago became a center for the manufacture of farm implements, Louisville of textiles, and Cleveland of iron.

For the North and the West, the period from 1800 through 1860 was one of enormous growth. Population increased sixfold. Settlement extended beyond the Mississippi by 1860 and was spreading east from the Pacific Ocean as well. By then, Cincinnati, St. Louis, and Chicago had populations exceeding a hundred thousand, and Buffalo, Louisville, San Francisco, Pittsburgh, Detroit, Milwaukee, and Cleveland has surpassed forty thousand. Thus commerce, urbanization, and industrialization overtook the farmers' frontier, wedding western areas to the Northeast. By the midcentury, farming was also challenged by a booming manufacturing sector. And agriculture itself was becoming not only mechanized but also more market-oriented.

Economic development changed the American landscape and the way people lived. Canals, railroads, steamboats, and telegraph lines linked economic activities hundreds and thousands of miles apart. The market economy brought sustained growth and cycles of boom and bust. Hard times and unemployment became frequent occurrences.

At the same time, commercial and industrial growth altered production and consumption. The market economy changed farm work as farmers began to purchase goods formerly produced by wives and daughters and farm families geared production to faraway markets. Farm women increasingly contributed wages and income from market sales to the family farm. In New England many farm daughters left to become the first factory workers in the new textile industry. As the master-journeyman-apprentice system faded away, workplace relations became more impersonal and conditions harsher. Immigrants began to form a new industrial group, and some workers organized labor unions.

The American people, too, were changing. Immigration and western expansion made the population and society more diverse. Urbanization, commerce, and industry produced significant divisions among Americans, affecting the home as well as the workshop. The South was not totally insulated from these changes, but its dependence on slave rather than free labor set it apart. Above all else, slavery defined the South.

Suggestions for Further Reading

General

Stuart Bruchey, *The Roots of American Economic Growth, 1607–1861: An Essay in Social Causation* (1965); David Klingaman and Richard Vedder, eds., *Essays in Nineteenth-Century History* (1975); Otto Mayr and Robert C. Post, eds., *Yankee Enterprise: The Rise of the American System of Manufactures* (1981); Douglass C. North, *Economic Growth of the United States, 1790–1860* (1966).

Transportation

Robert G. Albion, *The Rise of New York Port, 1815–1860* (1939); Carter Goodrich, *Government Promotion of American Canals and Railroads, 1800–1890* (1960); Harry N. Scheiber, *Ohio Canal Era: A Case Study of Government and the Economy, 1820–1861* (1969); Ronald E. Shaw, *Erie Water West: Erie Canal 1797–1854* (1966); George R. Taylor, *The Transportation Revolution, 1815–1860* (1951); James A. Ward, *Railroads and the Character of America, 1820–1887* (1986).

Commerce and Manufacturing

Alfred D. Chandler, Jr., *The Visible Hand: Managerial Revolution in American Business* (1977); Thomas C. Cochran, *Frontiers of Change: Early Industrialization in America* (1981); Robert F. Dalzell, Jr., *Enterprising Elite: The Boston Associates and the World They Made* (1987); Louis Hartz, *Economic Policy and Democratic Thought: Pennsylvania, 1776–1860* (1954); David J. Jeremy, *Transatlantic Industrial Revolution: The Diffusion of Textile Technologies Between Britain and America, 1790s–1830s* (1981); Stanley I. Kutler, *Privilege and Creative Destruction: The Charles River Bridge Case* (1971); Merritt Roe Smith, *Harpers Ferry Armory and the New Technology* (1977); Barbara M. Tucker, *Samuel Slater and the Origins of the American Textile Industry, 1790–1860* (1984).

Agriculture

Jeremy Atack and Fred Bateman, *To Their Own Soil: Agriculture in the Antebellum North* (1987); Allen G. Bogue, *From Prairie to Corn Belt: Farming on the Illinois and Iowa Prairies in the Nineteenth Century* (1963); Clarence Danhof, *Change in Agriculture: The Northern United States, 1820–1870* (1969); John Mack Faragher, *Sugar Creek: Life on the Illinois Prairie* (1986); Paul W. Gates, *The Farmer's Age: Agriculture, 1815–1860* (1962); Benjamin H. Hibbard, *A History of Public Land Policies* (1939); Joan M. Jensen, *Loosening the Bounds: Mid-Atlantic Farm Women, 1750–1850* (1986); Robert Leslie Jones, *History of Agriculture in Ohio to 1880* (1983).

The Western Frontier

Ray A. Billington and Martin Ridge, *Westward Expansion,* 5th ed. (1982); John Mack Faragher, *Women and Men on the Overland Trail* (1979); William H. Goetzmann, *Exploration and Empire: The Explorer and the Scientist in the Winning of the American West* (1966); Julie Roy Jeffrey, *Frontier Women: The Trans-Mississippi West, 1840–1880* (1979); Theodore J. Karamanski, *Fur Trade and Exploration: Opening the Far Northwest, 1821–1852* (1983); John D. Unruh, Jr., *The Overland Emigrants and the Trans-Mississippi West, 1840–1860* (1979); David J. Wishart, *The Fur Trade of the American West, 1807–1840* (1979).

Workers

Mary H. Blewett, *Men, Women, and Work: Class, Gender, and Protest in the New England Shoe Industry, 1780–1910* (1988); Alan Dawley, *Class and Community: The Industrial Revolution in Lynn* (1977); Thomas Dublin, *Women at Work: The Transformation of Work and Community in Lowell, Massachusetts, 1826–1860* (1979); Alice Kessler-Harris, *Out to Work; A History of Wage-earning Women in the United States* (1982); W. J. Rorabaugh, *The Craft Apprentice: From Franklin to the Machine Age in America* (1986); Steven J. Ross, *Workers on the Edge: Work, Leisure, and Politics in Industrializing Cincinnati, 1788–1890* (1985); Norman Ware, *The Industrial Worker, 1840–1860* (1924); Sean Wilentz, *Chants Democratic: New York City and the Rise of the American Working Class, 1788–1850* (1984).

He was weeping, sobbing. In a humble voice he had begged his master not to give him to Mr. King, who was going away to Alabama, but it had done no good. Now his voice rose and he uttered "an absolute cry of despair." Raving and "almost in a state of frenzy," he declared that he would never leave the Georgia plantation that was home to his father, mother, wife, and children. He would kill himself, he said, before he lost his family and all that made life worth living.

To Fanny Kemble, watching from the doorway, it was a horrifying and disorienting scene. One of the most famous British actresses ever to tour America, Fanny had grown up breathing England's antislavery tradition as naturally as the air. In New England, she had become friends with enlightened antislavery thinkers. Then the man she married took her away from New England to a Georgia rice plantation.

Pierce Butler, Fanny's husband, was everything that a Philadelphia gentleman should be. He had lived all his life in the North, though part of his family's fortune had always sprung from southern slavery. When Fanny chose him, he had seemed an attractive exemplar of American culture. Yet now he shattered his slave's hopes without hesitation. Butler advised the distraught black man not to "make a fuss about what there was no help for." Only with tears and vehement pleas was she able to convince Butler to keep the slave family together. He finally agreed as a favor to her, not on principle or because she had a right to be consulted.

This incident, which occurred in 1839, illustrates both the similarities between South and North and the differences that were beginning to emerge. Although racism existed in the North, its influence was far more visible in the South. And although some northerners, like Pierce Butler, were undisturbed by the idea of human bondage, a growing number considered it shocking and backward. After the Revolution, these northerners, possessing few slaves and influenced by the revolutionary ideal of natural rights, had adopted gradual emancipation laws.

While the North grew and changed between 1800 and 1860, economically the South merely grew. New lands were settled and new states peopled, but southern growth only reinforced existing economic patterns.

10

SLAVERY AND THE GROWTH OF THE SOUTH, 1800–1860

One force behind the South's growth was soaring world demand for cotton. John Stobart's painting shows a steam packet, heavily laden with bales of cotton, arriving in New Orleans. *Courtesy Maritime Heritage Prints.*

Steadily, the South emerged as the world's most extensive and vigorous slave economy. Its people were slaves, slaveholders, and nonslaveholders rather than farmers, merchants, mechanics, and manufacturers. Its well-being depended on agriculture alone, rather than on agriculture, plus commerce and manufacturing. Its population was almost wholly rural rather than rural and urban.

Migration, Growth, and the Cotton Boom

Between 1800 and 1860, the South grew dramatically. Small farmers and slaveowning planters migrated westward and brought new territory under cultivation. Farms and plantations spread across the landscape as human labor, both voluntary and coerced, built a vastly larger, slaveholding society.

The attraction of rich, new lands drew thousands of southerners across the Appalachian Mountains. Both small farmers and ambitious slaveowners poured across the mountains, pushing the Indians off their lands in the Gulf region. The floodtide of migration reached Alabama and Mississippi in the 1830s, then spilled into Texas in the 1850s. The earliest settlers were often yeomen—small farmers who generally owned no slaves. Yeomen pioneered the southern wilderness, moving into undeveloped regions and building their log cabins. They came first as herders of livestock and then as farmers. After the War of 1812, they moved in successive waves down the southern Appalachians into new Gulf lands. The herdsmen, who fattened their cattle and pigs on the abundant natural vegetation in the woods, generally moved on as farmers filled up an area and broke ground for crops. These yeomen farmers forced many herdsmen farther west and eventually across the Mississippi.

Some yeomen acquired large tracts of level land and became wealthy planters. Others clung to the beautiful mountainous areas they loved. As they moved, they tended to stick to the climate and soils they knew best. Yeomen could not afford the richest bottomlands, which were swampy and required expensive draining, but they acquired land almost everywhere else.

For slaveholding southerners, another powerful motive impelled westward movement: the chance to profit from a spectacular cotton boom. Southern planters were not sentimentalists who held onto their slaves for noneconomic reasons. Like other Americans, they were profit-oriented. But the cotton boom caused nonmechanized, slave-based agriculture to remain highly profitable in the South, sustaining the plantation economy.

Rise of the Cotton South

This had not always seemed likely. At the time of the Revolution, slave-based agriculture was not very profitable in the Upper South. Persistent debt hung heavily over Virginia's tobacco growers. Farther south, slaves grew rice and some indigo, but cotton was a profitable crop only for sea-island planters, who grew the luxurious long-staple variety. The short-staple cotton that grew readily in the interior was unmarketable because its sticky seeds lay tangled in the fibers.

Then England's burgeoning textile industry changed the southern economy. English mills consumed more and more cotton. Sea-island cotton was so profitable between 1785 and 1795 that thousands of farmers in the interior tried growing the short-staple variety. Most of this cotton was grown in the hope that some innovation would make the crop salable to the English. Eli Whitney responded to the need in 1793 with a simple machine that removed the seeds from the fibers. By 1800, cotton was spreading rapidly westward from the seaboard states.

The voracious appetite of English mills caused a meteoric rise in cotton production (see maps, page 180). Despite occasional periods of low prices, the demand for cotton surged ahead every decade. This inspired southerners with capital to buy more land, buy more slaves, and plant ever more cotton. Cotton growers boosted production so successfully that by 1825 the South was the world's dominant supplier of cotton. By the 1850s, the South sent Britain more than 70 percent of all the cotton it imported.

Thus the antebellum South, or Old South before the Civil War, became primarily a cotton South. Tobacco continued to be grown in Virginia and North Carolina, and rice and sugar were very important in certain coastal areas. But cotton was the largest crop and the force behind the South's hunger for new territory.

Small slaveowners and planters (those who owned at least twenty bondsmen) sought out alluvial bottomland and other fertile soils, eager to grasp the opportunity for wealth that came with the cotton boom. As demand for cotton increased, slaveowners pushed feverishly to grow more. Their desire to plant more cotton and buy more slaves often caused men with new wealth to postpone the enjoyment of luxuries. Many first-generation planters lived for decades in their original log cabin, improved only by clapboards or a frame addition. Yet the planters' wealth put ease and refinement within their grasp, and for the lucky, riches and high social status could come quickly.

The rise of new aristocrats in the Gulf and the migration of aspiring slaveholders across the Appalachians meant another kind of migration— involuntary movement—for black southerners. Cotton planters in the Gulf region generated a steady demand for more slaves, but Congress had closed the international slave trade in 1808. Despite some smuggling, slave labor from abroad was essentially unavailable. Thus new slaves for the Lower South had to come from the older states of the Upper South.

As it happened, slaveowners there often had more slaves than they needed. Their slave population had grown, but tobacco prices had fallen and soil exhaustion had become a serious problem. Thus planters in Virginia and North Carolina were shifting toward wheat and corn, crops that were less labor-intensive. Slaveowners on worn-out tobacco lands were glad to sell excess slaves to the expanding black belt areas of the cotton South.

Consequently, the expansion of slaveholding

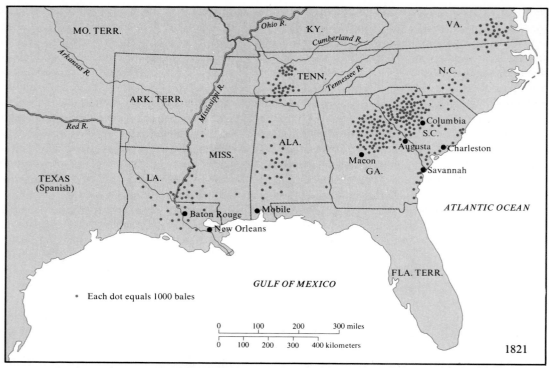

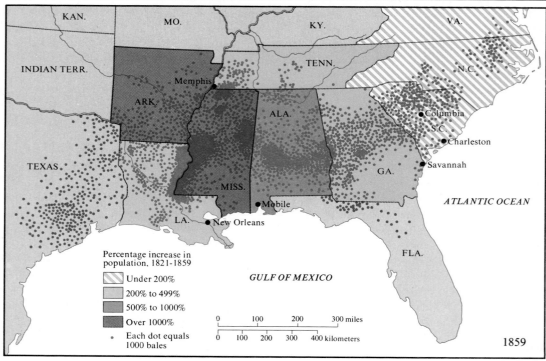

Cotton Production in the South

across the Appalachians caused a large interregional movement of the black population. Between 1810 and 1820 alone, 137,000 slaves were forced to move from North Carolina and the Chesapeake states to Alabama, Mississippi, and other western regions. From 1820 to 1860, an estimated 2 million persons were sold in this interregional slave trade. Each year, thousands of African-American families were disrupted to serve the needs of the cotton economy.

Thus the South was growing and expanding, driven by excitement over new lands and energies related to the cotton boom. To white southerners, the period from 1800 to 1860 was a time of great change and progress, no less so than in the North. But the South was different. The distinguishing features of its social system were those of an agricultural and a slave society.

An Agrarian Society

The South did share some of the diversity of the bustling, urbanizing, commercial North. It had merchants, artisans, and craftsmen in the larger cities and men of commerce who promoted railways and transportation improvements. But the largest patterns of southern development reflected the dominance of agriculture and slavery and the prominence of rural slaves, slaveholders, and yeomen farmers in the population.

In the South, population distribution remained thin. Cotton growers spread out over as large an area as possible in order to maximize production and income. Because farms were

Population Distribution far apart, rather than clustered around villages, southern society remained predominantly rural.

Population density, low even in the older plantation states, was extremely low in the frontier areas being brought under cultivation. In 1860, there were only 2.3 people per square mile in Texas, 15.6 in Louisiana, and 18.0 in Georgia. By contrast, the Northeast averaged 65.4 persons per square mile,

and in some places the density was much higher. Massachusetts had 153.1 people per square mile.

Society in such rural areas was characterized by relatively weak institutions, for it takes people to create and support organized activity. Where the concentration of people was low, it was difficult to finance and operate schools, churches, libraries, or even hotels, restaurants, and other urban amenities. Southerners were strongly committed to their churches, and some believed in the importance of universities, but all such institutions were far less developed than in the North.

The southern cities were likewise smaller and less developed than those in the North. As exporters, southerners did not need large cities; a small

Weak Urban Sector group of merchants working in conjunction with northern brokers sufficed to ship the cotton overseas and to import necessary

supplies and luxuries. As planters, southerners invested most of their capital in slaves. They had little money left to build factories—another source of urban growth. A few southerners did invest in iron or textiles on a small scale. But the largest southern "industry" was lumbering, and the largest factories were cigar factories, where slaves finished tobacco products.

More important, the South did not develop a unified market economy or regional transportation network, as the North did. Far less money was spent on canals, turnpikes, or railroads. As a result, urban growth after 1820 was far less vigorous than in the North. In 1860, the population of Charleston was only 41,000, Richmond 38,000, and Mobile 29,000. New Orleans, by far the largest southern city, had only 169,000 residents; it was at an economic disadvantage because it was not part of the national railroad network.

Thus the South was only semideveloped in comparison with other sections of the country. Its white people were prospering, but neither as rapidly nor as independently as residents of the North. To prosper, southern planters increased their acreage and hoped for continued high demand from foreign customers—decisions that worked to the ultimate disadvantage of the region. Subsistence farmers merely worked harder and hoped to grow a bit more.

Farmers, Planters, and Free Blacks

A large majority of white southern families (three-quarters in 1860) owned no slaves. Some of them lived in towns and ran stores or businesses, but most were yeomen farmers who owned their own land and grew their own food. They were the typical whites, but typical in a society of extremes. The social distance between different groups of whites could be great; still greater was the distance between whites and blacks.

Southern yeomen farmers occupied a relatively autonomous position within the slavery-based, staple-crop economy that was expanding around them. Independent and motivated by a hearty share of frontier individualism, they provided for themselves in the traditional way of American farm families, prospering slowly from improvements on their acreage or the settlement of new and better land. And this meant steady progress for thousands of yeomen as the South expanded.

But the lives of most southern yeomen, as compared to northern farmers, had not been transformed by improvements in transportation. Because few railroads penetrated the southern interior, yeomen generally had little connection with the market or its type of progress. Families might raise a small surplus to trade for needed items or spending cash, but they were not particularly concerned about larger cash income. They valued instead their self-reliance and freedom from others' control. Absorbed in an isolated but demanding rural life, they formed an important, though sometimes silent, part of southern society.

The yeomen enjoyed a folk culture based on family, church, and community. They spoke with a drawl, and their inflections were reminiscent of their Scottish and Irish backgrounds. Once a year they flocked to religious revivals, which they called protracted meetings or camp meetings, and in between they enjoyed events such as house-raisings, log-rollings, quilting bees, and corn shuckings. Such community events provided a fellowship that was especially welcome to isolated rural dwellers.

Folk Culture of the Yeoman

Beyond these basic facts, historians know little about the yeomen. Because their means were modest, they did not generate the voluminous legal papers—wills, contracts, and inventories of estates—that document the activities of the rich. Only a few letters have found their way into libraries and archives. It is reasonable to suppose, though, that yeomen held a variety of opinions and pursued individual goals. Many of them did aspire to wealth and were eager to join the race for slaves, land, and profits from cotton. Others were content with their independence, recreation, family life, and religion. But whether they strove to become rich or were satisfied with their status, they worked hard.

Toil was also the lot of two other groups of white southerners: landless whites and free blacks. From 25 to 40 percent of the white workers in the South were laborers who owned no land. Their property consisted of a few household items and some animals—most often pigs—that could feed themselves on the open range. In addition to unskilled laborers in the countryside and towns, the landless included some immigrants, especially the Irish, who did heavy and dangerous work such as building railroads and digging ditches.

Landless Whites

The white farm laborers were people struggling to become yeomen. They faced low wages or, if they rented, were dependent on the unpredictable market price for their crops. Some fell into debt and were frequently sued; others managed to climb into the ranks of yeomen. When James and Nancy Bennitt of North Carolina succeeded in their ten-year struggle to buy land, they decided to avoid the unstable market in cotton as much as possible; instead, they raised extra corn and wheat as sources of cash.

Nearly a quarter of a million free blacks lived in the South in 1860. Their situation was generally worse than the yeoman's and often little better than the slave's. The free blacks of the Upper South were usually descendants of men and women emancipated by their owners in the 1780s and 1790s, a period of postrevolutionary idealism that coincided with a decline in tobacco prices. Usually, they did not own land and had to labor in someone else's field, frequently beside slaves. By law they could

Free Blacks

not own a gun or liquor, violate curfew, assemble except in church, testify in court, or (everywhere after 1835) vote. Despite these obstacles, a minority bought land, and others found jobs as artisans, draymen, boatmen, and fishermen. A few owned slaves, who were almost always their wives and children, purchased from bondage.

Farther south, in the cotton and Gulf regions, a large proportion of free blacks were mulattos, the privileged offspring of wealthy planters. Some received a good education and financial backing from their fathers, who recognized a moral obligation to them. In a few cities such as New Orleans and Mobile, extensive interracial sex had produced a mulatto population that was recognized as a distinct class. These mulattos formed a society of their own and sought a status above slaves and other freedmen, if not equal to planters. But outside New Orleans, Mobile, and Charleston, such groups were rare, and most mulattos encountered disadvantages more frequently than they enjoyed benefits from their light skin tone.

At the opposite end of the spectrum from free blacks were the slaveholders. As a group, slaveowners lived well, on incomes that enabled them to enjoy superior housing, food, clothing, and luxuries. But most did not live on the opulent scale that legend suggests. A few statistics tell the story: 88 percent of southern slaveholders had fewer than twenty slaves; 72 percent had fewer than ten; 50 percent had fewer than five. Thus the average slaveholder was not a man of great wealth but an aspiring farmer. Rather than a polished aristocrat, he was more often a person of humble origins, with little formal education and many rough edges to his manner.

The wealth of the greatest planters gave ambitious men something to aspire to. Most planters lived in spacious, comfortable farmhouses, but some did live in mansions. Most slaveowners sat down at mealtimes to an abundance of tempting country foods—pork and ham, beef and game, fresh vegetables and fruits, tasty breads and biscuits, cakes and jams—but the sophisticated elite consumed such delights as "gumbo, ducks and olives, *supreme de volaille,* chickens in jelly, oysters, lettuce salad, chocolate cream, jelly cake, claret cup, etc."

Slaveholding men held the dominant position in society and, especially among the wealthiest and oldest families, they justified their dominance through a paternalistic ideology. Instead of stressing the acquisitive aspects of commercial agriculture, they focused on *noblesse oblige.* They viewed themselves as custodians of the welfare of society as a whole and of the black families who depended on them. The paternalistic planter viewed himself not as an oppressor but as the benevolent guardian of an inferior race. He developed affectionate feelings toward his slaves (as long as they kept in their place) and was genuinely shocked at outside criticism of his behavior.

Southern Paternalism

The letters of Paul Carrington Cameron, North Carolina's largest slaveholder, illustrate this mentality. After a period of sickness among his one thousand North Carolina slaves, Cameron wrote, "I fear the Negroes have suffered much from the want of proper attention and kindness under this late distemper . . . no love of lucre shall ever induce me to be cruel, or even to make or permit to be made any great exposure of their persons at inclement seasons." On another occasion, he described to his sister the sense of responsibility he felt: "I cannot better follow the example of our venerated Mother than in doing my duty to her faithful old slaves and their descendants."

There is no doubt that the richest southern planters saw themselves in this way. It was comforting to do so, and slaves, accommodating themselves to the realities of power, encouraged their masters to think that their benevolence was appreciated. Paternalism also provided a welcome defense against abolitionist criticism. Still, for most planters, paternalism affected the manner and not the substance of their behavior. It was a matter of style. Its softness and warmth covered harsher assumptions: blacks were inferior; planters should make money.

Relations between men and women in the planter class were similarly paternalistic. Typically, an upper-class southern woman was raised and educated to be the subordinate companion of men. Her proper responsibility was home management. She was not to venture into politics and other worldly affairs. In a social system based on the coercion of an entire race, no women could be allowed to challenge

Elite Women's Role

society's rules, on sexual or racial relations. If she defied or questioned the status quo, she risked universal condemnation.

Within the domestic circle, the husband reigned supreme. For the fortunate women, like North Carolina diarist Catherine Devereux Edmondston, whose marriage joined two people of shared tastes and habits, the husband's authority weighed lightly or not at all. But other women were acutely conscious of that authority. "He is master of the house," wrote South Carolina's Mary Boykin Chesnut. "To hear is to obey . . . all the comfort of my life depends upon his being in a good humor." In a darker mood, Chesnut once observed that "there is no slave . . . like a wife." Unquestionably, there were some, possibly many, close and satisfying relationships between men and women in the planter class, but many women were dissatisfied.

The upper-class southern woman had to clear several barriers in the way of happiness. Making the right choice of a husband was especially important. Once married, she lost most of her legal rights to her husband, became part of his family, and was expected to get along with numerous in-laws during extended visits. On the plantation, she was expected to oversee the cooking and preserving of food, manage the house, care for the children, and attend sick slaves. As a woman, she was forbidden to travel and visit unless accompanied by a man. All the circumstances of her future life depended on the man she chose.

Childbearing brought grief and sickness, as well as joy, to southern women. In 1840, the birthrate for southern women in their fertile years was almost 20 percent higher than the national average. At the beginning of the nineteenth century, the average southern woman could expect to bear eight children; by 1860, the figure had decreased only to six, and one or more miscarriages were likely among so many pregnancies. The high birthrate took a toll on women's health, for complications of childbirth were a major cause of death. Moreover, a mother had to endure the loss of many of the infants she bore. In the South in 1860, almost five out of ten children died before the age of five, and in South Carolina more than six in ten failed to reach the age of twenty.

Slavery was another source of trouble, a source of problems that women had to endure but were not supposed to notice. "Violations of the moral law . . . made mulattoes as common as blackberries," protested a woman in Georgia, but wives had to play "the ostrich game." "A magnate who runs a hideous black harem," wrote Mrs. Chesnut, "under the same roof with his lovely white wife, and his beautiful accomplished daughters . . . poses as the model of all human virtues to these poor women whom God and the laws have given him. From the height of his awful majesty, he scolds and thunders at them, as if he never did wrong in his life."

In the early 1800s, some southern women, especially Quakers, had spoken out against slavery. Although most white women did not criticize the "peculiar institution," they often approached it differently from men, seeing it less as a system and more as a series of relationships with individuals. Perhaps southern men sensed this, for they wanted no discussion of the slavery issue by women. In the 1840s and 1850s, as national and international criticism of slavery increased, southern men published a barrage of articles stressing that women should restrict their concerns to the home.

But southern women were beginning to chafe at their customary exclusion from financial matters. A study of women in Petersburg, Virginia, has revealed behavior that amounted to an implicit criticism of the institution of marriage and the loss of autonomy it entailed. During several decades before 1860, the proportion of women who had not married, or not remarried after the death of a spouse, grew to exceed 33 percent. Likewise, the number of women who worked for wages, controlled their own property, or even ran businesses increased. In managing property, these women benefited from legal reforms, beginning with Mississippi's Married Women's Property Act of 1839, that were not designed to increase female independence. Rather, the law gave women some property rights in order to protect families from ruin caused by the husband's indebtedness. But some women saw the resulting opportunity and took it.

Restrictions on freedom and the use of education were not limited to upper-class women. For a large category of southern men and women, freedom was wholly denied and education in any form was not allowed. Male or female, slaves were expected to accept bondage and ignorance as their condition.

Slaves and the Conditions of Their Servitude

For African-Americans, slavery was a curse unrelieved by blessings, except the strengths they developed to survive it. Slaves knew a life of poverty, coercion, toil, heartbreak, and resentment. They had few hopes that were not denied; often they had to bear separation from their loved ones; and they were despised as an inferior race. That they endured and found loyalty and strength among themselves is a tribute to their courage, but it could not make up for a life without freedom or opportunity.

Southern slaves enjoyed few material comforts beyond the bare necessities. Their diet was plain and limited, although generally they had enough to eat. The basic ration was corn-

Slaves' Diet, Clothing, and Housing

meal, fat pork, molasses, and occasionally coffee. Many masters allowed slaves to tend gardens, which provided the variety and extra nutrition of greens and sweet potatoes. Fishing and hunting benefited some slaves. Despite the occasional supplements of green vegetables and fish, their diet was nutritionally deficient; many slaves suffered from beriberi and pellagra. Clothing too was plain, coarse, and inexpensive. The few clothes issued to slaves were made either of light cotton or a coarse, heavy material called osnaburg. Because shoes were normally not issued until the weather became cool, slaves frequently contracted parasitic diseases such as hookworm.

Slaves typically lived in small one-room cabins with a door and possibly a window opening but no glass. Logs chinked with mud formed the walls; dirt was the only floor; and a wattle-and-daub or stone chimney vented the fireplace, which provided heat and light. Bedding consisted of heaps of straw, straw mattresses, or wooden bedframes lashed to the walls with rope. A few crude pieces of furniture and cooking utensils completed the furnishings of most cabins. The gravest drawback of slave cabins

was not their appearance and lack of comfort but their unhealthfulness. In each small cabin lived one or two whole families. Crowding and lack of sanitation fostered the spread of infection and contagious diseases.

Hard work was the central fact of the slaves' existence. In Gulf Coast cotton districts, long hours and large work gangs suggested factories in the

Slaves' Work Routines

field rather than the small-scale, isolated work patterns of slaves in the eighteenth-century Chesapeake. Overseers rang the morning bell before dawn, making it possible for slaves to be in the fields at first light. Except in urban settings and on some rice plantations, where slaves were assigned daily tasks to complete at their own pace, working from "sun to sun" became universal in the South. These long hours and hard work were at the heart of the advantage of slave labor. As one planter put it, slaves were the best labor because "you could command them and *make* them do what was right." White workers, by contrast, were few and could not be *driven*; "they wouldn't stand it."

Planters aimed to keep all their laborers busy all the time. Profit took precedence over paternalism's "protection" of women: slave women did heavy field work, often as much as the men and even during pregnancy. Old people—of whom there were few—were kept busy caring for young children, doing light chores, or carding, ginning, or spinning cotton. Children had to gather kindling for the fire, carry water to the fields, or sweep the yard. But slaves had a variety of ways to keep themselves from being worked to death. It was impossible for the master to supervise every slave every minute, and slaves slacked off when they were not being watched.

Of course, slaves could not slow their labor too much, because the owner enjoyed a monopoly on force and violence. Whites throughout the South

Physical and Mental Abuse of Slaves

believed that Negroes "can't be governed except with the whip." Evidence suggests that whippings were less frequent on small farms than on large plantations, but the reports of former slaves show that a large majority even of small farmers plied the

Coercion was the essence of slavery. To enforce their will, masters relied on whips and instruments like this pronged collar to inflict pain or restrict the slaves' movements. A slave girl in nineteenth-century New Orleans had to wear the collar shown as punishment for attempting to run away. The painting suggests that such sights were not unusual. *Painting: The Historic New Orleans Collection, Museum/Research Center; slave collar: Massachusetts Historical Society.*

lash. These beatings symbolized authority to the master and tyranny to the slaves, who made them a benchmark for evaluating a master. In the words of former slaves, a good owner was one who did not "whip too much," whereas a bad owner "whipped till he's bloodied you and blistered you."

As this testimony suggests, terrible abuses could and did occur. The master wielded virtually absolute authority on his plantation, and courts did not recognize the word of a chattel. Pregnant women were whipped, and there were burnings, mutilations, tortures, and murders. Yet the physical cruelty of slavery may have been less in the United States than elsewhere in the New World. In sugar-growing or mining regions of the Western Hemisphere in the 1800s, slaves were regarded as an expendable resource to be replaced after seven years. Treatment was so poor and families so uncommon that death rates were high and the heavily male slave population did not replace itself but instead rapidly shrank in size. In the United States, by contrast, the slave population showed a steady natural increase, as births exceeded deaths, and each generation grew larger.

The worst evil of American slavery was not its physical cruelty but the fact of slavery itself: coercion, loss of freedom, belonging to another person with virtually no hope for change. A woman named Delia Garlic cut to the core when she said, "It's bad to belong to folks that own you soul an' body. I could tell you 'bout it all day, but even then you couldn't guess the awfulness of it." American slaves hated their oppression, and contrary to some whites' perceptions, they were not grateful to their oppressors. Although they had to be subservient and speak honeyed words in the presence of their masters, they talked quite differently later on among themselves. The evidence of their resistant attitudes comes from their actions and from their own life stories.

Chapter 10: Slavery and the Growth of the South, 1800–1860

Former slaves reported some kind feelings between masters and slaves, but the overwhelming picture was one of antagonism and resistance.

Slaves' Attitudes Toward Whites
Slaves mistrusted kindness from whites and suspected self-interest in their owners. A woman whose mistress "was good to us Niggers" said her owner was kind "'cause she was raisin' us to work for her." Christmas presents of clothing from the master did not mean anything, observed another, "'cause he was going to [buy] that anyhow."

Slaves were sensitive to the thousand daily signs of their degraded status. One man recalled the general rule that slaves ate cornbread and owners ate biscuits. If blacks did get biscuits, "the flour that we made the biscuits out of was the third-grade shorts." A woman reported that on her plantation "Old Master hunted a heap, but us never did get none of what he brought in." If the owner took slaves' garden produce to town and sold it for them, the slaves suspected him of pocketing part of the profits.

Suspicion and resentment often grew into hatred. According to a former slave from Virginia, "the white folks treated the nigger so mean that all the slaves prayed God to punish their cruel masters." When a yellow fever epidemic struck in 1852, many slaves saw it as God's retribution. As late as the 1930s, an elderly woman named Minnie Fulkes cherished the conviction that God was going to punish white people for their cruelty to blacks. She described the whippings that her mother had had to endure and then exclaimed, "Lord, Lord, I hate white people and the flood waters goin' to drown some more."

Slave Culture and Everyday Life

The force that helped slaves to maintain such defiance was their culture. They had their own view of the world, a body of beliefs and values born of both their past and their present, as well as the fellowship and support of their own community. With power overwhelmingly in the hands of whites, it was not possible for slaves to change their world. But drawing strength from their culture, they could resist their condition and struggle on against it.

Slave culture changed significantly after the turn of the century. Between 1790 and 1808, when Congress banned further importation of slaves, there was a rush to import Africans. After that the proportion of native-born blacks rose steadily, reaching 96 percent in 1840 and almost 100 percent in 1860. With time the old African culture faded farther into memory as an African-American culture matured.

In one sense, African influences remained primary, for African practices and beliefs reminded the slaves that they were and ought to be different from their oppressors and thus

Remnants of African Culture
encouraged them to resist. The most visible aspects of African culture were the slaves' dress and recreation. Some slave men plaited their hair into rows and fancy designs; slave women often wore their hair "in string"—tied in small bunches with a string or piece of cloth. A few men and many women wrapped their heads in kerchiefs of the styles and colors of West Africa. For entertainment slaves made musical instruments with carved motifs that resembled some African stringed instruments. Their drumming and dancing clearly followed African patterns.

Many slaves continued to see and believe in spirits. Whites also believed in ghosts, but the belief was more widespread among slaves. It closely resembled the African concept of the living dead—the idea that deceased relatives visited the earth for many years until the process of dying was complete. Slaves also practiced conjuration, voodoo, and quasi-magical root medicine. By 1860, the most notable conjurers and root doctors were reputed to live in South Carolina, Georgia, Louisiana, and other isolated coastal areas of heavy slave importation.

These cultural survivals provided slaves with a sense of their separate past. Black achievement in music and dance was so exceptional that whites felt entirely cut off from it; in this one area some whites became aware that they did not "know" their slaves.

Sunday was a precious time for slaves to worship, rest, play, and spend time with the members of their families. *The Historic New Orleans Collection, Museum/Research Center.*

Conjuration and folklore directly fed resistance; slaves could cast a spell or direct the power of a hand (a bag of articles belonging to the person to be conjured) against the master. Not all masters felt confident enough to dismiss such a threat.

In adopting Christianity, slaves fashioned it, too, into an instrument of support and resistance. Theirs was a religion of justice quite unlike that of the propaganda their masters pushed at them. Former slaves scorned the preaching arranged by their masters. "You ought to have heard that preachin'," said one man. "'Obey your master and mistress, don't steal chickens and eggs and meat,' but nary a word about havin' a soul to save." The slaves believed that Jesus cared about their souls and their present plight. They rejected the idea that in heaven whites would have "the colored folks . . . there to wait on 'em." Instead, when God's justice came, the slaveholders would be "broilin' in hell for their sin."

For slaves Christianity was a religion of personal and group salvation. Beyond seeking personal guidance, blacks prayed "for deliverance of the slaves." Some waited "until the overseer got behind a hill" and then laid down their hoes and called on God to free them. Others held fervent secret prayer meetings that lasted far into the night. From such activities many slaves gained the unshakable belief that God would end their bondage. This faith and the joy and emotional release that accompanied their worship sustained blacks.

Slaves also developed a sense of racial identity. The whole experience of southern blacks taught them that whites despised their race. Blacks naturally drew together, helping each other in danger, need, and resistance. "We never told on each other," one woman declared. Although some slaves did tell on others, former slaves were virtually unanimous in denouncing those who betrayed the group or sought personal advantage through allegiance to whites. And because most slaves lived on small units, there was no overriding class system within the black community.

Slaves' Religion

The main source of support for individuals was the family. Slave families faced severe dangers. At any moment, the master could sell a husband or wife, give a slave child away as a wedding present, or die in debt, forcing a division of his property. Many families were broken up in such ways. Others were uprooted in the trans-Appalachian expansion of the South. When the Union Army registered thousands of black marriages in Mississippi and Louisiana in 1864 and 1865, 25 percent of the men over forty reported that they had been forcibly separated from a previous wife. Probably a substantial minority of slave families suffered disruption of one kind or another.

Slaves' Family Life

But this did not mean that slave families could not exist. American slaves clung tenaciously to the personal relationships that gave meaning to life, for although American law did not protect slave families, masters permitted them. In fact, slaveowners expected slaves to form families and have children. As a result, there was a normal ratio of men to women, young to old.

Following African kinship taboos, African-Americans avoided marriage between cousins (a frequent occurrence among aristocratic slaveowners). Adapting other West African customs to the circumstances of their captivity, they did not condemn unwed mothers, although they did expect a young girl to form a stable marriage after one pregnancy, if not before. By naming their children after relatives of past generations, African-Americans emphasized their family histories. If they chose to bear the surname of a slaveowner, it was often not their current master's name but that of the owner under whom their family had begun in America.

Slaves abhorred interference in their family lives. Some of their strongest protests sought to prevent the breakup of a family. Rape was a horror for both men and women. Some husbands faced death rather than permit their wives to be sexually abused, and women sometimes fought back. In other cases slaves seethed with anger at the injustice but could do nothing except soothe each other with human sympathy and understanding. Significantly, blacks condemned the guilty party, not the victim.

Slave men did not dominate their wives in a manner similar to white husbands, but it is misleading to say that slave women enjoyed equality of power in sex roles and family life. The larger truth is that all black people, men and women, were denied the opportunity to provide for or protect their families. Slavery's cruelties put black men and women in the same dilemma. Under the pressures of bondage, they had to share the responsibilities of parenthood. Each might have to stand in for the other and assume extra duties. Similarly, uncles, aunts, and grandparents sometimes raised the children of those who had been sold away.

Sex Roles in Slavery

In two other respects, however, distinct gender roles remained very important in slave families and experience. First, after work in the fields was done, men's activities focused on traditional "outdoor" tasks while women did "indoor" work. Second, the life cycle and pattern of work routines frequently placed slave women in close associations with each other, which heightened their sense of sisterhood. Female slaves lived significant portions of their lives as part of a group of women, a fact that emphasized the gender-based element of their experience.

Slaves brought to their efforts at resistance the same common sense, determination, and practicality that characterized their family lives. American slavery produced some fearless and implacable revolutionaries. Gabriel Prosser's conspiracy apparently was known to more than a thousand slaves when it was discovered in 1800, just before it was put into motion. A similar conspiracy in Charleston in 1822, headed by a free black named Denmark Vesey, involved many of the most trusted slaves of leading families. The most famous rebel of all, Nat Turner, rose in violence in Southampton County, Virginia, in 1831.

Resistance to Slavery

The son of an African woman who passionately hated her enslavement, Nat was a precocious child who learned to read at a very young age. Encouraged by his first owner to study the Bible, he enjoyed some special privileges but also knew changes of masters and hard work. In time, young Nat became a preacher. He also developed a tendency toward mysticism and became increasingly withdrawn. After nurturing his plan for several years, Turner led a band of rebels from house to house in the predawn darkness of August 22, 1831. The group severed limbs and crushed skulls with axes or killed their victims with guns. Before they were stopped, Nat Turner and his followers had slaughtered sixty whites of both sexes and all ages. About two hundred blacks, including Turner, lost their lives as a result of the rebellion.

But most slave resistance was not violent because the odds against revolution were especially poor in North America. Consequently, slaves directed their energies toward creating means of survival and resistance. A desperate slave could run away for good, but probably in more instances slaves ran off temporarily to hide in the woods. Every day that a slave "lay out" in this way, the master lost a day's labor. Most owners chose not to mount an exhaustive search and sent word instead that the slave's grievances would be redressed. The runaway would then return to bargain with the master. Most owners would let the matter pass, for, like the owner of a valuable cook, they were "glad to get her back."

Other modes of resistance had the same object: to resist but survive under bondage. Appropriating food (stealing, in the master's eyes) was so common that even whites sang humorous songs about it. Blacks were also alert to the attitudes of individual whites and learned to ingratiate themselves or play off one white person against another. Field hands frequently tested a new overseer to intimidate him or win more favorable working conditions.

Harmony and Tension in a Slave Society

Not only for blacks but for whites, too, slave labor stood at the heart of the South's social system, and its importance grew as the century advanced. Slavery affected the organization of society, the values of individuals, and—increasingly—every aspect of politics in the region.

Ever since the seventeenth century, slavery had placed severe restrictions on black southerners, but these deepened as the 1800s advanced. In all things, from their workaday movements to Sunday worship, slaves fell under the supervision of whites. Courts held that a slave "has no civil right" and could not even hold property "except at the will and pleasure of his master." When slaves revolted, legislators tightened the legal straitjacket: after the Nat Turner insurrection of 1831, for example, they prohibited owners from teaching their slaves to read. As the sectional crisis developed, fears of slave revolt grew and restrictions on slaves increased accordingly.

Slavery imposed responsibilities on nonslaveholders, as well as on slaveowners. All white male citizens bore an obligation to ride in patrols to discourage slave movements at night. White ship captains and harbor masters were required to scrutinize the papers of blacks who might be attempting to escape bondage. Urban residents who did not supervise their domestic slaves as closely as planters did found themselves subject to criticism for endangering the community. And the South's few manufacturers often felt pressure to use slave rather than free labor.

Slavery had a deep effect on southern values because it was the main determinant of wealth in the South. Ownership of slaves guaranteed the labor to produce cotton and other crops on a large scale. Slaves were therefore vital to the acquisition of a fortune. In fact, for southern society as a whole, slaveholding indicated wealth in general with remarkable precision. Important economic enterprises not based on slavery were so rare that variations in wealth from county to county followed very closely variations in slaveholding.

Slavery as the Basis of Wealth and Social Standing

It was therefore not surprising that slaveholding was the main determinant of a white man's social position. Wealth in slaves was also the foundation on which the ambitious built their reputations. Ownership of slaves brought political power: a solid majority of political officeholders were slaveholders, and the most powerful of them were generally large slaveholders. Lawyers and newspaper editors were sometimes influential, but they did not hold independent positions in the economy or society. Dependent on the planters for business and support, they served planters' interests and reflected their outlook.

Slavery's influence spread throughout the social system until even the values and mores of non-slaveholders bore its imprint. For one thing, the availability of slave labor tended to devalue free labor. Consequently, nonslaveholders preferred to work for themselves rather than to hire out. Whites who had to sell their labor tended to resent or reject tasks that seemed degrading. This kind of thinking engendered an aristocratic value system ill suited to a newly established democracy.

In modified form, the attitudes characteristic of the planter elite gained a considerable foothold among the masses. The ideal of the aristocrat emphasized lineage, privilege, power, pride, and refinement of person and manner. Some of those qualities were in short supply in the recently settled, expanding cotton kingdom, however; they mingled with and were modified by the tradition of the frontier. In particular, independence and defense of one's honor were highly valued by planter and frontier farmer alike. Thus, instead of gradually disappearing, as it did in the North, duelling hung on in the South and gained an acceptance that spread throughout the society.

Aristocratic Values and Frontier Individualism

Other aristocratic values that marked the planters as a class were less acceptable to the average citizen. Planters believed that they were better than other people. In their pride, they expected not only to wield power but to receive special treatment. By the 1850s, some planters openly rejected the democratic creed, vilifying Thomas Jefferson for his statement that all men are equal.

Belief in its own superiority shaped the outlook of the southern elite for generations, but this attitude was never acceptable to the individualistic members of the yeoman class. Independent and proud of their position, yeomen resisted any infringement of their rights. They believed that they were as good as anyone and knew that they lived in a nation in which democratic ideals were gaining strength. Thus there were occasional conflicts between aristocratic pretensions and democratic zeal.

Yeomen farmers and citizens resented their underrepresentation in state legislatures, corrup-

tion in government, and undemocratic control over local government. After vigorous debate, the reformers won most of their battles. Five southern states—Alabama, Mississippi, Tennessee, Arkansas, and Texas—adopted white manhood suffrage and other reforms, including popular election of governors, legislative apportionment based on the white population, and locally chosen county government. Only South Carolina and Virginia effectively defended property qualifications for office, legislative malapportionment, appointment of county officials, and selection of the governor by the lawmakers. The formal structure of government was more democratic than many planters would have wished.

Movements for Electoral Reform

Slaveowners knew that an open structure could permit troubling issues to arise. In Virginia, nonslaveholding westerners raised a basic challenge to the slave system in the year following the Nat Turner rebellion. Advocates of gradual abolition forced a two-week legislative debate on slavery, arguing that the institution was injurious to the state and inherently dangerous. When the House of Delegates finally voted, the motion favoring abolition lost by just 73 to 58. This was the last major debate on slavery in the antebellum South.

With such tension in evidence, it was perhaps remarkable that slaveholders and nonslaveholders did not experience frequent and serious conflict. Why were class confrontations among whites so infrequent? Historians who have considered this question have given many answers. One of the most important factors was race. The South's racial ideology stressed whites' superiority to blacks and declared that race, not class, was the social dividing line. Besides, in a rural society family bonds and kinship ties are valued, and some of the poor nonslaveholding whites were related to the rich new planters. The experience of frontier living must also have created a relatively informal, egalitarian atmosphere. Moreover, the South was an expanding, mobile society in which yeomen and planters rarely depended on each other. Yeomen farmed mainly for themselves; planters farmed for themselves and for the market.

But suppression of dissent also played a significant, and increasingly greater, role. White southern-

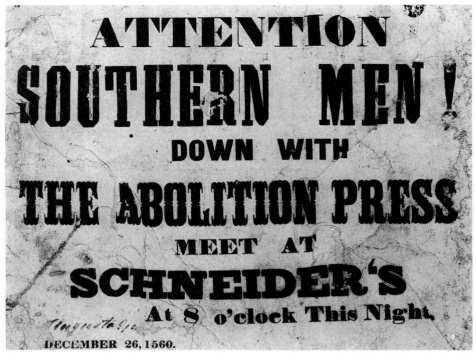

ATTENTION SOUTHERN MEN!

DOWN WITH THE ABOLITION PRESS

MEET AT SCHNEIDER'S

At 8 o'clock This Night,

DECEMBER 26, 1560.

Run off in haste and anger, with a misprinted date, this handbill illustrates the determination of southern slaveholders in Augusta, Georgia, to tolerate no criticism of their peculiar institution. *Library of Congress.*

ers who criticized the slave system out of moral conviction or class resentment were intimidated, attacked, or legally prosecuted. Southern cities impounded abolitionist literature and sought to bar any antislavery influences. Intellectuals developed elaborate justifications for slavery as newspapers railed at any antislavery threat. By the 1850s, the defense of slavery's interests dominated discussion, and all groups in society felt pressure to uphold the slave system.

Still, there were signs that the relative lack of conflict between slaveholders and nonslaveholders was coming to an end. As the region grew older, nonslaveholders saw their opportunities beginning to narrow; meanwhile, wealthy planters enjoyed an expanding horizon. The risks of cotton production were becoming too great and the cost of slaves too high for many yeomen to rise in society. Thus from 1830 to 1860, the percentage of white southern families holding

Hardening of Class Lines

slaves declined steadily from 36 to 25 percent. At the same time, the monetary gap between the classes widened. In 1860, slaveowners' share of the South's agricultural wealth remained at between 90 and 95 percent. The average slaveholder was almost fourteen times as rich as the average nonslaveholder.

Urban artisans and mechanics felt the pinch acutely. Their numbers were few; their place in society was hardly recognized; and in bad times they were often the first to lose work. Moreover, they faced stiff competition from urban slaves, whose masters wanted them to hire their time and bring in money by practicing a trade. White workers demanded that economic competition from slaves be forbidden. This demand was always ignored—the powerful slaveowners would not tolerate interference with their property or the income they derived from it. But the angry protests of white workers resulted in harsh restrictions on *free* black workers and craftsmen.

Pre–Civil War politics reflected these tensions. Facing the prospect of a war to defend slavery, slaveowners expressed growing fear about the loyalty of nonslaveholders and discussed schemes to widen slave ownership. In North Carolina, a prolonged and increasingly bitter controversy over the combination of high taxes on land and low taxes on slaves erupted; a class-conscious nonslaveholder named Hinton R. Helper attacked the institution of slavery in his book *The Impending Crisis,* published in New York in 1857. Discerning planters knew that such fiery controversies lay close at hand in every southern state.

But for the moment, slaveowners stood secure. They held from 50 to 85 percent of the seats in state legislatures and a similarly high percentage of the South's congressional seats. In addition to their near-monopoly on political office, they had established their point of view in all the other major social institutions. Professors who criticized slavery had been dismissed from colleges; school books that contained "unsound" ideas had been replaced. And almost all the clergy had given up preaching against the institution. In fact, except for a few obscure persons of conscience, southern clergy had become slavery's most vocal defenders. Society as southerners knew it seemed to be stable.

In the nation generally, however, society was anything but stable. Change had become one of the major characteristics of the northern economy and society, as the rise of the market and industry produced a more diverse population. The American people were changing, and the currents of change would eventually affect the South.

Suggestions for Further Reading

Southern Society

W. J. Cash, *The Mind of the South* (1941); Clement Eaton, *The Growth of Southern Civilization, 1790–1860* (1961); Clement Eaton, *Freedom of Thought in the Old South* (1940); William W. Freehling, *Prelude to Civil War* (1965); Eugene D. Genovese, "Yeoman Farmers in a Slaveholders' Democracy," *Agricultural History,* 49 (April 1975), 331–342; William Sumner Jenkins, *Pro-Slavery Thought in the Old South* (1935); Peter Kolchin, *Unfree Labor: American Slavery and Russian Serfdom* (1987); Robert McColley, *Slavery and Jeffersonian Virginia* (1964); Donald G. Mathews, *Religion in the Old South* (1977); James Hebron Moore, *The Emergence of the Cotton Kingdom in the Old Southwest: Mississippi, 1770–1860* (1987); Frederick Law Olmsted, *The Slave States,* ed. Harvey Wish (1959); Frederick F. Siegel, *The Roots of Southern Distinctiveness: Tobacco and Society in Danville, Virginia, 1780–1865* (1987); Charles S. Sydnor, *The Development of Southern Sectionalism, 1819–1848* (1948); Ralph A. Wooster, *Politicians, Planters, and Plain Folk* (1975); Ralph A. Wooster, *The People in Power* (1969); Gavin Wright, *The Political Economy of the Cotton South* (1978); Bertram Wyatt-Brown, *Southern Honor* (1982).

Slaveholders and Nonslaveholders

Bennet H. Barrow, *Plantation Life in the Florida Parishes of Louisiana, as Reflected in the Diary of Bennet H. Barrow,* ed. Edwin Adams Davis (1943); Malcolm Bell, Jr., *Major Butler's Legacy: Five Generations of a Slaveholding Family* (1987); Ira Berlin, *Slaves Without Masters* (1974); Randolph B. Campbell, "Intermittent Slave Ownership: Texas as a Text Case," *Journal of Southern History,* 30, No. 1 (February 1985), 15–30; William J. Cooper, *The South and the Politics of Slavery, 1828–1856* (1978); Everett Dick, *The Dixie Frontier* (1948); Clement Eaton, *The Mind of the Old South* (1967); Drew Faust, *A Sacred Circle: The Dilemma of the Intellectual in the Old South* (1977); John Hope Franklin, *The Free Negro in North Carolina, 1790–1860* (1943); Luther P. Jackson, *Free Negro Labor and Property Holding in Virginia, 1830–1860* (1942); Michael P. Johnson and James L. Roark, *Black Masters* (1984); Frances Anne Kemble, *Journal of a Residence on a Georgia Plantation in 1838–1839* (1863); Robert Manson Myers, ed., *The Children of Pride* (1972); James Oakes, *The Ruling Race* (1982); Frank L. Owsley, *Plain Folk of the Old South* (1949); J. Mills Thornton III, *Politics and Power in a Slave Society: Alabama, 1800–1860* (1978).

Southern Women

Carol Bleser, *The Hammonds of Redcliffe* (1981); Jane Turner Censer, *North Carolina Planters and Their Children, 1800–1860* (1984); Catherine Clinton, *The Plantation Mistress* (1982); Elizabeth Fox-Genovese, *Within the Plantation Household* (1988); Jean E. Friedman, *The Enclosed Garden* (1985); Jacqueline Jones, *Labor of Love, Labor of Sorrow* (1985); Suzanne Lebsock, *Free Women of Petersburg* (1984); Elisabeth Muhlenfeld, *Mary Boykin Chesnut* (1981); Mary D. Robertson, ed., *Lucy Breckinridge of Grove Hill* (1979); Ann Firor Scott, *The Southern Lady* (1970); Deborah G. White, *Arn't I a Woman?* (1985); C. Vann Woodward and Elisabeth Muhlenfeld, eds., *The Private Mary Chesnut* (1985).

Conditions of Slavery

Kenneth F. Kiple and Virginia H. Kiple, "Black Tongue and Black Men," *Journal of Southern History*, XLIII (August 1977), 411–428; Ronald L. Lewis, *Coal, Iron, and Slaves* (1979); Richard G. Lowe and Randolph B. Campbell, "The Slave Breeding Hypothesis," *Journal of Southern History*, XLII (August 1976), 400–412; Willie Lee Rose, ed., *A Documentary History of Slavery in North America* (1976); Todd L. Savitt, *Medicine and Slavery* (1978); Kenneth M. Stampp, *The Peculiar Institution* (1956); Robert S. Starobin, *Industrial Slavery in the Old South* (1970).

Slave Culture and Resistance

Herbert Aptheker, *American Negro Slave Revolts* (1943); John W. Blassingame, *The Slave Community* (1979); Judith Wragg Chase, *Afro-American Art and Craft* (1971); Paul D. Escott, *Slavery Remembered: A Record of Twentieth-Century Slave Narratives* (1979); Eric Foner, ed., *Nat Turner* (1971); Eugene D. Genovese, *From Rebellion to Revolution* (1979); Eugene D. Genovese, *Roll, Jordan, Roll* (1974); Herbert G. Gutman, *The Black Family in Slavery and Freedom, 1750–1925* (1976); Vincent Harding, *There Is a River* (1981); Charles Joyner, *Down by the Riverside* (1984); Lawrence W. Levine, *Black Culture and Black Consciousness* (1977); Stephen B. Oates, *The Fires of Jubilee* (1975); Albert J. Raboteau, *Slave Religion* (1978); Robert S. Starobin, *Denmark Vesey* (1970); Sterling Stuckey, *Slave Culture* (1987).

Chapter 10: Slavery and the Growth of the South, 1800–1860

In 1844, English immigrant George Martin of Rochester, New York, a carpenter, fell ill at the age of thirty-three and suddenly had a sense of his own mortality. "A very few years hence and not one of us will be among the living," he wrote his brother in England. "You cannot imagine what the feeling is," he went on, "to think that you will die . . . in a foreign land far from your kindred and home, and no friendly hand to close your eyes." Eight years later, in 1852, George Martin's worst fears were realized. Save for his wife, Betsy, and their children, he died among strangers, away from kin and old friends.

George and Betsy Martin came to the United States in 1834 from an agricultural hamlet twenty-two miles from London. George thought New York harbor "the most beautiful that ever was seen." After two days of touring New York City, the Martins traveled by canal boat, railroad, and lake steamer to their new home on the north shore of Lake Ontario in Upper Canada. They moved permanently to Rochester in 1838, when George found work as a carpenter. Opportunities were good in Canada he wrote his father, but "there is more spirit of enterprise" in the United States.

11

DIVERSITY AND CONFLICT: PEOPLE AND COMMUNITIES, 1800–1860

When he died in 1852, George Martin left very little. His spare time and money had gone into building his own house in Rochester, but it was unfinished. His relatives in England paid $500 to complete it, so that his widow and children would have a place to live. In the last four years of his life, Martin had become openly intolerant of ethnic diversity; his neighbors and fellow workmen, the butt of his anger, did nothing to help his family after his death.

The United States had changed so much and so rapidly in the decades before George Martin's death that most Americans, like him, were newcomers and strangers where they lived and where they worked. The largest cities grew to enormous size and numbered diverse ethnic, religious, and racial populations in the hundreds of thousands. Millions of immigrants settled in the expanding nation, and countless new and old Americans moved internally as the nation stretched from ocean to ocean.

As the market economy and economic opportunity attracted immigrants and energized the native-born, the American people drew apart. Increasingly, they lived in towns and cities, where diversity became the rule. And the nature of community was changing in the United States. Civic and public institutions had to offer services, such as education, once provided by private families. The face of the city changed too. Opulent mansions existed within sight of notorious slums, and both wealth and poverty reached extremes unknown before in agrarian America.

Private space—the family—also experienced change. With the growth of commerce and industry, the home began to lose its function as a workplace. Especially among the middle and upper classes, the home became woman's domain, a haven from man's world. Working-class women found no such refuge. At the same time, birth control was more widely practiced and families were smaller.

To a great degree, many Americans were uncomfortable with the new direction of American life. Antipathy toward immigrants was common among native-born Americans, who feared competition for jobs. Some blacks fought unceasingly for equality, and many Indians tried unsuccessfully to resist forced removal. In a society growing ever more diverse and complex, conflict became common.

Although the United States remained an agricultural country, the traditional economy and society were yielding to the spreading influence of the market economy, urban growth, and immigration. This process of change continued through the rest of the nineteenth century, accelerating and intensifying in the last three decades. But the path that led to the great industrial, urban, pluralist society had begun before the Civil War.

Country Life

Communities and life within them changed significantly in the first half of the nineteenth century. Within a generation, many frontier settlements became sources, rather than recipients, of migration. Villages in western New York state had lured the sons and daughters of New England in the first two decades of the century. But in the 1820s and 1830s, young people moved from New York villages to the new frontier in the Old Northwest. Later, Ohio and Michigan towns and farms would send their young people farther west. Similarly, migrants from the Upper South went to Illinois and Ohio as people on the move farther south settled the Gulf states.

Although they lived in isolation on individual farms, farm families found a sense of community in the neighborhood and village. The farm village was the center of rural life. But rural social life was not limited to trips to the village; families gathered on each other's farms to do as a community what they could not do individually. Barnraising was among the activities that regularly brought people together. In preparation for the event, the farmer and an itinerant carpenter built a platform and cut beams, posts, and joists. When the neighbors arrived by buggy and wagon, they put together the sides and raised them into position. After the roof was up, everyone celebrated with a communal meal and perhaps with singing, dancing, and folk games. Similar gatherings took place at harvest time and on special occasions.

Women especially sought to counter rural isolation. Farm men had frequent opportunities to mix at general stores, markets, and taverns and in hunting and fishing. Some women, too, met at market, but more typically they came together at regular work and social gatherings: after-church dinners; sewing, quilting, and cornhusking bees; and preparations for marriages and baptisms. These were times to exchange experiences and thoughts, offer each other support, and swap letters, books, and news.

Traditional country bees had their town counterparts. Fredrika Bremer, a Swedish visitor to the United States, described a sewing bee in 1849 in Cambridge, Massachusetts, at which neighborhood women made clothes for "a family who had lost all their clothing by fire." Yet town bees were neither the all-day family affairs typical of the countryside nor held as often. Life was changing, and town dwellers purchased their goods at the store.

Increasingly, Americans were conscious of such changes. One response was an interest in utopian communities, which offered an antidote to the market economy and to the untamed growth of large

IMPORTANT EVENTS

1819	Indian "civilization act"
1823	Hartford Female Seminary established by Catharine and Mary Beecher
1824	President Monroe proposes removal of Indians
1827	*Freedom's Journal* first published
1830s –50s	Urban riots
1831	*Cherokee Nation* v. *Georgia*
1831–38	Trail of Tears

1835–42	Second Seminole War
1837	Boston employs paid policemen
1837–48	Horace Mann heads the Massachusetts board of education
1841–47	Brook Farm
1842	Knickerbocker baseball club formed
1845	Start of the Irish potato famine
1846–47	Mormon trek to the Great Salt Lake
1847–57	Peak period of immigration before the Civil War

urban communities and an opportunity to restore tradition and social cohesion. Whatever their particular philosophy, utopians sought order and regularity in their daily lives and a cooperative rather than a competitive environment.

The Shakers, who derived their name from the way they danced and swayed at worship services, were an early, lasting utopian experiment. Founder **Shakers** Ann Lee brought this offshoot of the English Quakers to America in 1774. Shakers believed that the end of the world was near and that sin entered the world through sexual intercourse. They regarded existing churches as too worldly and considered the Shaker family the instrument of salvation.

In 1787, the Shakers "gathered in" at New Lebanon, New York, to live, worship, and work communally. Other colonies soon followed. At its peak, between 1820 and 1860, the sect had about six thousand members living in twenty settlements in eight states. It was the largest and most permanent of the utopian experiments. Though economically conservative, the Shakers were social radicals. They abolished individual families, practiced celibacy, and pioneered new roles for women. Each colony

was one large family. The Shaker ministry was headed by a woman, Lucy Wright, during its period of greatest growth. Celibacy, however, led to the withering away of the communities.

The most successful communitarians were the Mormons. Organized by Joseph Smith in 1830 as the Church of Jesus Christ of Latter-day Saints, the **Mormon Community of Saints** church spread from its birthplace in New York and established communities dedicated to Christian cooperation. Fleeing persecution in Ohio, Illinois, and Missouri because of their claims of continuous divine revelation and their newly adopted practice of polygyny, the Mormons trekked across the continent in 1846 and 1847 to found a New Zion in the Great Salt Lake Valley. There, under Brigham Young, head of the Twelve Apostles (their governing body), they established a cohesive community of Saints—a heaven on earth. The Mormons created agricultural settlements and distributed land according to family size. An extensive irrigation system, constructed by men who contributed their labor according to the quantity of land they received and the amount of water they expected to use, transformed the arid

Shaker meetinghouse at Pleasant Hill, Kentucky, 1820, designed by Micajah Burnett. Marked by a simplicity and beauty of design, the meetinghouse exemplifies the Shaker sense of order. Their code of behavior required separate entrances for men and women. *Linda Butler.*

valley into a rich oasis. As the colony developed, the church elders came to control water, trade, industry, and even the territorial government of Utah.

Not all utopian communities were founded by religious groups. Robert Owen's New Harmony was a well-known, short-lived attempt to found a socialist utopia in Indiana. A wealthy Scottish industrialist, Owen established the cooperative community in 1825. According to his plan, its nine hundred members were to exchange their labor for goods at a communal store. Handicrafts (hat and boot making) flourished at New Harmony, but its textile mill, the economic base of the community, failed after Owen gave it to the community to run. By 1827, the experiment had ended.

More successful were the New Englanders who lived and worked at the Brook Farm cooperative in West Roxbury, Massachusetts. Inspired by the transcendental philosophy that the spiritual rises above

Brook Farm the worldly, its members rejected materialism and sought satisfaction in a rural communal life combining spirituality, work, and play. Though short-lived (1841–1847), Brook Farm played a significant part in the romantic movement in the United States. There Nathaniel Hawthorne, Ralph Waldo Emerson, and the editor of the *Dial* (the leading transcendentalist journal), Margaret Fuller, joined Henry David Thoreau, James Fenimore Cooper, and others in creating what is known today as the American Renaissance—the flowering of a national literature. In poetry and prose, these romanticists favored faith and emotion over reason. Rebelling against convention, both social and literary, they celebrated the American character and experience.

Utopian communities were a reaction against contemporary society; they attempted to recapture the cohesiveness of traditional agricultural and artisan life. Utopians resembled Puritan perfectionists: like the Separatists of seventeenth-century New England, they sought to start anew in their own colonies. Communal work and life offered alternatives to the market economy and urbanizing society.

City Life

Everywhere cities were growing, especially in the North. The transportation revolution and the expansion of commerce and manufacturing, fed by immigration and internal migration, caused the population of cities to rise geometrically. Between 1800 and 1860, the number of Americans increased from 5.3 million to 31.4 million. As the population expanded, the frontier receded, and small rural settlements became towns. In 1800, the nation had only 33 towns with 2,500 or more people and only 3 with more than 25,000. By 1860, 392 towns exceeded 2,500 in population, 35 had more than 25,000, and 9 exceeded 100,000 (see maps below and on page 200).

New York City became the nation's premier urban place. It grew from 60,500 in 1800 to 813,600 in 1860. That year, the combined population of New York City and Brooklyn exceeded 1 million. Many were just passing through; a majority would not stay ten years. Although contemporary bird's-eye views of New York depict an almost pastoral urban life, the city emitted energy and aromas that make twentieth-century cities seem sanitized in comparison. It was an immigrant port city, mostly Irish and German by the 1850s.

In the 1820s, New York City literally burst its boundaries. Up to that time, New Yorkers could still envision the city as a village, because in an hour's walk they could reach every corner. Mass transit,

New York City

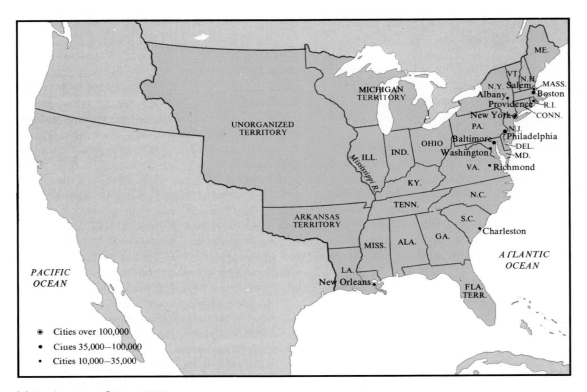

Major American Cities, 1820

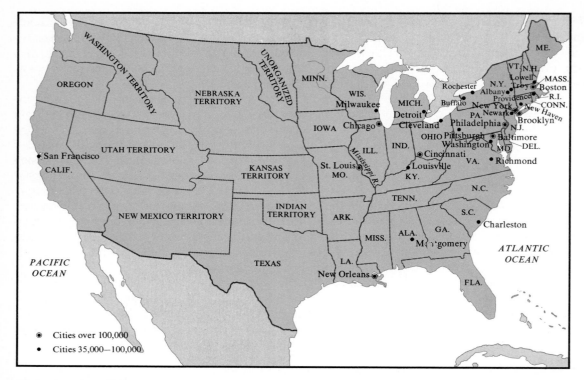

Major American Cities, 1860

however, made it possible for cities to expand. Horse-drawn buses appeared in New York in 1827, and the Harlem Railroad, completed in 1832, ran the length of Manhattan. By the 1850s, all big cities had horse-drawn streetcars.

By twentieth-century standards, early-nineteenth-century cities certainly were disorderly, unsafe, and unhealthy. Expansion occurred so rapidly that few cities could handle the problems it brought. For example, migrants from rural areas were used to relieving themselves and throwing refuse in any vacant area. In the city, such waste spread disease, created water pollution, and gave off obnoxious odors.

New York City solved part of the problem in the 1840s by abandoning wells in favor of reservoir water piped into buildings and outdoor fountains. In some districts, scavengers and refuse collectors carted away garbage and human waste, but in much of the city it just rotted on the ground. Only one-quarter of New York City's streets had sewers by 1857.

New York and other cities did not have the taxing power to raise the sums needed for providing adequate services to all. The best the city could do was to charge the cost of sewers, street paving, and water mains to adjoining property. Thus the spread of new services and basic sanitation depended on residents' ability or willingness to pay, and so those most in need of the services often got them last. Another solution was to depend on private companies. This worked well with gas service. Baltimore first chartered a private gas company in 1816; by the midcentury, all major cities were lit by private gas suppliers. The private sector, however, failed to supply the water that the cities needed. It did not have the capital to build adequate systems and laid pipe only in commercial and well-to-do residential areas, ignoring the poor. As cities grew, water service did not keep pace. Eventually, city governments had to take over.

Probably the most important and widespread service was the public school. In 1800, there were no public schools outside New England; by 1860,

     Chapter 11: Diversity and Conflict: People and Communities, 1800–1860

Horace Mann and Public Schools

every state had some public education. Massachusetts took the lead, especially under Horace Mann, secretary of the state board of education from 1837 to 1848. Under Mann, Massachusetts established a minimum school year of six months, increased the number of high schools, formalized the training of teachers, and emphasized secular subjects and applied skills rather than religious training.

Horace Mann's preaching on behalf of free state education changed schooling throughout the nation. "If we do not prepare children to become good citizens," Mann prophesied, "then our republic must go down to destruction." The abolition of ignorance, Mann claimed, would end misery, crime, and suffering. "The only sphere . . . left open for our patriotism," he wrote, "is the improvement of our children—not the few, but the many; not a part of them but all."

In laying the basis of free public schools, Mann also broadened the scope of education. Previously, education had focused on literacy, religious training, and discipline. Under Mann's leadership, the school curriculum became more secular and appropriate for future clerks, farmers, and workers. Students studied geography, American history, arithmetic, and science. Moral education was retained, but direct religious indoctrination was dropped.

Mann and others responded to the changes wrought by a market economy, urbanization, and immigration. The typical city dweller was a newcomer, whether from abroad or from a country district. The new public schools would take the nation of strangers and inculcate them with common values, ones shared by many native Protestant political leaders. The basic texts—McGuffey's readers—used the Protestant scriptures to teach children to accept their position in society. A good child, McGuffey taught, does not envy the rich: "it is God who makes some poor and others rich." Catholics, immigrants, blacks, and working-class people sought community control of the schools, but they lost out to state control under Protestant educators.

Theater was a major institution in American life. After a church, a theater was often the second public building constructed in town. Large cities

Leisure Activities

boasted of two or more theaters that catered to different classes. In New York City, the Park Theater enjoyed the patronage of the carriage trade, the Bowery drew the middle class, and the Chatham attracted workers. The opera house generally became the playhouse of the upper class. Yet some theater cut across class lines. Shakespeare was performed so often and appreciated so widely that even illiterate theatergoers knew his blank verse well.

Sports, like theater, increasingly involved city dwellers as spectators. Horse racing, boxing, pedestrianism (walking races), and, in the 1850s, baseball began to attract large urban crowds. Entertainment became part of specialized commerce; one purchased a ticket—to the theater, the circus, P. T. Barnum's American Museum, the racetrack, or the ballpark.

Sports and recreation mirrored the growing divisions in American urban society. They had become less spontaneous; increasingly they involved organization and formal rules and attracted spectators who paid an admission fee. Most important, they frequently depended on exclusive associations and clubs, which advanced the interests of particular groups. In 1829, for instance, a group of Ohio merchants organized the Cincinnati Angling Club, with a formal constitution and bylaws, and limited the membership to twenty-five. A group of Wall Street office workers formed the Knickerbocker Club in 1842 and in 1845 set down formal rules for the game of baseball. Their written rules were widely adopted and are the basis for the game of baseball today.

Middle- and upper-class Americans formed clubs and associations to avoid being strangers to each other and to defend themselves against the culture of other groups—immigrants,

City Life

migrants, blacks, and artisans— that spilled onto the city streets. Many native-born New Yorkers felt alienated in the city of their birth. Some neighborhoods seemed dominated by foreigners, others by artisans. In the 1840s, even a youth culture developed in the Bowery. Older New Yorkers feared the "Bowery boy," whose ostentatious dress and behavior seemed threatening. The Bowery boy had close-cut hair in the back and long locks in front, greased into a roll. He wore a broad-brimmed black hat, an open shirt collar, a black frock coat that reached below the knee, and as much jewelry as he could afford. His swaggering step, especially when he had a girl-friend on his arm, frightened many in the middle class.

Voluntary associations and clubs offered the middle and upper classes an opportunity to recapture the city. Some, like the Masonic order, provided comfort and leisure activity to middle- and upper-class members. The Masons offered everything that the bustling city did not: an elaborate hierarchy, an orderly system of deference between ranks, and harmony and shared values. Masons marched in the parades that were a regular part of the city's public and political life. Most parades contained artisan and working-class organizations, and the Masons believed that they, too, had a stake in the street life of the city.

Most working people spent much of their lives outdoors—they worked, paraded, and carried out ordinary social and domestic affairs on the streets. Young people courted there, neighbors argued, and ethnic groups defended their turf. Urban streets served as a political arena. Extreme behavior found a home there as well; mob violence took place in the streets.

Inequality, urbanization, and immigration gave rise to urban conflict as rioting and incidents of violence became frequent. The colonial tradition of crowd action, in which disfran-
Urban Riots chised people took to the streets, had diminished in the first three decades of the nineteenth century. In the 1830s and 1840s riots again became commonplace. "Gentlemen of property and standing," unnerved by antislavery proponents, sacked abolitionist and antislavery organizations. In the 1840s, "respectable" citizens waged war against the Mormons, driving them from Illinois and Missouri. Workers raged against new migrants to the cities and other symbols of the new industrial order. In Philadelphia, for instance, native-born workers fought Irish weavers in 1828, and whites and blacks rioted on the docks in 1834 and 1835. Philadelphia's disturbances climaxed in the riots of 1844, in which mostly Protestant skilled workers fought Irish Catholics. Other cities, too, became battlegrounds as

nativist riots peaked in the 1850s. By 1840, more than 125 people had died in urban riots, and by 1860 more than 1,000.

Public disorder spread in the city. To keep order and provide for public safety, Boston supplemented (1837) and New York replaced (1845) part-time watchmen and constables with uniformed policemen. Nonetheless, middle-class men and women did not venture out alone at night, and during the day they stayed clear of many city districts. And the influx of immigrants to the cities worsened social tensions by pitting people of different backgrounds against each other in the contest for jobs and housing. Ironically, in the midst of the dirt, the noise, the crime, and the conflict rose the opulent residences of the very rich.

Extremes of Wealth

Some observers, notably the young French visitor Alexis de Tocqueville, viewed the United States before the Civil War as a place of equality and opportunity. Tocqueville thought that American equality—the relative fluidity of the United States social order—derived from Americans' geographic mobility. Migration offered people opportunities to start anew regardless of where they came from or who they were. Prior wealth or family mattered little; a person could be known by deeds alone. Talent and hard work, many Americans believed, found their just reward in such an atmosphere.

But other observers recorded the rise of a new aristocracy based on wealth and power and the growth of class and ethnic divisions. Among those who disagreed with the egalitarian
Differences view of American life was *New*
in Wealth *York Sun* publisher Moses Yale Beach, author of twelve editions of *Wealth and Biography of the Wealthy Citizens of New York City*. In 1845, Beach listed 750 New Yorkers with assets of $100,000 or more. John Jacob Astor led the list of 19 millionaires with a fortune of $25 million. Ten years later, Beach reported that more than 1,000 New Yorkers were worth $100,000—28 of them were millionaires. Tocqueville himself, ever sensitive to the conflicting trends

The infamous Five Points section of New York City's Sixth Ward, probably the worst slum in pre–Civil War America. Immodestly dressed prostitutes cruise the streets or gaze from windows, while a pig roots for garbage in their midst. *The New-York Historical Society*.

in American life, had described the growth of an American aristocracy based on industrial wealth. The rich and well educated "come forward to exploit industries," Tocqueville wrote, and become "more and more like the administrators of a huge empire. . . . What is this if not an aristocracy?"

Wealth throughout the United States was becoming concentrated in the hands of a relatively small number of people. In New York City between 1828 and 1845, the wealthiest 4 percent of the city's population increased their holdings from an estimated 63 percent to 80 percent of all individual wealth. By 1860, the top 5 percent of American families owned more than half the nation's wealth.

A cloud of uncertainty hung over working men and women. Many were afraid that during hard times they would become unemployed. They feared the competition of immigrant and slave labor. They feared the insecurities and indignities of poverty, chronic illness, disability,

Urban Poverty

old age, widowhood, and desertion. And they had good reason.

Poverty and squalor stalked the urban working class as cities grew. Cities were notorious for the dilapidated districts where newly arrived immigrants, indigent free blacks, the working poor, and thieves, beggars, and prostitutes lived. New York City's Five Points, a few blocks from City Hall, became the worst slum in pre–Civil War America. The neighborhood was predominantly Irish and black. Ill suited to human habitation and lacking such amenities as running water and sewers, Five Points exemplified the worst of urban life.

A world apart from Five Points and the people of the streets lived the upper-class elite society of Philip Hone, one-time mayor of New York. Hone's diary, meticulously kept from 1826 until 1851, records the activities of an American aristocrat. On February 28, 1840, for instance, Hone attended a masked ball at the Fifth Avenue

The Urban Elite

mansion of Henry Breevoort, Jr., and Laura Carson Breevoort. The ball began at the fashionable hour of 10 P.M., and the five hundred ladies and gentlemen who filled the mansion wore costumes adorned with ermine and gold. Few balls attained such grandeur, but at one time or another similar parties were held in Boston, Philadelphia, Baltimore, and Charleston.

Much of this new wealth was inherited. For every John Jacob Astor who made millions in the western fur trade, there were ten who built additional wealth on money they had inherited or married. Many of the wealthiest bore the names of the colonial commercial elite—Beekman, Breevoort, Roosevelt, Van Rensselaer, and Whitney. These rich New Yorkers were not an idle class; they devoted energy to increasing their fortunes and power. Hardly a major canal, railroad, bank, or mill venture lacked the names and investments of the fashionable elite. Wealth begot wealth, and family ties through inheritance and marriage were essential in that world.

More modest in wealth, though hard working, were those in the expanding middle class. The growth and specialization of trade had rapidly increased their numbers, and they were a distinct part of the urban scene. The men were businessmen or professionals, the women homemakers. Middle-class families enjoyed the fruits of the advances in consumption—wool carpeting, fine wallpaper, rooms full of furniture, and indoor toilets. If they dreamed of entering Philip Hone's world, they were mindful to keep their distance from the working class and the poor.

The Middle Class

![arrow]

Women and the Family

Economic change and urbanization transformed women and families in the nineteenth century; work, class, gender roles, ethnicity, race, and religion created greater distinctions among families and among women. In the eighteenth century, the range of differences among females had been

much less; they had much more in common then.

Increasingly, women's and men's work grew apart. As manufacturing left the home, so did wage workers, except for those doing putting-out work. On farms, there was still an overlap between women's and men's work, but in the new stores and workshops tasks diverged. Specialization in business and production accompanied specialization in work tasks; men acquired new, narrow skills that they applied outside the home in set ways with purposefully designed tools and systems. Authority within the workplace, removed from the household, became formal and impersonal.

Some women shared these experiences for brief periods in their lives. New England farm daughters, who were the first textile mill workers, performed new, specialized tasks. The new urban department stores hired young women as clerks and cash runners. Many women worked for a few years as teachers. Paid employment represented a stage in their lives, a brief period before they left their paternal households and entered their marital households.

Working Women

Working-class women—the poor, widows, free blacks—worked for wages to support themselves and their families. Leaving their parental homes as early as the age of twelve or thirteen, they earned wages most of their lives. Unlike men and New England farm daughters, however, most of these women did not work in the new shops and factories. Instead, they worked as domestic servants in other women's homes and as laundresses, seamstresses, cooks, and boarding-house keepers. Few of the available occupations allowed them to support themselves or a family at an acceptable level. Widowhood, especially, was synonymous with poverty.

Increasingly, work took on greater gender meaning and segregation. Most women's work centered, as it always had, on the home. As the urban family lost its significance in the production of goods, household upkeep and child rearing grew in importance and required women's full-time attention. Education, religion, morality, domestic arts, and culture began to overshadow the economic functions of the family. These areas came to be known as the woman's sphere. For a woman to achieve mastery in these areas was to live up to the middle-class ideal of the cult of domesticity of the nineteenth century.

Middle-class American women and men placed great importance on the family. The role of the mother was to ensure the nation's future by rearing her children and providing the home with a spiritual and virtuous environment. The family was to be a moral institution characterized by selflessness and cooperation. Thus women were idealized as the embodiment of self-sacrificing republicanism. This view was in sharp contrast to the world outside the home—a sphere identified with men and dominated by base self-interest. In the rapidly changing world, in which single men and women left their parental homes and villages, and factories and stores replaced traditional means of production and distribution, the family was supposed to be a rock of stability and traditional values.

The domestic ideal limited the paying jobs available to middle-class women outside the home. Most paid work was viewed with disapproval because it conflicted with the ideal of domesticity. One occupation came to be recognized as consistent with the genteel female nature: teaching. In 1823, Catharine and Mary Beecher established the Hartford Female Seminary and added philosophy, history, and science to the traditional women's curriculum of domestic arts and religion. A decade later, Catharine Beecher campaigned to establish training seminaries for female teachers. Viewing formal education as an extension of women's nurturing role, Beecher had great success in spreading her message. By the 1850s, teaching was a popular vocation for women, and women—usually unmarried—constituted the majority of teachers in most cities. Their pay, however, was often half that of male teachers.

While woman's work outside the home remained limited, family size was shrinking due to a number of factors. Increasingly, small families were viewed as desirable. Children would have greater opportunities in smaller families; parents could pay more attention to them and would be better able to educate them and help them financially. Besides, contemporary marriage manuals stressed the harmful effects of too many births on a woman's health; too many children weakened women physically and overworked them as mothers.

Decline in the Birthrate

All this evidence suggests that wives and husbands made deliberate decisions to limit the size of families. In areas where farmland was relatively expensive, families were smaller than in other agricultural districts. It appears that parents who foresaw difficulty in setting up their children as independent farmers chose to have fewer children. Similarly, in urban areas, children, as consumers and not producers, were more an economic burden than an asset.

How did men and women limit the size of their families in the early nineteenth century? Many married later, thus shortening the period of childbearing. Women had their last child at a younger age, suggesting that family planning was becoming more common. Many couples used traditional forms of birth control, such as coitus interruptus, or withdrawal of the male before completion of the sexual act. Medical devices, however, were beginning to compete with this ancient practice. Cheap rubber condoms were widely adopted when they became available in the 1850s. Some couples used the rhythm method—attempting to confine intercourse to a woman's infertile periods. Knowledge of the "safe period," however, was uncertain even among physicians. Another method was abstinence, or less frequent sexual intercourse. For those desiring to terminate a pregnancy, surgical abortions became common after 1830. By 1860, however, twenty states had outlawed abortions.

Birth Control

Significantly, the birth-control methods that women themselves controlled—douching, the rhythm method, abstinence, and abortion—were the ones that were increasing in popularity. The new emphasis on women's domesticity encouraged women's autonomy in the home and gave women greater control over their own bodies. According to the cult of domesticity, the refinement and purity of women ruled the household, including the bedroom.

Sarah Ripley of Massachusetts, a young girl in the eighteenth century and an adult in the nineteenth, revealed in her diaries the changes that American society was experiencing. Daughter of a Greenfield

Sarah Ripley Stearns shopkeeper, Ripley had a privileged childhood. After completing boarding school, she returned home to work as an assistant in her father's store. In 1812, after a five-year courtship, she married Charles Stearns. "I have now . . . left the protection of my parents and given up the name I have always borne," she recorded in her diary. "May the grace of God enable me to fulfill . . . the great and important duties which now dissolve [fall] on me." Yet she missed the bustle of the shop, as she confessed in her diary.

Sarah Ripley Stearns's life was not a settled one; change was everywhere. During the six years after her marriage, she bore three children, moved three times, became a widow, and found an anchor in religion. For Stearns, as well as for other middle-class women, social interaction within the church made it possible to extend the bounds of ideal domesticity. For example, she and her neighbors sponsored a school society and a juvenile home. Such benevolent society work not only aided poor children, but also provided its female participants with experience in organizing and chairing meetings, raising funds, and cultivating an extended women's network.

Women who made the decision to stay single rejected both the cult of domesticity and the traditional pattern in which women moved as **Single Women** dependents from their fathers' households to those of their husbands. Louisa May Alcott (1832–1888), the author of *Little Women* (1868), sought independence and financial security for herself. Alcott worked as a seamstress, governess, teacher, housemaid, and author; her writing brought her success. "Things go smoothly, and I think I shall come out right," she wrote her father in 1856. "I like the independent feeling; and though not an easy life, it is a free one, and I enjoy it."

Louisa May Alcott had forsworn marriage, risking the opprobrium of being a spinster. She and other women took a path of independence that made them less dependent on men. They chose to pursue vocational identities outside of home and marriage, to explore their own personal growth, and to follow their own abilities. Given the difficulty women had in finding work that would allow them to be self-supporting, they undertook their independence at great risk. Nonetheless, there was a significant increase in single women in the first three quarters of the nineteenth century.

Independent white women helped establish new roles for women. They were responding to changes and opportunities offered by the market economy and expanding cities. Immigration, too, had an enormous impact in remaking American life; ethnic and religious diversity became a hallmark of nineteenth-century America.

Immigrant Lives in America

No less than gender, ethnic and religious differences divided Americans. In numbers alone, immigrants drastically altered the United States. Five million strangers came to the states between 1820 and 1860. They came from all continents, though Europeans made up the vast majority. The peak period of pre–Civil War immigration was from 1847 through 1857; in those eleven years, 3.3 million immigrants entered the United States, 1.3 million from Ireland and 1.1 million from the German states. By 1860, 15 percent of the white population was foreign-born.

This massive migration had been set in motion decades earlier. In Europe, around the turn of the nineteenth century, the Napoleonic wars had begun one of the greatest population shifts in history; it was to last more than a hundred years. War, revolution, famine, industrialization, and religious persecution led many Europeans to leave home. The United States beckoned, offering them economic opportunity and religious freedom.

American institutions, both public and private, actively recruited European emigrants. Western states lured potential settlers in the interest of promoting their economies. In the **Promotion of Immigration** 1850s, for instance, Wisconsin appointed a commissioner of emigration, who advertised the state's advantages in American and European newspapers. Wisconsin also opened an office in New York and hired European agents to compete with other states and with firms for immigrants' attention.

Large construction projects and mines needed strong young laborers. Textile mills and cities attracted young women workers. Europeans' awareness of the United States heightened as employers, states, and shipping companies advertised the opportunities to be found across the Atlantic. With regularly scheduled sailing ships plying the ocean after 1848, the cost of transatlantic travel was within easy reach of millions of Europeans.

So they came, enduring the hardships of travel and of settling in a strange land. The journey was difficult. The average transatlantic crossing took six weeks; in bad weather it could take three months. Disease spread unchecked among people huddled together like cattle in steerage. More than seventeen thousand immigrants, mostly Irish, died from "ship fever" in 1847. On disembarking, immigrants became fair game for the con artists and swindlers who worked the docks. In 1855, in response to the immigrants' plight, New York State's commissioners of emigration established Castle Garden as an immigrant center. There immigrants were somewhat sheltered from fraud. Authorized transportation companies maintained offices in the large rotunda and assisted immigrants with their travel plans.

Most immigrants, like the George Martin family, gravitated toward cities, since only a minority had farming experience or the means to purchase land and equipment. Many stayed in New York itself. By 1855, 52 percent of the city's 623,000 inhabitants were immigrants. Boston, an important entry port for the Irish, took on a European tone. Throughout the 1850s, the city was about 35 percent foreign-born, and the Irish constituted more than two-thirds of this segment. In the South, too, major cities had large immigrant populations. In 1860, New Orleans was 44 percent foreign-born, Savannah 33 percent, and the border city of St. Louis, 61 percent. On the West Coast, San Francisco had a foreign-born majority.

Some immigrants, however, did settle in rural areas. In particular, German, Dutch, and Scandinavian farmers gravitated toward the Midwest. Greater percentages of Scandinavians and Netherlanders took up farming than did other nationalities; both groups came mostly as religious dissenters and migrated in family units. The Dutch, under such leaders as Albertus C. Van Raalte, fled persecution in their native land to establish new and more pious communities—Holland and Zeeland, Michigan, among them.

Not all immigrants found success in the United States; hundreds of thousands returned to their homelands with disappointment. Before the potato blight hit Ireland, recruiters lured many Irish to swing picks and shovels on American canals and railroads and to work in construction. Among them was Michael Gaugin, who had the misfortune to arrive in New York City during the financial panic of 1837. Gaugin, for thirteen years an assistant engineer in the construction of a Dublin canal, had been attracted to the United States by the promise that "he should soon become a wealthy man." Within two months of arriving in the United States, Gaugin became a pauper. In August 1837, he declared that he was "now without means for the support of himself and his family . . . and has already suffered great deprivation since he arrived in this country; and is now soliciting means to enable him to return with his family home to Ireland."

Immigrant Disenchantment

Such experiences did not deter Irish men and women from coming to the United States. Ireland was the most densely populated European country and among the most impoverished. From 1815 on, small harvests prompted a steady stream of Irish to emigrate to America. Then, in 1845 and 1846, potatoes—the basic Irish food—rotted in the fields. From 1845 to 1849, death from starvation, malnutrition, and typhus spread. In all, 1 million died and about 1.5 million fled.

Irish Immigrants

In the 1840s and 1850s, a total of 1.7 million Irish men and women entered the United States. At the peak of Irish immigration, from 1847 to 1854, 1.2 million came. Between 1820 and 1854, except for two years, the Irish constituted the largest single group of immigrants annually. By the end of the century, there were more Irish in the United States than in Ireland.

The new Irish immigrants differed greatly from those who had left Ireland to settle in the American colonies. In the eighteenth century, the Scotch-Irish had predominated, and their journey had involved moving from one part of the British Empire to another. The nineteenth-century Roman Catholic Irish travelers to America, however, moved from colonial Ireland to an independent republic, and the political and religious differences made their cultural adaptation that much more difficult. In comparison with the Scotch-Irish, the new immigrants from Ireland tended to be younger, increasingly female, and mostly from the rural provinces.

In the urban areas, where they clustered in poverty, most Irish immigrants met growing anti-immigrant, anti-Catholic sentiment. "No Irish Need Apply" signs were common. During the colonial period, white Protestant settlers had feared "popery" as a system of tyranny and had discriminated against the few Catholics in America. After the Revolution, anti-Catholicism receded; but in the 1830s, the trend reversed, and anti-Catholicism appeared wherever the Irish did. Attacks on the papacy and the church circulated widely in the form of libelous texts like *The Awful Disclosures of Maria Monk* (1836), which alleged sexual orgies among priests and nuns. Nowhere was anti-Catholicism more open and nasty than in Boston, though such sentiments were widespread.

Anti-Catholicism

The native-born who embraced anti-Catholicism were motivated largely by anxiety. They feared that a militant Roman church would subvert American society, that unskilled Irish workers would displace American craftsmen, and that the slums inhabited in part by the Irish were undermining the nation's values. Every American problem from immorality and alcoholism to poverty and economic upheaval was blamed on immigrant Irish Catholics. Friction increased as Irish-American men fought back by entering politics.

In 1854, Germans replaced the Irish as the single largest group of arriving immigrants. Potato blight also sent many from the German states to the United States in the 1840s, but other hardships contributed to the steady stream. Many came from areas where small landholdings made it hard to eke out a living and to pass on land to their sons. Others were craftsmen displaced by the industrial revolution. These refugees were joined by middle-class Germans who emigrated to the United States after the abortive revolution of 1848.

German Immigrants

Unlike the Irish, who tended to congregate in towns and cities, Germans settled everywhere. Many came on cotton boats, disembarked at New Orleans, and traveled up the Mississippi. In the South, they became peddlers and merchants; in the North and West, they worked as farmers, urban laborers, and businessmen. They, more than the Irish, tended to migrate in families and groups; that tendency helped maintain German culture.

Native-born Americans treated immigrants from the German states with greater respect than they did the Irish. Stereotypes of Germans often included such terms as "industrious," "hard-working," "self-reliant," and "intelligent." Many believed that Germans would "harmonize" better with American culture. This contrasted with the almost universal dislike of the Irish, as most Americans seemed to accept the negative British stereotypes of Irish people.

Nonetheless, Germans, too, met antiforeign attitudes. More than half the German immigrants were Catholic, and their Sabbath practices differed from those of Protestants. On Sundays, many urban German immigrant families gathered at beer gardens to eat and drink beer, to dance, sing, and listen to band music, and sometimes to play cards. Protestants were outraged by such violations of the Lord's Day.

These immigrants' persistence in using the German language and their different religious beliefs set them apart. Besides the Catholic majority, a significant number of German immigrants were Jewish. And even the German Protestants—mostly Lutherans—founded their own churches and often educated their children in German-language schools. Not all Germans, however, were religious. The failure of the revolution in 1848 had sent to the United States a whole generation of liberals and freethinkers, some of whom were socialists, communists, and anarchists.

Not all immigrants came to the United States voluntarily. After the annexation of Texas, the Mexican War, and the Gadsden Purchase (which in 1853 added southern Arizona and New Mexico), many Hispanics found themselves in the United States, some against their will, because of boundary changes. The development of Texas apart from Mexico after 1836, the discovery of gold in Califor-

Hispanics

nia, and the extension of railroads broke the linkage of the Southwest with Mexico and reoriented the Southwest toward the United States.

Hispanic culture continued in the region, but Anglos and European immigrants seized economic and political power. Anglos overwhelmed Hispanics in Texas and in California. Hispanics retained their language, Roman Catholic religion, and community through newspapers, mutual aid societies, and the church, but they lost power and status. In Nueces County, Texas, at the time of the Texas Revolution (1836), Mexicans held all the land; twenty years later, they had lost it all. Although many Hispanics had fought for Texas independence, the settlers coming in tended to treat Mexicans as inferior people. Within two generations, Hispanics became second-class citizens and strangers in their own land.

For immigrants, conflict centered on the desire to be part of American society, although in some cases, on their own terms. Once here, they claimed their right to a fair economic and political share. Indians, however, like Hispanics in the Southwest, defended what they conceived of as prior rights. Their land, their religion, their way of life came under constant attack because they were most often viewed as obstacles to expansion and economic growth.

Indian Resistance and Removal

The clash between Indians and the larger society was inherited from the colonial past. Population growth, westward expansion, the transportation revolution, and market orientation underlay the designs and demands on Indian land. Under the Constitution, the federal government had the responsibility for dealing with Indians. For better or worse, there had to be a federal Indian policy. As territorial expansion came at the Indians' expense, it was for the worse. The result was removal of the great Indian nations to lands west of the Mississippi.

While the population of other groups increased by leaps and bounds, the Indian population shrank.

War, forced removal, disease, and malnutrition reduced many tribes by half. In the 1830s alone, more than half of the Pawnees, Omahas, Ottoes, Missouris, and Kansas died.

As the colonial powers in North America had done, the United States treated Indian tribes as sovereign nations, until Congress ended the practice in 1871. In its relations with tribal leaders, the government followed the ritual of international protocol. Indian chiefs and delegations visiting Washington were received with the appropriate pomp and ceremony. Agreements between a tribe and the United States were signed, sealed, and ratified like any international pact.

In practice, however, Indian sovereignty was a fiction. Protocol seemed to acknowledge independence and mutual respect, but treaty negotiations exposed the sham. Essentially, treaty making was a process used by the American government to acquire Indian land. Differences in power made it less than the bargaining of two equal nations. Treaties were often made between victors and vanquished. In a context of coercion, many old treaties gave way to new ones, in which the Indians ceded their traditional holdings in return for different lands in the West.

The War of 1812 snuffed out whatever realistic hopes eastern Indian leaders might have had of resisting American expansion by warfare. Armed resistance persisted and was bloody on both sides. Resistance, however, only delayed the inevitable. The Shawnee chiefs Prophet and Tecumseh led the most significant movement against the United States, but after Tecumseh's death, Prophet failed to sustain the movement.

The experiences of Prophet and other Shawnees were typical of the wanderings of an uprooted people. When the Shawnees gave up 17 million acres in Ohio in the 1795 Treaty of Greenville, they scattered to Indiana and eastern Missouri. After the War of 1812, Prophet's Indiana group withdrew to Canada. In 1822, other Shawnees sought Mexican protection and moved from Missouri to present-day eastern Texas. With the United States government promoting western removal, Prophet returned from Canada and led a group to the new Shawnee lands established in eastern Kansas in 1825. When Missouri achieved statehood, the Shawnees there

Prophet

were forced to move to Kansas. In the 1830s, Shawnees in Ohio were removed to Kansas and were joined there by others expelled from Texas. By 1854, Kansas was open to white settlement, and the Shawnees had to cede back seven-eighths of their land.

Removal had a profound impact on all Shawnees. The men had to give up their traditional role as providers; their methods of hunting and knowledge of woodland animals were useless in prairie Kansas. Shawnee women played a greater role as providers as grains became the tribe's dietary staple. Yet, remarkably, the Shawnees preserved their language and culture in the face of these drastic changes.

In the 1820s, under pressure, Indians in Ohio, southern Indiana and Illinois, southwestern Michigan, most of Missouri, central Alabama, and southern Mississippi ceded their lands.

Indian Policy They gave up nearly 200 million acres for pennies an acre. But white settlers wanted more Indian land, and they wanted the Indians to assimilate. One instrument that served both purposes was the Indian agency system, which monopolized trade with Indians in a designated locality and paid out the rations, supplies, and annuities that Indians received in exchange for abandoning their land. With time, the tribes became dependent on these government payments.

Ever since the early days of European colonization, assimilation of Native Americans through education and Christianity had been an important goal. It found renewed interest as the United States expanded westward. In 1819, under missionary lobbying, Congress appropriated $10,000 annually for the "civilization of the tribes adjoining the frontier settlements." This "civilization act" was a means to teach Indians to live like white settlers. Protestant missionaries administered the "civilizing fund" and established mission schools.

To settlers eyeing Indian land, assimilation through education was too slow a process, and Indians themselves questioned the instruction. Some tribes found the missionary message repugnant. The Creek nation permitted the schools only after being assured that there would be no preaching. Zealous missionaries, however, violated the agreement, preaching to the Creeks and their black slaves. In response, a band of Creeks sacked the school.

It became apparent in the 1820s that neither economic dependency, nor education, nor even Christianity, could force Indians to cede much more land voluntarily to meet the demands of expansionists. Attention focused on Cherokees, Creeks, Choctaws, Chickasaws, and Seminoles in the South because much of their land remained intact after the War of 1812 and because they aggressively resisted white encroachment.

In his last annual message in December 1824, President James Monroe suggested to Congress that all Indians be moved beyond the Mississippi River.

Indian Removal Three days later, the president sent a special message to Congress proposing removal. The southern tribes unanimously rejected Monroe's offer.

Pressure from Georgia had prompted Monroe's policy. Most Cherokees and some Creeks lived in northwestern Georgia, and in the 1820s, the state accused the federal government of not fulfilling its 1802 promise to remove the Indians in return for the state's renunciation of its claim to western lands. Georgia sought complete expulsion and was satisfied neither by Monroe's removal messages nor by further Creek cessions. In 1826, the Creek nation, under federal pressure, ceded all but a small strip of its Georgia acreage. Governor George M. Troup, however, wanted all the Creek land. When President John Quincy Adams threatened to send the army to protect the Indians' claims, Troup countered with his own threats. Only the removal of the Georgia Creeks to the West in 1826 prevented a clash between the state and the federal government.

If "civilizing" Indians was the goal, none met that test better than the Cherokees. During the Cherokee renaissance from 1819 to 1829, the tribe became economically self-

Cherokees sufficient and politically self-governing. The twelve thousand to fifteen thousand adult Cherokees in the 1820s came to think of themselves as a nation. During that decade, they created a formal government with a bicameral legislature, elected representatives, a

French genre painter Alfred Boisseau recorded the passage of the Choctaw through Louisiana from Mississippi to Indian Territory. With dignity they made the forced march. *New Orleans Museum of Art, gift of Mr. William E. Groves.*

court system, a salaried bureaucracy, and a written constitution, modeled after that of the United States. Cherokee land laws, however, differed from United States law. The tribe owned all land, and complex provisions covered the sale of land (forbidden to outsiders). Nonetheless, the Cherokees assimilated American cultural patterns well. By 1833, they held fifteen hundred black slaves, whose legal status under the Cherokees was the same as that of slaves held by southern whites. Moreover, missionaries had been so successful that the Cherokees could be considered a Christian community.

Although the tribe developed a way of life similar to that of an American state, it failed to win acceptance from southerners. Georgia pressed the Cherokees to sell the 7,200 square miles of land they held in the state. Most Cherokees, however, preferred to stay where they were. Then, in 1828 and 1829, Georgia annulled the Cherokee constitution, extended the state's sovereignty over the tribe, and ordered the tribal lands seized.

In 1829, the Cherokees turned to the federal courts to defend their treaty with the United States and prevent Georgia's seizure of their land. In *Cherokee Nation* v. *Georgia* (1831), Chief Justice John Marshall ruled that under the federal Constitution an Indian tribe was neither a foreign nation nor a state and therefore had no standing in federal courts. Nonetheless, said Marshall, the Indians had an unquestioned right to their lands; they could lose title only by voluntarily giving it up. A year later, in *Worcester* v. *Georgia*, Marshall defined the Cherokee position more clearly. The Indian nation was, he declared, a distinct political community in which "the laws of Georgia can have no force" and into which Georgians could not enter without permission or treaty privilege.

President Andrew Jackson had little sympathy for the Indians and ignored the Supreme Court's ruling. Keen to open up new lands for settlement, he was determined to remove the Cherokees at all

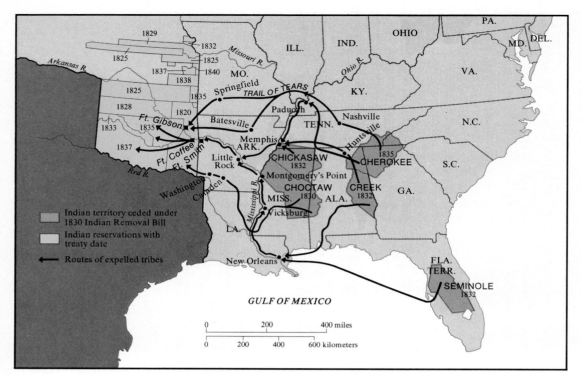

Removal of the Indians from the South, 1820–1840 *Source: Acknowledgment is due to Martin Gilbert and George Weidenfeld and Nicholson Limited for permission to reproduce the map above, taken from American History Atlas.*

costs. In the Removal Act of 1830, Congress provided Jackson with the funds he needed to negotiate new treaties and resettle the resistant tribes west of the Mississippi.

The infamous Trail of Tears (see map) had begun. The Choctaws in the winter of 1831 and 1832 were the first to go. Soon other tribes joined the trail: the Creeks in Alabama in 1836 and the Chickasaws in 1837.

Trail of Tears

The Cherokees, having fought through the courts to stay, found themselves divided. Some recognized the hopelessness of further resistance and accepted removal as the only chance to preserve their civilization. The leaders of this minority signed a treaty in 1835, in which they agreed to exchange their southern home for western land. But when the time for evacuation came in 1838, most Cherokees refused to move. President Martin Van Buren then sent federal troops to round up the Indians. About twenty thousand Cherokees were evicted, held in detention camps, and marched to present-day Oklahoma under military escort. Nearly one-quarter died of disease and exhaustion on the Trail of Tears. When the forced march to the West ended, the Indians had traded about 100 million acres of land east of the Mississippi for 32 million acres west of the river, plus $68 million. Only a few scattered remnants of the tribes, among them the Seminoles, remained in the East and South.

What was the impact of removal? Change had been thrust on these tribes so suddenly and drastically that they had to transform much of their culture. In the West, they occupied an alien environment; they had no generational ties with the new land. Many could not be at peace with the land or get used to the strange animals and plants they found there. Many Indians became dependent on government payments for survival. Finally, removal brought new internal conflicts that would ultimately shatter Cherokee tribal unity.

In the Southeast, a small band of Seminoles suc-

Chapter 11: Diversity and Conflict: People and Communities, 1800–1860

cessfully resisted removal and remained in Florida. In 1832, in the Treaty of Payne's Landing, some of the Seminole tribal leaders agreed

Second Seminole War

to relocate to the West within three years. A minority under Osceola refused to vacate their homes, and in 1835 they initiated a fierce guerrilla war against the federal troops. The army in turn waged an unsuccessful effort to exterminate the Seminoles. In 1842, the United States finally abandoned the Seminole War; it had cost the lives of fifteen hundred soldiers and $20 million. Most of Osceola's followers agreed to move west to Indian Territory in 1858, but many Seminoles remained in the Florida Everglades, prideful that they had successfully resisted conquest.

A complex set of attitudes drove whites to force Indian removal. Most merely wanted Indian lands. Others were aware of the injustice but believed that Indians must inevitably give way to white settlement. Some, like John Quincy Adams, believed that the only way to preserve Indian civilization was to remove the tribes and establish a buffer zone between Indians and whites. Others hoped to "civilize" Indians and assimilate them slowly into American culture. Whatever the source of white behavior in the United States, the outcome was the devastation of Native American peoples and their cultures.

Another minority experienced insecurity and struggled for recognition and legal rights. Like most Indians, they, too, were involuntarily a part of American society. Unlike Indians, however, they wished to be fully a part of the American people.

Free People of Color

No black person was safe, wrote the abolitionist and former slave Frederick Douglass after the Philadelphia riot of 1849. "His life—his property—and all that he holds dear are in the hands of a mob." Between 1832 and 1849, five major antiblack riots occurred in Philadelphia. Mobs stormed black dwellings and churches, set them on fire, and killed the people inside. The mobs intimidating free blacks could be made up of slave hunters seeking runaways but were as likely to kidnap a free black as a slave. Or they could represent civil authority. In 1829 in Cincinnati, frightened by the growing black population, officials drove as many as two thousand blacks from the city by enforcing a law requiring cash bonds to ensure good behavior. Free blacks faced insecurity daily.

Under federal law, the blacks' position was uncertain. The Fifth Amendment specified that "no person shall . . . be deprived of life, liberty, or property, without due process of law." Yet the racist theory of the eighteenth century that defined a republic as being only for whites seemed to exclude blacks. This exclusion was reflected in early federal legislation. In 1790, naturalization was limited to white aliens, and in 1792, the militia was limited to white male citizens. Moreover, Congress approved the admission to the Union of states whose constitutions restricted the rights of blacks. After the admission of Missouri in 1821, every new state admitted until the Civil War banned blacks from voting. When the Oregon and New Mexico territories were organized, public land grants were limited to whites.

In the North, blacks faced legal restrictions nearly everywhere. Only in Massachusetts, New Hampshire, Vermont, and Maine could blacks vote on an equal basis with whites throughout the pre–Civil War period. Blacks gained the right to vote in Rhode Island in 1842, but they had lost it earlier in Pennsylvania and Connecticut. No state but Massachusetts permitted blacks to serve on juries; four midwestern states and California did not allow blacks to testify against whites. In Oregon, blacks could not own real estate, make contracts, or sue in court.

Legal status was important, but practice and custom were crucial. Although Ohio repealed its law barring black testimony against whites in 1849, the

Exclusion and Segregation of Blacks

exclusion persisted as custom in southern Ohio counties. Throughout the North, free people of color were either excluded from or segregated in public places. Hotels and restaurants were closed to blacks, as were most theaters and churches. Probably no practice inflicted greater injury than the general discrimination in hiring. Counting houses, retail stores, and factories refused to hire black men except as janitors and general handymen. New England textile mills hired only whites.

Free people of color faced especially severe legal and social barriers in the southern slave states, where their presence was often viewed as an incentive to insurrection. Indeed, southern states responded to fear of mass rebellion by tightening the restrictions on free blacks and forcing them to leave small towns and interior counties. After the Nat Turner rebellion in 1831, the position of free blacks weakened further. Within five years, nearly all the southern states prohibited the freeing of any slaves without legislative or court approval; by the 1850s, Texas, Mississippi, and Georgia had banned manumission altogether.

Southern Free Blacks

To restrict free blacks and encourage them to migrate north, southern states adopted elaborate "black codes." Blacks, who provided most of the South's skilled labor, encountered licensing requirements and bans restricting work opportunities. Virginia and Georgia banned black river captains and pilots. Some states forbade blacks to assemble without a license; some prohibited blacks from being taught to read and write. In the late 1830s, when these black codes were first enforced with vigor, free blacks increasingly moved northward, even though northern states discouraged the migration.

In spite of these obstacles, the free black population rose dramatically in the first part of the nineteenth century, from 108,000 in 1800 to almost 500,000 in 1860. Nearly half lived in the North, occasionally in rural settlements, but more often in cities like Philadelphia, New York, and Cincinnati. Baltimore had the largest free black community; sizable free black populations also existed in New Orleans, Charleston, and Mobile.

The ranks of free blacks were constantly increased by ex-slaves. Some, like Frederick Douglass and Harriet Tubman, were fugitives. Tubman, a slave on the eastern shore of Maryland, escaped to Philadelphia in 1849, when her master's death led to rumors that she would be sold out of the state. Within the next two years, she returned twice to free her two children, her sister, her mother, and her brother and his family. Other slaves were voluntarily freed by their owners. Some, like a Virginia planter named Sanders, who settled his slaves as freedmen in Michigan, sought to cleanse their souls by freeing their slaves in their wills. Some freed elderly slaves after a lifetime of service rather than support them in old age.

In response to their oppression, free blacks founded strong, independent self-help societies to meet their unique needs and fight against their less-than-equal status. In every African-American community, people organized churches, fraternal and benevolent associations, literary societies, and schools. Many leaders believed that these mutual aid societies would encourage thrift, industry, and morality and thus equip the members to improve their lot. No amount of effort could counteract white prejudice, however.

Founding of Black Institutions

The network of societies among urban free black men and women provided a base for black protest. From 1830 to 1835, and thereafter irregularly, free blacks held national conventions, with delegates drawn from city and state organizations. Under the leadership of the small black middle class, which included a Philadelphia sail manufacturer, James Forten, and an orator, the Reverend Henry Highland Garnet, the convention movement served as a forum to attack slavery and agitate for equal rights. The struggle was joined by new militant black newspapers, such as *Freedom's Journal* (1827) and the *Weekly Advocate* (1837).

Although ending slavery and attaining equal rights remained at the top of blacks' agenda, the mood of free blacks began to shift in the late 1840s and 1850s. Some were swept up in a tide of black nationalism that stressed racial solidarity and unity, self-help, and a growing interest in Africa. Before this time, efforts to send African-Americans "back to Africa" had originated with whites seeking to solve racial problems by ridding the United States of blacks. But in the 1850s, blacks held emigrationist conventions of their own under the leadership of Henry Bibb and Martin Delany. With the coming of the Civil War and emancipation, however, all but a few African-Americans lost interest in migrating to Africa.

Black Nationalism

The United States in 1860 was a far more diverse and turbulent society than it had been in 1800. The market economy, urbanization, and immigration had altered the ways people lived and worked. Economic growth created new jobs, but inequality increased everywhere. Cities housed both ostentatious wealth and abject poverty, and violence and disorder became commonplace.

In the midst of these changes, middle-class families sought to insulate their homes from the competition of the market economy. Many women found fulfillment in the domestic ideal, although others found it confining. More and more, middle-class urban women became associated with nurturing roles, first in homes and schools, then in churches and reform societies. Working-class women had more modest goals: escaping poverty and winning respect.

In Europe, famine and religious and political oppression sent millions of people across the Atlantic. They were drawn to the United States by the promise of jobs and political and religious toleration. Yet most found the going rough, even though conditions were often better than in their native lands. In the process, they changed the profile of the American people. Competition and diversity bred intolerance and prejudice. None were to feel that more painfully than Indians and free blacks, who were most often made to feel like aliens in their own land.

As the economy and society changed, conflict became commonplace and entered the public arena. The utopian communities, conflict over public space, the backlash against immigrants, black protest, and Indian resistance were manifestations of the divisions in America. But conflict took other forms as well, as in the widespread reform movements that came to characterize American life from the 1820s through the 1850s. Through reform and politics, many Americans sought to harness and control the forces of change.

Suggestions for Further Reading

Rural and Utopian Communities

Leonard J. Arrington and Davis Bitton, *The Mormon Experience: A History of the Latterday Saints* (1979); Priscilla J. Brewer, *Shaker Communities, Shaker Lives* (1986); Don H. Doyle, *The Social Order of a Frontier Community: Jacksonville, Illinois, 1825–1870* (1978); Laurence Foster, *Religion and Sexuality: Three American Communal Experiments of the Nineteenth Century* (1981); Steven Hahn and Jonathan Prude, eds., *The Countryside in the Age of Capitalist Transformation* (1985); Joan M. Jensen, *Loosening the Bonds: Mid-Atlantic Farm Women, 1750–1850* (1986); Wallace Stegner, *The Gathering of Zion: The Story of the Mormon Trail* (1964); Anthony F. C. Wallace, *Rockdale: The Growth of an American Village in the Early Industrial Revolution* (1978).

Urban Communities and Inequality

Melvin A. Adelman, *A Sporting Time: New York City and the Rise of Modern Athletics, 1820–1870* (1986); Stuart M. Blumin, *The Urban Threshold: Growth and Change in a Nineteenth-Century American Community* (1976); Lawrence A. Cremin, *American Education: The National Experience, 1783–1876* (1980); Susan G. Davis, *Parades and Power: Street Theater in Nineteenth-Century Philadelphia* (1986); Karen Halttunen, *Confidence Men and Painted Women: A Study of Middle-Class Culture in America, 1830–1870* (1982); Carl Kaestle, *Pillars of the Republic: Common Schools and American Society, 1780–1860* (1982); Gary B. Nash, "The Social Evolution of Preindustrial American Cities, 1700–1820: Reflections and New Directions," *Journal of Urban History,* 13 (February 1987), 115–145; Edward Pessen, *Riches, Class and Power Before the Civil War* (1973); Christine Stansell, *City of Women: Sex and Class in New York, 1789–1860* (1986); Stephen Thernstrom, *Poverty and Progress: Social Mobility in a Nineteenth Century City* (1964); Alexis de Tocqueville, *Democracy in America,* 2 vols. (1835–1840); Richard C. Wade, *The Urban Frontier: 1790–1830* (1957).

Women and the Family

Lee Virginia Chambers-Schiller, *Liberty, A Better Husband: Single Women in America: The Generations of 1780–1840* (1984); Nancy F. Cott, *The Bonds of Womanhood: "Woman's Sphere" in New England, 1780–1835* (1977); Carl N. Degler, *At Odds: Women and the Family in America from the Revolution to the Present* (1980); Hasia R. Diner, *Erin's Daughters in America: Irish Immigrant Women in the Nineteenth Century* (1983); Linda Gordon, *Woman's Body, Woman's Rights: A Social History of Birth Control in America* (1976); Suzanne Lebsock, *The Free Women of Petersburg: Status and Culture in a Southern Town, 1784–1860* (1984); Mary P. Ryan, *Cradle of the Middle Class: The Family in Oneida County, New York, 1790–1865* (1981); Kathryn Kish Sklar, *Catharine Beecher: A Study in American Domesticity* (1973); Robert V. Wells, *Revolutions in Americans' Lives* (1982); Barbara Welter, "The Cult of True Womanhood, 1820–1860," *American Quarterly,* 18 (Summer 1966), 151–174.

Immigrants

Rowland Berthoff, *British Immigrants in Industrial America* (1953); Kathleen Neils Conzen, *Immigrant Milwaukee: 1836–1860* (1976); Arnoldo De León, *The Tejano Community, 1836–1900* (1982); Charlotte Erickson, *Invisible Immigrants* (1972); Robert Ernst, *Immigrant Life in New York City, 1825–1863* (1949); John Gjerde, *From Peasants to Farmers: The Migration from Balestrand, Norway, to the Upper Middle West* (1985); Oscar Handlin, *Boston's Immigrants: A Study in Acculturation,* rev. ed. (1959); Walter D. Kamphoefner, *The Westfalians: From Germany to Missouri* (1987); Dale T. Knobel, *Paddy and the Republic: Ethnicity and Nationality in Antebellum America* (1986); Philip Taylor, *The Distant Magnet: European Emigration to the United States of America* (1971); Mark Wyman, *Immigrants in the Valley: Irish, Germans, and Americans in the Upper Mississippi, 1830–1860* (1984).

Indians

Robert F. Berkhofer, Jr., *The White Man's Indian* (1978); Grant Foreman, *Indian Removal: The Emigration of the Five Civilized Tribes of Indians,* rev. ed. (1953); Michael D. Green, *The Politics of Indian Removal: Creek Government and Society in Crisis* (1982); Florette Henri, *The Southern Indians and Benjamin Hawkins, 1796–1816* (1986); Charles Hudson, *The Southeastern Indians* (1976); William G. McLoughlin, *Cherokee Renascence in the New Republic* (1986); Francis P. Prucha, *The Great Father: The United States Government and the American Indians,* 2 vols. (1984); Francis P. Prucha, *American Indian Policy in the Formative Years* (1967); Herman J. Viola, *Thomas L. McKenney: Architect of America's Early Indian Policy: 1816–1830* (1974); J. Leitch Wright, Jr., *Creeks and Seminoles: The Destruction and Regeneration of the Muscogulge People* (1986).

Free People of Color

Ira Berlin, *Slaves Without Masters: The Free Negro in the Antebellum South* (1974); Leonard P. Curry, *The Free Black in Urban America, 1800–1850* (1981); Luther Porter Jackson, *Free Negro Labor and Property Holding in Virginia, 1830–1860* (1942); David M. Katzman, *Before the Ghetto: Black Detroit in the Nineteenth Century* (1973); Rudolph M. Lapp, *Blacks in Gold Rush California* (1977); Leon Litwack, *North of Slavery: The Negro in the Free States, 1790–1860* (1961); Gary B. Nash, *Forging Freedom: The Formation of Philadelphia's Black Community, 1720–1840* (1988); Julie Winch, *Philadelphia's Black Elite: Activism, Accommodation, and the Struggle for Autonomy, 1787–1848* (1988); Arthur Zilversmit, *The First Emancipation: The Abolition of Slavery in the North* (1967).

The Tappan brothers, Arthur and Lewis, amassed a fortune from the War of 1812 through the 1840s. Born in Massachusetts in the 1780s, they were merchants and investors whose businesses included dry goods, textile mills, an importing house, the *New York Journal of Commerce,* and the Mercantile Agency (the first commercial-credit rating agency in the United States). Their wealth grew with the expansion of the market economy.

They shunned the balls and elaborate dinners of the urban elite. Instead, they lived by their mother's Calvinist tenet that this world was preparation for the next. Both believed that they would have to submit their accounts to God and that "luxurious living" would count against them. Nonetheless, they spent large sums, contributing generously to evangelical churches and missions, to temperance and antigambling societies, to Bible printing, to the Antimasons, and to antislavery.

The lives of the Tappan brothers and many other reformers were changed by one overriding issue: antislavery. Drawn to abolitionism by their religious concerns and the work of William Lloyd Garrison, Arthur and Lewis Tappan became the leaders of religious antislavery. They deservedly earned their reputations as being among the most committed reformers in the period from the 1820s through the 1850s, which became known as an age of reform.

12

REFORM, POLITICS, AND EXPANSION, 1824–1844

Reform was, in part, a response to the unsettling effect of the enormous transformation that the United States experienced after the War of 1812. Population growth, immigration, internal migration, urbanization, the market economy, growing inequality, loosening family and community ties, the advancing frontier, and territorial expansion all contributed to the remaking of the country. Many people felt that they were no longer masters of their own fate and that the changes in society were undermining traditional values.

Religious reformers such as the Tappans sought to find order or to impose it on a society in which economic change and discord had reached a crescendo. Prompted by the evangelical ardor of the Second Great Awakening and convinced of their moral rectitude, they crusaded for individual improvement. Everywhere benevolent and reform societies multiplied. Reform soon took on a much more active role than benevolent work and became an instrument for restoring discipline and order in a changing society. Women were prominent in the reform movement, and the role of women in public life became an issue in itself.

As reform organizations spread, they turned to the government as an effective instrument of social and economic change. Temperance, institutional reform, and most notably Antimasonry and abolition brought new voters into politics. The line between social reform and politics was not always distinguishable. Opponents were no less concerned with social problems. What set them apart from reformers was their skepticism about human perfectibility and their distrust of institutions and power. To them, coercion was the greater evil. They sought to reverse, not shape, change.

Two issues in particular provided the bridge between reform and politics: the brief Antimasonry frenzy and the crusade for immediate emancipation. Antimasons organized the first third-party movement, but abolition eventually overrode other concerns. No single issue evoked the depth of passion that slavery did. Territorial expansion in the 1840s and 1850s made it even more politically explosive.

Political leaders attempted to grapple with change. In the late 1820s, the opponents of religious reform found a champion in Andrew Jackson and a home in the Democratic party. Yet the Jacksonians saw themselves as reformers; they responded to change by attempting to foster individualism and to restore restraint in government. They fought special privileges and the Second Bank of the United States with the same vigor as the Tappan brothers opposed sin. President Jackson sought to restrain the national government, believing that a strong federal government restricted individual freedom by favoring one group over another. In response, reformers rallied around the new Whig party, which became the vehicle for humanitarian reform. Democrats and Whigs competed in the second party system, which was marked by strong organizations, intensely loyal followings, religious and ethnic differences, and popular bases among the electorate.

During the economically prosperous 1840s, both parties eagerly promoted westward expansion to further their goals. The idea of expansion from coast to coast seemed to Americans to be the inevitable manifest destiny of the United States. In the 1850s and 1860s, the politics of territorial expansion and the antislavery movement collided, with explosive results.

From Revival to Reform

The prime motivating force behind organized benevolence and reform was probably religion. Starting in the late 1790s, a tremendous religious revival, the Second Great Awakening, galvanized Protestants, especially women. The Awakening began in small villages in the East, intensified after the War of 1812, then spread over western New York, and continued to grow through the late 1840s. Under its influence, Christians tried to right the wrongs of the world.

Revivals were the lifeblood of evangelical Christianity, and they drew converts to a religion of the heart, not the head. In 1821, Charles G. Finney, "the father of modern revivalism," experienced a soul-shaking conversion, which, he said, brought him "a retainer from the Lord Jesus Christ to plead his cause." In everyday language, he told his audiences that "God has made man a moral free agent." In other words, evil was avoidable; Christians were not doomed by original sin. Hence anyone could achieve salvation. The Second Great Awakening also raised people's hopes for the Second Coming of the Christian messiah and the establishment of the Kingdom of God on earth. Revivalists set out to speed the Second Coming by creating a heaven on earth. They joined the forces of good and light—reform—to combat those of evil and darkness.

Regardless of theology, all shared a belief in individual improvement and self-reliance as moving forces. In this way, the Second Great Awakening bred reform, and evangelical Protestants became missionaries for both religious and secular salvation. Wherever they preached, voluntary reform societies arose. Evangelists organized an association for each issue—temperance, education, Sabbath

Second Great Awakening

1790s–1840s	Second Great Awakening		**1832–33**	Nullification crisis
1820s	Model penitentiaries		**1836**	Republic of Texas established Specie Circular Van Buren elected president
1825	House of Representatives elects John Quincy Adams president		**1837**	Financial panic
1826	American Society for the Promotion of Temperance founded		**1838–39**	U.S.–Canada border tensions
			1839–43	Hard times
1828	Tariff of Abominations Jackson elected president		**1840**	Whigs under Harrison win presidency
1830	Webster-Hayne debate		**1841**	Tyler assumes the presidency Oregon fever
1830s–40s	Second party system			
1831	*Liberator* begins publication First national Antimason Convention		**1844**	Polk elected president
			1845	Texas admitted to the Union
1832	Veto of Second Bank of the United States recharter Jackson re-elected		**1848**	Woman's Rights Convention, Seneca Falls, New York
			1851	Maine adopts Prohibition

observance, and later antislavery; collectively, these groups formed a national web of benevolent and moral reform societies.

Women were the earliest converts, and they tended to sustain the Second Great Awakening. When Finney led daytime prayer meetings in Rochester, New York, for instance, pious middle-class women visited families while the men were away at work. Slowly, they brought those families and husbands into the churches and under the influence of reform. Women more than men tended to feel personally responsible for the increasingly secular orientation of the expanding market economy. Many women felt guilty for neglecting their religious duties, and the emotionally charged conversion experience set them on the right path again.

Role of Women

Beyond conversion, the great impact of the Second Great Awakening was the spread of women's involvement in benevolent activities to ameliorate the growing social ills. In the cities, women responded both to inner voices and to the growing inequality, turbulence, and strains of change around them. By the turn of the nineteenth century, most of the expanding cities had women's benevolent societies to help needy women and orphans. Increasingly, the spread of poverty and vice that accompanied urbanization touched the hearts of women, especially those caught up in the fervor of revival.

An 1830 exposé of prostitution in New York City revealed the diverging concerns and responses of reform men and women, on the one hand, and political organizations, on the other hand, and demonstrated the convergence of urban problems, revival, and reform. In response to the report on how prostitution had taken hold in New York City, prominent male leaders united to defend the city's good name. Women, on the other hand, moved by the plight of "fallen women" and supported by the Tappans, responded by forming two new societies concerned with prostitutes and prostitution.

The Female Moral Reform Society led the crusade against prostitution. During the 1830s, the New York–based association expanded its activities and geographical scope as the American Female Moral Reform Society. By 1840, it had 555 affiliated societies across the nation. These women not only fought the evils of prostitution but also assisted poor women and orphans and entered the political sphere. In New York State in the 1840s, the movement fostered public morality by successfully crusading for criminal sanctions against seducers and prostitutes.

As the pace of social change increased in the 1830s and 1840s, so did efforts at reform. In western New York and Ohio, Finney's preaching was a catalyst to reform. Western New York experienced such continuous and heated waves of revivalism that it became known as the "burned-over" district. The opening of the Erie Canal and the migration of New Englanders carried the reform ferment farther westward. There, revivalist institutions—Ohio's Lane Seminary and Oberlin College were the most famous—sent committed graduates out into the world to spread the gospel of reform. Evangelists also organized grassroots political movements. In the late 1830s and 1840s, they rallied around the Whig party in an attempt to use government as an instrument of reform.

Temperance and Asylums

One of the most successful reform efforts was the campaign against the consumption of alcohol. As a group, American men liked to drink alcoholic spirits. They gathered in public houses, saloons, and rural inns to gossip, discuss politics, play cards, escape work and home pressures, and drink. And though respectable women did not drink in public, many regularly tippled alcohol-based patent medicines promoted as cure-alls.

This certificate of membership in a temperance society, for display, announced the virtues of the household to all visitors. In this illustration, the man signs with the support of wife and child; demon rum and its accompanying evils were banished from this home. *Library of Congress.*

Why then did temperance become such a vital issue? And why were women especially active in the movement? Like all reform, temperance had a strong religious base. To evangelicals, the selling of whiskey was a chronic symbol of Sabbath violation, for workers commonly labored six days a week, then spent Sunday at the public house drinking and socializing. Alcohol was seen as a destroyer of families. Temperance literature was laced with domestic images—abandoned wives, prodigal sons, drunken fathers. Outside the home, the habit of drinking could not be tolerated in the new world of the factory. Employers complained that drinkers took "St. Monday" as a holiday to recover from Sunday.

Demon rum thus became a major target of reformers. As the movement gained momentum, they shifted their emphasis from temperate use of spirits to voluntary abstinence and finally to legally enforced prohibition. The American Society for the Promotion of Temperance, organ-

Temperance Societies

ized in 1826 to urge drinkers to sign a pledge of abstinence, shortly afterward became a pressure group for state prohibition legislation. Within a few years, more than a million people had taken the pledge. By the 1840s, the annual per capita consumption of alcohol had fallen from more than five gallons to less than two gallons. Furthermore, many northern states, beginning with Maine in 1851, prohibited the manufacture and sale of alcohol except for medicinal purposes.

Another aspect of the temperance movement was the attack on gambling. People gathered at taverns to drink and gamble, and reformers believed that both drinking and gambling undermined independence and self-reliance. Of special concern in the nineteenth century was the spread of lotteries.

Lotteries had been brought by English colonists to the New World at the turn of the eighteenth century. In the New World, lotteries were a useful way of selling extremely valuable property in an age when few single buyers could raise the large purchase price. Hundreds of small investors could participate in a lottery for the prize, enabling a merchant to dispose of inventory or a homeowner to sell a house. Local governments used lotteries to ease the tax burden by raising money for capital improvements. The Continental Congress had tried to use a grand lottery to raise $1.5 million to wage revolutionary war against England, but it failed to raise the anticipated revenue.

Lotteries

Lotteries became a target of reform, and between 1830 and 1860 every state in the Union banned them. To some, lotteries were among such vices as slavery and alcohol. Other opponents objected to the abuses inherent in the common pattern of states delegating their lottery powers to private sponsors. For instance, a Pennsylvania investigation (1831) revealed that a state-authorized lottery to raise $27,000 a year for internal improvement generated enormous profits for the lottery company. On $5-million annual sales, the state received its $27,000 and the sponsors $800,000.

Another important part of the reform impulse was the development of new social institutions. The age of reform prompted the establishment and construction of asylums and other institutions to house prisoners, the insane and ill, orphans, delinquent children, and the poor. Many believed that such institutions would provide the victims of instability and turbulence with an environment of order, stability, and discipline, thus giving them an opportunity to become self-reliant and responsible.

The penitentiary movement exemplified this approach. In the 1820s, New York and Pennsylvania offered similar models for reforming criminals. Both systems sought to remove criminals from evil societal and individual influences and to place them in an ordered, disciplined regimen. It was commonly believed that criminals came from unstable families, in which lack of discipline and restraint led to vice and drink. Idleness was believed to be both a symptom and a cause of individual corruption and crime; thus the clock governed a prisoner's day, and idleness was banished.

Penitentiaries

Similar approaches were employed by societies promoting other asylums, from insane asylums and hospitals to orphanages and houses of refuge. Doctors linked mental illness to the stress and strain of contemporary urban life. The prescribed treatment was to remove individuals from families and society, to isolate them among strangers. The asylum would impose discipline and order on patients, but in a humane fashion. In response to organized reform societies, states began to erect asylums for the insane in the 1830s. They built them in tranquil, rural settings, away from the turbulent cities.

Antimasonry

Far more intense than the asylum movement, though of shorter duration, was the crusade against Masonry. The Antimasonry movement arose overnight in 1826, in the burned-over district of western New York, and it stirred political activity before virtually disappearing in the 1830s. Like other reforms, it sought political change. Indeed, it became more of a political than a reform movement. It created the first third-party movement and brought new white voters into politics at a time when male suffrage was being extended. Antimasons sought to liberate society from what they considered a secret, powerful, antirepublican fraternity. The political arena quickly absorbed Antimasonry, and its short life illustrates the close tie between politics and reform from the 1820s through the 1840s.

Antimasonry was a reaction to Freemasonry, which had come to the United States from England in the eighteenth century. Freemasonry was a secret middle- and upper-class fraternity that attracted the sons of the Enlightenment with its emphasis on individual belief in a deity (as opposed to organized religion) and on brotherhood (as opposed to one church). In the early nineteenth century, Freemasonry attracted many commercial and political leaders.

Opponents of Masonry charged that the order's secrecy was antidemocratic and antirepublican, as was its elite membership and its use of regalia and such terms as "knights" and "priests." As church leaders took up the moral crusade against Masonry, evangelicals labeled the order satanic. Antimasons argued that Masonry threatened the family because it encouraged men to spend time at the lodges, neglecting the family for alcohol and ribald entertainments.

The Morgan affair was the catalyst for Antimasonry as an organized movement. In 1826, William Morgan, a disillusioned Mason, wrote an exposé of Masonry, to which his **Morgan** printer David Miller added a **Affair** scathing attack on the order. On September 12, 1826, before the book appeared, a group of Masons abducted Morgan outside the jail in Canandaigua, New York. It was widely believed that some Masons murdered Morgan, whose body was never found.

What energized the Antimasonry crusade was that its worst fears about Masonry as a conspiracy seemed to be confirmed. Many of the officeholders in western New York, especially prosecutors, were Masons, and they appeared to obstruct the investigation of Morgan's abduction. Public outcry and opposing political factions pressed for justice, and a series of notorious trials from 1827 through 1831 led many to suspect a conspiracy. The cover-up became as much the issue as distrust of Masonry itself, and the movement spilled over to other states. In the Morgan affair, Antimason claims of a secret conspiracy seemed to be justified.

As a moral crusade, however, Antimasonry crossed over into politics almost immediately. The issue itself was a political one because the perceived obstruction of justice was a signal element. Antimasonry attracted the lower and middle classes, pitting them against higher-status Masons and exploiting the general public's distrust and envy of local political leaders.

Unwittingly, the Masons stoked the fires of Antimasonry. The silence of the order seemed to condone the murder of Morgan, and the construction of monumental lodges advertised their determination to remain a public force. When editors who were Masons ignored the crusade against Masonry, the Antimasons started their own newspapers. The struggle aroused further public interest in politics.

Antimasonry spread as a popular movement and introduced the convention system in place of caucuses for choosing political candidates. To defend public morality and the republic, **Convention** the Antimasons held conventions **System** in 1827. The following year the conventions supported the National Republican candidate and opposed Andrew Jackson because he was a Mason. In 1831, the Antimasons held the first national political convention in Baltimore and a year later nominated in convention William Wirt as their presidential candidate. Thus the Antimasons became one rallying point for those opposed to President Jackson.

By the mid-1830s, Antimasonry had lost force as a moral and political movement. A single-issue party, it declined along with Freemasonry. Yet the movement left its mark on the politics of the era. It inspired and welcomed wider participation in the political process. Moreover, the revivalist and reform impulses in movements such as Antimasonry further stimulated or awakened disagreements about values and ideology—disagreements that were reinforced by conflicts over wealth, religion, and status. These differences helped polarize politics and shape parties as organizations to express those differences. The Antimasons contributed specifically to party development by pioneering the convention system and by stimulating grassroots involvement.

Abolitionism and the Women's Movement

Sparked by territorial expansion, the issue of slavery eventually became so overpowering that it consumed all other reforms. Passions grew so heated that they threatened the nation itself. Above all else, those who advocated immediate emancipation saw slavery as a moral issue—evidence of the sinfulness of the American nation.

Before the 1830s few whites advocated the immediate abolition of slavery. Some, most notably the Quakers who had led the first antislavery movement in the eighteenth century, hoped that moral suasion would convince slaveholders to free their chattels. Others favored gradual abolition coupled with the resettling of blacks in Africa. The American Colonization Society had been founded in 1816 with this in mind.

Only free blacks pushed for an immediate end to slavery. By 1830, there were at least fifty black abolitionist societies in major African-American communities. These associations **Black** assisted fugitive slaves, attacked **Antislavery** slavery at every turn, and re- **Movement** minded the nation that its mission as defined in the Declaration of Independence remained unfulfilled. A free black press helped to spread their word. Black abolitionists Frederick Douglass, Sojourner Truth, and Harriet Tubman then joined forces with white reformers in the American Anti-Slavery Society. These crusaders also stirred European support for their militant and unrelenting campaign.

In the 1830s, a small minority of white reformers made immediate, complete, and uncompensated emancipation their primary commitment. William Lloyd Garrison, though clearly not **William** the most representative, was the **Lloyd** most prominent and uncom- **Garrison** promising immediatist. Recruited to the abolitionist cause in 1828 by Benjamin Lundy, a gradualist, Garrison broke with the moderate abolitionists in 1831. That year, contributions from the Tappans and others helped him

publish the first issue of the *Liberator,* which was to be his major weapon against slavery for thirty-five years. "I am in earnest—I will not equivocate—I will not excuse—I will not retreat a single inch—*and I will be heard*," he wrote in the first issue. Garrison's refusal to work with anyone who even indirectly delayed emancipation left him isolated from most people opposed to slavery. Still, through sheer force of rhetoric, Garrison helped to make antislavery a national issue.

Most benevolent workers and reformers kept their distance from the immediatists. Many thought the intensity of the immediatist approach was unchristian. They shared the view **Immediatists** that slavery was a sin, but they believed that it had to be eradicated slowly. If they moved too fast, if they attacked sinners too harshly or conflicted too much with community customs and beliefs, they would destroy the harmony and order that they sought to bring in benevolent and reform work.

Immediatists' greatest recruitment successes came from defending their own constitutional and natural rights, not those of slaves. Wherever they went, immediatists found their civil rights in danger, especially their right of free speech. For example, Southern mobs seized and destroyed much of the propaganda mailed by the American Anti-Slavery Society (organized by the immediatists in 1833), and the state of South Carolina (with the approval of the United States postmaster general) intercepted and burned abolitionist literature that entered the state. In 1837, Elijah P. Lovejoy, an abolitionist editor, was murdered in Alton, Illinois, by a mob that had come to sack his office.

The opposition saw many dangers in abolitionism. At a rally in Boston's Faneuil Hall in August 1835, former Federalist Harrison Gray Otis portrayed abolitionists as subversives. He attacked Garrison's American Anti-Slavery Society as a "dangerous association," a "revolutionary society" with branches in every community in the nation. Otis predicted that the abolitionists would soon turn to politics, causing unpredictable "trouble and calamity." "What will become of the union?" Otis asked. Others believed that the immediatist attack on colonization undermined the best solution. Keeping blacks in America, they believed, eventually would foment slave rebellions and lead to racial amalgamation.

Another civil rights confrontation developed in Congress. Exercising their constitutional right to petition Congress, abolitionists mounted a campaign to abolish slavery and the **Gag Rule** slave trade in the District of Columbia. But Congress responded in 1836 by adopting the so-called gag rule, which automatically tabled abolitionist petitions, effectively preventing debate on them. In a dramatic defense of the right of petition, former President John Quincy Adams, then a Massachusetts representative, took to the floor repeatedly to defy the detested gag rule and eventually succeeded in getting it repealed in 1844. Public outrage at the gag rule, censorship of the mails, and Lovejoy's murder broadened the base of antislavery support in the North.

Frustration with the federal government also fed northern support for antislavery. By and large, politicians and government officials sought to avoid the question of slavery. The Missouri Compromise of 1820 had been an effort to make debate on the slave or free status of new states unnecessary. Censorship of the mails and the gag rule were similar attempts to keep the issue out of the political arena. Yet the more national leaders, especially Democrats, sought to avoid the matter, the more they hardened the resolve of the antislavery forces.

The effect of the unlawful, violent, and obstructionist tactics used by proslavery advocates and anti-immediatists cannot be overestimated. This opposition, however, helped unify the abolition movement by forcing the factions to work together for mutual defense. At the outset, antislavery was not a unified movement. Its adherents were divided over Garrison's emphasis on "moral suasion" versus the more practical political approach of James G. Birney, the Liberty party's candidate for president in 1844 (see page 235). They disagreed about the place of free black people in American society and split on other reforms, especially the rights of women.

Women had less success when it came to their own position in society. At its inception, the American Anti-Slavery Society resembled most other benevolent societies; it was gender segregated, with

Women Abolitionists women in a subordinate role. Slowly over time, the pattern changed. By the late 1840s, women abolitionists were breaking free of the domestic sphere—many of them were single women—and becoming genuine colleagues to men in the movement. Men like Garrison came to accept their women colleagues' contributions in providing moral direction. Lydia Child, Maria Chapman, and Lucretia Mott all joined the American Anti-Slavery Society executive committee; Child edited its official organ, the *National Anti-Slavery Standard,* from 1841 to 1843, and Chapman co-edited it from 1844 until 1848.

Negative reaction to the growing involvement of women in reform movements led some women to re-examine their position in society. In 1837, two antislavery lecturers, Angelina and Sarah Grimké, became particular objects of controversy. Natives of South Carolina, they moved north in the 1820s to speak and write against slavery. They were received with hostility for speaking before mixed groups of men and women. This reaction turned the Grimkés' attention from slavery to women's condition. The two attacked the concept of "subordination to man," insisting that men and women had the "same rights and same duties." Sarah Grimké's *Letters on the Condition of Women and the Equality of the Sexes* (1838) and her sister's *Letters to Catharine E. Beecher* (1838) were the opening volleys in the war against the legal and social inequality of women.

Unlike other reform movements, which succeeded in building a broad base of individual and organizational support, the movement for women's **Women's Rights** rights was limited. Some men joined the ranks, notably Garrison and ex-slave Frederick Douglass, but most actively opposed the movement. The Woman's Rights Convention at Seneca Falls, New York, in 1848, led by Elizabeth Cady Stanton and Lucretia Mott, issued a much-published indictment of the injustices suffered by women. The Seneca Falls Declaration of 1848 paralleled the 1776 Declaration of Independence, asserting as a self-evident truth "that all men and women are created equal." The document listed the record of male tyranny against women and the inequalities

Leisure in America, **1850**

SHARED EXPERIENCE

Between 1800 and 1860, the American population increased from 5.3 to 31.4 million. Large cities grew even larger, villages became small towns, and the frontier and the countryside sprouted countless new settlements. People were able to interact more frequently with other people, and recreational activities often became social events, shared with participants beyond the family circle.

New York City, by 1810 the most populous city in the United States, provided the ultimate example of a burgeoning metropolis, growing from 60,500 people in 1800 to 813,600 in 1860. A view of Central Park painted by Winslow Homer during the winter of 1859–1860 provides a small glimpse of that crowded city. Recreational space had become limited, and skating time with the family had to be enjoyed in the midst of scores of like-minded neighbors.

Capitalizing on the growing concentrations of would-be patrons, entrepreneurs organized concerts in cities throughout the young nation. Jenny Lind (1820–1887) was perhaps the most famous singer of the

nineteenth century, renowned for the purity of her voice and its remarkable range. Already extremely successful on European opera stages, Lind toured the United States between 1850 and 1852, visiting 137 cities in all. P. T. Barnum, the circus impresario who managed the initial leg of her tour, publicized his star so well that thousands of enthusiasts surrounded her New York hotel within minutes of her arrival in America. Currier and Ives produced a lithograph of her first appearance on an American stage, at Castle Garden in Manhattan's Battery Park.

Lind's fame was so complete that her name was affixed to various items of clothing and furniture, and china-head dolls mimicking her hair style and facial features were widely manufactured. She also inspired larger tokens of devotion; one San Francisco fan, disappointed when Lind failed to include his town on her itinerary, consoled himself by building a theater and naming it after her.

Out-of-the-way locations were not without their own concert performances. Itinerant musicians, particularly in the South, traveled from farm to farm, playing for small family groups. Eastman Johnson's 1866 painting *Fiddling His Way* evokes a sense of the quiet pleasure such visits provided. Fiddles and banjos provided much of the music in rural America. Banjos, in particular, produced a music that was uniquely American in sound and style, a hybrid of African and European influences.

First page: Winslow Homer, *Skating in Central Park, 1859–60,* 1860. Previous page, top: Currier and Ives lithograph, *First Appearance of Jenny Lind in America,* 1850. Previous page, bottom: Jenny Lind doll, ca. 1860. This page, right: Banjo, ca. 1840–1860. Below: Eastman Johnson, *Fiddling His Way,* 1866.

Despite the rapidly changing demographics, life in the country and on the frontier was frequently still an isolated one. To combat the loneliness of widely separated homesteads, families gathered for harvestings, barn-raisings, and communal bees. At a quilting bee, for instance, young and old came together to socialize, gossip, eat, court, and, incidentally, make quilts. Ordinarily, the top of the quilt had already been pieced together; the partygoers helped stitch the top to the cotton batting and backing underneath.

Although the quilt shown in the painting below looks like a simple affair, others displayed far more elaborate designs, often patterned after natural forms. See the detail of a design known as "peony and prairie flower," at right. The lovely meticulousness of this work suggests that the quiet domestic pleasures had not gone out of style in American homes.

Above: Detail of quilt, stitched by Parnel R. Grumley, 1847. Below: Artist unknown, *Quilting Party*, 1854.

and indignities that women suffered from the government and the law. If women had the vote, these early advocates of women's rights argued, they could protect themselves and realize their potential as moral and spiritual leaders.

Jacksonianism and the Beginnings of Modern Party Politics

The distinction between reform and politics eroded in the 1820s and after as reform pushed its way into politics. Politicians no less than reformers sought to control and direct change in an expanding, urbanizing, market-oriented nation. They, too, shared the unease caused by change and the corruption in private and public life. After a brief flirtation with single-party politics after the War of 1812, the United States entered a period of intense and heated political competition. By the 1830s, politics had become the great nineteenth-century American pastime.

The election of 1824, in which John Quincy Adams and Andrew Jackson faced each other for the first time, heralded the start of a new, more open political system. From 1800 through 1820, the presidential system in which a congressional caucus chose Jefferson, Madison, and Monroe as the Republican nominees had worked well. Such a system restricted voter involvement, but this was not a drawback at first, because in 1800 the people in only five of sixteen states voted for their presidential electors. (In most, state legislators designated the electors.) By 1824, however, eighteen out of twenty-four states chose electors by popular vote.

End of the Caucus System

In 1824, the caucus chose William H. Crawford, secretary of the treasury. But other Republicans, encouraged by the opportunity to appeal directly to the voters in most states, challenged Crawford as sectional candidates. Secretary of State John Quincy Adams drew support from New England, and westerners backed Speaker of the House Henry Clay of Kentucky. Secretary of War John C. Calhoun looked to the South for support and hoped to win Pennsylvania as well. Andrew Jackson, a popular military hero whose political views were unknown, was nominated by resolution of the Tennessee legislature and had the most widespread support. By boycotting the deliberations of the caucus and by attacking it as being undemocratic, these men and their supporters ended the role of the congressional caucus in nominating presidents.

Andrew Jackson led in both electoral and popular votes in the four-way presidential election of 1824, but no one received a majority in the electoral college (see map, page 226). Adams finished second, and Crawford and Clay trailed far behind. (Calhoun dropped out of the race before the election.) Under the Constitution, the selection of a president in such circumstances fell to the House of Representatives, on the basis of one vote to a state. Clay, who had received the fewest votes, was dropped; Crawford, a stroke victim, never received serious consideration. Clay, as Speaker of the House and leader of the Ohio Valley states, backed Adams, who received the votes of thirteen out of twenty-four state delegations. Clay became secretary of state in the Adams administration—the traditional steppingstone to the presidency. With angry Jacksonians denouncing the arrangement as a "corrupt bargain" in which the office had been stolen from the front runner, the Republican party divided. The Adams wing emerged as the National Republicans, and the Jacksonians became the Democratic-Republicans (shortened to Democrats).

The Jacksonians immediately laid plans for 1828, while John Quincy Adams took the oath as the sixth president. Adams proposed a strong nationalist policy emphasizing Henry Clay's American System of protective tariffs, a national bank, and internal improvements. Adams believed that the federal government should take an activist role not only in the economy, but also in education, science, and the arts; accordingly, he proposed a national university in Washington, D.C.

Brilliant as a diplomat and secretary of state, Adams was inept as president. He underestimated the lingering effects of the Panic of 1819 and the ensuing bitter opposition to a national bank and protective tariffs. Meanwhile, supporters of Andrew

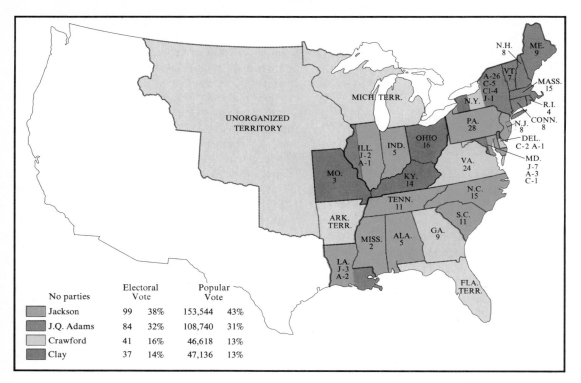

No parties	Electoral Vote		Popular Vote	
Jackson	99	38%	153,544	43%
J.Q. Adams	84	32%	108,740	31%
Crawford	41	16%	46,618	13%
Clay	37	14%	47,136	13%

Presidential Election, 1824

Jackson sabotaged Adams's administration at every opportunity.

The 1828 campaign between Adams and Jackson was an intensely personal conflict. Whatever principles the two men stood for were obscured by the mudslinging on both sides. A month after the election, Rachel Jackson died, and the president-elect attributed his wife's death to the abuse heaped upon him in the campaign. He never forgave her "murderers."

Jackson polled 56 percent of the popular vote and won in the electoral college, 178 to 83. For him and his supporters, the will of the people had been served, as it had not been in 1824. Through a lavishly financed coalition of state parties, political leaders, and newspaper editors, a popular movement elected a president. An era ended, and the Democratic party became the first truly political party in the United States. Well-organized parties became the hallmark of nineteenth-century American politics.

Andrew Jackson was nicknamed "Old Hickory," after the toughest American hardwood. A rough-and-tumble, ambitious man, he rose from humble birth to become a wealthy planter and slaveholder. Jackson was the first American president from the West and the first not born into comfortable circumstances; he was a self-made man at ease among both frontiersmen and southern planters. Though he had a violent temper and was often vindictive, he could charm those opposed to him and allay their suspicions. He had an instinct for politics and picked issues and supporters shrewdly.

Andrew Jackson

Jackson and his Democratic supporters offered a distinct alternative to the strong national government Adams had advocated. The Democrats represented a wide range of beliefs but shared some common ideals. Fundamentally, they sought to foster the Jeffersonian concept of an agrarian society, har-

Democrats

Chapter 12: Reform, Politics, and Expansion, 1824–1844

Jacques Amans's 1840 oil portrait of former President Andrew Jackson. Jackson appears to look into the viewer's eyes, suggesting the directness that earned so deep a loyalty from his supporters. *The Historic New Orleans Collection Museum/Research Center.*

kening back to the belief that a strong central government was the enemy of individual liberty, a tyranny to be feared. Thus, like Jefferson, they favored limited central government.

Jacksonians feared the concentration of economic power as much as the concentration of political power and viewed government intervention in the economy as a boon to special-interest groups and the rich. Consequently, they sought to restore the independence of the individual—the artisan and the yeoman farmer—by ending federal support of banks and corporations and restricting the use of paper currency.

Finally, Jackson and his supporters were hostile to reform as a movement and an ideology. Reformers were increasingly calling for an activist and interventionist government as they organized to turn their programs into legislation. But Democrats tended to oppose programs such as educational reform and the establishment of public education. They believed, for instance, that public schools restricted individual liberty by interfering with parental responsibility and undermined freedom of religion by replacing church schools. Nor did Jackson share reformers' humanitarian concerns.

Jackson and the Jacksonians considered themselves reformers in a different way. In following Jefferson's notion of restraint in government and in emphasizing individualism, Jackson and his followers sought to bring back old republican virtues, prizing such individual traits as industriousness, prudence, and economy. No less than the reformers, Jackson sought to restore a harmony and unity that had been displaced by economic and social change.

Like Jefferson, Jackson strengthened the executive branch of government at the same time as he tended to weaken the federal role. Given his popularity and the strength of his personality, this concentration of power in the presidency was perhaps inevitable; but his deliberate policy of combining the roles of party leader and chief of state centralized even greater power in the White House. Invoking the principle that rotating officeholders would make government more responsive to the public will, Jackson used the spoils system to reward loyal Democrats with appointments to office. Though he removed fewer than one-quarter of federal officeholders in his two terms, his use of patronage nevertheless strengthened party organization and loyalty.

Jackson himself stressed his rejection of elitism and special favors, his use of rotation in office, and his belief in popular government. He declared repeatedly that sovereignty resided with the people and not with the states or with the courts. Summoning the electorate to support him, he confidently claimed to represent the people's will. In this context, Jackson was a reformer; he returned government to majority rule. Yet it is hard to distinguish between Jackson's belief in himself as the instrument of the people and simple egotism and demagogic arrogance. After all, his opponents, too, claimed to represent the people.

Jackson invigorated the philosophy of limited government. In 1830, he vetoed the Maysville Road bill, which would have provided a federal subsidy to construct a sixty-mile turnpike from Maysville to Lexington, Kentucky. Jackson insisted that a federally subsidized internal improvement confined to one state was unconstitutional and that such projects were properly a state responsibility. The veto undermined Henry Clay's American System and personally embarrassed Clay because the project was in his home district.

The Nullification and Bank Controversies

Jackson had to face more directly the question of the proper division of sovereignty between state and central government. The slave South, especially South Carolina, was fearful of federal power. To protect their interests, South Carolinian political leaders articulated the doctrine of *nullification,* according to which a state had the right to overrule federal legislation. The act that directly inspired this doctrine was the passage of the protectionist 1828 Tariff of Abominations. In his unsigned *Exposition and Protest,* John C. Calhoun argued that in any disagreement between the federal government and a state, a special state convention—like the conventions called to ratify the Constitution—would decide the conflict by either nullifying or accepting the federal law. Only the power of nullification could protect the minority against the tyranny of the majority, Calhoun asserted.

In public, Calhoun let others take the lead in advancing nullification. As Jackson's running mate in 1828, he avoided publicly identifying with nullification and thus embarrassing the ticket. As vice president, he hoped to win Jackson's support as the Democratic presidential heir apparent. Thus a silent Calhoun presided over the Senate and its packed galleries when Senators Daniel Webster of New Hampshire and Robert Y. Hayne of South Carolina debated nullification in January 1830. The debate explored North-South frictions and the nature of the Union. Though debating Hayne, Webster aimed

Webster-Hayne Debate

his remarks at Calhoun as he depicted the nation as a compact of people, not merely states. In this climax of his career as a debater, he invoked two images. One, which he hoped he would not see, was the outcome of nullification: "states dissevered, discordant, belligerent; on a land rent with civil feuds, or drenched . . . in fraternal blood!" The other was a patriotic vision of a great nation flourishing under the motto "Liberty and Union, now and forever, one and inseparable."

Though sympathetic to states' rights, Jackson rejected the idea of state sovereignty. Moreover, he was deeply committed to union. Thus he shared Webster's dread and distrust of nullification. Soon after the Webster-Hayne debate, the president made his position clear at a Jefferson Day dinner with the toast: "Our Federal Union, it *must* and *shall* be preserved." Calhoun, when his turn came, offered: "The Federal Union—next to our liberty the most dear."

South Carolina invoked its theory of nullification against the Tariff of 1832. Although this tariff had the effect of reducing some duties, it retained high taxes on imported iron, cottons, and woolens. A majority of southern representatives supported the new tariff, but South Carolinians refused to go along. In their view, their constitutional right to control their own destiny had been sacrificed to the demands of northern industrialists. They feared the consequences of accepting such an act; it could set a precedent for congressional legislation on slavery. In November 1832, a South Carolina state convention nullified the tariff, making it unlawful for officials to collect duties in the state after February 1, 1833.

Nullification Crisis

"Old Hickory" responded with toughness. On December 10, 1832, Jackson issued his own proclamation, nullifying nullification. He moved troops to federal forts in South Carolina and prepared United States marshals to collect the required duties. At Jackson's request, Congress passed the Force Act, which supposedly renewed Jackson's authority to call up troops; it was actually a scheme to avoid the use of force by collecting duties before ships reached South Carolina. At the same time, Jackson extended the olive branch by recommending tariff reductions. Calhoun, disturbed by South Carolina's

Chapter 12: Reform, Politics, and Expansion, 1824–1844

drift toward separatism, resigned as vice president and became a United States senator from South Carolina. In the Senate, he worked with Henry Clay to draw up the compromise Tariff of 1833. Quickly passed by Congress and signed by the president, the revision lengthened the list of duty-free items and reduced duties over the next nine years. Satisfied, South Carolina's convention repealed its nullification law and in a final salvo nullified Jackson's Force Act. Jackson ignored the gesture.

The nullification controversy represented a genuine debate on the true nature and principles of the republic. Each side believed it was upholding the Constitution. Neither side won a clear victory, though both claimed to have done so. Another issue, that of a central bank, would define the powers of the federal government more clearly.

At stake was the rechartering of the Second Bank of the United States, whose twenty-year charter expired in 1836. One of the bank's functions was to

Second Bank of the United States act as a clearing-house for state banks, keeping them honest by refusing to accept their notes if they had insufficient gold in reserve. Most state banks resented the central bank's police role; by presenting state bank notes for redemption all at once, the Second Bank could easily ruin a state bank. Moreover, state banks, with less money in reserve, found themselves unable to compete on an equal footing with the Second Bank.

Many state governments regarded the national bank, with its headquarters in Philadelphia, as unresponsive to local needs. Westerners and urban workers remembered with bitterness the bank's conservative credit policies during the Panic of 1819. Although the Second Bank served some of the functions of a central bank, it was still a private profit-making institution, and its policies reflected the self-interest of its owners. To many westerners, the bank's eastern, conservative president, Nicholas Biddle, symbolized all that was wrong with the bank.

Although the bank's charter would not expire until 1836, Biddle got Congress to approve an early rechartering. This strategy, encouraged by Henry Clay, the National Republican presidential candidate, was designed to create public pressure to force Jackson to sign the bill or to secure a veto override. The plan backfired when Jackson, in July 1832, vetoed the rechartering bill and the Senate failed to override. Jackson's veto message was an emotional attack on the undemocratic nature of the bank. The bank became the major symbol and issue in the presidential campaign of 1832, and Jackson used it to attack special privilege and economic power.

In 1833, after his sweeping victory and second inauguration, Jackson moved not only to dismantle the Second Bank of the United States but to ensure that it would not be resurrected.

Jackson's Second Term He deposited federal funds in favored state-chartered ("pet") banks; without federal money, the Second Bank shriveled. When its federal charter expired in 1836, it became just another Pennsylvania-chartered private bank. In 1841, it closed its doors.

In the aftermath of the fight against the bank, Congress in 1836 passed the Deposit Act. Under this act, the secretary of the treasury designated one bank in each state and territory to provide the services formerly performed by the Bank of the United States. The act provided that the federal surplus in excess of $5 million be distributed to the states as interest-free loans beginning in 1837.

The surplus had derived from wholesale speculation in public lands. Purchasers bought public land on credit, borrowed from banks against the land to purchase additional acreage, and repeated the cycle. Jackson feared that the speculative craze threatened the state banks while shutting out settlers, who could not compete with speculators in bidding for the best land.

Following his hard-money instinct and his opposition to paper currency, President Jackson ordered Treasury Secretary Levi Woodbury to issue the **Specie Circular.** It provided that after August 15, 1836, only specie—gold or silver—or Virginia land scrip would be accepted as payment for federal lands. By ending credit sales, the circular significantly reduced public land purchases and the budget surplus. As a result, the government suspended the loan payments to the states soon after they were begun.

The policy was a disaster on many fronts. Although federal land sales dropped sharply, speculation continued as available land for sale became a scarce commodity. The ensuing increased demand for specie squeezed banks, and many suspended specie payment (the redemption of bank notes for specie). This led to further credit contraction as banks issued fewer notes and gave less credit. In the waning days of Jackson's administration, Congress voted to repeal the circular, but the president pocket-vetoed the bill. Finally, in May 1838, a joint resolution of Congress overturned the circular. Restrictions on land sales ended, but the speculative fervor was over. The federal government did not revive loans to states.

From George Washington to John Quincy Adams, presidents had vetoed nine bills; Jackson vetoed twelve. Previous presidents believed that vetoes were justified only on constitutional grounds, but Jackson stressed policy disagreement as well. He made the veto an important weapon in controlling Congress, since senators and representatives had to consider the possibility of a presidential veto on any bill. In effect, he made the executive a rival branch of government equal to Congress.

The Whig Challenge and the Second Party System

At one time, historians described the 1830s and 1840s as the Age of Jackson, and the personalities of the leading political figures dominated historical accounts. Increasingly, however, historians have viewed these years as an age of popularly based political parties and reformers, for only when the passionate concerns of reformers and abolitionists spilled into politics did party differences become paramount and party loyalties solidify. For the first time, grassroots political groups, organized from the bottom up, set the tone of political life.

In the 1830s, the Democrats' opponents found shelter under a common umbrella, the Whig party. Resentful of Jackson's domination of Congress, the

Whigs Whigs borrowed their name from the British party that had opposed the tyranny of Hanoverian monarchs in the eighteenth century. From the congressional elections of 1834 through the 1840s, they and the Democrats competed nearly equally. They fought at every level—city, county, and state—and achieved a stability previously unknown in American politics. The rise of political party competition in this period—commonly called the Second Party System—was a renewal of the organized political competition that had marked the First Party System of the Republicans and Federalists.

The two parties took different approaches to numerous fundamental issues during these years. Although both favored economic expansion, the Whigs sought it through an activist government and the Democrats through limited central government. Thus the Whigs supported corporate charters, a national bank, and paper currency, all of which the Democrats opposed. The Whigs also favored more humanitarian reforms than did the Democrats—public schools, abolition of capital punishment, temperance, and prison and asylum reform.

In general, Whigs were more optimistic than Democrats and more enterprising. They did not hesitate to help one group if doing so would promote the general welfare. The chartering of corporations, they argued, expanded economic opportunity for everyone, including laborers and farmers. Meanwhile, the Democrats, distrustful of the concentration of economic power and of moral and economic coercion, held fast to their Jeffersonian principle of limited government.

Ironically, the basic economic issues of the era were not the key determinants of party affiliation. Instead, religion and ethnicity determined party membership. In the North, the Whigs' concern for energetic government and humanitarian and moral reform won the favor of native-born and British-American evangelical Protestants, as well as the relatively small number of free black voters. Democrats, on the other hand, tended to be foreign-born Catholics and nonevangelical Protestants, both groups that preferred to keep religious and secular affairs separate.

The Whig party thus became the vehicle of re-

Chapter 12: Reform, Politics, and Expansion, 1824–1844

vivalist Protestantism. Indeed, Whigs practiced a kind of political revivalism. Their rallies resembled camp meetings; their speeches echoed evangelical rhetoric; their programs embodied the perfectionist beliefs of reformers. In unifying evangelicals, the Whigs alienated members of other faiths. The evangelicals' ideal Christian state had no room for Catholics, Mormons, Unitarians, Universalists, or religious freethinkers. Sabbath laws and temperance legislation threatened the religious freedom and individual liberty of these groups, which generally opposed state interference in moral and religious questions. As a result, more than 95 percent of Irish Catholics, 90 percent of Reformed Dutch, and 80 percent of German Catholics voted Democratic.

Whigs and Reformers

Jackson hand-picked Vice President Martin Van Buren to head the Democratic ticket in the presidential election of 1836. The Whigs, who in 1836 had not yet coalesced into a national party, entered three sectional candidates: Daniel Webster of New England, Hugh White of the South, and William Henry Harrison of the West. By splintering the vote, they hoped to throw the election into the House, but Van Buren comfortably captured the electoral college, even though he held only a 25,000-vote edge out of a total of 1.5 million votes cast.

Van Buren took office just weeks before the American credit system collapsed. The economic boom of the 1830s was over. In May 1837, New York banks stopped redeeming paper currency with gold, responding to the impact of the Specie Circular. Soon all banks suspended payments in hard coin. Suspension of specie began a cycle that led to banks curtailing loans and reduced business confidence. The credit contraction only made things worse; after a brief recovery, hard times set in and persisted from 1839 to 1843.

Martin Van Buren and Hard Times

Unfortunately, Van Buren followed Jackson's hard-money policies. He curtailed federal spending, thus accelerating deflation, and opposed the Whigs' advocacy of a national bank, which would have expanded credit. Even worse, Van Buren proposed a new regional treasury system for holding government deposits, replacing banks; Van Buren wanted to prevent further government losses from failing banks. The treasury branches would accept and pay out only gold and silver coin; they would not accept paper currency or checks drawn on state banks. Van Buren's independent treasury bill was passed in 1840. By creating a constant demand for hard coin, it deprived banks of gold and added to the general deflation.

With the nation in hard times, the Whigs confidently prepared for the election of 1840. The Democrats renominated President Van Buren. The Whigs rallied behind the military hero General William Henry Harrison, conqueror of Prophet Town, or Tippecanoe Creek, in 1811, and his running mate, John Tyler of Virginia. In a huge turnout, in which 80 percent of eligible voters cast ballots, Harrison won the popular vote by a narrow margin but swept the electoral college 234 to 60.

Election of 1840

Unfortunately for the Whigs, the sixty-eight-year-old Harrison died within a month of his inauguration. His successor, John Tyler, a former Democrat who had left the party in opposition to Jackson's nullification proclamation, turned out to be more a Democrat than a Whig. He consistently opposed the Whig congressional program, vetoing bills that provided for protective tariffs, a revived Bank of the United States, and internal improvements. Two days after Tyler's second veto of a bank bill, the entire cabinet, except Secretary of State Daniel Webster, resigned. Webster, involved in negotiating a new treaty with Great Britain, left shortly thereafter. Tyler became a president without a party, and the Whigs lost the presidency without an election.

Hard times in the late 1830s and early 1840s deflected attention from the renewal of Anglo-American tensions. Northern commercial rivalry with Britain, the default of state governments and corporations on British-held debts during the Panic of 1837, rebellion in Canada, boundary disputes, southern alarm over West Indian emancipation, and American expansionism—all caused Anglo-American conflict.

Anglo-American Tensions

A major dispute with Great Britain emerged over the imprecisely defined border between Maine and

Using many of the techniques of twentieth-century politics, General William Henry Harrison ran a "log cabin and hard cider" campaign—a popular crusade—against Jackson heir, President Martin Van Buren. This campaign handkerchief shows Harrison welcoming two of his comrades to his log cabin, with a barrel of cider outside. *The New-York Historical Society.*

New Brunswick. In the winter of 1838 and 1839, Canadian lumbermen moved into the disputed area. Shortly afterward, Maine attempted to expel them. After the Canadians captured the Maine land agent, both sides mobilized their militia and Congress authorized a call-up of fifty thousand men. Fortunately, war was avoided. General Winfield Scott, who was dispatched to Aroostook, Maine, arranged a truce between the warring state and province, and the two sides compromised on their conflicting claims in the Webster-Ashburton Treaty (1842).

The border conflict with Great Britain prefigured an issue that became prominent in national politics in the second half of the 1840 decade: the westward expansion of the United States. Tyler's succession to power in 1841 and a Democratic victory in the presidential election of 1844 ended an activist fed-

eral government in the domestic sphere for the rest of the decade. Attention turned to the debate over territorial expansion.

Manifest Destiny

Americans had been hungry for new lands ever since the colonists first turned their eyes westward. There lay fertile soil, valuable minerals, and the chance for a better life or a new beginning. Agrarian Democrats saw the West as an antidote to urbanization and industrialization. Enterprising Whigs looked to the new commercial opportunities the West offered. Equally important was a fierce national pride and a desire to acquire western lands to secure the nation from external enemies. Finally, Americans idealistically believed that westward expansion would extend American freedom and democracy "to less fortunate people." In the 1840s, *manifest destiny*—the belief that American expansion westward was inevitable, divinely ordained, and just—served the nation's expansionists (see map, page 234).

Manifest destiny was more than simply self-serving; it contained an undercurrent of racism. Indians were perceived as savages best confined to small areas in the West. Mexicans and Central and South Americans were also seen as inferior peoples, to be controlled or conquered. Thus the same racism that justified slavery in the South and discrimination in the North supported expansion in the West.

Among the long-standing objectives of expansionists was the Republic of Texas. Originally part of Mexico, Texas attracted thousands of Americans in the 1820s and 1830s. The Mex-

Republic of Texas ican government's extremely generous land policy enticed settlers into the area. In return for the right to settle in Texas, immigrants were expected to become Mexican citizens and adopt the Catholic religion.

By 1835, thirty-five thousand Americans, including many slaveholders, lived in Texas. These new settlers ignored local laws and oppressed native Mexicans, and when the Mexican government attempted to tighten its control over the region, Anglos and insurgent Hispanics rebelled. At the Alamo in San Antonio in 1836, fewer than two hundred Texans made a heroic stand against three thousand Mexicans under General Antonio López de Santa Anna. All the defenders of the mission died in the battle, and "Remember the Alamo" became the Texans' rallying cry. The desires of Texans to avenge the defeat at the Alamo and to secure their independence were fulfilled later in 1836, through Sam Houston's victory in the Battle of San Jacinto.

Americans were generally delighted with the revolution's success, but joy did not mean that the Texas request for annexation into the Union was welcomed. Texas was a slave republic and this made annexation a potentially explosive political issue. President Jackson delayed recognition of

Texas until after the election of 1836, and President Van Buren ignored annexation altogether. Texans then talked about developing close ties with the British and extending their republic all the way to the Pacific Coast. President Tyler feared that a Texas alliance with the British might threaten American independence. He was also committed to expansion and hoped to build support in the South by enlarging the area of slavery. Therefore, he pushed for annexation. But in a sectional vote, the Senate in April 1844 rejected a treaty of annexation.

Just as southerners sought expansion to the Southwest, northerners looked to the Northwest. In 1841, "Oregon fever" struck thousands. Lured by the glowing reports of mis-

Oregon Fever sionaries, migrants organized hundreds of wagon trains and embarked on the Oregon Trail. The 2,000-mile journey took six months or more, but within a few years five thousand settlers had arrived in the fertile Willamette Valley, south of the Columbia River.

Since the Anglo-American convention of 1818, Britain and the United States had jointly occupied the disputed Oregon Territory. Beginning with the administration of President John Quincy Adams, the United States had tried to fix the boundary at the 49th parallel, but Britain refused. Time only increased the American appetite. In 1843, a Cincinnati convention demanded that the United States obtain the entire Oregon Country, up to its northernmost border of 54°40′. Soon "Fifty-four Forty or Fight" had become the rallying cry of American expansionists.

The expansion into Oregon and the rejection of the annexation of Texas, both favored by antislavery forces, heightened southern pessimism. Southern leaders became anxious about

Election of 1844 their diminishing ability to control the debate over slavery. They persuaded the 1844 Democratic convention to adopt a rule that the presidential nominee had to receive two-thirds of the convention votes. In effect, the southern states acquired a veto, and they used it to block Van Buren as the nominee; most southerners objected to Van Buren's antislavery stance and opposition to Texas annexation. Instead, the party chose House Speaker James K. Polk, a hard-money Jacksonian and

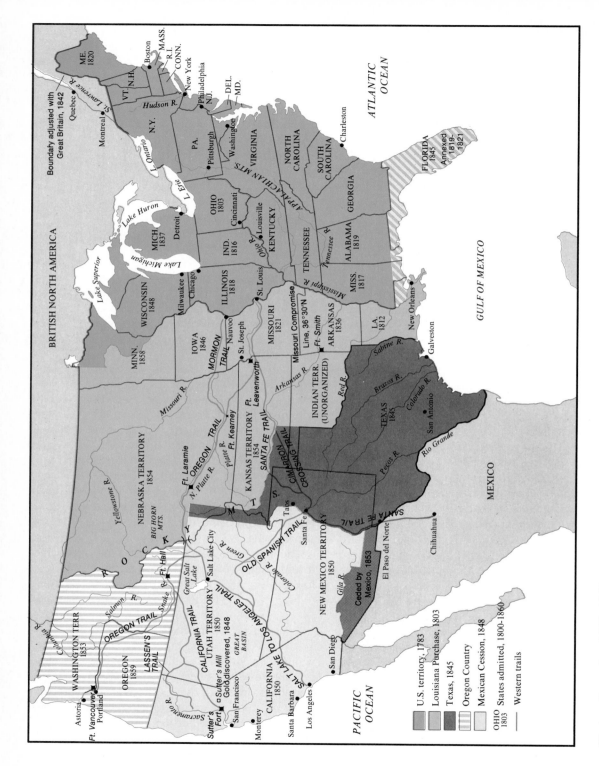

Western Expansion, 1800–1860

expansionist from Tennessee. The Whig leader Henry Clay, the Whig nominee, believed that the Democrats would provoke a war with Great Britain or Mexico. He favored expansion through negotiation, not force.

The Democrats captured the executive mansion with 170 electoral votes to 105 (they won the popular vote by just 38,000 out of 2.7 million). Polk carried New York's 36 electoral votes by just 6,000 votes; abolitionist James G. Birney, the Liberty party candidate, drew almost 16,000 votes away from Clay, handing New York and the election to Polk. Thus abolitionist forces unwittingly influenced the choice of a slaveholder as president.

Interpreting Polk's victory as a mandate for annexation, President Tyler proposed in his last days in office that Texas be admitted by joint resolution of Congress. Proslavery and antislavery congressmen debated the extension of slavery into the territory, and the resolution passed the House 120 to 98 and the Senate 27 to 25. Three days before leaving office, Tyler signed the measure. Mexico immediately broke relations with the United States; war loomed.

Politics, the reform spirit, and expansionism commingled in the 1830s and 1840s. Reform imbued with revivalism sought to bring order in a rapidly changing society. But reformers had no monopoly on claims of republican virtue; their opponents, too, claimed descent from the revolutionary values that held individual liberty dear. Once reform forced itself into politics, it sparked a broader-based interest. Political organization and conflict stimulated even greater interest in campaigns and political issues. Expansion and territorial questions further intensified conflict. Eventually, however, one issue absorbed nearly all attention and created a crisis in the Union: slavery.

Suggestions for Further Reading

Religion, Revivalism, and Reform

Michael Barkun, *Crucible of the Millennium: The Burned-over District of New York in the 1840s* (1986); Terry Bilhartz,

Urban Religion and the Second Great Awakening: Church and Society in Early National Baltimore (1986); Whitney R. Cross, *The Burned-Over District* (1950); Clifford S. Griffen, *Their Brother's Keepers: Moral Stewardship in the United States, 1800–1865* (1960); Keith J. Hardman, *Charles Grandison Finney, 1792–1875: Revivalist and Reformer* (1987); Paul E. Johnson, *A Shopkeeper's Millennium: Society and Revivals in Rochester, New York, 1815–1837* (1978); William G. McLoughlin, *Revivals, Awakenings, and Reform: An Essay on Religion and Social Change in America, 1607–1977* (1978); Randolph A. Roth, *The Democratic Dilemma: Religion, Reform, and the Social Order in the Connecticut Valley of Vermont, 1791–1850* (1987); Richard D. Shiels, "The Scope of the Second Great Awakening: Andover, Massachusetts, as a Case Study," *Journal of the Early Republic,* 5 (Summer 1985), 223–246; Timothy L. Smith, *Revivalism and Social Reform in Mid-Nineteenth Century America* (1957); Alice Felt Tyler, *Freedom's Ferment* (1944); Ronald G. Walters, *American Reformers, 1815–1860* (1978).

Temperance, Asylums, and Antimasonry

Paul Goodman, *Towards a Christian Republic: Antimasonry and the Great Transition in New England, 1826–1836* (1988); Gerald N. Grob, *Mental Institutions in America: Social Policy to 1875* (1973); Kathleen Smith Kutolowski, "Antimasonry Reexamined: Social Bases of the Grass-Roots Party," *Journal of American History,* 71 (September 1984), 269–293; W. J. Rorabaugh, *The Alcoholic Republic: An American Tradition* (1979); Charles E. Rosenberg, *The Care of Strangers: The Rise of America's Hospital System* (1987); David J. Rothman, *The Discovery of the Asylum: Social Order and Disorder in the New Republic* (1971); Ian R. Tyrrell, *Sobering Up: From Temperance to Prohibition in Antebellum America, 1800–1860* (1979); William Preston Vaughn, *The Antimasonic Party in the United States, 1826–1843* (1983).

Women and Reform

Barbara J. Berg, *The Remembered Gate: Origins of American Feminism: The Woman and the City, 1800–1860* (1977); Anne M. Boylan, "Women in Groups: An Analysis of Women's Benevolent Organizations in New York and Boston, 1797–1840," *Journal of American History,* 71 (December 1984), 497–523; Ellen C. Du Bois, *Feminism and Suffrage: The Emergence of an Independent Woman's Movement in America, 1848–1869* (1978); Barbara Leslie Epstein, *The Politics of Domesticity: Women, Evangelism, and Temperance in Nineteenth-Century America* (1981); Elisabeth Griffith, *In Her Own Right: The Life of Elizabeth Cady Stanton* (1984); Nancy A. Hewitt, *Women's Activism and Social Change: Rochester, New York, 1822–1872* (1984); Gerda Lerner, *The Grimké Sisters of South Carolina* (1967); Ian R. Tyrrell, "Women and Temperance in Antebellum America, 1830–1860," *Civil War History,* 28 (June 1982), 128–152.

Antislavery and Abolitionism

David Brion Davis, *Slavery and Human Progress* (1984); Frederick Douglass, *Life and Times of Frederick Douglass* (1881); Aileen S. Kraditor, *Means and Ends in American Abolitionism: Garrison and His Critics on Strategy and Tactics* (1967); Lewis Perry and Michael Fellman, eds., *Antislavery Reconsidered* (1979); Benjamin Quarles, *Black Abolitionists* (1969); Leonard L. Richards, *The Life and Times of Congressman John Quincy Adams* (1986); Leonard L. Richards, *"Gentlemen of Property and Standing": Anti-Abolition Mobs in Jacksonian America* (1970); Ronald G. Walters, *The Antislavery Appeal: American Abolitionism After 1830* (1976); Bertram Wyatt-Brown, *Lewis Tappan and the Evangelical War Against Slavery* (1969).

Andrew Jackson and the Jacksonians

Lee Benson, *The Concept of Jacksonian Democracy: New York as a Test Case* (1964); Donald B. Cole, *Martin Van Buren and the American Political System* (1984); Mary W. M. Hargreaves, *The Presidency of John Quincy Adams* (1985); Richard B. Latner, *The Presidency of Andrew Jackson* (1979); John Niven, *Martin Van Buren* (1983); Edward Pessen, *Jacksonian America: Society, Personality, and Politics,* rev. ed. (1979); Robert V. Remini, *The Legacy of Andrew Jackson: Essays on Democracy, Indian Removal, and Slavery* (1988); Robert V. Remini, *The Life of Andrew Jackson* (1988); Robert V. Remini, *Andrew Jackson and the Bank War* (1967); John William Ward, *Andrew Jackson: Symbol for an Age* (1955); Harry L. Watson, *Jacksonian Politics and Community Conflict: The Emergence of the Second American Party System in Cumberland County, North Carolina* (1981); Major L. Wilson, *The Presidency of Martin Van Buren* (1984).

Democrats and Whigs

Ronald P. Formisano, *The Transformation of Political Culture: Massachusetts Parties, 1790s–1840s* (1983); Daniel Walker Howe, *The Political Culture of the American Whigs* (1979); Merrill D. Peterson, *The Great Triumvirate: Webster, Clay, and Calhoun* (1987); James Roger Sharp, *The Jacksonians Versus the Banks: Politics in the States After the Panic of 1837* (1970).

Manifest Destiny and Foreign Policy

John M. Belohlavek, *"Let the Eagle Soar!" The Foreign Policy of Andrew Jackson* (1985); Norman B. Graebner, ed., *Manifest Destiny* (1968); Thomas R. Hietala, *Manifest Design: Anxious Aggrandizement in Late Jacksonian America* (1985); Reginald Horsman, *Race and Manifest Destiny* (1981); Frederick Merk, *Manifest Destiny and Mission in American History* (1963); David M. Pletcher, *The Diplomacy of Annexation: Texas, Oregon, and the Mexican War* (1973); Paul A. Varg, *United States Foreign Relations, 1820–1860* (1979).

He was free at last. Escaping from slavery in Virginia, Anthony Burns had stowed away on a ship and safely reached Boston. Breathing the free air in a city well known for its abolitionists, Burns seemed out of danger. He found a job in a clothing store, and his future for once looked bright.

Then Burns made a serious mistake. He wrote a letter and tried to route it to his brother, still enslaved in Virginia. Their master intercepted the letter and left for Boston, intending to seize his wayward human property. In so doing, he counted on government enforcement of the Fugitive Slave Act. In May 1854, a deputy marshal arrested Burns. Predictably, Boston's abolitionists went into action, organizing public protests at Faneuil Hall. Then, in an attempt to free Burns by force, someone fired a shot and killed a deputy.

President Franklin Pierce decided on emphatic enforcement of federal law. "Incur any expense," Pierce telegraphed officials, "to insure the execution of the law." To demonstrate his determination, he sent marines, cavalry, and artillery to Boston and ordered a federal ship to stand ready to return Burns to Virginia. On June 2, a formidable contingent of troops marched Burns to the harbor through streets draped in black and hung with American flags at half mast. At a cost of $100,000, a single black man was sent back into slavery through the power of federal law.

The polarizing effects of this demonstration of federal support for slavery reached far and wide. In Boston, conservatives found that the spectacle of the national government enforcing bondage had radicalized them. A textile manufacturer, Amos A. Lawrence, observed that "we went to bed one night old fashioned, conservative, Compromise Union Whigs & waked up stark mad Abolitionists." New England states passed personal liberty laws designed to impede or block federal power. The southern states, in turn, reacted with outrage at every sign of northern "faithlessness" about the Fugitive Slave Act. The slavery issue was driving the sections apart. Northerners feared that the Slave Power was dominating American government, and white southerners demanded that their rights be upheld.

13

SLAVERY AND AMERICA'S FUTURE: THE ROAD TO WAR, 1845–1861

What brought these issues to center stage more than anything else was territorial expansion. Between 1845 and 1853, the United States added Texas, the West Coast, and the Southwest to its domain and launched the settlement of the Great Plains. But each time the nation expanded, it confronted a thorny issue—whether new territories and states should be slave or free. Disagreements on this question were too violent for compromise. A host of political leaders, including Henry Clay, Lewis Cass, Stephen A. Douglas, and Presidents Jackson and Van Buren, tried from the 1830s through the 1850s to postpone or compromise disagreements about slavery in the territories. But these disputes injected into national politics the bitterness surrounding slavery. Indeed, battles over slavery in the territories broke the second party system apart and then shaped a realigned system that emphasized sectional enmity. Sectional parties replaced nationwide organizations, which had tried to compromise differences.

As parties clamored for support, the feeling grew in both North and South that America's future was at stake. The new Republican party charged that southerners were taking over the federal government and trying to make slavery legal in every part of the Union. Republicans believed that America's future depended on the free labor of free men, whose rights were protected by a government devoted to liberty. By contrast, southern leaders charged the North with lawless behavior and failure to respect the Constitution. To these southerners, slavery was the foundation of white equality and republicanism, and a government that failed to protect slavery seemed un-American and unworthy of their loyalty.

Not all citizens were obsessed with these conflicts. In fact, the results of the 1860 presidential election indicated that most voters hoped for neither disunion nor civil war. Yet within six months they had both. What had begun as a dark cloud over the territories grew into a storm. Both sections felt threatened and anxious and believed that the future hung in the balance. At the last minute, neither the victorious Republican party nor defensive southern slaveholders could agree on any of the desperate compromises proposed and thus a vast civil war began.

Conflict Begins: The Mexican War

Territorial expansion surged forward under the leadership of President James K. Polk. The annexation of Texas just before his inauguration had not cooled Polk's interest in acquiring California and the Southwest, and he desired Oregon as well. But though Polk was an effective president, he was unaware of the price that expansion would exact in domestic harmony. The addition of a huge domain to the nation's boundaries had major side effects. It divided the Whig party, drove southern Whigs into a full embrace of slavery, and brought into the open an aggressive new southern theory about slavery's position in the territories. It also elicited northern protests and proposals that revealed profound disagreement between the sections.

Although his supporters had belligerently demanded all of the Oregon Territory, Polk found as president that diplomacy had its advantages. Congress's annexation of Texas had outraged Mexican leaders, who severed relations with the United States. Knowing that war with Mexico could break out at any time, Polk decided to try to avoid a conflict with Great Britain in the Northwest. Dropping the demand for a boundary at 54°40', he kept up pressure on the British to accept the 49th parallel. Eventually, in 1846, Great Britain agreed. In the Oregon Treaty, the United States gained all of present-day Oregon, Washington, and Idaho and parts of Wyoming and Montana.

Toward Mexico, Polk was much more aggressive. He ordered American troops to defend the border claimed by Texas—but contested by Mexico—and offered to buy a huge tract of land in the Southwest from the resentful Mexicans. After purchase failed, Polk resolved to ask Congress for a declaration of war and set to work compiling a list of grievances. This task became unnecessary when word arrived that Mexican forces had engaged a body of American troops in disputed territory. American blood had been shed. Eagerly, Polk declared that "war exists by the act of Mexico itself" and summoned the nation to arms.

Congress voted to recognize a state of war be-

1846	War with Mexico Oregon Treaty Wilmot Proviso	**1856**	Preston Brooks attacks Charles Sumner in Senate chamber "Bleeding Kansas" Buchanan elected president
1847	Lewis Cass proposes idea of popular sovereignty	**1857**	*Dred Scott* v. *Sanford* Lecompton Constitution
1848	Taylor elected president Free-Soil party formed	**1858**	Voters reject Lecompton Constitution Lincoln-Douglas debates Freeport Doctrine
1849	California applies for admission to Union as free state		
1850	Compromise of 1850	**1859**	John Brown raids Harpers Ferry
1852	Publication of *Uncle Tom's Cabin* Pierce elected president	**1860**	Democratic party splits in half Lincoln elected president Crittenden Compromise fails South Carolina secedes from Union
1854	Kansas-Nebraska Act Republican party formed Democrats lose ground in congressional elections	**1861**	Six more southern states secede Confederacy established Attack on Fort Sumter

tween Mexico and the United States in May 1846, but controversy grew. Public opinion about the war was sharply divided, with southwesterners enthusiastic and New Englanders strenuously opposed. In Congress, Whigs charged that Polk had "literally provoked" an unnecessary war and "usurped the power of Congress by making war upon Mexico." The aged John Quincy Adams passionately opposed the war and a tall young Whig from Illinois, named Abraham Lincoln, questioned its justification. Moreover, a small minority of antislavery Whigs agreed with abolitionists—the war was no less than a plot to extend slavery.

These charges fed fear of the Slave Power. Abolitionists long had warned that there was a Slave Power—a slaveholding oligarchy in control of the South and intent on controlling the nation. The Slave Power's assault on northern liberties, abo-

Idea of a
Slave Power

litionists argued, had begun in 1836, when Congress passed the gag rule. Many white northerners, even those who saw nothing wrong with slavery, had viewed John Quincy Adams's stand against the rule as a valiant defense of free speech and the right to petition. The battle over free speech first made the idea of a Slave Power credible.

Now the Mexican War increased fears of this sinister power. Antislavery northerners asked why claims to all of Oregon had been abandoned but a questionable war begun for slave territory. Steadily these arguments had an effect on northern opinion. But the impact of events on southern opinion and southern leaders was even more dramatic.

At first, many southern leaders criticized the war with Mexico. Southern Whigs attacked the Democratic president for causing the war, and southern congressmen did not immediately see defens·

Wilmot Proviso slavery as the paramount issue. But no southern Whig could oppose it once slavery became the central issue. That happened in August 1846, when a Democratic representative from Pennsylvania, David Wilmot, offered an amendment to a military appropriations bill. Wilmot attached a condition, or proviso, to the bill: that "neither slavery nor involuntary servitude shall ever exist" in any territory gained from Mexico. His proviso did not pass both houses of Congress, but it immediately transformed the debate.

John C. Calhoun drew up resolutions on the territories that staked out a radical, new southern position. According to these resolutions, the territories belonged to all the states, and the federal government could do nothing to limit the spread of slavery there. Southern slaveholders had a constitutional right, Calhoun claimed, to take their slaves anywhere in the territories. This position, which quickly became orthodox for every southern politician, was a radical reversal of history. The founding fathers, under the Articles of Confederation, had excluded slavery from the Northwest Territory. Moreover, the Constitution authorized Congress to make "all needful rules and regulations" for the territories, and the Missouri Compromise had barred slavery from most of the Louisiana Purchase. But southern leaders now demanded protection for slavery.

In the North, meanwhile, the Wilmot Proviso soon became a rallying cry for abolitionists and Free-Soilers. Eventually, the legislatures of fourteen northern states endorsed it—and not because all its supporters were abolitionists. Like Wilmot, most white northerners were racists, not abolitionists, but it was possible to be racist and an opponent of slavery. Fear of the Slave Power was building a potent antislavery movement that united abolitionists and antiblack voters. The latter's concern was to protect themselves, not southern blacks, from the Slave Power.

Des___ ___ofound disagreement at home, events o___ ___eld went well for American troops, ___ious wars, were mainly volunteers ___ states. General Zachary Taylor's ___ occupied Monterrey, securing ___ (see map). Polk then ordered ___ ___y and a small detachment to

invade the remote and relatively unpopulated provinces of New Mexico and California. Taking Santa Fe without opposition, Kearny pushed into California, where he joined forces with rebellious American settlers, led by Captain John C. Frémont, and a couple of United States naval units. A quick victory was followed by reverses, but American soldiers soon re-established their dominance in distant and thinly populated California.

Meanwhile, General Winfield Scott's daring invasion of Mexico City brought the war to an end. On February 2, 1848, representatives of both countries signed the Treaty of Guadalupe **Treaty of Guadalupe Hidalgo** Hidalgo. The United States gained California and New Mexico (including present-day Nevada, Utah, and Arizona) and recognition of the Rio Grande as the southern boundary of Texas. In return, the American government agreed to settle the claims of its citizens against Mexico and to pay Mexico a mere $15 million.

The cost of the war included thirteen thousand American and fifty thousand Mexican dead, plus Mexican-American enmity lasting into the twentieth century. But the domestic cost was even higher. As sectional distrust and bitterness grew, party unity for both Democrats and Whigs began to loosen.

In the presidential election of 1848, slavery in the territories was the one overriding issue. Both parties tried to push this question into the background, but it dominated the conventions, **Election of 1848 and Popular Sovereignty** the campaign, and the election. The Democrats tried to avoid sectional conflict by nominating General Lewis Cass of Michigan for president and General William Butler of Kentucky for vice president. Cass had devised the idea of *popular sovereignty* for the territories—letting residents in the territories decide the question of slavery for themselves. His party's platform declared that Congress did not have the power to interfere with slavery and criticized those who pressed the question. The Whigs nominated General Zachary Taylor, who was a southern slaveholder, as well as a military hero, with Congressman Millard Fillmore of New York as his running mate. Their convention similarly refused to assert that Congress had power over slavery in the

sion by the Slave Power, and northern fears about slavery's influence deepened. Opposition to the fugitive slave law grew dramatically. Between 1855 and 1859, seven states—Connecticut, Rhode Island, Massachusetts, Michigan, Maine, Ohio, and Wisconsin—passed personal liberty laws. These laws interfered with the Fugitive Slave Act by providing counsel for alleged fugitives and requiring trial by jury. Southerners saw the personal liberty laws as signs of bad faith. Finally, the Kansas-Nebraska Act had a devastating impact on political parties.

The act divided the Whig party into northern and southern wings that could no longer cooperate as a national organization. One of the two great parties in the second party system was now gone. The Democrats survived, but their support in the North fell drastically in the 1854 elections. Moreover, anger over the territorial issue created a new political party. During the summer and fall of 1854, antislavery Whigs and Democrats, Free-Soilers, and other reformers throughout the Old Northwest met to form a new Republican party, dedicated to keeping slavery out of the territories. The Republicans' influence rapidly spread to the East, and they won a stunning victory in the 1854 elections by capturing a majority of House seats in the North.

The New Republican Party

For the first time, too, a sectional party had gained significant power in the political system. When Whigs and Democrats had competed throughout the country, the national base of each had moderated sectional conflict. Party leaders compromised to achieve unity and subordinated sectional differences to partisan needs. But now the Whigs were gone, and politics in the 1850s would never be the same.

Nor were Republicans the only new party. An anti-immigrant organization, the American party, also seemed likely for a few years to replace the Whigs. This party, popularly known as the Know-Nothings (because its members at first kept their purposes secret, answering all queries with the words "I know nothing"), exploited nativist fear of foreigners. By the mid-1850s, the American party was powerful and growing; in 1854 so many new congressmen won office with anti-immigrant, as well as antislavery, support

Know-Nothings

that Know-Nothings could claim that they outnumbered Republicans. But like the Whigs, the Know-Nothings could not keep their northern and southern wings together, and they melted away after 1856. That left the field to the Republicans.

Republicans, Know-Nothings, and Democrats were all scrambling to attract former Whig voters. The demise of that party ensured a major realignment of the political system, with nearly half the old electorate up for grabs. To woo these homeless Whigs, the remaining parties stressed a variety of issues, chosen to appeal to the Whigs for one reason or another. Immigration, temperance, homestead bills, the tariff, internal improvements—all played an important role in attracting voters during the 1850s.

Realignment of Political System

The Republicans appealed strongly to groups interested in the economic development of the West. Commercial agriculture was booming in the Ohio–Mississippi–Great Lakes area, but residents of that region needed more canals, roads, and river and harbor improvements to reap the full benefit of their labors. There was also widespread interest in a federal land-grant program that would provide free western land to homesteaders. Whigs had favored and Democrats had opposed all these things. Following long-standing party principles, Democratic presidents vetoed internal improvements bills and a homestead bill as late as 1859. Seizing their opportunity, the Republicans added internal improvements and land-grant planks to their platform. They also backed higher tariffs as an enticement to industrialists and businessmen.

Republican Appeals

Another major feature of the realigned political system was ideology. In the North, Republicans attracted many voters through effective use of ideology. They spoke to the image that northerners had of themselves, their society, and their future when they preached "Free Soil, Free Labor, Free Men." These phrases resonated with traditional ideals of equality, liberty, and opportunity under self-government—the heritage of republicanism.

"Free Soil, Free Labor, Free Men" seemed to fit in with a northern economy that was energetic, expanding, and prosperous. In the eyes of many, free labor was the key to northern progress. Any hard-working, virtuous person, it was thought, could improve his condition and gain economic independence by applying himself to opportunities that the country had to offer. Republicans pointed out that the South, which relied on slave labor and had little industry, appeared backward and retrograde in comparison. Praising both laborers and opportunity, the Republicans captured much of the spirit of the age in the North.

Thus, the Republican party attracted support from a variety of sources. Opposition to the extension of slavery had brought the party together, but party members carefully broadened their appeal by adopting the causes of other groups. They were wise to do so. As the newspaper editor Horace Greeley wrote in 1860, "an Anti-Slavery man *per se* cannot be elected." But, he added, "a Tariff, River-and-Harbor, Pacific Railroad, Free Homestead man, *may* succeed *although* he is Anti-Slavery." As these elements joined the Republican party, they also learned more about the dangers of slavery, and thus the process of party building deepened the sectional conflict.

A similar process was under way in the South. The disintegration of the Whig party had left many southerners at loose ends politically. Some of these people gravitated to the American **Southern** party, but not for long. By advocating states' rights, Democratic leaders managed to convert most of the formerly Whig slaveholders. Democrats spoke to the class interests of slaveholders, and the slaveholders responded.

Southern Democrats

In the South, however, yeomen rather than slaveholders were the heart of the party. Thus, Democratic politicians, though often slaveowners themselves, had lauded the common man and argued that their policies advanced his interests. Yeomen were told that a well-ordered South was the true defender of constitutional principles, and that runaway change in the North was threatening to subvert the nation. And according to the southern version of republicanism, white citizens in a slave society enjoyed liberty and social equality because the black race was enslaved. As Jefferson Davis put it in 1851, slavery elevated every white person's status and allowed the nonslaveholder to *"stand upon the broad level of equality with the rich*

man." Slaveholders warned that the overriding issue was "shall negroes govern white men, or white men govern negroes?"

These arguments had their effect, and racial fears and traditional political loyalties helped keep the political alliance between yeoman farmers and planters intact through the 1850s. No viable party emerged in the South to replace the Whigs. The result was a one-party system there that emphasized sectional issues. In the South, as in the North, political realignment sharpened sectional divisions.

In both sections, political leaders argued that opportunity was threatened. The *Montgomery* (Alabama) *Mail* warned southern whites that the Republicans intended "to free the negroes and force amalgamation between them and the children of the poor men of the South." Republicans warned northern workers that if slavery entered the territories the great reservoir of opportunity for decent people without means would be poisoned. These charges aroused fears and anxieties in both sections. But events in Kansas did even more to deepen the conflict. Put into practice, the Kansas-Nebraska Act spawned hatred and violence. Abolitionists and religious groups sent armed Free-Soil settlers to make Kansas free; southerners sent their reinforcements to establish slavery and prevent "northern hordes" from stealing Kansas. Clashes between the two groups caused bloodshed, and soon the whole nation was talking about "Bleeding Kansas."

Politics in the territory resembled war more than democracy. When elections for a territorial legislature were held in 1855, thousands of proslavery **Bleeding** Missourians invaded the polls and ran up a large but unlawful major-**Kansas** ity for slavery candidates. The legislature that resulted promptly legalized slavery, and in response Free-Soilers called an unauthorized convention and created their own government and constitution. A proslavery posse sent to arrest the Free-Soil leaders sacked the town of Lawrence; in revenge, John Brown, a zealot who saw himself as God's instrument to destroy slavery, murdered five proslavery settlers. Soon armed bands of guerrillas roamed the territory.

Bleeding Kansas

The passion generated by this conflict erupted in

The earliest known photograph of John Brown, probably taken in 1846 in Massachusetts, shows him pledging his devotion to an unidentified flag, possibly an abolitionist banner. Already Brown was aiding runaway slaves and pondering ways to strike at slavery. *Ohio Historical Society.*

candidate, John C. Frémont, won eleven of sixteen free states; Republicans had become the dominant party in the North. The Know-Nothing candidate, Millard Fillmore, received more than 20 percent of the vote, but this election was his party's last hurrah. The future battle was between a sectional Republican party and an increasingly divided Democratic party.

Slavery and the Nation's Future

For years, the issue of slavery in the territories had convulsed Congress, and for years the members of Congress had tried to settle the issue with vague formulas. In 1857, a different branch of government stepped onto the scene with a different approach. The Supreme Court addressed this emotion-charged subject and attempted to lay controversy to rest with a definitive verdict.

A Missouri slave named Dred Scott had sued his owner for his freedom. Scott based his suit on the fact that his former owner, an army surgeon, had

Dred Scott Case
taken him for several years into Illinois, a free state, and into the Wisconsin Territory, from which slavery had been barred by the

Missouri Compromise. Scott first won and then lost his case as it moved on appeal through the state courts, into the federal system, and finally to the Supreme Court.

Was a black person like Dred Scott a citizen and eligible to sue? Had residence in free territory made him free? Did Congress have the power to prohibit slavery in a territory or to delegate that power to a territorial legislature?

Each of these questions was answered by Chief Justice Roger B. Taney in *Dred Scott* v. *Sanford.* Taney wrote that Scott was not a citizen of either Missouri or the United States; that residence in a free territory did not make Scott free; and, most important, that Congress lacked the power to bar slavery from a territory, as it had done in the Missouri Compromise. The latter point suggested that

the chamber of the United States Senate in May 1856, when Charles Sumner of Massachusetts denounced "the Crime against Kansas." In doing so, Sumner bitterly assailed the president, the South, and Senator Andrew P. Butler of South Carolina. Soon afterward Butler's nephew, Representative Preston Brooks, approached Sumner at the latter's Senate desk, raised his arm, and began to beat Sumner over the head with a cane. Voters in the North and the South seethed; the country was becoming polarized.

The election of 1856 showed how far the polarization had gone. When Democrats met to select a nominee, they chose James Buchanan of Pennsylvania, whose chief virtue was that he had been serving as ambassador in Britain for four years. Thus he had not been embroiled in territorial controversies. This anonymity and superior party organization helped Buchanan win the election, but he owed his victory to southern support. Republican

the basic ideas of the Wilmot Proviso, and probably popular sovereignty, were invalid.

The Slave Power seemed to have gained vital constitutional ground. Black Americans were especially dismayed, for Taney's decision also declared that the founding fathers had never intended that black people be citizens. Though historically erroneous (black people had been citizens in several of the original states), the Dred Scott decision seemed to shut the door permanently on black people's hopes for justice and equal rights.

A storm of angry reaction broke in the North. The decision alarmed a wide variety of northerners—abolitionists, would-be settlers in the West, and those who hated black people but feared the influence of the South. Every charge against the aggressive Slave Power seemed now to be confirmed. "There is such a thing as THE SLAVE POWER," warned the *Cincinnati Daily Commercial.* And the *Cincinnati Freeman* asked, "What security have the Germans and the Irish that their children will not, within a hundred years, be reduced to slavery in this land of their adoption?" Echoed the *Atlantic Monthly,* "Where will it end?"

To Abraham Lincoln, the territorial question affected every citizen. "The whole nation," he declared as early as 1854, "is interested that the best use shall be made of these Territories. We want them for homes of free white people. This they cannot be, to any considerable extent, if slavery shall be planted within them." The territories must be reserved, he insisted, "as an outlet for *free white people everywhere."* After the Dred Scott decision, Lincoln charged, it was clear that slavery's advocates were trying to "push it forward, till it shall become lawful in *all* the states . . . *North* as well as *South."* He further asserted that the next step in the unfolding Slave Power conspiracy would be a Supreme Court decision "declaring that the Constitution does not permit a State to exclude slavery from its limits." This charge was not mere imagination, for cases soon were in the courts challenging state laws that gave freedom to slaves brought within their borders.

Lincoln's most eloquent statement against the Slave Power was his famous "House Divided"

Abraham Lincoln on the Slave Power

speech. In it, Lincoln declared: "I do not expect the Union to be dissolved—I do not expect the House to fall—but I do expect it to cease to be divided. It will become all one thing or all the other. Either the opponents of slavery will arrest the further spread of it, and place it where the public mind shall rest in the belief that it is in the course of ultimate extinction; or its advocates will push it forward, till it shall become alike lawful in all the States, old as well as new, North as well as South." Lincoln warned repeatedly that the latter possibility was well on the way to realization, and events convinced countless northerners that slaveholders were close to their goal of making slavery a national institution.

Politically, the force of Republican arguments offset the difficulties that the Dred Scott decision posed for party leaders. By endorsing southern constitutional theories, the Court had invalidated the central position of the Republican party: no extension of slavery. Republicans could only repudiate the decision, appealing to a "higher law," or hope to change the personnel of the Court. They did both and probably gained politically as public fear of the Slave Power increased.

Meanwhile, Stephen Douglas, a northern Democrat, faced an awful dilemma. He had to find a way to ease the fear of northerners without alienating southern Democrats. Douglas chose to stand by his principle of popular sovereignty, which encountered a second test in Kansas in 1857. There, after Free-Soil settlers boycotted an election, proslavery forces met at Lecompton and wrote a constitution that permitted slavery. New elections to the territorial legislature, however, returned an antislavery majority, and the legislature promptly called for a popular vote on the new constitution, which was defeated by more than 10,000 votes. Despite this overwhelming evidence that Kansans did not want slavery, President Buchanan tried to force the Lecompton Constitution through Congress. Douglas threw his weight against a document the people had rejected. He gauged their feelings correctly, for in 1858 Kansas voters rejected the constitution a third time. But his action infuriated southern Democrats.

In his well-publicized debates with Abraham Lincoln, his challenger for the Illinois Senate seat in

1858, Douglas further alienated the southern wing of his party. Speaking at Freeport,

Stephen Douglas Proposes the Freeport Doctrine

Illinois, he attempted to revive the notion of popular sovereignty with some tortured extensions of his old arguments. Asserting that the Supreme Court had not ruled on the powers of a *territorial* legislature, Douglas claimed that a territorial legislature could bar slavery either by passing a law against it or by doing nothing. Without the patrol laws and police regulations that support slavery, he reasoned, the institution could not exist. This argument, called the Freeport Doctrine, temporarily shored up Douglas's crumbling position in the North, but it alarmed southern Democrats. Some, like William L. Yancey of Alabama, studied the trend in northern opinion and concluded that southern rights would be safe only in a separate nation.

The immediate consequence for politics, however, was the likelihood of division in the Democratic party. Northern Democrats could not support the territorial protection for slavery that southern Democrats insisted was their constitutional right. Thus the territories continued to generate wider conflict, even though the issue had little practical significance. In territories outside Kansas, the number of settlers was small, and everywhere the number of blacks was negligible—less than 1 percent of the population in Kansas and New Mexico. Nevertheless, the general public in both North and South moved from anxiety to alarm and anger. The situation had become explosive.

The Breakup of the Union

One year before the 1860 presidential election, violence inflamed passions further when John Brown led a small band of whites and blacks in an attack on Harpers Ferry, Virginia. Hoping to trigger a slave rebellion, Brown failed miserably and was quickly captured, tried, and executed. Yet his attempted insurrection struck fear into the South. Then it came to light that Brown had financial backing from several prominent abolitionists, and northern intellectuals praised him as a hero and a martyr. These disclosures and northern praise of Brown multiplied southerners' fears and anger many times over. The unity of the nation was now in peril.

Many observers feared that the election of 1860 would decide the fate of the Union. By that year, the Democratic party was the only remaining organization that was truly national in scope. "One after another," wrote a Mississippian, "the links which have bound the North and South together, have been severed . . . [but] the Democratic party looms gradually up, its nationality intact, and waves the olive branch over the troubled waters of politics." At its 1860 convention, however, the Democratic party broke in two.

Stephen A. Douglas wanted the party's presidential nomination, but he could not afford to alienate northern opinion by accepting the southern position on the territories.

Splintering of the Democratic Party

Southern Democrats like William L. Yancey, on the other hand, were determined to have their rights recognized, and they moved to block Douglas's nomination. When Douglas marshaled a majority for his version of the platform, delegates from eight slave states walked out of the convention hall in Charleston. Efforts at compromise failed, and so the Democrats presented two nominees: Douglas for the northern wing, Vice President John C. Breckinridge of Kentucky for the southern. The Republicans nominated Abraham Lincoln. A Constitutional Union party, formed to preserve the nation but strong only in the Upper South, nominated John Bell of Tennessee.

The results of the balloting were sectional in character, with Lincoln the winner but with Douglas, Breckinridge, and Bell together receiving most of the votes. Douglas had broad-based support but won few states;

Election of 1860

Breckinridge carried nine southern states, with his strength concentrated in the Deep South; Bell won pluralities in Virginia, Kentucky, and Tennessee. Lincoln prevailed in the North, but in the states that ultimately remained loyal to the Union, he won only a plural-

These soldiers, photographed in 1859, were helping the Federal government protect slavery. The Richmond Grays, a militia company in the 1st Regiment, Virginia Volunteers, helped suppress John Brown's raid. Eighteen months later many of these men were wearing gray for the Confederacy. *The Valentine Museum, Richmond, Virginia.*

ity, not a majority (see table). He gained his victory in the electoral college.

Given the heterogeneous nature of Republican voters, it is likely that many of them did not view the issue of slavery in the territories as paramount. But opposition to extending slavery was the core issue of the Republican party, and Lincoln's alarm over slavery's growing power in the nation was genuine. The slavery issue would not go away. While abolitionists and Free-Soilers in the North worked to keep the Republicans from compromising on their territorial stand, proslavery advocates and secessionists whipped up public opinion in the South and shrewdly manipulated state conventions.

Lincoln made the crucial decision not to soften his party's position on the territories. His refusal to compromise probably derived both from his convictions and from his concern for the unity of the Republican party. Although many conservative Republicans—eastern businessmen and former Whigs who did not feel strongly about slavery—hoped for a compromise, the original and strongest Republicans—antislavery voters and "conscience Whigs"—would not abandon free soil. Lincoln chose to preserve the unity of his party and to take a stand against slavery.

Southern leaders in the Senate were willing, conditionally, to accept a compromise formula drawn up by Senator John J. Crittenden of Kentucky. Crittenden had suggested that the two sections divide the territories between them at 36°30'. But the southerners would agree to this *only* if the Republicans did too. When Lincoln ruled out concessions on the territorial issue, Crittenden's peacemaking effort collapsed. Virginians called for a special convention in Washington, to which several states sent representatives. But this gathering, too, failed to find a suitable formula or to reach unanimity on disputed questions.

Furthermore, political leaders in the North and the South misjudged each other. Lincoln and other prominent Republicans believed that southerners were bluffing when they threatened secession; they expected a pro-Union majority in the South to assert itself. On their side, moderate southern leaders had become convinced, with more accuracy, that

PRESIDENTIAL VOTE IN 1860		
	Lincoln	Other Candidates
Entire United States	1,866,452	2,815,617
North plus border and southern states that rejected secession prior to war[1]	1,866,452	2,421,752
North plus border states that fought for union[2]	1,864,523	1,960,842

Note the large vote for other candidates in the righthand column.
[1] Kentucky, Missouri, Maryland, Delaware, Virginia, North Carolina, Tennessee, Arkansas
[2] Kentucky, Missouri, Maryland, Delaware

Source: From David Potter, Lincoln and His Party in the Secession Crisis. *Copyright 1942, 1967 by Yale University Press. Reprinted by permission.*

northern leaders were not taking them seriously and that a posture of strength was necessary to win respect for their position. Thus, southern leaders who hoped to preserve the Union did not offer compromise, for fear of inviting aggression. Northern leaders who loved the Union believed compromise would be unnecessary and unwise. With such attitudes controlling leaders' actions, the prospects for a solution were dim.

Meanwhile the Union was being destroyed. On December 20, 1860, South Carolina passed an ordinance of secession amid jubilation and cheering.

Secession of South Carolina

This step marked the inauguration of a strategy known as separate-state secession. Foes of the Union, knowing the difficulty of persuading all the southern states to challenge the federal government simultaneously, had concentrated their hopes on the most extreme proslavery state. With South Carolina out of the Union, they hoped other states would follow and build momentum toward disunion.

Southern extremists soon got their way. Overwhelming their opposition, they quickly called conventions and passed secession ordinances in six other states: Mississippi, Florida,

Confederate States of America

Alabama, Georgia, Louisiana, and Texas. By February 1861, these states had joined with South Carolina to form a new government in Montgomery, Alabama: the Confederate States of America. Choosing Jefferson Davis as their president, they began to function independently of the United States.

Yet this apparent unanimity of action was deceiving. Confused and dissatisfied with the alternatives, many voters who had cast a ballot for president stayed home rather than vote for delegates who would consider secession. In some conventions, the vote to secede had been close, the balance tipped by the overrepresentation of plantation districts. Furthermore, the conventions were noticeably reluctant to seek ratification of their acts by the people. Four states in the Upper South—Virginia, North Carolina, Tennessee, and Arkansas—flatly rejected secession and did not join the Confederacy until after the fighting had started. In Kentucky and Missouri, popular sentiment was too divided for decisive action; these slave states remained under Union control, along with Maryland and Delaware (see map, page 252).

Misgivings about secession were not surprising, since it posed new and troubling issues for southerners, not the least of them being the possibility of war and the question of who would be sacrificed. A careful look at election returns indicates that slaveholders and nonslaveholders were beginning to part company politically. Heavily slaveholding counties gave strong support to secession, but many counties with few slaves took an antisecession position or were staunchly Unionist. In other words, nonslaveholding yeomen were beginning to

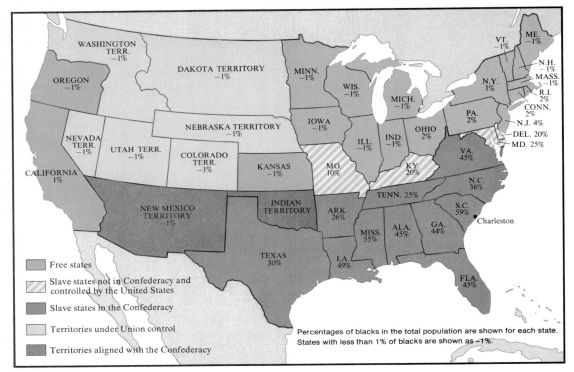

The Divided Nation—Slave and Free Areas, 1861

Legend:
- Free states
- Slave states not in Confederacy and controlled by the United States
- Slave states in the Confederacy
- Territories under Union control
- Territories aligned with the Confederacy

Percentages of blacks in the total population are shown for each state. States with less than 1% of blacks are shown as –1%.

act on their class interests. Finally, there was still considerable love for the Union in the South.

The dilemma facing President Lincoln on inauguration day in March 1861 was how to maintain the authority of the federal government without provoking war in the states that had left the Union. He decided to proceed cautiously; by holding onto federal fortifications, he reasoned, he could assert federal sovereignty while waiting for a restoration of relations. But Jefferson Davis, who could not claim to lead a sovereign nation if its ports and military facilities were under foreign control, would not cooperate. A collision was inevitable.

It came in the early morning hours of April 12, 1861, at Fort Sumter in Charleston harbor. A federal garrison there was running low on food. Lin-

Attack on Fort Sumter

coln notified the South Carolinians that he was sending a ship to resupply the fort. For the Montgomery government, the alternatives were to attack the fort or to acquiesce to Lincoln's authority. Accordingly, orders were sent to obtain surrender or attack the fort. Under heavy

bombardment for two days, the federal garrison finally surrendered. Confederates then permitted the soldiers, none of whom had been killed, to sail away on unarmed vessels while the residents of Charleston celebrated. The bloodiest war in America's history thus began in a deceptively gala spirit.

Throughout the 1840s and 1850s, many able leaders had worked diligently to avert armed conflict. Most people in both the North and the South had hoped to keep the nation together. As late as 1858, even Jefferson Davis had declared, "This great country will continue united." He had explained sincerely that the United States "is my country and to the innermost fibers of my heart I love it all, and every part." Why, then, had the war occurred?

Slavery was an issue that could not be compromised. The conflict over slavery was fundamental and beyond adjustment. Too many powerful emotions were engaged in attacking or defending it. Too many important interests and principles were involved in maintaining or destroying it. It was deeply entwined with almost every major policy question of the present and the future. Ultimately, each section regarded slavery as too important to ignore.

Even after extreme views were put aside, the North and the South had fundamentally different attitudes toward the institution. The logic of Republican ideology tended in the direction of abolishing slavery, though Republicans denied any such intention. Similarly, the logic of arguments by southern leaders led toward establishing slavery everywhere, though southern leaders denied that they sought any such thing. Lincoln put the problem succinctly. Soon after the 1860 election, he assured his old friend Alexander Stephens of Georgia that the Republican party would not attack slavery in the states where it existed. But Lincoln continued, "You think slavery is *right* and ought to be expanded; while we think it is *wrong* and ought to be restricted. That I suppose is the rub."

The issue of slavery in the territories made conflict impossible to avoid. Territorial expansion generated disputes so frequently that the nation never gained a breathing space. As the conflict recurred, it deepened its influence on policy and its effect on the government. Every southern victory increased fear of the Slave Power, and each increase in Free-Soil sentiment made alarmed slaveholders more insistent in their demands.

Concerns about slavery had driven all the other conflicts, but the fighting began with this central issue shrouded in confusion. How would the Civil War affect slavery, its place in the law, and black people's place in society?

Suggestions for Further Reading

Politics: General

Thomas B. Alexander, *Sectional Stress and Party Strength* (1967); Maurice G. Baxter, *One and Inseparable: Daniel Webster and the Union* (1984); Paul Bergeron, *The Presidency of James K. Polk* (1987); Ray Allen Billington, *The Protestant Crusade, 1800–1860* (1938 and 1964); Stanley W. Campbell, *The Slave Catchers* (1968); Avery O. Craven, *The Coming of the Civil War* (1942); Don E. Fehrenbacher, *The Dred Scott Case* (1978); Holman Hamilton, *Prologue to Con-*

flict: *The Crisis and Compromise of 1850* (1964); Michael F. Holt, *The Political Crisis of the 1850s* (1978); James M. McPherson, *Battle Cry of Freedom* (1988); Stephen E. Maizlish and John J. Kushma, eds., *Essays on American Antebellum Politics, 1840–1860* (1982); Roy F. Nichols, *The Disruption of American Democracy* (1948); Russell B. Nye, *Fettered Freedom* (1949); Merrill D. Peterson, *The Great Triumvirate: Webster, Clay, and Calhoun* (1987); David M. Potter, *The Impending Crisis, 1848–1861* (1976); Joel H. Silbey, *The Transformation of American Politics, 1840–1960* (1967); Gerald W. Wolff, *The Kansas-Nebraska Bill* (1977).

The South and Slavery

William L. Barney, *The Secessionist Impulse* (1974); Daniel W. Crofts, *Reluctant Confederates: Upper South Unionists in the Secession Crisis* (1989); Drew G. Faust, *The Ideology of Slavery* (1981); Drew G. Faust, *A Sacred Circle: The Dilemma of the Intellectual in the Old South* (1978); Eugene D. Genovese, *The World the Slaveholders Made* (1969); Eugene D. Genovese, *The Political Economy of Slavery* (1967); William Sumner Jenkins, *Pro-Slavery Thought in the Old South* (1935); John Niven, *John C. Calhoun and the Price of Union* (1988); David M. Potter, *The South and the Sectional Conflict* (1968); Thomas E. Schott, *Alexander H. Stephens of Georgia* (1988); J. Mills Thornton III, *Politics and Power in a Slave Society* (1978).

The North and Antislavery

Eugene H. Berwanger, *The Frontier Against Slavery* (1967); Louis Filler, *The Crusade Against Slavery, 1830–1860* (1960); Eric Foner, *Free Soil, Free Labor, Free Men* (1970); William E. Gienapp, *The Origins of the Republican Party, 1852–1856* (1986); Henry V. Jaffa, *Crisis of the House Divided* (1959); Robert W. Johannsen, *The Frontier, the Union, and Stephen A. Douglas* (1989); Aileen S. Kraditor, *Means and Ends in American Abolitionism* (1969); Lewis Perry and Michael Fellman, eds., *Antislavery Reconsidered* (1979); Jeffrey Rossbach, *Ambivalent Conspirators* (1982); Alice Felt Tyler, *Freedom's Ferment* (1944); Ronald G. Walters, *American Reformers* (1978).

The Mexican War and Foreign Policy

K. Jack Bauer, *Zachary Taylor* (1985); Reginald Horsman, *Race and Manifest Destiny* (1981); Ernest M. Lander, Jr., *Reluctant Imperialists: Calhoun, the South Carolinians, and the Mexican War* (1980); Robert E. May, *The Southern Dream of a Caribbean Empire, 1854–1861* (1973); Frederick Merk, *The Oregon Question* (1967); David M. Pletcher, *The Diplomacy of Annexation: Texas, Oregon, and the Mexican War* (1973); John H. Schroeder, *Mr. Polk's War: American Opposition and Dissent* (1973); Otis A. Singletary, *The Mexican War* (1960).

Moncure Conway, a Virginian who had converted to abolitionism and settled in New England, saw the Civil War as an opportunity to bring justice to human affairs. He urged northerners to accept slavery's challenge and defeat it, so that "the rays of Freedom and Justice" could shine throughout America. Then the United States would stand as a beacon not only of commercial power, but also of moral righteousness.

Conway's idealism was far removed from the motives that drove most federal soldiers to march grimly to their death. Although slaves believed that they were witnessing God's "Holy War for the liberation," Union troops often took a different perspective. When a Yankee soldier ransacked a slave family's cabin, the mother exclaimed, "Why you nasty, stinkin' rascal. You say you come down here to fight for the niggers, and now you're stealin' from 'em." The soldier replied, "You're a G____ D____ liar, I'm fightin' for $14 a month and the Union."

Southerners, too, acted from limited and pragmatic motives, fighting in self-defense or out of regional loyalty. A Union officer interrogating Confederate prisoners noticed the poverty of one captive. Clearly, the man was no slaveholder, so the officer asked him why he was fighting. "Because y'all are down here," replied the Confederate.

14

TRANSFORMING FIRE: THE CIVIL WAR, 1861–1865

For each of these people and millions of others, the Civil War was a life-changing event. It obliterated the normal circumstances of life, sweeping millions of men into training camps and battle units. Armies numbering in the hundreds of thousands marched over the South, devastating once-peaceful countrysides. Families struggled to survive without their men; businesses tried to cope with the loss of workers. Women in both North and South faced added responsibilities in the home and moved into new jobs in the work force. Nothing seemed untouched.

Change was more drastic in the South, where the leaders of the secession movement had launched a revolution for the purpose of keeping things unchanged. Never were men so mistaken. The Civil War forced changes in every phase of southern society, and the leadership of Jefferson Davis, president of the Confederate States of America, resulted in policies more objectionable to the elite than any proposed by President Lincoln.

War altered the North as well, but not as deeply. Because most of the fighting took place on southern soil, most northern farms and factories remained physically unscathed. The drafting of workers and the changing needs for products slowed the pace of industrialization somewhat, but factories and businesses remained busy. Workers lost ground to inflation, but the economy hummed. A new probusiness atmosphere dominated the United States Congress. To the discomfort of many, the powers of the federal government and the president increased during the war.

Ultimately, the Civil War forced new social and racial arrangements on the nation. Its greatest effect was to compel leaders and citizens to deal with an issue that they had often tried to avoid: slavery. This issue had, in complex and indirect ways, given rise to the war; now the war forced Americans to grapple with it.

The South Goes to War

In the first bright days of the southern nation, few foresaw the changes that were in store. Lincoln's call for troops to put down the Confederate insurrection stimulated an outpouring of regional loyalty that unified the classes. In the South, half a million men volunteered to fight for the Confederate cause. There were so many would-be soldiers that the Confederate government could not arm them all.

The ground swell of popular support for the Confederacy generated a mood of optimism and gaiety. Confident recruits boasted of whipping the

Battle of Bull Run

Yankees and returning home in time for dinner, and the first major battle of the war only increased such cockiness. On July 21, 1861, 30,000 federal troops attacked 22,000 southerners at a stream called Bull Run, near Manassas Junction, Virginia. Both armies were ill trained, and confusion reigned on the battlefield. But 9,000 Confederate reinforcements and a timely stand by General Thomas Jackson (thereafter known as "Stonewall" Jackson) won the day for the South. Union troops fled back to Washington in

disarray, and shocked northern congressmen and spectators, who had been following the battle from two miles away, suddenly feared that their capital would be taken.

In the wake of Bull Run, the North undertook a massive build-up of troops in northern Virginia. Lincoln gave command of the army to General George B. McClellan, who proved to be better at organization and training than at fighting. McClellan devoted the fall and winter of 1861 to readying a formidable force of a quarter of a million men. The North also moved to blockade southern ports in order to choke off the Confederacy's avenues of commerce and supply. At first, the Union blockade was woefully inadequate. But the Union Navy gradually increased the blockade's effectiveness, though it never completely bottled up southern commerce.

In the late summer and fall of 1861, Union naval power came ashore in the South. Federal squadrons captured Cape Hatteras and Hilton Head, part

Union Naval Campaign

of the Sea Islands off Port Royal, South Carolina (see map, page 256). A few months later, similar operations secured Albemarle and Pamlico sounds, Roanoke Island, and New Bern in North Carolina. The coastal victories, especially those off the coast of South Carolina, caused frightened planters to abandon their lands and flee. Their slaves thus became the first to escape slavery through military action. Ironically, the federal government, unwilling at first to wage a war against slavery, did not acknowledge the slaves' freedom.

With the approach of the spring of 1862, the military outlook for the Confederacy darkened again. In April 1862, ships commanded by Admiral David

Grant's Campaign in Tennessee

Farragut smashed through log booms on the Mississippi River and fought their way upstream to capture New Orleans. In northern Tennessee, land forces won significant victories for the Union. There, General Ulysses S. Grant captured Fort Henry and Fort Donelson, securing two prime routes into the Confederacy's heartland. A path into Tennessee, Alabama, and Mississippi now lay open before the Union Army.

On April 6, Confederate General Albert Sidney

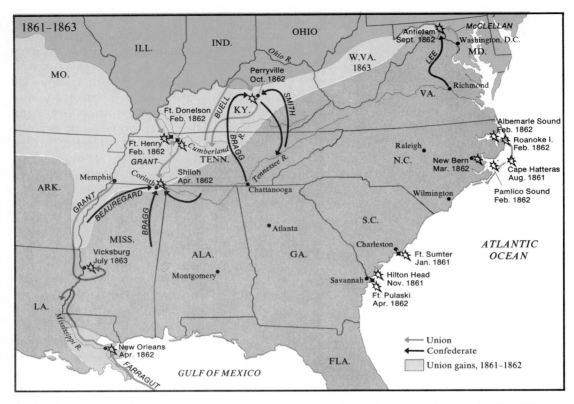

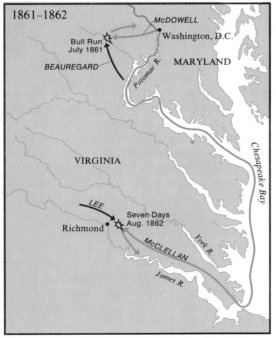

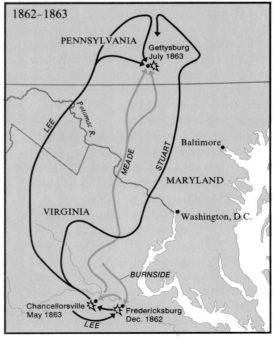

The Civil War, 1861–1863

1861	Battle of Bull Run General McClellan organizes Union Army Union blockade begins First confiscation act		Food riots in southern cities Battle of Chancellorsville Battle of Gettysburg and surrender of Vicksburg Draft riots in New York City
1862	Capture of Fort Henry and Fort Donelson Capture of New Orleans Battle of Shiloh Confederacy enacts conscription McClellan attacks Virginia Second confiscation act Confederacy mounts offensive Battle of Antietam	**1864**	Battle of Cold Harbor Lincoln requests party plank abolishing slavery General Sherman enters Atlanta Lincoln re-elected Jefferson Davis proposes Confederate emancipation Sherman marches through Georgia
1863	Emancipation Proclamation National Banking Act Union enacts conscription Black soldiers join Union Army	**1865**	Congress approves Thirteenth Amendment Hampton Roads Conference Lee surrenders at Appomattox Lincoln assassinated

Johnston caught Grant's army at Pittsburg Landing in southern Tennessee. The Confederates inflicted heavy damage, but Johnston was killed. The next day, a reinforced Union Army forced the enemy to withdraw to Corinth, Mississippi. There was no clear victor in the Battle of Shiloh, but destruction reigned. Northern troops lost 13,000 of 63,000 men; southerners sacrificed 11,000 out of 40,000.

The losses at Shiloh foreshadowed the enormous costs of the war. Never before in Europe or America had such massive forces pummeled each other with weapons of such destructive power. Yet the armies in the Civil War seemed virtually indestructible. Even in the bloodiest engagements, the losing army was never destroyed, even though thousands of men died. The improved range of modern rifles multiplied casualties, and because medical knowledge was rudimentary, minor wounds often led to death through infection.

The scope and duration of the conflict began to have unexpected effects. Tens of thousands of Con-

federate soldiers had volunteered for just one year's service, planning to return home in the spring of 1862 to plant their crops. To keep southern armies in the field, the War Department of the Confederacy offered bounties and furloughs to all who would re-enlist. When "the spirit of volunteering . . . died out," the Confederate government enacted the first national conscription law in American history. Thus, the war forced an unprecedented change on the states that had seceded out of fear of change.

Confederacy Resorts to a Draft

With their ranks reinforced, southern armies moved into heavier fighting. The Confederacy had relocated its capital from Montgomery, Alabama, to Richmond, Virginia. General McClellan sailed his troops to the York peninsula and advanced on Richmond from the east. But General Stonewall Jackson and General Robert E. Lee managed to stave off McClellan's attacks. First, Jackson maneuvered into the Shenandoah Valley, behind Union forces, and

Antietam was the bloodiest day of the war. Nearly 6,000 men died—far more than in the War of 1812 and the Mexican War combined—and another 17,000 were wounded. The northern victory helped prevent European recognition of the Confederacy. *Tharpe Collection of American Military History.*

threatened Washington, drawing some of the federals away from Richmond to protect their own capital. Then, in a series of engagements culminating in the Seven Days' battles, Lee held McClellan off. On August 3, McClellan withdrew to the Potomac, and Richmond was safe for almost two more years.

Buoyed by these results, Jefferson Davis conceived an ambitious plan to turn the tide of the war and compel the United States to recognize the Confederacy. He ordered a general offensive, sending Lee north to Maryland and General Kirby Smith and General Braxton Bragg to Kentucky. The South would go on the offensive and take the war north. The plan was promising, but every part of the offensive failed. In the bloodiest single day of fighting, September 17, 1862, McClellan turned Lee back in the Battle of Antietam, near Sharpsburg, Maryland. Smith and Bragg had to withdraw from Kentucky. The entire effort collapsed.

Davis Orders an Offensive

But southern armies were not exhausted. General James E. B. ("Jeb") Stuart executed a daring cavalry raid into Pennsylvania on October 10 through 12, and Lee decimated General Ambrose Burnside's soldiers as they charged his fortified positions at Fredericksburg, Virginia, on December 13. Nevertheless, the Confederacy had marshaled all its strength for a breakthrough and had failed.

Profoundly disappointed, Davis admitted to a committee of Confederate representatives that southerners had entered "the darkest and most dangerous period we have yet had."

War Transforms the South

Even more than the fighting, changes in civilian life robbed southerners of their gaiety and nonchalance. The war fundamentally altered southern society. One of the first traditions to fall was the southern preference for local government.

The South had been an area of limited government. States' rights had been its motto, but by modern standards the state governments were weak and sketchy affairs. To withstand the massive power of the North, the South had to centralize. No one saw the necessity of centralization more clearly than Jefferson Davis. If the states insisted on fighting separately, said Davis, "we had better make terms as soon as we can."

From the outset, Davis pressed to bring all arms, supplies, and troops under his control. He advocated conscription when the states failed to enroll enough new soldiers. He took a strong

**Central-
ization
of Power
in the South** leadership role toward the Confederate congress, which raised taxes and later passed a tax-in-kind—a tax paid not in money, but in wheat, corn, oats, cotton, and other farm products. Where opposition arose, the government suspended the writ of habeas corpus and imposed martial law. In the face of a political opposition that cherished states' rights, Davis proved unyielding.

Soon the Confederate administration in Richmond was taking virtually complete control of the southern economy. Because it controlled the supply of labor through conscription, the administration could regulate industry, compelling factories to work on government contracts to supply government needs. In addition, the Confederate congress passed laws giving the central government almost full control of the railroads; in 1864, shipping, too, came under extensive regulation. New statutes even limited corporate profits and dividends. A large bureaucracy sprang up to administer these operations; by the war's end, the southern bureaucracy was proportionally larger than its northern counterpart.

The mushrooming bureaucracy expanded the cities. Clerks and subordinate officials, many of them women, crowded the towns and cities where

**Effects
of War on
Southern
Cities and
Industries** Confederate departments had their offices. These sudden population booms stretched the existing housing supply and stimulated new construction. The pressure was especially great in Richmond, whose population increased two and a half times.

Another prime cause of urban growth was industrialization. Because of the Union blockade, the traditionally agricultural South became interested in industry. Davis exulted that southerners were manufacturing their own goods, thus "becoming more and more independent of the rest of the world." Indeed, though the Confederacy started almost from scratch, it achieved tremendous feats of industrial development.

As a result of these changes, southerners adopted new ways. Women, sheltered in the patriarchal antebellum society, gained substantial new

**Change
in the
Southern
Woman's
Role** responsibilities. The wives and mothers of soldiers became heads of households and undertook what had previously been considered men's work. In slaveowning families, women assumed management roles. In the cities, white women, who had been virtually excluded from the labor force, found a limited number of new, respectable, paying jobs. "Government girls" staffed the Confederate bureaucracy, and female schoolteachers became a familiar sight for the first time in the South. Such experiences undermined the image of the omnipotent male and gave thousands of women new confidence in their abilities.

The Confederate experience introduced and sustained many other new values. Legislative bodies yielded power to the executive branch of government, which could act more decisively in time of war. The traditional emphasis on aristocratic lineage gave way to respect for achievement and bravery under fire. Finally, sacrifice for the cause discouraged the pursuit of pleasure.

For the elite such sacrifice was symbolic, but for millions of ordinary southerners it was terrifyingly real. Mass poverty descended on the South, afflict-

**Human
Suffering
in the South** ing for the first time a large minority of the white population. Many yeoman families had lost their breadwinners to the army. As a South Carolina newspaper put it, "The duties of war have called away from home the sole supports of many, many families. . . . Help must be given, or the poor will suffer." The poor sought help from relatives, neighbors, friends, anyone. Sometimes they took their cases to the Confederate government.

Other factors aggravated the effect of the labor shortage. The South was in many places so sparsely populated that the conscription of one skilled craftsman could work a hardship on the people of an entire county. Often, they begged in unison for the exemption or discharge of the local miller, tanner, wheelwright, or potter. Most serious, however, was the loss of a blacksmith.

Inflation became a problem as prices increased by almost 7,000 percent. Indeed, rising prices imperiled those who could no longer provide for themselves. As early as 1861 and 1862, newspapers were reporting that "the poor of our . . . country will be unable to live at all" and that "want and starvation are staring thousands in the face." As their fortunes declined, people of once-modest means looked around them and found abundant evidence that all classes were not sacrificing equally. They saw that the wealthy gave up only their luxuries, while many poor families went without necessities. They saw that the government contributed to these inequities through policies that favored the upper class. Until the last year of the war, for example, prosperous southerners could avoid military service by hiring substitutes. Well over fifty thousand upper-class southerners purchased such substitutes.

Anger at such discrimination exploded in October 1862, when the Confederate congress exempted from military duty anyone who was supervising at least twenty slaves.

Inequities of the Confederate Draft Immediately, protests arose from every corner of the Confederacy, and North Carolina's legislators formally condemned the law. Its defenders argued, however, that the exemption preserved order and aided food production, and the statute remained on the books.

Dissension spread as growing numbers of citizens concluded that the struggle was "a rich man's war and a poor man's fight." Alert politicians and newspaper editors warned that class resentment was building to a dangerous level; letters to Confederate officials during this period contained a bitterness that suggested the depth of the people's anger. "If I and my little children suffer [and] die while there Father is in service," threatened one woman, "I invoke God Almighty that our blood rest upon the South." War was magnifying social tensions in the Confederacy.

The Northern Economy Copes with War

With the onset of war, the tidal wave of change rolled over the North just as it did over the South. Factories and citizens' associations geared up to support the war, and the federal government and its executive branch gained power they had never had before. The energies of an industrializing, capitalist society were harnessed to serve the cause of the Union. Idealism and greed flourished together, but the northern economy proved its awesome productivity.

At first, the war was a shock to business. With the sudden closing of southern markets, firms could no longer predict the demand for their goods, and many companies had to redirect

Initial Slump in Northern Business their activities in order to remain open. Southern debts became uncollectible, jeopardizing not only northern merchants, but many western banks as well. In farming regions, families struggled with an aggravated shortage of labor. For reasons such as these, the war initially caused an economic slump.

Overall, the war slowed industrialization in the North, but its economic impact was not all negative. Certain entrepreneurs, such as wool producers, benefited from shortages of competing products, and soaring demand for war-related goods swept some businesses to new heights of production. To feed the hungry war machine, the federal government pumped unprecedented amounts of money into the economy. As a result, firms producing weapons, munitions, uniforms, boots, camp equipment, saddles, ships, and other war necessities prospered.

War production also promoted the development of heavy industry in the North. The output of coal rose substantially. Iron makers improved the quality of their product while boosting

Effects of War on Northern Industry and Agriculture the production of pig iron. Although new railroad construction slowed, the manufacture of rails increased. Of considerable significance for the future were the railroad industry's adoption of a standard gauge for track and foundries' development of new and less expensive ways to make steel.

Another strength of the northern economy was the complementary relationship between agriculture and industry. The mechanization of agriculture had begun before the war. Wartime recruitment and conscription, however, gave western farmers an added incentive to purchase labor-saving ma-

Despite initial problems, the task of supplying a vast war machine kept the northern economy humming. This photograph shows the west side of Hudson Street, New York City, in 1865. *The New-York Historical Society*.

chinery. The shift from human labor to machines created new markets for industry and expanded the food supply for the urban industrial work force. Finally, farm families whose breadwinners went to war did not suffer as they did in the South. "We have seen," one magazine observed, "a stout matron whose sons are in the army, cutting hay with her team . . . and she cut seven acres with ease in a day, riding leisurely upon her cutter."

Northern industrial and urban workers did not fare as well. Jobs were plentiful following the initial slump, but inflation took much of a worker's pay. Studies of the cost of living indicate that between 1860 and 1864 consumer prices rose by at least 76 percent; wages rose by only 42 percent. Consequently, workers' families suffered a substantial decline in their standard of living.

Concurrent with the decline in real income was a loss of job security. To increase production, some

employers replaced workers with labor-saving machines. Other employers urged the government to liberalize immigration procedures so that they could import cheap labor. Workers responded by forming unions and sometimes by striking. Skilled workers organized to combat the loss of their jobs and status to machines; women and unskilled workers, excluded by the craftsmen, formed their own unions. In recognition of the increasingly national scope of business activity, thirteen groups—including coal miners and railway engineers—formed national unions during the Civil War.

New Militancy Among Northern Workers

Employers reacted negatively to this new spirit among workers. Manufacturers, for example, formed statewide or craft-based associations to pool information. These employers compiled blacklists of union members and required new workers to sign "yellow dog" contracts, or promises not to join a union. To put down strikes, they hired strikebreakers from the ranks of the poor— blacks, immigrants, and women—and sometimes received additional help from federal troops.

Troublesome as unions were, they did not prevent many employers from making a profit. The highest gains came from profiteering on government contracts. Unscrupulous businessmen took advantage of the sudden immense demand for goods for the army by selling clothing and blankets made of "shoddy"—wool fibers reclaimed from rags or worn cloth. Shoddy goods often came apart in the rain; most of the shoes purchased in the early months of the war were worthless, too. Contractors sold inferior guns for double the usual price and tainted meat for the price of good meat. Corruption was so widespread that it led to a year-long investigation by the House of Representatives.

Legitimate enterprises also made healthy profits. The output of woolen mills increased so dramatically that dividends in the industry nearly tripled.

Wartime Benefits to Northern Business
Some cotton mills made record profits on what they sold, even though they reduced their output. Railroads carried immense quantities of freight and passengers, increasing their business to the point that railroad stocks doubled or even tripled in value.

In fact, railroads were a leading beneficiary of government largesse. In the 1850s, Congress had failed to resolve the question of a northern versus a southern route for the first transcontinental railroad. With the South out of Congress, the northern route quickly prevailed. In 1862 and 1864, Congress chartered two corporations, the Union Pacific Railroad and the Central Pacific Railroad, and assisted them financially in connecting Omaha, Nebraska, with Sacramento, California. For each mile of track laid, the railroads received a loan ranging from $16,000 to $48,000, plus twenty square miles of land along a free 400-foot-wide right of way. Overall, the two corporations gained approximately 20 million acres of land and nearly $60 million in loans.

Higher tariffs also pleased many businessmen. Northern businesses did not uniformly favor high import duties; some manufacturers desired cheap imported raw materials more than they feared foreign competition. But northeastern congressmen traditionally supported higher tariffs, and after southern lawmakers left Washington, they had their way: the Tariff Act of 1864 raised tariffs generously. As one might expect, some healthy industries made artificially high profits by raising their prices to a level just below that of the foreign competition. By the end of the war, tariff increases averaged 47 percent, and rates were more than double those of 1857.

Wartime Society in the North

The outbreak of war stimulated patriotism in the North, just as it initially had in the South. Northern society, which had felt the stresses associated with urban growth, industrialization, and immigration, found a unifying cause in the preservation of the nation. Throughout thousands of towns and communities, northern citizens had participated in local government and local office holding. They worked in their government and felt it worked for them. Secession threatened to destroy this American system of representative government, and northerners rallied to its defense.

But there were other aspects of the northern response to war. The frantic wartime activity, the booming economy, and the Republican alliance with business combined to create a new atmosphere in Washington. The balance of opinion shifted against wage earners and toward large corporations; the notion spread that government should aid businessmen but not interfere with them. Noting the favorable atmosphere, railroad builders and industrialists took advantage of government loans, grants, and tariffs.

As long as the war lasted, the powers of the federal government and the president continued to grow. At the beginning of the conflict, Lincoln launched a major shipbuilding program without waiting for Congress to assemble. The lawmakers later approved his decision, and Lincoln continued to act in ad-

Wartime Powers of the U.S. Executive

vance of Congress when he deemed it necessary. In one striking exercise of executive power, Lincoln suspended the writ of habeas corpus for all people living between Washington and Philadelphia. There was scant legal justification for this act, but Lincoln's motive was practical: to ensure the loyalty of Maryland. Lincoln also used his wartime authority to bolster his political power. He and his generals proved adept at arranging furloughs for soldiers who could vote in close elections. Needless to say, the citizens in arms whom Lincoln helped to vote usually voted Republican.

Among the clearest examples of the wartime expansion of federal authority were the National Banking Acts of 1863, 1864, and 1865. Prior to the Civil War the nation did not have a uniform currency. Banks operating under state charters issued no fewer than seven thousand different kinds of notes. Under the new laws, Congress established a national banking system empowered to issue a maximum number of national bank notes. At the close of the war in 1865, Congress laid a prohibitive tax on state bank notes and forced most major state institutions to join the national system.

The increasing scale of things may have been best sensed by soldiers, whose first experiences with large organizations were often unfortunate. Blankets, clothing, and arms were often of poor quality. Vermin were commonplace. Hospitals were badly managed at first. Rules of hygiene in large camps were badly written or unenforced; latrines were poorly made or carelessly used. Indeed, conditions were such that 224,000 Union troops died from disease or accidents, far more than the 140,000 who died in battle.

Such conditions would hardly have predisposed the soldier to sympathize with changing social attitudes on the home front. Amid the excitement of moneymaking, a gaudy culture of vulgar display flourished in the largest cities. A writer for the New York *Herald* observed, "This war has entirely changed the American character. . . . The individual who makes the most money—no matter how—and spends the most—no matter for what—is considered the greatest man. . . . The world has seen its iron age, its silver age, its golden age, and its brazen age. This is the age of shoddy."

Self-Indulgence Versus Sacrifice in the North

Yet strong elements of idealism coexisted with ostentation. After initial uncertainty about whether to let the South go, abolitionists campaigned to turn the war into a war against slavery. Free black communities and churches both black and white responded to the needs of slaves who flocked to the Union lines. They sent clothing, ministers, and teachers in generous measure to aid the runaways.

Northern women, like their southern counterparts, took on new roles. Those who stayed home organized more than ten thousand soldiers' aid societies, rolled innumerable bandages, and raised $3 million. Thousands served as nurses in front-line hospitals, where they pressed for better care of the wounded. The professionalization of medicine since the Revolution had created a medical system dominated by men; thus, able female nurses had to fight both military regulations and professional hostility to win the chance to make their contribution. In the hospitals, they quickly proved their worth, but only the wounded welcomed them. Even Clara Barton, the most famous female nurse, was ousted from her post during the winter of 1863.

Thus, northern society embraced strangely contradictory tendencies. Materialism and greed flourished alongside idealism, religious conviction, and self-sacrifice. While wealthy men purchased 118,000 substitutes and almost 87,000 commutations at $300 each to avoid service in the Union Army, other soldiers risked their lives out of a desire to preserve the Union or extend freedom. It was as if several different wars were under way, each of them serving different motives.

The Strange Advent of Emancipation

At the very highest levels of government, there was a similar lack of clarity about the purpose of the war. Through the first several months of the struggle, both Davis and Lincoln studiously avoided references to slavery, the crux of the matter. Davis told southerners that they were fighting for constitutional liberty. He knew that stressing slavery might alienate nonslaveholders. Lincoln, hoping that a pro-Union majority would assert itself in the South, recognized that the mention of slavery would end any chance of coaxing the seceded states back into the Union. Moreover, not all Republicans were vitally interested in the slavery issue. An early presidential stand making the abolition of slavery, and not the preservation of the Union, the war's objective could split the party.

Lincoln first broached the subject of slavery in a major way in March 1862, when he proposed that the states consider emancipation on their own. He asked Congress to pass a resolution promising aid to any state that decided to emancipate, and he appealed to border-state representatives to consider seriously the idea of emancipation. What Lincoln was talking about was gradual emancipation, with compensation for slaveholders and colonization of the freed slaves outside the United States; until well into 1864, Lincoln steadfastly promoted an impractical scheme to colonize blacks in some region like Central America. The plan was extremely conservative, and since the states would make the decision voluntarily, no responsibility for it would attach to Lincoln.

Lincoln's Plan for Gradual Emancipation

Others wanted to go much further. A group of congressional Republicans known as the Radicals had, from the early days of the war, concerned themselves with slavery. In August 1861, at the Radicals' instigation, Congress passed its first confiscation act. Designed to punish the Confederate rebels, the law confiscated all property used for "insurrectionary purposes"— that is, if the South used slaves in a hostile action, those slaves were declared seized and liberated from their owners' possession. A second confiscation act (July 1862) was much more drastic: it confiscated the property of all those who supported the rebellion, even those who merely resided in the South and paid Confederate taxes. Their slaves were "forever free of their servitude, and not again [to be] held as slaves."

Confiscation Acts

Lincoln chose not to go that far. He stood by his proposal of voluntary gradual emancipation by the states and made no effort to enforce the second confiscation act. His stance brought a public protest from Horace Greeley, editor of the powerful *New York Tribune*. In an open letter to the president, Greeley wrote, "We require of you . . . that you execute the laws. . . . We think you are strangely and disastrously remiss . . . with regard to the emancipating provisions of the new Confiscation Act." Lincoln's reply was an explicit statement of his complex and calculated approach to the question. "I would save the Union," announced Lincoln. "If I could save the Union without freeing *any* slave I would do it, and if I could save it by freeing *all* the slaves I would do it; and if I would save it by freeing some and leaving others alone I would also do that. What I do about slavery, and the colored race, I do because I believe it helps to save the Union."

When he wrote those words, Lincoln had already decided to take a new step: issuance of the Emancipation Proclamation. He waited until an opportune time. On September 22, 1862, shortly after the Battle of Antietam, Lincoln issued the first part of his two-part proclamation. Invoking his powers as commander-in-chief of the armed forces, he announced that on January 1, 1863, he would emancipate the slaves in states whose people "shall then be in rebellion against the United States." The proclamation was less a declaration of the right of slaves to be free than it was a threat to southerners to end the war. Lincoln may not actually have expected southerners to give up their effort, but he was careful to offer them the option, thus putting the onus of emancipation on them.

Emancipation Proclamations

Lincoln's designation of the areas in rebellion on January 1 is worth noting. He excepted from his list every Confederate county or city that had fallen under Union control. Those areas, he declared, "are, for the present, left precisely as if this proclamation were not issued." Lincoln also did not liberate slaves in the border slave states that remained in the Union.

"The President . . . has proclaimed emancipation only where he has notoriously no power to execute it," complained the *New York World*. The exceptions, said the paper, "render the proclamation not merely futile, but ridiculous." Even Secretary of State William H. Seward, a moderate Republican, said sarcastically, "We show our sympathy with slavery by emancipating slaves where we cannot reach

Nearly 180,000 black men fought in the Union army, providing a vital infusion of strength for the northern cause. These soldiers in the 2nd U.S. Colored Light Artillery participated in the Battle of Nashville in December 1864. *Chicago Historical Society.*

them and holding them in bondage where we can set them free."

As a moral document, the Emancipation Proclamation, which in fact freed no slaves, was inadequate. As a political document, it was nearly flawless. Because the proclamation defined the war as a war against slavery, radicals could applaud it. Yet at the same time, it protected Lincoln's position with conservatives, leaving him room to retreat if he chose and forcing no immediate changes on the border slave states. The president had not gone as far as Congress, and he had taken no position that he could not change later if necessary.

In June 1864, however, Lincoln gave his support to the constitutional end of slavery. On the eve of the Republican national convention, he called the party's chairman to the White House and instructed him to have the party "put into the platform as the keystone, the amendment of the Constitution abolishing and prohibiting slavery forever." It was done; the party called for a new amendment, the thirteenth. Lincoln showed his commitment by lobbying Congress for quick approval of the measure.

He succeeded, and the proposed amendment went to the states for ratification or rejection. Lincoln's strong support for the Thirteenth Amendment—an unequivocal prohibition of slavery—constitutes his best claim to the title of Great Emancipator.

Yet Lincoln soon clouded that clear stand, for in 1865 the newly re-elected president considered allowing the defeated southern states to re-enter the Union and delay or defeat the amendment. In February, he and Secretary of State Seward met with three Confederate commissioners at Hampton Roads, Virginia. With the end of the war in sight, Lincoln was apparently contemplating the creation of a new and broader party based on a postwar alliance with southern Whigs and moderates. The cement for the coalition would be concessions to planter interests.

Hampton Roads Conference

Pointing out that the Emancipation Proclamation was only a war measure, Lincoln predicted that the courts would decide whether it had granted all, some, or none of the slaves their freedom. Seward observed that the Thirteenth Amendment was not yet ratified; re-entry into the Union would allow the southern states to vote against it and block it. Lincoln spoke in favor of ratification with a five-year delay. He also promised to seek $400 million in compensation for slaveholders. This financial aid would be an economic incentive for planters to rejoin the Union and would provide capital to ease the transition to freedom for both races. Such proposals were opposed in the North. In the South they were not discussed because of Davis's total commitment to independence.

Before the war was over, the Confederacy, too, addressed the issue of emancipation. Ironically, a strong proposal in favor of liberation came from Jefferson Davis, who was willing to sacrifice slavery to achieve independence. After considering the alternatives for some time, in the fall of 1864 Davis advocated the purchase and arming of slave soldiers and insisted that such soldiers, and later their wives and children, must be freed.

Davis's Plan for Emancipation

Confederate emancipation began too late to revive southern armies or win diplomatic advantages with antislavery Europeans. But Lincoln's Emancipation Proclamation stimulated a vital infusion of forces into the Union armies. Beginning in 1863, slaves shouldered arms for the North. Before the war was over, 134,000 slaves (and 52,000 free blacks) had fought for freedom and the Union. Their participation was crucial to northern victory, and it discouraged recognition of the Confederacy by foreign governments.

The Disintegration of Confederate Unity

During the final two years of fighting, both northern and southern governments waged the war in the face of increasing opposition at home. The unrest was connected to the military stalemate: neither side was close to victory in 1863. But protest also arose from fundamental stresses in the social structures of the North and the South.

One ominous development was the increasing opposition of planters to their own government, whose actions often had a negative effect on them. Not only did the Richmond government impose high taxes and a tax-in-kind, but Confederate military authorities also impressed slaves to build fortifications. And when Union forces advanced on plantation areas, Confederate commanders sent detachments through the countryside to burn stores of cotton that lay in the enemy's path. Such interference with plantation routines and financial interests was not what planters had expected of their government, and they resisted.

The Confederate constitution, drawn up by the leading political thinkers of the South, had in fact granted substantial powers to the central government, especially in time of war. But for many planters, states' rights had become virtually synonymous with complete state sovereignty. In effect, years of opposition to the federal government within the Union had frozen southerners in a defensive posture. Now they erected the barrier of states' rights as a defense against change. Planters sought a guarantee that their plantations and their lives would remain untouched; they were deeply committed neither to building a southern nation nor to winning independence. If the Confederacy had been allowed to depart from the Union in peace and continue as a semideveloped cotton-growing region, they would have been content. When secession revolutionized their world, they could not or would not adjust to it.

Meanwhile, at the bottom of southern society, there were other difficulties. Food riots occurred in the spring of 1863 in Atlanta, Macon, Columbus, and Augusta, Georgia, and in Salisbury and High Point, North Carolina. On April 2, a crowd assembled in the Confederate capital of Richmond to demand relief from Governor John Letcher. A passerby, noticing the excitement, asked a young girl, "Is there some celebration?" "There is," replied the girl. "We celebrate our right to live. We are starving. As soon as enough of us get together we are going to the bakeries and each of us will take a loaf of bread." Soon they did just that, sparking a riot that Davis himself had to quell at gunpoint.

Food Riots in Southern Cities

Throughout the rural South, ordinary people resisted more quietly—by refusing to cooperate with impressments of food, conscription, or tax collection. "In all the States impressments are evaded by every means which ingenuity can suggest, and in some openly resisted," wrote a high-ranking commissary officer. Farmers who did provide food refused to accept certificates of credit or government bonds in lieu of cash, as required by law. Conscription officers increasingly found no one to draft—men of draft age were hiding out in the forests.

Such civil discontent was certain to affect the Confederate armies. Spurred by concern for their loved ones and resentment of the rich man's war, large numbers of men did indeed leave the armies, supported by their friends and neighbors. The problem of desertion became so acute that by November 1863 Secretary of War James Seddon admitted that one-third of the army could not be accounted for. The situation was to worsen.

Desertions from the Confederate Army

The gallantry of those who stayed on in Lee's army and the daring of their commander made the start of the 1863 campaign deceptively positive. On May 2 and 3 at Chancellorsville, Virginia, 130,000 members of the Union Army of the Potomac bore down on fewer than 60,000 Confederates. Acting as if they enjoyed being outnumbered, Lee and Stonewall Jackson boldly divided their forces, ordering 30,000 men under Jackson on a day-long march westward and to the rear for a flank attack. Jackson arrived at his position late in the afternoon to witness unprepared Union troops "laughing, smoking," playing cards, and waiting for dinner. "Push right ahead," Jackson said, and his weary but excited corps swooped down on the federals and drove their right wing back in confusion. The Union forces left Chancellorsville the next day defeated. Although Stonewall Jackson had been fatally wounded, it was a remarkable southern victory.

Battle of Chancellorsville

But two critical battles in July 1863 brought crushing defeat for the Confederacy and a turning point for the war. After finding an advantageous approach to Vicksburg, General Ulysses S. Grant laid siege to that vital western fortification. If Vicksburg fell, United States forces would control the Mississippi, cutting the Confederacy in half and gaining an open path into its interior. Meanwhile, Lee proposed a Confederate invasion of the North. Both movements drew toward conclusion early in July.

In the North, Lee's troops streamed through western Maryland and into Pennsylvania, threatening both Washington and Baltimore. The possibility of a major victory near the Union capital became more and more likely. But along the Mississippi, Confederate prospects darkened. Davis and Secretary of War Seddon repeatedly wired General Joseph E. Johnston to concentrate his forces and attack Grant's army. "Vicksburg must not be lost, at least without a struggle," they insisted. Despite the prodding of his superiors, Johnston did nothing to relieve the garrison. In the meantime, Grant's men were supplying themselves by drawing on the agricultural riches of the Mississippi River valley. With such provisions, they could continue their siege indefinitely. In these circumstances, the fall of Vicksburg was inevitable, and on July 4, 1863, its commander surrendered.

On the same day, a battle that had been raging since July 1 concluded at Gettysburg, Pennsylvania. On July 1 and 2, Union and Confederate forces had both made gains in furious fighting. Then on July 3, Lee ordered a direct assault on Union fortifications atop Cemetery Ridge. Full of foreboding, General James Longstreet warned Lee that "no 15,000 men ever arrayed for battle can take that position." But Lee, hoping success might force the Union to accept peace with independence, stuck to his plan. His brave troops rushed the position, and a hundred momentarily breached the enemy's line. But most fell in heavy slaughter. On July 4, Lee had to withdraw, having suffered tremendous casualties in his troops: almost 4,000 killed and approximately 24,000 missing and wounded.

Battle of Gettysburg

Although southern soldiers displayed a courage and dedication at Gettysburg that would never be forgotten, the results were disastrous. Intelligent southerners knew that defeat lay ahead. The defeats of July 1863 also quickened the pace of the Confederacy's internal disintegration. Southern leaders began to realize that they were losing the support of the common people. Moreover, a few newspapers and politicians began to call for peace negotiations.

By 1864, much of the opposition to the war had moved entirely outside politics. Southerners were simply giving up the struggle, withdrawing their cooperation from the government. Deserters joined with ordinary citizens who were sick of the war to dominate whole towns. Secret societies dedicated to reunion sprang up. Active dissent spread through the South but was particularly common in upland and mountain regions. The government was losing the support of its citizens.

Antiwar Sentiment in the North

In the North, opposition to the war was similar in many ways, but not as severe. There was concern over the growing centralization of government, and war-weariness was a frequent complaint. Discrimination and injustice in the draft sparked protest among poor citizens, just as they did in the South. But the Union was so much richer than the South in human resources that none of these problems ever threatened the stability of the government. Fresh recruits were always available, and food and other necessities were not subject to severe shortages.

Furthermore, Lincoln possessed a talent that Davis lacked: he knew how to stay in touch with the ordinary citizen. Through letters to newspapers and to soldiers' families, he reached the common people and demonstrated that he had not forgotten them. Their grief was also his, for the war was his personal tragedy. His words helped to contain northern discontent but could not remove it.

Much of the wartime protest sprang from politics. The Democratic party was determined to regain power. Party leaders attacked the war, the **Peace Democrats** expansion of federal powers, inflation and the high tariff, and the improved status of blacks. They also denounced conscription and martial law and defended states' rights and the in-

terests of agriculture. In the 1862 congressional elections, the Democrats made a strong comeback, and during the war, peace Democrats influenced New York State and won majorities in the legislatures of Illinois and Indiana.

Led by outspoken men like Clement L. Vallandigham of Ohio, the peace Democrats were highly visible. Vallandigham criticized Lincoln as a dictator who had suspended the writ of habeas corpus without congressional authority and arrested thousands of innocent citizens. Vallandigham stayed within legal bounds, but his attacks were so damaging to the war effort that military authorities arrested him. Fearing that Vallandigham might seem a martyr, the president decided against a jail term and exiled him to the Confederacy.

Lincoln believed that antiwar Democrats were linked to secret organizations that harbored traitorous ideas. Likening such groups to a poisonous snake striking at the government, Republicans sometimes branded them—and by extension the peace Democrats—as Copperheads. Though Democrats were connected with these organizations, most engaged in politics rather than treason.

More violent opposition to the government came from ordinary citizens facing the draft, especially the urban poor, who were inducted in disproportionate numbers. Enrolling officers received rough treatment **New York City Draft Riot** in many parts of the North, and riots occurred in Ohio, Indiana, Pennsylvania, Illinois, and Wisconsin, and in such cities as Troy, Albany, and Newark. By far the most serious outbreak of violence occurred in New York City, in July 1863, where three days of rioting left seventy-four people dead. The riots had racist and class overtones. Many working-class whites feared an influx of black labor from the South, and Irish immigrants resented being forced to serve in the place of others.

Once inducted, northern soldiers felt many of the same anxieties and grievances as their southern counterparts. Federal troops, too, had to cope with loneliness and concern for their loved ones, disease, and the tedium of camp life. Thousands of men slipped away from authorities. Given the problems plaguing the draft and the discouragement in the North over lack of progress in the war, it is not

Chapter 14: Transforming Fire: The Civil War, 1861–1865

surprising that the Union Army struggled with a desertion rate as high as that of the Confederates.

Discouragement and war-weariness neared their peak during the summer of 1864. At that point, the Democratic party nominated the popular General George B. McClellan for president and put a qualified peace plank into its platform. Lincoln concluded that it was "exceedingly probable that this Administration will not be re-elected." The fortunes of war, however, soon changed the electoral situation.

Northern Pressure and Southern Will

The year 1864 brought to fruition the North's long-term diplomatic strategy. From the outset, the North's paramount diplomatic goal had been to prevent recognition of the Confederacy by European nations and the military and economic aid it would bring. Confederate leaders, believing that England was dependent on southern cotton, hoped to secure recognition through "King Cotton" diplomacy. Because British cotton mills had a 50-percent cotton surplus when the war began and because England developed new sources for cotton during the war, the South's strategy failed. The British government watched the battlefield and refused to be stampeded into acknowledging the Confederacy. France, though sympathetic to the South, was unwilling to act without the British.

Northern Diplomatic Strategy

More than once, the Union strategy nearly broke down. A major crisis occurred in 1861, when the overzealous commander of an American frigate stopped the British steamer *Trent* and abducted two Confederate ambassadors. The British reacted strongly, but Lincoln and Seward were able to delay any action until public opinion cooled and they could back down and return the ambassadors. In a series of confrontations, the United States protested against the building and sale of warships to the Confederacy. A few ships built in Britain, notably the *Alabama*, reached open water to serve the Confederacy. In less than two years, the *Alabama* destroyed or captured more than sixty northern ships. But soon the British government began to bar delivery to the Confederacy of warships such as the Laird rams—formidable vessels whose pointed prows were designed to break the Union blockade.

Back on American battlefields, the northern victory was far from won. Most engagements had demonstrated the advantages enjoyed by the defense. As General William Tecumseh Sherman recognized, the North had to "keep the war South until they are not only ruined, exhausted, but humbled in pride and spirit." Yet military authorities agreed that deep invasion was extremely difficult. The farther an army penetrated enemy territory, the more vulnerable its own communications and support became. Moreover, noted the Prussian expert Karl von Clausewitz, if the invader encountered a "truly national" resistance, his troops would be "everywhere exposed to attacks by an insurgent population."

General Grant decided to test these obstacles—and southern will—with an innovation of his own: the strategy of raids. Raids were nothing new, but what Grant had in mind were raids on a massive scale. He proposed to use whole armies, not just cavalry. Federal armies, abandoning their lines of support, would live off the land while they laid waste all resources useful to the Confederacy. After General George H. Thomas's troops won the Battle of Chattanooga in November 1863, the heartland of the South lay open. Moving to Virginia, Grant entrusted General Sherman with a hundred thousand men for a raid deep into the South, toward Atlanta.

Jefferson Davis countered by placing the army of General Johnston in Sherman's path. Davis's political strategy depended on the demonstration of military strength and a successful defense of Atlanta. With the federal elections of 1864 approaching, Davis hoped that a display of strength and resolution by the South would defeat Lincoln and elect a president who would sue for peace.

When Johnston slowly but steadily fell back toward Atlanta, Davis pressed his commander for assurances that Atlanta would be held. From a purely military point of view, Johnston was conducting the defense skillfully, but Davis replaced him with the one-legged General John Hood. Hood attacked but was beaten, and Sherman's army occupied Atlanta on September 2, 1864. The victory buoyed northern spirits, assured Lincoln's re-election, and cleared the way for Sherman's march from Atlanta to the sea.

As he moved across Georgia, Sherman cut a path fifty to sixty miles wide. A Georgia woman described the "Burnt Country" this way: "The fields were trampled down and the road was lined with carcasses of horses, hogs, and cattle that the invaders, unable either to consume or to carry with them, had wantonly shot down to starve our people and prevent them from making their crops. The stench in some places was unbearable." Such devastation diminished the South's material resources. More important, it was bound to damage further the faltering southern will to resist.

In Virginia, the preliminaries to victory proved to be protracted and ghastly. Throughout the spring and summer of 1864, Grant hurled his troops at Lee's army and suffered appalling

Heavy Losses Force Lee's Surrender losses: almost 18,000 casualties in the Battle of the Wilderness, more than 8,000 at Spotsylvania, and 12,000 in the space of a few hours at Cold Harbor (see map). Before the last battle, Union troops pinned scraps of paper bearing their names and addresses to their backs, certain that they would be mowed down as they rushed Lee's trenches. In four weeks in May and June, Grant lost as many men as were enrolled in Lee's entire army. Although costly, Grant's strategy prepared the way for eventual victory. Lee's army shrank until offensive action was no longer possible, while at the same time the Union Army kept replenishing its forces with new recruits.

The end finally came in the spring of 1865. Grant kept battering at Lee, who tried but failed to break through the federal line east of Petersburg on March 25. With the numerical superiority of Grant's army now upward of two to one, Confederate defeat was inevitable. On April 2, Lee abandoned Richmond and Petersburg. On April 9, hemmed in by federal troops, short of rations, and with fewer than thirty thousand men left, Lee surrendered to Grant. At Appomattox Courthouse, the Union general treated his rival with respect and paroled the

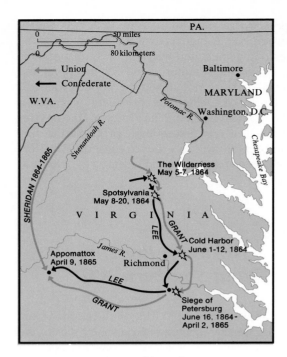

The War in Virginia, 1864–1865

defeated troops. Within weeks, Jefferson Davis was captured, and the remaining Confederate forces laid down their arms and surrendered. The war was over at last.

Lincoln did not live to see the last surrenders. On the evening of Good Friday, April 14, he went to Ford's Theatre in Washington, where an assassin named John Wilkes Booth shot him at pointblank range. Lincoln died the next day. The Union lost its wartime leader. For many, relief at the war's end was tempered by uncertainty about the future.

Costs and Effects

The costs of the Civil War were enormous. The total number of casualties exceeded 1 million—a frightful toll for a nation of 31 million. Approximately 364,222 federal soldiers died,

Casualties 140,070 of them from wounds suffered in battle. Another 275,175 Union soldiers were wounded but survived. On the Confederate side, an estimated 258,000 lost their lives, and almost as many suffered wounds. More men died in the Civil War than in all the other American wars combined, before Vietnam.

Although precise figures on enlistments are impossible to obtain, it appears that the Confederate armies claimed the services of 700,000 to 800,000 men. Far more, possibly 2.3 million, served in the Union armies. All these men were taken from home, family, and personal goals and had their lives disrupted in ways that, for those who survived the war, were not easily repaired.

Property damage and financial costs were also enormous, though difficult to tally. Federal loans and taxes during the conflict totaled almost $3 billion, and interest on the war debt was $2.8 billion. The Confederacy borrowed more than $2 billion but lost far more in the destruction of homes, fences, crops, livestock, and other property. Scholars have noted that small farmers lost just as much, proportionally, as planters whose slaves were emancipated.

Financial Cost of the War

Estimates of the total cost of the war exceed $20 billion—five times the total expenditure of the federal government from its creation to 1861. The northern government increased its spending by a factor of seven in the first full year of the war; by the last year, its spending had soared to twenty times the prewar level. By 1865, the federal government accounted for more than 26 percent of the gross national product.

These changes were more or less permanent. In the 1880s, interest on the war debt still accounted for approximately 40 percent of the federal budget and Union soldiers' pensions for as much as 20 percent. Thus, although many southerners had hoped to separate government from the economy, the war made such separation impossible. Although federal expenditures shrank after the war, they stabilized at twice the prewar level, or at 4 percent of the gross national product. Wartime emergency measures had brought the banking and transportation systems under federal control, and the government had put its power behind manufacturing and business interests through tariffs, loans,

and subsidies. Industrialization and large organizations arrived to stay, and in political terms, national power increased permanently. Extreme forms of the states' rights controversy were dead, although Americans continued to favor a state-centered federalism.

Despite all these changes, one crucial question remained unanswered: what was the place of black men and women in American life? The Union victory provided a partial answer: slavery as it had existed before the war could not persist. But what would replace it? African-Americans eagerly awaited an answer, which would have to be found during Reconstruction.

Suggestions for Further Reading

The War and the South

Thomas B. Alexander and Richard E. Beringer, *The Anatomy of the Confederate Congress* (1972); Richard E. Beringer et al., *Why the South Lost the Civil War* (1986); Robert F. Durden, *The Gray and the Black: The Confederate Debate on Emancipation* (1972); Paul D. Escott, *Many Excellent People* (1985); Paul D. Escott, *After Secession: Jefferson Davis and the Failure of Confederate Nationalism* (1978); Paul D. Escott, " 'The Cry of the Sufferers': The Problem of Poverty in the Confederacy," *Civil War History*, XXIII (September 1977), 228–240; Eli N. Evans, *Judah P. Benjamin* (1987); J. B. Jones, *A Rebel War Clerk's Diary*, 2 vols., ed. Howard Swiggett (1935); Stanley Lebergott, "Why the South Lost," *Journal of American History*, 70 (June 1983), 58–74; Ella Lonn, *Desertion During the Civil War* (1928); Malcolm C. McMillan, *The Disintegration of a Confederate State* (1986); Larry E. Nelson, *Bullets, Ballots, and Rhetoric: Confederate Policy for the United States Presidential Contest of 1864* (1980); Harry P. Owens and James J. Cooke, eds., *The Old South in the Crucible of War* (1983); Charles W. Ramsdell, *Behind the Lines in the Southern Confederacy*, ed. Wendell H. Stephenson (1944); James L. Roark, *Masters Without Slaves* (1977); Emory M. Thomas, *The Confederate Nation* (1979); Emory M. Thomas, *The Confederacy as a Revolutionary Experience* (1971); Emory M. Thomas, *The Confederate State of Richmond* (1971); William A. Tidwell, *Come Retribution: The Confederate Secret Service and the Assassination of Lincoln* (1989); Bell Irvin Wiley, *The Life of Johnny Reb* (1943); Bell Irvin Wiley, *The Plain People of the Confederacy* (1943); W. Buck Yearns, ed., *The Confederate Governors* (1985).

The War and the North

Ralph Andreano, ed., *The Economic Impact of the American Civil War* (1962); Robert Cruden, *The War That Never Ended* (1973); Wood Gray, *The Hidden Civil War* (1942); Randall C. Jimerson, *The Private Civil War* (1988); Frank L. Klement, *The Copperheads in the Middle West* (1960); Susan Previant Lee and Peter Passell, *A New Economic View of American History* (1979); James M. McPherson, *Battle Cry of Freedom* (1988); Phillip S. Paludan, *"A People's Contest": The Union and the Civil War, 1861–1865* (1989); George Winston Smith and Charles Burnet Judah, *Life in the North During the Civil War* (1966); George Templeton Strong, *Diary,* 4 vols., ed. Allan Nevins and Milton Hasley Thomas (1952); Paul Studenski, *Financial History of the United States* (1952); Bell Irvin Wiley, *The Life of Billy Yank* (1952).

Women

John R. Brumgardt, ed., *Civil War Nurse: The Diary and Letters of Hannah Ropes* (1980); Beth Gilbert Crabtree and James W. Patton, eds., *"Journal of a Secesh Lady": The Diary of Catherine Ann Devereux Edmondston, 1860–1866* (1979); Jacqueline Jones, *Labor of Love, Labor of Sorrow* (1985); George C. Rable, *Civil Wars: Women and the Crisis of Southern Nationalism* (1989); C. Vann Woodward and Elisabeth Muhlenfeld, ed., *Mary Chesnut's Civil War* (1981).

Blacks

Ira Berlin, ed., *Freedom,* Series II, *The Black Military Experience* (1982); David W. Blight, *Frederick Douglass' Civil War* (1989); Dudley Cornish, *The Sable Arm* (1956); Barbara Jeanne Fields, *Slavery and Freedom on the Middle Ground* (1985); James M. McPherson, *The Negro's Civil War* (1965); James M. McPherson, *The Struggle for Equality* (1964); Clarence L. Mohr, *On the Threshold of Freedom* (1986); Benjamin Quarles, *The Negro in the Civil War* (1953).

Military History

Bern Anderson, *By Sea and by River* (1962); Nancy Scott Anderson and Dwight Anderson, *The Generals* (1987); Bruce Catton, *Grant Takes Command* (1969); Thomas L. Connelly and Archer Jones, *The Politics of Command* (1973); Benjamin Franklin Cooling, *Forts Henry and Donelson* (1988); Burke Davis, *Sherman's March* (1980); William C. Davis, ed., *The Image of War,* multivolume (1983–1985); Shelby Foote, *The Civil War, a Narrative,* 3 vols. (1958–1974); William A. Frassanito, *Grant and Lee: The Virginia Campaigns, 1864–1865* (1983); Douglas Southall Freeman, *R. E. Lee,* 4 vols. (1934–1935); Herman Hattaway and Archer Jones, *How the North Won* (1983); Lawrence Lee Hewitt, *Port Hudson, Confederate Bastion on the Mississippi* (1988);

Archer Jones, *Confederate Strategy from Shiloh to Vicksburg* (1961); Gerald F. Linderman, *Embattled Courage* (1989); James Lee McDonough, *Chattanooga* (1984); Grady McWhiney and Perry D. Jamieson, *Attack and Die* (1982); J. B. Mitchell, *Decisive Battles of the Civil War* (1955); Reid Mitchell, *Civil War Soldiers* (1988); Harry W. Pfanze, *Gettysburg: The Second Day* (1988); Robert Garth Scott, *Into the Wilderness with the Army of the Potomac* (1987); Stephen W. Sears, *George B. McClellan* (1988); Stephen Z. Starr, *The Union Cavalry in the Civil War,* 3 vols. (1985); Emory M. Thomas, *Bold Dragoon: The Life of J.E.B. Stuart* (1987).

Diplomatic History

Stuart L. Bernath, *Squall Across the Atlantic* (1970); David P. Crook, *The North, the South, and the Powers, 1861–1865* (1974); Charles P. Cullop, *Confederate Propaganda in Europe* (1969); Frank J. Merli, *Great Britain and the Confederate Navy* (1970); Frank L. Owsley and Harriet Owsley, *King Cotton Diplomacy* (1959); Gordon H. Warren, *Fountain of Discontent* (1981).

Abraham Lincoln and the Union Government

Gabor S. Borit, ed., *The Historian's Lincoln* (1989); LaWanda Cox, *Lincoln and Black Freedom* (1981); Richard N. Current, *The Lincoln Nobody Knows* (1958); David Donald, *Charles Sumner and the Rights of Man* (1970); Ludwell H. Johnson, "Lincoln's Solution to the Problem of Peace Terms, 1864–1865," *Journal of Southern History,* XXXIV (November 1968), 441–447; Peyton McCrary, *Abraham Lincoln and Reconstruction: The Louisiana Experiment* (1978); Stephen B. Oates, *With Malice Toward None* (1977); James G. Randall, *Mr. Lincoln* (1957); Benjamin P. Thomas, *Abraham Lincoln* (1952); Hans L. Trefousse, *The Radical Republicans* (1969); Glyndon G. Van Deusen, *William Henry Seward* (1967); T. Harry Williams, *Lincoln and His Generals* (1952); T. Harry Williams, *Lincoln and the Radicals* (1941).

Saturday, May 16, was a beautiful spring day in 1868. Sunlight and balmy weather bathed the nation's capital. As the morning passed, a crowd gathered in the Senate chamber. Foreign dignitaries filled the diplomatic box, and spectators packed the Senate galleries. Outside the chamber, thousands milled about.

Precisely at noon, the chief justice of the United States entered the Senate. All principals in this solemn drama were present before the High Court of Impeachment except the accused: Andrew Johnson, president of the United States. Johnson, who never appeared to defend himself in person, waited at the White House as Chief Justice Salmon Chase ordered the calling of the roll. To each senator, he put the questions, "How say you? Is the respondent, Andrew Johnson, President of the United States, guilty or not guilty of a high misdemeanor, as charged in this article?" Thirty-five senators answered, "Guilty"; nineteen, "Not guilty." The thirty-five votes for conviction were one short of the required two-thirds majority. The United States had come within one vote of removing the president from office.

How had this extraordinary event come about? What had brought the executive and legislative branches of government into such severe conflict? An unprecedented

15

RECONSTRUCTION BY TRIAL AND ERROR, 1865–1877

problem, the reconstruction of the Union, furnished the occasion; deepening differences over the proper policy to pursue had led to the confrontation.

In 1865, at the end of the war, such an event seemed most unlikely. Although he was a southerner from Tennessee, Johnson had built his career on criticizing the wealthy planters and championing the South's small farmers. When an assassin's bullet thrust him into the presidency, many former slaveowners believed that they had reason to fear Johnson. In the North, the Radicals felt confident that he would deal sternly with the South. When one of them suggested the exile or execution of ten or twelve leading rebels to set an example, Johnson had replied, "How are you going to pick out so small a number? Robbery is a crime; rape is a crime; treason is a crime; and crime must be punished."

Moreover, fundamental change was already under way in the South. During his army's last campaign, General William T. Sherman had issued

Special Field Order No. 15, which set aside for Negro settlement the Sea Islands and all abandoned coastal lands thirty miles to the interior, from Charleston to the Saint John's River in northern Florida. Black refugees quickly poured into these lands; by the middle of 1865, forty thousand freed people were living in their new homes.

Before the year ended, however, these signs of change were reversed. Although Jefferson Davis was imprisoned for two years, no Confederate leaders were executed, and southern aristocrats soon came to view Andrew Johnson as their friend and protector. Johnson pardoned rebel leaders liberally, allowed them to take high offices, and ordered government officials to reclaim the freedmen's land and give it back to the original owners.

The unexpected outcome of Johnson's program led Congress to examine his policies and design new plans for Reconstruction. Out of negotiations in Congress and clashes between the president and the legislators, there emerged first one, and then two, new plans for Reconstruction. Before the process was over, the nation had adopted the Fourteenth and Fifteenth Amendments and impeached its president.

Blacks benefited from having greater control over their personal lives and took the risks of voting and participating in politics. But they knew that the success of Reconstruction also depended on the determination and support of the North. Southern opposition to Reconstruction grew steadily. Most frightful was a secret terrorist organization, the Ku Klux Klan. By the early 1870s, the failure of Reconstruction was apparent. Republican leaders and northern voters had to decide how far they would persist in their efforts to reform the South.

Thus the nation stumbled, by trial and error, toward a policy that attempted to reconstruct the South. Congress insisted on equality before the law for black people and gave black men the right to vote. It took the unprecedented step of impeaching the president. But more far-reaching measures to advance black freedom never had much support in Congress, and when suffrage alone proved insufficient to remake the South, the nation soon lost interest. Reconstruction proclaimed anew the American principle of human equality but failed to secure it in reality.

Equality: The Unresolved Issue

For America's former slaves, Reconstruction had one paramount meaning: a chance to explore freedom. A southern white woman admitted in her diary that the black people "showed a natural and exultant joy at being free." The slaves on one Texas plantation jumped up and down and clapped their hands as one man shouted, "We is free—no more whippings and beatings!" A few blacks gave in to the natural desire to do what had been impossible before. One grandmother who had long resented her treatment "dropped her hoe" and ran to confront the mistress. "I'm free!" she yelled at her. "Yes, I'm free! Ain't got to work for you no more!" Others left the plantation, either to search for family members or just to exercise their new-found freedom of movement.

Most freedmen reacted more cautiously and shrewdly, taking care to test the boundaries of their new condition. One sign of this shrewd caution was the way freedmen evaluated potential employers. If a white person had been relatively considerate to blacks in bondage, blacks reasoned that he might prove a desirable employer in freedom. Other blacks left their plantation all at once, for, as one put it, "that master am sure mean."

In addition to a fair employer, the freedmen wanted land of their own. Land represented their chance to farm for themselves and to have an independent life. It represented compensation for their generations of travail in bondage. A northern observer noted that freedmen made "plain, straight-forward" inquiries as they settled the land set aside for them by Sherman. They wanted to be sure the land "would be theirs after they had improved it."

Blacks' Desire for Land

No one could say how much of a chance the whites, who were in power, would give to blacks. During the war, the federal government had refused at first to arm black volunteers. Necessity forced a change in policy; because the war was going badly, the administration authorized black

1865	Johnson begins Reconstruction; Confederate leaders regain power Black codes; Congress refuses to seat southern representatives	**1870**	Enforcement Act
		1871	Enforcement Act of 1871; Ku Klux Klan Act
1866	Civil Rights Act; Congress approves Fourteenth Amendment Freedmen's Bureau renewed; *Ex parte Milligan* Most southern states reject Fourteenth Amendment	**1872**	Amnesty Act; Liberal Republicans organize Debtors urge government to keep greenbacks in circulation Grant re-elected
		1873	*Slaughter-House* cases; Panic of 1873
1867	Military Reconstruction Act; Tenure of Office Act Constitutional conventions called in southern states	**1875**	Civil Rights Act Congress requires that after 1878 greenbacks be convertible into gold
1868	House impeaches Johnson; Senate acquits him Fourteenth Amendment ratified Ulysses S. Grant elected president	**1876**	*United States* v. *Cruikshank; United States* v. *Reese* Presidential election disputed
1869	Congress approves Fifteenth Amendment (ratified in 1870)	**1877**	Congress elects Hayes; Black Exodusters migrate to Kansas

enlistments. By the spring of 1863, black troops were proving their value. "They fight like fiends," said one observer.

Black leaders hoped that military service would secure equal rights for their people. If black soldiers turned the tide, asked one man, "Would the nation refuse us our rights . . . ? Would it refuse us our vote?" Wartime experience suggested that it would. Despite their valor, black soldiers faced persistent discrimination. For example, the government paid white privates $13 per month, plus a clothing allowance of $3.50. Black troops earned $10 per month, less $3 deducted for clothing. Blacks resented this injustice so deeply that in protest two regiments refused to accept any pay, and eventually Congress remedied the discrimination.

The general attitude of northerners on racial questions was mixed. Abolitionists and many Republicans helped black Americans fight for equal rights, and they won some victories. In 1864, the federal courts accepted black testimony, and New York City desegregated its streetcars. One state, Massachusetts, enacted a comprehensive public accommodations law. Nevertheless, there were many signs of resistance to racial equality. The Democratic party fought hard against equality, charging that Republicans favored race mixing and were undermining the status of the white worker. Voters in three states—Connecticut, Minnesota, and Wisconsin—rejected black suffrage in 1865. For African-Americans, the conflicting signals from the North raised a question: how much opportunity would freedom bring? The answer depended on the evolution of policy in Washington.

Johnson's Reconstruction Plan

Through 1865, the formation of Reconstruction policy rested solely with Andrew Johnson, for shortly before he became president, Congress recessed and did not reconvene until December. In the nearly eight months that intervened, Johnson devised his own plan and put it into operation. He decided to form new state governments in the South by using his power to grant pardons.

Johnson had a few precedents to follow. In December 1863, Lincoln had proposed a "10-percent" plan for captured portions of Louisiana; a state government could be established as soon as 10 percent of those who had voted in 1860 took an oath of future loyalty. Only high-ranking Confederate officials would be denied a chance to take the oath. Radicals bristled, however, at such a mild plan, and a majority of Congress (in the Wade-Davis bill, which Lincoln pocket-vetoed) favored stiffer requirements and stronger proof of loyalty. At the time of his death, Lincoln had given general approval to a plan drafted by Secretary of War Edwin M. Stanton, which would have imposed military authority and provisional governors as steps toward new state governments.

Johnson began with the plan Stanton had drafted. Johnson's advisers split evenly on the question of voting rights for freedmen in the South. Johnson said he favored black suffrage, but only if the southern states adopted it voluntarily. A champion of states' rights, he regarded this decision as too important to be taken out of the hands of the states.

Such conservatism had an enduring effect on Johnson's policies, but at first it appeared that his old enmity toward the planters might produce a plan for radical changes in class relations among whites. As he appointed provisional governors in the South, Johnson also proposed rules that would keep the wealthy planter class out of power. He required every southern voter to swear an oath of loyalty as a condition of gaining amnesty or pardon. Some southern whites, however, faced special difficulties in regaining their rights.

Johnson barred certain classes of southerners from taking the oath and gaining amnesty. Former federal officials who had violated their oaths to support the United States and had aided the Confederacy could not take the oath. Nor could graduates of West Point or Annapolis who had resigned their commissions to fight for the South. The same was true for high-ranking Confederate officers and Confederate political leaders. Also barred were all southerners who aided the rebellion and whose taxable property was worth more than twenty thousand dollars. Such individuals had to apply personally to the president for pardon and restoration of political rights; otherwise, they risked legal penalties, including confiscation of their land. Thus, it appeared that the leadership class of the Old South would be removed from power and replaced by a new leadership of deserving yeomen.

Johnson's provisional governors began the Reconstruction process by calling constitutional conventions. The delegates chosen for these conventions had to draft new constitutions eliminating slavery and invalidating secession. After ratification of these constitutions, new governments could be elected, and the states would be restored to the Union with full congressional representation. But no southerners could participate in this process who had not taken the oath of amnesty or who had been ineligible to vote on the day the state seceded. Freedmen, being in the latter category, could not participate in the conventions.

But the plan did not work as Johnson had envisioned. Surprisingly, Johnson played a role in its subversion. He pardoned many aristocrats and chief rebels. By the time the southern states drafted their constitutions and elected public officials, Confederate leaders were in powerful positions. Johnson decided to stand behind his new governments and declare Reconstruction completed. Thus, in December 1865, many Confederate congressmen traveled to Washington to claim seats in the United States Congress, and Alexander Stephens, vice president of the Confederacy, returned to the capital as senator-elect.

Many northerners frowned on the election of such prominent rebels, and other results of Johnson's program also sparked negative comment in

Blacks Codes the North. Some of the state conventions were slow to repudiate secession; others only grudgingly admitted that slavery was dead. Of great concern to northern politicians was the enactment of the black codes. In these laws, southern state legislatures defined the status of freedmen. Some legislatures merely revised sections of the slave codes by substituting the word *freedman* for *slave*. Typical codes compelled African-Americans to carry passes and to observe a curfew. In some cases, restrictions kept blacks out of many desirable occupations and forced them to live in housing provided by a landowner. There were also vagrancy laws, and restrictive labor contracts bound supposedly free laborers to the plantation. Finally, states often denied blacks access to public institutions such as schools and orphanages.

Thus, it was not surprising that northern congressmen decided to take a close look at the results of Johnson's plan. On reconvening, they voted not to admit the newly elected southern representatives, whose credentials were subject, under the Constitution, to congressional scrutiny. The House and Senate established an important joint committee to examine Johnson's policies and advise on new ones. Reconstruction entered a second phase, one in which Congress would play a strong role.

The Congressional Reconstruction Plan

Northern congressmen disagreed on what to do, but they did not doubt their right to play a role in Reconstruction. The Constitution mentioned neither secession nor reunion, but it did assign to Congress the duty to guarantee to each state a republican government. Under this provision, the legislators thought, they could devise policies for Reconstruction.

They soon found that other constitutional questions had a direct bearing on the policies they followed. What, for example, had rebellion done to the relationship between southern states and the Union? Lincoln had always insisted that the Union

remained unbroken. In contrast, congressmen who favored vigorous Reconstruction measures tended to argue that war *had* broken the Union. The southern states had committed legal suicide and reverted to the status of territories, they argued, or the South was a conquered nation subject to the victor's will. Moderate congressmen held that the states had forfeited their rights through rebellion and had thus come under congressional supervision.

These diverse theories mirrored the diversity of Congress itself. Northern legislators fell into four major categories: Democrats, conservative Republicans, moderate Republicans, and **The Radicals** other Republicans called Radicals. Although the Republican party had a majority, there was considerable distance between conservative Republicans, who desired a limited federal role in Reconstruction and were fairly happy with Johnson's actions, and the Radicals. The Radicals, led by Thaddeus Stevens, Charles Sumner, and George Julian believed that it was essential to democratize the South, establish public education, and ensure the rights of freedmen. They favored black suffrage, often supported land confiscation and redistribution, and were willing to exclude the South from the Union for several years, if necessary, to achieve their goals. Between the conservative Republicans and the Radicals lay the moderates, who held the balance of power.

Through their actions, Johnson and the Democrats forced these diverse Republican factions to come together. The president and the northern Democrats, insisting that Reconstruction was over and that the southern delegates should be seated in Congress, refused to cooperate with conservative or moderate Republicans. Moreover, Johnson refused to support an apparent compromise on Reconstruction. Under its terms, Johnson would agree to two modifications of his program. The life of the Freedmen's Bureau, which Congress established in March 1865 to feed the hungry, negotiate labor contracts, and start schools, would be extended by one bill; and a civil rights bill would be passed to counteract the black codes. This bill gave federal judges the power to remove from southern courts cases in which blacks were treated unfairly. Its provisions applied to discrimination by private persons, as well as by government officials. As the first major bill to enforce the Thirteenth Amendment's abolition of slavery, it was a significant piece of legislation.

But in the spring of 1866, Johnson destroyed the compromise by vetoing both bills (they were later repassed) and condemning Congress's action. In doing so, he questioned the legitimacy of congressional involvement in policymaking. All hope of working with the president was now gone. Instead of a compromise program, the various Republican factions drew up a new Reconstruction plan. It took the form of a proposed amendment to the Constitution—the fourteenth—and it represented a compromise between radical and conservative elements of the party.

Of the four points in the amendment, the fourth won nearly universal agreement: the Confederate debt was declared null and void and the war debt of the United States guaranteed. The **Fourteenth Amendment** third section, prohibiting prominent Confederates from holding any national or state political office, also gained fairly general support. Only by a two-thirds vote of each house of Congress could these political penalties be removed.

The section of the Fourteenth Amendment that would have by far the greatest legal significance in later years was the first. On its face, this section was an effort to strike down the black codes and guarantee basic rights to freedmen. It conferred citizenship on freedmen and prohibited states from abridging their constitutional "privileges and immunities." Similarly, the amendment barred any state from taking a person's life, liberty, or property "without due process of law" and from denying "equal protection of the laws." These clauses were phrased broadly enough to become in time powerful guarantees of black Americans' civil rights.

The second section of the amendment revealed the political motives that had produced the document. Northerners, in Congress and out, disagreed about whether black citizens should have the right to vote. What was more, Republicans feared that emancipation, which made every former slave five-fifths of a person instead of three-fifths for purposes of congressional representation, might increase the South's power in Congress. If it did, and if blacks were not allowed to vote, the former secessionists would gain seats in Congress.

Most northerners had never planned to reward the South for rebellion, and Republicans in Congress were determined not to hand over power to their political enemies. So they offered the South a choice. According to the second section of the Fourteenth Amendment, states did not have to give black men the right to vote. But if they did not do so, their representation would be reduced proportionally. If they did enfranchise black men, their representation would be increased proportionally—but Republicans would be able to appeal to the new black voters.

Although the Fourteenth Amendment dealt with the voting rights of black men, it ignored female citizens. When legislators defined them as nonvoting citizens, prominent women's leaders such as Elizabeth Cady Stanton and Susan B. Anthony decided that it was time to end their alliance with abolitionists. Thus the independent women's rights movement grew.

In 1866, however, the major question in Reconstruction politics was how the public would respond to the amendment. Would the northern public support Congress's plan or **Southern Rejection of the Fourteenth Amendment** the president's? Johnson did his best to block the Fourteenth Amendment and to convince northerners to reject it. Condemning Congress for its refusal to seat southern representatives, the president urged state legislatures in the South to vote against ratification. Every southern legislature except Tennessee's rejected the amendment by a large margin. In the North, Johnson arranged a National Union convention to publicize his program. Then he boarded a special train for a "swing around the circle" that carried his message far into the Midwest. But increasingly, audiences rejected his views and jeered at him.

The election of 1866 was a resounding victory for Republicans in Congress. Men whom Johnson had denounced won re-election by large margins, and the Republican majority increased. Radical and moderate Republicans gained strength. Thus, Republican congressional leaders received a mandate to continue with their Reconstruction plan.

Recognizing that nothing could be accomplished under the existing southern governments and with blacks excluded from the electorate, Congress, in 1867, passed the Military Reconstruction Act.

Military Reconstruction Act of 1867 The act called for new governments in the South and a return to military authority until they were set up. It barred from political office the Confederate leaders listed in the Fourteenth Amendment. It guaranteed freedmen the right to vote in elections for state constitutional conventions and for subsequent state governments. In addition, each southern state was required to ratify the Fourteenth Amendment; to ratify its new constitution; and to submit its new constitution to Congress for approval. Thus, black people gained an opportunity to fight for a better life through the political process, but their only weapon was the ballot. The law required no redistribution of land and guaranteed no basic changes in southern social structure.

Congress's role as the architect of Reconstruction was not quite over. To restrict Johnson's influence and safeguard its plan, Congress enacted a number of controversial laws. First, it set the date for its own reconvening—an unprecedented act, for the president traditionally summoned the legislature to Washington. Then, it limited Johnson's power over the army by requiring the president to issue military orders through the General of the Army, Ulysses S. Grant, who could not be sent from Washington without the Senate's consent. Finally, Congress passed the Tenure of Office Act, which gave the Senate power to interfere with changes in the president's cabinet. Designed to protect Secretary of War Stanton, who sympathized with the Radicals, this law violated the tradition that a president controlled his own cabinet.

Johnson took several belligerent steps of his own. He issued orders to military commanders in the South limiting their powers and increasing the powers of the civil governments he had created in 1865. He also removed any officers who conscientiously enforced Congress's new law. Finally, in August 1867, he tried to remove Stanton. With that attempt, the confrontation reached its climax.

The House Judiciary Committee, which had twice before considered impeaching the president, again initiated the action. The 1868 indictment concentrated on Johnson's violation of **Impeachment of President Johnson** the Tenure of Office Act. Modern scholars, however, regard his systematic efforts to impede enforcement of the Military Reconstruction Act as a far more serious offense.

Johnson's trial in the Senate lasted more than three months. The prosecution, led by Radical Thaddeus Stevens and others, argued that Johnson was guilty of "high crimes and misdemeanors." But they also advanced the novel idea that impeachment was a political matter, not a judicial trial of guilt or innocence. The Senate ultimately rejected such reasoning, which would have transformed impeachment into a political weapon against any chief executive who disagreed with Congress. Although a majority of senators voted to convict Johnson, the prosecution fell one vote short of the necessary two-thirds majority. Johnson remained in office for the few months left in his term, and his acquittal established the precedent that only serious misdeeds merited removal from office.

In 1869, in an effort to write democratic principles and colorblindness into the Constitution, the Radicals presented the Fifteenth Amendment for ratification. This measure forbade **Fifteenth Amendment** states to deny the right to vote "on account of race, color, or previous condition of servitude." The wording fell short of an outright guarantee of the right to vote because many northern states denied the suffrage to women and to men who were illiterate or too poor to pay taxes. Ironically, the votes of four southern states—compelled by Congress to approve the amendment as an added condition to rejoining the Union—proved necessary to impose even this language on parts of the North. Although several states outside the South refused to ratify, the Fifteenth Amendment became law in 1870.

Reconstruction Politics in the South

From the start, white southerners resisted Reconstruction. Their opposition to change appeared in the black codes and other policies of the Johnson governments, as well as in private **White Resistance** attitudes. Many whites set their faces against emancipation, and the former planter class proved especially unbending. In 1866, a Georgia newspaper frankly declared, "Most of the white citizens believe that the institution of slavery was right, and . . . they will believe that the condition, which comes nearest to slavery, that can now be established will be the best."

Fearing the end of their control over slaves, some planters attempted to postpone freedom by denying or misrepresenting events. Former slaves reported that their owners "didn't tell them it was freedom" or "wouldn't let [them] go." To hold onto their workers, some landowners claimed control over black children and used guardianship and apprentice laws to bind black families to the plantation. Whites also blocked blacks from acquiring land and used force to keep blacks submissive.

After President Johnson encouraged the South to resist congressional Reconstruction, many white conservatives worked hard to capture the new state governments. Elsewhere, large numbers of whites boycotted the polls in an attempt to defeat Congress's plans. Since the new constitutions had to be approved by a majority of registered voters, registered whites could defeat them by sitting out the elections. This tactic was tried in North Carolina and succeeded in Alabama, forcing Congress to base ratification on a majority of those voting.

Very few black men stayed away from the polls. Enthusiastically, they seized the opportunity to participate in politics, voting solidly Republican. Most agreed with one man who felt that he should "stick to the end with the party that freed me."

With a large black turnout, and with prominent Confederates barred from politics under the Fourteenth Amendment, a new southern Republican party came to power in the constitutional conventions. Among Republican delegates were some blacks, northerners who had moved to the South, and native southern whites who favored change. Together, they brought the South's fundamental law into line with progressive reforms that had been adopted in the rest of the nation. The new constitutions were more democratic. They eliminated property qualifications for voting and holding office, and they made elective the state and local offices that had been appointive. They provided for public schools and institutions to care for the mentally ill, the blind, the deaf, the destitute, and the orphaned, and they ended imprisonment for debt.

The conventions also broadened women's rights in possession of property and divorce. Usually, the main goal was not to make women equal with men but to provide relief to thousands of suffering debtors. In families left poverty-stricken by the war, the husband had usually contracted the debts. Thus, giving women legal control over their own property provided some protection to their families. Some delegates, however, wanted to expand women's rights further. Blacks in particular called for laws to provide for women's suffrage, but they were ignored by their white colleagues.

Under these new constitutions, the southern states elected new governments. Again, the Republican party triumphed, bringing new men into positions of power. The ranks of state **Triumph of** legislators in 1868 included some **Republican** black southerners for the first **Governments** time in history. Congress's second plan for Reconstruction was well under way. It remained to be seen what these new governments would do and how much change they would bring to society.

There was one possibility of radical change through these new governments. That possibility depended on the disfranchisement of substantial numbers of Confederate leaders. If the Republican regimes used their new power to exclude many whites from politics as punishment for rebellion, they would have a solid electoral majority based on black voters and their white allies. Land reform and the assurance of racial equality would be possible. But none of the Republican governments even gave this serious consideration.

Why did the new legislators shut the door on the possibility of deep and thoroughgoing reform? First, they appreciated the realities of power and the depth of racial enmity. In most states whites were the majority of the population, and former slaveowners controlled the best land and other sources of economic power. James Lynch, a leading black politician from Mississippi, candidly explained why Negroes shunned "the folly of" disfranchisement. Unlike northerners, who "can leave when it becomes too uncomfortable," former slaves "must be in friendly relations with the great body of the whites in the state." Second, blacks believed in the principle of universal suffrage and the Christian goal of reconciliation. Far from being vindictive toward the race that had enslaved them, they treated leading rebels with generosity and appealed to white southerners to adopt a spirit of fairness and cooperation. For these, as well as other reasons, southern Republicans quickly restored the voting rights of former Confederates. Thus, the South's Republican party committed itself to a strategy of winning white support. To put the matter another way, the Republican party condemned itself to defeat if white voters would not cooperate.

But for a time, both Republicans and their opponents, who called themselves Conservatives or Democrats, moved to the center and appealed for support from a broad range of groups. Some propertied whites accepted congressional Reconstruction as a reality and declared that they would try to compete under the new rules. As these Democrats angled for some black votes, Republicans sought to attract more white voters. Both parties found an area of agreement in economic policies.

The Reconstruction governments devoted themselves to stimulating industry. This policy reflected northern ideals, but it also sprang from a growing southern interest in industrialization. Accordingly, Reconstruction legislatures designed many tempting inducements to investment. Loans, subsidies, and exemptions from taxation for periods of up to ten years helped to bring new industries into the region. The southern railroad system was rebuilt and expanded. Coal and iron mining laid the basis for Birmingham's steel plants, and the number of manufacturing establishments nearly doubled between 1860 and 1880. However, this emphasis on big business interests produced higher state debts and taxes, took money from schools, and multiplied possibilities for corruption.

Industrialization

Policies appealing to black voters never went beyond equality before the law. In fact, the whites who controlled the southern Republican party were reluctant to allow blacks a share of offices proportionate to their electoral strength. Aware of their weakness and the level of hostility in the South, black leaders did not push

Other Republican Policies

for revolutionary change. They failed to advocate the confiscation and redistribution of land and, with the exception of some urban mulattos, did not press for civil rights. Instead, they led the fight to establish schools in the region. The schools established, however, were segregated, setting the precedent for segregated theaters, trains, and other public accommodations.

Within a few years, as centrists in both parties met with failure, the other side of white reaction to congressional Reconstruction began to dominate. Some conservatives had always favored fierce opposition to Reconstruction through pressure and racist propaganda. Charging that the South had been turned over to ignorant blacks, conservatives deplored "black domination." The cry of "Negro rule" now became constant.

Such attacks were gross distortions. Blacks were a minority in eight out of ten state conventions (transplanted northerners were a minority in nine out of ten). Of the state legislatures, only in the lower house in South Carolina did blacks ever constitute a majority; generally, their numbers among officials were far below their proportion in the population. Sixteen African-Americans won seats in Congress before Reconstruction was over, but none was ever elected governor, and only eighteen served in a high state office such as lieutenant governor, treasurer, superintendent of education, or secretary of state. Thus, blacks participated in politics but did not dominate or control events.

Conservatives also stepped up their propaganda against the allies of black Republicans. *Carpetbagger* was a derisive name for whites who had come from the North. It suggested an evil and greedy northern politician, recently arrived with a carpetbag, into which he planned to stuff ill-gotten gains before fleeing. There were a few northerners who deserved this unsavory description. But of the thousands of northerners who settled in the postwar South, only a small portion entered politics. Most of them wanted to democratize the South and introduce northern ways, such as industry, public education, and the spirit of enterprise.

Carpetbaggers and Scalawags

Conservatives invented the term *scalawag* to discredit any native white southerner who cooperated with the Republicans. A substantial number of southerners did so, including some wealthy and prominent men. Most scalawags were men from mountain areas and small farming districts— average white southerners who saw that they could benefit from the opportunities promoted by Republicans. Banding together with freedmen, they pursued common class interests and hoped to make headway against the power of long-dominant planters. Yet this black-white coalition was usually vulnerable to the issue of race, and scalawags shied away from support for racial equality.

Taxation was a major problem for the Reconstruction governments. Financially, the Republicans, despite their achievements, were doomed to be unpopular. Republicans wanted to continue prewar services, repair war's destruction, stimulate industry, and support new ventures such as public schools. But the Civil War had destroyed much of the South's tax base. Thus, an increase in taxes was necessary to maintain traditional services, and new ventures required even higher taxes.

Corruption was another powerful charge levied against the Republicans. Unfortunately, it was true. Many carpetbaggers and black politicians sold their votes. Although white Democrats often shared in the guilt and some Republicans strove to stop corruption, Democrats convinced many voters that scandal was the inevitable result of a foolish Reconstruction program based on blacks and carpetbaggers.

All these problems damaged the Republicans, but in many southern states the deathblow came through violence: the murders, whippings, and intimidation by terrorist groups, which most often used the name Ku Klux Klan. Terrorism against blacks occurred throughout Reconstruction, but after 1867, white violence became more organized and purposeful. The Ku Klux Klan rode to frustrate Reconstruction and keep the freedmen in subjection. Nighttime visits, whippings, beatings, and murders became common, and in some areas virtually open warfare developed.

Ku Klux Klan

Although the Klan persecuted blacks who stood up for their rights as laborers or people, its main purpose was political. Lawless nightriders made active Republicans the target of their attacks. Promi-

nent white Republicans and black leaders were killed in several states. After blacks who worked for a South Carolina scalawag started voting, terrorists visited the plantation and "whipped every nigger man they could lay their hands on." Klansmen also attacked Union League Clubs (Republican organizations that mobilized the black vote) and teachers who were aiding the freedmen.

Klan violence was not spontaneous; certain social forces gave direction to racism. In North Carolina, for example, Alamance and Caswell counties were the sites of the worst Klan violence. They were in the Piedmont, where slim Republican majorities rested on cooperation between black voters and whites of the yeoman class. In a successful effort to restore Democratic control, wealthy and powerful men organized a campaign of terror in the two counties. These men served as Klan leaders at the county and local levels, recruited members, and planned atrocities.

Elsewhere in the South, Klan violence was all too common. At least 10 percent of the black leaders who had been delegates to the constitutional conventions of 1867 and 1868 were attacked, seven fatally. In Eutaw, Alabama, a Klan raid left four dead and fifty-four wounded. South Carolina Klansmen lynched eight blacks at the Union County jail and committed "at least eleven murders and hundreds of whippings" in York County. According to historian Eric Foner, the Klan "made it virtually impossible for Republicans to campaign or vote in large parts of Georgia." Clearly, "violence had a profound effect on Reconstruction politics."

Thus, a combination of difficult fiscal problems, Republican mistakes, racial hostility, and terror brought down the Republican regimes, and in most southern states so-called Radical Reconstruction was over after only a few years. The most lasting failure of Reconstruction governments, however, was not political but social. The new governments failed to alter the South's social structure or its distribution of wealth and power. Exploited as slaves, freedmen remained vulnerable to exploitation during Reconstruction. Without land of their own, they had to depend on white landowners, who could use their economic power to compromise blacks' political freedom.

Failure of Reconstruction

Since they were armed only with the ballot, southern blacks had little chance to effect major changes.

The Social and Economic Meaning of Freedom

Black southerners entered upon life after slavery with hope and determination, but they had too much experience with white people to assume that all would be easy. Expecting to meet with hostility, black people tried to gain as much as they could from their new circumstances. Often the most valued changes were personal ones—alterations in location, employer, or surroundings.

One of the first decisions that many made was whether to leave the old plantation or remain. This meant making a judgment about where the chances of liberty and progress would be greatest. Former slaves drew on their experiences in bondage. "Most all the Negroes that had good owners stayed with them," said one man. Not surprisingly, cruel slaveholders usually saw their former chattels walk off en masse.

On new farms or old, the newly freed men and women reached out for valuable things in life that had been denied them. One of these was education. Whatever their age, blacks hungered for knowledge. When they gained freedom, they started schools and filled classrooms both day and night. Young children brought infants to school with them, and adults attended at night or after "the crops were laid by." The federal government and northern reformers assisted this quest for education. In its brief life, the Freedmen's Bureau founded more than four thousand schools, and idealistic men and women from the North established others and staffed them ably.

Education for Blacks

Blacks and their white allies also realized that higher education was essential. Between 1866 and 1869, the American Missionary Association founded seven colleges, including Fisk and Atlanta universities. The Freedmen's Bureau helped to establish Howard University in Washington, D.C., and northern religious groups supported dozens of seminaries, colleges, and teachers' colleges. By the late 1870s, black churches had joined in the effort, founding numerous colleges despite their smaller financial resources. Although some of the new institutions did not survive, they brought knowledge to those who would educate others and laid a foundation for progress.

Even during Reconstruction, blacks were choosing many highly educated individuals as leaders. Many blacks who won public office in that period came from the prewar elite of free people of color. This group had benefited from its association with wealthy whites, who were often blood relatives. Some planters had given their mulatto children outstanding educations. The two black senators from Mississippi, Blanche K. Bruce and Hiram Revels, for example, were both privileged in their educations. Bruce was the son of a planter, who had provided tutoring on his plantation; Revels was the son of free North Carolina mulattos, who had sent him to Knox College in Illinois. These men and many self-educated former slaves brought experience as artisans, businessmen, lawyers, teachers, and preachers to political office.

While elected officials wrestled with the political tasks of Reconstruction, millions of former slaves concentrated on improving life at home, on their farms, and in their neighborhoods. They devoted themselves to reuniting their families, moving away from the slave quarters, and founding black churches. Given the eventual failure of Reconstruction, the practical gains that blacks made in their daily lives often proved the most enduring.

The search for long-lost family members was awe inspiring. With only shreds of information to guide them, thousands of black people embarked on odysseys in search of a husband, wife, child, or parent. By relying on the black community for help and information, many succeeded in their quest. Others walked through several states and never found loved ones.

Reunification of Black Families

For husbands and wives who had belonged to different masters, freedom meant the opportunity to establish homes together for the first time. It also meant that wives would not be ordered to work in the fields, and that parents finally would be able to raise their children without interference from whites.

Many black people wanted to minimize all contact with whites. To avoid contact with intrusive whites, who were used to supervising and controlling them, blacks abandoned the slave quarters and fanned out into distant corners of the land they worked. Some moved away to build new homes in the woods. Others established small all-black settlements that still can be found today along the backroads of the South.

The other side of this movement away from whites was closer communion within the black community. Freed from the restrictions and regulations of slavery, blacks could build their own institutions as they saw fit. The secret church of slavery now came out into the open. Within a few years, independent black branches of the Methodist and Baptist churches had attracted the great majority of black Christians in the South.

Founding of Black Churches

The desire to gain as much independence as possible carried over into the freedmen's economic arrangements. Since most former slaves lacked money to buy land, they preferred the next best thing—renting the land they worked. But many whites would not consider renting land to blacks; there was strong social pressure against it. Because few blacks had the means to rent a farm, other alternatives had to be tried.

Northerners and officials of the Freedmen's Bureau favored contracts between owners and laborers. To northerners who believed in "free soil, free labor, free men," contracts and wages seemed the key to progress. For a few years, the Freedmen's Bureau helped to draw up and enforce such contracts, but they proved unpopular with both blacks and whites. Owners often filled the contracts with detailed requirements that reminded blacks of their circumscribed lives under slavery. Disputes frequently arose over efficiency, lost time, and other matters. Besides, times were hard, and the failure of Confederate banks had left the South with a shortage of credit facilities.

Black farmers and white landowners therefore turned to a system of sharecropping: black families worked for part of the crop while living on the landowner's property. The landlord or a merchant "furnished" food and supplies, and the sharecropper, landowner, and furnishing merchant all received payment from the crop. Naturally, landowners tried to set the laborers' share at a low level. Typical arrangements left half the crop to the landowner and half to the sharecropper.

Rise of the Sharecropping System

The sharecropping system originated as a desirable compromise. For landowners, it eased problems with cash and credit. Blacks accepted it because it gave them a reasonable amount of freedom from daily supervision. Sharecropping later proved to be a disaster, both for blacks and for the South. Since blacks were living in a discriminatory society, the system placed them at the mercy of unscrupulous owners and merchants, who had many opportunities to cheat them. As for the South, sharecropping led to an overspecialization in cotton just as the worldwide demand for the crop began to grow more slowly.

The End of Reconstruction

The North had never made a total commitment to racial equality, and by the early 1870s, it was evident that even the North's partial commitment was weakening. New issues were capturing people's attention, and soon voters began to look for reconciliation with southern whites. In the South, Democrats won control of one state after another, and they threatened to defeat Republicans in the North as well. Before long, the situation had returned to "normal" in the eyes of southern whites.

The Supreme Court, after first re-establishing its power, took part in the northern retreat from Reconstruction. During the Civil War, the Court had been cautious and reluctant to assert itself. The *Dred Scott* decision had sparked such a violent reaction and the Union's wartime emergency was so great that the Court had refrained from blocking or interfering with government actions.

But in 1866, a similar case, *Ex parte Milligan*, reached the Court through proper channels. Lambdin P. Milligan of Indiana had participated in a plot to free Confederate prisoners of war and overthrow state governments; for these acts, a military court had sentenced Milligan, a civilian, to death. Milligan challenged the authority of the military tribunal, claiming that he had a right to a civil trial. In sweeping language, the Supreme Court declared that military trials were illegal when civil courts were open and functioning, thus indicating that it intended to reassert itself as a major force in national affairs.

Supreme Court Decisions on Reconstruction

In the 1870s, interpretations by the Supreme Court drastically narrowed the meaning and effectiveness of the Fourteenth Amendment. In 1873, the Court decided *Bradwell* v. *Illinois*, a case in which Myra Bradwell, a female attorney, had been denied the right to practice law in Illinois because of her gender. Pointing to the Fourteenth Amendment, Bradwell's attorneys contended that the state had unconstitutionally abridged her "privileges and immunities" as a citizen. The Supreme Court rejected her claim, alluding to women's traditional role in the home.

The next day, in the *Slaughter-House* cases, the Court made its restrictive reading of the Fourteenth Amendment even clearer. The *Slaughter-House* cases had begun in 1869, when the Louisiana legislature granted one company a monopoly on the slaughtering of livestock in New Orleans. Rival butchers in the city promptly sued. Their attorney, former Supreme Court Justice John A. Campbell, argued that the Fourteenth Amendment had revolutionized the constitutional system by bringing individual rights under federal protection. Campbell thus expressed an original and central goal of the Republican party: to nationalize civil rights and guard them from state interference.

The Court not only rejected Campbell's argument but dealt a stunning blow to both the scope of the Fourteenth Amendment and the hopes of African-Americans. The justices interpreted the "privileges and immunities" of citizens so narrowly that they reduced them almost to trivialities. Although the Fourteenth Amendment clearly protected citizens' rights, the Court declared that state citizenship and national citizenship were separate.

National citizenship involved only such things as the right to travel freely from state to state and to use the navigable waters of the nation, and only these narrow rights were protected by the Fourteenth Amendment. With this interpretation, the words "No state shall make or enforce any law which shall abridge the privileges or immunities of citizens of the United States" disappeared for decades as a meaningful or effective part of the Constitution. The Supreme Court also concluded that the butchers who sued had not been deprived of their rights or property in violation of the "due process" clause of the amendment. Thus, the justices dismissed Campbell's central contention: that the Fourteenth Amendment guaranteed the great basic rights of the Bill of Rights against state action. In so doing, the Court limited severely the amendment's potential for securing and protecting the rights of black citizens.

In 1876, the Court regressed even further by emasculating the enforcement clause of the Fourteenth Amendment and revealing deficiencies inherent in the Fifteenth Amendment. In *United States* v. *Cruikshank*, the Court dealt with Louisiana whites who were indicted for attacking a meeting of blacks and conspiring to deprive them of their rights. The justices ruled that the Fourteenth Amendment did not empower the federal government to redress the misdeeds of private individuals against other citizens; only flagrant discrimination by the states was covered. In *United States* v. *Reese*, the Court noted that the Fifteenth Amendment did not guarantee a citizen's right to vote but merely listed certain impermissible grounds for denying suffrage. Thus, a path lay open for southern states to disfranchise blacks for supposedly nonracial reasons—lack of education, lack of property, or lack of descent from a grandfather qualified to vote before the Military Reconstruction Act. (So-called grandfather clauses became a way of including illiterate whites in the electorate yet excluding blacks, because the grandfathers of most blacks had been slaves before Reconstruction and unable to vote.)

The retreat from Reconstruction continued steadily in politics as well. In 1868, Ulysses S. Grant, running as a Republican, defeated a Democrat, Horatio Seymour, in a presidential campaign that revived sectional divisions. In office, Grant some-

Election of 1868 times called out federal troops to stop violence or enforce acts of Congress, but only when he had to. He hoped to avoid confrontation with the South, to erase the image of dictatorship that his military background summoned up.

In 1870 and 1871, the violent campaigns of the Ku Klux Klan moved Congress to pass two Enforcement Acts and an anti-Klan law. These laws, for the first time, made acts by individuals against the civil and political rights of others a federal offense. They permitted martial law and suspension of the writ of habeas corpus to combat murders, beatings, and threats by the Klan. Federal troops and prosecutors used them with only partial success, for a conspiracy of silence frustrated some prosecutions.

Some conservative but influential Republicans opposed the anti-Klan laws, basing their opposition on the charge that the laws infringed on states' rights. It was striking that some Republicans were echoing an old and standard line of the Democrats. This opposition foreshadowed a more general revolt within Republican ranks in 1872.

Disenchanted with Reconstruction, in 1872 a group calling itself the Liberal Republicans bolted the party and nominated Horace Greeley, the well-known editor of the *New York Tribune*, for president. The Liberal Republicans were a varied group, including civil service reformers, foes of corruption, and advocates of a lower tariff. They were united by two popular, widespread attitudes: distaste for federal intervention in the South and a desire to let market forces and the "best men" determine events in the South. The Democrats also gave their nomination to Greeley in 1872. The combination was not enough to defeat Grant, but it reinforced his desire to avoid confrontation with white southerners.

Liberal Republican Revolt

The Liberal Republican challenge reflected dissatisfaction with Grant's administration. Corruption within the administration had become widespread, and Grant foolishly defended some culprits. As a result, Grant's popularity and his party's popularity declined. In the 1874 elections, Democrats recaptured the House of Representatives.

Congress's resolve on southern issues weakened steadily. By joint resolution, it had removed the political disabilities of the Fourteenth Amendment from many former Confederates.

Amnesty Act In 1872, it adopted a sweeping Amnesty Act, which pardoned most of the remaining rebels and left only five hundred excluded from political participation. A Civil Rights Act passed in 1875 purported to guarantee black people equal accommodations in public places, such as inns and theaters, but it was weak and contained no effective provisions for enforcement. Moreover, by 1876, the Democrats had regained control of all but three of the southern states (see dates of reestablishment of conservative rule in map).

Meanwhile, new concerns were catching the public's eye. Industrialization had surged forward, hastening change in national life. Only eight years after the war, industrial production had increased by an impressive 75 percent. For the first time, nonagricultural workers outnumbered farmers, and only Britain had a greater industrial output.

Then the Panic of 1873 occurred, throwing 3 million people out of work and focusing attention on economic and monetary problems. The clash between capital and labor became the major issue of the day. Disturbed by the strikes and industrial violence that accompanied the panic, businessmen became increasingly concerned about the defense of property. Debtors and the unemployed sought easy-money policies to spur economic expansion.

The monetary issue aroused strong controversy. Civil War greenbacks had the potential to expand the money supply and lift prices if they were kept in circulation. In 1872, Democratic farmers and debtors had urged such a policy, but they were overruled by "sound money" men. Now, hard times swelled the ranks of "greenbackers"—voters who favored greenbacks and easy money. In 1874, Congress voted to increase the number of greenbacks in circulation, but Grant vetoed the bill. The next year, Congress passed a law requiring that after 1878 greenbacks be convertible into gold. The law limited the inflationary impact of the greenbacks and aided creditors, not debtors such as hard-pressed farmers.

Greenbacks Versus Sound Money

By 1876, it was obvious to most political observers that the North was no longer willing to pursue

Chapter 15: Reconstruction by Trial and Error, 1865–1877

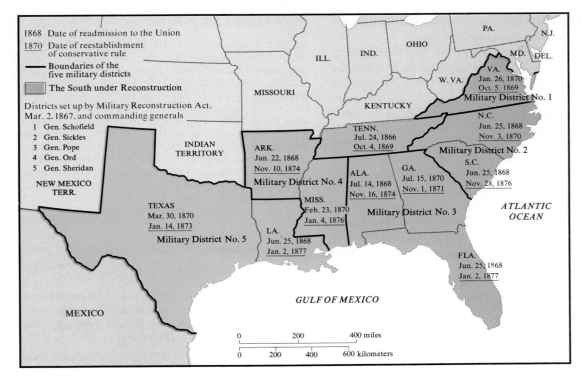

1868 Date of readmission to the Union
1870 Date of reestablishment
      of conservative rule
───── Boundaries of the
      five military districts
▨ The South under Reconstruction

Districts set up by Military Reconstruction Act,
Mar. 2, 1867, and commanding generals
  1 Gen. Schofield
  2 Gen. Sickles
  3 Gen. Pope
  4 Gen. Ord
  5 Gen. Sheridan

NEW MEXICO
TERR.

PA.
N.J.
OHIO
MD. DEL.
ILL.
IND.
MISSOURI
W. VA.
VA.
Jan. 26, 1870
Oct. 5, 1869
Military District No. 1
KENTUCKY
N.C.
Jun. 25, 1868
Nov. 3, 1870
Military District No. 2
INDIAN
TERRITORY
ARK.
Jun. 22, 1868
Nov. 10, 1874
Military District No. 4
TENN.
Jul. 24, 1866
Oct. 4, 1869
ALA.
Jul. 14, 1868
Nov. 16, 1874
GA.
Jul. 15, 1870
Nov. 1, 1871
S.C.
Jun. 25, 1868
Nov. 28, 1876
TEXAS
Mar. 30, 1870
Jan. 14, 1873
Military District No. 5
MISS.
Feb. 23, 1870
Jan. 4, 1876
Military District No. 3
ATLANTIC
OCEAN
LA.
Jun. 25, 1868
Jan. 2, 1877
FLA.
Jun. 25, 1868
Jan. 2, 1877
GULF OF MEXICO
MEXICO

0   200   400 miles
0   200   400   600 kilometers

The Reconstruction

the goals of Reconstruction. The results of a disputed presidential election confirmed this fact. Samuel J. Tilden, Democratic governor of New York, ran strongly in the South and took a commanding lead in both the popular vote and the electoral college over Rutherford B. Hayes, the Republican nominee. Tilden won 184 electoral votes and needed only one more for a majority. Nineteen votes from Louisiana, South Carolina, and Florida were disputed; both Democrats and Republicans claimed to have won in those states, despite fraud on the part of their opponents. One vote from Oregon was undecided due to a technicality.

Election of 1876

To resolve this unprecedented situation, on which the Constitution gave no guidance, Congress established a fifteen-member electoral commission. In the interest of impartiality, membership on the commission was to be balanced between Democrats and Republicans. But one independent Republican, Supreme Court Justice David Davis, re-

fused appointment in order to accept his election as a senator. A regular Republican took his place, and the Republican party prevailed 8 to 7 on every decision, a strict party vote. Hayes would become the winner if Congress accepted the commission's findings.

Congressional acceptance was not a certainty, and many citizens feared that the crisis might lead to another civil war. Democrats, however, acquiesced in the election of Hayes. Scholars have found that negotiations went on between some of Hayes's supporters and southerners who were interested in federal aid to railroads, internal improvements, federal patronage, and removal of troops from southern states. But the most recent studies suggest that these negotiations did not have a deciding effect on the outcome. Neither party was well enough organized to implement and enforce a bargain between the sections. Northern and southern Democrats decided that they could not win and failed to contest the election. Thus, Hayes became president, and southerners looked forward to the withdrawal of federal troops from the South. Reconstruction was unmistakably over.

Southern Democrats rejoiced, but black Americans grieved over the betrayal of their hopes for equality. After 1877, the hope for many African-Americans was "to go to a territory by ourselves." In some southern states, thousands gathered up their possessions and migrated to Kansas. They were known as Exodusters, disappointed people still searching for their share in the American dream.

Black Exodusters

Thus, the nation ended more than fifteen years of bloody civil war and controversial reconstruction without establishing full freedom for black Americans. Their status would continue to be a major issue. As the nation turned away from the needs of black citizens, a majority of its people and its government focused attention on the problems related to industrialism.

<hr>

Suggestions for Further Reading

National Policy, Politics, and Constitutional Law

Richard H. Abbott, *The Republican Party and the South, 1855–1877* (1986); Herman Belz, *Emancipation and Equal Rights* (1978); Michael Les Benedict, *A Compromise of Principle: Congressional Republicans and Reconstruction, 1863–1869* (1974); David W. Bowen, *Andrew Johnson and the Negro* (1989); William S. McFeely, *Grant* (1981); William S. McFeely, *Yankee Stepfather: General O. O. Howard and the Freedmen* (1968); Eric L. McKitrick, *Andrew Johnson and Reconstruction* (1966); James M. McPherson, *The Abolitionist Legacy* (1975); Kenneth M. Stampp, *The Era of Reconstruction* (1965); Mark W. Summers, *Railroads, Reconstruction, and the Gospel of Prosperity* (1984).

The Freed Slaves

Roberta Sue Alexander, *North Carolina Faces the Freedmen* (1985); Edmund L. Drago, *Black Politicians and Reconstruction in Georgia* (1982); Paul D. Escott, *Slavery Remembered* (1979); Leon Litwack, *Been in the Storm So Long* (1979); Willie Lee Rose, *Rehearsal for Reconstruction* (1964); Clarence Walker, *A Rock in a Weary Land* (1982).

Politics and Reconstruction in the South

Richard N. Current, *Those Terrible Carpetbaggers* (1988); W. E. B. Du Bois, *Black Reconstruction* (1935); Paul D. Escott, *Many Excellent People: Power and Privilege in North Carolina, 1850–1900* (1985); W. McKee Evans, *Ballots and Fence Rails: Reconstruction on the Lower Cape Fear* (1966); Eric Foner, *Reconstruction: America's Unfinished Revolution, 1863–1877* (1988); Eric Foner, *Nothing but Freedom* (1983); William C. Harris, *The Day of the Carpetbagger* (1979); Michael Perman, *The Road to Redemption* (1984); Allen Trelease, *White Terror* (1967); Ted Tunnell, *Carpetbagger from Vermont* (1989); Ted Tunnell, *Crucible of Reconstruction* (1984); Michael Wayne, *The Reshaping of Plantation Society* (1983); Sarah Woolfolk Wiggins, *The Scalawag in Alabama Politics, 1865–1881* (1977).

Women, Family, and Social History

Ellen Carol Dubois, *Feminism and Suffrage* (1978); Herbert G. Gutman, *The Black Family in Slavery and Freedom, 1750–1925* (1976); Elizabeth Jacoway, *Yankee Missionaries in the South* (1979); Jacqueline Jones, *Labor of Love, Labor of Sorrow* (1985); Jacqueline Jones, *Soldiers of Light and Love* (1980); Robert C. Kenzer, *Kinship and Neighborhood in a Southern Community* (1987).

The End of Reconstruction

Michael Les Benedict, "Southern Democrats in the Crisis of 1876–1877," *Journal of Southern History*, LXVI, No. 4 (November 1980), 489–524; William Gillette, *Retreat from Reconstruction, 1869–1879* (1980); William Gillette, *The Right to Vote* (1969); Keith Ian Polakoff, *The Politics of Inertia* (1973); C. Vann Woodward, *Reunion and Reaction* (1951).

Reconstruction's Legacy for the South

Robert G. Athearn, *In Search of Canaan* (1978); Jay R. Mandle, *The Roots of Black Poverty* (1978); Nell Irvin Painter, *Exodusters* (1976); Howard Rabinowitz, *Race Relations in the Urban South, 1865–1890* (1978); Roger L. Ransom and Richard Sutch, *One Kind of Freedom* (1977); Laurence Shore, *Southern Capitalists* (1986); Peter Wallenstein, *From Slave South to New South* (1987); C. Vann Woodward, *Origins of the New South* (1951).

They called themselves Dine', which meant "The People." White Americans called them *Navahos*. Whatever their name, they were a civilization that lived in what would become northern Arizona and New Mexico, and they devoted their lives to achieving *k'e*—a universal harmony of love, peace, and cooperation. They tried to achieve *k'e* by living in unity with the land and all other objects of nature.

White people did not understand Navaho beliefs. When they moved into territory inhabited by Navahos and other Native Americans, they wanted more than they needed simply to survive. They wanted to remove minerals for industry, cut down forests for lumber, and grow crops to sell at distant markets. The Indians did not understand why white people urged them to adopt these practices and change their lives by creating material wealth. When confronted with native resistance to their wishes, whites responded with brutal violence.

The withering of Indian subsistence cultures, coercive government policies, and the triumph of market economies exemplifies what happened when white Americans transformed the western frontier in the late nineteenth century. Settlement of the West proceeded at a furious pace. Between 1870 and 1890, the population living between the Mississippi River and the Pacific Ocean swelled from 7 million to nearly 17 million. By 1890, farms, ranches, mines, towns, and cities could be found in almost every region of what was to become the continental United States. That year, the superintendent of the census acknowledged that a frontier line of settlement no longer existed.

In popular thought, the frontier represented the birthplace of American self-confidence and individualism. Conquering the continent's vast wilderness and bringing forth food and raw materials from it filled white Americans with a sense of power and a faith that anyone eager and persistent enough could succeed. That self-confidence, however, was easily transformed into the arrogant belief that Americans were somehow special, and individualism often exerted itself at the expense of racial minorities and people without property.

Most Americans rarely thought about conserving resources because there always seemed to be more territory to exploit and bring into the

16

THE TRANSFORMATION OF THE WEST AND SOUTH, 1877–1892

A Sioux Indian camp in South Dakota, 1891. The Sioux led a nomadic life, carrying out their subsistence economy in harmony with the natural environment. When they packed up and moved on, they left the landscape almost undisturbed. This photograph shows the temporary situation characteristic of their camps. *Library of Congress.*

market economy. The fading of the frontier, though of great symbolic importance, had little direct impact on people's behavior, because vast stretches of land remained unsettled. Millions of people continued to stream into the West, and more land in the South fell under cultivation. Although life in the West was less romantic and comfortable than settlers might have hoped and the unreconstructed South failed to fulfill its potential, the western and southern frontiers gave Americans the feeling that they would always have a second chance.

The Transformation of Native American Cultures

Historians have sometimes defined the American frontier as "the edge of the unused," implying that the frontier faded when open land began to be used for farming or the building of cities. The definition is misleading because Native Americans were using the land long before white Americans migrated there.

Numerous western tribes differed in culture, but the economies of all were based to some extent on four activities: crop raising; livestock raising; hunting, fishing, and gathering; and **Subsistence** raiding. Corn was the most com-**Cultures** mon crop; sheep and horses were the livestock; and buffalo were the objects of hunts. Tribes raided each other for food, hides, and slaves. The goal of all these activities was subsistence, the maintenance of life at its most basic level. Indians tried to balance their economic systems to achieve subsistence. Thus, if a buffalo hunt failed, a tribe could still feed itself on crops being grown; if crops failed, a tribe could still hunt buffalo and steal food from another tribe. Indians also traded with each other and with whites.

1862	Homestead Act; Morrill Land Grant Act	**1889**	Statehood granted to North Dakota, South Dakota, Washington, and Montana
1869	First transcontinental railroad, the Union Pacific, completed	**1890**	Census Bureau announces closing of the frontier
1876	Custer's Last Stand (Battle of Little Big Horn)		Statehood granted to Wyoming and Idaho
1878	Timber and Stone Act	**1896**	*Plessy* v. *Ferguson*
1881	Helen Hunt Jackson, *A Century of Dishonor*		Development of Rural Free Delivery Statehood granted to Utah
1883	*Civil Rights Cases* Standardization of national time zones	**1899**	*Cummins* v. *County Board of Education*
1887	Dawes Severalty Act; Hatch Act		

For Indians on the Plains, much of everyday life focused on the buffalo. For centuries they had cooked and preserved buffalo meat; fashioned hides into clothing, shoes, and blankets; used sinew for thread and bowstrings; carved tools from bones; and made horns into implements. In the Southwest, Native Americans placed great value on sheep, goats, and horses. Old Man Hat, a Navaho, advised, "The herd is money. . . . You know that you have some good clothing; the sheep gave you that. And you've just eaten different kinds of food; the sheep gave that food to you. Everything comes from the sheep." To the Navahos, the herds were means to achieving security.

This world of subsistence and ecological balance began to dissolve when whites, perceiving buffalo as well as Indians as hindrances to their ambitions

Slaughter of Buffalo on the Plains, endeavored to remove both. To help destroy the buffalo, railroads sponsored hunts for eastern sportsmen, who rode on slow-moving trains and shot at the bulky targets. Some hunters collected one to three dollars offered by tanneries for hides; others did not even stop to pick up their kill. By the 1880s, only a few

hundred remained of the estimated 13 million buffalo that had existed in 1850. The scarcity of buffalo upset the subsistence system by leaving Indians less food to supplement their diets if their crops failed or were stolen.

When white Americans first extensively encountered western Indians in the mid-nineteenth century, they considered the native tribes as separate nations with which they could make treaties. Thus, the government made treaties with various tribes, ensuring peace and nominally defining boundaries of white and native lands. But the agreements seldom promised the Indians any future land rights; rather, whites assumed that eventually they could settle wherever they wished. Treaties made one week were violated the next. Some tribes acquiesced; others resisted with attacks on settlements, herds, and troops. Whites responded with murders of individuals and massacres of entire villages. At Sand Creek, Colorado, in 1864 United States troops murdered about 150 Cheyennes, mostly women and children.

By the 1870s, federal officials and humanitarians, seeking peaceful means of dealing with western tribes, began emphasizing policies that in some ways would treat Native Americans similarly to blacks and immigrants. Instead of being considered foreign nations, Indian tribes were to be "civilized" and "uplifted" through education. They were also to be inculcated with the values of the white mobility ethic: hard work, ambition, thrift, and materialism. To achieve this transformation, however, Indians would have to abandon their traditional cultures.

From the 1860s to the 1880s, the federal government tried to force Indians onto reservations, where, it was thought, they could best be civilized.

Reservation Policy Reservations usually consisted of the areas of a tribe's previous territory that were least desirable to whites. In assigning Indians to specific territories, the government promised protection from white encroachment and agreed to provide food, clothing, and other necessities.

Reservation policy had troublesome consequences. First, Indians had no say over their own affairs on reservations. Supreme Court decisions in 1884 and 1886 denied Indians the right to become United States citizens, leaving them unprotected by the Fourteenth and Fifteenth Amendments, which had given blacks rights of citizenship. Second, it was impossible to protect reservations from white farmers, miners, and herders, who continually sought even remote Indian lands for their own purposes. Third, the government disregarded variations among tribes, even concentrating tribes habitually at war with each other on the same reservation. Rather than acting as civilizing communities, reservations became more like antebellum slave quarters.

Not all tribes succumbed to forces that undermined their way of life. The Pawnees, for example, resisted heavy trading with the whites, as well as the liquor that traders used to addict

Indian Resistance many Indians and tempt them into disadvantageous deals. Even as they became dependent on whites, some tribes tried to preserve their traditional cultures. Navahos traded for food in order to restore their subsistence way of life, and Pawnees agreed to leave their Nebraska homelands for a reservation in the hope that they could hunt buffalo and grow corn as they once had done.

Native Americans also actively defended their homelands against white intrusion and violence in a series of bloody conflicts and revolts. The most famous battle occurred on June 25, 1876, when twenty-five hundred Dakota Sioux, led by Chiefs Sitting Bull, Rain-in-the-Face, and Crazy Horse, annihilated white troops led by the rash Colonel George A. Custer near the Little Big Horn River in southern Montana. There were other Indian victories, but white troops eventually overwhelmed armed Indian resistance.

These conditions, the publication of Helen Hunt Jackson's *A Century of Dishonor* (1881), and unfavorable comparison with Canada's management of Indian affairs kindled new efforts to reform Indian policy in the 1880s. In Canada, tribespeople had been given the rights of British subjects and were defended against whites by the Royal Mounted Police. Canadian officials were also more tolerant of tribal customs.

The reformers especially deplored Indians' sexual division of labor. Women seemed to do all the vital work—tending crops, rearing children, cooking, curing hides, making tools and clothes—and seemed to be servile to men, who hunted but otherwise were idle. Groups such as Women's National Indian Association and the Indian Rights Association wanted Indian men to bear more responsibilities and become like the heads of white middle-class households. Although reformers urged that Indian women be treated more respectfully by their menfolk, the effect of their reforms would have been—and sometimes was—reduced economic independence of Indian women.

Prodded by reformers, Congress in 1887 reversed its reservation policy and passed the Dawes Severalty Act, which dissolved community-owned tribal lands and granted land allotments to individual families. The

Dawes Severalty Act act also awarded citizenship to all who accepted allotments and authorized the government to sell unallotted land and to set aside proceeds for the education of Indians. These provisions applied to most western tribes, the exception being Pueblo peoples, who had retained land rights granted to them by the Spanish.

United States Indian policy, as carried out by the Indian Bureau of the Interior Department, now took on three main features. First, land was distributed to individual families in the belief that they would acquire white people's values by learning how to manage their own property. Second, bureau officials believed that Indians would lose their "barbaric" habits more quickly if their children were removed and educated in boarding schools away from the old reservations. Third, officials tried to suppress what they believed were dangerous religious ceremonies by providing money for white church groups to establish religious schools among the Indians and teach them to become good Christians.

In one crucial respect, the Dawes Act effectively accomplished what whites wanted and Indians feared: it reduced Indian control over land. In spite of some protection against such practices, eager speculators induced Indians to part with their newly acquired property. Between 1887 and the 1930s, Indian landholdings dwindled from 138 million acres to 52 million.

The Dawes Act had other drawbacks as well. The boarding-school program affected thousands of children, but most returned to their reservations rather than submit to assimilation into white society. Efforts to suppress religious observances only forced them under cover. By the end of the century, Native Americans became what historian Richard White has labeled "a population without control over resources, sustained in its poverty by payments controlled by the larger society, and subject to increasing pressure to lose their group identity and disappear."

The Exploitation of Natural Resources

In the years just before the Civil War, eager prospectors began to comb remote forests and mountains looking for gold, silver, iron, coal, timber, oil, and copper. The mining frontier advanced rapidly, drawing thousands of people to California, Nevada, Idaho, Montana, and Colorado. Prospectors tended to be restless optimists, willing to tramp mountains and deserts, searching for precious metals. They shot game for food and financed their explorations by convincing merchants to advance credit for equipment in return for a share of the lode yet to be discovered.

The ultimate goal was to sell large amounts of minerals, but extracting substances from the ground involved high expenses for excavation and transportation. Thus individual prospectors who did discover veins of metal normally sold their claims to mining syndicates that had ample capital to bring in engineers, heavy machinery, railroad lines, and work crews. Although discoveries of gold and silver first drew attention to the West and its resources, mining companies usually moved into these states to exploit less romantic but equally lucrative metals.

Mining and Lumbering

Lumber production—another large-scale extractive industry—required vast amounts of forest land. To obtain timber lands, lumber companies exploited a law meant to stimulate western settlement, the Timber and Stone Act (1878). This measure, which applied to land in California, Nevada, Oregon, and Washington, allowed private citizens to buy at the low price of $2.50 per acre 160-acre plots "unfit for cultivation" and "valuable chiefly for timber." Taking advantage of the act, lumber companies hired seamen from waterfront boarding houses to register claims to timberland and turn them over to the companies. By 1900, claimants had bought over 3.5 million acres under Timber and Stone Act provisions, but most of that land belonged to corporations.

While lumbermen were acquiring timberlands in the Northwest, oilmen were beginning to sink wells in the Southwest. Before 1900, most of the nation's petroleum came from the Appalachians and the Midwest, but promising developments were under way in southern California and eastern Texas. Although most oil and kerosene were still used for lubrication and lighting, discoveries in the Southwest were to become a vital new source of fuel in the twentieth century.

Much of the western frontier was a man's world. In 1880, white men outnumbered white women by more than two to one in Colorado, Nevada, and Arizona. Yet many communities had

The mining boom often created towns so fast that there was no time to remove rubble. This photograph of Leadville, near the gold and silver mines at the head of the Arkansas River, shows how the community grew up around a settler's cabin, which remained in the middle of the main street. *Colorado Historical Society*.

Frontier Society substantial numbers of women. Most women who went to the mining frontier did so for the same reasons as men: to find a fortune. They usually accompanied a husband or father and seldom prospected themselves. Even so, many women realized their own opportunities in the towns, where they provided cooking, laundering, and, in some cases, sexual services for the miners. While they pursued new opportunities and freedoms, women also helped to bolster family and community life by campaigning against vice.

Many of the mining and lumber communities contained small numbers of Chinese, Mexicans, Indians, and blacks. Most Chinese migrated to work on American railroads, but some were employed in the camps to do cooking and cleaning. Blacks also held such jobs. Mexicans and Indians often had been the original settlers of land coveted by whites. Each of these minority groups encountered prejudice. California imposed a tax on foreign miners and denied blacks, Indians, and Chinese the right to testify or submit evidence in court. Just as land treaties with Indians were frequently broken, any claims that Mexicans might have had to land sought by white miners were often ignored or stolen.

Development of the nation's natural resources raised serious questions about what belonged to all the people, as represented by the federal government, and what belonged to private interests. Two factors worked at cross-purposes. First, much of the undeveloped territory west of the Mississippi was public domain, and some people believed that the federal government, as owner, should receive some return from the exploitation of it. But the government, lacking both motivation and the means to dig mines, sink wells, and cut forests, sold the land to private interests that would take the initiative.

The developers of natural resources were seldom interested in landowning. They wanted trees,

Use of Public Lands

Chapter 16: The Transformation of the West and South, 1877–1892 not forest land that would become useless once the trees had been cut down. They wanted oil, not the scrubby plain that would be worthless if—as often happened—wells were dug but no oil was found. To avoid purchase costs, oilmen and iron miners often leased property from private owners or from the government and paid royalties on the minerals extracted. Some lumbermen simply cut trees on public lands without paying a cent and used trickery to buy land cheaply under the Timber and Stone Act. Even when the government tried to prevent fraud, many communities resisted in fear that such crackdowns would slow local economic growth.

Development of the mining and forest frontiers, and the farms and cities that followed, brought western territories to the threshold of statehood. In

Admission of New States 1889, Republicans seeking to solidify their control of Congress pushed through an omnibus bill granting statehood to North Dakota, South Dakota, Washington, and Montana. Wyoming and Idaho were admitted in 1890. Congress denied statehood to Utah until 1896, when the Mormon majority agreed to abandon polygamy.

The mining towns and lumber camps in these states spiced American folk culture and fostered a go-getter optimism that distinguished the American spirit. The lawlessness and hedonism of places like Deadwood, in Dakota Territory, and Tombstone, in Arizona Territory, gave the West notoriety and romance. But violence and eccentricity were far from common. Most miners and lumbermen worked seventy hours a week and had no time, energy, or money for drinking, gambling, or gunfights. Women worked as long or longer as teachers, cooks, laundresses, storekeepers, and housewives; only a few were sharpshooters or dance-hall queens.

The Age of Railroad Expansion

On May 10, 1869, the whole country celebrated a major event at Utah's Promontory Point. There, the Central Pacific Railroad, built 689 miles eastward from Sacramento, California, met the Union Pacific Railroad, built 1,086 miles westward from Omaha, Nebraska, to form the nation's first transcontinental rail route.

The completion of the transcontinental railroad was part of a rapid expansion in the nation's rail system. Between 1865 and 1890, total track in the United States grew from 35,000 to 200,000 miles (see map, page 296). By 1910, the nation had one-third of all railroad track in the world.

The economic consequences of railroads were immense. After 1880, when durable steel rails began to replace iron rails, railroads helped to boost

Effects of Railroad Construction the nation's steel industry to international leadership. Moreover, railroad expansion spawned a number of related industries, including coal production, passenger and freight car manufacture, and depot construction.

Railroads also altered Americans' conceptions of time and space and spurred a movement for standardization. First, by overcoming barriers of distance, railroads in effect transformed space into time. Instead of using geographical distance to measure the separation of places, it became easier to use the amount of time it took to travel from one place to the other. Second, railroad scheduling necessitated nationwide agreement on time. Before railroads, each locale had had its own time. Community church bells and steeple clocks had struck twelve when the sun was overhead, and people had set their own clocks accordingly. But because the sun was not overhead at exactly the same moment everywhere, there were variations in time from place to place. To achieve some regularity, railroads created their own time zones. By 1880, there still were nearly fifty different standards, but in 1883 railroads finally agreed—without consulting anyone in government—to establish four standard time zones for the whole country. Most communities adjusted their clocks, and railroad time became national time.

Third, railroad construction brought about technological and organizational reforms. By the late 1880s, almost all lines had adopted standard-gauge rails so that their tracks could connect with one another. Westinghouse air brakes, automatic car

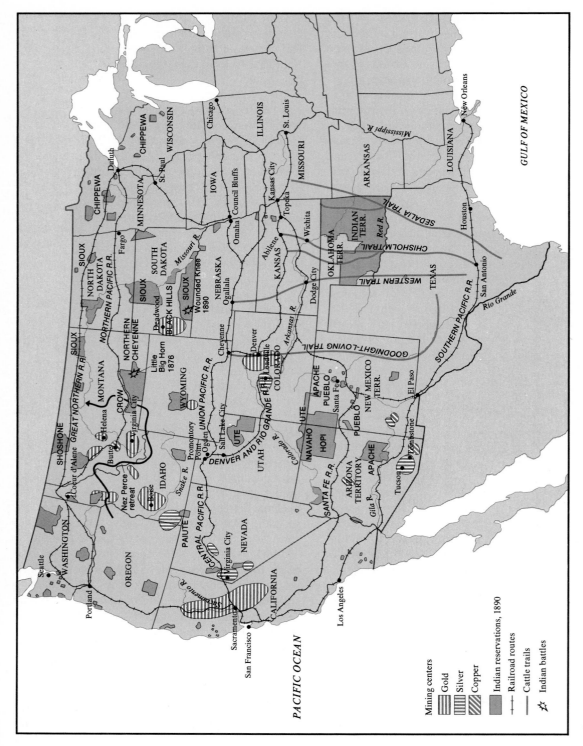

Mining centers

▥ Gold
▤ Silver
▨ Copper

▦ Indian reservations, 1890
┼┼┼ Railroad routes
— Cattle trails
☆ Indian battles

The American West, 1860–1890

Three generations of a homesteading family overflow their primitive sod home on the Oklahoma frontier. This photograph reveals how dry and vacant the scrub Plains were, yet it also suggests a quiet confidence among the people who lived there. *University of Oklahoma Western History Collection.*

couplers, and other devices made rail transportation safer and more efficient. Organizational advances included systems for coordinating complex passenger and freight schedules and the adoption of uniform freight-classification systems.

Railroads accomplished these feats with the help of some of the largest government subsidies in American history. Railroad executives argued that

Government Subsidy of Railroads

their activities benefited the public and that the government should aid them by giving them land from the public domain. Sympathetic governments at the national, state, and local levels responded by providing railroad companies with massive subsidies. Indeed, the federal government gave the railroads more than 180 million acres of land; state grants amounted to about 50 million acres. Capitalists sought and accepted these grants, as well as other subsidies, while at the same time arguing against government interference. Yet without public help,

few railroads could have prospered sufficiently to attract private investment.

Farming the Plains

Settlement of the Plains and the West involved the greatest migration in American history. Most, though not all, migrants came from the eastern states or Europe. They were lured by offers of cheap land and credit from states and railroads eager to promote settlement. Between 1870 and 1910, the nation's population rose from 40 million to 92 million, and total urban population swelled by more than 400 percent. As a result, demand for farm products grew rapidly. Moreover, developments in transportation and storage made the possibilities for commercial farming—growing crops for profit—more favorable than ever.

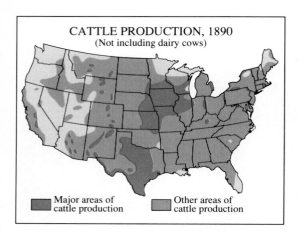

CATTLE PRODUCTION, 1890
(Not including dairy cows)

Major areas of cattle production · Other areas of cattle production

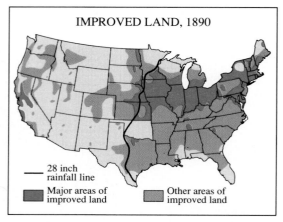

IMPROVED LAND, 1890

— 28 inch rainfall line · Major areas of improved land · Other areas of improved land

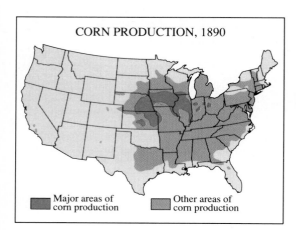

CORN PRODUCTION, 1890

Major areas of corn production · Other areas of corn production

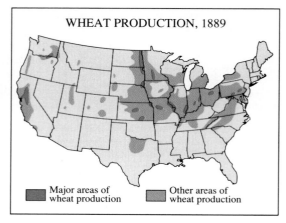

WHEAT PRODUCTION, 1889

Major areas of wheat production · Other areas of wheat production

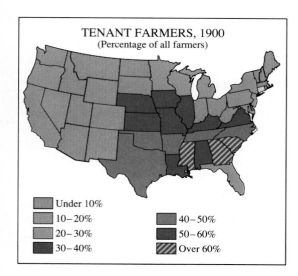

TENANT FARMERS, 1900
(Percentage of all farmers)

Under 10% · 10–20% · 20–30% · 30–40% · 40–50% · 50–60% · Over 60%

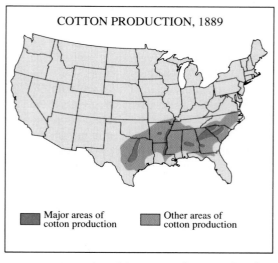

COTTON PRODUCTION, 1889

Major areas of cotton production · Other areas of cotton production

Agricultural Regions, 1889 and 1900 *Source: From Charles A. Paullin,* Atlas of the Historical Geography of the United States. *Used by permission of Carnegie Institution of Washington.*

Life on the Plains, however, was much harder than the advertisements suggested. Migrants often encountered scarcities of essentials they had once taken for granted. The open prairies contained little lumber for housing and fuel. Pioneer families were forced to build houses of sod and to burn manure for heat. Water was as scarce as timber.

Hardships of Life on the Plains

Even more formidable than the terrain of the Plains was the climate. The expanse between the Missouri River and the Rocky Mountains divides climatologically along a line running from Minnesota southwest through Oklahoma, then south, bisecting Texas. East of this line, annual rainfall averages about 28 inches, enough for most crops (see map). West of the line, life-giving rain was never certain.

Weather seldom followed predictable cycles on either side of the line. In the summer, weeks of torrid heat and parching winds would suddenly yield to violent storms that washed away crops and property. Winter blizzards piled up mountainous snowdrifts that halted all outdoor movement. In March and April, melting snow swelled streams, and flood waters threatened millions of acres. In the fall, a week without rain could turn dry grasslands into tinder, and the slightest spark could ignite a raging prairie fire.

Even when the climate was favorable, nature could be cruel. Weather that was good for crops was also good for breeding insects. In the 1870s and 1880s, swarms of grasshoppers virtually ate up entire farms. Heralded only by the rising din of buzzing wings, a cloud of insects a mile long would smother the land and devour everything in sight: plants, seeds, tree bark, and clothes. As one farmer lamented, the "hoppers left behind nothing but the mortgage."

Settlers of the Plains also had to contend with social isolation, a factor accentuated by the pattern of settlement. Under the Homestead Act of 1862, for example, settlers received rectangular-shaped tracts of 160 acres. At most, four families could live near each other, but only if they congregated around a shared four-corner boundary intersection. In practice, farmers usually

Social Isolation

lived back from their boundary lines, and at least half a mile separated farmhouses.

Many observers wrote about the loneliness and monotony of life on the Plains. Men might find escape by working outdoors and taking occasional trips to sell crops or buy supplies. Women were more isolated, confined by domestic chores to the household, where, as one writer remarked, they were "not much better than slaves. It is a weary, monotonous round of cooking and washing and mending and as a result the insane asylum is 1/3d filled with wives of farmers."

Farm families survived by depending on their resolve and by organizing churches and clubs where they could socialize a few times a month. By the early 1900s, two external developments had combined to bring rural settlers into closer contact with modern consumer society. First, starting in the 1870s and 1880s, mail-order houses—Montgomery Ward and Sears Roebuck—expanded and made new industrial products available to almost everyone. Second, during the 1890s, scores of rural communities petitioned Congress for extension of the postal service, and in 1896 the government made Rural Free Delivery (RFD) widely available. Farmers would no longer lack news and information; they could receive letters, newspapers, advertisements, and catalogues at home nearly every day. In 1913, the postal service inaugurated parcel post, which enabled people to receive packages, such as orders from Ward's and Sears, more easily.

Mail-Order Companies and Rural Free Delivery

In the years after the Civil War, the extension of the farming frontier, the growth of national and international markets for food, and the expansion of railroad routes brought about an agricultural revolution. But that transformation would not have been possible, nor would the Plains have been conquered, without the expanded use of machinery. When the Civil War drew men away from farms in the upper Mississippi River valley, the female and male laborers who remained behind began using reapers and other implements to meet the demand for grain and to take advantage of high prices. After the war, continued demand and high prices encouraged

Mechanization of Agriculture

TIME AND COST OF FARMING AN ACRE OF LAND BY HAND AND BY MACHINE, 1890

Crop	Hours Required		Labor Costs	
	Hand	Machine	Hand	Machine
Wheat	61	3	$3.65	$ .66
Corn	39	15	$3.62	$1.51
Oats	66	7	$3.73	$1.07
Loose hay	21	4	$1.75	$ .42

Source: Ray Allan Billington, Westward Expansion: A History of the American Frontier, 2nd ed. (New York: Macmillan, 1960), p. 697. Copyright © 1960 Macmillan Publishing Company. Reprinted with permission.

farmers to depend more on machines, and inventors worked to develop new implements for farm use. Machines dramatically reduced the per-acre time and cost of farming various crops (see table).

At the same time, Congress and scientists were making efforts to improve existing crops and develop new ones. The 1862 Morrill Land Grant Act gave each state public lands to sell in order to finance agricultural and industrial colleges. Another law, the Hatch Act of 1887, provided for agricultural experiment stations in every state, further encouraging the advancement of farming technology.

Legislative and Scientific Aid to Farmers

Meanwhile, scientific advances were enabling farmers to use the soil more efficiently. Agricultural researchers developed the technique of dry farming, a system of plowing and harrowing that prevented precious moisture from evaporating. Botanists perfected varieties of "hard" wheat, whose seeds could withstand northern winters, and millers invented an efficient process for grinding those tougher wheat kernels into flour. Californian Luther Burbank developed a wide range of new plants by crossbreeding, and Tuskegee Institute's chemist George Washington Carver created hundreds of new products from peanuts, soybeans, sweet potatoes, and cotton wastes. Scientists also developed means of combating plant and animal diseases. Although turbulent times for farmers lay just ahead, development of the agricultural hinterland by settlement, science, and technology made America "the garden of the world."

The Ranching Frontier

While commercial farming was spreading, one of the West's most romantic industries, cattle ranching, was evolving. Early in the nineteenth century, huge herds of cattle, originally introduced by the Spanish and developed by Mexican ranchers, roamed southern Texas and bred with cattle brought by American settlers. The resulting longhorn breed multiplied and became valuable by the 1860s, when the East's as well as the West's growing population increased the demand for food and railroads made the transportation of beef more feasible. By 1870, drovers were herding thousands of Texas cattle northward to railroad connections in Kansas, Missouri, and Wyoming (see map, page 296). On these long drives, mounted cowboys (as many as 25 percent of whom were blacks) tended the herds, which fed on open grassland along the way.

The long drive gave rise to its own romantic lore, but it was not very efficient. In trekking fifteen hundred miles, the cattle became sinewy and tough. Herds traveling through Indian lands and farmers' fields were sometimes shot at and later prohibited from such trespass by state laws. The ranchers' only solution was to eliminate long drives by raising herds nearer to railroad routes.

Cattle raisers needed vast stretches of land where their herds could graze, and they wanted to incur as little expense as possible in using such land. Thus,

Open-Range Ranching

they often bought a few acres bordering streams and turned their herds loose on adjacent public domain that no one wanted to own because it lacked water access. By this method, called open-range ranching, a cattle raiser could control thousands of acres by owning only a hundred or so.

Roundups provided easterners with colorful images of western life: bellowing cattle, mounted rope-swinging cowboys, the smell of singed hides and smoky campfires. But roundups and open-range ranching were short-lived because they were too successful. Opportunities for profit first provided new fortunes for Civil War veterans in Texas and other states. As national and international demand for beef kept rising, ranchers and investment capital flowed into the Plains. Soon cattle began to overrun the range.

By the 1880s, ranchers, largely in response to the problem of overgrazing, began to fence in "their" pastures—even though they had no legal title to the land. Fences destroyed the open range and often provoked disputes between cattle raisers and sheep raisers, and between ranchers and farmers, who claimed use of the same land. In 1885, President Grover Cleveland ordered the removal of illegal fences on public lands and Indian reservations. Enforcement was slow, but the order signaled that the free use of public domain was ending.

Open-range ranching made beef a staple of the American diet and created a few fortunes, but its extralegal features could not survive the rush of history. By 1890, big businesses were taking over the cattle industry and applying scientific methods of breeding and feeding. Most ranchers owned or leased the land they used, though some illegal fencing continued. The cowboy became just another corporate wage earner, though the myth of his freedom and individualism grew rather than faded.

The South After Reconstruction

In 1880, four times as many farmers lived in the South as on the Plains. Ravaged by the Civil War, which had killed one-third of all draft animals and destroyed half of the region's farm equipment, southern agriculture recovered slowly. Rather than diversify, farmers concentrated on cotton growing even more heavily than before the war. High prices for seed and implements, declining prices for crops, taxes, and, most of all, debt trapped many families in poverty.

Some southern leaders made attempts to industrialize, but their efforts were only partially successful. By 1900, for example, most southern industries were mere subsidiaries of northern firms. Whether interested in an industrialized New South or in agriculture, southerners were generally dependent on northern capital.

During and after Reconstruction, a significant shift in the nature of agriculture swept through the South. Between 1860 and 1880, the total number of farms in southern states more than doubled. The number of landowners, however, did not increase, and the size of the average farm actually decreased—from 347 to 156 acres. The result was that a larger proportion of southern farmers rented, rather than owned, their farms. Southern agriculture was dominated by sharecropping and tenant farming. More than one-third of the farmers counted in 1880 were sharecroppers and tenants, and the proportion increased to two-thirds by 1920.

Sharecropping and tenant farming entangled millions of southerners in a web of humiliation. At its center was the crop lien, which worked in

Crop-Lien System

the following way. Currency was scarce, and most farmers were too poor ever to have cash on hand. Forced to borrow in order to buy necessities, they could offer as collateral only what they could grow. Thus, a farmer in need of supplies would deal with a nearby "furnishing merchant," who would exchange supplies for a certain portion, or lien, of the farmer's forthcoming crop. In the fall, after the crop was harvested and brought to market, the merchant collected his debt.

The prices charged to credit customers averaged 30 to 40 percent higher than prices charged to cash customers. Credit customers also had to pay interest ranging from 33 to 200 percent on the advances they received. Suppose, for example, that a farmer needed a 20-cent bag of seed and had no cash. The furnishing merchant would extend credit for the purchase but would also boost the price to 28 cents. At year's end that 28-cent loan would have accumulated interest, raising the farmer's debt to, say, 42 cents—more than double the item's original cost. The farmer, having pledged more than his crop's worth against scores of such debts, fell behind in payments. His only choice was to commit the next year's crop to the merchant and sink deeper into debt. If he fell too far behind, he could be evicted.

The lien system caused hardship in former plantation areas, where black and white tenants and sharecroppers grew cotton for the same markets that had existed before the Civil War. But in the southern backcountry, which in the antebellum era had contained small farms, relatively few slaves, and diversified agriculture, problems of crop liens were compounded by other economic changes.

New spending habits of backcountry farmers reflected the most important of these changes. In 1884, Jephta Dickson of Jackson County in the northern Georgia hills bought $53.37 worth of flour, meal, peas, meat, corn, and syrup from one merchant and $2.53 worth of potatoes, peas, and sugar from another. Such expenditures would have been rare in the upcountry before the Civil War, when most farmers grew almost all the food they needed. But after the war, yeoman farmers like Jephta Dickson shifted from semi-subsistence agriculture to more commercialized farming—in the South that meant cotton raising—because their indebtedness forced them to grow a crop that would bring in cash. As backcountry yeomen put more acres under cotton cultivation, they raised less of what they needed on a day-to-day basis and were forced more frequently into positions where they were at the mercy of merchants.

Poor whites of the rural South also perceived a political threat to their status (real and imagined)

from newly enfranchised blacks. Wealthy white landowners and merchants fanned these fears, using racism to keep poor whites and blacks divided and to prevent protests over economic distress from threatening their power.

The majority of the nation's black people lived in the South, worked in agriculture, and found that under freedom they faced the same disadvantages they had faced under slavery. In 1880, 90 percent of all southern blacks depended for a living on farming or personal and domestic service—the same occupations they had held as slaves.

Conditions of Blacks

Pushed into sharecropping and burdened with crop liens, blacks also had to contend with new forms of social and political oppression. With slavery dead, white supremacists fashioned new ways to keep blacks in a position of inferiority. As part of this effort, southern leaders instituted racist measures to discourage blacks from voting and to legally segregate them from whites.

The end of Reconstruction had not stopped blacks from voting. Although threats and intimidation against them increased, blacks still formed the backbone of the Republican party and some still won elective offices. White politicians, however, began to seek ways to reduce the "Negro vote." Beginning with Georgia in 1877, southern states levied taxes of one to two dollars on all citizens wishing to vote. These poll taxes were prohibitive to most black voters, who were so deeply in debt to furnishing merchants and landlords that they never had cash for any purpose. Other schemes disfranchised black voters who could not read. For example, voters might be required to deposit ballots for different candidates in different ballot boxes. In order to do so correctly, voters had to be able to read instructions. Although aimed at blacks, these measures also disqualified many poor whites.

Racial discrimination also stiffened in social affairs. A widespread informal system of separation had governed race relations in the antebellum South. After the Civil War, this system was formalized in law. In a series of cases during the 1870s, the Supreme Court opened the door to discrimination by ruling

Spread of Jim Crow Laws

that the Fourteenth Amendment protected citizens' rights only against infringement by state governments. If blacks wanted protection under the law, the Court said, they must seek it from the states.

The climax to these rulings came in 1883, when in the *Civil Rights Cases* the Court struck down the 1875 Civil Rights Act, which had prohibited segregation in public facilities such as streetcars, hotels, theaters, and parks. Subsequent lower-court cases in the 1880s established the principle that blacks could be restricted to "separate-but-equal" facilities. The Supreme Court upheld the separate-but-equal doctrine in *Plessy* v. *Ferguson* (1896) and officially applied it to schools in *Cummins* v. *County Board of Education* (1899).

Thereafter, segregation laws—known as Jim Crow laws—piled up throughout the South, confronting black people with daily reminders of their inferior status. State and local laws restricted blacks to the rear of streetcars, separate drinking and toilet facilities, and separate sections of hospitals, asylums, and cemeteries. Segregation reached such extremes that Atlanta required separate Bibles for black witnesses swearing before court.

In industry, breezes of change were being stimulated by new manufacturing initiatives, but there, too, a distinctively southern quality prevailed. Two of the South's leading industries

Industrial- ization of the South

in the late nineteenth century relied on traditional staple crops, cotton and tobacco. In the 1870s, textile mills began to appear in the Cotton Belt. Manned cheaply by poor whites eager to escape crop liens, and aided by low taxes, such mills grew rapidly. By 1900, the South had four hundred mills; twenty years later the region was replacing New England in textile-manufacturing supremacy. Proximity to raw materials and cheap labor also aided the tobacco industry, and the invention in 1880 of a cigarette-making machine immensely enhanced the marketability of tobacco.

Cigarettes were manufactured in cities by black and white workers; textile mills were concentrated in small towns and developed their own exploitative labor system. Financed mostly by local investors, mills employed women and children from nearby poor white families and paid fifty cents a day

Textile mills, such as this one in Greensboro, North Carolina, represented the growing industrialization of the New South around 1900. Here, low-paid millworkers are shown feeding cotton into machines. *Library of Congress.*

for twelve or more hours of work. Many companies built villages around their mills and controlled housing, stores, schools, and churches. Criticism of the company was forbidden, and attempts at union organization were squelched.

Northern and European capitalists sponsored other southern industries. In the Gulf states, the lumber industry became significant, and iron and steel production made Birmingham, Alabama a boom city. Yet in 1900, the South remained as rural as it had been in 1860. The emergence of a New South would have to await another era.

As the continent filled in and the West and South were transformed, white Americans exhibited their best and worst characteristics. The development of the West was accomplished with courage and creativity. The optimistic conquerors, however, displayed a wastefulness, violence, and greed that tarnished the American image by overwhelming Native American culture and sacrificing environmental balance for market profits. In the South, careless exploitation exhausted the soil and left poor farmers downtrodden. Industrialization failed to lessen the dominance of southern staple-crop agriculture, and by 1900, the South was more dependent economically on the North than it had been before the Civil War.

Suggestions for Further Reading

The Western Frontier

Ray A. Billington and Martin Ridge, *Westward Expansion,* 5th ed. (1982); Robert V. Hine, *The American West,* 2nd ed. (1984); Julie Roy Jeffrey, *Frontier Women* (1979); Patricia Limerick, *The Legacy of Conquest: The Unbroken Past of the American West* (1987); Frederick Merk, *History of the Westward Movement* (1978); Rodman W. Paul, *The Far West and the Great Plains in Transition, 1859–1900* (1988); Rodman W. Paul and Richard W. Etulain, *The Frontier and the American West* (1977); Richard Slotkin, *The Fatal Environment: The Myth of the Frontier in the Age of Industrialization* (1985); Henry Nash Smith, *Virgin Land: The American West as Symbol and Myth* (1950); Roberta B. Sollid, *Calamity Jane* (1958); Kent Ladd Steckmesser, *The Western Hero in History and Legend* (1965).

Railroads

Alfred D. Chandler, ed., *Railroads: The Nation's First Big Business* (1965); Robert W. Fogel, *Railroads and Economic Growth* (1964); Alan Trachtenberg, *The Incorporation of America* (1982); O. O. Winther, *The Transportation Frontier* (1964).

Indians

Ralph K. Andrist, *The Long Death: The Last Days of the Plains Indians* (1964); Francis Paul Prucha, *The Great Father: The United States Government and the American Indians* (1984); Edward H. Spicer, *Cycles of Conquest: The Impact of Spain, Mexico, and the United States on the Indians of the Southwest* (1962); Robert M. Utley, *The Indian Frontier of the American West, 1846–1890* (1984); Wilcomb E. Washburn, *Red Man's Land/White Man's Law* (1971).

Ranching and Settlement of the Plains

Lewis Atherton, *The Cattle Kings* (1961); Allan G. Bogue, *From Prairie to Corn Belt* (1963); Everett Dick, *The Sod-House Frontier* (1937); Gilbert C. Fite, *The Farmer's Frontier* (1963); Walter Prescott Webb, *The Great Plains* (1931).

The New South

Orville Vernon Burton and Robert C. McMath, Jr., eds., *Toward a New South?: Post–Civil War Southern Communities* (1982); Thomas D. Clark and Albert D. Kirwan, *The South Since Appomattox* (1967); Dewey Grantham, Jr., *The Democratic South* (1963); Steven Hahn, *The Roots of Southern Populism: Yeoman Farmers and the Transformation of the Georgia Upcountry, 1850–1890* (1983); J. Morgan Kousser, *The Shaping of Southern Politics* (1974); Howard N. Rabinowitz, *Race Relations in the Urban South, 1865–1890* (1978); Theodore Saloutos, *Farmer Movements in the South, 1865–1933* (1960); C. Vann Woodward, *The Strange Career of Jim Crow* (1966); C. Vann Woodward, *Origins of the New South,* rev. ed. (1951); Gavin Wright, *Old South, New South* (1986).

It was the spring of 1882, and Conrad Carl, who for nearly thirty years had been a tailor in New York City, was appearing before a group of United States senators to explain changing work conditions in the tailoring business. Admitting that his testimony would probably cost him his job, Carl nevertheless testified candidly. When he first began tailoring, Carl explained, he and his wife and children had pieced together garments by hand. The pace of their work was relaxed, yet he was able to save a few dollars each year. Then, said Carl, "in 1854 or 1855 . . . the sewing machine was invented and introduced, and it stitched very nicely, nicer than the tailor could do; and the bosses said: 'We want you to use the sewing machine; you have to buy one.' "

Carl and his fellow tailors used their meager savings to buy machines, hoping they could earn more by producing more. But their employers cut wages instead of raising them. The tailors "found that we could earn no more than we could without the machine; but the money for the machine was gone now, and we found that the machine was only for the profit of the bosses; that they got their work quicker, and it was done nicer."

Conrad Carl's testimony to the Senate committee was one worker's view of the industrialization that was relentlessly overtaking American society. The forces prevailing in the new order were both inspiring and ominous. The factory and the machine broke down manufacturing into minute, routinized tasks and organized work according to the dictates of the clock. Corporations merged and amassed frightening power in the quest for productivity and profits. Defenders of the new system devised new social and economic theories to justify it, while critics tried to counteract what they thought were abuses of power. Workers, who had long thought of themselves as valued producers, were caught in the changing modes of production and fought to avoid becoming slaves to machines.

Industrialization was and is a complex process whose chief feature is the production of goods by machine rather than by hand. American industrialization had the following characteristics:

1. Involvement of an increasing proportion of the work force in manufacturing
2. Concentration of production in large, intricately organized factories

17

THE MACHINE AGE, 1877–1920

3. Accelerated technological innovation, emphasizing new inventions and applied science
4. Expanded markets, no longer merely local and regional in scope
5. Growth of a nationwide transportation network based on the railroad, and an accompanying communications network based on the telegraph and telephone
6. Increased accumulation of capital for investment in the expansion of production
7. Growth of large enterprises and specialization in all forms of economic activity
8. Rapid increase in population
9. Steady increase in the size and predominance of cities

In 1860, about one-fourth of the American labor force worked in manufacturing and transportation; more than half did so in 1920. The number of people gainfully employed rose from 17.4 million in 1880 to 41.6 million in 1920. In 1870, Western Union handled more than 9 million telegraph messages on 112,000 miles of wire; by 1900, it processed over 63 million messages on 933,000 miles of wire. At the dawn of the twentieth century, the United States was not only the world's largest producer of raw materials and food, but the most productive industrial nation as well.

Economic growth furnished jobs and income to millions of families who had left American farms and European villages in search of a better existence. But industry's emphasis on productivity and profitability often kept wages at or below subsistence levels and harnessed workers to monotonous routines. Fearful that American industrialism might create a class of helpless proletarians who had lost control over their economic livelihoods, laborers fought to retain independent work habits and to be paid a living wage.

Technology and the Quest for Wealth

In 1876, Thomas A. Edison and his associates moved into a long wooden shed in Menlo Park, New Jersey, where Edison intended to turn out "a minor invention every ten days and a big thing every six months or so." He envisioned his laboratory as an invention factory, where creative people would pool their ideas and skills to fashion marketable products. Edison, and others like him, helped to make the years between 1865 and 1900 an age of invention. Indeed, the work of inventors was an integral part of American industrialization (see map, page 308).

Perhaps the biggest of his "big thing" projects began in 1878, when he formed the Edison Electric Light Company and embarked on a search for a cheap, efficient means of indoor lighting. Edison's major contribution was the perfecting—in 1879—of an incandescent bulb, which used a filament in a vacuum. At the same time, he worked out a system of power production and distribution—an improved dynamo and a parallel circuit of wires—that would provide cheap, convenient lighting to a large number of customers.

Birth of the Electrical Industry

Aware that he had to make his ideas marketable, Edison acted as his own publicist. During the 1880 Christmas season, he illuminated Menlo Park with forty incandescent bulbs, and in 1882, he built a power plant that would light eighty-five buildings in New York's Wall Street financial district. When this Pearl Street Station began service, a *New York Times* reporter marveled that working in his office at night "seemed almost like writing in daylight."

Edison's system had a major limitation: it used direct current at low voltage and could thus send electric power only a mile or two. George Westinghouse, an inventor from Schenectady, New York, solved this problem. Westinghouse used alternating current and transformers to reduce high-voltage power to lower voltage levels, thus making transmission over long distances cheaper.

Once Edison and Westinghouse had made their breakthroughs, others helped distribute their inventions to a wide market. Samuel Insull, Edison's private secretary, deftly attracted investments and organized Edison power plants across the country. In the late 1880s and early 1890s, financiers Henry Villard and J. P. Morgan consolidated patents in electric lighting and merged equipment-manufacturing companies into the General Electric Company. Equally important, General Electric and

IMPORTANT EVENTS

1873–78	Hard times
1877	Widespread railroad strikes
1879	Henry George, *Progress and Poverty*
	Edison perfects the incandescent light bulb
1884–85	Hard times
1886	Haymarket riot; American Federation of Labor founded
1888	Edward Bellamy, *Looking Backward*
1890	Sherman Anti-Trust Act
1892	Homestead Steel strike
1893–97	Hard times
1894	Pullman strike
1895	*United States* v. *E. C. Knight Co.*
1896	*Holden* v. *Hardy*
1901	U.S. Steel Corporation founded
1905	*Lochner* v. *New York*
	Industrial Workers of the World founded
1908	*Muller* v. *Oregon*
	First Ford Model T built
1913	First moving assembly line begins operation at Ford

Westinghouse Electric established research laboratories that paid practical-minded scientists to find new uses for electricity.

A number of inventors worked independently and tried to sell their handiwork to manufacturing companies. One such inventor was Granville T. Woods, an African-American electrical and mechanical engineer from Columbus, Ohio. Working in machine shops, Woods patented thirty-five devices vital to electronics and communications. Among his inventions were an automatic circuit breaker, an electric incubator, an electromagnetic brake, and various instruments to aid communications between railroad trains.

The era's most visionary manufacturer was Henry Ford. In the 1890s, he worked as an electrical engineer in Detroit's Edison Company and in his spare time experimented with a gasoline-burning internal combustion engine to power a vehicle. Like Edison, Ford had a scheme as well as a product. His plan was to reduce production costs by producing millions of identical cars in exactly the same

Mass Production of the Automobile

way. The key was mass production, and the watchword was *flow*. On Ford's assembly lines, production was broken down so that each worker had responsibility for only one task, constantly repeated. There was a continuous flow of these tasks until the finished product was assembled. In 1908, the first year the famous Model T was built, Ford sold 10,000 cars. By 1914, the year after the first moving assembly line was inaugurated, 248,000 Fords were sold. Many of them sold for $490 apiece, only about one-fourth of what they would have cost a decade earlier.

Even $490 was beyond the means of many workers, who earned at best $2 a day. In 1914, however, Ford tried to spur productivity, prevent high turnover among his employees, and head off unionization by offering his workers combined wages and profit sharing of $5 a day. "This is neither charity nor wages," he explained, "but profit sharing and efficiency engineering." Moreover, rising automobile production meant more jobs, higher earnings, and higher profits in such related industries as oil, paint, rubber, and glass.

Although the timing of mechanization varied

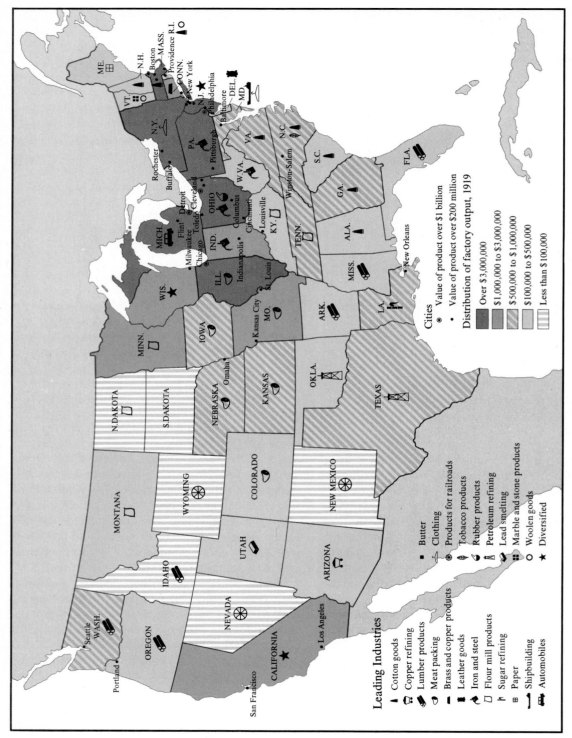

Industrial Production, 1919 *Source: © American Heritage Publishing Co., Inc., American Heritage Pictorial Atlas of United States History; data from U.S. Bureau of the Census, Fourteenth Census of the United States, 1920. Vol. IX: Manufacturing (Washington: U.S. Government Printing Office, 1921).*

The assembly line at the Ford Motor plant shows how the process of production was broken down into simple, repetitive tasks—here, the fashioning of auto seats. Rather than building the entire product, specialized crews worked on individual parts that later were assembled into the whole automobile. *Ford Motor Company.*

from one industry to another, a host of machines and processes helped to alter the nation's economy and everyday life between 1865 and 1900. The telephone and typewriter revolutionized communications. Sewing machines made mass-produced clothing available to almost everyone. Refrigeration changed American dietary habits by making it easier to preserve food. Streetcars, elevated railroads, and subways extended city limits and enabled people to live farther from their workplaces.

All these inventions and more thrust the United States into the vanguard of industrial nations. But other effects were less positive. Industrial expansion and mechanization not only destroyed time-honored crafts but subordinated workers to rigid schedules and repetitive routines. The scramble for patents resulted in as much waste as technological advancement. Entrepreneurs spent huge sums hop-

ing to profit from inventing something slightly different from what already existed and tried to monopolize new discoveries by confining research to their own labs. Finally, bigness and consolidation in industry engulfed the individual.

The Triumph of Industrialism

In the industrial sector, higher profits resulted from higher production at lower costs. As railroads and technological innovations made large-scale production more economical, sizable factories began to replace small ones. Only large factories could afford to buy new machines and operate them at full capacity. And large factories could best take advantage of discount rates for shipping products in bulk and for buying raw materials in quantity. Economists call such advantages *economies of scale*.

Machines and large factories made such economies possible, but profitability was as much a matter of organization as of mechanics. Thus, by the 1890s, engineers and managers planned every work task to increase output economically and efficiently. Their efforts not only allowed standardization of tasks and quality in mass production but also reduced the skill level and independent judgment of workers involved in production.

New
Emphasis
on Efficiency

Of those who espoused systems of efficient production, the most influential was engineer Frederick W. Taylor. In 1898, Taylor took his stopwatch to the Bethlehem Steel Company to illustrate how his principles of scientific management worked. His experiments involved identifying the "elementary operations of motions" used by specific workers, selecting better tools, and devising "a series of motions which can be made quickest and best." Applying the technique to the shoveling of ore, Taylor designed fifteen kinds of shovel and prescribed the proper motions for using each one. As a result, he reduced a crew of 600 men to 140.

Taylor's writings helped make time studies and scientific management a national obsession. Workers' skills became less valued, and managers increasingly controlled the pace and scale of output. Time, as much as quality, became the measure of acceptable work, and science rather than tradition determined the right ways of doing things. As integral features of the assembly line, where work was divided into specific time-determined tasks, employees had become another kind of interchangeable part.

At the same time, large manufacturers were adding new marketing techniques to their technological and organizational innovations. Meat processor Gustavus Swift used branch slaughterhouses and refrigeration to enlarge the market for fresh meat. James B. Duke, whose American Tobacco Company made cigarettes a big business, saturated communities with billboards and free samples and of-

New
Marketing
Techniques

fered premium gifts to retailers for selling more cigarettes. Companies such as International Harvester and Singer Sewing Machine set up systems for servicing their products and introduced financing schemes to permit customers to buy the machines more easily. In many instances, marketing innovations enabled producers to sell directly to retailers and so eliminate the costs that wholesaling entailed.

The Corporate Consolidation Movement

Neither the wonders of industrial production nor the new techniques of market promotion masked unsettling factors in the American economy. Competition and the race for higher productivity and new markets had costs, as well as benefits. New technology demanded that factories operate at near-capacity in order to produce goods most economically. But the more manufacturers produced, the more they had to sell. And in order to sell more, they had to reduce prices. In order to profit more, they expanded production further and often reduced wages. In order to expand, they had to borrow money. In order to repay the money, they had to produce and sell even more. This circular process strangled small firms that could not keep pace and thrust workers into conditions of constant uncertainty. The same cycle affected trade, banking, and transportation.

This environment encouraged rapid growth, but optimism could dissolve at the hint that debtors were unable to meet their obligations. In the final third of the nineteenth century, financial panics afflicted the economy at least once a decade, depressing wages and prices, destroying businesses, and putting workers out of jobs. Economic hard times that began in 1873, 1884, and 1893 hovered over the nation for several years in each instance. Business leaders failed to agree on what caused the declines. In an effort to combat the uncertainty of the business cycle, many corporate leaders turned to more centralized and cooperative forms of economic power, notably corporations, pools, trusts, and holding companies.

In the nineteenth century, corporations, with their limited liability for stockholders, were the best instruments for raising the capital needed for industrial expansion. Moreover, in the 1880s and 1890s, corporations received broad judicial protection when the Supreme Court ruled that they, like individuals, were protected by the Fourteenth Amendment. States could not deny corporations equal protection of the laws and could not deprive them of rights or property without due process of law.

As economic disorder and the urge for profits mounted, corporation managers began to seek stability in new and larger forms of economic concentration. At first, such efforts were **Pools, Trusts, and Holding Companies** tentative and informal, consisting mainly of cooperative agreements among firms that made the same product or offered the same service. Through these arrangements, called *pools*, competing companies tried to control the market by agreeing how much each should produce and what prices should be charged. Such "gentlemen's agreements" worked during good times, when there was enough business for all; but during slow periods, the desire for profits often tempted pool members to evade their commitments. The Interstate Commerce Act of 1887 outlawed pools, but by then their usefulness was already fading.

John D. Rockefeller disliked pools, calling them "ropes of sand." In 1879, one of his lawyers, Samuel Dodd, devised a more stable means of dominating the market. Since state laws prevented one corporation from holding stock in another corporation, Dodd adapted an old device called a *trust*, which in law existed as an arrangement that allowed responsible individuals to manage the financial affairs of a person unwilling or unable to handle them alone. Dodd reasoned that stockholders of companies could be lured or forced into turning over control of their stock "in trust" to a board of trustees, which could then supervise all operations under the name of one company. This device allowed Rockefeller to integrate the management of his Standard Oil Company of Ohio with that of other companies he controlled, strengthening his grip on the petroleum industry.

In 1888, New Jersey adopted new incorporation laws allowing corporations chartered there to own property in other states and to own stock in other corporations. This reform led to the creation of the *holding company*, which owned a partial or complete interest in other companies. Holding companies could, in turn, merge their constituent companies' assets, as well as their management. Thus, Rockefeller incorporated the holding company of Standard Oil of New Jersey, merging the assets of forty constituent companies. Holding companies also encouraged *vertical integration*. This allowed companies to take over several levels of production and distribution, including control of raw materials and transportation, as well as manufacturing.

Mergers became the answer to industry's search for order. Between 1889 and 1903, some three hundred combinations were formed, most of them trusts and holding companies. By far the most spectacular was the U.S. Steel Corporation, formed in 1901 and financed by J. P. Morgan. This new enterprise, made up of iron-ore properties, freight carriers, wire mills, plate and tubing companies, and other firms, was capitalized at more than $1.4 billion.

The merger movement created a new species of businessmen, whose vocation was financial organizing rather than producing a particular good or service. Shrewd operators sought opportunities for combination, formed corporations, and then persuaded producers to sell their firms to the new company. These financiers usually raised money by selling stock and borrowing from banks. Investment bankers like J. P. Morgan and Jacob Schiff piloted the merger movement, inspiring awe with their financial power and organizational skills.

The Gospel of Wealth

Business leaders turned to consolidation under new corporate forms to promote growth and to cut down competition. But the American public be-

Social Darwinism lieved in open competition. It thus became necessary for the defenders of monopolistic companies to find a means to justify their size and power. They turned to the doctrine of Social Darwinism, a philosophy that loosely adapted Charles Darwin's theory of the origin of species to the principles of laissez faire (the doctrine opposing government interference in economic affairs). Human society had evolved naturally, Social Darwinists reasoned, and any interference with existing institutions would only hamper progress and aid the weak. In a free society operating according to the principle of survival of the fittest, power would flow naturally to the most capable. Holding and acquiring of property were therefore inalienable rights, and wealth was a mark of well-deserved power and responsibility.

This philosophy required that people be left free to accumulate and dispose of wealth. In fact, however, new corporate forms, with their domination of production and finance, prevented most individuals who did not already have wealth from acquiring it. To compensate for this inconsistency, Social Darwinists reasoned that wealth carried moral responsibilities. Thus, captains of industry strongly believed that they had an obligation to provide for the needs of those less fortunate or less capable. Steel baron Andrew Carnegie, who proclaimed his philanthropic activities to be the "Gospel of Wealth," believed that he and other powerful industrialists were trustees for society's wealth and that his duty was to fulfill that trust in humane ways.

Such philanthropy, however, had limits. John D. Rockefeller once stated, "I believe it is my duty to make money and . . . to use the money I make for the good of my fellow man according to the dictates of my conscience." This belief implied a right for economic elites to define what they believed was good and necessary for society. It meant that the wealthy could and should endow churches, hospitals, and schools. But it also meant that government should not force the rich, through taxation or regulation, to become more humanitarian.

Paradoxically, business executives who exalted individual initiative and independence also pressed for government assistance. They denounced any measures that might aid unions or regulate factory

Government Assistance to Business conditions; such legislation, they said, thwarted natural economic laws. At the same time, though, they lobbied for subsidies, loans, and tax relief that would encourage business growth. Tariffs were by far the largest form of government assistance to industry. By putting high import duties on competing goods from abroad, Congress enabled American producers to keep the prices of their goods relatively high. Industrialists argued that tariff protection encouraged the development of new products and the founding of new enterprises. But tariffs also forced consumers to pay artificially high prices for many products.

Whatever their inconsistencies, business leaders took great pride in the achievements of their era. Many accepted credit for the meteoric rise of the American standard of living—national wealth rose by 550 percent between 1860 and 1900, and per capita income increased by 150 percent—and they scoffed at charges that only the wealthy were benefiting. They also warned that government intervention in the business system—in the form of regulation, taxation, or aid to the poor—would stall or even reverse progress. Others disagreed.

Dissenting Voices

Writers who attacked trusts argued within the same framework of values as did corporate leaders who defended the new economic system. While defenders insisted that trusts were the natural and efficient outcome of economic development, critics charged that trusts were unnatural because they were created by greed and inefficient because they stifled opportunity. Underlying such charges was an ardent fear of monopoly. Those who feared monopoly believed that large corporations could exploit consumers by fixing prices, demean workers by cutting wages, destroy opportunity by eliminating small businesses, and threaten democracy by corrupting politicians.

Many believed that there was a better way to achieve progress. By the mid-1880s, a number of young professors, troubled by the growing size of industrial and financial firms, began to challenge Social Darwinism and laissez faire. Some, like pioneering sociologist Lester Ward, attacked the application of evolutionary theory to social and economic relations. In *Dynamic Sociology* (1883), Ward argued that human control of nature, not natural law, accounted for the advance of civilization. To Ward, a system that guaranteed survival only to the fittest was wasteful and brutal; instead, he reasoned, cooperative activity, fostered by planning and government intervention, was the best means to unity and happiness for all. Economists Richard Ely, John R. Commons, and Edward Bemis agreed that natural forces should be harnessed for the public good. Instead of the laissez-faire system, they preferred one of positive assistance by the state.

While academics recommended intervening in the natural economic order, others proposed more utopian schemes for combating monopolies. Reformer Henry George, the author

Utopian Economic Schemes

of *Progress and Poverty* (1879), declared that inequality stemmed from the ability of a few to profit from rising property values. These values rose, George argued, without any effort on the part of owners, simply because a growing population increased demand for living and working space, especially in cities. To restore equality, George proposed to tax the "unearned increment"—the rise in land values caused by increased market demand rather than by owners' improvements—and to eliminate all other taxes. By confiscating undue profits, George insisted, this "single tax" would end monopolistic tendencies and ensure social progress.

Unlike George, who approved of private ownership, novelist Edward Bellamy envisioned a socialist state in which government would own and oversee the means of production and distribution and unite all people under moral laws. Bellamy outlined his vision in *Looking Backward, 2000–1887*, published in 1888. The novel depicted Boston in the year 2000 as a peaceful community where all people belonged to one industrial army. Each person was paid not with money, but with credits enabling him or her to obtain consumer goods and entertainment. By portraying a utopian world, free of lawyers, politics, and class divisions, Bellamy tried to convince readers that a "principle of fraternal cooperation" could replace vicious competition and wasteful monopoly.

Meanwhile, public clamor against monopolies and trusts began to prod legislators into action. By 1900, fifteen states had constitutional provisions outlawing trusts, and twenty-seven

Antitrust Legislation

had laws forbidding pools. Most were states in the South and West, responding to antimonopolistic pressure exerted by various farm organizations. But problems of definition and enforcement mounted. State attorneys general lacked staff and judicial support for a concerted attack on big business, and corporations always found ways to evade restrictions. Consequently, a need for national legislation became more pressing.

Throughout the 1880s, both major parties moved toward such legislation, and in 1890 Congress passed the Sherman Anti-Trust Act. The law made illegal "every contract, combination in the form of trust or otherwise, or conspiracy in the restraint of trade." People found guilty of violating the law faced fines and jail terms, and those wronged by illegal combinations could sue for triple damages. However, the law was purposely vague because that was the only way it could have been passed in Congress. It did not define clearly what a restraint of trade was. It also consigned interpretation of its provisions to the courts, which at that time were strong allies of business.

Judges—particularly Supreme Court justices—blurred distinctions between reasonable and unreasonable restraints of trade. When in 1895 the United States government prosecuted the so-called Sugar Trust for owning 98 percent of the nation's sugar-refining capacity, eight of nine Supreme Court justices ruled that control of manufacturing did not necessarily mean control of trade (*United States* v. *E. C. Knight Co.*).

This interpretation left the antitrust act with only token power to combat industrial bigness. Ironically, the Sherman Act did serve government officials as a tool for breaking up labor unions: courts that did not consider monopolistic production a restraint of trade willingly applied antitrust provisions to strikes that affected trade.

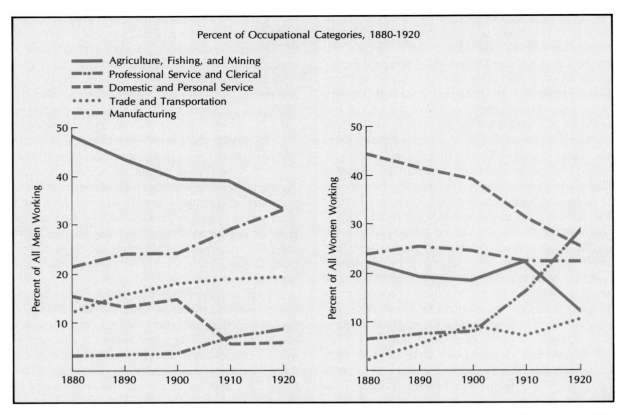

Percent of Occupational Categories, 1880–1920

Percent of Occupational Categories, 1880–1920 *Source: U.S. Bureau of the Census,* Census of the United States, 1880, 1890, 1900, 1910, 1920 *(Washington: U.S. Government Printing Office).*

Mechanization and the Changing Status of Labor

By 1880, when almost 5 million Americans worked in manufacturing, construction, and transportation, the status of labor had shifted dramatically from what it had been a generation earlier, when there were only 1.5 million workers in those industries. Most workers could no longer accurately be termed producers, as craftsmen and farmers had traditionally considered themselves. The enlarged working class consisted mainly of employees, people who worked only when someone else hired them. Whereas producers were paid by consumers according to the quality of what they produced, employees were paid wages based on time spent on the job.

As mass production subdivided manufacturing into small tasks, workers spent their time repeating one specialized operation. No longer was it up to the worker to decide when to begin and end the workday, when to rest, and what tools and techniques to use. Especially as assembly-line production spread, employees lost their independence. Workers reacted to industrialization by struggling to retain old customs, such as appointing a fellow worker to read aloud while they worked. Employers sought to make workers more docile.

As machines and assembly-line production reduced the need for skilled workers, employers cut wage costs by hiring more women and children.

Employment of Women Between 1880 and 1900, the number of employed women grew from 2.6 million to 8.6 million, and their occupational patterns underwent major changes (see figure). First, the

Families in need of extra income often sent children to work in textile mills and other factories, where numerous unskilled jobs existed. Children such as the textile workers above operated machines and did jobs such as sorting and carrying at wages that were a fraction of those paid to adults. *Library of Congress.*

proportion of women engaged in domestic and personal service jobs (maids, cooks, laundresses), traditionally the most common form of female employment, dropped dramatically as other types of jobs opened. Many new jobs were in manufacturing, usually menial positions in textile mills and food-processing plants that paid women as little as $1.56 a week for seventy hours of labor.

Second and more important, a major shift was occurring that set the trend among female workers for much of the twentieth century. The numbers and percentages of women in clerical jobs—clerks, typists, bookkeepers, salespersons—skyrocketed. By 1920, nearly half of all clerical workers were women; in 1880, only 4 percent of such workers had been women. Previously, when the work demanded many different skills, such as accounting, drafting, recordkeeping, letter-writing, and others, men had dominated office positions. New inventions, for instance, the typewriter and the adding machine, intensified the division of labor so that only narrow skills were needed for clerical jobs.

Companies eagerly hired women who had taken courses in typing and shorthand in school and who desired the better pay and conditions that these jobs offered over factory and domestic work.

Although most working children toiled on their parents' farms, the number in nonagricultural occupations tripled between 1870 and 1900. In 1890, more than 18 percent of all children between the ages of ten and fifteen were gainfully employed.

Employment of Children

Mechanization created a number of light unskilled tasks (such as running errands and helping machine operators) that children could handle at a fraction of adult wages. Conditions were especially harsh for child laborers in the South, where burgeoning textile mills needed unskilled workers. Mill owners induced poor white families, who otherwise might not have had any jobs or income, to bind their children over to the factories at miserably low wages.

Several states, especially in the Northeast, had laws limiting the ages and hours of child labor, but such laws had little effectiveness. Since state statutes did not affect firms engaged in interstate commerce, most large companies fell outside state regulation. It was difficult to enforce age requirements, and many parents lied about their children's ages to help them get jobs to supplement the family income. By 1900, tougher laws and further automation had reduced the number of children working in manufacturing, but many more worked in street trades—shining shoes and peddling newspapers—and as helpers in stores.

Though working conditions loomed as the major issue laborers had to face, the problem of wages was often the immediate catalyst of worker unrest. Many employers believed in the "iron law of wages," which dictated that employees be paid according to the conditions of supply and demand. In practice, this meant that employers did not have to raise wages—and could even cut them—as long as there were people who would accept low pay. Employers justified the system with references to individual freedom: a worker who did not like the wages being paid was free to quit and find a job elsewhere. Courts reinforced the principle, denying workers the right to organize and bargain collectively and saying instead that whatever wages an employee received should be the result of an individual deal between employee and employer.

Even steady employment was insecure. Repetitive tasks using high-speed machinery dulled concentration, and the slightest mistake could cause injury. Industrial accidents rose steadily before 1920, killing or maiming hundreds of thousands of people each year. As late as 1913, after factory owners had installed safety devices, some twenty-five thousand people died in industrial mishaps, and close to a million were injured.

Industrial Accidents

Families stricken by industrial accidents suffered acutely because disability insurance and pensions were almost nonexistent. Laissez-faire attitudes stifled protective legislation for workers, and employers would not take responsibility for employees' well-being. As one railroad manager told his workers, "The regular compensation of employees covers all risk or liability to accident. If an employee is disabled . . . the right to claim compensa-

tion is not recognized." The only recourse for a stricken family was to sue and prove in court that the killed or injured worker did not realize the risks involved and had not caused the accident.

Reformers, including union leaders, lobbied Congress to pass laws to ease working conditions, but the Supreme Court limited their impact by narrowly defining what jobs were dangerous and which workers needed protection. Initially, in *Holden* v. *Hardy* (1896), the Court upheld a law regulating the working hours of miners because their work was so dangerous that overly long hours would increase the threat of injury. In *Lochner* v. *New York* (1905), however, the Court struck down a law limiting bakery workers to a sixty-hour week and a ten-hour day. In response to the argument that a state had authority to protect workers' health and safety, the Court ruled that baking was not a dangerous enough occupation to justify restricting the right of workers to sell their labor freely.

Courts Restrict Labor Reform

Then, in *Muller* v. *Oregon* (1908), the Court used a different rationale to uphold a law limiting working hours for women to ten a day. Labor legislation for women was necessary, the Court asserted, because a woman's health "becomes an object of public interest and care in order to preserve the strength and vigor of the race." As a result, women were barred from many occupations, such as printing and transportation, which required long or nighttime hours.

Throughout the nineteenth century, workers confronting mechanization reacted in different ways. Some bent to the demands of the factory, the machine, and the time clock. Some tried to blend old ways of working into the new system. Some never adjusted and wandered from job to job. Others, however, turned to organized resistance.

In many ways, the year 1877 was a historical watershed. In July a series of strikes broke out among railroad workers, who were protesting wage cuts. Violence spread across Pennsylvania and Ohio all the way to Chicago and St. Louis. Venting their anger, rioters attacked railroad property, derailing trains and burning rail yards. State militia companies, commanded and or-

Strikes of 1877

ganized by employers, broke up picket lines and fired into threatening crowds. In several communities, factory workers, wives, and even local merchants aided the strikers, while railroads enlisted strikebreakers to replace union men. After more than a month of unprecedented carnage that reached from Maryland to Illinois, Texas, and California, President Rutherford B. Hayes sent federal troops to restore order and end the strikes. His action marked the first significant use of troops to quell labor unrest.

The Union Movement

The union movement had precedents but few successes. Craft unions of skilled workers in a particular trade dated from the early nineteenth century, but their emphasis on exclusive membership left them without broad power. The National Labor Union, which flourished briefly after its founding in 1866, died during the hard times of the 1870s. The only broad-based labor organization to survive that depression was the Knights of Labor. Founded in 1869 by Philadelphia garment cutters, the Knights opened their doors to other workers during the 1870s. Under the leadership of Terence V. Powderly, the Knights recruited women, blacks, immigrants, and unskilled and semiskilled workers, who were excluded from craft unions. Membership mushroomed from 10,000 in 1879 to 730,000 in 1886.

Strikes presented a dilemma for the Knights. Some leaders, including Powderly, feared that the pursuit of immediate goals through strikes would detract from the union's long-range objective: a Bellamy-type cooperative society. However, other leaders, and much of the rank and file, did engage in militant actions, such as demanding higher wages and union recognition from railroads in the Southwest in 1886. Railroad baron Jay Gould refused to negotiate with the Knights, and a strike began on March 1 in several Texas communities, spreading to Kansas, Missouri, and Arkansas. As violence increased, Powderly denounced the strikers' radical action, and as the more militant craft

unions broke away, membership in the Knights of Labor dwindled. The union survived in only a few small towns. The special interests of craft unions overcame the Knights' general and often vague appeal, and dreams of labor unity faded.

As the hard times of the 1870s subsided and better conditions returned in the early 1880s, a number of labor groups, including the Knights, began to campaign for an eight-hour workday. This effort by laborers to regain control of their work gathered momentum in Chicago, where anarchists (radicals who advocated extreme action against authority), as well as various craft unions, agitated for the cause. On May 1, 1886, a day of mass strikes and the largest spontaneous labor demonstration in the country's history, Chicago police were mobilized to prevent disorder, especially among striking workers at the huge McCormick reaper factory. The day passed calmly, but two days later, police stormed an area near the McCormick plant and broke up a battle between striking unionists and nonunion strikebreakers. Police shot and killed two unionists and wounded several others.

Haymarket Riot

The next evening, labor groups rallied at Haymarket Square, near downtown Chicago, to protest police brutality. As a company of police officers approached the meeting, a bomb exploded near their front ranks, killing seven and injuring sixty-seven. Mass arrests followed. Eventually eight men, all anarchists, were tried and convicted of the bombing, though there was no evidence of their guilt. Four were executed and one committed suicide in prison. The remaining three were pardoned in 1893 by the governor of Illinois, John P. Altgeld, who believed that they had been victims of the "malicious ferocity" of the courts.

The Haymarket bombing drew public attention to the growing discontent of labor but also revived middle-class fear of radicalism. In several cities, police forces and armories were strengthened. Manufacturers countered worker militancy by agreeing to use their employer associations to resist strikes and by purchasing strike insurance.

The newly formed American Federation of Labor was the major workers' organization to emerge after the 1886 upheavals. A combination of national

This engraving of the Haymarket riot in Chicago in May of 1886 shows labor demonstrators pelting police with bricks and the officers threatening to retaliate. The day after this incident, a bomb exploded near a police brigade, and police fired into the surrounding crowd, killing seven men. *The Bettman Archive.*

American Federation of Labor craft unions, the AFL initially had about 140,000 members, most of whom were skilled native-born workers. Led by Samuel Gompers, the pragmatic head of the Cigar Makers' Union, AFL unions avoided the ideal of worker solidarity but pressed for specific goals, such as higher wages, shorter hours, and the right to bargain collectively. They also avoided party politics, choosing instead to follow Gompers's dictum of supporting labor's friends and opposing its enemies regardless of party. By 1917, the organization included 111 national unions, 27,000 local unions, and 2.5 million members.

The AFL and the labor movement in general staggered in the early 1890s, when once again labor violence evoked public fears. In July 1892, Henry C. Frick, the stubborn president of Carnegie Steel Company, closed the plant in Homestead, Pennsylvania, when the AFL-affiliated Amalgamated Asso-

ciation of Iron and Steelworkers struck over pay cuts. Shortly afterward, angry workers attacked and routed three hundred Pinkerton guards hired to protect the plant. State militia were summoned, and after five months the strike failed.

In 1894, workers at the Pullman Palace Car Company walked out in protest over exploitative policies at the company town near Chicago. **Pullman Strike** The paternalistic company head, George Pullman, owned and controlled all land and buildings, the school, bank, and water and gas systems. One laborer grumbled, "We are born in a Pullman house, fed from the Pullman shop, taught in the Pullman school, catechized in the Pullman church, and when we die we shall be buried in the Pullman cemetery and go to the Pullman hell."

One thing Pullman would not do was negotiate with workers. When the hard times that began in 1893 threatened his business, Pullman managed to maintain profits and pay dividends to stockholders by cutting wages 25 to 40 percent while holding firm on rents and prices in the company town. Workers, squeezed into debt and deprivation, sent a committee to Pullman in May 1894 to protest his policies. Pullman reacted by firing three members of the committee. Enraged workers, most of whom had joined the American Railway Union, called a strike. Pullman retaliated by closing the plant. When the American Railway Union, led by the charismatic young organizer Eugene V. Debs, voted to aid the strikers by boycotting all Pullman cars, Pullman stood firm. The railroad owners' association then enlisted the aid of U.S. Attorney General Richard Olney, who obtained a court injunction to prevent the union from "obstructing the railways and holding up the mails." President Grover Cleveland sent federal troops to Chicago, supposedly to protect the mail but in reality to crush the strike. Within a month the strike was over, and Debs was jailed for six months for contempt in defying the injunction.

After 1900, an increasing number of battles occurred between workers and employers in the mining industry. Out of the western mining struggles emerged the Industrial Workers of the World (IWW), a radical labor organization, founded in 1905, which fused the vision of worker solidarity with the tactics of strikes and sabotage. Using the rhetoric of class conflict—"The final aim is revolution"—the IWW attracted far greater attention than its small membership warranted.

During the half-century following the Civil War, only a small fraction of American workers belonged to unions. Part of labor's weakness was caused by the failure of union organizers to take an interest in large segments of the industrial labor force and to intentionally exclude others. Many unions, for example, were openly hostile toward women. Of the 6.3 million employed women in 1910, only 125,000 were in unions. Yet female employees could organize and fight employers as strenuously as men could.

Women and the Labor Movement

Since the early years of industrialization, female workers had formed their own unions. Some, such as the Collar Laundry Union of Troy, New York,

organized in the 1860s, succeeded in carrying out strikes and achieving higher wages. The first inclusive women's labor federation was the Women's Trade Union League (WTUL), founded in 1903. The WTUL worked for protective legislation for female workers, sponsored educational activities, and campaigned for women's suffrage. In 1909, it joined with the International Ladies Garment Workers Union in support of a massive strike against New York City sweatshops. Although the WTUL had forceful working-class leaders—notably Agnes Nestor, a glove maker, Rose Schneiderman, a cap maker, and Mary Anderson, a shoe worker—it was dominated by middle-class women who had humane but generally nonmilitant reasons for helping working women. In the early 1920s, the WTUL fought a constitutional amendment guaranteeing equal rights to women, arguing that women needed protection from exploitation more than they needed equality. Such reasoning fit the assertion of males, who argued that women belonged in their own sphere at home, out of the work force and out of unions. As the WTUL gradually backed away from active union organization, it lost the support of working-class women, and by 1930 it had virtually dissolved.

Organized labor also excluded most immigrant and black workers. Some trade unions welcomed skilled immigrants but only the Knights of Labor and the IWW had firm policies of accepting immigrants and blacks. Blacks were among the organizers of the coal miners' union, and they had a presence in other unions involving trades in which blacks were a significant part of the work force. But often blacks could belong only to segregated local unions in the South, and the majority of northern AFL unions had exclusion policies as well. Resentments, already fueled by long-held prejudices, increased when blacks and immigrants worked as strikebreakers.

Immigrants, Blacks, and the Labor Movement

For most American workers, then, the machine age had mixed results. Industrial wages rose between 1877 and 1914, boosting purchasing power and creating a mass market for standardized goods. Yet in 1900, most employees worked sixty hours a week at wages that averaged twenty cents an hour for skilled work and ten cents an hour for unskilled work. Moreover, as wages rose, living costs increased even faster. The industrial transformation had thrust the United States into international leadership in economic capability. But in factories as well as on farms, some people were beginning to question whether a system based on ever-greater profits was the best way for Americans to achieve the nation's democratic destiny.

Suggestions for Further Reading

General

Daniel J. Boorstin, *The Americans: The Democratic Experience* (1973); Thomas C. Cochran and William Miller, *The Age of Enterprise* (1942); Ray Ginger, *The Age of Excess* (1965); Samuel P. Hays, *The Response to Industrialism* (1975).

Technology and Invention

Roger Burlingame, *Henry Ford* (1957); Sigfried Giedeon, *Mechanization Takes Command* (1948); Matthew Josephson, *Edison* (1959); Leo Marx, *The Machine in the Garden: Technology and the Pastoral Ideal* (1964); Elting E. Morison, *Men, Machines, and Modern Times* (1966); Nathan Rosenberg, *Technology and American Economic Growth* (1972); Harold I. Sharlin, *The Making of the Electrical Age* (1963); Peter Temin, *Steel in Nineteenth Century America* (1964).

Industrialism, Industrialists, and Corporate Growth

W. Eliot Brownlee, *Dynamics of Ascent: A History of the American Economy,* 2nd ed. (1979); Stuart Bruchey, *Growth of the Modern Economy* (1973); Alfred D. Chandler, *The Visible Hand: The Managerial Revolution in American Business* (1977); Alfred D. Chandler, *Strategy and Structure: Chapters in the History of American Industrial Enterprise* (1966); Thomas C. Cochran, *Business in American Life* (1972); David F. Hawkes, *John D.: The Founding Father of the Rockefellers* (1980); Matthew Josephson, *The Robber Barons* (1934); Edward C. Kirkland, *Industry Comes of Age* (1961); Harold C. Livesay, *Andrew Carnegie and the Rise of Big Business* (1975); Daniel Nelson, *Managers and Workers: Origins of the New Factory System in the United States, 1800–1920* (1975); Glen Porter, *The Rise of Big Business* (1973).

Attitudes Toward Industrialism

Sidney Fine, *Laissez Faire and the General Welfare State* (1956); Louis Galambos and Barbara Barron Spence, *The Public Image of Big Business in America* (1975); Richard Hofstadter, *Social Darwinism in American Thought*, rev. ed. (1955); T. Jackson Lears, *No Place of Grace: Antimodernism and the Transformation of American Culture* (1981); Robert McCloskey, *American Conservatism in the Age of Enterprise* (1951); John L. Thomas, *Alternative America: Henry George, Edward Bellamy, Henry Demarest Lloyd, and the Adversary Tradition* (1983).

Work and Labor Organization

Melvin Dubofsky, *Industrialism and the American Worker* (1975); Melvin Dubofsky, *We Shall Be All: A History of the Industrial Workers of the World* (1969); Sarah Eisenstein, *Give Us Bread, Give Us Roses: Working Women's Consciousness in the United States, 1890 to the First World War* (1983); Leon Fink, *Workingmen's Democracy: The Knights of Labor and American Politics* (1982); Philip S. Foner, *The Great Labor Uprising of 1877* (1977); Herbert G. Gutman, *Work, Culture and Society in Industrializing America* (1976); Stuart Bruce Kaufman, *Samuel Gompers and the Origins of the American Federation of Labor* (1973); Alice Kessler-Harris, *Out to Work: A History of Wage Earning Women in the United States* (1982); Susan Levine, *Labor's True Women: Carpet Weavers, Industrialization, and Labor Reform in the Gilded Age* (1984); Harold Livesay, *Samuel Gompers and Organized Labor in America* (1978); Milton Meltzer, *Bread and Roses: The Struggle of American Labor, 1865–1915* (1967); Stephen Meyer III, *The Five Dollar Day: Labor Management and Social Control in the Ford Motor Company, 1908–1921* (1981); David Montgomery, *The Fall of the House of Labor: The Workplace, the State, and American Labor Activism, 1865–1925* (1987); David Montgomery, *Workers' Control in America: Studies in the History of Work, Technology, and Labor Struggles* (1979); Barbara Mayer Wertheimer, *We Were There: The Story of Working Women in America* (1977); Irwin Yellowitz, *Industrialization and the American Labor Movement* (1977).

For nearly thirty years, Frank Ventrone had successfully pursued his dream, until one night his world literally shattered. In the 1880s, Ventrone had emigrated from southern Italy, to Providence, Rhode Island. By saving money and buying property, Ventrone became a prominent businessman in the city's fast-growing Italian immigrant community. Ventrone's biggest success was a pasta business, which furnished the community's staple food. But this business was also the source of his trouble.

In the summer of 1914, food prices were rising, and Ventrone followed the trend by increasing the price of his pasta. Angered by the threat to their over-burdened incomes, people of Providence's Italian section vented their frustration against Ventrone. On a warm August weekend, they marched through the neighborhood, broke windows in a block of property owned by Ventrone, entered his business establishment, and dumped his stock of macaroni into the street. When police arrived to quell the disturbance, ri-oters resisted with catcalls and violence, insisting that the matter was an internal one to be resolved by the community. The next Monday, Ventrone's agent met with community members and agreed to lower his prices. Ventrone had overstepped the bounds of ethnic loyalty and suffered as a result.

18

THE CITY AND EVERYDAY LIFE, 1877–1920

The Providence "macaroni riot," with its various dimensions—the trans-fer of immigrant cultures from Old World to New, the mobility of some people from rags to respectability, the continued poverty of others, the eruption of violence—was just one of millions of events that came to characterize life in an American city. Between 1870 and 1920, the driving forces behind the changing nature of American society were industrializa-tion and urbanization.

Demographically, the population shifts were dramatic. In the United States of 1880, seven out of ten Americans lived on farms or in towns with fewer than twenty-five hundred people. By 1920, a milestone had been reached: a majority of people—51.4 percent—dwelled in cities. Thus, for most people, the idyllic serenity of rural America gave way to clanging trolleys, smoky air, crowded streets, and a jumble of languages.

Change was both rapid and striking for those who moved from the country to the city. They found that a new society of street corners, saloons, shops, and commercial amusements replaced the village church and the general store. People tended to spend more time with their peers and less with their families. Moreover, the spread of railroad, postal, telephone, and electrical service drew even isolated communities into the orbit of a consumer-oriented society. American ingenuity combined with technology, mass production, and mass marketing to fashion and advertise myriad goods that had not previously existed or had been the exclusive property of the wealthy. This new material well-being enabled Americans of differing status to join communities of consumers—communities defined not by place or class, but by common possession. It also accentuated differences between those who could afford such goods and services and those who could not.

Transportation and Industrial Growth in the Modern City

By 1900, the modern American city was reaching maturity. From Boston to Los Angeles, developed areas sprawled outward several miles from the original central core. No longer did walking distance determine a city's size, and no longer did different social groups live physically close together: poor near rich, immigrant near native, black near white. Instead, cities divided into distinct districts: working-class neighborhoods, black ghettos, a ring of suburbs, and business districts.

New Shape of the City

Two forces, mass transportation and economic change, were responsible for this new arrangement. Steam-powered commuter railroads had appeared in a few cities during the 1850s and 1860s, but not until the late 1870s did inventors begin to mechanize mass transit. The first power-driven devices were cable cars, carriages that traveled over

Mechanization of Mass Transportation

tracks by clamping onto a moving underground wire. In the 1880s, cable-car lines operated in Chicago, San Francisco, and many other cities. By the 1890s, however, electric-powered streetcars were replacing early forms of mass transit. Between 1890 and 1902, total mileage of electrified track in American cities grew from 1,300 to 22,000 miles.

In a few cities, streetcar companies elevated part of their track onto stilts, enabling vehicles to travel above jammed downtown districts without interference from other traffic. In Boston, New York, and Philadelphia, transit firms dug underground passages for their cars, also to avoid tie-ups and delays. Elevated railroads and subways were extremely expensive to construct. Thus, they appeared only in the few cities where companies could amass enough capital to build them and where there were enough riders to ensure profits.

Mass-transit lines launched millions of urban dwellers into outlying neighborhoods and created a commuting public. Those who could afford the fare—usually five cents a ride—could live outside the crowded, dirty central city but return there for work, shopping, and entertainment. Working-class families, whose incomes rarely topped a dollar a day, found the fare too high and could not benefit from the streetcars. But for the growing middle class, a home in a quiet, tree-lined neighborhood became a real possibility. Real-estate development boomed around the periphery of scores of cities. Between 1890 and 1920, for example, developers in the Chicago area opened 800,000 new lots—enough to house at least three times the city's population in 1890.

Beginnings of Urban Sprawl

Urban sprawl was essentially unplanned. Investors who bought land in anticipation of settlement paid little attention to the need for parks, traffic control, and public services. Construction of mass transit was guided by the profit motive and thus served the urban public unevenly. Streetcar lines serviced mainly those neighborhoods that promised the most riders—those whose fares, in other words, would provide dividends for stockholders.

Public transportation altered commercial, as well as residential, patterns. As consumers moved outward, businesses followed. Branches of downtown

1860s–90s	Horatio Alger stories	**1890s**	Electric trolleys replace horse-driven mass transit
1867	First law passed regulating tenements (New York)	**1896**	Frank Merriwell series begins
1869	Alcott, *Little Women*	**1898**	Race riot in Wilmington, North Carolina
1876	Twain, *Tom Sawyer*	**1900s**	Rise in popularity of vaudeville
1880s	Acceptance of germ theory of disease	**1903**	First baseball World Series
	"New" immigrants from eastern and southern Europe begin to arrive in large numbers	**1905**	Intercollegiate Athletic Association formed
1883	Pulitzer buys *New York World*	**1908**	Race riot in Springfield, Illinois
1884	Twain, *Huckleberry Finn*	**1915**	*Birth of a Nation*, film directed by D. W. Griffith
1886	First settlement house opened	**1920**	Majority (51.4 percent) of Americans live in cities
1889	Edison invents the motion-picture camera and viewing device		

department stores and banks joined groceries, theaters, drugstores, taverns, and specialty shops to create neighborhood shopping centers. Meanwhile, the urban core became the work zone, where offices, stores, warehouses, and factories loomed over streets clogged with traffic.

Cities also became the main arenas for industrial growth, generating and attracting concentrations of economic power. As centers of resources, labor, transportation, and communications, cities provided everything that factories needed. Once mass production became possible, capital accumulated by the cities' commercial enterprises fed industrial investment, and urban populations furnished consumers for new products. Thus, urban growth and industrialization wound together in a mutually beneficial spiral. The further industrialization advanced, the more opportunities it created for work and investment in cities. Increased opportunity drew more people to cities;

Urban-Industrial Development

as workers and as consumers, they in turn fueled further industrialization.

Urban and industrial growth transformed the national economy and freed the United States from dependence on European capital and manufactured goods. Imports and foreign investments still flowed into the United States. But by the early 1900s, cities and their factories, stores, and banks were converting America from a debtor, agricultural nation into a major industrial, financial, and exporting power.

Peopling the Cities: Migrants and Immigrants

The population of a place can grow in three ways: by extension of its borders to annex land and

The first contact with America that most immigrants had was on Ellis Island, just offshore of New York City. Upon debarking from their ships, the immigrants were herded into pens where they were registered and then into rooms where medical personnel examined them for disease. As the photograph suggests, the experience could be quite dehumanizing. *Brown Brothers.*

than in rural areas, so that in cities there was not much of a gap annually between the number of people who were born and those who died.

Migration and immigration made by far the greatest contribution to urban population growth. Each year, millions of people were on the move, many of them lured by the cities' promise of opportunity. Although many farm families left rural America for the nation's cities, most urban newcomers were from Europe. Many immigrants did not intend to stay. Instead, they hoped to make enough money to return home and live there in greater comfort and security. For every hundred foreigners who entered the country, around thirty left. Still, most of the 26 million immigrants who arrived between 1870 and 1920 stayed, and the great majority settled in cities, where they helped to shape modern American culture.

Major Waves of Migration and Immigration

The United States had been the destination of immigrants from northern and western Europe since the 1840s, but after 1880 a second wave of mass immigration began from new sources. Though northern and western Europeans continued to arrive, the new wave contained mainly people from eastern and southern Europe, along with smaller contingents from Canada, Mexico, and Japan (see figure and map, page 326). Two-thirds of the newcomers who arrived in the 1880s were from Germany, England, Ireland, and Scandinavia; between 1900 and 1909 two-thirds were from Italy, Austria-Hungary, and Russia. By 1910, arrivals from Mexico were beginning to outnumber arrivals from Ireland, and large numbers of Japanese had moved to the West Coast and Hawaii.

The New Immigration

Many Americans feared that the strange customs, Catholic and Jewish religions, illiteracy, and poverty of "new" immigrants made them less desirable and assimilable than "old" immigrants, whose languages and beliefs seemed less alien. In reality, however, old and new immigrants resembled each other more closely than many Americans wished to believe. The majority of both groups were young—between fifteen and thirty-nine years old—and male. Both groups had lived in a world where their family was the focus of everything they did. Deci-

people; by natural increase, an excess of births over deaths; and by migration, an excess of in-migrants over out-migrants. Between the 1860s and early 1900s, many cities annexed nearby suburbs, thereby increasing their populations. The most notable consolidation occurred in 1898, when New York City, which had previously consisted only of Manhattan and the Bronx, merged with Brooklyn, Staten Island, and part of Queens and grew overnight from 1.5 million to more than 3 million people. The major effect of annexation, however, was to enlarge the physical size of cities. Annexed vacant land did, of course, provide space where new city dwellers could live.

How Cities Grew

Natural increase did not account for very much of any city's population growth. In the late nineteenth century, death rates declined in most regions of the country, but birthrates also fell. In urban areas, birthrates decreased more rapidly

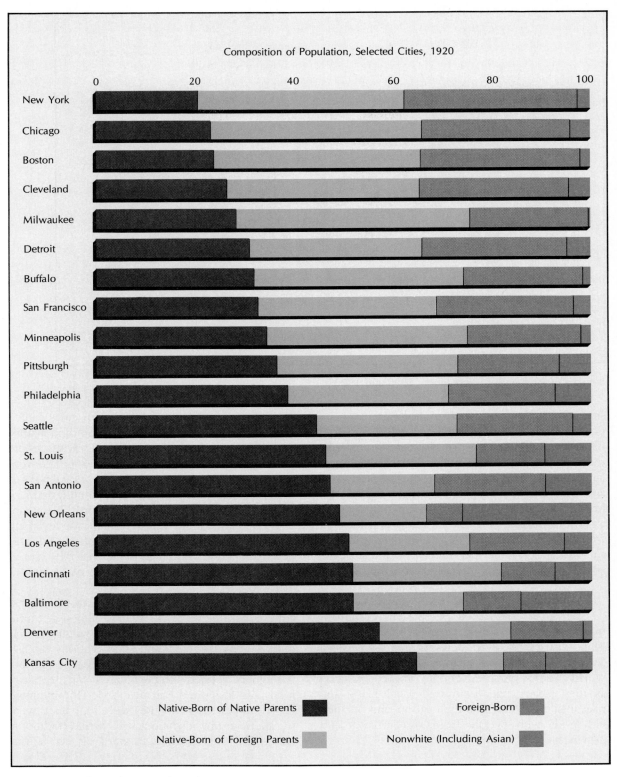

Composition of Population, Selected Cities, 1920

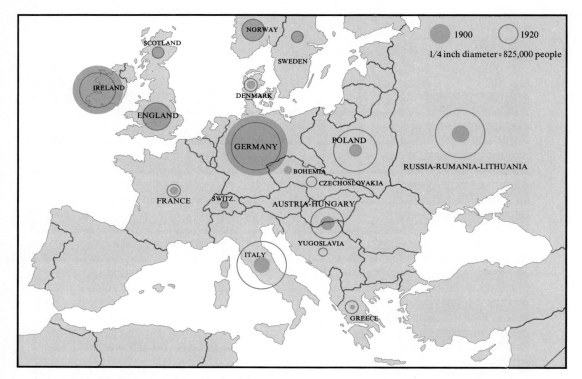

Sources of Foreign-Born Population, 1900 and 1920

sions of whether and when to emigrate had been made to match family needs, and family bonds and interests continued to prevail once immigrants reached the New World. Those leaving the homeland almost always knew where they wanted to go and how to get there because they received aid from relatives who had already immigrated.

Most important, perhaps, all immigrants brought with them memories of their homelands. In new surroundings, where the language was a struggle, immigrants anchored their lives in **Immigrant** what they knew best: their culture. **Cultures** Many immigrant neighborhoods consisted of enclaves of Italians from the same province, Japanese from the same island district, or Russian Jews from the same *shtetl* (village). In these transplanted communities, Old World customs persisted. People practiced religion as they always had, held traditional feasts and pageants, married within their group, and pursued old feuds with people from rival villages and provinces.

Yet the very diversity of American cities forced immigrants to modify their attitudes and habits. Few newcomers could avoid contact with people different from themselves, and few could prevent such contacts from altering their traditional ways of life. Although many foreigners identified themselves by their village or region of birth and organized their mutual aid and fraternal societies along these lines, other immigrant institutions, such as newspapers and churches, found that they had to appeal more broadly to the entire nationality in order to survive.

Mostly, there was a combination of Old World culture with New World reality. Although immigrants struggled to maintain native languages and to pass them down to younger generations, English was taught in the schools and needed on the job. Foreigners cooked ethnic meals using American foods and fashioned European-style clothing from American fabrics. When they were ill, Italians went to American physicians but still carried traditional amulets in their pockets to ward off evil spirits.

The Chinese expanded their traditional gambling games to include poker. Music, especially, revealed adaptations. Mexican ballads acquired new themes that reflected adventures of border crossing and hardships of labor in the United States. Eventually, most immigrants grew accustomed to trusting American institutions.

The influx of so many immigrants between 1870 and 1920 transformed the United States from a basically Protestant nation into a society of Protestants, Catholics, and Jews. Newcomers from Italy, Hungary, and what would become Czechoslovakia, Yugoslavia, and Poland joined Irish and Germans to boost the proportion of Catholics in several midwestern and eastern cities, and German and Russian immigrants gave New York one of the largest Jewish populations in the world. In the Southwest, Catholic Mexicans constituted more than half of the population of El Paso.

In the 1880s, another group of migrants began to move into American cities. Thousands of rural African-Americans moved northward and westward, fleeing crop liens, violence, and political oppression and seeking better employment. Although the numbers of black urban dwellers would grow much larger after 1915, thirty-two cities contained ten thousand or more blacks by 1900, and 79 percent of all blacks outside the South lived in cities. African-American migrants resembled foreign immigrants in their rural backgrounds and economic motivations, but they differed in several important ways. Because few factories would employ them, most black workers found jobs in the service sector—cleaning, cooking, and carting. Because the majority of jobs in domestic and personal service were traditionally female jobs, black women outnumbered black men in many cities.

African-American Migration to the Cities

Each of the three major migrant groups that peopled American cities—native whites, foreigners, and native blacks—contributed to the making of modern American culture. The rich cultural variety that was nurtured in the cities included American folk music and literature, Italian and Mexican cuisine, Irish comedy, Yiddish theater, and African-American jazz and dance. Like their predecessors, newcomers in the late nineteenth century changed their environment as much as they were changed by it.

Living Conditions in the Inner City

Population growth created intense pressures on the public and private sectors of the city. Masses of people jammed inner-city districts, where they were known less for their cultural contributions than for the problems they bred. American cities seemed to harbor all the afflictions that plague modern society: poverty, disease, crime, decay, and other unpleasant conditions that develop when large numbers of people live close together. Although technology, science, private enterprise, and public authority did not relieve all of these problems, some remarkable successes were achieved. In the late nineteenth century and in the early twentieth, construction of buildings, homes, streets, sewers, and schools proceeded at a furious pace. American cities set world standards for fire protection and water purification. Yet hardship and other ills awaited solution.

One of the most persistent shortcomings of American cities has been their failure to provide adequate housing to all who need it. The failure has roots in nineteenth-century urban development. In spite of massive construction in the 1880s and the early 1900s, population growth outpaced the supply of housing. This condition especially affected working-class families. As cities grew, landlords took advantage of shortages in low-cost rental housing by splitting up existing buildings to house more people, constructing multiple-unit tenements, and hiking rents. Low-income families adjusted to high costs and short supply by sharing space and expenses. Thus, it became common in many big cities for a one-family apartment to be occupied by two or three families or by one family and a number of paying boarders.

Housing Problems

Inside many buildings, living conditions were inhumane. The largest rooms were barely ten feet wide, and interior rooms either had no windows at all or opened onto narrow shafts that bred vermin and rotten odors. Few buildings had indoor plumbing, and the only source of heat was dangerous, polluting coal-burning stoves.

In several places, housing problems aroused concerned citizens to mount reform campaigns. New York State took the lead in 1867, 1879, and 1901 by legislating light, ventilation, and safety codes for new tenement buildings. A few reformers, such as Jacob Riis and Lawrence Veiller, advocated housing low-income families in model tenements, with more spacious, airier rooms and better facilities. Model tenements, however, required landlords and investors to accept lower profits—a sacrifice few were willing to make. Neither reformers nor public officials would consider government financing of better housing, fearing that such a step would undermine private enterprise. Still, the codes and commissions that resulted from reform campaigns did strengthen the power of local government to regulate housing construction.

Housing reforms had only limited success, but scientific and technological advances enabled city dwellers and the nation in general to live in greater comfort and safety. When the germ theory of disease became generally accepted in the 1880s, cities established more efficient systems of water purification and sewage disposal. Public health regulations helped to control such dread diseases as cholera, typhoid fever, and diphtheria. Modernized firefighting equipment and electric streetlighting made the cities safer places in which to live. None of those improvements, however, eased the burden of poverty.

Since colonial days, Americans have never agreed on how much responsibility the general public should assume for poor relief. In the late nineteenth and early twentieth **Response** centuries, many people held to **to Poverty** traditional beliefs that anyone could escape poverty through hard work and clean living. Such reasoning bred fears that assistance to poor people would encourage paupers to depend on public relief rather than practice self-reliance. As cases of poverty increased, this attitude hardened, and city governments discontinued direct grants of food, fuel, and clothing

to needy families. Instead, cities either provided relief in return for work on public projects or sent special cases to state-run institutions such as almshouses, orphanages, and homes for the blind, deaf, and mentally ill.

Yet close observation of the poor caused some welfare workers to conclude that people's environments, rather than personal shortcomings, caused poverty. This new attitude, which had been gaining ground since the mid-nineteenth century, fueled drives for building codes, factory regulations, and public health measures. Nevertheless, most middle- and upper-class Americans remained wedded to the view that in a society of abundance only the unfit were poor and that relief of poverty should be tolerated but never encouraged.

Even more than crowding and pauperism, crime and disorder alarmed Americans and nurtured fears that urban growth, especially the growth of slums, threatened the nation. The **Crime and** more cities grew, it seemed, the **Violence** more they shook with violence. While homicide rates in other urban-industrial nations like England and Germany declined, those in America rose alarmingly: 25 per million people in 1881; 107 per million in 1898. Pickpockets, swindlers, sneak thieves, and holdup men roamed every city.

Despite the fear of urban crime waves, it is possible that as a greater proportion of the population concentrated in cities, crime merely became more conspicuous and sensational rather than more prevalent. To be sure, urban wealth and the mingling of different kinds of people provided new opportunities for thievery, petty larceny, vice, and violent settling of grudges. Native whites were quick to blame Irish bank-robbery gangs, German pickpockets, and Italian Black Hand murderers for urban disorder, but there is little evidence that more immigrants than natives populated the rogues' gallery.

One thing does seem certain; city life in this period supported a thesis that there is a tradition of violence in the United States. Cities served as arenas for many of the era's worst riots. Besides the violence that often erupted during strikes or times of depression, there were race riots: Wilmington, North Carolina, 1898; Atlanta, Georgia, 1906; Springfield, Illinois, 1908. In cities of the Southwest and the Pacific coast, Chinese and Mexican immigrants often felt the sting of intolerance.

Solving the mounting problems of city life seemed to many Americans to demand greater government action. Thus, city governments passed more laws and ordinances that regulated housing, provided poverty relief, and expanded police power. Yet public responsibility always ended at the boundaries of private property. Eventually, some advances in housing construction, sanitation, and medical care did reach slum dwellers. But for most people, the only hope was that their children would do better or that opportunities would be better somewhere else.

Promises of Mobility

Between the Civil War and the First World War, Baptist minister Russell Conwell delivered the same sermon more than six thousand times to untold millions across the United States. Titled "Acres of Diamonds," his immensely popular lecture affirmed the belief that any American could achieve success. People did not have to look very far for riches, Conwell preached; acres of diamonds lay at everyone's feet. Night after night, Conwell declared to his audiences that it was one's "Christian and Godly" duty to attain riches. But how possible was it for people to significantly improve their lot?

Basically, there were three ways a person could get ahead: occupational advancement (and the higher income that accompanied it); acquisition of property (and the potential for greater wealth it represented); and migration to an area of better conditions and greater opportunity. These options were open chiefly to white men. Although many women worked, owned property, and migrated, their economic standing was usually defined by the men in their lives—husbands, fathers, or other kin. Women could improve their economic status by marrying men with wealth or potential, but other avenues were mostly closed to them. Men and women who were African-American, American Indian, Mexican-American, or Asian-American had even fewer opportunities for success. Pinned to the bottom of society by prejudice, these groups were forced to accept their imposed station.

To large numbers of people, however, urban and industrial expansion of the late nineteenth century should have offered broad opportunity for occupational mobility. Thousands of

Occupational Mobility small businesses were needed to supply goods and services to burgeoning urban populations. And corporations required a variety of managerial and clerical personnel. Relatively few Americans traveled the rags-to-riches path, but considerable movement occurred along the path from rags to moderate success.

Rates of occupational mobility in American communities between 1870 and 1920 were slow but steady. Some people slipped from a higher to a lower rung of the occupational ladder, but rates of upward movement almost always doubled downward rates. Though patterns were far from consistent, immigrants generally experienced lower rates of upward mobility and higher rates of downward mobility than the native-born. Still, regardless of birthplace, the chances for a white male to rise occupationally over the course of his career or to have a higher-status job than his father were relatively good.

In addition to or instead of advancing occupationally, a person could achieve social mobility by acquiring property. But property was not easy

Acquisition of Property to acquire in turn-of-the-century America. Banks and savings institutions were far stricter in their lending practices than they would become after the 1930s, when the federal government began to insure real-estate financing. Mortgage loans carried relatively high interest rates and short repayment periods. Nevertheless, a general rise in wage rates enabled many families to amass savings, which could be used as down payments on property. By 1900, 36.3 percent of urban American families owned their homes, the highest home ownership rate among all Western nations except Denmark, Norway, and Sweden.

Finally, each year millions of families tried to improve their living conditions by packing up and moving elsewhere. In general, Americans followed

Residential Mobility the maxim that movement means improvement. From Boston to San Francisco, from Minneapolis to San Antonio, no more than half

By the beginning of the twentieth century, several cities were developing dense ghettos of African-American residents. This photograph of frame tenements in Washington, D.C., shows the poor housing that blacks were forced to occupy. Yet within these districts, blacks participated in an active street life and nurtured their own social, cultural, and economic institutions.   *George Eastman House, International Museum of Photography.*

the families residing in a city at any one time could be found there ten years later.

In addition to population movement between cities, extraordinary numbers of people moved from one residence to another within the same city. Today, one in every five families moves in a given year. A hundred years ago, the proportion was closer to one in four, or even one in three. Population turnover affected almost every neighborhood and every ethnic and occupational group.

Rapid residential flux undermined the stability of even the most homogeneous neighborhoods. Rarely did a single nationality make up a clear majority in any large area, even when that area was known as Little Italy, Jewtown, Polonia, or Greektown. Residential change dispersed immigrants from their original areas of settlement into many different neighborhoods. In New York, Boston, and other eastern ports, ethnically homogeneous dis-

Ethnic Neighborhoods and Ghettos

tricts did exist, and people tended to change residences within those districts rather than move away from them. Elsewhere, however, most immigrant families lived dispersed in ethnically mixed neighborhoods rather than in ghettos.

In most places, an area's institutions and enterprises, more than the people who actually lived there, identified a district as an ethnic neighborhood. A Bohemian Town, for example, received its nickname because it was the location of Swoboda's Bakery, Cermak's Drug Store, Knezacek's Meats, St. Wenceslaus Church, and the Bohemian Benevolent Association. Such institutions gave a district an ethnic identity even though surrounding neighborhoods were mixed and unstable.

If the term *ghetto* is defined as a place of enforced residence from which escape is at best difficult, only nonwhites in this era had a true ghetto experience. Wherever Asians and Mexicans immigrated, they encountered discrimination in housing, employment, and other facets of public life. Although these groups often preferred to remain separate in Chinatowns and *barrios*, white Americans made every effort to keep them confined.

Prejudice and discrimination not only trapped blacks at the bottom of the occupational ladder but also operated in housing markets to limit residential opportunities. Whites organized protective associations that pledged not to sell homes to blacks and occasionally used violence to scare away black families that did move into white neighborhoods. Such efforts seldom worked. Whites who lived on the edge of black neighborhoods often fled, leaving homes and apartments to be sold and rented to black occupants. By 1920, in Chicago, Detroit, Cleveland, and other cities outside of the South, two-thirds or more of the total black population lived in only 10 percent of the residential area. Within these districts, blacks nurtured cultural institutions that helped them adjust to urban life. But the ghettos also bred frustration, the result of stunted opportunity and racial bigotry. Color, more than any other factor, made the urban experiences of blacks different from those of whites.

All groups, however, including blacks, could and did move—if not from one part of the city to another, then from one city to another. Americans were always seeking greener pastures, and the hope that things might be better somewhere else acted as a safety valve, relieving some of the tensions and frustrations that simmered inside the city. At times, these emotions erupted into violence; more often, people simply left.

The Rise of Urban Boss Politics

The sudden growth and mounting rivalry among social and economic interest groups that occurred in the late nineteenth century mired cities in a governmental swamp. Burgeoning populations, business expansion, and technological change created urgent needs for water, sewers, police and fire protection, schools, parks, and other services. Such needs strained governments beyond their capacities. Furthermore, city governments approached these needs in a disorganized fashion.

Power thrives on confusion, and out of this governmental chaos arose the political machine. Unlike political parties, which ideally exist for higher purposes than merely electing their candidates to office, machines were organizations whose main goals were the rewards— whether money, influence, or prestige—of getting and keeping political power. In order to achieve such goals, a machine had to win popular support. Machine politicians routinely used bribery and graft to further their ends. But they could not have succeeded if they had not provided relief, security, and municipal services to large numbers of people. By doing so, machine politicians accomplished things that other agencies had been unable or unwilling to attempt.

Political Machines

Machines were also beneficiaries of new urban conditions. As cities grew larger and economically more complex, business leaders either vied to use government to advance their own interests or withdrew from local affairs to pursue their interests in interurban or interregional economic organizations. At the same time, hordes of newcomers, often unskilled and foreign-born, crowded into cities. As they acquired citizenship and voting rights, the men of these groups became a substantial political force. These circumstances bred a new kind of leader: the political boss. Conflicting interest groups needed brokers who could by-pass governmental stalemates, and urban newcomers had needs that required government attention. Bosses and machines filled these needs.

The system rested on a popular base and was held together by loyalty and service. City machines were coalitions of smaller machines that derived power directly from neighborhoods, particularly inner-city neighborhoods inhabited by native and immigrant working classes. In return for votes, bosses provided jobs, built parks, distributed food to the needy, and helped when someone ran afoul of the law. Such personalized service cultivated mass attachment to the boss; never before had government or public leaders assumed such responsibility for people in need.

In order to finance their largess and support their system, bosses exchanged favors for votes or money. Power over local government enabled machines to control the letting of contracts, the granting of utility or streetcar franchises, and the distribution of city jobs. Recipients of city business and jobs were expected to repay the machine with a portion of their profits or salaries and to cast supporting votes on election day. Machines constructed public buildings, sewer systems, mass transit lines, and more that otherwise might not have been built; but bribes and kickbacks made such projects costly to taxpayers. Machines dispersed favors to illegal businesses, as well as to legitimate ones. Payoffs from gambling, prostitution, and illegal liquor traffic became important sources of machine revenue.

Civic Reform

While bosses were consolidating their power, others were attempting to destroy political machines and improve the quality of urban life. This urban reform effort, which paralleled its agrarian counterpart and laid the foundation for national reforms of the Progressive era, shared the strengths and weaknesses of the American liberal tradition of government activism.

Urban reform partly derived from the industrial system's emphasis on eliminating waste and inefficiency. Business-minded reformers believed that government could be made more efficient if it were run like a business. They thought that the only way to prevent civic decay was to elect officials who would hold down expenses and prevent corruption. Thus, their major goals were to reduce city budgets, make employees work longer, and cut taxes.

In order to introduce sound business principles to government, civic reformers supported a number of structural changes, such as the city-manager

Structural Reforms in Government and commission forms of government and nonpartisan, citywide election of officials. Each of these reforms was meant to remove politics from government. Experts would control decision making at the local level,

and the ward and neighborhood power bases of the bosses would be undermined. Reformers saw only the waste and corruption that machines bred. Most failed to understand that bosses succeeded because they met people's needs.

A few reformers did move beyond structural changes to a genuine concern for social problems. Mayors like Detroit's Hazen S. Pingree (1889–1896), Toledo's Samuel "Golden Rule" Jones (1897–1904), and Cleveland's Thomas L. Johnson (1901–1909) worked to provide jobs for poor people, reduce charges by transit and utility companies, and establish greater governmental responsibility for the welfare of all citizens. Some supported public ownership of gas, electric, and telephone companies, a quasi-socialist reform that alienated their business allies. But most civic reformers could not match the bosses' political savvy and soon found themselves out of power.

Seeds of social reform nevertheless were beginning to sprout outside of politics. Convinced that laissez-faire ideology was not applicable in a complex urban-industrial world and

Social Reform driven by an urge to identify and address urban problems, a number of men and women, mostly young and middle-class, embarked on campaigns for social betterment. These urban social reformers operated within a variety of fields. Housing reformers wanted local government to pass building codes to ensure safety in tenements. Protestant reformers influenced by the Social Gospel movement, which emphasized social responsibility as a means to salvation, built churches in slum neighborhoods and urged businesses to be socially responsible. Educational reformers saw public schools as a means of preparing immigrants and their children for citizenship by teaching them American values, as well as the English language.

Perhaps the most ambitious and inspiring feature of the urban reform movement was the settlement house (the first one opened in 1886). Patterned after London's Toynbee Hall and mostly led by women, settlements were efforts by educated, middle-class young adults to bridge the gulf between classes by going to live in slum neighborhoods. Early settlement founders, such as Jane Addams, Florence Kelley, and Graham Taylor, wanted to improve the lives of slum dwellers by helping them to obtain education, appreciation of the arts, better jobs, and better housing. Settlement houses provided neighborhood residents with a wide array of activities, ranging from vocational classes and childcare for working mothers to exhibitions of ethnic art. Because of their efforts in areas such as the establishment of school nurses, the passing of building safety codes, construction of public playgrounds, and support for labor unions, settlement workers often became reform leaders in cities and in the nation. Although the neighborhood residents they served sometimes mistrusted them because they were outsiders to working-class and immigrant cultures, settlement workers made valuable contributions to inner-city life.

Urban reformers wanted to save cities, not abandon them. They believed that urban life could be improved by restoring feelings of service and cooperation among all citizens. They often failed to realize, however, that cities were places of great diversity and that different people had different views of what reform actually meant. Distributing city jobs on the basis of civil service exams rather than party loyalty meant progress to government reformers, but to working-class men it signified reduced employment opportunities. Moral reformers tried to prohibit the sale of alcoholic beverages to prevent working-class breadwinners from wasting their wages and ruining their health, but European immigrants saw such crusades as interference in their long-held wine- and beer-drinking customs. Thus, in early urban reform, idealism merged with naiveté and insensitivity.

It is important to note, however, that important decisions and accomplishments affecting urban life were made outside of the context of bossism and reform. Sanitation, garbage disposal, streetlighting, bridge and street building, and other such needs posed problems that required technical, not political or humanitarian, creativity.

To solve their problems, cities increasingly depended on engineers, who, next to teachers, had become the largest profession in the country by 1900. These individuals applied technical expertise in establishing systems for incinerating refuse, for dumping trash while still en-

Engineering Reforms

suring safe water supplies, for constructing sewers and transporting sewage, and for instituting regular streetcleaning (including snow removal). Engineers also sponsored studies of local problems and advised officials on budgetary matters and contracts. They had similar influence in matters of streetlighting, parks, fire protection, and more.

The Legacy of Urbanism

Urban America seldom functioned smoothly; in fact, there really was no coherent urban community, but only a collection of subcommunities. As a result of immigration and urbanization, the United States became a culturally pluralistic society—not a melting pot but a salad bowl. Literary critic Randolph Bourne dubbed the United States "a cosmopolitan federation of national colonies." This kind of reasoning produced hyphenated identifications: people considered themselves Irish-American, Italo-American, Polish-American, and the like.

Cultural Pluralism

Pluralism and its attendant interest-group loyalties made politics an important institution. If America was not a melting pot, then different groups were competing with each other for power, wealth, and status. When lack of skills, education, capital, and influence closed paths to success, immigrants turned to politics to protect their interests and to open new opportunities. American cities became arenas in which different groups formed coalitions to achieve their goals. But such coalitions were fragile, and their membership shifted according to the issue in question.

Adherents of diverse cultural traditions fought about how much control government should exercise over people's lives. The most provocative issue concerned use of leisure time and celebration of Sunday, the Lord's day. In the Puritan tradition, the native-born supported blue laws designed to prevent desecration of the Sabbath by prohibiting various commercial and recreational activities. European immigrants,

Cultural-Political Alignments

accustomed to feasting and playing after church, fought the closing of saloons and other restrictions on the only day they had free for fun and relaxation. Similar splits developed over public versus parochial schools and prohibition versus free availability of liquor.

Such efforts at government control generally failed, however, because too many people had a stake in the country's cultural diversity. By 1920, immigrants and their offspring outnumbered natives in many cities, and the national economy depended on new workers and consumers. These new Americans had transformed the United States into an urban nation; they had given American culture its rich and varied texture; and they had laid foundations for the liberalism that would characterize future American politics.

Standards of Living

If the affluence of a society can be measured by how quickly the society converts luxuries into commonplace articles of everyday life, the United States was indeed becoming affluent in the years between 1880 and 1920. In 1880, for example, only wealthy women could afford silk stockings and only residents of Florida, Texas, and California could enjoy fresh oranges. In 1921, however, Americans of all regions ate 248 crates of oranges per 1,000 people and bought 217 million pairs of silk stockings. How did people afford these goods? How did changes in standards of living come about?

What people can afford depends on their resources and incomes. Data for the period from 1880 to 1920 are incomplete, but there is no doubt that incomes rose. As always, the **Rising** rich got richer. But incomes also **Personal** rose among the middle classes. **Income** For example, the average pay for clerical workers rose by 36 percent between 1890 and 1910 (see table, page 335). In the early 1900s, employees of the federal executive branch were averaging $1,072 a year, and college professors $1,100—not handsome sums but

much more than manual workers received. With these incomes, the middle class could afford relatively comfortable housing. A six- or seven-room house cost around $3,000 to buy or build and $15 to $20 per month to rent.

Wages for industrial workers increased as well, though they varied widely and income figures were deceiving. On the average, annual wages of factory workers rose from $486 in 1890 to $630 in 1910, or about 35 percent. Hourly rates in industries with large female work forces were lower than in industries with predominantly male employees. Regional variations, too, were wide. Nevertheless, wages for all moved upward (see table). Pay for farm laborers followed the same trend, though wages remained relatively low because generally those workers received room and board along with their pay.

Wage increases mean little, however, if living costs rise as fast as or faster than wages, and that is what happened. According to one economic index, **Cost of Living** the weekly cost of living for a typical wage earner's family of four rose by more than 47 percent between 1889 and 1913. Very rarely did the income for a particular working-class occupation rise at the same rate as the cost of living.

How then could working-class Americans afford the new goods and services that the industrial age offered? Some working-class families increased their incomes and partook at least partially in the consumer society by sending children and women into the labor market. In a household where the father made $600 a year, the wages of other family members might lift total income to $800 or $900. Many families also rented household space to boarders and lodgers, a practice that could yield up to $200 a year. These means of increasing family income enabled people to spend more and save more.

Scientific developments eased some of life's struggles, and their impact on living standards increased after 1900. Advances in medical care and improved living conditions **Higher Life** sharply reduced death rates and **Expectancy** extended the life span. Between 1900 and 1920, life expectancy rose by six years and the death rate dropped by 24 percent (see table). During the same period, there

AMERICAN LIVING STANDARDS, 1880–1920

	1880	1890	1900	1910	1920
Income and earnings:					
Annual income:					
Clerical worker		$848		$1,156	
Public school teacher		$256		$492	
Industrial worker		$486		$630	
Farm laborer		$233		$336	
Hourly wage:					
Soft-coal miner		$0.18[a]		$0.21	
Iron worker		$0.17[a]		$0.23	
Shoe worker		$0.14[a]		$0.19	
Paper worker		$0.12[a]		$0.17	
Labor statistics					
Number of people in labor force	17.4 million	28.5 million			41.7 million
Average workweek, manufacturing		60 hours		51 hours	47.4 hours
Food costs					
10 pounds potatoes		$0.16		$0.17	
1 dozen eggs		$0.21		$0.34	
1 pound bacon		$0.12½		$0.25	
Demographic data					
Life expectancy at birth:					
Women			48.3 years		54.6 years
Men			46.3 years		53.6 years
Death rate per 1,000 people			172		130
Birthrate per 1,000 people	39.8		32.3		27.7
Other					
Number of students in public high schools		203,000			2.3 million
Advertising expenditures	$20 million		$95 million		$500 million
Telephones per 100 people		0.3[b]	2.1[c]		12.6[d]

[a] 1892   [b] 1891   [c] 1901   [d] 1921

were significant declines in death rates from typhoid, diphtheria, influenza (except for a harsh epidemic in 1918 and 1919), tuberculosis, and intestinal ailments—diseases that had been the scourge of earlier generations. However, deaths from cancer, diabetes, and heart disease increased significantly. Americans also found more ways to kill: although the suicide rate remained about the same, the number of homicides and automobile deaths rose dramatically between 1900 and 1920.

Not only were amenities and luxuries more readily available in the early 1900s than they had been half a century earlier, but the means to upward mobility seemed more accessible as well. The spread of public education—particularly high schools—helped equip young people to achieve a standard of living higher than that of their parents. More than ever before, education was becoming the key to success. Yet the inequality that had pervaded earlier eras remained. Race, sex, religion, and ethnicity still determined one's access to power.

Family Life

Although the overwhelming majority of Americans continued to live their lives within a family, this basic social institution underwent considerable strain during the industrial era. As American society became more affluent and complex, it generated new institutions—schools, social clubs, political organizations, and others—that competed with the family to provide nurture, education, companionship, and security. Many popular and scholarly writers warned that rising divorce rates, the entrance of large numbers of women into the work force, and loss of parental control over children spelled peril for home and family. Yet the family retained its fundamental usefulness as a cushion in a hard, uncertain world.

Throughout modern Western history, most people have lived in two overlapping kinds of basic units: household and family. A *household* is a residential unit, a group of related or unrelated people who live in the same abode. A *family* is a group of people related by kinship, some of whom typically live together. The distinction between household and family is important in describing how Americans lived in the late nineteenth and early twentieth centuries.

Family and Household Structures

At the most elementary level, Americans between 1877 and 1920 grouped themselves in traditional ways. As in the past, the vast majority of households consisted of *nuclear families*—usually, a married couple with or without children. About 15 to 20 percent of households consisted of *extended families*—usually, a married couple with or without children, plus a combination of one or more relatives such as grandparents, grandchildren, aunts, uncles, in-laws, or cousins. About 5 percent of households consisted of people who lived alone.

The relative size of nuclear families did change over time, however. In 1880, the birthrate was 39.8 live births per 1,000 people; by 1900, it had dropped to 32.3, and by 1920, to 27.7. Several reasons can be offered to explain this decline. First, the United States was becoming an urban nation, and birthrates in cities generally are lower than in rural areas. On farms, where children could work at home or in the fields at an early age, each child born contributed to the family work force. In the wage-based urban economy, children could not contribute significantly to the family income for many years, and a new child simply represented another mouth to feed. Second, as diet and medical care improved, infant mortality fell and families did not have to have many children just to ensure that some would survive. Third, it appears that decisions to limit family size resulted from growing consciousness that people could improve the quality of life for themselves and their children if their families were smaller than their ancestors' families.

Declining Birthrates

Although fertility among blacks, immigrants, and rural dwellers was consistently higher than among white native urban dwellers, birthrates of all groups fell. As a result, families with six or eight children became less common; three or four became more usual. The nuclear family tended to reach its maximum size and then decline in size faster than in earlier eras.

In spite of the predominance of the nuclear family, the household typically expanded and contracted over the lifetime of a given family. First, family size fluctuated as children were born and later left home. Second, the process of leaving home made for huge numbers of young people—and some older people—who lived as boarders and lodgers, especially in cities. Middle- and working-class families commonly took in boarders to help pay the rent or to occupy unused rooms vacated by grown children.

Boarding

Housing reformers charged that boarding caused overcrowding and loss of privacy. Yet for those who

Better diets and improved living conditions increased life expectancy so that the numbers and proportions of older people in the American population grew. As a result, even though generations became more separated from each other, children were more likely than those of previous generations to have their grandparents alive to dote on them, as this photograph from Horton, Kansas, in 1907 reveals. *Jules A. Bourquin, Kansas Collection, University of Kansas Libraries.*

immigrants and others in need. At a time when welfare and service agencies were rare, the family continued to be the institution to which people could turn. Even when relatives did not live together, they often lived nearby and could help each other with childcare, meals, shopping, advice, and consolation. Family members also obtained jobs for each other.

Importance of Kinship

Obligations of kinship, however, were not always welcome or even helpful. Immigrant families often put pressure on last-born children to stay at home and care for aging parents, a practice that stifled opportunities for education, marriage, and economic independence. Tensions also developed when one relative felt that another was not helping out enough. Kinship, for better or worse, nevertheless gave people a means of coping with the many stresses caused by an urban industrial society.

At the turn of the century, family life and its functions were both changing and holding firm. New institutions were assuming tasks formerly performed by the family. Schools were making education more of a community responsibility. Employment agencies, personnel offices, labor unions, and legislatures were taking responsibility for employee recruitment and job security. In addition, migration and a soaring divorce rate seemed to be splitting families apart. Yet in the face of these changes, the family remained a resilient institution.

boarded the practice was highly useful. Boarding gave a household flexibility, bringing in extra income. For immigrants and young people who had left home, it was a transitional stage, providing them with a quasi-family environment until they set up their own households.

Some households included extended family members who lived as quasi-boarders. Especially in communities where economic hardship or rapid growth made housing expensive or scarce, newlyweds tended to live with the husband's or wife's parents until they could afford their own place. Often a family would take in a widowed parent or an unmarried sibling who would otherwise have had to live alone. For immigrants and migrants, the family served as a refuge in a strange new place.

Kinship had important functions, especially for

The New Leisure and Mass Culture

On December 2, 1889, as hundreds of workers paraded through Worcester, Massachusetts, in support of shorter working hours, a group of carpenters hoisted a banner that proclaimed, "Eight Hours for Work, Eight Hours for Rest, Eight Hours for What We Will." That last phrase, "for What We Will," was significant, for it marked recognition of a special segment of everyday life that belonged to the individual. Increasingly, leisure activities filled this time segment.

American inventors had always tried to create labor-saving devices, but not until the late 1800s did technological development truly save time.

Increase in Leisure Time

Mechanization and assembly-line production helped to cut the average workweek for manufacturing workers from sixty hours in 1890 to forty-seven in 1920. These reductions meant not only shorter workdays but also freer weekends. By the 1920s, white-collar workers and farmers also had more free time than in the past. To be sure, thousands still spent twelve- or fourteen-hour shifts in steel mills and sweatshops and had no time or energy for leisure. Nevertheless, Americans in the early 1900s were enmeshed in the business of play.

The vanguard of this trend was sports. Football and especially baseball were popular among males. In 1845, baseball's rules had been codified. By the 1880s, professional baseball was a big business. In 1887, more than 51,000 people paid to watch a championship series between St. Louis and Detroit. In 1903, the National League and competing American League began a World Series between their championship teams. About the time that baseball was becoming entrenched as the national pastime, football began to attract public attention.

Sports

Football first gained popularity at the intercollegiate level, among those who could afford a college education. Soon colleges hired nonstudents—called "tramp athletes"—to play on their teams. Winning at virtually any cost became important; in 1905, 18 players died and more than 150 were seriously injured. Such violence stirred President Theodore Roosevelt, who convened a White House conference to discuss ways of eliminating brutality and foul play. The conference founded the Intercollegiate Athletic Association (renamed the National College Athletic Association in 1910) to police college sports and to make them less violent.

Meanwhile, college women, believing that to succeed intellectually they needed to be active and healthy, engaged in such sports as rowing, track, and swimming. Eventually, basketball became the most popular sport among college women. Invented in 1891 as a winter sport for men, basketball was given women's rules (that limited dribbling and running and encouraged passing) in the 1890s, and intercollegiate games became common.

There were, of course, sports enjoyed by both sexes. Croquet, which swept the nation after the Civil War, was popular among middle- and upper-class people. Bicycling achieved a popularity rivaling that of baseball. Like croquet, bicycling brought men and women together. Especially on the bicycle-built-for-two, it provided a combination of courtship and exercise. Moreover, the bicycle played an influential role in freeing women from the constraints of Victorian fashions. In order to ride bikes, women had to wear divided skirts and simple undergarments. Gradually, freer styles of cycling costumes began to have an influence on everyday fashions.

The rise of American show business paralleled the rise of sports and similarly became a mode of leisure created by and for common people.

Circuses

Circuses—traveling shows of acrobats and animals—had existed since the 1820s. But after the Civil War, railroads enabled circuses to reach more of the country, and the popularity of the big show increased enormously. Circuses offered two main attractions: so-called freaks of nature, both human and animal, and the temptation and conquest of death. More important was the sheer astonishment aroused by the trapeze artists, lion tamers, high-wire artists, acrobats, and clowns.

Several branches of American show business matured with the growth of cities. Popular drama, musical comedy, and vaudeville all gave Americans a chance to escape from the harsh

Popular Drama and Musical Comedy

realities of life into melodrama, adventure, and comedy. Plots were simple, and the heroes and villains instantly recognizable. For urbanized people increasingly distant from the frontier, popular plays brought to life the mythical Wild West and Old South. Virtue, honor, and justice always triumphed in melodramas, reinforcing the popular belief that even in an uncertain and disillusioning world, goodness would prevail.

Musical comedies raised audiences' spirits with song, humor, and dance. American musical comedy grew out of the lavishly costumed operettas popular in Europe. By introducing American themes (often involving ethnic groups), folksy humor, and catchy tunes and dances, these shows launched the nation's most popular songs and entertainers. George M. Cohan, the master of American musical comedy after the turn of the century, helped to reinforce national morale during the First World War with songs like "Yankee Doodle Dandy" and "You're a Grand Old Flag."

Vaudeville

The French term *vaudeville* first referred to light drama with musical interludes, but in the United States vaudeville became a unique entertainment form. Vaudeville was probably the most popular entertainment in early-twentieth-century America because its variety made it attractive to mass audiences. Shows included magic and animal acts, juggling, stunts, comedy (especially ethnic humor), and song and dance. Around 1900, the number of vaudeville theaters and troupes skyrocketed. The most famous promoter, Florenz Ziegfeld, brilliantly packaged popular entertainment in a stylish format—the Ziegfeld Follies—and gave the nation a new model of femininity, the Ziegfeld Girl, whose graceful dancing and alluring costumes were meant to suggest a haunting sensuality.

Comic opera star Lillian Russell, vaudeville singer and comedienne Fanny Brice, and burlesque queen Eva Tanguay attracted intensely loyal fans, commanded handsome fees, and won respect for their genuine talents. In contrast to the demure Victorian female, they conveyed pluck and creativity. But show business, which provided new economic opportunities for women, African-Americans, and immigrants, also indulged in stereotyping and exploitation.

Blacks and Immigrants in Vaudeville

Before the 1890s, the chief form of commercial entertainment open to black performers was the minstrel show. By the end of the century, however, minstrel shows had given way to more sophisticated musicals, and blacks had begun to break into vaudeville. As stage sets shifted from the plantation to the city, music shifted from folk tunes to ragtime. Pandering to the prejudice of white audiences, composers and performers of both races ridiculed blacks. Even Burt Williams, a highly paid black comedian and dancer who was one of the era's most talented performers, achieved his tormented success mainly by playing the stereotypical roles of darky and dandy.

Much of the uniqueness of American mass entertainment came from its ethnic flavor. Indeed, immigrants were the core of American show business. Vaudeville particularly drew on and embellished ethnic humor, exaggerating dialects and other national traits. Skits and songs reinforced ethnic stereotypes and made fun of ethnic groups, but such distortions were more self-conscious and sympathetic than those directed at blacks.

Movies

Shortly after 1900, live entertainment began to yield to an even more accessible form of amusement: moving pictures. Perfected by Thomas Edison in the late 1880s, movies began as slot-machine peepshows in penny arcades and billiard parlors. Eventually, images were projected onto a screen so large that audiences could view them, and a new medium was born.

By 1910, motion pictures had become an art form, thanks to creative directors like D. W. Griffith. Griffith's most famous work, *The Birth of a Nation* (1915), an epic film about the Civil War and Reconstruction, fanned racial prejudice by depicting blacks as threatening white moral values; its exaltation of the Ku Klux Klan also helped to revive the hooded empire. But the film's innovative techniques—close-ups, fade-outs, and battle scenes—gave viewers heightened drama and excitement. From the beginning, movies were popular among all classes.

The still camera, modernized by inventor George Eastman, enabled ordinary people to make their own photographic images; and the phonograph, another of Edison's inventions, brought musical performances to the home. The spread of movies, photography, and phonograph records meant that access to live performances no longer limited people's exposure to art and entertainment.

To some extent, new amusements and pastimes had a homogenizing influence, bringing together disparate ethnic and social groups into a common experience. Parks, ball fields, vaudeville shows, and movies were designed for and appealed to everyone; they were nonsectarian and apolitical. Yet various groups adopted leisure institutions in their own way. For example, in some communities working-class immigrant groups used parks and amusement parks as locations for traditional family and ethnic gatherings. Thus, as Americans learned

By the end of the nineteenth century, recreation of all sorts became a value of, and attainable by, almost all classes for the first time in American history. Note the free-spirited relaxation of these bathers on a Coney Island beach; their poses contrast markedly with the stiff formality of people on city streets and the serious concentration of people at work. *Library of Congress.*

to play, their leisure—like their work and politics—was shaped by pluralistic forces.

The Transformation of Mass Communications

With so many new things to do and buy, how did Americans decide what they wanted? Two new types of communication influenced consumer tastes and mass opinion. Modern advertising molded people's needs and consumption patterns, and popular journalism spread mass culture throughout the country.

A society of scarcity does not need advertising. When demand exceeds the supply of goods and services, producers have no trouble selling what they market. But in a society of abundance such as industrial America, supply frequently outstrips demand, making necessary a means of creating or increasing demand. The aim of advertising is to *invent* a demand by convincing whole groups that everyone in that group should buy a specific product. Indeed, the growth in the late nineteenth century of large companies that mass-produced consumer goods gave advertisers the task of creating "consumption communities"—bodies of consumers loyal to a particular brand name.

Advertising

The major vehicle for advertising was the newspaper. In 1879, Wanamaker's department store placed the first full-page ad, and at about the same time newspapers began to allow advertisers to print pictures of products. Such attention-getting techniques transformed advertising into news. More than ever before, people read newspapers to find out what was for sale, as well as what was happening.

Just as advertising became news, news became a form of advertising, or at least of publicity. Canny publishers made people crave news just as they craved amusements and con-

Yellow Journalism sumer goods. Joseph Pulitzer, a Hungarian immigrant who bought the *New York World* in 1883,
pioneered journalism as a branch of mass culture. Believing that newspapers should be "dedicated to the cause of the people rather than to that of the purse potentates," Pulitzer filled the *World* with stories of disasters, crimes, and scandals. Sensational headlines, set in large bold type like that used for advertisements, screamed from every page. Pulitzer's journalists not only reported news but sought it out—and sometimes even created it. He also popularized the comics, and the yellow ink they were printed in gave his emphasis on the sensational nickname "yellow journalism." The success enjoyed by Pulitzer caused others, most notably William R. Hearst, to adopt his techniques.

Pulitzer and his rivals fanned popular interest even more by emphasizing sports and women's news. Newspapers had always reported on sporting events, but yellow-journalism papers gave such stories far greater prominence by printing separate, expanded sports sections. A special section devoted to household tips, fashion, decorum, and club news captured the interest of female readers. Like crime and disaster stories, sports and women's sections helped to make news a mass commodity.

By the early twentieth century, communications media, like the mass consumption of goods, were becoming commonplace. Alongside newspapers, mass-circulation magazines offered human-interest stories, muckraking exposés, titillating fiction, and eye-catching ads to a growing mass market. In addition, the total number of books published more than quadrupled between 1880 and 1917. This rising popular consumption of news and books reflected growing literacy (94 percent in 1920).

Other forms of communication were also expanding. By 1920, increasing numbers of people were using the telephone and sending telegrams and letters. Little wonder, then, that the term *com-munity* took on new dimensions. More than ever before, people in different parts of the country knew about and discussed the same news event. America was becoming a mass society.

Popular Literature

American culture has long focused one eye on an increasingly complex technological future while casting the other at a sentimentalized, simpler past. When modern wonders such as telephones, high-speed printing presses, phonographs, and cameras made information and entertainment more accessible, people demanded diversions that reaffirmed traditional values of optimism, individualism, and freedom. Thus in 1914, just when they were beginning to appreciate automobiles, movies, and electricity, Americans made Edgar Rice Burroughs's *Tarzan of the Apes* a best seller.

Since the 1840s, low-priced, paperbound adventure novels had circulated widely among the literate public. After the Civil War, such books, called

Dime Novels dime novels, became the most widely read variety of American literature, especially among youth.
These publications offered three types of stories. The first evoked the Wild West. Intertwining fact and fiction, writers such as Zane Grey wove adventure stories around famous folk heroes like Buffalo Bill Cody, the Lone Ranger, and Wild Bill Hickok. During the 1880s, however, many authors, recognizing the lure and growing impact of city life, began to give their tales urban settings and themes. Detective thrillers became the leading type of popular urban fiction. Just before the end of the century, science fiction and character heroes came to the fore.

One popular writer, Horatio Alger, moved beyond the fantasies of dime novels and offered readers a formula for contending with new social and economic forces. Alger began

Moral Messages of Popular Fiction writing boys' stories in the 1860s. As his titles attest, each story emphasizes the virtues of self-reliance and hard work. Alger's heroes begin their lives in poverty and call on ambition, honesty, courage, thrift, and luck to overcome obstacles and achieve success. But his message was more than an exhortation to morality and frugality. The moral of Alger's stories was that success came to those who were not only virtuous but also alert enough to capitalize on a lucky break.

A few years before Alger's death in 1899, one of America's most popular character heroes, Frank Merriwell, was created by Gilbert Patten (using the pen name of Burt Standish). Frank Merriwell's adventures had a common theme that accorded with the way many Americans liked to think of themselves and their nation: he attempted and accomplished the impossible. Merriwell's name symbolized American virtues. According to Patten, "I took the three qualities I most wanted him to represent—frank and merry in nature, well in body and mind—and made the name Frank Merriwell."

Young women found escape and inspiration in sentimental tales about growing up and about animals. One of the most widely read novels was Louisa May Alcott's *Little Women,* published in two parts in 1868 and 1869. It recreated the domestic delights and moral trials of four girls, who were based on Alcott and her sisters. A generation later, romantic novels about animals, like Anna Sewell's *Black Beauty* (1890) and Kate Douglas Wiggins's *Rebecca of Sunnybrook Farm* (1903), became best sellers.

Popular literature for adults also oozed sentimentality. The best-selling titles of the late nineteenth century included romances about chivalry and honor. *Ben Hur* (1880), General Lew Wallace's powerful religious melodrama set in the Roman Empire, sold 2 million copies by 1933 and heralded a rage for historical fiction. Works about self-help and inspiration, both perennial themes in American popular literature, also flourished.

While some popular writers focused on escapism, others tried to introduce realism into romance. During the 1870s and 1880s, a number of "local-color" writers began producing works that depicted the people and environment of a particular region more realistically. This movement was centered in the South, whose writers felt compelled to rebuild the region's na-

Local Colorists

tional image. Joel Chandler Harris, who created the popular Uncle Remus stories, Mary Noailles Murfree, who located her tales in Appalachia, and George Washington Cable, who captured the aura of exotic New Orleans, all produced authentic characters and dialects. Regional writers of the Far West and Midwest included Bret Harte, who spun tales about the California mining experience and Constance Fenimore Woolson, who wrote about lumbering and fur-trading districts of the Great Lakes.

One local colorist, Mark Twain (the pen name of Samuel Clemens), moved beyond romance and adventure and in so doing won recognition from both intellectuals and the masses. He was best known for his books about the American West: *Tom Sawyer* (1876) and *Huckleberry Finn* (1884). These antisentimental novels were realistic portrayals of western life and of human weakness. Twain was sensitive to both the comic and the tragic sides of life, and his writing reflected the dynamic energy and materialism of his era.

Literary Classics

A number of Twain's contemporaries shunned the falseness of escape writing and focused instead on the moral tests that life holds. Realists like William Dean Howells, Edith Wharton, and Henry James wrote chiefly about upper-class Americans, but other realists examined the lives of ordinary folk and in so doing opened new literary vistas. These writers, sometimes called naturalists, often viewed life in terms of the survival of the fittest; they portrayed ruthless struggles for survival and power in frank detail. Their descriptions of slum life, sexual immorality, and violence portrayed a side of life avoided by local colorists.

The escapism of popular fiction and the realism of serious fiction, though seemingly at odds, offered similar commentaries on American society of the early twentieth century. It was no coincidence that Frank Merriwell replaced Horatio Alger's heroes in popular fiction around 1900: by then Americans knew that it took more than honesty, energy, and a timely rescue to become rich. Naturalist writers, for example, saw that the new demands that an industrial age placed on individuals threatened traditional American values of family, practicality, and moral restraint.

Suggestions for Further Reading

Urban Growth

Howard P. Chudacoff and Judith E. Smith, *The Evolution of American Urban Society,* 3rd ed. (1988); Kenneth T. Jackson, *The Crabgrass Frontier: The Suburbanization of the United States* (1985); Jon Teaford, *City and Suburb: The Political Fragmentation of Metropolitan America, 1850–1970* (1979); Sam Bass Warner, Jr., *The Urban Wilderness* (1982); Sam Bass Warner, Jr., *Streetcar Suburbs* (1962).

Immigration, Ethnicity, and Religion

Aaron I. Abell, *American Catholicism and Social Action* (1960); Josef J. Barton, *Peasants and Strangers: Italians, Rumanians, and Slovaks in an American City* (1975); John Bodnar, *The Transplanted* (1985); John Bodnar et al., *Lives of Their Own: Blacks, Italians, and Poles in Pittsburgh, 1900–1960* (1982); John W. Briggs, *An Italian Passage* (1978); Jack Chen, *The Chinese of America* (1980); John B. Duff, *The Irish in the United States* (1971); Elizabeth Ewen, *Immigrant Women in the Land of Dollars* (1985); Mario T. Garcia, *Desert Immigrants: The Mexicans of El Paso, 1880–1920* (1981); Nathan Glazer and Daniel P. Moynihan, *Beyond the Melting Pot,* rev. ed. (1970); Caroline Golab, *Immigrant Destinations* (1977); Milton Gordon, *Assimilation in American Life* (1964); Victor Greene, *For God and Country: The Rise of Polish and Lithuanian Ethnic Consciousness in America* (1975); Oscar Handlin, *The Uprooted,* 2nd ed. (1973); John Higham, *Strangers in the Land: Patterns of American Nativism* (1955); Yusi Ichioka, *The Issei: The World of the First Japanese Immigrants, 1885–1924* (1988); Harry Kitano, *Japanese Americans: The Evolution of a Subculture* (1969); Matt S. Maier and Felciano Rivera, *The Chicanos* (1972); Ewa Morawska, *For Bread with Butter: Life-Worlds of East Europeans in Johnstown, Pennsylvania, 1890–1940* (1986); Humbert S. Nelli, *The Italians of Chicago* (1970); Moses Rischin, *The Promised City: New York's Jews* (1962); Judith E. Smith, *Family Connections* (1985); Werner Sollors, *Beyond Ethnicity* (1986).

Urban Needs and Services

Robert H. Bremner, *From the Depths: The Discovery of Poverty* (1956); Lawrence A. Cremin, *American Education: The Metropolitan Experience* (1988); Thomas L. Philpott, *The Slum and the Ghetto* (1978); James F. Richardson, *The New York Police* (1970); Barbara Gutmann Rosencrantz, *Public Health and the State* (1972); Mel Scott, *American City Planning Since 1890* (1969); Christopher Tunnard and Henry Hope Reed, *American Skyline* (1955); David B. Tyack, *The One Best System: A History of American Urban Education* (1974).

Mobility and Race Relations

Howard P. Chudacoff, *Mobile Americans* (1972); Clyde Griffen and Sally Griffen, *Natives and Newcomers* (1977); Jacqueline Jones, *Labor of Love, Labor of Sorrow: Black Women, Work and the Family from Slavery to the Present* (1985); David M. Katzman, *Before the Ghetto* (1973); Thomas Kessner, *The Golden Door* (1977); Kenneth L. Kusmer, *A Ghetto Takes Shape* (1976); Gilbert Osofsky, *Harlem: The Making of a Ghetto* (1966); Howard N. Rabinowitz, *Race Relations in the Urban South* (1978); Allan H. Spear, *Black Chicago* (1967); Stephan Thernstrom, *The Other Bostonians: Poverty and Progress in the American Metropolis* (1973); Olivier Zunz, *The Changing Face of Inequality: Urbanization, Industrial Development and Immigrants in Detroit, 1880–1920* (1982).

Boss Politics

John M. Allswang, *Bosses, Machines and Urban Voters* (1977); Alexander B. Callow, Jr., ed., *The City Boss in America* (1976); Bruce M. Stave and Sondra Stave, eds., *Urban Bosses, Machines, and Progressive Reformers* (1984).

Urban Reform

John D. Buenker, *Urban Liberalism and Progressive Reform* (1973); James B. Crooks, *Politics and Progress* (1968); Melvin Holli, *Reform in Detroit* (1969); C. H. Hopkins, *The Rise of the Social Gospel in American Protestantism* (1940); Roy M. Lubove, *The Progressives and the Slums* (1962); Martin J. Schiesl, *The Politics of Efficiency: Municipal Administration and Reform in America* (1977).

Family and Individual Life Cycles

W. Andrew Achenbaum, *Old Age in the New Land* (1979); Howard P. Chudacoff, *How Old Are You? Age Consciousness in American Culture* (1989); Carl N. Degler, *At Odds: Women and the Family in America* (1980); Michael Gordon, ed., *The American Family in Social-Historical Perspective,* 3rd ed. (1983); Carole Haber, *Beyond Sixty-five: Dilemmas of Old Age in America's Past* (1983); Tamara K. Hareven, *Family Time and Industrial Time: The Relationship Between the Family and Work in a New England Industrial Community* (1981); Joseph Kett, *Rites of Passage: Adolescence in America* (1979); Ellen K. Rothman, *Hands and Hearts: A History of Courtship in America* (1986).

Mass Entertainment and Leisure

Robert Clyde Allen, *Vaudeville and Film, 1895–1915: A Study in Media Interaction* (1977); Gunther Barth, *City People* (1980); Allen Guttmann, *A Whole New Ball Game: An Interpretation of American Sports* (1988); John F. Kasson, *Amusing the Million: Coney Island at the Turn of the Century* (1978); Donald J. Mrozek, *Sport and American Mentality, 1880–1910* (1983); Joseph A. Musselman, *Music in the Cultured Generation: A Social History of Music in America, 1870–1900* (1971); Kathy Peiss, *Cheap Amusements: Working Women and Leisure in Turn-of-the-Century New York* (1986); Benjamin G. Rader, *American Sports* (1983); Roy Rosenzweig, *Eight Hours for What We Will! Workers and Leisure in an Industrial City, 1870–1920* (1983); Robert Sklar, *Movie-Made America* (1976); Robert C. Toll, *On with the Show: The First Century of Show Business in America* (1976).

Advertising and Journalism

Stephen Fox, *The Mirror Makers: A History of American Advertising and Its Creators* (1984); George Juergens, *Joseph Pulitzer and the New York World* (1966); Frank L. Mott, *American Journalism,* 3rd ed. (1962); Daniel Pope, *The Making of Modern Advertising* (1983); W. A. Swanberg, *Citizen Hearst* (1961); Bernard A. Weisberger, *The American Newspaperman* (1961).

Popular Literature

John G. Cawelti, *Apostles of Success in America* (1965); John L. Cutler, *Patten and His Merriwell Saga* (1934); Frank L. Mott, *Golden Multitudes: The Story of Best Sellers in the United States* (1947); Moses Rischin, ed., *The American Gospel of Success* (1965); Henry Nash Smith, *Mark Twain* (1962); John W. Tebbel, *From Rags to Riches: Horatio Alger, Jr., and the American Dream* (1963).

The platform written by the newly organized People's party that met in Omaha, Nebraska, in July 1892 bristled with discontent. Those who drafted the platform charged that the nation had been "brought to the verge of moral, political, and material ruin." They further asserted that from the "womb of governmental injustice we breed the two great classes–tramps and millionaires."

Most members of the People's party, called Populists (from *populus*, the Latin word for "people"), were farmers who believed that new, large-scale modes of production threatened their rights to equality and freedom. Like labor unions and socialists, Populists protested that the economic system was creating irresponsible concentrations of power and wealth that crushed small producers and dominated government. Thus, they gathered in Omaha to preserve a sense of cooperation and justice against the greed of market competition and the despotism of big business.

In some ways, the Populists were right. Corruption and greed tugged at the fabric of democracy, and the era's venality prompted novelists Mark Twain and Charles Dudley Warner to dub the 1870s and 1880s the Gilded Age. Officeholders used their positions to amass personal fortunes and dispense patronage appointments to their supporters. Although Congress did grapple with important issues, many of its accomplishments were either weak compromises or favors to special interests. Meanwhile, the judiciary, by defending vested rights of property against state and federal interference, supported big business. The presidency was filled by a series of honest, respectable men who seldom took the initiative; when they did, they often found themselves beaten back by Congress and the courts.

During the 1870s and 1880s, the influence of powerful special interests became a basic ingredient of politics, and it infused politics with corruption. Vote fraud, bribery, and unfair advantage roused reformers and defined several major legislative issues. Another ingredient was exclusion, because the majority of Americans—including women, southern blacks, Indians, illiterate whites, and unnaturalized immigrants—could not vote. Special interests, corruption, and exclusion were part of a delicate equilib-

19

GILDED AGE POLITICS, 1877–1900

rium consisting of a stable party system and a regional balance of power.

Then, in the 1890s, two developments shattered the equilibrium: the rural discontent that accompanied the transformation of the West and South reached its climax, and a deep economic depression bared flaws in the industrial system. Amid these crises, the presidential campaign of 1896 stirred Americans as they had not been stirred for a generation. A new party arose; old parties split; sectional unities dissolved; and questions about the nation's future congealed around a single election. The nation emerged from the turbulent 1890s with new political alignments. These alignments prepared the way for the new century and for reforms designed to overcome the injustices that the People's party had listed in its Omaha platform.

The Nature of Politics

Historian Henry Adams, grandson and great-grandson of presidents, wrote that in American political history the period between 1870 and 1895 "was poor in purpose and barren in results." From the voters' perspective, however, politics appeared anything but barren. At no other time in the nation's history was public interest in elections higher. Consistently, 80 to 90 percent of eligible voters (white and black in the North, mostly white males in the South) cast ballots in local and national elections. Even among those who could not vote, politics was the prime form of mass entertainment, outdistancing baseball, vaudeville, and circuses. Voting was only the last stage in a process that included rallies, parades, picnics, and speeches, all of which were as much public amusement as civic responsibility.

Politics was a personal, as well as a community, activity. People formed strong loyalties to individual politicians and parties. These allegiances were usually so evenly distributed that no major faction or party gained lasting control. Between 1877 and 1897, Republicans held the presidency for three terms, and Democrats for two. The

Party Allegiances

same party controlled the presidency and both houses of Congress for only three two-year spans: Republicans twice and Democrats once. The balance persisted despite the admission of six territories to statehood during this period.

Republicans and Democrats competed avidly for office, but internal quarrels split both parties. Among Republicans, factional feuds and personal rivalries often took precedence over national concerns. On one side stood the "Stalwarts," led by New York's pompous Senator Roscoe Conkling, who sought party influence and government jobs for his supporters. On the other side stood the "Half Breeds," led by James G. Blaine of Maine. Blaine pursued influence as much as Conkling did but attempted to disguise his aims by courting support from independents. On the sidelines were the more idealistic liberals, or "Mugwumps" (an Indian term meaning "undisciplined chiefs"), who disliked the political roguishness that tainted their party and believed that only righteous, dedicated men like themselves should govern. Meanwhile, Democrats tended to separate into white-supremacy southerners, immigrant-stock urban machine members, and business interests favoring low tariffs. Like Republicans, Democrats eagerly pursued the spoils of office.

Party Factions

National Issues

In Congress, however, the parties split over long-standing political and economic issues, such as sectional controversies, patronage, railroad regulation, tariffs, and currency. Long after Reconstruction ended, Americans were haunted by conflicts and disruptions that had followed the Civil War. Republicans tried to capitalize on war memories by "waving the bloody shirt," blaming Democrats for starting the painful war. In the South, Democrats also waved the bloody shirt, blaming Republicans for interfering in regional affairs. The use of such appeals persisted well into the 1880s.

Sectional Conflict

1873	Coinage of silver dollars ends	1890	McKinley Tariff
1873–78	Economic hard times		Sherman Silver Purchase Act
1876	Hayes elected president		"Mississippi Plan"
	United States v. *Reese*		Federal budget surpasses $1 billion
1877	*Munn* v. *Illinois*	1892	Populist convention in Omaha
1878	Bland-Allison Act		Cleveland elected president
	Anthony amendment on women's	1893	Repeal of the Sherman Silver
	suffrage defeated in Congress		Purchase Act
1880	Garfield elected president	1893–97	Depression
1881	Garfield assassinated; Arthur	1894	Pullman strike
	assumes the presidency		Coxey's march
1883	Pendleton Civil Service Act	1895	Cleveland deals with bankers to save
1884	Cleveland elected president		the gold reserve
1886	*Wabash* case	1896	McKinley elected president
1887	Interstate Commerce Act	1897	Dingley Tariff
1888	Harrison elected president		*Maximum Freight Rate* case
		1898	Louisiana enacts first grandfather
			clause
		1900	Gold Standard Act
			McKinley re-elected

Politicians were not the only ones who attempted to profit by keeping the war alive. In the 1880s and 1890s, the Grand Army of the Republic, an organization of Union Army veterans numbering more than 400,000, allied with the Republican party and pressured Congress into legislating generous pensions for former soldiers and their widows. Many pensions were deserved. Union soldiers had been poorly paid, and thousands of women had been widowed. But for many veterans, the war's emotional wake provided an opportunity to profit at public expense.

Few politicians could afford to oppose Civil War pensions, but a number of reformers attempted to dismantle the spoils system. The practice of award-

Civil Service Reform
ing government jobs to party workers, regardless of their qualifications, flourished after the Civil War. As construction of buildings, the postal service, the diplomatic corps, and other government activities expanded, so did the number of jobs on public payrolls. Elected officials scrambled to control new appointments as a means of cementing support for themselves and their parties. In return for the comparatively short hours and high pay of government jobs, appointees pledged their votes and a portion of their earnings.

A system so susceptible to corruption vexed a

growing number of independents, who began advocating appointments and promotions based on merit rather than on connections. The movement grew during the 1870s, when scandals in the Grant administration bared defects of the spoils system. It reached full flower in 1881, with the formation of the National Civil Service Reform League. The same year, Charles Guiteau, a frustrated and demented jobseeker, assassinated President James Garfield, and the murder hastened the drive for civil service reform.

Late in 1882, Congress passed the Pendleton Civil Service Act, and President Chester Arthur signed it early in 1883. The measure outlawed political contributions by officeholders and created the Civil Service Commission to oversee competitive examinations for government positions. The act, however, gave the commission jurisdiction over only some 10 percent of federal jobs—though the president could expand the list.

In the 1880s, railroads provided an example of how economic development caused political problems at both the state and the national levels. As the nation's rail network expanded, so did competition. In their quest for customers, railroad lines reduced rates to outmaneuver rivals, but rate wars soon cut into profits and wild vacillations of rates angered shippers and farmers.

Ironically, while rates generally were falling, complaints about excessively high rates were rising. Railroads often boosted rates as high as possible on noncompetitive routes to compensate for unprofitably low rates on competitive routes, making pricing disproportionate to distance. Charges on short-distance shipments served by only one line could be far higher than those on long-distance shipments served by competing lines. Railroads also gave reduced rates to large shippers and offered free passenger passes to important customers and politicians.

During the 1870s, such favoritism stirred farmers, shippers, and reform politicians to demand that government regulate railroad practices, especially rates. By 1880, fourteen states had **Railroad** established commissions to limit **Regulation** the freight and storage charges of state-chartered lines. Railroads bitterly fought these measures, but in 1877 the Supreme Court upheld the principle of rate regulation in *Munn* v. *Illinois.*

State agencies, however, could not control large, interstate lines, a limitation affirmed in the *Wabash* case of 1886, when the Supreme Court declared that only Congress could limit rates involving interstate commerce. Congress responded in 1887 by passing the Interstate Commerce Act. The act prohibited pools, rebates, and long haul–short haul rate discrimination; and it also directed that "all charges . . . shall be reasonable and fair." It also created the Interstate Commerce Commission (ICC) and gave the ICC power to investigate railroads, issue "cease-and-desist" orders against illegal practices, and seek court aid to enforce compliance. However, the provisions for enforcement left the railroads room for evasion, and federal judges chipped away at ICC powers. In the *Maximum Freight Rate* case of 1897, the Supreme Court ruled that the ICC did not have power to set rates, and in the *Alabama Midlands* case the same year, the Court overturned prohibitions against long haul–short haul discrimination.

Initially, Congress had created and raised tariff rates to protect American manufactured goods and some agricultural products from European competition. But tariffs quickly became a **Tariff Policy** tool with which special interests could protect and enhance profits. By the 1880s, separate tariffs covered more than four thousand items, and resulting revenues were producing an embarrassing surplus in the federal Treasury. Although a few economists and farmers argued for free trade, most politicians still claimed that high tariffs were necessary to support industry and preserve jobs.

The Republican party, claiming responsibility for economic growth, put protective tariffs at the core of its policies. Democrats complained that tariffs made prices artificially high, benefiting interests—such as woolen manufacturers—whose products were protected, while hurting farmers, whose crops were not protected, and consumers, who had to buy manufactured goods. Although Democrats generally saw the need for some protection of manufactured goods and raw materials, they favored lower tariff rates to encourage foreign trade and reduce the Treasury surplus.

Privileged interests and their congressional allies fought off objections and maintained control over tariff policy. When in 1894, House Democrats, supported by President Grover Cleveland, passed a bill to reduce tariff rates, Senate Republicans, aided by southern Democrats eager to protect their region's infant industries, added some six hundred amendments restoring most cuts. In 1897, a new tariff bill, the Dingley Act, raised rates further, although it expanded reciprocity provisions. Introduced in the McKinley Tariff of 1890, reciprocity gave the president authority to remove items from the free list if their countries of origin placed unreasonable tariffs on American goods.

The currency controversy was even more tangled than the tariff issue. It involved opposing reactions to the fall in prices caused by increased industrial and agricultural production after the Civil War. Farmers, most of whom were debtors, suffered because they had to make fixed mortgage and interest payments while prices for their crops were dropping. Correctly perceiving that an insufficient money supply made debts more expensive relative to other costs, farmers favored schemes like the coinage of silver to increase the amount of currency in circulation. Creditors, on the other hand, believed that overproduction had caused prices to decline. They favored a more stable, limited money supply backed only by gold as a means of maintaining the confidence of investors in the American economy.

Monetary Policy

But the issue involved more than economics. The creditor-debtor conflict translated into haves versus have-nots. It also involved a sectional cleavage: western silver-mining areas and agricultural regions of the South and West against the more conservative industrial Northeast.

Before 1870, the government had coined both silver and gold dollars. A silver dollar weighed sixteen times more than a gold dollar, meaning that gold was officially worth sixteen times as much as silver. Gold discoveries after 1848, however, had increased the supply and lowered gold's market price relative to that of silver. Producers of silver, which was now worth more than one-sixteenth the value of gold, preferred to sell their metal on the open market rather than to the government. Sil-

ver dollars disappeared from circulation—owners hoarded them rather than spend them—and in 1873, Congress officially stopped coining silver dollars. At about the same time, European nations also stopped buying silver. Thus, the United States and many of its trading partners adopted the gold standard, meaning that their currency was backed chiefly by gold.

Within a few years, new mines in the American West began to flood the market with silver, and its price dropped. Gold became worth more than sixteen times what silver was worth. It became profitable to spend silver dollars, and it would have been worthwhile to sell silver to the government in return for gold, but the government was no longer buying silver. Debtors, who saw silver as a means of expanding the currency supply, now joined with silver producers to denounce the "Crime of '73" and press for the resumption of coinage at the old 16-to-1 ratio.

Congress, split into silver and gold factions, tried to neutralize the issue with compromise legislation: the Bland-Allison Act of 1878, which required the Treasury to buy between $2 million and $4 million worth of silver each month; and the Sherman Silver Purchase Act of 1890, which fixed the monthly purchase of silver in weight (4.5 million ounces) rather than in dollars. But neither act satisfied the different interest groups. The Sherman Act, passed partially in response to economic decline in the mid-1880s, failed to expand the money supply: as the price of silver dropped, the government, required only to buy a certain weight of silver, could spend less to purchase the stipulated number of ounces. Thus, the money supply was not increased as substantially as had been hoped.

While debates over tariffs and money raged, supporters of women's suffrage began to pressure Congress and state legislatures more fervently than ever before. In 1878, Susan B. Anthony, the staunch fighter for human rights who had been rebuffed by the courts when she tried to vote in 1872, convinced Senator A. A. Sargent of California, a proponent of women's suffrage, to introduce a constitutional amendment stating that "the right of citizens of the United States to vote shall not be denied or abridged by the

Women's Suffrage

United States or by any state on account of sex." The bill was killed by a Senate committee, but supporters, such as the National Woman Suffrage Association (NWSA), got it reintroduced many times during the next eighteen years. On the few occasions when the bill reached the Senate floor, it was voted down by senators, who expressed fears that suffrage would interfere with women's family responsibilities and ruin female virtue.

While NWSA and others fought for the vote on the national level, the American Woman Suffrage Association worked for constitutional amendments at the state level. (The two suffrage groups joined in 1890 to form the National American Woman Suffrage Association.) Between 1870 and 1910, there were seventeen referenda in eleven states (all but three of which were west of the Mississippi River) to legalize women's suffrage. These attempts seldom succeeded, but women did attain partial victories: by 1890, nineteen states allowed women to vote on school issues, and three granted suffrage on tax and bond issues.

Throughout the Gilded Age, legislators did address some basic issues, but they focused chiefly on protection of private property and stability of the investment climate. The needs of debtors, farmers, laborers, women, racial minorities, and others who believed themselves disadvantaged found increased expression. But Congress and the state legislatures excluded their interests while catering to the interests of those who already had social and economic privileges.

The Presidency in Eclipse

American presidents in the years between 1877 and 1900 contrasted sharply with forceful predecessors like Andrew Jackson and Abraham Lincoln. Proper, honorable, and honest, Presidents Rutherford Hayes (1877–1881), James Garfield (1881), Chester Arthur (1881–1885), Grover Cleveland (1885–1889, 1893–1897), Benjamin Harrison (1889–1893), and William McKinley (1897–1901) won public respect but seldom provoked strong positive or negative emotions. None of the era's presidents was an inspiring personality, nor could he dominate the factional chieftains of his party.

Rutherford B. Hayes avoided such controversial issues as the tariff and sectional rivalry. He did, however, exercise some presidential power, though mainly in support of privileged business interests. Thus, he took a conservative position on currency by supporting the gold standard and in 1877 ordered troops to quell the railroad strikes. Hayes pleased civil service advocates by appointing reformer Carl Schurz to the cabinet and battling New York's patronage king, Senator Roscoe Conkling. But Hayes demanded that his own appointees contribute to Republican coffers for the 1878 elections.

Hayes, Garfield, and Arthur

When Hayes declined to run for re-election in 1880, Republicans chose James A. Garfield—like Hayes, an Ohio congressman and Civil War hero. After defeating Democrat Winfield Scott Hancock by just 40,000 votes out of more than 9 million, Garfield spent most of his brief presidency trying to secure an independent position among party potentates. His chance to make lasting contributions ended with his assassination in 1881.

Garfield's vice president and successor was New York politician Chester A. Arthur, a spoilsman fired by Hayes in 1877. His elevation to the presidency made reformers shudder; yet he became a dignified and temperate executive. Arthur urged Congress to modify outdated tariff rates, spoke in favor of federal regulation of railroads, and vetoed a number of bills that excessively benefited privileged interests. But his ideas for reducing the tariff and building up the navy were frustrated by party politics within Congress. In 1884, he lost the Republican nomination to James G. Blaine.

The Democrats named New York's Governor Grover Cleveland to run against Blaine. On election day, Cleveland beat Blaine by only 23,000 popular votes; his tiny margin of 1,149 votes in New York gave him that state's 36 electoral votes, enough for a 219-to-182-vote victory in the electoral college. Cleveland may have won New York because in the campaign's last week a local Protestant minister publicly equated Democrats with "rum, Romanism, and rebellion" (drinking, Catholicism, and the Civil War). Democrats eagerly publicized the slur among

New York's large Irish-Catholic population, urging voters to protest by turning out for Cleveland.

Cleveland, the first Democratic president since James Buchanan (1857–1861), exerted more vigorous leadership than had his immediate predecessors. He used the veto extensively against outrageous pension bills and expanded the civil service. His most forceful action was his unsuccessful campaign for tariff reform. Worried about the growing Treasury surplus, Cleveland urged Congress to cut duties on raw materials and manufactured goods. When advisers warned him that his stand might weaken his chances for re-election, the president retorted, "What is the use of being elected or re-elected, unless you stand for something?" But Cleveland's firmness did not prevail. The Mills tariff bill of 1888, passed by the House in response to Cleveland's wishes, was killed by the Senate.

Cleveland and Harrison

In 1888, the Democrats renominated Cleveland, and the Republicans ran Benjamin Harrison, the grandson of President William Henry Harrison (1841). The campaign was less savage than in 1884, though far from clean. Bribery and multiple voting helped Harrison win Indiana by 2,300 votes and New York by 14,000. (Democrats also indulged in bribery and vote fraud, but Republicans were more successful at it.) Those crucial states assured Harrison's victory. Although Cleveland outpolled Harrison by 90,000 popular votes, Harrison carried the electoral vote by 233 to 168.

Harrison was the first president since 1875 whose party had majorities in both houses of Congress. However, he had little control over legislators. He professed support for civil service and appointed Theodore Roosevelt a civil service commissioner. Harrison also signed the Dependents' Pension Act, which provided disability pensions to all Union veterans of the Civil War and granted aid to veterans' widows (if they had to depend on their own labor for support) and to their minor children. The bill nearly doubled the number of pensioners, from 490,000 to 966,000. As a result of the pension act and other grants and appropriations, the federal budget surpassed $1 billion in 1890 for the first time in the nation's history.

Cleveland and Harrison ran against each other again in 1892. This time Cleveland attracted heavy contributions from business and beat Harrison by 380,000 popular votes and by 277 to 145 electoral votes.

In office once more, Cleveland took bolder steps to meet problems of currency, tariffs, and labor unrest. But his actions reflected a narrow orientation toward the interests of business and bespoke political weakness. In order to protect the nation's gold reserve, which was shrinking during the Panic of 1893, Cleveland enlisted aid from bankers, who in 1895 bailed out the nation on terms highly favorable to themselves. Contrary to his campaign promises, however, he made little effort to line up support for tariff reform in the Senate. And when 120,000 boycotting railroad workers paralyzed western trade in the Pullman strike of 1894, Cleveland bowed to requests for federal troops from railroad managers and Attorney General Richard Olney. Throughout Cleveland's second term, events—particularly economic downturn and Populist ferment—seemed too much for the president.

Stirrings of Agrarian Unrest

While the government labored to sustain order and prosperity, inequities in the new agricultural and industrial order were creating the first rumblings of a mass movement that was to shake American society. The agrarian revolt began when farmers' alliances formed in Texas in the late 1870s, then spread across the Cotton Belt and Plains in the 1880s. The movement caught on chiefly in areas where farm tenancy, crop liens, furnishing merchants, railroads, banks, weather, and insects threatened the ambitions and economic well-being of hopeful farmers. Once under way, it inspired visions of a truly cooperative, democratic society.

Agricultural expansion in the West and South exposed millions of people to the hardships of rural life. Uncertainties might have been more bearable if rewards had been more promising, but such was not the case. As growers put more land under cultivation, as mechanization boosted productivity, and as foreign competition increased, supplies exceeded demand for agricultural products. Consequently, prices for staple crops steadily declined. Meanwhile, transportation, storage, and commission fees remained high relative to other prices. Costly seed, fertilizer, manufactured goods, taxes, and mortgage interest combined with social isolation to trap many farm families in disadvantageous and sometimes desperate circumstances.

Even before the full impact of these developments was felt, small farmers had begun to organize to relieve mounting distress. With aid from **Grange Movement** Oliver H. Kelley of the Department of Agriculture, farmers founded a network of local organizations called Granges in almost every state during the late 1860s and early 1870s. By 1875, the Grange had nearly 20,000 local branches and more than 1 million members. Strongest in the Midwest and South, Granges served chiefly as social organizations, sponsoring meetings and educational events to help ease the loneliness of farm life.

As membership flourished, Granges moved beyond social functions into economic and political action. At its 1874 convention, the national Grange proposed to avoid high retail prices by forming local cooperatives to buy equipment and supplies directly from manufacturers. Granges also encouraged the formation of sales cooperatives, whereby farmers would pool their grain and dairy products and then divide the profits. In politics, Grangers used their numbers to some advantage, electing sympathetic legislators and pressing for laws to regulate transportation and storage rates.

Despite their efforts, Granges declined in the late 1870s. A requirement that cooperatives run on a cash-only basis excluded large numbers of farmers, who rarely had any cash. Efforts to regulate business and transportation withered when corporations won court support against "Granger laws." Thus, after a brief assertion of influence, the Grange reverted to an organization of farmers' social clubs.

Rural activism then shifted to Farmers' Alliances, two networks of organizations—one in the Plains and one in the South—that by 1890 constituted a

Mary E. Lease (1850–1933), a fiery and controversial speaker for the Farmers' Alliance and Populist party in Kansas. Tall and intense, she had a deep, almost hypnotic voice that made her an effective publicist for the farmers' cause. *Library of Congress.*

Farmers' Alliances genuine mass movement. The first Alliances sprang up in Texas, where hard-pressed small farmers rallied against crop liens, furnishing merchants, and railroads in particular, and against "money power" in general. Adopting an effective system of traveling lecturers to recruit members, Alliance leaders extended the movement to other southern states. By 1889, the Southern Alliance boasted more than 3 million members, including the powerful Colored Farmers' National Alliance, which claimed more than 1 million black members. A similar movement flourished in the Plains, where, by the late 1880s, 2 million members were organized in Kansas, Nebraska, and the Dakotas.

Alliance members not only pushed the Grange concept of cooperation, but also proposed a scheme to alleviate the most serious rural problems: lack of cash and credit. Their plan called for

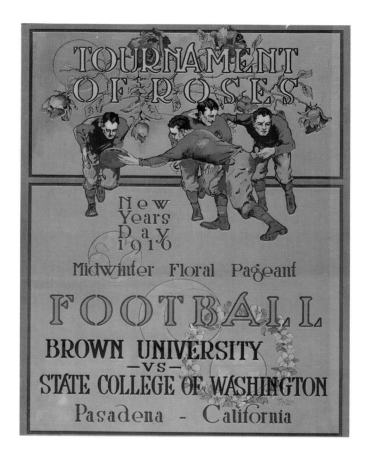

Leisure in America, 1900

A VIGOROUS NATION

By the end of the nineteenth century, the dynamism of the United States was palpable. The country was extending its borders, accumulating wealth, admitting thousands of immigrants, harnessing new technologies, and undergoing rapid changes in social mobility and mores. This energy led to the development of new forms of entertainment and recreation as well as an increase in the amount of time that could be devoted to play.

Football originally drew its audience from the upper classes. By the 1900s, however, the sport was attracting a broader class of supporters; informal games were often played in yards and playgrounds. College football was early tarnished by accusations of unnecessary violence and unscrupulous play, but by 1906 the organization that became the National College Athletic Association had instituted new rules to make the game less brutal and more open (extending the distance to be gained for a first down, for instance, and legalizing the forward pass).

In 1910, more than 2,000 theater companies operated in the United States. Most companies used the same group of actors for a succession of productions, and many presented a new play every week, a pace that often forced resident actors to rely on a limited number of "stock" characterizations. Yet the quality of some productions, particularly those in the large cities, was quite high. Immigrant cultures greatly influenced the American theater; New York City had a number of foreign-language companies, including Kessler's Second Avenue Theatre, which presented musical, comedic, and dramatic productions in Yiddish.

Thomas Edison invented a primitive phonograph in 1877, which he further refined in the late 1880s. Early Edison gramophones played cylinders, not discs; each cylinder had to be an original recording. The development of record discs in 1893 proved a major breakthrough for the recording industry; recordings could now be produced in large quantities, pressed from master molds made of steel. The First World War introduced new technological advances, including the electronic amplifier, which led to the first

Previous page: Rose Bowl poster, 1916. Top: Kessler's Second Avenue Theatre program, 1927. Bottom, left: Edison gramophone, 1903. Bottom, right: Sheet music, 1904.

"all-electric" phonograph in 1925. Sound quality advanced dramatically, and phonographs began to be fixtures in American parlors.

Before the phonograph achieved popularity, sheet music provided the primary means of enjoying popular music at home. After the phonograph became a common household item, however, publishers printed sheet music only if the recording of a song was successful.

Traveling carnivals featuring mechanical rides, games, and sideshows wound their colorful way through the rural areas and small towns of the nation. The ferris wheel and the carousel were a carnival's centerpieces. Between 1875 and 1935,

Right: Giraffe, carved by Daniel Muller, made by Gustav A. Dentzel Carousel Co., before 1903. Below: John Sloan, *Traveling Carnival, Santa Fe,* **1924.**

10,000 carousels were built in the United States, many by the Gustav A. Dentzel Company of Philadelphia. Sadly, by 1980 only 315 carousels still existed.

An exhibition on a much larger scale, a world's fair, showcased a host nation's technological advances and artistic triumphs, drawing crowds of domestic and international visitors. The 1904 World's Fair, held in St. Louis, commemorated the centenary anniversary of the Louisiana Purchase with a focus on education.

A new form of mass media took hold in the last half of the nineteenth century: dime novels became the most popular form of American fiction. These inexpensive paperbound books (most cost a nickel, not a dime) told satisfyingly melodramatic and moralistic stories—good always bested evil. Beadle and Adams was the first and the principal publisher of dime novels; the cover of one of its 1887 efforts featured a black cowboy rescuing the protagonist, Arizona Joe ("a living character of today"), from an Indian attack. Western themes were common; as the country expanded, American readers loved action stories about the wild frontier.

Above: St. Louis World's Fair poster, 1904. Left: Dime novel, 1887.

Subtreasury Plan the federal government to construct warehouses in every major agricultural county. At harvest time, farmers could store crops in these "subtreasuries" while awaiting higher prices, and the government would loan farmers Treasury notes amounting to 80 percent of the market price the stored crops would bring. Farmers could use these Treasury notes as legal tender to pay debts and make purchases. Once stored crops were sold, farmers would pay back the loans, plus a small interest and storage fees.

Growing membership and rising confidence drew Alliances more deeply into politics. By 1890, farmers had elected a number of officeholders sympathetic to their programs— **Rise of** especially in the South. In the Mid- **Populism** west, Alliance candidates often ran on independent third-party tickets and achieved some success in Kansas, Nebraska, and the Dakotas. During the summer of 1890, the Kansas Alliance held a "convention of the people" and nominated candidates who swept the fall elections. Formation of this People's party gave a name to the Alliances' political activism. Two years later, after overcoming regional differences, the People's party held a convention in Omaha, drafted a platform, and nominated a presidential candidate.

The Omaha platform was one of the most comprehensive reform documents in American history. Most of its planks addressed three central issues: transportation, land, and money. Frustrated with weak state and federal regulation, Populists demanded government ownership of railroad and telegraph lines. They urged the federal government to reclaim all land owned for speculative purposes by railroads and foreigners. The monetary plank called for a flexible currency system based on free and unlimited coinage of silver, which would increase the money supply and enable farmers to pay debts more easily. Other planks advocated a graduated income tax, postal savings banks, direct election of United States senators, and shorter hours for workers. As its presidential candidate, the party nominated James B. Weaver of Iowa, a former Union general.

Although Weaver lost badly in 1892, he garnered more than 1 million popular votes (8 percent of the total), winning majorities in four states and 22 electoral votes. Not since 1856 had a third party won so many votes in its first national effort. The party's central dilemma—whether to stand by its ideals at all costs or compromise those ideals in order to gain power—still loomed ahead. But in the early 1890s, rural dwellers in the South and West foresaw a promising future. Amid hardship and desperation, millions of people had begun to believe that they could overcome corporate power with a cooperative democracy in which government would ensure equal opportunity.

The Depression of the 1890s

Early in 1893, shortly before Grover Cleveland became president for the second time, a relatively minor but ominous economic event occurred: the Philadelphia and Reading Railroad went bankrupt. Like other railroads, the Philadelphia and Reading had borrowed heavily to lay track and build stations and bridges. But overexpansion cut into revenues. Profits dwindled, and the company was unable to pay its debts.

The same problem nagged manufacturers. For example, output at McCormick farm machinery factories was nine times greater in 1893 than it had been in 1879, but revenues had only tripled. To compensate, the company tried to boost profits by buying more machines and squeezing more work out of fewer laborers. This strategy, however, only enlarged the debt and increased unemployment.

Banks suffered too. As primary lending agents, banks found their problems compounded when customers defaulted. Failure of the National Cordage Company in May 1893 set off a chain reaction of business and bank closings. During the first four months of 1893, 28 banks failed. By June, the number reached 128. In 1894, one adviser warned President Cleveland, "We are on the eve of a very dark night." He was right; between 1893 and 1897, the nation suffered the worst economic depression it had yet experienced.

As the depression deepened, currency problems

reached a critical stage. The Sherman Silver Purchase Act of 1890 had committed the government to buy 4.5 million ounces of silver each month. Payment was to be in gold, at the ratio of one ounce of gold to every sixteen ounces of silver. But the western mining boom made silver more plentiful, and its value relative to gold fell. Thus, every month the government exchanged gold, whose worth remained fairly constant, for less-valuable silver. Fearful that the dollar, which was based on Treasury holdings in silver and gold, was losing value, merchants at home and abroad began to cash in paper money and securities for gold. As a result, the nation's gold reserve dwindled, falling below the psychologically significant level of $100 million in April 1893.

Currency Problems

President Cleveland, promising to protect the gold reserve, called a special session of Congress to repeal the Sherman Silver Purchase Act. Repeal, however, failed to stop the run on the Treasury. By early 1895, gold reserves had fallen to $41 million. In desperation, Cleveland accepted an offer of 3.5 million ounces of gold in return for $62 million worth of federal bonds from a banking syndicate led by J. P. Morgan. When bankers resold the bonds to the public, they profited handsomely at the nation's expense. Cleveland claimed that the gold reserves had been saved, but discontented farmers, workers, silver miners, and even some members of Cleveland's own party saw only humiliation in the president's actions. Moreover, the deal between Cleveland and Morgan did not end the depression.

In the final years of the century, new gold discoveries in Alaska, good harvests, and industrial growth brought better times. But the depression of the 1890s had hastened the crumbling of an old system and the emergence of a new one. The processes of industrial development and technological change had been under way for some time, but the organizational features of the new business system—consolidation and a trend toward bigness—were just beginning to solidify when the depression hit.

Effect of New Economic Structures

The national economy had reached the point of interdependence, at which the fortunes of a business in one part of the country or the world had repercussions elsewhere. By the 1890s, many companies had expanded too rapidly; when contraction occurred, their reckless investments inevitably crumbled and they pulled other industries down with them. In 1893, for example, five hundred banks and sixteen thousand businesses toppled into bankruptcy. European economies also slumped, and more than ever before the fortunes of one country affected those of other countries.

To complicate matters, American farmers had to contend not only with fluctuating transportation rates and falling crop prices at home, but also with foreign agricultural products. When farmers fell into debt and lost purchasing power, their depressed condition in turn affected the economic health of railroads, farm-implements manufacturers, banks, and other businesses. The downward spiral reversed late in 1897, but the depression left deep scars.

Depression-Era Protests

The depression bared problems in the industrial system. For half a century, technological and organizational changes had been widening the gap between employers and employees. By the 1890s, workers' protests against exploitation threatened economic and political upheaval. In 1894, when the American economy plunged, there were more than thirteen hundred strikes and countless riots. Violence reached an alarming pitch, and radical rhetoric escalated. Contrary to the fears of business leaders, all protesters were not anarchists or communists from Europe come to sabotage American democracy. The disaffected included thousands of men and women who believed that in a democracy their voices should be heard.

Socialism was part of this undercurrent. Socialists generally agreed with Karl Marx, the father of communism, that whoever controlled the means of production held power to determine how well people lived. Marx predicted that workers throughout the world would become so discontented that they would revolt and seize factories, farms, banks,

Socialism

and transportation lines. The societies resulting from this revolution would end exploitation and establish a new order of social justice and equality.

American socialism suffered from internal disagreements and lack of strong leadership. Daniel DeLeon, the West Indian–born head of the Socialist Labor party, and other leaders failed to attract the mass of unskilled workers. American socialists often focused on ideals while neglecting the everyday needs of workers. Besides, most workers sought individual improvement rather than the betterment of all workers, hoping that they or their children would raise their status through education or the acquisition of property, or by becoming their own bosses.

Events in 1894 triggered changes within the socialist movement. That year, the government's quashing of the Pullman strike and of the newly formed American Railway Union created a new, inspiring socialist leader. Eugene V. Debs, the railway union president, had become a socialist while serving a six-month prison term for defying an injunction against the strike. When released, Debs became the leading spokesman for American socialism, combining visionary Marxism with Jeffersonian and Populist antimonopolism. Debs captivated huge audiences with passionate eloquence and indignant attacks on the free enterprise system.

In 1894, however, it was not the tall, animated Debs but a short, quiet businessman from Massillon, Ohio, who captured public attention. His name was Jacob S. Coxey, and he had a vision. Coxey had become convinced that, to help debtors, the government should issue paper money unbacked by gold—purposeful inflation, in other words. As the depression spread, Coxey recommended a federal public works program financed by an issue of $500 million of this "legal tender" paper money to relieve unemployment and revive consumer spending. He planned to publicize his scheme by leading a march from Massillon to Washington, D.C., gathering a "commonweal army" of unemployed workers along the way.

Coxey's Army

Coxey's troops, including women and children, entered the capital on April 30. The next day, the citizen army of five hundred people marched to the Capitol, armed with "war clubs of peace." When Coxey and a few others vaulted the wall surrounding the Capitol grounds, mounted police moved in and routed the crowd. Coxey tried to speak from the Capitol steps, but police dragged him away. As arrests and clubbings continued, Coxey's dreams of a demonstration of 400,000 jobless workers dissolved. Like the strikes, the people's first march on Washington had yielded to police muscle.

Coxey's march was an expression of frustration by people who were seeking relief from uncertainty. Unlike socialists, who wished to alter the economic system, Coxey commonwealers merely wanted more jobs and better living standards. Yet the brutal reactions of officials reveal how threatening the dissenters, from Coxey to Debs, must have seemed to the defenders of special interests.

Populists and the Silver Crusade

Populists, too, were part of the protest activism. In 1892, their presidential candidate had received more than 1 million votes, and as late as 1894, Populist candidates were making good showings in local and state elections in the West and South. Like previous third parties, Populists were underfinanced and underorganized. They had strong and colorful candidates but not enough of them to wrest control from the major parties. Moreover, the two major parties fought to destroy Populist voting strength, especially in the South.

By the 1890s, the threat of biracial political dissent posed by the Farmers' Alliances prompted southern white Democrats to take urgent action.

Curtailment of Black Voting

During the 1880s, southern legislatures had enacted several measures to curtail black voting, including poll taxes and literacy tests. Not satisfied that these measures would thwart a coalition of black and white voters in the Populist party and fearful that northern Republicans might revive federal supervision of elections, southern states tried more directly to prevent all blacks from voting.

Disfranchisement was accomplished in clever and devious ways. In 1876, the Supreme Court had affirmed that the Fifteenth Amendment prohibited states from denying the vote to people "on account of race, color, or previous condition of servitude." But, said the Court, Congress had no control over state elections beyond provisions set by the Fifteenth Amendment (*United States* v. *Reese*). Subsequently, state legislatures found ways to exclude black voters without ever mentioning race, color, or previous condition of servitude. The "Mississippi Plan," adopted in 1890, for example, required all voters to pay a poll tax eight months before an election, to keep and present the receipt at election time, and to prove that they could read and interpret the state constitution. Registration officials applied much stiffer standards to blacks than to whites. In 1898, Louisiana enacted the first grandfather clause, which established literacy and property qualifications for voting but exempted sons and grandsons of those eligible to vote before 1867. The law effectively excluded blacks from voting because few could meet the qualifications and none had been able to vote before 1867. Other southern states initiated similar measures. These and other restrictions proved effective. By the early 1900s, blacks had lost political rights in every southern state except Tennessee.

To a large extent, white fears were unjustified, for fundamental factors impeded the acceptance of blacks by white Populists. Most white farmers could not put aside their racism. Many came from families that had supported the Ku Klux Klan during Reconstruction; some had once owned slaves, and they considered blacks to be a permanently inferior people who would never be able to act for themselves. And poor whites seemed to take comfort in the belief that there would always be people worse off than they were. Thus, Populists seldom addressed the needs of black farmers and used white-supremacist rhetoric to avoid charges that they encouraged racial mingling.

On the national level, the Populist crusade against "money power" settled on the issue of silver. Many people saw silver as a simple solution to the nation's complex ills. To them, free silver meant the end of special privileges for the rich and

Free Silver

the return of government to the people. Using this reasoning, Populists adopted free coinage of silver as their political battle cry. But as the elections of 1896 approached, they faced the dilemma of what strategy to use to translate their few previous electoral victories into larger success. Would they lose their identity by joining with sympathetic factions of the major parties, or would they remain independent as a third party and settle for, at best, minor successes?

The Election of 1896

The presidential election of 1896 brought the nation's political turbulence to a climax. Each party was divided. Republicans, under the direction of Marcus Alonzo Hanna, a prosperous Ohio industrialist, had only minor problems. Since early 1895, Hanna had been maneuvering to win the nomination for Ohio's governor, William McKinley. By the time the party convened in St. Louis in 1896, Hanna had corralled enough delegates to succeed. The Republicans' only distress occurred when the party adopted a moderate platform supporting gold, rejecting a prosilver stance proposed by Senator Henry M. Teller of Colorado. Teller, who had been among the party's founders forty years earlier, walked out of the convention in tears, taking a small group of prosilver Republicans with him.

McKinley and Bryan

At the Democratic convention, silver delegates paraded through the Chicago Amphitheatre wearing silver badges and waving silver banners. "All the silverites need is a Moses," remarked a *New York World* reporter. They found one in William Jennings Bryan of Nebraska. Bryan, a former congressman whose support for free coinage of silver had annoyed President Cleveland, was only thirty-six years old, avidly religious, and highly distressed by what the depression had done to midwestern farmers. As a member of the party's resolutions committee, Bryan helped write a platform calling for free coinage of silver.

When the committee presented the platform to

the full convention, Bryan rose to speak on its be-half. His now-famous closing words ignited the del-egates:

> Having behind us the producing masses of this nation and the world, supported by the commer-cial interests, the laboring interests, and the toilers everywhere, we will answer their [the wealthy classes'] demand for a gold standard by saying to them: You shall not press down upon the brow of labor this crown of thorns, you shall not crucify mankind upon a cross of gold.

The speech could not have been more timely. Indeed, Bryan planned it to be so. Friends who had been pushing Bryan for the presidential nomina-tion now had no trouble enlisting support. Bryan won the nomination, a group of gold Democrats split from the party, and the "great campaign" had begun in earnest.

Bryan's nomination presented the Populist party with a dilemma. Should Populists join Democrats in support of Bryan, or should they nominate their own candidate and preserve their party's independ-ence? Each faction had its supporters. In the end, the convention compromised, first naming Tom Watson of Georgia as vice-presidential nominee to preserve party identity and then nominating Bryan for president.

The election results revealed that the political standoff had finally ended. McKinley, symbol of Re-publican pragmatism and new economic order,

Election Results beat Bryan by more than 600,000 popular votes and by 271 to 176 in the electoral college. It was the most lopsided presidential elec-tion since 1872.

Democrats and Populists had tried to rally the nation. But lean campaign finances and an obses-sion with silver undermined Bryan's effort. Silver, especially, prevented Populists from building the urban-rural coalition that would have given them political breadth. Urban workers shied away from the silver issue because they feared that high prices would result. Labor leaders like Samuel Gompers of the AFL, though partly sympathetic, would not join with Populists because they viewed farmers as businessmen, not as workers. And socialists such as Daniel DeLeon denounced Populists because, un-

William McKinley (1843–1901) ran for president in 1896 on a platform that linked business prosperity with national prestige and economic well-being. *Library of Congress.*

like socialists, they still believed in free enterprise. The Populist crusade collapsed in 1896.

The Populists made a concerted effort to combat special privilege and corruption but foundered be-cause too many people were benefiting from a generally expanding economy. Ironically, by 1920 many Populist reform goals would be achieved, in-cluding regulation of railroads, banks, and utilities; shorter working hours; a variant of the subtreasury system; a graduated income tax; direct election of senators; and the secret ballot.

As president, McKinley signed the Gold Standard Act (1900), which required that all paper money be backed by gold. He also supported the Dingley

The McKinley Presidency Tariff of 1897, which raised duties even higher—though it did expand reciprocity provisions. During McKinley's presidency, domestic tensions subsided. An upward swing of the business cycle and increased money supply from new gold discoveries helped restore prosperity. Freed from care of the economy, McKinley turned his attention to foreign affairs. Good times and victory in war enabled McKinley to beat Bryan again in 1900.

The 1896 election ended the old equilibrium and realigned national politics. The Republican party had become the party of the majority of voters by emphasizing economic progress and broadening its social base to include urban workers. The Democratic party had miscalculated on the silver issue and had held its support only in the South. After 1896, however, party loyalties were not as potent as they once had been. Suspicions of party politics increased, to the point at which some people chose not to vote at all, and voter participation rates declined. A new kind of politics was brewing, one in which technical experts and scientific organization would attempt to supplant the back-room deals and favoritism that had characterized the previous age.

Suggestions for Further Reading

General

Sean Denis Cashman, *America in the Gilded Age* (1984); Ray Ginger, *The Age of Excess*, 2nd ed. (1975); H. Wayne Morgan, *From Hayes to McKinley* (1969); Nell Irvin Painter, *Standing at Armageddon: The United States, 1877–1919* (1987); Alan Trachtenberg, *The Incorporation of America: Culture and Society in the Gilded Age* (1982); R. Hal Williams, *Years of Decision: American Politics in the 1890s* (1978).

Parties and Political Issues

Beverly Beeton, *Women Vote in the West: The Suffrage Movement, 1869–1896* (1986); John H. Dobson, *Politics in the Gilded Age* (1972); Eleanor Flexner, *Century of Struggle: The Women's Rights Movement in the United States* (1959); Elisabeth Griffith, *In Her Own Right: The Life of Elizabeth Cady Stanton* (1984); Ari A. Hoogenboom, *Outlawing the Spoils: The Civil Service Movement* (1961); Morton Keller, *Affairs of State* (1977); Paul Kleppner, *The Third Electoral System, 1853–1892* (1979); Paul Kleppner, *The Cross of Culture* (1970); Michael E. McGerr, *The Decline of Popular Politics* (1986); Walter T. K. Nugent, *Money and American Society* (1968); A. M. Paul, *Conservative Crisis and the Rule of Law: Attitudes of Bar and Bench, 1887–1895* (1969); John G. Sproat, *The Best Men: Liberal Reformers in the Gilded Age* (1968).

Currents of Protest

William M. Dick, *Labor and Socialism in America* (1972); John P. Diggins, *The American Left in the Twentieth Century* (1973); Ray Ginger, *Bending Cross: A Biography of Eugene Victor Debs* (1969); Nick Salvatore, *Eugene V. Debs: Citizen and Socialist* (1982); Carlos A. Schwantes, *Coxey's Army* (1985); David Shannon, *The Socialist Party of America* (1955).

Populism and the Election of 1896

Paolo Coletta, *William Jennings Bryan: Political Evangelist* (1964); Paul W. Glad, *McKinley, Bryan, and the People* (1964); Paul W. Glad, *The Trumpet Soundeth: William Jennings Bryan and His Democracy* (1964); Lawrence Goodwyn, *Democratic Promise: The Populist Moment in America* (1976); Sheldon Hackney, *Populism to Progressivism in Alabama* (1969); Steven Hahn, *The Roots of Southern Populism* (1983); John D. Hicks, *The Populist Revolt* (1931); Richard Hofstadter, *The Age of Reform: From Bryan to FDR* (1955); J. Morgan Kousser, *The Shaping of Southern Politics* (1974); Walter T. K. Nugent, *The Tolerant Populists* (1963); Norman Pollack, *The Populist Response to Industrial America* (1962); Allan Weinstein, *Prelude to Populism: Origins of the Silver Issue* (1970).

Writing to his friend Henry Ford in 1912, Edison observed that

> in a lot of respects we Americans are the rawest and crudest of all. Our production, our factory laws, our charities, our relations between capital and labor, our distribution—all wrong, out of gear. We've stumbled along for a while, trying to run a new civilization in old ways, but we've got to start to make this world over.

Americans had always been preoccupied with reforming their society, with "making it over," and from the 1890s through the end of the First World War, the reform spirit intensified.

By the 1910s, many reformers were calling themselves progressives, and a new political party by that name had formed to embody their principles. Since that time, historians have used the term *progressivism* to refer to the reform spirit in general, while disagreeing about the movement's meaning and membership. Actually, the period between 1895 and 1920 was marked by a series of movements, each aimed at renovating or restoring American society, its values, and its institutions. Collectively, the reforms constituted the Progressive era.

20

THE PROGRESSIVE ERA, 1895–1920

The urge for reform had many sources. Industrialization had brought unprecedented productivity and awesome technology. But it had also included labor strife, waste of natural resources, and abuse of corporate power. Rapidly growing cities facilitated the amassing and distribution of goods, services, and cultural amenities but also magnified problems of poverty, disease, crime, and political corruption. Massive influxes of immigrants and the rise of a new class of managers and professionals shook the foundations of old social classes. And the depression that crippled the country in the 1890s made many leading citizens realize what working people had known for some time: the central promise of American life was not being kept. Equality of opportunity was a myth.

Progressives tried to surmount these problems by organizing ideas and actions around three basic themes. First, they sought to end abuses of power. Trustbusting, consumers' rights, and good government became vital political issues. Second, progressives aimed to supplant corrupt power with the power of reformed institutions, such as schools, charities, medical clinics, and the family. Third, they wanted to apply principles of science and efficiency on a nationwide scale to all economic, social, and political institutions. Their aim was to minimize social and economic disorder and to establish cooperation, especially between business and government.

The Progressives

The Progressive era emerged out of the new political atmosphere that formed after the tumultuous election of 1896 and the issues raised by urban reformers during the previous fifty years. As the twentieth century dawned, the loyalty that political parties had once commanded eroded, and voter turnouts declined. Parties and elections, it seemed, were losing their function of providing Americans with a means of influencing government policies.

The political system was opening up to various interest groups, each of which championed its own brand of reform. These organizations included professional associations, such as the
Issues American Bar Association; wom-
of Reform en's organizations, such as the National American Woman Suffrage Association; issue-oriented lobbies, such as the National Consumers League; civic clubs, such as the National Municipal League; and associations oriented toward minority groups, such as the Society of American Indians. Members of these organizations hoped to advance their own interests and to educate others about their goals. They made politics much more fragmented and issue-focused than in earlier eras.

Although ideas of moral regeneration, political democracy, and antimonopolism lingered from the rural-based Populist movement, the prevailing issues of the Progressive era were mostly urban. The progressive quest for social justice, educational and legal reform, and streamlining of government extended existing urban-reform goals. Formation of the National Municipal League in 1895 and the National Civic Federation in 1900 signaled the beginning of the new reform era. The National Municipal League served as a forum for debates on urban reform issues, such as nonpartisan elections and municipal ownership of public utilities. The National Civic Federation broadened discussion of social reforms, such as workers' compensation and arbitration of labor disputes.

Organizations and individuals that accepted the three progressive themes—opposition to abuse of power, reform of social institutions, quest for cooperation and scientific efficiency—existed in almost all levels of society, but the new middle class of professional men and women formed the vanguard of reform. Offended by inefficiency and immorality in business, government, and human relations, these people set out to apply scientific techniques they had learned in their professions to problems of the larger society.

Many middle-class progressive reformers were motivated by personal indignation at corruption and injustice and felt frustrated by abusers of power. This feeling was voiced by the journalists whom Theodore Roosevelt dubbed muckrakers (alluding to a character in John Bunyan's *Pilgrim's Progress*, who rejected a crown for a muckrake). These writers fed the public's taste for scandal and sensation by investigating and attacking social, economic, and political wrongs. Their fact-filled articles and books exposed such offenses as the sale of tainted meat, fraudulent insurance, and prostitution. Lincoln Steffens's articles in *McClure's*, later published as *The Shame of the Cities* (1904), ranked among the highlights of muckraker journalism. Other well-known muckraking efforts included Upton Sinclair's *The Jungle* (1906), a novel that attacked the meat-packing industry, and Ida M. Tarbell's scathing history of Standard Oil (1904).

Middle-class indignation also revealed itself in opposition to party politics. Male political reformers (women could not vote) had a distaste for
the bargaining and self-serving
Political that they believed infected boss-
Reformers ridden parties. They felt, as journalist William Allen White did, that machines and bosses should "be reduced to mere political scrap iron by the rise of the people." When reformers referred to "the people," however, all too often they meant white middle-class people like themselves. To improve the political process, these progressives urged that candidates be nominated through direct primaries instead of party caucuses, and they also called for nonpartisan

1893	Anti-Saloon League founded	**1910**	Mann-Elkins Act
1895	Booker T. Washington's Atlanta Compromise speech		Mann (White Slave Traffic) Act Ballinger-Pinchot controversy
1898	*Holden* v. *Hardy*	**1912**	Roosevelt runs for president on the Progressive (Bull Moose) ticket
1901	McKinley assassinated; Roosevelt assumes the presidency		Wilson elected president
1904	*Northern Securities* case	**1913**	Sixteenth and Seventeenth amendments ratified
	Roosevelt elected president		Underwood Tariff
1905	Niagara Falls Convention		Federal Reserve Act
	Lochner v. *New York*	**1914**	Federal Trade Commission Act
1906	Hepburn Act		Clayton Anti-Trust Act
	Pure Food and Drug Act	**1916**	Wilson re-elected
1908	Taft elected president		Federal Farm Loan Act
1909	NAACP founded	**1919**	Eighteenth Amendment ratified
	Payne-Aldrich Tariff	**1920**	Nineteenth Amendment ratified

elections to prevent the fraud and bribery bred by party loyalties.

To involve more people and make legislators more responsible, they advocated three reform devices: the initiative, which would empower voters to propose new laws on their own; the referendum, which would enable voters to accept or reject a law; and the recall, which would allow voters to remove officials and judges from office before their terms were up. The goal was efficiency. Government would be reclaimed by replacing the favoritism of the boss system with rational, accountable management chosen by a responsible electorate.

Progressive reformers recoiled from party politics, not from government. They turned to government for aid in achieving most of their goals, for they were convinced that only government offered them the leverage they needed. Science and the scientific method—planning, control, predictability—were central to their values. Just as corporations applied scientific management to achieve

economic efficiency, progressives used expertise and planning to achieve social and political efficiency.

The progressive spirit also stirred some elite business leaders. Successful executives, such as Alexander Cassatt of the Pennsylvania Railroad,

Upper-Class Reformers

supported some government regulation and political reforms to protect their interests from more radical political elements. Others were humanitarians who worked unselfishly for social justice. Business leaders guided organizations like the Municipal Voters League and the U.S. Chamber of Commerce, which supported limited political and economic reform. They aimed to stabilize society by organizing schools, hospitals, and local government like efficient businesses. Women of elite classes often led reform organizations such as the YWCA, which sponsored aid and education for growing numbers of unmarried working women, and the Women's Christian Temperance Union, which participated in numerous causes besides those linked with drinking.

Not all progressive reformers had middle- or upper-class standing. During this era, vital elements of what would become modern American liberalism grew out of the working-class urban experience. By 1900, many urban workers were pressing for government intervention to ensure safety and promote welfare. They wanted improvements in housing and health, safe factories, shorter working hours, workers' compensation, and other "bread and butter" reforms. Often, these were the very people who were or who supported political bosses, supposedly the enemies of reform. Workers knew that bosses needed to cultivate support among their constituents and would cater to everyday needs. In fact, bossism was not necessarily at odds with humanitarianism.

Working-Class Reformers

After 1900, voters from inner-city districts populated by working-class families elected a number of progressive legislators who had trained in the arena of machine politics. The chief goal of these legislators was to establish government responsibility for alleviating hardship that resulted from urban-industrial growth. They opposed such reforms as prohibition, Sunday closing laws, and civil service, all of which conflicted with their constituents' interests.

Some deeply frustrated workers wanted more than progressive reform: they wanted a different society. These people turned to the socialist movement. Some factions had more impact than others. The radical union known as the Industrial Workers of the World—the IWW, or "Wobblies"—reached out to unskilled laborers, promising to unite all workers by enabling them to control their own factories. However, IWW membership probably never exceeded 150,000, and the organization faded during the First World War, when federal prosecution—and persecution—sent many of its leaders to jail.

Socialists

The majority of socialists united behind Eugene V. Debs. Although Debs was never able to develop a consistent program beyond opposition to war and to bourgeois materialism, he was a spellbinding speaker for the radical cause. His speaking tours touched increasing numbers of disenchanted workers and intellectuals. As a candidate for the Socialist party, Debs won 400,000 votes for the presidency in 1904, and in 1912, at the pinnacle of his and his party's career, he polled more than 900,000.

With stinging rebukes of exploitation and unfair privilege, Debs and other socialists made attractive overtures to reform-minded people. Some, such as settlement-house worker and child-labor reformer Florence Kelley, joined the socialist cause. But most progressives avoided radical attacks on free enterprise. Municipal ownership of public utilities was as far as they would go toward changing the system. Indeed, progressives had too much at stake in the capitalist system to overthrow it.

It would be a mistake to assume that a progressive spirit touched all of American society between 1895 and 1920. Large numbers of people, heavily represented in Congress, disliked government interference in economic affairs—except when it strengthened the tariff—and saw nothing wrong with existing power structures. In Washington, "old-guard" Republicans like Senator Nelson W. Aldrich of Rhode Island and House Speaker Joseph Cannon of Illinois championed this ideology. Outside government, this outlook was represented by leaders of big business, such as J. P. Morgan, John D. Rockefeller, and E. H. Harriman.

Progressive reformers operated from the center of the ideological spectrum. Moderate, concerned, sometimes contradictory, they believed on the one hand that the laissez-faire system was obsolete and on the other that a radical shift away from the fundamentals of capitalism was dangerous. Like Jeffersonians, they believed in the conscience and will of the people; like Hamiltonians, they opted for a strong central government to act in the interest of conscience.

Governmental and Legislative Reform

By the turn of the century, professionals and intellectuals were accepting the notion that government could and should exert more power to ensure justice and well-being. They were becoming convinced that public power was needed to counteract inefficiency, corruption, and exploitation. But before reformers could effectively use such power, they would have to capture government from the politicians whose greed had soiled the democratic system.

Reformers first attacked this problem in cities by trying to recast government through structural changes such as civil service, nonpartisan elections, and tighter scrutiny of public expenditures. After 1900, reform momentum brought into being city manager and city commission forms of government and public ownership of utilities (to prevent gas, electric, telephone, and streetcar companies from profiting at the public's expense).

Reformers discovered, however, that the city was too small an arena for the changes they sought. State and federal governments offered more promising opportunities for effecting reform through legislation. Because of their faith in a strong, fair-minded executive, progressives looked to governors and other elected officials to extend and protect reforms that had been achieved at the local level.

The reform movement produced a number of skillful governors who used executive power to achieve change. Their ranks included Braxton Bragg Comer of Alabama and **Progressive Governors** Hoke Smith of Georgia, who introduced business regulations and other reforms in the South; Albert Cummins of Iowa and Hiram Johnson of California, who battled railroads, which dominated their states; and Woodrow Wilson of New Jersey, whose administrative reforms were copied by other governors. Such men were not saints, however. Smith supported disfranchisement of blacks, and Johnson worsened discrimination against Japanese-Americans.

The most notable progressive governor was Wisconsin's Robert M. La Follette. A self-made, small-town lawyer, La Follette rose through the ranks of the state Republican party to the governorship in 1900. As governor, he initiated a multipronged reform program that included direct primaries, more equitable taxes, and regulation of railroad rates. He also established commissions staffed with experts, whose investigations supplied La Follette with facts and figures that he used in fiery speeches to muster public support for his policies. After three terms as governor, La Follette was elected senator and carried his progressive ideals into national politics.

Not all state leaders were as successful as La Follette. To be sure, the crusade against party politics and corruption did accomplish some permanent changes. By 1916, all but three states had direct primaries, and many states had adopted the initiative, referendum, and recall. Political reformers achieved a major goal in 1913, when the states ratified the Seventeenth Amendment, which provided for the direct election of United States senators (formerly elected by state legislatures). But political reforms did not always bring about desired results. Party bosses, better organized and more experienced than reformers, were still able to control elections. Moreover, political reformers found that the courts aided entrenched power in stifling change.

New state laws aimed at bettering social welfare had greater impact than political reforms, especially in factories. Broadly interpreting their powers **Progressive Legislation** to protect the health and safety of their citizens, many states enacted factory inspection laws. By 1916, nearly two-thirds of the states required compensation for most victims of industrial accidents. Under pressure from the National Child Labor Committee, nearly every state set a minimum age for employment (varying from twelve to sixteen) and prohibited employers from letting children work more than eight or ten hours a day. Such laws, however, were hard to enforce. Several groups also joined forces to limit working hours for women. After the Supreme Court upheld Oregon's ten-hour limit in 1908, many more states passed laws protecting female workers. In addition, efforts of the American Association for Old Age Security began to succeed in 1914, when Arizona established old-age pensions. The courts struck down the law, but interest in pensions remained, and in the 1920s many states enacted laws to provide for needy elderly people.

Defenders of laissez faire and free enterprise opposed most of the new regulatory measures. They were motivated by self-interest or a belief that such government programs undermined individual initiative and responsibility. The National Association of Manufacturers coordinated the battle against regulation of business and working conditions. Legislators friendly to special interests connived to weaken new laws by failing to fund their enforcement.

The reformers themselves were not always certain about what was progressive, especially in human behavior. The main problem seemed to be whether it was possible to create a desirable moral climate through legislation. Some reformers, such as members of the Social Gospel movement, believed that only church-based inspiration and humanitarian work, rather than legislation, could transform society. Other people viewed state intervention as necessary to achieve purity, especially in drinking habits and sexual behavior.

Moral Reform

Formation of the Anti-Saloon League in 1893 marked a new turn in the long campaign against drunkenness and its effects on society. This organization joined with the Women's Christian Temperance Union (founded in 1873) to publicize the fact that alcoholism caused liver disease and other health problems. The league was especially successful in shifting the focus away from individual responsibility for temperance to the saloon and the alleged link between the drinking that saloons encouraged and the accidents, poverty, and threat to industrial productivity that resulted from drinking. Consequently, numerous city wards, towns, counties, and states restricted the sale and consumption of alcohol. In 1918, prohibitionists induced Congress to pass the Eighteenth Amendment (ratified in 1919 and implemented in 1920), forbidding the manufacture, sale, and transportation of intoxicating liquors.

Public outrage seethed after 1900, when muckraking journalists exposed interstate and international rings that kidnapped young women and forced them to become prostitutes, a practice called white slavery. Middle-class moralists, already alarmed by a perceived link between immigration and prostitution, prodded governments to investigate the problem and recommend corrective legislation. In 1910, Congress passed the Mann, or White Slave Traffic, Act, prohibiting interstate and international transportation of women for immoral purposes. By 1915, nearly every state had outlawed brothels and the soliciting of sex.

Like prohibition, the Mann Act reflected growing sentiment that state and national governments could improve human behavior by restricting it. Reformers believed that the source of evil was not original sin, but the social environment. If evil were human-made, then it could be destroyed by humans.

New Ideas in Education, Law, and the Social Sciences

Reformers had long envisioned education as a means of bettering society. In 1883, psychologist G. Stanley Hall, whose ideas strongly influenced educator and philosopher John Dewey, noted that the experiences of modern urban schoolchildren differed greatly from those of their farm-bred parents and grandparents. In the early nineteenth century, school curricula chiefly taught moralistic pieties. *McGuffey's Reader*, used throughout the nation, contained homilies such as "One deed of shame is succeeded by years of penitence." Hall and Dewey, however, asserted that modern education had to prepare children for productive lives. The child, not subject matter, should be the focus of school policy, and schools should serve as community centers and instruments of social progress. Above all, said Dewey, education must relate directly to experience. Children should be encouraged to discover for themselves. Knowledge relevant to students' lives should replace rote memorization and outdated subjects. To Dewey, personal growth, not mastery of a given body of knowledge, was the goal of human existence.

Progressive Education

Personal growth also became the driving principle behind college education. The purpose of American colleges and universities had traditionally been to train a select few for the professions of law, medicine, teaching, and religion. But in the late 1800s, institutions of higher education multiplied, spurred by public aid and an increase in the number of people who could afford tuition. Furthermore, curricula expanded as educators sought to

Growth of Colleges and Universities

The objective of progressive education was to free children from the rigid classroom of the past, where pupils sat quietly at attention, and allow them to learn by doing. Subject matter was no longer the major focus of the learning process; progressives made children the center of attention. *Library of Congress.*

make learning attractive to more students and to keep up with technological and social changes. Harvard University, under President Charles W. Eliot, pioneered in substituting electives for required courses and experimenting with new teaching methods.

As colleges and universities expanded, so did the enrollment of women. Between 1890 and 1920, the number of females enrolled in institutions of higher learning swelled from 56,000 to 283,000, accounting for 47.3 percent of total enrollment. Their numbers disproved earlier objections that women were unfit for higher learning because they were mentally and physically inferior to men. But discrimination lingered in admissions and in curricular policies. Most women were encouraged to take home economics courses rather than science and mathematics, and most medical schools refused to admit women.

Law, like education, exhibited new emphases on experience and scientific principles. An influential

Progressive Legal Thought

proponent of the new point of view was Harvard scholar Roscoe Pound, whose writings urged that social experience should influence legal thinking. In practice, Oliver Wendell Holmes, Jr., associate justice of the Supreme Court between 1902 and 1932, led the attack on the concept of law as universal and unchanging. Holmes's view that law should reflect society's needs challenged the practice of invoking precedents in an inflexible way—a practice that often obstructed social legislation. Louis D. Brandeis, a brilliant lawyer who later joined Holmes on the Supreme Court, carried legal reform one step further by insisting that judges' opinions be based on factual, scientifically gathered information about social realities.

New legal thought, however, met some resistance. Judges raised on laissez-faire economic theory continued to overturn the kind of law progressives thought necessary for effective reform. Thus, in 1905, the Supreme Court revoked a New York law limiting bakers' working hours (*Lochner* v. *New York*). As in other cases in which it struck down reform, the Court's majority argued that the Fourteenth Amendment protected an individual's right to make contracts without government interference and that this protection superseded reform sentiments. Judges also weakened federal regulations by invoking the Tenth Amendment, which prohibited the federal government from interfering in matters reserved for state supervision. Thus, the judiciary's use of constitutional principles governing freedom of contract and the division of government powers impeded reform.

However, the judiciary during the Progressive era was not entirely negative. Courts upheld some regulatory measures, particularly those affecting the safety of the general public. A string of decisions, beginning with *Holden* v. *Hardy* (1898) in which the Supreme Court upheld Utah's mining regulations, supported the use of state police powers to protect health, safety, and morals. Judges also recognized federal police powers and the authority of Congress over interstate commerce in sustaining such federal legislation as the Pure Food and Drug Act, the Meat Inspection Law, and the Mann Act.

Meanwhile, social scientists joined with physicians and with organizations such as the National Consumers League (NCL) to bring about some of the most far-reaching of progressive reforms: those in public health. Founded by Josephine Shaw, a socially prominent Massachusetts widow, the NCL initially worked to improve the wages and conditions of young women employed in department stores. After settlement worker Florence Kelley became NCL's general secretary, the organization expanded its activities to include women's suffrage, protection of child laborers, and removal of potential health hazards. Local branches supported such consumer protection measures as the licensing of food vendors and inspection of dairies. They also urged city governments to fund neighborhood clinics that provided health education and medical care to the poor. Their efforts spurred a movement for consumer

National Consumers League and Public Health Reform

and health awareness that has continued to the present.

Between the end of the nineteenth century and the First World War, a new breed of men and women pressed for institutional change, as well as for political reform. Largely middle-class in background, trained by new professional standards, and confident that new ways of thinking would bring progress, these people helped to broaden government's role in meeting the needs of a mature industrial society. Their questioning extended beyond their immediate goals and jostled conventional attitudes toward race and gender.

Challenges to Racial and Sexual Discrimination

W. E. B. Du Bois, the forceful black scholar and teacher, ended an essay in his book *The Souls of Black Folk* (1903) with a call that heralded the twentieth-century civil rights movement. "By every civilized and peaceful method," he wrote, "we must strive for the right which the world accords to men."

By "men," Du Bois meant all human beings, not just one sex. But his statement and its context suggest the dilemma that vexed the two largest groups of underprivileged Americans in the early 1900s: women and nonwhites. Both lived in a society dominated by white native-born males. Both suffered from disfranchisement, discrimination, and humiliation. And for both groups, the progressive challenge to old ideas and customs gave impetus to their struggle for rights, but it posed a dilemma as well. Should women and blacks strive to become just like white men, with white men's values and power, as well as their rights? Or was there something unique about racial and sexual identity that should be retained at the risk of sacrificing some gains?

Black leaders differed over how—and whether—to achieve assimilation. In the wake of emancipation, ex-slave Frederick Douglass had urged "ultimate assimilation through self-assertion, and on no

College students in a physics class at Hampton Institute, in Virginia. Founded in 1868, Hampton Institute was one of the first colleges for black men and women. *Museum of Modern Art.*

other terms." Other blacks, who favored isolation from the cruel white society, supported migration back to Africa or establishment of all-black communities in Oklahoma Territory and Kansas. Still others advocated militancy.

Most blacks, however, could neither escape nor conquer white society. They had to find other routes to improvement. Self-help, a strategy articulated by educator Booker T. Washington, was one of the most popular alternatives. Born in 1856 to slave parents, Washington worked his way through school and in 1881 founded Tuskegee Institute in Alabama, a vocational school for blacks. There, he developed the philosophy that blacks' hopes for assimilation lay in at least temporarily accommodating themselves to whites. Rather than fighting for political rights, he said, blacks should work hard, acquire property, and prove that they were worthy of their rights. Washington voiced his views in a widely acclaimed speech at the Atlanta Exposition in 1895, a speech that became known as the Atlanta Compromise. Whites, including progressives, welcomed Washington's policy of accommodation.

But to some blacks, Washington seemed to favor second-class citizenship. In 1905, a group of "anti-Bookerites" convened near Niagara Falls and pledged a more militant pursuit of such rights as unrestricted voting, equal access to economic opportunity, integration, and equality before the law. The spokesperson for the Niagara movement was W. E. B. Du Bois, a vociferous critic of the Atlanta Compromise. A New Englander with a Ph.D. from Harvard, Du Bois blended the backgrounds of a progressive and a black elite. He had an undergraduate degree from all-black Fisk University and had studied in Germany. Du Bois used scientific methods to compile fact-filled sociological studies of black ghetto dwellers, and he wrote poetically for the cause of civil rights. Du Bois treated Washington politely, but he could not accept submission to white domination.

Du Bois showed that accommodation was an unrealistic strategy, but his own solution may have been just as fanciful. A blunt elitist, Du Bois believed that an intellectual vanguard of cultivated, highly trained blacks, which he called the Talented Tenth, would save the race by setting an example to whites and uplifting other blacks. Such sentiment had more attraction for middle-class white liberals than for black sharecroppers. Thus, when Du Bois and his allies formed the National Association for the Advancement of Colored People (1909), which aimed to use legal redress in the courts to end racial discrimination, the leadership consisted chiefly of white progressives.

Whatever strategy they pursued—accommodation or agitation—African-Americans faced continued oppression. Indeed, under the administration of Woodrow Wilson (1913–1921), discrimination within the federal government expanded; southern cabinet members supported racial separation in rest rooms, restaurants, and offices of government buildings and balked at hiring black workers.

Native Americans also took steps to advance their interests. In 1911, they formed the Society of American Indians (SAI). The SAI consisted of educated, middle-class Indian men and women who worked for better education, civil rights, and healthcare. As part of an effort to cultivate native pride and offset Anglo images of Native Americans represented in Wild West shows, the SAI sponsored American Indian Days.

The SAI's emphasis on racial pride, however, was squeezed between pressures for assimilation of Indians on the one side and tribal allegiance on the other. Its small membership had trouble representing the diverse Indian peoples of America, and its attempt to establish a governing body in which all tribes were represented faltered. At the same time, the goal of achieving acceptance into white society proved elusive, and attempts to redress grievances through legal action bogged down for lack of funds. Ultimately, the SAI had to rely on rhetoric and moral exhortation, which had little effect on poor and powerless Indians. Torn by doubts and internal disputes, the association folded in the early 1920s.

During this time, the progressive challenge to social relations stirred women to seek liberation from the home. Their struggle raised questions of identity. What tactics should women use to achieve equality, and what should be their role in society? Could women achieve equality with men and at the same time change male-dominated society? Answers involved a subtle but important shift in women's politics. Before 1910 or so, those engaged in the quest for women's rights referred to themselves as "the woman movement." This label characterized women striving to move beyond the home into social and welfare activities, higher education, and paid labor. Like some black and Indian leaders, they argued that legal and voting rights were needed to accompany such moves. These women's rights advocates based their claims on the theory that women's special, even superior, traits as guardians of morals and the family would humanize all of society.

"The Woman Movement"

The women's club movement defined a particularly female dimension of progressive era reform. Started as literary and educational organizations, women's clubs consisted of middle-class women who began entering public affairs in the late 1800s. Because they were excluded from office holding, these reformers were drawn less to efforts to revise government than to drives for social betterment. As governments began assuming functions formerly filled by women in households, families, and voluntary associations, they drew women into the political arena more than ever before. But rather than press for reforms such as trustbusting and direct primaries, women tended to work for goals such as regulation of children's and women's labor, housing reform, education improvement, and pure food and drug laws. Such efforts were not confined to white women. The National Association of Colored Women, founded in 1895, was the nation's first black social service organization, establishing a variety of activities, ranging from nurseries to retirement homes.

Women's Clubs

Around 1910, however, some of those concerned with women's place in society began using a new term to refer to their efforts: feminism. Whereas members of the woman movement spoke of duties and moral purity, feminists spoke of rights and self-development. Feminism focused es-

Feminism

pecially on economic and sexual independence. In 1898, Charlotte Perkins Gilman previewed feminist goals in her book *Women and Economics*, declaring that domesticity and female innocence were obsolete and attacking male monopoly on economic opportunity. She argued that women must enter the modern age by taking paid jobs in industry and the professions.

Feminists also supported what they called "sex rights," meaning a single sexual standard for men and women. A number of them joined the birth-control movement led by Margaret Sanger. As a visiting nurse in New York's East Side immigrant neighborhoods, Sanger distributed information about contraception in the hope of preventing unwanted pregnancies among poor women. Her crusade captured the attention of middle-class women who wanted to limit their own families and to control the growth of immigrant masses. It also roused opposition from men and women who saw birth-control as a threat to the family and morality. In 1914, foes caused Sanger to be indicted for sending obscene literature (articles on contraception) through the mails, forcing her to flee the country for a year. Sanger persevered and in 1921 formed the American Birth Control League, which enlisted physicians and social workers to convince judges to allow distribution of birth-control information. Most states still prohibited sale of contraceptives, but the issue had entered the realm of public discussion.

Feminist debates over work and class pervaded the suffrage movement. Until the 1890s, the suffrage crusade was led by elite women who believed that the political system needed more representation from refined and educated persons, such as themselves, and that working-class women would defer to the betters of their sex on political matters. But feminists ardently opposed this logic. To them, achievement rather than wealth and refinement was the major criterion for public influence. Thus, women should have the vote not necessarily to increase the role of elites in public life, but to promote and protect women's economic roles. This rationale implicitly (sometimes explicitly) advocated that all women work for pay, especially outside the home.

Regardless of theoretical arguments, suffragists

Women's Suffrage

achieved some successes. By 1912, nine states, all in the West, allowed women to vote in state and local elections, and women pressed increasingly for national suffrage. Tactics ranged from the moderate but persistent propaganda campaigns of the National American Woman Suffrage Association, led by Carrie Chapman Catt, to picketing and marching by the National Woman's party, led by feminist Alice Paul. All these activities heightened public awareness. More decisive, however, was women's participation during the First World War as factory laborers, medical volunteers, and municipal workers. Their efforts convinced legislators that women could shoulder public responsibilities and gave final impetus to the adoption of the Nineteenth Amendment in 1920.

All the activities by women's clubs, suffragists, and feminists failed to create an interest group united or powerful enough to dent political, economic, and social systems run by men. Like blacks, women knew that voting rights meant little until people's attitudes changed. The progressive era helped women to clarify issues that concerned them, but major reforms would await the future.

Theodore Roosevelt and the Revival of the Presidency

The Progressive era's theme of reform drew attention to government, especially the federal government, as the foremost agent of change. At first, however, the federal government seemed incapable of assuming such responsibility. Dominated by two political parties that resembled private clubs more than bodies of impartial statesmen, the federal government acted mainly for special interests when it acted at all. Then suddenly, in September 1901, the climate changed. The assassination of President McKinley vaulted Theodore Roosevelt, the vice president, into the White House.

Political manager Mark Hanna had warned fellow Republicans against nominating Roosevelt for the vice presidency in 1900. "Don't any of you realize," Hanna asked after the nominating convention, "that

Theodore Roosevelt (1858–1919) liked to think of himself as a great outdoorsman and believed that he and his country should serve as examples of "manliness." *California Museum of Photography, University of California, Riverside.*

there's only one life between that madman and the Presidency?" As governor of New York, Roosevelt angered party bosses by showing sympathy for regulatory legislation, so Republican leaders rid themselves of their pariah by pushing him into national politics.

As president, Roosevelt became a progressive hero. At heart, though, he was a conservative. His brash patriotism, admiration for big business, and dislike of anything he considered effeminate recalled the previous era of unbridled expansion, when raw power prevailed in social and economic affairs. Yet Roosevelt came to similar conclusions as the progressives. His sense of history convinced him that the kind of small government Jefferson had hoped for would not suffice in the industrial era. Instead, economic development necessitated a Hamiltonian system of government, powerful enough to guide national affairs.

Roosevelt's presidency inaugurated the federal regulation of economic affairs that has characterized twentieth-century America. He first turned his attention to big business, where the combination movement had produced giant trusts that controlled almost every sector of the economy. Although Roosevelt has a reputation as a trustbuster, he actually believed in consolidation as the most efficient means to achieve material progress. Rather than return to uncontrolled competition, he preferred to distinguish between good and bad trusts and to prevent bad ones from manipulating markets. Thus he instructed the Justice Department to use antitrust laws to prosecute railroad, meat-packing, and oil trusts, which he believed had unscrupulously exploited the public. Roosevelt's policy triumphed in 1904, when the Supreme Court ordered the dissolution of the Northern Securities Company, the huge railroad combination created by J. P. Morgan and his powerful business allies. In general, however, Roosevelt favored cooperation between business and government. He also exerted pressure on business to regulate itself.

Regulation of Trusts

Moreover, Roosevelt pushed for regulatory legislation, especially after 1904, when he won a resounding electoral victory by garnering the votes of progressives and businesspeople alike. In 1906, he succeeded in getting passage of the Hepburn Act, which imposed stricter control over railroads and expanded the powers of the Interstate Commerce Commission. The act gave the ICC more authority to set railroad rates, though it did allow the courts to overturn rate decisions.

As he had done in securing passage of the Hepburn Act, Roosevelt showed a willingness to compromise on legislation to ensure pure food and drugs. For decades, reformers had been urging government regulation of patent medicines and processed meat. The outcry against fraud and adulteration heightened in 1906, with the publication of Upton Sinclair's *The Jungle*, a fictionalized exposé of Chicago meat-packing plants. On reading the novel, Roosevelt ordered an investigation. Finding Sinclair's descriptions accurate, he supported the Pure Food and Drug Act and the Meat Inspection Act, both of which passed in 1906. Like the Hepburn Act, these

Pure Food and Drug Laws

laws reinforced government regulation. But as part of the compromise to obtain their passage, the government had to pay for inspections and meatpackers could appeal adverse decisions in court.

Roosevelt's policy on labor issues resembled his stance toward business. When, for example, the United Mine Workers struck in 1902, the president intervened by using the progressive tactics of investigation and arbitration. Mine workers wanted higher wages and an eight-hour day, but owners stubbornly refused to recognize the union or arbitrate grievances. As winter approached and fuel shortages threatened, Roosevelt warned that he would use federal troops to reopen the mines and so forced management to accept arbitration of the dispute by a special commission. The commission decided in favor of higher wages and reduced hours but also declared that owners did not have to recognize the union, though management did have to deal with grievance committees elected by the miners. The decision, according to Roosevelt, created a "square deal" for all. The strike settlement illustrated Roosevelt's belief that the president or his agents should have a say in which labor demands were legitimate and which were not.

On the issue of conservation, Roosevelt displayed the same mix of flamboyant executive action and quiet compromise that he applied to other domestic matters. He built a repu-

Conservation tation as a determined conservationist, using presidential authority to add almost 150 million acres to the national forests and to preserve vast areas of water and coal from private plunder. In 1902, he used his influence to secure passage of the National Reclamation Act, sponsored by Senator Francis G. Newlands of Nevada, which set aside proceeds of western public land sales for the purpose of financing irrigation projects. True to the progressive spirit, Roosevelt wanted a "well-conceived plan" for resource management. But compromises and factors beyond his control weakened his scheme. Timber and mining companies shunned supervision of their wasteful practices, and Congress never authorized enough funds to enforce federal regulations.

During his last year in office, Roosevelt moved further away from the Republican party's traditional alliance with big business. He lashed out at the irresponsible actions of "malefactors of great wealth" and supported stronger regulation of business and heavier taxation of the rich. Having promised in 1904 that he would not seek re-election, Roosevelt backed Secretary of War William Howard Taft for the nomination in 1908, hoping that Taft would continue to pursue Roosevelt initiatives. Democrats nominated William Jennings Bryan for the third time, but the "Great Commoner" lost again.

Early in 1909, Roosevelt went to Africa to shoot game, leaving Taft to face political problems that his predecessor had managed to postpone. Foremost among them were tariff rates,

Taft Admin- which had risen to excessive
istration levels. Honoring Taft's pledge to cut rates, the House passed a bill sponsored by Representative Sereno E. Payne that provided for numerous downward revisions. Senate protectionists prepared to amend the House bill and revise rates upward, but progressives, led by La Follette, fought back. Taft was caught between reformers, who claimed that they were carrying on in Roosevelt's antitrust spirit, and protectionists, who still controlled the Republican party. In the end, Senator Nelson W. Aldrich of Rhode Island and other protectionists restored many of the cuts, and Taft signed the Payne-Aldrich Tariff. To many progressives, Taft had failed the test of filling Roosevelt's shoes.

Progressive and conservative wings of the Republican party were rapidly drifting apart. Soon after the tariff controversy, a group of insurgents in the House challenged Speaker "Uncle Joe" Cannon, whose power over committee assignments and the scheduling of debate could make or break a piece of legislation. Taft first supported and then abandoned the insurgents, who nevertheless managed to liberalize procedures by enlarging the important Rules Committee and removing its appointments from Cannon's control. Meanwhile, Taft also angered conservationists by allowing Secretary of the Interior Richard A. Ballinger to remove 1 million acres of forest and mineral land from the reserved list and to fire Gifford Pinchot, the government's chief forester, when he protested a questionable sale of coal lands in Alaska.

In reality, Taft was as sympathetic to reform as Roosevelt. He prosecuted more trusts than Roosevelt, expanded the national forest reserves, signed the Mann-Elkins Act of 1910, which bolstered the regulatory powers of the ICC, and supported such labor reforms as the eight-hour day and mine safety legislation. The Sixteenth Amendment, which legalized federal income tax, and the Seventeenth Amendment, which provided for the direct election of United States senators, were initiated during Taft's presidency (and ratified in 1913). Like Roosevelt, Taft was forced to compromise with big business, but he lacked Roosevelt's ability to maneuver and publicize the issues he supported.

Thus in 1910, when Roosevelt returned from Africa, he found his party worn and tormented. Reformers, angered by Taft's apparent insensitivity to their cause, formed the National Progressive Republican League and rallied behind La Follette for president in 1912. Another wing of the party remained loyal to Taft. Roosevelt, disappointed by Taft's performance, began to speak out and to rekindle public attention. When La Follette became ill early in 1912, Roosevelt, proclaiming himself fit as a "bull moose," threw his hat into the ring for the Republican presidential nomination.

Taft's supporters controlled the convention and nominated him for a second term, but Roosevelt forces formed a third party—the Progressive, or Bull Moose, party—and nominated the former president. Meanwhile, Democrats endured forty-six ballots before selecting as their candidate New Jersey's progressive governor, Woodrow Wilson. The Socialists, by now an organized and growing party, again nominated Eugene V. Debs.

Woodrow Wilson and the Extension of Reform

Wilson won the election with 42 percent of the popular vote, though he did capture 435 out of 531 electoral votes. Roosevelt received about 27 percent of the popular vote. Taft finished a poor third, polling 23 percent of the popular vote and only 8 electoral votes. Debs won 902,000 votes, 6 percent

of the total, but no electoral votes. Thus, fully three-quarters of the electorate supported some alternative to the restrained approach to government that Taft represented.

The campaign had featured sharp debate over the fundamentals of progressive government. On one side stood Roosevelt with a system called the New Nationalism. Roosevelt foresaw a new era of national unity, in which governmental authority would balance and coordinate economic activity. He would not destroy big business, which he saw as an efficient way to organize production. Rather, he would establish regulatory commissions, groups of experts who would protect citizens' interests and ensure wise use of concentrated economic power.

New Nationalism and New Freedom

Wilson offered a more idealistic scheme in his New Freedom. He believed that concentration of economic power threatened individual liberty and that monopolies had to be broken so that the marketplace could again become open. But he did not want to restore laissez faire. Like Roosevelt, Wilson sought to enhance governmental authority to protect and regulate but he stopped short of the cooperation between big business and big government inherent in Roosevelt's New Nationalism.

Roosevelt and Wilson stood closer together than their rhetoric implied. Both men strongly supported equality of opportunity (though chiefly for whites), conservation of natural resources, fair wages, and social betterment for all classes. Perhaps more important, both wanted to expand government activity through strong personal leadership and bureaucratic reform. Thus, even though he received a minority of the total vote in 1912, Wilson could interpret the election results as a popular mandate to subdue trusts and broaden the federal government's concern for social reform.

As president, Wilson had to blend New Freedom ideals with New Nationalism precepts, and in so doing he set the direction of federal economic policy for much of the twentieth century. The corporate merger movement had proceeded so far that restoration of free competition was impossible. Thus, Wilson could only acknowledge economic

Wilson's Policy on Business Regulation

concentration and try to prevent its abuse by expanding government's regulatory powers. His administration moved toward that end with the passage, in 1914, of the Clayton Anti-Trust Act and a bill creating the Federal Trade Commission (FTC). The Clayton Act extended the Sherman Anti-Trust Act of 1890 by outlawing quasi-monopolistic practices such as price discrimination (through which a company tried to destroy competition by lowering prices in some regions but not in others) and interlocking directorates (management of two or more competing companies by the same executives). The FTC was to investigate corporations and issue cease-and-desist orders against unfair trade practices. As in ICC rulings, accused companies could appeal FTC orders in the courts. Nevertheless, the FTC represented a further step in the protection of consumers.

Wilson increased federal regulation of finance with the Federal Reserve Act of 1913. The law established the nation's first central banking system since Andrew Jackson had destroyed the Second Bank of the United States. Twelve newly created district banks would hold the reserves of member banks throughout the nation. (The act created many banks rather than one, to allay the agrarian fear of a monolithic eastern banking power.) District banks would lend money to member banks at a low interest rate, called the discount rate. By adjusting this rate, the reserve bank could loosen or tighten credit. Monetary affairs would no longer depend on the supply of gold, and interest rates would be fairer, especially for small borrowers.

Perhaps the only act of Wilson's first administration that promoted free competition was the Underwood Tariff, passed in 1913. For years, rising prices had thwarted consumers' desires for the material benefits of the industrial age. Some prices were unnaturally high because government tariffs had discouraged the importation of cheaper foreign products. The Underwood Tariff encouraged imports by drastically reducing or eliminating tariff rates. To recover revenues lost due to reductions, the act levied a graduated income tax on United States residents—an option made possible when the Sixteenth Amendment was ratified. The income tax was tame by today's standards. Since incomes under $4,000 were ex-

Tariff and Tax Reform

empt, almost all factory workers and farmers escaped the tax. People and corporations earning $4,000 to $20,000 had to pay a 1-percent tax, and rates for higher incomes rose gradually to a maximum of 6 percent on earnings over $500,000.

In 1916, the First World War and the approaching presidential campaign prompted Wilson to support stronger reforms. Concerned that food shortages might result if farmers could not borrow money to sustain production, the president gave his backing to the Federal Farm Loan Act. The measure created twelve federally supported banks that would lend money at moderate interest rates to farmers. To stave off railroad strikes that might disrupt transportation at a time of national emergency, Wilson pushed passage of the Adamson Act that same year. The act mandated an eight-hour day and time-and-a-half payments for overtime for railroad laborers. Finally, Wilson courted the support of social reformers by backing laws that banned child labor and provided workers' compensation for federal employees who suffered injury or illness.

In selecting a candidate to oppose Wilson in 1916, Republicans snubbed Theodore Roosevelt, who wanted the nomination, in favor of Charles Evans Hughes, former reform governor of New York and Supreme Court justice. Wilson ran on a platform of peace, progressivism, and preparedness. Many voters were attracted by the Democratic party's campaign slogan, "He Kept Us Out of War." Hughes led a fractured party, and he could not muzzle Roosevelt, whose bellicose speeches suggested that Republicans would drag Americans into the world war. Wilson received 9.1 million votes to Hughes's 8.5 million, and the president barely won the electoral college by a 277-to-254 count.

Election of 1916

Wilson's second term and American involvement in the First World War brought a shift away from competition toward interest-group politics and government regulation. During his first term, Wilson had become convinced that laws—and not regulatory commissions, which could easily fall under the influence of the very interests they were meant to regulate—should govern social and economic behavior. The wartime crisis, however, required government coordination of production and cooperation between public and private sectors.

The Progressive Era
in Perspective

The Progressive era was characterized by a welter of confusing and sometimes contradictory goals. Certainly, there was no single progressive movement. On the national level, reform programs ranged from Roosevelt's New Nationalism, with its faith in big government as a coordinator of big business, to Wilson's New Freedom, with its promise to dissolve economic concentrations and legislate open competition. At state and local levels, reformers pursued causes as varied as neighborhood improvement, government reorganization, public ownership of utilities, betterment of working conditions, and moral revival.

The failure of many progressive initiatives testifies to the strength of opposition to reform, as well as to ambiguities within the reform movements themselves. By asserting constitutional and liberty-of-contract maxims, courts struck down some key progressive legislation, most notably the federal law prohibiting child labor. In states and cities, adoption of the initiative, referendum, and recall did not encourage greater participation in government; either those mechanisms were seldom used or they became tools of special interests. On the federal level, new regulatory agencies rarely had resources for thorough investigations; they had to obtain information from the companies they were meant to police. Thus, in many respects, progressives failed to redistribute power. In 1920, as in 1900, government remained under the influence of business and industry.

Yet in spite of all their weaknesses, the numerous reform movements of the Progressive era did refashion the nation's future. Trustbusting, however faulty, forced industrialists to become more sensitive to public opinion, and reforms initiated by insurgents in Congress partially diluted the power of dictatorial politicians. Progressive legislation gave government important tools to protect consumers. The income tax was a first step toward building government revenues and redistributing wealth. But perhaps most important, progressives challenged old ways of thinking: they raised questions

about the quality of American life. Even though these questions remained unresolved, they made the nation more aware of its principles and promises.

Suggestions for
Further Reading

General

John W. Chambers, *The Tyranny of Change: America in the Progressive Era* (1980); Arthur Ekirch, *Progressivism in America* (1974); Louis Filler, *The Muckrakers*, rev. ed. (1980); Richard Hofstadter, *The Age of Reform: From Bryan to FDR* (1955); William R. Hutchinson, *The Modernist Impulse in American Protestantism* (1976); Gabriel Kolko, *The Triumph of Conservatism* (1963); David W. Noble, *The Progressive Mind*, rev. ed. (1981); Nell Irvin Painter, *Standing at Armageddon: The United States, 1877–1919* (1987); Robert Wiebe, *The Search for Order* (1968).

Regional Studies

Dewey Grantham, *Southern Progressivism: The Reconciliation of Progress and Tradition* (1983); Richard L. McCormick, *From Realignment to Reform: Political Change in New York State, 1893–1910* (1981); George E. Mowry, *The California Progressives* (1951); David P. Thelen, *Robert La Follette and the Insurgent Spirit* (1976); C. Vann Woodward, *Origins of the New South* (1951).

Legislative Issues and Reform Groups

Norman H. Clark, *Deliver Us from Evil: An Interpretation of American Prohibition* (1976); Allen F. Davis, *Spearheads for Reform: The Social Settlements and the Progressive Movement, 1890–1914* (1967); Ruth Rosen, *The Lost Sisterhood: Prostitution in America, 1900–1918* (1982); James H. Timberlake, *Prohibition and the Progressive Crusade* (1963); Walter I. Trattner, *Crusade for the Children* (1970). For works on socialism, see the listings under "Currents of Protest" at the end of Chapter 19.

Education, Law, and the Social Sciences

Jerold S. Auerback, *Unequal Justice: Lawyers and Social Change in Modern America* (1976); Lawrence Cremin, *The Transformation of the School: Progressivism in American Education* (1961); David W. Marcell, *Progress and Pragma-*

tism: James, Dewey, Beard, and the American Idea of Progress (1974); Philippa Strum, *Louis D. Brandeis, Justice for the People* (1984); David Tyack and Elizabeth Hansot, *Managers of Virtue: Public School Leadership in America, 1820–1980* (1982).

Women

Lois Banner, *Women in Modern America: A Brief History*, 2nd ed. (1984); Ruth Borden, *Women and Temperance* (1980); Nancy F. Cott, *The Grounding of American Feminism* (1987); Carl N. Degler, *At Odds: Women and the Family in America* (1980); Eleanor Flexner, *Century of Struggle: The Women's Rights Movement in the United States* (1959); Linda Gordon, *Woman's Body, Woman's Right: A Social History of Birth Control in America* (1976); Aileen Kraditor, *The Ideas of the Women's Suffrage Movement* (1965); Ellen Condliffe Lagemann, *A Generation of Women: Education in the Lives of Progressive Reformers* (1970); William L. O'Neill, *Everyone Was Brave: The Rise and Fall of Feminism in America* (1969); Rosalind Rosenberg, *Beyond Separate Spheres: Intellectual Roots of Modern Feminism* (1982); Elyce J. Rotella, *From Home to Office: U.S. Women and Work, 1870–1930* (1981); Sheila M. Rothman, *Woman's Proper Place* (1978).

Blacks

John Dittmer, *Black Georgia in the Progressive Era, 1900– 1920* (1977); Louis R. Harlan, *Booker T. Washington: The Wizard of Tuskegee, 1901–1915* (1983); Jacqueline Jones, *Labor of Love, Labor of Sorrow: Black Women, Work and the Family from Slavery to the Present* (1985); Charles F. Kellogg, *NAACP* (1970); August Meier, *Negro Thought in America, 1880–1915* (1963); Elliot M. Rudwick, *W. E. B. Du Bois* (1969).

Roosevelt, Taft, and Wilson

John M. Blum, *Woodrow Wilson and the Politics of Morality* (1956); John M. Blum, *The Republican Roosevelt*, 2nd ed. (1954); Paolo E. Coletta, *The Presidency of William Howard Taft* (1973); John Milton Cooper, Jr., *The Warrior and the Priest: Woodrow Wilson and Theodore Roosevelt* (1983); Arthur S. Link, *Wilson*, 5 vols. (1947–1965); Arthur S. Link, *Woodrow Wilson and the Progressive Era* (1954); Edmund Morris, *The Rise of Theodore Roosevelt* (1979).

Nicaragua? Panama? Mexico? Where should a canal linking the Gulf of Mexico and the Pacific Ocean be dug? Navy Captain Robert W. Shufeldt knew exactly where—the Isthmus of Tehuantepec in southern Mexico. Such an interoceanic canal, he argued, would become an extension of the Mississippi River. The canal would permit a boat "to load in Saint Louis and discharge her freight in California with but little more than the risk of inland navigation." Indeed, it would "convert . . . the Gulf of Mexico into an American lake." Shufeldt dreamed, too, that the new waterway would help extend "our Empire" to Asia. The Pacific, "the ocean bride of America," would marry West to East. "Let us see to it that no rival flag floats upon [America's] Pacific bosom."

After leading a survey expedition, Shufeldt recommended a canal of 140 locks, deep and wide enough to accommodate nine-tenths of the world's commerce. But the United States Inter-Oceanic Canal Commission rejected Tehuantepec in favor of Nicaragua, whose Lake Nicaragua provided a much larger water supply. In the end, Panama, not Nicaragua, became the canal site—but not until the early twentieth century and under less-than-peaceful circumstances (see page 388).

Shufeldt contented himself with the thought that the "controlling influence" of the United States "upon this hemisphere" ensured its control of a canal, wherever located. He soon turned his expansionist zeal elsewhere. In the 1870s and 1880s, he sailed his United States Navy vessels to Asia, the Middle East, and Africa in search of markets for the increased production of American factories and farms. Most Americans heard little about Shufeldt's global exploits. But the American people did not make foreign policy—the men who governed in Washington, D.C., did, and they were expansionists and imperialists.

This chapter explores the sources of American expansionism and the building, managing, and protecting of an overseas empire in the late nineteenth and early twentieth centuries. The United States empire ultimately stretched from Latin America to Asia, and it faced threats from restless nationalists, commercial competitors, and other imperial nations. The global American empire also aroused critics at home. These anti-imperialist dissenters engaged imperialists in a momentous debate, es-

21

THE QUEST FOR EMPIRE, 1865–1914

pecially at the turn of the century, over the fundamental course of American foreign policy.

Most Americans applauded *expansionism*—the outward movement of goods, dollars, ships, people, and ideas—as a traditional feature of their nation's history. But many became uneasy with *imperialism*—the imposition of control over other peoples, denying them the freedom to make their own decisions and undermining their sovereignty. Imperial control could be imposed in several ways, both formally (by annexation, colonialism, or military occupation) and informally (by economic domination, political manipulation, or the threat of intervention). As the informal methods indicate, imperialism did not refer only to the taking of territory, although that is how most Americans have interpreted the term.

Expansionism and Imperialism Defined

Many Americans in the late nineteenth century disparaged territorial imperialism as unbefitting the United States and opposed joining the scramble for colonies in Asia and Africa. Would not an overseas territorial empire undermine institutions at home, invite perpetual war, and violate honored principles? The United States grew more interested in the "annexation of trade" than in the annexation of territory, as Secretary of State James G. Blaine declared in 1890. Expansionism raised two key questions: when did it become nonterritorial imperialism, and when, to remain successful, did it require colonies? By the early twentieth century, the United States possessed a fair number of colonies and Americans had become imperialists—although more informal than formal imperialists.

In this expansionist era, the federal government did not always adequately fund the vehicles of expansion, and most Americans were too caught up in the daily bustle of life to give much attention to foreign matters. Still, the direction of American foreign policy after the Civil War became unmistakable. Americans intended to exert their influence beyond the continental United States and to reach for more land, more markets, and more international power. A pattern of accelerating activity abroad culminated in the tumultuous decade of the 1890s, when doubters' voices were drowned out by shouts for war and foreign territory.

The Domestic Roots of Expansionism and Empire

The Civil War had temporarily interrupted expansionism, but after that conflict, leaders worked to heal sectional wounds and put the nation back on its traditional expansionist course. The 1876 centennial celebration emphasized national unity. Confederate and Union soldiers met to exchange captured flags. Pride welled up when American machines earned top marks at world fairs. Patriotic societies like the Daughters of the American Revolution (founded in 1890) championed nationalism.

Nationalism

The inflated rhetoric of American exceptionalism and manifest destiny revived. To Reverend Josiah Strong, author of the influential book *Our Country* (1885), Americans were a special, God-favored Anglo-Saxon race destined to lead others. To Social Darwinists, Americans stood as a superior people who would surely overcome all competition and thrive.

With such chauvinistic attitudes, Americans scouted new frontiers to conquer. Secretary of State William H. Seward wanted Cuba; President Grant coveted Santo Domingo; and others envisioned new outposts in the Pacific Ocean. Religious leaders contemplated the conversion of "natives" to Christianity. Businesspeople and farmers talked of untapped overseas markets. Nationalists spoke of exporting America's superior political principles and practices to other peoples and of building an enlarged modern navy of the first order.

The arguments for expansion and empire seemed all the more urgent when Americans anticipated the closing of the frontier at home. In 1893, Frederick Jackson Turner of the University of Wisconsin postulated his frontier thesis, the idea that an ever-expanding continental frontier had shaped the American character. That "frontier has gone, and with its going has closed the first period of American history." Although he did not say so explicitly, some thought Turner believed that a new frontier had to be found overseas.

Turner's Frontier Thesis

Foreign policy has always sprung from the domestic setting of a nation—its needs, wants, moods, and ideals. The leaders who guided America's expansionist foreign relations were the same people who kindled the spirit of national growth at home. They understood the close relationship between domestic developments and foreign relations—that, for example, railroads made it possible for Iowa farmers to transport their crops to seaboard cities and then on to foreign markets. The farmers' livelihood thus became tied to world market conditions, the outcomes of foreign wars, and the viability of the principle of freedom of the seas.

The threads of domestic and foreign events and policies became densely interwoven in other ways. Periodic depressions fostered the belief that the country's surplus production must be sold in foreign markets to restore and sustain economic well-being at home. Tariff increases designed to protect American industry and agriculture from foreign competition adversely affected those who sold to America, prompting them to enact retaliatory tariffs on American products. And the massive influx of immigrants also raised diplomatic, as well as domestic, questions. Ideas of racial superiority, moreover, influenced American policies toward Asian and Latin American peoples of color, who were considered inferior.

Unlike domestic policy, foreign policy is seldom shaped by the people. The spokesmen for expansion and empire belonged to what scholars have labeled the foreign policy elite, or opinion leaders. Better read and better traveled than most Americans, more cosmopolitan than provincial in outlook, and politically active, these opinion leaders believed that the prosperity and security of the United States depended on the exertion of American influence abroad. This elite group, which included Theodore Roosevelt, Henry Cabot Lodge, and John Hay, dominated the making of foreign policy and increasingly urged not only expansionism, but also both formal and informal imperialism. The members of the political elite who, like President Grover Cleveland, favored economic expansion and United States hegemony (that is, dominance) in South America, but not the annexation of overseas territory, gradually lost ground.

Foreign Policy Elite

With a mixture of self-interest and idealism typical of American thinking on foreign policy, advocates of empire believed that imperialism benefited both Americans and those who came under their control. When they intervened in other lands or lectured weaker states, Americans defended their behavior on the grounds that they were extending the blessings of liberty and prosperity to less fortunate people. To critics at home and abroad, however, American paternalism appeared hypocritical. They charged that to coerce foreigners to behave like Americans violated cherished American ideals. The persistent American belief that other people cannot solve their own problems and that only the American model of development is appropriate produced what historian William Appleman Williams has called "the tragedy of American diplomacy."

Factory, Farm, and Foreign Affairs

Many businesspeople and farmers savored expansion and ultimately endorsed empire. They looked to profits from foreign sales. Fear generated foreign trade as well, for the nation's farms and factories produced more than Americans could consume. Foreign commerce, it was assumed, served as a safety valve to avert or relieve economic depression.

The tremendous economic growth of the United States after the Civil War stimulated foreign trade. In 1865, United States exports totaled $234 million; in 1914, $2.5 billion. In the 1870s, the United States began to enjoy a long-term favorable balance of trade (exporting more than it imported). Most American products went to Britain, Europe, and Canada, but increasing amounts flowed to new markets in Latin America and Asia. Agricultural goods accounted for about two-thirds of the total exports in 1900. Manufactured goods led foreign sales for the first time in 1913, when the United States ranked third behind only Britain and Germany in such exports.

Growth of Foreign Trade

IMPORTANT EVENTS

1861–69	Seward is secretary of state
1866	Transatlantic cable completed
	France withdraws from Mexico
1867	Alaska and Midway acquired
1868	Burlingame Treaty with China
1871	*Alabama* claims settled
1883	Advent of New Navy
1889	First Pan-American Conference
1890	Mahan, *The Influence of Sea Power upon History*
1893	Hawaiian revolution begins
1895	Crisis over Venezuela
	Cuban revolution begins
1896	McKinley elected president
1898	Sinking of the *Maine*
	Spanish-American-Cuban-Filipino War
	Hawaii and Wake Island annexed
1899	Senate passes Treaty of Paris
	First Open Door note
	Outbreak of Philippine Insurrection
1900	Second Open Door note
	McKinley re-elected
1901	Theodore Roosevelt becomes president
	Philippine insurrection suppressed
	Hay-Pauncefote Treaty
1903	Panama breaks from Colombia
	United States granted canal rights in Panama
	Platt Amendment
1904	Roosevelt Corollary
1905	Portsmouth Conference
	Taft-Katsura Agreement
1906	San Francisco segregates Asian schoolchildren
	United States invades Cuba
1907	Great White Fleet
	Gentleman's agreement with Japan
1908	Root-Takahira Agreement
1912	U.S. troops occupy Nicaragua
1914	First World War begins
	Panama Canal opens

America's large businesses looked to foreign markets, especially in the 1890s, when it became clear that industrial production was outdistancing consumption. In the 1870s and 1880s, about two-thirds of all American petroleum was exported, and in succeeding decades the figure was about one-half. By the turn of the century, 15 percent of America's iron and steel and 50 percent of its copper were sold abroad, making many workers in those industries dependent on exports. George Westinghouse marketed his air brakes in Europe, and almost as many Singer sewing machines were exported as were sold at home. In addition, direct American investments abroad reached $3.5 billion by 1914, placing the United States among the top four investor countries.

United States economic expansion was especially impressive in Latin America, arousing Washington's diplomatic interest in its neighbors to the south.

Economic Expansion in Latin America United States exports to Latin America exceeded $50 million in the 1870s and $300 million in 1914. Investments by United States citizens in Latin America amounted to a towering $1.26 billion in 1914. In 1899, two of the largest banana

Singer sewing machines joined many other American products in penetrating global markets. In 1890 three-quarters of the sewing machines sold in the world were Singers. The caption for this company-sponsored photograph of the king of Ou (Caroline Islands, in the Pacific) read: "The Herald of Civilization—Missionary Work of the Singer Manufacturing Company." *Courtesy, Robert B. Davies,* Peacefully Working to Conquer the World.

importers merged to form the United Fruit Company. Owning much of the land (more than 1 million acres in 1913) and the railroad and steamship lines of Central America, United Fruit became a major economic and political force in the region. As for Mexico, United States capitalists came to own its railroads and mines. By 1910, Americans controlled 43 percent of Mexican property and produced more than half that nation's oil.

Economic expansion abroad became both a reason and a mechanism for exerting political influence. Indeed, by the early twentieth century United States economic interests were influencing policies on taxes and natural resources in countries like Cuba and Mexico. American interests were responsible for drawing Hawaii into the United States imperial net and for spreading American cultural values abroad. Religious missionaries and Singer

executives, for example, joined hands in promoting the "civilizing medium" of the sewing machine. "The world is to be Christianized and civilized," declared Josiah Strong. "And what is the process of civilizing but the creating of more and higher wants. Commerce follows the missionary."

In the United States, most people championed economic expansion. Anti-imperialists, however, drew the line between expansionism and imperialism: profitable and fair trade relationships, yes; exploitation, no. Some also cautioned against letting American business activity abroad draw the United States into unwanted diplomatic crises and wars. But it did.

Looking Outward, 1860s–1880s

One of the chief architects of the United States empire was William H. Seward. As secretary of state (1861–1869), he envisioned a large, coordinated American empire encompassing **William H.** Canada, the Caribbean, Cuba, Cen- **Seward** tral America, Mexico, Hawaii, Iceland, Greenland, and Pacific islands. It would be built not by war, but by a natural process of gravitation toward the attractive, republican United States; commerce would hurry the process. To ensure the unity of this empire, Seward appealed for a canal across Central America, a transcontinental American railroad to link up with Asian markets, and a telegraph system to speed communications.

Most of Seward's plans were blocked by a combination of anti-imperialists and political foes. Anti-imperialists like Senator Carl Schurz and E. L. Godkin, editor of the magazine *The Nation*, believed that the country already had enough unsettled land and that creating a showcase of democracy and prosperity at home would best persuade other peoples to adopt American institutions and principles. Some anti-imperialists, sharing the racism of the times, opposed the annexation of territory populated by "inferior" dark-skinned people, such as Santo Domingo or Cuba.

Although political foes sought to punish Seward

by denying him his imperial dreams, he did enjoy some successes. When an American naval officer seized the Midway Islands in 1867, Seward laid claim to them for the United States. That same year, he paid Russia $7.2 million for the 591,000 square miles of Alaska. He also shepherded the Burlingame Treaty (1868) through the Senate. This treaty with China provided for free immigration between the two countries. The secretary's forceful handling of French interference in Mexico also enhanced his reputation. In 1861, Napoleon III had placed Archduke Ferdinand Maximilian of Austria on the throne in Mexico. Preoccupied with the Civil War, Seward could do little to help the Mexicans dislodge the intruding Europeans. But in 1866, as American troops headed for the Mexican border, Seward cited the Monroe Doctrine and told the French to get out. Napoleon, troubled at home and now opposed by both Mexicans and Americans, abandoned his venture.

Seward's dream of a world knit together into a giant communications system was satisfied. In 1866, an underwater transatlantic cable linked European and American telegraph networks. Americans also strung telegraph lines to Latin America, reaching Chile in 1890. Information about markets, diplomatic crises, and war flowed steadily and quickly.

Seward's successor, Hamilton Fish (1869–1877), inherited the knotty and emotional problem of the *Alabama* claims. The *Alabama* and other vessels built by Great Britain for the Confederacy during the Civil War had preyed on Union shipping. Senator Charles Sumner demanded that Britain pay $2 billion in damages or cede Canada to the United States, but Fish patiently took the question to the bargaining table. In 1871, Britain and America signed the Washington Treaty, whereby the British apologized and agreed to the creation of a tribunal, which later awarded the United States $15.5 million. Disputes over fishing rights along the North Atlantic coast and the hunting of seals in the Bering Sea near Alaska also dogged Anglo-American relations and would continue to do so for decades. Yet the two powers were coming to the conclusion that rapprochement rather than confrontation best served their interests.

The convening in 1889 of the first Pan-American Conference in Washington, D.C., bore witness to growing ties between the United States and Latin America. Secretary of State Blaine sponsored the meeting to improve commercial relations. The Latin American conferees toured United States factories and then negotiated several general agreements. To perpetuate inter-American cooperation, they founded the Pan American Union.

Anglo-American Relations

Pan-American Conference

As the United States acquired new territories and markets and extended its influence abroad, the call went out for an improved and enlarged navy. Captain Alfred T. Mahan became a major popularizer for the "New Navy." Because foreign trade was vital to United States well-being, he argued, the nation required an efficient navy to protect its shipping; in turn, a navy required colonies for bases. Mahan's widely read book, *The Influence of Sea Power upon History* (1890), sat on every serious expansionist's shelf. Theodore Roosevelt consulted Mahan, sharing his belief in the linkage of trade, navy, and colonies.

New Navy

Until its modernization, the American navy was in a sorry state. Many of its wooden ships were rotting. But in 1883, Congress authorized construction of the first steel-hulled warships. Gradually, the United States Navy shifted from sail to steam and from wood to steel. New Navy ships like the *Maine*, the *Oregon*, and the *Boston* thrust the United States into naval prominence. Many of the steel vessels were named for states and cities to kindle patriotism and local support for naval expansion. The enlarged navy gave the United States the tools to expand and build a greater empire.

Crises in the 1890s: Hawaii, Venezuela, and Cuba

When the United States became engaged in a number of crises in the 1890s, the New Navy warships were put to the test. For decades, the Hawaiian Islands had commanded American attention. This major Pacific way station became important for trade with Asia and had long been a site of missionary work. Its undeveloped but strategic port of Pearl Harbor tempted naval expansionists, and the vast sugar plantations of the islands attracted American entrepreneurs. In 1875, the United States signed a treaty granting Hawaiian sugar duty-free entry into the American market; the Hawaiian sugar industry boomed and became dependent on mainland business. When Congress revised the tariff laws in the early 1890s, however, it eliminated the special provision for Hawaiian sugar. American planters in Hawaii suffered losses as sugar exports to the United States declined. To gain exemption from American tariffs, a group of planters called the Annexation Club plotted a revolution.

In January 1893, the white minority overthrew the native monarch, Queen Liliuokalani. Their success stemmed in part from the support of the chief

Annexation of Hawaii

American diplomat in Honolulu, John L. Stevens, who saw to it that sailors from the warship *Boston* encircled the royal palace. Stevens informed Washington that the "Hawaiian pear is now fully ripe, and this is the golden hour . . . to pluck it." Against the protests of Japan, whose nationals accounted for about 40 percent of Hawaii's population (Americans constituted only 5 percent), President Benjamin Harrison sent a treaty of annexation to the Senate. But incoming President Grover Cleveland, who disapproved of forced annexation, withdrew it. Five years later, during the Spanish-American-Cuban-Filipino War, President William McKinley successfully maneuvered annexation through Congress.

The Venezuelan crisis of 1895 also gave the United States an opportunity to express its expansive mood. For decades, Venezuela and Great

Venezuelan Crisis

Britain had squabbled over the border between Venezuela and British Guiana. The disputed territory contained rich gold deposits and the mouth of the Orinoco River, the commercial gateway to northern South America. Venezuela asked for American help. President Cleveland decided that the "mean and hoggish" British had to be warned away. In July 1895, Secretary of State Richard Olney sent the British a brash message. After lecturing the British about the Monroe Doc-

trine, Olney declared: "To-day the United States is practically sovereign on this continent, and its fiat is law upon the subjects to which it confines its interposition."

This statement of United States hegemony did not impress the British, who rejected American interference in what they considered a local issue. American jingoistic nationalists clamored for action. But neither London nor Washington wanted war. The British, seeking international friends to counter intensifying competition from Germany, quietly retreated from the crisis. In 1896, an Anglo-American arbitration board divided the disputed territory. Throughout the deliberations, Venezuela was barely consulted. Thus, the United States displayed a trait common to imperialists: a disregard for the rights and sensibilities of small nations.

In 1895, another crisis rocked Latin America: the Cuban revolution against Spain. From 1868 to 1878, the Cubans had battled their mother country.

Cuban Revolution

Slavery was abolished but independence denied. The Cuban insurgents waited for another chance. José Martí, one of the heroes of Cuban history, collected money, arms, and men in the United States. As in the case of Hawaii, a change in American tariff policy hastened the revolution. The Wilson-Gorman Tariff (1894) imposed a duty on Cuban sugar, which had been entering the United States duty-free. The Cuban economy, highly dependent on exports, was thrown into turmoil.

From American soil, Martí launched a revolution that became gruesome in its human and material costs. Rebels burned sugar-cane fields and razed mills. The Spanish retaliated under the command of Valeriano Weyler, soon dubbed "Butcher." He instituted a policy of "reconcentration": an estimated 300,000 Cubans of all ages were herded into fortified towns and camps to separate the insurgents from their many supporters. Hunger, starvation, and disease in the resettlement camps led to mass deaths; tens of thousands perished. The island's economy deteriorated badly, and American investments of $50 million became jeopardized.

As tragic stories of atrocity and destruction reached the United States—and were played up by the American yellow press—people grew angry with the Spanish and sympathetic toward the insurrectionists. In late 1897, a new government came to power in Madrid. The Spanish modified reconcentration and promised that Cuba would be given some autonomy.

President William McKinley had come to office an imperialist. The 1896 Republican platform on which he ran demanded both an enlarged American empire (Hawaii, the Virgin Islands, and a Nicaraguan canal) and Cuban independence. In his annual message in December 1897, McKinley surveyed the Cuban crisis, ruling out American intervention while Spain was walking the path of reform. McKinley wanted to avoid war if at all possible.

Events in the first few months of 1898 sabotaged the Spanish reforms and exhausted American patience. Early in January, antireform pro-Spanish loyalists and army personnel rioted in Havana. After the riots, Washington officials ordered the battleship *Maine* to Havana harbor to demonstrate United States concern and protect American citizens. On February 15, explosions ripped the *Maine*, killing 260 American officers and crew. Americans were quick to blame Spain for the disaster.

Sinking of the *Maine*

Spain's image in the United States had been further undermined a week earlier, when William Randolph Hearst's inflammatory *New York Journal* published a stolen private letter from Enrique Dupuy de Lôme, the Spanish minister in Washington. In the letter, de Lôme scorned McKinley and revealed Spanish determination to fight on in Cuba. In March, an irritated McKinley asked for $50 million in defense funds, and Congress complied unanimously. The naval board created to investigate the sinking of the *Maine* then reported that a mine had caused the explosion. (A study by Admiral Hyman G. Rickover in 1976 blamed the explosion on an internal accident.) The panel did not assign responsibility, but restless Americans blamed Spain.

The impact of these events greatly reduced McKinley's diplomatic options. He decided to send Spain an ultimatum. In late March, the United States insisted that Spain accept an armistice, end reconcentration, and designate McKinley as arbiter. Implicit was the demand that Spain grant Cuba its independence. Yet no Spanish government could have given up Cuba and remained in office. Nonetheless, Madrid abolished reconcentration and accepted an armistice on the condition that the insurgents agree first.

Wanting more, McKinley began to write a war message to Congress. After completing it, however, he received the news that Spain had gone one step further and declared a unilateral armistice. McKinley hesitated, but he could no longer tolerate the chronic disorder just ninety miles off the American coast. On April 11, the president asked Congress for authorization to use force, as "an impartial neutral," to effect "a rational compromise between the contestants."

The Spanish-American-Cuban-Filipino War

Congress debated for more than a week and then on April 19 declared Cuba free and independent, directing the president to use force to remove Spanish authority from the island. The legislators also passed the Teller Amendment, which disclaimed any American intention to annex Cuba. McKinley beat back a congressional amendment to recognize the rebel government, for he believed that the Cubans were not ready for self-government and would need a period of American tutoring.

The motives of the Americans who favored war were mixed and complex. McKinley's April message expressed a humanitarian impulse to stop the bloodletting, concern for commerce and property, and the need to end the nightmarish anxiety once and for all. Republican politicians advised McKinley that they would lose the upcoming congressional elections unless the Cuban question was solved. Many businesspeople, who had been hesitant before the crisis of early 1898, joined many farmers in the belief that removing Spain from Cuba would open new markets for surplus production—a belief to which the depression of the 1890s had given urgency.

Motives for War

Inveterate imperialists saw the war as an opportunity to fulfill what Senator Henry Cabot Lodge called the "large policy." Naval enthusiasts could prove the worth of the New Navy. Conservatives, alarmed by violent labor strikes and populism, welcomed war as a national unifier. Some of those too young to remember the Civil War looked on war as an adventure. Anglo-Saxon supremacists like politician Albert Beveridge shouted, "God's hour has struck!" Underlying all explanations for this war was the spirit and reality of expansionism, which had been moving the nation ever outward in the last half of the nineteenth century.

Secretary of State John Hay called it a "splendid little war," but it was hardly splendid. More than 5,400 Americans died, but only 379 of them in combat. The rest fell to malaria and **Conditions in the Army** yellow fever spread by mosquitoes. Food was bad and medical care was unsophisticated. Black troops, about 10,000 in number, saw no relief from racism and Jim Crow. Their regiments were segregated, and they were constantly insulted.

Before Americans began to fight and die in Cuba, the first news of war came from faraway Asia. It surprised many Americans, ignorant of the steady United States push into the Pacific, **Dewey in the Philippines** the dreams of farmers and businesspeople for a huge market in China, and the foreign policy elite's knowledge of the Spanish colony of the Philippines. On May 1, 1898, Commodore George Dewey's New Navy ship the *Olympia*, leading an American squadron, steamed into Manila Bay, the Philippines, and wrecked the Spanish fleet. Dewey became an instant hero. His sailors had to be handed volumes of the *Encyclopaedia Britannica* to acquaint them with this strange land, but officials in Washington knew that Manila ranked with Pearl Harbor as a choice harbor.

Facing rebels and Americans in both Cuba and the Philippines, Spanish resistance collapsed rapidly. American ships had early blockaded Cuban ports to prevent Spain from reinforcing and resupplying its army on the island. On July 3, the Spanish Caribbean squadron, trapped in Santiago harbor, made a desperate attempt to escape but was destroyed by American warships. American troops did not get into a ground war until after June 22, the day several thousand of them landed near Santiago de Cuba and laid siege to the western city. On July 17, the Spanish garrison at Santiago capitulated. Several days later, American forces assaulted the Spanish island colony of Puerto Rico. And Manila could not withstand the pressure from Americans and from the Filipino insurgents led by Emilio Aguinaldo. Losing on all fronts, Madrid sued for peace. Spain and the United States signed an armistice on August 12.

In Paris in December, American and Spanish negotiators agreed on the peace terms: independence for Cuba, cession of the Philippines, Puerto Rico, and Guam (an island in the **Treaty of Paris** Pacific) to the United States, and American payment of $20 million to Spain for the new American territories. Filipino nationalists tried to persuade American officials to set their nation free but were rebuffed. The American empire now stretched deep into Asia. The annexation of Wake Island and Hawaii in 1898 and Samoa in 1899 gave American traders, missionaries, and naval promoters other steppingstones to China. Puerto Rico provided a long-desired base in the Caribbean that could help protect an American-built isthmian canal.

Taste of Empire: Imperialists and Anti-Imperialists Debate

During the war, the *Washington Post* noted that the "taste of empire is in the mouth of the people." But as the debate over the Treaty of Paris intensified, it became evident that many Americans found the taste sour. Anti-**Anti-Imperialist Arguments** imperialists like William Jennings Bryan, Andrew Carnegie, and Senator George Hoar argued vigorously against annexing the Philippines. They were disturbed that a war to free Cuba had led to an empire that reached into Asia. Their arguments varied. Some appealed to principle, citing the Dec-

"Declined with thanks" reads this 1900 *Puck* magazine cartoon. President William McKinley measures Uncle Sam, fattened by several imperialist meals, as a group of anti-imperialists led by Carl Schurz futilely attempts to administer an antidote. The message was clear: the United States would continue to expand. *Library of Congress.*

laration of Independence and the Constitution: the conquest of people against their will violated the concept of self-determination. Others protested that the dispatch of troops overseas by the president, as commander-in-chief, greatly increased the power of the presidency and subverted the constitutional checks-and-balances system. Still others argued that the United States could acquire markets without having to subjugate foreign peoples. And reform-minded critics emphasized domestic priorities over foreign ventures.

The imperialists answered their critics by sketching a scenario of American greatness: merchant ships plying the waters to Asian markets; naval vessels cruising the Pacific to protect

Arguments for Empire American interests; missionaries uplifting inferior peoples. Furthermore, insurgents were beginning to resist American rule, and it was cowardly to

pull out under fire. Germany and Japan, two major international competitors, seemed ready to seize the Philippines if the United States did not. National honor dictated that Americans keep what they had shed blood to take.

The anti-imperialists entered the debate with many handicaps. Possession of the Philippines was an accomplished fact; the anti-imperialists' role was thus a negative one. Then, too, they were internally divided, never able to launch an effective campaign. Although many of them belonged to the Anti-Imperialist League, they differed on so many domestic issues that it was difficult for them to speak with one voice on a foreign question. They were also inconsistent: Carnegie would accept colonies if they were not acquired by force; Hoar voted for the annexation of Hawaii but against that of the Philippines.

On February 6, 1899, the Senate passed the

Taste of Empire: Imperialists and Anti-Imperialists Debate

Treaty of Paris by a 57-to-27 vote. All but two Republicans voted with their president; twenty-two Democrats voted no, but ten voted for the treaty. The latter group was probably influenced by Bryan, who had served as a colonel during the war; he urged a favorable vote in order to end the war and then push for Philippine independence. An amendment promising independence as soon as the Filipinos formed a stable government was defeated only by the tie-breaking ballot of the vice president.

Asian Troubles: Open Door in China, Filipino Insurrection, and Japan

Meanwhile, the Germans, Japanese, Russians, French, and British were creating spheres of interest (see map) in China. Within their spheres, the imperial powers built fortified bases, leased territory, and claimed exclusive economic privileges. American religious leaders, whose missions in China had doubled to one thousand in the 1890s, and business interests, which saw trade opportunities threatened, petitioned Washington to halt the dismemberment before they were closed out. What good were the Philippines as steppingstones to China if there was nothing left to step into?

Secretary of State Hay recognized that the United States could not force the imperial powers out of China, but he was determined to protect American commerce. In September 1899, **Open Door Policy** Hay sent the imperial nations a note asking them to respect the principle of equal trade opportunity—an Open Door—for all nations in their spheres. Germany, France, and the others sent evasive replies, privately complaining that the United States was seeking for free the trade rights that the others had gained and maintained at considerable cost. Then in 1900, a secret Chinese society called the Boxers revolted against the foreigners in their midst and laid siege to the foreign legations in Beijing (Peking). The United States joined the imperialists in sending troops to Beijing to lift the siege. Hay, in a second Open Door note, dated July 3, 1900, instructed the other nations to preserve China's territorial integrity. He also called again for "equal and impartial trade."

Hay's foray into Asian politics settled little, but the Open Door policy became a central element in United States diplomacy. Actually, the Open Door had long been an American principle, for as a trading nation, the United States opposed barriers to international commerce and demanded equal access to markets. After 1900, when the United States began to emerge as the premier world trader, the Open Door policy became an instrument first to pry open markets and then to dominate them—not just in China, but throughout the world. The Open Door, however, was not just a policy; it was also an ideology. The tenets of this ideology were that America's domestic well-being required exports, that foreign trade would suffer interruption unless the United States intervened abroad to implant American principles and keep foreign markets open, and that the closing of any area to American products, citizens, or ideas threatened the survival of the United States itself.

In the Philippines, meanwhile, the United States antagonized its new colonials. Emilio Aguinaldo, the Philippine nationalist leader, believed that **Philippine Insurrection** Dewey had promised independence for his country. But after the victory, Aguinaldo was ordered out of Manila and isolated from decisions affecting his nation. American racial slurs and paternalistic attitudes infuriated nationalistic Filipinos, and they felt betrayed by the Treaty of Paris.

In January 1899, Aguinaldo proclaimed an independent Philippine Republic. Soon, the Filipinos took up arms. Before the Philippine Insurrection was suppressed in 1901, more than 5,000 Americans and more than 200,000 Filipinos lay dead. The defeat of the Filipinos was followed by the Americanization of the islands and the growth of the Philippine economy as a satellite of the United States economy. In 1916, the Jones Act promised Filipino independence, but not until thirty years later was Aguinaldo's dream realized.

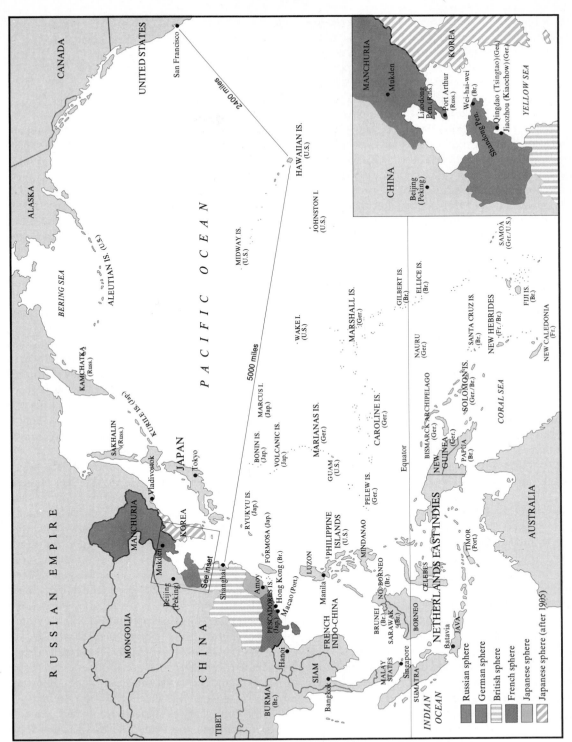

Imperialism in Asia: Turn of the Century

Within the map:

CANADA

UNITED STATES

ALASKA

San Francisco

2400 miles

HAWAIIAN IS. (U.S.)

MIDWAY IS. (U.S.)

JOHNSTON I. (U.S.)

P A C I F I C   O C E A N

BERING SEA

ALEUTIAN IS. (U.S.)

KAMCHATKA (Russ.)

SAKHALIN (Russ.)

KURILE IS. (Jap.)

Vladivostok

JAPAN

Tokyo

KOREA

R U S S I A N   E M P I R E

MONGOLIA

MANCHURIA

Mukden

Beijing (Peking)

Shanghai

C H I N A

TIBET

BURMA (Br.)

Bangkok

SIAM

FRENCH INDO-CHINA

Hanoi

RYUKYU IS. (Jap.)

FORMOSA (Br.)

Amoy

Hong Kong (Br.)

Macao (Port.)

PESCADORES IS. (Jap.)

See inset

MALAY STATES

Singapore

SUMATRA

BRUNEI (Br.)

SARAWAK (Br.)

NO. BORNEO (Br.)

BORNEO

CELEBES

JAVA

Batavia

NETHERLANDS EAST INDIES

TIMOR (Port.)

PHILIPPINE ISLANDS (U.S.)

LUZON

Manila

MINDANAO

BONIN IS. (Jap.)

VOLCANIC IS. (Jap.)

MARCUS I. (Jap.)

MARIANAS IS. (Ger.)

GUAM (U.S.)

PELEW IS. (Ger.)

CAROLINE IS. (Ger.)

WAKE I. (U.S.)

MARSHALL IS. (Ger.)

GILBERT IS. (Br.)

ELLICE IS. (Br.)

NAURU (Ger.)

Equator

BISMARCK ARCHIPELAGO (Ger.)

NEW GUINEA (Ger.)

PAPUA (Br.)

SOLOMON IS. (Ger./Br.)

SANTA CRUZ IS. (Br.)

NEW HEBRIDES (Fr./Br.)

FIJI IS. (Br.)

SAMOA (Ger./U.S.)

NEW CALEDONIA (Fr.)

CORAL SEA

AUSTRALIA

INDIAN OCEAN

5000 miles

Legend:
- Russian sphere
- German sphere
- British sphere
- French sphere
- Japanese sphere
- Japanese sphere (after 1905)

Inset:

MANCHURIA

CHINA

Beijing (Peking)

Mukden

Liaodong Pen. (Russ.)

Port Arthur (Russ.)

Wei-hai-wei (Br.)

Shandong Pen.

Qingdao (Tsingtao) (Ger.)

Jiaozhou (Kiaochow) (Ger.)

KOREA

YELLOW SEA

387

Possession of the Philippines meant American participation in the turbulent politics of Asia. The major contender for influence in the area was Japan, and the Open Door policy did not stop its advances. When competition for Manchuria and Korea led to the Russo-Japanese War (1904–1905), Japan scored quick victories over the stunned Russians. President Theodore Roosevelt mediated the crisis at the Portsmouth Conference in New Hampshire in 1905. The peace settlement, he hoped, would preserve a balance of power in Asia. It did not. Later that year, in the Taft-Katsura Agreement, the United States conceded Japanese hegemony over Korea in return for Japan's pledge not to undermine the American position in the Philippines. To alert Japan to American naval power and to persuade Congress to increase the navy's budget, Roosevelt in 1907 sent the "Great White Fleet" on a world tour. Duly impressed, the Japanese began to build a bigger navy of their own.

Japanese-American Rivalry

Troubles with Japan boiled to the surface in 1906, when the San Francisco School Board ordered the segregation of all Chinese, Koreans, and Japanese in a special school. Tokyo protested this discrimination against its citizens. The following year, President Roosevelt quieted the crisis by striking a gentleman's agreement with Tokyo restricting Japanese immigration to the United States; San Francisco then rescinded its offending segregation order.

Despite the Root-Takahira Agreement (1908), in which the United States recognized Japan's interests in Manchuria and Japan again pledged the security of American possessions in the Pacific, Japanese-American relations deteriorated. Japan became alarmed by President William Howard Taft's ineffective attempt at dollar diplomacy, inducing American bankers to join an international consortium to build a Chinese railway. *Dollar diplomacy* was an effort to use private funds to serve American diplomatic goals and at the same time to garner profits for American financiers. Realizing neither purpose, Taft's venture seemed only to embolden the Japanese. In 1915, Japan issued its Twenty-one Demands, further solidifying and extending its power over China.

The Fruits and Tasks of Empire in Latin America

If the United States seemed feeble in Asia, it showed strength in Latin America (see map). Although the Teller Amendment outlawed annexation, it did not rule out American control of postwar Cuba. American troops remained there until 1902. American officials also wrote the Platt Amendment (1903) and then forced the Cubans to append it to their constitution. A frank avowal of United States hegemony, the Platt Amendment provided that Cuba could not make a treaty with another nation that might impair its independence. In short, all treaties had to be approved by the United States. Most important, Cuba granted the United States "the right to intervene" to preserve the island's independence and to maintain domestic order. (Marines were sent to Cuba to quell a revolution in 1906 and kept there until 1909; they returned briefly in 1912; and they occupied Cuba again from 1917 to 1922.) Cuba was also required to lease a naval base (Guantánamo) to the United States. These conditions helped foster strong anti-Yankee views among Cuban nationalists.

Platt Amendment for Cuba

Panama was the site of one of Theodore Roosevelt's boldest expansionist ventures. Americans had a long-standing fascination with an isthmian canal. But three obstacles had to be overcome. First, the Clayton-Bulwer Treaty with Britain (1850) provided for joint control of a Central American canal. Roosevelt persuaded the British, who were cultivating United States friendship, to step aside (Hay-Pauncefote Treaty of 1901). Second, Colombia was driving a hard bargain in talks about a canal to be cut through its province of Panama. Roosevelt urged Panamanian rebels to declare independence from Colombia, and he sent American warships to the isthmus to ensure the success of the rebellion. In 1903, the United States signed a treaty with the new nation of Panama: the United States was awarded a canal zone and long-term rights to its control;

Panama Canal

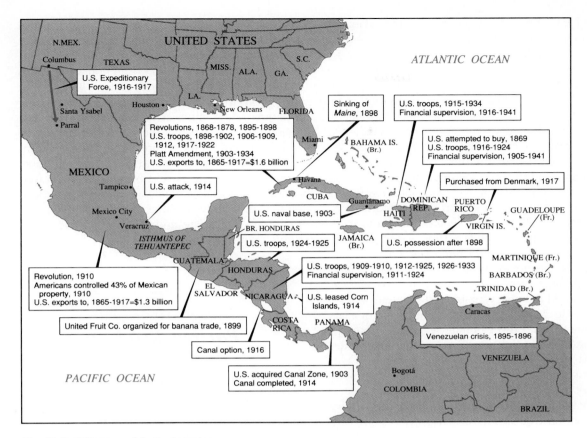

The United States and Latin America

Panama was guaranteed its independence. Third, the cost of constructing a canal was enormous. Roosevelt, having overcome the British and Colombian problems, pressed an obliging Congress for substantial funds.

The completion of the Panama Canal in 1914 marked a major technological achievement. The special bearings and gears used to operate the locks were manufactured by a Wheeling, West Virginia, firm; Pittsburgh factories and shops made the various bolts and steel girders; and the General Electric Company produced the electrical apparatus. People greeted the canal's opening the way people in the 1960s hailed the landing on the moon.

The rest of the Caribbean became an American lake. "Speak softly and carry a big stick," Roosevelt intoned. Worried that Latin American nations that

Roosevelt Corollary had defaulted on huge debts owed to Europeans were sparking European intervention (as when England, Germany, and Italy sent warships to Venezuela in 1902), the president in 1904 decided to issue the Roosevelt Corollary to the Monroe Doctrine. He warned Latin Americans to stabilize their politics and finances. "Chronic wrongdoing," he lectured them, might require "intervention by some civilized nation" (the United States). "In flagrant cases of such wrongdoing or impotence," the United States would have to assume the role of "an international police power." Roosevelt and his successors were not bluffing. From 1900 to 1917, United States troops intervened in Cuba, Panama, Nicaragua, the Dominican Republic, Mexico, and Haiti. United States officials took over customhouses to control tariff revenues, renegotiated foreign debts with American banks, trained national guards, and ran elections.

The United States set out to police its neighbors to the south in the name of order. Whether it be achieved by the landing of marines, the development of a national guard, a managed electoral process, a manipulated economy, or dollar diplomacy, Americans deemed order necessary to guarantee United States security and prosperity. After the United States began building the Panama Canal, Washington would not tolerate disturbances that might threaten this vital waterway. Order was also seen as essential to American commerce and investment. Finally, order seemed imperative to Americans eager to remake Latin American societies in the image of the United States.

One of the assumptions that governed United States policy toward Europe was that European nations should not intervene in Western Hemispheric affairs; the Monroe Doctrine, European officials now knew, had power behind it. Another assumption of American policy toward Europe was that the United States should stand outside continental embroilments. A third was that America's best interests lay in cooperation with Great Britain.

A major offshoot of the German-British rivalry was London's quest for American friendship. The makings of the "great rapprochement" had been

Anglo-American Rapprochement

developing since the late nineteenth century. When the British supported Americans in the war of 1898, stepped aside in the Hay-Pauncefote Treaty (1901) to permit the building of an American canal, virtually endorsed the Roosevelt Corollary, and withdrew their warships from the Caribbean, Americans warmed toward them. The British overtures paid off in 1917, when the United States threw its arms and men into the First World War on the British side.

From the Civil War to the First World War, expansionism and imperialism rested at the core of American foreign policy. By 1914, Americans held extensive interests in a world made smaller by modern technology. Ideas of racial supremacy, the belief that the nation needed foreign markets to absorb surplus production so that the domestic economy could thrive, a mission to uplift the less

fortunate, and emotional appeals to national greatness—all fed the appetite for foreign adventure and commitments.

The outward reach of American policy from Secretary of State Seward to President Wilson met opposition from domestic critics, congressional doubters, other imperial nations, and proud and resentful nationalists; but the trend was never seriously diverted. In the future, Americans who sincerely believed that they had been helping others to enjoy a better life would come to feel betrayed when their foreign clients questioned American tutelage or openly rebelled. But August 1914 presented an immediate and different problem: the outbreak of war in Europe.

Suggestions for Further Reading

General

Robert L. Beisner, *From the Old Diplomacy to the New, 1865–1900*, 2nd ed. (1986); Charles S. Campbell, *The Transformation of American Foreign Relations, 1865–1900* (1976); Willard B. Gatewood, Jr., *Black Americans and the White Man's Burden* (1975); John A. S. Grenville and George B. Young, *Politics, Strategy, and American Diplomacy* (1967); David Healy, *United States Expansionism* (1970); Patricia Hill, *The World Their Household* (1985) (on women missionaries); Paul Kennedy, *The Rise and Fall of the Great Powers* (1987); Walter LaFeber, *The New Empire* (1963); Ernest R. May, *American Imperialism* (1968); Milton Plesur, *America's Outward Thrust* (1971); David M. Pletcher, *The Awkward Years* (1962); Emily Rosenberg, *Spreading the American Dream* (1982); Rubin F. Weston, *Racism in United States Imperialism* (1972); William Appleman Williams, *The Tragedy of American Diplomacy*, new ed. (1988).

Theodore Roosevelt and Other Expansionists

Howard K. Beale, *Theodore Roosevelt and the Rise of America to World Power* (1956); John M. Blum, *The Republican Roosevelt* (1954); John M. Cooper, Jr., *The Warrior and the Priest: Woodrow Wilson and Theodore Roosevelt* (1983); Lewis L. Gould, *The Presidency of William McKinley* (1981); William H. Harbaugh, *The Life and Times of Theodore Roosevelt* (1975); Frederick Marks III, *Velvet on Iron* (1979) (on Roosevelt); Edmund Morris, *The Rise of Theodore Roosevelt* (1979); Ernest N. Paolino, *The Foundations of the American Empire* (1973) (on Seward); William C. Widenor, *Henry Cabot Lodge and the Search for an American Foreign Policy* (1980). For works on Woodrow Wilson, see the listings at the end of Chapter 22.

Economic Expansion

See the works by Beisner, Campbell, and LaFeber cited above; William H. Becker, *The Dynamics of Business-Government Relations* (1982); Robert B. Davies, *Peacefully Working to Conquer the World: Singer Sewing Machines in Foreign Markets, 1854–1920* (1976); Tom Terrill, *The Tariff, Politics, and American Foreign Policy, 1874–1901* (1973); Mira Wilkins, *The Emergence of the Multinational Enterprise* (1970); William Appleman Williams, *The Roots of the Modern American Empire* (1969).

The American Navy

Benjamin F. Cooling, *Gray Steel and Blue Water Navy* (1979); Frederick C. Drake, *The Empire of the Seas* (1984) (on Shufeldt); Kenneth J. Hagan, ed., *In Peace and War*, 2nd ed. (1984); Kenneth J. Hagan, *This People's Navy* (1990); Walter R. Herrick, *The American Naval Revolution* (1966); Peter Karsten, *The Naval Aristocracy* (1972); Robert Seager II, *Alfred Thayer Mahan* (1977); Ronald Spector, *Admiral of the New Empire* (1974) (on Dewey).

The Spanish-American-Cuban-Filipino War

Graham A. Cosmas, *An Army for Empire* (1971); Gerald F. Linderman, *The Mirror of War: American Society and the Spanish-American War* (1974); Ernest R. May, *Imperial Democracy* (1961); Joyce Milton, *The Yellow Journalists* (1989); Julius Pratt, *Expansionists of 1898* (1936); David F. Trask, *The War with Spain in 1898* (1981).

Anti-Imperialism and the Peace Movement

Robert L. Beisner, *Twelve Against Empire* (1968); Kendrick A. Clements, *William Jennings Bryan* (1983); Charles DeBenedetti, *Peace Reform in American History* (1980); C. Roland Marchand, *The American Peace Movement and Social Reform, 1898–1918* (1973); Thomas J. Osborne, *"Empire Can Wait": American Opposition to Hawaiian Annexation, 1893–1898* (1981); David S. Patterson, *Toward a Warless World* (1976); E. Berkeley Tompkins, *Anti-Imperialism in the United States* (1970). See also works listed at the end of Chapter 22.

Relations with Cuba and Latin America

Samuel F. Bemis, *The Latin American Policy of the United States* (1943); David Healy, *Drive to Hegemony: The United States in the Caribbean, 1898–1917* (1989); Walter LaFeber, *Inevitable Revolutions* (1983) (on Central America); Walter LaFeber, *The Panama Canal* (1979); Lester D. Langley, *The United States and the Caribbean, 1900–1970* (1980); Lester D. Langley, *Struggle for the American Mediterranean* (1980); David McCullough, *The Path Between the Seas* (1977) (on the Panama Canal); Allan R. Millett, *The Politics of Intervention* (1968) (on Cuba); Louis A. Pérez, Jr., *Cuba* (1988); Dexter Perkins, *The Monroe Doctrine, 1867–1907* (1937); Ramon Ruiz, *Cuba* (1968); Karl M. Schmitt, *Mexico and the United States, 1821–1973* (1974); Josefina Vázquez and Lorenzo Meyer, *The United States and Mexico* (1985).

Asia and the Pacific

Charles S. Campbell, *Special Business Interests and the Open Door Policy* (1951); Warren I. Cohen, *America's Response to China*, 3rd ed. (1989); Michael Hunt, *The Making of a Special Relationship* (1983) (on China); Jane Hunter, *The Gospel of Gentility: American Women Missionaries in Turn-of-the-Century China* (1984); Akira Iriye, *Across the Pacific* (1967); Jerry Israel, *Progressivism and the Open Door* (1971); Robert McClellan, *The Heathen Chinee: A Study of American Attitudes Toward China, 1890–1905* (1971); Thomas J. McCormick, *China Market* (1967); Charles E. Neu, *The Troubled Encounter* (1975) (on Japan); Merze Tate, *The United States and the Hawaiian Kingdom* (1965); Paul A. Varg, *The Making of a Myth: The United States and China, 1897–1912* (1968); Marilyn Blatt Young, *The Rhetoric of Empire* (1968).

The Philippines: Insurrection and Colony

John M. Gates, *Schoolbooks and Krags: The United States Army in the Philippines, 1898–1902* (1973); Brian M. Linn, *The U.S. Army and Counterinsurgency in the Philippine War, 1898–1902* (1989); Glenn A. May, *Social Engineering in the Philippines* (1980); Stuart C. Miller, *"Benevolent Assimilation"* (1982); Daniel B. Schirmer, *Republic or Empire?* (1972); Peter Stanley, *A Nation in the Making* (1974); Richard E. Welch, *Response to Imperialism: American Resistance to the Philippine War* (1972).

Britain and Canada

Kenneth Bourne, *Britain and the Balance of Power in North America, 1815–1908* (1967); Charles S. Campbell, *From Revolution to Rapprochement: The United States and Great Britain, 1783–1900* (1974); Adrian Cook, *The Alabama Claims* (1975); Bradford Perkins, *The Great Rapprochement* (1968).

"Oh my God, what am I to do?" murmured Woodrow Wilson. Just moments before, he had been holding Ellen Axson Wilson's hand when she died after years of suffering kidney disease. Two days earlier, on August 4, 1914, as he kept vigil at her bedside, the president had drafted a message offering American mediation to end the menacing war that the European nations had just begun. Seldom have such painful personal and official burdens fallen on a president at the same time. In his bereavement, when the partner who had always helped him in previous crises was gone, Wilson also faced momentous decisions about America's place in the First World War. Wilson had long believed that individuals and nations should demonstrate the "dignity of self-control." Now both personal and national self-control seemed elusive.

The Great War in Europe shocked Woodrow Wilson and the American people. For years, Americans had witnessed and participated in the international competition for colonies, markets, and weapons supremacy. But full-scale war seemed unthinkable in the modern age of progress. "Civilization is all gone, and barbarism come," moaned one social reformer after hearing the gruesome news from the European battlefields.

22

AMERICA AT WAR, 1914–1920

For almost three years, President Wilson kept America out of the world war. He sought to protect American interests as a neutral trader and to improve the nation's military posture, all the while lecturing the belligerents to rediscover their humanity and to respect international law. But American neutrality, lives, and property fell victim to British and German naval warfare. In early 1917, with his characteristic crusading zeal, the president asked Congress for a declaration of war. America joined the battle not just to win the war, but to reform the postwar world.

The American people, even after more than a decade of progressive reform, remained heterogeneous and fractious during the war. In 1914, confrontations between labor and capital—like the Ludlow Massacre in Colorado, in which two women and eleven children were killed when state militia attempted to break a miners' strike—still claimed headlines. Racial antagonisms were evidenced by Wilson's decision to segregate federal buildings in Washington, D.C., the continued lynchings of blacks (fifty-

The Wilson family: from left to right, Margaret, Ellen Axson Wilson (1860–1914), Eleanor, Jessie, and President Woodrow Wilson (1856–1924). Ellen Wilson died just as the First World War was breaking out. The president married again in 1915. *Library of Congress.*

one in 1914), and race riots. Ethnic groups eyed one another suspiciously. German-Americans were denounced as traitors, and war hawks harassed pacifists. Many women articulated the case for equality between the sexes and for female suffrage, while many men restated the case for traditional subordination. And the federal government itself, eager to arouse patriotism, trampled on civil liberties to silence critics. Thus, the war experience accentuated the nation's social divisiveness.

America's participation in the war also wrought massive changes and accelerated trends already in motion. Wars are emergencies, and during such times the normal way of doing things surrenders to the extraordinary and the exaggerated. This period witnessed greater powers for the presidency, the military draft, unprecedented centralization and integration of the economy, increased standardization of products, and unusual cooperation between

government and business. The war experience also helped cause the splintering and fading of the progressive movement.

The United States came out of the war a major power in a disrupted and economically hobbled world. Yet Americans, who had marched to battle as if on a crusade, grew disillusioned. They recoiled from the spectacle of the victors squabbling over the spoils, and they chided Wilson for failing to deliver his promised "peace without victory." As in the 1890s, Americans engaged in a fundamental national debate about foreign policy. The president appealed for American membership in a new international organization, the League of Nations, which he touted as a vehicle for reforming world politics. But the Senate killed his diplomatic offspring, fearful that it might entangle Americans once again in Europe's problems, impede the growth of the American empire, and compromise the country's traditional unilateralism in international affairs. On many fronts, then, during the era of the First World War, Americans were at war with themselves.

Neutrality and Unneutrality

The war that erupted in August 1914 grew from years of European competition over trade, colonies, allies, and armaments. Two powerful alliance systems had formed: the Triple Alliance, consisting of Germany, Austria-Hungary, and Italy, and the Triple Entente, comprising Britain, France, and Russia. All had imperial ambitions, but Germany seemed particularly bold as it rivaled Britain for world leadership. Strategists said that Europe enjoyed a balance of power, but a series of crises in the Balkans (southeastern Europe) propelled the European nations into battle.

Slavic nationalists in the Balkans sought to attach to Serbia, an independent Slavic nation, regions like Bosnia, a province of the Austro-Hungarian Empire (see map, page 396). In June 1914, at Sarajevo, Bosnia, the heir to the Austro-Hungarian throne was assassinated by a member of the Black Hand, a Slavic terrorist group using Serbia as a base. Austria-Hungary, long worried that a large Slavic state—an enlarged Serbia—would grow on its southern border, consulted Germany, which urged toughness. Serbia called upon its Slavic friend Russia for help. Russia looked to its ally France. When Austria-Hungary declared war against Serbia, Russia began to mobilize its armies.

Outbreak of the First World War

Certain that war was coming its way, Germany struck first, declaring war against Russia on August 1 and against France two days later. After Germany slashed into Belgium to get at France, Britain declared war against Germany on August 4. Eventually, Turkey joined the Central Powers of Germany and Austria-Hungary, and Japan and Italy teamed up with the Allies of Britain, France, and Russia. Japan took advantage of the European war to seize Germany's Chinese sphere of influence, Shandong, and to expand Tokyo's power in China. The world was aflame.

President Wilson at first sought to distance America from the conflagration by proclaiming neutrality. He also asked Americans to refrain from taking sides. But Wilson's lofty appeal for American neutrality and unity at home collided with three realities. First, ethnic groups in the United States naturally took sides. Many German-Americans and anti-British Irish-Americans (Ireland was then trying to break free from British rule) cheered for the Central Powers. Americans of British and French ancestry applauded the Allies. Anglo-American traditions, as well as the sheer number of Americans with roots in the Allied nations, drew a majority to the Allied cause.

Ethnic Ties to Europe

Second, America's economic links with the Allies also rendered neutrality difficult. England had long been one of the nation's best customers. Now, the British flooded the United States with new orders for products, including arms. In 1914, American exports to England and France totaled $753 million; in 1916, the figure spurted to $2.75 billion. In the same period, however, exports to Germany dropped from $345 million to $29 million. Much of the American-Allied trade was financed through private American loans, amounting to $2.3 billion during the period of neutrality. In stark contrast, Germany received only $27 million.

Trade and Loans

At first frowning on the transactions, the Wilson administration came to see the sales to the Allies and the loans that made them possible as being necessary to the economic health of the United States. From Germany's perspective, however, the links between the American economy and the Allies meant that the United States had become the quite unneutral Allied arsenal and bank. Under international law, Britain (which controlled the seas) could buy contraband (war-related goods) and noncontraband from neutrals. Thus, it was Germany's responsibility, not America's, to stop the trade in ways that international law prescribed—by an effective blockade of the enemy's territory or the seizure of all goods from belligerent (British) ships and contraband from neutral (American) ships.

The third reason neutrality did not work derived from the pro-Allied sympathies of Wilson adminis-

1914	U.S. troops invade Mexico	**1918**	Wilson announces Fourteen Points
	First World War begins		Sedition Act
			Eugene Debs imprisoned
1915	Germany declares war zone around		U.S. troops at Château-Thierry
	British Isles		U.S. troops intervene in Russia
	German U-boat sinks *Lusitania*		Flu epidemic
	Bryan resigns in protest		Republicans win congressional
			elections
1916	Gore-McLemore resolution loses		Armistice
	U.S. troops invade Mexico again		
	Sussex torpedoed	**1919**	Paris Peace Conference at Versailles
	National Defense Act		May Day bombs
	Wilson re-elected		Red Summer; Chicago race riot
			Steel strike
1917	Germany declares unrestricted		Wilson suffers stroke
	submarine warfare		Senate rejects Treaty of Paris
	Zimmermann telegram		*Schenck* v. *United States*
	Russian Revolution		
	United States enters First World War	**1920**	Palmer Raids (Red Scare)
	Selective Service Act		
	Espionage Act		
	Race riot in East St. Louis, Illinois		
	War Industries Board created		

tration officials. Wilson believed that a German victory "would change the course of our civilization and make the United States a military nation." The president's chief advisers and diplomats—his assistant, Edward House, Secretary of State Robert Lansing, and the Ambassador to London, Walter Hines Page—held similar anti-German views, which often translated into pro-Allied policies.

Pro-Allied Sympathies

The president and his aides also believed that Wilsonian principles stood a better chance of international acceptance if Britain, rather than the Central Powers, sat astride the postwar world. "Wilsonianism"—the cluster of ideas espoused by Wilson—consisted of traditional American principles. Wilson's ideal world was to be open in every sense: no barriers to commerce, no impediments to dem-

Wilsonianism

ocratic politics, no secret diplomatic deals. Empires were to be opened up in keeping with the principle of self-determination, and armaments were to be reduced. Wilson envisioned a free market, nonexploitative capitalism, and political constitutionalism for all nations to ensure the good society and world peace. Wilson also articulated the traditional belief in American exceptionalism. America, he believed, had a mission to reform international relations and other societies. American progressivism was to be projected onto the world. "We created this Nation," he declared "not to serve ourselves, but to serve mankind."

To say that American neutrality was never a real possibility, given ethnic loyalties, economic ties, and Wilsonian preferences, is not to claim that Wilson sought to enter the war. He emphatically wanted to keep the United States out. But the United States finally did enter the war. Why?

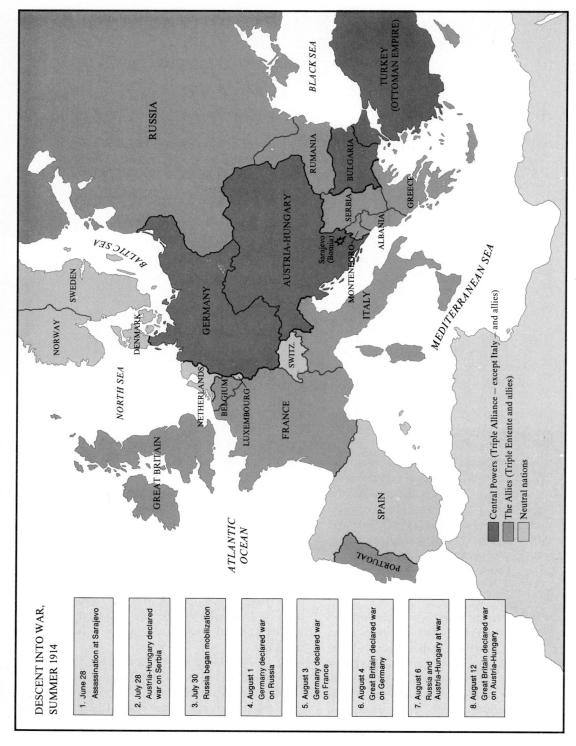

DESCENT INTO WAR,
SUMMER 1914

1. June 28
Assassination at Sarajevo

2. July 28
Austria-Hungary declared
war on Serbia

3. July 30
Russia began mobilization

4. August 1
Germany declared war
on Russia

5. August 3
Germany declared war
on France

6. August 4
Great Britain declared war
on Germany

7. August 6
Russia and
Austria-Hungary at war

8. August 12
Great Britain declared war
on Austria-Hungary

Central Powers (Triple Alliance — except Italy — and allies)

The Allies (Triple Entente and allies)

Neutral nations

RUSSIA

BLACK SEA

TURKEY
(OTTOMAN EMPIRE)

RUMANIA

BULGARIA

GREECE

SERBIA

AUSTRIA-HUNGARY

Sarajevo
(Bosnia)

ALBANIA

MONTENEGRO

ITALY

MEDITERRANEAN SEA

SWEDEN

BALTIC SEA

NORWAY

DENMARK

GERMANY

SWITZ.

NORTH SEA

NETHERLANDS

BELGIUM

LUXEMBOURG

FRANCE

GREAT BRITAIN

ATLANTIC
OCEAN

SPAIN

PORTUGAL

Europe Goes to War

Americans got caught in the Allied–Central Power crossfire. The British, "ruling the waves and waiving the rules," declared a blockade of water entrances to Germany; defined a broad list of contraband (including foodstuffs), which was not supposed to be shipped to Germany by neutrals; mined the North Sea; and harassed neutral shipping by seizing cargoes. American vessels bearing goods for Germany seldom reached their destination. To counter German submarines, the British flouted international law by arming their merchant ships and flying neutral (sometimes American) flags. Wilson frequently protested British violations of neutral rights, but London often deftly defused American criticism by paying for confiscated cargoes. Provocative German actions made British behavior seem less serious by comparison.

British Naval Policy

Germany struggled to lift the blockade and to end American-Allied commerce. Unable to win the war on land, German leaders looked for victory at sea by using submarines. In February 1915, Berlin announced that it was creating a war zone around the British Isles; all enemy ships in the area would be sunk. Neutral vessels were warned to stay out so as not to be attacked by mistake, and passengers from neutral nations were warned to stay off enemy ships. Wilson informed Germany that the United States was holding it to "strict accountability" for any losses of American life and property.

Wilson interpreted international law in the strictest sense. Such law held that an attacker had to warn a passenger or merchant ship before attacking, so that passengers and crew could disembark safely into lifeboats. That rule predated the emergence of the submarine—whose effectiveness was based on surprise—as a major weapon. But Wilson refused to make adjustments. Berlin frequently complained to Wilson that he was denying the Germans the one weapon they could use to break the British economic stranglehold, disrupt the Allies' substantial connection with American producers and bankers, and win the war.

The Submarine and International Law

Wilson, the Submarine, and War

During the next few months, the U-boats sank ship after ship. In May, the *Lusitania* , a luxurious British passenger liner, left New York City with more than twelve hundred passengers aboard. It also carried a cargo of food and contraband, including 4.2 million rounds of rifle ammunition. Before "Lucy's" departure, the newspapers carried an unusual announcement from the German embassy: travelers on British vessels were warned that Allied ships in war-zone waters "are liable to destruction." On May 7, off the Irish coast, submarine U-20 unleashed torpedoes at the vessel. The *Lusitania* sank quickly, taking to their deaths 1,198 people, 128 of them Americans.

A stunned Wilson argued that, even if the ship was carrying armaments, the sinking was a brutal assault on innocent people. But he ruled out a military response. Secretary of State William Jennings Bryan advised that Americans be prohibited from travel on belligerent ships and that passenger vessels be prohibited from carrying war goods. Bryan also urged Wilson to forward protest notes to both London and Berlin. Wilson rejected Bryan's counsel and sent a note to Berlin insisting on the right of Americans to sail on belligerent ships and demanding that Germany cease its inhumane submarine warfare. When the president refused to ban American travelers from belligerent ships, Bryan resigned in protest. The pro-Allied Robert Lansing was elevated to the top diplomatic post. To criticism that he was pursuing a double standard favoring the Allies, Wilson responded that the British were taking cargoes and violating property rights, but the Germans were taking lives and violating human rights.

Reaction to the Sinking of the *Lusitania*

Seeking to avoid war with America, Germany ordered its U-boat commanders to halt attacks on passenger liners. But in mid-August, another British vessel, the *Arabic*, was sunk and two Americans lost their lives. The Germans hastened to pledge that never again would an unarmed passenger ship be attacked without warning. But the sinking of the *Arabic* fueled the debate about American passengers on belligerent vessels. Why not require Americans to sail on American craft? asked critics.

In early 1916, Congress began to debate the Gore-McLemore resolution, which would prohibit Americans from traveling on armed merchant vessels or on ships carrying contraband. The resolution, it was hoped, would prevent incidents like the sinking of the *Lusitania* from hurtling the United States into war. But Wilson refused to tolerate any restrictions on American travel. After heavy politicking, both the House and the Senate rejected the resolution.

Gore-McLemore Resolution

In March 1916, an attack on the *Sussex*, a French vessel crossing the English Channel, took the United States a step closer to war. Four Americans on that ship were injured. Stop the marauding submarines, Wilson lectured Berlin, or he would sever diplomatic relations. Again the Germans backed off, pledging not to attack merchant vessels without warning.

Sentiment for peace remained strong, as evidenced by Wilson's victory on a peace platform in the 1916 election. After his triumph, Wilson futilely labored to bring the belligerents to the conference table. In early 1917, he advised them to temper their acquisitive war aims, appealing for a "peace without victory."

In early February 1917, Germany startled the Wilson administration by launching unrestricted submarine warfare. All vessels, belligerent or neutral, warship or merchant, would be attacked if sighted in the declared war zone. This bold decision represented a calculated risk that submarines could impede munitions shipments from America to England and thus defeat the Allies before Americans could be mobilized and ferried across the Atlantic to enter the fight. Wilson quickly broke diplomatic relations with Berlin.

Unrestricted Submarine Warfare

With this German challenge to American neutral rights and economic interests came a German threat to American security. In late February, the British intercepted, decoded, and handed to the American government a telegram addressed to the German minister in Mexico from the German foreign secretary, Arthur Zimmermann. The minister was instructed to tell the Mexican government that, if it joined a military alliance against the United States, Germany would help Mexico recover the territories it had been forced to give up to its northern neighbor in 1848.

Mexican Revolution and Zimmerman Telegram

American officials took the message seriously because at the time Mexican-American relations were extremely tense. The Mexican Revolution, a bloody civil war with strong anti-American overtones, had spilled across the Rio Grande, and the Mexican government was threatening to nationalize American properties. Wilson had twice ordered American troops onto Mexican soil: in 1914, at Vera Cruz, to avenge a slight to the American uniform and flag; and again in 1916, in northern Mexico, where General John J. Pershing spent months trying to capture the elusive Pancho Villa after his raid on an American border town.

Soon after learning of Zimmermann's ploy, Wilson asked Congress for "armed neutrality" to defend American lives and commerce. He requested the specific authority to arm American merchant ships and the more general power to "employ any other instrumentalities or methods that may be necessary." In the midst of the debate, Wilson released Zimmermann's telegram to the press; Americans expressed outrage. Still, antiwar senators saw the armed-ship bill as a blank check for the president to move the country to war, and they filibustered it to death. Wilson proceeded to arm America's commercial vessels anyway. The action came too late to prevent the sinking of several American ships. War cries echoed across the nation.

On April 2, 1917, the president stepped before a hushed Congress. Passionately and eloquently, Wilson explained American grievances: Germany's violation of the principle of freedom of the seas, disruption of American commerce, the attempt to stir up trouble in Mexico, and

Wilson's War Message

violation of human rights by killing innocent Americans. Wilson's most famous words rang out: "The world must be made safe for democracy." Congress quickly declared war against Germany by a vote of 373 to 50 in the House and 82 to 6 in the Senate. The first woman ever to sit in Congress, Montana's Representative Jeannette Rankin, elected in 1916, cast a ringing "no" vote that won her high ranking in the pantheon of American pacifism. "Peace is a woman's job," she believed.

For principle, for morality, for honor, for commerce, for security—for all these reasons the United States took up arms against Germany. The submarine was certainly the culprit that drew the nation into the maelstrom. Yet Wilson's critics did not think that the U-boat alone was responsible for the American descent into war. They emphasized Wilson's rigid definition of international law, which did not take account of the submarine's tactics. They faulted his contention that Americans could travel anywhere, even on a belligerent ship loaded with contraband, in time of war. They criticized his policies as unneutral. But they lost the debate.

In the most general sense, America went to war to reform world politics, not to destroy Germany. By early 1917, Wilson seemed to believe that after the war America would not be able to claim a seat at the peace conference unless it had been a combatant. At the peace conference, Wilson intended to put into constitutional form the principles he thought essential to a stable world order—principles that would promote democracy and the Open Door and outlaw revolution and aggression. In the end, Wilson decided for war to gain an American-fashioned peace.

Taking Up Arms and Winning the War

Even before the war decision, the United States had been preparing for combat. Encouraged by such groups as the National Security League and the Navy League and by mounting public outrage against Germany's submarine warfare, the president in 1915 began to plan a substantial military build-up. As the debate over preparedness swirled about the nation's capital, Wilson took a new bride, the widowed Edith Bolling Galt, and went on a two-week honeymoon.

Meanwhile, antiwar critics vowed to block preparedness. Some pacifist progressives became active in an antiwar coalition, the American Union Against Militarism. Jane Addams and Carrie Chapman Catt founded the Women's Peace party, and both Andrew Carnegie and Henry Ford worked for peace. Socialists like Eugene Debs added their voices to the peace movement. But the peace movement was splintered, and it could not prevent passage of the National Defense Act of 1916.

Peace Movement

To raise an army after the declaration of war, Congress in May 1917 passed the Selective Service Act, requiring the registration of all males between the ages of twenty and thirty (later changed to eighteen and forty-five). National service, proponents believed, would not only prepare the country for battle but also promote efficiency, order, democracy, personal sacrifice, and nationalism. Critics, on the other hand, feared that "Prussianism," not democratization, would be the likely outcome.

The Draft

On June 5, 1917, more than 9.5 million men signed up for the "great national lottery." By war's end, 24 million men had been registered by local draft boards. More than 4.8 million men served in the armed forces, and 2 million of them fought in France. About 16 percent of the male labor force was drawn into military service. Besides those inducted, hundreds of thousands volunteered for military service. However, more than 300,000 men evaded the draft by failing to show up when called, and 4,000 were classified as conscientious objectors.

The typical soldier was a draftee between twenty-one and twenty-three years of age, white, single, and poorly educated (most had not attended high school). Perhaps as many as 18 percent were foreign-born, and 400,000 were black. On college campuses, 150,000 students entered the Student Army Training Corps or similar navy and marine units. Women served as navy clerks or in the U.S. Army Signal Corps or Nurse Corps.

American leaders worried that the young soldiers, once away from their homes, would be tempted by vice—especially by the houses of prostitution and saloons that quickly surrounded training centers. To protect the supposed novices with "invisible armor," the government created the Commission on Training Camp Activities to coordinate the work of the YMCA and other groups that dispensed food, showed movies, held athletic contests, and distributed books. Men in uniform were not permitted to drink. Alarmed by the spread of venereal disease, commission officials declared "sin-free" zones around military bases.

Commission on Training Camp Activities

Jim Crow was in the army too. Fearing "arrogant, strutting representatives of black soldiery in every community," as Senator James K. Vardaman of Mississippi snarled, many politicians opposed the drafting of blacks. But the army needed men, white and black. The NAACP, believing that a war to make the world safe for democracy might blur the color line at home, urged blacks to join the armed forces. Military leaders, however, segregated facilities, discouraged blacks from becoming officers, and assigned black recruits to menial labor. Racist slang echoed through the camps. In Houston, Texas, angry black soldiers took up arms against whites who had been goading them, killing thirteen. After brief "trials," thirteen blacks were executed; another six were hanged after an unsuccessful appeal of their death sentences; others were court-martialed and given long prison terms.

In Europe, the head of the American Expeditionary Forces (AEF), General John J. Pershing, insisted that his troops remain an independent American army. He was not about to put his AEF "doughboys" under the leadership of Allied commanders, who had become wedded to unimaginative trench warfare, producing military stalemate and ghastly casualties on the Western front. Zigzag trenches, fronted by barbed wire and mines, stretched across France. Beyond the muddy

trenches lay "no man's land." When ordered out, soldiers would charge the German lines, also a maze of trenches. Machine guns mowed them down; chlorine gas, first used by Germany in 1915, poisoned them. Little was gained. At the Battle of the Somme in 1916, the British and French suffered 600,000 dead or wounded to earn only 125 square miles (the Germans lost 500,000 men).

The influx of American men and materiel decided the outcome of the First World War. With both sides virtually exhausted, the Americans in France tipped the balance toward the Allies. Actually, the American forces did not engage in much combat until 1918. In March 1918, after knocking Russia out of the war, closing the eastern front, and shifting troops to France, the Germans launched a major offensive. By May, Kaiser Wilhelm's forces had stormed to within fifty miles of Paris. American troops helped blunt the German advance at Cantigny. In June, the United States Second Division fought the Germans at Château-Thierry in the Belleau Wood; before American soldiers won, 5,183 of the 8,000 marines died or were wounded. Americans also played a role in the Second Battle of the Marne, an Allied victory that seemed to turn the tide against the Germans. In September, the Allies began their massive Meuse-Argonne offensive. More than a million Americans joined British and French troops in weeks of fierce combat. More than 26,000 Americans died in that campaign before the Allies claimed the Argonne Forest on October 10.

Americans in Combat in France

American victories in the fall of 1918 spelled doom for Germany. Its ground war a shambles, its submarine warfare a dismal failure, and its troops and cities mutinous, Germany—abandoned by Turkey and Austria—sued for peace. The armistice was signed on November 11, 1918. The belligerents then counted their awesome casualties: 8 million soldiers and 6.6 million civilians dead and 21.3 million people wounded. More than 200,000 of the wounded were American soldiers, and more than 50,000 Americans died in battle. (Another 62,000 American soldiers died from disease—many from the worldwide flu epidemic of 1918.)

Casualties

An American soldier of Company K, 110th Infantry Regiment, receives aid during fighting at Verennes, France. *National Archives.*

President Wilson welcomed the armistice, which was signed on his terms. The combatants agreed that the president's Fourteen Points, which he had enunciated in January, would guide the peace negotiations. The Allies initially balked, but Wilson scared them into acceptance by threatening a separate peace with Germany. The Fourteen Points summarized "Wilsonianism." The first five called for diplomacy in the "public view," freedom of the seas, lower tariffs, reductions in armaments, and the decolonization of empires. Points six through thirteen appealed for self-determination for national groups in Europe. To Wilson, the fourteenth point was the most important, the mechanism for achieving all the others: "a general association of nations," or League of Na-

The Fourteen Points

tions. Having won the war, Wilson set out to win the peace and build a stable world order based on American principles.

The Home Front

"It is not an army that we must shape and train for war," declared the president, "it is a nation." The United States was a belligerent for only nineteen months, but the war had a tremendous impact on domestic America. The federal government quickly geared the economy to war needs and marshaled public opinion for the sacrifices and adjustments imposed by belligerency. As never before, the state intervened in American life.

The federal government and private business became partners during the war. Dollar-a-year executives flocked to the nation's capital from major companies; they retained their corporate salaries while serving in official administrative and consulting capacities. Early in the war, the government relied on several industrial committees for advice on purchases and prices. But evidence of self-interested businesspeople cashing in on the national interest aroused public protest. The committees were disbanded in July 1917 in favor of the War Industries Board (WIB). The government, however, continued to work closely with business through trade associations. Business-government cooperation was also stimulated by the suspension of antitrust laws; by cost-plus contracts, which guaranteed companies a healthy profit and a means to pay higher wages to head off labor strikes; by the virtual abandonment of competitive bidding; and by a floor placed under prices to ensure profits.

Business-Government Cooperation

Hundreds of new government agencies, staffed largely by businesspeople, came into being to wage the war. Some of the agencies placed unprecedented controls on the economy. The Food Administration, led by Herbert Hoover, undertook programs to improve production and conserve food through voluntary action; it also set prices and regulated distribution. Americans were urged to grow "victory gardens" in their backyards and to eat meatless and wheatless meals. The Railroad Administration took over the snarled and financially troubled railway industry. When strikes threatened the telephone and telegraph companies, the federal government seized and ran them.

The largest and potentially most powerful of the wartime agencies was the War Industries Board. Designed as a clearinghouse to coordinate the national economy and headed after early 1918 by financier Bernard Baruch, the WIB faced the enormous task of satisfying both Allied and domestic needs. It made purchases, allocated supplies, and fixed prices. Although the WIB seemed all-powerful, in reality it

War Industries Board

had to conciliate competing interest groups and compromise with the businesspeople whose advice it so valued.

The mobilized economy delivered enough men and materiel to France to ensure the defeat of the Central Powers. About a quarter of all American production was diverted to war needs. Farmers enjoyed boom years as they put more acreage into production and watched prices go up. Induced to produce more at a faster pace, farmers mechanized as never before. Wartime demand also brought increased productivity and profits to some industries. Steel production in 1917, for example, was twice the prewar figure.

Nonetheless, mistakes were made. Weapons deliveries fell short of demand; the bloated bureaucracy of the War Shipping Board failed to build enough ships. As the mercury dipped in the severe winter of 1917–1918, millions of Americans found that they could not get coal, because the coal companies had held back on production to raise prices and railroads did not have enough coal cars. And the government, by adopting liberal credit policies and fixing prices at high levels, encouraged inflation. The wholesale price index was 98 percent higher in 1918 than it had been in 1913. Loopholes in the tax laws permitted corporate leaders to enjoy huge war profits.

For labor unions, the war seemed to offer opportunities for recognition and better pay. Samuel Gompers, president of the American Federation of Labor, threw the AFL's loyalty to the Wilson administration, promising to deter strikes. He and other moderate labor leaders were rewarded with appointments to high-level wartime government agencies. The National War Labor Board, created to mediate labor disputes, ruled out strikes and lockouts but required management to deal with already organized unions. From roughly 2.7 million in 1916, union membership climbed to more than 4 million in 1919. The AFL could not curb strikes by the radical Industrial Workers of the World (IWW) or rebellious AFL locals. In the nineteen war months, more than six thousand strikes expressed workers' discontent with their wages, working conditions, and inflation. Laborers benefited from the full-employment wartime economy,

Wartime Labor

When men trooped off to war, women filled industrial jobs as never before. These women are trimming shell fuses in a munitions plant. *The Bettman Archive.*

which increased their total earnings. Given the high cost of living, however, workers saw little improvement in their economic standing.

With 16 percent of the male work force in the military and a declining immigration rate, the call went out to women, blacks, and Mexican-Americans to fill job vacancies.

Women in the Work Force Although the number of women in the work force increased slightly, the real story was that many shifted from one job to another, sometimes into formerly male domains. Some white women quit domestic service for work in factories and left textile mills for employment in firearms plants. Twenty percent or more of all workers in the wartime manufacture of electrical machinery, airplanes, and food were women. As white women took advantage of the new opportunities, black women took some of their places in domestic service and in textile factories. Overall, most working women remained concentrated in sex-segregated occupations ("women's jobs").

The movement of women into jobs that had been the preserve of males generated controversy. Some male workers complained that women were destabilizing the work environment with their higher productivity; women answered that they were used to seasonal employment and piecework and hence worked at a faster pace. Some men protested that women were undermining the wage system by working for lower pay; women pointed out that male-dominated companies discriminated against them and unions denied them membership. Finally, male employees resented the spirit of independence evident among women whose labor was now greatly valued.

When the war was over, women lost many of the gains they had made. The attitude that women's proper sphere was the home changed very little. Some married working women found that their husbands and children resented the disruption of home life. Reformers complained that working mothers were neglecting their children. Day nurseries were scarce and beyond the means of most working-class families, and few employers provided childcare facilities. Whether married or single—and the great majority of working women were unmarried—women lost their jobs to the returning veterans.

Black Migration to the North Wartime mobilization wrought significant changes for the black community. Wartime jobs in the North provided an escape from southern social, political, and economic oppression. During the war years, southern blacks undertook a great migration to northern cities to work in railroad yards, packing houses, steel mills, shipyards, and coal mines. Between 1910 and 1920, about half a million black Americans uprooted themselves to move north. Most were young (in their early twenties) unmarried males seeking economic opportunity.

New jobs and improved opportunities could not erase the fact that blacks, both North and South, continued to be a minority in a white society. When the United States entered the First World War, there was not one black judge in the entire country and segregation was social custom. The Ku Klux Klan began to revive, and racist films like D. W. Griffith's *The Birth of a Nation* (1915) fed prejudice. Lynching statistics exposed the wide gap between American declarations of humanity in the war and the American practice of inhumanity at home: between 1914 and 1920, 382 blacks were lynched, some of them in military uniform.

Northern whites who resented the "Negro invasion" vented their anger in riots. In East St. Louis, Illinois, in July 1917, whites opposed to black employment in a defense plant rampaged through the streets; nine whites and about forty blacks lost their lives. In the bloody "Red Summer" of 1919, race riots rocked two dozen cities and towns. The worst race war occurred in Chicago, where thirty-eight people died in a riot after a black youth swimming at a segregated white beach was hit by a rock and drowned. W. E. B. Du Bois vowed to continue the struggle against segregation: "We return. We return from fighting. We return fighting."

The Attack on Civil Liberties

"Woe be to the man that seeks to stand in our way in this day of high resolution," warned President Wilson. Dissenters who questioned his war decision and the draft soon faced an official and unofficial campaign to silence them. The targets of abuse were the hundreds of thousands of Americans and aliens who refused to support the war. To ensure conformity, Wilson created the Committee on Public Information (CPI).

Led by George Creel, a progressive journalist, the CPI was a propaganda agency, pure and simple. Employing some of the nation's most talented writers and scholars, the CPI set out to shape and mobilize public opinion by means of anti-German tracts, speeches, films, and "self-censorship" of the press. The CPI encouraged people to spy on their neighbors and report any suspicious behavior. Exaggeration, fearmongering, distortion, and half-truths were the stuff of the CPI's "mind mobilization."

Committee on Public Information

The Wilson administration also guided through an obliging Congress the Espionage Act (1917) and the Sedition Act (1918). The first statute forbade "false statements" designed to impede the draft or

Silencing Critics promote military insubordination and banned from the mails materials considered treasonous. The Sedition Act made it unlawful to obstruct the sale of war bonds and to use "disloyal, profane, scurrilous, or abusive" language against the government, the Constitution, the flag, and the military uniform. These loosely worded laws gave the government wide latitude to crack down on those with whom it differed. More than two thousand people were prosecuted under the acts, and many others were intimidated into silence. Among them was the Socialist party leader, Eugene Debs, who received a ten-year sentence for his criticism of the war.

State and local governments, as well as private organizations and citizens, joined the campaign. Officials banned what they considered "pro-German" books from public schools. Everywhere, teachers who questioned the war faced dismissal by hostile school boards. In Tulsa, a mob whipped IWW members and then poured tar into their bleeding sores. A German-American miner in Illinois was wrapped in a flag and lynched. And at Columbia University, antiwar Professor J. M. Cattell, a distinguished psychologist, was fired. His colleague Charles Beard, a prowar historian, resigned in protest: "If we have to suppress everything we don't like to hear, this country is resting on a pretty wobbly basis."

The point was just that: Wilson and his officers tried to crush what they did not like to hear. In particular, the administration concentrated on the IWW and the Socialist party. The war emergency and the frank opposition of those two radical organizations gave progressives and conservatives alike an opportunity to throttle their political rivals. Soon after the declaration of war, government agents raided union meetings and arrested IWW leaders. The army was sent into western mining and lumber regions to put down IWW strikes on the pretense that they were pro-German. Under the immigration acts, alien members of the IWW were deported. Town after town evicted the "Wobblies," and by the end of the war most of the union's leaders were in jail. The Socialist party fared little better.

The Supreme Court, itself attuned to the pulse of the times, upheld the Espionage Act. Justice Oliver

Wendell Holmes, in *Schenck* v. *United States* (1919), expressed the Court's unanimous opinion that in time of war the First Amendment could be restricted: "Free speech would not protect a man falsely shouting fire in a theater and causing panic." If words "are of such a nature as to create a clear and present danger that they will bring about the substantial evils that Congress has a right to prevent," Holmes went on, free speech could be limited. In another case, *Abrams* v. *United States* (1919), the Court upheld the Sedition Act.

The Red Scare

In the last few months of the war, guardians of Americanism began to label dissenters not only pro-German but pro-Bolshevik. After the Bolshevik Revolution in the fall of 1917, American hatred for the Kaiser's Germany was readily transferred to Communist Russia. When the new Russian government made peace with Germany in early 1918, Americans grew angry that the closing of the eastern front would give the Germans the chance to move troops west. Many lashed out at American radicals, casually applying the term "Red" to people of varying beliefs, such as anarchists, Wobblies, Socialists, pacifists, Communists, union leaders, and reformers.

An early sign of the Wilson administration's anti-Bolshevism was the president's ordering of five thousand American troops to northern Russia in June 1918. Then, a month later, he **Intervention** sent another ten thousand sol-**in Russia** diers to Siberia, where they joined other Allied contingents. Wilson did not consult Congress. He announced that the military expeditions were intended to guard Allied supplies and Russian railroads from German seizure and to rescue a group of Czechs who wished to return to their homeland to fight the Germans. Wilson worried that the Japanese were building influence in Siberia and closing the Open Door. But he also hoped to smash the infant Bolshevik government. Besides trying to subvert Lenin's regime

by military means, Wilson joined an economic blockade of Russia, sent arms to anti-Bolshevik forces, refused to recognize the Bolshevik government, and later blocked Russian participation in the Paris Peace Conference. These interventions embittered Washington-Moscow relations—a legacy that would persist deep into the twentieth century.

At home, too, the Wilson administration moved against radicals and others imprecisely defined as Bolsheviks or Communists. After the war, Americans were edgy. The war had disrupted race relations, the workplace, and the family; postwar unemployment loomed; and in 1919, the Russian Communists established the Comintern to promote world revolution. Already hardened by wartime violations of civil liberties, Americans found it easy to blame their postwar troubles on new scapegoats.

A rash of labor strikes in 1919 helped spark the Red Scare. All told, more than 3,300 strikes, involving 4 million laborers, occurred that year, including a Seattle general strike in January. **Labor Strikes,** On May 1 (May Day), bombs were **1919** sent through the mails to prominent Americans. Most of the devices were intercepted and dismantled. Police never captured the conspirators. The common and not unreasonable assumption was that anarchists and others bent on the destruction of the American way of life were responsible. Next came the Boston police strike in September; some thought it part of a Bolshevik conspiracy. The governor of Massachusetts, Calvin Coolidge, gained fame by proclaiming that nobody had the right to strike against the public safety. State guardsmen were brought in to replace the striking police force.

Especially ominous was the September walkout of 250,000 steel workers, many of whom still put in twelve-hour days seven days a week and went home to squalid living quarters. In defeating the strike, management hired agents to club strikers, employed strikebreakers, and depicted strike leaders as Bolsheviks. One of the leaders of the steel strike was William Z. Foster, a radical who later joined the Communist party. His presence in a labor movement seeking legitimate bread-and-butter goals permitted political and business leaders to dismiss the steel strike as a foreign threat orchestrated by American radicals. There was actually no conspiracy; the American left was badly splintered and incapable of mounting a threat to established order.

But Attorney General A. Mitchell Palmer claimed that the "blaze of revolution" was "burning up the foundations of society." To stamp out the radical fire, Palmer created a new Bureau of Investigation and appointed J. Edgar Hoover to run it. Hoover organized a file of thousands of index cards bearing the names of alleged radical individuals and organizations. During 1919, agents jailed IWW members; and in December, Palmer saw to it that 249 alien radicals, including the anarchist Emma Goldman, were deported to Soviet Russia. Again, state and local governments took their cue from Washington. The New York State legislature expelled five duly elected Socialist members. States passed peacetime sedition acts, under which hundreds of people were arrested.

A. Mitchell Palmer

The Red Scare reached a climax in January 1920, when the attorney general staged his Palmer Raids. Using information gathered by Hoover, government agents in thirty-three cities broke into meeting halls, poolrooms, and homes without search warrants. More than four thousand people were thrown into overcrowded jails and denied counsel. Of this number, nearly six hundred were deported.

Palmer Raids

Palmer's disregard for elementary civil liberties soon drew criticism. Civil libertarians and lawyers pointed out that Palmer's blatant tactics ignored the Constitution, that many of the arrested "Communists" had committed no crimes, and that some were not even radicals. Palmer's call for a peacetime sedition act alarmed leaders of many political persuasions. His dire prediction that major violence would mar May Day 1920 proved mistaken. Palmer's exaggerations simply exceeded the truth so far that he lost credibility.

The campaign against free speech in the period from 1917 through 1920 left casualties. Critics, radical or otherwise, became afraid to speak their minds. Debate, so essential to democracy, was curbed. Reform suffered as reformers either joined in the anti-radicalism or became victims of it. The radical movement was badly weakened, the IWW becoming virtually extinct and the Socialist party

paralyzed. The government's war on its critics and disrespect for the Bill of Rights left an indelible blot on Wilson's political record.

The Peace Conference and League Fight

As the Red Scare was threatening American democracy, Woodrow Wilson was struggling to make his Fourteen Points a reality. When the president departed for the Paris Peace Conference at the palace of Versailles in December 1918, he faced obstacles erected by his political enemies, by the Allies, and by himself. Some observers suggested that the ambitious and very confident Wilson underestimated his task. During the 1918 congressional elections, Wilson had urged a vote for the Democrats as a sign of support for his peace goals. But the American people, probably voting less in response to foreign policy issues than to domestic questions like inflation, did just the opposite. The Republicans gained control of both houses, signaling trouble for Wilson in two ways. First, any peace treaty would have to be submitted for approval to a potentially hostile Senate; second, Wilson's stature had been diminished in the eyes of foreign leaders. Wilson aggravated his political problems by not naming a senator to his advisory American Peace Commission, refusing to take any prominent Republican with him to Paris, and failing to consult with the Senate Foreign Relations Committee before he sailed for Paris.

Another obstacle in Wilson's way was the Allies' determination to impose a harsh, vengeful peace on the Germans. Georges Clemenceau of France, David Lloyd George of Britain, and Vittorio Orlando of Italy—with Wilson, the Big Four—were formidable adversaries. They had signed secret treaties during the war and expected to enlarge their empires at Germany's expense. They scoffed at the headstrong, self-impressed president who wanted to deny them the spoils of war.

The victors demanded that Germany pay a huge reparations bill. Wilson called for a small indemnity, fearing that a resentful and economically hobbled Germany might turn to Bolshevism or disrupt the postwar community in some other way. Unable to moderate the Allied position, the president reluctantly gave way, agreeing to a clause blaming the war on the Germans and to the creation of a reparations commission to determine a figure (later set at $33 billion).

Paris Peace Conference

As for decolonization (the breaking up of empires) and the principle of self-determination, Wilson only partially overcame the land-grabbing mood of the conference. The conferees placed former German and Turkish colonies under the control of other imperial nations in a League-administered "mandate" system: a halfway station between outright imperial domination and independence. France and Britain obtained parts of the Middle East, and Japan gained authority over Germany's colonies in the Pacific. In other compromises, Japan was granted influence over China's Shandong peninsula, and France was permitted occupation rights in Germany's Rhineland. Elsewhere in Europe, however, Wilson's prescriptions fared better. Out of Austria-Hungary and Russia came the new independent states of Austria, Hungary, Yugoslavia, Czechoslovakia, and Poland. Wilson and his colleagues also built a *cordon sanitaire* of new westward-looking nations (Finland, Estonia, Latvia, and Lithuania) around Russia to quarantine the Bolshevik contagion.

Wilson worked harder on the charter for the League of Nations than on anything else. In the long run, he believed, the League would moderate the harshness of the Allied peace terms and temper imperial ambitions. He devised a League that reflected the power of major nations like the United States: an influential council of five permanent members (great powers) and elected delegates from smaller states; an assembly for discussion; and a World Court. The backbone of the League covenant was the collective security provision, contained in Article 10. In this provision, League members agreed to "respect and preserve" each other's territorial integrity.

League of Nations

Americans vigorously debated the treaty, and criticisms mounted: Wilson had bastardized his own principles, conceded Shandong to Japan, and personally killed a provision affirming the racial equality of all peoples. The treaty did not mention freedom of the seas, and tariffs were not reduced. Negotiations had been conducted in private, and reparations promised to be punishing. Moreover, Article 10 raised serious questions: would the United States be obligated to use armed force to ensure collective security?

The Treaty Debate

Wilson pleaded for understanding. Did his opponents not realize that compromises were necessary, given the adamant resistance of the Allies, who had threatened to jettison the conference unless Wilson made concessions? Did they not recognize that the League would rectify wrongs? Could they not see that membership in the League would give the United States "leadership in the world"? Senator Henry Cabot Lodge remained unimpressed. A Harvard-educated Ph.D. and partisan Republican, he ridiculed Wilson's charter as poor scholarship. Lodge packed the Foreign Relations Committee with League critics. He introduced reservations to the treaty; one stated that Congress had to approve any obligation under Article 10.

In September 1919, Wilson embarked on a speaking tour of the United States. Growing more exhausted every day, he dismissed his critics as "absolute, contemptible quitters." In Colorado, while delivering another passionate speech, the president collapsed. A few days later, in Washington, D.C., he suffered a stroke that paralyzed his left side. Although his mind remained alert, he became grumpy and peevish, fearful of displaying weakness and unable to conduct the heavy business of the presidency. Told by advisers to placate senatorial critics so that the treaty would have a chance of passing, Wilson stubbornly refused to compromise. From Democrats in the Senate he demanded loyalty—a vote against all reservations.

The Senate first tested the treaty's strength in November. In two votes, one on the treaty with reservations and one without, the Senate rejected it. A group of sixteen "Irreconcilables" determined to defeat any treaty and voted "nay" each time. Republicans either opposed the treaty altogether or

Senate Rejection of the Treaty

favored reservations; Democrats, on the whole, voted for the treaty without reservations. Again in March 1920, the treaty fell short of the necessary two-thirds vote. Had Wilson permitted Democrats to compromise, he could have achieved his fervent wish for American membership in the League of Nations.

Who or what was responsible for the defeat of the treaty? At the core of the debate lay a basic issue of American foreign policy: whether the United States would endorse collective security or continue to travel the path of unilateralism, articulated in George Washington's Farewell Address and the Monroe Doctrine. Wilson lost because, in a world dominated by imperialist states unwilling to subordinate their acquisitive ambitions to an international organization, Americans preferred their traditional nonalignment and freedom of choice over commitments to collective action. Wilson failed to create a new world order through reform; he had promised more than he could deliver.

The Experience of War

America emerged from the war years an unsettled mix of the old and the new. The war exposed the heterogeneity of the American people and the deep divisions among them: white versus black, nativist versus immigrant, capital versus labor, "dry" versus "wet," men versus women, radical versus progressive or conservative, pacifist versus interventionist, and nationalist versus internationalist. Race riots, labor strikes, the suppression of civil liberties, the Red Scare, and the League fight—all underscored the distempers of the times. Wearied by these conflicts, Americans, after 1920, sought relief in "normalcy."

During the war, the federal government intervened in the economy and influenced people's everyday lives as never before. In the period from 1916 to 1919, annual federal expenditures increased by 2,500 percent, and war expenses ballooned to $33.5 billion. The total cost of the war was probably triple that figure, since

Enlarged Federal Role

future generations would have to pay veterans' benefits and interest on loans. Wartime policies nourished the continued growth of oligopoly through the suspension of antitrust laws, and cooperation between business and government encouraged the growth of trade associations. A 1920 Supreme Court decision not to dissolve the giant U.S. Steel Corporation symbolized the persistent trend toward bigness. After a short postwar recession, business power revived to dominate the next decade.

America's changed place in world affairs also held significance for later generations. By 1920, the United States had become the world's leading economic power, producing 40 percent of its coal, 70 percent of its petroleum, and half its pig iron. Rising to first rank in world trade, the United States also shifted from a debtor to a creditor nation, becoming the world's leading banker.

The international system born in these years was unstable and fragmented. Espousing decolonization, nationalist leaders like Ho Chi Minh of Indochina and Mohandas K. Gandhi of India took to heart the Wilsonian principle of self-determination and vowed to achieve independence for their peoples. Communism became a new and disruptive force in world politics, and the Russians bore a grudge against those invaders who had tried to thwart their revolution. The new states in Central and Eastern Europe proved weak, dependent on outsiders for security. The Germans bitterly resented the harsh peace settlement. And the war debts and reparations problems dogged international order for years.

Unstable International System

The war experience also changed Americans' mood. The war was grimy and ugly. People recoiled from the photographs of bodies dangling from barbed wire, poison-gas victims, and battle-shocked faces. American soldiers were eager to return home. Apparently tired of idealism and cynical about their ability to right wrongs, they craved the latest baseball scores. Still, for the doughboys, the army years were memorable, a turning point in their lives.

Those progressives who had believed that entry into the war would deliver the millennium now marveled at their naiveté. Many lost their enthusiasm for crusades, and many others turned away in disgust from the bickering of the victors. Woodrow Wilson himself had remarked soon after taking office in 1913, before the Great War, that "there's no chance of progress and reform in an administration in which war plays the principal part." From the perspective of 1920, looking back on distempers at home and abroad, Wilson would have to agree with other Americans that progress and reform had been dealt blows.

Suggestions for Further Reading

General

LeRoy Ashby, *William Jennings Bryan* (1987); John W. Chambers, *The Tyranny of Change* (1980); Ellis W. Hawley, *The Great War and the Search for a Modern Order* (1979); Henry F. May, *The End of American Innocence* (1964); Emily S. Rosenberg, *Spreading the American Dream* (1982); Bernadotte Schmitt and Harold E. Vedeler, *The World in the Crucible: 1914–1919* (1984); Ronald Steel, *Walter Lippmann and the American Century* (1980); David P. Thelan, *Robert M. La Follette and the Insurgent Spirit* (1976); John A. Thompson, *Reformers and War* (1987).

Woodrow Wilson, His Diplomacy, and the First World War

Thomas A. Bailey and Paul B. Ryan, *The Lusitania Disaster* (1975); Kendrick A. Clements, *Woodrow Wilson, World Statesman* (1987); John W. Coogan, *The End of Neutrality* (1981); Patrick Devlin, *Too Proud to Fight* (1975); Robert H. Ferrell, *Woodrow Wilson and World War I* (1985); Lloyd C. Gardner, *Safe for Democracy: The Anglo-American Response to Revolution, 1913–1923* (1984); Ross Gregory, *The Origins of American Intervention in the First World War* (1971); Manfred Jonas, *The United States and Germany* (1984); N. Gordon Levin, Jr., *Woodrow Wilson and World Politics* (1968); Arthur S. Link, ed., *Woodrow Wilson and a Revolutionary World, 1913–1921* (1982); Arthur S. Link, *Woodrow Wilson: Revolution, War and Peace* (1979); Arthur S. Link, *Wilson*, 5 vols. (1947–1965); Ernest R. May, *The World War and American Isolation, 1914–1917* (1959); Barbara Tuchman, *The Zimmermann Telegram* (1958); Edwin A. Weinstein, *Woodrow Wilson: A Medical and Psychological Biography* (1981).

The American Military and the First World War

Arthur E. Barbeau and Florette Henri, *The Unknown Soldiers: Black American Troops in World War I* (1974); John W. Chambers, *To Raise an Army* (1987); J. Garry Clifford, *The Citizen Soldiers* (1972); Edward M. Coffman, *The War to End All Wars* (1968); Harvey A. DeWeerd, *President Wilson Fights His War* (1968); Marvin E. Fletcher, *The Black Soldier and Officer in the United States Army, 1891–1917* (1974); Thomas C. Leonard, *Above the Battle* (1978); Bernard C. Nalty, *Strength for the Fight* (1989); Donald Smythe, *Pershing* (1986); David Trask, *The United States in the Supreme War Council* (1961); Russell F. Weigley, *The American Way of War* (1973).

The Home Front

Allan M. Brandt, *No Magic Bullet* (1985) (on venereal disease); Valerie Jean Conner, *The National War Labor Board* (1983); Alfred W. Crosby, *America's Forgotten Pandemic: The Influenza of 1918* (1990); Robert D. Cuff, *The War Industries Board* (1973); Maurine W. Greenwald, *Women, War, and Work* (1980); David M. Kennedy, *Over Here* (1980); Seward W. Livermore, *Politics Is Adjourned* (1966); Stephen L. Vaughn, *Holding Fast the Inner Lines* (1979) (on CPI); Neil A. Wynn, *From Progressivism to Prosperity: World War I and American Society* (1986).

Black Americans on the Home Front

Robert V. Haynes, *A Night of Violence: The Houston Riot of 1917* (1976); James R. Grossman, *Land of Hope* (1989); Florette Henri, *Black Migration* (1975); Carole Marks, *Farewell—We're Good and Gone* (1989); Elliot M. Rudwick, *Race Riot at East St. Louis, July 2, 1917* (1964); William M. Tuttle, *Race Riot: Chicago in the Red Summer of 1919* (1970).

Wartime Dissent, Civil Liberties, and the Red Scare

David Brody, *Labor in Crisis: The Steel Strike of 1919* (1965); Charles Chatfield, *For Peace and Justice: Pacifism in America, 1914–1941* (1971); Stanley Coben, *A. Mitchell Palmer* (1963); Charles DeBenedetti, *Origins of the Modern Peace Movement* (1978); Sondra Herman, *Eleven Against War* (1969); Donald Johnson, *The Challenge to American Freedoms* (1963); C. Roland Marchand, *The American Peace Movement and Social Reform, 1898–1918* (1973); Paul L. Murphy, *World War I and the Origin of Civil Liberties* (1979); Robert K. Murray, *Red Scare* (1955); H. C. Peterson and Gilbert C. Fite, *Opponents of War, 1917–1918* (1968); Richard Polenberg, *Fighting Faiths* (1987) (on the *Abrams* case); William Preston, *Aliens and Dissenters: Federal Sup-*

pression of Radicals, 1903–1933 (1966); James Weinstein, *The Decline of Socialism in America, 1912–1923* (1967).

The Bolshevik Revolution and United States Intervention

Peter G. Filene, *Americans and the Soviet Experiment, 1917–1933* (1967); John L. Gaddis, *Russia, the Soviet Union, and the United States,* 2nd ed. (1990); George F. Kennan, *The Decision to Intervene* (1958); George F. Kennan, *Russia Leaves the War* (1956); Betty M. Unterberger, *The United States, Revolutionary Russia, and the Rise of Czechoslovakia* (1989); William Appleman Williams, *American-Russian Relations, 1781–1947* (1952).

Paris Peace Conference and League Fight

Lloyd Ambrosius, *Woodrow Wilson and the American Diplomatic Tradition* (1987); Thomas A. Bailey, *Woodrow Wilson and the Great Betrayal* (1945); Thomas A. Bailey, *Woodrow Wilson and the Lost Peace* (1944); Inga Floto, *Colonel House in Paris* (1973); Herbert Hoover, *The Ordeal of Woodrow Wilson* (1958); Warren F. Kuehl, *Seeking World Order* (1969); Arno Mayer, *Politics and Diplomacy of Peacemaking* (1967); Ralph A. Stone, *The Irreconcilables* (1970); Arthur Walworth, *Wilson and the Peacemakers* (1986); William C. Widenor, *Henry Cabot Lodge and the Search for an American Foreign Policy* (1980).

The Aftermath of War

Stanley Cooperman, *World War I and the American Mind* (1970); Malcolm Cowley, *Exile's Return* (1951); Paul Fussell, *The Great War and Modern Memory* (1975); Stuart I. Rochester, *American Liberal Disillusionment in the Wake of World War I* (1977); Stephen R. Ward, ed., *The War Generation: Veterans of the First World War* (1975).

Edward Albert Filene's most famous innovation was the "Automatic Bargain Basement," a section of his Boston department store in which prices automatically declined when merchandise failed to sell after a given period. Copied and elaborated by merchants across the country, the "bargain basement" became synonymous with the concept of offering goods in large variety at low prices. Filene believed his merchandising idea would give consumerism a good name and cause his store to be overrun with customers looking for values rather than bargains.

But E. A. Filene was more than just a conscientious retailer. In his numerous writings, as well as in his marketing innovations, Filene set the tone for much of the American outlook of the 1920s. He believed that mass production was about to create a world of abundance, in which trouble-free prosperity would ensure freedom and peace. The basis of prosperity, he wrote in 1929, was "the buying power of the masses." As prosperity spread throughout the world, it would "become a bulwark against war." Filene was also a reformer; he established unemployment and medical insurance for his employees, sponsored a program for city betterment in Boston, endowed a foundation, and supported high wages for all workers. But most of all, Filene had deep faith in the benefits of consumerism.

23

THE NEW ERA OF THE 1920s

Filene only had to look around him to justify his faith, for during the 1920s the flower of consumerism reached full bloom. Although poverty dogged small farmers, workers in declining industries, and nonwhites living in urban slums, the majority of the population enjoyed a high standard of living. Spurred by advertising and new forms of credit, Americans eagerly bought automobiles, radios, real estate, and stocks. As in the Gilded Age, government policies supported the interests of business. Congress, the Supreme Court, and three Republican presidents all directed their efforts toward maintaining a favorable climate for profits. Yet important reforms were accomplished at state and local levels of government.

In many ways, the decade was a time of complexities. Its frivolous stunts, contests, and fads were balanced by an outburst of creativity in literature, music, and art and by significant advances in science and technology. Changes in work habits, family responsibilities, and healthcare fostered new uses of time and new attitudes about proper behavior. Material bounty and increased leisure time enticed Americans into a variety of new amusements. Winds of change also stirred up waves of reaction. New, more liberal, values repelled various groups, such as the Ku Klux Klan, immigration restrictionists, and religious fundamentalists.

However, troubling clouds were gathering. The consumer culture that dominated everyday life caused Americans to ignore rising debts and other increasingly negative economic signs. Just before the decade closed, the whole system came crashing down.

Big Business Triumphant

The decade of business ascendancy did not begin very brightly. Besides political wrangling over ratification of the Treaty of Paris and the Red Scare, the nation suffered a frightening economic decline. For two years after the First World War, heavy consumer spending drove prices up. Then, in 1920, people stopped buying. Export trade and industrial output dropped as wartime orders ended. Farm income also plunged as the result of falling exports. Unemployment, around 2 percent in 1919, passed 12 percent in 1921. Railroad and mining industries suffered declining profits, and layoffs spread through New England as textile companies abandoned outdated factories for the raw materials and cheap labor of the South.

Recovery began in 1922 and continued unevenly until 1929. Electric motors were responsible for much of the expansion. By 1929, electricity powered 70 percent of American in-
Postwar Economic Recovery dustry. Assembly-line production also contributed to economic health, adding countless new consumer products to the market. As Americans acquired more spending money and as leisure time expanded, service industries boomed. More people could afford the goods and services of department stores, restaurants, and movie theaters. This new consumerism was fueled by refined methods of credit, especially the installment plan.

Behind the prosperity, an economic revolution was peaking. First, the consolidation movement that had bred trusts and holding companies reached a new stage. Although Progressive-era trustbusting had harnessed big business to some extent, it had not halted *oligopoly*—control of a whole industry by a few large firms. By the 1920s, oligopolies dominated not only production, but also marketing, distribution, and even financing. In such businesses as automobile manufacturing, steel production, meat processing, and railroads, a few sprawling companies predominated. Oligopolistic firms, like General Electric, General Motors, and U.S. Steel, developed management techniques to maximize profits and minimize market uncertainties.

The organizational movement that had begun around 1900 also matured in the 1920s. Myriad business and professional associations sprang up to protect members' interests. Retailers and small manufacturers formed trade associations to pool information and coordinate planning. Farm bureaus and cooperative associations promoted scientific agriculture, lobbied for government protection, and tried to stabilize markets. Lawyers, engineers, and social scientists cooperated with business to promote economic growth. Big business had begun to dominate American economic life in the late nineteenth century, but these consolidated, corporate forms of activity now pervaded so many segments of the economy that in many ways they marked the real separation of the twentieth century from the nineteenth. In this outburst of expansion, many Americans shed their fear of big business, swayed in part by testimonials of pro-business propagandists. "Among the nations of the earth today," one writer proclaimed in 1921, "America stands for one idea: *Business*."

Government reflected this outlook. In 1921, Congress reduced taxes on corporations and wealthy individuals, and in 1922 it raised tariff rates. Presidents Warren G. Harding, Calvin
Government Support of Business Coolidge, and Herbert Hoover appointed strong cabinet officers, who pursued policies favorable to business. Agencies such as the Federal Trade Commission and the Interstate Commerce Commission cooperated with corporations

IMPORTANT EVENTS

1919	Eighteenth Amendment ratified	**1923–24**	Exposure of government scandals
1920	Nineteenth Amendment ratified Harding elected president First commercial radio broadcast	**1924**	National Origins Act Coolidge elected president
		1925	Scopes trial
1920–21	Postwar deflation and depression	**1927**	Sacco and Vanzetti executed
1921	Immigration quotas established Sacco and Vanzetti convicted		Lindbergh's transatlantic flight Babe Ruth hits 60 home runs
1922	Economic recovery	**1928**	Hoover elected president
1923	Harding dies Coolidge assumes the presidency Peak of Ku Klux Klan activity Equal rights amendment introduced	**1929**	Stock market crashes; depression begins

more than they regulated them. And the Supreme Court, by voiding restrictions on child labor in *Bailey* v. *Drexel Furniture Company* (1922) and overturning a minimum wage law for women in *Adkins* v. *Children's Hospital* (1923), upheld business and struck down reform. Other Supreme Court decisions ruled that a striking union could be prosecuted for illegal restraint of trade but that trade associations could gather and disseminate antiunion information.

Organized labor, which had gained ground during the Progressive era, suffered other setbacks during the 1920s. Public opinion, influenced by

Suppression of Labor Unions

prosperity and probusiness rhetoric, turned against workers who disrupted everyday life with strikes. The federal government frequently stifled union attempts to exercise power. The Justice Department, for instance, used troops and court injunctions to end strikes by steel, mine, and railroad workers. Meanwhile, large corporations counteracted the appeal of unions by offering pensions, profit sharing, and company-sponsored social and sporting events—

a policy known as welfare capitalism. Employers also received aid from legislators in establishing measures that ensured open shop conditions (prohibiting mandatory employment of union members) over closed, or union, shop employment. In such a climate, union membership fell from 5.1 million in 1920 to 3.6 million in 1929.

A Business-minded Presidency

A Republican elected in 1920, at a time when the country wanted to avoid national and international crusades, President Warren G. Harding symbolized

Harding Administration

the decade's goodwill toward business. He chose some capable assistants, notably Secretary of State Charles Evans Hughes, Secretary of Commerce Herbert Hoover, Secretary of the Treasury Andrew Mellon, and Secretary of Agriculture Henry C. Wallace. Harding also backed some important reforms. He helped streamline the budget, supported antilynching legislation, approved bills assisting farm cooperatives and liberalizing farm credit, and, unlike his predecessor, Wilson, was generally tolerant on civil liberties issues.

Harding's problem was that he appointed some predatory friends to positions from which they infested the government with corruption. Charles Forbes of the Veterans Bureau served time in Leavenworth prison after being convicted of fraud and bribery in connection with government contracts. Attorney General Harry Daugherty was implicated in a scheme of accepting bribes and in other fraudulent acts; he escaped prosecution only by refusing to testify against himself. In the most notorious case of all, Secretary of the Interior Albert Fall had accepted bribes to lease government property to private oil companies. For his role in the affair, called the Teapot Dome scandal, after a Wyoming oil reserve that had been turned over to Mammoth Oil Company, Fall was fined $100,000 and spent a year in prison. He was the first cabinet officer to be so disgraced.

In June 1923, few Americans knew how corrupt Harding's administration had become. The president, however, was disillusioned. Amid rumors of mismanagement and crime, he told journalist William Allen White, "My God, this is a hell of a job. I have no trouble with my enemies. . . . But my friends, my God-damned friends . . . they're the ones that keep me walking the floor nights." On a speaking tour that summer, Harding became ill and died in San Francisco on August 2. Harding's successor, Vice President Calvin Coolidge, a former governor of Massachusetts, had first attracted national attention by his firm stand against striking Boston policemen in 1919, a policy that won him the vice-presidential nomination in 1920.

Coolidge had great respect for private enterprise, and his presidency coincided with extraordinary business prosperity. Aided by Andrew Mellon, whom he retained as secretary of the treasury, and other cabinet officers, his administration balanced the budget, reduced government debt, lowered income-tax rates (especially for the rich), and began construction of a national highway system. The only disruptions arose over

Coolidge Prosperity

Basically a shy and introverted person, Calvin Coolidge was content to give business free rein in its pursuit of profits. This cartoon shows Coolidge playing music for a lively performance by big business. *Culver Pictures.*

farm policy. Responding to farmers' complaints of falling prices, Congress twice passed bills to establish government-backed price supports for staple crops (the McNary-Haugen bills of 1927 and 1928). But Coolidge vetoed the measure both times.

"Coolidge prosperity" was the determining issue in the presidential election of 1924. That year, both major parties ran candidates who accepted business supremacy. Republicans nominated Coolidge with little dissent. At their national convention, Democrats first debated heatedly whether to condemn the Ku Klux Klan, voting 542 to 541 against condemnation. Then they endured 103 ballots before settling on John W. Davis, a corporation lawyer from New York. Remnants of the progressive movement, along with various farm, labor, and Socialist groups, formed a new Progressive party and nominated Robert M. La Follette, the aging reformer from Wisconsin. Coolidge beat Davis by

15.7 million to 8.4 million popular votes and 382 to 136 electoral votes. La Follette finished a poor third, receiving a respectable but ineffective 4.8 million popular votes and only 13 electoral votes.

Extensions of Reform

The triumph of business influence prompted some political analysts to claim that progressivism had died. They were partly right; concern for social and economic justice that had moved the previous generation faded in the 1920s. Yet many of the Progressive era's achievements were sustained and expanded in these years. Federal trustbusting declined, but regulatory commissions and other government agencies still monitored business activities and worked to reduce wasteful practices. In Congress, a corps of reformers kept progressive causes alive by supporting labor legislation, federal aid to farmers, and a government-owned hydroelectric dam at Muscle Shoals, Alabama.

Extension of Progressive Reforms

Most reforms, however, occurred at state and local levels. Following initiatives begun before the First World War, thirty-four states instituted or expanded workers' compensation laws in the 1920s. At the same time, many states established old-age pensions and other welfare programs. In cities, social scientists gathered data and drew maps in a systematic effort to identify and solve urban problems. Planning became a common feature of urban government; by 1926, every major city and many smaller ones had planning and zoning commissions that aimed to harness physical growth to the common good. Social workers continued to strive for better housing and poverty relief. During the 1920s, the nation's state houses, city halls, and universities trained a new generation of reformers, who would eventually influence national affairs during the New Deal government of the 1930s.

Indian affairs stirred some reform interest, though the generally apathetic stance of the federal government forced reformers to take adversary positions toward federal officials. No longer a threat to whites' ambitions, largely because of reduced numbers, Native Americans had become like other minorities: objects of discrimination and of pressures to assimilate. Severalty, the policy of allotting land to individual Indians rather than to tribes, had failed. Indian farmers suffered from poor soil, lack of irrigation, poor medical care, and white cattle thieves. Attached to their land, natives showed little desire to move to cities. Whites remained insensitive to Indian culture.

Indian Affairs

Some reformers realized that citizenship would have to come at the Indians' pace and with their consent. Organizations such as the Indian Rights Association, the American Indian Defence Association, and the General Federation of Women's Clubs worked to obtain racial justice and social services for Indians. Under President Hoover, expenditures were increased for health, education, and welfare. Yet much of the money went to enlarge the bureaucracy rather than into Indian hands, and paternalism continued to characterize policy toward Native Americans.

Certain continuities characterized women's politics even after the achievement of suffrage in 1920, when the Nineteenth Amendment was ratified. Rather than become enmeshed in party politics, women tended to remain tied to voluntary organizations, whose specialized memberships helped develop modern pressure-group politics. Whether their issue was birth control, education, or opposition to lynching, women in these associations tried to publicize their cause and lobby legislators rather than elect their own candidates.

Women and Politics

Still, women now were voters and as such faced a dilemma in electoral politics. Given that male party leaders were not likely to yield their power and would welcome only those women who accepted a party's platform and candidates, should women form their own party? The National Woman's party, which before suffrage had been the champion of feminism, still stressed female solidarity in the quest for equal rights. Other groups, such as the League of Women Voters, tried to avoid creating a female voting bloc, preferring instead to lobby for issues of interest to women while integrating women into politics with men—rather than constantly struggling against men. To the dismay of women's political groups, however, female voters participated in elections in the same small proportions as did men. Like men, they seemed caught up in the diversions of the new era's materialism.

Materialism Unbound

Poor Richard's Almanack would have sold poorly in the 1920s. Few Americans of that era had much interest in the virtues of thrift and sobriety that Benjamin Franklin had preached. They grew more attracted to acquisition, amusement, and salesmanship. Instead of heeding traditional homilies like "Waste not, want not," they succumbed to the advice of an advertising executive: "Make the public want what you have to sell. Make 'em pant for it." Although poverty and social injustice still blighted the country, many people shared the belief, as journalist Joseph Wood Krutch put it, that "the future was bright and the present was good fun at least."

Indeed, between 1919 and 1929, the gross national product—the total value of goods and services produced in the United States—swelled by 40 percent. Wages and salaries also increased (though not as much), while the cost of living remained relatively stable. As a result, people had more purchasing power, and they spent as Americans had never spent before. By 1929, two-thirds of all Americans lived in dwellings that had electricity, one-fourth of all families owned electric vacuum cleaners, and one-fifth had electric toasters. Many could afford these and other items, such as radios, washing machines, and movie tickets, only because more than one family member worked or because the breadwinner took a second job. Nevertheless, new products and services were available to more people than just the rich.

Expansion of the Consumer Society

Of all the era's technological and economic wonders, the automobile was the vanguard. During the 1920s, automobile registrations soared from 8 million to 23 million. Mass production and competi-

Effects of the Automobile

tion brought down prices, making cars affordable even to some working-class families. By 1926, a Ford Model T cost under $300 and a Chevrolet sold for $700—at a time when workers in manufacturing earned about $1,300 a year and clerical workers about $2,300.

The motor car altered society as much as the railroad had seventy-five years earlier. Public officials were forced to pay more attention to safety regulations and traffic control. The growing choice of models and colors allowed owners to suit their personal tastes in a growing mass society. Most important, the car was the ultimate symbol of social equality.

More than ever, the taste for automobiles and other goods and services was whetted by advertising. By 1929, total advertising earnings reached $3.4 billion, more than was spent on all types of formal education. For many, advertising became the language of a new gospel. In his best-selling *The Man Nobody Knows* (1925), advertising executive Bruce Barton called Jesus "the founder of modern business" because he "picked up twelve men from the bottom ranks of business and forged them into an organization that conquered the world."

Advertising

Although daily newspaper circulation declined during the 1920s, more than 10 million families owned radios at the decade's end. A new advertising medium had been discovered. Station KDKA in Pittsburgh pioneered in commercial radio broadcasting beginning in 1920; by 1922, there were 508 such stations. By 1929, the National Broadcasting Company, which had begun to assemble a network of radio stations three years earlier, was charging advertisers $10,000 to sponsor an hour-long show. Commercial intermissions at movie houses and highway billboards also reminded viewers to buy.

Cities, Migrants, and Suburbs

The expansion of consumerism bespoke not only an economically mature nation, but also an urbanized one. By the 1920s, the city had become the

"Everyone owns a car but us"~

You, too, can own an automobile without missing the money, and *now*, is the time to buy it—through the easiest and simplest method ever devised:

Ford Weekly Purchase Plan

Thousands of families, who thought a car was out of the question because of limited incomes, found that they could easily, quickly and surely buy a car of their own under this remarkable plan

You can own an automobile, and you *should*. It will mean so much to you. It will add much to the happiness of your family that is worth while. It will bring the most glorious pleasures into your life. It will increase your chances for success. It will give you and your family a social and business prestige that will be invaluable—and which you, and every family, should enjoy. A car is a symbol of success—a mark of achievement, and it brings opportunities to you that you would probably never secure otherwise. You should have a car of your own, and you can.

The Ford Plan makes it possible for anyone to own an automobile. It is so easy, simple and practical that many who could easily pay "spot cash" take advantage of it—and buy their car from weekly earnings. The plan is simply wonderful! Before you realize it, you are driving your own automobile. If you have felt that you did not make enough to buy a car, you must read The Ford Plan. Send for it. See how easy it is to get a car of your own, now, and pay for it without missing the money. It seems almost too good to be true, doesn't it? *But it is true.* Get the book—at once. Simply mail the coupon. *Mail it today!*

Give your family the advantages which others have. Get a car of your own. The Ford Plan book tells you "how" you can buy a car and pay for it without missing the money. Get it! Read it!

Mail Coupon Now. This Book Will be Sent to By return Mail.

COUPON
FORD MOTOR COMPANY
Dept. B-3 Detroit, Michigan
Please send me your book, "The Ford Plan" which fully explains your easy plan for owning an automobile.

Name ....

R. F. D. Box or St. & No. ....

Town .... State ....

Ford Motor Company
Detroit

IT IS EASY TO OWN A CAR BY USING THIS PLAN

By the 1920s, the automobile was affordable, especially through installment payments such as the "Ford Weekly Purchase Plan." As this advertisement so vividly illustrates, Americans were made to feel that they needed an automobile for the pleasure and status it would bring. *Library of Congress.*

Continuing Urbanization locus of national experience, and urban expansion occurred across the nation. Cities in warm climates, such as Miami and San Diego, underwent the most explosive growth. The trend toward urbanization continued during the 1920s, as an estimated 6 million Americans left their farms for nearby or distant cities. African-Americans accounted for a sizable portion of the migrants. Crushed by tenant farming and lured by industrial jobs, 1.5 million blacks moved cityward, accelerating a trend that began a decade earlier. Black populations of New York, Chicago, Detroit, and Houston doubled. Forced by necessity and discrimination to seek the cheapest housing, newcomers squeezed into ghettos—low-rent districts from which escape

was difficult at best. When overcrowding burst the boundaries of the ghetto and African-Americans spilled over into nearby white neighborhoods, racial violence often resulted.

In response partly to their new urban experiences and partly to race riots and threats, thousands of blacks in northern cities joined movements that glorified black independence. The most influential of these black **Marcus Garvey** nationalist groups was the Universal Negro Improvement Association (UNIA), headed by Marcus Garvey, a Jamaican immigrant, who believed that blacks should separate themselves from corrupt white society. Proclaiming "I am the equal of any white man," Garvey cultivated racial pride through militant mass meetings and parades. He also promoted black capitalism. His newspaper, the *Negro World*, refused to publish ads for hair straighteners and skin-lightening cosmetics, and his Black Star shipping line was intended to help blacks emigrate to Africa.

The UNIA declined in the mid-1920s, when the Black Star line went bankrupt (unscrupulous dealers had sold the line dilapidated ships) and when antiradical fears prompted government prosecution (ten of the organization's leaders were arrested on charges of anarchism and Garvey was deported for mail fraud). Black middle-class leaders like W. E. B. Du Bois opposed the UNIA. Nevertheless, the association attracted a huge following, and it served notice that blacks had their own aspirations, which they could and would translate into action.

The newest immigrants to American cities came from Mexico and Puerto Rico. As in the nineteenth century, Mexicans moved north to work as agricultural laborers in the Southwest, **Mexican and Puerto Rican Immigrants** but in the 1920s a large number also flowed into growing cities, such as Denver, San Antonio, Los Angeles, and Tucson. Like other immigrant groups, they generally lacked resources and skills, and men greatly outnumbered women. Victims of Anglo prejudice, they crowded into low-rent, inner-city districts. Yet their communities, called *barrios*, provided an environment in which immigrants could sustain customs and values of the homeland and develop institutions to help them adapt to American society.

The 1920s also saw a great influx of Puerto Ricans to the mainland. A shift in the island's economy from sugar to coffee production had created a surplus population willing to move and attracted by contracts from American employers seeking cheap labor. Most Puerto Rican migrants came to New York City, where they formed barrios in parts of Brooklyn and Manhattan. Puerto Rican and Mexican communities contained some educated elites—doctors, lawyers, and business owners—who served as ethnic leaders.

As urban growth peaked, suburban growth accelerated. Although towns had existed around the edges of urban centers since the nation's earliest years, prosperity and easier transportation—mainly the automobile—made the urban fringe more accessible in the 1920s. Between 1920 and 1930, suburbs of Chicago, Cleveland, and Los Angeles grew five to ten times as fast as the central cities. Most suburbs were middle- and upper-class bedroom communities.

Growth of the Suburbs

The bulging cities and suburbs fostered the new mass culture that gave the decade its character. Most of the consumers who jammed shops, movie houses, and sporting arenas and who embraced fads like crossword puzzles and marathon dancing were city and suburban dwellers. Cities and suburbs were the places where people defied law and convention by patronizing speakeasies (illegal saloons), wearing outlandish clothes, and listening to jazz. Yet the ideal of small-town society survived. While millions thronged cityward and intellectuals carped that small towns stifled personal growth, Americans reminisced about the innocence and simplicity of a world gone by. This was the dilemma of a modern nation: how could one anchor oneself in a world of rampant material and social change?

New Rhythms of Everyday Life

Amid all the change, Americans developed new social values and new ways of using time. Increasingly, people were splitting their daily lives into three distinct compartments: work, family, and leisure. Each type of time was altered in the 1920s. For many people, time on the job shrank. Among industrial workers, the five-and-a-half-day workweek (half a day on Saturday) was becoming common. Many white-collar employees enjoyed two days off and worked a forty-hour week. Annual vacations were becoming a standard job benefit for white-collar workers, whose numbers grew by 40 percent.

Family time is harder to measure, but certain figures suggest important changes. As birth control became more widely practiced, birthrates dropped noticeably between 1920 and 1930. As a result, family size decreased. During the same period, the divorce rate rose. In 1920, there was 1 divorce in every 7.5 marriages; in 1929, the national ratio was 1 in 6, and in many cities it was 2 in 7. Lower birthrates, more divorces, and a longer life expectancy meant that adults were devoting a smaller portion of their lives to parental and other family tasks.

The availability of ready-to-wear clothes, preserved foods, and mass-produced furniture meant that family members needed less time for providing household necessities. Wives still spent most of their day cleaning, cooking, mending, and raising children, but new machines lightened some of their tasks. Instead of being a producer of food and clothing, as women had been in the past, the wife became chief consumer, shopping and making sure that the family spent its money wisely.

Household Management

In addition, the ready availability of washing machines, hot water, and commercial soap put great pressure on wives to keep everything clean. Advertisers tried to coax women into buying products by making them feel guilty for not giving enough attention to cleaning the home, caring for children, and tending to personal hygiene. Thus, while the industrial and service sectors became more specialized as a result of technological advances, housewives retained a wide variety of tasks and added new ones as well.

While family time shifted and work time decreased, nonwork and nonfamily activities expanded. High school enrollment quadrupled between 1910 and 1929; by 1929, more than one-third of all high school graduates went on to college. As the use of electricity spread, people stayed up later at night to read or listen to the radio. They filled expanding leisure time with automobile rides, sports events, motion pictures, shopping, and other forms of amusement.

With more people spending time away from work and family, new values were inevitable. Especially among middle-class people, but also among those of the working class, clothes

Social Values became a means of personal expression and freedom. Both men and women wore more casual styles and gayer colors than their parents would have considered. The line between inappropriate and acceptable behavior blurred as smoking, swearing, and frankness about sex became more common. Thousands who had never read psychoanalyst Sigmund Freud's theories were certain that he prescribed an uninhibited sex life as the key to mental health. Birth-control advocate Margaret Sanger gained a large following in respectable circles. Newspapers, magazines, motion pictures, and popular songs made certain that Americans did not suffer from "sex starvation."

Other trends contributed to the breakdown of old values. Because child-labor laws and laws that made school attendance compulsory kept children in school longer than was common in earlier generations, schools and peer groups played a greater role in socializing children. In earlier times, different age groups had common activities: children worked with older people in the fields, and young apprentices worked with older journeymen and craftsmen. Now, however, graded school classes, sports, clubs, and other activities constantly brought together children who were the same age, separating them from the company and influence of adults. In addition, parents tended to rely less on family tradition and more on childcare manuals in raising children. Old-age homes, public health clinics, and workers' compensation reduced family responsibilities even further.

Despite shrinkage in the employment opportunities that had been created by the First World War, women continued to stream into the labor force. By

Jobs for Women 1930, 10.8 million women held paying jobs, an increase of more than 2 million since the war's end. The sex segregation that had long characterized occupations continued; most female workers held jobs at which few men worked. More than a million women were teachers and nurses. Some 2.2 million were typists, bookkeepers, and office clerks, a tenfold increase since 1920; another 736,000 were store clerks. Almost 2 million women worked in factories, but their numbers grew very little during the decade. Whatever the employment, wages paid to women seldom equaled more than half of the wages paid to men.

Entry into work outside the home extended women's family roles. Although they worked for a combination of reasons, the economic needs of their families shaped most women's job experiences. The consumerism of the 1920s prompted many working-class and middle-class families to satisfy their wants by sending women and children into the labor force. In previous eras, most of these extra wage earners had been young and single. In the 1920s, the number of employed married women swelled from 1.9 million to 3.1 million (though this figure includes countless widows, divorcées, and abandoned women who held jobs). The vast majority of married women remained out of the work force (only 12 percent were employed in 1930), but they did so because social pressures and the demands of housework and childcare prevented them from joining. Black women were the exception; their proportions in the work force were twice those of white women. Extended kin, such as grandmothers and aunts, helped with childcare while black mothers took outside employment.

Feminists in the 1920s focused on the issue of women in the labor force. Women's earlier functions as producers of food and clothes, said feminists, had lapsed into passive roles

Economic Feminism as child nurturers and homemakers; the result was economic dependency. The way to restore married women's sense of worth in a money-oriented society was through gainful employment. Moreover, feminists believed that women should challenge the sexual division of labor. They also tended to oppose protective legislation that limited hours and improved conditions in industries dominated by female workers. Instead, feminists heeded the call for equal pay and equal opportunity voiced by Alice Paul, leader of the National Woman's party, who in 1923 supported an equal rights amendment to the Constitution. But other women, especially in the working class, had doubts. They did not trust the competitive, individualistic environment of job markets, and they had been raised in cultures that assigned women the responsibility of maintaining cooperation within their families and neighborhoods.

Employed or not, women were exposed to alternative images of femininity. Short skirts and bobbed hair, regarded as signs of sexual freedom,

Alternative Images of Femininity became common among office workers, store clerks, and college coeds. Several studies claimed that sexual experimentation, including premarital sex, increased among young women during the decade. The most popular models of female behavior were not chaste, modest heroines, but movie vamps like Clara Bow, known as the "It Girl," and Gloria Swanson, known for torrid love affairs on and off the screen. Not every woman was a flapper, as the young independent-minded woman was called, but many women were asserting social equality with men.

These new trends represented a sharp break with the more restrained culture of the nineteenth century. But social change, as always, did not proceed smoothly. As the decade wore on, various groups prepared to defend the older, more familiar values against the new threats.

Lines of Defense

In the spring of 1920, the leader of a revived organization decided to hire two public relations experts to recruit members. Using modern advertising techniques, the promoters canvassed communities in the South, Southwest, and Midwest, where they found thousands of men eager to join. By 1923, the organization, the Ku Klux Klan, claimed 5 million members.

The Klan was the most sinister reactionary movement of the 1920s. Reconstituted in 1915 by William J. Simmons, an Atlanta evangelist and insurance

Ku Klux Klan salesman who wanted to purify southern culture, the new Invisible Empire revived the hoods, intimidating tactics, and mystical terms of its forerunner. The new Klan, however, was broader in membership and objectives than the old. Its chapters fanned outward from the deep South and for a time wielded frightening power in all other regions of the country. Unlike the first Klan, which terrorized mostly emancipated blacks, the new Klan directed its venom toward a variety of groups.

Assuming the role of moral protectors, Klan members meted out vigilante justice to blacks, presumed bootleggers, wife beaters, and adulterers; they forced schools to adopt Bible readings and stop teaching the theory of evolution; and they campaigned against Catholic and Jewish political candidates. By the mid-1920s, however, the Invisible Empire was on the wane, outnumbered by immigrants and their offspring and rocked by scandal. (In 1925, Indiana Grand Dragon David Stephenson allegedly kidnapped and raped a woman, who later died either from taking poison or from an infection caused by bites on her body; Stephenson was convicted of second-degree murder on the grounds that he was responsible for her suicide.)

The Ku Klux Klan had no monopoly on bigotry; intolerance still pervaded American society. Since the 1880s, a number of groups had been urging an end to free immigration. Huge influxes of Catholic and Jewish immigrants, nativists charged, clogged inner-city slums, upset traditional norms with their drinking habits, and stubbornly held to alien religious and political beliefs.

Fear of radicalism, left over from the Red Scare of 1919, fueled antiforeign sentiments. The most notorious outburst of hysteria occurred in 1921,

Sacco and Vanzetti when a court convicted Nicola Sacco and Bartolomeo Vanzetti, two immigrant anarchists, of murdering a guard and paymaster during a robbery in South Braintree, Massachusetts. Sacco and Vanzetti's main offenses seem to have

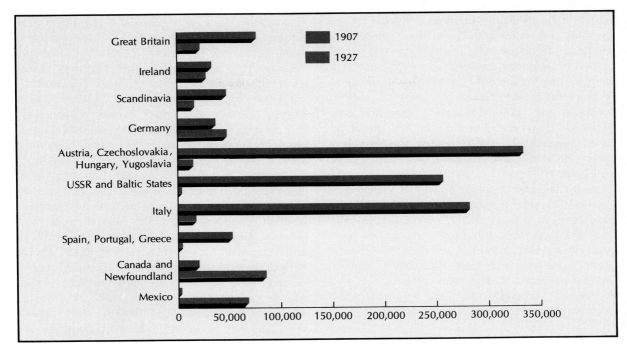

Immigration, 1907 and 1927

been their political beliefs and Italian origin, since evidence failed to prove their involvement in the robbery. Nevertheless, Judge Webster Thayer openly sided with the prosecution, privately calling the defendants "those anarchist bastards." The execution of the two in August 1927 chilled those who had looked to the United States as the land that nurtured freedom of belief.

Meanwhile, Congress responded to the mounting pressure to restrict immigration by enacting laws that set yearly immigration quotas for each nationality. The quotas favored northern and western Europeans, reflecting the prejudices of the nativists against new immigrants from southern and eastern Europe. The Emergency Quota (Johnson) Act of 1921 stipulated that annual immigration of a given nationality could not exceed 3 percent of the number of immigrants from that nation residing in the United States in 1910. This law, meant to be temporary, did not satisfy restrictionists' aims, and so Congress replaced it with the National Origins Act of 1924. The new law set the

Immigration Quotas

quota at 2 percent of each nationality residing in the United States in 1890. Congress amended the National Origins Act in 1927, moving the base year to 1920 and fixing a limit of 150,000 immigrants a year—including 65,721 from Great Britain and 25,957 from Germany but only 5,802 from Italy and 2,712 from Russia. The laws excluded Asians but set no quotas for peoples from the Western Hemisphere. Soon Canadians, Mexicans, and Puerto Ricans became the largest groups of newcomers (see figure).

The impulse to ensure moral purity also stirred religious fundamentalists, especially those concerned about the theory of evolution. In 1925, the Tennessee legislature passed a law forbidding public school instructors to teach the theory that humans had evolved from lower forms of life rather than from Adam and Eve. Shortly afterward, a Dayton, Tennessee, high school teacher, John Thomas Scopes, was arrested for violating the law (he had volunteered to serve in a test case). Scopes's trial that summer became a headline

Scopes Trial

event, with William Jennings Bryan, former secretary of state and three-time presidential candidate, arguing for the prosecution, and a team of civil liberties lawyers, headed by Clarence Darrow, arguing for the defense. Hordes of news correspondents crowded into town, and radio stations broadcast the trial. Although Scopes was convicted—clearly he had broken the law—modernists claimed victory. The testimony, they believed, showed fundamentalism to be at odds with secular social trends.

Americans' emotional responses to events during the 1920s were part of an attempt to sustain old, local ways in a fast-moving, materialistic world. Even as they worried about losing old values, however, most Americans tried to adjust to the new order in one way or another. They went to movies, listened to music on the radio, attended sporting events, and generally attempted to find release from societal pressures in a world of leisure.

The Age of Play

During the 1920s Americans developed an almost insatiable thirst for recreation. Entrepreneurs responded quickly. The decade marked the flowering of fads, frivolities, and what contemporaries called ballyhoo—a blitz of publicity that lent exaggerated importance to some person or event. New games and fancies were particularly attractive to middle-class families. In the early 1920s, the Chinese tile game of mahjong was the rage. By the mid-1920s, people were turning to crossword puzzles; a few years later fun seekers adopted miniature golf as their new craze. Throughout the decade, dance crazes such as the Charleston riveted public attention, aided by radio music and the growing popularity of jazz.

Besides engaging in leisure activities, Americans were avid spectators, particularly of movies and sports. In 1922, movies attracted 40 million viewers a week; by 1930, the number had reached 100 million—at a time when total population was just over 120 million and total weekly church atten-

Movies

dance was under 60 million. The introduction of sound in *The Jazz Singer* in 1927 and of color a few years later made movies even more attractive and realistic. The most popular films were mass spectacles, such as Cecil B. De Mille's *The Ten Commandments* (1923); lurid dramas, such as *A Woman Who Sinned* (1924); and slapstick comedies. Ironically, the comedies, with their poignant satire of the human condition, carried the most thought-provoking messages.

Spectator sports also boomed. Each year, millions packed stadiums and parks to watch athletic events. By the late 1920s, gate receipts from college football alone surpassed $21 million. In an age when technology and mass production had robbed experiences and objects of their uniqueness, sports provided unpredictability and drama that people craved. Baseball, with its drawn-out suspense, infinite variety of plays, and potential for statistics keeping, attracted a huge following. Newspapers and radio captured and exaggerated the drama of sports, feeding news to an eager public and often overpromoting events with unrestrained narrative.

Sports, movies, and the news gave Americans a galaxy of heroes. As society became more anonymous and the individual less significant, people clung to heroic personalities as a

Sports Heroes

means of identifying with the unique. Boxing, football, and baseball produced the biggest sports heroes. Heavyweight champion Jack Dempsey, a powerful brawler from Manassa, Colorado, attracted the first of many million-dollar gates in his fight with Georges Carpentier in 1921. Harold "Red" Grange, running back for the University of Illinois football team, thrilled thousands and became the idol of sportswriters. Baseball's major hero was George Herman "Babe" Ruth, who began his career as a pitcher but found that he could use his prodigious strength to better advantage hitting home runs. Ruth hit 29 of them in 1919, 54 in 1920, 59 in 1924, and 60 in 1927—each year a record. His exaggerated gestures on the field, defiant life style, and boyish grin endeared him to millions and made him a national legend.

If Americans identified with the physical exploits of sports stars, they fulfilled a yearning for romance and adventure through adulation of movie stars.

Rudolph Valentino became the idol of men and women alike in *The Sheik*, his most famous movie. With flashing eyes and wanton smile, Valentino carries a swooning woman to his tent. This immensely popular movie earned a million dollars for Paramount Pictures. *Museum of Modern Art, Film Stills Archive.*

Movie Stars and Public Heroes Films and the personal lives of Douglas Fairbanks, Gloria Swanson, Charlie Chaplin, and others were discussed in parlors and pool halls across the country. Perhaps the decade's most ballyhooed personality was Rudolph Valentino, whose Latin machismo made women swoon and prompted men to copy his pomaded hairdo and slick sideburns.

News promoters created their own heroes beyond athletics and entertainment. Flagpole sitters, marathon dancers, and other record seekers regularly occupied front pages. The most notable news hero was Charles A. Lindbergh, the pilot whose daring nonstop solo flight across the Atlantic in 1927 was cheered by millions. A modest, independent midwesterner whom writers dubbed the Lone Eagle, Lindbergh accepted fame but did not try to profit from it. Because his quiet personality contrasted so starkly with the ballyhoo that surrounded him, Americans honored him even more fervently.

In part, adulation of Lindbergh may have reflected guilt over betrayal of traditional virtues of restraint and moderation, for in their quest for fun and individual expression— **Prohibition** liberties that Prohibition seemed to deny—Americans became lawbreakers and supporters of crime. The Eighteenth Amendment (1919) and federal law that prohibited the manufacture, sale, and transportation of alcoholic beverages worked well at first. Per capita consumption of liquor dropped, arrests for drunkenness diminished, and the price of illegal booze rose higher than the average worker could afford.

But after 1925, the noble experiment broke down in cities, where desire for personal freedom overwhelmed weak enforcement.

Criminal organizations were quick to capitalize on this fact. The most notorious of such mobs belonged to Al Capone, a burly tough who seized control of illegal liquor and vice **Al Capone** organizations in Chicago and exercised his influence through bribery, intimidation, and violence. It is important to recognize that Prohibition and its weak enforcement did not create organized crime. Gangs like Capone's had provided illegal goods and services long before the 1920s. As Capone explained it, "Prohibition is a business. All I do is supply a public demand."

Thus, during the 1920s, Americans were caught between two value systems. On the one hand, the Puritan tradition of hard work, sobriety, and restraint—"Waste not, want not"—still prevailed, especially in rural areas, where new diversions were unavailable. On the other hand, a liberating age of play beckoned. At no previous time in American history had so many opportunities for recreation existed.

Cultural Currents

Tension between value systems pulled artists and intellectuals in new directions. Rejection of old beliefs prompted experimentation in literature, art, and music. Fear that materialism and conformity were being fostered by mass society gave this movement a bitterly critical tinge. Yet critics seldom voiced a radical message; they had no urge to destroy modern society, but only to protect the individual from vulgar forces.

Many of the era's leading literary figures, finding vulgar materialism hostile to their art, became disillusioned and were known as the Lost Generation. A number of them moved **Literature** to Europe. Others remained in **of Alienation** America but assailed what they saw happening around them. Along with innovative forms of expression and realistic portrayals of emotions, these writers also produced biting social commentary. The dominant themes of social criticism were middle- and upper-class materialism and the impersonality of modern society. F. Scott Fitzgerald's novels and Eugene O'Neill's plays exposed Americans' overemphasis on money. The powerful antiwar sentiments of John Dos Passos' *Three Soldiers* (1921) and Ernest Hemingway's *Farewell to Arms* (1929) were skillfully interwoven with passionate critiques of the impersonality of modern relationships.

A spiritual discontent quite different from that of white writers inspired a new generation of young black artists. Middle class and well educated, these writers often rejected the amal- **Harlem** gamation of black and white **Renaissance** cultures, exalting the militantly assertive "New Negro," proud of his or her African heritage. Most of them lived in Harlem, the black section of upper Manhattan. In this "Negro Mecca," black intellectuals and artists, aided by a few white patrons, celebrated modern black culture in what became known as the Harlem Renaissance.

Harlem in the 1920s nurtured a number of gifted writers, among them Langston Hughes, whose poems captured the mood and rhythm of blues and jazz; Countee Cullen, a poet with moving lyrical skills; and Claude McKay, whose militant verses invoked rebellion against bigotry. Jean Toomer's poems and his novel *Cane* (1923) portrayed black life with passionate realism, and Alain Locke's essays gave direction to the artistic renaissance. The movement also embraced visual artists, including James A. Porter, whose paintings became part of every important exhibition of black artists, and Augusta Savage, who sculpted busts of many famous black personalities.

Issues of identity vexed many participants in the Harlem Renaissance. Although black intellectuals and artists took pride in their African heritage and culture, they also realized that black Americans had to assert themselves and come to terms with themselves as Americans. Thus, Locke urged that the New Negro should "lay aside the status of beneficiary and ward for that of a collaborator and participant in American civilization."

The Jazz Age, as the decade of the 1920s is sometimes called, owed its name to music that grew out of black urban culture. Evolving from African and black American folk music, early **Jazz** jazz communicated unrestrained freedom that blacks seldom knew in their public, working, and political lives. With its emotional rhythms and emphasis on improvisation, jazz blurred the distinction between composer and performer and created new intimacy between performer and audience. Jazz also endowed America with its most distinctive art form.

In many ways, the 1920s were the most creative years that the nation had yet experienced. Influenced by jazz and experimental writing, painters such as Georgia O'Keeffe and John Marin tried to forge a unique American style of painting. European composers and performers still dominated classical music, but Americans such as Henry Cowell, who pioneered electronic music, and Aaron Copland, who built orchestral and vocal works around native folk motifs, began careers that later won wide acclaim. George Gershwin blended jazz, classical, and folk musical forms in his serious compositions, musical dramas, and numerous hit tunes. In architecture, Frank Lloyd Wright's "prairie-style" houses, churches, and schools reflected the magnificence of the American landscape. At the beginning of the decade, essayist Harold Stearns had complained that "the most . . . pathetic fact in the social life of America today is emotional and aesthetic starvation." By 1929, such a contention was hard to support.

The Election of 1928 and the End of the New Era

Whatever doubts intellectuals may have had about materialism in the 1920s faded before the confident rhetoric of politics. Herbert Hoover epitomized that confidence in his speech accepting the Republican nomination for president in 1928. "We in America today," he boasted, "are nearer to the final triumph over poverty than ever before in the history of any land. . . . We have not yet reached the

goal, but, given a chance to go forward with the policies of the last eight years, we shall soon, with the help of God, be in sight of the day when poverty will be banished from this nation."

As Hoover's opponent, Democrats chose Governor Alfred E. Smith of New York, whose career contrasted markedly with that of Hoover. Whereas Hoover had rural, native, Protestant, business roots and had never **Al Smith** run for public office, Smith was an urbane, gregarious politician of immigrant stock whose career was rooted in New York City's Tammany Hall. Smith was the first Roman Catholic to run for president on a major party ticket. As such, he had considerable appeal among urban ethnic groups, who were voting in increasing numbers, but he lost southern and rural votes for the same reason.

Although Smith waged a spirited campaign, Hoover, who stressed the nation's prosperity, won the popular vote by 21 million to 15 million and the electoral vote by 444 to 87. But Smith's candidacy had important effects on the Democratic party. Smith carried the nation's twelve largest cities, which formerly had given majorities to Republican candidates, and lured millions of foreign-stock voters to the polls for the first time. From 1928 on, the Democratic party would solidify this urban base, which, when combined with its traditional strength in the South, made the party a formidable force in national elections.

Democrats and Republicans both had reasons to be encouraged in 1928. In his inaugural address, Hoover proclaimed a New Day, "bright with hope." **Hoover's Administration** His cabinet, composed mostly of businessmen, included six millionaires devoted to the existing order. To the lower ranks of government, Hoover appointed mostly young professionals who agreed with him that scientific methods could be applied to solve national problems.

If the Hoover administration was optimistic, so were most Americans. Reverence for what Hoover called "the American system" ran high. The belief that individuals were responsible for their own condition and that unemployment or poverty suggested a personal failing was widespread. Prevailing thought also held that changes in the business cycle were natural and therefore not to be tampered with.

This confidence was jolted in the fall of 1929, when stock prices suddenly plunged. Analysts explained the drop as a temporary condition caused

Stock Market Crash

by a "lunatic fringe." But on October 24, Black Thursday, panic selling set in. The price of many stocks hit record lows; some sellers could find no buyers. At noon, banking leaders met at the headquarters of J. P. Morgan and Company to halt the skid. To restore faith, they put up $20 million and ceremoniously began buying stocks like U.S. Steel. The mood changed and some stocks rallied.

But as news of Black Thursday spread across the country, fearful investors decided to sell their stocks rather than risk further drops. On Black Tuesday, October 29, stock prices plummeted again. The market settled into a grim pattern of declines and weak rallies. Hoover, who had never approved of what he called the "fever of speculation," assured Americans that the economy was sound. He shared the popular assumption that the stock market's ills could be quarantined and that the economy was strong enough to endure until the stock market righted itself.

Instead of reversing, the crash ultimately helped to unleash a devastating depression. The economic downturn did not come suddenly; it was more like

Over-production

a leak in a punctured tire than a blowout. There were several interrelated causes of the weak economy and ultimately the Great Depression. The first was overproduction. Throughout the 1920s, farmers produced more and more to compensate for declining crop prices and mounting debts. Industries like coal, railroads, and textiles were in distress long before 1929; the automobile and construction industries also faced troubles early. These weaknesses meant that by 1929 major sectors of the economy were not expanding; owners were not investing funds to build new plants and hire more workers. Instead, unsold inventories were stacking up in warehouses, and laborers were being laid off.

The onset and severity of the depression can also be attributed to underconsumption. Production (supply) had outstripped consumption (demand).

Under-consumption

Wages and mass purchasing power had lagged behind the industrial surge of the 1920s; workers who produced the new consumer goods ultimately could not afford to buy them. Farmers suffered economic distress and had to trim their purchases. As industries declined, they held wages down and sent home laborers, who lacked the money to buy goods.

Underconsumption also resulted from the unequal distribution of income. Between 1920 and 1929, average per capita disposable income rose about 9 percent, but the income of the wealthiest 1 percent rose 75 percent, accounting for most of the increase. Much of this increase was put into luxuries, savings, and stock market investments instead of being spent on consumer goods.

American business was unbalanced because oligopolies dominated each industry. In 1929, the top two hundred nonfinancial corporations con-

Oligopolies

trolled 49 percent of corporate wealth. Many corporations built pyramid-like empires supported by shady, though legal, manipulation of assets. When one part of the edifice collapsed, the entire structure crumbled.

The depression also derived from pell-mell, largely unregulated, speculation on the stock market. Corporations and banks invested huge sums in

Speculation on the Stock Market

stocks, and some even speculated in their own issues. Brokers sold stocks to buyers who put up little cash, borrowed in order to purchase, and then used as collateral for loans the stocks that they had bought but not fully paid for. When stock prices collapsed, so did brokerage firms, banks, and investment companies.

International economic troubles constitute a fifth explanation for the crash and depression. As the world's leading creditor and trader, the United

International Economic Troubles

States was deeply involved in the world economy. Billions of dollars in loans had flowed to Europe during the First World War and during postwar reconstruction. Yet in the late 1920s, American investors were beginning to invest more of their money at home in the lucrative stock market. Europeans, unable to borrow more funds and unable to sell their goods easily in the American market because of high tariffs, began to buy less from the United States and to default on their debts. Pinched at home, they raised their own tariffs, further disabling international commerce, and withdrew their investments from America.

Finally, government policies and practices contributed to the crash and depression. The federal government failed to regulate wild speculation. It neither checked corporate power nor raised income taxes to encourage a more equitable distribution of income. The Federal Reserve Board pursued easy credit policies, even though it knew that easy money was financing the speculative mania.

Failure of Federal Policies

In 1929, conventional wisdom, based on the experience of previous depressions, held that little could be done to correct economic problems; they simply had to run their course, like a common cold. So people waited for the deflation to bottom out, never realizing that the era of expansion and frivolity had come to an end and that the nation's culture and politics, as well as its economy, would have to be rebuilt.

Suggestions for Further Reading

Overviews of the 1920s

Frederick Lewis Allen, *Only Yesterday* (1931); Paul A. Carter, *Another Part of the Twenties* (1977); Ellis Hawley, *The Great War and the Search for a Modern Order* (1979); William E. Leuchtenburg, *The Perils of Prosperity* (1958).

Business and the Economy

Irving L. Bernstein, *The Lean Years: A History of the American Worker, 1920–1933* (1960); James J. Flink, *The Car Culture* (1975); Stephen Fox, *The Mirror Makers: A History of American Advertising and Its Creators* (1984); John Rae,

The Road and the Car in American Life (1971); Robert Zieger, *Republicans and Labor, 1919–1929* (1969).

Politics and Law

Christine Bolt, *American Indian Policy and American Reform* (1987); David Burner, *The Politics of Provincialism* (1968); Nancy F. Cott, *The Grounding of American Feminism* (1988); Paula Elder, *Governor Alfred E. Smith: The Politician as Reformer* (1983); Allan J. Lichtman, *Prejudice and the Old Politics: The Presidential Election of 1928* (1979); Donald R. McCoy, *Calvin Coolidge* (1967); Alpheus Mason, *The Supreme Court from Taft to Warren* (1958); Robert K. Murray, *The Harding Era* (1969); George Tindall, *The Emergence of the New South* (1967); Joan Hoff Wilson, *Herbert Hoover: The Forgotten Progressive* (1975).

Blacks and Latinos

Rodolfo Acuna, *Occupied America: A History of Chicanos* (1980); E. D. Cronon, *Black Moses: The Story of Marcus Garvey* (1955); Matt S. Meier and Feliciano Rivera, *The Chicanos* (1972); Gilbert Osofsky, *Harlem: The Making of a Ghetto* (1965); Ricardo Romo, *East Los Angeles: History of a Barrio* (1983); Virginia E. Sanchez, *From Colonia to Community: The History of Puerto Ricans in New York, 1917–1948* (1983); Alan Spear, *Black Chicago* (1967); Judith Stein, *The World of Marcus Garvey* (1986).

Women and the Family

W. Andrew Achenbaum, *Shades of Gray: Old Age, American Values, and Federal Policies Since 1920* (1983); William H. Chafe, *The American Woman: Her Changing Social, Economic, and Political Role* (1972); Howard P. Chudacoff, *How Old Are You? Age Consciousness in American Culture* (1989); Ruth Schwartz Cowan, *More Work for Mother* (1983); Linda Gordon, *Woman's Body, Woman's Right: A Social History of Birth Control in America* (1976); Lois Scharf, *To Work and to Wed* (1980); Susan Strasser, *Never Done: A History of American Housework* (1982); Winifred D. Wandersee, *Women's Work and Family Values, 1920–1940* (1981).

Lines of Defense

David M. Chalmers, *Hooded Americanism: The History of the Ku Klux Klan* (1965); Norman F. Furnis, *The Fundamentalist Controversy* (1954); John Higham, *Strangers in the Land: Patterns of American Nativism* (1955); Kenneth T. Jackson, *The Ku Klux Klan and the City* (1967); G. L. Joughin and E. M. Morgan, *The Legacy of Sacco and Vanzetti* (1948); Andrew Sinclair, *Prohibition: The Age of Excess* (1962).

Mass Culture

Erik Barbouw, *A Tower of Babel: A History of Broadcasting in the United States to 1933* (1966); Robert Creamer, *Babe* (1974); Kenneth S. Davis, *The Hero, Charles A. Lindbergh* (1959); Susan J. Douglas, *Inventing American Broadcasting* (1987); Paula Fass, *The Damned and the Beautiful: American Youth in the 1920s* (1977); Harvey J. Levenstein, *Revolution at the Table: The Transformation of the American Diet* (1988); Randy Roberts, *Jack Dempsey, The Manassa Mauler* (1979); Robert Sklar, *Movie-made America* (1976).

Literature and Thought

Mary Campbell, *Harlem Renaissance: Art of Black America* (1987); George H. Douglas, *H. L. Mencken* (1978); Gloria T. Hull, *Color, Sex and Poetry: Three Woman Writers of the Harlem Renaissance* (1987); Nathan I. Huggins, *Harlem Renaissance* (1971); David L. Lewis, *When Harlem Was in Vogue* (1981); Roderick Nash, *The Nervous Generation: American Thought, 1917–1930* (1969); Kenneth M. Wheller and Virginia L. Lussier, eds., *Women, the Arts, and the 1920s in Paris and New York* (1982).

Butch Beuscher was fifty-six years old when he was laid off from the job he had held for twenty-nine years. The year was 1931, and businesses and farms across the country were collapsing. Butch's wife, Tessie, was a part-time seamstress, but since her customers were also unemployed or irregularly employed, her earnings declined until they rarely exceeded three or four dollars a week. Four of the Beuschers' ten children still lived at home. As their income plummeted, the family lived off money borrowed on a partially paid-up insurance policy, Tessie's earnings, and credit from the grocery store. Their unpaid bills mounted, as did the overdue notices for their home mortgage and property-tax payments. Then, in the fall of 1933, Butch announced that the family would have to face facts. "We ought to try to get relief," he said. Tessie gasped at the suggestion that they apply to the government for welfare, but there was no alternative.

Statistics begin to tell the story of the Great Depression's human tragedy. Between 1929 and 1933, a hundred thousand businesses failed; corporate profits fell from $10 billion to $1 billion; and the gross national product was cut in half. Banks failed by the thousands. Americans who believed that saving was a virtue discovered that their deposits had disappeared with the banks.

24

THE GREAT DEPRESSION AND THE NEW DEAL, 1929–1941

Americans lost jobs as well as savings. Each day, thousands of men and women received severance slips. The number of unemployment workers increased from at least 4 million at the beginning of 1930 to 13 million (one-fourth of the work force) in early 1933. And millions more were underemployed. Unemployment placed strains on relations within the family. Blacks and other minorities sank deeper into destitution. Working women heard renewed calls for their return to the home in order to open places for males in the labor market. Overall, the economic catastrophe aggravated old tensions: labor versus capital, white versus black, male versus female.

Elected amid prosperity and optimism, President Herbert Hoover spent the years from late 1929 to his departure from office in early 1933 presiding over a gloomy and sometimes angry nation. Although he activated the federal government more than any of his predecessors had done in an economic crisis, he opposed direct relief payments for the unemployed. When Hoover refused to take measures strong enough to relieve people's hardships, voters turned him out of office in the election of 1932. His successor in the White House was Franklin D. Roosevelt, the governor of New York.

From the first days of his presidency, Roosevelt displayed a buoyancy and a willingness to experiment that helped restore public confidence in the government and the economy. He acted not only to reform the banks and securities exchanges, but also to provide central planning for industry and agriculture and direct government relief for the jobless. After shoring up the banks, Roosevelt proposed a succession of laws to aid landowning farmers, blue-collar workers, business and local governments facing bankruptcy, the unemployed, the elderly, and even impoverished writers and artists. This sweeping legislation was based on the concept of "pump priming," or deficit financing, to stimulate economic activity by pouring billions of federal dollars into the economy. Roosevelt's New Deal aroused opposition from both the left and the right. Ultimately, however, Roosevelt prevailed, vastly expanding both the scope of the federal government and the popularity of the Democratic party and in the process establishing America's welfare system.

During these years, several million workers seized the chance to organize for better wages and working conditions. The new Congress of Industrial Organizations (CIO) established unions in major industries, such as automobiles, steel, and meat packing. African-Americans also registered political and economic gains, but some federal agencies worked against them. On the other hand, black advisers took posts in the White House, and Native Americans discovered that New Dealers respected their culture and tribal rights.

Two-and-a-half million additional women workers joined the labor force during the 1930s. But female workers were segregated in low-income jobs, and New Deal legislation excluded many women from Social Security coverage and minimum-wage protection. Still, there was progress on the political front, as a "women's network" of government and Democratic party officials worked effectively in Washington for social welfare and social justice.

Roosevelt was re-elected in 1936, but soon afterward his fortunes began to wane. The spate of relief and reform legislation came to an end in 1938, but by that time the New Deal had transformed the United States. Although the New Deal was not a revolution, its legacy is evident today. Farmers, for example, still plant according to federal crop allotments, and the elderly and disabled still collect Social Security payments. One goal the New Deal did not accomplish was putting back to work all the people who wanted jobs. That had to wait until the United States entered the Second World War in 1941.

▼

Hard Times: America's Worsening Depression, 1929–1933

As the Great Depression deepened in the early 1930s, its underlying causes—problems such as overproduction and underconsumption—grew more severe. So, too, did another cause: instability in the banking industry. What happened to America's banks illustrates the cascading nature of the depression. Banks tied into the stock market or foreign investments were badly weakened; some failed. When nervous Americans made runs on banks to salvage their threatened savings, they created a powerful momentum—panic. In 1929, the number of bank failures reached 659; in 1930, it more than doubled, to 1,350. The next year proved still worse: 2,293 banks shut their doors, and another 1,453 folded in 1932.

During these years, people's diets deteriorated, malnutrition became common, and the undernourished became ill more easily. Some people quietly queued up at Red Cross and Salvation Army soup kitchens or in bread lines. Others ate only potatoes, crackers, or dandelions, or scratched through garbage cans for bits of food. Millions of Americans were not only hungry and ill, but also cold. Unable to afford fuel, they huddled in unheated tenements and

Deterioration of Health

IMPORTANT EVENTS

1931	Scottsboro affair Moratorium on First World War debts and reparations	**1936**	*United States* v. *Butler* invalidates AAA Roosevelt defeats Landon
1932	Reconstruction Finance Corporation established Bonus March Franklin D. Roosevelt elected president	**1937**	United Auto Workers' sit-down strikes Court-packing plan *N.L.R.B.* v. *Jones and Laughlin* upholds Wagner Act Memorial Day Massacre Farm Security Administration
1933	13 million American unemployed National bank holiday Agricultural Adjustment Act Tennessee Valley Authority National Industrial Recovery Act Prohibition repealed	**1937–39**	Business recession
		1938	AFL expels CIO unions Fair Labor Standards Act 10.4 million Americans unemployed
1934	Townsend's Old Age Revolving Pensions plan Huey Long's Share Our Wealth Society Indian Reorganization Act Democratic victories in congressional elections	**1940**	Roosevelt defeats Willkie
		1941	March on Washington Movement Fair Employment Practices Committee (FEPC) established
1935	Emergency Relief Appropriation Act Works Progress Administration *Schecter* v. *United States* invalidates NIRA National Labor Relations (Wagner) Act Social Security Act Committee for Industrial Organization (CIO) organized		

shacks. Families doubled up in crowded apartments, but some who were unable to pay the rent were evicted, furniture and all. Makeshift urban communities, bitterly called "Hoovervilles," sprouted up, constructed from packing boxes and other debris.

In the countryside, economic hardship deepened. Between 1929 and 1933, farm income was cut in half. Although farm prices dropped 60

Plight of Farmers percent, production decreased only 6 percent as individual farmers struggled to make up for lower prices by producing more, thereby creating an excess. The surplus that so depressed agricultural prices could not be exported because foreign demand had shrunk. Drought, foreclosure, clouds of hungry grasshoppers, and bank failures further plagued American farmers. Some became tran-

Plagued by dust storms and evictions, thousands of tenant farmers and sharecroppers were forced to leave their land during the Great Depression. Known as "Okies" and "Arkies," they headed for California with their few belongings. These refugees from drought-stricken Oklahoma were stalled on a New Mexico highway. *Library of Congress.*

sients in search of jobs or food. Dispossessed tenant farmers—husbands, wives, and children—walked the roads of the South. Hundreds of thousands of other people jumped aboard freight trains or hitchhiked. The California Unemployment Commission reported in 1932 that an "army of homeless" had trooped into the state and moved constantly from place to place, forced by one town after another to move on.

Across America, economic woe changed marriage patterns and family life. People postponed marriage, and married couples postponed having children. Divorces also declined, **Marriage** but desertions rose as husbands, **and Family** unable to provide for their **Patterns** families, simply took off. Families were beset in other ways as well. With less opportunity for outside recreation, family members were forced to spend more time to-gether, which increased the tension in families suffering unemployment and living in crowded quarters.

Most Americans met the crisis not with protest or violence but with bewilderment and an inability to fix the blame. They scorned businesspeople and bankers, of course, but often they **Farmers'** blamed themselves as well. Some **Holiday** people were angry, and scattered **Association** protests raised the specter of popular revolt. Farmers in the Midwest prevented evictions and slowed foreclosures on farm properties by harassing sheriffs, judges, and lawyers. They also conspired at auctions to bid very low on foreclosed land and then turned over the property to its relieved former owners. In Nebraska, Iowa, and Minnesota, farmers protesting low prices put up barricades, stopped trucks, and dumped milk and vegetables on the road. Some of these demonstrations were organized by the Farmers' Holiday Association, whose leader, Milo Reno, encouraged farmers to take a holiday—to keep their products off the market until they commanded a better price.

Isolated protests also sounded in cities and in mining regions. In Chicago, Los Angeles, and Philadelphia, the unemployed marched on city halls. In Harlan County, Kentucky, miners struck against wage reductions. Mine owners responded with strikebreakers, bombs, the National Guard, the closing of relief kitchens, and evictions from company-owned housing.

The most spectacular confrontation shook Washington, D.C., in the summer of 1932. Congress was considering a bill authorizing immediate issuance of bonuses, totaling $2.4 billion, **Bonus** already allotted to First World War **Expeditionary** veterans but not due for payment **Force** until 1945. To lobby for the bill, fifteen thousand unemployed veterans and their families converged on the capital, calling themselves the Bonus Expeditionary Force (BEF). They camped in crude shacks on vacant lots and in empty government buildings. President Hoover threw his weight against the bonus bill, but the House passed it. The showdown came in the Senate, which voted "no" after much debate. Many of the bonus marchers then left Washington, but several thousand stayed on during the summer.

In July, General Douglas MacArthur, assisted by Major Dwight D. Eisenhower and Major George S. Patton, met the veterans and their families with cavalry, tanks, and bayonet-bearing soldiers. The BEF hurled back stones and bricks. What followed shocked the nation. Men and women were chased down by horsemen; children were tear-gassed; shacks were set afire. When presidential hopeful Franklin D. Roosevelt heard about the attack on the Bonus Army, he turned to his friend Felix Frankfurter and said: "Well, Felix, this will elect me."

With capitalism on its knees, American Communists in various parts of the nation organized "unemployment councils" to arouse class consciousness and to agitate for jobs and food. In March 1930, they conducted ur-**Communist** ban demonstrations, some of **Party** which ended in violent clashes with local police. The following year, using the slogan "Fight—Don't Starve," they led a hunger march on Washington, D.C. Their tangles with authority publicized the real human tragedy of the depression. Still, total party membership in 1932 remained small—twelve thousand. The Socialist party fared better. More reformist than radical, the Socialists ran well in municipal elections after the stock market crash but scored few victories. Indeed, few despairing Americans looked to left-wing parties and doctrines, protest marches, or violence for relief from their misery. They turned instead to their local, state, and federal governments.

Hoover Holds the Line

When urgent daily appeals for government relief for the jobless reached the White House, Hoover at first became defensive, if not hostile. He rejected direct relief because he believed it would undermine character and individualism. To a growing number of Americans, Hoover seemed heartless and inflexible. True to his beliefs, the president urged people to help themselves and their neighbors. He applauded private voluntary relief through charitable agencies. Yet when the need was greatest, donations declined. State and urban officials found their treasuries drying up too. Meanwhile, those calling for federal action got no sympathy from Secretary of the Treasury Andrew Mellon, who advised Hoover to "let the slump liquidate itself. Liquidate labor, liquidate stocks, liquidate the farmers, liquidate real estate. . . . It will purge the rottenness out of the system."

As the depression intensified, Hoover's opposition to federal action diminished. He met with business and labor leaders, winning pledges from them **Hoover's** to maintain wages and production **Anti-** and to avoid strikes. He urged **depression** state governors to increase their **Remedies** expenditures for public works. And he created the President's Organization on Unemployment Relief (POUR) to generate private contributions for relief of the destitute. Unfortunately, POUR accomplished little.

If POUR proved ineffective, Hoover's spurring of federal public works projects (including the Hoover and Grand Coulee dams) did provide some jobs. Help also came from the Federal Farm Board (created by the Agricultural Marketing Act of 1929), which supported agriculture prices by lending money to cooperatives to buy products and keep them off the market. But the board soon found itself short of funds, and unsold surplus commodities jammed warehouses. To retard the collapse of the international monetary system, Hoover announced a moratorium on the payment of First World War debts and reparations (1931).

The president reluctantly asked Congress to charter the Reconstruction Finance Corporation (RFC). Created in 1932 and eventually empowered
Reconstruction Finance Corporation with $2 billion, the RFC was designed to make loans to banks, insurance companies, and railroads and later to state and local governments. The theory behind the RFC was that it would lend money to large entities at the top of the economic system, and benefits would filter down to people at the bottom. It did not work; banks continued to collapse and small companies to go into bankruptcy.

Despite warnings from prominent economists, Hoover had also signed the Hawley-Smoot Tariff (1930). A congressional compromise serving special interests, the tariff raised
Hawley-Smoot Tariff duties by about one-third. Hoover argued that the tariff would help farmers and manufacturers by keeping foreign goods off the American market. Actually, the tariff further weakened the economy. Since foreign nations had a harder time selling their products in the United States, they found it more difficult to earn money to buy American products.

Like most of his contemporaries, Hoover believed that a balanced budget was sacred and deficit spending sinful. In 1931, he appealed for a decrease in federal expenditures and an increase in taxes. The following year, he supported a sales tax on manufactured goods. The sales tax was defeated, but the Revenue Act of 1932 raised corporate, excise, and personal income taxes. Hoover seemed

caught in a contradiction: he urged people to spend to spur recovery, but his tax policies deprived them of spending money.

Although Hoover expanded public works projects and approved loans to some institutions, he vetoed a variety of relief bills presented to him by
Hoover's Traditionalism the Democratic Congress. In rejecting a public power project for the Tennessee River, he argued that its cheap electricity would compete with power from private companies. Hoover also demonstrated his traditionalism by his handling of Prohibition. Although Prohibition was not and could not be enforced, Hoover resisted the mounting public pressure for repeal. Opponents argued not only that Prohibition encouraged crime, but that its repeal would stimulate economic recovery in Milwaukee and St. Louis, increase demand for grain, and revive the nation's old beer, liquor, and pretzel factories. But the president would not, he said, tamper with the Constitution, and the liquor industry, having no socially redemptive value, was best left depressed. (After Hoover left office in 1933, Prohibition was repealed through the ratification of the Twenty-first Amendment.)

During his presidency, Hoover held the line. Clinging to his old viewpoints, he stretched government activities as far as he thought he could without violating his principles. Still, because Hoover mobilized the resources of the federal government as never before, some historians have depicted him as a bridge to the New Deal of the 1930s. If nothing else, he prepared the way for massive federal activity by giving private enterprise the opportunity to solve the depression—and to fail in the attempt.

▼

Franklin D. Roosevelt and the Election of 1932

Herbert Hoover and the Republican party faced dreary prospects in 1932. The president kept pointing to international causes for the economic crisis when Americans were less concerned with abstract explanations than with tomorrow's meal. He grumbled and grew impatient with critics. But what soured public opinion most was that Hoover seemed not to lead at a time when innovative generalship was required. So unpopular had he become by 1932 that Republicans who did not want to be associated with a loser ran independent campaigns.

Franklin D. Roosevelt enjoyed a different reputation. Born into the upper class of tradition and privilege, the smiling, ingratiating governor of New York appealed to people of all classes, races, and regions, and he spoke to the American penchant for optimism. He had served for eight years as the assistant secretary of the navy under Woodrow Wilson and in 1920 had been the robust vice-presidential candidate of the Democratic party. The Democratic ticket went down to defeat, but Roosevelt suffered a more devastating loss the following year, when he was struck by polio and totally paralyzed in both legs.

Franklin D. Roosevelt

What should Roosevelt do next? Should he retire from pubic life, a rich invalid? His answer and his wife Eleanor's was no. Throughout the 1920s, Franklin and Eleanor contended with his new handicap. Rejecting self-pity, Roosevelt worked to rebuild his body. People who had known him before commented that polio had made him a "twice-born man" and that his fight against the dread disease had given him "new moral and physical strength."

For her part, Eleanor Roosevelt began to shape her own career in public life, giving speeches and participating in the activities of the League of Women Voters, the Women's Trade Union League, and the Democratic party. Two of her strongest commitments came to be equal opportunity for women and for African-Americans. She also wanted to alleviate the suffering of the poor. On these issues, she served as her husband's conscience.

Eleanor Roosevelt

Roosevelt was elected to the first of two terms as governor of New York in 1928. Thus, his governorship coincided with Hoover's presidency, and both coincided with the onset of the Great Depression. But whereas Hoover appeared hardhearted and unwilling to help the jobless, Roosevelt seemed just the opposite. He

Roosevelt as Governor of New York

In November 1930, Franklin D. Roosevelt (1882–1945) was re-elected governor of New York by 735,000 votes and immediately became a leading contender for the Democratic presidential nomination. Note Roosevelt's leg braces, rarely shown in photographs. *The Bettmann Archive.*

urged unemployment insurance and direct relief payments for the jobless. As governor of New York, Roosevelt advocated creating jobs in publicly funded reforestation, land reclamation, and hydroelectric power projects. He endorsed and worked for old-age pensions and protective legislation for labor unions. With this record, Roosevelt became an obvious prospect for the 1932 Democratic presidential nomination.

To prepare a national political platform, Roosevelt surrounded himself with a brain trust of lawyers and university professors. Bigness was unavoidable in the modern American economy, these experts reasoned; thus, the cure for the nation's ills was not to go on a rampage of trustbusting but to place large corporations, monopolies, and oligopolies under effective government regulation. "We are no longer afraid of bigness," declared Rexford G. Tugwell, a professor at Columbia University, speaking in the tradition of Theodore Roosevelt's New Nationalism.

Roosevelt's Brain Trust

Roosevelt and his brain trust agreed that it was essential for the government to restore purchasing power to farmers, blue-collar workers, and the middle classes, and that the way to do so was to cut production. If the demand for a product remained constant and the supply were cut, they reasoned, the price would rise. Producers would make higher profits, and workers would earn more money. This method of combating a depression has been called the economics of scarcity. Roosevelt and Hoover both campaigned as fiscal conservatives committed to the balanced budget. But unlike Hoover, Roosevelt also advocated immediate and direct relief to the unemployed. Finally, Roosevelt and his advisers demanded that the federal government engage in centralized economic planning and experimentation to bring about recovery.

Upon accepting the Democratic nomination, Roosevelt called for a "new deal for the American people." The two party platforms differed little, but the Democrats were willing to abandon Prohibition and to launch federal relief. More people went to the polls in 1932 than in any election since the First World War. In a crisis-ridden moment, Americans calmly, even routinely, followed tradition and exchanged

1932 Election Results

one government for another. Roosevelt's 22.8 million popular votes far outdistanced Hoover's 15.8 million. Democrats also won overwhelming control of the Senate and the House.

On the afternoon of March 2, 1933, President-elect Roosevelt and his family and friends boarded a train for Washington, D.C., and the inauguration ceremony. Roosevelt was carrying with him rough drafts of two presidential proclamations, one summoning a special session of Congress and the other declaring a national bank holiday, suspending banking transactions throughout the nation.

Launching the New Deal and Restoring Confidence

"First of all," declared the newly inaugurated president, "let me assert my firm belief that the only thing we have to fear is fear itself—nameless, unreasoning, unjustified terror." In his inaugural address, Roosevelt scored his first triumph as president, instilling hope and courage in the rank and file. He attacked the nation's bankers, accusing them of having "fled from their high seats in the temple of our civilization." He invoked "the analogue of war," asserting that, if need be, "I shall ask the Congress for the one remaining instrument to meet the crisis—broad Executive power to wage a war against the emergency, as great as the power that would be given to me if we were in fact invaded by a foreign foe."

On March 5, Roosevelt declared a four-day national bank holiday and summoned Congress to an emergency session. Congress convened on March 9 to launch what observers would call the First Hundred Days. This was also the beginning of what historians would call the First New Deal (1933–1934). Roosevelt's first measure, the Emergency Banking Relief Bill, was introduced on March 9, passed sight unseen by unanimous House vote, approved 73 to 7 in the Senate, and signed by the president that evening. The act confirmed Roosevelt's emergency actions and provided for the reopening, under Treasury

Launching the First New Deal

Department license, of banks that were solvent and the reorganization and management of those that were not. It also prohibited the hoarding and export of gold. It was, however, a conservative law that upheld the status quo and left the same bankers as before in charge.

On March 10, another conservative New Deal bill was introduced in Congress; ten days later it became law. Called the Economy Act, its purpose was to balance the federal budget by chopping veterans' benefits and allowances by $400 million and reducing the pay of federal employees by $100 million. Although this legislation was deflationary and would decrease rather than increase the amount of money in circulation, the important point was that Roosevelt had acted and had done so boldly.

On Sunday evening, March 12, the president broadcast the first of his fireside chats, and 60 million people heard his comforting voice on their radios. His message: banks were once again safe places for depositors' savings. On Monday morning, the banks opened their doors, but instead of queuing up to withdraw their savings, people were waiting outside to deposit their money. The bank runs were over. People had regained confidence in their political leadership, their banks, and even their economic system.

First Fireside Chat

Four days after the first fireside chat, Roosevelt sent to Congress the Agricultural Adjustment bill to restore farmers' purchasing power. If overproduction was the cause of farmers' problems—falling prices and mounting surpluses—then the government had to encourage farmers to grow less food. Under the domestic allotment plan, the government would pay farmers to reduce their acreage or plow under crops already in the fields. Farmers would receive payments based on parity, a system of regulated prices for corn, cotton, wheat, rice, hogs, and dairy products that would allow them the same purchasing power that they had during the prosperous period of 1909 to 1914. In effect, the government was making up the difference between the actual market value of farm products and the income farmers needed to make a profit. The funds for the subsidies would come from taxes levied on the processors of agricultural commodities. Against

Agricultural Adjustment Act

vehement opposition, the Agricultural Adjustment Act (AAA) was passed on May 12. A month later, Congress also passed the Farm Credit Act, providing short- and medium-term loans that enabled many farmers to refinance their mortgages and hang on to their homes and land.

Meanwhile, other relief measures were enacted as well. On March 21, the president requested three kinds of massive relief: a job corps called the Civilian Conservation Corps (CCC), direct cash grants to the states for relief payments to needy citizens, and public works projects. Ten days later, Congress approved the CCC, which ultimately put 2.5 million young men between the ages of eighteen and twenty-five to work planting trees, clearing camp areas and beaches, and building bridges, dams, reservoirs, fish ponds, and fire towers. Then on May 12, Congress passed the Federal Emergency Relief Act, which authorized $500 million in aid to state and local governments.

Civilian Conservation Corps

Roosevelt's proposed plan for public works became Title II of the National Industrial Recovery Act (NIRA). Passed on June 16, NIRA established in the Public Works Administration (PWA) a fund of $3.3 billion to hire the unemployed to build roads, sewage and water systems, public buildings, ships, naval aircraft, and a host of other projects. The purpose of the PWA was to prime the economic pump to spur economic recovery.

If the AAA was the agricultural cornerstone of the New Deal, the National Industrial Recovery Act was the industrial cornerstone. The NIRA was a testimony to the New Deal belief in national planning as opposed to an individualistic, intensely competitive, laissez-faire economy. It was essential, the planners argued, for businesses to end cutthroat competition and raise prices by limiting production. Like the War Industries Board during the First World War, the NIRA exempted businesses from antitrust laws by establishing the National Recovery Administration (NRA). Under the auspices of the NRA, competing businesses met with representatives of workers and consumers to draft codes of fair competition, which limited production and established prices. Finally, Section 7(a) of the NIRA

Economic Planning under the NIRA

guaranteed the right of workers to unionize and to bargain collectively.

One of the boldest programs enacted by Congress during this period concerned the badly depressed Tennessee River valley, which ran through Tennessee, North Carolina, Kentucky, Virginia, Mississippi, Georgia, and Alabama. For years, progressives had advocated government operation of the Muscle Shoals electric power and nitrogen facilities on the Tennessee River. Roosevelt's Tennessee Valley Authority (TVA), established in May 1933, was a much broader program. Its dams would not only control floods but also generate hydroelectric power, reclaim and reforest land, and prevent soil erosion. The TVA would produce and sell nitrogen fertilizers to private citizens and nitrate explosives to the government, dig a 650-mile navigation channel from Knoxville to Paducah, and construct public power facilities as a yardstick for determining fair rates for privately produced electric power. The goal of the TVA was nothing less than enhancement of the economic well-being of the entire Tennessee River valley.

Congress finally adjourned on June 16. During the First Hundred Days, Roosevelt had delivered fifteen messages to Congress, and fifteen significant laws had been enacted (see table, page 439), including the Federal Securities Act, to compel brokers to tell the truth about new securities issues, and the Banking Act of 1933, to set up the Federal Deposit Insurance Corporation for insuring bank deposits. On April 19, the United States had abandoned the gold standard, no longer guaranteeing the gold value of the dollar abroad. Freed from the gold standard, the Federal Reserve System could expand the supply of currency in circulation, thus enabling monetary policy to become another weapon for economic recovery.

End of the First Hundred Days

Throughout the remainder of 1933 and the spring and summer of 1934, more New Deal bills became law. Indeed, there seemed to be something for everybody. Here was interest-group democracy at work, with government benefits accruing not only to business, but also to agriculture and labor, to farm- and homeowners, to corpo-

Interest-Group Democracy

rations and city governments, and to the jobless. In the midst of this coalition of interests was President Roosevelt, the artful broker, and this broker state was working. Following New Deal legislation, the unemployment figure fell steadily from 13 million in 1933 to 9 million in 1936. Net farm income rose from just over $3 billion in 1933 to $5.85 billion in 1935. Manufacturing salaries and wages also increased, jumping from $6.25 billion in 1933 to almost $13 billion in 1937.

There was no doubt about the popularity of either the New Deal or Roosevelt. In the 1934 congressional elections, the Democrats gained ten seats in the House and ten in the Senate. The New Deal, according to Arthur Krock of the *New York Times*, had won "the most overwhelming victory in the history of American politics." As for Roosevelt, "he has been all but crowned by the people," wrote William Allen White.

Reactions Against the First New Deal

There was more than one way to read employment and income statistics and election returns. For example, although unemployment had dropped from a high of 13 million (25 percent) in 1933 to 9 million (16.9 percent) in 1936, it had been only 1.5 million (3.2 percent) in 1929. And although manufacturing wages and salaries had reached almost $13 billion in 1937, that figure was almost $1.5 billion less than the total for 1929. In other words, regardless of the New Deal's successes, it had a long way to go before reaching predepression standards.

With the arrival of partial economic recovery, many businesspeople and conservatives became vocal critics of the New Deal. Some charged that there was too much taxation and government regulation. Others criticized the deficit financing of relief and public works. According to still others, the New Deal was subverting individual initiative and self-reliance by providing welfare payments.

Conservative Critics of the New Deal

NEW DEAL ACHIEVEMENTS

	Labor	Agriculture	Business and Industrial Recovery	Relief	Reform
1933	Section 7(a) of NIRA	Agricultural Adjustment Act Farm Credit Act	Emergency Banking Act Economy Act Beer and Wine Revenue Act Banking Act of 1933 (guaranteed deposits) National Industrial Recovery Act	Civilian Conservation Corps Federal Emergency Relief Act Home Owners Refinancing Act Public Works Administration Civil Works Administration	TVA Federal Securities Act
1934	National Labor Relations Board				Securities Exchange Act
1935	National Labor Relations (Wagner) Act	Resettlement Administration Rural Electrification Administration		Works Progress Administration and National Youth Administration	Banking Act of 1935 Social Security Act Public Utilities Holding Company Act Revenue Act (wealth tax)
1937		Farm Security Administration			
1938	Fair Labor Standards Act	Agricultural Adjustment Act of 1938			

Source: Adapted from Charles Sellers, Henry May, and Neil R. McMillen, A Synopsis of American History, *6th ed. Copyright © 1985 by Houghton Mifflin Company. Reprinted by permission.*

If businesspeople saw the government as their enemy, others thought the government favored business too much. Critics argued that the NRA favored industry's needs over those of workers and consumers. Farmers, labor unions, individual entrepreneurs, and antitrust critics complained that the NRA set prices too high and favored large producers over small businesses. The federal courts also began to scrutinize the constitutionality of the legislation in cases brought by critics.

The AAA, too, came under attack because it encouraged cutbacks in production. In 1933, farmers had plowed under 10.4 million acres of cotton and slaughtered 6 million pigs—at a time when people were ill clothed and ill fed. Although for landowning farmers the program was successful, to the average person such waste was shocking. Tenant farmers and sharecroppers were also supposed to receive government payments for taking crops out of cultivation, but very few of them, especially if they were black, received what they were entitled to. Furthermore, the AAA's hopes that landlords would keep their tenants on the land even while cutting production were not fulfilled. In the South, the number of sharecropper farms dropped from 776,278 in 1930 to 541,291 in 1940. The result was a homeless population. Joining the migration were the "Okies" and "Arkies," who took to the road in the mid-1930s to escape the "Dust Bowl" areas of Oklahoma, Arkansas, and the rest of the Great Plains.

As dissatisfaction mounted, so did the appeal of various demagogues. Father Charles Coughlin, a Roman Catholic priest whose weekly radio sermons offered a curious combination of anticommunism, anticapitalism, and anti-Semitism, was one of the best-known demagogues. Coughlin opposed the AAA's plowing under of crops and slaughtering of livestock, and began to criticize the New Deal for having "out-Hoovered Hoover."

Demagogic Attacks on the New Deal

Another challenge to the New Deal came from Dr. Francis E. Townsend. Under Townsend's Old Age Revolving Pensions plan, the government would pay monthly pensions of $200 to all citizens over the age of sixty on condition that they spent the money in the same month they received it.

Townsend claimed that his plan would not only aid the aged but cure the depression by pumping enormous purchasing power into the economy. The plan was fiscally impossible, but it addressed a real need.

Then there was Huey Long, "the Kingfish," perhaps the most successful demagogue in American history. In 1928, Long was elected governor of Louisiana with the slogan "Every Man a King, But No One Wears a Crown." As a United States senator (elected in 1930), Long at first supported the New Deal, but he found the Economy Act and the NRA too conservative and began to believe that Roosevelt had fallen captive to big business. Long countered in 1934 with the Share Our Wealth Society, which advocated the seizure by taxation of all incomes over $1 million and all inheritances over $5 million. With those funds, the government would furnish each family a homestead allowance of $5,000 and an annual income of $2,000. By mid-1935, Long's movement claimed 7 million members, and few doubted that Long aspired to the presidency. An assassin's bullet extinguished his ambition in September 1935, but the Share Our Wealth movement persisted.

Some politicians of the 1930s, like Floyd Olson, the governor of Minnesota, declared themselves Socialists. Olson sought a third party that would "preach the gospel of government and collective ownership of the means of production and distribution." In Wisconsin, the left-wing Progressive party re-elected Robert La Follette, Jr., to the Senate in 1934, sent seven of the state's ten representatives to Washington, and placed La Follette's brother Philip in the governorship. And the old muckraker Upton Sinclair won the Democratic gubernatorial nomination in California in 1934 on the platform End Poverty in California (EPIC).

Left-Wing Critics of the New Deal

Perhaps the most controversial alternative to the New Deal was the Communist Party of the United States of America (CPUSA). Membership in the CPUSA remained small until 1935, when the party leadership changed its strategy. Proclaiming that "Communism is Twentieth Century Americanism," the CPUSA disclaimed any intention of overthrowing the United States government and began to cooperate with left-wing labor unions, student groups, and writers' organizations. At its high point for the decade in 1938, the CPUSA had 55,000 members.

In addition to challenges from the right and the left, the New Deal was threatened by the Supreme Court. Many New Deal laws had been hastily drafted and enacted, and the ma-

Supreme Court Decisions Against the New Deal

jority of the justices feared that this legislation had vested too much power in the presidency. In May 1935, the Court unanimously struck down the NIRA (*Schechter* v. *United States*) on the grounds that it gave excessive legislative power to the White House and that the commerce clause of the Constitution did not give the federal government authority to regulate intrastate businesses. Roosevelt's industrial recovery program was dead. In January 1936, his farm program met a similar fate when the Court invalidated the AAA (*United States* v. *Butler*), deciding that agriculture was a local problem and thus, under the Tenth Amendment, subject to state, not federal, action.

As Roosevelt looked ahead to the presidential election of 1936, he saw that he was in danger of losing his capacity to lead and to govern. His coalition of all interests was breaking up, radicals and demagogues were offering Americans alternative programs, and the Supreme Court was dismantling the New Deal. In the spring and summer of 1935, Roosevelt took the initiative once more, and the New Deal scored some of its biggest victories. So impressive was the new legislation, which had reforming the economy as its primary thrust, that some historians have called it the Second New Deal.

The Second New Deal and the Election of 1936

The first triumph of the Second New Deal was an innocuous-sounding but momentous law called the Emergency Relief Appropriation Act, which Con-

Works Progress Administration

gress passed and Roosevelt signed in April 1935. The act authorized the president to issue executive orders establishing massive public works programs for the jobless, including the Works Progress Administration (WPA). Later renamed the Work Projects Administration, the WPA ultimately employed more than 8.5 million people on a total of 1.4 million projects. By the time it was terminated in 1943, the WPA had built more than 650,000 miles of highways, streets, and roads, 125,000 public buildings, and 8,000 parks, as well as numerous bridges, airports, and other structures. But the WPA did more than lay bricks. Its Federal Theatre Project brought plays, vaudeville shows, and circuses to cities and towns across the country, and its Federal Writers' Project hired writers like John Cheever, Claude McKay, John Steinbeck, and Richard Wright to write local guidebooks and regional and folk histories.

Besides the WPA, the Emergency Relief Appropriation Act funded other relief and public works measures. The Resettlement Administration (RA) resettled destitute families and organized rural homestead communities and suburban greenbelt towns for low-income workers. The Rural Electrification Administration (REA) distributed electricity to isolated rural areas. And the National Youth Administration (NYA) sponsored work relief programs for young adults and part-time jobs for students.

As significant as these achievements were, Roosevelt wanted new legislation, some of it aimed at controlling the activities of big business. The Supreme Court had condemned the government-business cooperation that had been the foundation of the First Hundred Days. Businesspeople had become increasingly critical of Roosevelt and the New Deal. Now Roosevelt determined that if big business would not cooperate with government, government should "cut the giants down to size" through antitrust suits and heavy corporate taxes. In June 1935, he asked Congress to enact five major bills: a labor bill sponsored by Senator Robert Wagner, a Social Security bill, a banking bill, a measure to regulate public-utilities holding companies, and a "soak-the-rich" tax bill.

The summer of 1935 constituted the Second

Hundred Days. On July 5, the National Labor Relations (Wagner) Act granted workers the right to unionize and bargain collectively with management. The act empowered the National Labor Relations Board to ensure democratic union elections and to eradicate unfair labor practices by employers, such as the firing of workers for union membership.

Roosevelt's Second Hundred Days

On August 15, Roosevelt signed the Social Security Act, which established a cooperative federal-state system of unemployment compensation and old-age insurance. According to the law, workers who paid Social Security taxes out of their wages would receive retirement benefits at the age of sixty-five. Social Security was a conservative measure: the government did not pay for old-age benefits; workers and their bosses did. The tax was regressive because the more workers earned, the less they were taxed proportionally, and it was deflationary because it took out of people's pockets money that it did not repay for years. Finally, the law excluded many people from coverage—farm workers, domestic servants, and many hospital and restaurant workers. Nevertheless, the act was a milestone. It acknowledged the government's responsibility to establish a system of insurance for the aged, dependent children, the disabled, and the temporarily unemployed.

Social Security Act

In the next two weeks, Roosevelt gained the remainder of what he had asked for, including the Revenue (Wealth Tax) Act of 1935. The Wealth Tax Act, which some critics saw as the president's attempt to "steal Huey's thunder," did not result in a redistribution of income, though it did increase the income taxes paid by the wealthy. It also imposed a new tax on excess business profits and increased taxes on inheritances, large gifts, and profits from the sale of property.

The Second Hundred Days indicated not only that the president was once again in charge but that he was set to run for re-election. The campaign was less heated than might have been expected, however. The Republican nominee, Governor Alf Landon of Kansas, criticized

Election of 1936

Roosevelt, but he did not advocate wholesale repeal of the New Deal. When the ballots were counted, Roosevelt had won a landslide victory, polling 27.8 million votes to Landon's 16.7 million. The Democrats carried every state but Maine and Vermont and won huge majorities in the House and Senate.

The Democratic victory in 1936 stemmed from what observers have called the "New Deal coalition." The growing strength of the party in the cities converged with the New Deal's response to social distress to make Roosevelt the champion of the urban masses, as well as many farmers. Labor, especially the new unions of the Congress of Industrial Organizations (CIO), was an integral part of the coalition. And black voters in northern cities, most of whom had been Republicans prior to the 1930s, now cast their lot with the Democratic party. Finally, the party included the "Solid South," the eleven states of the Confederacy that had voted Democratic since the end of Reconstruction. The Democratic party had become the dominant half of the two-party system.

New Deal Coalition

Roosevelt's Second Term: Court Packing and Other Failures

Despite the bold and unprecedented steps of his first term, Roosevelt faced a darkening horizon during his second term. The economy faltered again between 1937 and 1939, bringing renewed unemployment and suffering. And Europe drew closer to war, threatening to drag the United States into the conflict. To gain support for his foreign and military policies, Roosevelt began to court conservative politicians, who were long-time opponents of his domestic reforms. The eventual result was the demise of the New Deal.

In several instances, Roosevelt caused his own defeat. The Supreme Court had invalidated much of the work of the First Hundred Days; now Roosevelt feared it would do the same with the Second Hundred Days. Four of the justices steadfastly opposed the New Deal, three generally approved of it, and two were swing votes. Hoping to create a more progressive federal judiciary, Roosevelt, in February 1937, sent his Judiciary Reorganization bill to Congress.

What Roosevelt requested was the authority to add a federal judge whenever an incumbent who had already served at least ten years failed to retire within six months of reaching the age of seventy. He wanted the power to name up to fifty additional federal judges, including six to the Supreme Court. Roosevelt envisioned using the bill to create a Supreme Court sympathetic to the New Deal. Opposition to Roosevelt's attempt to pack the Court was widespread and vocal. Liberals joined Republicans and some conservative Democrats in resisting the bill. In the end, Roosevelt had to concede defeat. The bill he signed into law in August made pensions available to retiring judges but denied him the power to increase the number of judges.

Roosevelt's Court-packing Plan

This episode had an ironic final twist. During the public debate over court packing, the two swing-vote justices began to vote in favor of liberal, pro–New Deal rulings. In the spring of 1937, the Court upheld the Wagner Act (*N.L.R.B.* v. *Jones & Laughlin Steel Corp.*), ruling that Congress's power to regulate interstate commerce involved also the power to regulate the production of goods for interstate commerce and the Social Security Act. Moreover, the new pensions encouraged judges past the age of seventy to retire, and the president appointed seven new associate justices in the next four years, including such notables as Hugo Black, Felix Frankfurter, and William O. Douglas.

Another New Deal setback was the renewed economic recession of 1937–1939. Roosevelt had never abandoned his commitment to the balanced budget. In 1937, confident that most of the problems of the depression had been solved, he began to order drastic cutbacks in government spending. At the same time, the Federal Reserve Board, concerned about a 3.6-percent inflation rate, tightened credit. The two actions sent the economy into a tailspin: unemployment

Recession of 1937–1939

climbed from 7.7 million in 1937 to 10.4 million in 1938. Soon, Roosevelt was forced to resume deficit financing.

In the spring of 1938, with conflict over events in Europe commanding more and more of the nation's attention, the New Deal came to an end. Roosevelt sacrificed further domestic reforms in return for conservative support of his programs of military rearmament and preparedness. The last significant New Deal laws enacted were the National Housing Act of 1937, which established the U.S. Housing Authority, and in 1938, a new Agricultural Adjustment Act and the Fair Labor Standards Act, which established the minimum wage and the forty-hour workweek for many, but by no means all, workers.

Industrial Workers and the Rise of the CIO

From the New Deal, working people gained the right to organize labor unions and bargain collectively with their bosses. On enactment, Section 7(a) of the NIRA inspired the vigorous recruitment of union members. By October 1933, an additional 1.5 million workers had enlisted in unions, bringing total membership to 4 million. With the passage of the Wagner Act in mid-1935, labor union recruiting received another big boost; within three years, total membership surpassed 7 million.

These gains did not always come easily. Management put up determined resistance in the 1930s, relying upon the police or hiring armed thugs to intimidate workers and break up strikes. Labor confronted yet another obstacle in the AFL craft unions' traditional skepticism and hostility toward industrial unions. Craft unions typically consisted of skilled workers in a particular trade, such as carpentry or plumbing. Industrial unions, on the other hand, represented all the workers, skilled and unskilled, in a given industry. The organizational gains in the 1930s were far

Rivalry Between Craft and Industrial Unions

more impressive in industrial unions than in craft unions, with hundreds of thousands of workers organizing in such industries as autos, garments, rubber, and steel.

Attempts to reconcile the craft and industrial union movements failed, and in late 1935, John L. Lewis of the United Mine Workers resigned as vice president of the AFL. He and other industrial unionists within the AFL formed the Committee for Industrial Organization (CIO). In 1938, the AFL expelled the CIO unions, and the CIO reorganized itself as the Congress of Industrial Organizations. By that time CIO membership stood at 3.7 million, surpassing AFL membership, which was 3.4 million.

The CIO, which in the 1930s evolved into a pragmatic, "bread and butter" labor organization, organized millions of workers who had never before had an opportunity to join a **Sit-down** union. One of these unions, the **Strikes** United Auto Workers (UAW), scored a major victory in late 1936. The union demanded recognition from General Motors, Chrysler, and Ford. When GM refused, the workers launched a sit-down strike. Beginning in the Fisher Body plant in Flint, Michigan, they refused to leave the building. To discourage the strikers, GM managers turned off the heat. When that tactic failed, they called the police, who were met by a barrage of iron bolts, coffee mugs, and pop bottles. When the police resorted to tear gas, the strikers turned the plant's water hoses on them.

The strike lasted for weeks. GM obtained a court order to evacuate the plant, but the strikers continued, risking imprisonment and fines. With the support of their families, neighbors, and a women's organized "emergency brigade" that delivered food and supplies to the strikers, the UAW prevailed. In 1937, GM agreed to recognize the union. Chrysler signed a similar agreement, but Ford held out for four more years. As a tactic, the sitdown strike spread to all kinds of laborers, including textile, glass, and rubber workers, dime-store clerks, janitors, dressmakers, and pie bakers.

In 1937, the Steel Workers Organizing Committee (SWOC) signed a contract with the nation's largest steelmaker, U.S. Steel, that guaranteed an eight-hour day and a forty-hour week. Other **Memorial Day Massacre** steel companies refused to go along, however. Confrontations between these so-called little steel companies and the SWOC led to violence. On Memorial Day in Chicago, strikers and their families had joined with sympathizers in a peaceful picket line in front of the Republic Steel plant. Suddenly and without provocation, the police opened fire. They continued to shoot into the crowd even as people turned away and began to run.

As senseless as the Memorial Day Massacre was—ten people had been killed—its occurrence was not surprising. During the 1930s, industries had hired private police agents and accumulated large stores of arms and ammunition for use in deterring workers from organizing and joining unions. Through it all, the CIO continued to enroll new members. By the end of the decade, the CIO had succeeded in organizing most of the nation's mass-production industries.

<hr/>

Mixed Progress for People of Color

The depression sank the vast majority of blacks deeper into the mire of fear, political disfranchisement, segregation, and privation. In 1930, about three-fourths of all blacks lived in **Blacks in the Depression** the South. Almost all were prohibited from voting or serving on juries; they were denied access to hospitals, universities, and public parks; and they were not hired except for the most menial jobs. Blacks living in rural areas (56.9 percent in 1930) were sharecroppers, tenants, or wage hands. Black life expectancy was more than ten years lower than white life expectancy. And the specter of the lynch mob's noose was a growing threat to black people. In 1929, seven black men were lynched; in 1933, when the depression was at its worst, twenty-four.

Racism also plagued blacks living in the North. Southern blacks who migrated to northern cities discovered that employers discriminated against them. Black unemployment rates ran high; in Pittsburgh, 48 percent of black workers were jobless in 1933, compared with 31 percent of white laborers.

Blacks were aware that Herbert Hoover shared prevailing white racial attitudes. Hoover sought a lily-white GOP and was attempting to push blacks out of the Republican party in order to attract white southern Democrats. In 1930, the president showed his racial insensitivity by nominating Judge John J. Parker of North Carolina to the Supreme Court. Ten years earlier, Parker had endorsed the disfranchisement of blacks. Pressure from the NAACP and the AFL helped to defeat Parker's nomination in the Senate.

Then came Scottsboro, a civil rights case that symbolized the ugliness of race relations in the depression era. One afternoon in March 1931, when a

Scottsboro Trials freight train pulled in at Paint Rock, near Scottsboro, Alabama, armed sheriff's deputies arrested nine blacks, charging them with roughing up some white hoboes and throwing them off the train earlier in the day. Two white women who were removed from the same train claimed that the blacks had raped them. Medical evidence later showed that the women were lying, perhaps to save themselves from arrest as prostitutes. But within two weeks, eight of the so-called Scottsboro boys were convicted of rape by all-white juries and sentenced to death.

After several trials, Haywood Patterson, the first defendant, was ordered to die. But a Supreme Court ruling intervened, this time because it was evident that in Alabama blacks were systematically excluded from juries. Patterson faced a new trial in 1936. Found guilty again, he was given a seventy-five-year jail sentence. Four of the other youths were sentenced to life imprisonment. Not until 1950 were all five out of jail—four by parole and Patterson by escaping from his work gang.

Blacks coped with their white-circumscribed environment and fought back against racism in a variety of ways. The NAACP, though internally divided, lobbied quietly against a long list of injustices, and A. Philip Randolph's Brotherhood of Sleeping Car Porters defended the rights of black workers. In Harlem, the militant Harlem Tenants League fought rent increases and evictions, and in some cities black consumers began to boycott white merchants. But America's white leaders made few concessions.

With the election of Franklin D. Roosevelt, blacks' attitudes toward government changed, as did their political affiliation. For black Americans, Franklin D. Roosevelt would become the most appealing president since Abraham Lincoln. Part of the reason was the courageous way he bore his physical disability. Blacks, who suffered from a handicap of their own—racism—knew what courage was. Moreover, Roosevelt seemed a decided improvement over Hoover. When they saw pictures of black visitors at the White House and read about Roosevelt's Black Cabinet, they were heartened. Most important, through the WPA and other relief programs, the New Deal aided black people in their struggle for economic survival.

The Black Cabinet, or black brain trust, was unique in United States history. Never before had there been so many black advisers at the White

Black Cabinet House, and never had they been highly trained professionals. There were black lawyers, journalists, and Ph.D.s; black experts on housing, labor, and social welfare. William H. Hastie and Robert C. Weaver, holders of advanced degrees from Harvard, served in the Department of the Interior. Mary McLeod Bethune, a college president, was director of the Division of Negro Affairs of the National Youth Administration. There were also among the New Dealers some whites who had committed themselves to first-class citizenship for African-Americans. Foremost among these people was Eleanor Roosevelt.

The president himself, however, remained uncommitted to black civil rights. Fearful of alienating southern whites, he never endorsed a federal law

Antiblack Effects of the New Deal against lynching nor abolition of the poll tax. Furthermore, some New Deal programs functioned in ways that were definitely hostile to black Americans. The AAA, rather than benefiting black tenant farmers and sharecroppers actually forced many of them off the land. The Federal Housing Administration (FHA) refused to guarantee mortgages on houses purchased by blacks in white neighborhoods. The CCC was racially segregated, as was much of the TVA.

Finally, waiters, cooks, hospital orderlies, janitors, farm workers, and domestics, many of whom were black, were excluded from Social Security coverage and from the minimum-wage provisions of the Fair Labor Standards Act of 1938.

Confronted with the mixed message of the New Deal, many blacks turned only reluctantly to the Democratic party, while others, concluding that ultimately they could depend only on themselves, organized self-help and direct-action movements. Nowhere was the trend toward direct action more evident than in the March on Washington Movement in 1941. In that year, billions of federal dollars flowed into American industry as the nation prepared for the possibility of another world war. The government funds generated thousands of new jobs, but discrimination deprived blacks of their fair share. One executive notified black job applicants that the "Negro will be considered only as janitors and in other similar capacities." So in early 1941, A. Philip Randolph, president of the Brotherhood of Sleeping Car Porters, proposed that blacks march on the nation's capital to demand equal access to jobs in defense industries. Fearing that the march might provoke riots and Communists might infiltrate the movement, Roosevelt announced that if the march were canceled, he would issue an executive order prohibiting discrimination in war industries and in the government. The result was Executive Order No. 8802, issued on June 25, 1941, which established the Fair Employment Practices Committee (FEPC).

During the early 1930s, another group, American Indians, sank further into malnutrition and disease. In Oklahoma, where the Choctaws, Cherokees, and Seminoles lived with more than twenty other tribes on infertile soil, three-fourths of all Indian children were undernourished. Tuberculosis swept through the reservations. At the heart of the problem was a 1929 ruling by the comptroller general of the United States that landless tribes were ineligible for federal aid. Not until 1931 did the Indian Bureau take steps to relieve the suffering.

The New Deal took a very different approach from earlier administrations to fulfilling its duty to Native Americans. As a result, Indians benefited more directly than blacks from the New Deal.

A New Deal for American Indians

Roosevelt appointed John Collier commissioner of Indian affairs. In the 1920s, as founder of the American Indian Defense Association, Collier had crusaded for tribal landownership and an end to the allotment policy established by the Dawes Severalty Act of 1887. Since 1887, total Indian landholdings had declined from 138 million acres to 48 million acres, 20 millions of which were arid or semiarid.

Passed by Congress in 1934, the Indian Reorganization (Wheeler-Howard) Act aimed to reverse this process by restoring lands to tribal ownership and forbidding future division of Indian lands into individual parcels. Other provisions of the act enabled tribes to obtain loans for economic development and to establish self-government. Under Collier, the Bureau of Indian Affairs also encouraged the perpetuation of Indian religions and cultures.

Mexican-Americans also suffered extreme hardship during the depression, but no government programs benefited them. During these years, many Mexicans and Mexican-Americans packed up their belongings and moved south of the border, sometimes willingly and sometimes deported by immigration officials or forced out by California officials eager to purge them from the relief rolls. According to the federal census, the Mexican-born population dropped from 617,000 in 1930 to 377,000 in 1940. One reason was that many employers had changed their minds about the desirability of hiring Mexican-American farm workers. Before the 1930s, farmers had boasted that Mexican-Americans were a cheap, docile labor supply and would not join unions. But in the 1930s, Mexican-Americans belied their image by engaging in prolonged and sometimes bloody strikes.

Depression Hardships for Mexican-Americans

The New Deal offered little help to these Mexican-Americans. The AAA was created to assist property-owning farmers, not migratory farm workers. The Wagner Act did not cover farm workers' unions, nor did the Social Security Act or the Fair Labor Standards Act cover farm laborers. One New Deal agency, the Farm Security Administration (FSA), was established in 1937 to help farm workers, in part by setting up migratory labor camps. But the FSA came too late to help Mexican-Americans,

Violence erupted in October 1933 in California's San Joaquin Valley. When Mexican farm workers struck, growers evicted them and their families and also fired upon workers holding strike meetings at Pixley and Arvin, killing three. This group of Mexican women was bound for the picket line to protest for food relief for the hungry families. *Library of Congress.*

most of whom had by that time been replaced by dispossessed white farmers.

Women, Work, and the Depression

In *It's Up to the Women* (1933), Eleanor Roosevelt wrote that during depressions, wives and mothers often had to bear a heavier responsibility than husbands and fathers. Many women

Wives and Mothers Face the Depression followed the maxim "Use it up, wear it out, make it do, or do without." Women bought day-old bread and cheap cuts of meat; they relined old coats with blankets and saved string, rags, and broken crockery for possible future use. In short, many families with reduced incomes were able to maintain their standard of living only because of astute women shoppers or because women substituted their own labor in the home for the goods and services that they used to purchase.

While they were cutting corners to make ends meet, women were also seeking paid work outside the home. In 1930, more than 10.5 million women were paid workers; ten years later, the female labor force topped 13 million. Despite these statistics, most Americans believed that women should not work outside the home, that they should strive instead to be good wives and mothers, and that women who worked were doing so for "pin money" to buy frivolous things.

Another popular argument of the 1930s held that male unemployment stemmed directly from women in the work force. When a Gallup poll in 1936 asked whether wives should work if their husbands had jobs, 82 percent of the respondents (including 75 percent of the women) answered no. Severe job discrimination resulted from these attitudes. Most insurance companies, banks, and public utilities had policies against married women working, and from 1932 to 1937, federal law prohibited more than one family member from working for the civil service. Because wives usually earned less than their husbands, they were the ones who quit their government jobs.

Such thinking missed the point, for two reasons. First, women were heavily concentrated in certain occupations, or "women's jobs." Men rarely sought "feminized" jobs, such as teaching, nursing, and clerical work, and probably would not have been hired had they applied for such work. Second, most women workers (72 percent in 1930) were single, not married; they were thus self-supporting.

Other women workers were married; they worked to keep their families from slipping into poverty. Married women constituted 35 percent of the work force in 1940, an increase from 29 percent in 1930 and 15 percent in 1900. But working wives' help with family expenses did not improve their status. As the sociologists Robert and Helen Lynd observed at the time, "The men, cut adrift from their usual routine, lost most of their sense of time and dawdled helplessly and dully about the streets; while in the homes the women's world remained largely intact and the round of cooking, house-cleaning, and mending became if anything more absorbing." Even while women were making increased contributions to the family, their husbands, including those without jobs, still exercised authority as family decision makers.

The New Deal did take into account women's needs, but only if reminded forcefully to do so by the women activists who advised the government.

Women in the New Deal There was in Washington a women's network of government and Democratic party officials who were united by their attitudes toward social reform and the role of women in politics and government. The network's most prominent member was Eleanor Roosevelt, who was her husband's valued adviser. Frances Perkins, the secretary of labor, was the nation's first woman cabinet officer. Other historic New Deal appointments included the first woman federal appeals judge and the first women ambassadors.

Even with increased participation by women, however, New Deal provisions for women were mixed. The maximum-hour and minimum-wage provisions mandated by the NRA won women's applause. Women workers in the lowest-paying jobs, many of them laboring under sweatshop conditions, had the most to gain from these standards. At the same time, some NRA codes mandated pay differentials based on gender, so that women's minimum wages were lower than men's. Federal relief agencies, such as the Civil Works Administration, put only one woman to work for every eight to ten men placed in relief jobs. A popular New Deal program, the Civilian Conservation Corps, was limited to young men. And women who were low-income workers, especially in agriculture and domestic service, were not protected by the 1935 Social Security Act or the 1938 Fair Labor Standards Act.

The Election of 1940 and the Legacy of the New Deal

As the presidential election of 1940 approached, many people wondered whether Roosevelt would run for a third term (no president had ever served more than two terms). Roosevelt himself seemed undecided until May 1940, when Adolf Hilter's military advances in Europe apparently convinced him to stay on. The Republican candidate was Wendell Willkie, a utilities executive who had been an anti–New Deal Democrat throughout most of the 1930s.

Willkie campaigned against the New Deal, contending that its meddling in the affairs of business had failed to return the nation to prosperity. He also criticized the government's lack of military preparedness. But Roosevelt pre-empted the defense issue by beefing up military and naval contracts. When Willkie reversed his approach and accused Roosevelt of being a warmonger, the president promised, "Your boys are not going to be sent into any foreign wars."

Willkie never did come up with an effective campaign issue, and on election day Roosevelt received 27 million votes to Willkie's 22 million. In the electoral college, Roosevelt buried Willkie 449 to 82. Although the New Deal was over at home, Roosevelt was still riding a wave of public approval.

Any analysis of the New Deal must begin with Franklin Delano Roosevelt. Assessments of his career varied widely during his presidency. Most **Franklin D. Roosevelt Assessed** historians have considered him a truly great president, citing his courage, his buoyant self-confidence, his willingness to experiment, and his capacity to inspire the nation during the most somber days of the depression. Those who have criticized him have charged that he was too pragmatic and that he failed to formulate a bold and coherent strategy of economic recovery and political and economic reform.

Although scholars have debated Roosevelt's performance, they all agree that he transformed the presidency. "Only Washington, who made the office, and Jackson, who remade it," Clinton Rossiter, the political scientist, observed, "did more than Roosevelt to raise it to its present condition of strength, dignity, and independence." Scholars in a later era would charge that Roosevelt had initiated "the imperial presidency." But whether for good or ill, Roosevelt strengthened not only the presidency, but also the whole federal government. "For the first time for many Americans," the historian William Leuchtenburg has written, "the federal government became an institution that was directly experienced. More than state and local governments, it came to be *the* government."

The New Deal laid the foundation of America's welfare system on which subsequent presidential administrations would build. For the first time, the federal government acknowledged a responsibility to bring relief to the jobless and the needy, and for the first time it resorted to deficit spending in order to stimulate the economy. The New Deal also brought about limited change in the nation's power structure. Beginning in the 1930s, business interests had to share their political clout with others. Labor gained influence in Washington, and farmers got more of what they wanted from Congress and the White House. But there was no real increase in the power of African-Americans and other minorities. If people wanted their voices to be heard, they had to organize in labor unions, trade associations, or other special-interest lobbies.

Origins of America's Welfare System

The New Deal failed in its fundamental purpose: to put people back to work. As late as 1939, more than 10 million men and women were still jobless.

New Deal's Failure to Solve Unemployment

That year, unemployment was 19.1 percent; over the next two years, it fell no lower than 14.6 percent. What plagued the nation throughout the 1930s was underconsumption: people and businesses did not purchase enough goods to sustain high levels of employment. In the end, it was not the New Deal but massive government spending during the Second World War that put people back to work. In 1941, as a result of mobilization for war, unemployment dropped to 9.9 percent, and in 1944, at the height of the war, only 1.2 percent of the labor force lacked jobs.

In some ways, the New Deal's most lasting accomplishments were its programs to ameliorate the suffering of unemployment. The United States has experienced several economic recessions since 1945, but American presidents, including Republicans, have "primed the pump" during these periods of slump. Before the New Deal, the United States had endured a major depression every fifteen or twenty years. But since the New Deal, thanks to unemployment compensation, Social Security, and other measures, the national nightmare of the Great Depression has not recurred.

<hr>

Suggestions for Further Reading

Hoover and the Worsening Depression

William W. Barber, *Herbert Hoover, the Economists, and American Economic Policy, 1921–1933* (1986); Michael A. Bernstein, *The Great Depression: Delayed Recovery and Economic Change in America 1929–1939* (1988); David Burner, *Herbert Hoover* (1979); Martin L. Fausold, *The Presidency of Herbert C. Hoover* (1985); Susan Kennedy, *The Banking Crisis of 1933* (1973); Charles Kindleberger, *The World in Depression, 1929–1939* (1973); James S. Olson, *Herbert Hoover and the Reconstruction Finance Corporation, 1931–1933* (1977); Albert B. Romasco, *The Poverty of Abundance: Hoover, the Nation, the Depression* (1965); Jordan A. Schwarz, *Interregnum of Despair* (1970); Richard N. Smith, *An Uncommon Man* (1984).

The New Deal

Paul K. Conkin, *The New Deal,* 2nd ed. (1975); Peter Fearon, *War, Prosperity, and Depression* (1987); Otis L. Graham, Jr., *Encore for Reform: The Old Progressives and the New Deal* (1967); Ellis W. Hawley, *The New Deal and the Problem of Monopoly* (1966); William E. Leuchtenburg, *Franklin D. Roosevelt and the New Deal* (1963); Robert S. McElvaine, *The Great Depression* (1984); James S. Olson, *Saving Capitalism: The Reconstruction Finance Corporation and the New Deal,*

1933–1940 (1988); Albert U. Romasco, *The Politics of Recovery: Roosevelt's New Deal* (1983); Harvard Stikoff, ed., *Fifty Years Later: The New Deal Evaluated* (1985).

Franklin D. Roosevelt

James MacGregor Burns, *Roosevelt: The Lion and the Fox* (1956); Kenneth S. Davis, *FDR: The New Deal Years, 1933–1937* (1986); Frank Freidel, *Franklin D. Roosevelt,* 4 vols. (1952–1973); Joseph P. Lash, *Eleanor and Franklin* (1971); William E. Leuchtenburg, *In the Shadow of FDR* (1983); Arthur M. Schlesinger, Jr., *The Age of Roosevelt,* 3 vols. (1957–1960).

Voices from the Depression

James Agee, *Let Us Now Praise Famous Men* (1941); Ann Banks, ed., *First-Person America* (1980); Robert S. McElvaine, ed., *Down and Out in the Great Depression: Letters from the Forgotten Man* (1983); Studs Terkel, *Hard Times: An Oral History of the Great Depression* (1970); Tome E. Terrill and Jerrold Hirsch, eds., *Such as Us: Southern Voices of the Thirties* (1978).

Alternatives to the New Deal

Alan Brinkley, *Voices of Protest: Huey Long, Father Coughlin, and the Great Depression* (1982); Harvey Klehr, *The Heyday of American Communism* (1984); Mark Naison, *Communists in Harlem During the Depression* (1983); James T. Patterson, *Congressional Conservatism and the New Deal* (1967); Leo Ribuffo, *The Old Christian Right: The Protestant Far Right from the Great Depression to the Cold War* (1983); Frank A. Warren, *An Alternative Vision: The Socialist Party in the 1930s* (1976); T. Harry Williams, *Huey Long* (1969).

Labor

John Barnard, *Walter Reuther and the Rise of the Auto Workers* (1983); Irving Bernstein, *A Caring Society: The New Deal, the Worker, and the Great Depression* (1985); Irving Bernstein, *Turbulent Years: A History of the American Worker, 1933–1941* (1969); Melvin Dubofsky and Warren Van Tine, *John L. Lewis: A Biography* (1977); Sidney Fine, *Sit-Down: The General Motors Strike of 1936–1937* (1969); August Meier and Elliott Rudwick, *Black Detroit and the Rise of the UAW* (1979); David Milton, *Politics of U.S. Labor: From the Great Depression to the New Deal* (1980).

Agriculture

David E. Conrad, *The Forgotten Farmers: The Story of Sharecroppers in the New Deal* (1965); Theodore M. Saloutos, *The American Farmer and the New Deal* (1982); John L. Shover, *Cornbelt Rebellion: The Farmer's Holiday Association* (1965); Walter J. Stein, *California and the Dust Bowl Migration* (1973); Donald Worster, *Dust Bowl: The Southern Plains in the 1930s* (1979).

People of Color

Francisco E. Balerman, *In Defense of LaRaza: The Los Angeles Mexican Consulate and the Mexican Community, 1929–1936* (1982); Dan T. Carter, *Scottsboro,* rev. ed. (1979); Abraham Hoffman, *Unwanted Mexican Americans in the Great Depression: Repatriation Pressures, 1929–1939* (1974); Laurence C. Kelly, *The Assault on Assimilation: John Collier and the Origins of Indian Policy Reform* (1983); John B. Kirby, *Black Americans in the Roosevelt Era: Liberalism and Race* (1980); Donald J. Lisio, *Hoover, Blacks, and Lily-Whites* (1985); Donald L. Parman, *The Navajos and the New Deal* (1975); Mark Reisler, *By the Sweat of Their Brow: Mexican Immigrant Labor in the United States, 1900–1940* (1976); Harvard Stikoff, *A New Deal for Blacks* (1978); Nancy J. Weiss, *Farewell to the Party of Lincoln, Black Politics in the Age of FDR* (1983); Robert L. Zangrando, *The NAACP Crusade Against Lynching, 1909–1950* (1980).

Women

Julia Kirk Blackwelder, *Women of the Depression: Caste and Culture in San Antonio, 1929–1939* (1984); Glen H. Elder, Jr., *Children of the Great Depression: Social Change in Life Experience* (1974); Lois Scharf, *To Work and to Wed: Female Employment, Feminism, and the Great Depression* (1980); Winifred Wandersee, *Women's Work and Family Values, 1920–1940* (1981); Susan Ware, *Holding Their Own, American Women in the 1930s* (1982); Susan Ware, *Beyond Suffrage: Women in the New Deal* (1981).

Cultural and Intellectual History

Daniel Aaron, *Writers on the Left: Episodes in American Literary Communism* (1961); Andrew Bergman, *We're in the Money: Depression America and Its Films* (1971); Jerre Mangione, *The Dream and the Deal: The Federal Writers' Project, 1935–1943* (1972); Alice Goldfarb Marquis, *Hopes and Ashes: The Birth of Modern Times, 1929–1939* (1986); David P. Peeler, *Hope Among Us Yet: Social Criticism and Social Solace in Depression America* (1987); Richard H. Pells, *Radical Visions and American Dreams: Culture and Social Thought in the Depression Years* (1973); Warren I. Susman, "The Culture of the Thirties," in Warren I. Susman, *Culture as History* (1984), 150–183.

On December 24, 1921, prisoner #9653 strode out of Atlanta's federal penitentiary. After a train ride to Washington, D.C., he entered the White House to meet the man who had just pardoned him. "Well," said President Warren G. Harding, "I have heard so damned much about you, Mr. Debs, that I am now very glad to meet you personally." By releasing Eugene V. Debs, the most prominent of the jailed antiwar critics, Harding was saying that the United States was liquidating the war and returning to what he called "normalcy."

The president took several other steps in November 1921 to demonstrate his resolve to put the war behind the nation. He buried the Unknown Soldier in Arlington Cemetery to initiate, he said, "a new and lasting era of peace." He signed peace treaties with the defeated Central Powers, until then technically still at war with the United States because the Senate had rejected the Treaty of Paris. That month, too, he opened an international conference in Washington, where the United States insisted on a major reduction in naval armaments to ensure a stable world order.

Harding's desire to shove the war into the past and his emphasis on avoiding new entanglements with Europe should not be interpreted to mean that Americans cut themselves off from international affairs after the First World War. To be sure, many Americans had become disillusioned with their war experience. But they remained quite active in the world in the 1920s. The most useful description of interwar foreign policy is *independent internationalism*. That is, the United States was active on a global scale to protect its far-flung interests but retained its independence of action, its traditional unilateralism.

At the same time, many Americans called themselves *isolationists*. By that label they meant that they wanted to isolate themselves from Europe's political squabbles, from military alliances and interventions, and from commitments like the League of Nations, which might restrict their freedom of choice. Americans, then, were isolationists in their desire to avoid war but independent internationalists in their behavior.

The desire to avoid war led American leaders to search for nonmilitary means of exercising power. In the aftermath of the First World War,

25

DIPLOMACY IN A BROKEN WORLD, 1920–1941

Americans had grown disenchanted with military methods of achieving order and protecting American prosperity and security. American diplomats thus increasingly emphasized conferences, moral lectures and calls for peace, nonrecognition of disapproved regimes, arms control, and economic and financial ties in accord with the principle of the Open Door. They pulled the marines out of Latin America and fashioned a Good Neighbor policy for it.

The United States, however, failed to create a stable world order, largely because severe economic problems undercut stability. The debts and reparations bills left over from the First World War bedeviled leaders in the 1920s, and the Great Depression of the 1930s further disrupted world trade and finance. The depression also spawned revolutions in Latin America and political extremism, militarism, and war in Europe and Asia. As Nazi Germany and Japan traveled the road to another world war, the United States sought neutrality.

Yet in the late 1930s, Americans, along with President Franklin D. Roosevelt, changed their minds. They believed that Germany and Japan had become unacceptable menaces to the national interest. Roosevelt first appealed for American military preparedness and then worked to abandon neutrality in favor of aiding Britain and France. To deter Japanese expansion in the Pacific, the United States cut off supplies of vital American products. However, economic warfare had the effect not of containing Japan, but rather of intensifying antagonisms. Japan's surprise attack on Pearl Harbor in December 1941 finally brought the United States into the Second World War.

A fundamental clash of orders or systems explains why diplomacy failed and war came. On the one hand, Germany and Japan preferred a world divided into closed spheres of influence. On the other, the United States sought conditions that would ensure it continued international stature and domestic well-being: a liberal, capitalist world order in which all nations enjoyed the freedom to trade with and invest in all other nations. The United States also prided itself on its democratic system; Germany and Japan embraced authoritarian regimes with strong military influence. Because of such different objectives and outlooks, conflict, if not war, was certainly inevitable.

During the era of independent internationalism, the United States government sent marines to intervene abroad, especially in the Caribbean and Central America. The violent interventions and occupations, however, were hardly as fun-filled as this recruiting poster suggested. And, anti-imperialist critics asked, once you are on the jaguar's back, how do you get off? *Library of Congress.*

The Search for Peace and Order in the 1920s

Europe lay in shambles at the end of the First World War. In the years 1914 to 1921, Europe suffered 60 million casualties from world war, civil war, massacre, epidemic, and famine. Crops, livestock, factories, trains, forests, bridges—little was spared. The plight of Europeans drew American sympathy and aid. The American Relief Administration delivered food to needy Europeans, including Soviet citizens wracked by famine in 1921 and 1922.

IMPORTANT EVENTS

1921	Washington Conference opens
1922	Mussolini comes to power in Italy
1924	Dawes Plan for German reparations
	United States troops leave the Dominican Republic
1926	United States troops occupy Nicaragua
1927	Jiang Jieshi attacks Communists in China
1928	Kellogg-Briand Pact
1929	Onset of the Great Depression
	Young Plan for German reparations
1930	Hawley-Smoot Tariff
1931	Japan seizes Manchuria
1932	Stimson Doctrine
1933	Hitler comes to power in Germany
	United States recognizes Soviet Russia
	Good Neighbor policy announced
1934	Batista comes to power in Cuba
	Reciprocal Trade Agreements Act
	Export-Import Bank founded
1935	Italy invades Ethiopia
	Neutrality Act

1936	Outbreak of Spanish Civil War
	Neutrality Act
1937	Neutrality Act
	Roosevelt's quarantine speech
1938	Mexico nationalizes American-owned oil companies
	Munich Conference
1939	Nazi-Soviet pact
	Germany invades Poland
	Second World War begins
	United States repeals arms embargo
	Soviets invade Finland
1940	Committee to Defend America by Aiding the Allies formed
	Tripartite Pact
	Destroyer-bases deal
	America First Committee formed
	Selective Training and Service Act
1941	Lend-Lease Act
	Germany attacks the Soviet Union
	United States freezes Japanese assets
	Atlantic Charter
	Greer incident
	Japan attacks Pearl Harbor
	United States enters Second World War

American pacifists joined American humanitarians in trying to create international stability. During the 1920s and 1930s, peace societies advocated numerous strategies to ensure world order: cooperation with the League of Nations, membership in the World Court, disarmament and arms reduction, curbs on exploitative business ventures, arbitration of international disputes, the outlawing of war, and strict neutrality in

Peace Movement

times of belligerency. Organizations like the Fellowship of Reconciliation and the Women's International League for Peace and Freedom strove to remind Americans of the carnage of the First World War and the futility of war as a solution to international problems.

At the time, the Washington Conference (November 1921–February 1922) seemed a substantial step toward arms control. The United States discussed with eight other nations (Britain,

Washington Conference Japan, France, Italy, China, Portugal, Belgium, and the Netherlands) limits on naval armaments. Britain, the United States, and Japan—the three major naval powers—were facing a costly naval arms race, and they welcomed the opportunity to deflect it. In the Five-Power Treaty, the delegates set a ten-year moratorium on the construction of capital ships (battleships and aircraft carriers) and established a total tonnage ratio of 5:5:3:1.75:1.75 among the five top nations—Britain, the United States, Japan, France, and Italy. The first three nations actually agreed to dismantle some existing vessels to meet the ratio. They also pledged not to build new fortifications in their Pacific possessions (such as the Philippines for the United States). The Nine-Power Treaty reaffirmed the Open Door in China, recognizing Chinese sovereignty. In the Four-Power Treaty, the United States, Britain, Japan, and France agreed to respect each other's Pacific possessions.

The treaties represented a rare example of mutual disarmament. But they did not limit submarines, destroyers, or cruisers; nor did they provide enforcement powers for the Open Door declaration. Subsequent conferences in the 1930s produced meager results, and rearmament rather than disarmament became the thrust of the times.

Peace advocates also placed their hopes on the Kellogg-Briand Pact of 1928, a treaty eventually signed by sixty-two nations. The signatories agreed to "condemn recourse to war for **Kellogg-** the solution of international con-**Briand Pact** troversies, and renounce it as an instrument of national policy." The treaty's backers billed it as a first step toward international cooperation and the outlawry of war. Although weak, the pact reflected popular sentiment that war was barbaric and wasteful.

The League of Nations, also looked to as a peacemaker, was conspicuously feeble, not because the United States refused to join, but because its members by and large chose not to use it to settle disputes. Starting in the mid-1920s, American officials participated discreetly in League meetings on public health, prostitution, drug trafficking, and other questions. Individual American jurists served on the World Court in Geneva, although the United States also refused to join that institution.

Instability: The World Economy and the Great Depression

While Europe struggled to recover from the ravages of the First World War, United States economic influence became conspicuous around the world. Then the world economy collapsed in the 1930s, after the Great Depression hit. Cordell Hull, secretary of state from 1933 to 1944, often said that economic conditions defined the character of international relations. Hull pointed to political extremism, resurgent militarism, and increased military expenditures as products of maimed economies. Indeed, the depression so disoriented world politics that it ranks as one of the main causes of the Second World War.

For those leaders who believed that American economic expansion would stabilize world politics, the prominent United States position in the international economy seemed oppor-**U.S.** tune. By the late 1920s, the United **Economic** States produced about half the **Expansion** world's industrial goods, ranked first among exporters, and acted as the financial capital of the world. During the period from 1914 to 1930, private investments abroad grew fivefold, to more than $17 billion. Much of this economic activity was facilitated by the United States government through the overseas offices of the Department of Commerce, which gathered important market information. The federal government also stimulated and monitored foreign loans made by American investors.

Europeans warily watched American economic expansion while they branded Americans stingy for their handling of war debts and reparations. Twenty-eight nations became en-**War Debts** tangled in the web of inter-Allied debts, which totaled $26.5 billion, about half of it owed to the United States. Europeans urged Americans to erase the debts as a magnanimous contribution to the war effort. But American leaders insisted on repayment.

The debt question was linked to Germany's $33-billion reparations bill. Hobbled by inflation and economic disorder, Germany began to default on its payments. Americans grew

German Reparations worried that German economic troubles would spawn radicalism. To keep Germany afloat, American bankers loaned millions of dollars to the floundering nation. A triangular relationship developed: American investors' money flowed to Germany; German reparations payments went to the Allies; the Allies then paid some of their debts to the United States. The American-crafted Dawes Plan of 1924 greased the financial tracks by reducing Germany's annual payments, extending the repayment period, and providing still more loans. The United States also gradually scaled down Allied obligations, cutting the debt by half during the 1920s.

The triangular arrangement, however, depended on continued German borrowing in the United States, and in 1928 and 1929 American lending abroad declined sharply in the face of more lucrative opportunities in the stock market. The American-negotiated Young Plan of 1929, which reduced Germany's reparations, salvaged little as the international economy sputtered and collapsed. By 1931, when Hoover declared a moratorium on payments, the Allies had paid back only $2.6 billion. Wracked by the Great Depression, they defaulted on the rest.

By the early 1930s, United States economic power had failed to sustain a healthy world economy. Americans might have worked for a

Economic Nationalism comprehensive, multinational settlement. Instead of raising tariff rates, as they did in 1922 (the Fordney-McCumber Act) and 1930 (the Hawley-Smoot Act), they might have lowered them so that Europeans could sell their goods in the United States and thus earn dollars to pay off their debts. By 1932, about twenty-five nations had retaliated against the American tariff by imposing similar restrictions on American imports. In short, economic nationalism gained momentum. The selfish and vengeful Europeans might have trimmed Germany's huge indemnity. The Germans might have borrowed less from abroad and taxed themselves more. The Soviets might have agreed to pay rather than repudiate Russia's $4-billion indebtedness. Many nations, in short, shared responsibility for the economic cataclysm.

Calling the protective tariff the "king of evils," Secretary of State Hull successfully pressed Congress to pass the Reciprocal Trade Agreements Act

Reciprocal Trade Agreements Act in 1934. This important piece of legislation, which would guide American economic foreign policy thereafter, empowered the president to reduce American tariffs by as much as 50 percent through special agreements with foreign countries. The central feature of the act was the *most-favored-nation principle*, whereby the United States was entitled to the lowest tariff rate set by a nation with which it had an agreement. In 1934, Hull also sponsored the creation of the Export-Import Bank, a government agency that provided loans to foreigners for the purchase of American goods. But Hull's ambitious programs—examples of America's independent internationalism—brought only mixed results in the short term.

Sphere of Influence in Latin America

In United States policy toward Latin America, the interwar themes of independent internationalism, isolationism, nonmilitary means, economic expansion, and the destabilizing impact of the Great Depression became prominent. Before the First World War, the United States had thrown an imperial net over much of the region. By the 1920s, North American–built schools, roads, telephones, and irrigation systems were evident in Latin America. United States financial advisers supervised government budgets in the Caribbean, and in 1920, American soldiers were occupying Cuba, the Dominican Republic, Haiti, Panama, and Nicaragua.

Imperial behavior, however, drew mounting criticism at home and abroad. Manuel Ugarte, a famous Argentine writer, asserted that the United States had become a new Rome.

Criticism of American Imperialism Congressional critics complained about the denial of self-determination to Latin Americans and the dispatch of troops abroad without a congressional declaration of war. Businesspeople feared the destruction of property by angry Latin Americans. And in 1932, Secretary of State Henry L. Stimson, who was concerned about Japanese incursions in China, worried that similar United States intervention in Latin America would render his protests meaningless because of the double standard.

Turning away pragmatically from unpopular military intervention, the United States tried other methods of maintaining its influence in Latin America: Pan-Americanism, support for strong native leaders, the training of national guards, economic penetration, Export-Import Bank loans, and political subversion. Although the process began before his presidency, Franklin D. Roosevelt gave it a name in 1933: the Good Neighbor policy. It meant that the United States would be less blatant in its domination—less willing to defend exploitative business practices, less eager to send in military expeditions, and less wary of consultation with Latin Americans.

The training of national guards went hand in hand with support of dictators. Some Latin American dictators rose to power through the ranks of a national guard trained by the United States. For example, before the United States withdrew its troops from the Dominican Republic in 1924, American personnel created a guard. One of its first officers was Rafael Leonidas Trujillo, who became president in 1930 through fraud and intimidation. He ruled the Dominican Republic with an iron fist until his assassination in 1961. "He may be an S.O.B.," Roosevelt supposedly remarked, "but he is our S.O.B."

In Nicaragua, the experience was similar. United States troops occupied Nicaragua from 1912 to 1925 and returned in late 1926 during a civil war. Washington claimed that it was only trying to stabilize Nicaragua's politics, but critics at home and abroad saw the situation as a case of United States imperialism. Nationalistic Nicaraguan opposition, led by César Augusto Sandino, who denounced the Monroe Doctrine as meaning "America for the Yankees," helped prompt Washington to end the occupation.

In 1933, the United States Marines departed, but they left behind a powerful national guard headed by General Anastasio Somoza. With American backing, the Somoza family ruled Nicaragua from 1936 to 1979 through corruption, political suppression, and torture.

The marines' occupation of black Haiti from 1915 to 1934 also produced a very negative legacy. United States officials censored the Haitian press, manipulated elections, wrote the constitution, jailed or killed thousands of protesters, managed government finances, and created a national guard. The National City Bank of New York became the owner of the Haitian Banque Nationale, and the United States became Haiti's largest trading partner.

Black leaders in the United States decried this blatant manipulation of foreigners. James Weldon Johnson of the NAACP reported that Haitians forced to work without pay to build roads "were in the same category with the convicts in the negro chain gangs" of the American South. Not until 1929, when Haitians protested violently against American rule and an official investigative commission told President Hoover that the occupation had failed to bring benefits to the Haitian people, did Washington decide to withdraw its soldiers.

The Cubans, too, grew restless under United States domination. By 1929 United States investments in the Caribbean nation totaled $1.5 billion. Furthermore, the United States military maintained a naval base at Guantánamo Bay. Still, during the Cuban revolution of 1933, in open defiance of United States warships cruising offshore, Professor Ramon Grau San Martín became president. Grau declared the Platt Amendment, which allowed the United States to intervene in Cuban affairs, null and void. His government also seized some American-owned mills, did not repay United States bank loans, and talked of land reform. The United States responded by refusing to recognize the Grau government and by successfully plotting in 1933 and 1934 with an army sergeant, Fulgencio Batista, to overthrow it. During the dictatorial Batista era, which lasted until 1959, Cuba protected United States investments and granted the United States military sites. In return,

Good Neighbor Policy

National Guard in the Dominican Republic

Somoza and Sandino in Nicaragua

Occupation of Haiti

Cuban Revolution of 1933

Havana received military aid, loans, the abrogation of the Platt Amendment, and a favorable sugar tariff.

The pattern was different in Mexico. In 1917, the Mexicans adopted a new constitution specifying that all "land and waters" and all subsoil raw mate-

**Confronta-
tion with
Mexico**

rials (like oil) belonged to the Mexican nation. This nationalistic document represented a threat to North American landholdings and petroleum interests. A weak, un-developed Latin American nation on the United States border had issued a direct challenge to the hemisphere's hegemonic power.

Washington and Mexico City wrangled for years over the rights of American economic interests. Then, in 1938, Mexico boldly expropriated the property of all foreign-owned petroleum companies. The United States countered by reducing purchases of Mexican silver and encouraging a business boycott of the upstart nation. But President Roosevelt decided to compromise because he feared that the Mexicans would sell their oil to Germany and Japan. In 1941, the United States conceded that Mexico owned its raw materials and Mexico compensated American companies for their lost property. United States power had been diminished, and Mexico became an inspiring symbol for other Latin American nationalists.

The Good Neighbor policy paid off in the Declaration of Panama (1939), wherein Latin American governments drew a security line around the hemisphere and warned aggressors away. In exchange for more trade and foreign aid, Latin Americans also reduced their sales of raw materials to Germany, Japan, and Italy and increased shipments to the United States. On the eve of the Second World War, then, the United States's sphere of influence was virtually intact, and most Latin American regimes backed United States diplomatic objectives.

Upheaval in Europe

In depression-wracked Germany, where 6 million workers were unemployed in the early 1930s, Adolf Hitler came to power in 1933. Like Benito

**Hitler's
Germany**

Mussolini, who had gained control of Italy in 1922, Hitler was a fascist. Fascism (called Nazism, or National Socialism, in Germany) was a collection of ideas and prejudices that included supremacy of the state over the individual; of dictatorship over democracy; of authoritarianism over freedom of speech; of a regulated, state-oriented economy over a free market economy; and of militarism and war over peace. The Nazis vowed not only to revive German economic and military strength but to cripple communism and to "purify" the German "race" by subjugating and ultimately destroying Jews.

In 1933, resentful of the punitive terms of the 1919 Treaty of Paris, Hitler pulled Germany out of the League of Nations, ended reparations payments, and began to rearm. Secretly laying plans for the conquest of neighboring states, he watched admiringly as Mussolini's troops invaded the African nation of Ethiopia in 1935. The next year, Hitler ordered his troops into the Rhineland, an area that the Treaty of Paris had declared demilitarized. Germany's timid neighbor France did not resist this aggressive action.

Soon, the aggressors began to join hands. In the fall of 1936, Italy and Germany formed an alliance called the Rome-Berlin Axis. Shortly afterward, Germany and Japan united against the Soviet Union in the Anti-Comintern Pact. Britain and France responded to these events with a policy of appeasement, hoping to curb Hitler's expansionist appetite by permitting him a few nibbles. But the policy eventually proved disastrous; Hitler continually raised his demands.

In those hair-trigger times, a civil war in Spain turned into an international struggle. From 1936 to 1939, the Loyalist Republicans battled the fascist-

**Spanish
Civil War**

backed insurgents under Francisco Franco. Hitler and Mussolini sent military aid to Franco; the Soviet Union assisted the Loyalists. France and Britain held to the fiction of a nonintervention pledge that even Italy and Germany had signed. About three thousand American volunteers, known as the Lincoln Battalion, joined the fight on the side of the Republicans. When Franco won in 1939, his victory tightened the grip of fascism on the European continent.

Early in 1938, Hitler once again tested the limits

The bold, militaristic Adolf Hitler (1889–1945) ruled Germany from 1933 to 1945. Here he salutes march-ers in Nuremberg, 1937. The anti-Semitic Hitler denounced the United States as a "Jewish rubbish heap" of "inferiority and decadence" that was "incapable of conducting war." *Hugo Jaeger,* Life *magazine,* © *Time Warner Inc.*

of European patience when he sent his soldiers into Austria to annex that nation. In September of the same year, he seized the Sude-ten region of Czechoslovakia. Ap-peasement reached its peak that month at the Munich Conference, when France and Britain, without consulting the helpless Czechs, agreed to allow Hitler this one last territorial bite. British Prime Minister Neville Chamberlain returned home to proclaim "peace in our time." But in March 1939, Hitler swallowed the rest of Czechoslovakia. Poland was next on his list. Scuttling appeasement, London and Paris an-nounced that they would stand by their ally Poland. Undaunted, Berlin signed the Nazi-Soviet Pact with Moscow and launched attacks against Poland on September 1. Britain and France declared war on Germany two days later. The Second World War had begun.

As the world spiraled toward war, the Soviet

Munich and Poland

Union played a key role and posed a special problem in American foreign relations. Following precedent, the Republican admin-istrations of the 1920s had not rec-ognized the Soviet government, arguing that the Bolsheviks had refused to pay more than $600 million for confiscated American-owned property and had repudiated Russian debts. Yet American businesses began to enter the Soviet marketplace, and by 1930, the Soviet Union had become the larg-est buyer of American farm and industrial equip-ment.

Relations with the Soviet Union

In the early 1930s, however, trade began to slump. To stimulate business and help the United States pull out of the depression, some busi-nesspeople began to lobby for diplomatic recogni-tion of the Soviet Union. President Roosevelt agreed that a change in policy was necessary. Prac-ticing personal, one-on-one diplomacy, Roosevelt negotiated in 1933 with Soviet Commissar for Foreign Affairs Maxim Litvinov. They hammered out agreements, some of them vague in language: United States recognition, future discussion of the debts question, a Soviet promise to forgo propagandistic or subversive activities in the United States, and religious freedom and legal rights for Americans in the Soviet Union. Within a few years, however, Soviet-American relations had once again become embittered. Especially upsetting to Americans was the Nazi-Soviet Pact and the Soviet Union's grabbing of half of Poland.

Isolationism, Roosevelt, and the Neutrality Acts

As authoritarianism, racial hatred, and military expansion descended on Europe and Asia in the 1930s, Americans reasserted their isolationist beliefs. A 1937 Gallup poll found that nearly two-thirds of the people asked about the First World War thought that American participation had been a mistake. Conservative isolationists feared higher taxes and increased federal power if the nation went to war again. Liberal isolationists spoke of the need to give domestic problems priority and to spend less on the military. Critics of many persuasions predicted that in attempting to spread democracy abroad Americans would lose it at home. Many Americans resented the fact that some Europeans looked to the United States to do what they themselves refused to do: block Hitler.

Isolationism was a national phenomenon that cut across socioeconomic, ethnic, party, and sectional lines and attracted a majority of the American people. Some liberal isolationists, critical of business practices at home, charged that corporate "merchants of death" were undermining the national interest by assisting the aggressors. From 1934 to 1936, a congressional committee, chaired by Senator Gerald P. Nye, held hearings on the role of business interests in the American deci-

Isolationist Thought

sion to enter the First World War. The hearings did not prove that businesspeople and financiers had dragged reluctant Americans into that war, but they did uncover evidence that corporations in the 1920s and 1930s had bribed foreign politicians to improve arms sales, had lobbied against arms control, and had signed contracts with Nazi Germany and fascist Italy.

President Franklin D. Roosevelt shared isolationist views in the early 1930s. Like his famous older cousin Theodore, Franklin as a young man had believed that the United States should exert leadership in the world community and flex its military muscle to ensure American security and prosperity. He was an expansionist and interventionist, but during the interwar period, like most Americans, he talked less about preparedness and more about disarmament and the horrors of war.

Roosevelt revealed his and the nation's preference to avoid European squabbles when he signed a series of neutrality acts. Congress sought to protect the nation by stopping contacts that had compromised American neutrality two decades earlier. The Neutrality Act of 1935 prohibited arms shipments to either side in a war once the president had declared the existence of belligerency. The Neutrality Act of 1936 forbade loans to belligerents. After a joint resolution in 1937 declared the United States neutral in the Spanish Civil War, Roosevelt embargoed arms shipments to both sides. The Neutrality Act of 1937 introduced the cash-and-carry principle: warring nations wishing to trade with the United States would have to pay cash for their purchases and carry the goods away in their own ships. The act also forbade Americans from traveling on the ships of belligerent nations.

Neutrality Acts

Expressing prevailing isolationist opinion and making a pitch for the pacifist vote in the upcoming election, Roosevelt gave a stirring speech in August 1936 in Chautauqua, New York: "I have seen war. . . . I have seen blood running from the wounded. I have seen men coughing out their gassed lungs. . . . I have seen the agony of mothers and wives. I hate war." He promised that the United States would remain distant from European conflict. During the Czech crisis of 1938, Roosevelt actually endorsed appeasement. The United States, he wrote to Hitler, had "no political involvements in Europe."

But Roosevelt became deeply troubled by the arrogant behavior of the "three bandit nations"—Germany, Italy, and Japan. He expressed disgust with Nazi persecution of the Jews and with Japanese slaughter of Chinese civilians. Privately, he snarled against the refusal of the British and French to collar Hitler in their own backyards, and he worried that the United States was militarily ill prepared to confront the aggressors.

The United States did not neglect its military. Roosevelt's New Deal public works programs included millions for the construction of new ships. In 1935, the president requested the largest peacetime defense budget in American history; three years later, in the wake of Munich, he asked Congress for funds to build up the air force. The president also began to cast about for ways to encourage the British and French to show more backbone. One result was his agreement in January 1939 to sell bombers to France.

In his annual message early in 1939, the president lashed out at the international lawbreakers. Soon afterward, he failed to persuade Congress to repeal the arms embargo and per-

Repeal of the Arms Embargo mit the sale of munitions to belligerents on a cash-and-carry basis. When Europe fell into the abyss of war in September 1939, Roosevelt both declared neutrality and pressed again for repeal of the arms embargo. After much debate, Congress in November lifted the embargo on contraband and approved cash-and-carry exports of arms. Roosevelt was ready to aid the Allies—short of entering the war.

Japan, China, and a New Order in Asia

If United States power was massive in Latin America and limited in Europe, it was minuscule in Asia. Still, the United States had interests in Asia that needed defense: the Philippines and Pacific islands, religious missions, trade and investments, and the Open Door in China. Americans came to believe that Japan threatened these interests because the Japanese seemed bent on subjugating China and unhinging the Open Door doctrine of equal trade and investment opportunity. Although Americans saw themselves as China's special friend, many Chinese nationalists complained that America joined other imperialists in undermining Chinese sovereignty.

In 1927, Jiang Jieshi (Chiang Kai-shek) emerged as the leader of China, having ousted Communists from the nationalistic Guomindang party and

Rise of Jiang Jieshi in China forced Mao Zedong and his followers to flee to the hills. Americans applauded this display of anti-Bolshevism and Jiang's conversion in 1930 to Christianity. Warming to Jiang, United States officials signed a treaty in 1928 restoring control of tariffs to the Chinese. American gunboats and marines remained in China, however.

The Japanese grew increasingly suspicious of United States–Chinese ties. In the early twentieth century, Japanese-American relations were seldom cordial. As the Japanese intruded

Japanese Seizure of Manchuria more and more into China, they collided with America's Open Door policy. Relations deteriorated further after the Japanese military seized Manchuria in September 1931 (see map). Only nominally a Chinese region, Manchuria was important to the Japanese both as a buffer against the Soviets and as a vital source of coal, iron, timber, and food. Although the seizure of Manchuria violated the Nine-Power Treaty and the Kellogg-Briand Pact, the United States did not have the power to compel Japanese withdrawal. The American response, therefore, went no further than a moral lecture called the Stimson Doctrine (1932), which declared that the United States would not recognize any impairment of China's sovereignty or of the Open Door policy.

Hardly cowed by protests from Western capitals, Japan continued to harry China. In mid-1937, a full-scale Sino-Japanese war erupted. In an effort to help China, Roosevelt refused to declare the exis-

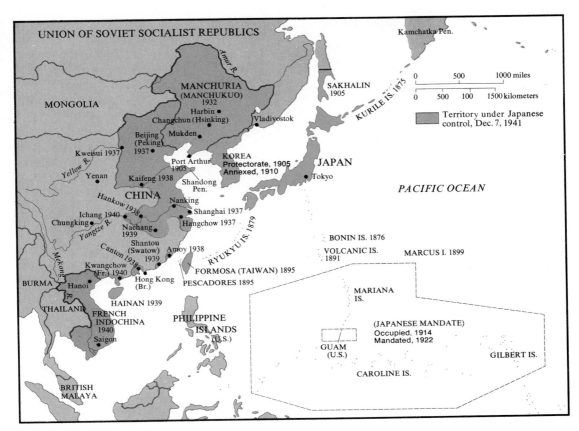

Japanese Expansion Before Pearl Harbor

tence of war, thus not invoking the Neutrality Acts and so allowing the Chinese to buy weapons in the United States. In a stirring speech denouncing the aggressors in October 1937, he called for a "quarantine" to curb the "epidemic of world lawlessness." Yet Roosevelt had formulated no program to halt the Japanese.

Japan's declaration of a "New Order" in Asia "banged, barred, and bolted" the Open Door, as one American official observed. Alarmed, the Roosevelt administration found small ways to assist China and thwart Japan in 1938 and 1939. Military equipment flowed to the Chinese, as did a $25-million loan. Secretary of State Hull declared a moral embargo on the shipment of airplanes to Japan. The United States Navy continued to grow, helped by a billion-dollar congressional appropriation in 1938. In mid-1939, the United States ab-

rogated the 1911 Japanese-American trade treaty; yet America continued to ship oil, cotton, and machinery to Japan. The administration hesitated to initiate economic sanctions because such economic pressure might spark a Japanese-American war at a time when Germany posed the more serious threat.

▼

Collision Course, 1939–1941

Polls showed that Americans strongly favored the Allies and that most supported aid to Britain and France; but the great majority emphatically wanted the United States to stay out of the Second World

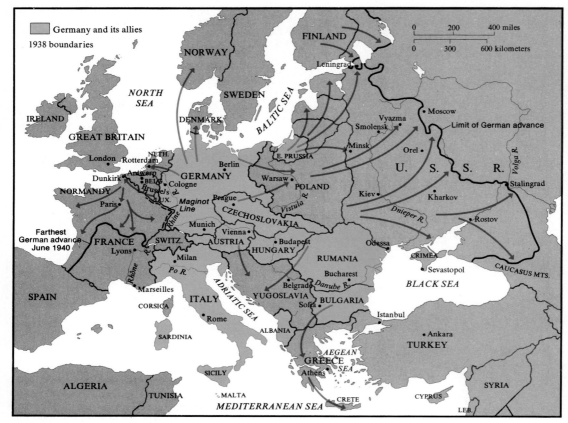

The German Advance, 1939–1942

War. Troubled by this conflicting advice—defeat Hitler, aid the Allies, but stay out of war—the president between 1939 and 1941 gradually moved the nation from neutrality to undeclared war and then to war itself.

During those tense months of inching toward belligerency, isolationist sentiment declined. Alarmed by the swift defeat of one European nation after another, some liberals left the isolationist fold, which became more and more the province of conservatives. Die-hard isolationists organized the America First Committee in the fall of 1940; interventionists, meanwhile, joined the Committee to Defend America by Aiding the Allies (formed in mid-1940). Roosevelt charged that some isolationists were pro-Nazi subversives—"conscious disorganizers or unwitting dupes." Debate raged.

In September 1939, Poland succumbed to German storm troopers in two weeks (see map). In November, Soviet forces marched into Finland, **Fall of France** prompting Roosevelt to denounce "this dreadful rape"; by March 1940, Finland had been defeated. The following month, Germany invaded Denmark and Norway and a month later the Netherlands and Belgium. In May 1940, several German divisions attacked France. By early June, they had pushed French and British forces to the English Channel. At Dunkirk, more than 300,000 Allied soldiers, leaving their equipment on the beaches, frantically escaped to Britain on a flotilla of small boats. Would Britain be next?

In the meantime, Roosevelt began to aid the beleaguered Allies. In May 1940, he had ordered the sale of surplus First World War equipment to Britain and France. In July, he cultivated bipartisan sup-

Chapter 25: Diplomacy in a Broken World, 1920–1941

port by naming Republicans Henry L. Stimson and Frank Knox, ardent backers of aid to the Allies, secretaries of war and of the navy, respectively. In September, by executive agreement, he traded fifty old American destroyers for leases to eight British bases, including Newfoundland, Bermuda, and Jamaica. Two weeks later, Roosevelt signed into law the hotly debated and narrowly passed Selective Training and Service Act, the first peacetime military draft in American history.

Roosevelt claimed that the United States could keep out of the war if America enabled the British to win. The United States must become the "great arsenal of democracy." In January 1941, the administration sent the controversial Lend-Lease bill to Congress. Because Britain was broke, the president said, the United States should lend rather than sell weapons, much as a neighbor lends a garden hose to fight a fire. The bill cleared Congress in March 1941, and $7 billion was appropriated. By the end of the war, the amount had reached $50 billion, more than $31 billion of it for England.

Lend-Lease Act

To ensure the safe delivery of Lend-Lease goods, Roosevelt ordered the navy to patrol halfway across the Atlantic and sent American troops to Greenland. In June 1941, Hitler struck the Soviet Union. In July, arguing that Iceland was essential to the defense of the Western Hemisphere, Roosevelt dispatched four thousand marines there. He also sent Lend-Lease aid to the Soviet Union. If the Soviets could hold off the more than two hundred German divisions engaged in the east, Britain would gain some breathing time.

In August 1941, British Prime Minister Winston Churchill and Roosevelt met for four days off Newfoundland. At this conference, the two leaders issued the Atlantic Charter, a set of war aims reminiscent of Wilsonianism: collective security, disarmament, self-determination, economic cooperation, and freedom of the seas. Later, on January 1, 1942, twenty-six nations signed the Declaration of the United Nations, pledging allegiance to the charter.

Atlantic Charter Conference

In September 1941, the American destroyer *Greer* was fired on (but not hit) by a German submarine. Using the incident to his advantage, Roosevelt protested German "piracy" before a national radio audience. The president also announced a policy he had privately promised to Churchill: American naval vessels would now convoy British merchant ships all the way to Iceland and shoot German submarines, the "rattlesnakes of the Atlantic," on sight. Roosevelt failed to mention that the *Greer* had been tailing a German U-boat, giving its position to British airplanes. The next month, another American destroyer, the *Reuben James*, was torpedoed, with the loss of more than a hundred American lives. Congress responded by scrapping the cash-and-carry policy and authorizing armed American merchant ships to transport munitions to England.

In retrospect, it seems ironic that the Second World War came to the United States by way of Asia, where Roosevelt so wanted to avoid it in order to concentrate American resources on the defeat of Germany. In September 1940, after Germany, Italy, and Japan had signed the Tripartite Pact, Roosevelt slapped an embargo on shipments of aviation fuel and scrap metal to Japan. The next summer, Washington responded to the Japanese occupation of French Indochina by freezing Japanese assets in the United States. The action made it virtually impossible for Japan to secure goods, including much needed oil, from the United States.

Cutoff of Trade with Japan

Tokyo recommended a high-level meeting between President Roosevelt and Prime Minister Prince Konoye, but the United States rejected the idea. American officials insisted that the Japanese first agree to respect China's sovereignty and territorial integrity and to honor the Open Door policy—in short, to get out of China. Roosevelt told his advisers to string out Japanese-American talks and so gain time to fortify the Philippines and check the fascists in Europe.

By breaking the Japanese code through Operation Magic, Americans learned that Tokyo had committed itself to war with the United States if shipments of oil did not resume. In late November, the Japanese rejected American proposals that they withdraw from Indochina. On December 1, decoding experts informed the president that Japanese

December 7, 1941. The daring Japanese attack on Pearl Harbor, Hawaii, caught the United States by surprise. Rescuers struggle to save survivors of a crippled American warship, the USS *West Virginia*. *U.S. Army.*

task forces were being ordered into battle. Secretary Stimson explained later that the United States let Japan fire the first shot so as "to have the full support of the American people" and "so that there should remain no doubt in anyone's mind as to who were the aggressors."

The Japanese plotted a daring raid on Pearl Harbor in Hawaii. A flotilla of Japanese aircraft carriers crossed 3,000 miles of ocean undetected. On the morning of December 7, Japanese planes swept down on the unsuspecting American naval base and nearby airfields, killing more than 2,400 people, sinking or damaging eight battleships, and smashing aircraft (three American Pacific aircraft carriers, at sea, escaped the disaster). Roosevelt was distressed that his proud navy had been caught by

Pearl Harbor

surprise, but like many Americans he felt relief after the weeks of tension.

How could the stunning attack on Pearl Harbor have happened? Americans asked. Roosevelt did not, as some critics charged, conspire to leave the fleet vulnerable to attack so that the United States could enter the Second World War through the "back door" of Asia. The base was not ready—not on red alert—because a message of warning from Washington, mistakenly transmitted by a slow method, arrived too late. Base commanders were relaxed, thinking Hawaii too far from Japan to be a target for all-out attack. They expected the assault to come in British Malaya, Thailand, or the Philippines. The terrible tragedy at Pearl Harbor stemmed from mistakes, not conspiracy.

On December 8, referring to the previous day as

a "date which will live in infamy," Roosevelt asked Congress for a declaration of war against Japan. The vote was unanimous in the Senate and 388 to 1 in the House. Three days later, Germany and Italy declared war against the United States. Winston Churchill was pleased that America was now fully at war. "Hitler's fate was sealed," he wrote in his memoirs. "Mussolini's fate was sealed. As for the Japanese, they would be ground to powder."

The war was now a global conflict. As they had so many times before, Americans flocked to the colors. Isolationists now joined the president in spirited calls for victory. "We are going to win the war, and we are going to win the peace that follows," Roosevelt predicted.

▼

Suggestions for Further Reading

General and 1920s Foreign Policy

Thomas H. Buckley, *The United States and the Washington Conference, 1921–1922* (1970); Warren I. Cohen, *Empire Without Tears* (1987); Frank Costigliola, *Awkward Dominion* (1984) (on Europe); Robert H. Ferrell, *American Diplomacy in the Great Depression* (1957); Bruce Kent, *The Spoils of War* (1989); Arnold A. Offner, *The Origins of the Second World War* (1975); Emily S. Rosenberg, *Spreading the American Dream* (1982); Michael S. Sherry, *The Rise of American Airpower* (1987); Raymond Sontag, *A Broken World, 1919–1939* (1971).

The Peace Movement and the Kellogg-Briand Pact

Charles Chatfield, *For Peace and Justice: Pacifism in America, 1914–1941* (1971); Charles DeBenedetti, *The Peace Reform in American History* (1980); Charles DeBenedetti, *Origins of the Modern American Peace Movement, 1915–1929* (1978); Robert H. Ferrell, *Peace in Their Time* (1952); Lawrence Wittner, *Rebels Against War* (1984).

The United States in the World Economy

Frederick Adams, *Economic Diplomacy* (1976); Derek H. Aldcroft, *From Versailles to Wall Street, 1919–1929* (1977); Herbert Feis, *The Diplomacy of the Dollar, 1919–1932* (1950); Lloyd C. Gardner, *Economic Aspects of New Deal*

Diplomacy (1964); Michael J. Hogan, *Informal Entente* (1977) (on Anglo-American relations); Charles Kindleberger, *The World in Depression* (1973); Stephen J. Randall, *United States Foreign Oil Policy, 1919–1948* (1986); Mira Wilkins, *The Maturing of Multinational Enterprise* (1974); Joan Hoff Wilson, *American Business and Foreign Policy, 1920–1933* (1971).

Latin America

Bruce J. Calder, *The Impact of Intervention* (1984) (on the Dominican Republic); Alton Frye, *Nazi Germany and the American Hemisphere, 1933–1941* (1967); Irwin F. Gellman, *Good Neighbor Diplomacy* (1979); David Green, *The Containment of Latin America* (1971); Walter LaFeber, *Inevitable Revolutions* (1983) (on Central America); Lester D. Langley, *The United States and the Caribbean, 1900–1970* (1980); Neil Macaulay, *The Sandino Affair* (1967); Louis A. Pérez, *Cuba* (1988); Louis A. Pérez, *Cuba Under the Platt Amendment* (1986); Stephen G. Rabe, *The Road to OPEC* (1982) (on Venezuela); Robert I. Rotberg, *Haiti* (1971); Karl M. Schmitt, *Mexico and the United States, 1821–1973* (1974); Bryce Wood, *The Making of the Good Neighbor Policy* (1961).

Isolationism and Isolationists

Warren I. Cohen, *The American Revisionists* (1967); Wayne S. Cole, *Roosevelt and the Isolationists, 1932–1945* (1983); Wayne S. Cole, *America First* (1953); Manfred Jonas, *Isolationism in America, 1935–1941* (1966); Richard Lowitt, *George W. Norris*, 3 vols. (1963–1978); John Wiltz, *In Search of Peace: The Senate Munitions Inquiry, 1934–1936* (1963).

Europe, the Coming of World War II, and Roosevelt

Edward Bennett, *Recognition of Russia* (1970); James MacGregor Burns, *Roosevelt: The Lion and the Fox* (1956); J. Garry Clifford and Samuel R. Spencer, Jr., *The First Peacetime Draft* (1986); James V. Compton, *The Swastika and the Eagle* (1967); Robert Dallek, *Franklin D. Roosevelt and American Foreign Policy, 1932–1945* (1979); Robert A. Divine, *The Reluctant Belligerent*, 2nd ed. (1979); Robert A. Divine, *Roosevelt and World War II* (1969); Waldo H. Heinrichs, Jr., *Threshold of War* (1988); Manfred Jonas, *The United States and Germany* (1984); Warren F. Kimball, *The Most Unsordid Act: Lend-Lease, 1939–1941* (1969); Thomas R. Maddux, *Years of Estrangement* (1980) (on relations with the Soviet Union); David Reynolds, *The Creation of the Anglo-American Alliance, 1937–1941* (1982); David F. Schmitz, *The United States and Fascist Italy, 1922–1944* (1988); Richard Steele, *Propaganda in an Open Society: The Roosevelt Administration and the Media, 1933–1941* (1985).

China, Japan, and the Coming of War in Asia

Dorothy Borg and Shumpei Okomoto, eds., *Pearl Harbor as History* (1973); R. J. C. Butow, *Tojo and the Coming of War* (1961); Warren I. Cohen, *America's Response to China*, 3rd ed. (1990); Roger Dingman, *Power in the Pacific* (1976); Herbert Feis, *The Road to Pearl Harbor* (1950); Akira Iriye, *The Origins of the Second World War in Asia and the Pacific* (1987); Akira Iriye, *Across the Pacific* (1967); Akira Iriye, *After Imperialism* (1965); Charles Neu, *The Troubled Encounter* (1975); Paul W. Schroeder, *The Axis Alliance and Japanese-American Relations, 1941* (1958); Jonathan Utley, *Going to War with Japan* (1985).

Pearl Harbor

Martin V. Melosi, *The Shadow of Pearl Harbor* (1977); Gordon W. Prange, *Pearl Harbor* (1986); Gordon W. Prange, *At Dawn We Slept* (1981); John Toland, *Infamy* (1982); Roberta Wohlstetter, *Pearl Harbor* (1962).

Elliott Johnson was dining with three friends in a Chinese restaurant in Portland, Oregon, when he learned of the attack. It was December 7, 1941. Bursting through the doors of the kitchen came the restaurant owner; the portable radio he was carrying told the news of the Japanese bombing of Pearl Harbor. "We immediately went to the marine recruiting headquarters," recalled Johnson. But before he could enlist, the recruiter barked at him: "Step out of line, you're getting a Dear John letter from the President." The next day, Johnson received the letter; and on January 12, he was inducted into the army.

Two-and-a-half years later, as a lieutenant in charge of an artillery company, Johnson participated in the D-Day invasion of Europe. On the morning of June 6, 1944, Johnson and his men were aboard a 300-foot-long "landing ship tank" (LST). While the craft was approaching Normandy beach, Johnson saw another LST take "a direct hit and go up in a huge ball of flames" and "there were bodies floating, face down, face up." The young naval officer at the helm of Johnson's LST announced that he "wasn't gonna take us up that beach. . . . So I ended up taking my gun out on him. Shoved it in his mouth. . . . He finally got us to where we were in about three feet of water and he said, 'I just can't go any more.' Fine, let down the ramp."

26

THE SECOND WORLD WAR AT HOME AND ABROAD, 1941–1945

Like many soldiers, sailors, and marines, Elliott Johnson found that during the Second World War his life changed in profound ways. For one thing, it took the war "to hammer it home to me: I am totally averse to killing and warfare. I saw it with my own eyes and it didn't do a dadratted thing." Contrary to Johnson, most home-front Americans believed that war was a proper instrument of national policy. But whether overseas or at home, few disagreed that the Second World War was a watershed in the country's development.

For forty-five months, Americans fought abroad to subdue the aggressors. After military engagements against fascists in North Africa and Italy, American troops joined the dramatic crossing of the English Channel on D-Day in June 1944. The massive invasion forced the Germans to retreat through France to Germany. They finally capitulated in May 1945. In the Pacific, Americans drove the Japanese from one island after another before turning to the just-tested atomic bombs, which demolished Hiroshima and Nagasaki and helped spur a Japanese surrender in August 1945.

Throughout the war, the Allies—Britain, the Soviet Union, and the United States—were held together by their common goal of defeating Germany. But they squabbled over many issues: when the second, or western, front would be opened; how a new international organization would be structured; how Eastern Europe, liberated from the Germans, would be reconstructed; how Germany itself would be governed after defeat. At the end of the war, Allied leaders seemed more intent on keeping and expanding their own nations' spheres of influence than on building a community of mutual interest. The prospects for postwar international cooperation seemed bleak, and the advent of an atomic age with nuclear weapons frightened people everywhere.

At home, Americans united behind the war effort, collecting scrap iron, rubber, and old newspapers and planting victory gardens. The federal government mobilized all traditional sectors of the economy—industry, finance, agriculture, and labor—as well as a couple of new ones: higher education and science. For this was a scientific and technological war, supported by the development of new weapons like the atomic bomb.

For millions of Americans, the war was a time to relocate in other parts of the country. Not only did 16 million men and women serve in the armed forces, but blacks, Mexican-Americans, and whites migrated to war-production centers in the North and the West. Employers' negative attitudes toward women workers eased during the Second World War, and millions of married middle-class women took jobs in war industries.

Winning the Second World War

"We are now in the midst of a war, not for conquest, not for vengeance, but for a world in which this Nation, and all that this Nation represents, will be safe for our children." President Roosevelt was speaking just two days after the surprise attack on Pearl Harbor. Americans believed with Roosevelt that they were defending their homes and families against aggressive and satanic Japanese and Nazis.

America's men and women responded to Roosevelt's call to the colors. In 1941, even though Selective Service had been functioning for a full year, the grand total of people serving on active duty was only 1,801,000. In 1945, the number of women and men serving in the army, navy, and marines peaked at 12,124,000. Such a massive force was necessary to fight a world war on two fronts.

Despite Americans' nearly unanimous support for the war effort, various government leaders worried that public morale would lag during a lengthy war. Thus, the army hired prominent Hollywood director Frank Capra to produce a series of propaganda films called *Why We Fight*. In these widely distributed films and in the popular mind, the Allies were heroic partners in a common struggle against evil.

Actually, wartime relations among the United States, Great Britain, and the Soviet Union ran hot and cold. Although winning the war claimed top priority, Allied leaders knew that military decisions had political consequences. If one ally became desperate, for instance, it might sue for a separate peace. Moreover, the position of troops at the end of the war might determine the politics of the region they occupied. Thus, an undercurrent of suspicion ran beneath the surface of Allied cooperation.

Roosevelt, British Prime Minister Winston Churchill, and Soviet Premier Josef Stalin differed over the opening of a second, or western, front. Stalin **Second-** pressed for a British-American **Front** landing on the northern coast of **Controversy** Europe to draw German troops away from the eastern front, but Churchill would not agree. The Soviets therefore did most of the fighting and dying on land, while the British and Americans concentrated on getting Lend-Lease supplies across the Atlantic and harassing the Germans from the air with attacks on factories and civilians alike.

Roosevelt was particularly sensitive to the Soviet burden. And he feared that the Soviet Union might be knocked out of the war, leaving Hitler free to

IMPORTANT EVENTS

1941	Japan attacks Pearl Harbor; United States enters Second World War
1942	National War Labor Board established War Production Board established Internment of more than 110,000 Japanese-Americans in "relocation centers" Bataan Death March Battles of Coral Sea and Midway Allied invasion of North Africa Synthetic-rubber program begins
1943	Russian victory at Stalingrad Strikes by soft-coal and anthracite miners War Labor Disputes (Smith-Connally) Act Race riots in Detroit and 46 other cities Allied invasion of Italy Teheran Conference
1944	Roosevelt requests Economic Bill of Rights War Refugee Board established Supreme Court upholds internment of Japanese-Americans Normandy landings (D-Day) Dumbarton Oaks Conference Roosevelt re-elected United States retakes the Philippines
1945	Yalta Conference Battles of Iwo Jima and Okinawa Roosevelt dies; Truman assumes the presidency United Nations founded Germany surrenders Potsdam Conference Atomic bombs devastate Hiroshima and Nagasaki Japan surrenders

send his goose-stepping soldiers into England. In 1942, Roosevelt told the Soviets that they could expect the Allies to open a second front later that year. The move across the English Channel, later tagged Operation OVERLORD, was exactly what Stalin sought to take pressure off his wracked country. But Churchill, fearing heavy British losses in a premature invasion, balked; he favored a series of small jabs at the enemy's Mediterranean forces.

Churchill won the debate. Instead of attacking France, the western Allies invaded North Africa in November 1942. "We are striking back," the cheered president declared. News from the Soviet Union also buoyed Roosevelt. In the battle for Stalingrad (September 1942 to January 1943), probably the turning point of the European war, the Red Army defeated the Germans, forcing Hitler's divisions to retreat. But in early 1943, Stalin was again told that the second front would be delayed. He was not mollified by the Allied invasion of Italy in the summer of 1943. When Italy surrendered in September, it capitulated to American and British officers; Soviet officials were not invited to participate. Stalin grumbled that the arrangement smacked of a separate peace.

With the Grand Alliance badly strained, Roosevelt sought reconciliation through personal diplomacy. The three Allied leaders met in Teheran, Iran, in December 1943. Stalin dismissed Churchill's repetitious justifications for further delaying the second front. Roosevelt, too, had had enough; with Stalin, he rejected Churchill's proposal for another peripheral attack, this time through the Balkans to Vienna. The three finally agreed to launch OVERLORD in early 1944.

Like a coiled spring bursting free, the second front opened in the dark morning hours of June 6, 1944: D-Day. Two hundred thousand Allied troops under the command of General **D-Day** Dwight D. Eisenhower scrambled ashore in Normandy, France, in the largest amphibious landing in history. After digging in at now-famous places like Utah and Omaha beaches and gaining reinforcements, Allied forces broke through disorderly German lines and gradually pushed inland, reaching Paris in August. That same month another force invaded southern France and threw the stunned Germans back.

Allied troops soon spread across the countryside, liberating France and Belgium and entering Germany itself in September. In December, German panzer divisions counterattacked in Belgium's Ardennes Forest, hoping to push on to Antwerp to halt the flow of Allied supplies through that major Belgian port. After weeks of heavy fighting in what has come to be called the Battle of the Bulge—because of the noticeable dent in the Allied line—the Allies pushed the enemy back once again. Meanwhile, battle-hardened Soviet troops marched through Poland and cut a path to the German capital, Berlin. American forces crossed the Rhine in March 1945 and captured the heavily industrial Ruhr valley. Some units peeled off to enter Austria and Czechoslovakia, where they met up with Soviet soldiers.

As the Americans marched east, a new president took office in Washington. Franklin D. Roosevelt died on April 12, and Harry S Truman became the commander-in-chief. Eighteen days later, in bomb-ravaged Berlin, defended largely by teenage boys and old men, Adolf Hitler killed himself. On May 8, Germany surrendered.

Allied strategists had devised a "Europe first" formula: knock out Germany first and then concentrate on an isolated Japan. Nevertheless, the Pacific theater claimed headlines throughout the war, for the American people regarded Japan as their country's chief enemy. By mid–1942, Japan had seized the Philippines, Guam, Wake, Hong Kong, Singapore, Malaya, and the Netherlands East Indies. In the Philippines in 1942, Japanese soldiers forced American and Filipino prisoners, weak from insufficient rations, to walk sixty-five miles, clubbing, shooting, or starving to death about ten thousand of them. The Bataan Death March intensified American hatred of the Japanese.

In April 1942, Americans began to hit back. They bombed Tokyo, and in May, in the momentous Battle of the Coral Sea, carrier-based United States planes halted a Japanese advance toward Australia (see map). The next month, American forces defeated the Japanese at Midway, sinking four of the enemy's valuable aircraft carriers. The Battle of Midway was a turning point in the Pacific war, breaking the Japanese momentum and relieving the threat to Hawaii. Thereafter, Japan was never able to match American manpower, sea power, air power, or economic power.

The American strategy was to "island-hop" toward Japan itself, skipping the most strongly fortified points whenever possible and taking weaker ones. Americans also set **American** out to sink the Japanese merchant **Offensive** marine, in an effort to strand the **in the Pacific** Japanese armies in their island outposts and to cut off raw materials from the factories of the home islands. The first American offensive was at Guadalcanal in the Solomon Islands in 1942. Over the next few years, American troops attacked the Gilberts in 1943 and the Marianas and Philippines in 1944, reclaiming the Philippines. Then, in early 1945, both sides took heavy losses at Iwo Jima and Okinawa. In desperation, Japanese pilots began suicide (*kamikaze*) attacks, flying their planes directly into American ships.

Hoping to avoid a humiliating unconditional surrender (and to preserve the emperor's sovereignty), Japanese leaders refused to admit defeat. They hung on while American bombers leveled their cities. In one staggering attack on Tokyo on May 23, 1945, 83,000 people died.

Impatient for victory, American leaders began to plan a fall invasion of the Japanese islands, an expedition that was sure to bring high casualties. But a secret program, known as the Manhattan Project,

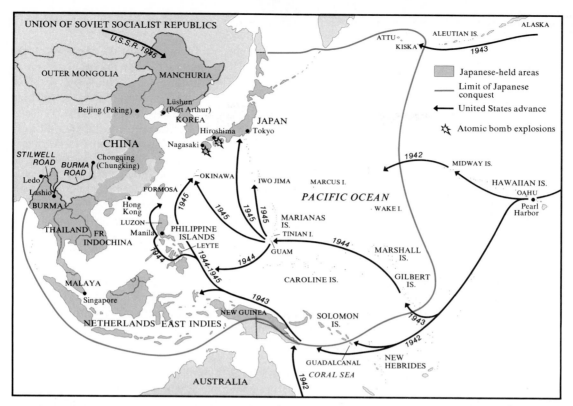

The Pacific War *Source: From Paterson et al.,* American Foreign Policy: A History, *copyright 1988, p. 398. Reprinted by permission of D.C. Heath and Company.*

led to the successful development of an atomic bomb by American scientists. On August 6, the Japanese city of Hiroshima was destroyed by an atomic blast that killed approximately 130,000 people. Three days later, another atomic attack flattened Nagasaki, killing at least 60,000 people. Four days later, the Japanese, who had been sending out peace feelers since June, surrendered. The victors promised that the Japanese emperor could remain as the nation's titular head. Formal surrender ceremonies were held September 2 aboard the battleship *Missouri.* The Second World War was over.

Most Americans agreed with President Truman that the atomic bombing of two Japanese cities had been necessary to end the war as quickly as possible and to save American lives. Use of the bomb to

Why the Atomic Bomb Was Used achieve victory had, in fact, been the primary assumption of the Manhattan Project. At the highest government levels and among atomic scientists, alternatives had been discussed: detonate the bomb on an unpopulated Pacific island, with international observers as witnesses; blockade and bomb Japan conventionally; follow up Tokyo's peace feelers; encourage a Soviet declaration of war. But Truman's aides had rejected these options on the grounds that they would take too long and would not convince the tenacious Japanese that they had been beaten.

Diplomatic considerations also sped the decision to use the bomb. Leaders envisioned the real and psychological power that the bomb would bestow on the United States. It might serve as a deterrent against aggression; it might intimidate the Soviet Union into making concessions in Eastern Europe; it might end the war in the Pacific before the Soviet Union could claim a role in the management of Asia. "If it explodes," Truman remarked, "I'll certainly have a hammer on those boys [the Soviets]."

▼

Economic Effects of the War at Home

The Second World War was won at great cost not only abroad but also on the American home front. While the guns boomed in Europe and Asia, the war changed American lives and institutions. One month after Pearl Harbor, President Roosevelt established the War Production Board (WPB). First on the WPB's list of tasks was the conversion from civilian to military production. Factories had to be expanded and new ones built. Furthermore, whole new industries, the best known of which was synthetic rubber, had to be created. (Japan had captured 90 percent of the world's supply of crude rubber.) The WPB was so successful that the production of durable goods more than tripled.

To gain the cooperation of business, the WPB and other government agencies met business more than halfway. The government guaranteed profits in the form of cost-plus-fixed-fee contracts, generous tax write-offs, **Government** **Incentives** and exemption from antitrust **to Business** prosecution. It also allowed prime contractors to distribute subcontracts as they saw fit.

From mid-1940 through September 1944, the government awarded contracts totaling $175 billion, no less than two-thirds of which went to the top one hundred corporations. General Motors received 8 percent of the total; big awards also went to other automobile companies, as well as to aircraft, steel, electrical, and chemical companies. Although no one had yet coined the expression "military-industrial complex," as President Dwight D. Eisenhower would do in 1961, the web of military-business interdependence had begun to be woven.

In science and higher education, the big also got bigger. To develop radar and do other research, Massachusetts Institute of Technology received contracts valued at $117 million. California Institute of Technology was in second place with contracts totaling $83 million, followed by Harvard, Columbia, the University of California, Johns Hopkins, and the University of Chicago. The most spectacular result of a government contract with a university was the atomic bomb; its testing was run by the University of California at Berkeley.

Big labor also grew bigger during the war. Union membership ballooned from 8.5 million in 1940 to 14.75 million in 1945. In 1942, to minimize labor-management conflict, President Roosevelt created the National War Labor Board (NWLB), sometimes referred to as the Supreme Court for labor disputes. Unions were permitted to enroll as many new members as possible, but workers were not required to join a union. Thus, the NWLB forged a compromise between the unions' demand for a closed shop, in which only union members could be hired, and management's interest in open shops.

When the NWLB attempted to limit wage increases to increases in the cost of living, there were wildcat strikes and other work stoppages that **Wartime** tripled the production time lost in **Labor Strikes** 1943. The worst labor disruptions of 1943 came in the coal fields, where 450,000 soft-coal miners and 80,000 anthracite miners struck. To discourage further work stoppages, Congress passed the War Labor Disputes (Smith-Connally) Act of June 1943. The act conferred on the president the authority to seize and operate any strikebound plant deemed necessary to the national security, and it established a mandatory thirty-day cooling-off period before any new strike could be called. The Smith-Connally Act also gave the NWLB the legal authority to settle labor disputes for the duration of the war.

Agriculture, too, made an impressive contribution to the war effort, especially through the introduction of labor-saving machinery to replace the men and women who had gone to the front or migrated to war-production centers. Farming was in the midst of a transition from the family farm to

B-17 pilots return from a training flight in their Flying Fortress Pistol Packin' Mama. WAF pilots ferried the planes for the Air Corps. *U.S. Air Force Photo.*

the large-scale, mechanized agribusiness dominated by banks, insurance companies, and farm co-ops. The Second World War accelerated the trend, for wealthy financial institutions were better able than family farmers to pay for expensive new machinery. Like business and labor, agriculture was becoming more consolidated as it contributed to the war effort.

At the head of the burgeoning national economy stood the federal government, whose size and importance, like that of business and labor, was mush-

Growth in the Federal Government

rooming: from 1940 to 1945 the federal bureaucracy expanded from 1.1 million workers to 3.4 million. The WPB and the NWLB were only two of a host of new agencies that sprang up: others included the Office of Price Administration, the War Manpower Commission, the Office of War Mobilization, the Office of War Information, and the Office of Scientific Research and Development. The national debt skyrocketed from $49 billion in 1941 to $259 billion in 1945.

The federal government was, of course, also responsible for mobilizing the military. During the war years, 16.4 million men and women served in

The Military

the armed forces. The largest branch of the services was the army, which, at the war's conclusion in 1945, had 8.3 million soldiers, including 100,000 WACS (Women's Army Corps). Although women were prohibited from engaging in combat duty, they worked at a variety of noncombat jobs, not only in the WACS but as WAVES (Women Accepted for Volunteer Emergency Service) in the navy, as pilots in the WASPS (Women Air Service Pilots), and as members of the Coast Guard and the Marine Corps Women's Reserve. The WASPS taught basic flying, towed aerial targets for gunnery practice, and flight-tested military aircraft.

American troops served overseas for an average of about sixteen months. Some never returned: total deaths exceeded 405,000; total wounded, 670,000. In terms of human life, the cost of the war was second only to that of the Civil War. Still, compared with losses suffered by other nations, United

States figures were low; less than 1 percent of the population was killed or wounded in the war. The Soviet Union lost 8 percent of its population—about 20 million people.

Civil Liberties and the Internment of Japanese-Americans

Once the United States entered the war, American leaders had to consider whether enemy agents were operating within the nation's borders and threatening the war effort. It was clear that not all Americans were enthusiastic supporters of the nation's involvement in the war. After Pearl Harbor, several thousand "enemy aliens" were arrested and taken into custody, some of them Nazi agents who had accumulated firearms, short-wave radios, and codes in the course of their work. Other people had conscientious objections to the war. During the Second World War, conscientious objectors (COs) had to have a religious (as opposed to moral or ethical) reason for refusing military service. About 25,000 qualified COs accepted noncombat service, most of them as medical corpsmen. An additional 12,000 were placed in civilian public service camps, where they worked in forestry or conservation or as orderlies in public health hospitals. Approximately 5,500, three-fourths of whom were Jehovah's Witnesses, refused to participate in any way; they were imprisoned.

The one enormous exception to the nation's generally creditable wartime civil liberties record was the internment in 1942, in "relocation centers," of more than 110,000 Japanese-Americans. Of these people, 70,000 were Nisei, or native-born citizens of the United States. Their imprisonment was not based on suspicion or evidence of treason. Their crime was their ethnic origin—the fact that they were of Japanese descent. Charges of criminal behavior were never brought against Japanese-

Internment in "Relocation Centers"

Americans; none was ever indicted or tried for espionage, treason, or sedition.

"It was really cruel and harsh," recalled Joseph Y. Kurihara, a citizen and a veteran of the First World War. "To pack and evacuate in forty-eight hours was an impossibility. Seeing mothers completely bewildered with children crying from want and peddlers taking advantage and offering prices next to robbery made me feel like murdering those responsible."

The internees were sent to flood-damaged lands at Relocation, Arkansas; to the intermountain terrain of Wyoming and the desert of western Arizona; and to other arid and desolate spots in the West. Although the names were evocative—Topaz, Utah; Rivers, Arizona; Heart Mountain, Wyoming; Tule Lake and Manzanar, California—the camps themselves were bleak and demoralizing. Behind barbed wire stood tarpapered wooden barracks where entire families lived in a single room furnished only with cots, blankets, and a bare light bulb. Toilets and dining and bathing facilities were communal; privacy was almost nonexistent. Besides their freedom, the Japanese-Americans lost property valued at $500 million, along with their positions in the truck-garden, floral, and fishing industries. Indeed, their economic competitors were among the most vocal proponents of their relocation.

The Supreme Court upheld the government's policy of internment. In wartime, the Court said in the *Hirabayashi* ruling (1943), "residents having ethnic affiliations with an invading enemy may be a greater source of danger than those of different ancestry." And in the *Korematsu* case (1944), the Court, with three justices dissenting, approved the removal of the Nisei from the West Coast. One dissenter, Justice Frank Murphy, denounced the decision as the "legalization of racism." The most damning appraisal of all came from Circuit Court Judge William Denman, who in an earlier ruling had written that "the identity of this doctrine with that of the Hitler generals . . . justifying the gas chambers of Dachau is unmistakable."

In 1983, forty-one years after he had been placed in a government camp, Fred Korematsu had the satisfaction of hearing a federal judge rule that he—and by implication all detainees—had been the victim of "unsubstantiated facts, distortions and misrepresentations of at least one military commander whose views were affected by racism." A year earlier, the government's special Commission on Wartime Relocation and Internment of Civilians had recommended compensating the victims of this policy. In 1988, Congress voted to award $20,000 and a public apology to the surviving 60,000 Japanese-American internees. The following year, the government decided to stagger the payments over a three-year period, with the first 25,000 internees to receive their payment in 1990.

Jobs and Racism on the Home Front

For other people of color in America, the Second World War proved to be a mixed blessing, providing both the benefits of employment and the insults of racism. For many black Americans, the war was a turning point at which they determined to make a stand against racial discrimination. Several factors highlighted African-American involvement in the war: the presence of nearly 1 million black men and women in the armed services; the mass migration of blacks, particularly from the rural South to the urban North and West, to work in war industries; and the participation of black people in all kinds of wartime activities—buying war bonds, serving as air-raid wardens, and volunteering for the Red Cross.

Although blacks served in segregated units, they made some real advances in the direction of racial equality during these years. For the first time, the War Department sanctioned the **Black Troops** training of blacks as pilots. After instruction at Tuskegee Institute in Alabama, pilots served with heroism in such all-black units as the Ninety-ninth Pursuit Squadron, winner of eighty Distinguished Flying Crosses. Some blacks reached positions of leadership. In 1940, Colonel Benjamin O. Davis became the first black brigadier general. Wherever black people were offered opportunities to distinguish themselves, they proved that they could do the job.

Set against these accomplishments, however, were serious failures in race relations. Race riots instigated by whites occurred on military bases, and white civilians assaulted black soldiers and sailors throughout the South. When the War Department issued an order in mid-1944 forbidding racial segregation in military recreation and transportation, the *Montgomery Advertiser* replied, "Army orders, even armies, even bayonets, cannot force impossible and unnatural social relations upon us."

Experiences such as these caused black soldiers and sailors to wonder what, in fact, they were fighting for. They recalled the remark of the governor of Tennessee, when blacks urged him to appoint African-Americans to local draft boards: "This is a white man's country. . . . The Negro had nothing to do with the settling of America." They noted that the Red Cross separated blood taken from whites and blacks, as if there were some difference. But most telling was the charge that American racism differed little from German racism.

At the same time, there were positive reasons for blacks to participate in the war effort. Perhaps this was an opportunity, as the NAACP believed, "to persuade, embarrass, compel and shame our government and our nation . . . into a more enlightened attitude toward a tenth of its people." Proclaiming that in the Second World War they were waging a "Double V" campaign (for victory at home and abroad), blacks were more militant than before and readier than ever to protest. Membership in civil rights organizations soared.

Because of the war, blacks found new opportunities in industry. To secure defense jobs, 1.2 million blacks migrated from the South to the industrial cities of the North and West in **Black War** the 1940s. Almost three-fourths **Workers** settled in the urban-industrial states of California, Illinois, Michigan, New York, Ohio, and Pennsylvania. More than half a million became active members of CIO unions. Finally, black voters in northern cities were beginning to constitute a vital swing vote not only in presidential contests, but in local and state elections as well.

However, along with the benefits of urban life

"above and beyond the call of duty"

DORIE MILLER
*Received the Navy Cross
at Pearl Harbor, May 27, 1942*

The first African-American hero of the Second World War was Dorie Miller, who won the Navy Cross. Miller's citation for bravery read: "Without previous experience [he] . . . manned a machine gun in the face of serious fire during the Japanese attack on Pearl Harbor, December 7, 1941, on the battleship *Arizona,* shooting down four enemy planes." *Library of Congress.*

came liabilities. The migrants had to make enormous emotional and cultural adjustments, and white hostility and ignorance made their task difficult. In 1942, more than half of all northern whites believed that blacks should be segregated in separate schools and neighborhoods. Such attitudes caused many people to fear that the summer of 1943 would be like 1919, another Red Summer. And indeed, almost 250 racial conflicts exploded in forty-seven cities that year.

Race Riots of 1943

The worst of the 1943 race riots bloodied the streets of Detroit in June. At the end of thirty hours of rioting, twenty-five blacks and nine whites lay dead.

The federal government did practically nothing to prevent further racial violence. From President Roosevelt down, most federal officials put the war first and domestic reform second. But government neglect did not discourage African-Americans and their century-old civil rights movement. By the war's end, they were ready—politically, economically, and emotionally—to wage the struggle for voting rights and for equal access to public accommodations and institutions.

Not all racial violence was directed against blacks. To some whites, people of Mexican origin were as despicable as those whose roots were African. In 1942, American farms and war industries needed workers, and the United States and Mexico had agreed to the *bracero* program, whereby Mexicans were admitted to the United States on short-term work contracts. Although the newcomers suffered racial discrimination and segregation, they seized the economic opportunities that had become available. In Los Angeles, seventeen thousand people of Mexican descent found shipyard jobs where before the war none had been available to them.

In 1943, whites, most of whom were sailors and soldiers, attacked Mexican-Americans in the Los Angeles zoot-suit riot. Mexican-American teenagers had joined street gangs (*pachucos*), adopted duck-tail haircuts, and donned zoot suits: long coats (called "drapes") with wide, padded shoulders, pegged pants, wide-brimmed hats, and long watch chains. Whites' anger boiled over in June, and for four days mobs invaded Mexican-American neighborhoods. Not only did white policemen look the other way during these assaults, but the city of Los Angeles passed an ordinance that made it a crime to wear a zoot suit within city limits.

Such experiences made life difficult for people of Mexican descent within the United States. Although the war opened up brief economic opportunities for Mexican-Americans, the war years were not the transformational experience for this ethnic group as they were for African-Americans.

A Milestone for Women

If the Second World War was a turning point for African-Americans, it was equally or even more so for American women. War temporarily ended the depression-era hostility toward working women. Well over 6 million women entered the labor force during the war years, increasing the number of working women by 57 percent in less than five years. Moreover, the typical newcomer was not a young, single woman; she was married and over the age of thirty-five.

But statistics tell only part of the story. There was a change in attitude toward heavy labor for women. In the early months of the war, employers had still **Women in War Production** insisted that women were not suited for industrial jobs. "Almost overnight," said Mary Anderson, head of the Women's Bureau of the Department of Labor, "women were reclassified by industrialists from a marginal to a basic labor supply for munitions making." Women became riveters, lumberjacks, welders, crane operators, toolmakers, shell loaders, cowgirls, blast-furnace cleaners, locomotive greasers, police officers, and taxi drivers.

The new employment opportunities increased women's geographic and occupational mobility. Especially noteworthy were the gains made by black women: more than 400,000 quit work as domestic servants to enjoy the better working conditions, higher pay, and union benefits of industrial employment. More than 7 million women moved from their original counties of residence to new locations during the war. Many sought jobs in the rapidly expanding aircraft industry, which increased its employment of women from 4,000 in December 1941 to 310,000 two years later.

Public opinion quickly changed from hostility to support of women's war work. Newspapers and magazines, radio and movies proclaimed Rosie the Riveter a war hero. But very few people asserted that women's war work should bring about a permanent shift in sex roles. Once the victory was won, women should go back to nurturing their husbands and children, leaving their jobs to returning GIs. Wartime surveys showed, however, that many of the women wanted to remain in their jobs. Eighty percent of New York's women workers felt that way, as did 75 percent of Detroit's female laborers.

Although women increased their wages when they acquired better jobs, they still received lower pay than men, even for the same work. In 1945, **Discrimination Against Women and Children** women in manufacturing earned only 65 percent of what men were paid. And working women, particularly working mothers, suffered in other ways as well. Perhaps the most persistent problem was the near-absence of supportive services such as child-care centers and communal kitchens. Some of the most serious wartime social problems were a direct result of the lack of such services. During the war, there were increases in juvenile delinquency, venereal disease, teenage pregnancy, and the incidence of "eight-hour orphans," or "latchkey children," left alone while their mothers worked eight-hour shifts in war plants.

While millions of women were entering the work force, hundreds of thousands of women were getting married. From 1939 to 1942, the marriage **Increase in Marriage, Divorce, and Birth Rates** rate rose from 73 marriages per 1,000 unmarried women to 93 per 1,000. Some couples scrambled to get married so they could spend time together before the man was sent overseas. These hasty marriages often did not survive long military separations. As a result, divorces soared too, from 25,000 in 1939 to 359,000 in 1943 and 485,000 in 1945. As might be expected, the birthrate also climbed: total births rose from just over 2.4 million in 1939 to 3.1 million in 1943. Many of these births were "goodbye babies," conceived as a hedge against the future before the father left for the war, a guarantee that the family would be perpetuated if he died in battle overseas.

Ironically, women's efforts to hold their families together during the war posed problems for returning fathers. Women war workers had brought home the wages; they had taken over the budgeting of expenses and the writing of checks. In countless ways, they had proved they could hold the reins in their husbands' absence. Some men had difficulty accepting the idea that their families could survive and even prosper without them.

What of the women who wanted to remain in the labor market? Many were forced by employers, or by their husbands, to quit. Others chose to leave their jobs for a year or two but then returned to work. And throughout the rest of the 1940s and 1950s, millions more who had never worked took jobs.

The Decline of Liberalism and the Election of 1944

Another wartime trend was the decline of political liberalism. Even before Pearl Harbor, liberals had suffered major defeats. Some Democrats hoped to revive the reform movement during the war, but Republicans and conservative Democrats were on guard against such a move.

Part of the Democrats' problem was that the war years, unlike the 1930s, were a time of full employment. Once people had acquired jobs and gained some economic security, they began to be more critical of New Deal policies. The New Deal coalition had always had the potential for fragmentation. Southern white farmers had little in common with northern blacks or white factory workers. And in northern cities, blacks and whites who had voted for Roosevelt in 1940 were competing for jobs and housing and would soon collide in race riots.

With impressive Republican gains in the 1942 congressional elections, the alliance of conservative southern Democrats and Republicans became a formidable threat to New Deal programs. In 1942 and 1943, the conservative coalition actually abolished several New Deal relief and social welfare agencies, among them the Civilian Conservation Corps and the Work Projects Administration.

But though enfeebled, liberalism was far from dead. The liberal agenda began with a pledge to secure full employment. Roosevelt emphasized the concept in his Economic Bill of Rights, delivered as part of his 1944 State of the Union address. Every American had a right, the president declared, to a decent job, to sufficient food, shelter, and clothing, and to financial security in unemployment, illness, and old age. If to accomplish those goals the government had to operate at a deficit, Roosevelt was willing to do so. But first he had to be re-elected.

In 1944, the Republicans were optimistic about their prospects for regaining the presidency. New York's Governor Thomas E. Dewey, who won the nomination on the first ballot, was a moderate who did not advocate repeal of the essentials of the New Deal—Social Security, unemployment relief, collective bargaining, and price supports for farmers. Despite rumors of ill health, Roosevelt was elected for a fourth term.

It was the urban vote that returned Roosevelt to the White House. Wartime population shifts had much to do with the cities' new political clout. New workers—notably southern whites who had been lifelong Democrats and southern blacks who had never before voted—had migrated to the urban industrial centers (see map). Added to the urban vote was a less obvious factor. Many voters seemed to be exhibiting what has been called "depression psychosis." Fearful that hard times would return once war contracts were terminated, they remembered New Deal relief programs and voted for Roosevelt. Finally, many Americans wanted Roosevelt's experienced hand to guide the nation, and the world, to a lasting international peace. But Roosevelt's death rendered that choice moot. His running mate in 1944, Harry S Truman, would be the president to deal with the postwar world.

Wartime Diplomacy

The lessons of the post–First World War period weighed heavily on the minds of American diplomats throughout the war. Americans vowed to make a peace that would ensure a postwar world free from depression, totalitarianism, and war. Thus, American goals included the Open Door and lower tariffs; self-determination for liberated peoples; avoidance of the debts-reparations tangle that

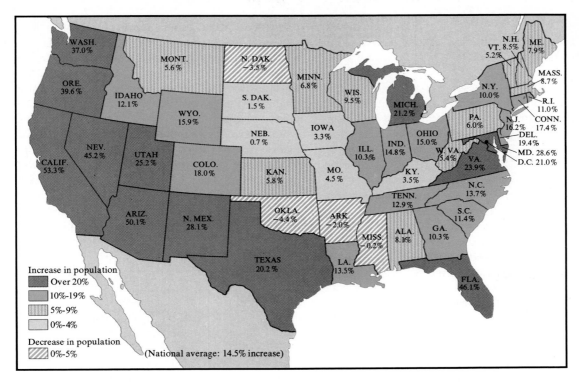

A Nation on the Move, 1940–1950 *Source: U.S. Bureau of the Census,* Portfolio of United States Census Maps, 1950 *(Washington: U.S. Government Printing Office, 1953), p. 4.*

had plagued Europe after the First World War; expansion of the United States sphere of influence; and management of world affairs by what Roosevelt once called the Four Policemen: Russia, China, Great Britain, and the United States.

Although the major Allies concentrated on defeating the aggressors, their suspicions of one another undermined cooperation. For the Al-

Allied Disagreement over Eastern Europe

lies, Eastern European questions proved the most difficult. The Soviets sought to fix their boundaries where they had stood before Hitler attacked in 1941. In the case of Poland, this meant that the part of the country that the Soviets had invaded and captured in 1939 would become Soviet territory. The British and Americans hesitated, preferring to deal with Eastern Europe at the end of the war. Yet in October 1944, Churchill and Stalin, without Roosevelt's participation, struck a bargain: the

Soviet Union would gain Rumania and Bulgaria as a sphere of influence; Britain would have the upper hand in Greece; and the two would share authority in Yugoslavia and Hungary.

Poland was a special case. In 1943, Moscow had broken off diplomatic relations with the conservative Polish government-in-exile in London. The Poles had angered Moscow when they asked the International Red Cross to investigate German charges that the Soviets had massacred thousands of Polish army officers in the Katyn Forest in 1940. (The Soviets did not accept responsibility for the massacre until 1990.) Then an uprising in Warsaw in August 1944 complicated matters still further. Taking advantage of the nearness of Soviet troops, the Warsaw underground rose against the occupying Germans. To the dismay of the world community, Soviet armies stood aside as German troops slaughtered 166,000 people and devastated the city. Finally, in late 1944 and early 1945, the Soviets spawned a pro-Communist government in Lublin. Thus, near the end of the war, Poland had two competing governments, one in London and another in Lublin.

Early in the war, the Allies had begun talking about a new international organization. At Teheran in 1943, Roosevelt called for an institution controlled by the Four Policemen.

Creation of the United Nations Organization The next year, in a Washington, D.C., mansion called Dumbarton Oaks, American, British, Soviet, and Chinese representatives conferred on the details. The conferees approved a preliminary charter for a United Nations Organization, providing for a supreme Security Council dominated by the great powers and a weak General Assembly. The Security Council would have five permanent members, each with veto power; Britain had insisted that France be one of them. Meanwhile, the Soviet Union, hoping to counter pro-British and pro-American blocs in the General Assembly, sought separate membership for each of its sixteen Soviet republics. This issue was not resolved at Dumbarton Oaks, but the meeting proved a success nevertheless.

Diplomatic action on another problem, Nazi treatment of the Jews, proved to be a tragic failure. Even before the war, Nazi officials had targeted Jews throughout Europe for extermination. By the war's end, about 6 million Jews had been forced into concentration camps and systematically killed by firing squads, unspeakable tortures, and gas chambers. Many others who survived the Holocaust could never forget the terror.

Jewish Refugees from the Holocaust

During the Great Depression, the United States and other nations had refused to relax their immigration restrictions to save Jews fleeing persecution. Bureaucrats applied the rules so strictly—requiring legal documents that fleeing Jews could not possibly provide—that otherwise qualified refugees were kept out of the country. From 1933 to 1945, less than 40 percent of the German-Austrian quota was filled.

Even the tragic voyage of the *St. Louis* did not change government policy. The vessel left Hamburg in mid-1939 with 930 desperate Jewish refugees who lacked proper immigration documents. Denied entry to Havana, the *St. Louis* headed for Miami, where Coast Guard cutters prevented it from docking. The ship was forced to return to Europe. Some of those refugees took shelter in countries that were later overrun by Hitler's legions.

When evidence mounted that Hitler intended to exterminate the Jews, British and American representatives met in Bermuda (1943) but came up with no plans. Secretary of State Cordell Hull made a discouraging report to the president, emphasizing "the unknown cost of moving an undetermined number of persons from an undisclosed place to an unknown destination." Appalled, Secretary of the Treasury Henry Morgenthau, Jr., charged that the State Department's foot-dragging made the United States an accessory to murder. Early in 1944, stirred by Morgenthau's well-documented plea, Roosevelt created the War Refugee Board, which set up refugee camps in Europe and saved thousands from death.

But American officials waited too long to act, and they missed a chance to destroy the gas chambers and ovens at the extermination camp at Auschwitz in occupied Poland. They had aerial photographs and diagrams of the camp, but they argued that bombing it would detract from the war effort or prompt the Germans to step up the anti-Jewish terror. In 1944, American planes bombed synthetic oil and rubber plants in the industrial sector of Auschwitz but left untouched the gas chambers and crematoria that were only five miles away.

The Yalta Conference and a Flawed Peace

With the war in Europe nearing an end, Roosevelt urged another summit meeting. The three Allied leaders met at Yalta, on the Crimea, in early February 1945. Controversy has surrounded the conference ever since. Roosevelt was obviously ill, and critics of the Yalta agreements later charged that Roosevelt was too weak to resist the demands of a

On April 11, 1945, prisoners in the Buchenwald concentration camp rose up against their SS jailers and liberated themselves. The inmates were in control when American troops arrived the next day. During the grisly years preceding the end of the war, the Nazis had murdered well over 6 million people in camps such as this. *Margaret Bourke-White,* Life *magazine,* © *Time Warner Inc.*

guileful Stalin. The evidence suggests, however, that Roosevelt was mentally alert and that he managed to sustain his strength during negotiations.

Each of the Allies entered into the conference with definite goals. Britain sought a place for France in occupied Germany, a curb on Soviet influence in Poland, and protection for the vulnerable British Empire. The Soviet Union wanted reparations from Germany to assist in the massive task of rebuilding at home, possessions in Asia, continued influence in Poland, and a permanently weakened Germany. The United States lobbied for the United Nations Organization, where it believed it could exercise influence; for a Soviet

Allied Goals at Yalta

declaration of war against Japan; for recognition of China as a major power; and for compromise between rival factions in Poland.

Military positions at the time of the conference helped to shape the final agreements. Soviet troops had occupied much of Eastern Europe, including Poland, and the Soviets were set against the return of the Polish government-in-exile from London. Under Roosevelt's leadership, Stalin and Churchill reached a compromise: a boundary favorable to the Soviet Union in the east, postponement of the western boundary issue, and the creation of a "more broadly based" coalition government that would include members of the London government-in-exile. Free elections would be held sometime in the future. The agreement was vague, but given

Soviet occupation of Poland, Roosevelt considered it "the best I can do."

As for Germany, the Big Three agreed that it would be divided into four zones, the fourth to go to France. On the question of reparations, Stalin wanted a precise figure, but Churchill and Roosevelt said that they would first have to determine Germany's ability to pay. Without the British, the Americans and Soviets agreed that an Allied committee would consider the sum of $20 billion as a basis for discussion in the future.

Other issues found trade-offs. Stalin promised to declare war on Japan two or three months after Hitler's defeat. The Soviet premier also consented to sign a treaty of friendship and alliance with Jiang Jieshi (Chiang Kai-shek), America's ally in China, rather than with the Communist Mao Zedong. In return, the United States agreed to the Soviet Union's taking of the southern part of Sakhalin Island and Lüshun (Port Arthur). Regarding the new world organization, Roosevelt and Churchill granted the Soviets three votes in the General Assembly. (Fifty nations officially launched the United Nations Organization in May.) Finally, the conferees accepted the Declaration of Liberated Europe, pledging to establish order and to rebuild economies by democratic methods.

Yalta marked the high point of the Grand Alliance; each of the Allies came away with something. But as the great powers jockeyed for influence at the close of the war, **Potsdam Conference** neither the spirit nor the letter of Yalta held firm. The crumbling of the alliance became evident at the Potsdam Conference, which took place between July 17 and August 2, 1945. Roosevelt had died in April. Truman, who replaced him, was a novice at international diplomacy and less patient with the Soviets.

Despite major differences, the Big Three did agree on general policies toward Germany: complete disarmament, the elimination of industry used for military production, and the dissolving of Nazi institutions and laws. In a compromise over reparations, they decided that each occupying nation should take reparations from its own zone, but they could not agree on a total figure. To resolve other issues, such as peace treaties with Italy, Finland, and Hungary, the Big Three created the Council of Foreign Ministers.

Hitler once said, "We may be destroyed, but if we are, we shall drag a world with us—a world in flames." True to Hitler's words, modern warfare had made rubble of European and Asian cities. And the human suffering was immense. Everywhere, ghostlike people wandered about, searching desperately for food and mourning those who would never come home. Russia had lost 20 million people; Poland 5.8 million; Germany 4.5 million. In all, about 35 million Europeans died as a result of the war. In Asia, untold millions of Chinese and 2 million Japanese died.

Only one major combatant escaped these grisly statistics: the United States. Its cities were not burned and its fields were not trampled. American **Postwar Strength of the United States** deaths from the war—405,399—were few compared with the losses of other nations. In fact, Americans came out of the Second World War more powerful than they had gone in. They alone had the atomic bomb. What is more, only the United States had the capital and economic resources to spur international recovery. America was, gloated Truman, a "giant."

Because of events at home and abroad, life for many Americans in 1945 was fundamentally different from what it had been before Pearl Harbor. The Academy Award–winning film for 1946, *The Best Years of Our Lives,* dwelled on some of these changes as it told the painful story of the postwar readjustments faced by three veterans and their families and friends. Not only veterans' lives had been changed by the experiences of war. With the advent of the Cold War, millions of younger men would also be inducted into the armed forces during the next thirty years. War and the expectation of war would become part of American life.

The Second World War was a powerful engine of social change in the United States. The gains made during the war by blacks and women were overdue, but other changes were less welcome. The war had stimulated the trend toward bigness not only in business and labor, but also in government. In the next few years, government agencies that had been conceived as temporary would become permanent and would grow in size and influence. And the seeds of the military-industrial complex were sown in these years. For better or worse—and clearly there were elements of both—the Second World War was indeed a watershed in the nation's history.

Suggestions for Further Reading

Fighting the War

Stephen A. Ambrose, *Eisenhower: Soldier, General of the Army, President-Elect* (1983); Stephen A. Ambrose, *The Supreme Commander* (1970); Hanson Baldwin, *Battles Lost and Won* (1966); A. Russell Buchanan, *The United States in World War II*, 2 vols. (1964); Peter Calvocoressi and Guy Wint, *Total War* (1972); John W. Dower, *War Without Mercy: Race and Power in the Pacific War* (1986); R. Ernest Dupuy, *World War II* (1969); Kent R. Greenfield, *American Strategy in World War II* (1963); B. H. Liddell Hart, *History of the Second World War* (1970); Max Hastings, *OVERLORD: D-Day and the Battle of Normandy* (1984); D. Clayton James, *A Time for Giants: Politics of the American High Command in World War II* (1987); D. Clayton James, *The Years of MacArthur, 1941–1945* (1975); Eric Larabee, *Commander in Chief* (1987); Richard M. Leighton and Robert W. Coakley, *Global Logistics and Strategy, 1940–1945*, 2 vols. (1955–1968); Samuel Eliot Morison, *The Two-Ocean War* (1963); Samuel Eliot Morison, *Strategy and Compromise* (1958); Forrest C. Pogue, *George C. Marshall*, 4 vols. (1963–1987); Ronald Schaffer, *Wings of Judgment: American Bombing in World War II* (1985); Ronald H. Spector, *Eagle Against the Sun: The American War with Japan* (1984); Russell F. Weigley, *The American Way of War* (1973); Gordon Wright, *The Ordeal of Total War, 1939–1945* (1968).

Grand Alliance Diplomacy

Robert Beitzel, *The Uneasy Alliance* (1972); Russell Buhite, *Decisions at Yalta* (1986); James MacGregor Burns, *Roosevelt: The Soldier of Freedom* (1970); Winston S. Churchill, *The Second World War*, 6 vols. (1948–1953); Diane Clemens, *Yalta* (1970); Robert Dallek, *Franklin D. Roosevelt and American Foreign Policy, 1932–1945* (1979); Robert A. Divine, *Roosevelt and World War II* (1969); Herbert Feis, *Churchill, Roosevelt, and Stalin* (1957); George C. Herring, *Aid to Russia, 1941–1946* (1973); Akira Iriye, *Power and Culture: The Japanese-American War, 1941–1945* (1981); Gabriel Kolko, *The Politics of War* (1968); William R. Louis, *Imperialism at Bay: The United States and the Decolonization of the British Empire* (1978); William H. McNeill,

America, Britain, and Russia (1953); Vojtech Mastny, *Russia's Road to the Cold War* (1979); Arthur D. Morse, *While Six Million Died* (1968); Keith Sainsbury, *The Turning Point* (1985); Gaddis Smith, *Diplomacy During the Second World War, 1941–1945*, 2nd ed. (1985); Michael Stoff, *Oil, War, and American Security* (1980); Mark Stoler, *The Politics of the Second Front* (1977); David S. Wyman, *The Abandonment of the Jews: America and the Holocaust, 1941–1945* (1984).

The Home Front

John Morton Blum, *V Was for Victory: Politics and American Culture During World War II* (1976); Alan Clive, *State of War: Michigan in World War II* (1979); John Costello, *Virtue Under Fire: How World War II Changed Our Social and Sexual Attitudes* (1985); Mark Jonathan Harris et al., *The Homefront* (1984); Richard R. Lingeman, *Don't You Know There's a War On?* (1970); Gerald D. Nash, *The American West Transformed: The Impact of the Second World War* (1985); Geoffrey Perrett, *Days of Sadness, Years of Triumph: The American People, 1939–1945* (1973); Richard Polenberg, *War and Society* (1972); Studs Terkel, ed., *"The Good War": An Oral History of World War Two* (1984).

Mobilizing for War

David Brinkley, *Washington Goes to War* (1988); Bruce Catton, *The War Lords of Washington* (1948); George Q. Flynn, *The Mess in Washington: Manpower Mobilization in World War II* (1979); Eliot Janeway, *The Struggle for Survival* (1951); Paul A. C. Koistinen, *The Hammer and the Sword: Labor, the Military, and Industrial Mobilization, 1920–1945* (1979); William M. Tuttle, Jr., "The Birth of an Industry: The Synthetic Rubber 'Mess' in World War II," *Technology and Culture,* 22 (1981), 35–67; Harold G. Vatter, *The U.S. Economy in World War II* (1985); Gerald T. White, *Billions for Defense: Government Finance by the Defense Plant Corporation During World War II* (1980).

Farmers and Workers, Soldiers and Sailors

Melvyn Dubofsky and Warren H. Van Tine, *John L. Lewis: A Biography* (1977); Lee Kennett, *G.I.: The American Soldier in World War II* (1987); Nelson Lichtenstein, *Labor's War at Home: The CIO in World War II* (1983); Bill Mauldin, *Up Front,* rev. ed. (1968); Joel Seidman, *American Labor from Defense to Reconversion* (1953); Samuel A. Stouffer et al., *The American Soldier*, 2 vols. (1949); Walter W. Wilcox, *The Farmer in the Second World War* (1947).

Japanese-American Internment

Commission on Wartime Relocation and Internment of Civilians, *Personal Justice Denied* (1982); Roger Daniels, *Concen-*

tration Camps U.S.A. (1971); Bill Hosokawa, *Nisei: The Quiet Americans* (1969); Peter Irons, *Justice at War* (1983); Thomas James, *Exile Within: The Schooling of Japanese-Americans, 1942–1945* (1987); John Tateishi, ed., *And Justice for All: An Oral History of the Japanese-American Detention Camps* (1984); Jacobus tenBroek et al., *Prejudice, War and the Constitution* (1954); Michi Weglyn, *Years of Infamy* (1976).

Politics

James C. Foster, *The Union Politic: The CIO Political Action Committee* (1975); Maurice Isserman, *Which Side Were You On? The American Communist Party During the Second World War* (1982); Roland Young, *Congressional Politics in the Second World War* (1956).

African-Americans and Wartime Violence

A. Russell Buchanan, *Black Americans in World War II* (1977); Dominic J. Capeci, Jr., *Race Relations in Wartime Detroit* (1984); Dominic J. Capeci, Jr., *The Harlem Riot of 1943* (1977); Lee Finkle, *Forum for Protest: The Black Press During World War II* (1975); Phillip McGuire, ed., *Taps for a Jim Crow Army: Letters from Black Soldiers in World War II* (1982); Mauricio Mazon, *The Zoot-Suit Riots* (1984); Patrick S. Washburn, *A Question of Sedition: The Federal Government's Investigation of the Black Press During World War II* (1986); Neil A. Wynn, *The Afro-American and the Second World War* (1976).

Women at War

Karen T. Anderson, *Wartime Women: Sex Roles, Family Relations, and the Status of Women During World War II* (1981); D'Ann Campbell, *Women at War with America* (1984); William H. Chafe, *The American Woman: Her Changing Social, Economic, and Political Roles, 1920–1970* (1972); Sherna Berger Gluck, *Rosie the Riveter Revisited* (1987); Chester W. Gregory, *Women in Defense Work During World War II* (1974); Susan M. Hartmann, *The Home Front and Beyond* (1982); Margaret Randolph Higgonet et al., eds., *Behind the Lines: Gender and the Two World Wars* (1987); Ruth Milkman, *Gender at Work: The Dynamics of Job Discrimination by Sex During World War II* (1987); Leila J. Rupp, *Mobilizing Women for War: German and American Propaganda, 1939–1945* (1978).

The Atomic Bomb and Japan's Surrender

Gar Alperovitz, *Atomic Diplomacy*, rev. ed. (1985); Barton J. Bernstein, ed., *The Atomic Bomb* (1976); Robert J. C. Butow, *Japan's Decision to Surrender* (1954); Herbert Feis, *The Atomic Bomb and the End of World War II* (1966); Gregg Herken, *The Winning Weapon* (1980); Richard Rhodes, *The Making of the Atomic Bomb* (1987); Martin J. Sherwin, *A World Destroyed* (1975); Leon V. Sigal, *Fighting to a Finish* (1988).

President Harry S Truman was exhausted on March 13, 1947, as his official plane flew him from Washington to his Florida vacation spot in Key West. The day before, in a controversial speech to a joint session of Congress, the president had announced the Truman Doctrine. Without mentioning the Soviet Union by name, he equated its policies with the former "totalitarian regimes" of Germany and Japan. "I believe," he said, "that it must be the policy of the United States to support free peoples who are resisting attempted subjugation by armed minorities or by outside pressures." These words became the backbone of containment, a doctrine that in the coming years would lead the United States into armed conflict in Asia, the Middle East, and Latin America.

Truman had acceded to the presidency upon the death of Franklin D. Roosevelt in April 1945. The new president's immediate response to this challenge was a deep feeling of inadequacy. "I'm not big enough for this job," he confided to a friend. Even an experienced, well-respected president would have faced an enormous task in guiding the nation's transition from war to peace. But Truman was little more than an obscure politician. During his few months as vice president, this former senator from Missouri had been kept in the dark about crucial foreign and military policies. Indeed, Roosevelt had not even told Truman about the atomic bomb project.

27

THE COLD WAR AND AMERICAN POLITICS, 1945–1953

The Cold War was a central theme of Truman's presidency both at home and abroad. Just a week after his Truman Doctrine speech, a presidential executive order announced the establishment of the Employee Loyalty Program. Henceforth, all agency heads in the executive branch had to ensure that each employee under their jurisdiction was a loyal American. In doubtful cases, the agency's director had to appoint a loyalty board to hear the evidence and make recommendations. People already on the job who were accused of disloyalty were presumed to be guilty, not innocent.

In foreign affairs, the theme of anticommunism revealed itself in Cold War policies that protected and expanded American overseas interests, challenged the Soviet Union, created alliance systems, rebuilt Western Europe and Japan, drew the United States into civil wars, and favored a military build-up over diplomacy. While much of Asia and Europe lay in ruins and civil wars and colonial rebellions rocked many areas, the United States and the Soviet Union scrambled to win friends and to drive in economic and strategic stakes.

Truman saw the Soviet threat as global and decided to project American power on a worldwide scale. This new globalism brought the United States into crisis after crisis. Just five years after the Second World War, the Cold War turned hot on the peninsula of Korea. Although the threat of world war did not materialize, the Korean conflict significantly accelerated the process toward globalism. The United States began to enlarge its military power and to develop new nuclear weapons.

On the domestic front, the new president got a crash course in the intricacies of governing the United States. In 1945, the nation's reconversion from war to peace was not smooth, and Truman managed to anger liberals, conservatives, farmers, consumers, and union members during his first year as president. In 1948, however, Truman confounded political experts by winning the presidency in his own right. He had continued to espouse the New Deal and to be loyal to the welfare system fashioned in the 1930s. He was also the first president ever to pledge federal support for racial equality.

As Truman's victory indicated, however, politics were volatile. The key domestic issues of the period—black civil rights and the anti-Communist witch-hunt called McCarthyism—were the most highly charged of all. The outbreak of the Korean War in June 1950 intensified discontent at home. The military stalemate frustrated war-weary citizens, inflation began another upward climb, and evidence of corruption surfaced in the White House. Truman's popularity plummeted. In 1952, Americans cast their presidential votes for a war hero, General Dwight D. Eisenhower.

The Sources of the Cold War

After overseeing the final stages of Germany's and Japan's defeat, President Truman participated in the rapid deterioration of Soviet-American relations—

the Cold War. In this new conflict, competitive ideologies, propaganda, reconstruction programs, military alliances, atomic arms development, and spheres of influence condemned the world once again to instability and fear.

Some conflict was inevitable after the Second World War because the international environment was so unsettled. First, the world was in serious economic trouble. Across Europe and Asia, factories, bridges, transportation and communications systems, and houses had been reduced to rubble. Agricultural production was low, and displaced persons wandered around in search of food and family members. How would this devastated world be pieced back together? America and the Soviet Union each offered a different model. Second, the collapse of Germany and Japan created power vacuums that drew the two major powers into collision as they sought to claim influence in countries where the enemy had once held sway. Third, political turmoil within nations spurred Soviet-American competition. Fourth, empires were disintegrating. In this process of decolonization, the European imperial nations were forced to withdraw by nationalist rebels and by their own financial constraints. New nations were born in the Middle East and Asia, and America and the Soviet Union competed to win them as friends who might provide military bases, resources, and markets. Conflict also seemed inevitable because of the shrinkage of the globe. The advent of the "air age" made the world more compact. Nations were brought closer together by faster travel; at the same time, they became more vulnerable to surprise attack from the air. The Americans and the Soviets once again collided as they strove to establish defensive positions, sometimes far from home.

Although conflict may have been inevitable because of those international conditions, the Cold War may not have been. The national policies of the United States and the Soviet Union and their leaders' conduct of diplomacy worsened rather than resolved postwar conflict. Each country saw the other as the world's bully. If Americans feared "communist aggression," Soviets feared "capitalist encirclement." In mirror image, each side saw the other as the obstacle to international peace.

1945	Yalta Conference		Berlin blockade and airlift
	Roosevelt dies		Truman elected president
	Truman assumes presidency	**1949**	North Atlantic Treaty Organization
	Germany surrenders		founded
	Potsdam Conference		Russia explodes an atomic bomb
	Japan surrenders		Communist victory in China
1946	Crisis over Iran	**1950**	Klaus Fuchs arrested as an atomic
	Churchill's Iron Curtain speech		spy
	Strikes by coal miners		Alger Hiss convicted of perjury
	Baruch Plan		McCarthy alleges presence of
	Inflation reaches 18.2 percent		Communists in government
	Republicans win both houses of		NSC-68
	Congress		Point Four Program launched
1947	Truman Doctrine		Korean War begins
	Truman's Employee Loyalty Program		Julius and Ethel Rosenberg arrested
	Communist takeover in Hungary		Marines land at Inchon
	Taft-Hartley Act		Internal Security (McCarran) Act
	Kennan's "Mr. X" article		China enters the Korean War
	Marshall Plan announced	**1951**	Armistice talks begin in Korea
	To Secure These Rights issued by President's Committee on Civil Rights		*Dennis et al.* v. *United States*
	National Security Act	**1952**	Eisenhower elected president
	Rio Pact		Republicans win both houses of
1948	Communist coup in Czechoslovakia		Congress
	State of Israel founded	**1953**	Korean War ends
	Committee on Equality of Treatment and Opportunity in the Armed Services formed		

"We are in this thing all over the world to the extent few people realize," Secretary of State James F. Byrnes (1945–1947) told Truman's cabinet. Why were Americans "all over the world"? One reason was that they had determined never to repeat the experience of the 1930s: they vowed to have no more depressions that would spawn political extremism and in turn produce war, no more Munichs, no more appeasement. It seemed to Americans in the 1940s that Nazi Germany had been replaced by the Soviet Union, that communism was simply the flip side of the totalitarian coin. The popular term "Red fascism" captured this sentiment.

American officials also knew that the nation's economic well-being depended on an activist foreign policy. In the postwar years, the United States was the largest supplier of goods to world markets. That trade was jeopardized by the postwar economic paralysis of Europe and by discriminatory trade practices that violated the Open Door doctrine. "Any serious failure to maintain this flow,"

The Sources of the Cold War

People and governments in the postwar world faced the awesome task of rebuilding. In Berlin, which had been reduced to rubble, the future of subsequent generations depended upon their success. *William Vandivert,* Life *magazine,* © *Time Warner Inc.*

declared an assistant secretary of state, "would put millions of American businessmen, farmers, and workers out of business." Indeed, exports constituted about 10 percent of the gross national product (GNP). Finally, the United States needed to export in order to pay for imports such as zinc, tin, and manganese. Economic expansionism, so much a part of pre–Cold War history, thus remained a central feature of postwar foreign relations.

New strategic theory also propelled the United States toward an activist, expansionist, globalist diplomacy. As American strategists saw it, if the

American Strategic Thinking

United States was to be ready for a military challenge in the postwar air age, the nation's defenses had to begin far beyond its own borders. Therefore, the United States acquired overseas bases to guard the approaches to the Western Hemisphere. Overseas bases also per-

mitted the launching of attacks with might and speed.

President Truman, who shared the strategists' assumptions, had a personality that tended to increase international tensions. Whereas Roosevelt had been ingratiating, patient, and evasive, Truman was brash, impatient, and direct. He seldom displayed the appreciation of subtleties so essential to successful diplomacy. In his first meeting with V. M. Molotov, the Soviet commissar of foreign affairs, Truman sharply berated the Soviet Union for violating the Yalta accords, a charge Molotov denied. When Truman shot back that the Soviets should honor their agreements, Molotov stormed out of the room. The president was pleased with his "tough method": "I gave it to him straight 'one-two to the jaw.'" This simplistic display of toughness became a trademark of American Cold War diplomacy.

As for the Soviets, they were not easy to get along with either. Dean Acheson, a high-ranking diplomat from 1945 to 1947 and secretary of state from 1949 to 1953, found them rude

American Anti-Soviet Views

and abusive. Indeed, Premier Josef Stalin's blunt *nyets* stung American ears. But more than Soviet style bothered Americans. Soviet territorial ambitions—and successes— included a portion of eastern Poland, the Baltic states of Lithuania, Latvia, and Estonia, and parts of Finland and Rumania. In Eastern Europe, Soviet officials began to suppress non-Communists.

For their part, the Soviets remembered how the hostile West had attempted to ostracize them before. Driven by memories of the past, by fear of a revived Germany, by the huge task of reconstruction, and by Marxist-Leninist doctrine, the Soviets suspected capitalist nations of plotting once again to extinguish the Communist flame. They protested that the Americans were surrounding them with hostile bases and practicing atomic and dollar diplomacy.

"After World War II," Senator J. William Fulbright remembered, "we were sold on the idea that Stalin was out to dominate the world." This view pitted a generous United States against a selfish Soviet Union. But Fulbright came to believe that the Soviets probably never intended to dominate the world. With a weak military establishment, a hobbled economy, and obsolete technology, they lacked the capability to do so. Knowing this, American leaders did not expect the Soviets to attack Western Europe or to start a war they obviously could not sustain. The Soviet Union was a regional power in Eastern Europe, not a global menace.

American officials nonetheless exaggerated the Soviet threat, and the reasons for this approach sum up the American global perspective early in the Cold War. First, President Truman

Question of the Soviet Threat

liked things in black and white. Nuances, ambiguities, and counterevidence were often glossed over to satisfy Truman's penchant for the simple answer. Second, military officers often overplayed the Soviet threat to persuade Congress to pass larger defense budgets. Third, some Americans fixed their attention, as

they had since the Bolshevik Revolution of 1917, on the utopian Communist goal of world revolution rather than on actual Soviet behavior. Fourth, American leaders feared that the terrible postwar conditions of poverty and social unrest abroad would leave United States strategic and economic interests vulnerable to political disorders that the Soviets might exploit. In other words, Americans feared less a direct Soviet attack and more the Soviets' potential seizing of opportunities to challenge American interests, perhaps through subversion. Last and overall, the United States, flushed with its own strength, took advantage of the postwar power vacuum to expand its overseas interests and shape a peace on American terms.

Cold War Crises and the Containment Doctrine

One of the first Soviet-American clashes came in Poland in 1945, when the Soviets refused to admit conservative Poles from London to the Communist government in Lublin, as agreed at

Soviet Domination of Eastern Europe

Yalta. The Soviets also snuffed out civil liberties in the former Nazi satellite of Rumania. They allowed free elections to be held in Hungary and Czechoslovakia, but as the Cold War progressed and they came to fear American power more and more, they encouraged Communist coups. First Hungary (1947) and then Czechoslovakia (1948) succumbed to Soviet subversion. Yugoslavia was a unique case: its independent Communist government successfully broke with Stalin in 1948.

To justify their actions, the Soviets complained that the United States was reviving Russia's traditional enemy, Germany. Soviet leaders also charged that the United States was pursuing a double standard—intervening in the affairs of Eastern Europe but expecting the Soviet Union to stay out of Latin America and Asia. The Soviets pointed to the lack of free elections in United States–backed Latin American dictatorships. Americans insisted that their spheres of influence were far more open, their methods far less repressive than the Soviets'. But protest as Washington did, it was unable to roll back Soviet influence in Eastern Europe.

Another issue that divided America and the Soviet Union was the atomic bomb. The Soviets believed that the Americans were practicing "atomic diplomacy"—maintaining a frightening nuclear monopoly and bragging about it to scare the Soviets into diplomatic concessions. At a stormy foreign ministers' conference in London in the fall of 1945, Soviet diplomat V. M. Molotov asked Secretary of State James F. Byrnes if he had an atomic bomb in his side pocket. Byrnes replied that southerners "carry our artillery in our hip pocket. If you don't cut out all this stalling and let us get down to work, I am going to pull an atomic bomb out of my hip pocket and let you have it."

Atomic Diplomacy

In this atmosphere of suspicion and distrust, the two powers could not agree on the international control of atomic energy. The American proposal, called the Baruch Plan, provided for America's abandoning of its monopoly after the world's fissionable materials had been brought under the authority of an international agency. The Soviets retorted that this plan denied them the right to develop their own bomb while the United States continued its supremacy.

The two adversaries also collided over Iran. By wartime agreement, British, American, and Soviet troops occupied Iran. When American petroleum companies asked the Iranian government for an oil concession, Moscow sniffed a capitalist plot on its border. In March 1946, the date agreed on for troop withdrawal, the Soviets stayed on in violation of the wartime treaty. Americans angrily accused them of intending to take over Iran. Iranian and Soviet diplomats managed to negotiate a settlement in April: Soviet soldiers would leave Iran in exchange for an oil concession. Americans claimed a Cold War victory, believing that their tough words had forced the Soviets to withdraw. In 1947, they turned the tables on the Soviets by persuading the Iranians to go back on their promise of a Soviet oil concession. Moscow cried that it had been double-crossed.

Crisis in Iran

Soviets and Americans clashed on every front in 1946. Since they could not agree on the unification of Germany, they built up their zones independently. The new World Bank and International Monetary Fund, created at the 1944 Bretton Woods Conference to stabilize trade and finance, also became tangled in the Cold War struggle. The Soviets refused to join because the United States dominated both institutions. In early 1946, Washington extended a $3.5 billion loan to Great Britain but turned down a similar Soviet request.

When in early February 1946, Stalin gave a pre-election speech depicting a world threatened by capitalist acquisitiveness, the American chargé d'affaires in Moscow, George F. Kennan, concluded that Soviet fanaticism made even a temporary understanding impossible. Kennan's pessimistic "long telegram" to Washington fed the growing belief that only toughness would work with the Soviets. On March 5, Winston Churchill made his stirring Iron Curtain speech, warning that Eastern European countries were being cut off from the West by the Soviet Union.

The Cold War escalated further on March 12, 1947, when in response to a request from the British, who could no longer afford to fund their Greek client government, the president asked Congress for $400 million in aid to Greece and Turkey. Both these countries were threatened by economic dislocation and Communist political pressure. The United States must help "free peoples who are resisting attempted subjugation by armed minorities or by outside pressures," Truman declared; it was time to contain the Communist menace. The president's statement quickly became known as the Truman Doctrine. Critics correctly pointed out that there was no evidence that the Soviet Union was involved in the civil war in Greece. Nevertheless, the money was appropriated and the insurgents defeated.

Truman Doctrine

In July 1947, George F. Kennan, now director of the State Department's policy-planning staff, offered another statement of what became known as the containment doctrine. Writing under the name "Mr. X" in the magazine *Foreign Affairs*, this expert on Soviet affairs advocated a "policy of firm containment, designed to confront the Russians with unalterable counterforce at every point where they show signs of encroaching upon the interests of a peaceful and stable world." Such a counterforce, Kennan argued, would check Soviet expansion and eventually foster a "mellowing" of Soviet behavior. Together with the Truman Doctrine, Kennan's article became a key manifesto of Cold War policy. Critic Walter Lippmann complained that the policy did not distinguish between areas vital and peripheral to American security.

Lippmann was happier with a program announced by Secretary of State George C. Marshall (1947–1949) on June 5, 1947. Under the Marshall
Marshall Plan Plan, the United States would finance a massive European recovery program. Although Marshall did not exclude Eastern Europe or the Soviet Union, few American leaders believed that the Soviets and their allies would want to join an American-dominated project. And, indeed, they did not join. Launched in 1948, the Marshall Plan sent $12.4 billion to Western Europe before the program ended in late 1951 (see map, page 492). To stimulate business at home, the legislation provided that the foreign aid dollars must be spent in the United States.

The Marshall Plan was a mixed success. In Europe, it caused inflation, failed to solve a serious balance-of-payments problem, and took only tentative steps toward economic integration. But it also sparked impressive Western European industrial production and investment and started the region toward self-sustaining economic growth. By 1952, the focus of the program had shifted from recovery to military assistance.

To strengthen the nation's defenses, Truman worked with Congress to streamline the government's administrative structure under the National Security Act (July 1947). The act created the Department of Defense, the National Security Council (NSC) to advise the president, and the Central Intelligence Agency (CIA) to conduct spying and information gathering. By the early 1950s, the CIA had expanded its functions to include covert (secret) operations aimed at overthrowing unfriendly foreign leaders and stirring up economic trouble in "the camp of the enemy."

American officials also reached out to find new foreign friends and build new bases. In 1946, the United States granted the Philippines indepen-dence but maintained its old military, economic, and political ties. The next year, American diplomats created the Rio Pact—a military alliance with Latin American countries. Under this and other agreements, the Truman administration sent several military advisory missions to Latin America and to Greece, Turkey, Iran, China, and Saudi Arabia. In May 1948, Truman recognized the new state of Israel, which had been carved out of the British-held territory of Palestine after years of Arab-Jewish dispute. America's perceived need for international allies, along with the president's desire for Jewish-American votes in the upcoming election, helped speed the decision.

One of the most electric moments in the Cold War came in June 1948, when the Soviets cut off Western access to the jointly occupied city of Ber-
Berlin Blockade and Airlift lin, located well inside the Soviet zone of Germany. Before the Soviets' bold move, the Americans, French, and British had agreed to fuse their zones into what became known as West Germany. The three allies planned to integrate West Germany, including the three sectors of Berlin under their control, into the Western European economy, complete with a reformed German currency. The Soviets, fearing a resurgent Germany tied to the American Cold War camp, may have sparked the Berlin crisis to stimulate negotiations. But if they thought Truman would compromise, they guessed wrong. The president ordered a massive airlift of food, fuel, and other supplies to the isolated city. Finally, in May 1949, their image badly damaged, the Soviets lifted the blockade. They had spurred the very result they feared: the creation of the Federal Republic of Germany (West Germany) that month. In retaliation, they founded the German Democratic Republic (East Germany).

On April 4, 1949, believing that a military shield should be added to the economic shield of the Marshall Plan, the United States, Canada, and much
Creation of NATO of Western Europe founded the North Atlantic Treaty Organization (NATO) (see map, page 492). The treaty aroused considerable debate at home, for not since 1778 had the United States entered a formal European military alliance. Critics protested that NATO would provoke an

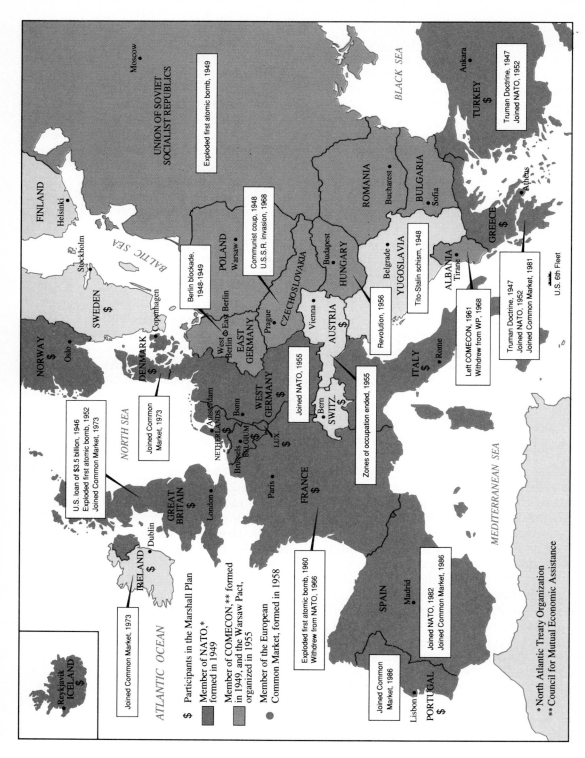

Divided Europe

arms race with the Soviet Union, cause American soldiers to be stationed in Europe, and allow the president power to commit troops to combat without a congressional declaration of war. Truman responded that NATO would give Europeans the will to resist communism. And it would function as a "tripwire," bringing the full force of the United States to bear on the Soviet Union if it dared to cross the East-West line with troops. The Senate ratified the treaty in July. Truman then asked for a $1.5 billion Mutual Defense Assistance Act; Congress consented, as it did to all of Truman's major foreign policy requests.

Just before passage of the military aid bill (September 1949), the Soviet Union exploded an atomic bomb, breaking the American nuclear monopoly. In early 1950, Truman responded by ordering production of the hydrogen bomb. In May, Congress endorsed funds for technical assistance to developing nations, to draw them into the American sphere of influence (a plan called the Point Four Program, after the fourth point of Truman's 1949 inaugural address).

A month earlier, the National Security Council had delivered to the president a top-secret document numbered NSC-68. Predicting continued tension with the Communists and describing a "shrinking world of polarized power," the report appealed for an enlarged military budget to counter the Soviet global design that Americans perceived. Administration officials worried about how to sell this strong prescription to the voters and a budget-conscious Congress. "We were sweating over it, and then—with regard to NSC-68—thank God Korea came along," recalled one of Dean Acheson's aides.

NSC-68

▼

The Cold War in Asia

When the Korean War erupted in mid-1950, it came in the wake of vast changes in Asia. The Second World War had accelerated the process of decolonization. Occupied with defending themselves and then with rebuilding after the war, imperial countries were no longer able to resist their colonies'

demands for independence. Britain gave up India and what are now Pakistan and Bangladesh in 1947 and Burma and Ceylon in 1948. The Dutch reluctantly let go of Indonesia in 1949. Only the French fought on in Indochina, finally retiring from that outpost in 1954.

The defeat of Japan brought about the division of its empire among the victors. Korea was divided between the United States and the Soviet Union. The Pacific islands (the Marshalls, Marianas, and Carolines) came under American control. Half of Sakhalin went to the Soviets, as agreed at Yalta, and Formosa (Taiwan) was returned to the Chinese. As for Japan itself, the United States monopolized its reconstruction. General Douglas MacArthur, the director of the American occupation, wrote a democratic constitution for Japan, revitalized its economy, and destroyed the weapons of the Japanese military.

Reconstruction of Japan

Although United States supremacy in Japan was an established fact, the Soviets would not recognize it. Thus, after squabbling with Moscow for years over a peace treaty with Japan, the United States finally signed a separate peace in 1951. The treaty restored Japan's sovereignty, ended the occupation, granted the United States a military base at Okinawa, and permitted American troops to be stationed in Japan. Tokyo and Washington also initialed a defense pact. The people who had been called beasts after their surprise attack on Pearl Harbor were now American allies.

Meanwhile, America's Chinese ally was faltering. The United States was feeding and fueling Jiang Jieshi's (Chiang Kai-shek's) Nationalist army in its battle against Mao Zedong and Zhou Enlai's Communists. Immediately after the Second World War American troops had occupied northern China, flown Nationalist soldiers to Manchuria, and stayed on to advise Generalissimo Jiang. Despite $3 billion in American aid from 1945 to 1949, Jiang proved a weak and unreliable friend. His government was corrupt and out of touch with the peasants, who were attracted to the Communists by promises of land redistribution. He also tolerated a grossly unfair tax system.

Chinese Civil War

Still, American leaders saw Jiang as the only alternative to Mao. In the *White Paper* of 1949—a government report written to explain America's efforts to contain communism through aid to Jiang—Secretary of State Dean Acheson asserted that the "Communist leaders have . . . publicly announced their subservience to a foreign power." Actually, Americans had overestimated Mao's dependence on the Soviet Union. The Soviets had given Mao little support; indeed they preferred a weak China under Jiang to a strong China under Mao. Truman's refusal to allow talks with the Communists, however, left Mao little choice; he leaned toward the Soviets.

In the fall of 1949, after numerous military setbacks, Jiang fled to the island of Formosa, and Mao proclaimed the People's Republic of China. For several reasons, the United States decided not to recognize the new government. American officials were alarmed by a Sino-Soviet treaty of friendship signed in February 1950, and Mao's followers had harassed Americans and seized American owned property in China. Furthermore, Mao was now openly hostile to the United States. Secretary Acheson believed that Mao would conquer Formosa, thus eliminating Jiang, and that frictions between Beijing and Moscow would ultimately convince Mao to sever his ties with the Soviets.

Nonrecognition of the People's Republic of China

Reaching for some way to offset Jiang's collapse, the National Security Council urged the president to fortify "friendly and independent" states in Asia as a bulwark against Communist expansion. In February 1950, the United States recognized the French puppet regime of Bao Dai in Vietnam and a few months later decided to extend aid to the beleaguered French there. In April, the National Security Council sent the president its alarming report NSC-68. And in May, more funds went to Jiang Jieshi in Formosa.

A Rough Transition at Home

As the Truman administration struggled with the Cold War abroad, it also faced the huge task of economic conversion from war to peace. Even before the end of the Second World War, cutbacks in production had caused layoffs. Workers at Ford Motor Company's massive Willow Run plant outside Detroit, where nine thousand Liberator bombers had been produced, were let go in the spring of 1945. Ten days after the victory over Japan, 1.8 million people received pink slips and 640,000 filed for unemployment compensation. Postwar unemployment peaked in March 1946, when 2.7 million people were seeking work. Swelling the ranks of those seeking jobs were millions of discharged soldiers and sailors.

Postwar Job Layoffs

Despite high unemployment in the immediate postwar period, the United States was not teetering on the brink of a depression. People had plenty of savings to spend in 1945 and 1946, and suddenly there were new houses and cars for them to buy. Easy credit and the availability of new products from such war-inspired industries as synthetic rubber and electronics promoted the buying spree. As a result, though war production began to wind down in 1944, the gross national product continued to rise in 1945. The nation's postwar economic problem was not depression but inflation. Throughout 1945 and 1946, prices skyrocketed; the inflation rate for 1946 was 18.2 percent.

Meanwhile, though prices were spiraling upward, many people were earning less real income than they had earned during the war. The wartime Little Steel formula had limited workers to cost-of-living pay increases, and the end of war production had eliminated much of their overtime work. But while wages and salaries had declined slightly in 1946, net profits reached all-time highs. Indignant that they were not sharing in the increased prosperity, more than 4.5 million men and women left their jobs to strike in 1946. Workers forced nationwide shutdowns in the coal, automobile, steel, and electric industries and halted railroad and maritime transportation.

Upsurge in Labor Strikes

John L. Lewis's United Mine Workers was among the most powerful unions to walk off the job. Coal was the nation's primary source of energy in 1946. When soft-coal production stopped on April 1, steel and automobile output plummeted, railroad service was canceled, thousands of people were laid off, and twenty-two states reinstituted wartime "dim-outs" to conserve coal. The miners' demands were legitimate—higher wages, a federal safety code, and a royalty of ten cents per ton to finance health services and welfare and pension funds. A two-week truce in May failed to produce a solution, and so on May 21, with time running out and the country still desperate for coal, Truman ordered the seizure of the mines. Lewis and the government reached an accord a week later, and the miners returned to work. But within six months the agreement collapsed, and once again the government placed the operation of the mines under its direct control.

There was no doubt in 1946 about the growing unpopularity of labor unions and their leadership. Many Americans believed that the unions were re-

Truman's Attack on the Unions

sponsible for strikes that not only restricted the output of consumer goods and inflated prices, but also threatened the national security. In May, when a nationwide rail-

road strike was threatened, Truman hopped aboard the antiunion bandwagon. A special board appointed to mediate the dispute had managed to satisfy eighteen of the disgruntled unions, but two held out for a better settlement. In exasperation, Truman made a dramatic appearance before a joint session of Congress. If the government seized a strikebound industry, he said, and the workers in that industry refused to honor a presidential order to return to work, "I [would] request the Congress immediately to authorize the President to draft into the Armed Forces of the United States all workers who are on strike against their government." He also requested authority to strip strikers of seniority benefits, to take legal action against union leaders, and to fine and even imprison them for contempt. Truman's speech alienated not only railroad workers, but union members in general. Many dedicated themselves to defeating Truman in the 1948 presidential election.

Truman fared little better in his direction of the Office of Price Administration. Now that the war was over, powerful interests wanted OPA controls lifted. Consumers were impatient with short-

Consumer Discontent

ages and black-market prices, and manufacturers and farmers wanted to jack up prices legally. Yet when most controls expired in mid-1946 and inflation rose higher, people became angry.

Republicans made the most of public discontent. "Got enough meat?" asked Republican Congressman John M. Vorys of Ohio. "Got enough houses? Got enough OPA? . . . Got enough inflation? . . . Got enough debt? . . . Got enough strikes?" When the votes were tabulated in the 1946 congressional election, the Republicans had won a majority in both houses of the Eightieth Congress. The White House in 1948 seemed within their grasp.

The Eightieth Congress and the Election of 1948

The politicians who ruled the Eightieth Congress, both Republicans and southern Democrats, were committed conservatives. Although they supported Truman's foreign policy, they perceived the Republican landslide as a mandate to reverse the New Deal, to curb the power of government and of labor. Truman had had little success with the Seventy-ninth Congress; he would have even less success with this one. Ironically, however, the Eightieth Congress helped him win the presidency in 1948. For if Truman had alienated labor, farmers, and liberals, the Eightieth Congress made them livid.

One extremely unpopular measure was the Taft-Hartley Act, which Congress adopted over Truman's veto in 1947. A revision of the Wagner Act of

Taft-Hartley Act

1935, it prohibited the union, or closed, shop, in which only union members could be hired. It also permitted the states to ban the

closed shop by passing "right-to-work" laws. In addition, the law forbade union contributions to political funds in federal elections, required union leaders to sign affidavits stating they were not Communists, and mandated an eighty-day cooling-off period in strikes that imperiled the national se-

Few pollsters predicted that President Harry S Truman (1884–1972) would win in 1948. The *Chicago Tribune* announced his defeat before all the returns were in. Here a victorious Truman pokes fun at the premature headline. *The Bettmann Archive.*

curity. Truman's veto therefore vindicated him in the eyes of labor.

Throughout 1947 and into 1948, the Eightieth Congress offended numerous interest groups, which in turn swung back to Truman. For example, the president asked Congress for continued price supports for farmers; the Eightieth Congress responded with weakened price supports. The president requested nationwide health insurance; the Eightieth Congress refused. It was the same with federal funding of public housing and aid to public education; with broadened and increased unemployment compensation, old-age and survivors' benefits, and the minimum wage; with funds for land reclamation, irrigation, and public power; and with antilynching, anti–poll tax, and fair employment legislation. Truman proposed; Congress rejected or ignored his requests.

Republicans seemed oblivious to public opinion. Not since 1928 had they been so confident of capturing the presidency, and most political experts agreed. "Only a political miracle," stated *Time*, "or

Campaign of 1948 extraordinary stupidity on the part of the Republicans can save the Democratic party." At their national convention, Republicans strengthened their position by nominating for president and vice president the governors of two of the nation's most populous states: Thomas E. Dewey of New York and Earl Warren of California.

Truman, who received the Democratic nomination, found himself fighting more than just Republicans. Leftist elements of the party, especially those critical of the Truman Doctrine, started a new Progressive party under the leadership of former vice president Henry Wallace. Segregationists, angered over the Democratic party's adoption of a civil rights plank, formed the States Rights Democratic party (Dixiecrats) and nominated Governor Strom Thurmond of South Carolina. If Wallace's candidacy did not destroy Truman's chances, experts said, the Dixiecrats certainly would.

But Truman had ideas of his own. He called the Eightieth Congress into special session and demanded that it enact all the planks in the Republican platform. If Republicans really wanted to transform their ideals into law, said Truman, this was the time to do it. After Congress had met for two weeks and accomplished nothing of significance, Truman took to the road. Traveling more than 30,000 miles by train, he delivered scores of whistle-stop speeches denouncing the "do-nothing" Eightieth Congress. Still, no amount of furious campaigning by Truman seemed likely to change the predicted outcome.

As the votes were counted early into the morning, it became clear that Truman had confounded the experts. The final tally was 24.1 million popular votes, 303 electoral votes, for Truman; 21.9 million popular votes, 189 electoral votes, for Dewey. Rather than the predicted 5 million votes apiece, Wallace and Thurmond polled just a little over 1 million each. Not only had Truman won four more years in the White House, but the Democrats had also regained control of Congress.

Truman on Civil Rights

The postwar years were a period of gathering strength for African-Americans. Truman and other politicians knew that they would have to compete for the growing black vote in urban-industrial states like California, Illinois, Michigan, Ohio, Pennsylvania, and New York. Many Republicans cultivated the black vote. Thomas Dewey, who as governor of New York had pushed successfully for the establishment of a fair employment practices commission, was particularly popular with blacks. In Harlem, which had gone Democratic by a 4-to-1 margin in 1938, Dewey won by large margins in 1942 and 1946.

Certainly, then, Truman had political reasons for supporting black civil rights. But he also felt a moral obligation to blacks. For one thing, he believed it was only fair that each American, regardless of race, should enjoy the full rights of citizenship. More than that, Truman was horrified by a report that police in Aiken, South Carolina, had gouged out the eyes of a black sergeant just

three hours after he had been discharged from the army. Several weeks later, on December 5, 1946, Truman signed an executive order establishing the President's Committee on Civil Rights.

A year later, the committee delivered its report, *To Secure These Rights*. Among the committee's recommendations, which became the agenda for the civil rights movement for the next twenty years, were the enactment of federal antilynching, antisegregation, and anti–poll tax laws. *To Secure These Rights* also called for laws guaranteeing voting rights and equal employment opportunity, and for the establishment of a permanent commission on civil rights and a civil rights division within the Department of Justice. Although Congress failed to act and evidence suggests that Truman's motive may have been the black vote in 1948, his action was significant. For the first time since Reconstruction, a president acknowledged the federal government's responsibility to protect African-Americans and strive for racial equality.

President's Committee on Civil Rights

Truman took this responsibility seriously and in 1948 issued two executive orders demanding an end to racial discrimination in the federal government. One proclaimed a policy of "fair employment throughout the federal establishment" and created the Employment Board of the Civil Service Commission to hear charges of discrimination. The other ordered the racial desegregation of the armed forces and appointed the Committee on Equality of Treatment and Opportunity in the Armed Services to oversee this change.

Blacks also benefited from a series of Supreme Court decisions. The trend toward judicial support of civil rights had begun in the late 1930s, when the NAACP established its Legal Defense Fund. At the time, the NAACP was trying to destroy the separate-but-equal doctrine by insisting on its literal interpretation. In higher education, the NAACP figured, the cost of racially separate schools was prohibitive. "You can't build a cyclotron for one [black] student," the president of the University of Oklahoma acknowledged. As a result of NAACP lawsuits in the 1930s and 1940s,

Supreme Court Decisions on Civil Rights

black students won admission to professional and graduate schools at a number of state universities. The NAACP also scored notable victories in several other cases. In 1944, in *Smith* v. *Allwright*, the Supreme Court outlawed the whites-only primaries held by the Democratic party in some southern states, branding them a violation of the Fifteenth Amendment. Two years later, the Court declared segregation in interstate bus transportation unconstitutional. And in *Shelley* v. *Kraemer* (1948), the Court held that a racially restrictive covenant (a private agreement among white homeowners not to sell to blacks) violated the equal protection clause of the Fourteenth Amendment.

A change in social attitudes accompanied these gains in black political and legal power. Books such as Gunnar Myrdal's *An American Dilemma* (1944) and Richard Wright's *Native Son* (1940) and *Black Boy* (1945) had increased white awareness of the social injustice that plagued blacks. A new black middle class had emerged, composed of college educated activists, veterans, and union workers. Blacks and whites were working together in CIO unions and with service organizations such as the National Council of Churches. In 1947, a black baseball player, Jackie Robinson, cracked the major-league color barrier.

Cold War pressures also benefited blacks. As the Soviet Union was quick to point out, the United States could not pose as the leader of the free world, or condemn the denial of human rights behind the Iron Curtain, so long as it condoned racism at home. Nor could it convince new African and Asian nations of its dedication to human rights if African-Americans were subjected to segregation, disfranchisement, and racial violence. To win the support of nonaligned nations, the United States would have to live up to its own ideals.

McCarthyism

A common misconception about the postwar era is that anti-Communist hysteria began in 1950 with the speeches of Senator Joseph R. McCarthy. Actually, anticommunism had been part of the American political temper since the First World War and the Red Scare of 1919 and 1920. The Cold War heightened anti-Communist fears at home, and McCarthy manipulated these fears to his own advantage. He was the most successful and frightening redbaiter the country had ever seen.

To a great extent, President Truman initiated the postwar anti-Communist crusade. Truman was bothered by the revelation in 1945 that classified government documents had been found in the offices of *Amerasia*, a little-known magazine whose editors sympathized with the Chinese Communists. He was also bothered by a report that Soviet spies operating in Canada had transmitted atomic secrets to a Soviet agent.

Spurred by these revelations, Truman in March 1947 ordered investigations into the loyalty of the more than 3 million employees of the United States government. In 1950, the government began discharging people deemed "security risks." Some were purged because they were allegedly homosexuals or alcoholics; others became victims of guilt by association. None were allowed to confront their accusers.

Truman's Loyalty Probe

The wellspring of this fear of communism was the Cold War, and Truman was not alone in peddling fear. Conservatives and liberal Democrats joined him. Republicans used the same technique to attack the Democratic candidates for president in 1948 and 1952; liberal Democrats used it to discredit the far-left, pro-Wallace wing of their party. In many ways, the anti-Communist hysteria of the late 1940s was a phenomenon created by professional politicians and promoted by labor union officials, religious leaders, Hollywood moguls, and other influential figures.

People began to point accusing fingers at each other. Hollywood film personalities who had been ardent left-wingers were blacklisted. Schoolteachers and college professors were fired for expressing dissenting viewpoints, and in some communities "pro-Communist" books were removed from school libraries. In labor union elections and in struggles to dominate local parent-teacher associations, redbaiting became a convenient tactic for discrediting the opposition.

Although the hysteria was unwarranted, there

Congressman Richard M. Nixon appeared to take little satisfaction in the newspaper headline proclaiming Alger Hiss's perjury conviction in early 1950. As a member of the House Un-American Activities Committee, Nixon had led the investigation into charges that Hiss had been a Communist party member and a spy in the 1930s. *The Bettmann Archive.*

was cause for alarm—especially in 1949. In that year, the Soviets exploded their first atomic bomb, and the Chinese Communists, finally victorious in the civil war, proclaimed the People's Republic of China. Furthermore, a former State Department official, Alger Hiss, was on trial for perjury for swearing to a grand jury that he had never passed classified documents to his accuser, former American Communist spy Whittaker Chambers, and had not seen Chambers since 1936. When Truman and Secretary of State Acheson came to his defense, some people began to suspect that the Democrats had something to hide. In 1950, Hiss was convicted

Hiss Trial

of perjury. That same year, the British arrested Klaus Fuchs, a nuclear scientist, for turning over to Soviet agents secrets from the atomic bomb project at Los Alamos, New Mexico.

It was in this atmosphere that on February 9, 1950, Senator Joseph McCarthy mounted a rostrum in Wheeling, West Virginia, and gave a name to the hysteria: McCarthyism. The State Department, he asserted, was "thoroughly infested with Communists," and the most dangerous person in the State Department was Dean Acheson. Reporters wrote that the senator claimed to have a list of 205

McCarthy's Attack on the State Department

Communists working in the State Department; later, McCarthy lowered the figure to "57 card-carrying members," then raised it to 81. No matter the number. What McCarthy needed was a winning campaign issue, and he had found it. Republicans, distraught over losing what had appeared to be a sure victory in 1948, were eager to support his attack.

Widespread support for anti-Communist measures was also apparent in the adoption, over Truman's veto, of the Internal Security (McCarran) Act of 1950. The act made it unlawful for anyone to "contribute to the establishment . . . of a totalitarian dictatorship," required members of "Communist-front" organizations to register with the government, and prohibited them from holding defense jobs or traveling abroad. In a telling decision in 1951 (*Dennis et al.* v. *United States*), the Supreme Court upheld the Smith Act, under which eleven Communist leaders had been convicted and imprisoned.

McCarthy and McCarthyism gained momentum throughout 1950. Nothing seemed to slow the senator down, not even attacks by other Republicans. Seven Republican senators broke with their colleagues and publicly condemned McCarthy for his "selfish political exploitation of fear, bigotry, ignorance, and intolerance." A Senate committee reported that his charges against the State Department were "a fraud and a hoax." But McCarthy had much to sustain him, including Julius and Ethel Rosenberg's 1950 arrest for conspiracy to commit espionage; during the war, at the Los Alamos atomic laboratory, they allegedly had recruited and supervised a spy. (Both were convicted, and in 1953 they were executed.) Perhaps even more helpful to McCarthy than the Rosenberg case was the outbreak of war in Korea in June 1950.

The Korean War and Its Global Consequences

In the early morning hours of June 25, 1950, thousands of troops under the banner of the Democratic People's Republic of Korea (North Korea) moved across the 38th parallel into the Republic of Korea (South Korea). For years, the two Koreas had skirmished along the border drawn for them by the great powers in 1945. Both regimes sought reunification of the divided country, but each on its own terms. Now it appeared that the North Koreans, heavily armed by the Soviets, would realize their goal by force.

President Truman, after huddling with his advisers, decided to intervene. He ordered General MacArthur to send arms to South Korea and to attack North Korean forces from the air. Thinking beyond Korea, he directed the Seventh Fleet to patrol the waters between the Chinese mainland and Jiang's sanctuary, Formosa, thus inserting the United States once again into Chinese politics. Finally, on June 30, Truman ordered American troops into battle. After the United Nations Security Council, in the Soviet delegate's absence, voted to assist South Korea, MacArthur became United Nations commander.

Truman acted decisively for war because he believed, in line with the Cold War mentality of the time, that the Soviets had masterminded the North Korean attack. But unanswered questions dog the thesis that Moscow started the Korean War. When the Security Council voted to aid South Korea, the Soviet delegate was absent because he was protesting the United Nations' refusal to seat the People's Republic of China. If the Soviets did foment the war in Korea, it is surprising that their delegate was not present to veto aid to South Korea. Then, too, why did the Soviets give so little aid to the North Koreans once the war broke out? And why, when they were scoring important propaganda points by advocating peaceful coexistence, would they destroy their gains by igniting a war? Did the war, as some scholars have suggested, begin as a Korean civil conflict rather than as part of the Soviet-American confrontation?

In June 1950, such questions were not being asked. Truman and his aides never doubted that the Soviet Union was testing their policy of containment, that American prestige was at stake, and that failure to act in Korea would prompt Soviet aggression in Iran or Berlin. Having bragged about toughness against communism, Truman could not refrain from acting against North Korea.

Origins of the Korean War

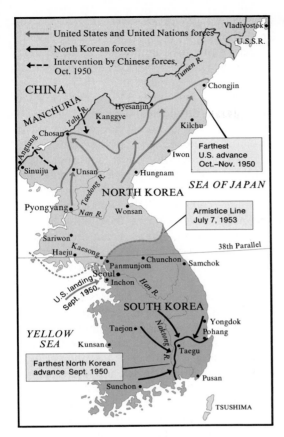

The Korean War, 1950–1953 *Source: From Paterson et al.,* American Foreign Policy: A History, *copyright 1988, p. 378. Reprinted by permission of D.C. Heath and Company.*

At first the war went badly. Within weeks of its outbreak, the North Koreans pushed the South Koreans and Americans into the tiny Pusan perimeter at the base of South Korea. Then, **Inchon** on September 15, 1950, MacArthur launched an amphibious landing at Inchon, several hundred miles behind enemy lines (see map). The operation was so successful that it enabled American leaders to redefine their goal from the containment of North Korea to the unification of Korea by force.

During the weeks following the Inchon landing, American troops drove deeply into North Korea. In early November, American aircraft began strikes against bridges on the Yalu River, the border between North Korea and the People's Republic of

Chinese Entry into the Korean War China. The Chinese watched warily; Mao issued public warnings that China could not permit the continued bombing of its transportation links with Korea or the annihilation of North Korea itself. MacArthur and officials in Washington shrugged off the warnings. In late October, Americans tangled with some Chinese soldiers, who pulled back quickly after the encounter. This may have been one of many signals to the United States that American advances to the Chinese border should halt or else China would enter the war. A month later, an unmoved MacArthur sent his Eighth Army northward in a new offensive. On November 26, tens of thousands of Chinese troops counterattacked, surprising the general's forces and driving them southward. Embarrassed, MacArthur demanded that Washington order a massive air attack on China. Truman, after reflecting on the costs and consequences of a wider war, rejected MacArthur's advice.

By March 1951, the military lines had stabilized around the 38th parallel. Truman contemplated negotiations, and the Soviets stated publicly that they favored a political settlement. **Truman Fires MacArthur** MacArthur had other ideas. The general was making reckless public statements, calling for an attack on China or for Jiang's return to the mainland. He also hinted that the president was practicing appeasement and denounced limited war (war without nuclear weapons, confined to one place). On April 10, Truman fired the general for insubordination. MacArthur returned home to a hero's welcome and Truman's popularity sagged. The chairman of the Joint Chiefs of Staff, General Omar Bradley, spoke against MacArthur's provocative ideas. Escalation, Bradley pointed out, could bring the Soviet Union into battle and exhaust America's resources in an Asian war that promised no victory when there were allies in Europe to be protected.

Armistice talks began in July 1951, but the fighting and dying went on for two more years. Dwight D. Eisenhower, elected president in November 1952, went to Korea in December to fulfill a campaign pledge, but his **The POW Question** postelection visit brought no settlement. The sticking point in the negotiations was the fate of the prisoners of war (POWs): thousands of North Korean and Chinese captives did not want to return home. On July 23, 1953, an armistice was finally signed. The combatants agreed to hand the POW question over to a special panel of neutral nations (which later gave prisoners their choice of staying or leaving). The North Korean–South Korean line was set close to the 38th parallel, the prewar boundary. Thus ended a frustrating war—a limited war that Americans, accustomed to victory, had not won. No celebrations greeted news of the end of the war. The experience was indeed sobering, as was the casualty list of 34,000 Americans dead in battle and 103,000 wounded. The total of killed and wounded for all combatants in the Korean War was 1.9 million.

The Korean War had major political consequences. Bipartisanship in foreign policy eroded further, and the powers of the presidency grew as Congress deferred to Truman time and again. Truman had never gone to Congress for a declaration of war, for he believed that as commander-in-chief he had the authority to send troops to Korea. The war also set off a great national debate. Conservative critics of globalism suggested that America should reduce its overseas commitments and draw its defense line in the Western Hemisphere. But Republican John Foster Dulles countered that "a defense that accepts encirclement quickly decomposes." The advocates of global defense won the debate. Increased aid flowed to allies around the world, and defense budgets remained high.

Debate over Globalist Policy

Wartime Discontent and the Election of 1952

As the 1952 presidential election approached, the Democrats foundered. Added to frustration with the war and hysteria over communism was the revelation of influence-peddling by some of Truman's cronies. Known as "five-percenters," these presidential appointees had offered government con-

tracts in return for 5 percent kickbacks. One employee of the executive branch admitted under oath, "I have only one thing to sell and that is influence." Once again, the Democratic party seemed doomed.

What sealed the fate of the Democratic party was the Republican candidate, General Dwight D. Eisenhower. "Ike" was a bona fide war hero who seemed to embody the virtues Americans most admired: integrity, decency, lack of pretense, and the ability to rise from humble beginnings. His Democratic opponent was Adlai Stevenson, the thoughtful, literate, and witty governor of Illinois. From the outset, it was never much of a contest. Eisenhower promised to end the Korean War. He remained cautiously silent on the subject of McCarthyism, but his running mate did not. Richard M. Nixon scrambled for political points by referring to Stevenson as "Adlai the appeaser . . . who got a Ph.D. from Dean Acheson's College of Cowardly Communist Containment." The result was a landslide: Eisenhower won almost 34 million popular votes and 442 electoral votes, compared with the Democrats' 27 million popular and 89 electoral votes. Moreover, Eisenhower's coattails were long enough to carry other Republicans to victory; the party gained control of both houses of Congress.

The Republican Ticket

Although Truman was highly unpopular when he left office in 1953, historians now rate him among the nation's ten best presidents. He came to office suddenly and with little experience, but in eight years he greatly strengthened the powers of the presidency. At the onset of the Cold War, he announced policies to contain any presumed threat of Soviet expansion. During his presidency, the Central Intelligence Agency, National Security Council, Council of Economic Advisers, and a unified Department of Defense were all created. Truman's main problems stemmed from his overreaction to the alleged threat of Communist subversion in government. His loyalty program ruined innocent people's lives and careers. In drumming up support for his foreign and military policies, Truman presented a frightening picture to the American people of the Communists' aims, and with his rhetoric he helped

Truman's Presidential Legacy

prepare the way for McCarthyism. Finally, he sent American troops to fight in Korea without a declaration of war from Congress.

At the same time, Truman was a New Dealer who fought for social welfare programs and legislation for farmers and workers. His Fair Deal, most of which was enacted during subsequent presidential administrations, included first-class citizenship for African-Americans. When he left office in 1953, he had set the United States on a course from which it would not veer in the future, and he had cast a long shadow across the country's twentieth-century history.

Suggestions for Further Reading

Origins of the Cold War and Policy Toward Europe

Stephen Ambrose, *Rise to Globalism*, 5th ed. (1988); Richard J. Barnet, *The Alliance* (1983); Scott L. Bills, *Empire and Cold War: The Roots of US–Third World Antagonism, 1945–47* (1990); Leonard Dinnerstein, *America and the Survivors of the Holocaust* (1982); John L. Gaddis, *The United States and the Origins of the Cold War, 1941–1947* (1972); James L. Gormly, *The Collapse of the Grand Alliance* (1987); Francis Harbutt, *The Iron Curtain* (1986); Michael Hogan, *The Marshall Plan* (1987); Laurence S. Kaplan, *The United States and NATO* (1984); Walter LaFeber, *America, Russia, and the Cold War, 1945–1984*, 5th ed. (1985); Melvyn Leffler, "The American Concept of National Security and the Beginnings of the Cold War, 1945–1948," *American Historical Review*, 89 (1984), 346–381; Alan Milward, *The Reconstruction of Western Europe* (1984); Thomas G. Paterson, *Meeting the Communist Threat* (1988); Thomas G. Paterson, *On Every Front: The Making of the Cold War* (1979); Thomas G. Paterson, *Soviet-American Confrontation* (1973); Thomas G. Paterson, ed., *Cold War Critics* (1971); Gaddis Smith, *Dean Acheson* (1972); William Taubman, *Stalin's American Policy* (1982); Imanuel Wexler, *The Marshall Plan Revisited* (1983); Daniel Yergin, *Shattered Peace* (1977).

Truman Doctrine, Containment, and the Middle East

John L. Gaddis, *Strategies of Containment* (1982); Howard Jones, *A New Kind of War* (1989); Bruce R. Kuniholm, *The Origins of the Cold War in the Near East* (1980); Deborah Larson, *Origins of Containment* (1985); William R. Louis, *The British Empire in the Middle East, 1945–1951* (1984); Aaron D. Miller, *Search for Security* (1980); Michael B. Stoff, *Oil, War, and American Security* (1980); Samuel F. Wells, Jr., "Sounding the Tocsin: NSC-68 and the Soviet Threat," *International Security*, 4 (1979), 116–158; Lawrence S. Wittner, *American Intervention in Greece, 1943–1949* (1982).

China, Japan, and Asia

Robert M. Blum, *Drawing the Line* (1982); Dorothy Borg and Waldo Heinrichs, eds., *Uncertain Years* (1980); Russell Buhite, *Soviet-American Relations in Asia, 1945–1954* (1982); Warren I. Cohen, *America's Response to China*, 2nd ed. (1980); Herbert Feis, *Contest over Japan* (1967); Akira Iriye, *The Cold War in Asia* (1974); E. J. Kahn, Jr., *The China Hands* (1975); Gary May, *China Scapegoat: The Diplomatic Ordeal of John Carter Vincent* (1979); Charles E. Neu, *The Troubled Encounter: The United States and Japan* (1975); Michael Schaller, *The American Occupation of Japan* (1985); William W. Stueck, Jr., *The Road to Confrontation: American Policy Toward China and Korea, 1947–1950* (1981); Christopher Thorne, *Allies of a Kind* (1978); Tang Tsou, *America's Failure in China, 1941–1950* (1963); Nancy B. Tucker, *Patterns in the Dust: Chinese-American Relations and the Recognition Controversy, 1949–1950* (1983).

Politics of the Truman Administration

Barton J. Bernstein, ed., *Politics and Policies of the Truman Administration* (1970); Robert J. Donovan, *Conflict and Crisis: The Presidency of Harry S Truman, 1945–1948* (1977); Andrew J. Dunar, *The Truman Scandals and the Politics of Morality* (1984); Alonzo L. Hamby, *Beyond the New Deal: Harry S Truman and American Liberalism* (1973); Donald R. McCoy, *The Presidency of Harry S Truman* (1984); William E. Pemberton, *Harry S Truman* (1989); Gary Reichard, *Politics as Usual* (1988).

The Truman Administration and the Economy

Jack Stokes Ballard, *The Shock of Peace: Military and Economic Demobilization After World War II* (1983); Richard O. Davies, *Housing Reform During the Truman Administration* (1966); R. Alton Lee, *Truman and Taft-Hartley* (1966); Arthur F. McClure, *The Truman Administration and the Problems of Postwar Labor* (1969); Allen J. Matusow, *Farm Policies and Politics in the Truman Years* (1967).

Civil Rights

William C. Berman, *The Politics of Civil Rights in the Truman Administration* (1970); Richard M. Dalfiume, *Desegregation* of the U.S. Armed Forces (1969); Donald R. McCoy and Richard T. Ruetten, *Quest and Response: Minority Rights and the Truman Administration* (1973); Mark V. Tushnet, *The NAACP's Legal Strategy Against Segregated Education* (1987); Jules Tygiel, *Baseball's Great Experiment: Jackie Robinson and His Legacy* (1983).

McCarthyism

David Caute, *The Great Fear* (1978); Larry Ceplair and Steven Englund, *The Inquisition in Hollywood* (1983); Robert Griffith, *The Politics of Fear: Joseph R. McCarthy and the Senate* (1970); Maurice Isserman, *If I Had a Hammer . . . : The Death of the Old Left and the Birth of the New Left* (1987); Stanley I. Kutler, *The American Inquisition* (1982); Victor Navasky, *Naming Names* (1980); William L. O'Neill, *A Better World: Stalinism and the American Intellectuals* (1983); David M. Oshinsky, *A Conspiracy So Immense: The World of Joe McCarthy* (1983); Richard Gid Powers, *Secrecy and Power: The Life of J. Edgar Hoover* (1987); Ronald Radosh and Joyce Milton, *The Rosenberg File* (1983); Thomas C. Reeves, *The Life and Times of Joe McCarthy* (1982); Walter and Miriam Schneir, *Invitation to an Inquest,* rev. ed. (1983); Ellen W. Schrecker, *No Ivory Tower: McCarthyism in the Universities* (1986); Athan Theoharis, *Seeds of Repression: Harry S Truman and the Origins of McCarthyism* (1971); Athan Theoharis and John Stuart Cox, *The Boss: J. Edgar Hoover and the Great American Inquisition* (1988); Allen Weinstein, *Perjury: The Hiss-Chambers Case* (1978).

The Korean War

Clay Blair, *The Forgotten War* (1988); Ronald J. Caridi, *The Korean War and American Politics* (1969); Bruce Cumings, *The Origins of the Korean War* (1980); Rosemary Foote, *The Wrong War* (1985); John Halliday and Bruce Cumings, *Korea: The Unknown War* (1989); Max Hastings, *The Korean War* (1987); Burton I. Kaufman, *The Korean War* (1986); Peter Lowe, *The Origins of the Korean War* (1986); Callum A. MacDonald, *Korea* (1987); Glenn D. Paige, *The Korean Decision* (1968); Michael Schaller, *Douglas MacArthur* (1989); Robert R. Simmons, *The Strained Alliance* (1975); John W. Spanier, *The Truman-MacArthur Controversy and the Korean War* (1959); Allen Whiting, *China Crosses the Yalu* (1960).

The signs of patriotism were everywhere. Whether scoring victories over Soviet athletes at the Olympics or marveling at the nation's powerful military machine, Americans celebrated their country as the best place on earth. And to trumpet that difference—the Presbyterian minister George M. Docherty sermonized on February 7, 1954—religion should be enlisted. With President Dwight D. Eisenhower sitting in his congregation that day, the Reverend Docherty implored political leaders to insert "under God" after "one nation" in the pledge of allegiance. The president agreed, and Congress hastened to make the change.

This episode conjoining religion, patriotism, and politics befitted the 1950s, an age of consensus. In that decade, Americans generally shared a belief in anticommunism and economic progress. Republican President Eisenhower, hardly the passive, ill-informed chief executive the Democrats tried to depict, was active in articulating the two beliefs and devising programs to satisfy them. But he moved cautiously and preferred a hidden-hand style to conspicuous displays of political arm-twisting.

Believing that Communists posed a mortal danger to the American system, the Eisenhower administration expanded Truman's loyalty program, endorsed restrictive legislation, and purged the State Department. The president was reluctant to confront directly Senator Joseph McCarthy, whose anti-Communist tactics proved reckless. To maintain economic growth, Eisenhower pursued staunchly Republican goals: a balanced budget, reduced government spending, lower taxes, low inflation, private enterprise, a return of power to the states, and modest federal efforts to stimulate economic development. Eisenhower officials did not attempt to roll back the New Deal and the Fair Deal. In fact, however reluctantly, they expanded the welfare state.

Holding to their consensus thinking, white Americans celebrated their economic system for providing a high standard of living. But recurrent recessions and continued poverty in the midst of plenty raised doubts that economic progress had bestowed its benefits on all. An infant civil rights movement especially challenged the consensus view. Not only were most blacks at the bottom of the economic ladder; they were also being denied

28

AN AGE OF FRAGILE CONSENSUS, 1953–1961

their constitutional rights. How would blacks be brought into the consensus? The president, Congress, southern whites, and black civil rights activists gave different answers as they debated the Supreme Court's 1954 *Brown* decision on desegregation.

In foreign affairs, Eisenhower essentially continued Truman's Cold War policies, applying the containment doctrine worldwide. To wage the Cold War, the administration relied on the threat of nuclear weapons and on interventions, some of them by the Central Intelligence Agency (CIA). Many of the CIA's covert operations were directed against governments in the Third World, where new states were emerging from colonialism into nationhood. Americans feared that revolutionary nationalism and unrest in Third World countries would be exploited by Communists linked to a Soviet-led international conspiracy. And Latin America nationalists, seeking to end their countries' economic dependency upon North Americans, challenged United States hegemony. The United States, then, intervened abroad not just to stop communism but also to protect American economic interests.

Consensus and the Politics of the Eisenhower Presidency

Smiling Ike, with his folksy style, displays of confusion, garbled syntax, and frequent escapes from the Oval Office to the golf course, fueled Democratic charges that he failed to lead—"the bland leading the bland." But it was not that simple. Dwight D. Eisenhower was no stranger to hard work. His style was to play down his political role and highlight his role as chief of state. Eisenhower relied considerably upon staff work, delegated authority to departments, and shied away from close involvement in the legislative process. Sometimes this meant that he was not well informed on details, giving the impression that he was out of touch with his own

government. But this very popular president was not out of touch at all.

During Eisenhower's presidency, most Americans clung to the status quo. Demand for reform was deemed by many to be both unnecessary and unpatriotic. The country was engaged in a moral struggle with communism, people believed, and during such a crusade one should support, not criticize, the government. The historian Henry Steele Commager regretted that he saw conformity everywhere— "the uncritical and unquestioning acceptance of America as it is." A weak minority on the left advocated checks on the political power of corporations, and a noisy minority on the right vilified the government for a supposedly wishy-washy campaign against communism. But both liberal Democrats and moderate Republicans avoided extremism, satisfied to be occupying "the vital center." Along with this attitude of conformity went trust in and respect for established authority. Americans, like their leaders, feared mass movements, even those with democratic goals like the civil rights movement, as threats to stability.

The Consensus Mood

Scholars of the 1950s who subscribed to the consensus proclaimed the "end of ideology" in America. Since the early twentieth century, historians had told the American story as one of conflict—rich against poor, North against South, farmer against industrialist and banker. They focused on rebellions, strikes, moral crusades, and wars. The consensus historians of the 1950s, on the other hand, wrote about stability, continuity, and cultural wholeness. Although they did not deny the existence of conflict in the nation's past, they ascribed it less to flaws in society than to psychologically disturbed personalities. Among the people whom historians like Richard Hofstadter identified as maladjusted were abolitionists, feminists, Populists, and progressive reformers. The consensus interpretation thus shifted the emphasis away from society's faults— slavery, sexism, political corruption—and placed it on the critics who demanded reform.

Consensus Historiography

In this age of consensus, President Eisenhower approached his duties with a philosophy of "dy-

IMPORTANT EVENTS

1952	Eisenhower elected president United States explodes the first H-bomb	**1957**	Eisenhower Doctrine Little Rock desegregation crisis Civil Rights Act *Sputnik* launched
1953	Stalin dies Rosenbergs executed Oppenheimer case Termination policy for Native Americans	**1958**	United States intervenes in Lebanon NASA established Quemoy-Matsu crisis again National Defense Education Act Adams resigns over scandal
1954	St. Lawrence Seaway project started *Brown* decision CIA intervention in Guatemala Quemoy-Matsu crisis Senate condemns Senator McCarthy	**1960**	Sit-in in Greensboro, North Carolina SNCC formed U-2 incident Kennedy elected president
1955	Montgomery bus boycott begins	**1961**	Eisenhower warns against "military-industrial complex"
1956	Highway Act Soviets invade Hungary Suez crisis Eisenhower re-elected		

namic conservatism," meaning that he would be "conservative when it comes to money and liberal when it comes to human beings." Eisenhower's was "an Administration representing business and industry," admitted Secretary of the Interior Douglas McKay. The president and his appointees gave priority to reducing the federal budget, but they did not always succeed. (Fixed costs, such as Social Security benefits, interests payments on the national debt, and veterans' pensions, always inhibit budget cutting efforts.) Eisenhower officials recognized that they could not dismantle New Deal and Fair Deal programs because doing so would have been politically impossible. However, the administration did try to remove the government from agriculture, but the effort failed. Despite several changes in federal farm price support policy, the government found

"Dynamic Conservatism"

itself spending more money and stockpiling increased amounts of surplus farm commodities.

Eisenhower made more headway with other issues. In 1954, Congress passed legislation to begin the St. Lawrence Seaway project—the construction of a canal between Montreal and Lake Erie. This inland waterway was intended to spur the economic development of the Midwest by linking the Great Lakes to the Atlantic Ocean. That year, too, Eisenhower signed into law amendments to the Social Security Act that raised benefits and added 7.5 million workers, largely self-employed farmers, to the program's coverage. The Housing Act of 1954, the first of many such measures during the decade, provided federal funds for the construction of houses for low-income families displaced by urban renewal projects. Congress also obliged the president in 1954 with tax reform that increased deductions and raised business depreciation allowances

On July 4, 1961, residents of a Chicago neighborhood posed in front of their flag-draped homes. Patriotism was a prominent characteristic of the age of consensus. *National Archives.*

and with the Atomic Energy Act, which granted private companies the right to own reactors and nuclear materials for the production of electric power.

The Eisenhower administration presided over a dramatic change in the lives of Native Americans. In 1953, Congress adopted *termination*: the liquidation of Indian reservations and an end to federal services. Another act of that year made Indians subject to state laws. Native Americans were not asked if they approved of these departures from policies established a century before. Eisenhower officials applauded the changes be-

Termination Policy for Native Americans

cause they would reduce federal costs and serve states' rights. Critics, including most Indians, denounced termination as another attempt to grab Indian lands and further exploit Native Americans. Between 1954 and 1960, the federal government withdrew its benefits from sixty-one tribes. About one in eight Indians abandoned their reservations. Many found themselves joining the ranks of the urban poor in low-paying jobs. By the time termination was halted in the 1960s, so much human tragedy had struck Native Americans that observers compared their plight to the distress their forebears had endured in the late nineteenth century.

In the 1954 congressional elections, voters

revealed that, although they still liked Ike, they remained loyal to the Democratic party. The Democrats gained control of both houses of Congress, and Lyndon B. Johnson became the new Senate majority leader. An energetic, pragmatic politician from Texas, he tried to work with the Republican White House to achieve legislation. A notable accomplishment was the Highway Act of 1956, which launched the largest public works program in American history. This law authorized the spending of $31 billion over the next thirteen years to build a 41,000-mile interstate highway system, intended to permit the military to move around the nation more easily and to assist commerce. The interstate highways invigorated the tourist industry and spurred the growth of the suburbs.

Interstate Highway System

Eisenhower suffered a heart attack in September 1955, but soon regained his strength and declared his intention to run again. The Democrats nominated Adlai E. Stevenson once more. Eisenhower won a landslide victory in 1956—35.6 million votes and 457 electoral votes to Stevenson's 26 million and 73. Still, the Democrats continued to dominate the Congress.

Election of 1956

Eisenhower faced rising federal expenditures in his second term, in part because of the tremendous expense of America's global activities. In the first three years of his presidency, he had managed to trim the budget, largely by controlling defense spending. But he discovered that he had to tolerate deficit spending to achieve his goals. In all, Eisenhower balanced only three of his eight budgets. One reason for the administration's resort to deficit spending was the need to cushion the impact of three recessions—in the years 1953–1954, 1957–1958, and 1960–1961. A sluggish economy and unemployment (it peaked in 1958 at 7.6 percent) also reduced the tax dollars collected by the federal government.

A series of setbacks in 1958 marked the low point for the administration. Besides a lingering recession, scandal unsettled the White House. The president's chief aide, Sherman Adams, resigned in September under charges of influence-

Setbacks of 1958

peddling. Then came large Republican losses in the 1958 congressional elections. The Democrats, helped by the Adams affair, economic slump, discontent among farmers, and their exaggerated claims that the administration had let the United States fall behind in the arms race, took the Senate 64 to 34 and the House 282 to 154. Often at odds with Congress, Eisenhower cast vetoes against the bills that he thought would plunge the nation into even greater debt, which stood at $286 billion by the end of 1960.

The Decline of McCarthyism

During Eisenhower's first term, one of the most vexing problems for the administration was the conduct of Senator Joseph R. McCarthy (see pages 499–500). The Wisconsin senator's no-holds-barred search for subversives in government turned up none, but it did affront political fair play, decency, and civil liberties. The president privately labeled McCarthy a "pimple on the path of progress," but he avoided directly confronting him. Eisenhower feared that a showdown would splinter the Republican party. Instead, the president spoke against unnamed "demagogues thirsty for personal power" and hoped the media and Congress would bring McCarthy down.

Eisenhower on McCarthy

While Eisenhower tried his quiet strategy to undermine the senator, his administration practiced its own brand of anticommunism. In 1953, Eisenhower broadened Truman's loyalty program and denied clemency to Julius and Ethel Rosenberg. The two, having received the death penalty for espionage, were then executed. Late that year, at the urging of the chairman of the Atomic Energy Commission, the president suspended the security clearance of J. Robert Oppenheimer, the celebrated physicist who had directed the atomic bomb proj-

Administration Anti-Communist Activities

ect at Los Alamos during the Second World War. Oppenheimer's "crimes" were not that he was either disloyal or a security risk, but rather that he could not remember well the details of a 1943 conversation with a friend on Soviet interest in atomic secrets and that he had opposed the government's crash program to develop the hydrogen bomb. In 1954, the Communist Control Act demonstrated that both liberals and conservatives shared the consensus on anticommunism. In effect making membership in the Communist party illegal, the measure passed the Senate unanimously and the House 265 to 2.

As for Senator McCarthy, he finally undercut himself by taking on the United States Army in front of millions of television viewers. At issue was the senator's wild accusation that the army was shielding and promoting Communists. The Army-McCarthy hearings, held by a Senate subcommittee in 1954, became a showcase for his abusive treatment of witnesses. McCarthy alternately ranted and, appearing drunk, slurred his words. Finally, after he had maligned a young lawyer who was not even involved in the hearings, Joseph Welch, counsel for the army, asked, "Have you no sense of decency, sir?" The gallery erupted in applause. In December 1954, in a 67-to-22 vote, the Senate condemned McCarthy, not for defiling the Bill of Rights, but for sullying the dignity of the Senate with his contemptuous behavior. He remained a senator, but exhaustion and alcohol took their toll. He died in 1957 at the age of forty-eight.

Army-McCarthy Hearings

President Eisenhower's reluctance to discredit McCarthy publicly gave the senator, other right-wing members of Congress, and some private and public institutions enough rein to divide and damage the nation and destroy the careers of many innocent people. Eisenhower's own government-sponsored McCarthyism demoralized and frightened federal workers, some of whom were driven from public service. The anti-Communist campaigns of the 1950s also discouraged people from freely expressing themselves and hence from debating critical issues of the time. Fear and a contempt for the Bill of Rights, in short, helped sustain the consensus.

An Awakened Civil Rights Movement

In May 1954, the NAACP won a historic victory that stunned the white South and encouraged blacks to challenge prejudice on several fronts. In *Brown* v. *Board of Education of Topeka*, the Supreme Court grouped cases from several states under one hearing. Written by Chief Justice Earl Warren, the Court's unanimous decision concluded that "in the field of public education the doctrine of 'separate but equal' has no place. Separate educational facilities are inherently unequal." Such facilities, Warren wrote, produced in black children "a feeling of inferiority . . . that may affect their hearts and minds in a way unlikely ever to be undone." Blacks were being "deprived of the equal protection of the laws guaranteed by the Fourteenth Amendment." A year later, the Court ordered the desegregation of schools "with all deliberate speed." This vague timetable encouraged the Southern states to resist.

Brown v. Board of Education of Topeka

Some border states quietly implemented the order, and Southern moderates advocated a gradual rollback of segregation. But the forces of resistance soon came to dominate, urging southern communities to defy the Court. Business and professional people created White Citizens' Councils for the express purpose of resisting the order. Known familiarly as "uptown Ku Klux Klans," the councils used their economic power against black civil rights activists. The Klan itself experienced another resurgence. One of the most effective resistance tactics was the enactment of state laws that paid tuition for white children who left public for private schools. In some cases, desegregated public schools were ordered closed.

Eisenhower, who personally disapproved of segregation, objected to "punitive or compulsory federal law." He also feared that the ugly public confrontations likely to follow rapid desegregation would jeopardize Republican inroads in the South. Thus, Eisenhower did not state forthrightly that the federal govern-

Eisenhower on Civil Rights

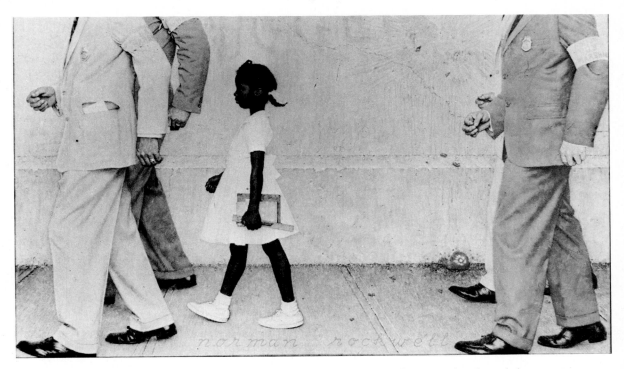

In 1957, escorted to school by federal marshals, black students in Little Rock, Arkansas, endured racial slurs, spittings, and other attempts at humiliation—three years after the Supreme Court's *Brown* decision against segregation in public schools. This depiction is by the noted illustrator Norman Rockwell. *Courtesy of the Norman Rockwell Museum at Stockbridge, MA. By permission of the Norman Rockwell Estate Licensing Company.*

ment would enforce the Court's decision as the nation's law. Instead, he spoke ambiguously and so encouraged massive resistance.

Dramatic events in Little Rock, Arkansas, forced the president to stop sidestepping the issue. In September 1957, Governor Orval E. Faubus intervened to halt a local plan for the gradual desegregation of Little Rock's Central High School. Faubus mobilized the Arkansas National Guard to block the entry of black students. Eisenhower made no effort to impede Faubus's actions. Late that month, after bowing to a federal judge's order, Faubus withdrew the guardsmen. As hundreds of jeering whites threatened to storm the school, eight black children slipped inside Central High. The next day, fearing violence, Eisenhower federalized the Arkansas National Guard and dispatched paratroopers to Little Rock to ensure the children's safety. Troops

Crisis in Little Rock, Arkansas

patrolled the school for the rest of the year, but in response, the Little Rock officials closed all public high schools in 1958 and 1959 rather than desegregate them.

Elsewhere, blacks did not wait for Supreme Court or White House decisions to claim equal rights. In December 1955, Rosa Parks, a seamstress, refused to give up her seat to a white man on a public bus in Montgomery, Alabama. Jim Crow practices required that blacks sit at the back of the bus and, when asked, surrender their seats to whites. Mrs. Parks's arrest ignited a yearlong black boycott of the city's bus system. In a stirring speech that launched the boycott, a protest leader, Martin Luther King, Jr., declared: "If we are wrong, the Constitution is wrong. If we are wrong, God Almighty is wrong. If we are wrong, Jesus of Nazareth was merely a utopian dreamer. . . . If we are wrong, justice is a lie."

Montgomery Bus Boycott

Martin Luther King, Jr., was an Atlanta-born, twenty-six-year-old Baptist minister who had recently earned a Ph.D. at Boston University. Disciplined and analytical, he insisted on nonviolent peaceful protest in the spirit of India's leader Mohandas Gandhi. Although he was jailed and a bomb blew out the front of his home, King persisted. What King gave to blacks was the "absence of fear," recalled black leader Bayard Rustin. In 1957, King became president of the Southern Christian Leadership Conference, organized to coordinate civil rights activities.

Martin Luther King, Jr.

With the aid of a 1956 Supreme Court decision that declared Alabama's Jim Crow laws unconstitutional, Montgomery blacks triumphed. They and others across the nation won again in 1957, when Congress passed the Civil Rights Act, which created the U.S. Commission on Civil Rights. This measure, like a voting rights act passed three years later, proved ineffective. Critics claimed that Washington was more interested in quieting the civil rights question than in addressing it.

African-Americans themselves tried new tactics. On February 1, 1960, four black students from North Carolina Agricultural and Technical College in Greensboro sat down at a department store lunch counter and ordered coffee. Though they were denied service and were verbally abused, they refused to budge. Thus began the sit-in movement, which spread from the South to the North, rolling back segregation in many public places. Inspired by the sit-ins, some activists met on Easter weekend in 1960 and organized the Student Nonviolent Coordinating Committee (SNCC). In the face of angry white mobs, SNCC members challenged the status quo.

The Sit-ins

Eisenhower-Dulles Foreign Policy and the Cold War

Dwight D. Eisenhower had had more experience in foreign affairs than in domestic affairs before he became president. He had lived and traveled in Europe, Asia, and Latin America. During the Second World War, General Eisenhower came to know Europe well, negotiated with world leaders, and made tough decisions of international consequence. After the war, he served as army chief of staff and NATO supreme commander and learned the essentials of nuclear weapons development and secret intelligence operations. Like most Americans, Eisenhower accepted the Cold War consensus about the threat of communism and the need for a global watch by the United States.

For the most part, Eisenhower and Secretary of State John Foster Dulles continued Truman's containment policy but introduced some memorable phrases to distinguish their administration from Truman's. Thinking containment too defensive a concept, Dulles invented *liberation*. (He did not, however, explain precisely how the countries of Eastern Europe could be freed from Soviet control.) *Massive retaliation* was the administration's phrase for the nuclear obliteration of the Soviet state or its assumed client, the People's Republic of China, if they took aggressive actions. The ability of the United States to make such a threat was thought to provide *deterrence,* or the prevention of hostile Soviet behavior.

Eisenhower-Dulles Policies

Related to both massive retaliation and deterrence was the *New Look* of the American military. Eisenhower and Dulles emphasized air power and nuclear weaponry and de-emphasized conventional forces. The president's preference for heavy weapons stemmed in part from his desire to trim the federal budget ("more bang for the buck" in the words of the time). With this huge military arsenal, the United States in the 1950s practiced *brinkmanship:* not backing down in a crisis, even if it meant taking the nation to the brink of war. Eisenhower also popularized the *domino theory*, according to which small, weak nations would fall to communism like a row of dominoes if they were not propped up by the United States. Adopting a globalist perspective on wrenching changes in the Third World, the Eisenhower administration conducted a diplomacy of holding the line—against the Soviet Union, Communist China, neutralism,

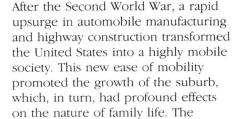

Leisure in America, **1950**

THE OPEN ROAD

After the Second World War, a rapid upsurge in automobile manufacturing and highway construction transformed the United States into a highly mobile society. This new ease of mobility promoted the growth of the suburb, which, in turn, had profound effects on the nature of family life. The privacy of suburban residences tended to separate individual families; as a result, recreation once again became essentially a family affair.

Even when families traveled, they traveled together in a car, an enforced proximity that was not without its stresses and strains. Norman Rockwell poked fun at family excursions in his 1947 painting *The Outing.* A happy family group drives off to the lake in frame one; frame two finds them heading home later that day in a state of considerably greater disrepair.

Previous page: Norman Rockwell, *The Outing,* 1947. Left: The Wigwam Motel, Holbrook, Arizona, built ca. 1955. Below: Randy's Donuts, Inglewood, California, built 1953.

Still, the automobile could introduce families to exotic and far-ranging pleasures. National parks, ocean resorts, and amusement parks drew many carloads of visitors. Roadside enterprises quickly adopted new guises to attract the tourists rolling by, and the sights seen during a journey soon became almost as entertaining as the destination itself.

Some highway businesses assumed wildly inventive forms. A Holbrook, Arizona, motel offered families the chance to spend the night in a room built in the shape of a wigwam. The fact that these concrete tepees fronted a busy highway seems not to have discouraged customers seeking an authentic Old West experience. And Randy's Donuts in Inglewood, California, found a rather impressive way of reminding hungry motorists that a doughnut might hit the spot.

Along with the automobile, another household possession introduced Americans to new landscapes: television quickly captured hearts and minds. In 1946, only 8,000 American families had a television set, but by 1950, 3.9 million families owned at least one. By 1960, that figure had climbed to 46.3 million.

Above: Toy bus, ca. 1955. Right: Buttons, ca. 1955. Below: Television set, ca. 1950.

The television broadcast industry swung into high gear in 1948; until 1958, most programming was live. Television shows had a profound impact on American fads and affections, and merchandisers jumped to capitalize on a show's popularity. Inspired by *The Jackie Gleason Show,* which ran from 1952 to 1970, a miniature "Honeymooners" bus featured Ralph Kramden at the wheel; Loudmouth, a June Taylor dancer, Poor Soul, and Reginald Van Gleason III peered from the passenger windows. (Reruns of "The Honeymooners" serial were still a staple of American television four decades after its debut.)

Children's television inspired countless toys, gadgets, and accessories. *Howdy Doody* starred a freckle-faced puppet and his human sidekick, Buffalo Bob, alongside a studio audience of noisy youngsters. Until its demise in 1960, the show entertained and instructed children for thirteen years. *The Mickey Mouse Club* aired from 1955 to 1959, five days a week. Its combination of cartoons, child performers, and adventure serials entranced young viewers so thoroughly that its theme song and a few of its stars became permanent fixtures of American popular culture.

Above: Chita Rivera in Broadway production
of *West Side Story,* 1957. Right: Album
covers, 1957–1959.

Although television lured away some of the
audiences for theatrical productions and movies,
these older forms of entertainment produced
their great successes in the 1950s. The Broadway
musical *West Side Story,* which opened in 1957,
melded romance, drama, singing, and dancing in
its contemporary reinterpretation of the Romeo
and Juliet story.

Finally, the introduction of inexpensive long-
playing records (LPs) in 1948 revolutionized the
music industry. Earlier 78s accommodated only
5 minutes of playing time per side. Now listeners
could enjoy as much as 20 minutes of music at
one sitting. Fans of artists like Pat Boone, Sarah
Vaughn, Rosemary Clooney, and Nat "King" Cole
rushed to buy records that played longer and
with higher fidelity.

communism, socialism, nationalism, and revolution everywhere.

After the death of Stalin in 1953, Eisenhower hoped for a relaxation in Soviet-American relations but instead witnessed alternating thaws and freezes.

Nuclear Arms Race The nuclear arms race accelerated as the two superpowers developed new military technology and nuclear delivery systems. In November 1952, the United States detonated the first hydrogen bomb. In March 1954, the biggest bomb the United States has ever tested destroyed the Pacific island of Bikini. This fifteen-megaton H-bomb was 750 times as powerful as the atomic bomb that leveled Hiroshima.

The Soviets, who tested their first H-bomb in 1953, shocked Americans in October 1957 by propelling the first man-made satellite, *Sputnik*, into outer space. Just two months earlier, Soviet technicians had fired the first intercontinental ballistic missile (ICBM). Americans now felt vulnerable to air attack and inferior to the Soviets in rocket technology. But the United States soon tested its own ICBMs. Moreover, it enlarged its fleet of long-range bombers (the B-52s) and deployed intermediate-range missiles in Europe targeted against the Soviet Union. By the end of 1960, Americans had also produced submarines that carried Polaris missiles. To ensure future technological advancement, the National Aeronautics and Space Agency (NASA) was created in 1958. That same year, Eisenhower signed the National Defense Education Act, establishing a program that loaned money to college students and provided funds for upgrading instruction in mathematics, the sciences, and foreign languages.

Through flights by the CIA's U-2 spy planes, American officials knew that the Soviets had deployed very few ICBMs. Yet critics charged that Eisenhower had allowed the United States to fall behind in the missile race. The "missile gap" was actually a false notion inspired in part by political partisanship. As the 1950s closed, the United States enjoyed overwhelming strategic dominance because of its "triad" of long-range bombers, submarine-launched ballistic missiles, and ICBMs.

Still, President Eisenhower grew increasingly uneasy about the arms race. He feared nuclear war, and the cost of the new weapons made it difficult to balance the budget. He also doubted the need for more and bigger nuclear weapons. How many times, he once asked, "could [you] kill the same man?" Spurred by such thoughts and by neutralist and Soviet appeals, the president cautiously initiated arms control proposals, such as his "open skies" proposal designed to reduce the chances for surprise attack. But because he did not trust the Soviets, arms control talks never became a top priority. To satisfy world opinion about radioactive fallout, however, the two powers unilaterally suspended atmospheric testing from late 1958 to the fall of 1961, when the Soviet Union resumed it. The United States began testing again at the same time, but underground.

As the nuclear arms race accelerated, the Soviet Union and the United States waged the Cold War. The year 1955 provided a brief respite from the intensity of the competition. The superpowers agreed to end their ten-year joint occupation of Austria, making it an independent neutral state. In addition, Eisenhower and Soviet leader Nikita Khrushchev journeyed to Geneva for high-level talks. This first summit meeting in ten years produced no important resolutions, but the conferees "disagreed so nicely," as one reporter put it.

Events in Eastern Europe soon returned the Cold War to its accustomed acrimony. In 1956, Khrushchev called for "peaceful coexistence" between capitalists and Communists,

Hungarian Uprising denounced Stalin, and suggested that Moscow would tolerate different brands of communism. Soon revolts against Soviet power erupted in Poland and Hungary. When a new Hungarian government announced that Hungary was withdrawing from the Soviet-dominated Warsaw Pact (formed in 1955), Moscow sent in troops. In November, Soviet soldiers and tanks battled students and workers in the streets of Budapest and crushed the rebellion. The Eisenhower administration found itself unable to aid the rebels without igniting a third world war. All the United States could do was to welcome Hungarian immigrants in greater numbers than American quota laws allowed.

Hardly had the turmoil in Eastern Europe subsided when the divided city of Berlin once again became a Cold War flash point. The Soviets were angry that American bombers capable of carrying nuclear warheads had been placed in West Germany. They were also upset that West Berlin had become an escape route for disaffected East Germans. In 1958, Khrushchev boldly announced that the Soviet Union would recognize East German control of all of Berlin unless East and West began talks on German reunification and rearmament. The Americans, unwilling to give up their hold on West Berlin, sought to strengthen West German ties with NATO. The two sides talked of war; finally Khrushchev backed away from his ultimatum, resolving to discuss the issue at future conferences.

Berlin and Germany were on the agenda of a summit meeting planned for Paris in May 1960. But two weeks before the conference, an American U-2 spy plane crashed 1,200 miles inside the Soviet Union. Moscow announced that it had been shot down. At first, Washington denied that its planes flew over Soviet territory, but Soviet officials exposed that lie by displaying the captured CIA pilot, Francis Gary Powers, his aircraft, and the pictures he had been snapping of Soviet military installations. Moscow demanded an apology, Washington refused, and the Soviets walked out of the Paris summit.

U-2 Incident

While West and East sparred over Europe, both kept a wary eye on the People's Republic of China (PRC). Despite growing evidence of a Sino-Soviet split, most American officials continued to think of communism as a unified world movement. The United States refused to open diplomatic relations with the Chinese government and continued to give aid to Jiang Jieshi (Chiang Kai-shek) on Formosa, which the People's Republic claimed as part of its territory. Washington worried about PRC calls for anti-imperialist rebellions in the Third World and its support for revolutionaries in Indochina (see Chapter 30).

Tense Sino-American Relations

In 1954 and 1955, a crisis brought the two nations to the brink of war. Just a few miles off the Chinese coast sat two tiny islands, Quemoy and Matsu, that Jiang's forces used as bases for com-

Quemoy and Matsu

mando raids against the PRC. In the fall of 1954, China bombarded the islands. Eisenhower decided to defend the outposts and let it be known that he was considering the use of nuclear weapons. Massive retaliation over such an insignificant issue? "Let's keep the Reds guessing," advised John Foster Dulles. But what if they guessed wrong? asked critics. Congress passed the Formosa Resolution (1955), which authorized the president to send troops to Formosa and adjoining islands. Two years later, the United States installed on Formosa missiles capable of carrying nuclear warheads. In 1958, war again loomed over Quemoy and Matsu. The crisis passed, but American defense of the islands became an issue in the election of 1960 at home.

Interventions in the Third World

Other challenges increasingly drew the Eisenhower administration's attention and resources. In the 1940s, as a result of changes wrought by the Second World War, a cavalcade of new nations began to alter the international community. From 1943 to 1989, ninety-six countries cast off their colonial bonds, twenty-four of them during the Eisenhower years (see map).

These profound stirrings arose in what is now known as the Third World, a general term applied to the parts of the global community belonging to neither of the other two "worlds": the United States and its allies in the capitalist "West" and the Soviet Union and its allies in the Communist "East." Third World nations on the whole are nonwhite, nonindustrialized, and located in the southern half of the globe—Asia, Africa, the Middle East, and Latin America. With Cold War lines drawn fairly tightly in Europe by the early 1950s, Soviet-American rivalry shifted increasingly to the Third World. Much was at stake. Third World nations possessed strategic raw materials. They also attracted foreign investment and provided markets, especially for American products and technology. The great powers

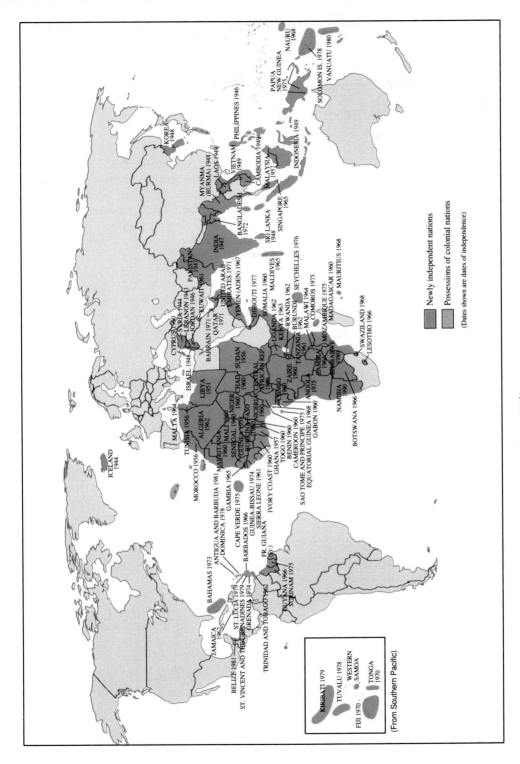

The Rise of the Third World: Newly Independent Nations Since 1943

ICELAND 1944

MOROCCO 1956
TUNISIA 1956
ALGERIA 1962
MALTA 1964
CYPRUS 1960
SYRIA 1944
LEBANON 1943
JORDAN 1946
ISRAEL 1948
KUWAIT 1961
BAHRAIN 1971
QATAR 1971
UNITED ARAB EMIRATES 1971
YEMEN (ADEN) 1967
LIBYA 1951

KOREA 1948
MYANMA (BURMA) 1948
LAOS 1949
VIETNAM 1949
PHILIPPINES 1946
CAMBODIA 1949
MALAYSIA 1957
INDONESIA 1949
SINGAPORE 1965

PAPUA NEW GUINEA 1975
NAURU 1968
SOLOMON IS. 1978
VANUATU 1980

INDIA 1947
PAKISTAN 1947
BANGLADESH 1972
SRI LANKA 1948
MALDIVES 1965

MAURITANIA 1960
MALI 1960
NIGER 1960
CHAD 1960
SENEGAL 1960
GAMBIA 1965
GUINEA-BISSAU 1974
GUINEA 1958
BURKINA FASO
SIERRA LEONE 1961
IVORY COAST 1960
GHANA 1957
TOGO 1960
BENIN 1960
NIGERIA 1960
CAMEROON 1960
SAO TOME AND PRINCIPE 1975
EQUATORIAL GUINEA 1968
GABON 1960
CENTRAL AFRICAN REP.
SUDAN 1956
SOMALIA 1960
DJIBOUTI 1977
UGANDA 1962
KENYA 1963
RWANDA 1962
BURUNDI 1962
TANZANIA 1961
MALAWI 1964
COMOROS 1975
MADAGASCAR 1960
MAURITIUS 1968
SEYCHELLES 1976
CONGO 1960
ZAIRE 1960
ANGOLA 1975
ZAMBIA 1964
MOZAMBIQUE 1975
ZIMBABWE 1980
NAMIBIA 1990
BOTSWANA 1966
SWAZILAND 1968
LESOTHO 1966

CAPE VERDE 1975

ANTIGUA AND BARBUDA 1981
DOMINICA 1978
BAHAMAS 1973
BARBADOS 1966
JAMAICA 1962
BELIZE 1981
ST. LUCIA 1979
ST. VINCENT AND THE GRENADINES 1979
GRENADA 1974
TRINIDAD AND TOBAGO 1962
FR. GUIANA (Fr.)
GUYANA 1966
SURINAM 1975

(From Southern Pacific)

KIRIBATI 1979
TUVALU 1978
FIJI 1970
WESTERN SAMOA
TONGA 1970

Newly independent nations

Possessions of colonial nations

(Dates shown are dates of independence)

looked to these new states for support in the United Nations and for sites to be used as military and intelligence bases.

Many Third World states, like India, Ghana, and Egypt, did not wish to take sides in the contest between the great powers. To the dismay of both Washington and Moscow, they proudly declared themselves neutral, or nonaligned, in the Cold War. Dulles declared neutralism immoral, a first step along the road to communism.

If this negative view of neutralism inhibited United States efforts to strengthen its links with the Third World, so did America's domestic race relations. In August 1955, the ambassador from India sat down in a restaurant at the Houston International Airport. Texas law, however, required that whites and blacks be served in separate dining facilities. The dark-skinned diplomat, who had seated himself in a white-only area, was told to move. The insult stung deeply and was not soon forgotten.

American Racism as a Handicap

Because such embarrassments were not uncommon in the 1950s, Dulles complained that segregationist practices were becoming a "major international hazard," a threat to United States efforts to gain the friendship of Third World countries. Americans stood publicly condemned as a people who did not honor the ideal of equality. Thus, when the attorney general appealed to the Supreme Court to strike down segregation in public schools, he stated that racial discrimination "furnished grist for the Communist propaganda mills."

United States hostility toward revolution also obstructed the American quest for influence in the Third World. Despite its own history, the United States has been uncomfortable with and openly hostile toward significant twentieth-century revolutions. Although Americans in the 1950s paid lip service to the Spirit of '76, they were intolerant of revolutionary disorder—in part because Third World revolutions were directed against their Cold War allies, but also because such upheavals threatened American investments, markets, and military bases. During rev-

American Intolerance of Revolution

olutionary crises, therefore, the United States usually threw its support to its European allies or to the conservative propertied classes in the Third World.

Still another obstacle in America's relations with the rising Third World was the country's great wealth. Foreigners both envied and resented the "people of plenty." American products drew attention at international trade fairs and were coveted items at native marketplaces. Finally, many foreign peoples resented the ample profits that American corporations extracted from them. For all these reasons, the United States often found itself not the model of revolution, but the target.

The Soviet Union enjoyed only a slight edge, if any, in the race to win friends in the Third World. It was true that Communist ideology encouraged anticolonialism and that the Soviet Union was free of association with the long years of Western European imperialism. But though Moscow kept up a heavy drumbeat of propaganda, it could not easily explain away its subjugation of Eastern European countries. The Soviet invasion of Hungary in 1956 earned Russia international condemnation. Khrushchev toured India and Burma in the mid-1950s, but those nations refused to become Soviet clients. They were not about to replace one imperial master with another. Like Americans, the Soviets ultimately concluded that Third World nations were playing the two superpowers against each other in order to garner larger amounts of aid and arms.

Obstacles to Soviet Influence

Americans nonetheless often interpreted Third World anti-imperialism, political instability, and attacks on foreign-owned property as Soviet inspired, rather than as profound expressions of nationalism or internal racial, class, religious, and ethnic divisiveness. American leaders either simplistically labeled radicals, nationalists, reformers, and neutralists as Communists or assumed that they were susceptible to Communist influence. To thwart these presumed enemies, the United States resorted to alignments with undemocratic but friendly regimes.

The United States also utilized the CIA to meet Third World challenges. In the 1950s and later, the

CIA bribed foreign politicians, subsidized foreign newspapers, hired mercenaries, conducted sabotage, sponsored labor unions, dispensed "disinformation" (false information), plotted the assassination of foreign leaders like Cuba's Fidel Castro, and staged coups. The CIA helped overthrow the governments of Iran (1953) and Guatemala (1954) but failed in attempts to topple regimes in Indonesia (1958) and Cuba (1961). The CIA and other parts of the American intelligence community followed the principle of "plausible deniability": covert operations should be conducted and the decisions that launched them concealed so that the president could deny any knowledge of them. Thus, President Eisenhower denied the United States role in Guatemala, even though he ordered the operation.

CIA Covert Operations

In Latin America, long a United States sphere of influence, where poverty, overpopulation, illiteracy, economic sluggishness, and foreign exploitation fed discontent, anti-American feelings grew. In 1951 the leftist Jacobo Arbenz Guzmán was elected president of Guatemala, a poor country whose largest landowner was the American-owned United Fruit Company. United Fruit was a major force throughout Latin America. To fulfill his promise of land reform, Arbenz expropriated United Fruit's uncultivated land and offered compensation. United Fruit dismissed the offer and began to rally official Washington against what the company called a Communist threat to Guatemala.

CIA in Guatemala

United States officials cut off aid to Guatemala, and the CIA began a secret plot to subvert its government. When Arbenz learned that the CIA was working against him, he turned to Moscow, thus reinforcing American suspicions. The CIA airlifted arms into Guatemala, dropping them at United Fruit facilities, and in June 1954, CIA-supported Guatemalans struck from Honduras. American planes bombed the capital; the invaders drove Arbenz from power; and the new pro-American regime returned United Fruit's land. Latin Americans wondered what had happened to the Good Neighbor policy.

In the Middle East, the Eisenhower administration also confronted challenges to United States influence. American stakes there included the survival of the Jewish state of Israel and extensive oil holdings. Oil-rich Iran was a special friend, for the ruling shah had granted American oil companies a 40-percent interest in a new petroleum consortium in return for CIA help in the overthrow of his rival, Mohammed Mossadegh (1953).

American Interests in the Middle East

The major threat to American interests in the Middle East came from Egypt, where the Arab nationalist Gamal Abdul Nasser rose to power determined to push the British out of the Suez Canal Zone and the Israelis out of Palestine. The United States was caught in a double bind. It did not wish to anger the Arabs, for fear of losing oil holdings. Nor did it wish to lose its ally Israel, which was supported at home by a vocal Jewish-American lobby. But when Nasser declared neutrality in the Cold War, Dulles lost patience with him. In July 1956, American officials withdrew their offer to help finance the Aswan Dam, a project to provide inexpensive electricity and water for thirsty Egyptian farmlands. Nasser quickly nationalized the British-owned Suez Canal, intending to use its profits to build the dam.

Fearing interruption of the Middle East oil trade, from which Western Europe received 75 percent of its oil, the British and French conspired with Israel to bring down Nasser. On October 29, 1956, the Israelis invaded the Suez, joined two days later by Britain and France. Eisenhower, who had not been consulted, fumed. He bluntly told London, Paris, and Tel Aviv to pull out. The troops withdrew; Egypt paid $81 million for the canal; and the Soviets built the Aswan Dam.

In early 1957, in an effort to improve the deteriorating Western position in the Middle East and protect American interests there, the president proclaimed what became known as the Eisenhower Doctrine. The United States would intervene in the Middle East, he said, if any government threatened by a Communist takeover

Eisenhower Doctrine

Vice President Richard M. Nixon's "goodwill tour" of Latin America, in the spring of 1958, frequently aroused anti–United States demonstrations. In Caracas, Venezuela, protesters surrounded his automobile and threatened his life—providing yet another example of growing anti-Americanism in the Third World. *The Bettmann Archive.*

asked for help. Fourteen thousand American troops scrambled ashore in Lebanon the next year to quell an internal political dispute. Some critics protested that the United States was wrongfully acting as the world's policeman. Others complained that Eisenhower had failed miserably to thwart challenges to American power or win Cold War allies in the Third World.

The Election of 1960 and the Eisenhower Record

The election of 1960 was one of the closest and most spirited in the twentieth century. Although

Democratic candidate John F. Kennedy shared the two fundamental tenets of the **John F.** 1950s consensus, he asserted that **Kennedy** he could expand the benefits of economic progress and win foreign disputes through more vigorous leadership. People often contrasted his youth (forty-three years old) with Eisenhower's age (seventy years old). Handsome and intelligent, Kennedy was born to wealth, graduated from Harvard, and served as a congressman before joining the Senate in 1953. His running mate in 1960 was Senator Lyndon B. Johnson of Texas, who was added to the ticket to hold white southerners in the Democratic party as the civil rights issue heated up. Republican candidate Richard M. Nixon, the forty-seven-year-old vice president from California, and his running mate,

Ambassador Henry Cabot Lodge of Massachusetts, expected a rugged campaign.

Kennedy, exploiting the media to great advantage, ran a risky, yet ultimately brilliant, race. Knowing his major liability was his Roman Catholicism, he addressed that issue head-on. He traveled to the Bible Belt to tell a group of Houston ministers that he respected the separation of church and state and would take his orders from the American people, not the pope. Seeing a major opportunity in the black vote, and calculating that Johnson could keep the white South loyal to the Democrats, Kennedy appealed to black voters. A major asset to Kennedy was the unsavory image that Nixon presented in the nation's first televised debate between presidential candidates; he came across as surly and heavy-jowled. Nixon was also hurt by the tepid endorsement he received from Eisenhower.

How and Why Kennedy Beat Nixon

Foreign policy became a major issue. Nixon claimed that because Kennedy lacked experience in foreign affairs he could not stand up to Khrushchev. Kennedy shot back, "I was not the Vice President of the United States who presided over the Communization of Cuba." Kennedy hit hard on Cuba, while Nixon played on the senator's statement that Quemoy and Matsu were not worth defending. Kennedy's most effective theme was that Eisenhower and Nixon had let American prestige and power slip. The Democratic candidate offered Cold War victory instead of stalemate, and he vowed to secure Third World countries as allies.

In an election that saw the highest voter participation (62.8 percent) in half a century, Kennedy defeated Nixon by the razor-slim margin of 118,000 votes. The electoral college margin, 303 to 219, was much closer than the numbers suggest. Slight shifts in the popular vote in Illinois and Texas, two states where electoral fraud may have helped produce narrow Democratic majorities, would have made Nixon president. Although Kennedy's Catholicism lost him votes, especially in the Midwest, it also gained him about 80 percent of Catholic voters. Religious bigotry did not decide the election, and Kennedy became the first Roman Catholic president.

Just before leaving office in early 1961, Eisen-hower issued a warning to the nation. Because of the Cold War, he observed, the United States had been "compelled to create a permanent industry of vast proportions," as well as a standing army of 3.5 million. "Now this conjunction of an immense military establishment and a large arms industry is new in the American experience." In it, he went on, resides the "potential for the disastrous rise of misplaced power." The demands of national security, he said, had created a powerful interest group that threatened the very existence of liberty. No doubt Eisenhower was thinking about a 1960 congressional report that showed that there were 1,400 retired military officers above the rank of major, including 261 generals and admirals, employed by the one hundred leading defense contractors. Eisenhower urged Americans to guard against the "military-industrial complex." They did not.

The "Military-Industrial Complex"

Assessments of the Eisenhower administration used to emphasize its conservatism, passive style, limited achievements, and hesitancy to confront difficult issues. They pointed to Eisenhower's reluctance to take strong stands, keep abreast of events, or inspire needed reforms.

Eisenhower Presidency Assessed

In recent years, scholars have been researching in the now declassified documents of the consensus era, and interpretations are changing. Many have begun to stress Eisenhower's influential style, command of policymaking, sensibly moderate approach to most problems, political savvy, and great popularity. Many historians now argue that he was not an aging bystander in the 1950s but a competent, pragmatic, compassionate leader.

The record of Eisenhower's presidency is mixed. At home, he failed to deal with problems that would wrack the country in the next decade: racism, poverty, urban decay. He dragged his feet on civil rights. He exacerbated the damage done by McCarthyism by refusing to come down hard on the reckless senator, and the president's own loyalty program was excessive. The economy suffered recessions and a growth rate of only 2.5 percent. Eisenhower never solved the farm problem, and he never moved his party to the moderate Republicanism that he championed. In foreign policy, he found no way to relax Cold War tensions, and in the end, he accelerated the nuclear arms race that he so disliked. He unleashed the CIA upon the Third World and failed to adjust American diplomacy to the immense changes there. On the other hand, in comparison with his successors, Eisenhower was cautious. He kept military budgets under control and managed crises so that the United States avoided major military ventures abroad. Americans respected him.

Suggestions for Further Reading

An Age of Fragile Consensus

Paul A. Carter, *Another Part of the Fifties* (1983); John Diggins, *The Proud Decades: 1941–1960* (1989); Ronald Lora, *Conservative Minds in America* (1971); Elaine T. May, *Homeward Bound: American Families in the Cold War Era* (1988); George H. Nash, *The Conservative Intellectual Movement in America* (1976); William O'Neill, *American High* (1986); Richard H. Pells, *The Liberal Mind in a Conservative Age* (1985); Alan M. Wald, *The New York Intellectuals* (1987).

Eisenhower and the Politics of the 1950s

Stephen E. Ambrose, *Eisenhower: The President* (1984); Piers Brendon, *Ike* (1986); Robert F. Burk, *Dwight D. Eisenhower* (1986); Larry W. Burt, *Tribalism in Crisis: Federal Indian Policy, 1953–1961* (1982); Barbara B. Clowse, *Brainpower for the Cold War: The Sputnik Crisis and the National Defense Education Act of 1958* (1981); Donald L. Fixico, *Termination and Relocation: Federal Indian Policy, 1945–1970* (1986); Richard Fried, *Nightmare in Red* (1990); Fred I. Greenstein, *The Hidden-Hand Presidency* (1982); Peter Lyons, *Eisenhower* (1974); Herbert Parmet, *Eisenhower and the American Crusades* (1972); Herbert Parmet, *Richard Nixon and His America* (1990); Nicol C. Rae, *The Decline and Fall of the Liberal Republicans* (1989); Gary W. Reichard, *Politics as Usual* (1988); Gary W. Reichard, *The Reaffirmation of Republicanism* (1975).

The Civil Rights Movement and Martin Luther King, Jr.

Numan V. Bartley, *The Rise of Massive Resistance* (1969); John Bloom, *Class, Race, & the Civil Rights Movement* (1987); Taylor Branch, *Parting the Waters: America in the King Years, 1954–1963* (1988); Robert F. Burk, *The Eisenhower Administration and Black Civil Rights* (1984); William H. Chafe, *Civilities and Civil Rights* (1980) (on the Greensboro sit-in); Charles W. Eagles, ed., *The Civil Rights Movement in America* (1986); David J. Garrow, *Bearing the Cross* (1986) (on King and SCLC); Elizabeth Huckaby, *Crisis at Central High, Little Rock, 1957–1958* (1980); Richard Kluger, *Simple Justice* (1975) (on the Brown decision); Robert J. Norrell, *Reaping the Whirlwind: The Civil Rights Movement in Tuskegee* (1985); Stephen B. Oates, *Let the Trumpet Sound* (1982) (on King); Howell Raines, *My Soul Is Rested* (1977); Harvard Sitkoff, *The Struggle for Black Equality, 1954–1980* (1981); Robert Weisbrot, *Freedom Bound* (1990).

Eisenhower-Dulles Foreign Policy

Michael Beschloss, *MAYDAY* (1986) (on the U-2 crisis); Henry W. Brands, Jr., *Cold Warriors* (1988); Blanche W. Cook, *The Declassified Eisenhower* (1981); Robert A. Divine, *Eisenhower and the Cold War* (1981); Michael Guhin, *John Foster Dulles* (1972); Townsend Hoopes, *The Devil and John Foster Dulles* (1973); Richard Immerman, ed., *John Foster Dulles and the Diplomacy of the Cold War* (1990); Burton I. Kaufman, *Trade and Aid* (1982); Richard A. Melanson and David A. Mayers, ed., *Reevaluating Eisenhower* (1986).

Nuclear Arms Race

Howard Ball, *Justice Downwind: America's Nuclear Testing Program in the 1950s* (1986); Paul Boyer, *By the Bomb's Early Light* (1986); Robert A. Divine, *Blowing in the Wind: The Nuclear Test Ban Debate, 1954–1960* (1978); Lawrence Freedman, *The Evolution of Nuclear Strategy*, 2nd ed. (1990); Gregg Herken, *Counsels of War* (1985); Richard G. Hewlett and Jack M. Hall, *Atoms for Peace and War, 1953–1961* (1989); Jerome Kahan, *Security in the Nuclear Age* (1975); Walter A. McDougall, *. . . The Heavens and the Earth* (1985); Michael Mandelbaum, *The Nuclear Question* (1979); Richard Smoke, *National Security and the Nuclear Dilemma* (1988).

The United States and the Third World

Richard J. Barnet, *Intervention and Revolution*, rev. ed. (1972); Chester L. Cooper, *The Lion's Last Roar: Suez, 1956* (1978); Richard Immerman, *The CIA in Guatemala* (1982); Gabriel Kolko, *Confronting the Third World* (1988); Walter LaFeber, *Inevitable Revolutions* (1983); William Roger Lewis and Roger Owen, eds., *Suez 1956* (1989); Gail E. Meyer, *Egypt and the United States* (1980); Stephen G. Rabe, *Eisenhower and Latin America* (1988).

"The remarkable thing," recalled Chuck Faust, "was that I had never expected to do anything other than follow in my father's footsteps as a farmer in central Kansas." But when Chuck was seventeen years old, a historic event changed his life forever: Pearl Harbor. The following spring, just days after graduating from Salina High School, Chuck enlisted in the army.

When Chuck Faust returned home in 1945, his mind was fixed not on farming but on college. While overseas, he had read about the GI Bill, which would pay living expenses and tuition for college-bound veterans. Soon after being discharged from the army, Chuck married his high school sweetheart, Annie Kempton, and the two moved to Lawrence, Kansas. For the next four years, the Fausts lived in a leftover Quonset hut near the University of Kansas campus. By graduation time, their first child, an early member of the postwar baby boom, had been born.

Like many Americans, Chuck and Annie Faust were determined to succeed so that their children could grow up in grassy suburban yards and attend good public schools. By the end of the 1950s, the Fausts had added three more children to their family. Moreover, Chuck's income had enabled them to buy a comfortable home in a Kansas City suburb. The Fausts and their baby-boom children had joined the suburban middle class.

29

AMERICAN SOCIETY DURING THE BABY BOOM, 1945–1964

Material comfort was the hallmark of the postwar middle classes. Whether considered in terms of income levels or life styles, more Americans were better off than ever before—and most counted on their good fortune to continue. The baby boom was the most obvious expression of postwar optimism. From 1946 through 1964, 75.9 million babies were born in the United States, compared with only 44.4 million during the period of depression and war from 1929 through 1945.

Beginning with its vast size, this generation of newborns was different. For example, as parents were rearing these millions of children, "family togetherness" took on almost religious significance. Moreover, as this age group grew older, it had a successive impact on housing, elementary and secondary education, fads and popular music, higher education, and the adult job market.

Fueling Americans' postwar optimism was the twenty-five-year economic boom that began in 1946. Its cornerstones were the automobile, housing, and defense industries. To many people, it seemed that the American dream had come true. Even though the nation's economic progress was disrupted four times by recessions (1950, 1953, 1957, and 1959–1960), most Americans enjoyed an increasingly comfortable standard of living throughout this period. Whatever the nation's shortcomings, Americans boasted that they enjoyed political self-determination through the vote and social mobility through the melting pot. And public education guaranteed a better life to all who were willing to study and work hard.

The exceptions to the dream went unnoticed by most Americans. The lack of equal opportunities for women was concealed by an emphasis on femininity, piety, and family togetherness. Affluent families ignored evidence of poverty in society by indulging in their own pleasures and pursuing numerous ways to enjoy their leisure time. Yet in the early 1960s, nearly one of every four Americans was poor. Not until the publication of Michael Harrington's *The Other America* in 1962 did people become aware of this contradiction in their midst.

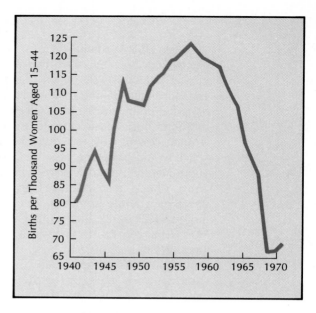

Birthrate, 1940–1970 *Source: Adapted from U.S. Bureau of the Census,* Historical Statistics of the United States, Colonial Times to 1970, *Bicentennial Edition (Washington, D.C.: U.S. Government Printing Office, 1975), p. 49.*

The Postwar Booms: Business and Babies

As Americans entered the postwar era, many wondered whether it would resemble another postwar epoch, the Roaring Twenties. Most Americans expected a replay not of the 1920s, however, but of the 1930s. After all, it was the war that had created jobs and prosperity; surely, the end of war would bring a slump.

Neither prediction came true. In 1945, the United States entered one of its longest, steadiest periods of growth and prosperity. The keys to this success were increasing output and increasing demand. Between 1945 and 1970, the American economy grew at an average rate of 3.5 percent per year. Even with occasional recessions, the gross national product seldom faltered, rising from just under $210 billion in 1946 to almost $1 trillion in 1970.

When the economy produced more, Americans

generally brought home bigger paychecks and had more money to spend. Between 1946 and 1950, per capita real income rose 5.9 percent—but that was only the beginning. In the 1950s, it jumped another 15.2 percent; in the 1960s, the increase was even greater—31.7 percent. The result was a noticeable increase in the standard of living. To the vast majority of Americans, such prosperity was a vindication of the American system of free enterprise.

Increased Purchasing Power

The baby boom was both a cause and an effect of prosperity. In 1950, 3.5 million babies were born, a sizable jump from the 2.5 million born in 1940. It was natural for the birthrate to soar immediately after the Second World War. What was unusual was that it continued to do so throughout the late 1940s and 1950s (see figure), reversing the downward trend in birthrates that had prevailed for 150 years.

Baby Boom

The baby boom spelled business for builders, manufacturers, and school systems. "Take the 3,548,000 babies born in 1950," wrote Sylvia F. Por-

IMPORTANT EVENTS

1946	Beginning of the baby boom Spock, *Baby and Child Care* More than 1 million GIs enroll in colleges
1948	Kinsey, *Sexual Behavior in the Human Male*
1949	National Housing Act
1952	Peale, *The Power of Positive Thinking* Ellison, *Invisible Man*
1953	Kinsey, *Sexual Behavior in the Human Female*
1955	Salk polio vaccine approved for use AFL-CIO merger *Rebel Without a Cause*
1956	Highway Act Ginsberg, *Howl*
1957	Soviet Union launches *Sputnik* Kerouac, *On the Road*
1958	National Defense Education Act
1962	Harrington, *The Other America*
1970	Gross national product reaches $977.1 billion

ter in her syndicated newspaper column. "Bundle them into a batch, bounce them all over the bountiful land that is America. What do you get?" Porter's answer: "Boom. The biggest, boomiest boom ever known in history. Just imagine how much these extra people, these new markets, will absorb. . . . Our factories must expand just to keep pace."

Of the three cornerstones of the postwar economic boom, two were related to the upsurge in births. The first was a construction boom to provide houses and schools for all these children. Office buildings, shopping centers, factories, airports, and stadiums also sprang up across the country. Much of this construction took place in suburbs. The postwar suburbanization of America would have been impossible without the second cornerstone, automobile manufacturing, for in the sprawling new communities a car was a necessity.

Auto Sales

The third cornerstone of the postwar economic boom was military spending. When the Defense Department was established in 1949, the nation was spending just over $13 billion a year on defense. By 1953, the Defense Department's budget was more than $50 billion. Except for a short dip from 1954 to 1956, it has been going up

Military Spending

ever since. Some of the money spent on defense went into weapons research.

The invention of the transistor in 1948 inaugurated the computer revolution and stunning advances in electronics. Businesses and governments were so eager to buy electronic data-processing machines that sales zoomed from $25 million in 1953 to $1 billion in 1960. By the early 1960s, thousands of computers had been produced and sold.

The evolution of electronics was a trade-off for the American people. Computers brought about a rapid rise in productivity through the automation of numerous industries. But in doing so, they stimulated technological unemployment. The spread of electronic technology also promoted the concentration of ownership in industry. Sophisticated technology was expensive to develop or purchase. Often, only large corporations could afford it; small corporations were shut out of the market. Indeed, large corporations with capital and experience in high-technology fields expanded into related industries.

Not all expansion was a matter of diversification into related fields. Beginning in the early 1950s, a third great merger wave swept American business. But unlike the first two waves, in the 1890s and

Babies meant big business for companies that produced baby foods, toys, and clothing. "In its first year as a consumer," read the caption for this 1958 *Life* photo, "baby is a potential market for $800 worth of products." *Yale Joel,* Life *magazine,* © *1958 Time Warner, Inc.*

Conglomer-ate Mergers 1920s, which tended toward vertical and horizontal integration respectively, the new wave was distinguished by conglomerate mergers. A *conglomerate* merged companies in totally unrelated fields as a hedge against instability in a particular market or industry. The new wave of mergers resulted in unprecedented concentration of industry.

Even the labor movement experienced a merger. In 1955, the American Federation of Labor and the Congress of Industrial Organizations put aside their differences and established the AFL-CIO. Union membership remained fairly constant, however, increasing from just under 18 million at the time of the merger to only 20.7 million fifteen years later. Most new jobs were opening up not in the heavy industries that hired blue-collar workers, but in the union-resistant white-collar service trades.

The postwar economic boom was a good time for unionized blue-collar workers, many of whom not only benefited from real increases in wages, but also enjoyed a middle-class life

Union Workers' Benefits style, which until then had been the exclusive province of white-collar workers, businesspeople, and professionals. Because most union jobs paid well, these workers could obtain mortgages for suburban homes, especially if their spouses were also employed. Many enjoyed job security, paid vacations, and retirement plans. And they were more secure against inflation. In 1948, General Motors and the United Auto Workers agreed on automatic cost-of-living adjustments

(COLAS) in workers' wages, a practice that spread to other industries.

The trend toward economic consolidation brought changes in agriculture, as well as in business and labor. While new machines such as **Agricultural Consolidation** mechanical cotton, tobacco, and grape pickers and crop-dusting planes revolutionized farming methods, the increased use of fertilizers and pesticides raised the total value of farm output from $28.8 billion in 1946 (in constant dollars) to $54.2 billion in 1970. Meanwhile, labor productivity tripled. The resulting improvement in profitability drew large investors into agriculture. By the 1960s, it took money—sometimes big money—to become a farmer. In many cases, only banks, insurance companies, and other large businesses could afford the necessary land, machinery, and fertilizer.

By no means did all the effects of economic growth benefit the average American. In agriculture, the movement toward consolidation threatened the survival of the family farm. From 1945 to 1970, the nation's farm population declined from 24.4 million to just under 10 million. When the harvesting of cotton in the South was mechanized in the 1940s and 1950s, more than 4 million people were displaced. One result was a shift of this poverty to the North and the cities.

The significant changes that postwar growth produced in industry and agriculture were matched by changes in Americans' buying habits and life styles. For many Americans, the postwar economic boom brought what the economist John Kenneth Galbraith called the affluent society.

The Affluent Society

As America's productivity grew by leaps and bounds in the postwar years, so did its appetite for goods and services. During the depression and Second World War, many Americans had dreamed of buying a home or a car. In the affluent postwar years, they satisfied their deferred desires. Families purchased not one but sometimes two cars and equipped their new homes with dishwashers, television sets, and stereophonic sound systems. When they lacked cash to buy what they wanted, they borrowed money. Credit to support the nation's shopping spree grew from over $8 billion worth of short- and intermediate-term loans in 1946 to $127 billion in 1970. Here was the economic basis of the consumer culture.

As Americans consumed goods and services, they were using up the world's resources. Consumption of crude petroleum soared 118 percent from 1946 to 1970. Electricity use jumped too, from 270 billion kilowatt-hours to 1.6 trillion. By the mid-1960s, the United States, with only 5 percent of the world's population, produced and consumed more than one-third of the world's goods and services.

Advances in public health were a particularly happy effect of postwar prosperity. The average life span increased from 66.7 years in 1946 to 70.9 in **Improvements in Public Health** 1970. (Racial differences, however, continued to be significant. In 1970, whites lived more than six years longer than blacks.) Regular prenatal and pediatric care led to a major reduction in the infant mortality rate. At the same time, the discovery of wonder drugs such as streptomycin (1945) and Aureomycin (1948) reduced deaths from influenza and postsurgical infection. The Salk polio vaccine, approved for public use in 1955, in seven years reduced the number of reported cases of polio by 97 percent.

Millions of Americans began their search for the affluent society by migrating to the Sunbelt. This mass migration had started during the Second **Growth of the Sunbelt** World War, when GIs and their families were ordered to new duty stations and war workers moved to the shipyards and aircraft factories of San Diego and other cities of the West and South. Soon, the Sunbelt encompassed most of America's southern rim, the area running from southern California across the Southwest and the South all the way to the Atlantic coast. The economic bases of the Sunbelt's spectacular growth were easy to identify: agribusiness, the aerospace industry, the oil industry, real-estate development, recreation, and defense spending.

Industry was also drawn to the southern rim by right-to-work laws, which outlawed the closed union shop, and by low taxes and low heating bills, which reduced overhead expenses.

The millions of people who left the chilly industrial cities of the North and East for sunnier climes in the 1940s and 1950s strengthened the political clout of the Sunbelt. In a book published in the 1960s, Kevin Phillips, a conservative Republican, predicted an emerging Republican majority based on the votes of the South and West. Richard Nixon's triumph in the presidential election of 1968 seemed to support Phillips's thesis. So did the tendency of political parties to nominate Sunbelt candidates for national office. (The nation's five most recently elected presidents have hailed from the Sunbelt—two from Texas, two from California, and one from Georgia.)

The economic boom that made for the political pre-eminence of the Sunbelt also brought increased security for whole classes of Americans. The expanding economy combined with federal welfare legislation to reduce poverty. But even with the reduction in poverty, there was little redistribution of income.

The Other America

In the postwar age of abundance, most Americans found it especially hard to acknowledge the presence of poverty in their midst. But according to the Bureau of Labor Statistics, in 1962 about 42.5 million Americans (nearly one out of every four people) were poor. These Americans earned less than $4,000 per year for a family of four, or $2,000 per year for a single person living alone. Age, race, sex, education, and marital status were all factors in their poverty. One-fourth of the poor were over the age of sixty-five. More than one-third of the poor were under the age of eighteen. One-fifth were people of color, including almost half the nation's black population and more than half the Native American population. Two-thirds lived in households headed by a person with an eighth-grade education or less, and one-fourth lived in households headed by a single woman. For all these people, there was little reason for hope.

In the years after 1945, while millions of Americans, most of them white, were settling in the suburbs, the poor were congregating in the inner cities. By 1970, the black population, which had been 48.6 percent urban in 1940, had become 81.3 percent urban. Joining African-Americans in the exodus to the cities were poor whites from the southern Appalachians, who moved to Cincinnati, Baltimore, St. Louis, Detroit, and Chicago. Latin Americans were arriving in growing numbers from Mexico, Puerto Rico, the Dominican Republic, Colombia, Ecuador, and Cuba.

Poor People in the Inner Cities

Next to African-Americans, the largest group of urban newcomers were the Mexican-Americans, or Chicanos. Millions came during and after the war as farm workers, and increasingly, they remained to make their lives in the United States. Despite the initiation in 1953 of Operation Wetback, a program to find and deport illegal aliens, Mexicans continued to enter the country in large numbers, many of them illegally. Many settled in cities. According to the 1960 census, more than 500,000 Mexican-Americans had migrated to the barrios of the Los Angeles–Long Beach area since 1940. If estimates of uncounted illegal aliens were added to the census figure, the total was far higher. The same was true of the barrios in southwestern and northern cities.

Mexican-Americans

American Indians made up the country's poorest group, with an average annual income that was half the amount of the poverty level. Indians moved to the cities in the 1950s and 1960s, particularly after Congress, in 1953, adopted the policy of termination. Accustomed to the life of the reservation, many had difficulty adjusting to the urban environment. Tragically, many groups that migrated to cities, instead of finding a place to prosper, found only a dumping ground for the poor.

American Indians

Not all the poor, however, lived in cities. By 1960, 30 percent lived in small towns and 15 percent on farms. Tenant farmers and sharecroppers, both black and white, suffered economic hardship. Mi-

Despite America's postwar economic boom, many people still lived in poverty. In 1945, these black farm workers in Belleglade, Florida, had little hope for the future. Fifteen years later, their plight was unchanged, as the historic television documentary "A Harvest of Shame" (1960) made clear. *National Archives.*

gratory farm workers lived in abject poverty. Elderly people tended to be poor regardless of where they lived.

Women made up a large segment of the poor. They had limited opportunities for well-paying employment and faced extensive occupational segregation: low-paying positions were

Women in Poverty

labeled women's work and jobs that paid better were reserved for men. In 1945, many women wanted to remain in the factories and shipyards, but they were pushed out to make way for returning veterans. Those who tried later to return to industrial work were discouraged. Moreover, many women's jobs were not covered by either the minimum wage or Social Security. Finally, if divorce, desertion, or death did rend a family, it was usually the woman who was left to bear responsibility for the health and welfare of the children. Many ex-husbands did not make their child-support

payments. And on welfare, or on a salary that paid women sixty cents for each dollar a man got, many single mothers and their children slipped into poverty.

One of the least-known effects of economic hardship on the poor has been physical and emotional illness. A study done in the late 1950s in New Haven, Connecticut, found that the rate of treated psychiatric illness was three times as high for the lowest fifth of income earners as it was for the upper-middle and upper classes. Psychiatrists at Cornell University's Medical School described the "low social economic status individual" as "rigid, suspicious," and having "a fatalistic outlook on life. . . . They are prone to depression, have feelings of futility, lack of belongingness . . . and a lack of trust in others." During the economic recession of 1960, a social worker from Rochester, New York, bemoaned a sharp rise in "marital discord and desertions of families by the father, increased welfare dependency, increased crime, especially robberies, burglaries and muggings, and alcoholism." Ironically, all of this suffering was occurring in a nation that was being heralded as the affluent society.

The Growth of Suburbs

A combination of motives drew people to the suburbs. Many wanted to leave behind the sounds and smells of the city and be closer to nature. They also wanted homes with yards so that, as one suburbanite put it, "every kid [would have] an opportunity to grow up with grass stains on his pants." Or they wanted the privacy and quiet that detached homes provided, as well as family rooms, extra closets, and utility rooms. Many were also looking for a community of like-minded people, a place where they could have a measure of political influence. Big-city government was dense and impenetrable. In the suburbs, citizens could become involved in government and have an impact, particularly on the education their children received. Indeed, the general welfare of their children seemed to be a major concern of suburbanites.

Government funding and policies helped families to settle in the suburbs. Low-interest GI mortgages and Federal Housing Administration (FHA) mortgage insurance made the difference for people who would otherwise have been unable to afford a home. Such easy credit combined with postwar prosperity to produce a construction boom. From 1945 to 1946, housing starts climbed from 326,000 to more than 1 million, and in 1950, they approached 2 million. Never before had new starts exceeded 1 million; not until the early 1980s would they dip below that level.

Housing Boom

At the same time, highway construction opened up rural lands for the development of suburban communities. In 1947, Congress authorized the construction of a 37,000-mile chain of highways, and in 1956, President Dwight D. Eisenhower signed the Highway Act, which launched a 41,000-mile nationwide network. Fed-

Highway Construction

eral funds spent on highways swelled from $79 million in 1946 to $4.6 billion in 1970. State and local highway expenditures also mushroomed. Of special interest to the South, the highways carried the fast-moving trucks that accelerated the integration of the region into the national economy.

The spurt in highway construction combined with the sprawl of suburbia to produce the *megalopolis*. The term was first used by urban experts in the early 1960s, to refer to the almost uninterrupted metropolitan complex stretching along the northeastern seaboard of the United States. Beginning in Boston and extending 600 miles south through New York, Philadelphia, Baltimore, and Washington, "Boswash" encompassed parts of eleven states and a population of 49 million people, all tied together by interstate highways. Other megalopolises that took shape after the Second World War were "Chipitts," a band of heavy industry and dense population stretching from Chicago to Pittsburgh, and "San-San," the area from San Francisco to San Diego.

Middle-class whites benefited more than other Americans from the government-supported housing and highway boom. For example, the FHA refused to guarantee suburban home loans to the poor, people of color, Jews, and other "inharmonious racial and ethnic groups." And some federal programs actually worsened conditions for the poor. The National Housing Act of 1949 was designed to provide for urban redevelopment (slum clearance), the construction of public housing for low-income people, and FHA mortgages for home buyers. Under the program, however, the slums were replaced not with low-income housing, but with parking lots, shopping centers, luxury highrise buildings, highways, and factories. The planned 810,000 housing units for the poor were constructed not in four years, but in twenty.

Socially, the suburban emphasis on family togetherness tended to isolate families. Writing in 1957, sociologist David Riesman criticized "the decentralization of leisure in the suburbs . . . as the home itself, rather than the neighborhood, becomes the chief gathering place for the family—either in the 'family room' with its games, its TV, its informality, or outdoors around the barbecue." The floor plan of

Critics of Suburban Life

the ranch-style home, at whose center was the television set, was suited to the stay-at-home life style.

Riesman was only one of many critics of suburban living. Other observers denounced the suburbs for breeding conformity. The word *suburbia*, Scott Donaldson wrote in *The Suburban Myth* (1969), had "unpleasant overtones, suggesting nothing so much as some kind of scruffy disease." And C. Wright Mills, a sociologist, castigated white-collar suburbanites, who "sell not only their time and energy but their personalities as well. They sell . . . their smiles and their kindly gestures."

When all the pluses and minuses were tallied, however, most residents of suburbia seemed to prefer family togetherness to any other life style of which they were aware. Most of the college students interviewed by Riesman in the 1950s looked forward to living in the suburbs.

Ideals of Motherhood and the Family

Change, some of it caused by the publication of Dr. Benjamin Spock's *Baby and Child Care* (1946), had also occurred within the American family. The book, which quickly became a bible for new parents, answered many common questions about child rearing. Unlike earlier manuals, however, *Baby and Child Care* urged mothers (but not fathers, because Spock assigned them little formal role in child rearing) always to think of their children first. Dr. Spock's predecessors during the previous thirty years had advised mothers to consider their own needs, as well as their children's. But women who embraced Dr. Spock's teachings tried to be mother, teacher, psychologist, and buddy to their children. If they failed in any of these prescribed roles, guilt often resulted.

Dr. Spock on Child Rearing

At the same time, Philip Wylie, author of the book *Generation of Vipers*, denounced such selfless behavior as Momism. In the guise of sacrificing for her children, Wylie wrote, Mom was pursuing "love of herself." She smothered her children with affection so that they would become emotionally dependent on her and would not want to leave home. Some medical experts agreed. But women were caught in a double bind, for if they pursued a life outside the home, they were accused of being "imitation men" or "neurotic" feminists. Echoing the psychoanalyst Sigmund Freud, critics of working mothers contended that a woman could be happy and fulfilled only through domesticity.

Women's Conflicting Roles

A reason for women's dilemma was the conflicting roles a woman was expected to fulfill. On the one hand, the home was premised on a full-time housewife who, with little regard for her own needs, provided her husband and children with a haven from the outside world. On the other hand, women continued the wartime trend toward work outside the home. The female labor force rose from 16.8 million in 1946 to 31.6 million in 1970. These women entered the job market lacking the support of an organized women's movement and without challenging sex-role stereotypes. Many of them were their families' sole source of income; they had to work. Still others took jobs not to challenge male dominance, but to earn additional family income, enjoy adult company, or bolster their self-esteem. Despite the cult of motherhood, most new entrants into the job market were married and had children.

GI Bill

Immediately after the Second World War, many American families moved into abandoned military housing on college campuses. Accompanied by wives and babies, former GIs were getting an education. The legislation making it possible was the Servicemen's Readjustment Act of 1944, or GI Bill of Rights, which provided living allowances and tuition payments to college-bound veterans. More than 1 million veterans enrolled in 1946, so that almost one out of every two students was a GI. Despite dire predictions to the contrary, the veterans succeeded as students.

Family Togetherness

These veterans were determined to provide economic security for their families. Men and women of their generation had grown up during the economic deprivation of the 1930s. Having also experienced separation from family and friends caused by the Second World War, they became exponents of "family togetherness."

Such togetherness included family watching of television, outings to parks and beaches, and Little League games.

Most American families were preoccupied with education. But in 1957, the Soviet launching of *Sputnik*, the first earth-orbiting satellite, made education a matter of national secu-

Education of the Baby-Boom Generation

rity. The Soviet success challenged American military and technological superiority, based ultimately on the nation's school system. Congress responded in 1958 with the National Defense Education Act (NDEA), which funded public school programs in mathematics, foreign languages, and science, as well as fellowships and loans to college students. Parents were quick to endorse the new programs. After all, public education was "the engine of democracy," a guarantee of both upward social mobility and military superiority.

Just as education became intertwined with national security, religion became synonymous with patriotism. As President Eisenhower put it, "Recognition of the Supreme Being is the first, the most basic expression of Americanism." In America's Cold War with the godless Soviet Union, ministers, priests, and rabbis became foot soldiers in the battle for souls. Religious leaders emphasized family togetherness in their appeals for new converts. "The family that prays together stays together" was a famous slogan used during the 1950s and 1960s. The Bible topped the best-seller lists, and books with religious themes, such as the Reverend Norman Vincent Peale's *The Power of Positive Thinking* (1952), sold in the millions. Evangelist Billy Graham exhorted television viewers and stadium audiences throughout the country. Membership in religious organizations increased from 74 million in 1946 to 131 million in 1970.

Although Americans were eager to improve their minds and souls, they were not ready until the 1960s to liberate themselves sexually. When Dr. Alfred Kinsey, director of the Insti-

Sex in Postwar America

tute for Sex Research at Indiana University, published his pioneering book *Sexual Behavior in the Human Male* (1948), the American public was shocked. On the basis of interviews

with numerous men, Kinsey estimated that 95 percent of American men had engaged in masturbation, premarital or extramarital intercourse, or homosexual behavior. Five years later, Kinsey caused even more of a disturbance with *Sexual Behavior in the Human Female*, which revealed that 62 percent of women masturbated and 50 percent had intercourse before marriage. Sex was nothing new, of course, but its existence was seldom acknowledged in polite conversation or respectable publications—and most Americans preferred that situation.

Middle-Class America at Play

The prosperity that marked the postwar era was reflected in the materialistic values and pleasures of the period. Having satisfied their basic needs for food, clothing, and shelter, growing numbers of Americans turned their attention to luxury items. Indeed, the quest of middle-class families for the latest conveniences made shopping a form of recreation.

Of the new luxuries, television was the most revolutionary in its effects. One man who grew up in the postwar era recalled the purchase of the first

TV Enters American Homes

family television set in 1950. "And so the monumental change began in our lives and those of millions of other Americans. More than a year passed before we again visited a movie theater. Money which previously would have been spent for books was saved for the TV payments. Social evenings with friends became fewer and fewer still because we discovered we did not share the same TV program interests."

Entertainment was television's number one product. Situation comedies and action series were among the most popular shows. Topping these categories in the 1950s were "I Love Lucy," starring Lucille Ball, and "Dragnet," a detective series. Family togetherness was a theme of "Father Knows Best" and "Leave It to Beaver." As daily average television viewing in the United States increased (five hours in 1956), critics worried that television's distorted presentation of the world would significantly define people's sense of reality.

As television brought the world into their living rooms, Americans began to read newspapers and news magazines a little less carefully and to listen to radio a lot less frequently. But despite the lure of television, book readership went up. One reason for the increased consumption of literature was the mass marketing of inexpensive paperbound books. Pocket Books hit the market in 1939; soon, westerns, detective stories, and science fiction filled the newsstands, supermarkets, and drugstores. The comic book, which had become popular in 1939 with the introduction of Superman, became another drugstore standard. Reprints of hardcover books and condensed books also did well.

One obvious casualty of the stay-at-home suburban culture was the motion picture. From 1946 to 1948, Americans had attended movies at the rate of nearly 90 million a week. By 1950, the figure had dropped to 60 million a week; by 1960, to 40 million. Thus, the postwar years saw the steady closing of movie theaters—with the notable exception of the drive-in, which appealed to car-oriented suburban families, as well as to teenagers.

There was one crucial exception to the downturn in moviegoing. By the late 1950s, the first children of the postwar baby boom had become adolescents, and although their par-

Rise of Youth Subculture

ents preferred to stay home and watch television, they themselves flocked to the theaters. No less than 72 percent of moviegoers during the 1950s were under the age of thirty. Hollywood responded to this youthful new audience with films portraying young people as sensitive and intelligent and adults as boorish and hostile. *Rebel Without a Cause* (1955), starring James Dean, was one such movie. The cult of youth had been born.

Soon, the music industry was catering to teens with cheap 45 rpm records. Bored with the era's syrupy music, young Americans welcomed the driving energy and hard beat of

Rock 'n' Roll

rock 'n' roll. Bill Haley, the Everly Brothers, and Buddy Holly thrilled teenagers with their music. Elvis Presley horrified their parents with his suggestive gyrations; but with the release of his first single

Elvis Presley's performances upset some parents, but they thrilled young people, who cheered the gyrations of "Elvis the Pelvis." This 1956 photo captured Presley rocking through the song "Hillbilly Heartbreak." *UPI/ Bettmann Archives.*

("Heartbreak Hotel") in 1956, he became the idol of millions of girls and boys. Although the roots of rock 'n' roll lay in black rhythm-and-blues, most white stars did not acknowledge the debt. Presley's hit tune "Hound Dog," for example, had originally been performed by the black singer Big Mama Thornton, but Thornton received little credit for her contribution. Among the black rock-'n'-roll stars of the 1950s were Chuck Berry and Little Richard.

While white performers copied black rhythm-and-blues, serious black jazz artists like Charlie Parker and Dizzy Gillespie were experimenting with bebop. In the 1950s, jazz became increasingly fused with classical themes, compositions, and instrumentation. Intellectuals began to study this art form, which had once been looked down on as vulgar.

America's cultural influence grew worldwide in the 1950s and 1960s. In dance, Martha Graham was lauded in international circles, and in painting, Jackson Pollock became the pivotal figure of the abstract expressionist movement, which in the 1950s established New York City as the center of the art world. Rather than work with the traditional painter's easel, Pollock spread his canvas on the floor, where he was free to walk around it, "work from the four sides and literally be in the painting." In the 1960s, artists of the Pop Art movement satirized the consumer society, using commercial techniques to depict everyday objects. Andy Warhol painted Campbell soup cans; other artists did blowups of ice-cream sundaes, hamburgers, and comic-strip panels.

Consumerism was evident in Americans' postwar play and in the era's fads. Slinky, selling for a dollar, began loping down people's stairs in 1947; Silly Putty was introduced in 1950. The 1950s also had 3-D movies and Hula-Hoops. Although most crazes were short-lived, they created multimillion-dollar industries and effectively promoted dozens of movies and television shows. Other postwar crazes are still with us—Scrabble, paint-by-number sets, and Barbie dolls, to name just a few. Many of these toys and games succeeded because they were activities that brought the whole family together.

Needless to say, the consensus society of the 1950s and early 1960s was not receptive to social criticism. The filmgoing public preferred noncontroversial doses of Doris Day and Rock Hudson and Dean Martin and Jerry Lewis. Readers bought novels and retreated into the criminal underworld, the Wild West, or science fiction fantasy. Even serious artists tended to ignore the country's social problems.

There were exceptions. Ralph Ellison's *Invisible Man* (1952) gave white Americans a glimpse of the psychic costs to black Americans of exclusion from the white American dream. Two films—*Gentleman's Agreement* (1947) and *Home of the Brave* (1949)—examined anti-Semitism and white racism. And in the 1950s, one group of writers repudiated the conventional world of the middle class and the suburbs. Rejecting the same

Beat Generation

social niceties that Kinsey had challenged, the writers of the Beat (for "beatific") Generation flaunted their freewheeling sexuality and consumption of drugs. The Beats produced some memorable prose and poetry, including Allen Ginsberg's long poem *Howl* (1956) and Jack Kerouac's novel *On the Road* (1957), and they offered American youth an alternative to their parents' materialism and righteous self-congratulation. Although the Beats were mostly ignored during the 1950s, millions of young Americans discovered their writings and lifestyle in the 1960s.

One of the most influential books of the postwar years was the best seller *The Affluent Society* (1958), by economist John Kenneth Galbraith. Galbraith's thesis dovetailed with the prevalent belief that economic growth would bring prosperity to everyone. Some would have more than others, of course, but in time everybody would have enough. "Production has eliminated the more acute tensions associated with [economic] inequality," Galbraith wrote. Not until Chapter 23 did the author mention poverty; when he did, he dismissed it as not "a universal or massive affliction," but "more nearly an afterthought."

Only in the 1960s would comfortable Americans of the middle class discover that millions of poor people lived in America (see Chapter 31). Politically and culturally, the 1960s were vastly different from the consensus years that preceded them. Ironically, the products of suburbia—the children of the baby boom—were the ones who formed the vanguard of the assault not only on poverty, but also on the whole value system of the American middle class.

Suggestions for Further Reading

The Baby Boom

Richard A. Easterlin, *Birth and Fortune* (1980); Landon Y. Jones, *Great Expectations: America and the Baby Boom Generation* (1980); Michael P. Nichols, *Turning Forty in the '80s* (1986).

The Affluent Society

Carl Abbott, *The New Urban America*, rev. ed. (1987); David P. Calleo, *The Imperious Economy* (1982); John Kenneth Galbraith, *The Affluent Society* (1958); John Kenneth Galbraith, *American Capitalism* (1952); David M. Potter, *People of Plenty* (1954); Kirkpatrick Sale, *Power Shift: The Rise of the Southern Rim and Its Challenge to the Eastern Establishment* (1975); Robert Sobel, *The Last Bull Market* (1980); Harold G. Vatter, *The U.S. Economy in the 1950s* (1963).

Farmers and Workers

Gilbert C. Fite, *American Farmers* (1981); James R. Green, *The World of the Worker* (1980); John L. Shover, *First Majority—Last Minority: The Transforming of Rural Life in America* (1976); Philip Taft, *The A.F. of L. from the Death of Gompers to the Merger* (1959).

The Other America

Joseph H. Cash and Herbert T. Hoover, eds., *To Be an Indian: An Oral History* (1971); Harry M. Caudill, *Night Comes to the Cumberland* (1963); J. Wayne Flint, *Dixie's Forgotten People: The South's Poor Whites* (1979); Leo Grebler et al., *Mexican-American People* (1970); Michael Harrington, *The Other America*, rev. ed. (1981); Herman P. Miller, *Rich Man, Poor Man* (1971); Dorothy K. Newman et al., *Politics and Prosperity: Black Americans and White Institutions, 1940–75* (1978); James T. Patterson, *America's Struggle Against Poverty, 1900–1985* (1986); David S. Walls and John B. Stephenson, eds., *Appalachia in the Sixties* (1972).

Suburbia

Robert Fishman, *Bourgeois Utopias* (1987); Mark I. Gelfand, *A Nation of Cities* (1975); Dolores Hayden, *Redesigning the American Dream* (1984); Kenneth T. Jackson, *Crabgrass Frontier: The Suburbanization of the United States* (1985); Zane L. Miller, *Suburb* (1982); John B. Rae, *The American Automobile* (1965); William H. Whyte, *The Organization Man* (1956); Gwendolyn Wright, *Building the Dream: A Social History of Housing in America* (1981).

The Spread of Education

Keith W. Olson, *The GI Bill, the Veterans, and the Colleges* (1974); Diane Ravitch, *The Troubled Crusade: American Education, 1945–1980* (1983); Joel Spring, *The Sorting Machine: National Educational Policy Since 1945* (1976).

Motherhood, Work, and Family Togetherness

William H. Chafe, *The American Woman: Her Changing Social, Economic, and Political Role, 1920–1970* (1972); Ruth Schwartz Cowan, *More Work for Mother* (1983); Carl Degler, *At Odds: Woman and the Family in America from the Revolution to the Present* (1980); Benita Eisler, *Private Lives: Men and Women of the Fifties* (1986); Betty Friedan, *The Feminine Mystique* (1963); Cynthia Harrison, *On Account of Sex: The Politics of Women's Issues, 1945–1968* (1988); Susan M. Hartmann, *The Homefront and Beyond: American Women in the 1940s* (1982); Eugenia Kaledin, *Mothers and More: American Women in the 1950s* (1984); Susan Estabrook Kennedy, *If All We Did Was to Weep at Home: A History of White Working-Class Women in America* (1979); Glenna Matthews, *"Just a Housewife"* (1987); Elaine Tyler May, *Homeward Bound: American Families in the Cold War Era* (1988); Leila J. Rupp and Verta Taylor, *Survival in the Doldrums: The American Women's Rights Movement, 1945 to the 1960s* (1987); Susan Strasser, *Never Done: A History of American Housework* (1982).

Popular Culture

Chuck Berry, *Chuck Berry* (1987); Peter Biskind, *Seeing Is Believing: How Hollywood Taught Us to Stop Worrying and Love the Fifties* (1983); Paul A. Carter, *Another Part of the Fifties* (1983); Kenneth C. Davis, *Two-Bit Culture: The Paperbacking of America* (1984); James Gilbert, *A Cycle of Outrage: America's Reaction to the Juvenile Delinquent* (1986); Charlie Gillett, *The Sound of the City: The Rise of Rock and Roll*, rev. ed. (1983); Serge Guilbaut, *How New York Stole the Idea of Modern Art* (1982); Gerald Nicosia, *Memory Babe: A Critical Biography of Jack Kerouac* (1983); Jane and Michael Stern, *Elvis World* (1987); John Tytell, *Naked Angels: The Lives and Literature of the Beat Generation* (1976).

Television

Erik Barnouw, *Tube of Plenty*, rev. ed. (1982); George Comstock et al., *Television and Human Behavior* (1978); Todd Gitlin, *Inside Prime-Time* (1983); Frank Mankiewicz and Joel Swerdlow, *Remote Control: Television and the Manipulation of American Life* (1978).

The Joint Chiefs of Staff memorandum lay on the table. Its recommendation: add another 100,000 to the 80,000 American troops already in Vietnam, because the war was not going well. "Is there anyone here of the opinion we should not do what the memorandum says?" asked President Lyndon B. Johnson of his advisers, assembled for a tense meeting on the morning of July 21, 1965. Only Under Secretary of State George W. Ball was openly critical, advising, "Take our losses, let their government fall apart, negotiate, discuss, knowing full well there will be a probable takeover by the Communists." Yet Johnson recoiled from the thought that a small, primitive country like Vietnam could deny the United States victory.

The next day, Johnson huddled with the military brass. The generals told him that more men, more bombings, and more money were needed to keep America's South Vietnamese ally in power against the North Vietnamese and Vietcong. "But if we put in 100,000 men won't they put in an equal number, and then where will we be?" Johnson asked. When an admiral claimed that if the United States did not back the faltering South Vietnamese regime, allies around the world would lose faith in America's word, Johnson knew better: "We have few allies really helping us now." And have the bombing raids hurt the enemy? Not really, the generals answered, but if more sites were added to the target list, they would. Johnson grew worried: "Isn't this going off the diving board?"

In late July, a troubled President Johnson nonetheless decided to give the Joint Chiefs of Staff what they wanted. A major decision of the Vietnam War, it meant that the United States was assuming, for the first time, primary responsibility for fighting the war. Fearing a national debate, Johnson muted the decision's importance when he announced it. By the end of 1965, 184,000 American combat troops were at war in Vietnam. Yet Congress had not passed a declaration of war. Ball later concluded that Johnson's July decision was "the greatest single error that America had made in its national history."

Vietnam, either because of the searing war experience itself or because of the lessons Americans later drew from that experience, bedeviled the Kennedy, Johnson, Nixon, and Ford presidencies. Other concerns

30

VIETNAM AND THE COLD WAR: AMERICAN FOREIGN POLICY, 1961–1977

crowded the international agenda in the 1960s and 1970s: continued Soviet-American competition for global influence, with dramatic swings from conciliation to confrontation in the Cold War; an accelerating nuclear arms race; turmoil in the Third World, much of it anti-American; eruptions in the Middle East; mean-spirited Cuban-American hostilities; and disorder in the world economy. But Vietnam, where Cold War and Third World issues seemed to merge, at least in American thinking, dominated United States foreign policy. Kennedy enlarged the United States presence in Southeast Asia; Johnson Americanized the war; Nixon struggled to pull American troops out of the war without losing it; and Ford and his successors had to deal with the aftermath of America's longest war. As he wound down the American combat role in Vietnam, Nixon also inched toward détente with the Soviet Union and China and intervened in Third World disputes to protect American interests that he thought threatened.

Throughout the 1960s and 1970s, Americans became uneasy not only about the troubled position of the United States in world affairs, but also about the disorder wrought at home by foreign entanglements. Foreign policy and domestic developments had been traditionally interconnected, and foreign policy had always sprung from the domestic setting of the nation—its needs, wants, moods, and ideals. Yet the experience of the Vietnam War called into question those needs, wants, moods, and ideals because a majority of Americans came to see the effects of the war as a threat to their economic well-being, social stability, moral standards, and political system.

Kennedy's Quest for Cold War Victory

John F. Kennedy's diplomacy owed much to the past. He remembered the tragedy of appeasement in the 1930s, as well as the triumph of containment in the 1940s. America had turned back Nazism and

Kennedy as Cold War Activist had contained communism, Kennedy argued, and now, in the 1960s, communism would be routed. That there would be no halfway measures was apparent in Kennedy's inaugural address: "Let every nation know that we shall pay any price, bear any burden, meet any hardship, support any friend, oppose any foe to assure the survival and the success of liberty."

Soviet Premier Nikita S. Khrushchev matched Kennedy's rhetoric with an endorsement of "wars of national liberation" in the Third World. The Soviet leader also bragged about Soviet intercontinental ballistic missiles (ICBMs), raising American anxiety over Soviet capabilities. Intelligence data soon proved that there was no "missile gap"— except the one in America's favor. Nonetheless, Kennedy sought to fulfill his campaign commitment to a military build-up based on the principle of *flexible response*. Junking Eisenhower's concept of massive retaliation, which emphasized nuclear weapons, Kennedy sought ways to meet any kind of warfare, from guerrilla combat in the jungles to a nuclear showdown. In this way, he reasoned, he could contain both the Soviet Union and Third World revolutionary movements. In 1961, the military budget shot up 15 percent; ICBM arsenals swelled further; and plans were laid to increase NATO's nuclear firing power. Although Kennedy could claim credit for the Limited Test Ban Treaty with the Soviet Union (1963), his read legacy was an accelerated arms race.

During this time Berlin continued to claim headlines. The Soviets again demanded negotiations to end the Western occupation of Berlin. But Kennedy saw the historic city as "the great **Berlin Crisis** testing place of Western courage and will." Instead of negotiating, he asked Congress in 1961 for an additional $3.2 billion for defense and the authority to call up reservists. Events took an ugly turn in August 1961, when the Soviets erected the Berlin Wall, a concrete-and-barbed-wire barricade designed to halt the exodus of East Germans into West Berlin. Yet another example of Soviet repression, the wall inspired protests all over the non-Communist world. The crisis passed. When Kennedy visited the wall in 1963, he stirred a mass rally of West Berliners with the words "Ich bin ein Berliner" ("I am a Berliner").

But it was over Cuba that Kennedy had his most serious confrontation with the Soviet Union (see map, page 538). Cuba became an obsession of American policymakers in 1959, when Fidel Castro and rebels of his 26th of July Movement ousted America's long-time ally Fulgencio Batista. President Eisenhower had made a last-minute attempt in late 1958 to install a friendly military regime in order to deny the Cuban revolutionaries their hard-fought triumph.

The Cuban Revolution

From the start, Castro was determined to break the economic power of American business, which owned 3 million acres of Cuba's land and controlled 40 percent of its sugar production and 90 percent of its telephone and electric service. The Castro government nationalized some American-owned property, suspended promised elections, indulged in a barrage of anti-American rhetoric, and, early in 1960, signed a trade treaty with the Soviet Union. In mid-1960, President Eisenhower reduced American purchases of Cuban sugar. Castro's response was large-scale seizures of American-owned companies. Soon, the Cuban premier began to appeal to the Soviet Union for support.

In March 1960, Eisenhower had ordered the CIA to train Cuban exiles for an invasion of their homeland. Just before he left office, Eisenhower broke diplomatic relations with Castro and advised Kennedy to advance plans for the invasion. Kennedy, who preferred victory over compromise, never attempted to negotiate Cuban-American troubles with Castro. Instead, he listened to the CIA. The picture sketched by the CIA appealed to Kennedy: Cuban exiles would land at the Bay of Pigs and secure a beachhead; the Cuban people would rise up against Castro; a revolutionary council organized in the United States would enter Havana in triumph. When the Bay of Pigs attack began in April 1961, however, the Cuban people did not rise up in sympathy with the invaders, and within two days the poorly planned and poorly executed invasion collapsed.

Bay of Pigs

Kennedy did not suffer defeat easily. Soon, he and his advisers set about finding other means to unseat Castro. As part of a plan called Operation Mongoose, government agents worked to disrupt the island's trade and continued to aid anti-Castro groups in Miami. The CIA plotted with organized crime leaders to assassinate Castro. The United States also tightened its economic blockade of Cuba and engineered its eviction from the Organization of American States.

Cuba soon became the site of one of the scariest crises of the Cold War. Had there been no Bay of Pigs invasion, no Operation Mongoose, no assassination plots, and no program of diplomatic and economic isolation, there probably would have been no missile crisis. For Castro, American hostility represented a real threat to Cuba's independence. For the Soviets, American actions challenged the only pro-Communist regime in Latin America. In an attempt to counter any new American intervention and to improve the Soviet position in the nuclear arms race, Castro and Khrushchev devised a daring plan: installation of Soviet missiles and nuclear bombers in Cuba.

Cuban Missile Crisis

Although the Kennedy administration was aware of a military build-up on the island, it was not until October 14, 1962, that a U-2 plane photographed sites for medium-range missiles that could reach the United States. Whether the Soviets had acted to protect Cuba, to improve their own nuclear capability, or to force the United States to pull its missiles out of Turkey remains debatable. In any case, the president organized an executive committee and ordered it to find a way to remove the missiles from Cuba. Some members advised a surprise air strike. Robert Kennedy scotched that idea; he wanted no Pearl Harbors on his brother's record. The Joint Chiefs of Staff recommended a full-scale military invasion, but that risked a prolonged war with Cuba, a Soviet attack against Berlin, or even nuclear holocaust. Soviet expert Charles Bohlen urged quiet, direct negotiations with Soviet officials. Secretary of Defense Robert S. McNamara proposed the formula that the president found most acceptable: a naval quarantine of Cuba that left the administration free to attack or negotiate, depending on the Soviet response.

Over national television on October 22, Kennedy

IMPORTANT EVENTS

1960	Kennedy elected president
1961	Peace Corps founded
	Alliance for Progress
	Bay of Pigs invasion
	Berlin crisis
	American military build-up
1962	Cuban missile crisis
1963	Limited Test Ban Treaty
	Diem assassinated in Vietnam
	Kennedy assassinated; Johnson assumes presidency
1964	Tonkin Gulf incident and resolution
	Johnson elected president
1965	Johnson Americanizes Vietnam War
1967	Peace rallies across the nation
	Six-Day War in the Middle East
1968	Tet offensive in Vietnam
	My Lai massacre
	Vietnam peace talks open in Paris
	Nixon elected president

1969	543,400 U.S. troops in Vietnam
	Nixon begins withdrawal of troops
	Nixon Doctrine
	Détente policy announced
1970	Invasion of Cambodia
1971	*Pentagon Papers* released
1972	Nixon visits China
	SALT-I Treaty
	Nixon re-elected
1973	Vietnam cease-fire agreement
	Allende ousted in Chile
	Arab-Israeli War
	Arab oil embargo
	War Powers Resolution
1974	Nixon resigns; Ford becomes president
1975	Vietnam War ends
	Civil war in Angola

informed the Soviets of American policy and demanded their retreat. American warships headed for the Caribbean, B-52s loaded with nuclear bombs took to the skies, and American military forces around the globe went on alert. Khrushchev first replied that the missiles would be withdrawn if Washington pledged never to attack Cuba again. Then he demanded the removal of American Jupiter missiles from Turkey. Kennedy accepted the first condition but rejected the second. On October 28, Khrushchev finally accepted the American pledge to respect Cuban sovereignty; in return, he promised to ship the missiles back to the Soviet Union. The Soviet missiles in Cuba were dismantled, and Kennedy privately promised to with-

draw the Jupiters from Turkey, as was done. This was, said many, Kennedy's finest hour.

But critics have raised questions. Was the crisis really necessary? Why did the president attempt to solve the crisis with public brinkmanship instead of private negotiations? Was he motivated by the forthcoming congressional elections? Finally, critics have claimed that the strategic balance of power was not seriously altered by the placement of Soviet missiles in Cuba. Perhaps Kennedy risked doomsday when he did not need to?

In the Cuban missile crisis, the Soviets were forced to back down. Exposed as nuclear inferiors, the Soviets vowed to catch up—and they managed to do so by the late 1960s. The crisis did produce

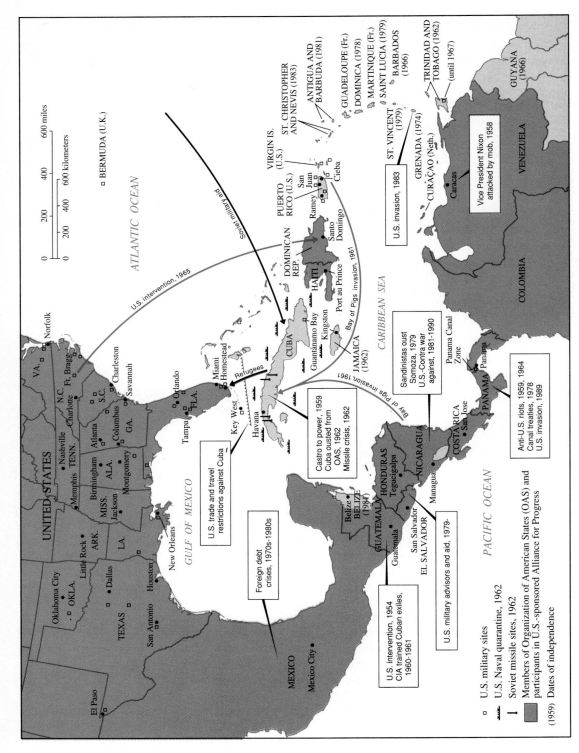

The United States in the Caribbean and Central America

Map labels

BERMUDA (U.K.)

ATLANTIC OCEAN

600 miles

600 kilometers

0   200   400   600 miles
0   200   400   600 kilometers

ANTIGUA AND BARBUDA (1981)
ST. CHRISTOPHER AND NEVIS (1983)
GUADELOUPE (Fr.)
DOMINICA (1978)
MARTINIQUE (Fr.)
SAINT LUCIA (1979)
BARBADOS (1966)
TRINIDAD AND TOBAGO (1962) (until 1967)
GUYANA (1966)

VIRGIN IS. (U.S.)

Soviet military aid

PUERTO RICO (U.S.)
San Juan
Ramey
Cieba

ST. VINCENT (1979)
GRENADA (1974)
CURAÇAO (Neth.)
Caracas

U.S. invasion, 1983

VENEZUELA

Vice President Nixon attacked by mob, 1958

COLOMBIA

U.S. intervention, 1965

DOMINICAN REP.
HAITI
Port au Prince
Santo Domingo

Bay of Pigs invasion, 1961

CARIBBEAN SEA

CUBA
Guantánamo Bay
Kingston
JAMAICA (1962)

Norfolk
VA.
Ft. Bragg
N.C.
Charleston
S.C.
Savannah
Charlotte
GA.
Atlanta
Orlando
TENN.
Nashville
ALA.
Birmingham
Columbus
Montgomery
MISS.
Jackson
Memphis
ARK.
Little Rock
LA.
New Orleans
FLA.
Tampa
Miami
Homestead
Key West
Refugees
Havana

UNITED STATES

Castro to power, 1959
Cuba ousted from OAS, 1962
Missile crisis, 1962

U.S. trade and travel restrictions against Cuba

GULF OF MEXICO

Foreign debt crises, 1970s-1980s

Oklahoma City
OKLA.
Dallas
TEXAS
San Antonio
Houston
El Paso

MEXICO
Mexico City

Sandinistas oust Somoza, 1979
U.S.-Contra war against, 1981-1990

Panama Canal Zone
Panama
PANAMA

Anti-U.S. riots, 1959, 1964
Canal treaties, 1978
U.S. invasion, 1989

BELIZE (1981)
Belize
GUATEMALA
Guatemala
HONDURAS
Tegucigalpa
NICARAGUA
Managua
COSTA RICA
San José
EL SALVADOR
San Salvador

U.S. military advisors and aid, 1979-

U.S. intervention, 1954
CIA trained Cuban exiles, 1960-1961

PACIFIC OCEAN

Bay of Pigs invasion, 1961

Legend

□ U.S. military sites

⊥ U.S. Naval quarantine, 1962

Soviet missile sites, 1962

Members of Organization of American States (OAS) and participants in U.S.-sponsored Alliance for Progress

(1959) Dates of independence

"This flag will be returned to this Brigade in a free Havana," President Kennedy promised CIA-trained commandos after their release from Cuban jails in December 1962. The men had been captured during the failed 1961 Bay of Pigs invasion. Under Kennedy, the United States government undertook an array of projects to undermine the Cuban Revolution and topple its charismatic leader Fidel Castro. *Wide World Photos.*

some relaxation in Soviet-American relations. The superpower leaders installed a Teletype "hot line" between Washington and Moscow, signed the Limited Test Ban Treaty in 1963, and refrained from further confrontation in Berlin.

In the Third World, Kennedy called for "peaceful revolution" based on the concept of nation building. Drawing on the ideas of the economist Walt W. Rostow, who joined the Kennedy administration, the president determined to win favor in Third World countries by helping them through the infant stages of nationhood with programs aimed at improving agriculture, transportation, and communications. In 1961, he launched the Alliance for Progress in Latin America. That same year, he also

Peace Corps

created the Peace Corps, to send teachers, agricultural specialists, and health workers into developing nations throughout the world. But the Peace Corps's humanitarian purpose competed with the administration's political needs. Periodic conflicts arose between corps members in the field, who identified with Third World peoples' desire for neutralism, and headquarters in Washington, where the goal was aligning those peoples with American foreign policy.

Besides such development programs, Kennedy relied on counterinsurgency: the training of native troops and police forces by American military and technical advisers. The assumption was that American soldiers—particularly the Special Forces units, or Green Berets—would help provide a protective shield against insurgents while American civilian personnel worked on economic projects.

Nation building and its interventionist methods did not succeed. Americans assumed that they could simply transfer their own model of capitalism and government to foreign cultures. But many foreigners resented American meddling in their affairs. And because monetary aid was usually funneled through a self-interested elite, it often did not reach the very poor. To people who preferred the relatively quick solutions of a managed economy, moreover, the American emphasis on private enterprise seemed inappropriate. "In the end," the presidential adviser and historian Arthur M. Schlesinger, Jr., later wrote, counterinsurgency proved "a ghastly illusion. Its primary consequence was to keep alive the American belief in [America's] capacity and right to intervene in foreign lands."

Descent into the Longest War: Vietnam

The belief in the right to influence the internal affairs of other countries led to disaster in Southeast Asia. How Vietnam became the site of America's longest war (1950 to 1975), how the world's most powerful nation failed to subdue a peasant people, and how those people suffered enormous losses of life and property and yet persisted in their struggle is one of the most remarkable and tragic stories of modern history.

The story begins with the French takeover of Vietnam during the late nineteenth century (see "Vietnam Chronology"). For decades, the French exploited the colony for its rice, **French Imperialism in Vietnam** rubber, tin, and tungsten, beating back peasant rebellions. All the while, Vietnamese nationalists grew in strength. They were led by Ho Chi Minh. Born in 1890, Ho moved to France before the First World War. At the close of the war, he joined the French Communist party to use it as a vehicle for Vietnamese independence.

Not until the Second World War, when the Japanese moved into Indochina, did French authority collapse. Seizing their chance, the Vietminh, an anti-imperialist coalition organized by Ho and other patriots, began guerrilla warfare in northern Vietnam. The Vietminh teamed up with agents of the American Office of Strategic Services (OSS) to harass the Japanese and their French collaborators. OSS officers who worked with Ho in Vietnam were impressed by his determination to drive outsiders from his country and by his frequent references to the United States as a revolutionary model. When Ho declared Vietnam's independence on September 2, 1945, his words sounded familiar: "We hold these truths to be self-evident. That all men are created equal."

The United States did not recognize Vietnamese independence for several reasons. Americans wanted France's cooperation in the emerging Cold **American Rejection of Vietnamese Independence** War, and besides, Southeast Asia was an economic asset. Its rice could feed America's soon-to-be ally Japan, and it was the world's largest producer of natural rubber and a rich source of other commodities. In addition, the area seemed strategically vital to the defense of Japan and the Philippines. Finally, Ho Chi Minh was a Communist, who, it was assumed, would assist Soviet expansionism. Vietnam thus became another test in the containment of communism.

Because of France's attempt to restore colonial rule, Vietnam was initially seen as a French problem. But when Jiang Jieshi (Chiang Kai-shek) went **American Support for the French** down to defeat in China, the United States was aroused to action. The Truman administration made two crucial decisions in early 1950. First, it recognized the French puppet government of the former emperor Bao Dai. Thus in Vietnamese eyes the United States became a colonial power, an ally of the hated French. Second, the administration agreed to send weapons, and ultimately military advisers, to the French. By 1954, the United States had provided more than $2 billion in military assistance and was bearing three-fourths of the cost of the war.

1861–87	French consolidate colonial rule in Indochina	1954	Dienbienphu crisis Geneva Conference and Accords Temporary partition of Vietnam United States backs Diem government
1890	Ho Chi Minh born		
1920	Ho Chi Minh joins Communist party		
1940	Japan occupies Indochina	1955	Diem, with American support, rejects Geneva Accords
1941	Vietminh organized OSS cooperates with Vietminh	1956	Diem begins crackdown on opponents
1945	Ho declares independence for Democratic Republic of Vietnam	1957	Anti-Diem insurgents begin terrorist attacks
1946	Anticolonial war against France begins	1959	North Vietnam begins sending aid to Communists in the South
1950	United States recognizes Bao Dai's government United States sends military aid to French for war in Vietnam	1960	National Liberation Front (Vietcong) organized in the South
		1961	President Kennedy decides to increase American military role in Vietnam

Note: For Vietnam events after 1961, see "Important Events," page 537.

Despite American aid, the French lost steadily to the Vietminh. Finally, in early 1954, Ho's forces surrounded the French fortress at Dienbienphu, in northwest Vietnam. What would **Dienbienphu** the United States do? President Eisenhower moved deliberately. Although Americans had been advising the French, they had not committed American forces to the war. If the president introduced American air power and it did not save the French, would American troops be required next?

Nonetheless, Eisenhower worried aloud at the prospect of a Communist victory, comparing the weak nations of the world to a row of dominoes, all of which would topple if just one fell (this became known as the domino theory). Washington pressed the British to help, but they refused. At home, members of Congress warned the administration to avoid any commitment of the American military, especially in the absence of allied backing. On May

7, the weary French defenders at Dienbienphu surrendered.

To add to the administration's problems, the French wanted out of the war. They agreed to peace talks at Geneva, where France, the United States, the Soviet Union, Britain, the People's Republic of China, Laos, and **Geneva** **Accords** Cambodia joined the two competing Vietnamese regimes of Bao Dai and Ho Chi Minh. The 1954 Geneva Accords, signed by France and Ho's Democratic Republic of Vietnam, temporarily divided Vietnam at the 17th parallel, with Ho's government confined to the North. National elections would be held in 1956, and the country would then be unified. In the meantime, neither North nor South was to join a military alliance or permit foreign military bases on its soil.

Certain that the Geneva agreements would ultimately mean Communist victory, the United States refused to accept the accords and set about sabotaging them. Soon after the conference, a CIA team entered Vietnam and began secret operations against the North, including commando raids across the 17th parallel. In the South, the United States and Ngo Dinh Diem became allies. A Catholic in a Buddhist nation, Diem lacked popular support. But with American aid and a fraudulent election, he outmaneuvered his opponents, including Bao Dai. When Ho called for national elections in keeping with the Geneva agreements, Diem and Eisenhower refused, fearing that the charismatic Vietminh leader would win. In September 1954, the United States, Britain, France, Australia, New Zealand, the Philippines, Thailand, and Pakistan formed an anti-Communist pact called the Southeast Asia Treaty Organization (SEATO). In a special protocol, SEATO extended protection to South Vietnam.

Ngo Dinh Diem

Meanwhile, Diem sought dictatorial power. He abolished village elections and appointed to public office people beholden to him. He threw dissenters into jail and shut down newspapers that criticized his regime. Communists and non-Communists alike struck back. Encouraged by Ho's regime in the northern capital of Hanoi, southern insurgents embarked on a program of terror, assassinating hundreds of Diem's village officials. In late 1960, southern Communists organized the National Liberation Front, or Vietcong. The Vietcong attracted other anti-Diem groups in the South. The war against imperialism had become a two-part Vietnamese civil war: Ho's North versus Diem's South, and Vietcong guerrillas versus the Diem government.

In the United States, newly elected President Kennedy decided to stand firm in Vietnam. He had suffered the humiliations of the Bay of Pigs and the Berlin Wall and feared further criticism if the United States backed down in Asia (where he was already seeking negotiations to end civil war in Laos). But more important, he sought a Cold War victory. By late 1963, South Vietnam had 16,700 American "advisers" stationed within its borders, and 489 of them were killed that year. Also in 1963, an American project called the

Kennedy's Escalation

Strategic Hamlet Program aimed to separate peasants from the Vietcong by relocating villagers to barbed-wire compounds. Meanwhile, Buddhist priests began protests, charging Diem with religious persecution. Protesting monks poured gasoline over their robes and ignited themselves in the streets of Saigon.

Diem, American officials decided, had to be removed. Through the CIA, the United States quietly encouraged disaffected South Vietnamese generals to stage a coup. The generals struck in early November 1963. Diem was captured and murdered—only a few weeks before Kennedy himself met death by an assassin's bullet.

With new governments in Saigon and Washington, some analysts thought it was time for reassessment. The Vietcong, United Nations General Secretary U Thant, France, and others called for a coalition government in South Vietnam. But the new American president, Lyndon B. Johnson, would have none of it; he sought victory.

Johnson and the War Without Victory

Johnson saw the world in simple terms—them against us—and privately disparaged both his allies and his enemies. Vietnam was a "raggedy-ass fourth-rate country," and his critics at home "rattlebrains." Johnson sometimes lied or exaggerated, creating what became known as a credibility gap. He also held firmly to fixed ideas about American superiority, the menace of communism, and the necessity of global intervention.

By early 1964, the Vietcong controlled nearly half of South Vietnam. Because the new Saigon government was shaky and seemed to be leaning toward neutralism, United States officials cooperated in a second coup. In neighboring Laos, American bombers hit supply routes connecting the Vietcong with the North Vietnamese. Laos, where the CIA had manipulated politics for years and where in 1962 non-Communists and Communists agreed to a neutralist government, was increasingly drawn into a wider Southeast Asian war. The bombings were kept secret from the American Congress and people.

An incident in the Gulf of Tonkin, off the coast of North Vietnam, accelerated American war making (see map, page 544). On August 2, 1964, the U.S.S. *Maddox*, participating in South Vietnamese commando raids against North Vietnam, came under attack from northern patrol boats, which suffered heavy damage. The unharmed *Maddox* sailed away. On August 4, now joined by another destroyer, the *Maddox* moved again toward the North Vietnamese shore. During bad weather, sonar technicians reported what they thought were enemy torpedoes; the two destroyers began firing ferociously. Yet when the captain of the *Maddox* asked his crew members what had happened, not one had seen or heard hostile gunfire.

Tonkin Gulf Incident

President Johnson, however, seized the chance to go on national television and announce retaliatory air strikes against North Vietnam. He then secured from Congress the Tonkin Gulf Resolution, which authorized the president to "take all necessary measures to repel any armed attack against the forces of the United States and to prevent further aggression." The vote was 466 to 0 in the House and 88 to 2 in the Senate. Over time, the Tonkin Gulf Resolution would come to serve as the declaration of war that Congress never voted.

After winning the presidency in his own right in the fall of 1964, Johnson directed the military to plan for stepped-up bombing of North Vietnam and Laos. After a Vietcong attack on an American airfield at Pleiku in February 1965, Johnson ordered carrier-based jets to ravage the North. Soon, Operation Rolling Thunder—a sustained bombing program above the 17th parallel—was under way. Before the longest war was over, more bombs would fall on Vietnam than American aircraft had dropped in the Second World War. The president also sent more American troops to Vietnam. America's troop commitment increased from 184,000 at the end of 1965 to 543,400 in 1969.

The "Americanization" of the war in Vietnam under Johnson troubled growing numbers of Americans, especially as increased television coverage brought the ugliness of combat into their homes every night. The pictures and stories were not pretty. Innocent civilians were caught in the line of fire; refugees flooded "pacification" camps; villages considered friendly to the enemy were burned to the ground. To expose and destroy Vietcong hiding places, pilots sprayed chemical defoliants like Agent Orange over the landscape to denude it. Stories of atrocities made their way home. Most gruesome was the My Lai massacre in March 1968 (not made public until twenty months later because of a military cover-up). An American unit, frustrated by its inability to pin down an elusive enemy and eager to avenge the loss of some buddies, shot to death more than two hundred unarmed Vietnamese civilians, most of them women and children.

Although many incidents of the deliberate shooting of civilians, torturing and killing of prisoners, taking of Vietnamese ears as trophies, and burning of villages have been recorded, most American soldiers were not committing atrocities. They were trying instead to save their young lives (their average age was only nineteen) and serve the United States mission by killing enemy troops. Many of these Americans made up the rear-echelon forces that supported the "grunts" in the field. Wherever they were, soldiers met an inhospitable environment, for no place in Vietnam was secure. The enemy was everywhere yet nowhere, often burrowed into elaborate underground tunnels or melded into the population, where every Vietnamese might be a Vietcong terrorist.

American Soldiers in Vietnam

Hundreds of thousands of the 2.8 million Vietnam veterans suffered post-traumatic stress disorder after returning home. This illness of nightmares and extreme nervousness was different from the shell shock of the First World War or the battle fatigue of the Second. Doctors reported that the disorder stemmed primarily from the fact that soldiers saw so many children, women, and elderly people killed. Sometimes, GIs themselves inadvertently killed these people, not always able to distinguish the innocent from the enemy; sometimes, they vengefully killed them and later felt guilt.

Post-traumatic Stress Disorder

Southeast Asia and the Vietnam War

Wounded American soldiers after a battle in Vietnam. *Larry Burrows,* Life *magazine, © 1971 Time Warner, Inc.*

As the war ground on to no discernible conclusion, the army in Vietnam grew troubled and morale sagged. Desertions and absent-without-official-leave (AWOL) cases increased, especially in the early 1970s, when no GI wanted to be the last man killed in the war. Racial tensions intensified between whites and blacks. Drug abuse became serious. "Fragging," the murder of an officer by soldiers using hand grenades or other weapons, also increased. "Grenades leave no fingerprints. Nobody's going to jail," recalled a soldier.

At home, thousands of young men expressed their opposition to the war by fleeing the draft. By the end of 1972, more than thirty thousand draft resisters were living in Canada, and thousands had gone into exile in Sweden and Mexico or lived under false identities in the United States. During the war, half a million men committed draft violations, including a quarter-million who never registered and thousands who burned their draft cards in protest.

As American military engagement in Vietnam escalated, so did protest at home. As early as April 1965, twenty-five thousand people marched on the White House, and in October the National Committee to End the War in Vietnam mobilized more than eighty thousand in nationwide demonstrations. In October 1967, a hundred thousand people marched on Washington, thousands of them reaching the steps of the Pentagon. Within the administration, too, disenchantment rose. Secretary of Defense Robert McNamara worked quietly to scale back the American military presence in Vietnam, but when he failed to persuade President Johnson, he resigned. "Ho Chi Minh is a tough old S.O.B.," McNamara told his aides. "And he won't quit no matter how much bombing we do."

Johnson dug in, snapping at his critics and

vowing to continue the battle, cheered by opinion polls that showed Americans actually favoring escalation over withdrawal. At times, he halted the bombing to encourage Ho Chi Minh to negotiate. Such pauses, however, were often accompanied by increases in American troop strength. American terms were unacceptable to Ho. They included nonrecognition of the Vietcong, withdrawal of northern soldiers from the South, and an end to North Vietnamese military aid to the Vietcong; in short, an abandonment of Ho's lifelong dream of an independent, unified Vietnam.

Defeat, Withdrawal, and the Legacy of Vietnam

In January 1968, a shocking event forced Johnson to reappraise his position. During Tet, the Vietnamese lunar new year, Vietcong and North Vietnamese forces struck all across South Vietnam, hitting and capturing provincial capitals. In Saigon, Vietcong raiders actually penetrated the American embassy compound. American and South Vietnamese units eventually regained much of the lost ground, inflicting heavy casualties on the enemy. But the Tet offensive jolted Americans. If all of America's firepower and dollars and half a million troops could not defeat the Vietcong, could anything?

Tet Offensive

The Tet offensive and its impact on public opinion hit the White House like a thunderclap. The new secretary of defense, Clark Clifford, told Johnson that the war could not be won, even if the 206,000 more soldiers requested by the army were sent to Vietnam. Strained by exhausting sessions with advisers, realizing that further escalation would not bring victory, and faced with serious opposition within the Democratic party, Johnson changed course. In a television appearance on March 31, he announced that he had stopped the bombing of most of North Vietnam and asked Hanoi to begin negotiations. Then he surprised the nation by dropping out of the presidential race. The United States, knowing it could not win, would at least try not to lose.

In July 1969, the new president, Richard M. Nixon, announced the Nixon Doctrine: the United States would help those nations that helped themselves. This doctrine reflected official Washington's realization that it could no longer afford to sustain so many overseas commitments, as well as the growing assumption that the United States would have to rely more on allied regional powers (like Iran in the Middle East) to maintain an anti-Communist world order. In Southeast Asia, the doctrine was implemented as "Vietnamization"—building up South Vietnamese forces to replace American troops. Nixon began a gradual withdrawal of American troops from Vietnam, decreasing their number to 139,000 by the end of 1971. But he also increased the bombing of the North, hoping to pound Hanoi into making concessions. Nixon's national security adviser, Henry A. Kissinger, called it jugular diplomacy.

Nixon Doctrine

In April 1970, South Vietnamese and American forces invaded Cambodia in search of arms depots and enemy forces that used the neutral nation as a sanctuary. This escalation sparked protests on college campuses across the nation. In June, the Senate joined the protest against Nixon's broadening of the war by terminating the Tonkin Gulf Resolution of 1964. Still, Nixon continued the "secret" bombing of Cambodia.

Cambodia and Antiwar Protests

Nixon's troubles at home mounted in mid-June 1971, when the *New York Times* began to publish the *Pentagon Papers*, a top-secret, official study of United States decisions in the Vietnam War. In 1967, Secretary McNamara had ordered preparation of the study to preserve the documentary record of the United States relationship with Vietnam. The *Pentagon Papers* revealed that American leaders had frequently lied to the American people.

Nixon and Kissinger continued to escalate the war, ordering "protective reaction strikes" against the North; acceleration of the CIA's Operation Phoenix (the assassination of thousands of enemy civilians in the South); the bombing of Cambodia; and the mining of Haiphong harbor in North Viet-

The agony of war. On the left is Marine Lance Corporal James Farley in Danang, after a Vietcong ambush killed American troops. On the right is President Lyndon B. Johnson (1908–1973), photographed in the wake of the Tet offensive and his decision not to run again for the presidency. *Left: Larry Burrows,* Life *magazine, © 1965 Time Warner, Inc.; right: Jack Kightlinger.*

nam. In December 1972, a massive air strike, called the Christmas bombing, hit the North. The air terror punished the Vietnamese; but twenty-six American planes, including fifteen B-52 bombers, were lost.

In Paris, meanwhile, peace talks, which began in 1968, seemed to be going nowhere. But Kissinger was meeting privately with Le Duc Tho, the chief delegate from North Vietnam. On **Cease-Fire** January 27, 1973, Kissinger and Le **Agreement** Duc Tho signed a cease-fire agreement. The United States promised to withdraw all its troops within sixty days. Other troops would stay in place, and a coalition government that included the Vietcong would eventually be formed in the South. Pleased that a peace had been made, critics nonetheless noted that the terms of the agreement could have been accepted in 1969 and more than twenty thousand American lives could have been spared. To prevent a future Vietnam, Congress, in November 1973, passed the War Powers Resolution: the president could commit American troops abroad for no more than sixty

days; after that period, he had to obtain congressional approval.

Leaving behind some advisers, the United States pulled its troops out of Vietnam and reduced, but did not end, its aid program. Both North and South soon violated the cease-fire, and full-scale war erupted once more. As many had predicted, the feeble South Vietnamese government could not hold out. On April 29, 1975, the South Vietnamese government collapsed. Ho's dream of a united, independent Vietnam was finally realized.

The overall costs of the war were immense. More than fifty-eight thousand Americans and more than a million Asians died. In monetary terms, the war cost the United States more than $150 billion, and billions more would be paid in future veterans' benefits. At home, the war brought inflation, political schism, attacks on civil liberties, and retrenchment from reform programs. The war also had negative consequences internationally: delay in moving toward better relations with the Soviet Union and China, friction with allies, and the alienation of Third World nations.

Meanwhile, in South Vietnam, Cambodia, and Laos, Communists assumed power and instituted repressive governments. Acute hunger afflicted the people of those devastated lands. Soon, refugees were crowding aboard unsafe vessels in an attempt to escape their battered homelands. Many of these "boat people" emigrated to the United States, where Americans, reluctant to be reminded of their defeat in Asia, received them with mixed feelings. But thoughtful Americans realized that the United States, which had relentlessly bombed, burned, and defoliated once-rich agricultural lands, bore considerable responsibility for the plight of the Southeast Asian peoples.

Gradually, debate developed about the causes and consequences of the war. Hawkish leaders who argued about the meaning of the war claimed that America's ignoble failure in Vietnam undermined the nation's credibility and tempted enemies to exploit opportunities at the expense of United States interests. They pointed to a Vietnam syndrome—a mood suspicious of foreign entanglements—which would inhibit the United States from exercising its power. They advised that next time the military should be permitted to do its job, free from the constraints of whimsical public opinion, stab-in-the-back journalists, and meddlesome politicians. America lost in Vietnam, they asserted, because the American people lost their guts and will at home.

The Lessons of Vietnam Debated

Others drew different lessons. Some people blamed the war on strong-willed presidents like Johnson and pusillanimous Congresses that had conceded too much power to the executive branch, as evident in the Tonkin Gulf Resolution. Trim the powers of the imperial presidency, they counseled, and America would become less interventionist. Others took a more hardheaded, even fatalistic, view: as long as the United States remained an industrial giant, with strong ideological, strategic, economic, and political needs that could be satisfied only through activism abroad, then the nation would continue to be expansionist and interventionist. Still others found fault with the containment doctrine: it failed to make distinctions between areas peripheral and areas vital to the national security and relied too heavily on military means. Furthermore, containment could not work without political stability and an effective and popular government in the country where it was being applied.

Public discussion of the Vietnam War was also stimulated by veterans, who called for better benefits to deal with posttraumatic stress disorder and the effects of the chemicals with which they had come in contact in Vietnam. Many returning veterans were also stung by the unsympathetic glances of Americans who did not want to be reminded of the unpleasant war or who blamed them for losing a war that could not be won. The veterans began to demand respect, arguing that the leaders who ordered them to Southeast Asia, not the GIs, should be held responsible for the negative results of the long war.

Nixon, Kissinger, and Détente

As the war wound down, Nixon and Kissinger pursued a grand strategy designed to promote a global balance of power, or "equilibrium." The first part of the strategy, announced in 1969, was détente: measured cooperation with the Soviets through negotiations within a general environment of rivalry. The purpose of détente, like that of the containment doctrine, which it resembled, was to check Soviet expansion and limit a Soviet arms build-up. The second part of the strategy was to curb revolution and radicalism in the Third World so as to resist threats to American interests. Critics faulted the Nixon-Kissinger policy for blaming Third World troubles on the Soviet Union rather than on unstable local conditions and for its arrogant assumption that the United States had the ability and the right to manipulate a disorderly world. Rather than decreasing the need for intervention, said critics, the new design actually increased it.

Détente

Nixon and Kissinger pursued détente with energy and fanfare. They expanded trade relations with the Soviet Union; a 1972 deal sent $1 billion worth of American grain to the Soviets at bargain prices. To slow the costly arms race, the Nixon administration initiated Strategic Arms Limitations Talks (SALT) with the Soviets. In 1972, the talks produced a SALT treaty that limited antiballistic missile (ABM) systems. The defensive ABM systems made offensive missiles less vulnerable to attack—and hence encouraged the other side to build more missiles to overcome ABM protection. Limiting ABMs was thus a step toward halting a spiraling arms race. A second agreement placed a five-year freeze on the number of offensive nuclear missiles each side could have. At the time of the agreement, the Soviets held an advantage in total missiles, but the United States had more warheads per missile because of its MIRVs (multiple independently targeted re-entry vehicles). In short, the United States had a 2-to-1 advantage in deliverable warheads. Because SALT did not restrict MIRVs, the nuclear arms build-up continued.

SALT Talks

Nixon and Kissinger also cultivated détente with the People's Republic of China, ending almost three decades of Sino-American hostility. In February 1972, the president made a historic trip to China. The Chinese Communists welcomed him because they sought to improve trade and hoped that friendlier Chinese-American relations would make the Soviets—a foe of China—more cautious. Nixon reasoned the same way. Official diplomatic recognition and exchange of ambassadors came in 1979.

Opening to China

Turmoil in the Third World

Tortuous events in the Middle East revealed how fragile the Nixon-Kissinger grand strategy was. When Nixon took office in 1969, the Middle East was, in the president's words, a "powder keg." In the Six-Day War (1967), Israel had used American weapons to score victories against Egypt and Syria. The Israelis had seized the West Bank and the an-

cient city of Jerusalem from Jordan, the Golan Heights from Syria, and the Sinai peninsula from Egypt (see map, page 550). To further complicate matters, Palestinian Arabs, many of them expelled from their homes in 1948, when the nation of Israel was created, had organized the Palestine Liberation Organization (PLO) and pledged to destroy Israel.

On October 6, 1973, Egypt and Syria attacked Israel. In spite of détente, Moscow, backing Egypt, and Washington, backing Israel, headed for a confrontation: both superpowers put their armed forces, including nuclear forces, on alert. At the same time, in an attempt to pressure Americans into taking a pro-Arab stance, the Organization of Petroleum Exporting Countries (OPEC) imposed an embargo on shipments of oil to the United States.

The 1973 War in the Middle East

Faced with an energy crisis at home from dramatically higher oil prices, the Nixon administration had to find a way to end Mideast hostilities. Kissinger arranged a cease-fire and undertook "shuttle diplomacy," flying back and forth repeatedly between Middle Eastern capitals in an exhausting search for a settlement. In March 1974, OPEC lifted the oil embargo. The next year, Kissinger persuaded Egypt and Israel to accept a United Nations peace-keeping force in the Sinai. But other problems, including Israel's insistence on building settlements in occupied lands and Arab threats to destroy the Jewish state, remained.

In Latin America, Nixon continued Cold War interventionist policies. In 1970, after the people of Chile elected a Marxist president, Salvador Allende, Nixon mobilized the CIA, which began secret operations to disrupt the Chilean economy, funneled money to newspapers critical of Allende, and apparently encouraged military officers to stage a coup. In 1973, a military junta ousted and killed Allende and installed an authoritarian regime in his place.

Intervention in Chile

In Africa, Nixon-Kissinger maneuvers proved less successful. During the 1960s and early 1970s, the CIA channeled funds to some of the groups fighting for the liberation of Angola from Portuguese colonial rule—while Washington publicly supported Por-

Angola

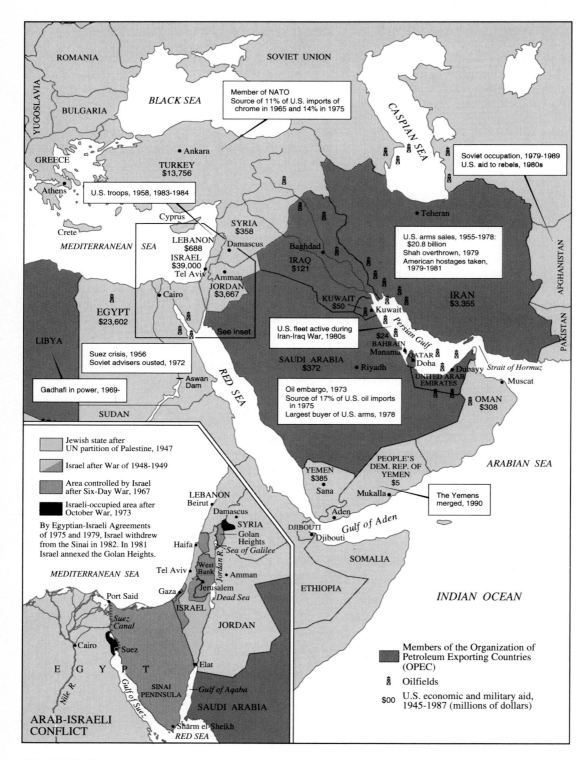

ROMANIA

SOVIET UNION

BLACK SEA

Member of NATO
Source of 11% of U.S. imports of
chrome in 1965 and 14% in 1975

CASPIAN SEA

Soviet occupation, 1979-1989
U.S. aid to rebels, 1980s

YUGOSLAVIA

BULGARIA

GREECE

Ankara

Athens

TURKEY
$13,756

Teheran

AFGHANISTAN

U.S. troops, 1958, 1983-1984

Cyprus

Crete

SYRIA
$358

LEBANON
$688

Damascus

Baghdad

U.S. arms sales, 1955-1978:
$20.8 billion
Shah overthrown, 1979
American hostages taken,
1979-1981

MEDITERRANEAN SEA

ISRAEL
$39,000

IRAQ
$121

Tel Aviv

Amman

PAKISTAN

JORDAN
$3,667

Cairo

KUWAIT
$50

IRAN
$3,355

EGYPT
$23,602

Kuwait

LIBYA

See inset

U.S. fleet active during
Iran-Iraq War, 1980s

$24
BAHRAIN
Manama

Persian Gulf

Suez crisis, 1956
Soviet advisers ousted, 1972

SAUDI ARABIA
$372

Riyadh

QATAR
Doha

Dubayy

Strait of Hormuz

Muscat

UNITED ARAB
EMIRATES

RED SEA

Aswan
Dam

Gadhafi in power, 1969-

OMAN
$308

Oil embargo, 1973
Source of 17% of U.S. oil imports
in 1975
Largest buyer of U.S. arms, 1978

SUDAN

PEOPLE'S
DEM. REP. OF
YEMEN
$5

ARABIAN SEA

YEMEN
$385

Sana

Mukalla

The Yemens
merged, 1990

Jewish state after
UN partition of Palestine, 1947

Israel after War of 1948-1949

LEBANON
Beirut

Aden

Gulf of Aden

Area controlled by Israel
after Six-Day War, 1967

Damascus

Israeli-occupied area after
October War, 1973

SYRIA
Golan
Heights

DJIBOUTI

Djibouti

By Egyptian-Israeli Agreements
of 1975 and 1979, Israel withdrew
from the Sinai in 1982. In 1981
Israel annexed the Golan Heights.

Haifa

Sea of Galilee

SOMALIA

MEDITERRANEAN SEA

Tel Aviv

West
Bank

Amman

INDIAN OCEAN

Port Said

Gaza

Jerusalem

Jordan R.

Dead Sea

Suez
Canal

ISRAEL

JORDAN

Cairo

Suez

E G Y P T

Elat

Members of the Organization of
Petroleum Exporting Countries
(OPEC)

Nile R.

SINAI
PENINSULA

Gulf of Aqaba

Oilfields

Gulf of Suez

SAUDI ARABIA

$00

U.S. economic and military aid,
1945-1987 (millions of dollars)

ARAB-ISRAELI
CONFLICT

Sharm el-Sheikh

RED SEA

The Middle East

tugal. After Angola won its independence in 1975, civil war erupted. The United States, which stepped up covert aid, and South Africa, which sent troops, backed one faction while the Soviets helped another. When Congress learned about the secret aid, it voted to cut all funds. Kissinger complained that the Soviets would gain a foothold in Africa. But many members of Congress argued that Americans could not decide the outcome of an African civil war; that the United States should not be aligned with the white racist regime of South Africa; and that diplomacy should have been tried. After a leftist government came to power in Angola, Washington took a keener interest in the rest of Africa, building economic ties, sending arms to friendly black nations, and distancing the United States from the white minority governments in Rhodesia (now Zimbabwe) and South Africa.

If disputes in the Middle East, Latin America, and Africa bedeviled the Nixon-Kissinger grand design for world order, global economic issues also heightened political disorder. **International Economic Instability** Kissinger explained that "international political stability requires international economic stability." But in the 1970s, there was little economic stability. Indeed, national economies were affected by a global recession, high oil prices, and increased tariff rates. Economists coined the term "Fourth World" for poor, less-developed Third World countries that lacked profit-making raw materials, relied heavily on food imports to combat famines, and built up large debts owed to governments and private banks. Third and Fourth World countries—often called the "South"— insisted that the wealthier, industrial "North" share economic resources.

As a major participant in the world economy, the United States could not escape these problems. Although America's economic standing had declined since the olympian days of the 1940s and 1950s, Americans remained the richest people in the world. The United States produced about one-third of the world's goods and services. In the mid-1970s, American investments abroad totaled more than $133 billion. The need to protect such interests explains in part why the United States was an interventionist power.

Multinational corporations became a symbol and a target of the conspicuous American economic position overseas. American-based multinationals **Multinational Corporations** like Exxon and General Motors actually enjoyed budgets and incomes larger than those of most countries. These giant firms brought home profits and exported American culture, but they aroused criticism. American workers protested that these global oligopolies stole their jobs when they moved factories abroad in search of cheaper labor. People of the "South" complained that multinationals exploited them, robbing their natural resources; that they corrupted politics; that they sometimes provided "cover" for CIA agents; and that they evaded taxes by clever manipulations of their books.

Multinational officers and government officials defended these enterprises, pointing out that they invested in risky ventures that brought economic progress, including the transfer of technology. Multinationals, they insisted, helped rationalize a chaotic world economy. Nonetheless, many countries passed laws requiring a certain percentage of native ownership. India, for example, legislated that its nationals own a majority of voting shares in industrial firms. Other countries simply nationalized multinational properties.

Another question that pitted "North" against "South" was the Law of the Sea Treaty, patiently composed in the 1970s through extended negotiations. Developing nations argued **Law of the Sea Treaty** that the rich seabed resources of petroleum and minerals should be shared among all nations as a "common heritage of mankind." The industrial states tended to prefer private enterprise or national exploitation, reaping the profits and raw materials for themselves. In the early 1980s, the global community finally hammered out a compromise between international and national controls and rights, but the United States rejected the treaty in 1983. Angry Third World nations railed against what they perceived as selfish economic imperialism, whereas many American allies who supported the compromise predicted a chaotic future of competing claims of ownership, territorial disputes, and threats to freedom of navigation. Like other international economic issues, this one promised a future of political instability.

Faced with so many international troubles, the Nixon administration clung to the now traditional globalist belief that the United States faced ubiquitous threats from Communists, radicals of all kinds, nationalists, and neutralists, and therefore that interventionism was a necessary burden. Thus, in the mid-1970s, some 686,000 American military personnel were stationed abroad; the United States had military links with ninety-two nations; American arms sales overseas climbed to $10 billion; and the CIA was active on every continent. These global activities were undertaken not only to impress Moscow with American might and will, but to serve as a counterrevolutionary force against nationalist stirrings, which threatened American economic and strategic interests. Nixon, his successor Gerald Ford, and Kissinger stood in a long line of leaders who counterpoised American power against foreign peoples determined to decide their own fate—such as against the Vietnamese, who, in their dogged pursuit of independence and social revolution, collided so directly with Americans that the societies, politics, and economies of both Vietnam and the United States suffered terribly.

Suggestions for Further Reading

General and Soviet-American Relations

Stephen Ambrose, *Rise to Globalism*, 4th ed. (1985); Richard J. Barnet, *The Alliance* (1983); John L. Gaddis, *Strategies of Containment* (1982); Raymond L. Garthoff, *Détente and Confrontation: American-Soviet Relations from Nixon to Reagan* (1985); Alexander L. George and Richard Smoke, *Deterrence in American Foreign Policy* (1974); Robert C. Johansen, *The National Interest and the Human Interest* (1980); Paul Kennedy, *The Rise and Fall of the Great Powers* (1987); Gabriel Kolko, *Confronting the Third World* (1988); Walter LaFeber, *America, Russia, and the Cold War, 1945–1985*, 5th ed. (1985); Thomas G. Paterson, *Meeting the Communist Threat* (1988); Alvin Z. Rubenstein and Donald E. Smith, eds., *Anti-Americanism in the Third World* (1985); Adam B. Ulam, *Dangerous Relations* (1983).

Kennedy and Johnson Diplomacy

Warren I. Cohen, *Dean Rusk* (1980); Doris Kearns, *Lyndon Johnson and the American Dream* (1976); Montague Kern et al., *The Kennedy Crises* (1984); Richard D. Mahoney, *JFK: Ordeal in Africa* (1983); Herbert S. Parmet, *JFK* (1983); Thomas G. Paterson, ed., *Kennedy's Quest for Victory* (1989); Gerald T. Rice, *The Bold Experiment: JFK's Peace Corps* (1985); Arthur M. Schlesinger, Jr., *Robert Kennedy and His Times* (1978); Arthur M. Schlesinger, Jr., *A Thousand Days* (1965); Thomas J. Schoenbaum, *Waging Peace and War* (1988).

Latin America and Cuba

Graham Allison, *Essence of Decision: Explaining the Cuban Missile Crisis* (1971); Samuel Baily, *The United States and the Development of South America, 1945–1975* (1977); Jules Benjamin, *The United States and the Origins of the Cuban Revolution* (1990); Cole Blasier, *Hovering Giant* (1974); Herbert Dinerstein, *The Making of a Missile Crisis* (1976); Jorge I. Domíguez, *To Make a World Safe for Revolution: Cuba's Foreign Policy* (1989); Trumbull Higgins, *The Perfect Failure* (1987) (on the Bay of Pigs invasion); Walter LaFeber, *Inevitable Revolutions* (1983) (on Central America); Walter LaFeber, *The Panama Canal* (1979); Morris Morley, *Imperial State and Revolution* (1987) (on Cuba); Louis A. Pérez, *Cuba* (1988); Stephen G. Rabe, *The Road to OPEC: United States Relations with Venezuela* (1982); Tad Szulc, *Fidel* (1986).

Middle East

Stephen Green, *Living by the Sword: America and Israel in the Middle East, 1968–87* (1988); George Lenczowski, *The Middle East in World Affairs*, 4th ed. (1980); William B. Quandt, *Decade of Decision: American Policy Toward the Arab-Israeli Conflict, 1967–1976* (1977); Barry Rubin, *Paved with Good Intentions* (1980) (on Iran); Steven L. Spiegel, *The Other Arab-Israeli Conflict* (1985); Robert W. Stookey, *America and the Arab States* (1975).

The Vietnam War and Southeast Asia

Loren Baritz, *Backfire* (1985); Larry Berman, *Lyndon Johnson's War* (1989); William C. Berman, *William Fulbright and the Vietnam War* (1988); Melanie Billings-Yun, *Decision Against War: Eisenhower and Dien Bien Phu, 1954* (1988); Jeffrey J. Clarke, *United States Army in Vietnam* (1989); Frances FitzGerald, *Fire in the Lake* (1972); Lloyd C. Gardner, *Approaching Vietnam* (1988); Leslie H. Gelb and Richard K. Betts, *The Irony of Vietnam* (1979); William C. Gibbons, *The U.S. Government and the Vietnam War* (1986–87); Daniel C. Hallin, *The "Uncensored War"* (1986); George C. Herring,

America's Longest War, 2nd ed. (1986); Gary Hess, *The United States' Emergence as a Southeast Asian Power* (1987); Arnold R. Isaacs, *Without Honor: Defeat in Vietnam and Cambodia* (1983); George McT. Kahin, *Intervention* (1986); Stanley Karnow, *Vietnam* (1983); Gabriel Kolko, *Anatomy of a War* (1986); Guenter Lewy, *America in Vietnam* (1978); Andrew Rotter, *The Path to Vietnam* (1987); William Shawcross, *Sideshow* (1979) (on Cambodia); Ronald H. Spector, *United States Army in Vietnam* (1983).

The Vietnam Legacy

Walter H. Capps, *The Unfinished War* (1982); John Hellman, *American Myth and the Legacy of Vietnam* (1986); Herbert Hendin and Ann P. Haas, *Wounds of War: The Psychological Aftermath of Combat in Vietnam* (1984); Myra MacPherson, *Long Time Passing: Vietnam and the Haunted Generation* (1984); Norman Podhoretz,*Why We Were in Vietnam* (1982); Harrison E. Salisbury, ed., *Vietnam Reconsidered* (1984); Harry G. Summers, Jr., *On Strategy* (1982).

Nixon, Kissinger, and Détente

Stephen Ambrose, *Nixon* (1987); Richard J. Barnet, *The Giants: Russia and America* (1977); Seymour M. Hersh, *The Price of Power* (1983); Stanley Hoffmann, *Primacy or World Order* (1978); Roger Morris, *Uncertain Greatness* (1977); Franz Schurmann, *The Foreign Politics of Richard Nixon* (1987); Richard Stevenson, *The Rise and Fall of Détente* (1985); John Stoessinger, *Henry Kissinger* (1976); Tad Szulc, *The Illusion of Peace* (1978).

The CIA and Counterinsurgency

Philip Agee, *Inside the Company* (1975); Douglas S. Blaufarb, *The Counterinsurgency Era* (1977); Loch Johnson, *America's Secret Power* (1989); Mark Lowenthal, *U.S. Intelligence* (1984); Victor Marchetti and John D. Marks, *The CIA and the Cult of Intelligence* (1974); Thomas Powers, *The Man Who Kept the Secrets* (1979); John Prados, *Presidents' Secret Wars* (1986); John Ranelagh, *The Agency* (1986); John Stockwell, *In Search of Enemies* (1978).

Nuclear Arms Race and SALT

Desmond Ball, *Politics and Force Levels: The Strategic Missile Program of the Kennedy Administration* (1980); Samuel B. Payne, Jr., *The Soviet Union and SALT* (1980); David N. Schwartz, *NATO's Nuclear Dilemmas* (1983); Glenn T. Seaborg, *Kennedy, Khrushchev, and the Test Ban* (1981); Stanford Arms Control Group, *International Arms Control*, 2nd ed. (1984).

The World Economy and "North-South" Issues

Richard J. Barnet, *The Lean Years* (1980); Richard J. Barnet and Ronald Müller, *Global Reach: The Power of the Multinational Corporations* (1974); David P. Calleo, *The Imperious Economy* (1982); Alfred E. Eckes, *The U.S. and Global Struggle for Minerals* (1979); Charles A. Jones, *The North-South Dialogue* (1983); Robert K. Olsen, *U.S. Foreign Policy and the New International Economic Order* (1981); William Paddock and Paul Paddock, *Time of Famines* (1976); Joan E. Spero, *The Politics of International Economic Relations*, 2nd ed. (1981); Herman Van Der Wee, *The Search for Prosperity: The World Economy, 1945–1980* (1986).

The first dreadful flash from Dallas clattered over newsroom Teletype machines across the country at 1:34 P.M., Eastern Standard Time. People still remember precisely where they were and what they were doing on November 22, 1963, when they heard that President John F. Kennedy had been shot and killed. For them, time stopped at that moment in what psychologists called flashbulb memory, the freeze-framing of an exceptionally emotional event down to the most incidental detail.

For four days in late November 1963, Americans wept, prayed, and stared at their television sets, numbed by the unbelievable. Throughout the afternoon and night before the funeral, 250,000 people trod silently past the coffin in the Capitol Rotunda. On the fourth day, a million people lined the streets of Washington and millions more watched on television as the president's body was borne by horse-drawn caisson to Arlington Cemetery.

"In retrospect," the British journalist Godfrey Hodgson has written, "people looked back to Friday, November 22, 1963, as the end of a time of hope, the beginning of a time of troubles." What was ironic about America's outpouring of grief was that the Kennedy administration had failed in many of its goals. In the final months of his presidency, Kennedy had been criticized for being ineffectual in domestic affairs and reckless in foreign affairs. But John Kennedy's assassination was a national tragedy. In their grief, Americans remembered how he had inspired their hopes for peace, prosperity, and social justice.

In the early 1960s, hope had run especially high among the nation's poor. Kennedy's presidency coincided with and was spurred by the modern African-American civil rights movement, and his call for a New Frontier had inspired liberal Democrats, idealists, and brave young activists to work to eliminate poverty, segregation, and voting rights abuses. Americans also supported Kennedy's desire to court the Third World and prevail in the Cold War. Lyndon B. Johnson, Kennedy's successor in the White House, presided over the Great Society, and Congress responded to his urgings with a flood of legislation. The 1960s saw more economic, political, and social reform than any period since the New Deal. But even during these years of liberal triumphs, anger occasionally flared into vio-

31

REFORM AND CONFLICT: A TURBULENT ERA IN AMERICA, 1961–1973

lence. Beginning with the assassination in 1963, ten years of events ensued—including race riots, the murders of other political and civil rights leaders, and the war in Vietnam—that shattered the Kennedy and Johnson optimism.

In the cities, many blacks were angry that they still lived in poverty and segregation despite the civil rights movement and the passage of landmark civil rights laws. Their discontent exploded during the "long hot summers" of the 1960s. In July 1967, for example, twenty-six people were killed in Newark, New Jersey, in warfare between blacks, the police, and army troops. This event was followed a week later by the Detroit race riot, which led to the deaths of forty-three persons. The next year, the National Advisory Commission on Civil Disorders, chaired by Governor Otto Kerner of Illinois, released its report on the causes of the race riots. "The nation is rapidly moving toward two increasingly separate Americas . . . a white society principally located in suburbs . . . and a Negro society largely concentrated within large central cities."

This social turbulence, along with the growing movement opposing the Vietnam War, brought down the presidency of Lyndon B. Johnson and gave rise to Black Power, the radical politics of the New Left, and a revived women's movement, not to mention the "hippie" counterculture. Johnson's departure from office did not produce calm. Richard M. Nixon, who was elected president in 1968, polarized the nation still further.

The Civil Rights Movement and Kennedy's New Frontier

He was, as Norman Mailer wrote of President John F. Kennedy, "our leading man." The handsome, vigorous new chief executive was young, the first president born in the twentieth century. Perceived by the public as an intellectual, he had a genuinely inquiring mind; as a patron of the arts, he brought wit and sophistication to the White House.

In a departure from the Eisenhower administration's staid, conservative image, the new president, elected in 1960, surrounded himself with young men of intellectual verve who proclaimed that they had fresh ideas for invigorating the nation. The writer David Halberstam called these men "the best and the brightest." Secretary of Defense Robert McNamara, aged forty-four, had been an assistant professor at Harvard at twenty-four and later the whiz kid president of the Ford Motor Company. Kennedy's special assistant for national security affairs, McGeorge Bundy, aged forty-one, had become a dean at Harvard at thirty-four with only a bachelor's degree. Kennedy himself was only forty-three, and his brother Robert, the attorney general, was thirty-five.

"The Best and the Brightest"

Kennedy's program, the New Frontier, was immensely ambitious and promised more than Kennedy could deliver: an end to racial discrimination, federal aid to farmers and to education, medical care for the elderly, and government action to halt the recession that had the country in its grip. Longtime members of Congress saw him and his administration as publicity hungry. By August 1961, eight months into his first year, it was evident that Kennedy lacked the ability to move Congress.

Despite his rhetoric, Kennedy pursued civil rights without vigor. Thus, black civil rights activists had to continue their struggle for equality without strong overt support from the White House. The tactic they used most often was nonviolent civil disobedience. Volunteers organized by the Southern Christian Leadership Conference (SCLC), headed by Martin Luther King, Jr., deliberately violated segregation laws by sitting in at white-only lunch counters, libraries, and bus stations in parts of the South. When arrested they went to jail as an act of conscience. The Congress of Racial Equality (CORE) initiated the Freedom Rides. In May 1961, the "Freedom Riders," an integrated group of thirteen persons, boarded buses and braved attacks by southern white mobs for daring to desegregate interstate transportation. Meanwhile, black students in the South were joining the Student Non-Violent Coordinating Committee (SNCC). More than any other volunteers, it was these field workers who walked the dusty back

Civil Rights Movement

A historic moment for the civil rights movement was the March on Washington, August 28, 1963, as 250,000 people stood together for racial equality. The Reverend Martin Luther King, Jr., is about to deliver his "I Have a Dream" speech. *Francis Miller,* Life *magazine,* © *1963 Time Warner, Inc.*

roads of Mississippi and Georgia, encouraging African-Americans to resist segregation and register to vote.

As the civil rights movement gained momentum, President Kennedy gradually made a commitment to first-class citizenship for blacks. In September 1962, he ordered United States marshals to protect and assist James Meredith, the first black student to attend the University of Mississippi. And in June 1963, Kennedy finally requested legislation to outlaw segregation in public accommodations. When more than 250,000 people, black and white, gathered at the Lincoln Memorial for a March on Washington that August, they did so with the knowledge that President Kennedy was at last on their side.

Meanwhile, television news programs brought civil rights struggles into American homes. The story was sometimes grisly. In 1963, Medgar Evers, director of the NAACP in Mississippi, was murdered in his own driveway. That same year, police in Birmingham, Alabama, attacked nonviolent civil rights demonstrators, including many children, with snarling dogs, fire hoses, and cattle prods. Then two horrifying events helped to convince reluctant politicians that action on civil rights was

long overdue. In September, white terrorists exploded a bomb during Sunday-morning services at Birmingham's Sixteenth Street Baptist Church. Sunday school was in session, and four black girls were killed. A little more than two months later, on November 22, 1963, John Kennedy was assassinated in Dallas.

Historians have wondered what John Kennedy would have accomplished had he lived. Although his legislative achievements were meager, he inspired idealism in Americans.

Kennedy in Retrospect Thousands of Americans joined the Peace Corps, volunteering to spend two years of their lives in this Kennedy-created program. Kennedy also created a sense of national purpose through his vigorous support of the space program. In recent years, however, some writers have described not Kennedy's idealism, but his recklessness in world events, such as authorizing CIA assassination attempts on the life of Cuba's Premier Fidel Castro. It is clear, however, that Kennedy had begun to grow as president during his last few months in office. He made a moving appeal for racial equality and called for an easing of Cold War tensions.

IMPORTANT EVENTS

1960	Kennedy elected president	**1967**	Race riots in Newark, Detroit, and other cities
1961	Freedom Rides		
	Establishment of the first President's Commission on the Status of Women	**1968**	U.S.S. *Pueblo* captured by North Korea
1962	SDS's Port Huron Statement		Tet offensive
	Baker v. *Carr*		Martin Luther King, Jr., assassinated
1963	Friedan, *The Feminine Mystique*		Race riots in 168 cities and towns
	March on Washington		Antiwar protests escalate
	Birmingham, Alabama, Baptist church bombed		Robert F. Kennedy assassinated
	Kennedy assassinated; Johnson assumes the presidency		Violence at Democratic convention
			Nixon elected president
1964	Economic Opportunity Act	**1969**	Stonewall riot
	Civil Rights Act of 1964		*Apollo 11* moon landing
	First of the "long hot summers"		Woodstock festival
	Free Speech Movement		Moratorium Day
	Johnson elected president	**1970**	United States invades Cambodia
1965	Malcolm X assassinated		Students killed at Kent State University and Jackson State University
	Voting Rights Act of 1965		
	Medicare	**1971**	*Pentagon Papers*
	Elementary and Secondary Education Act		Twenty-sixth Amendment ratified, giving vote to eighteen-year-olds
	Watts race riot	**1972**	Nixon visits China and Russia
1966	National Organization for Women (NOW) established		Equal Rights Amendment (ERA) approved by Congress
	Miranda v. *Arizona*		Nixon re-elected
		1973	*Roe* v. *Wade*

Johnson and the Great Society

The new president, Lyndon B. Johnson, made civil rights his top legislative priority. "No memorial oration or eulogy," he told a joint session of Congress five days after the assassination, "could more elo-

Civil Rights Act of 1964

quently honor President Kennedy's memory than the earliest passage of the civil rights bill." It was fortunate for the civil rights movement that Johnson, a southerner, had become president. Within months Johnson had signed into law the Civil Rights Act of 1964. The act outlawed discrimination on the basis of race, color, religion, sex, or national origin not only in public accommodations, but also in employment. An Equal Employment

Opportunity Commission was established the same year to investigate and judge complaints of job discrimination. The act also authorized the government to withhold funds from public agencies that discriminated on the basis of race, and it gave the attorney general powers to guarantee voting rights and end school segregation.

Johnson enunciated another priority in January 1964, in his first State of the Union address: "The administration today, here and now, declares unconditional war on poverty." Eight months later, he signed into law the Economic Opportunity Act of 1964, which allocated almost $1 billion to fight poverty. The act became the opening salvo in Johnson's War on Poverty.

In the year following Kennedy's death, Johnson sought to govern by consensus, appealing to the shared values and aspirations of the majority of the nation. Judging by his lopsided victory over his Republican opponent in 1964, Senator Barry Goldwater of Arizona, he succeeded. Johnson garnered 61 percent of the popular vote and the electoral votes of all but six states.

Election of 1964

The Democrats also won staggering majorities in both the House and the Senate. Johnson knew that the moment for further reform had arrived. "Hurry, boys, hurry," he told his staff just after the election. "Get that legislation up to the Hill and out. Eighteen months from now ol' Landslide Lyndon will be Lame-Duck Lyndon." Congress responded in 1965 and 1966 with the most sweeping reform legislation since 1935.

Three bills enacted in 1965 were legislative milestones. The Medicare program insured the elderly against medical and hospital bills. The Elementary and Secondary Education Act became the first general program of federal aid to education. The Voting Rights Act of 1965 empowered the attorney general to supervise voter registration in areas where fewer than half the minority residents of voting age were registered. In 1960, only 29 percent of the South's black population was registered to vote; when Johnson left office in 1969, the proportion was approaching two-thirds. Even in the most resistant states, that trend continued. Only 6.7 percent of Mississippi's black citizens were registered to vote in 1964; in 1968, the figure was 59.4 percent.

Other accomplishments during Johnson's presidency included establishment of the Department of Housing and Urban Development; water and air quality improvement acts; liberalization of immigration laws; and appropriations for the most ambitious federal housing program since 1949, including rent supplements to low-income families. In 1968, Johnson signed his third civil rights act, banning racial and religious discrimination in the sale and rental of housing. Another provision of this legislation, known as the Indian Bill of Rights, extended those constitutional protections to reservation Indians living under tribal self-government.

Even more ambitious was Johnson's War on Poverty. Because the gross national product had increased, Johnson and his advisers reasoned that the government could expect a "fiscal dividend" of several billion dollars in additional tax revenues. They decided to spend the extra money to wipe out poverty through education and job training programs. Beginning with the $1-billion appropriation in 1964, the War on Poverty evolved in 1965 and 1966 to include the Job Corps, which was to provide marketable skills, work experience, remedial education, and counseling for young people; Project Head Start, geared to preparing low-income preschoolers for grade school; and Upward Bound, aimed at high school students from low-income families who aspired to a college education. Other antipoverty programs were Legal Services for the Poor; Volunteers in Service to America (VISTA); and the Model Cities program, which directed federal funds toward upgrading employment, housing, education, and health in targeted neighborhoods.

War on Poverty

The War on Poverty, in tandem with a rising gross national product, substantially alleviated hunger and suffering in the United States. For one thing, the War on Poverty directly attacked the debilitating housing, health, and nutritional conditions from which the poor suffered. Moreover, between 1965 and 1970, federal spending for Social Security, health, welfare, and education more than doubled. During the same years, the GNP leaped from $685 billion to $977 billion. The result was a startling reduction

Successes in Reducing Poverty

in the number of poor people, from 25 percent of the population in 1962 to 11 percent in 1973.

Despite the War on Poverty's successes, the period of liberal ascendancy it represented was short-lived; its legislative achievements occurred from 1964 to 1966. Disillusioned with America's deepening involvement in Vietnam, many of Johnson's allies began to reject both him and his liberal consensus. But one branch of government continued the liberal tradition—the Supreme Court.

The Warren Court

In the volatile 1960s, the Supreme Court was disposed by political sentiment and a belief in judicial activism to play a major role in the resurgence of liberalism. Its liberal majority included Chief Justice Earl Warren. After the 1954 and 1955 school desegregation cases, the Warren Court did not disturb the political waters for the remainder of the 1950s. Beginning in 1962, however, the Court began handing down a series of liberal decisions. In *Baker* v. *Carr* (1962) and subsequent rulings, it declared that the principle of "one person, one vote" must prevail at both state and national levels. This decision required the reapportionment of state legislatures so that each representative would serve the same number of constituents. The Court also outlawed required prayers and Bible readings in public schools, explaining that such practices placed an "indirect coercive pressure upon religious minorities."

The Court also attacked the constitutional basis of McCarthyism, ruling in 1965 that a person need not register with the government as a member of a subversive organization, for to do so would violate constitutional safeguards against self-incrimination. It also ruled on birth control, holding in *Griswold* v. *Connecticut* (1965) that a state law prohibiting the use of contraceptives by married persons violated "a marital right of privacy" and was unconstitutional. The Court upheld the Civil Rights Act of 1964 and the Voting Rights Act of 1965. In other rulings that par-

Civil Rights Rulings

ticularly upset conservatives, the Court decreed that books, magazines, and films could not be banned as obscene unless they were "found to be utterly without redeeming social value."

Perhaps most controversial was the Court's transformation of the criminal justice system. Beginning with *Gideon* v. *Wainwright* (1963), the Court ruled that a poor person charged with a felony had the right to a state-appointed lawyer. In *Escobedo* v. *Illinois* (1964), it decreed that the accused had the right to counsel during interrogation and could remain silent. And in *Miranda* v. *Arizona* (1966), it added that police had to inform criminal suspects that they could see a lawyer and remain silent and that any statements they made could be used against them.

Despite demands for Warren's removal, most constitutional historians judge him to have been perhaps the most influential chief justice in the nation's history. Whether or not one approved of the Warren Court, which ended with Warren's retirement in 1969, there was no denying its impact on the American people.

Race Riots and the Movement Toward Black Power

Even as the civil rights movement registered legal and constitutional victories, some activists began to grumble that the federal government was not to be trusted. During the Mississippi Summer Project of 1964, hundreds of college-age volunteers from the North had joined SNCC and CORE field workers to establish "freedom schools" for black children. Many of these volunteers believed that the Federal Bureau of Investigation was hostile to the civil rights movement, and they charged that FBI Director J. Edgar Hoover was a racist. They were also disturbed by rumors, later confirmed, that Hoover had wiretapped and bugged the hotel room where Martin Luther King, Jr., was staying and planted allegations in the newspapers about his sexual improprieties.

Indeed, some FBI informants had not only joined the Ku Klux Klan, but reportedly had also become leaders of the terrorist group. One of them had organized several atrocities, including the bombing of Birmingham's Sixteenth Street Baptist Church in 1963. Small wonder that during the summer of 1964 there was an upsurge in racist violence in the South, particularly in Mississippi. White vigilantes bombed and burned two dozen black churches there, and three civil rights workers were murdered in Philadelphia, Mississippi, by a group that included sheriff's deputies.

Violent Attacks on Civil Rights Workers

Meanwhile, northern blacks began to consider their situation. They knew that their neighborhoods were deteriorating. Their neighborhoods were more segregated than ever, for whites had responded to the black migration from the South by fleeing to the suburbs. Their median income was little more than half that of whites, and their unemployment rate was twice that of whites. For African-American males between the ages of eighteen and twenty-five, it was five times as high. Many black families, particularly those headed solely by women, lived in perpetual poverty. Such were the conditions in 1964 that caused the first of the "long hot summers" of race riots in northern cities. In Harlem and Rochester, New York, and in several cities in New Jersey black anger boiled over.

If 1964 was fiery and violent, 1965 was even more so. In August, blacks gutted the Los Angeles neighborhood of Watts; thirty-four people were killed (see map). Other cities exploded in riots between 1966 and 1968. Unlike the race riots of 1919 and 1943, those in the 1960s were not provoked by white mobs. Instead, blacks exploded in anger over their joblessness and lack of opportunity, looting white-owned stores, setting fires, and throwing rocks. "What white Americans have never fully understood," stated the Kerner Commission in its report several years later, "but what the Negro can never forget—is that white society is deeply implicated in the ghetto. White institutions created it, white institutions maintain it, and white society condones it."

Explosion of Black Anger

It was obvious that many blacks, especially in the North, had begun to question whether the nonviolent civil rights movement had ever addressed their needs. In 1963 Martin Luther King, Jr., had appealed to whites' humanitarian instincts in his "I have a dream" speech. But another voice was beginning to be heard, one that urged blacks to seize their freedom "by any means necessary." It was the voice of Malcolm X, a one-time pimp and street hustler who, while in prison, had converted to the Nation of Islam religion, commonly known as the Black Muslims.

The Black Muslims, a small sect that espoused black pride along with separatism from white society, condemned the "white devil" as the chief source of evil in the world. They attempted to dissociate themselves from white society, exhorted blacks to lead sober lives and practice thrift, and advocated violence in self-defense. By the early 1960s, Malcolm X had become their chief spokesperson, and his advice was straightforward: "If someone puts a hand on you, send him to the cemetery."

Malcolm X

Malcolm X was murdered in a hail of bullets in February 1965; his assassins were Black Muslims who believed that he had betrayed their cause. It was true that he had modified some of his ideas just before his death. He had met whites who were not devils, he said, and he had expressed cautious support for the nonviolent civil rights movement. Still, for both blacks and whites, Malcolm X symbolized black defiance and self-respect.

A year after Malcolm X's murder, Stokely Carmichael, chairman of SNCC, called on blacks to assert Black Power. Carmichael believed that in order to be truly free from white oppression, blacks had to control their own institutions—businesses, politics, schools. Soon organizations that had been committed to racial integration and nonviolence began to embrace Black Power. SNCC and CORE purged white members and repudiated integration, arguing that black people needed power, not white friendship.

Black Power

The wellspring of this new militance was black nationalism, the concept that black peoples everywhere in the world shared a unique history and cultural heritage that set them apart from

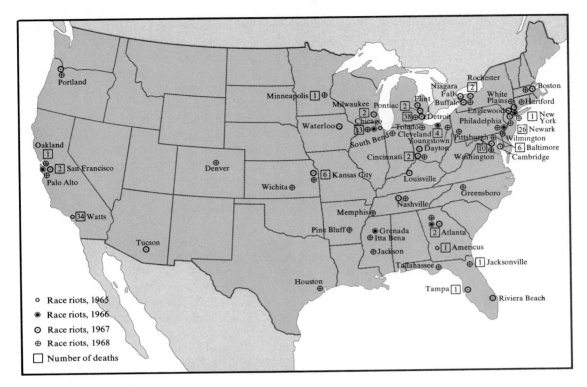

Race Riots, 1965–1968

whites. College students pressed for black studies programs, and blacks began to call themselves black or Afro-American rather than Negro.

To white America, one of the most fearsome of the new black groups was the Black Panther party. Armed and wearing leather jackets, Panther leaders dedicated themselves to destroying capitalism. At the same time, a vocal minority of whites from the baby-boom generation set out to "change the system."

The New Left and the Counterculture

In the fall of 1964, Mario Savio returned to Berkeley, California, from Mississippi, where he had been working in the SNCC summer project. Savio and other students became convinced that the same

power structure that dominated blacks' lives also controlled the bureaucratic machinery of the university. "Last summer I went to Mississippi to join the struggle there for civil rights. This fall I am engaged in another phase of the same struggle, this time in Berkeley. . . . The same rights are at stake in both places," Savio wrote.

In many ways, the University of California in 1964 was a model university, with a worldwide reputation for excellence. Its chancellor, the economist Clark Kerr, had likened the university to a big business. But that was what bothered some students. Berkeley, a "multiversity" with tens of thousands of students, had become hopelessly impersonal. "I am a student," rang one lament of the Free Speech Movement. "Do not fold, spindle, or mutilate."

The struggle at Berkeley began in September 1964, when the university administration banned civil rights and antiwar recruitment in Sproul Plaza,

Free Speech Movement

the students' traditional gathering place. Militant students defied Kerr's ban; the administration suspended them or had them arrested. On October 1, several thousand students surrounded a police car in which a militant was being held, immobilizing it for thirty-two hours. Then, in December, the Free Speech Movement seized and occupied the main administration building. The governor dispatched state police to Berkeley, and more than eight hundred people were arrested. Angry students shut down classes for several days in protest. By the end of the decade, the activism born at Berkeley would spread to hundreds of other campuses.

Two years earlier, another group of students had gathered in Port Huron, Michigan, for a national meeting of Students for a Democratic Society **Students for a Democratic Society (SDS)** (SDS). Like their leaders, Tom Hayden and Al Haber, most SDS members were white college students, the children of middle-class Americans. In their platform, the Port Huron Statement, they condemned racism, poverty amid plenty, and the Cold War. SDS sought nothing less than the revitalization of democracy through the return of power to the people.

Inspired by the Free Speech Movement and SDS, a minority of students joined the New Left. Although they were united in their hatred of racism and the Vietnam War, the New Left **New Left** was not a single organization or movement. Some people in the New Left were Marxists, others black nationalists, anarchists, or pacifists. Some believed in pursuing social change through negotiation; others were revolutionaries who rejected compromise.

In the wake of the New Left appeared a phenomenon that observers called the counterculture. Revolutionary figures like Mao Zedong and Fidel Castro became campus idols. Millions of students experimented **Counter-cultural Revolution** with marijuana, amphetamines, and hallucinogenic drugs. But it was music more than anything else that reflected the new attitudes. Long before the Beatles sang "you say you want a revolution," it was evident that their music had inspired one. Soon, music was the chief vehicle for the counterculture's assault on the status quo. Bob Dylan promised revolutionary answers "blowin' in the wind," and young people cheered Jimi Hendrix, who sang of life in a drug-induced "purple haze," and Janis Joplin, who brought African-American blues to white Americans.

Rock festivals became cultural happenings. The most famous of them, Woodstock (1969), in upstate New York, attracted 400,000 people. The huge crowd endured several days of rain and mud together, without shelter and without violence. Some among them began to dream of a peaceful "Woodstock nation," based on love, drugs, and rock music.

While some youths sought alternative experiences through drugs and music, others tried to construct alternative ways of life. Among the most conspicuous were the hippies. In the Haight-Ashbury section of San Francisco, "flower children" created an urban subculture as distinctive as that of any Chinatown or Little Italy. "Hashbury" inspired numerous other communal living experiments.

Just as the New Left attracted a minority of students, so the counterculture represented only a small proportion of American youth. But to disconcerted middle-class parents, hip- **Drugs and Sex** pies seemed to be everywhere. Parents carped about long hair, love beads, and patched jeans. They complained that "acid rock" was loud, discordant, even savage. They feared that their children would suffer lifelong damage from drugs. Most disturbing to parents were the casual sexual mores that young people were adopting, partly as a result of the availability of birth-control pills. For many young people, living together no longer equaled living in sin; and as attitudes toward premarital sex changed, so did notions about pornography, homosexuality, sex roles, and familial relationships.

The militancy of the 1960s also helped inspire the gay rights movement. Throughout the 1950s and much of the 1960s, many homosexuals had feared that disclosing their sexual **Gay Rights Movement** preference would cause them to lose not only their jobs, but even their friends and families. In June 1969, that attitude began to change. In New York

City's Greenwich Village, a riot erupted between police and the patrons of the Stonewall Inn, a gay bar. Police who raided the bar were not prepared for the volley of beer bottles that greeted them. Rioting continued into the night. As John D'Emilio, the historian, has written: "Stonewall thus marked a critical divide in the politics and consciousness of homosexuals and lesbians. A small, thinly spread reform effort suddenly grew into a large, grass-roots movement for liberation."

For both cultural and political reasons, the slogan "Make Love, Not War" became popular in the 1960s. As the war in Vietnam escalated, the New Left and the counterculture discovered a common cause. Students held teach-ins on the war—open forums for discussion among students, professors, and guest speakers. Marches and demonstrations against the war became a popular protest tactic. In addition to the young men who had fled the draft by moving to other countries, others protested, violently and nonviolently, at local draft board offices.

By this time, growing numbers of Americans, young and old, had quit believing their elected leaders. President Johnson claimed the United States was fighting for honorable reasons, and by 1968 almost half a million American soldiers were stationed in Vietnam. But increasing numbers of people were wondering what goal could justify the Vietnam War.

1968: A Year of Protest, Violence, and Loss

As stormy and violent as the years from 1963 through 1967 had been, many Americans were still trying to downplay the nation's distress in the hope that it would go away. But in 1968, a series of shocks hit them even harder. The first hit in 1968, when the U.S.S. *Pueblo*, a navy intelligence ship, was captured by the North Koreans. A week later came the Tet offensive in Vietnam. For the first time, many Americans believed that they might lose the war. Meanwhile, American casualties in-creased. On July 4, 1968, total American fatalities surpassed thirty thousand.

Controversy over the war deepened. Within the Democratic party, two men rose to challenge John-son for the 1968 presidential nomination. One of them, Senator Eugene McCarthy of Minnesota, en-tered the New Hampshire primary solely to contest Johnson's war policies. On March 12, McCarthy won twenty of twenty-four convention delegates. Soon after, another Democrat, Senator Robert F. Kennedy of New York, entered the fray. On March 31, President Johnson went on national television and announced a scaling-down of the bombing in North Vietnam. Then he hurled a political thunder-bolt—he would not be a candidate for re-election.

Less than a week later, a white assassin named James Earl Ray shot and killed Martin Luther King, Jr., in Memphis. Ray's crime aroused instant rage in the nation's ghettos. Blacks rioted in 168 cities and towns, looting and burning white businesses and properties. Thirty-four blacks and five whites died in the violence. In Chicago, Mayor Richard Daley or-dered police to shoot to kill arsonists. Across the nation, hatred mounted on both sides.

Assassination of Martin Luther King, Jr.

In April and May, Gallup polls reported Robert Kennedy to be the front-running presidential candi-date among Democrats. In June, he won the Califor-nia primary. While Kennedy was celebrating his victory in a Los Angeles hotel, a young man stepped forward with a revolver and fired repeatedly. The assassin was an Arab nationalist named Sirhan Sirhan, who despised Kennedy for his unwavering support of Israel.

Assassination of Robert Kennedy

Violence erupted again in August at the Demo-cratic national convention in Chicago. The Demo-crats were divided, and adding to the dissension were the thousands of antiwar protesters and members of the Youth International Party ("Yip-pies") who had traveled to Chicago. The Chicago police force was still in the psychological grip of Mayor Daley's shoot-to-kill directive. Twelve thousand police were assigned to twelve-hour

Violence at the Democratic Convention

Violence erupted in Chicago's Grant Park during the 1968 Democratic convention. Police and National Guardsmen used tear gas and clubs to stop twelve thousand protesters from marching to the convention hall. *UPI/Bettmann Archives.*

shifts, and another twelve thousand army troops and National Guardsmen were on call. On Michigan Avenue, in front of the Conrad Hilton Hotel, they attacked, wading into ranks of demonstrators, reporters, and television camera operators. Throughout the nation, viewers watched as club-swinging police beat protesters to the ground. When onlookers rushed to shield the injured, they too were clubbed.

The Democratic convention nominated Vice President Hubert Humphrey for president and Senator Edmund Muskie of Maine for vice president. Like Johnson and Kennedy before him, Humphrey was a political descendant of the New Deal and an unstinting supporter of the war. Opposing Humphrey in the 1968 election were Richard M. Nixon, the Republican nominee, and Governor George Wallace of Alabama, who ran as the nominee of the American Independent party.

When the votes were tabulated, Nixon emerged the winner by the slimmest of margins. Wallace collected almost 10 million votes, or 13.5 percent of the total, the best performance by a third party since 1924. His strong showing made Nixon a minority president, elected with only 43.4 percent of the popular vote. Moreover, the Democrats maintained control of the House and the Senate.

Election of 1968

Still, the election had been a triumph for conservatism, as the combined vote for Nixon and Wallace was 57 percent. The war had hurt the Democrats' appeal, but even more politically damaging was the party's identification with the cause of racial justice. In 1968, Humphrey received only 35 percent of the white vote. Among the defectors from the New Deal coalition were northern, blue-collar, ethnic voters. "In city after city," one observer noted, "ra-

Chapter 31: Reform and Conflict: A Turbulent Era in America, 1961–1973

cial conflicts had destroyed the old alliance. The New Deal had unraveled block by block."

The Rebirth of Feminism

During the turbulence of the 1960s, another liberation movement gained momentum, at first quietly and then on the picket line. After the adoption of the Nineteenth Amendment in 1920, the women's rights movement had languished. But in the 1960s, feminism was reborn. Many women were dissatisfied with their lives, and in 1963, with the publication of *The Feminine Mystique*, they found a voice. Betty Friedan, the book's author, wrote that women across the country were deeply troubled by "the problem that has no name." Most women believed that "all they had to do was devote their lives from earliest girlhood to finding a husband and bearing children." The problem was that "this mystique of feminine fulfillment" left many wives and mothers feeling "empty" or "incomplete." Friedan quoted a young mother: "I've tried everything women are supposed to do—hobbies, gardening, pickling, canning, and being very social with my neighbors. . . . I love the kids and Bob and my home. . . . But I'm desperate. I begin to feel that I have no personality. . . . Who am I?"

The Feminine Mystique

Although President Kennedy had appointed only one woman to a policymaking post in his administration, she was an effective advocate of women's equal rights. Esther Peterson, assistant secretary of labor, urged Kennedy in 1961 to establish the first President's Commission on the Status of Women in the nation's history. Its report, *American Women*, issued in 1963, argued that every obstacle to women's full participation in society must be removed. By 1967, all fifty states had established commissions to promote women's equality, but the federal government was not enforcing the gender equality provisions of the Civil Rights Act of 1964. The need for action inspired the founding, in 1966, of the National Organization for Women (NOW). A reform organization, NOW battled for "equal rights in

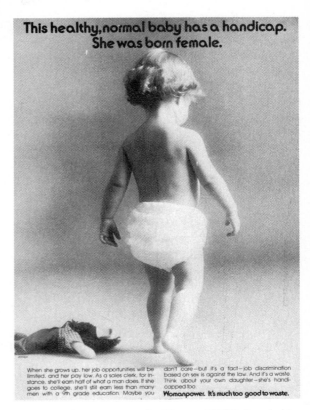

This healthy, normal baby has a handicap. She was born female.

When she grows up, her job opportunities will be limited, and her pay low. As a sales clerk, for instance, she'll earn half of what a man does. If she goes to college, she'll still earn less than many men with a 9th grade education. Maybe you don't care—but it's a fact—job discrimination based on sex is against the law. And it's a waste. Think about your own daughter—she's handicapped too. **Womanpower. It's much too good to waste.**

The National Organization for Women (NOW), founded in 1966, went from one thousand members in 1967 to forty thousand in 1974. NOW's advertisements about sexual inequality were simple and to the point. *NOW Legal Defense and Education Fund, Inc.*

partnership with men" by lobbying for legislation and testing laws in the courts.

Not long after NOW was formed, a new generation of radical feminists emerged. Most were white and well educated; many were the daughters of working mothers. They had also been raised in the era of sexual liberation, in which birth-control pills and other contraceptives were taken for granted. The intellectual ferment of their movement produced a new feminist literature. Feminists challenged everything from women's economic, political, and legal inequality to sexual double standards and sex-role stereotypes. Unlike the members of NOW, the radical feminists practiced direct action, as when they picketed the

Radical Feminism

1968 Miss America contest in Atlantic City. One woman auctioned off an effigy of Miss America: "Gentlemen, I offer you the 1969 model. . . . She walks. She talks. She smiles on cue. And she does the housework." Into the "freedom trash can" the pickets dumped false eyelashes, curlers, girdles, and *Playboy*. These feminists were protesting the view of women as servants and sex objects. They were also practicing "personal politics."

Many radical feminists had struggled earlier for black civil rights and against the Vietnam War. In these movements, they discovered that instead of making policy they were expected to make coffee, take minutes, and even provide sexual favors. Radicalized but wanting to put their political energies into antisexist causes, these feminists joined in consciousness-raising groups, where they discussed sensitive issues such as homosexuality and abortion. The issue of homosexuality caused a split in the women's movement, and in 1969 and 1970, NOW forced lesbians to resign from membership and offices in the organization. This rift was healed in 1971, largely because homosexuals had begun to fight back.

For working women in the 1960s, the major problems were sex discrimination in employment, lack of professional opportunities, unequal pay for equal work, lack of adequate day **Occupational** care for children, and prohibi-**Segregation** tions against abortion. An underlying cause of the disparity in pay was "occupational segregation," which became even more pronounced as women flooded entry-level jobs in female-dominated fields, such as secretarial and clerical work. Since many women with college educations were earning less than men with eighth-grade educations, it was natural that the two primary feminist goals of the 1960s were equal job opportunity and equal pay for equal work.

Despite opposition, women made impressive gains. They entered professional schools in record numbers: from 1969 to 1973, the number of women law students almost quad-**Legal** rupled and the number of women **Advances** medical students more than dou-**for Women** bled. Under Title IX of the Educational Amendments of 1972, female college athletes gained the right to the same financial support as male athletes. In the same year Congress approved the Equal Rights Amendment (ERA) and sent it to the states for ratification. (The ERA stated, "Equality of rights under the law shall not be denied or abridged by the United States or by any State on account of sex.") In 1973, the Supreme Court struck down state laws that made abortion a crime (*Roe* v. *Wade*). The Court also attacked sex discrimination. In a 1971 ruling (*Reed* v. *Reed*), it held that legislation differentiating between the sexes "must be reasonable, not arbitrary," and in 1973 (*Frontiero* v. *Richardson*), several justices went a step further in declaring that "classifications based on sex," like those based on race, were "inherently suspect." As a result of these victories, the women's movement gained new confidence.

Nixon and the Persistence of Chaos

Richard Nixon's presidency was born in chaos. In 1969, a hundred black students armed with rifles and shotguns seized the student union at Cornell University and occupied the building for thirty-six hours. Bloody confrontations occurred at Berkeley, San Francisco State, Wisconsin, and scores of other colleges and universities. In October 1969, three hundred Weathermen, members of an SDS splinter group, raced through Chicago's downtown district, smashing windows and attacking police officers in an attempt to incite armed class struggle. A month later, half a million people assembled peacefully at the Washington Monument on Moratorium Day to call for an end to the Vietnam War.

One bright spot for President Nixon in 1969 was the flight of *Apollo 11,* a manned spaceship, to the moon. After separating in space from the *Apollo* craft, the lunar module reached its **Moon** destination in mid-July, and on **Landing** July 20 astronaut Neil Armstrong made history by taking the first step onto the moon's surface. After gathering rock and soil samples, Armstrong and his flightmate, Edwin Aldrin, rendezvoused with the *Apollo* command ship, docked, and returned to earth.

But this was a momentary respite. On April 30,

1970, President Nixon announced that the United States had launched an "incursion" into Cambodia.

Kent State and Jackson State

Protest against the war escalated at home. On May 4, national guardsmen in Ohio killed four students at Kent State University. Ten days later, police and state highway patrolmen armed with automatic weapons blasted a women's dormitory at Jackson State, an all-black university in Mississippi, killing two students and wounding nine others. No evidence of student sniping could be found; the police had fired no tear gas or warning shots.

While police and soldiers waged official violence in 1970, revolutionaries conducted an unofficial campaign of terror. They bombed the New York offices of Mobil Oil, IBM, General Telephone and Electronics, and various banks. In March, a bomb factory exploded in Greenwich Village, blowing up at least three young revolutionaries. There were scores of politically motivated skyjackings.

Worst of all, as far as many Americans were concerned, was street crime. Sales of pistols, burglar alarms, and bulletproof vests soared, as did the demand for private guards and spe-

Fear of Crime

cial police. Conservatives accused liberals of causing the crime wave by coddling criminals.

In the wake of this new wave of riots and violent crime, Nixon became convinced that the nation was plunging into anarchy. He worried, as had Lyndon Johnson before him, that the antiwar movement was Communist-inspired. In June 1970, he ordered the FBI, the CIA, the National Security Agency, and the Defense Intelligence Agency to formulate a coordinated attack on "internal threats." "Everything is valid," a Nixon aide told the group, "everything is possible." Had it not been for FBI Director J. Edgar Hoover's refusal to cooperate in the illegal plot, the group would have had free rein to open mail, tap telephones, and break into citizens' homes and offices.

The administration also worked to put the Democratic party on the defensive. Vice President Spiro Agnew took to the road in September to warn the country of threats to its internal security posed "by a disruptive, radical, and militant

Politics of Divisiveness

minority." The campaign strategy was to portray Democrats as a rad-

ical fringe. But Republican attempts to discredit the Democrats failed.

Nixon's fortunes declined further in 1971. On June 13, the *New York Times* began to publish the *Pentagon Papers*, a top-secret Defense Department study of the Vietnam War. Nixon

Stagflation

also had to contend with inflation, a problem not entirely of his making. Rather, it was Lyndon Johnson's policy of guns and butter—massive deficit financing to support both the Vietnam War and the Great Society—that had fueled inflation. By January 1971, the United States was suffering from a 5.3-percent inflation rate and a 6-percent unemployment rate. Soon after this period, the word *stagflation* was coined to describe the coexistence of economic recession (stagnation) and inflation.

That January, Nixon shocked both critics and allies by declaring, "I am now a Keynesian." Like his Democratic predecessors, he would try to stimulate the economy through government spending. The budget for fiscal 1971 would have a built-in deficit of $23 billion, just slightly under the all-time high of $25 billion. Then in August, in an effort to correct the nation's balance-of-payments deficit, Nixon announced that he would devalue the dollar by allowing it to "float" in international money markets. Finally, to curb inflation, the president froze prices, wages, and rents for ninety days, and then set limits on their increase. Nixon's commitment to the controversial wage and price controls buckled the following year under pressure from businesses and unions.

The wage and price controls were just one sign of what surprised observers called Nixon's "great turnabout." Another was his announcement in July 1971 that he would travel the following year to the People's Republic of China, an enemy Nixon had denounced for years. It was clear that the president was preparing for the 1972 presidential election.

The Southern Strategy and the Election of 1972

Political observers believed that Nixon would have a hard time running for re-election on his first-term record. Having urged Americans to use "cool" words and "lower our voices," he had ordered Vice President Agnew to denounce the press and student protesters. Having espoused unity, he had practiced the politics of polarization. Having campaigned as a fiscal conservative, he had authorized near-record budget deficits. And having promised peace, he had widened the war in Southeast Asia.

Legislative achievements in Congress had come about more in spite of Nixon than because of him. The Twenty-sixth Amendment gave eighteen-year-olds the vote; Social Security payments and food-stamp funding were increased; and the Occupational Safety and Health Administration was established. Congress responded to the growing environmental movement by passing the Clean Air Act, the Water Quality Improvement Act, and the Resource Recovery Act.

Democratic Legislative Victories

In his campaign for re-election, Nixon was less interested in running on his record than in employing a "southern strategy" of political conservatism. A product of the Sunbelt himself, Nixon was attuned to the growing political power of that conservative region. Thus, he appealed to "the silent majority," the white suburbanites, blue-collar workers, Catholics, and ethnic groups of "middle America." As in the 1970 congressional elections, Nixon equated the Republican party with law and order and the Democratic party with permissiveness, crime, drugs, pornography, the hippie lifestyle, student radicalism, black militancy, feminism, homosexuality, and the dissolution of the family. Moreover, Attorney General John Mitchell had courted southern white voters by trying to delay school desegregation in Mississippi and to prevent extension of the 1965 Voting Rights Act.

Nixon's Southern Strategy

To a great extent, the campaign waged by Nixon's Democratic opponent, Senator George McGovern of South Dakota, handed victory to the president. When McGovern committed himself to a $30-billion cut in the defense budget, people began to fear that he was a neo-isolationist who would reduce the United States to a second-rate power. This and other McGovern proposals split the Democrats between his supporters—blacks, feminists, antiwar activists, and young militants—and old-guard urban bosses, labor and ethnic leaders, and southerners.

Nixon's victory in November was overwhelming. He polled 47 million votes, 60.7 percent of the votes cast. McGovern received only 29 million and won in just one state, Massachusetts, and the District of Columbia. Nixon's southern strategy was supremely successful: he carried all of the Deep South, which had once been solidly Democratic. He also gained a majority of the urban vote, winning over to his side such longtime Democrats as blue-collar workers, Catholics, and ethnics. Only blacks, Jews, and low-income voters stuck by the Democrats. Remarkably, the Democrats retained control of both houses of Congress and won two additional seats in the Senate.

Nixon's Landslide Victory

When John F. Kennedy delivered his inaugural address in 1961, he had challenged Americans to "pay any price, bear any burden, meet any hardship" to defend freedom and inspire the world. Twelve years later, Richard M. Nixon echoed that rhetoric: "Let us pledge to make these four years the best four years in America's history, so that on its 200th birthday America will be as young and vital as when it began, and as bright a beacon of hope for all the world." Largely because of the president's own actions, however, the next four years would be among the most dismal in the nation's history.

▼

Suggestions for Further Reading

The 1960s

William H. Chafe, *The Unfinished Journey: America Since World War II* (1986); Richard N. Goodwin, *Remembering America* (1988); Godfrey Hodgson, *America in Our Time* (1976); Allen J. Matusow, *The Unraveling of America: A History of Liberalism in the 1960s* (1984); Charles R. Morris, *A Time of Passion: America, 1960–1980* (1984); Geoffrey O'Brien, *Dream Time* (1988); Tom Shachtman, *Decade of Shocks: Dallas to Watergate, 1963–1974* (1983); Milton Viorst, *Fire in the Streets* (1979).

The Kennedy Administration

Thomas Brown, *JFK: History of an Image* (1988); David Burner, *John F. Kennedy and a New Generation* (1988); David Halberstam, *The Best and the Brightest* (1972); Jim F. Heath, *Decade of Disillusionment: The Kennedy-Johnson Years* (1975); Herbert S. Parmet, *J.F.K.—The Presidency of John F. Kennedy* (1983); Arthur M. Schlesinger, Jr., *A Thousand Days: John F. Kennedy in the White House* (1965); Theodore C. Sorenson, *Kennedy* (1965); Gary Wills, *The Kennedy Imprisonment* (1982).

Lyndon Johnson and the Great Society

Vaughn D. Bornet, *The Presidency of Lyndon B. Johnson* (1983); Paul K. Conkin, *Big Daddy from the Pedernales: Lyndon Baines Johnson* (1986); Ronnie Dugger, *The Politician* (1982); Lyndon B. Johnson, *The Vantage Point* (1971); Doris Kearns, *Lyndon Johnson and the American Dream* (1976); Sar A. Levitan and Robert Taggart, *The Promise of Greatness* (1976); Charles Murray, *Losing Ground: American Social Policy, 1950–1980* (1983); James T. Patterson, *America's Struggle Against Poverty, 1900–1985* (1986); Carl Solberg, *Hubert Humphrey* (1984).

Civil Rights and Black Power

Carl M. Brauer, *John F. Kennedy and the Second Reconstruction* (1977); Clayborne Carson, *In Struggle: SNCC and the Black Awakening of the 1960s* (1981); William H. Chafe, *Civilities and Civil Rights: Greensboro, North Carolina, and the Black Struggle for Freedom* (1980); Charles E. Fager, *Selma 1965*, rev. ed. (1985); David J. Garrow, *Bearing the Cross: Martin Luther King, Jr., and the Southern Christian Leadership Conference* (1986); Doug McAdam, *Freedom Summer* (1988); Malcolm X and Alex Haley, *The Autobiography of Malcolm X* (1965); August Meier and Elliott Rudwick, *CORE* (1973); Robert J. Norrell, *Reaping the Whirlwind: The Civil Rights Movement in Tuskegee* (1985); Stephen B. Oates, *Let the Trumpet Sound: The Life of Martin Luther King, Jr.* (1982); Harvard Sitkoff, *The Struggle for Black Equality, 1954–1980* (1981).

Warren Court

Alexander M. Bickel, *The Supreme Court and the Idea of Progress* (1970); Gerald Dunne, *Hugo Black and the Judicial Revolution* (1977); G. Theodore Mitau, *Decade of Decision: The Supreme Court and the Constitutional Revolution, 1954–1964* (1967); Bernard Schwartz, *Super Chief: Earl Warren and His Supreme Court* (1983).

The New Left and the Antiwar Movement

Wini Breines, *The Great Refusal: Community and Organization in the New Left* (1983); Todd Gitlin, *The Sixties: Years of Hope, Days of Rage* (1987); Todd Gitlin, *The Whole World Is Watching: Mass Media in the Making and Unmaking of the New Left* (1980); James Miller, *"Democracy Is in the Streets": From Port Huron to the Siege of Chicago* (1987); Thomas Powers, *Vietnam, the War at Home* (1984); W. J. Rorabaugh, *Berkeley at War* (1989); Kirkpatrick Sale, *SDS* (1973); Sohnya Sayres et al., eds., *The 60s, Without Apology* (1984); Nancy Zaroulis and Gerald Sullivan, *Who Spoke Up? American Protest Against the War in Vietnam, 1963–1975* (1984).

The Counterculture

Stanley Booth, *Dance with the Devil: The Rolling Stones and Their Times* (1984); Morris Dickstein, *Gates of Eden: American Culture in the Sixties* (1977); Philip Norman, *Shout! The Beatles in Their Generation* (1981); Charles Perry, *The Haight-Ashbury* (1984); Theodore Roszak, *The Making of a Counter Culture* (1969); Philip Slater, *The Pursuit of Loneliness*, rev. ed. (1976); Jon Weiner, *Come Together: John Lennon in His Time* (1984).

The Rebirth of Feminism

William H. Chafe, *The American Woman: Her Changing Social, Economic, and Political Role, 1920–1970* (1972); Sara Evans, *Personal Politics* (1978); Marian Faux, *Roe v. Wade* (1988); Betty Friedan, *The Feminine Mystique* (1963); Judith Hole and Ellen Levine, *Rebirth of Feminism* (1971); Alice Kessler-Harris, *Out to Work: A History of Wage-Earning Women in the United States* (1982); Kate Millett, *Sexual Politics* (1970); Robin Morgan, ed., *Sisterhood Is Powerful* (1970); Sheila M. Rothman, *Women's Proper Place* (1978); Gayle Graham Yates, *What Women Want: The Ideas of the Movement* (1975).

Year of Shocks: 1968

David Caute, *The Year of the Barricades* (1988); David Farber, *Chicago '68* (1988); Ronald Fraser et al., *1968: A Student Generation in Revolt* (1988); Charles Kaiser, *1968 in America* (1988); George Katsiaficas, *The Imagination of the New Left: A Global Analysis of 1968* (1987); Hans Koning, *Nineteen Sixty-Eight* (1987); Theodore H. White, *The Making of the President, 1968* (1969).

The Nixon Administration

Richard M. Nixon, *RN: The Memoirs of Richard Nixon* (1978); Leon E. Panetta and Peter Gall, *Bring Us Together: The Nixon Team and the Civil Rights Retreat* (1971); Raymond Price, *With Nixon* (1977); Jonathan Schell, *The Time of Illusion* (1975); Leonard Silk, *Nixonomics* (1972); Herbert Stein, *Presidential Economics* (1984); Garry Wills, *Nixon Agonistes* (1970).

Night watchman Frank Wills was making his rounds at the Watergate apartment-office complex in Washington, D.C., on June 17, 1972, when he noticed that two doors connecting the building to an underground garage had been taped to keep them from locking. Wills removed the tape, but when he returned thirty minutes later, he found it had been replaced. He promptly telephoned the police to report the illegal entry. At 2:30 A.M., police arrested five men who were attaching listening devices to telephones in the sixth-floor offices of the Democratic National Committee.

One of the men arrested was a former CIA employee who had become security coordinator of the Committee to Re-Elect the President (CREEP). The other four were anti-Castro Cubans from Miami. Unknown to the police, two other men had been in the Watergate building at the time of the break-in: E. Howard Hunt, a one-time CIA agent who had become CREEP's security chief, and G. Gordon Liddy, a former FBI agent serving on the White House staff. What were these men trying to find in the Democrats' offices? What did they hope to overhear on the telephones? Most important, who had ordered the break-in?

As the shoddy story of Watergate unfolded, Americans' disillusion intensified. Most had grown up believing their country

32

A DISILLUSIONED PEOPLE: WATERGATE, STAGFLATION, AND GLOBAL DECLINE, 1973–1981

was the most powerful, the most democratic, and the most bountiful in the history of humankind. By the early 1980s, far fewer Americans clung to such beliefs, and many wondered why they had not shed their innocence earlier. The Watergate scandal came to light at a time when Americans were still in anguish over their country's involvement in the Vietnam War. Perhaps for that reason, it was more traumatic than earlier national scandals. In 1974, it caused the first presidential resignation in American history.

While Americans worried about morality in government, economic events touched their lives even more deeply. First, economic stagnation, or recession, brought unemployment. Americans in the 1970s saw once-proud automobile and steel plants close. As a result of "deindustrialization," many jobs were jeopardized and some disappeared forever. Second, inflation eroded the purchasing power of workers' paychecks.

America's economic dominance in the world was also in decline. The

1973 Arab oil embargo led to the realization that the United States was not a fortress that could stand alone; it depended for its survival on imported oil. Long gasoline lines plagued Americans, and increases in foreign imports on store shelves constantly reminded them that the competition was gaining. The postwar economic boom was over.

Politicians seemed unable to cope with the floundering economy. President Gerald Ford's weak WIN (Whip Inflation Now) program of 1974 did not impress voters, who turned him out of office in 1976. Jimmy Carter, who defeated Ford, fared just as badly. Under Carter, inflation reached new heights and unemployment remained high.

Besides distress at home, Carter faced diplomatic crises that tested his ability to lead. At the start, he promised to apply some lessons of the Vietnam War: first, that the United States did not always have answers to the deep-seated problems of other nations; and second, that diplomatic, rather than military, means had a better chance of creating global stability. He also pledged to emphasize human rights issues and long-term planning on environmental questions that threatened international disorder. But his foreign affairs bureaucracy suffered divisiveness, and the president seemed to lurch from side to side. His accomplishments—SALT-II, the Camp David agreements, and the Panama Canal treaties—became overshadowed by the wrenching and lingering Iranian hostage crisis and renewed Cold War with the Soviets. By the end of the Carter administration, many Americans believed that he had let America's international prestige and power slip.

By 1980, economic uncertainty was higher than at any time since the 1930s. The 1970s were the first post–Second World War decade in which Americans' purchasing power declined. In addition, profound social change resulted as mass-production technologies gave way to a service and information-based economy, which required a more highly educated work force. A decade of inflation and declining real wages, plus the changing nature of the labor market, had shaken Americans' confidence that they could shape their personal destinies.

Women and people of color were particularly hard hit, for they were usually the last hired and the first to be laid off. Being generally less educated and skilled, they also suffered most from the shift to the service and information economy. Even when they had jobs, women and African-Americans were paid less than white men, and experts pointed to the growing "feminization" and "blackening" of poverty. The 1970s were also characterized by mounting opposition to the aspirations of both women and racial minorities. Still, women and minorities did achieve some victories. Women made educational gains and won legislative seats in Washington and in various state houses. Many African-Americans attended college, and growing numbers of black men and women were elected to political office.

Some Americans decided that if they could not reform society, they could at least develop their own individual potential. For them, the 1970s were the Me Decade. Millions of people took to jogging; others meditated, ate health food, or developed their assertiveness skills. But some observers thought that they detected an undercurrent of desperation. By 1980, public opinion polls disclosed that most Americans found the present worse than the past and believed that the future would be worse yet.

As the 1980 presidential election approached, Americans looked back on a decade of difficulties at home and abroad. It was in this context that Ronald Reagan rode a wave of conservatism into office. Reagan promised a return to old-fashioned morality and a balanced budget. He promised to restore American power on a global scale, expand the military establishment, and boldly confront America's adversaries. America could again be what it once was, he declared, and Americans believed him.

Nixon and the Watergate Scandal

Watergate actually began in 1971, when the White House established not only CREEP, but also the Special Investigations Unit, known familiarly as the

Plumbers, to stop the leaking of confidential information to the press. After Daniel Ellsberg released the *Pentagon Papers*, the Plumbers burglarized the office of his psychiatrist in an attempt to find information to discredit Ellsberg. The Plumbers broke into the Democratic National Committee's headquarters to photograph documents and install wiretaps. CREEP raised money to pay the Plumbers' expenses both before and after the break-ins.

The arrest of the Watergate burglars generated furious activity in the White House. Incriminating documents were shredded; E. Howard Hunt's name was expunged from the White House telephone directory; and President Nixon ordered his chief of staff, H. R. Haldeman, to discourage the FBI's investigation into the burglary on the pretext that it might compromise national security. Nixon also authorized CREEP payments in excess of $460,000 to keep Hunt and others from implicating the White House in the crime.

White House Cover-up

Because of White House efforts to cover up the scandal, the break-in went practically unnoticed by the electorate. Had it not been for the diligent efforts of reporters, government special prosecutors, federal judges, and congressional representatives, Nixon might have succeeded in disguising his involvement in Watergate. Slowly, however, the ball of lies and distortions began to unravel. In early 1973, U.S. District Court Judge John Sirica tried the burglars, one of whom implicated his superiors in CREEP and at the White House. From May until November, the Senate Select Committee on Campaign Practices, chaired by Senator Sam Ervin of North Carolina, heard testimony from White House aides. John Dean, the White House counsel, acknowledged not only that there had been a cover-up but also that the president had directed it. Another aide shocked the committee and the nation by disclosing that Nixon had had a taping system installed in the White House and that conversations about Watergate had been recorded.

Watergate Hearings and Investigations

Nixon feigned innocence. On April 30, 1973, he tried to distance himself from the cover-up by announcing the resignations of his two chief White House aides, John Ehrlichman and H. R. Haldeman.

Saturday Night Massacre

The president then appointed Archibald Cox, a Harvard law professor, to the new position of special Watergate prosecutor. But when Cox sought to obtain the White House tapes by means of a court order, Nixon decided to fire him. Both Attorney General Elliot Richardson and his deputy resigned rather than carry out the dismissal order. It thus fell to the next-ranking official in the Department of Justice to fire Cox. The public outcry provoked by the so-called Saturday Night Massacre (October 20, 1973) compelled the president to appoint a new special prosecutor, Leon Jaworski. When Nixon still refused to surrender the tapes, Jaworski took him to court.

Watergate Tapes

Throughout 1973 and 1974, enterprising reporters uncovered details of the break-in, the hush money, and the various people from Nixon on down who had taken part in the cover-up. White House aides and CREEP subordinates began to go on trial, with Nixon cited as their "unindicted co-conspirator." *Washington Post* reporters Carl Bernstein and Bob Woodward found an informant in the White House known as Deep Throat, who provided damning evidence against Nixon and his aides. As Nixon's story became less credible, his hold on the tapes became more tenuous. In late April 1974, the president finally released an edited version of the tapes.

The tapes, however, were replete with gaps. They swayed neither the public nor the House Judiciary Committee, which had begun to draft articles of impeachment against the president. Nixon was still trying to hang onto the tapes when on July 24 the Supreme Court unanimously ordered him to surrender the recordings to Judge Sirica. At about the same time, the Judiciary Committee began to conduct nationally televised hearings. After several days of testimony, the committee voted for impeachment on three of five counts: obstruction of justice through the payment of hush money to witnesses, lying, and withholding of evidence; defiance of a congressional subpoena of the tapes; and the use of the CIA, the FBI, and the Internal Revenue Service to deprive Americans of their constitutional rights to privacy and free speech.

On August 5, the president finally handed over

1972	Break-in at Watergate	1977	Human rights policy launched

1973	Trials of Watergate burglars
	Ervin Watergate hearings
	White House aides Ehrlichman and
	    Haldeman resign
	Wounded Knee confrontation
	War Powers Resolution
	Arab oil embargo
	Agnew resigns; Ford appointed vice
	    president
	Saturday Night Massacre
		1978	*Bakke* v. *University of California*
			Panama Canal treaties
			Egyptian-Israeli peace accord (Camp
			    David)
			California voters approve
			    Proposition 13
			Mass suicides in Guyana

1974	OPEC oil price increases
	Supreme Court orders Nixon to
	    release White House tapes
	House Judiciary Committee votes to
	    impeach Nixon
	Nixon resigns the presidency; Ford
	    becomes president
	Rockefeller appointed vice president
	Ford pardons Nixon
	Ford's WIN program
		1979	Three Mile Island nuclear accident
			Federal Reserve Board tightens
			    money supply
			American hostages seized in Iran
			SALT-II treaty
			Soviets invade Afghanistan

1975	Brown's Ferry nuclear accident
	Economic recession
		1980	Carter Doctrine
			Grain embargo and boycott of
			    Olympic Games against Soviets
			Economic recession
			Phased decontrol of oil prices and
			    deregulation of transportation
			    industries
			Race riots
			Reagan elected president

1976	Hyde Amendment on abortions Carter elected president	1981	American hostages in Iran released after 444 days

the complete tapes, which he knew would condemn him. Four days later, he resigned. Nixon's successor was Gerald R. Ford. Vice President Spiro Agnew had resigned in October 1973, after pleading no contest to charges on income-tax evasion and acceptance of bribes. In line with the provisions of the Twenty-fifth Amendment, Nixon had nominated Ford, minority leader of the House, to replace Agnew. Ford's congressional colleagues hailed the new president as a "decent" and "good" man, but his first substantive act was to pardon Nixon. Some people concluded that Ford and Nixon had struck a deal.

The Watergate scandal prompted the reform of abuses of presidential power, some of which dated from Franklin D. Roosevelt's administration. In

Post-Watergate Restrictions on Executive Power

1973, Congress passed the War Powers Act, which mandated that "in every possible instance" the president must consult with Congress before sending American troops into foreign wars. Under this law, the president could commit American troops abroad for no more than sixty days, after which he had to obtain congressional approval. In 1974, Congress produced the

Congressional Budget and Impoundment Control Act, which prohibited the impounding of federal money. Congress also attacked campaign fund-raising abuses and the misuse of government agencies. The Federal Election Campaign Act of 1972 had restricted campaign spending to no more than ten cents per constituent and required candidates to report individual contributions of more than a hundred dollars. In 1974, Congress enacted additional legislation that set ceilings on campaign contributions and expenditures for House, Senate, and presidential elections. Finally, to aid citizens who were victims of dirty-tricks campaigns, Congress strengthened the Freedom of Information Act, originally passed in 1966.

The Energy Crisis and the End of the Postwar Economic Boom

The fallout from Watergate was not the only problem confronting the nation in the early 1970s. More disruptive in the long run was the Arab oil embargo of 1973. Americans, who had grown up on cheap, abundant energy, made no effort to conserve it. By the fall of 1973, the country had to import one-third of its oil supplies.

Price increases ordered by the Organization of Petroleum Exporting Countries (OPEC) struck another blow at the United States. From January 1973 to January 1974, oil prices rose 350 percent. As people grappled with the price hikes, multinational oil companies prospered. Profits jumped 70 percent in 1973 and another 40 percent in 1974. The boost in the price of imported oil reverberated through the entire economy. Inflation jumped from 3.3 percent in 1972 to a frightening 11 percent in 1974.

OPEC Price Increases and Rising Inflation

At the same time, recession hit the auto industry. In Detroit, General Motors laid off 38,000 workers—6 percent of its domestic work force—indefinitely and put another 48,000 on leave for up to ten days at a time. The reason was obvious: sales of gas-guzzling American cars had plummeted as consumers rushed to purchase energy-efficient foreign subcompacts. Moreover, since the ailing American auto companies were not selling cars, they were not buying steel, glass, rubber, or tool-and-die products either. Soon, the recession in the auto industry spread to other manufacturers, who both quit hiring new workers and began laying off experienced employees.

Recession in the Auto Industry

Unlike earlier postwar recessions, this one did not fade away in a year or two. Part of the reason was the coexistence of inflation. In the earlier recessions, Democrats, as well as many Republicans, had held to a policy of neo-Keynesianism. That is, they had manipulated federal policies to minimize the swings in the business cycle—both fiscal policies, covering taxes and government spending, and monetary policies, including interest rates and the money supply. Thus, they hoped to keep employment up and inflation down. Beginning in the 1970s, however, joblessness and prices both began to rise sharply. Policies to correct one problem seemed only to worsen the other.

Even in the best of times, the economy would have been hard-pressed to produce jobs for the millions of baby-boomers who joined the labor market in the 1970s. As it was, economic activity created 26.5 million additional jobs during the decade, a remarkable increase of 32.3 percent. But because of deindustrialization, there was a shift in the occupational structure. As heavy industries collapsed, laid-off workers took jobs in fast-food restaurants, all-night gas stations, and convenience stores—but at half their former wages and with no provision of health insurance or retirement benefits. Thus, workers who once had held high-paying blue-collar jobs saw their middle-class standard of living slipping away.

The Shifting Occupational Structure

Other problems included a slower growth in productivity, or the average output of goods per

Richard M. Nixon bids farewell to his staff and the nation on August 9, 1974, the day he resigned the presidency—the first president ever to resign from the White House. *J.P. Laffont/Sygma.*

hour of labor. Between 1947 and 1965, American industrial productivity had averaged an increase of 3.3 percent a year, raising manufacturers' profits and reducing the cost of products to consumers. From 1966 to 1970, the annual productivity increase averaged only 1.5 percent; it fell further, to 1.4 percent between 1971 and 1975 and to a mere 0.2 percent between 1976 and 1980. Economists blamed the lack of business investment in state-of-the-art technology, the shift from an industrial to a service economy, and an alleged erosion of the work ethic. Whatever the causes, American goods cost more than those of foreign competitors.

Decreased Productivity

The lag in productivity was not matched by a decrease in workers' expectations. Wage increases regularly exceeded production increases, and some economists blamed the raises for inflation. Indeed, wages that went up seldom came down again. Managers of the nation's basic industries—steel, car, and rubber—complained that the automatic cost-of-living adjustments in their labor contracts left them little margin to restrain price hikes.

Another spur to inflation was easy credit, particularly between 1975 and 1979. Fearing an era of scarcity, many people went on a buying spree. Household and business borrowing more than tripled (from $94 billion to $328 billion). More people had credit cards. This credit explosion helped bid up the price of everything, from houses to gold. Some people, especially farmers, borrowed more than they could afford. The nation's farm debt in 1971 was $54.5 billion; by 1980, it was $165.8 billion. Overburdened with debts, many farmers faced bankruptcy in the 1980s.

Easy Credit and Inflation

Every expert had a scapegoat to blame for the nation's economic doldrums. Labor leaders cited foreign competition and called for tariffs to protect American goods. Some businesspeople and economists said the cost of obeying federal health and safety laws and pollution controls added to the price of goods. They urged officials to abolish the Environmental Protection Agency and the Occupational Safety and Health Administration. In addition, they pressed for deregulation of the oil, airline, and trucking industries on the theory that competition would bring down prices. Above all, critics attacked the federal government's massive spending programs; the mounting national debt, they said, was the sad result.

By the time Gerald Ford became president in 1974, OPEC price increases had pushed the inflation rate to 11 percent. Appalled, Ford created

Government Response to the Economic Crisis

WIN, a voluntary program that encouraged businesses, consumers, and workers to save energy and form grassroots anti-inflation organizations. WIN was much too weak to be effective.

Ford's ultimate response to inflation, like Nixon's, was to curb federal spending and encourage the Federal Reserve Board to raise its interest rates to banks and so tighten credit. As before, these actions prompted a recession—only this time it was the worst in forty years. Unemployment jumped to 8.5 percent in 1975, and because the economy had stagnated, the federal deficit for the fiscal year 1976 and 1977 hit a record $60 billion.

Neither Nixon nor Ford devised lasting solutions to the energy crisis. When OPEC ended the embargo, the crisis seemed to pass and with it passed

Nuclear Power

the incentive to prevent future shortages. But the energy crisis intensified public debate over nuclear power. For the sake of energy independence, advocates asserted, the United States had to rely more on nuclear energy. Environmental activists countered that the risk of nuclear accident was too great and that there was no safe way to store nuclear waste. Accidents in the nuclear power plants at Brown's Ferry, Alabama, in 1975 and at Three Mile Island, Pennsylvania, in 1979 gave credibility to the activists' cause. By 1979, however, ninety-six reactors were under construction

throughout the nation, and thirty more were on order.

Meanwhile, the combined effects of the energy crisis, stagflation, and the flight of industry and the middle class to the suburbs and the South were producing fiscal disaster in the nation's cities. Not since 1933, when Detroit defaulted on its debts, had an American city gone bankrupt. But in November 1975, New York City was near financial collapse. President Ford vowed "to veto any bill that has as its purpose a federal bail-out of New York City," but after the Senate and House Banking Committees approved loan guarantees, he relented, and the city was saved. New York was not alone in its financial problems; other cities in the North and East were in trouble, saddled with growing welfare rolls, deindustrialization, and a declining tax base.

Throughout the economic problems during Ford's term, Congress enjoyed new power. Watergate and the new criticism of the imperial presidency accounted for Congress's new self-confidence. There was also the fact that, for the first time in the nation's history, both the president and the vice president lacked the popular mandate of having been elected to office. One of Ford's first acts as president had been to select Nelson Rockefeller, former governor of New York, to be his vice president.

The Failed Promise of the Carter Presidency

While Ford struggled with a Democratic Congress, the Democratic party prepared for the presidential election of 1976. Against the background of Watergate secrecy and corruption, one

Election of 1976

candidate in particular promised honesty and openness. "I will never lie to you," pledged Jimmy Carter, an obscure former one-term governor of Georgia. When this born-again Christian promised voters efficiency and decency in government, they believed him. Carter secured the Democratic nomination and chose Senator Walter Mondale, a liberal from Minnesota as his running mate.

Neither Carter nor President Ford, the Republican nominee, inspired much interest, and on election day only 53.5 percent of the electorate voted. Nevertheless, an analysis of the turnout was instructive. One political commentator concluded that the vote was "fractured to a marked degree along the fault line separating the haves and have-nots." Carter gained nearly 90 percent of the black and Mexican-American vote and squeaked to victory by the slim margin of 1.7 million votes out of 80 million. Ford's appeal was strongest among middle- and upper-middle-class voters.

Carter's major domestic accomplishments were in energy, transportation, and conservation policy. To encourage domestic production of oil, he in-

Carter Administration stituted phased decontrol of oil prices. To moderate the social effects of the energy crisis, he called for a windfall-profits tax on excessive profits resulting from decontrol, and grants to the poor and elderly for the purchase of heating fuel. He deregulated the airline, trucking, and railroad industries and persuaded Congress to ease federal control of banks. His administration established a $1.6-billion "superfund" to clean up abandoned chemical-waste sites. And finally, he placed more than 100 million acres of Alaskan land under the federal government's protection as national parks, national forests, and wildlife refuges.

Despite these accomplishments, Carter soon alienated party members. Elected as an outsider, he remained one, failing to develop working relationships with congressional leaders. Moreover, his support of deregulation and his opposition to wage and price controls and gasoline rationing ran counter to the liberal Democratic position. Seeing inflation as a greater threat to the nation's health than either recession or unemployment, Carter announced that his top priority would be to cut federal spending, even though doing so would add to the jobless rolls. But inflation continued to rise.

By 1980, the economy was a shambles. Inflation had jumped in 1979 to 13.4 percent, and buyers around the world had lost confidence in the dollar, causing unprecedented increases in the price of

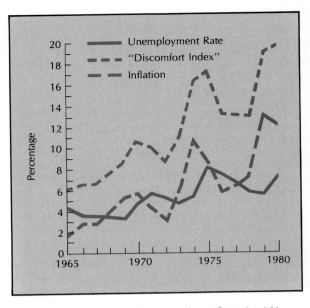

Discomfort Index (Unemployment plus Inflation), 1965–1980 *Source:* Economic Report of the President: 1980 *(Washington, D.C.: U.S. Government Printing Office, 1981), pp. 238, 263.*

gold. To steady the dollar and curb inflation, the Federal Reserve Board took

Economic Discomfort in 1980 drastic measures. First, the board cut the money supply—partly by selling Treasury securities to take money out of circulation—thus forcing borrowers to bid up interest rates sufficiently to dampen the economy and reduce inflation. Second, it raised the rate at which the Federal Reserve loaned money to banks. As a result of these actions, car loans became more difficult to obtain, mortgage interest rates leaped beyond 15 percent, and the prime lending rate (the rate charged to businesses) hit an all-time high of 20 percent. Worse still, by 1980 the nation was in a full-fledged recession, with an unemployment rate of 7.5 percent. And the combined high inflation and high unemployment rates had produced a staggering discomfort index of just under 20 percent (see figure).

The inability of Carter and the government to ameliorate the economic crisis, as well as the failure to gain the freedom of Americans held hostage in Iran, made the government appear ineffectual. In 1976, Carter had gibed at President Ford by saying, "Anything you don't like about Washington, I suggest you blame on him." In 1980, Carter was the incumbent, and many Americans blamed him for the nation's problems.

Carter and the World

President Carter was "deeply troubled," he said, "by the lies our people had been told" during the Vietnam War, and he asked Americans to put their "inordinate fear of Communism" behind them. His secretary of state, Cyrus R. Vance, said that he had learned from the Vietnam War that the United States could not "prop up a series of regimes that lacked popular support" and that "there can be no going back to a time when we thought there could be American solutions to every problem." Yet not all Americans agreed. Some wanted Carter to spare no expense to expand the military and to face down America's many adversaries. Others wanted less Cold War bluster, less military, and less interventionism.

In this environment of conflicting answers and lessons, Carter vowed to chart a new course. When he took office in 1977, he pledged to give as much attention to North-South as to East-West issues, to reduce the American military presence overseas, to cut back arms sales, and to slow the nuclear arms race. He also promised preventive diplomacy: advancing the peace process in the Middle East; mediating conflict in the Third World; and creating worldwide economic stability through agreements on the law of the sea, energy, and clean air and water. "The soul of our foreign policy," he explained, would be the championing of individual human rights abroad—the freedom to vote, worship, travel, speak out, and get a fair trial. A deeply religious man, Carter intended to infuse international relations with moral force.

Carter's Foreign Policy Goals

Almost from the start, Carter spoke and acted inconsistently, and his advisers squabbled among themselves. A major source of the problem was Zbigniew Brzezinski, his Polish-born national security adviser. The stern-faced Brzezinski was an old-fashioned Cold Warrior who viewed foreign crises in globalist terms—that is, he blamed them on the Soviet Union. Carter gradually listened more to Brzezinski than to Secretary of State Vance, a widely respected public servant who advocated quiet diplomacy to find avenues toward Soviet-American cooperation.

Under Carter, détente further deteriorated, and the Cold War revived. The president first angered the Soviets by demanding that they respect their citizens' human rights and tolerate dissent. Moscow told him to mind his own business. Then American officials denounced the Soviets for sponsoring Cuban troops in Angola, where a leftist government was struggling against South African and American-backed rebels.

A thaw came in 1979, when negotiations produced a new treaty, SALT-II, which acknowledged Soviet-American nuclear parity. The agreement placed a ceiling of 2,250 delivery vehicles (long-range bombers, ICBMs, and submarine-based missiles) on each side. The Soviet Union had to dismantle more than 250 existing delivery vehicles, but the United States could expand from its current 2,060 to the new ceiling. Critics from the right nonetheless charged that the treaty favored the Soviets and that verification of compliance was difficult; critics from the left protested that the treaty did not go far enough toward curtailing the arms race. To win votes from conservative senators, Carter proposed the construction of an expensive new MX missile system that would shuttle ICBMs back and forth along a vast maze of underground tunnels designed to confuse an attacker. The president did not get the votes for the treaty, but he did alarm the Soviets.

SALT-II

Meanwhile, events in Afghanistan led to a Soviet-American confrontation. In December 1979, the Red Army bludgeoned its way into the Soviets' southern neighbor to shore up a faltering Communist government under siege by Moslem rebels. An embittered Carter shelved SALT-II, suspended shipments of grain and high-technology equipment to Russia, and initiated an international boycott of the 1980 Summer Olympics in Moscow. The president also announced the Carter Doctrine: the United States would intervene, unilaterally and militarily if necessary, against Soviet aggression in the petroleum-rich Persian Gulf. But all of Carter's efforts proved fruitless: the Soviets refused to withdraw their forces from Afghanistan. (They did not leave until 1989.)

Carter met his toughest test in Iran, where in early 1979 the shah was toppled from his throne by revolutionaries under the leadership of the **Iranian Hostage Crisis** Ayatollah Ruhollah Khomeini, a wrathfully anti-American Moslem cleric. In November, after the exiled shah was admitted to the United States for medical treatment, mobs stormed the American embassy in Teheran and took American personnel as hostages, demanding the return of the shah for trial, as well as the return of his vast wealth. Although the Iranians released a few of the prisoners, fifty-two others languished more than a year under Iranian guard.

Carter would not return the shah to Iran or apologize for past American involvement there (such as the CIA's 1953 intervention that restored the shah to his throne). Unable to gain the hostages' freedom through diplomatic intermediaries, the president took steps to isolate Iran economically. He froze Iranian assets in the United States and appealed to American allies, largely in vain, to reduce trade with the Moslem state. In April 1980, Carter broke diplomatic relations with Iran and ordered a daring rescue mission that miscarried after an equipment breakdown in the Iranian desert; during the hasty withdrawal, two aircraft collided, killing eight American soldiers. The hostages were not freed until January 1981, after the United States unfroze Iranian assets and promised not to intervene again in Iran's internal affairs.

Elsewhere in the Middle East, Carter enjoyed some success. Through his tenacious personal diplomacy at a Camp David meeting in September **Camp David Agreements** 1978 with Egyptian and Israeli leaders, the president gained Israel's promise to withdraw from the Sinai, which it had occupied

On November 4, 1979, an Iranian mob encouraged by government officials seized the American embassy in Teheran and took Americans prisoner. Iranian demonstrators taunted the powerlessness of the United States. The crisis lasted 444 days. *Wide World Photos.*

since 1967. Other Arab states denounced the agreement for not requiring Israel to relinquish other occupied territories and for not guaranteeing a Palestinian homeland. But the treaty at least ended warfare along one boundary in that troubled area of the world.

Carter also had some success elsewhere in the Third World. His appointment of Andrew Young, a black civil rights activist and member of Congress, as ambassador to the United Nations earned goodwill among developing nations. Young believed that the United States should stay out of local disputes, even if Communists were involved. Third World leaders were shocked, however, when Carter forced Young to resign in 1979, after the ambassador had met privately with representatives of the Palestine Liberation Organization, which the United States had refused to recognize as a legitimate group.

In Nicaragua in 1979, leftist revolutionaries overthrew the dictatorial Somoza family, which had ruled the nation since 1936. The revolutionaries called themselves Sandinistas, after the Nicaraguan who had fought American marines in the early 1930s. Carter at first tried to tame their radicalism, but, failing, he recognized the new government. In early 1981, he shut off aid to Nicaragua to demonstrate disapproval of the Sandinistas' curbing of civil liberties, growing ties with Castro's Cuba, and assistance to rebels in El Salvador, where another regime friendly to the United States was threatened by internal upheaval. Elsewhere in Latin America, Carter in 1978 concluded two treaties that provided for the gradual return of the Canal Zone to Panama.

Latin America

Carter's diplomatic record never met his aspirations. More American military personnel were stationed overseas in 1980 than in 1976; the defense budget climbed; foreign arms sales grew from $8.3 billion in 1977 to $15.3 billion in 1980. Carter's human rights policy also proved inconsistent. He followed a double standard—that is, he applied the human rights test to some nations (the Soviet Union, Argentina, and Chile) but not to American allies (South Korea, the shah's Iran, and the Philippines).

Carter's performance did not satisfy those Americans who wanted superiority in foreign affairs—a reinstatement of the economic hegemony and the considerable military edge that the United States had had in the early days of the Cold War. As one Tennessee woman mused, "Growing up we learned in history that America was the best in everything. We had the respect of the whole world. But where can you go today and be respected for being American?" A broad segment of American public opinion agreed with her.

People of Color and New Immigrants

Carter, Nixon and Ford, presided over a nation in which many people of color saw their economic fortunes decline. Joblessness plagued blacks, Native Americans, and Hispanics. As a result of the sluggish economy, poverty was still a national problem in 1980, and blacks made up a disproportionate share of the poor. The weight of poverty fell heavily on black children. A 1981 Children's Defense Fund survey reported that black children in the United States were four times more likely than whites to be born in poverty, twice as likely to drop out of school before twelfth grade, five times as likely as white teenagers to be murdered, and three times as likely to be unemployed. Indeed, in 1980 the unemployment rate for black male teenagers in the inner cities hovered around 50 percent.

Tied to the high unemployment rate was the increase in the number of young black families headed by single women. Between 1960 and 1975, the number of fatherless black families rose by 130 percent. Many of these families were headed by unmarried teenagers who relied on welfare to support their children. Other mothers earned meager incomes as domestic servants, laundresses, or kitchen helpers. Like young black males, welfare mothers suffered from a sense of futility.

Some whites and even other blacks grumbled that poor blacks were responsible for their own poverty. But the job market was far different in the 1970s from what it had been twenty-five, fifty, or seventy-five years before. Most jobs required skills that the poor and undereducated did not have.

But even as the plight of the black poor worsened, the black middle class expanded. The number of black college students increased from 282,000 in 1966 to more than 1 million in 1976. By 1980, about one-third of all black high school graduates were going on to college, the same proportion as of white youths. At least at the upper levels of black society, the dream of equality was being realized.

Black Middle Class

As middle-class blacks were making gains, resentful whites complained that they were being victimized by "reverse discrimination." To meet federal affirmative action require-

White Backlash ments, some schools and companies had established quotas for minorities and women. In some cases the requirements for quota groups were lower than those for whites. When Allan Bakke, a white man, was denied admission to medical school, he sued, contending that less-qualified black applicants had been admitted in his place. In a 5-to-4 ruling in 1978, the Supreme Court outlawed quotas but upheld the principle of affirmative action (*Bakke* v. *University of California*).

Anger over affirmative action and busing combined with the effects of stagflation to produce an upsurge in racism in the 1970s. In Boston, where busing caused numerous riots, a group of white students protesting busing attacked a black passerby outside City Hall. "Get the nigger; kill him," one shouted, and they ran at him with the sharp end of a flagstaff flying an American flag. Tension rose not only in Boston, but all across the nation.

Blacks were tense too, and they showed it more openly than in the past. Charles Silberman wrote in *Criminal Violence, Criminal Justice* (1978) that "black Americans have discov-

Black Anger ered that fear runs the other way, that whites are intimidated by their very presence. . . . The taboo against expression of anti-white anger is breaking down, and 350 years of festering hatred has come spilling out." That hatred erupted several times in summer 1980, most notably in Miami and Chattanooga, after all-white juries acquitted whites of the murder of blacks. Miami's three days of rioting left eighteen dead and four hundred injured.

American Indians were every bit as angry as blacks. Their new militancy burst into the headlines in November 1969, when a small group of Indians seized Alcatraz Island in San Fran-

Indian Militancy cisco Bay. Arguing that an 1868 Sioux treaty entitled them to possession of unused federal lands, the Indians occupied the island until the summer of 1971. Two years later, members of the American

Indian Movement (AIM) seized eleven hostages and a trading post on the Pine Ridge Reservation at Wounded Knee, South Dakota, the place where troops of the 7th Cavalry had massacred the Sioux in 1890. Their seventy-one-day confrontation with federal marshals ended with a government agreement to examine the treaty rights of the Oglala Sioux.

Like many blacks, Indians were trapped in poverty. The unemployment rate among Indians was 40 percent in the late 1970s. Nine out of ten Indians lived in substandard housing, and the high school dropout rate averaged 53 percent. Being an Indian was also unhealthy: Native Americans suffered the highest incidence of alcoholism, tuberculosis, and suicide of any ethnic group in the United States.

Since 1924, Indians have had dual legal status as United States citizens and as members of tribal nations subject to special treaty agreements with the United States. Their dual status has

Indian Suits for Lost Lands proved a curse, in large part because the government has not honored its treaty commitments. In 1946, Congress established the Indian Claims Commission to compensate Indians for lands stolen from them. Under the legislation, lawyers for the Native American Rights Fund and other groups scored notable victories in the 1970s, including protection of Indians' hunting and fishing rights and restitution of their land and water. In 1971, President Nixon signed a bill returning to the Taos Pueblo the sacred forest of Blue Lake in New Mexico. In 1980, the Supreme Court ordered the government to pay $106 million, plus interest, to the Sioux Indian Nation for the Black Hills of South Dakota, stolen when gold was discovered there in the 1870s.

As Indians fought to regain old rights, Hispanics struggled to make a place for themselves in the United States. An influx of immigrants coupled with a high birthrate made His-

Hispanic-Americans panic peoples America's fastest-growing minority by the 1970s. Of the more than 20 million Hispanics living in the United States in the 1970s, 8 million were Mexican-Americans concentrated in Arizona, California, Colorado, New Mexico, and Texas. Several million Puerto Ricans and perhaps 1 million Cubans clustered principally on the East Coast.

Besides these officially acknowledged Hispanics, between 8 million and 12 million more undocumented workers, or illegal aliens, lived in the United States. Beginning in the mid-1960s, large numbers of poverty-stricken Mexicans began to cross the 2,000-mile border between Mexico and the United States. The movement north continued in the 1970s. By 1980, one out of every four Texans and one out of every five Californians was Mexican-American.

Poverty awaited these new immigrants. The median family income for Mexican-Americans in 1979 was $11,421, as compared with $16,284 for non-Hispanic families. Nineteen percent of Mexican-Americans lived below the poverty line. Puerto Ricans were worse off, with a median family income of about $8,300 and 30 percent of their number living in poverty. Although the problems that Hispanics contended with were similar to those confronting other nonwhites, Hispanics also faced a language barrier.

Most Hispanics preferred their family-centered culture to Anglo culture, and for that reason they resisted assimilation. "What we are saying," explained Daniel Villanueva, a television executive, "is that we want to be here, but without losing our language and our culture. They are a richness, a treasure that we don't care to lose."

Hispanic Cultural Pride

Like other minorities, Hispanics wanted power—"brown power." Cesar Chávez's United Farm Workers was the first Hispanic interest group to gain national attention. Another group, the militant Brown Berets, attracted notice for their efforts to provide meals to preschoolers and courses in Chicano studies and consciousness-raising to older students. And throughout the 1970s, the Mexican-American political party La Raza Unida was a potent force in the Southwest and in East Los Angeles. Still, for a group soon to become the nation's largest minority, Hispanics exercised a disproportionately small share of political power.

During the 1970s, millions of people of color immigrated to the United States. They came in record numbers from Indochina, Mexico, Central and South America, and the Caribbean. Between 1970 and 1980, the United States absorbed more than 4 million immigrants and refugees and perhaps twice that number of illegal aliens. Refugees of the Vietnam War arrived, and other immigrants came from the Philippines, Korea, Taiwan, India, the Dominican Republic, and Jamaica. In 1980, 160,000 boat people poured in from the islands of Cuba and Haiti. Although well-wishers were on hand to greet these people, the history of the nation's treatment of people of color, along with the severe recession that began in 1979, did not augur well for them.

New Influx of Immigrants

The arrival of so many newcomers put pressure on Congress to curtail the flow and perhaps provide amnesty for those aliens already living illegally in the United States. In 1978, Congress authorized the Select Commission on Immigration and Refugee Policy to undertake the first comprehensive re-examination of America's immigration policy since 1965. The commission conducted its study between 1979 and 1981, but legislative solutions would await congressional action in the 1980s.

Women's Struggles

In the 1970s, while civil rights struggles were engaging the energies of various racial and ethnic groups, increasing numbers of women were committing themselves to the struggle for equality with men. Feminists had scored some impressive legislative victories. In 1974, Congress passed the Equal Credit Opportunity Act, which enabled women to get bank loans and obtain credit cards on the same terms as men. Even more significant were women's gains, along with gains by blacks and other minorities, from affirmative action in hiring. As mandated by the Civil Rights Act of 1964 and the establishment of the Equal Employment Opportunity Commission, women and minorities applying for a job had to receive the same consideration as white males. In the field of criminal law, many states revised their statutes on rape, prohibiting

The 1970s saw the mass immigration of people from numerous Asian and Latin American countries to the United States. As evidenced by these smiling Boy Scouts, young Asian-Americans took quickly to the ways of their new country. *Leif Skoogfors/Woodfin Camp.*

lawyers from stressing the previous sexual experience of rape victims.

Still, women continued to encounter barriers in their quest for equality. One of the most formidable was the antifeminist, or "profamily," movement, which contended that men should **Antifeminist** lead and women should follow, **Movement** particularly within the family. The backlash against feminism became an increasingly powerful political force in the 1970s. In defense of the family, antifeminists campaigned against the Equal Rights Amendment (ERA), the gay rights movement, and abortion on demand. Anita Bryant and Phyllis Schlafly gained fame by arguing that all these issues were interrelated and that they endangered traditional American values.

Antifeminists stalled ratification of the Equal Rights Amendment, which, after quickly passing through thirty-five state legislatures, fell three states short of success in the late 1970s. Schlafly's

Equal Rights "STOP ERA" campaign falsely **Amendment** claimed that the ERA would abolish alimony and legalize homosexual marriage. The ERA debate was vicious at times. Refusing to acknowledge gender-based discrimination, Schlafly derided ERA advocates as "a bunch of bitter women seeking a constitutional cure for their personal problems."

Many antifeminists also participated in the antiabortion or "prolife," movement, which sprang up almost overnight in the wake of the Supreme Court's 1973 decision in *Roe* v. *Wade*. Along with Catholics, Mormons, and other religious opponents of abortion, the prolife movement supported the successful legislative efforts of Representative Henry Hyde of Illinois in 1976 to cut off most Medicaid funds for abortions. In the summer of 1980, the Supreme Court upheld the Hyde Amendment, deciding that the government had no obligation to make even medically necessary abortions available to the poor.

As activists in the women's struggle looked to the 1980s, they had to acknowledge certain harsh realities. One was the tight job market, created by the economic recessions of the 1970s. Added to job scarcity was the continuing problem of occupational segregation: women were concentrated in low-paying positions while most men enjoyed much higher incomes. By the end of the 1970s, female workers still took home only 59 cents to every male worker's dollar. Another disturbing trend was "the Superwoman Squeeze." According to a report by the Worldwatch Institute in 1980, most working wives and mothers, even those with full-time jobs, "retained an unwilling monopoly on unpaid labor at home."

Increased Burdens on Women

The Me Decade

At the beginning of 1980, the editors of *Time* magazine observed that the 1970s had been "erected upon the smoldering wreckage of the '60s." In the 1970s, the nation had turned apathetic, and perhaps nowhere was this new attitude more evident than among youth. During the 1960s, American youths had worked for change in the nation's social, political, and cultural life. But by the mid-1970s, their younger brothers and sisters rejected revolutionary idealism. Older Americans also turned their backs to a lost war, political scandal, and economic distress. As a theologian put it, Americans "have a beleaguered sense in their bones that the old order is dying. Very few want a radical alternative, but few also are working to develop a rationale for the system we've got." Instead, in the 1970s, Americans turned inward and concentrated on self-expression and personal improvement. Social commentator Tom Wolfe branded the 1970s the Me Decade.

In that decade, suggestions for realizing one's full potential were consumed as readily as jogging shoes and health foods. Transcendental Meditation (TM), a yogic discipline, drew 350,000 adherents and spawned more than two hundred teaching centers. Other new therapies and exotic religions flourished in the 1970s, as did such Eastern religions and practices of long standing as Zen and yoga.

As millions of Americans sought to fill spiritual and emotional voids through esoteric movements, millions more were drawn to traditional Christian beliefs. According to a 1977 survey, about 70 million Americans defined themselves as born-again Christians. Religious revivals and evangelical sects were not new, of course, but by the mid-1970s, they were a growth industry. In the latter years of the decade evangelicals were grossing $200 million annually in sales of religious books.

Spiritual Revival

Besides the relatively harmless human potential movements and the traditional religious enthusiasms, a dark undercurrent of cult-like adherence to charismatic leaders ran through the 1970s. Reverend Sun Myung Moon, Korean founder of the Unification Church, converted young Americans to his religion, a curious blend of Christianity, anticommunism, and worship of Moon as a messiah. Critics charged that Moon and his disciples brainwashed their converts. Brainwashing clearly marked Reverend Jim Jones's People's Temple, which in 1977 moved from California to Guyana, in South America. In November 1978, convinced that the United States was about to destroy the colony, the crazed leader ordered his followers to kill themselves with a mixture of Kool-Aid and cyanide. The mass murder and suicide of 911 Americans in Guyana added a satanic dimension to the history of American cults.

Messianic Cults

In the 1970s, Americans tried to develop not only their spiritual potential, but their physical potential as well. Perhaps America was no longer the best nation it could be, but Americans were determined to make themselves the healthiest individuals that they could. Membership in racquetball clubs and diet clinics boomed. As the decade drew to a close, Christopher Lasch, a history professor, condemned the nation's behavior as self-indulgent and apolitical. In *The Culture of Narcissism* (1979), Lasch branded

The Culture of Narcissism

Americans an emotionally shallow, anxiety-ridden people desperately trying to ignore the waning of their nation's power. He cited advertising and the human potential movement as causes of the nation's malaise. Yet there was little evidence that the trend was changing.

Ronald Reagan and the Election of 1980

By 1980, the nation's mood had turned conservative. In 1978, California voters approved a tax-cutting referendum called Proposition 13, which reduced property taxes and put stringent limits on state spending for social programs. On the national level, conservatives lobbied for a constitutional amendment to prohibit federal budget deficits and organized for the 1980 elections. One conservative campaign group, the National Conservative Political Action Committee (NCPAC), targeted a number of liberal senators for defeat. And a number of evangelical Christians joined with the economic conservatives, hoping to use the body politic in their fight against abortion, gay rights, sex in movies, and the ERA.

Resurgence of Conservatism

From the beginning, the front runner for the Republican presidential nomination was conservative Ronald Reagan, a former movie actor and two-term governor of California. Reagan appealed to both the traditional political conservatives and the new breed of social-issue conservatives. In the Democratic party, President Carter easily beat back Senator Edward Kennedy of Massachusetts for the nomination. As the incumbent, Carter had to accept political responsibility not only for high stagflation, but also for the Americans being held hostage in Iran. When the votes were counted, Reagan had won 51 percent of the popular vote and all but forty-nine electoral votes. Carter carried only six states and the District of Columbia. John Anderson, a Republican who ran as an independent, garnered 7 percent of the popular vote.

Election of 1980

As startling as Reagan's sweep was the capture of eleven Senate seats by Republican candidates, a victory that gave the party a majority in that house. Conservative advertising campaigns had succeeded in defeating several liberal senators. Republicans also gained thirty-three seats in the House of Representatives and four state governorships. It seemed clear that the Democrats would be running scared in the 1980s.

On January 20, 1981, Ronald Reagan was inaugurated president. He pledged to work for "an era of national renewal," for "a healthy, vigorous, growing economy that provides equal opportunities for all Americans." On the same day, after 444 days in captivity, the American hostages boarded an airplane that flew them from Teheran to freedom. Yellow ribbons welcomed the freed Americans, and the nation rejoiced. Seldom had a new administration had a more auspicious beginning.

Suggestions for Further Reading

Watergate

Seymour M. Hersh, "The Pardon: Nixon, Ford, Haig, and the Transfer of Power," *Atlantic Monthly*, 252 (1983), 55–78; J. Anthony Lukas, *Nightmare: The Underside of the Nixon Years* (1976); Kim McQuaid, *The Anxious Years: America in the Vietnam-Watergate Era* (1989); Arthur M. Schlesinger, Jr., *The Imperial Presidency* (1973); Theodore H. White, *Breach of Faith* (1975); Bob Woodward and Carl Bernstein, *The Final Days* (1976); Bob Woodward and Carl Bernstein, *All the President's Men* (1974).

Energy Shortages, Stagflation, and Other Economic Woes

Richard J. Barnet, *The Lean Years* (1980); Daniel Bell, *The Coming of the Post-Industrial Society* (1973); John M. Blair, *The Control of Oil* (1976); Barry Bluestone and Bennett Harrison, *The Deindustrialization of America* (1982); David P. Calleo, *The Imperious Economy* (1982); William Greider, *Secrets of the Temple: How the Federal Reserve Runs the Country* (1987); John P. Hoerr, *And the Wolf Finally Came: The Decline of the American Steel Industry* (1988); Robert Sherrill, *The Oil Follies of 1970–1980* (1983); Lester C. Thurow, *The Zero-Sum Society* (1980).

The Ford Administration

Gerald R. Ford, *A Time to Heal* (1979); Robert T. Hartmann, *Palace Politics* (1980); Ron Nessen, *It Sure Looks Different from the Inside* (1978); A. James Reichley, *Conservatives in an Age of Change: The Nixon and Ford Administrations* (1981); James L. Sundquist, *The Decline and Resurgence of Congress* (1981).

The Carter Administration

Griffin Bell, *Taking Care of the Law* (1982); Joseph A. Califano, *Governing America* (1981); Jimmy Carter, *Keeping Faith* (1982); Rosalynn Carter, *First Lady from Plains* (1984); Betty Glad, *Jimmy Carter* (1980); Erwin C. Hargrove, *Jimmy Carter as President* (1989); Haynes Johnson, *In the Absence of Power* (1980); Charles O. Jones, *The Trusteeship Presidency: Jimmy Carter and the United States Congress* (1988); Jody Powell, *The Other Side of the Story* (1984); Laurence H. Shoup, *The Carter Presidency and Beyond* (1980).

Carter's Foreign Policy

James A. Bill, *The Eagle and the Lion* (1988) (on Iran); Zbigniew Brzezinski, *Power and Principle* (1983); Warren Christopher et al., *American Hostages in Iran* (1985); James Fallows, *National Defense* (1981); Ole R. Holsti and James N. Rosenau, *American Leadership in World Affairs: Vietnam and the Breakdown of Consensus* (1984); Anthony Lake, *Somoza Falling* (1989); Walter LaFeber, *The Panama Canal* (1978); David S. McLellan, *Cyrus Vance* (1985); A. Glenn Mower, Jr., *Human Rights and American Foreign Policy: The Carter and Reagan Experiences* (1987); Richard S. Newell, *The Struggle for Afghanistan* (1981); Kenneth A. Oye et al., *Eagle Entangled* (1979); Robert A. Pastor, *Condemned to Repetition* (1987) (on Nicaragua); William B. Quandt, *Camp David* (1986); Gaddis Smith, *Morality, Reason, and Power* (1986); Strobe Talbott, *Endgame* (1979) (on SALT-II); Cyrus R. Vance, *Hard Choices* (1983); Sandy Vogelgesang, *American Dream, Global Nightmare* (1980).

Women and the Family

Suzanne M. Bianchi, *American Women in Transition* (1987); Mary Francis Berry, *Why ERA Failed* (1986); Susan Brownmiller, *Against Our Will: Men, Women and Rape* (1975); Andrea Dworkin, *Right-Wing Women* (1983); Barbara Ehrenreich, *The Hearts of Men: American Dreams and the Flight from Commitment* (1983); Kenneth Keniston, *All Our Children: The American Family Under Pressure* (1977); Christopher Lasch, *Haven in a Heartless World: The Family Besieged* (1977); Kristin Luker, *Abortion and the Politics of Motherhood* (1984); Jane Mansbridge, *Why We Lost the ERA* (1986); Maggie Scarf, *Unfinished Business: Pressure Points in the Lives of Women* (1980); Winifred D. Wandersee, *On the Move: American Women in the 1970s* (1988).

People of Color and New Immigrants

Frank D. Bean and Marta Tienda, *The Hispanic Population of the United States* (1988); Nathan Caplan et al., *The Boat People and Achievement in America* (1989); James D. Cockcroft, *Outlaws in the Promised Land: Mexican Immigrant Workers and America's Future* (1986); John Crewdson, *The Tarnished Door: The New Immigrants and the Transformation of America* (1983); Reynolds Farley and Walter R. Allen, *The Color Line and the Quality of Life in America* (1987); Nancy Foner, ed., *New Immigrants in New York* (1987); Gil Loescher and John A. Scanlan, *Calculated Kindness: Refugees and America's Half-Open Door* (1986); J. Anthony Lukas, *Common Ground* (1985); Peter Matthiessen, *In the Spirit of Crazy Horse* (1983); David M. Reimers, *Still the Golden Door: The Third World Comes to America* (1985); Carol B. Stack, *All Our Kin: Strategies for Survival in a Black Community* (1975); Arnulfo D. Trejo, ed., *The Chicanos: As We See Ourselves* (1979); William Julius Wilson, *The Declining Significance of Race: Blacks and Changing American Institutions*, rev. ed. (1980).

The Me Decade

Peter Clecak, *America's Quest for the Ideal Self: Dissent and Fulfillment in the Sixties and Seventies* (1983); Jim Hougan, *Decadence: Radical Nostalgia, Narcissism, and Decline in the Seventies* (1975); Christopher Lasch, *The Culture of Narcissism* (1978); Edwin Schur, *The Awareness Trap: Self-Absorption Instead of Social Change* (1976); Steven M. Tipton, *Getting Saved from the Sixties* (1982); Tom Wolfe, "The 'Me' Decade and the Third Great Awakening," *New York*, 9 (1976), 26–40; Daniel Yankelovich, *New Rules: Searching for Self-Fulfillment in a World Turned Upside Down* (1981).

The New Conservatism and the Election of 1980

Sidney Blumenthal, *The Rise of the Counter-Establishment* (1986); Peter N. Carroll, *It Seemed Like Nothing Happened: The Tragedy and Promise of America in the 1970s* (1982); Alan Crawford, *Thunder on the Right* (1980); Elizabeth Drew, *Portrait of an Election* (1981); Thomas Byrne Edsall, *The New Politics of Inequality* (1984); Jack W. Germond and Jules Witcover, *Blue Smoke and Mirrors: How Reagan Won and Why Carter Lost the Election of 1980* (1981); Gillian Peele, *Revival and Reaction* (1984); David W. Reinhard, *The Republican Right Since 1945* (1983); Kirkpatrick Sale, *Power Shift: The Rise of the Southern Rim and Its Challenge to the Eastern Establishment* (1975); Peter Steinfels, *The Neo-Conservatives* (1979).

"Lying does not come easy to me," stated Lieutenant Colonel Oliver L. North in mid-July 1987. "I came here to tell the truth—the good, the bad and the ugly." In testimony before a special congressional committee investigating covert arms transactions with Iran and the contras, an American-launched band of counterrevolutionaries in Nicaragua, North said that he was simply a patriot and a gung-ho marine. "I'm not in the habit of questioning my superiors." North was a controversial witness. A former National Security Council aide, he had violated the law while working in the White House.

North had been dismissed from the White House staff on November 25, 1986. On the same day, Attorney General Edwin M. Meese III had announced that some money from a just-revealed secret arms deal with Iran may have gone to the contras fighting against the government of Nicaragua. Americans had mixed reactions to North. Both President Ronald Reagan and Vice President George Bush championed him as a national hero. However, the co-chair of the congressional investigating committee, Senator Daniel K. Inouye of Hawaii, charged that the Iran-contra scandal was "much more serious than Watergate" because it involved "the formulation and conduct of American foreign policy."

33

A TURN TO THE RIGHT: AMERICA SINCE 1981

Between May and August 1987, three-fourths of the American people watched the Iran-contra hearings on television. Many thousands felt moved to write the members of the congressional committee. A Latina school principal from California wrote: "I do not want anyone fighting in Latin America. . . . Help us not to send money for my *brown* son to kill his cousins or ancestors." On the other hand, a woman from New Jersey wrote: "I am as proud of Ollie as I am of my Father who served before and during World War II. . . . My father fought for all the freedoms we hold dear. This is just what Lt. Col. North was doing." Others considered North a menace to democracy.

The Iran-contra hearings focused attention on President Reagan's "management style," which his aides described as a "hands-off" approach. But others, both outsiders and insiders, saw Reagan as unengaged and uninformed. By 1987, the political satirists were in hot pursuit. The real question, went one gibe, was not "what did the President know and when did he know it?" but "what didn't the President know, and why didn't he know it?"

Such ridicule was at odds with the history of the first six years of Reagan's presidency. During his first term, the economy rebounded, and by 1984 his policies had lowered inflation, interest rates, and unemployment. As the 1984 election approached, many Americans also applauded Reagan's foreign policy, expressing their satisfaction that their nation was confronting the Russians with strong words, interventions, and a large military build-up. Patriotism was back in style. Reagan's support of prayer in the public schools and his opposition to abortion also bolstered his popularity. Many Americans agreed with his desire for a return to the morality that had dominated American culture before the 1960s.

Nonetheless, Reagan suffered severe criticism during his first term. Opponents lambasted his economic policies ("Reaganomics") as favoring the rich and penalizing the poor. Although unemployment mounted between 1981 and 1983, Reagan seemed to escape personal blame. Indeed, the president was a master at avoiding responsibility for both domestic and foreign policy problems. Representative Patricia Schroeder, a Colorado Democrat, gave this phenomenon a memorable label, saying that Reagan was "perfecting a Teflon-coated presidency. . . . He sees to it that nothing sticks to him." Reagan's victory in 1984 was never in doubt. The size of it, however—his forty-nine-state total—led observers to conclude that he had transformed American politics by forging a New Right coalition, which could dominate national politics for years to come.

Reagan's conservatism also shaped his foreign policy. He surrounded himself with people who believed that previous administrations had shown weakness in dealing with the Soviet Union, Cuba, Third World countries, and terrorists. The Reagan administration set out to swell the American military arsenal, denounce and intimidate the Soviets, unseat leftist governments through military intervention and covert operations, and settle on American terms civil wars in the Middle East and Latin America. Although many Americans and foreigners grew alarmed at the rapid acceleration of the nuclear arms race and at the application of mili-

tary power to political problems, most Americans approved of Reagan's harsh anti-Sovietism and emphasis on military strength.

On election day 1986, however, trouble started brewing for the administration. From Lebanon came a bizarre story that Robert McFarlane, the president's national security aide, had traveled to Iran with a Bible, a cake, and a planeload of weapons seeking the release of Americans held hostage in the Middle East. Also on that day, the Republicans lost control of the Senate, thus stripping the president of a crucial power base. Other setbacks followed, including additional scandals involving White House staffers, congressional overrides of presidential vetoes, and in a single day in October 1987, a 508-point crash in the stock market.

While middle- and upper-middle-class Americans worried about the declining value of their stocks, others worried about how to pay the rent or buy the next meal. Poverty deepened in the 1980s, especially for people of color and single-parent families, usually headed by women. In the 1980s, the United States was polarized racially and economically, and two new problems worsened societal divisions: AIDS (Acquired Immune Deficiency Syndrome) and the cocaine-derived drug known as crack.

Near the end of his presidency, Reagan did enjoy some foreign policy success, but this progress stemmed as much from changes abroad as from his own decisions. A younger generation of leaders under Mikhail S. Gorbachev came to power in the Soviet Union in 1985 and moved to modernize their nation's decaying economy, liberalize its suffocating political system, and reduce its expensive overseas activities. They also sought serious détente with the United States. Gorbachev and Reagan met at summits, visited each other's countries, and signed a treaty banning intermediate-range nuclear forces (INF) in Europe. Elsewhere, in war-embroiled Central America and the Middle East, Reagan had conspicuously failed to meet his objectives.

Reagan's influence waned during his final two years in office. But when the voters went to the polls in November 1988, the nation was at peace and both unemployment and inflation were low.

IMPORTANT EVENTS

1981
Prime interest rate at 21.5 percent
AIDS first observed in United States
Congress approves Reagan's budget cuts
Economic Recovery Tax Act
Soviet crackdown in Poland
Economic recession
Unemployment at 8 percent
United States steps up role in El Salvador
INF talks begin
CIA begins to train contras

1982
START negotiations begin
American troops ordered to Lebanon
Unemployment at 10.1 percent

1983
Prime interest rate at 10.5 percent
Strategic Defense Initiative ("Star Wars") announced
Unemployment at 10.2 percent
More than half of adult women hold jobs outside the home
Soviets shoot down Korean airliner
Terrorists kill American marines in Lebanon
Invasion of Grenada
American missiles deployed in Western Europe
Contadora peace plan for Central America

1984
American troops leave Lebanon
CIA mines Nicaraguan harbors
Unemployment drops to 7.1 percent
Reagan re-elected
Inflation falls to 4 percent

1985
Reagan Doctrine announced
Gorbachev comes to power in Soviet Union
United States economic embargo on Nicaragua
Geneva summit meeting

1986
Tax Reform Act
Immigration Reform and Control Act
Republicans lose control of Senate in congressional election
Iran-contra scandal breaks

1987
Washington summit meeting
One-day drop of 508 points in stock market prices
American trade deficit at $170 million

1988
Palestinian uprising on West Bank
Arias peace plan for Central America
Agreement on Soviet withdrawal from Afghanistan
Moscow summit meeting
INF Treaty signed
American warship downs Iranian airliner
Understanding AIDS mailed to 107 million households
Unemployment rate at 5.4 percent
Bush elected president
Bombing of Pan American flight

1989
Solidarity legalized in Poland; wins free elections
Prodemocracy demonstration throughout Eastern Europe
Communist oligarchs fall in Eastern Europe
Berlin Wall opened
United States invades Panama
Third World debt at more than $1.2 trillion

1990
Noriega surrenders
Elections in Nicaragua
Free elections held in East Germany and Eastern Europe
Washington summit
Iraq invades Kuwait; American troops sent to Middle East

Vice president George Bush was the beneficiary of the Reagan legacy, and as the Republican candidate, he rode it to victory.

During Bush's first year in office, the seemingly impossible happened—the Communist regimes of Eastern Europe toppled. In Poland, Hungary, Czechoslovakia, and Romania, Communists lost power. Even the Berlin Wall and the repressive government of East Germany's Erich Honecker failed to survive the popular onslaught.

Gorbachev's policies of *glasnost* (openness) and *perestroika* (fundamental restructuring) stimulated this dramatic change. Gorbachev kept Soviet troops in their barracks when people took to the streets in protest of their governments. Indeed, his tolerance of change in Eastern Europe whetted the appetites of Soviet citizens for greater liberalization at home. Gorbachev thus found himself confronted with secessionist movements in the Baltic republics of Lithuania, Latvia, and Estonia as well as with domestic political opponents who thought he was moving too slowly.

"Reaganomics"

Upon taking office, President Reagan wasted little time in announcing his plans for what he called "a new beginning." In February 1981, he launched a double-barreled attack on problems in the economy. First, he asked Congress for billions in spending cuts from domestic programs, including urban aid, Medicare and Medicaid, food stamps, welfare subsidies for the working poor, and school meals. In July, Congress met most of Reagan's demands. He initiated a second round of budget cuts in September, resulting, among other things, in the trimming of 1 million food-stamp recipients from government rolls.

Tax cuts constituted the second part of Reagan's economic plan. Reagan was a fervent believer in supply-side economics, which called for reductions in the income taxes of the affluent

Tax Cuts and of corporations in order to stimulate savings and investments. New capital would be invested, the argument went, and would produce new plants, new jobs, and new products. As prosperity returned, the profits at the top would trickle down to the middle classes and even to the poor at the bottom. Economic growth and expanding opportunities would again be the hallmarks of American society. Congress responded with a five-year, $750-billion tax cut, the largest ever in American history. The major feature of the Economic Recovery Tax Act was a 25-percent reduction in personal income taxes over the next three years. Other provisions increased business investment tax credits and depreciation allowances and lowered the maximum tax on all income from 70 to 50 percent. Wealthy people gained the most from these tax cuts.

Reagan also began an assault on federal environmental, health, and safety regulations; in his view, they needlessly sapped business profits and discouraged economic growth. The

Weakened Environmental Enforcement president appointed opponents of these regulations to enforce them. The administration claimed that slacker enforcement was necessary to reduce business costs and make American goods competitive in world markets, but environmentalists countered that such policy invited human disaster, such as toxic-waste poisoning or nuclear reactor accidents.

Reagan scored two notable economic successes during his first two years in office: the inflation rate plummeted, and so did the cost of borrowing money. The prime rate for bank

Falling Inflation loans, which had reached a record high of 21.5 percent in early 1981, dropped to 10.5 percent by early 1983. Inflation fell from 12.4 percent in 1980 to less than 7 percent in 1982. Oil led the way in price declines. In 1981, the United States was awash with oil, as world production exceeded demand by 2 million barrels a day.

But there was also a sobering explanation for the decline in inflation. By mid-1981, the nation was mired in a recession, which not only persisted, but also deepened. During the last three months of the year, the gross national product fell 5.3 percent, and sales of cars and houses dropped sharply. With declining economic activity, unemployment went up, soaring in October to 8 percent.

A year later, in October 1982, unemployment reached 10.1 percent, the highest rate since 1940.

Most of the jobless were adult men, particularly black men who suffered an unemployment rate of 19.8 percent. Many of the unemployed were blue-collar workers in such ailing "smokestack industries" as autos, steel, and rubber. Reagan and his advisers had hoped that his supply-side economics would produce demand-side results and that consumers would lift the economy out of the recession by spending their tax cuts. But as late as April 1983, unemployment stood at 10.2 percent.

Rising Un-employment

Agriculture, too, was faltering and near collapse. Farmers suffered not only from floods and droughts, but also from the debts they had incurred at high interest rates. Many lost their property through mortgage foreclosures and farm auctions, and others filed for bankruptcy.

The Election of 1984 and the Triumph of Reagan's Presidency

As he prepared for his 1984 re-election campaign, Reagan knew that most white men in the country supported him but the majority of women and people of color did not. The AFL-CIO, too, joined the anti-Reagan camp. Reagan had presided over the government's busting of the Professional Air Traffic Controllers Organization during the union's 1981 strike. He had also appointed people to the National Labor Relations Board who consistently voted against labor and for management. Still, the economy was showing signs of recovery, making Reagan's re-election prospects excellent.

In 1984, the gross national product rose 6.8 percent, the sharpest increase since 1951, and midyear unemployment fell to a four-year low of 7.1 percent. Although the economy was heating up, it did so without causing inflation to boil. Indeed, inflation—4 percent in 1984—fell to its lowest level since 1967. Another factor in Reagan's favor was people's percep-

Reagan's Re-election Assets

tion of him as a strong leader in foreign, as well as national, affairs. In addition, Reagan was the enthusiastic choice of both the political right and of social, cultural, and religious conservatives. He won the approval of millions of other Americans, who agreed with his television ads that "America is back" after two decades of turmoil and self-doubt.

The Democrats did not field a convincing alternative. In contrast to Reagan, the Democratic nominee—former Vice President Walter Mondale—did not inspire Americans. Most people identified him with the ineffectual Carter administration. The Democratic party's policies seemed timeworn, and its presidential candidate aroused little excitement. Besides, the party was in disarray—fragmented into numerous caucuses for union members, blacks, women, Jews, homosexuals, Hispanics, and other groups. Each group had its own agenda.

Democratic Divisions

What enthusiasm there was for the Democratic ticket arose from Mondale's historic selection of Congresswoman Geraldine Ferraro of New York as his vice-presidential running mate. Feminists hailed this choice, as did numerous women and men throughout the country. Ferraro showed herself to be an intelligent, indefatigable campaigner who won the respect of even her opponents.

Geraldine Ferraro

During the campaign, Mondale attempted to debate such issues as the federal deficit and the nuclear arms race, but Reagan preferred to invoke the theme of leadership and rely on slogans. Mondale chastised Reagan for the federal deficit, which had reached $175 billion in fiscal year 1984. But when Mondale announced that he would raise taxes to cut the deficit, he lost votes. Mondale also attacked Reagan's foreign policy as too militaristic and too interventionist. But Americans were attracted to Reagan's strident anti-Soviet rhetoric and his pledge to restore American global power.

Voters in 1984 had a clear choice, and in all but one state they chose the Republican ticket. Only Minnesota—Mondale's home state—kept the results from being unanimous. The election returns were the most convincing evidence yet that by 1984 the nation had taken a sharp turn to the right.

Reagan's Victory

The New Deal coalition was in shambles. The only groups still voting for the Democratic ticket were blacks, Hispanics, Jews, the poor, and the unemployed. Reagan scored solid victories with all other voting groups, including young people, northern and southern whites, high school and college graduates, Protestants and Catholics, and families with incomes exceeding $12,500.

In 1985, in his second inaugural address, Reagan announced that his "new American Emancipation" would "tear down economic barriers to liberate the spirit of enterprise" by eradicating the excesses of fifty years of Democratic liberalism. Whether Reagan had forged a lasting conservative coalition—one that would eventually repeal the New Deal—was debatable. What was not debatable was that he had succeeded in his principal aims during his first term and had restored the presidency to its central role in politics and the government.

Columnist David Broder noted, however, that "Reagan's issue-free, feel-good 1984 campaign created no policy mandate." For much of 1985, the newly re-elected president was on the defensive. The fiscal deficit particularly, caused public concern. During the 1980 campaign, Reagan had assailed Carter's $73.8-billion deficit, but in fiscal 1985 and 1986, the deficit exceeded $236 billion and $220 billion, respectively. Although Republicans blamed the deficit on the Democrats, almost half of the national debt accrued in the fiscal years 1982 through 1986, when Reagan sat in the White House and the Republicans controlled the Senate. Tax reductions and upwardly spiraling defense budgets increased the national debt by $954 billion during this five-year period. In response, Reagan and Congress reluctantly agreed to the Gramm-Rudman bill, which called for a balanced federal budget by fiscal 1991 through a gradual reduction of the annual deficit.

Mounting Fiscal Deficit

The trade deficit presented another economic problem. Between 1984 and 1986, the annual trade deficit increased from $102 billion to $169.8 billion. Protectionists, who favored charging tariffs on foreign goods imported into the United States, were especially angry with Japan, for its trade surplus with the United States amounted to $56.8 billion in 1986.

Trade Deficit

In 1985 and 1986, Reagan confronted other challenges more successfully. In 1986, following Warren Burger's decision to retire from the Supreme Court, Reagan nominated William Rehnquist to serve as chief justice and Antonin Scalia to fill Rehnquist's seat. The Senate confirmed both choices. Another victory for Reagan was the Tax Reform Act of 1986, which closed some flagrant tax loopholes, eliminated six million poor people from the tax rolls, and lowered the rates on personal income tax.

Until November 1986, Reagan's place in history was secure. But with the disclosures of the Iran-contra affair, his aura faded. The revelations sullied his last two years in office, placed his historical reputation in danger, and raised the Democrats' hopes for a presidential victory in 1988.

Reagan's Foreign Policy: The Soviets and the Nuclear Arms Race

Ronald Reagan's foreign policy was driven by five beliefs rooted in America's past. First, Reagan and his advisers saw the Soviet Union as malevolent and the source of the world's troubles. Charging that the Soviets were prepared "to commit any crime" to achieve a Communist world, the president blamed Third World disorders on Soviet intrigue. He rejected arguments that the civil wars in Central America derived from economic instability, poverty, and class oppression.

Reagan's Foreign Policy Views

Second, Reagan believed that a major American military build-up would thwart the Soviet threat and intimidate Moscow into negotiating on terms favorable to the United States. In sponsoring multi-trillion-dollar defense spending, the president pushed plans for the B-1 bomber, a much enlarged navy, production of poison gas, beefed-up special forces units for counterinsurgency, and the MX missile. In 1983, he also proposed an antimissile defense system in space (titled the Strategic Defense

Initiative, or SDI, but soon dubbed "Star Wars"). In 1985, the Pentagon was spending an average of $28 million an hour, twenty-four hours a day, seven days a week. And the military was sent abroad—to (among other places) the tiny Caribbean island of Grenada, where in 1983 American invaders drove from power a leftist government friendly with Cuba. A warmongering image soon settled around the Reagan administration.

Third, Reagan thought it important to change America's mood and gain public support for a more interventionist, militarized foreign policy. Using his exceptional communicating skills to stimulate emotional patriotism, Reagan asked for a "national reawakening" and pronounced the end of post-Vietnam "self-doubt." Most Americans shared Reagan's feeling that the United States had been ignobly retreating from global power and leadership. Reagan's rhetoric and actions made Americans feel good about themselves and their place in the world.

Fourth, Reagan and his advisers believed that nations must embrace private capitalism and "privatize" managed economies. They frequently lectured Third World countries on the virtue of private enterprise. Overall, the Reagan administration withdrew from the "North-South" dialogue.

The fifth driving force became known as the Reagan Doctrine. As the president declared in 1985, the United States would openly support anti-Communist movements wherever

Reagan Doctrine "freedom fighters" were battling the Soviets or Soviet-backed governments. The CIA funneled aid to Islamic rebels in Afghanistan and to the contras assaulting Nicaragua. Reagan vowed the overthrow of governments deemed hostile to United States interests.

In this atmosphere, Soviet-American relations became "white hot, thoroughly white hot," noted a Soviet leader. Actually, Reagan's first decision affecting the Soviets had been to lift the grain embargo imposed by President Carter after the Soviet invasion of Afghanistan. A grain deal worth about $3 billion was soon negotiated. Reagan thus fulfilled a campaign promise to American farmers eager to sell wheat and corn in foreign markets. But hostility resurfaced in late 1981, when the Soviets cracked down on the Solidarity labor movement in Poland. In response, Washington placed some restrictions on Soviet-American trade and hurled angry words at Moscow. Then in September 1983, when a South Korean commercial jet had strayed some 300 miles off course into Soviet air space, a Soviet fighter pilot shot it out of the sky. Two hundred and sixty-nine passengers died. Reagan immediately restricted American commercial flights to the Soviet Union.

Reagan's expansion of the military, his coolness toward arms control, his careless utterances about winning a limited nuclear war, his apparent quest for nuclear supremacy, and his insistence on placing new cruise and Pershing-II missiles in Western Europe stimulated a lively international debate. In late November 1981, talks began on limiting intermediate-range nuclear forces (INF) based in Europe. These INFs had a range of 300 to 3,400 miles and included both the Soviet SS-20 missiles targeted against Western Europe and the American cruise missiles and Pershing-IIs aimed at Russia. However, the INF talks collapsed in November 1983, after the first American cruise and Pershing-II missiles were installed in Western Europe.

Debate over Nuclear Weapons

As for the SALT talks, Reagan replaced those discussions with the Strategic Arms Reduction Talks (START). Begun in June 1982, START faltered in December of the next year. But these difficult negotiations stirred intense interest in the American public, which reacted with the largest peaceful protest in the nation's history. In June 1982, 1 million people marched through New York City to support a freeze in the nuclear arms race. The next year, the House of Representatives, over the opposition of the White House, passed a freeze resolution.

Because of such public opinion, pressure from NATO allies, worry that a more expensive and more dangerous nuclear arms race loomed, and the belief that reinvigorated American military power gave the United States a strong bargaining position, Reagan officials resumed discussions on strategic arms control with the Soviets in early 1985. The talks stalled because the Soviets insisted on limiting the Strategic Defense Initiative, and the Americans would not budge on the new and still untested program. At the 1985 Geneva summit meeting, Reagan and Gorbachev agreed in

In June 1988 President Ronald Reagan (1911–) traveled to Moscow for a summit meeting with Russian leader Mikhail Gorbachev. Here, in Moscow's Red Square, the two politicians take turns fawning over a baby. *Tass/Soufoto.*

principle that strategic weapons should be reduced by 50 percent. But summit meetings at Reykjavik, Iceland, in 1986, Washington in 1987, and Moscow in 1988 failed to produce a treaty.

In the twilight of the Reagan presidency, Soviet-American relations improved. Recognizing that the Soviet Union was stagnating, Gorbachev launched two ambitious programs of reform: *perestroika*, to restructure and modernize the highly bureaucratized, low-productivity Soviet economy, and *glasnost*, to liberalize the authoritarian political system. Soviet officials understood that a decrease in military spending through reduced international tensions would release resources for their reforms. People everywhere began to talk about the end of the Cold War.

Improved United States– Soviet Relations

In 1988, Gorbachev began to withdraw Soviet troops from Afghanistan (the last of them departed in early 1989) and to press the Soviet ally Vietnam to pull out of Cambodia. Late in the year, a deal was struck to withdraw Cuban troops from Angola. In 1988, too, the United States and the Soviet Union finally put into effect an INF treaty. They agreed to destroy all their land-based intermediate-range missiles in Europe (totaling 2,800) and soon began to do so. The Soviets and the Americans also established Nuclear Risk Reduction Centers in their capitals: the rooms, with direct hookups, operated around the clock to limit the chances that nuclear war could start by accident.

After George Bush took office in 1989, the Soviets broke the impasse in the START talks by dropping their demand that the United States abandon its research on the Strategic Defense Initiative. Earlier that year, the two superpowers agreed in principle to reductions of weapons in the negotiations on the conventional forces in Europe. In June 1990, Bush and Gorbachev held a friendly summit meeting in Washington, agreeing to speed up talks on arms reductions, improve trade relations, and ban the production of chemical weapons. Although they disagreed on the terms for a reunified Germany and Lithuanian independence, Bush declared, "We've moved a long, long way from the depths of the Cold War."

▼

Interventions in the Third World and Persistent Global Issues

The region of Guatemala, Honduras, El Salvador, Nicaragua, and Costa Rica was a traditional sphere of influence for the United States. But Reagan officials believed that the Soviet Union (with its ally Cuba) was fomenting disorder in the Third World, and especially in Central America. They saw El Salvador as a textbook case of Communist aggression. In that very poor country, revolutionaries challenged the government, which was dominated by the military and a small, landed elite. The regime used (or could not control) right-wing "death squads," which killed thousands of dissidents and other citizens, as well as some American missionaries who worked with landless peasants. Apparently concluding that the war against the rebels could be won quickly, Reagan eschewed negotiations and instead increased military assistance to the Salvadoran regime.

El Salvador

The controversial intervention in the Salvadoran civil war in the early 1980s sparked a debate that recalled the disagreement over Vietnam years before. Those who urged negotiations thought Reagan was wrong to interpret the conflict as an East-West contest. Oppression and poverty, not Communist plots, caused people to pick up guns to fight the regime, they argued. Resurrecting the discredited domino theory, Reagan warned that if the "Communists" were not stopped in El Salvador they would soon be at the Mexican-American border. When that argument convinced few, Reagan

turned to a strategic case. Central America, he said, hugs the Caribbean Sea—"our lifeline to the outside world." In time of war, the Soviets could cripple American shipping from Caribbean bases. All of this assumed, of course, that the Soviets or their client Communists were in fact trying to take over El Salvador; critics rejected that assumption.

Congress voted funds for the American involvement in El Salvador, especially after May 1984, when a United States–influenced election produced a government under José Napoleon Duarte, a graduate of the University of Notre Dame in South Bend, Indiana. Still, civilian deaths mounted and land reform languished. Although Duarte met with rebel leaders on occasion to talk peace, the civil war continued. A major rebel offensive in the fall of 1989 demonstrated that substantial United States assistance in the form of arms, economic aid, and CIA operatives had failed to deter the guerrillas.

Elsewhere in Central America, the Reagan administration intervened, threatening a regional war. Nicaragua was ruled by the leftist Sandinista government. To improve health and education, the Sandinistas invited several thousand Cubans to work in Nicaragua's hospitals and schools. Cuban military advisers helped them reorganize their army, and Soviet weapons were ordered. Reagan charged that Nicaragua was becoming a Soviet puppet and that it was sending arms to the rebels in El Salvador. He strove to topple the Nicaraguan government. The United States staged war games in neighboring Honduras, where major American bases were built. In 1981, the CIA also began to train, arm, and direct more than ten thousand counterrevolutionaries, called contras. From CIA-managed bases in Honduras and Costa Rica the contras crossed into Nicaragua to kill officials and innocent civilians and to destroy oil refineries, transportation facilities, and medical clinics.

Undeclared War Against Nicaragua

In the spring of 1984, it became known that the CIA had mined the harbors of Nicaragua, causing merchant ships to be blown up. The World Court ruled that Nicaragua had the right to sue the United States for damages. Both houses of Congress passed a nonbinding resolution to halt the mining operations. In mid-1984, Congress also voted to stop

American aid to the contras ("humanitarian" aid was later extended). In 1985, Reagan imposed an economic embargo on Nicaragua.

The United States, choosing to ignore the opportunities for negotiations that arose, decided on an undeclared war against well-armed Nicaragua. The Nicaraguans accepted the objectives of the peace plan, worked out in 1983 by the Contadora group (Mexico, Venezuela, Colombia, and Panama), and these objectives included the reduction of foreign military bases and advisers in Central America. But the Reagan administration snubbed the Contadora peace plan. It also snubbed the Arias plan (named for the president of Costa Rica), which in 1988 brought the contras and Sandinistas to the peace table for the first time and produced shaky agreements to build democratic institutions in Nicaragua.

In 1986, Congress once again voted military aid for the contras. This was also the year that the Iran-contra scandal broke. The president's national security adviser, John M. Poindexter, and an aide, Oliver North, in collusion with CIA Director William J. Casey, had diverted funds from a covert arms sale to Iran to the contras so that the counter-revolutionaries could buy guns. The diversion had occurred during the period when Congress had prohibited military assistance to the contras. At the time of these deals, Washington had been condemning Iran as a terrorist nation and demanding that America's allies not trade with the radical Islamic state. President Reagan looked bad no matter how "Irangate" or "Contragate" turned out: if he did not know that the National Security Council was running guns to both Iran and the contras, then he appeared incompetent. If he did know about the arrangement, then he was guilty of breaking his own pledge against aiding a government that supported terrorists and of violating the law banning military aid to the contras.

The contra war finally came to an end in early 1990. In an election monitored by six hundred international observers, Sandinista leader Daniel Ortega lost the presidency. The victorious candidate, Violeta Chamorro, was the leader of a coalition of anti-Sandinista elements backed by the United States and the widow of a martyred newspaper editor. Upon taking office, Chamorro found herself in charge of a bankrupt government in a country with rampant inflation. A decade of civil war had ravaged much of Nicaragua and left thousands dead.

In the 1980s, the Middle East continued to attract American attention but defy American solutions. An Iraqi-Iranian war threatened Persian Gulf shipping, and Moslem factions unleashed bruising attacks on one another. American leaders became upset that moderate Arab states like Jordan and Saudi Arabia were doing little to stabilize the region. Even an ally, Israel, gave the United States trouble. The Israelis repeatedly bombed suspected Palestine Liberation Organization (PLO) camps inside Lebanon, killing hundreds of civilians. In December 1981, without warning, Israel annexed the Syrian territory of the Golan Heights.

Then, in June 1982, Israeli troops invaded Lebanon, which was in the throes of a civil war. They cut their way to the capital, Beirut, inflicting massive damage. The beleaguered PLO and various Lebanese factions called upon Syria to contain the Israelis. Thousands of civilians died in the multifaceted conflict and a million people became refugees. In August, as part of a peacekeeping force, American marines entered Lebanon. Their mission ill defined, the American troops soon became embroiled in a war between Lebanese factions. In October 1983, terrorist bombs demolished a marine barracks, killing 240 American servicemen. The following February, Reagan recognized failure and pulled out the remaining marines.

Crisis in Lebanon

Still, the United States had commitments (the defense of Israel), political friends (Saudi Arabia), and enemies (Iran and Libya—American bombers hit the latter in 1986) that would continue to draw it into the Middle East. Besides, the region's oil supplies fueled Western economies. This was such a critical concern that in 1988 American warships escorted both American and foreign commercial ships through the Persian Gulf. An American warship erred tragically in July, when it shot down an Iranian jetliner, killing hundreds.

Washington, which openly sided with Israel in the Middle East, continued to offer peace plans; the goal was to persuade the Israelis to give back occupied territories and the Arabs to stop trying to push the Jews out of the Middle East. In 1988, Palestinians living on the West Bank began an uprising, called *Intifadah*, against Israeli forces, which had occupied the area since 1967. Israel used brute force to quell rock-throwing youths. But the uprising continued, and the PLO declared the West Bank and the Gaza Strip an independent Palestinian state. Israel refused to negotiate, but the United States decided to invigorate the stalled peace process by reversing its previous policy of refusing to talk with the PLO. In 1989, talks between American and PLO representatives opened after PLO leader Yasser Arafat renounced terrorism and accepted Israel's right "to exist in peace and security." In 1990, a new hard-line Israeli government vowed to crush the Intifadah.

Americans in the 1990s faced bewildering international problems that destabilized economies and societies, ensuring political disorder, threats to peace, and a decline of American power. Looming large among these problems, global economic issues bedeviled world order and endangered American prosperity.

Global Economic Issues

Third World nations, racked by slow economic growth, continued to sink into staggering debt. By 1989, they owed creditors, including American banks, more than $1.2 trillion. Burdened with such debt, many Third World countries had to reduce imports. This shift hurt Americans since it reduced American exports to developing nations.

The Third World debt crisis also contributed to America's trade deficit, which skyrocketed to $170 billion in 1987 (but dropped to $137 billion the following year). The United States became a debtor nation, constantly borrowing to pay for its persistent trade deficit. Many Americans partly blamed the Japanese, believing that they engaged in unfair trade practices, for the Japanese had penetrated American markets and bought considerable American property. Thus, some favored retaliatory protectionist measures, such as tariffs.

Furthermore, the global environment was deteriorating. Soil erosion hurt food production at a time when the world's population was growing

Global Environment Issues

rapidly. Toxic wastes, acid rain, shortages of clean water, the overcutting of forests, and the depletion of the earth's ozone layer speeded up environmental decline. In 1990, United Nations scientists reported that "greenhouse gases," such as carbon dioxide and chlorofluorocarbons, were creating a global warming trend by trapping heat within the earth's atmosphere. The possibility existed that within a hundred years the rising temperatures could cause a two-foot increase in sea levels.

In many parts of the world, hunger and famine took a ghastly human toll and contributed to political instability as governments struggled, and often failed, to satisfy their people's basic needs. In the early 1980s, experts estimated that annual hunger-related deaths numbered between 13 million and 18 million people. Drought-ravaged Africa continued to suffer throughout the decade and into the next.

The international drug traffic exacted a human toll as well, causing health problems and killing narcotics users in the United States. It enriched criminals, who sometimes gained political influence, as in Bolivia and Colombia, and corrupted governments, as in Mexico. American programs to eradicate crops of opium poppies (used to make heroin) in Asia and in Mexico and coca (used to make cocaine) in Latin America cost a great deal but failed.

International Drug Traffic

Terrorism continued to plague the world. Terrorists struck at will and without warning. In June 1985, Shiite Moslem terrorists from Lebanon hijacked an American jetliner; they killed one passenger, beat others, and held thirty-nine Americans hostage for seventeen days. In December 1988, a Pan American passenger plane (Flight 103) was destroyed by a terrorist bomb over Scotland. And although two Americans held hostage in Lebanon were released in 1990, others remained in captivity.

Terrorism

Across the globe, religious and racial tensions undermined stability and spawned war. Sikhs and Hindus fought one another in India; Christians and Moslems battled in Lebanon; and Roman Catholics and Protestants bloodied each other in Northern Ireland.

In the midst of all these problems, the United States was facing a future of uneasy relations with its allies. Once valuable allies like the Philippines were rocked by political unrest, imperiling military bases and intelligence-gathering stations.

South Africa posed special difficulties. There, a blatantly racist white minority ruled a predominantly black population through the segregationist policy of *apartheid*. Blacks

South Africa were kept poor, disenfranchised, and geographically segregated in townships that resembled prisons. At first, the Reagan administration refrained from criticizing the white government, preferring instead a policy of "constructive engagement." But a widespread and vocal antiapartheid movement in the United States triggered some official responses. Many major American corporations with holdings in South Africa ceased doing business there. Some states and cities passed divestment laws—laws requiring the withdrawal of dollars from American companies active in South Africa. In 1986, public American protest and congressional legislation forced the Reagan administration to impose economic restrictions against South Africa.

Some hope of a political solution to South Africa's problems appeared in 1990. The nation's new president, F. W. de Klerk, lifted a thirty-year ban on the African National Congress (ANC), the most prominent group struggling against apartheid. He also freed ANC leader Nelson Mandela, a political prisoner for twenty-seven years. For the first time, a dialogue began between the white minority government and representatives of the black majority.

In 1988, one of the most popular books in the United States was a historical work by Paul Kennedy, *The Rise and Fall of Great Powers*. The author argued that American power would continue to erode if the United States failed to achieve some critical goals. It had to restore its productive vitality and marketplace competitiveness and to reduce its huge federal debt. It needed to put more resources into long-term investment, limit its military spending to what it can afford, and curb its excessive global interventionism. In addition, it had to improve its educational system. The question was

whether the Bush administration would be up to the task of putting the nation's house in order.

▼

A Polarized People: American Society in the 1980s

In the 1980s, the rich got even richer, while the poor sank deeper into despair (see figure). As inequality grew, the gap widened between affluent

Increasing Inequality
whites and poor blacks, Indians, and Hispanics; between single-parent and dual-parent families; between the suburbs and the inner cities; and between the country's social and defense needs. Violent crime, particularly murders and gang warfare, grew alarmingly. So, too, did school dropout rates, crime rates, and child abuse.

Poverty in the 1980s stemmed from a variety of causes. Certainly, it was the result of economic recessions. The poverty rate in 1983 was 14 percent, or higher than in any year from 1969 through 1980. Blacks were much more likely than whites to be poor; in 1983, the poverty rate for whites was 12.2 percent and for blacks 35.7 percent. Similarly, women were more likely to be poor than men. However, in the 1980s, women's earnings rose to 70 percent of men's—a sizable gain from 62 percent in 1979. "Occupational segregation" accounted for much of the disparity between women's and men's earnings. Eighty percent of all women employees worked in such "female" occupations as clerking, selling, teaching, nursing, and waitressing.

Poverty also resulted from the changing structure of the labor market. With the rise of the service and information-based economy, entry-level manufacturing jobs disappeared in the

Changing Job Market
country's old industrial cities. In 1974, blue-collar jobs accounted for half of the employment of black males between the ages of twenty and twenty-four; by 1984, such jobs accounted for only one-fourth of their employment. Partly because of the

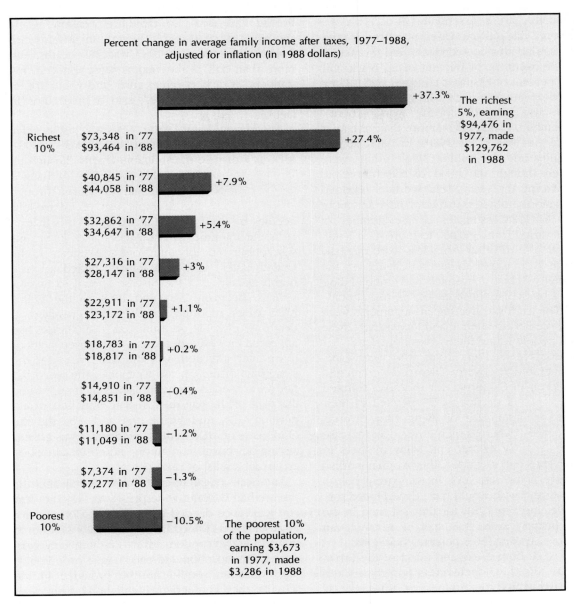

Percent change in average family income after taxes, 1977–1988, adjusted for inflation (in 1988 dollars)

Richest 10%	+37.3% — The richest 5%, earning $94,476 in 1977, made $129,762 in 1988
$73,348 in '77 / $93,464 in '88	+27.4%
$40,845 in '77 / $44,058 in '88	+7.9%
$32,862 in '77 / $34,647 in '88	+5.4%
$27,316 in '77 / $28,147 in '88	+3%
$22,911 in '77 / $23,172 in '88	+1.1%
$18,783 in '77 / $18,817 in '88	+0.2%
$14,910 in '77 / $14,851 in '88	−0.4%
$11,180 in '77 / $11,049 in '88	−1.2%
$7,374 in '77 / $7,277 in '88	−1.3%
Poorest 10%	−10.5% — The poorest 10% of the population, earning $3,673 in 1977, made $3,286 in 1988

Richer and Poorer: Changes in Average Family Income, 1977–1988 *Source: Congressional Budget Office.*

disappearance of jobs, poverty became more concentrated than before. Indeed, most of the increase in the underclass occurred in just a few cities—most notably, New York, Chicago, Detroit, and Philadelphia.

According to the sociologist William Julius Wilson, the issue of "the truly disadvantaged" became "one of the most important social issues of the remainder of the 20th century." Those who suffered most were children. By the mid-1980s, children, who constituted 27 percent of the nation, accounted for 40 percent of the poor. Frequently, these children were poor because their families had only one wage earner, and she was an unskilled single parent. Essentially, as a result of a high divorce rate and increased numbers of pregnancies among unwed teenagers and women in their early twenties, 54 percent of all black children, 29 percent of Hispanic children, and 18 percent of white children lived with one parent.

Life was also precarious for the "working poor," whose numbers increased by more than one-third during the first half of the 1980s. In 1985, 3.6 million families and 2.5 million single adults were poor even though the head of the household worked during the year. Social workers reported that the nation's homeless included more and more families. In 1988, estimates of the number of homeless varied from 350,000 to more than 1 million. About a third of the homeless were mentally ill people who found themselves living on the streets after psychiatric hospitals had emptied their wards in a burst of enthusiasm for "deinstitutionalization." The truth was that few arrangements were made for medical treatment, and increasingly these troubled people found themselves homeless.

Women were another group who were especially vulnerable to poverty. Divorced women and their children in California, for example, suffered a decline of 73 percent in their standard of living after divorce, whereas men enjoyed an increase of 42 percent. Many mothers in the 1980s thus had to work. Other women worked to preserve living standards in two-parent households that otherwise would have experienced substantial declines. In 1983, for the first time in the nation's history, more than half of all American women over twenty (50.5 percent) held jobs.

Working Women

Drugs were both cause and effect of the urban underclass. Mired in hopelessness, poverty-stricken people tried to find forgetfulness in drugs such as cocaine and its derivative, crack. In 1985, crack first struck New York City's poorest neighborhoods. Users included children eleven and twelve years old and increasing numbers of young single mothers. Child abuse and destroyed families were legacies of crack.

Tragic Effects of Drugs

The crack epidemic had other pernicious results. Children and youth became drug dealers. Many dealers who were too young to boast a driver's license had access to rapid-fire weapons. Gang shootouts were deadly. The toll in Los Angeles from such warfare in 1987 was 387 deaths, and more than half of the victims were innocent bystanders. "Crack, cocaine, guns, and youth are an extremely lethal mixture," said a prosecutor in Detroit.

Another epidemic of the 1980s was just as lethal as crack. First observed in the United States in 1981, AIDS is a disease transmittable chiefly through infected bodily fluids exchanged during sexual contact and through the multiple use of intravenous needles by drug users. Caused by a virus that attacks the immune system, AIDS makes its victims susceptible to deadly infections and cancers. In the United States, AIDS was initially linked to male homosexuality, but the disease spread to heterosexuals. Between 1981 and 1988, of the 57,000 AIDS cases reported, nearly 32,000 resulted in death. (Worldwide, an estimated 700,000 cases had appeared by 1990.) Because it takes seven years or more after infection with the AIDS virus for the symptoms of the disease to appear, the worst has not yet arrived. A study published in 1988 warned that half of the gay men in San Francisco would develop AIDS. And during 1988 and 1989, the rate of increase of AIDS in the United States was greater among newborns than among homosexual or heterosexual adults, or drug users.

AIDS

Americans began to confront AIDS only after the disease had become widespread. As they did, fear and ignorance divided communities. Conservative Protestant sects joined the Roman Catholic Church in warning that condom advertising implicitly sanctioned contraception and encouraged promiscuity. Sex education should not be provided in the schools, they contended, highlighting their deep belief that any sexual activity that did not conform to the canonical model of heterosexual matrimonial monogamy was wrong. Gay men expected little assistance from the conservative executive branch, but they were partly wrong. In June 1988, the government mailed a booklet entitled *Understanding AIDS* to 107 million households.

AIDS—along with such other sexually transmitted diseases as genital herpes and chlamydia—affected Americans' sexual behavior. Caution

An alarming spread in sexually transmitted diseases, including Acquired Immune Deficiency Syndrome (AIDS), occurred in the 1980s. Campaigns for "safe sex," exemplified by this New York City subway ad, urged people to use condoms. *Courtesy New York City Department of Health.*

replaced the mores of the "sexual revolution," which had liberated sexual practices in the 1960s and 1970s. "Safe Sex" campaigns urged the use of condoms.

In the 1980s, several minority groups, homosexuals among them, mobilized in opposition to the conservative agenda of the Reagan White House.

Opponents of Reagan's Conservatism

Ronald Reagan's most vocal critics were women and people of color. In 1983, the *New York Times* reported a "gender gap" between men's and women's opinions of Reagan's performance: far fewer women (38 percent) than men (53 percent) believed that Reagan deserved re-election. Reagan's opposition to the Equal Rights Amendment and abortion on demand had already won him the enmity of many feminists. But what really caused the gender gap to yawn widely were Reagan's social welfare, health, and education cuts.

Reagan's critics assailed him for failing to stop the "feminization of poverty" and for approving cuts in food stamps and school meals, which added to the woes of poor women and their children. The Reagan administration also opposed federally subsidized childcare and the feminist goal of equal pay for jobs of comparable worth. Why, women asked, should a teacher earn less than an electrician, if the two jobs require comparable skills and involve comparable responsibilities?

Black civil rights leaders joined feminists in assailing not only Reagan's economic policies, but also his presidential appointments. Whereas 12 percent of President Jimmy Carter's high-level job-holders were black and 12.1 percent women, Reagan's comparable totals were 4.1 percent black and 8 percent women. Reagan appointed four women to his cabinet, and he made history by appointing Sandra Day O'Connor the first woman associate justice of the Supreme Court; but blacks could find little to applaud in Reagan's performance. Reagan denounced the allegation that "we are taking a less active approach to protecting the civil rights of all Americans," but his record proved otherwise. Reagan's civil rights chief in the Justice Department fought in 1982 against renewing intact the Voting Rights Act of 1965, expressed opposition to busing and affirmative action, and was criticized for lax enforcement of fair-housing laws and laws banning sexual and racial discrimination in federally funded education programs.

Hispanic and Native Americans joined African-Americans in blasting the Reagan administration. The League of United Latin American Citizens censured Reagan for his "very, very dismal record" in dealing with their problems, and the National Tribal Chairmen's Association charged that under Reagan "the delivery of services by federal agencies to Indians was in a shambles." Even though poverty had begun to decline nationwide in the mid-1980s, it continued its rise for Hispanics and Indians.

In 1986, Congress passed the Immigration Reform and Control Act, which provided amnesty to undocumented foreign workers who had entered the United States before 1982. The

Immigration Reform

act's purpose was to discourage illegal immigration by placing sanctions on employers who hired undocumented workers, but it failed to stem the flow of Mexicans into the United States. Women,

men, and increasingly entire families continued to flee Mexico's economic woes and illegally enter the United States. In 1988 the number of new immigrants from Mexico approached the record numbers reached just before the reform law went into effect.

Still, if Reagan did not enjoy the support of women and people of color, he continued to be the choice of white men in both the North and the South. But buoying the Democrats' hopes for winning the presidency in 1988 was Reagan's dismal presidential performance beginning in November 1986. First, despite Reagan's active campaigning, the Republicans lost control of the Senate in the fall elections; later in the month came the Iran-contra scandal. Adding to Reagan's woes was the stock market crash of October 1987, which made Americans uneasy about the future.

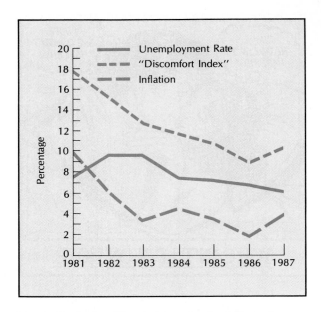

Discomfort Index (Unemployment plus Inflation), 1981–1987. *Source:* Economic Report of the President: 1987 *(Washington, D.C.: U.S. Government Printing Office, 1988).*

Reagan's Decline and Bush's Election

During his second term, President Reagan lost his mastery; the "great communicator" took on the appearance of a tired, bumbling old man. "WHO'S IN CHARGE HERE?" asked *Time* magazine. Half of the people in the country believed that Reagan was lying about what he knew regarding the Iran-contra scandal. And Congress in the spring of 1987 overrode Reagan's veto of a massive highway construction bill. "No one is afraid of him anymore," said one political observer.

Reagan's problems continued in 1987 and 1988. Not once, but twice, he failed to get his nominees for the Supreme Court confirmed by the Senate. Moreover, one close Reagan aide was convicted of violating federal ethics laws and another of perjury for lying to a congressional subcommittee and a federal grand jury. Then, on October 19, 1987, the stock market went into a nosedive and fell 508 points. In addition, the president suffered health problems, and both he and his wife had surgery. On top of these

Reagan's Political Woes

political and personal woes, a new scandal broke the following year. Federal prosecutors charged that Department of Defense procurement officers had leaked information to defense contractors in exchange for money and the promise of jobs after they left the Pentagon.

Yet, for a variety of reasons, the Democrats could not count on success in the 1988 elections. Reagan had calmed his anti-Soviet rhetoric and, in the summer of 1988, to the applause of most Americans, had traveled to the Soviet Union—the first American president to visit Moscow since Richard Nixon in 1972. More important from the voters' point of view, after the economic recession of 1981 and 1982, the United States had embarked on a six-year business recovery. The discomfort index, which had risen alarmingly in the 1970s and early 1980s, fell to more acceptable levels in the late 1980s (see figure). In April 1988, the unemployment rate dropped to its low for the decade—5.4 percent— without refueling inflation.

The competition for the 1988 Republican and Democratic presidential nominations was intense. On the Republican side, the host of campaigners

Inauguration day, 1989. President George Bush and his wife, Barbara, stroll down Pennsylvania Avenue. Bush's call for a "kinder, gentler nation" was vague, but the American people were willing to let him prove himself. *Dirck Halstead © 1989* Time *Magazine.*

Presidential Campaign of 1988 included Vice President George Bush, Senate Minority Leader Bob Dole, and Pat Robertson, a television evangelist. The nomination went to Bush, after bitter Republican in-fighting in state primaries.

Though it began with a half-dozen campaigners, the Democratic race narrowed to a two-person contest. Jesse Jackson, the first African-American candidate to win mass support in seeking the presidential nomination of a major political party, campaigned on his dream of forming a "Rainbow Coalition" of the "rejected"—blacks, women, and Hispanics. But his main rival, Governor Michael Dukakis of Massachusetts, won the nomination.

During the campaign, both Bush and Dukakis avoided a serious debate of the issues: childcare, drugs, environmental collapse, corruption in government, poverty, rising medical and educational costs, foreign policy, and the fiscal and trade deficits. Instead, the candidates relied on clichés and negative campaigning. Television dominated the presidential election as never before. Bush aimed his television appeals to the "Reagan Democrats" by pushing emotional ("hot button") items such as "patriotism" and the death penalty. With inflation and unemployment at low rates, Bush's victory seemed assured. His margin over Dukakis was substantial: 54 percent of the popular vote to 46 percent.

1989: A Year of Miracles

In January 1989, George Bush was inaugurated as the forty-first president of the United States. That same month, Lech Walesa's Solidarity trade union movement in Poland regained its legal status and began working with the Communist government to frame a new constitution. After adopting the constitution, the government allowed the first free elections in Poland since 1946. The election results were startling: Solidarity won 260 of the 261 seats in the parliament.

The End of the Communist Oligarchs

At the same time, a prodemocracy movement was spreading throughout Eastern Europe. Popular pressure in favor of change mounted, and leaders yielded to the will of the people. By July 1990, free elections had taken place in East Germany, Czechoslovakia, Hungary, Romania, and Bulgaria.

The shift in the German Democratic Republic (GDR) proved especially dramatic. It began in the summer of 1989, when Hungary opened its border with Austria. Thousands of East Germans traveled to Hungary and then fled to freedom into Austria. By the end of October, more than 200,000 East Germans had left their country, and Communist leader Erich Honecker had left office. In an effort to stop this hemorrhage, Honecker's successor decided to allow East Germans the right to travel to West Berlin. At midnight on November 9, the gates of the Berlin Wall, the archsymbol of repression, were opened. "It was one of those rare times," according to *Time*, "when the tectonic plates of history shift beneath men's feet, and nothing after is quite the same."

In contrast to the East European rebellions of the 1950s and 1960s, Soviet troops did not crush these uprisings. Instead, Gorbachev encouraged the process, telling crowds in Berlin that "life itself punishes delay." Most important of all, Gorbachev did not order Soviet troops to attack protesters.

Gorbachev's Role and Bush's Reaction

As the events in Europe unfolded, Bush adopted a wait-and-see posture. Choosing not to proclaim a "Cold War victory," he assured the Soviets that the United States would not exploit the remarkable changes under way.

Once the immediate joy over the spread of democracy started to subside, leaders and common people in both the East and the West began to deal with the questions associated with the changing face of Europe. How does a society move from a managed to a market economy? How much aid should the United States provide to such nations as Poland and Hungary? How would the reunification of Germany take place? Would a unified Germany be a member of NATO? If so, how would the fears of the Soviet Union be allayed?

In many ways, the most pressing problems came not from the nations of Eastern Europe, but from inside the Soviet Union itself. In 1989, dormant ethnic unrest erupted. In January 1990, violent clashes between Muslim Azerbaijanis and Christian Armenians forced Gorbachev to dispatch forty thousand troops to maintain order. Martial law was proclaimed in an effort to stop rioting in Uzbekistan and Tadzhikistan. Nationalist stirrings also became evident in Georgia, Moldavia, and the Ukraine. Then the largest Soviet republic, Russia, declared its sovereignty.

The Baltic Republics

The Baltic republics of Lithuania, Latvia, and Estonia posed a particularly grave challenge to Gorbachev. On the fiftieth anniversary of the Nazi-Soviet Pact that led to Stalin's annexation of the Baltic republics, a million Lithuanians, Latvians, and Estonians linked arms and formed a four-hundred-mile human chain of protest. Then, in March 1990, the Lithuanian parliament declared the republic's independence from the Soviet Union. Within months, Latvia and Estonia took similar action. Gorbachev sought a middle ground. He did not send in troops to crush the separatist movements but insisted that withdrawal from the Soviet Union could only take place through Soviet constitutional procedures. He also applied economic sanctions against Lithuania. Washington protested his actions but did not recognize Lithuania's independence.

Unlike the Soviet leader, President Bush decided to use force to solve one of his problems. The strongman president of Panama, General Manuel Noriega, was allegedly involved in the illegal drug trade between Colombia and the United States. In

When the gates of the Berlin Wall opened in November 1989, East and West Germans gathered to join in the demolition of the graffiti-covered structure, a prominent symbol of communist suppression and the Cold War. The twenty-eight-mile-long concrete wall had restricted the freedom of two-thirds of Berlin's inhabitants for nearly thirty years. *R. Bossu/Sygma.*

an effort to remove him from power, the United States tried several approaches: it encouraged the Panamanian military to oust him; it offered him asylum in another country if he would step down; it indicted him on drug-related charges; and it held back canal dues owed to Panama, as well as stopped all foreign aid to the Central American nation. Nothing worked. Noriega announced in the fall of 1989 that a "state of war" existed between the United States and Panama.

Two incidents spurred Bush to stronger action: an American marine was killed in Panama and Panamanian soldiers beat an American naval officer and threatened his wife. Concluding that "This guy [Noriega] is not going to lay off," Bush ordered the invasion of Panama on December 20, 1989. This invasion, dubbed Operation Just Cause, involved 22,500 Americans. It resulted in the deaths of more than 300 Panamanians and 23

Invasion of Panama

American soldiers. Noriega took sanctuary in the Vatican Embassy in Panama City. Church officials finally convinced him to surrender to American officials, and on January 4, 1990, Noriega was taken to Miami to await trial.

In the wake of the Panama invasion, Bush's popularity at home rose. Some observers, however, criticized the administration for violating both the United Nations Charter and the Charter of the Organization of American States.

Challenges for the 1990s

When George Bush was inaugurated, the American people prepared to greet a new presidency and a new decade. "Ronald Reagan leaves no Vietnam War, no Watergate, no hostage crisis," reported the

New York Times. "But he leaves huge question marks—and much to do." Inequality had escalated in the 1980s, as the poor got poorer and the rich got richer. The poorest Americans of all were children. In the 1980s, too, economics and racism had conspired to widen the gap among the races. The rising federal debt remained a problem. Furthermore, the effects of mismanagement and deception were beginning to show in certain industries, forcing the federal government to consider massive bailouts and threatening greater fiscal deficits. In 1989, Congress debated putting up $157 billion to rescue insolvent savings and loan associations; within a year, the bailout was estimated at $500 billion. America's nuclear weapons production system also needed to be cleaned and repaired; the estimated price tag was $150 billion. Finally, the country was losing control of its economic destiny. Between 1983 and 1989, foreigners invested $700 billion more in America than Americans invested abroad.

A number of challenges faced the United States abroad. Despite the capture of Noriega and some sensational seizures of narcotics, the United States was failing to halt the importation of illegal drugs. The Bush administration struggled to devise new policies to meet the rapid political and economic changes in Europe—especially the emergence of a reunified Germany and the formation of a single market by the European Community. Japan continued to challenge the United States for international economic pre-eminence.

As the Cold War waned, some American leaders anticipated a peace dividend—savings from the defense budget that could be directed to the repair of America's shaky infrastructure and social programs. But President Bush resisted military cutbacks, and Iraq's surprise invasion of Kuwait in August 1990 helped him prove his point. Bush ordered more than 100,000 American military personnel to the Middle East to deter an Iraqi attack against oil-rich Saudi Arabia, a long-time American ally; the Bush administration also orchestrated an international economic boycott of Iraq. These actions were undertaken to guarantee shipments of petroleum to Western nations and prevent a worldwide depression created by higher oil prices. As Bush sought to protect what he called "our way of life," some analysts, like former president Jimmy Carter, regretted that the United States had virtually abandoned energy conservation programs, leaving itself dependent on foreign oil and vulnerable to Middle East flare-ups.

According to President Bush, although the Cold War had receded, terrorism, hostage-taking, ethnic and religious tensions, fierce economic competition, unpredictable rulers, civil wars, and growing environmental crises made the world "a dangerous place," requiring American vigilance and engagement. The 1990s seemed to offer no respite from American globalism and hard, expensive choices at home and abroad.

<hr/>

Suggestions for Further Reading

Ronald Reagan and His Presidency

Terrel H. Bell, *The Thirteenth Man* (1988); Larry Berman, ed., *Looking Back at the Reagan Presidency* (1990); Paul Boyer, ed., *Reagan as President* (1990); Lou Cannon, *Reagan* (1982); Robert Dallek, *Ronald Reagan* (1984); Ronnie Dugger, *On Reagan* (1983); Anne Edwards, *Early Reagan* (1987); Paul D. Erickson, *Reagan Speaks: The Making of an American Myth* (1985); Jane Mayer and Doyle McManus, *Landslide: The Unmaking of the President, 1984–1988* (1988); Donald T. Regan, *For the Record* (1988); Michael Rogin, *Ronald Reagan, the Movie* (1987); Herman Schwartz, *Packing the Courts* (1988); Hedrick Smith, *The Power Game* (1988); John Kenneth White, *The New Politics of Old Values* (1988); Garry Wills, *Reagan's America* (1987).

Reagan's Domestic Policies

Jeffrey H. Birnbaum and Alan S. Murray, *Showdown at Gucci Gulch: Lawmakers, Lobbyists, and the Unlikely Triumph of Tax Reform* (1987); Joan Claybrook, *Retreat from Safety: Reagan's Attack on America's Health* (1984); Benjamin Friedman, *Day of Reckoning: The Consequences of American Economic Policy Under Reagan and After* (1988); Jonathan Lash, *A Season of Spoils: The Story of the Reagan Administration's Attack on the Environment* (1984); Charles Noble, *Liberalism at Work: The Rise and Fall of OSHA* (1986); Frances Fox Piven and Richard Cloward, *The New Class War* (1982); David Stockman, *The Triumph of Politics* (1986).

Foreign Policy and the Nuclear Arms Race

Ruth Adams and Susan Cullen, eds., *The Final Epidemic: Physicians and Scientists on Nuclear War* (1981); George W. Ball, *Error and Betrayal in Lebanon* (1984); Richard J. Barnet, *The Alliance: America, Europe, Japan* (1983); Seweryn Bialer and Michael Mandelbaum, eds., *Gorbachev's Russia and American Foreign Policy* (1988); Daniel P. Bolger, *Americans at War, 1975–1986* (1988); Dusko Doder and Louise Branson, *Gorbachev* (1990); Bernard Gwertzman and Michael T. Kaufman, eds., *The Collapse of Communism* (1990); Harvard Nuclear Study Group, *Living with Nuclear Weapons* (1983); Paul Kennedy, *The Rise and Fall of the Great Powers* (1988); Michael Klare and Peter Kornbluh, eds., *Low Intensity Warfare* (1988); David E. Kyvig, *Reagan and the World* (1990); David McDowell, *Palestine and Israel* (1990); National Academy of Sciences, *Nuclear Arms Control* (1985); John Newhouse, *War and Peace in the Nuclear Age* (1989); Joseph S. Nye, Jr., *Bound to Lead* (1990); Kenneth A. Oye et al., eds., *Eagle Resurgent?* (1987); Cheryl A. Rubenberg, *Israel and the American National Interest* (1986); Strobe Talbott, *The Master of the Game: Paul Nitze and the Nuclear Peace* (1988); Strobe Talbott, *Deadly Gambits: The Reagan Administration and the Stalemate in Nuclear Arms Control* (1984); Sanford J. Ungar, ed., *Estrangement* (1985).

The United States and Latin America

Cynthia J. Arnson, *Crossroads: Congress, the Reagan Administration, and Central America* (1989); Morris J. Blachman et al., eds., *Confronting Revolution* (1986); Raymond Bonner, *Weakness and Deceit: U.S. Policy and El Salvador* (1984); E. Bradford Burns, *At War in Nicaragua* (1987); Kenneth M. Coleman and George C. Herring, eds., *The Central America Crisis* (1985); Steven Emerson, *Secret Warriors: Inside the Covert Military Operations of the Reagan Era* (1988); Guy Gugliotta and Jeff Leen, *Kings of Cocaine* (1989); Roy Gutman, *Banana Diplomacy, 1981–1987* (1988) (on Nicaragua); J. Michael Hogan, *The Panama Canal in American Politics* (1986); Jane Hunter et al., *The Iran-Contra Connection* (1987); John J. Johnson, *Distant Neighbors* (1990); Walter LaFeber, *Inevitable Revolutions,* rev. ed. (1984); Abraham F. Lowenthal, *Partners in Conflict: The United States and Latin America* (1987); Hugh O'Shaughnessy, *Grenada* (1985); Robert A. Pastor, *Condemned to Repetition: The United States and Nicaragua* (1987); Lars Schoultz, *National Security and United States Policy Toward Latin America* (1987); Bob Woodward, *Veil: The Secret Wars of the CIA* (1987).

A Polarized Society in the 1980s

J. Larry Brown and H. F. Pizer, *Living Hungry in America* (1987); Leslie W. Dunbar, ed., *Minority Report: What Has Happened to Blacks, Hispanics, American Indians, and Other Minorities in the Eighties* (1984); Marian Wright Edelman, *Families in Peril* (1987); David T. Ellwood, *Poor Support: Poverty in the American Family* (1988); Michael Harrington, *The New American Poverty* (1984); Bennett Harrison and Barry Bluestone, *The Great U-Turn: Corporate Restructuring and the Polarizing of America* (1988); Jonathan Kozol, *Rachel and Her Children: Homeless Families in America* (1988); John Langone, *AIDS: The Facts* (1988); Frank Levy, *Dollars and Dreams: The Changing American Income Distribution* (1987); Harrell R. Rodgers, Jr., *Poor Women, Poor Families* (1986); Al Santoli, *New Americans* (1988); Hilda Scott, *Working Your Way to the Bottom: The Feminization of Poverty* (1985); Randy Shilts, *And the Band Played On: Politics, People and the AIDS Epidemic* (1987); Ruth Sidel, *Women and Children Last* (1986); Studs Terkel, *The Great Divide* (1988); E. Fuller Torrey, *Nowhere to Go: The Tragic Odyssey of the Homeless Mentally Ill* (1988); William Julius Wilson, *The Truly Disadvantaged: The Inner City, the Underclass, and Public Policy* (1987).

The Elections of 1984 and 1988

Lucius J. Barker and Ronald W. Walters, eds., *Jesse Jackson's 1984 Presidential Campaign* (1989); Thomas Ferguson and Joel Rogers, *Right Turn: The Decline of the Democrats and the Future of American Politics* (1986); Jack W. Germond and Jules Witcover, *Wake Us When It's Over: Presidential Politics of 1984* (1985); Peter Goldman and Tony Fuller, *The Quest for the Presidency, 1984* (1985); Xandra Kayden and Eddie Mahe, Jr., *The Party Goes On: The Persistence of the Two-Party System in the United States* (1986); Frances Fox Piven and Richard A. Cloward, *Why Americans Don't Vote* (1988).

Appendix

Historical Reference Books by Subject:
Encyclopedias, Dictionaries, Atlases, Chronologies, and Statistics

American History: General

Dictionary of American History (1976–1978); Robert H. Ferrell and John S. Bowman, eds., *The Twentieth Century: An Almanac* (1984); John D. Buenker and Edward R. Kantowicz, eds., *Historical Dictionary of the Progressive Era, 1890–1920* (1988); George H. Gallup, *The Gallup Poll: Public Opinion, 1935–1971* (1972) and *1972–1977* (1978); Bernard Grun, *The Timetables of History* (1975); Stanley Hochman, *Yesterday and Today* (1979); *International Encyclopedia of the Social Sciences* (1968–   ); R. Alton Lee, ed., *Encyclopedia USA* (1983–   ); Richard B. Morris, *Encyclopedia of American History* (1982); James S. Olson, *Historical Dictionary of the 1920s* (1988); Thomas Parker and Douglas Nelson, *Day by Day: The Sixties* (1983); Harry Ritter, *Dictionary of Concepts in History* (1986); Arthur M. Schlesinger, Jr., ed., *The Almanac of American History* (1983); *Scribner Desk Dictionary of American History* (1984); U.S. Bureau of the Census, *Historical Statistics of the United States* (1975); *Webster's New Geographical Dictionary* (1984); Philip P. Wiener, ed., *Dictionary of the History of Ideas* (1973).

American History: General Atlases

Geoffrey Barraclough, ed., *The Times Atlas of World History* (1979); W. P. Cumming et al., *The Discovery of North America* (1972); Robert H. Ferrell and Richard Natkiel, *Atlas of American History* (1987); Kenneth T. Jackson and James T. Adams, *Atlas of American History* (1978); Adrian Johnson, *America Explored* (1974); National Geographic Society, *Historical Atlas of the United States* (1988); Charles O. Paullin, *Atlas of the Historical Geography of the United States* (1932); U.S. Department of the Interior, *National Atlas of the United States* (1970). Other atlases listed under specific categories.

American History: General Biographies

Concise Dictionary of American Biography (1980); *Dictionary of American Biography* (1928–   ); John A. Garraty, ed., *Encyclopedia of American Biography* (1974); *National Cyclopedia of American Biography* (1898–   ). Other biographical works appear under specific categories.

African-Americans

Rayford W. Logan and Michael R. Winston, eds., *The Dictionary of American Negro Biography* (1983); W. A. Low and Virgil A. Clift, eds., *Encyclopedia of Black America* (1981); Bruce Kellner, *The Harlem Renaissance* (1984); Randall M. Miller and John D. Smith, eds., *Dictionary of Afro-American Slavery* (1988).

American Revolution

Mark M. Boatner III, *Encyclopedia of the American Revolution* (1974); Lester J. Cappon, ed., *Atlas of Early American History: The Revolutionary Era, 1760–1790* (1976); Douglas W. Marshall and Howard H. Peckham, *Campaigns of the American Revolution* (1976); Gregory Palmer, ed., *Biographical Sketches of Loyalists of the American Revolution* (1984); *Rand-McNally Atlas of the American Revolution* (1974).

Architecture

William D. Hunt, Jr., ed., *Encyclopedia of American Architecture* (1980).

Business and the Economy

Christine Ammer and Dean S. Ammer, *Dictionary of Business and Economics* (1983); Douglas Auld and Graham Bannock, *The American Dictionary of Economics* (1983); Douglas Greenwald, *Encyclopedia of Economics* (1982); John N. Ingham, *Biographical Dictionary of American Business Leaders* (1983); John N. Ingham and Lynne B. Feldman, *Contemporary American Business Leaders* (1990); William H. Mulligan, Jr., ed., *A Historical Dictionary of American Industrial Language* (1988); Glenn G. Munn, *Encyclopedia of Banking and Finance* (1973); Glenn Porter, ed., *Encyclopedia of American Economic History* (1980).

Cities and Towns

Charles Abrams, *The Language of Cities: A Glossary of Terms* (1971); John L. Androit, ed., *Township Atlas of the United States* (1979); Melvin G. Holli and Peter d'A. Jones, eds., *Biographical Dictionary of American Mayors, 1820–1980: Big City Mayors* (1981); Ory M. Nergal, ed., *The Encyclopedia of American Cities* (1980). See also "Politics and Government."

The Civil War

Mark M. Boatner III, *The Civil War Dictionary* (1988); Patricia L. Faust, *Historical Times Encyclopedia of the Civil War* (1986); Mark E. Neely, Jr., *The Abraham Lincoln Encyclopedia* (1982); Craig L. Symonds, *A Battlefield Atlas of the Civil War* (1983); U.S. War Department, *The Official Atlas of the Civil War* (1958); Jon L. Wakelyn, ed., *Biographical Dictionary of the Confederacy* (1977); Ezra J. Warner and W. Buck Yearns, *Biographical Register of the Confederate Congress* (1975). See also "Politics and Government" and "The South."

Conservation

Forest History Society, *Encyclopedia of American Forest and Conservation History* (1983).

Constitution and Supreme Court

Congressional Quarterly, *Guide to the Supreme Court* (1979); Leon Friedman and Fred I. Israel, eds., *The Justices of the United States Supreme Court, 1789–1978* (1980); Richard F. Hixson, *Mass Media and the Constitution* (1989); Robert J. Janosik, ed., *Encyclopedia of the American Judicial System* (1987); Leonard W. Levy et al., eds., *Encyclopedia of the American Constitution* (1986). See also "Politics and Government."

Crime and Police

William G. Bailey, *Encyclopedia of Police Science* (1987); Sanford H. Kadish, ed., *Encyclopedia of Crime and Justice* (1983); Michael Newton and Judy Ann Newton, *The FBI Most Wanted* (1989); Carl Sifakis, *The Encyclopedia of American Crime* (1982).

Culture and Folklore

Hennig Cohen and Tristram Potter Coffin, eds., *The Folklore of American Holidays* (1987); Richard M. Dorson, ed., *Handbook of American Folklore* (1983); M. Thomas Inge, ed., *Handbook of American Popular Culture* (1979–1981); J. F. Rooney, Jr. et al., eds., *This Remarkable Continent: An Atlas of United States and Canadian Society and Cultures* (1982); Marjorie Tallman, *Dictionary of American Folklore* (1959); Justin Wintle, ed., *Makers of Nineteenth Century Culture, 1800–1914* (1982). See also "Entertainment," "Mass Media and Journalism," "Music," and "Sports."

Education

Lee C. Deighton, ed., *The Encyclopedia of Education* (1971); Joseph C. Kiger, ed., *Research Institutions and Learned Societies* (1982); John F. Ohles, ed., *Biographical Dictionary of American Educators* (1978).

Entertainment

Tim Brooks and Earle Marsh, *The Complete Directory to Prime Time Network TV Shows, 1946–Present* (1979); Barbara N. Cohen-Stratyner, *Biographical Dictionary of Dance* (1982); John Dunning, *Tune in Yesterday* [radio] (1967); Stanley Green, *Encyclopedia of the Musical Film* (1981); *Notable Names in the American Theater* (1976); *New York Times Encyclopedia of Television* (1977); Andrew Sarris, *The American Cinema: Directors and Directions, 1929–1968* (1968); Anthony Slide, *The American Film Industry* (1986). See also "Culture and Folklore," "Mass Media and Journalism," "Music," and "Sports."

Foreign Policy and International Relations

Gerard Chaliand and Jean-Pierre Rageau, *Strategic Atlas* (1990); Alexander DeConde, ed., *Encyclopedia of American Foreign Policy* (1978); John E. Findling, *Dictionary of American Diplomatic History* (1989); *Foreign Affaris Chronology, 1978–1989* (1990); *International Geographic Encyclopedia and Atlas* (1979); Warren F. Kuehl, ed., *Biographical Dictionary of Internationalists* (1983); George T. Kurian, *Encyclopedia of the Third World* (1981); Jack C. Plano and Roy Olton, eds., *The International Relations Dictionary* (1988); Bruce W. Watson et al., eds., *United States Intelligence* (1990). See also "Peace Movements and Pacifism," "Politics and Government," "Wars and the Military," and specific wars.

Immigration and Ethnic Groups

American Jewish Yearbook (1899–   ); Stephanie Bernardo, *The Ethnic Almanac* (1981); Hyung-Chan Kim, ed., *Dictionary of Asian American History* (1986); Matt S. Meier, *Mexican American Biographies* (1988); Matt S. Meier and Feliciano Rivera, *Dictionary of Mexican American History* (1981); Sally M. Miller, ed., *The Ethnic Press in the United States* (1987); Stephan Thernstrom, ed., *Harvard Encyclopedia of American Ethnic Groups* (1980).

Labor

Gary M. Fink, ed., *Biographical Dictionary of American Labor Leaders* (1984); Gary M. Fink, ed., *Labor Unions* (1977); Philip S. Foner, *First Facts of American Labor* (1984).

Literature

James T. Callow and Robert J. Reilly, *Guide to American Literature* (1976–1977); *Dictionary of Literary Biography* (1978–   ); Eugene Ehrlich and Gorton Carruth, *The Oxford Illustrated Literary Guide to the United States* (1982); Jon Tuska and Vicki Piekarski, *Encyclopedia of Frontier and Western Fiction* (1983). See also "Culture and Folklore," "The South," and "Women."

Mass Media and Journalism

Robert V. Hudson, *Mass Media* (1987); William H. Taft, ed., *Encyclopedia of Twentieth-Century Journalists* (1986).

Medicine and Nursing

Vern L. Bullough et al., eds., *American Nursing* (1988); Martin Kaufman et al., eds., *Dictionary of American Medical Biography* (1984); Martin Kaufman et al., eds., *Dictionary of American Nursing Biography* (1988); George L. Maddox, ed., *The Encyclopedia of Aging* (1987).

Music

John Chilton, *Who's Who of Jazz* (1972); Edward Jablonski, *The Encyclopedia of American Music* (1981); Roger Lax and Frederick Smith, *The Great Song Thesaurus* (1984). See also "Culture and Folklore" and "Entertainment."

Native Americans

Michael Coe et al., *Atlas of Ancient America* (1986); *Handbook of North American Indians* (1978–   ); J. Norman Heard et al., *Handbook of the American Frontier: Four Centuries of Indian-White Relationships* (1987–   ); Barry Klein, ed., *Reference Encyclopedia of the American Indian* (1986); Paul Stuart, *Nation Within a Nation: Historical Statistics of American Indians* (1987); Helen H. Tanner, ed., *Atlas of Great Lakes Indian History* (1987); Carl Waldman, *Atlas of the North American Indian* (1985); Carl Waldman, *Encyclopedia of Native American Tribes* (1988).

The New Deal and FDR

Otis L. Graham, Jr., and Meghan R. Wander, eds., *Franklin D. Roosevelt: His Life and Times* (1985); James S. Olson, ed., *Historical Dictionary of the New Deal* (1985). See also "Politics and Government."

Peace Movements and Pacifism

Harold Josephson et al., eds., *Biographical Dictionary of Modern Peace Leaders* (1985); Ervin Laszlo and Jong Y. Yoo, eds., *World Encyclopedia of Peace* (1986); Robert S. Meyer, *Peace Organizations Past and Present* (1988). See also "Wars and the Military" and specific wars.

Politics and Government: General

Erik W. Austin, *Political Facts of the United States Since 1789* (1986); Mari Jo Buhle et al., eds., *Encyclopedia of the American Left* (1990); Jack P. Greene, ed., *Encyclopedia of American Political History* (1984); Leon Hurwitz, *Historical Dictionary of Censorship in the United States* (1985); Bernard K. Johnpoll and Harvey Klehr, eds., *Biographical Dictionary of the American Left* (1986); Edwin V. Mitchell, *An Encyclopedia of American Politics* (1968); Charles R. Ritter

et al., *American Legislative Leaders, 1850–1910* (1989); William Safire, *Safire's Political Dictionary* (1978); Arthur M. Schlesinger, Jr., and Fred I. Israel, eds., *History of American Presidential Elections, 1789–1968* (1971); Robert Scruton, *A Dictionary of Political Thought* (1982); Jay M. Shafritz, *The Dorsey Dictionary of American Government and Politics* (1989). See also "Cities and Towns," "Constitution and Supreme Court," "The States," and the next three sections.

Politics and Government: Congress

Congressional Quarterly, *Congress and the Nation, 1945–1976* (1965–1977); Kenneth C. Martis, *Historical Atlas of Political Parties in the United States Congress, 1789–1989* (1989); Kenneth C. Martis, *Historical Atlas of United States Congressional Districts, 1789–1983* (1982); U.S. Congress, *Biographical Directory of the United States Congress, 1774–1989* (1989).

Politics and Government: Election Statistics

Erik W. Austin and Jerome C. Clubb, *Political Facts of the United States Since 1789* (1986): Svend Peterson, *A Statistical History of the American Presidential Elections* (1963); Richard M. Scammon et al., eds., *America Votes* (1956–   ); G. Scott Thomas, *The Pursuit of the White House* (1987).

Politics and Government: Presidency and Executive Branch

Henry F. Graff, *The Presidents* (1984); Richard S. Kirkendall, ed., *The Harry S Truman Encyclopedia* (1989); Merrill D. Peterson, ed., *Thomas Jefferson: A Reference Biography* (1986); Robert Sobel, ed., *Biographical Directory of the United States Executive Branch, 1774–1977* (1977). See other categories for specific presidents.

Religion and Cults

Henry Bowden, *Dictionary of American Religious Biography* (1977); John T. Ellis and Robert Trisco, *A Guide to American Catholic History* (1982); Edwin S. Gaustad, *Historical Atlas of Religion in America* (1976); Samuel S. Hill, Jr., ed., *Encyclopedia of Religion in the South* (1984); Charles H. Lippy and Peter W. Williams, eds., *Encyclopedia of the American Religious Experience* (1988); J. Gordon Melton, *Biographical Dictionary of American Cult and Sect Leaders* (1986); J. Gordon Melton, *The Encyclopedia of American Religions* (1987); J. Gordon Melton, *The Encyclopedic Handbook of Cults in America* (1986); Mark A. Noll and Nathan O. Hatch, eds., *Eerdmans Handbook to Christianity in America* (1983).

Science and Technology

James W. Cortada, *Historical Dictionary of Data Processing* (1987); Clark A. Elliott, *Biographical Index to American Science: The Seventeenth Century to 1920* (1990); Charles C.

Gillispie, ed., *Dictionary of Scientific Biography* (1970–); National Academy of Sciences, *Biographical Memoirs* (1877–).

Social Issues, Organizations, and Reform

Louis Filler, *A Dictionary of American Social Reform* (1963); Louis Filler, *Dictionary of American Social Change* (1982); Robert S. Fogarty, *Dictionary of American Communal and Utopian History* (1980); Harold M. Keele and Joseph C. Kiger, eds., *Foundations* (1984); Mark E. Lender, *Dictionary of American Temperance Biography* (1984); Patricia M. Melvin, ed., *American Community Organizations* (1986); Alvin J. Schmidt, *Fraternal Organizations* (1980); Walter I. Trattner, *Biographical Dictionary of Social Welfare in America* (1986). See also "Crime and Police."

The South

Robert Bain et al., eds., *Southern Writers: A Biographical Dictionary* (1979); Kenneth Coleman and Charles S. Gurr, eds., *Dictionary of Georgia Biography* (1983); William Ferris and Charles R. Wilson, eds., *Encyclopedia of Southern Culture* (1986); David C. Roller and Robert W. Twyman, eds., *The Encyclopedia of Southern History* (1979); Walter P. Webb et al., eds., *The Handbook of Texas* (1952, 1976). See also "The Civil War," "Politics and Government," and "The States."

Sports

Ralph Hickok, *New Encyclopedia of Sports* (1977); Zander Hollander, *The NBA's Official Encyclopedia of Pro Basketball* (1981); Frank G. Menke and Suzanne Treat, *The Encyclopedia of Sports* (1977); *The NFL's Official Encyclopedic History of Professional Football* (1977); David L. Porter, *Biographical Dictionary of American Sports: Baseball* (1987), *Football* (1987), and *Outdoor Sports* (1988); David Wallechinsky, *The Complete Book of the Olympics* (1984). See also "Culture and Folklore."

The States

John Clayton, ed., *The Illinois Fact Book and Historical Almanac, 1673–1968* (1970); Roy R. Glashan, ed., *American Governors and Gubernatorial Elections, 1775–1978* (1979); Thomas A. McMullin and David Walker, *Biographical Directory of American Territorial Governors* (1984); Marie Mullaney, *Biographical Directory of the Governors of the United States, 1983–1987* (1988); John W. Raimo, ed., *Biographical Directory of American Colonial and Revolutionary Governors, 1607–1789* (1980); John W. Raimo, ed., *Biographical Directory of the Governors of the United States, 1978–1983* (1985); Robert Sobel and John W. Raimo, eds., *Biographical Directory of the Governors of the United States, 1789–1978* (1978); James W. Scott and Ronald L. De Lorme, *Historical Atlas of Washington* (1988); *The Worldmark Encyclopedia of the States* (1986). See also "Politics and Government," "The South," and "The West and the Frontier."

The Vietnam War

John S. Bowman, ed., *The Vietnam War* (1986); James S. Olson, ed., *Dictionary of the Vietnam War* (1988); Harry G. Summers, Jr., *Vietnam War Almanac* (1985). See also "Peace Movements and Pacifism" and "Wars and the Military."

Wars and the Military

William M. Arkin et al., *Encyclopedia of the U.S. Military* (1990); R. Ernest Dupuy and Trevor N. Dupuy, *The Encyclopedia of Military History* (1977); Holger H. Herwig and Neil M. Heyman, *Biographical Dictionary of World War I* (1982); Michael Kidrow and Dan Smith, *The War Atlas* (1983); Roger J. Spiller and Joseph G. Dawson III, eds., *Dictionary of American Military Biography* (1984); U.S. Military Academy, *The West Point Atlas of American Wars, 1689–1953* (1959); *Webster's American Military Biographies* (1978). See also "American Revolution," "The Civil War," "The Vietnam War," and "World War II."

The West and the Frontier

William A. Beck and Ynez D. Haase, *Historical Atlas of the American West* (1989); Doris O. Dawdy, *Artists of the American West* (1974–1984); Howard R. Lamar, ed., *The Reader's Encyclopedia of the American West* (1977); Doyce B. Nunis, Jr. and Gloria R. Lothrop, eds., *A Guide to the History of California* (1989); Don L. Thrapp, *Encyclopedia of Frontier Biography* (1988).

Women

Maggie Humm, *The Dictionary of Feminist Theory* (1990); Edward T. James et al., *Notable American Women, 1607–1950* (1971); Lina Mainiero, ed., *American Women Writers* (1979–1982); Barbara G. Shortridge, *Atlas of American Women* (1987); Barbara Sicherman and Carol H. Green, eds., *Notable American Women, The Modern Period* (1980); Angela H. Zophy and Frances M. Kavenik, eds., *Dictionary of American Women's History* (1989).

World War II

Marcel Baudot et al., eds., *The Historical Encyclopedia of World War II* (1980); Simon Goodenough, *War Maps: Great Land Battles of World War II* (1988); Robert Goralski, *World War II Almanac, 1931–1945* (1981); John Keegan, ed., *The Times Atlas of the Second World War* (1989); Thomas Parrish, ed., *The Simon and Schuster Encyclopedia of World War II* (1978); Louis L. Snyder, *Louis L. Snyder's Historical Guide to World War II* (1982); U.S. Military Academy, *Campaign Atlas to the Second World War: Europe and the Mediterranean* (1980); Peter Young, ed., *The World Almanac Book of World War II* (1981). See also "Wars and the Military."

Declaration of Independence in Congress, July 4, 1776

The unanimous declaration of the thirteen United States of America

When, in the course of human events, it becomes necessary for one people to dissolve the political bonds which have connected them with another, and to assume, among the powers of the earth, the separate and equal station to which the laws of nature and of nature's God entitle them, a decent respect to the opinions of mankind requires that they should declare the causes which impel them to the separation.

We hold these truths to be self-evident: That all men are created equal; that they are endowed by their Creator with certain unalienable rights; that among these are life, liberty, and the pursuit of happiness; that, to secure these rights, governments are instituted among men, deriving their just powers from the consent of the governed; that whenever any form of government becomes destructive of these ends, it is the right of the people to alter or to abolish it, and to institute new government, laying its foundation on such principles, and organizing its powers in such form, as to them shall seem most likely to effect their safety and happiness. Prudence, indeed, will dictate that governments long established should not be changed for light and transient causes; and accordingly all experience hath shown that mankind are more disposed to suffer, while evils are sufferable, than to right themselves by abolishing the forms to which they are accustomed. But when a long train of abuses and usurpations, pursuing invariably the same object, evinces a design to reduce them under absolute despotism, it is their right, it is their duty, to throw off such government, and to provide new guards for their future security. Such has been the patient sufferance of these colonies; and such is now the necessity which constrains them to alter their former systems of government. The history of the present King of Great Britain is a history of repeated injuries and usurpations, all having in direct object the establishment of an absolute tyranny over these states. To prove this, let facts be submitted to a candid world.

He has refused his assent to laws, the most wholesome and necessary for the public good.

He has forbidden his governors to pass laws of immediate and pressing importance, unless suspended in their operation till his assent should be obtained; and, when so suspended, he has utterly neglected to attend to them.

He has refused to pass other laws for the accommodation of large districts of people, unless those people would relinquish the right of representation in the legislature, a right inestimable to them, and formidable to tyrants only.

He has called together legislative bodies at places unusual, uncomfortable, and distant from the depository of their public records, for the sole purpose of fatiguing them into compliance with his measures.

He has dissolved representative houses repeatedly, for opposing, with manly firmness, his invasions on the rights of the people.

He has refused for a long time, after such dissolutions, to cause others to be elected; whereby the legislative powers, incapable of annihilation, have returned to the people at large for their exercise; the state remaining, in the mean time, exposed to all the dangers of invasions from without and convulsions within.

He has endeavored to prevent the population of these states; for that purpose obstructing the laws for naturalization of foreigners; refusing to pass others to encourage their migration hither, and raising the conditions of new appropriations of lands.

He has obstructed the administration of justice, by refusing his assent to laws for establishing judiciary powers.

He has made judges dependent on his will alone, for the tenure of their offices, and the amount and payment of their salaries.

He has erected a multitude of new offices, and sent hither swarms of officers to harass our people and eat out their substance.

He has kept among us, in times of peace, standing armies, without the consent of our legislatures.

He has affected to render the military independent of, and superior to, the civil power.

He has combined with others to subject us to a jurisdiction foreign to our constitution, and unacknowledged by our laws, giving his assent to their acts of pretended legislation:

For quartering large bodies of armed troops among us;

For protecting them, by a mock trial, from punishment for any murders which they should commit on the inhabitants of these states;

For cutting off our trade with all parts of the world;

For imposing taxes on us without our consent;

For depriving us, in many cases, of the benefits of trial by jury;

For transporting us beyond seas, to be tried for pretended offenses;

For abolishing the free system of English laws in a neighboring province, establishing therein an arbitrary government, and enlarging its boundaries, so as to render it at once an example and fit instrument for introducing the same absolute rule into these colonies;

For taking away our charters, abolishing our most valuable laws, and altering fundamentally the forms of our governments;

For suspending our own legislatures, and declaring themselves invested with power to legislate for us in all cases whatsoever.

He has abdicated government here, by declaring us out of his protection and waging war against us.

He has plundered our seas, ravaged our coasts, burned our towns, and destroyed the lives of our people.

He is at this time transporting large armies of foreign mercenaries to complete the works of death, desolation, and tyranny already begun with circumstances of cruelty and perfidy scarcely paralleled in the most barbarous ages, and totally unworthy the head of a civilized nation.

He has constrained our fellow-citizens, taken captive on the high seas, to bear arms against their country, to become the executioners of their friends and brethren, or to fall themselves by their hands.

He has excited domestic insurrection among us, and has endeavored to bring on the inhabitants of our frontiers the merciless Indian savages, whose known rule of warfare is an undistinguished destruction of all ages, sexes, and conditions.

In every stage of these oppressions we have petitioned for redress in the most humble terms; our repeated petitions have been answered only by repeated injury. A prince, whose character is thus marked by every act which may define a tyrant, is unfit to be the ruler of a free people.

Nor have we been wanting in our attentions to our British brethren. We have warned them, from time to time, of attempts by their legislature to extend an unwarrantable jurisdiction over us. We have reminded them of the circumstances of our emigration and settlement here. We have appealed to their native justice and magnanimity; and we have conjured them, by the ties of our common kindred, to disavow these usurpations, which would inevitably interrupt our connections and correspondence. They, too, have been deaf to the voice of justice and of consanguinity. We must, therefore, acquiesce in the necessity which denounces our separation, and hold them, as we hold the rest of mankind, enemies in war, in peace friends.

We, therefore, the representatives of the United States of America, in General Congress assembled, appealing to the Supreme Judge of the world for the rectitude of our intentions, do, in the name and by the authority of the good people of these colonies, solemnly publish and declare, that these United Colonies are, and of right ought to be, FREE AND INDEPENDENT STATES; that they are absolved from all allegiance to the British crown, and that all political connection between them and the state of Great Britain is, and ought to be, totally dissolved; and that, as free and independent states, they have full power to levy war, conclude peace, contract alliances, establish commerce, and do all other acts and things which independent states may of right do. And for the support of this declaration, with a firm reliance on the protection of Divine Providence, we mutually pledge to each other our lives, our fortunes, and our sacred honor.

JOHN HANCOCK
and fifty-five others

◣

Constitution of the United States of America and Amendments

Preamble

We the people of the United States, in order to form a more perfect union, establish justice, insure domestic tranquillity,

provide for the common defense, promote the general welfare, and secure the blessings of liberty to ourselves and our posterity, do ordain and establish this Constitution for the United States of America.

Article I

Section 1 All legislative powers herein granted shall be vested in a Congress of the United States, which shall consist of a Senate and a House of Representatives.

Section 2 The House of Representatives shall be composed of members chosen every second year by the people of the several States, and the electors in each State shall have the qualifications requisite for electors of the most numerous branch of the State Legislature.

No person shall be a Representative who shall not have attained to the age of twenty-five years, and been seven years a citizen of the United States, and who shall not, when elected, be an inhabitant of that State in which he shall be chosen.

Representatives and direct taxes shall be apportioned among the several States which may be included within this Union, according to their respective numbers, *which shall be determined by adding to the whole number of free persons, including those bound to service for a term of years and excluding Indians not taxed, three-fifths of all other persons.* The actual enumeration shall be made within three years after the first meeting of the Congress of the United States, and within every subsequent term of ten years, in such manner as they shall by law direct. The number of Representatives shall not exceed one for every thirty thousand, but each State shall have at least one Representative; *and until such enumeration shall be made, the State of New Hampshire shall be entitled to choose three, Massachusetts eight, Rhode Island and Providence Plantations one, Connecticut five, New York six, New Jersey four, Pennsylvania eight, Delaware one, Maryland six, Virginia ten, North Carolina five, South Carolina five, and Georgia three.*

When vacancies happen in the representation from any State, the Executive authority thereof shall issue writs of election to fill such vacancies.

The House of Representatives shall choose their Speaker and other officers; and shall have the sole power of impeachment.

Section 3 The Senate of the United States shall be composed of two Senators from each State, *chosen by the legislature thereof,* for six years; and each Senator shall have one vote.

Immediately after they shall be assembled in consequence of the first election, they shall be divided as equally as may be into three classes. The seats of the Senators of the first class shall be vacated at the expiration of the second year, of the second class at the expiration of the fourth year, and of the third class at the expiration of the sixth year, so that one-third

---

Passages no longer in effect are printed in italic type.

may be chosen every second year; *and if vacancies happen by resignation or otherwise, during the recess of the legislature of any State, the Executive thereof may make temporary appointments until the next meeting of the legislature, which shall then fill such vacancies.*

No person shall be a Senator who shall not have attained to the age of thirty years, and been nine years a citizen of the United States, and who shall not, when elected, be an inhabitant of that State for which he shall be chosen.

The Vice-President of the United States shall be President of the Senate, but shall have no vote, unless they be equally divided.

The Senate shall choose their other officers, and also a President *pro tempore,* in the absence of the Vice-President, or when he shall exercise the office of President of the United States.

The Senate shall have the sole power to try all impeachments. When sitting for that purpose, they shall be on oath or affirmation. When the President of the United States is tried, the Chief Justice shall preside: and no person shall be convicted without the concurrence of two-thirds of the members present.

Judgment in cases of impeachment shall not extend further than to removal from the office, and disqualification to hold and enjoy any office of honor, trust or profit under the United States: but the party convicted shall nevertheless be liable and subject to indictment, trial, judgment and punishment, according to law.

Section 4 The times, places and manner of holding elections for Senators and Representatives shall be prescribed in each State by the legislature thereof; but the Congress may at any time by law make or alter such regulations, except as to the places of choosing Senators.

The Congress shall assemble at least once in every year, and such meeting *shall be on the first Monday in December, unless they shall by law appoint a different day.*

Section 5 Each house shall be the judge of the elections, returns and qualifications of its own members, and a majority of each shall constitute a quorum to do business; but a smaller number may adjourn from day to day, and may be authorized to compel the attendance of absent members, in such manner, and under such penalties, as each house may provide.

Each house may determine the rules of its proceedings, punish its members for disorderly behavior, and with the concurrence of two-thirds, expel a member.

Each house shall keep a journal of its proceedings, and from time to time publish the same, excepting such parts as may in their judgment require secrecy; and the yeas and nays of the members of either house on any question shall, at the desire of one-fifth of those present, be entered on the journal.

Neither house, during the session of Congress, shall, without the consent of the other, adjourn for more than three days, nor to any other place than that in which the two houses shall be sitting.

Section 6 The Senators and Representatives shall receive a compensation for their services, to be ascertained by law and paid out of the treasury of the United States. They shall in all cases except treason, felony and breach of the peace, be privileged from arrest during their attendance at the session of their respective houses, and in going to and returning from the same; and for any speech or debate in either house, they shall not be questioned in any other place.

No Senator or Representative shall, during the time for which he was elected, be appointed to any civil office under the authority of the United States, which shall have been created, or the emoluments whereof shall have been increased, during such time; and no person holding any office under the United States shall be a member of either house during his continuance in office.

Section 7 All bills for raising revenue shall originate in the House of Representatives; but the Senate may propose or concur with amendments as on other bills.

Every bill which shall have passed the House of Representatives and the Senate, shall, before it become a law, be presented to the President of the United States; if he approve he shall sign it, but if not he shall return it with objections to that house in which it originated, who shall enter the objections at large on their journal, and proceed to reconsider it. If after such reconsideration two-thirds of that house shall agree to pass the bill, it shall be sent, together with the objections, to the other house, by which it shall likewise be reconsidered, and, if approved by two-thirds of that house, it shall become a law. But in all such cases the votes of both houses shall be determined by yeas and nays, and the names of the persons voting for and against the bill shall be entered on the journal of each house respectively. If any bill shall not be returned by the President within ten days (Sundays excepted) after it shall have been presented to him, the same shall be a law, in like manner as if he had signed it, unless the Congress by their adjournment prevent its return, in which case it shall not be a law.

Every order, resolution, or vote to which the concurrence of the Senate and House of Representatives may be necessary (except on a question of adjournment) shall be presented to the President of the United States; and before the same shall take effect, shall be approved by him, or being disapproved by him, shall be repassed by two-thirds of the Senate and House of Representatives, according to the rules and limitations prescribed in the case of a bill.

Section 8 The Congress shall have power

To lay and collect taxes, duties, imposts, and excises, to pay the debts and provide for the common defense and general welfare of the United States; but all duties, imposts and excises shall be uniform throughout the United States;

To borrow money on the credit of the United States;

To regulate commerce with foreign nations, and among the several States, and with the Indian tribes;

To establish an uniform rule of naturalization, and uniform laws on the subject of bankruptcies throughout the United States;

To coin money, regulate the value thereof, and of foreign coin, and fix the standard of weights and measures;

To provide for the punishment of counterfeiting the securities and current coin of the United States;

To establish post offices and post roads;

To promote the progress of science and useful arts by securing for limited times to authors and inventors the exclusive right to their respective writings and discoveries;

To constitute tribunals inferior to the Supreme Court;

To define and punish piracies and felonies committed on the high seas and offenses against the law of nations;

To declare war, grant letters of marque and reprisal, and make rules concerning captures on land and water;

To raise and support armies, but no appropriation of money to that use shall be for a longer term than two years;

To provide and maintain a navy;

To make rules for the government and regulation of the land and naval forces;

To provide for calling forth the militia to execute the laws of the Union, suppress insurrections, and repel invasions;

To provide for organizing, arming, and disciplining the militia, and for governing such part of them as may be employed in the service of the United States, reserving to the States respectively the appointment of the officers, and the authority of training the militia according to the discipline prescribed by Congress;

To exercise exclusive legislation in all cases whatsoever, over such district (not exceeding ten miles square) as may, by cession of particular States, and the acceptance of Congress, become the seat of government of the United States, and to exercise like authority over all places purchased by the consent of the legislature of the State, in which the same shall be, for erection of forts, magazines, arsenals, dockyards, and other needful buildings;—and

To make all laws which shall be necessary and proper for carrying into execution the foregoing powers, and all other powers vested by this Constitution in the government of the United States, or in any department or officer thereof.

Section 9   The migration or importation of such persons as any of the States now existing shall think proper to admit shall not be prohibited by the Congress prior to the year 1808; but a tax or duty may be imposed on such importation, not exceeding $10 for each person.

The privilege of the writ of habeas corpus shall not be suspended, unless when in cases of rebellion or invasion the public safety may require it.

No bill of attainder or ex post facto law shall be passed.

No capitation, or other direct, tax shall be laid, unless in proportion to the census or enumeration herein before directed to be taken.

No tax or duty shall be laid on articles exported from any State.

No preference shall be given by any regulation of commerce or revenue to the ports of one State over those of another; nor shall vessels bound to, or from, one State, be obliged to enter, clear, or pay duties in another.

No money shall be drawn from the treasury, but in consequence of appropriations made by law; and a regular statement and account of the receipts and expenditures of all public money shall be published from time to time.

No title of nobility shall be granted by the United States: and no person holding any office of profit or trust under them, shall, without the consent of the Congress, accept of any present, emolument, office, or title, of any kind whatever, from any king, prince, or foreign state.

Section 10   No State shall enter into any treaty, alliance, or confederation; grant letters of marque and reprisal; coin money; emit bills of credit; make anything but gold and silver coin a tender in payment of debts; pass any bill of attainder, ex post facto law, or law impairing the obligation of contracts, or grant any title of nobility.

No State shall, without the consent of Congress, lay any imposts or duties on imports or exports, except what may be absolutely necessary for executing its inspection laws: and the net produce of all duties and imposts, laid by any State on imports or exports, shall be for the use of the treasury of the United States; and all such laws shall be subject to the revision and control of the Congress.

No State shall, without the consent of Congress, lay any duty of tonnage, keep troops or ships of war in time of peace, enter into any agreement or compact with another State, or with a foreign power, or engage in war, unless actually invaded, or in such imminent danger as will not admit of delay.

Article II

Section 1   The executive power shall be vested in a President of the United States of America. He shall hold his office during the term of four years, and, together with the Vice-President, chosen for the same term, be elected as follows:

Each State shall appoint, in such manner as the legislature thereof may direct, a number of electors, equal to the whole number of Senators and Representatives to which the State may be entitled in the Congress; but no Senator or Representative, or person holding an office of trust or profit under the United States, shall be appointed an elector.

The electors shall meet in their respective States, and vote by ballot for two persons, of whom one at least shall not be an inhabitant of the same State with themselves. And they shall make a list of all the persons voted for, and of the number of votes for each; which list they shall sign and certify, and transmit sealed to the seat of government of the United States, directed to the President of the Senate. The President of the Senate shall, in the presence of the Senate and House of Representatives, open all the certificates, and the votes shall then be counted. The person having the greatest number of votes shall be the President, if such number be a majority of the whole number of electors appointed; and if there be more than one who have such majority, and have an equal number of votes, then the House of Representatives shall immediately choose by ballot one of them for President; and if no person have a majority, then from the five highest on the list said house shall in like manner choose the Presi-

dent. But in choosing the President the votes shall be taken by States, the representation from each State having one vote; a quorum for this purpose shall consist of a member or members from two-thirds of the States, and a majority of all the States shall be necessary to a choice. In every case, after the choice of the President, the person having the greatest number of votes of the electors shall be the Vice-President. But if there should remain two or more who have equal votes, the Senate shall choose from them by ballot the Vice-President.

The Congress may determine the time of choosing the electors and the day on which they shall give their votes; which day shall be the same throughout the United States.

No person except a natural-born citizen, *or a citizen of the United States at the time of the adoption of this Constitution,* shall be eligible to the office of President; neither shall any person be eligible to that office who shall not have attained to the age of thirty-five years, and been fourteen years a resident within the United States.

In cases of the removal of the President from office or of his death, resignation, or inability to discharge the powers and duties of the said office, the same shall devolve on the Vice-President, and the Congress may by law provide for the case of removal, death, resignation, or inability, both of the President and Vice-President, declaring what officer shall then act as President, and such officer shall act accordingly, until the disability be removed, or a President shall be elected.

The President shall, at stated times, receive for his services a compensation, which shall neither be increased nor diminished during the period for which he shall have been elected, and he shall not receive within that period any other emolument from the United States, or any of them.

Before he enter on the execution of his office, he shall take the following oath or affirmation:—"I do solemnly swear (or affirm) that I will faithfully execute the office of the President of the United States, and will to the best of my ability preserve, protect and defend the Constitution of the United States."

Section 2 The President shall be commander in chief of the army and navy of the United States, and of the militia of the several States, when called into the actual service of the United States; he may require the opinion, in writing, of the principal officer in each of the executive departments, upon any subject relating to the duties of their respective offices, and he shall have power to grant reprieves and pardons for offenses against the United States, except in cases of impeachment.

He shall have power, by and with the advice and consent of the Senate, to make treaties, provided two-thirds of the Senators present concur; and he shall nominate, and by and with the advice and consent of the Senate, shall appoint ambassadors, other public ministers and consuls, judges of the Supreme Court, and all other officers of the United States, whose appointments are not herein otherwise provided for, and which shall be established by law: but Congress may by law vest the appointment of such inferior officers, as they think proper, in the President alone, in the courts of law, or in the heads of departments.

The President shall have power to fill up all vacancies that may happen during the recess of the Senate, by granting commissions which shall expire at the end of their next session.

Section 3 He shall from time to time give to the Congress information of the state of the Union, and recommend to their consideration such measures as he shall judge necessary and expedient; he may, on extraordinary occasions, convene both houses, or either of them, and in case of disagreement between them, with respect to the time of adjournment, he may adjourn them to such time as he shall think proper; he shall receive ambassadors and other public ministers; he shall take care that the laws be faithfully executed, and shall commission all the officers of the United States.

Section 4 The President, Vice-President and all civil officers of the United States shall be removed from office on impeachment for, and on conviction of, treason, bribery, or other high crimes and misdemeanors.

Article III

Section 1 The judicial power of the United States shall be vested in one Supreme Court, and in such inferior courts as the Congress may from time to time ordain and establish. The judges, both of the Supreme and inferior courts, shall hold their offices during good behavior, and shall, at stated times, receive for their services a compensation which shall not be diminished during their continuance in office.

Section 2 The judicial power shall extend to all cases, in law and equity, arising under this Constitution, the laws of the United States, and treaties made, or which shall be made, under their authority;—to all cases affecting ambassadors, other public ministers and consuls;—to all cases of admiralty and maritime jurisdiction;—to controversies to which the United States shall be a party;—to controversies between two or more States;—*between a State and citizens of another State;*—between citizens of different States;—between citizens of the same State claiming lands under grants of different States, and between a State, or the citizens thereof, and foreign states, citizens or subjects.

In all cases affecting ambassadors, other public ministers and consuls, and those in which a State shall be party, the Supreme Court shall have original jurisdiction. In all the other cases before mentioned, the Supreme Court shall have appellate jurisdiction, both as to law and fact, with such exceptions, and under such regulations, as the Congress shall make.

The trial of all crimes, except in cases of impeachment, shall be by jury; and such trial shall be held in the State where said crimes shall have been committed; but when not committed within any State, the trial shall be at such place or places as the Congress may by law have directed.

Section 3 Treason against the United States shall consist only in levying war against them, or in adhering to their enemies, giving them aid and comfort. No person shall be convicted of treason unless on the testimony of two witnesses to the same overt act, or on confession in open court.

The Congress shall have power to declare the punishment of treason, but no attainder of treason shall work corruption of blood, or forfeiture except during the life of the person attainted.

Article IV

Section 1 Full faith and credit shall be given in each State to the public acts, records, and judicial proceedings of every other State. And the Congress may by general laws prescribe the manner in which such acts, records, and proceedings shall be proved, and the effect thereof.

Section 2 The citizens of each State shall be entitled to all privileges and immunities of citizens in the several States.

A person charged in any State with treason, felony, or other crime, who shall flee from justice, and be found in another State, shall on demand of the executive authority of the State from which he fled, be delivered up, to be removed to the State having jurisdiction of the crime.

No person held to service or labor in one State, under the laws thereof, escaping into another, shall, in consequence of any law or regulation therein, be discharged from such service or labor, but shall be delivered up on claim of the party to whom such service or labor may be due.

Section 3 New States may be admitted by the Congress into this Union; but no new State shall be formed or erected within the jurisdiction of any other State; nor any State be formed by the junction of two or more States, or parts of States, without the consent of the legislatures of the States concerned as well as of the Congress.

The Congress shall have power to dispose of and make all needful rules and regulations respecting the territory or other property belonging to the United States; and nothing in this Constitution shall be so construed as to prejudice any claims of the United States, or of any particular State.

Section 4 The United States shall guarantee to every State in this Union a republican form of government, and shall protect each of them against invasion; and on application of the legislature, or of the executive (when the legislature cannot be convened), against domestic violence.

Article V

The Congress, whenever two-thirds of both houses shall deem it necessary, shall propose amendments to this Constitution, or, on the application of the legislatures of two-thirds of the several States, shall call a convention for proposing amendments, which, in either case, shall be valid to all intents and purposes, as part of this Constitution, when ratified by the legislatures of three-fourths of the several States, or by conventions in three-fourths thereof, as the one or the other mode of ratification may be proposed by the Congress; provided *that no amendments which may be made prior to the year one thousand eight hundred and eight shall in any manner affect the first and fourth clauses in the ninth section of the first article;* and that no State, without its consent, shall be deprived of its equal suffrage in the Senate.

Article VI

All debts contracted and engagements entered into, before the adoption of this Constitution, shall be as valid against the United States under this Constitution, as under the Confederation.

This Constitution, and the laws of the United States which shall be made in pursuance thereof; and all treaties made, or which shall be made, under the authority of the United States, shall be the supreme law of the land; and the judges in every State shall be bound thereby, anything in the Constitution or laws of any State to the contrary notwithstanding.

The Senators and Representatives before mentioned, and the members of the several State legislatures, and all executive and judicial officers, both of the United States and of the several States, shall be bound by oath or affirmation to support this Constitution; but no religious test shall ever be required as a qualification to any office or public trust under the United States.

Article VII

The ratification of the conventions of nine States shall be sufficient for the establishment of this Constitution between the States so ratifying the same.

Done in Convention by the unanimous consent of the States present, the seventeenth day of September in the year of our Lord one thousand seven hundred and eighty-seven and of the Independence of the United States of America the twelfth. In witness whereof we have hereunto subscribed our names.

GEORGE WASHINGTON
and thirty-seven others

Amendments to the Constitution*

Amendment I

Congress shall make no law respecting an establishment of religion, or prohibiting the free exercise thereof; or abridging the freedom of speech, or of the press; or the right of the

---

*The first ten Amendments (the Bill of Rights) were adopted in 1791.

people peaceably to assemble, and to petition the government for a redress of grievances.

Amendment II

A well-regulated militia being necessary to the security of a free State, the right of the people to keep and bear arms shall not be infringed.

Amendment III

No soldier shall, in time of peace, be quartered in any house without the consent of the owner, nor in time of war, but in a manner to be prescribed by law.

Amendment IV

The right of the people to be secure in their persons, houses, papers, and effects, against unreasonable searches and seizures, shall not be violated, and no warrants shall issue but upon probable cause, supported by oath or affirmation, and particularly describing the place to be searched, and the persons or things to be seized.

Amendment V

No person shall be held to answer for a capital, or otherwise infamous crime, unless on a presentment or indictment of a grand jury, except in cases arising in the land or naval forces, or in the militia, when in actual service in time of war or public danger; nor shall any person be subject for the same offense to be twice put in jeopardy of life or limb; nor shall be compelled in any criminal case to be a witness against himself, nor be deprived of life, liberty, or property, without due process of law; nor shall private property be taken for public use without just compensation.

Amendment VI

In all criminal prosecutions, the accused shall enjoy the right to a speedy and public trial, by an impartial jury of the State and district wherein the crime shall have been committed, which district shall have been previously ascertained by law, and to be informed of the nature and cause of the accusation; to be confronted with the witnesses against him; to have compulsory process for obtaining witnesses in his favor, and to have the assistance of counsel for his defense.

Amendment VII

In suits at common law, where the value in controversy shall exceed twenty dollars, the right of trial by jury shall be preserved, and no fact tried by a jury shall be otherwise reexamined in any court of the United States, than according to the rules of the common law.

Amendment VIII

Excessive bail shall not be required, nor excessive fines imposed, nor cruel and unusual punishments inflicted.

Amendment IX

The enumeration in the Constitution, of certain rights, shall not be construed to deny or disparage others retained by the people.

Amendment X

The powers not delegated to the United States by the Constitution, nor prohibited by it to the States, are reserved to the States respectively, or to the people.

Amendment XI

[Adopted 1798]

The judicial power of the United States shall not be construed to extend to any suit in law or equity, commenced or prosecuted against one of the United States by citizens of another State, or by citizens or subjects of any foreign state.

Amendment XII

[Adopted 1804]

The electors shall meet in their respective States, and vote by ballot for President and Vice-President, one of whom, at least, shall not be an inhabitant of the same State with themselves; they shall name in their ballots the person voted for as President, and in distinct ballots the person voted for as Vice-President, and they shall make distinct lists of all persons voted for as President, and of all persons voted for as Vice-President, and of the number of votes for each, which lists they shall sign and certify, and transmit sealed to the seat of government of the United States, directed to the President of the Senate;—the President of the Senate shall, in the presence of the Senate and House of Representatives, open all the certificates and the votes shall then be counted;—the person having the greatest number of votes for President shall be the President, if such number be a majority of the whole number of electors appointed; and if no person have such majority, then from the persons having the highest numbers not exceeding three on the list of those voted for as President, the House of Representatives shall choose immediately, by ballot, the President. But in choosing the President, the votes shall be taken by States, the representation from each State having one vote; a quorum for this purpose shall consist of a member or members from two-thirds of the States, and a majority of all the States shall be necessary to a choice. And if the House of Representatives shall not choose a President whenever the right of choice shall devolve upon them, before *the fourth day of March* next following, then the Vice-President shall act as President, as in the case of the death or other constitutional disability of the President.

The person having the greatest number of votes as Vice-President shall be the Vice-President, if such number be a majority of the whole number of electors appointed; and if no person have a majority, then from the two highest numbers on the list the Senate shall choose the Vice-President; a quorum for the purpose shall consist of two-thirds of the whole number of Senators, and a majority of the whole number shall be necessary to a choice. But no person constitutionally ineligible to the office of President shall be eligible to that of Vice-President of the United States.

Amendment XIII

[Adopted 1865]

Section 1 Neither slavery nor involuntary servitude, except as a punishment for crime whereof the party shall have been duly convicted, shall exist within the United States, or any place subject to their jurisdiction.

Section 2 Congress shall have power to enforce this article by appropriate legislation.

Amendment XIV

[Adopted 1868]

Section 1 All persons born or naturalized in the United States, and subject to the jurisdiction thereof, are citizens of the United States and of the State wherein they reside. No State shall make or enforce any law which shall abridge the privileges or immunities of citizens of the United States; nor shall any State deprive any person of life, liberty, or property, without due process of law; nor deny to any person within its jurisdiction the equal protection of the laws.

Section 2 Representatives shall be apportioned among the several States according to their respective numbers, counting the whole number of persons in each State, excluding Indians not taxed. But when the right to vote at any election for the choice of Electors for President and Vice-President of the United States, Representatives in Congress, the executive and judicial officers of a State, or the members of the legislature thereof, is denied to any of the male inhabitants of such State, being twenty-one years of age and citizens of the United States, or in any way abridged, except for participation in rebellion, or other crime, the basis of representation therein shall be reduced in the proportion which the number of such male citizens shall bear to the whole number of male citizens twenty-one years of age in such State.

Section 3 No person shall be a Senator or Representative in Congress, or Elector of President and Vice-President, or hold any office, civil or military, under the United States, or under any State, who, having previously taken an oath, as a member of Congress, or as an officer of the United States, or as a member of any State legislature, or as an executive or judicial officer of any State, to support the Constitution of the United States, shall have engaged in insurrection or rebellion against the same, or given aid or comfort to the enemies thereof. Congress may, by a vote of two-thirds of each house, remove such disability.

Section 4 The validity of the public debt of the United States, authorized by law, including debts incurred for payment of pensions and bounties for services in suppressing insurrection or rebellion, shall not be questioned. But neither the United States nor any State shall assume or pay any debt or obligation incurred in aid of insurrection or rebellion against the United States, or any claim for the loss of emancipation of any slave; but all such debts, obligations, and claims shall be held illegal and void.

Section 5 The Congress shall have power to enforce, by appropriate legislation, the provisions of this article.

Amendment XV

[Adopted 1870]

Section 1 The right of citizens of the United States to vote shall not be denied or abridged by the United States or by any State on account of race, color, or previous condition of servitude.

Section 2 The Congress shall have power to enforce this article by appropriate legislation.

Amendment XVI

[Adopted 1913]

The Congress shall have power to lay and collect taxes on incomes, from whatever source derived, without apportionment among the several States, and without regard to any census or enumeration.

Amendment XVII

[Adopted 1913]

Section 1 The Senate of the United States shall be composed of two Senators from each State, elected by the people thereof, for six years; and each Senator shall have one vote. The electors in each State shall have the qualifications requisite for electors of [voters for] the most numerous branch of the State legislatures.

Section 2 When vacancies happen in the representation of any State in the Senate, the executive authority of such State shall issue writs of election to fill such vacancies: Provided, that the Legislature of any State may empower the executive thereof to make temporary appointments until the people fill the vacancies by election as the Legislature may direct.

Section 3 This amendment shall not be so construed as to affect the election or term of any Senator chosen before it becomes valid as part of the Constitution.

Amendment XVIII

[Adopted 1919; Repealed 1933]

Section 1 After one year from the ratification of this article the manufacture, sale, or transportation of intoxicating liquors within, the importation thereof into, or the exportation thereof from the United States and all territory subject to the jurisdiction thereof, for beverage purposes, is hereby prohibited.

Section 2 The Congress and the several States shall have concurrent power to enforce this article by appropriate legislation.

Section 3 This article shall be inoperative unless it shall have been ratified as an amendment to the Constitution by the legislatures of the several States, as provided by the Constitution, within seven years from the date of the submission thereof to the States by the Congress.

Amendment XIX

[Adopted 1920]

Section 1 The right of citizens of the United States to vote shall not be denied or abridged by the United States or by any State on account of sex.

Section 2 The Congress shall have power to enforce this article by appropriate legislation.

Amendment XX

[Adopted 1933]

Section 1 The terms of the President and Vice-President shall end at noon on the 20th day of January, and the terms of Senators and Representatives at noon on the 3d day of January, of the years in which such terms would have ended if this article had not been ratified; and the terms of their successors shall then begin.

Section 2 The Congress shall assemble at least once in every year, and such meeting shall begin at noon on the 3d day of January, unless they shall by law appoint a different day.

Section 3 If, at the time fixed for the beginning of the term of the President, the President-elect shall have died, the Vice-President-elect shall become President. If a President shall not have been chosen before the time fixed for the beginning of his term, or if the President-elect shall have failed to qualify, then the Vice-President-elect shall act as President

until a President shall have qualified; and the Congress may by law provide for the case wherein neither a President-elect nor a Vice-President-elect shall have qualified, declaring who shall then act as President, or the manner in which one who is to act shall be selected, and such persons shall act accordingly until a President or Vice-President shall have qualified.

Section 4 The Congress may by law provide for the case of the death of any of the persons from whom the House of Representatives may choose a President whenever the right of choice shall have devolved upon them, and for the case of the death of any of the persons from whom the Senate may choose a Vice-President whenever the right of choice shall have devolved upon them.

Section 5 Sections 1 and 2 shall take effect on the 15th day of October following the ratification of this article.

Section 6 This article shall be inoperative unless it shall have been ratified as an amendment to the Constitution by the Legislatures of three-fourths of the several States within seven years from the date of its submission.

Amendment XXI

[Adopted 1933]

Section 1 The eighteenth article of amendment to the Constitution of the United States is hereby repealed.

Section 2 The transportation or importation into any State, Territory, or Possession of the United States for delivery or use therein of intoxicating liquors, in violation of the laws thereof, is hereby prohibited.

Section 3 This article shall be inoperative unless it shall have been ratified as an amendment to the Constitution by conventions in the several States, as provided in the Constitution, within seven years from the date of submission thereof to the States by the Congress.

Amendment XXII

[Adopted 1951]

Section 1 No person shall be elected to the office of President more than twice, and no person who has held the office of President, or acted as President, for more than two years of a term to which some other person was elected President shall be elected to the office of President more than once. But this article shall not apply to any person holding the office of President when this article was proposed by the Congress, and shall not prevent any person who may be holding the office of President, or acting as President, during the term within which this article becomes operative from holding the office of President or acting as President during the remainder of such term.

Section 2 This article shall be inoperative unless it shall have been ratified as an amendment to the Constitution by the legislatures of three-fourths of the several States within seven years from the date of its submission to the States by the Congress.

Amendment XXIII

[Adopted 1961]

Section 1 The District constituting the seat of Government of the United States shall appoint in such manner as the Congress may direct:

A number of electors of President and Vice-President equal to the whole number of Senators and Representatives in Congress to which the District would be entitled if it were a State, but in no event more than the least populous State; they shall be in addition to those appointed by the States, but they shall be considered for the purposes of the election of President and Vice-President, to be electors appointed by a State; and they shall meet in the District and perform such duties as provided by the twelfth article of amendment.

Section 2 The Congress shall have the power to enforce this article by appropriate legislation.

Amendment XXIV

[Adopted 1964]

Section 1 The right of citizens of the United States to vote in any primary or other election for President or Vice-President, for electors for President or Vice-President, or for Senator or Representative in Congress, shall not be denied or abridged by the United States or any State by reason of failure to pay any poll tax or other tax.

Section 2 The Congress shall have the power to enforce this article by appropriate legislation.

Amendment XXV

[Adopted 1967]

Section 1 In case of the removal of the President from office or of his death or resignation, the Vice-President shall become President.

Section 2 Whenever there is a vacancy in the office of the Vice-President, the President shall nominate a Vice-President who shall take office upon confirmation by a majority vote of both Houses of Congress.

Section 3 Whenever the President transmits to the President pro tempore of the Senate and the Speaker of the House of Representatives his written declaration that he is unable to discharge the powers and duties of his office, and until he transmits to them a written declaration to the contrary, such powers and duties shall be discharged by the Vice-President as Acting President.

Section 4 Whenever the Vice-President and a majority of either the principal officers of the executive departments or of such other body as Congress may by law provide, transmit to the President pro tempore of the Senate and the Speaker of the House of Representatives their written declaration that the President is unable to discharge the powers and duties of his office, the Vice-President shall immediately assume the powers and duties of the office as Acting President.

Thereafter, when the President transmits to the President pro tempore of the Senate and the Speaker of the House of Representatives his written declaration that no inability exists, he shall resume the powers and duties of his office unless the Vice-President and a majority of either the principal officers of the executive department[s] or of such other body as Congress may by law provide, transmit within four days to the President pro tempore of the Senate and the Speaker of the House of Representatives their written declaration that the President is unable to discharge the powers and duties of his office. Thereupon Congress shall decide the issue, assembling within forty-eight hours for that purpose if not in session. If the Congress, within twenty-one days after receipt of the latter written declaration, or, if Congress is not in session, within twenty-one days after Congress is required to assemble, determines by two-thirds vote of both Houses that the President is unable to discharge the powers and duties of his office, the Vice-President shall continue to discharge the same as Acting President; otherwise, the President shall resume the powers and duties of his office.

Amendment XXVI

[Adopted 1971]

Section 1 The right of citizens of the United States, who are eighteen years of age or older, to vote shall not be denied or abridged by the United States or by any State on account of age.

Section 2 The Congress shall have power to enforce this article by appropriate legislation.

POPULATION OF THE UNITED STATES

Year	Number of States	Population	Percent Increase	Population Per Square Mile	Percent Urban/ Rural	Percent Male/ Female	Percent White/ Nonwhite	Persons Per House- hold	Median Age
1790	13	3,929,214		4.5	5.1/94.9	NA/NA	80.7/19.3	5.79	NA
1800	16	5,308,483	35.1	6.1	6.1/93.9	NA/NA	81.1/18.9	NA	NA
1810	17	7,239,881	36.4	4.3	7.3/92.7	NA/NA	81.0/19.0	NA	NA
1820	23	9,638,453	33.1	5.5	7.2/92.8	50.8/49.2	81.6/18.4	NA	16.7
1830	24	12,866,020	33.5	7.4	8.8/91.2	50.8/49.2	81.9/18.1	NA	17.2
1840	26	17,069,453	32.7	9.8	10.8/89.2	50.9/49.1	83.2/16.8	NA	17.8
1850	31	23,191,876	35.9	7.9	15.3/84.7	51.0/49.0	84.3/15.7	5.55	18.9
1860	33	31,443,321	35.6	10.6	19.8/80.2	51.2/48.8	85.6/14.4	5.28	19.4
1870	37	39,818,449	26.6	13.4	25.7/74.3	50.6/49.4	86.2/13.8	5.09	20.2
1880	38	50,155,783	26.0	16.9	28.2/71.8	50.9/49.1	86.5/13.5	5.04	20.9
1890	44	62,947,714	25.5	21.2	35.1/64.9	51.2/48.8	87.5/12.5	4.93	22.0
1900	45	75,994,575	20.7	25.6	39.6/60.4	51.1/48.9	87.9/12.1	4.76	22.9
1910	46	91,972,266	21.0	31.0	45.6/54.4	51.5/48.5	88.9/11.1	4.54	24.1
1920	48	105,710,620	14.9	35.6	51.2/48.8	51.0/49.0	89.7/10.3	4.34	25.3
1930	48	122,775,046	16.1	41.2	56.1/43.9	50.6/49.4	89.8/10.2	4.11	26.4
1940	48	131,669,275	7.2	44.2	56.5/43.5	50.2/49.8	89.8/10.2	3.67	29.0
1950	48	150,697,361	14.5	50.7	64.0/36.0	49.7/50.3	89.5/10.5	3.37	30.2
1960	50	179,323,175	18.5	50.6	69.9/30.1	49.3/50.7	88.6/11.4	3.33	29.5
1970	50	203,302,031	13.4	57.4	73.5/26.5	48.7/51.3	87.6/12.4	3.14	28.0
1980	50	226,545,805	11.4	64.0	73.7/26.3	48.6/51.4	86.0/14.0	2.76	30.0
1990	50	248,656,000[a]	8.9	70.3	NA/NA	48.7/51.3[b]	84.4/15.6[b]	2.64[b]	32.3[b]

NA = Not available.
[a] Projection.
[b] 1988 figure.

Immigration Totals by Decade

Years	Number	Years	Number
1820–1830	151,824	1911–1920	5,735,811
1831–1840	599,125	1921–1930	4,107,209
1841–1850	1,713,251	1931–1940	528,431
1851–1860	2,598,214	1941–1950	1,035,039
1861–1870	2,314,824	1951–1960	2,515,479
1871–1880	2,812,191	1961–1970	3,321,677
1881–1890	5,246,613	1971–1980	4,493,000
1891–1900	3,687,546	1981–1987	4,067,600
1901–1910	8,795,386	Total	53,723,220

Sources: *U.S. Bureau of the Census,* Historical Statistics of the United States, Colonial Times to 1970 (1975); *U.S. Bureau of the Census,* Statistical Abstract of the United States, 1989 (1989).

Major Sources of Immigrants by Country (in thousands)

Period	Germany	Italy	Britain (UK)	Ireland	Austria-Hungary	Canada	Russia (USSR)[a]	Mexico	Denmark, Norway, Sweden[b]	Caribbean (West Indies)
1820–1830	8	—	27	54	—	2	—	5	—	4
1831–1840	152	2	76	207	—	14	—	7	2	12
1841–1850	435	2	267	781	—	42	—	3	14	14
1851–1860	952	9	424	914	—	59	—	3	25	11
1861–1870	787	12	607	436	8	154	3	2	126	9
1871–1880	718	56	548	437	73	384	39	5	243	14
1881–1890	1,453	307	807	655	354	393	213	2[c]	656	29
1891–1900	505	652	272	388	593	3	505	—	372	—[d]
1901–1910	341	2,046	526	339	2,145	179	1,597	50	505	108
1911–1920	144	1,110	341	146	896	742	922	219	203	123
1921–1930	412	455	330	221	64	925	89	459	198	75
1931–1940	114	68	29	13	11	109	7	22	11	16
1941–1950	227	58	132	28	28	172	4	61	27	50
1951–1960	478	185	192	57	104	378	6	300	57	123
1961–1970	200	207	231	42	31	287	22	443	45	520
1971–1980	66	130	124	14	16	115	46	637	15	760
1981–1987	49	24	99	11	9	79	47	474	13	576
Total	6,981	5,323	5,032	4,743	4,332	4,037	3,500	2,692	2,512	2,444

Notes: Numbers are rounded. Dash indicates less than one thousand.
[a] Includes Finland, Latvia, Estonia, and Lithuania.
[b] Includes Iceland.
[c] Figure for 1881–1885 only.
[d] Figure for 1894–1900 only.

Sources: *U.S. Bureau of the Census*, Historical Statistics of the United States: Colonial Times to 1970 (1975); *U.S. Bureau of the Census,* Statistical Abstract of the United States, 1989 (1989).

THE AMERICAN FARM

Year	Farm Population (in thousands)	Percent of Total Population	Number of Farms (in thousands)	Total Acres (in thousands)	Average Acreage Per Farm	Corn Production (millions of bushels)	Wheat Production (millions of bushels)
1850	NA	NA	1,449	293,561	203	592[a]	100[a]
1860	NA	NA	2,044	407,213	199	839[b]	173[b]
1870	NA	NA	2,660	407,735	153	1,125	254
1880	21,973	43.8	4,009	536,082	134	1,707	502
1890	24,771	42.3	4,565	623,219	137	1,650	449
1900	29,875	41.9	5,740	841,202	147	2,662	599
1910	32,077	34.9	6,366	881,431	139	2,853	625
1920	31,974	30.1	6,454	958,677	149	3,071	843
1930	30,529	24.9	6,295	990,112	157	2,080	887
1940	30,547	23.2	6,102	1,065,114	175	2,457	815
1950	23,048	15.3	5,388	1,161,420	216	3,075	1,019
1960	15,635	8.7	3,962	1,176,946	297	4,314	1,355
1970	9,712	4.8	2,949	1,102,769	374	4,200	1,370
1980	6,051	2.7	2,428	1,042,000	427	6,600	2,400
1987	4,986	2.0	2,176	1,003,000	461	7,064	2,105

[a] Figure for 1849.
[b] Figure for 1859.
NA = Not available.

THE AMERICAN WORKER

Year	Total Number of Workers	Males as Percent of Total Workers	Females as Percent of Total Workers	Married Women as Percent of Female Workers	Female Workers as Percent of Female Population	Percent of Labor Force Unemployed	Percent of Workers in Labor Unions
1870	12,506,000	85	15	NA	NA	NA	NA
1880	17,392,000	85	15	NA	NA	NA	NA
1890	23,318,000	83	17	13.9	18.9	4 (1894 = 18)	NA
1900	29,073,000	82	18	15.4	20.6	5	3
1910	38,167,000	79	21	24.7	25.4	6	6
1920	41,614,000	79	21	23.0	23.7	5 (1921 = 12)	12
1930	48,830,000	78	22	28.9	24.8	9 (1933 = 25)	7
1940	53,011,000	76	24	36.4	27.4	15 (1944 = 1)	27
1950	59,643,000	72	28	52.1	31.4	5	25
1960	69,877,000	68	32	59.9	34.8	5.4	26
1970	82,049,000	63	37	63.4	42.6	4.8	25
1980	108,544,000	58	42	59.7	51.1	7.0	23
1987	119,865,000	55	45	59.1	55.4	6.1 (1983 = 9.5)	17

NA = Not available.

Territorial Expansion of the United States

Territory	Date Acquired	Square Miles	How Acquired
Original states and territories	1783	888,685	Treaty with Great Britain
Louisiana Purchase	1803	827,192	Purchase from France
Florida	1819	72,003	Treaty with Spain
Texas	1845	390,143	Annexation of independent nation
Oregon	1846	285,580	Treaty with Great Britain
Mexican Cession	1848	529,017	Conquest from Mexico
Gadsden Purchase	1853	29,640	Purchase from Mexico
Alaska	1867	589,757	Purchase from Russia
Hawaii	1898	6,450	Annexation of independent nation
The Philippines	1899	115,600	Conquest from Spain (granted independence in 1946)
Puerto Rico	1899	3,435	Conquest from Spain
Guam	1899	212	Conquest from Spain
American Samoa	1900	76	Treaty with Germany and Great Britain
Panama Canal Zone	1904	553	Treaty with Panama (returned to Panama by treaty in 1978)
Corn Islands	1914	4	Treaty with Nicaragua (returned to Nicaragua by treaty in 1971)
Virgin Islands	1917	133	Purchase from Denmark
Pacific Islands Trust (Micronesia)	1947	8,489	Trusteeship under United Nations (some granted independence)
All others (Midway, Wake, and other islands)		42	

Admission of States into the Union

State	Date of Admission	State	Date of Admission
1. Delaware	December 7, 1787	26. Michigan	January 26, 1837
2. Pennsylvania	December 12, 1787	27. Florida	March 3, 1845
3. New Jersey	December 18, 1787	28. Texas	December 29, 1845
4. Georgia	January 2, 1788	29. Iowa	December 28, 1846
5. Connecticut	January 9, 1788	30. Wisconsin	May 29, 1848
6. Massachusetts	February 6, 1788	31. California	September 9, 1850
7. Maryland	April 28, 1788	32. Minnesota	May 11, 1858
8. South Carolina	May 23, 1788	33. Oregon	February 14, 1859
9. New Hampshire	June 21, 1788	34. Kansas	January 29, 1861
10. Virginia	June 25, 1788	35. West Virginia	June 20, 1863
11. New York	July 26, 1788	36. Nevada	October 31, 1864
12. North Carolina	November 21, 1789	37. Nebraska	March 1, 1867
13. Rhode Island	May 29, 1790	38. Colorado	August 1, 1876
14. Vermont	March 4, 1791	39. North Dakota	November 2, 1889
15. Kentucky	June 1, 1792	40. South Dakota	November 2, 1889
16. Tennessee	June 1, 1796	41. Montana	November 8, 1889
17. Ohio	March 1, 1803	42. Washington	November 11, 1889
18. Louisiana	April 30, 1812	43. Idaho	July 3, 1890
19. Indiana	December 11, 1816	44. Wyoming	July 10, 1890
20. Mississippi	December 10, 1817	45. Utah	January 4, 1896
21. Illinois	December 3, 1818	46. Oklahoma	November 16, 1907
22. Alabama	December 14, 1819	47. New Mexico	January 6, 1912
23. Maine	March 15, 1820	48. Arizona	February 14, 1912
24. Missouri	August 10, 1821	49. Alaska	January 3, 1959
25. Arkansas	June 15, 1836	50. Hawaii	August 21, 1959

Presidential Elections

Year	Number of States	Candidates	Parties	Popular Vote	% of Popular Vote	Electoral Vote	Voter Participation[b]
1789	11	**George Washington**	No party			69	
		John Adams	designations			34	
		Other Candidates				35	
1792	15	**George Washington**	No party			132	
		John Adams	designations			77	
		George Clinton				50	
		Other candidates				5	
1796	16	**John Adams**	Federalist			71	
		Thomas Jefferson	Democratic-Republican			68	
		Thomas Pinckney	Federalist			59	
		Aaron Burr	Democratic-Republican			30	
		Other candidates				48	
1800	16	**Thomas Jefferson**	Democratic-Republican			73	
		Aaron Burr	Democratic-Republican			73	
		John Adams	Federalist			65	
		Charles C. Pinckney	Federalist			64	
		John Jay	Federalist			1	
1804	17	**Thomas Jefferson**	Democratic-Republican			162	
		Charles C. Pinckney	Federalist			14	
1808	17	**James Madison**	Democratic-Republican			122	
		Charles C. Pinckney	Federalist			47	
		George Clinton	Democratic-Republican			6	
1812	18	**James Madison**	Democratic-Republican			128	
		DeWitt Clinton	Federalist			89	
1816	19	**James Monroe**	Democratic-Republican			183	
		Rufus King	Federalist			34	
1820	24	**James Monroe**	Democratic-Republican			231	
		John Quincy Adams	Independent Republican			1	
1824	24	**John Quincy Adams**	Democratic-Republican	108,740	30.5	84	26.9
		Andrew Jackson	Democratic-Republican	153,544	43.1	99	
		Henry Clay	Democratic-Republican	47,136	13.2	37	
		William H. Crawford	Democratic-Republican	46,618	13.1	41	

Year	Number of States	Candidates	Parties	Popular Vote	% of Popular Vote	Electoral Vote	Voter Participation[b]
1828	24	**Andrew Jackson**	Democratic	647,286	56.0	178	57.6
		John Quincy Adams	National Republican	508,064	44.0	83	
1832	24	**Andrew Jackson**	Democratic	688,242	54.5	219	55.4
		Henry Clay	National Republican	473,462	37.5	49	
		William Wirt	Anti-Masonic	101,051	8.0	7	
		John Floyd	Democratic			11	
1836	26	**Martin Van Buren**	Democratic	765,483	50.9	170	57.8
		William H. Harrison	Whig			73	
		Hugh L. White	Whig	739,795	49.1	26	
		Daniel Webster	Whig			14	
		W. P. Mangum	Whig			11	
1840	26	**William H. Harrison**	Whig	1,274,624	53.1	234	80.2
		Martin Van Buren	Democratic	1,127,781	46.9	60	
1844	26	**James K. Polk**	Democratic	1,338,464	49.6	170	78.9
		Henry Clay	Whig	1,300,097	48.1	105	
		James G. Birney	Liberty	62,300	2.3		
1848	30	**Zachary Taylor**	Whig	1,360,967	47.4	163	72.7
		Lewis Cass	Democratic	1,222,342	42.5	127	
		Martin Van Buren	Free Soil	291,263	10.1		
1852	31	**Franklin Pierce**	Democratic	1,601,117	50.9	254	69.6
		Winfield Scott	Whig	1,385,453	44.1	42	
		John P. Hale	Free Soil	155,825	5.0		
1856	31	**James Buchanan**	Democratic	1,832,955	45.3	174	78.9
		John C. Frémont	Republican	1,339,932	33.1	114	
		Millard Fillmore	American	871,731	21.6	8	
1860	33	**Abraham Lincoln**	Republican	1,865,593	39.8	180	81.2
		Stephen A. Douglas	Democratic	1,382,713	29.5	12	
		John C. Breckinridge	Democratic	848,356	18.1	72	
		John Bell	Constitutional Union	592,906	12.6	39	
1864	36	**Abraham Lincoln**	Republican	2,206,938	55.0	212	73.8
		George B. McClellan	Democratic	1,803,787	45.0	21	
1868	37	**Ulysses S. Grant**	Republican	3,013,421	52.7	214	78.1
		Horatio Seymour	Democratic	2,706,829	47.3	80	
1872	37	**Ulysses S. Grant**	Republican	3,596,745	55.6	286	71.3
		Horace Greeley	Democratic	2,843,446	43.9	[a]	
1876	38	**Rutherford B. Hayes**	Republican	4,036,572	48.0	185	81.8
		Samuel J. Tilden	Democratic	4,284,020	51.0	184	
1880	38	**James A. Garfield**	Republican	4,453,295	48.5	214	79.4
		Winfield S. Hancock	Democratic	4,414,082	48.1	155	
		James B. Weaver	Greenback-Labor	308,578	3.4		
1884	38	**Grover Cleveland**	Democratic	4,879,507	48.5	219	77.5
		James G. Blaine	Republican	4,850,293	48.2	182	
		Benjamin F. Butler	Greenback-Labor	175,370	1.8		
		John P. St. John	Prohibition	150,369	1.5		

Year	Number of States	Candidates	Parties	Popular Vote	% of Popular Vote	Electoral Vote	Voter Participation[b]
1888	38	**Benjamin Harrison**	Republican	5,447,129	47.9	233	79.3
		Grover Cleveland	Democratic	5,537,857	48.6	168	
		Clinton B. Fisk	Prohibition	249,506	2.2		
		Anson J. Streeter	Union Labor	146,935	1.3		
1892	44	**Grover Cleveland**	Democratic	5,555,426	46.1	277	74.7
		Benjamin Harrison	Republican	5,182,690	43.0	145	
		James B. Weaver	People's	1,029,846	8.5	22	
		John Bidwell	Prohibition	264,133	2.2		
1896	45	**William McKinley**	Republican	7,102,246	51.1	271	79.3
		William J. Bryan	Democratic	6,492,559	47.7	176	
1900	45	**William McKinley**	Republican	7,218,491	51.7	292	73.2
		William J. Bryan	Democratic; Populist	6,356,734	45.5	155	
		John C. Wooley	Prohibition	208,914	1.5		
1904	45	**Theodore Roosevelt**	Republican	7,628,461	57.4	336	65.2
		Alton B. Parker	Democratic	5,084,223	37.6	140	
		Eugene V. Debs	Socialist	402,283	3.0		
		Silas C. Swallow	Prohibition	258,536	1.9		
1908	46	**William H. Taft**	Republican	7,675,320	51.6	321	65.4
		William J. Bryan	Democratic	6,412,294	43.1	162	
		Eugene V. Debs	Socialist	420,793	2.8		
		Eugene W. Chafin	Prohibition	253,840	1.7		
1912	48	**Woodrow Wilson**	Democratic	6,296,547	41.9	435	58.8
		Theodore Roosevelt	Progressive	4,118,571	27.4	88	
		William H. Taft	Republican	3,486,720	23.2	8	
		Eugene V. Debs	Socialist	900,672	6.0		
		Eugene W. Chafin	Prohibition	206,275	1.4		
1916	48	**Woodrow Wilson**	Democratic	9,127,695	49.4	277	61.6
		Charles E. Hughes	Republican	8,533,507	46.2	254	
		A. L. Benson	Socialist	585,113	3.2		
		J. Frank Hanly	Prohibition	220,506	1.2		
1920	48	**Warren G. Harding**	Republican	16,143,407	60.4	404	49.2
		James M. Cox	Democratic	9,130,328	34.2	127	
		Eugene V. Debs	Socialist	919,799	3.4		
		P. P. Christensen	Farmer-Labor	265,411	1.0		
1924	48	**Calvin Coolidge**	Republican	15,718,211	54.0	382	48.9
		John W. Davis	Democratic	8,385,283	28.8	136	
		Robert M. La Follette	Progressive	4,831,289	16.6	13	
1928	48	**Herbert C. Hoover**	Republican	21,391,993	58.2	444	56.9
		Alfred E. Smith	Democratic	15,016,169	40.9	87	
1932	48	**Franklin D. Roosevelt**	Democratic	22,809,638	57.4	472	56.9
		Herbert C. Hoover	Republican	15,758,901	39.7	59	
		Norman Thomas	Socialist	881,951	2.2		
1936	48	**Franklin D. Roosevelt**	Democratic	27,752,869	60.8	523	61.0
		Alfred M. Landon	Republican	16,674,665	36.5	8	
		William Lemke	Union	882,479	1.9		

Year	Number of States	Candidates	Parties	Popular Vote	% of Popular Vote	Electoral Vote	Voter Participation[b]
1940	48	**Franklin D. Roosevelt**	Democratic	27,307,819	54.8	449	62.5
		Wendell L. Willkie	Republican	22,321,018	44.8	82	
1944	48	**Franklin D. Roosevelt**	Democratic	25,606,585	53.5	432	55.9
		Thomas E. Dewey	Republican	22,014,745	46.0	99	
1948	48	**Harry S Truman**	Democratic	24,179,345	49.6	303	53.0
		Thomas E. Dewey	Republican	21,991,291	45.1	189	
		J. Strom Thurmond	States' Rights	1,176,125	2.4	39	
		Henry A. Wallace	Progressive	1,157,326	2.4		
1952	48	**Dwight D. Eisenhower**	Republican	33,936,234	55.1	442	63.3
		Adlai E. Stevenson	Democratic	27,314,992	44.4	89	
1956	48	**Dwight D. Eisenhower**	Republican	35,590,472	57.6	457	60.6
		Adlai E. Stevenson	Democratic	26,022,752	42.1	73	
1960	50	**John F. Kennedy**	Democratic	34,226,731	49.7	303	62.8
		Richard M. Nixon	Republican	34,108,157	49.5	219	
1964	50	**Lyndon B. Johnson**	Democratic	43,129,566	61.1	486	61.7
		Barry M. Goldwater	Republican	27,178,188	38.5	52	
1968	50	**Richard M. Nixon**	Republican	31,785,480	43.4	301	60.6
		Hubert H. Humphrey	Democratic	31,275,166	42.7	191	
		George C. Wallace	American Independent	9,906,473	13.5	46	
1972	50	**Richard M. Nixon**	Republican	47,169,911	60.7	520	55.2
		George S. McGovern	Democratic	29,170,383	37.5	17	
		John G. Schmitz	American	1,099,482	1.4		
1976	50	**Jimmy Carter**	Democratic	40,830,763	50.1	297	53.5
		Gerald R. Ford	Republican	39,147,793	48.0	240	
1980	50	**Ronald Reagan**	Republican	43,899,248	50.8	489	52.6
		Jimmy Carter	Democratic	35,481,432	41.0	49	
		John B. Anderson	Independent	5,719,437	6.6	0	
		Ed Clark	Libertarian	920,859	1.1	0	
1984	50	**Ronald Reagan**	Republican	54,455,075	58.8	525	53.1
		Walter Mondale	Democratic	37,577,185	40.6	13	
1988	50	**George Bush**	Republican	48,901,046	53.4	426	50.2
		Michael Dukakis	Democratic	41,809,030	45.6	111[c]	

Candidates receiving less than 1 percent of the popular vote have been omitted. Thus the percentage of popular vote given for any election year may not total 100 percent.

Before the passage of the Twelfth Amendment in 1804, the Electoral College voted for two presidential candidates; the runner-up became vice president.

Before 1824, most presidential electors were chosen by state legislatures, not by popular vote.

[a] Greeley died shortly after the election; the electors supporting him then divided their votes among minor candidates.

[b] Percent of voting-age population casting ballots.

[c] One elector from West Virginia cast her Electoral College presidential ballot for Lloyd Bentsen, the Democratic party's vice presidential candidate.

Presidents and Vice Presidents

1.	President	**George Washington**	1789–1797		22.	President	**Grover Cleveland**	1885–1889
	Vice President	John Adams	1789–1797			Vice President	Thomas A. Hendricks	1885–1889
2.	President	**John Adams**	1797–1801		23.	President	**Benjamin Harrison**	1889–1893
	Vice President	Thomas Jefferson	1797–1801			Vice President	Levi P. Morton	1889–1893
3.	President	**Thomas Jefferson**	1801–1809		24.	President	**Grover Cleveland**	1893–1897
	Vice President	Aaron Burr	1801–1805			Vice President	Adlai E. Stevenson	1893–1897
	Vice President	George Clinton	1805–1809		25.	President	**William McKinley**	1897–1901
4.	President	**James Madison**	1809–1817			Vice President	Garret A. Hobart	1897–1901
	Vice President	George Clinton	1809–1813				Theodore Roosevelt	1901
	Vice President	Elbridge Gerry	1813–1817		26.	President	**Theodore Roosevelt**	1901–1909
5.	President	**James Monroe**	1817–1825			Vice President	Charles Fairbanks	1905–1909
	Vice President	Daniel Tompkins	1817–1825		27.	President	**William H. Taft**	1909–1913
6.	President	**John Quincy Adams**	1825–1829			Vice President	James S. Sherman	1909–1913
	Vice President	John C. Calhoun	1825–1829		28.	President	**Woodrow Wilson**	1913–1921
7.	President	**Andrew Jackson**	1829–1837			Vice President	Thomas R. Marshall	1913–1921
	Vice President	John C. Calhoun	1829–1833		29.	President	**Warren G. Harding**	1921–1923
	Vice President	Martin Van Buren	1833–1837			Vice President	Calvin Coolidge	1921–1923
8.	President	**Martin Van Buren**	1837–1841		30.	President	**Calvin Coolidge**	1923–1929
	Vice President	Richard M. Johnson	1837–1841			Vice President	Charles G. Dawes	1925–1929
9.	President	**William H. Harrison**	1841		31.	President	**Herbert C. Hoover**	1929–1933
	Vice President	John Tyler	1841			Vice President	Charles Curtis	1929–1933
10.	President	**John Tyler**	1841–1845		32.	President	**Franklin D. Roosevelt**	1933–1945
	Vice President	none				Vice President	John N. Garner	1933–1941
11.	President	**James K. Polk**	1845–1849				Henry A. Wallace	1941–1945
	Vice President	George M. Dallas	1845–1849				Harry S Truman	1945
12.	President	**Zachary Taylor**	1849–1850		33.	President	**Harry S Truman**	1945–1953
	Vice President	Millard Fillmore	1849–1850			Vice President	Alben W. Barkley	1949–1953
13.	President	**Millard Fillmore**	1850–1853		34.	President	**Dwight D. Eisenhower**	1953–1961
	Vice President	none				Vice President	Richard M. Nixon	1953–1961
14.	President	**Franklin Pierce**	1853–1857		35.	President	**John F. Kennedy**	1961–1963
	Vice President	William R. King	1853–1857			Vice President	Lyndon B. Johnson	1961–1963
15.	President	**James Buchanan**	1857–1861		36.	President	**Lyndon B. Johnson**	1963–1969
	Vice President	John C. Breckinridge	1857–1861			Vice President	Hubert H. Humphrey	1965–1969
16.	President	**Abraham Lincoln**	1861–1865		37.	President	**Richard M. Nixon**	1969–1974
	Vice President	Hannibal Hamlin	1861–1865			Vice President	Spiro T. Agnew	1969–1973
	Vice President	Andrew Johnson	1865				Gerald R. Ford	1973–1974
17.	President	**Andrew Johnson**	1865–1869		38.	President	**Gerald R. Ford**	1974–1977
	Vice President	none				Vice President	Nelson A. Rockefeller	1974–1977
18.	President	**Ulysses S. Grant**	1869–1877		39.	President	**Jimmy Carter**	1977–1981
	Vice President	Schuyler Colfax	1869–1873			Vice President	Walter F. Mondale	1977–1981
	Vice President	Henry Wilson	1873–1877		40.	President	**Ronald Reagan**	1981–1989
19.	President	**Rutherford B. Hayes**	1877–1881			Vice President	George Bush	1981–1989
	Vice President	William A. Wheeler	1877–1881		41.	President	**George Bush**	1989–
20.	President	**James A. Garfield**	1881			Vice President	Dan Quayle	1989–
	Vice President	Chester A. Arthur	1881					
21.	President	**Chester A. Arthur**	1881–1885					
	Vice President	none						

Justices of the Supreme Court

	Term of Service	Years of Service	Life Span		Term of Service	Years of Service	Life Span
John Jay	1789–1795	5	1745–1829	Stephen J. Field	1863–1897	34	1816–1899
John Rutledge	1789–1791	1	1739–1800	*Salmon P. Chase*	1864–1873	8	1808–1873
William Cushing	1789–1810	20	1732–1810	William Strong	1870–1880	10	1808–1895
James Wilson	1789–1798	8	1742–1798	Joseph P. Bradley	1870–1892	22	1813–1892
John Blair	1789–1796	6	1732–1800	Ward Hunt	1873–1882	9	1810–1886
Robert H. Harrison	1789–1790	—	1745–1790	*Morrison R. Waite*	1874–1888	14	1816–1888
James Iredell	1790–1799	9	1751–1799	John M. Harlan	1877–1911	34	1833–1911
Thomas Johnson	1791–1793	1	1732–1819	William B. Woods	1880–1887	7	1824–1887
William Paterson	1793–1806	13	1745–1806	Stanley Matthews	1881–1889	7	1824–1889
*John Rutledge**	1795	—	1739–1800	Horace Gray	1882–1902	20	1828–1902
Samuel Chase	1796–1811	15	1741–1811	Samuel Blatchford	1882–1893	11	1820–1893
Oliver Ellsworth	1796–1800	4	1745–1807	Lucius Q. C. Lamar	1888–1893	5	1825–1893
Bushrod Washington	1798–1829	31	1762–1829	*Melville W. Fuller*	1888–1910	21	1833–1910
Alfred Moore	1799–1804	4	1755–1810	David J. Brewer	1890–1910	20	1837–1910
John Marshall	1801–1835	34	1755–1835	Henry B. Brown	1890–1906	16	1836–1913
William Johnson	1804–1834	30	1771–1834	George Shiras, Jr.	1892–1903	10	1832–1924
H. Brockholst Livingston	1806–1823	16	1757–1823	Howell E. Jackson	1893–1895	2	1832–1895
Thomas Todd	1807–1826	18	1765–1826	Edward D. White	1894–1910	16	1845–1921
Joseph Story	1811–1845	33	1779–1845	Rufus W. Peckham	1895–1909	14	1838–1909
Gabriel Duval	1811–1835	24	1752–1844	Joseph McKenna	1898–1925	26	1843–1926
Smith Thompson	1823–1843	20	1768–1843	Oliver W. Holmes	1902–1932	30	1841–1935
Robert Trimble	1826–1828	2	1777–1828	William R. Day	1903–1922	19	1849–1923
John McLean	1829–1861	32	1785–1861	William H. Moody	1906–1910	3	1853–1917
Henry Baldwin	1830–1844	14	1780–1844	Horace H. Lurton	1910–1914	4	1844–1914
James M. Wayne	1835–1867	32	1790–1867	Charles E. Hughes	1910–1916	5	1862–1948
Roger B. Taney	1836–1864	28	1777–1864	*Edward D. White*	1910–1921	11	1845–1921
Philip P. Barbour	1836–1841	4	1783–1841	Willis Van Devanter	1911–1937	26	1859–1941
John Catron	1837–1865	28	1786–1865	Joseph R. Lamar	1911–1916	5	1857–1916
John McKinley	1837–1852	15	1780–1852	Mahlon Pitney	1912–1922	10	1858–1924
Peter V. Daniel	1841–1860	19	1784–1860	James C. McReynolds	1914–1941	26	1862–1946
Samuel Nelson	1845–1872	27	1792–1873	Louis D. Brandeis	1916–1939	22	1856–1941
Levi Woodbury	1845–1851	5	1789–1851	John H. Clarke	1916–1922	6	1857–1945
Robert C. Grier	1846–1870	23	1794–1870	*William H. Taft*	1921–1930	8	1857–1930
Benjamin R. Curtis	1851–1857	6	1809–1874	George Sutherland	1922–1938	15	1862–1942
John A. Campbell	1853–1861	8	1811–1889	Pierce Butler	1922–1939	16	1866–1939
Nathan Clifford	1858–1881	23	1803–1881	Edward T. Sanford	1923–1930	7	1865–1930
Noah H. Swayne	1862–1881	18	1804–1884	Harlan F. Stone	1925–1941	16	1872–1946
Samuel F. Miller	1862–1890	28	1816–1890	*Charles E. Hughes*	1930–1941	11	1862–1948
David Davis	1862–1877	14	1815–1886	Owen J. Roberts	1930–1945	15	1875–1955

	Term of Service	Years of Service	Life Span		Term of Service	Years of Service	Life Span
Benjamin N. Cardozo	1932–1938	6	1870–1938	William J. Brennan, Jr.	1956–	—	1906–
Hugo L. Black	1937–1971	34	1886–1971	Charles E. Whittaker	1957–1962	5	1901–1973
Stanley F. Reed	1938–1957	19	1884–1980	Potter Stewart	1958–1981	23	1915–1985
Felix Frankfurter	1939–1962	23	1882–1965	Byron R. White	1962–	—	1917–
William O. Douglas	1939–1975	36	1898–1980	Arthur J. Goldberg	1962–1965	3	1908–
Frank Murphy	1940–1949	9	1890–1949	Abe Fortas	1965–1969	4	1910–1982
Harlan F. Stone	1941–1946	5	1872–1946	Thurgood Marshall	1967–	—	1908–
James F. Byrnes	1941–1942	1	1879–1972	*Warren C. Burger*	1969–1986	17	1907–
Robert H. Jackson	1941–1954	13	1892–1954	Harry A. Blackmun	1970–	—	1908–
Wiley B. Rutledge	1943–1949	6	1894–1949	Lewis F. Powell, Jr.	1971–1987	16	1907–
Harold H. Burton	1945–1958	13	1888–1964	*William H. Rehnquist*	1971–	—	1924–
Fred M. Vinson	1946–1953	7	1890–1953	John P. Stevens III	1975–	—	1920–
Tom C. Clark	1949–1967	18	1899–1977	Sandra Day O'Connor	1981–	—	1930–
Sherman Minton	1949–1956	7	1890–1965	Antonin Scalia	1986–	—	1936–
Earl Warren	1953–1969	16	1891–1974	Anthony M. Kennedy	1988–	—	1936–
John Marshall Harlan	1955–1971	16	1899–1971				

*Appointed and served one term, but not confirmed by the Senate.
Note: Chief justices are in italics.

Index

Agriculture (*cont.*)
impact of increased specialization on economy, 160–161; as foundation of American economy, 161; prior to transportation revolution, 163; governmental promotion of western, 165; State Department assistance in, 165; state of mid-19th-century, 170; and development of market economy, 172, 173, 175–176; mechanization of, 172, 173, 175, 260–261, 299–300; 19th-century commercial, 172–173; sharecropping system, 284; regions of, 296 (ill.); and migration to Plains, 297–299; in post–Reconstruction South, 301–302; declining profitability of, 351–352; economic reform for, 373, 434, 437, 440, 441; foreign markets and, 378, 412; during First World War, 402; promotion of scientific, 412; price supports for, 414; Mexican-American labor in, 417, 446–447; migration from farming communities, 417; overproduction in, 426; during Great Depression, 430, 432, 434; legacy of New Deal on, 430; legislation during Great Depression, 437, 440; during Second World War, 472, 474; movement of consolidation in, 525; during 1980s, 591
Aguinaldo, Emilio, 384, 386
AIDS, 601–602
Air brakes, 379
Air traffic controllers, 591
Akan States, 9
Alabama: Creek withdrawal to, 153; admission to statehood, 157; migration to, 178; slave migration to, 181; political reform in, 191; Indian land concessions in, 210; secession of, 251
Alabama (ship), 269, 381
Alabama Midlands case (1897), 348
Alaska: discovery of gold in, 354; sale of coal lands in, 371; purchase of, 381
Albany, New York, 268
Albany Congress, 73
Albemarle Sound, North Carolina, 255
Alcatraz Island, 581
Alcohol: consumption of, 220, 221; moral reformers and, 333, 364; immigrant cultures and use of, 334. *See also* Prohibition; Temperance movement
Alcott, Louisa May, 206, 342
Aldrich, Nelson W., 362, 371
Alger, Horatio, 341–342
Algiers, 147
Algonkians, 3, 5; clash with colonists, 16–17; slave trade in, 38

Alien and Sedition Acts (1798), 145; description of, 132–133; Jefferson and Madison's means of combating, 133–134; expiration of, 142; opposition to, 142
Alien Enemies Act (1798), 132
Alien Friends Act (1798), 132
Allende, Salvador, 549
Alliance for Progress in Latin America, 539
Altgeld, John P., 317
Amalgamated Association of Iron and Steelworkers, 318
Amans, Jacques, 227
Amerasia, 498
America First Committee, 462
American Anti-Slavery Society, 223, 224
American Association for Old Age Security, 363
American Bar Association, 360
American Birth Control League, 369
American Board of Customs Commissioners, 80, 82
American Colonization Society, 223
American Dilemma, An (Myrdal), 498
American Expeditionary Forces (AEF), 400
American Federation of Labor (AFL): formation of, 317–318; support of Wilson administration during First World War, 402; expulsion of industrial unions from, 444; membership in, 444; merger with Congress of Industrial Organizations, 524
American Federation of Labor–Congress of Industrial Organizations (AFL-CIO), 524, 591
American Female Moral Reform Society, 220
American Independent Party, 564
American Indian Days, 368
American Indian Defense Association, 415, 446
American Indian Movement (AIM), 581
American Indians. *See* Native Americans
American League, 338
American Missionary Association, 283
American Office of Strategic Services (OSS), 540
American party, 245, 246
American Peace Commission, 406
American Railway Union, 319, 355
American Relief Administration, 452
American Revolution: Jacobites during, 53; women camp followers in, 87, 98; impact of, 87–88; prerequisites for success, 88; threats posed by neutrals and loyalists during, 90–91; makeup of patriots involved in, 91; threats posed by African-Americans during, 91–92; loyalties of Indians during, 92–93, 99–101; initial military campaigns in, 93–94; British strategy, 94; military cam-

paigns in north, 96–100; slaves in Continental Army, 98; military campaigns in south, 100–102; and Treaty of Paris, 102; Indians as losers in, 102; nationalistic spirit created by, 105; economic changes resulting from, 117; war debts from, 127
American Society for Promotion of Temperance, 220–221
American System, 155, 225, 228
American system of manufacturing, 166
American Tobacco Company, 310
American Union Against Militarism, 399
American Woman Suffrage Association, 350
American Women, 565
Amnesty, for Southerners, 276
Amnesty Act (1872), 286
Amusement parks, 339
Anderson, John, 585
Anderson, Mary, 319, 477
Andros, Edmund, 45, 46
Anglicans: migration of merchants to New England, 43; in Massachusetts, 46; loyalist sentiment among clergy, 90
Angola, 549, 551, 578
Anne (Queen of England), 53
Annexation Club, 381
Anthony, Susan B., 278, 349
Antiballistic missile (ABM) systems, 549
Antibiotics, 525
Anti-Catholicism, 208
Anti-Comintern Pact, 457
Anticommunism: during Truman administration, 485, 486; origins of, 498; during Eisenhower administration, 509–510; during Nixon administration, 552
Antifederalists: opposition to Constitution by, 120–121; ethnic makeup of, 121; representation in First Congress, 124
Antifeminist movement, 583
Anti-Imperialist League, 385
Anti-imperialists: imperialists vs., 376–377; racism and, 380; arguments against empire, 384–386; Third World, 516
Anti-Klan laws, 286
Antimasonry movement, 218, 221–222
Anti-Saloon League, 364
Anti-Semitism, 532
Antislavery. *See* Abolitionism; Abolitionists
Antitrust legislation, 313, 370, 373, 408, 441
Antiwar sentiment: during Civil War, 266, 268–269; during Vietnam War, 543, 545, 546, 563, 566
Apaches, 14
Apartheid, 598
Apollo 11 (spaceship), 566

Five Points section (New York City), 203
Five-Power Treaty, 454
Fletcher, Benjamin, 66
Fletcher v. *Peck,* 155
Flexible response, 535
Florida: Spanish presence in, 13, 70; British control of, 73; ceding to U.S., 156; Seminole land claims to, 213; secession of, 251; election of *1876* and, 287
Folklore, slave, 187, 188
Foner, Eric, 282
Food Administration, 402
Food legislation, 370–371
Food shortages: during Civil War, 266; fear of, 373
Football, 338, 422
Forbes, Charles, 414
Force Act, 228, 229
Ford, Gerald, 552; and Vietnam War, 535; economic policy of, 571, 576; as successor to Nixon, 573; pardon of Nixon, 573; and election of *1976,* 577
Ford, Henry, 307, 359, 399
Ford Motor Company, 309 (ill.), 444, 494
Fordney-McCumber Act (1922), 455
Foreclosures, farm, 431, 432
Foreign investments, 430
Foreign policy: Washington's view regarding, 131; problems confronting early 19th-century America, 158; makers of, 378; relationship between domestic developments and, 378; expansionist, 378–381, 390; toward Europe, 390; basic tenets of U.S., 408; economic, 455; erosion of bipartisanship in, 502. *See also* Expansionism
Foreign policy elite, 378
Foreign Relations Committee, Senate, 406, 407
Foreign trade: with Europe, 378–379; with Latin America, 379–380; with China, 386; at outbreak of First World War, 394; and shift from debtor to creditor nation, 408; post–First World War decline in, 412; with Soviet Union, 458, 549; with Japan, 461, 463
Forests, national, 371
Formal imperialism, 377, 378
Formosa, 493, 494, 514, 582
Formosa Resolution (1955), 514
Fort Dearborn, 150
Fort Donelson, 255
Fort Duquesne, 73
Forten, James, 214
Fort Henry, 255
Fort McHenry, 153
Fort Necessity, 73
Fort Pitt, 74

Fort Stanwix, New York, 92, 116
Fort Sumter, South Carolina, 252
Fort Ticonderoga, 94, 99
Fort Washington, New York, 97
Forty-hour workweek, 443, 444
Forty-niners, 174
Foster, William Z., 405
Four–Power Treaty, 454
Fourteen Points, 401, 406
Fourteenth Amendment, U.S. Constitution, 274, 286; contents of, 278; Southern rejection of, 278; Supreme Court interpretations of, 285, 303, 310, 366; and Indians, 292; protection of corporations by, 311; equal protection clause of, 498
Fourth Amendment, U.S. Constitution, 124–125
Fourth World, 551
France; exploratory voyages of, 11; attempt to convert Native Americans, 13; trade with Indians, 39, 40; role in Beaver Wars, 39; expansion by, 39–40; relations with Indians, 41; colonialism of, 48; expulsion from North America, 70; hold on American frontier, 71; and Seven Years' War, 73; involvement in American Revolution, 100, 102; and Treaty of Paris, 102; during French Revolution, 123, 129; war with England (*1793*), 124; war debts owed to, 127; war with Britain, Spain, and Holland, 129, 130; Quasi-War with, 132; trade relations with, 147–149; occupation of Spain, 156; lack of dealings with Confederacy, 269; interest in Asia, 386; and outbreak of First World War, 394; in First World War combat, 400; First World War settlement with, 407; and disarmaments negotiations, 454; policy of appeasement toward Hitler, 457, 458; U.S. sale of bombers to, 460; German attack on, 462; U.S. aid to, 462; liberation of, 470; and Yalta Conference, 482; imperialism in Vietnam, 540
Franciscans, 37
Franco, Francisco, 457
Frankfurter, Felix, 433, 443
Franklin, Benjamin, 52, 79, 416; background of, 63; resistance to British, 74; identification with Stamp Act, 79; negotiation of Franco-American alliance of *1778,* 88; role in Declaration of Independence, 95; diplomacy during American Revolution, 100; as negotiator of Treaty of Paris, 102; as delegate to Constitutional Convention, 118
Franklin, Sally, 79
Fredericksburg, Virginia, 258

Free Banking, 169–170
Free blacks, 111, 182–183, 192; founding of institutions for, 111, 214; employment opportunities for, 111; family life of, 111; in North, 111, 214; in South, 182–183, 214; restrictions on, 192; population of, 214; involvement in abolitionism, 223. *See also* African–Americans
Freedmen: equality for, 274, 275; participation at constitutional conventions, 276; impact of black codes on, 277; Fourteenth Amendment and, 278; impact of Military Reconstruction Act on, 279; exploitation during Reconstruction, 282–283; social and economic changes for, 283–284. *See also* Reconstruction period
Freedmen's Bureau, 277, 283, 284
Freedom: individual, 164–165; for Southern women, 184; benefits for African-Americans, 275; social and economic meaning of, 283–284
Freedom of Information Act (1966), 574
Freedom Riders, 555
Freedom's Journal, 214
Free enterprise, 363
Freeholders, 20
Freemasonry, 222
Freeport Doctrine, 249
Free-Soilers, 240, 245, 246, 253
Free-Soil party, 241
Free speech: and immediatists, 223; Slave Power and, 239; during time of war, 405; post–First World War campaign against, 406
Free Speech Movement, 561, 562
Frémont, John C., 240, 247
French Revolution: American opinion regarding, 123; Americans' views regarding, 129
Freud, Sigmund, 419
Frick, Henry C., 318
Friedan, Betty, 565
Frontier, 173, 290, 377
Frontier lore. *See* Westward expansion
Frontiero v. *Richardson,* 566
Frontier thesis, 377
Fuchs, Klaus, 499
Fuel industry, 293
Fugitive Slave Act, 237, 242, 245
Fulbright, William J., 489
Fulkes, Minnie, 187
Fuller, Margaret, 108
Fulton, Robert, 161, 165
Furnishing merchants, 301–302
Fur trade, 204; with Indians, 37, 39–40, 174; importance to New England economy, 42; British control of, 73; Jefferson's interest in, 144; history of, 174
Fur trappers, 174

Gabriel's Rebellion, 137
Gadsden Purchase, 208
Gage, Thomas, 91, 93, 95
Gag rule, 224, 239
Galbraith, John Kenneth, 525, 532
Gallatin, Albert, 142
Galloway, Joseph, 88
Galt, Edith Bolling, 399
Gama, Vasco da, 11
Gambling, 221
Gandhi, Mohandas K., 408, 512
Garfield, James A., 348, 350
Garlic, Delia, 186
Garnet, Henry Highland, 214
Garrison, William Lloyd, 217, 223, 224
Garvey, Marcus, 417
Gaspée (ship), 82
Gas services, 200
Gates, Horatio, 99, 101
Gaugin, Michael, 207
Gay rights movement, 562–563, 583
Gaza Strip, 597
General Court (Massachusetts Bay), 22, 23
General Electric Company, 306–307, 389, 412
General Federation of Women's Clubs, 415
General Motors, 412, 444, 472, 524, 551, 575
Generation of Vipers (Wylie), 529
Genêt, Edmond, 129, 144
Geneva Accords (1954), 541–542
Gentleman's Agreement, 532
Geographic expansion. *See* Westward expansion
Geographic surveying, 165
Geologic surveying, 165
George, Henry, 313
George I (King of England), 53
George III (King of England), 83, 95, 96 (ill.)
Georgia: founding of, 39; revolutionary sentiment in, 91; borders of, 92; guerrilla warfare among patriots and loyalists in, 102; laws regarding slaveholding in, 110; war debts from American Revolution, 127; Tennessee, 136; population density in, 181; Indian land concessions in, 210, 211; ban on manumission in, 214; racial discrimination in, 214; secession of, 251; Civil War destruction in, 270; tax on voters in, 302
Germain, George, 94, 98, 100
German Democratic Republic (GDR). *See* East Germany
German immigrants: Palatine, 32; migration to Pennsylvania, 52, 53; in New York City, 199; 19th–century, 208; in cities, 324, 327; during First World War, 394
German Reformed, 53

Germantown, Pennsylvania, 99
Germany: migration to Pennsylvania from, 32; exportation of manufacture goods by, 378; conflict with Britain, 382; interest in Philippines, 385; interest in Asia, 386; pre–First World War relations with, 394, 396; and outbreak of First World War, 394; First World War combat, 396–400; attempt at military alliance with Mexico, 398; U.S. grievances with, 398–399; First World War settlement with, 406–408; First World War reparations, 434, 454–455; conflict with, 452; rise of fascism in, 457; pre–Second World War aggression of, 457–459, 462; Second World War combat with Allies, 468–470, 480; Allied troops in, 470; surrender of, 470; mass extermination of Jews by Nazis, 480; casualties of Second World War in, 482; settlement of Second World War with, 482–483, 490. *See also* East Germany; West Germany
Germ theory of disease, 328
Gerry, Elbridge, 132
Gershwin, George, 425
Gettysburg, Pennsylvania, 267
Ghana, 8, 516
Ghettos, 330–331, 417
Gibbons v. *Ogden*, 165
GI Bill, 521, 529
Gideon v. *Wainwright*, 559
Gilbert, Humphrey, 14
Gilbert Islands, 470
Gillespie, Dizzy, 531
Gilman, Charlotte Perkins, 369
GI mortgages, 528
Ginsberg, Allen, 532
Glasnost, 590
Glorious Revolution, 29, 46, 65
Godkin, E. L., 380
Golan Heights, 549
Gold Coast, 8
Goldman, Emma, 406
Gold mining, 174, 175, 293, 354
Gold rush, California, 174
Gold standard, 349, 350, 354, 357, 373, 438
Gold Standard Act (1900), 357
Goldwater, Barry, 558
Gompers, Samuel, 318, 357, 402
Good Neighbor policy, 456, 517
Gorbachev, Mikhail, 588, 590, 593–594
Gore-McLemore Resolution, 398
Gospel of wealth, 312
Gould, Jay, 317
Government: Enlightenment and view of, 62; colonists' view of, 76; promotion of economic growth following War of *1812*, 161; Jefferson's view of, 164–165; reform during Progressive movement,

362–364. *See also* City government; Federal government; Republican government; State government
Governors, 363
Graham, Billy, 530
Graham, Martha, 532
Grain, 56, 434
Grain Coast, 8
Grand Army of the Republic, 347
Grand Coulee Dam, 434
Grandfather clauses, 285, 356
Grange, Harold "Red," 422
Grange movement, 352
Granger laws, 352
Grant, Ulysses S., 270 (ill.), 279; military campaigns during Civil War, 255, 267, 269–271; election of, 285; as president, 286; scandal in administration of, 348; desire for Santo Domingo, 377
Grassroots politics: Antimasonry and, 222; beginnings of, 230
Grau San Martín, Ramon, 456
Great Awakening, 51, 66–67. *See also* Second Great Awakening
Great Basin, 3
Great Britain. *See* England
Great Depression: bank failures during, 353, 354, 429, 430; economy preceding, 426; causes of, 426–427, 449; business failures during, 429; unemployment during, 429, 433, 438; effects of, 429; government intervention in, 436–443; labor organizing during, 443–444; African-Americans during, 444–446; and women, 447–448; impact on foreign affairs, 452, 454
Great Lakes, 161, 162; navigation rights, 116; Rush–Bagot Treaty regarding, 156
Great Lakes campaigns (War of 1812), 150
Great Society, 554
Greece, 490
Greeley, Horace, 246, 264, 287
Greenbacks, 286
Green Berets, 539–540
Greene, Nathanael, 101
Greenhouse effect, 597
Greenland, 463
Greensboro, North Carolina, 303 (ill.)
Greer (U.S.S.), 463
Grenville, George, 76, 77
Grey, Zane, 341
Griffith, D. W., 339, 403
Grimké, Angelina, 224
Grimké, Sarah, 108, 224
Griswold v. *Connecticut*, 559
Gross national product, 416, 522
Guadalcanal, Solomon Islands, 470
Guam: cession to U.S., 384; Japanese seizure of, 470
Guantánamo Bay, Cuba, 388, 456

Guardianship, of black children, 280
Guatemala, 6, 517
Guilford Court House, North Carolina, 101
Guinea, 8, 34
Guiteau, Charles, 348
Gulf of Guinea, 8
Gulf of Mexico, 70, 71
Gullah, 36
Guyana suicides, 584
Guzmán, Jacobo Arbenz, 517

Habeas corpus, 263, 268
Haber, Al, 562
Haight-Ashbury culture, 562
Haiphong harbor, 546–547
Haiti, 137; U.S. intervention in, 389–390, 455, 456; immigrants from, 582
Halberstam, David, 555
Haldeman, H. R., 572
Haley, Bill, 531
Half Breeds, 346
Halfway Covenant, 42
Halifax, Nova Scotia, 95
Hall, G. Stanley, 364
Hamilton, Alexander, 50–51, 62–63, 115; campaign for ratification of Constitution by, 121; as first secretary of treasury, 126; profile of, 126–127; national debt plan, 127, 128; as member of Federalist faction, 129; conflict regarding Treaty of Alliance, 129; reaction to Democratic-Republican societies, 130; as author of Washington's Farewell Address, 131; allegiance of Adams's cabinet to, 132; conflict with Burr, 147
Hampton Institute, 367 (ill.)
Hampton Roads Conference, 265
Hancock, John, 69
Hancock, Winfield Scott, 350
Handsome Lake, 137–138
Hanna, Marcus Alonzo, 356
Hanna, Mark, 369–370
Harding, Warren G.: appointment of cabinet officers by, 412; as president, 413; election of, 413; and aftermath of First World War, 451; pardon of Debs, 451
Hard Labor Creek, South Carolina, 92
Harlan County, Kentucky, 433
Harlem Railroad, 200
Harlem Renaissance, 424
Harlem Tenants League, 445
Harmar, Gen. Josiah, 117
Harpers Ferry, Virginia, 249
Harriman, E. H., 362
Harrington, Michael, 522
Harris, Joel Chandler, 342
Harrison, Benjamin, 350, 351; on annexation of Hawaii, 382

Harrison, William Henry, 149, 150, 152, 153, 231, 232, 351
Harte, Bret, 342
Hartford Convention, 154
Hartford Female Seminary, 205
Harvard University, 62, 365, 472
Hastie, William H., 445
Hatch Act (1887), 300
Havana, Cuba, 383
Hawaii: annexation of, 244, 382, 384, 385; Japanese immigrants in, 324, 382; expansionist interest in, 380, 382
Hawkins, John, 14
Hawley-Smoot Tariff (1930), 434, 455
Hay, John, 384, 386; as member of foreign policy elite, 378
Hayden, Tom, 562
Hayes, Rutherford B., 350; election of 1876, 287–288; use of troops to quell labor unrest, 317
Haymarket Riot, 317, 318 (ill.)
Hayne, Robert Y., and nullification debate, 228
Hay-Pauncefote Treaty of 1901, 388
Headright system, 18, 19
Head Start, 558
Health. See Epidemics; Illness
Hearst, William Randolph, 341, 383
Heart disease, 335
Hegemony, 378, 382
Helper, Hinton R., 193
Hemingway, Ernest, 424
Hendrix, Jimi, 562
Henry, Patrick, 78; participation at First Continental Congress, 88; opposition to Constitution, 121
Henry the Navigator (Prince of Portugal), 11
Henry VII (King of England), 10
Henry VIII (King of England), 15
Hepburn Act (1906), 370
Hero worship, 422
Hessian troops, 97
High Court of Impeachment, 273
High Point, North Carolina, 266
High schools, 419. See also Schools
Highway Act (1956), 509, 528
Highway construction, 528
Hillsborough, Lord, 80–81
Hilton Head, South Carolina, 255
Hippies, 562
Hirabayashi case, 475
Hiroshima, Japan, 468, 471
Hispanic-Americans: 19th-century immigration of, 208–209; rebellion in Texas, 233; unemployment among, 580; culture of, 582; poverty of, 582. See also Cuban-Americans; Mexican-Americans; Puerto Ricans
Hispaniola, 11
Hiss, Alger, 499
Hitler, Adolf, 448, 457 (ill.), 482; prewar aggression of, 457–458; and con-

duct of Second World War, 468; suicide of, 470; mass extermination of Jews by, 480
Hoar, George, 384, 385
Hobb, Alfred C., 166
Ho Chi Minh, 408, 540–542, 545, 546
Hodgson, Godfrey, 554
Hofstadter, Richard, 506
Hog brokers, 169
Holden, Massachusetts, 84
Holden v. *Hardy,* 316, 366
Holding companies, 311
Holland: trade and colonization interests of, 29, 31; migration to Pennsylvania from, 32; role in slave trade, 34. See also Netherlands, The
Holland, Michigan, 207
Holly, Buddy, 531
Holmes, Oliver Wendell, Jr., 365, 405
Holocaust, 480, 481
Home of the Brave, 532
Homeowners agreements, 498
Homestead Act (1862), 299
Homosexuals, 566. See also Gay rights movement
Honduras, 517
Hone, Philip, 203–204
Honecker, Erich, 604
Hong Kong, 470
Hood, John, 270
Hooker, Thomas, 23
Hoover, Herbert, 402; appointments of, 412, 425; as commerce secretary, 413; election in 1928 of, 425; as president, 429–430; election in 1932 of, 430, 436; economic policy of, 433–434; as bridge to New Deal, 434; racial attitudes of, 445
Hoover, J. Edgar, 559, 567; as head of Bureau of Investigation, 406
Hoover dam, 434
Hoovervilles, 430
Hopewell, South Carolina, 116
Hopewell treaties, 116
Hospitals, 221, 263
"House Divided" speech (Lincoln), 248
Households, 336, 418
House of Burgesses, 18–19, 21, 41, 78
House of Commons (England), 64, 65, 76
House of Delegates (Maryland), 21
House of Representatives, U. S.: influence of Madison in, 124; on creation of role of president, 125; on assumption of state debts from American Revolution, 127; on Jay Treaty, 130; voting patterns in, 131; impeachment of Chase by, 142; impeachment of Pickering by, 142; selection of president by, 225; investigation of Civil War corruption, 262; committee to examine Johnson's policies, 277; results of 1874

International Monetary Fund, 490
Interregnum period, 29
Interstate commerce: Supreme Court decisions regarding, 165, 366, 443; regulation of, 348, 443
Interstate Commerce Act (1886), 348
Interstate Commerce Act (1887), 311
Interstate Commerce Commission (ICC), 348, 373; regulatory powers of, 370, 372; cooperation with corporations by, 412–413
Intervention: proposed U.S.-British declaration against European, 156; Monroe Doctrine's attempt to avoid, 156–157
Intifadah, 597
Intolerable Acts. *See* Coercive Acts
Inventions, 165
Invisible Man (Ellison), 532
Iowa, 432–433
Iran, 596; Soviet-U.S. clash over, 490; CIA role in, 517; U.S. interests in, 517; U.S. hostages in, 577, 579, 585
Iran-contra affair, 587–588, 595–596
Iraq, 606
Ireland, 394
Irish immigrants: migration to Pennsylvania, 32; labor in textile mills, 168, 170 (ill.), 171; as landless Southerners, 182; in New York City, 199; in Boston, 207; in 19th century, 207–208; discontent with Civil War, 268; in cities, 324; during First World War, 394
Iron: exportation of, 379; production of, 408
Iron Curtain speech, 490
Iron industry, 54, 170, 260, 281
Iroquois, 3, 5, 74; political structure of, 6; drawing of, 40 (ill.); neutrality of, 71, 73; erosion of power of, 93; settlement in Canada, 100; treaty with, 116; religious revival, 137–138
Iroquois Confederacy: Beaver Wars and, 39; neutrality of, 71; split during American Revolution, 99–100; land claims of, 116
Isabella of Castile (Queen of Spain), 10, 11
Islam, in African cultures, 6, 8. *See also* also Muslims
Isolation, on Plains, 299
Isolationism: definition of, 451; pre–Second World War, 459, 462
Israel: U.S. recognition of, 491; U.S. interests in, 517; wars, 549; and Camp David meeting, 579; and West Bank uprising, 596; invasion of Lebanon, 596
Isthmus of Tehuantepec, 376
Italian immigrants, 324, 327
Italy: and outbreak of First World War, 394; and disarmaments negoti-

ations, 454; pre–Second World War aggression of, 457; peace treaty with, 482
It's Up to the Women (Roosevelt), 447
Iwo Jima, 470

Jackson, Andrew, 226 (ill.), 350; role in War of *1812,* 149–150, 153; Indian policy of, 211–212; support by opponents of religious reform, 218; Freemasonry and, 222; in campaign of *1824,* 225; background of, 226; as president, 227–230; opposition to nullification doctrine, 228–229; and Second Bank of the United States, 229, 373; use of veto by, 230
Jackson, Helen Hunt, 292
Jackson, Jesse, 603
Jackson, Rachel, 226
Jackson, Thomas "Stonewall," 255, 257–258, 267
Jacksonians, 225–228
Jackson State University, 567
Jacobites, 53
Jamaica, 582
James, Henry, 342
James (Duke of York), 29, 31–32
James I (King of England), 15, 16, 18
James II (King of England), 45, 46
Jamestown, Virginia, 16, 18
Japan: interest in Philippines, 385; interest in Asia, 386; foreign policy with, 388, 460–461; relationship with China, 388, 394; build-up of navy, 388; in Russo-Japanese War, 388; interest in Korea and Manchuria, 388; restrictions in emigration to U.S., 388; interest in Siberia, 405; First World War settlement with, 407; attack on Pearl Harbor, 452, 464; conflict with, 452; and disarmaments negotiations, 454; aggression against China, 460–461, 463; U.S. trade with, 461, 463; in Second World War, 464–465, 470–471; U.S. entry into war with, 465; casualties of Second World War in, 482; division of empire, 493; U.S. peace treaty with, 493; U.S. reconstruction of, 493; in Indochina, 540
Japanese-Americans: in Hawaii, 324, 382; in cities, 324; internment of, 474–475
Jaworski, Leon, 572
Jay, John: participation at First Continental Congress, 88; as negotiator of Treaty of Paris, 102; campaign for ratification of Constitution by, 121; negotiation of trade and territorial issues with England, 130
Jay Treaty (1796), 130–131
Jazz, 424–425, 531

Jazz Singer, The, 422
Jefferson, Thomas, 141 (ill.), 191, 225; views regarding slave system, 60; role in Declaration of Independence, 95; views regarding architecture, 107; views regarding African-Americans, 111; as first secretary of state, 126; view of Bank of the United States, 128; as member of Republican faction, 129; conflict regarding Treaty of Alliance, 129; as vice president, 131; handling of Alien and Sedition Acts, 133; election of *1800,* 134; Republicanism of, 138, 154; inauguration of, 140, 141, 147; appointment of Supreme Court justices by, 142; consolidation of Republican power by, 142; and westward expansion, 144; election of *1804,* 144–145; actions regarding *Chesapeake* Affair, 148; suspension of Non-Importation Act, 148; view of individual freedom, 164–165
Jehovah's Witnesses, 474
Jeremiads, 43
Jeremiah, Thomas, 91
Jerusalem, 549
Jervis, John, 160, 162
Jesuit missionaries, 13, 24
Jewish immigrants: in colonies, 54; from Germany, 208; in cities, 324; opposition to, 420
Jews: expulsion from Spain, 10; and Nazi ideology, 457; Roosevelt and persecution of, 460; immigration quotas and, 480; mass extermination by Nazis, 480, 481; Israel lobby in U.S., 517
Jiang Jieshi (Chiang Kai-shek), 460, 482, 493, 494, 514, 540
Jim Crow laws, 302–303
Jobbers, 169
Job Corps, 437, 558
Johns Hopkins University, 472
Johnson, Andrew: and election of *1864,* 269; background of, 273; impeachment and acquittal of, 273, 279; Reconstruction plan of, 274, 276–277; and congressional Reconstruction plan, 277–280; attempt to block Fourteenth Amendment, 278; confrontation with Congress, 279; congressional actions to restrict, 279
Johnson, Elliot, 467
Johnson, Hiram, 363
Johnson, James Weldon, 456
Johnson, Lyndon B., 518; as Senate majority leader, 509; and Vietnam War, 534, 542–546; failures of presidency, 555; and civil rights, 557–558; election in *1964* of, 558; State of Union address of, 558

Moon landing, 566
Moral reform, 333, 364
Moratorium Day demonstration, 566
Moravians, 53
Morgan, Daniel, 101
Morgan, J. P., 270, 306, 311, 354, 362
Morgan, William, 222
Morgenthau, Henry, Jr., 481
Mormons: establishment of, 197–198; riots against, 202; abandonment of polygamy by, 295
Morrill Land Grant Act (1862), 300
Morris, Robert, 115
Morristown, New Jersey, 97
Morse, Samuel B., 162
Mortgage rates, 329
Mossadegh, Mohammed, 517
Most-favored-nation principle, 455
Motion picture industry, 339, 422, 423 (ill.), 531
Mott, Lucretia, 224
Movie stars, 423
Muckraking, 341, 360, 364
Mugwumps, 346
Mulattos, 110, 183; civil rights interests of, 281; education of, 283
Multinational corporations, 551
Munich Conference, 458
Municipal Voters League, 361
Munn v. *Illinois*, 348
Murfree, Mary Noailles, 342
Murphy, Frank, 475
Murray, Judith Sargent, 108
Muscle Shoals, Alabama, 415, 438
Music: African heritage in, 187, 425; immigrant adaptations to native, 327; jazz, 424–425; electronic, 425; rock 'n' roll, 431; as reflection of counterculture, 562
Musical comedies, 338–339
Muskie, Edmund, 564
Muskogeans, 3; division of labor among, 5; political structure of, 6
Muslims: in Africa, 6, 8; Spanish defeat of, 10
Mussolini, Benito, 457
Mutual Defense Assistance Act (1949), 493
MX missiles, 578
My Lai Massacre, 543
Myrdal, Gunnar, 498

Nagasaki, Japan, 468, 471
Napoleon: acquisition of Louisiana, 144; seizure of American ships by, 149; fall from power of, 153–154
Napoleonic wars, 147
Napoleon III, 381
Narcissism, 584–585
Narragansett Indians, 22, 23, 41
Nasser, Gamal Abdel, 517
Nation, The, 380
National Advisory Commission on Civil Disorders, 555

National Aeronautics and Space Agency (NASA), 513
National American Woman Suffrage Association, 350, 360, 369
National anthem, 153
National Anti-Slavery Standard, 224
National Association for the Advancement of Colored People (NAACP), 368, 476; urging blacks to enter First World War combat, 400; intervention of, 445; on Haitian intervention, 456; Supreme Court victories for, 497–498
National Association of Colored Women, 368
National Association of Manufacturers, 363–364
National bank, 128; opposition to, 225. *See also* Bank of the United States; Second Bank of the United States
National Banking Act of 1863, 263
National Banking Act of 1864, 263
National Banking Act of 1865, 263
National banking system, 263
National Broadcasting Company, 416
National Child Labor committee, 363
National City Bank of New York, 456
National Civil Federation, 360
National Civil Service Reform League, 348
National College Athletic Association, 338
National Committee to End the War in Vietnam, 545
National Conservative Political Action Committee (NCPAC), 585
National Consumers League (NCL), 360, 366
National Cordage Company, 353
National Council of Churches, 498
National Defense Act (1916), 399
National Defense Education Act (NDEA) (1958), 513, 530
National Guard: used in miners strike, 433; training in Latin American countries, 456
National Housing Act (1937), 443
National Housing Act (1949), 528
National Industrial Recovery Act (NIRA) (1933), 437–438, 441, 443
Nationalism: following War of *1812,* 154, 157, 159; railroad routes and, 162; black, 214, 560–561; following Civil War, 377
National Labor Relations Act (1935). *See* Wagner Act (1935)
National Labor Relations Board, 442, 591
National Labor Union, 317
National League, 338
National Municipal League, 360
National Organization for Women (NOW), 565
National Origins Act (1924), 421

National Origins Act (1927), 421
National Progressive League, 372
National Reclamation Act (1902), 371
National Recovery Administration (NRA), 437, 440, 448
National Republican party, 229
National Republicans, 225
National Road, 155, 161
National Security Act (1947), 491
National Security Council (NSC), 491, 493, 494, 502
National Security League, 399
National Socialism, 457
National Union convention, 278
National War Labor Board, 402, 472, 474
National Woman's party, 369, 415
National Woman Suffrage Association (NWSA), 350
National Youth Administration, 441, 445
Native Americans, 4 (ill.), 17 (ill.), 72 (ill.); disease in, 1, 14, 581; relations with English, 2; forerunners of, 2–5; agricultural economy of, 5, 6, 290–291; division of labor among, 5, 292; role of women, 5, 6, 10; economic and political organization of, 5–6; kinship structure of, 6; religious beliefs of, 6; conversion to Christianity, 13, 18, 24, 211, 377; trade with colonists, 13, 16, 37, 39; relations with New England settlers, 23–24, 37; Penn's relationship with, 32; role in fur trade, 37, 39–40, 174; slave trade in, 38–39; relations with French, 39–41; balance of power in North America and, 70; alliances in Seven Years' War, 73; uprising against British, 74; warfare in British colonial possessions, 74–75; revolutionary involvement among, 92–93, 99–101; as losers in American Revolution, 102; land claims of, 116, 210; involvement in War of 1812, 150–154, 209; eviction from western lands, 165, 291–293; role in settlement of West, 173, 294; right to cultural heritage, 209; government policy in dealing with, 209–210, 291–293, 415; forced resettlement of, 209–213; assimilation of, 210, 292, 293, 415; education of, 210, 292, 293; as slaveholders, 211; cultural differences with whites, 289, 415; subsistence cultures of, 290–291; massacres of, 291; reservation policy for, 292; in mining and lumber communities, 294; voting rights for, 345; advances during Progressive movement, 368; progressive reforms for, 415; during Great Depression and New Deal, 430, 446; termination

Panama (*cont.*)
389–390, 455, 457; return of Canal zone to, 580; invasion of, 605
Panama Canal, 388–390
Pan-American Conference (1889), 381
Pan American Union, 381
Panic of 1819, 175, 225, 229
Panic of 1837, 131, 169
Panic of 1857, 172
Panic of 1873, 286
Panic of 1893, 351
Paper currency, 231
Paraguay, 156
Parcel post, 299
Paris Peace Conference (1918–1919), 406–408
Parker, Charlie, 531
Parker, Capt. John, 93
Parker, John J., 445
Parks, 339
Parks, Rosa, 510
Park Theater, 201
Parliament (England), 29, 83; application of mercantilist principles to colonies, 43; theories of representation, 76; authority over colonies, 77, 80; repeal of Stamp Act, 79; repeal of Townshend duties, 82; passage of Coercive Acts, 85
Parochial schools, 334. *See also* Schools
Partisanship, as force in U.S. politics, 131
Patent laws, 165
Paternalism: Southern, 183; toward Native Americans, 415
Paterson, William, 118
Patrilineal descent, 6
Patriotism: from resistance to Townshend Acts, 81; American Revolution and, 90–91; stimulated by Civil War, 262; and age of consensus, 508 (ill.); during Reagan era, 588
Patronage, 227
Patten, Gilbert, 342
Patterson, Haywood, 445
Patton, George S., 433
Paul, Alice, 369, 420
Pawnees, 209, 292
Pawtucket, Rhode Island, 117, 168
Paxton Boys, 75
Paxton Township, Pennsylvania, 74–75
Payne, Sereno E., 371
Payne-Aldrich Tariff (1909), 371
Peace Corps, 539, 556
Peace movements, 453–454, 566–567
Peace of Utrecht, 71
Peale, Charles Willson, 141 (ill.)
Peale, Norman Vincent, 530
Peale, Rembrandt, 141 (ill.)
Pearl Harbor, Hawaii: strategic location of, 382; attack on, 452, 464, 468
Pendleton Civil Service Act, 348
Penitentiaries, 221
Penn, William, 32

Penn, Adm. William, 32
Pennsylvania: founding of, 32; suspension of charter of, 45; Scotch–Irish in, 53; resistance to British taxation in, 81; authority of colonial assembly in, 90; loyalists in, 97; abolishment of slavery in, 110; state constitution, 113; protest of whiskey tax in, 128; industrialization in, 170; rights of pre–Civil War African-Americans in, 213; lotteries in, 221; disillusionment with Civil War in, 268; labor unrest in, 316
Pennsylvania Journal, 83
Pennsylvania Railroad, 162
Pensacola Bay, Florida, 153
Pensions, 316, 347, 351. *See also* Old-age pensions
Pentagon Papers, 546, 567, 572
People's party, 345, 353
People's Republic of China: creation of, 494; and Korean War, 500, 501; conflict over Quemoy and Matsu, 514; Nixon's visit to, 549, 567; détente with, 549
People's Temple, 584
Pequot Indians, 23
Perestroika, 590
Perkins, Frances, 448
Perry, Oliver Hazard, 150
Persecution, religious, 32
Pershing, John J., 398, 400
Personal income: rise in, 163, 334; unequal distribution of, 426; changes in, 598, 599 (ill.)
Personal income tax: creation of, 373; increase during Great Depression, 434; and New Deal legislation, 442
Personal liberty laws, 245
Personal savings: growth in, 329; threat to, 430
Petersburg, Virginia, 184, 271
Petersham, Massachusetts, 84
Peterson, Esther, 565
Petroleum, 293, 517, 606; exportation of, 379; production of, 408; Mexican, 457; OPEC embargo of, 549, 571, 574, 576; from seabed, 551; price decline in, 590
Philadelphia, Pennsylvania, 50, 162; settlement of, 32; poverty in, 55; resistance to British taxation in, 79; activity during American Revolution in, 98; free blacks in, 111, 214; election day in *1815*, 146 (ill.); unemployment in, 164, 433; riots in, 202, 213; mass transportation in, 322
Philadelphia and Reading Railroad, 353
Philippines, 463, 598; annexation of, 384, 386, 388; cession to U.S., 384; insurrection in, 386; Japan's recognition of U.S. position in, 388; Al-

lied forces in, 470; Japanese seizure of, 470; immigrants from, 582
Philipse family, 66
Phillips, Kevin, 526
Phonograph, 339
Phrenology, 243
Pickering, John, 142
Pickering, Timothy, 147
Pierce, Franklin, 237, 243–244
Pike, Zebulon, 144
Pilgrims, 21–22
Pilgrim's Progress (Bunyan), 360
Pilots, 473 (ill.), 475
Pinchot, Gifford, 371
Pinckney, Charles Cotesworth, 132, 145, 148
Pinckney, Thomas: treaty with Spain negotiated by, 130; as running mate in *1796* election, 131
Pinckney, William, 148
Pinckney's Treaty, 130, 144
Pingree, Hazen S., 332
Pinta (ship), 11
Pioneers, 173–174
Pitt, William, 73, 80
Pittsburgh, Pennsylvania, 162, 444–445
Pittsburg Landing, Tennessee, 257
Pizarro, Francisco, 11
Plains: migration to, 297, 299; argicultural regions, 298 (ill.); quality of life on, 299; cattle ranching in, 300–301
Plan of Union, 73
Plantations: 18th-century, 58–59; in South, 161, 178; economy of, 179; family life on, 183–184
Planters: and relationship between sexes, 183–184; aristocratic values of, 191; opposition to Confederate government, 266; Johnson's relationship with, 276; attempt to gain control over black children during Reconstruction, 280; opposition to Reconstruction, 280
Platt Amendment (1903), 388, 457
Plattsburgh, New York, 153
Plausible deniability, 517
Pledge of Allegiance, 505
Plessy v. *Ferguson*, 303
Plows, 173
Pluralism, cultural, 333
Plymouth, Massachusetts, 21
Pocahontas, 16
Poindexter, John M., 596
Point Four Program, 493
Pokanokets, 22, 41
Poland: creation of, 407; German aggression against, 458, 462, 480; concentration camps in, 480; postwar authority over, 480, 489; casualties of Second World War in, 482; Soviet occupation of, 482; revolt against Soviet control of, 513; Solidarity labor movement in, 593, 604

Polio vaccine, 525
Polish immigrants, 327
Political barbecue, 146
Political caucuses: choosing candidates in, 222, 225; disbandment of, 225, 360
Political machines, 331–332
Political movements, 218, 221–222
Political parties: in first decades of 19th century, 158; Antimasons and, 218, 221–222; creation of modern, 226; renewal of competition among, 230; membership determinants of, 231; sectional, 238; impact of Kansas-Nebraska Act on, 245; realignment of, 245–247; corruption in, 345, 363; allegiances to, 346. *See also* Democratic party; Federalist faction; Republican faction; Republican party; Whig party
Political structure: of Indians, 6; of colonies, 45–46
Politics: in Chesapeake Bay region, 21; in 18th-century colonies, 64–67; post-Revolution exclusion of African-Americans, Indians, and women from, 105; avoidance of slavery issue in, 157, 159, 224; economic hard times and interest in, 157; reform movements and, 218, 220, 225; African-Americans in Reconstruction, 280, 281, 283; rise of urban boss, 331–333, 361, 362; influence of special interest on, 345; as form of mass entertainment, 346; women in, 415–416; decline in liberalism in, 478–479
Polk, James K.: election of *1844* and, 233, 235; as president, 238
Pollock, Jackson, 532
Poll tax, 356, 445
Polo, Marco, 10
Polygamy, 294
Polygyny, 34, 197
Polytheism, 6
Pomeioc, 5 (ill.), 9
Pontiac, 74
Pontiac's uprising, 74–75
Pools, 311
Poor Richard's Almanack (Franklin), 63, 416
Pop Art movement, 532
Popular sovereignty, 240, 242; interpretations of, 244; validity of, 248, 249
Population: in colonies, 41–42, 51–54; African-American, 51, 110–111, 214, 417; representation based on, 118–119; distribution, 175, 181; pre–Civil War density, 181; urban, 199, 321; of Native Americans, 209; shifts in U.S., 321, 330
Populism: and monetary policy, 335, 356; attack of corruption, 345; Omaha platform, 353; and racial

politics, 355–356; and election of 1896, 357
Porter, James A., 424
Porter, Sylvia F., 523
Port Huron Statement, 562
Portraiture, 107
Portsmouth, New Hampshire, 110
Portsmouth Conference (1905), 388
Portugal: exploratory voyages of, 11; role in slave trade, 34; role in Angola, 549, 551
Postal service, 299
Postmaster General, 125
Post-traumatic stress disorder, 543, 548
Potawatomis, 74; confederacy formed by, 116; and War of *1812*, 150, 153
Potomac River, 127
Potsdam Conference, 482
Poverty: urban, 55, 203, 219, 327–329, 526; as result of Civil War, 259–260; in southern agricultural communities, 301–302; efforts to relieve, 415; New Deal measures to counteract, 437, 440, 441; rural, 526–527; post–Second World War, 526–528; reduction in, 558–559; during *1960s* and *1970s*, 580; of Hispanic-Americans, 582; in *1980s*, 598
Powderly, Terence V., 317
Power loom, 168
Power of Positive Thinking, The (Peale), 530
Power of Sympathy, The (Brown), 106–107
Powhatan Confederacy, 16, 18
Preachers, 137
Predestination, 136
Pre-emption Act, 175
Prescott, Samuel, 93
Presidency: and Bill of Rights, 125; power of, 441; Franklin Roosevelt's role in strengthening, 449; power of, 502, 573
Presidential campaigns: of *1828*, 226; of *1832*, 229; of *1840*, 232 (ill.); of *1912*, 372; of *1896*, 383; of *1928*, 425; of *1932*, 436; of *1940*, 448; of *1948*, 496–497; of *1960*, 519; of *1968*, 563, 564; of *1972*, 568; of *1984*, 591; of *1988*, 603
Presidential elections: of *1796*, 131; of *1800*, 134 of *1804*, 144–145; of *1808*, 148; of *1812*, 154; of *1820*, 157; transition of power in, 158; of *1828*, 225, 228; of *1824*, 225; of *1836*, 231; of *1840*, 231; of *1844*, 233, 235; of *1860*, 238, 249–251; of *1848*, 240–241; of *1852*, 243; of *1856*, 247; of *1864*, 270; of *1868*, 285; of *1872*, 286; of *1876*, 287; of *1884*, 350; of *1892*, 351, 353; of *1888*, 351; of *1896*, 356, 360; of *1900*, 358; of *1912*, 362; of *1904*,

362, 370; of *1908*, 371; of *1916*, 373, 398; of *1920*, 413; of *1924*, 414–415; of *1928*, 425; of *1936*, 430, 442; of *1932*, 430; of *1940*, 448–449; of *1944*, 478–479; of *1948*, 495; of *1952*, 502; of *1960*, 518–519; of 1968, 526, 564; of *1972*, 567; of *1976*, 576–577; of *1980*, 585; of *1984*, 591; of *1988*, 603
Presidential vetos, 230
President's Commission on the Status of Women, 565
President's Committee on Civil Rights, 497
President's Organization on Unemployment Relief (POUR), 433–434
Presley, Elvis, 531
Price discrimination, 373
Primaries: nomination through, 360; increase in states having, 363; whites-only, 498
Princeton, New Jersey, 97
Printing press, 10
Privateering, 115
Proclamation of 1763, 75, 92
Professional Air Traffic Controllers Organization, 591
Progress and Poverty (George), 313
Progressive movement: issues in, 359–362; political reform in, 360–361; governmental and legislative reform as result of, 362–364; educational reform during, 364–365; advances in legal thought during, 365–366; public health reform during, 366; challenges to discrimination during, 366–369; revival of presidency during, 369–372; Wilson's extension of reform during, 372–274; impact of, 374; impact of First World War on, 393; expansion into *1920s*, 415
Progressive party, 372; formation of, 414; elections in *1934* and, 440
Prohibition: results of, 423–424; repeal of, 434, 436; and Hoover, 434
Project Head Start, 558
Propaganda: abolitionist, 223; First World War, 404
Property acquisition, 329
Property rights: Indian concepts of, 18; and voting rights, 109, 280; of women, 109, 184, 280
Prophet, 150–152, 209
Proposition 13 (California), 585
Proslavery theories, 243
Prosser, Gabriel, 137, 189
Prosser, Martin, 137
Prostitution, 219–220, 364
Protestant Association, 46
Protestant reform: religious, 136–137; in urban centers, 332 . *See also* Second Great Awakening

Slavery (*cont.*)
and conflict of, 105; revision of laws regarding, 110; politics and, 157, 159, 224, 245, 246; as emotional issue, 157; political balance in Senate committed to, 157; emotional attitudes toward, 157–158; in territories, 158, 238–242, 244, 245–249; as foundation of economic and social system in South, 159, 179, 190–191; tactics of advocates of, 224; war with Mexico and, 240; election of *1848* and, 240–241; theories advocating, 243; division of Union over, 247–249; North-South split in Union over, 249–253; avoidance of issue during Civil War, 263–264; in Cuba, 382. *See also* Abolitionism

Slaves: in Muslim Mediterranean, 8; introduction into Europe, 11; in New York State, 31; lifestyle in South Carolina, 36; white male authority over, 58; runaway, 58–60, 237, 242, 263; education of, 62; resistance among, 65, 91–93, 189–190, 237; in Continental Army, 98; in British army during American Revolution, 101; implications of revolutionary ideology for, 110; compensation for slaves who returned to England after American Revolution, 130; westward migration of, 136, 139, 159, 178, 179, 181; sale of excess, 179; as major investment in South, 181; labor conditions of, 184; diet of, 185; physical and mental abuse of, 185–186; attitude toward whites, 187; culture of, 187–188; owned by Cherokees, 211; prohibitions against freeing, 214; plan for emancipation of, 264–265; in Union Army, 266

Slave trade, 20, 33, 35 (ill.); European involvement in, 157; *1807* act closing foreign, 157, 179; interregional, 181

Smallpox: epidemics, 1, 14; inoculation against, 63

Smith, Adam, 164
Smith, Alfred E., 425
Smith, Hoke, 363
Smith, John, 16
Smith, Joseph, 197
Smith, Kirby, 258
Smith, Margaret B., 140
Smith-Connally Act (1943), 472
Smith v. *Allwright*, 498
Social Darwinism, 312, 313, 377
Social Gospel movement, 332, 364
Socialism: rise of, 354–355; and Progressive movement, 362; politicians and, 440
Social isolation, 299, 352

Socialist Labor party, 355, 372
Socialist party: and civil liberties during First World War, 404; and Red Scare, 405, 406; during Great Depression, 433
Social mobility, 329
Social reform: politics and, 218, 332; 19th-century, 220–222; urban, 332–333; and role of women, 448. *See also* Reform movements
Social Security Act (1935), 442, 443; jobs excluded from coverage, 430, 446, 448, 527; amendments to, 507
Social values, 419
Society of American Indians, 360, 368
Society of the Cincinnati, 107
Soil: exhaustion of, 172, 179; use of, 300
Solidarity labor movement, 593, 604
Somoza, Anastasio, 456
Sons of Liberty, 79, 81, 130
Soto, Hernando de, 12
Souls of Black Folk, The (Du Bois), 366
Sound money, 286
Soup kitchens, 430
South: basis of economy in, 159, 177–178, 239; regional specialization in, 161; development of transportation in, 181, 182; population density in, 181; rural society in, 181; paternalistic attitudes of slaveholders in, 183; class conflict and, 191–192; growing conflict with North, 238, 240–249; opposition to war with Mexico, 239–240; impact of Civil War on, 254, 258–260, 266–268; anti–Civil War sentiment in, 266, 268; opposition to Reconstruction, 274, 279–280; power in Congress after Civil War, 278; Reconstruction politics in, 280–283; post-Reconstruction, 301–304; support of Democratic party in, 442
South Africa, 598
South America. *See* Latin America
Southampton County, Virginia, 189
South Carolina: founding of, 33; slavery in, 36, 52, 60; trade in Indian slaves, 38; as royal colony, 45; antagonism between Africans and Indians in, 54; Stono Rebellion in, 65; Regulator movements in, 66; revolutionary sentiment in, 91, 92; American Revolution in, 100–101; laws regarding slaveholding in, 110; war debts of, 127; political reform in, 191; antiabolitionism in, 223; doctrine of nullification and, 228–229; secession of, 251; naval battles of Civil War off coast of, 255; Ku Klux Klan violence in, 282; election in *1876* and, 287
South Carolina Gazette, 83

South Dakota: statehood for, 295; agrarian movement in, 352
South East Asia Treaty Organization (SEATO), 542
Southern Christian Leadership Conference (SCLC), 555
Southern Railroad, 160
Soviet Union: relations with U.S., 405, 458–459, 485–491, 493, 513–516; détente with, 448–449, 578, 588; First World War debts, 455; aid to Spanish Loyalists, 457; signing of Nazi–Soviet Pact, 458, 459; German attack on, 463; and conduct of Second World War, 468; and Eastern Europe, 480, 590, 604; and casualties of Second World War, 482; and reparations, 482; and Yalta Conference, 482; territorial ambitions of, 489; U.S. view of, 489; development of atomic bomb by, 493, 499; relations with China, 493, 494; and Korean War, 500; launching of Sputnik, 513, 530; and U–2 incident, 514; erection of Berlin Wall, 535; arms control with, 535, 549, 593–594; Middle East policy of, 549; and Carter, 578; and Afghanistan, 578–579, 593, 594; and Reagan, 592–594; shooting of South Korean jet, 593. *See also* Russia
Spain, 10; colonialism of, 1, 12–14, 37; exploratory voyages of, 11–12; in Florida and Gulf of Mexico, 70, 71 loss of Florida to British, 73; involvement in American Revolution, 100; post–Revolution presence on U.S. borders, 116; Pinckney's treaty negotiated with, 130; Adams-Onis Treaty with, 156; French occupation of, 156; loss of Latin American territories by, 156; and Cuban revolution, 382–384; Cuban independence from, 384; civil war in, 457
Spanish-American-Cuban-Filipino War, 382–384
Special Forces units, 539–540
Special Investigations Unit (Plumbers), 571–572
Specie Circular, 229, 231
Spectator sports, 338, 422
Spirits, 187
Spock, Benjamin, 529
Spoils system, 227, 348
Sports, 338; in 19th-century urban life, 201; in 20th-century life, 422
Spotsylvania, Virginia, 270
Springfield, Illinois, 328
Springfield, Massachusetts, 105
Sputnik (satellite), 513, 530
Squanto, 22
Squatters, 175
Stagflation, 567, 585
Stalin, Josef, 489, 513; and conduct of